COMPANY LAW AND CORPORATE FI

COMPANY LAW AND CORPORATE FINANCE

EILÍS FERRAN, MA, PhD (Cantab), Solicitor
University Lecturer and Director of the
Centre for Corporate and Commercial Law,
University of Cambridge
Fellow and Director of Studies in Law,
St Catharine's College, Cambridge

OXFORD
UNIVERSITY PRESS

OXFORD
UNIVERSITY PRESS
Great Clarendon Street, Oxford OX2 6DP
Oxford University Press is a department of the University of Oxford.
It furthers the University's objective of excellence in research, scholarship,
and education by publishing worldwide in
Oxford New York
Athens Auckland Bangkok Bogotá Buenos Aires Calcutta
Cape Town Chennai Dar es Salaam Delhi Florence Hong Kong Istanbul
Karachi Kuala Lumpur Madrid Melbourne Mexico City Mumbai
Nairobi Paris São Paulo Singapore Taipei Tokyo Toronto Warsaw
with associated companies in Berlin Ibadan

Published in the United States
by Oxford University Press Inc., New York

First published 1999

British Library Cataloguing in Publication Data
Data available
Library of Congress Cataloging in Publication Data
Ferran, Eilís.
Company law and corporate finance / Eilís Ferran.
Includes bibliographical references.
1. Corporations—Finance—Law and legislation—Great Britain.
2. Corporations—Finance—Great Britain. I. Title
KD2094.F47 1999 346.41′066—dc21 99–23248
ISBN 0–19–876392–1 (hb).
ISBN 0–19–876393–X (pb).
3 5 7 9 10 8 6 4
Typeset in Utopia
by Hope Services (Abingdon) Ltd.
Printed in Great Britain
on acid-free paper by
T.J. International
Padstow, Cornwall

Preface

This book has its origins in my lectures for the Corporate Finance paper of the Cambridge University Master of Laws degree. In teaching that course over a number of years, it became apparent to me that whilst there existed a rich body of literature on English company law, ranging from excellent well-established practitioner and student textbooks through to the more recent materials examining the theoretical underpinnings of the subject, and also a vast array of relevant materials in economics and other disciplines, there was no book that looked at company law from the starting-point of the company as a vehicle for raising business finance and for the diversification of financial risk. In my view, these factors, more than any other, explain the popularity of the corporate form of business structure. Accordingly, it is with the idea of the company as a financing vehicle in mind, and against the background of the markets in which business takes place, that I have tried to examine the subject. The book's target audience is, first, students and academics who are interested in the operation of company law in its broadest sense—that is, as including self-regulation as well as the traditional sources of legislation and case law—in its practical context. It is aimed, secondly, at practising lawyers and other corporate finance professionals, as well as at managers of companies and investors. Although the ways in which academics and practitioners can contribute positively to each other's work is perhaps less well-recognised in this country than elsewhere, my personal experience has always been that practitioners do recognise the importance of knowing not just what the detailed rules are and how they apply in specific situations but also how those rules fit within a broader framework and what they seek to achieve. Especially at a time when English company law is undergoing its first fundamental review in over thirty years, it is reasonable to suppose that interest in these broader issues will extend far beyond the world of academia. This is a selective account of a vast subject but I hope that my choices about coverage and emphasis make sense given the starting point of the company as a financing vehicle

I am extremely grateful to Professor Len Sealy and Professor Barry Rider who, many years ago, first introduced me to the fascinations of company law. During the writing of this book I have been privileged to have had Len's advice and support as a colleague in the Law Faculty and the Centre for Corporate and Commercial Law in the University of Cambridge. Other Cambridge colleagues to whom I am indebted for their comments on draft chapters, answers to specific queries, suggestions and general support are Gareth Jones, Richard Hooley, Michael Kitson, Richard Nolan and Pippa Rogerson. The staff of the Squire Law Library, especially David Wills and Peter Zawada, assisted me in finding materials whilst the Faculty computer officers, Alan Edgar and Sarah

Hill, saved me from many potential disasters. The errors and omissions that remain despite the help of colleagues are, naturally, my own responsibility.

I would also like to record my thanks to the partners of Slaughter and May for giving me the opportunity to see how company law actually works in practice. This has both deepened my understanding of the subject and helped me to recognise areas where the existing law is inadequate or excessive. I am especially grateful to Nigel Boardman, Nilufer von Bismarck, John Crosthwait and Andrew Gibson.

I have benefited considerably from the interest, enthusiasm and insight of students taking the LLM Corporate Finance paper. I am grateful to them for providing a uniquely stimulating environment in which to voice and discuss half-formed views.

It took me longer to finish this book than I envisaged when I first discussed it with Richard Hart who was then at OUP. Richard's enthusiasm for the project was a great source of encouragement in the early years. Michaela Coulthard, ably assisted by Myfanwy Milton, took it through the later stages and into production with exemplary efficiency and cheerfulness. I am particularly grateful to them for allowing me to add an extra chapter on the future of company law in response to the publication, a fortnight after I had delivered the manuscript of the rest of the book, of the first consultation document to be published by the steering group established by the government to take forward the fundamental review of company law. I am also grateful to the publishers for preparing the tables and index.

Two life-changing events took place during the years that I was writing this book: the birth of my daughter, Aoife, in November 1994 and son, Oliver, in November 1997. My children ensure that all other preoccupations are kept in perspective. The book is dedicated to them and to my husband, Rod Cantrill, without whose support, encouragement and practical help in everything from childcare to understanding investment banking practices, it would not have been possible to complete it.

The law is stated as known to me on 31 January 1999 with brief references to some later developments added at proof stage. Chapter 19 summarises law reform proposals published in February 1999.

Eilís Ferran
9 June 1999

Contents

Table of Cases

CANADA

European Court of Justice

Hong Kong

IRELAND

NEW ZEALAND

South Africa

UK

US

Table of Statutes

Treaties

IRELAND

NEW ZEALAND

UK

USA

PART I

THE FRAMEWORK OF CORPORATE ACTIVITY

1

The Company and the Corporate Group

THE CORPORATE ENVIRONMENT

This book is concerned with the legal principles governing the financing of companies formed and registered under the Companies Act 1985 or former Companies Acts.[1] The great advantage that the corporate form has over firms which are sole traders or partnerships is with regard to financing: the corporate form is best suited to raising large amounts of business finance and to limiting, or diversifying, financial risk. Company law, then, can be seen as being essentially concerned with making available the corporate form, facilitating and regulating the process of raising capital, and imposing controls on persons whose power is derived from the finance that the use of the corporate form has put at their disposal. In approaching the subject from this direction, we are pointed towards its fundamental elements.[2] The discussion centres mainly on companies limited by shares, although it is possible under the Companies Act 1985 to form an unlimited company[3] or a company limited by guarantee.[4] The company limited by shares is the business structure that dominates economic life in the UK. At the end of 1997 there were over one million registered companies, most of which were limited companies.[5]

TYPES OF LIMITED COMPANY

Companies limited by shares are either public companies or private companies. Only about one per cent of the total number of registered companies are public companies,[6] although in terms of size of operations, market capitalisation, number of employees and the like, public companies tend to be much larger than private companies. The distinction between public and private

[1] Companies can also be formed by Royal Charter or by specific Acts of Parliament but incorporation by these methods is now uncommon. It is still possible to encounter references to incorporation as a privilege: eg, Mitchell, A, and Sikka, P, *Corporate Governance Matters* (Fabian Society Discussion Paper No 24) (1996) 1.

[2] Manne, HG, 'Our Two Corporations Systems: Law and Economics' (1967) 53 Virginia Law Review 259, 260; Posner, RA, *Economic Analysis of Law* (4th edn, 1992) 392.

[3] Companies Act 1985, s 1 (2)(c). An unlimited company is not subject to the maintenance of capital rules and is therefore free to return capital to its members. Occasionally limited companies re-register as unlimited, in accordance with the procedure in Companies Act 1985, ss 49–50, in order to return capital to members.

[4] Companies Act 1985, s 1 (2)(b). This form of corporate structure tends to be adopted by non-profit making organisations.

[5] *Companies in 1996–7* (DTI Report for the Year Ended 31 March 1997). Table A2 shows that there were only 3,900 unlimited companies.

[6] *Companies in 1996–7* (DTI Report for the Year Ended 31 March 1997), Table A2.

companies is enshrined in the Companies Act 1985. It is a requirement of the legislation that a company should make plain its status by its suffix: 'public limited company' ('plc' for short)[7] or 'private limited company' ('ltd' for short).[8] The fundamental point of distinction between public and private companies is that only public companies are allowed to raise capital by offering their shares and other securities to the investing public.[9] The Companies Act 1985 also distinguishes between public and private companies with regard to the rules relating to the raising and maintenance of share capital where, broadly speaking, private companies operate under more a relaxed regime than public companies. The more stringent rules applying to public companies are commonly derived from European Union law, which member states have been obliged to incorporate into their domestic legislation. Private companies can also opt out of some of the administrative obligations imposed by the Companies Act 1985, such as the requirement to hold an annual general meeting.[10]

For the purposes of exposition, it is often convenient to contrast a public company with a large number of shareholders, each of whom holds only a tiny fraction of its shares and virtually all of whom perform no managerial function, with a private company which has a few shareholders, all or most of whom are also involved in the management of the company. This habit should not be allowed to obscure the fact that there are many different types and sizes of company that can be accommodated under the 'public' and 'private' banners. There is no upper limit on the number of shareholders in a private company. It is possible to have private companies which have managerial structures similar to those of the paradigm public company, that is, where most shareholders are investors who do not participate directly in the management of the company. Equally, subject to satisfying the statutory requirement to have at least two shareholders,[11] the shareholder base of a public company can be very small. However, the burden of complying with more onerous requirements would usually deter the operators of a small business from seeking public company status at least until such time as it has established a sufficient reputation to make raising capital from external investors a viable financing option. In the context of public companies, it is important to recognise that there can be some companies where the shareholding is so widely dispersed that no one shareholder or group of shareholders holds more than a tiny fraction of its shares whilst there are others where one shareholder, or a group of shareholders, holds a significant portion of the share capital.[12] Commentators have noted that as dispersal of the shares increases, the portion of the shareholding that is needed in order to exercise some form of practical control decreases.[13]

[7] Or Welsh equivalents: Companies Act 1985, ss 25 (1) and 27.

[8] Or Welsh equivalents: Companies Act 1985, ss 25 (2) and 27. Certain private companies are exempt from the requirement relating to the use of 'limited': Companies Act 1985, s 30.

[9] Companies Act 1985, s 81.

[10] Companies Act 1985, s 366A.

[11] Companies Act 1985, s 1 (1).

[12] Herman, ES, *Corporate Control, Corporate Power* (1981) ch 3.

[13] Parkinson, JE, *Corporate Power and Responsibility* (1993) 59–63.

Companies where all, or most, of the shareholders participate in management are sometimes described as quasi-partnership companies, reflecting the fact that the management structure is akin to that of a partnership. Quasi-partnership companies tend to be private companies with just a few shareholders. The companies legislation does not specifically recognise the category of quasi-partnership companies, but in permitting private companies to opt out of certain administrative requirements it acknowledges that there may be companies for which the demarcations between one group of corporate actors (the directors) and another group (the shareholders) are unnecessary and inappropriate. Quasi-partnership companies have achieved recognition in case law concerned with the protection of minority shareholders. It is established that a relevant consideration in determining whether a petitioner is entitled to relief can be whether the company in question was established on the basis of mutual confidence between the parties and in the expectation that all, or some, of them would be involved in management.[14]

In its accounting requirements, the Companies Act 1985 distinguishes between 'small', 'medium' and 'large' companies and groups of companies, with the relevant criteria for this purpose being turnover, balance sheet totals and number of employees.[15] Many quasi-partnership companies will satisfy the criteria to be small companies for the purposes of the statutory accounting rules.

Another type of company that is recognised by the Companies Act 1985 is the company that is part of a larger group of companies. Corporate groups are subject to specific regulation in the context of accounting requirements. Certain other legislative rules also have a particular application to companies within a group.

Despite the recognition of different types of company for various purposes, in broad terms the framework of English company law is that the same rules apply to all companies regardless of the number of shareholders or employees, managerial structure or size of financial operations. From time to time there have surfaced proposals for a separate form of incorporation for small businesses[16] but legislation to that effect has not been forthcoming. A specific charge against English company law is that it is deficient in not containing more extensive rules relating specifically to corporate groups. This charge is considered in the closing sections of this chapter.[17]

[14] *Ebrahimi v Westbourne Galleries Ltd* [1973] AC 360, HL. Although Lord Wilberforce thought that references to quasi-partnership companies could be confusing, the terminology is convenient and is widely used. That a company has been run on a quasi-partnership basis is a claim that is often included in petitions for relief under Companies Act 1985, s 459: eg *Corbett v Corbett* [1998] BCC 93. See further Boros, EJ, *Minority Shareholders Remedies* (1995) 254–9 where the application of *Ebrahimi* (which was an application for winding up of the company under what is now Insolvency Act 1986, s 122 (1)(g)) to petitions for relief from unfairly prejudicial conduct under Companies Act 1985, s 459 is discussed with reference to quasi-partnership companies.

[15] Companies Act 1985, ss 247 and 249. Note also s 249A which exempts 'tiny' companies (based on turnover and balance-sheet totals) from the requirement for an independent audit.

[16] eg, *A New Form of Incorporation for Small Firms*, Cmnd 8171 (1981). See Sandars, WJ, 'Small Businesses—Suggestions for Simplified Forms of Incorporation'[1979] JBL 14. On the particular needs of small companies see further *Modern Company Law for a Competitive Economy: The Strategic Framework* (Company Law Review Steering Group Consultation Document) (1999), ch 5. 2.

[17] See below, at 38–43.

THE SOURCES OF COMPANY LAW

Legislation

The main piece of primary legislation relevant to companies is the Companies Act 1985. This is a large Act, divided into 27 parts containing in total 747 sections. The matters covered by the Companies Act include: the formation and registration of companies; juridical status and membership (Part I); allotment of shares and debentures (Part IV); share capital, its increase, maintenance and reduction (Part V); distribution of profits and assets (Part VIII); a company's management; directors and secretaries; their qualifications, duties and responsibilities (Part IX); enforcement of fair dealing by directors (Part X); company administration and procedure (Part XI); and registration of charges (Part XII). The Companies Act 1985 is supplemented by other statutes and statutory instruments including the Insolvency Act 1986, the Financial Services Act 1986 and the Public Offers of Securities Regulations 1995.[18] Much of this primary and secondary legislation gives effect to European law that has been imposed upon member states of the European Union with a view to harmonisation of legal requirements relating to companies and capital markets. Underlying European law is examined in context throughout the book.

A Company's Constitution and the Role of Contract

The shareholders of a company are permitted considerable flexibility in the regulation of their own affairs through the company's constitution. The Companies Act 1985 states that a company must have a constitution set out in two documents: the memorandum of association and the articles of association. The minimum contents of a memorandum are regulated. It must contain the name of the company, the situation of its registered office, its objects, its authorised share capital, the division of that share capital into shares of a fixed amount[19] and, if relevant, a statement of its status as a public company.[20] Apart from these requirements, a company is free to include additional information in its memorandum. The legislative direction that a company should have a memorandum in the form of one of the model memoranda provided by statutory instrument or as near to that form as circumstances permit[21] means only that companies should follow the formal layout and does not extend to prescription of the contents of the document.[22]

Whilst the memorandum contains the fundamental information about a company, it is usually the articles of association that contain the more detailed provisions regulating the company's internal relationships and its external dealings. There is, again, a model form of articles prescribed by statu-

[18] SI 1995/1537.

[19] Companies Act 1985, s 2.

[20] Companies Act 1985, s 1 (3)(a).

[21] Companies Act 1985, s 3. The relevant statutory instrument is the Companies (Table A to F) Regulations 1985 (SI 1985/805).

[22] *Gaiman v National Association for Mental Health* [1970] 2 All ER 362.

tory instrument, Table A,[23] but companies are free to adopt their own articles. Table A applies to the extent that a company does not exclude it nor make contrary provision.[24] The Companies Act 1985 gives legal effect to the memorandum and articles as a contract between the company and its shareholders and between the shareholders amongst themselves.[25]

Case Law

The Companies Act 1985, and related legislation, do not form a comprehensive code of the legal rules relating to companies. Important areas, such as the duties that the directors of a company owe by virtue of their position, are governed by case law, either alone or in conjunction with specific statutory requirements. At the time of writing the Government has launched a wide-ranging review of company law. The question of codification of parts of company law that are presently based on case law will feature as part of that review.[26]

Stock Exchange Requirements, Takeover Code and Codes of Practice on Corporate Governance

Companies that have outside shareholders[27] are in practice mindful of the expectations of those investors. Although failure to meet those expectations will not expose a company or its management to legal liability, the fact that widespread selling of shares by dissatisfied investors will trigger a fall in the company's share price usually ensures that investor expectations are not lightly disregarded. Where its shares have been admitted to dealings on a formal market, such as the London Stock Exchange, a company must comply with the obligations of that market in order not to jeopardise its position as a quoted company. The City Code on Takeovers and Mergers is a self-regulatory code governing the takeover of public companies in the UK. Although it is not backed by direct legal sanctions, if public companies that are involved in takeovers do not follow the Takeover Code they risk public censure, and access to the facilities of the securities markets, such as by the quotation of their shares on an organised exchange, may be withdrawn. For these reasons, from a commercial perspective compliance with stock exchange requirements, takeover rules and codes of practice that embody investor expectations on corporate governance can be just as important as satisfying the requirements of the companies legislation and case law. The significance of these 'quasi' or 'soft' law requirements is examined at appropriate points in

[23] The Companies (Table A to F) Regulations 1985 (SI 1985/805).

[24] Companies Act 1985, s 8 (2).

[25] Companies Act 1985, s 14.

[26] *Modern Company Law For a Competitive Economy* (DTI Consultative Document) (March 1998) para 3.4. For arguments for and against codification of directors' duties see: *Company Directors: Regulating Conflicts of Interests and Formulating a Statement of Duties: A Joint Consultation Paper* (Law Commission Consultation Paper No 153; Scottish Law Commission Discussion Paper No 105) (1998) pts 14 and 15.

[27] ie shareholders who are not involved in management and who are not connected to management through family, social or other ties.

the book. The introductory point that suffices here is that to develop a realistic view of the legal and regulatory environment in which companies which have external investors operate, it is necessary to look beyond the traditional legal sources of legislation and case law and to consider market regulation as well.

PROCESS OF INCORPORATION: INCORPORATION AS A PRIVILEGE?

A company is incorporated under the Companies Act 1985 by completing the relevant forms and submitting them, together with the appropriate fee, to the registrar of companies.[28] It is possible for one person acting alone to form a private company limited by shares or by guarantee.[29] A public company must have at least two members and each of them must take at least one share.[30] The registrar performs the administrative function of checking that the statutory requirements for registration have been complied with. If they have been, the application must be accepted unless the proposed company is being formed for an illegal purpose in which case the application should be rejected.[31] The registrar does not have a discretion to approve or refuse registration.[32] The process of incorporation is completed by the issue of a certificate of incorporation by the registrar.[33] This certificate constitutes conclusive evidence of compliance with the statutory registration requirements and of incorporation.[34] If a company formed for illegal purposes slips through the filter operated by the registrar, the Attorney-General, acting on behalf of the Crown, can seek judicial review to have the registration quashed.[35]

It was in 1844 that incorporation of a company by registration first became possible under English law.[36] Before then, company incorporation was by Royal Charter or specific Act of Parliament. When companies were formed by Charter or by specific Acts of Parliament it was realistic to regard the corporate form as a privilege or concession granted by the state to worthy individuals, but that description became meaningless once incorporation by an essentially administrative process became possible.[37] A modified version of the concession theory continues to be expressed in cases concerning the disqualification of directors under the Company Directors Disqualification Act 1986. In this version, involvement in the management of a company, as opposed to participation in the incorporation process, is viewed as a privilege granted by

[28] Companies Act 1985, ss 1 (1), 10–11.

[29] Companies Act 1985, s 1 (3A).

[30] Companies Act 1985, s 1 (3). A public company must have a share capital: s 1 (3).

[31] *R v Registrar of Companies ex p More* [1931] 2 KB 197, CA; *Bowman v Secular Society* [1917] AC 406, HL.

[32] *R v Registrar of Companies ex p Bowen* [1914] 3 KB 1161.

[33] Companies Act 1985, s 13.

[34] Companies Act 1985, s 13 (7).

[35] *R v Registrar of Companies ex p Attorney-General* (1980), reported [1991] BCLC 476, CA.

[36] Companies Registration and Regulation Act 1844. On the historical development of English law, see Davies, PL, *Gower's Principles of Modern Company Law* (6th edn, 1997) chs 2–3.

[37] Bratton, WW, 'The New Economic Theory of the Firm: Critical Perspectives from History' (1989) 1 Stanford Law Review 1471; Stokes, M, 'Company Law and Legal Theory' in Wheeler, S (ed), *The Law of the Business Enterprise* (1994) 80, 89 (reprinted from Twining, W (ed), *Legal Theory and Common Law* (1986) 155). Wheeler's own comments on the concession theory are at 6–8. See also Parkinson, JE, *Corporate Power and Responsibility* (1993) 25–32.

the state; the disqualification legislation is the mechanism whereby the state, acting in the public interest, can withdraw the concession from those who have shown themselves to be unfit for that purpose.[38]

JUSTIFICATIONS FOR THE LEGAL REGULATION OF COMPANIES

Companies are subject to extensive legal regulation in the conduct of their operations, far more so than businesses that are partnerships or sole traders. There is much discussion of the basis for the law's intervention in the affairs of companies. Although it is not the aim of this book to develop theoretical concepts of the company and the regulation of corporate power in any significant way,[39] a basic awareness of these issues may be helpful in considering the nature of the legal rules regulating corporate finance and the purposes that these rules seek to achieve. This awareness may also be helpful in identifying the type of questions that should properly be taken in account when law reform is under consideration.

Fiction Theory

The fiction theory of the company is that corporate personality is a fiction to which the law gives effect: companies are able to incur rights and obligations because the law endows them with capacity to act. The fiction theory provides a ready justification for state regulation of the activities of companies because the state can intervene to impose whatever restrictions it deems appropriate on those creatures whose very existence depends on the operation of law. The concession theory of incorporation can be seen to be an aspect of the fictional approach and, just as the establishment of incorporation by administrative act rapidly made it unrealistic to view incorporation as a privilege granted as a concession by the state, so too have legal developments undermined other aspects of a fiction-based analysis.[40] Consistent with fiction theory, it used to be the case that companies were regarded as having limited capacity: they were required by the companies legislation to state their objects in their constitution and the constitutional statement operated as a limit on capacity, with any purported act which was not authorised by the constitution being regarded as void. The rule of limited capacity was undermined by companies taking matters into their own hands by drafting ever-wider statements of their

[38] *Re Cedac Ltd* [1991] BCC 148, CA, 154 *per* Balcombe LJ; *Re Swift 736 Ltd* [1993] BCC 312, CA, 315 *per* Nicholls V-C; *Re Sevenoaks Stationers Ltd* [1991] Ch 164, CA, 176 *per* Dillon LJ; *Secretary of State for Trade and Industry v Davies* [1997] BCC 235, CA, 245–6 *per* Hobhouse LJ.

[39] These topics are amply covered by Parkinson, JE, *Corporate Power and Responsibility* (1993) and Cheffins, BR, *Company Law Theory, Structure and Operation* (1997). For an overview see Tomasic, R, Jackson, J, and Woellner, R, *Corporations Law Principles, Policy and Process* (3rd edn, 1996) 87–97.

[40] Stokes, M, 'Company Law and Legal Theory' in Wheeler, S (ed), *The Law of the Business Enterprise* (1994) 80 (reprinted from Twining, W (ed), *Legal Theory and Common Law* (1986) 155); Bratton, WW, 'The Nexus of Contract Corporation: a Critical Appraisal' (1989) 74 Cornell Law Review 407; Eisenberg, MA, 'The Structure of Corporation Law' (1989) 89 Columbia Law Review 1461.

objects. The result is that, nowadays, companies incorporated under the Companies Act 1985 typically have such long objects that their capacity is practically unlimited. This illustrates how the consequences of corporate personality can stem more from the actions of the human beings who are involved in the company—in the specific example, the action of the company's shareholders in adopting the constitution—than from the intervention of the state. It is generally accepted that it is now implausible to rest any justification for state intervention in a company's affairs on the fact that its existence is derived from a state concession or privilege.[41] Fiction theory is a model that does not fit with the realities of modern corporate practice.

Contractual Theory

An important economic model of the company views it as a nexus of contracts between the various constituencies, shareholders, managers, creditors and employees, who have an interest in the firm.[42] 'Contract' is used in a loose sense to include voluntary associations of whatever nature. Corporate legislation and judge-made rules on such matters as fiduciary duties are seen as a form of standard form contract which the constituencies can adopt or depart from as they think fit.[43] An example of the contractual approach to company law is to say that one of its distinctive features—limited liability for shareholders in limited companies—is a standard form provision which removes the need for costly negotiations in order to contract out of liability on a case-by-case basis.[44] In this model, corporate personality is no more than a convenient shorthand for the complex arrangements worked out between the various constituencies who have an interest in the company. As so stated, the contractual theory seems to rule out the existence of mandatory corporate law, but this is to oversimplify a complex and highly developed analytical model. Proponents of the contractual approach accept that some mandatory legislation may be justifiable but suggest that this should be kept to a minimum: wherever possible, the state should allow the parties who have an involvement in a company to make their own bargain in accordance with prevailing market forces.[45]

Although there is a large element of contract in company law, the contractual theory does not explain fully the present day structure and operation of

[41] Bratton, WW, 'The New Economic Theory of the Firm: Critical Perspectives from History' (1989) 1 Stanford Law Review 1471.

[42] Easterbrook, FH, and Fischel, DR, *The Economic Structure of Corporate Law* (1991) ch 1; Jensen, M, and Meckling, W, 'Theory of the Firm: Managerial Behavior, Agency Costs and Ownership Structure' in Putterman, L, (ed) *The Economic Nature of the Firm* (1986) 209, 215–16 (reprinted in abridged form from (1976) 3 *Journal of Financial Economics* 305).

[43] Easterbrook, FH, and Fischel, DR, *The Economic Structure of Corporate Law* (1991) 34.

[44] Posner, RA, *Economic Analysis of Law* (4th edn, 1992) 396.

[45] Easterbrook, FH, and Fischel, DR, *The Economic Structure of Corporate Law* (1991) 21–2. Cheffins, BR, *Company Law Theory, Structure and Operation* (1997) chs 3–4 analyses the arguments for and against state intervention. Ch 6 applies these arguments to company law rules. At 249, the author concludes: 'While mandatory rules have some important positive attributes, overall, lawmakers should be cautious in using this approach in dealing with issues affecting company participants.'

company law.[46] As well as the existence of a considerable amount of mandatory legislation,[47] the theory struggles to explain convincingly the basic fact of separate legal personality.[48] As a matter of legal analysis, the company is a legal entity which is itself capable of incurring rights and obligations. If a company were not something more than a convenient shorthand for a network of voluntary arrangements, and in the absence of some other legislative mechanisms such as are now being considered in relation to limited liability partnerships, its shareholders would automatically be fully liable for the debts of the business except to the extent of contractual exclusions worked out on an individual basis.[49] Another reason why it may be potentially misleading to overemphasise the existing role of contract in company law is that even in the paradigm case of a contractual relationship within a company, namely that between its shareholders which, according to the Companies Act 1985, is a contract on the terms of the company's constitution,[50] the contract is of a special type and lacks certain of the features that are normal to arrangements in contractual form.[51]

The normative role played by this analytical perspective is important. One of the most valuable aspects of the contractual theory is that it puts the spotlight firmly on the need to justify mandatory company law rules so as to ensure that businesses in corporate form are not subjected to regulation that does not produce beneficial outcomes measured in terms of economic efficiency or on the basis of other criteria.[52] Yet contractual theory, as a normative tool, is also open to criticism. It is based on the classical idea of contract in which the parties have personal autonomy and can fix their bargain as they please. That the general process of contracting really operates in this way is a notion that is widely discounted by specialists in that field.[53] More specifically, the idea of negotiation and bargain does not seem an entirely apt description of the dynamics of many typical relationships within a company: for example, a person who buys shares in a public company through an organised securities market does not engage in a process of negotiation with the company prior to making the investment; the investor's personal discretion is

[46] 'Nothing, however, beats a theory like a practice, and reference to practice makes the pure contractual corporation untenable': Bratton, WW, 'The Economic Structure of the Post-Contractual Corporation' (1992) 87 Northwestern Law Review 180, 185.

[47] Eisenberg, MA, 'The Structure of Corporation Law' (1989) 89 Columbia Law Review 1461, 1486.

[48] *Gas Lighting Improvement Co Ltd v IRC* [1923] AC 723, HL, 740–1 *per* Lord Sumner.

[49] Parkinson, JE, *Corporate Power and Responsibility* (1990) 32; Brudney, V, 'Corporate Governance, Agency Costs and the Rhetoric of Contract' (1985) 85 Columbia Law Review 1403.

[50] Companies Act 1985, s 14.

[51] *Bratton Seymour Service Co Ltd v Oxborough* [1992] BCC 471, CA, 475 *per* Steyn LJ. The statutory contract is unlike an ordinary contract in the following ways: (a) it derives its binding force not from a bargain struck between the parties but from the terms of the statute; (b) it is binding only in so far as it affects the rights and obligations between the company and its members acting in their capacity as members; (c) it can be altered by special resolution, ie without the consent of all of the contracting parties; (d) it is not defeasible on the grounds of misrepresentation, common-law mistake, mistake in equity, undue influence or duress; (e) it cannot be rectified on the grounds of mistake. Also, terms cannot be implied on the basis of business efficacy: *Stanham v National Trust of Australia* (1989) 15 ACLR 87, NSW SC-EqD, 90–1.

[52] Cheffins, BR, *Company Law Theory, Structure and Operation* (1997) ch 3.

[53] Beatson, J, *Anson's Law of Contract* (27th edn, 1998) 4–7.

limited to deciding whether to pay the price at which the shares are trading and, in making that decision, the investor may lack the knowledge and understanding of the implications of the investment that classical contract theory would ascribe to the maker of a bargain.[54] These considerations indicate that although removal of excessive regulation should be the driving factor in any reform process, it is also important not to overestimate the ability of persons who have an interest in a company to protect that interest by contract and by the operation of market forces.

Realist Theory

The realist view of the company is that a company is a real person brought into existence by the actions of a group of individuals acting together for a common purpose. As a real rather than a fictitious person, its existence does not depend on state intervention. As a real person, the company is deemed to have organs to think and act on its behalf. This view of the company was originally popularised by German theorists in the nineteenth century.[55] Its impact on the development of English company law has been greatest in the context of attributing knowledge and personal characteristics to a company although, even there, recent case law has shifted the focus away from an anthropomorphic approach towards a more functionally-orientated and context-driven assessment of the rule in question and its application to a company.[56] At a theoretical level, however, new life has been breathed into this theory with the suggestion that the recognition of the company as a distinct social entity, rather than as the product of private contract, could provide the basis for a shift towards a stakeholder model of company law. This would involve recognising that the duty of management to act in the interests of the company extends beyond looking after the collective interests of only one constituency, namely, the shareholders, and also embraces the interests of other groups, especially creditors and employees.[57]

Political Theory

This analytical perspective is linked to the previous one and also views the company as a social institution.[58] Here the argument is that political theory

[54] Stokes, M, 'Company Law and Legal Theory' in Wheeler, S (ed), *The Law of the Business Enterprise* (1994) 80, 91 (reprinted from Twining, W (ed), *Legal Theory and Common Law* (1986) 155); Brudney, V, 'Corporate Governance, Agency Costs and the Rhetoric of Contract' (1985) 85 Columbia Law Review 1403; Eisenberg, MA, 'The Structure of Corporation Law' (1989) 89 Columbia Law Review 1461.

[55] Gierke, O, *Political Theories of the Middle Ages* (translated with introduction by FW Maitland).

[56] *Meridian Global Funds Management Asia Ltd v Securities Commission* [1995] 2 AC 500, PC.

[57] Kay, J, and Silberston, A, 'Corporate Governance' (Aug 1995) *National Institute Economic Review* 84.

[58] Parkinson, JE, *Corporate Power and Responsibility* (1993) 21–41. Parkinson confines the discussion to large companies. It would hardly be appropriate to regard, say, a typical one-person company as an entity capable of wielding considerable power. The developing structure of English company law is increasingly imposing much more onerous obligations on public com-

about the legitimacy of private power has an application in relation to companies: although companies are private institutions, they are in a position to yield considerable power which could lead to damaging results if left unregulated. The state can intervene in company affairs in the public interest with a view to curbing misuse of power and achieving socially desirable outcomes. The political theory, either on its own or in combination with the reification of the company, is the main theoretical alternative to the contractual approach. It rejects the notion that a company is simply the creature of a private bargain between participants and, in particular, the suggestion that the role of management is simply to maximise profits for the benefit of shareholders. This theory suggests that, in the public interest, the management of a company should be legally required to act in a way that recognises the impact that the exercise of their powers can also have on employees, creditors and even the wider community.

Whilst some elements of existing company law are consistent with the stakeholder model of the company, this is more an aspirational vision of what companies and company law might be than an explanation of how they operate at present. Reservations that have been expressed about political theory as a normative tool include: that the legitimate public interests that company law should be designed to serve have not been not precisely articulated,[59] and that it is not clear that the interests of, say, employees would be better served by the full-scale reorganisation of company law than by the enactment of specific obligations and requirements in their favour. As is discussed at various points in this book, a general shift towards adoption of the stakeholder model would require fundamental aspects of company law to be redrawn.

DISTINCTIVE FEATURES OF THE COMPANY LIMITED BY SHARES

A company has three distinctive features: separate legal personality, limited liability and separation of equity investment and managerial responsibility.

Separate Legal Personality

A company is a legal person separate and distinct from the people who hold shares in it and the people who manage it. The company continues in existence even though managers and shareholders may come and go. It is the company, not its managers or shareholders, that acquires the contractual

panies (ie the form that larger companies in terms of turnover, assets, employees, etc are likely to adopt) than on private companies. There is scope for more opting out by shareholder consent to be permitted in relation to private companies (eg with regard to statutory powers such as Companies Act 1985, s 121 (altering share capital) and s 303 (removal of directors by ordinary resolution). At present it is not possible to contract out these powers but weighed voting rights can be employed to prevent their exercise: *Russell v Northern Bank Development Corpn Ltd* [1992] 1 WLR 588, HL (s 121); *Bushell v Faith* [1970] AC 1099, HL (s 303).

59 McGuinness, K, Rees, B, and Copp, S, 'Recent Perspectives on Company Law: A Review Article' (1998) 19 Co Law 290.

rights and undertakes the contractual liabilities that are involved in the running of the business. A contract between a company and a substantial shareholder, even one who controls all of the shares in the company, is a valid bilateral contract.[60] A company can have as one of its employees the controller of all its shares.[61] The property of the business is owned by the company, and its shareholders do not have an insurable interest in it.[62] If shareholders misappropriate the company's property they may be guilty of theft.[63] As a legal person, a company can incur tortious liability and can be prosecuted for committing crimes. The separate legal personality of the company distinguishes it from other business structures. Individuals who wish to conduct business can do so in an unincorporated firm (sole trader or partnership) or through the structure of a private company. Unincorporated firms do not have distinct legal personality. Contracts made in the name of an unincorporated firm benefit, and impose obligations on, the individuals whose business it is, and they are liable to be sued accordingly.

The leading case on corporate personality in English law is the decision of the House of Lords *Salomon v Salomon & Co Ltd*.[64] Mr Salomon was a boot and shoe manufacturer who had been in business for over thirty years as a sole trader. He then converted his business into the newly fashionable company limited by shares incorporated under the companies legislation of the time. Mr Salomon financed the company partly by investing in its shares and partly by lending to it and taking security. In the company's subsequent insolvency, the House of Lords held that Mr Salomon was entitled to enforce his security and thus to rank ahead of the company's unsecured trade creditors. This conclusion was based on the then equivalent of the Companies Act 1985, s 13 which states that, upon registration, a company is incorporated. This led their Lordships to conclude that an incorporated company was a legally different person from the persons who had formed the company. Accordingly, even though Mr Salomon controlled all the shares in the company, the contract between him and the company creating the security was a valid contract and gave rise to an enforceable security.

Separate legal personality is a foundation stone of company law but, as is self-evident, a corporate person cannot act itself. One of the major areas[65] of company law built on the foundation of corporate personality is the series of

[60] *Salomon v Salomon & Co Ltd* [1897] AC 22, HL.

[61] *Lee v Lee Air Farming Ltd* [1961] AC 12, HL. But whether a controlling shareholder can be viewed as an employee will depend on the context: *Buchan v Secretary of State for Employment* [1997] BCC 145 (director and controlling shareholder was not an employee for the purpose of receiving redundancy and other payments from the Secretary of State under Employment Protection (Consolidation) Act 1978, ss 106 and 122). Cp, *Secretary of State for Trade and Industry v Bottrill* [1999] BCC 177.

[62] *Macaura v Northern Assurance Co* [1925] AC 619, HL.

[63] *Re AG's Reference (No 2 of 1982)* [1984] QB 624, CA.

[64] [1897] AC 22, HL.

[65] There are also subsidiary aspects of the personification of the company, eg, the attribution of enemy status to a company in a time of war: eg, *Daimler v Continental Tyre Co* [1916] 2 AC 307, HL. This is done by identifying the characteristics of the controllers of the company and attributing them to the company. As Ottolenghi, S, notes ('From Peeping Behind the Corporate Veil to Ignoring it Completely'(1990) 53 MLR 338, 340) cases such as *Daimler* do not involve lifting the veil in the sense of imposing obligations on anyone other than the company.

principles which determine when acts which are done on behalf of a company are properly to be attributed to it. These principles are considered in Chapter 3.

Lifting The Veil of Incorporation

In limited circumstances company law is prepared to depart from the principle of separate legal personality in a process generally described as 'lifting the veil of incorporation'. When the veil of incorporation is lifted the shareholders rather than the company itself are regarded as the relevant actors and, therefore, the shareholders are personally responsible for any liabilities incurred. Specific statutory provisions authorise lifting the veil in particular circumstances: for example, if a public company carries on business for more than six months after the number of its shareholders has fallen below two, the remaining shareholder is personally liable (jointly and severally with the company) for any debts thereafter incurred if he knows that the company is carrying on business with only one shareholder.[66]

The courts can lift the veil. The precise scope of the courts' power in this respect has not been articulated[67] but it is established that the courts do not have a discretionary power to lift the veil in the interests of justice.[68] It is indisputable that the veil can be lifted where the corporate form is a façade which is being used in order to evade an existing legal obligation or to practise some other deception.[69] The Court of Appeal has identified the motives of the persons responsible for the use of the corporate structure as a relevant consideration in determining whether an arrangement involving a company is a façade, but has declined to give a comprehensive definition of the principles which should guide a court in determining whether an arrangement involving a company amounts to a façade.[70] It is understandable that the higher courts should resist any temptation to prescribe comprehensively the elements of a façade, since that would be an invitation to the unscrupulous to devise new and unenvisaged misuses of the corporate form, but the absence of fuller guidance at a senior judicial level, say in the form of a non-exhaustive list of relevant considerations, makes the law on this point vulnerable to the charge that it is unpredictable and arbitrary.[71]

[66] Companies Act 1985, s 24.

[67] Ottolenghi, S, 'From Peeping Behind the Corporate Veil to Ignoring it Completely' (1990) 53 MLR 338 reviews the authorities and the earlier literature in an attempt to provide a structure based on four categories. The author places the cases discussed in the text in the category of 'Ignoring the veil'. The article concedes that there can be no closed list of the circumstances in which the court will lift the veil.

[68] *Woolfson v Strathclyde Regional Council*, 1978 SLT 159, HL; *Adams v Cape Industries plc* [1990] Ch 433, CA; *Yukong Lines Ltd of Korea v Rendsburg Investments Corpn of Liberia* [1998] 1 WLR 294.

[69] *Woolfson v Strathclyde Regional Council*, 1978 SLT 159, HL, 161 *per* Lord Keith; *Adams v Cape Industries plc* [1990] Ch 433, CA, 544 *per* Slade LJ; *Re Polly Peck plc* [1996] 2 All ER 433, 447.

[70] *Adams v Cape Industries plc* [1990] Ch 433, CA, 540 *per* Slade LJ.

[71] Prentice, DD, 'Groups of Companies: the English Experience' in Hopt, KJ (ed), *Groups of Companies in European Laws* (1982) 99, 101. The plea 'is it not time to know just when a company is a "sham" and when the veil of incorporation *can* be "torn aside"?' (Lord Wedderburn,

An example of an attempt to use the corporate form to evade an existing obligation is provided by *Gilford Motor Co v Horne*,[72] where an individual attempted to side-step a restrictive covenant which had been imposed on him by his former employer by carrying on business through a limited company. The Court of Appeal held that the company was a façade and lifted the veil of incorporation so as to ensure that the restrictive covenant continued to bite. In that case the company was formed specifically to evade the restrictive covenant, but the veil can also be lifted in relation to a company which has an existing legitimate business but which is used by its controllers as a façade in a particular matter. *Re H*,[73] was a case where the corporate form was used to practise a deception, illustrates this point. Two companies were used by a number of individuals to perpetrate excise duty offences. The court granted an order restraining the individuals from dealing with their personal property and, because the companies had been used for fraud, the veil was pierced so as to include the companies' property within the scope of the order.

Whilst the courts will lift the veil in circumstances where a company is used to evade an existing obligation, they are not receptive to lifting the veil where the corporate form is adopted in order to limit the future obligations of its shareholders. The freedom to use incorporation as a means of reducing future legal liability is an inherent part of company law.[74] Lifting the veil to remove limited liability runs counter to a fundamental principle of company law and could have serious economic implications.

Lifting the veil of incorporation between companies that are in the same corporate group is considered later in this chapter.[75]

Limited Liability

Shareholders in companies limited by shares are liable to contribute only a limited amount to its assets. The minimum amount of the contribution is the par value of the shares—that is the value ascribed to the shares in the company's constitution[76]—but where shares are issued at a price higher than the par value (described as an issue at a premium) then the required contribution is par value plus the premium.[77] Company law does not impose mandatory

'Multinationals and The Antiquities of Company Law' (1984) 47 MLR 87) has gone unanswered, save that it can be gleaned from recent decisions that the fraud category will be strictly confined: *Ord v Belhaven Pubs Ltd* [1998] BCC 607, CA (where *Creasey v Breachwood Motors Ltd* [1993] BCLC 480 was said to be no longer authoritative); *Yukong Lines Ltd of Korea v Rendsburg Investment Corpn of Liberia (No 2)* [1998] 1 WLR 294 (noted Payne, J, 'Reaching the Man Behind the Company' [1998] CfiLR 147); *HR v JAPT* [1997] Pensions LR 99 (noted Mitchell, C, 'Beneficiaries' Rights Against Trustee Company Directors' [1998] CfiLR 133).

[72] [1933] Ch 935, CA. See also *Jones v Lipman* [1962] 1 All ER 442; *Re a Company* (1985) 1 BCC 99,421 CA.

[73] [1996] 2 All ER 391, CA.

[74] *Adams v Cape Industries plc* [1990] Ch 433, CA, 544 *per* Slade LJ. See also *Multinational Gas and Petrochemical Co v Multinational Gas and Petrochemical Services Ltd* [1983] Ch 258, CA, noted Lord Wedderburn, 'Multinationals and The Antiquities of Company Law' (1984) 47 MLR 87.

[75] See below, at 31–5.

[76] Par values of shares must be stated in the company's memorandum: Companies Act 1985, s 2 (5)(a).

[77] See, generally, Ch 8.

par values for shares, nor does it require companies to issue their shares at specific premiums. These are matters for companies to decide on an individual basis.[78] Many private companies start life with a nominal share capital of £100 divided into 100 £1 shares. The par values of shares in public companies is often much less than £1 because this can enhance liquidity, the argument being that, for example, 10 shares of 10p each will be easier to sell than one share of £1. Another reason for low par values is that there is a mandatory rule in the Companies Act 1985 that shares cannot be sold by the company at less than par.[79] When a public company is planning to raise capital by offering its shares for investment it will have in mind the price at which it intends to offer the shares but must take into account that the offer price may have to be adjusted downwards in response to market conditions at the time when the offer is made. To enable this fine-tuning to take place, the par value of shares must be virtually irrelevant, which means that there must be a large margin between intended premium at which the shares are to be offered and their par value.

Limited liability does not follow automatically from the principle of separate legal personality.[80] If it did, then unlimited companies in which the shareholders are liable to contribute to meet the company's debts in full could not exist. Corporate personality means that the company, not its shareholders, is the person responsible for the debts of the business. The extent to which the company can require its shareholders to provide the finance to meet the liabilities of the business is a logically distinct issue. The legislation of 1844[81] that first established the procedure for incorporating a company by an administrative registration process did not provide for limited liability of the shareholders. Limited liability did not become part of the law relating to companies incorporated by registration[82] until over ten years later when the Limited Liability Act 1855 was passed.[83]

People who lend to companies also have limited liability: they, too, are liable to contribute no more than the principal amount that they agreed to lend. The basic distinction between the shareholder and the lender is that, whilst both contribute a fixed amount, only the shareholder hopes for capital gain in respect of the investment. This distinction can easily become

[78] It may be a breach of duty by directors if they fail to offer new shares at the best price obtainable (*Shearer v Bercain* [1980] 3 All ER 295) but the company would not be in breach of any general requirement of company law in that event.

[79] Companies Act 1985, s 100.

[80] Blumberg, PI, *The Multinational Challenge to Corporation Law: The Search for a New Corporate Personality* (1993) 7.

[81] Joint Stock Companies Act 1844.

[82] The principle of limited liability already applied to companies incorporated by Charter or by specific Act of Parliament.

[83] On the struggle for limited liability in the UK: Davies, PL, *Gower's Principles of Modern Company Law* (6th edn, 1997) 40–6; Muscat, A, *The Liability of The Holding Company for the Debts of its Insolvent Subsidiaries* (1996) 103–6. The Limited Liability Act 1855 contained various safeguards including regulated minimum par values (£10) but most of these disappeared almost immediately when that Act was repealed and replaced by the Joint Stock Companies Act 1856. The historical background to limited liability in the USA is explored in Presser, SB, 'Thwarting the Killing of the Corporation: Limited Liability, Democracy and Economics' (1992) 87 Northwestern University Law Review 148, 155–6 and Blumberg, PI, *The Multinational Challenge to Corporation Law: The Search for a New Corporate Personality* (1993) 10–14.

blurred—preference shares can resemble debt finance by offering the investor only a limited capital return, lenders may make their profit on a loan by advancing less than the agreed principal on the basis that the full amount of the principal is to be repaid—but it suffices as a point of departure for the present discussion.[84] Provided the company remains solvent, lenders get back what they lent, but no more; it is the shareholders of a solvent company who are entitled to claim the residue remaining after all liabilities and claims have been met (hence shareholders can be described as the 'residual claimants'). The flip side of the contrast between a lender and a shareholder is the position in an insolvent company: there, in simple terms,[85] the order of repayment is: first, creditors who have taken security on the company's property, second, unsecured creditors and, finally, shareholders. Shareholders, at the bottom of the pile, have the least chance of recovering their investment but, because they benefit from limited liability, they do not have to make good any shortfall in the company's assets in the event of its insolvency. The risk of corporate insolvency is thus borne in part by its creditors.[86]

For shareholders limited liability operates as a shield against having to contribute over and above the fixed amount of the investment. The shielding effect of limited liability leads to a number of positive consequences which for convenience can be considered under the following headings, although they are inter-related: promotion of entrepreneurial activity; passive investment; portfolio diversification; cost of capital; transferability of shares; and insulation from tort liabilities.

Promotion of Entrepreneurial Activity

Limited liability encourages entrepreneurial activity because it allows people to limit the risks involved in conducting business. This is the main function of limited liability in quasi-partnership type companies where raising share capital from persons other than the controllers of the business, or their families, is not normally a realistic option.[87] The importance of this aspect of limited liability should not be over-stated because in a real-life situation it is likely to be whittled away by unlimited personal guarantees which some providers of debt finance to the business may demand from its controllers. To the extent that personal guarantees are given, contractual stipulation overrides the

[84] It has been argued that capital markets would nullify the practical impact of any widescale attempt to withdraw shareholders' limited liability by devising synthetic securities which replicated all of the advantages of shares but which did not adopt that legal form: Grundfest, JA, ' The Limited Future of Unlimited Liability: a Capital Markets Perspective' (1992) 102 Yale Law Journal 387.

[85] This rank order ignores such matters as the costs of the insolvency, priorities between secured creditors (see Ch 15), subordinated creditors (Ch 16), and different classes of shareholders (Ch 9).

[86] Some writers regard limited liability as a device for shifting risk from shareholders to creditors. See Posner, RA, *Economic Analysis of Law* (4th edn, 1992) 394 and Leebron, DW, 'Limited Liability, Tort Victims, and Creditors' (1991) 91 Columbia Law Review 1565, 1584; but contrast Cheffins, BR, *Company Law Theory, Structure and Operation* (1997) 497.

[87] Presser, SB, 'Thwarting the Killing of the Corporation: Limited Liability, Democracy and Economics' (1992) 87 Northwestern University Law Review 148, 163 argues that limited liability was developed in the nineteenth century to facilitate investment in smaller firms and that it 'reflects a traditional American policy to favour the small-scale entrepreneur'.

limited-liability position established by company law.[88] Yet not all creditors of the business will be in a position to demand personal guarantees. Some will lack the necessary bargaining strength whilst others may have no opportunity to bargain because they are the victim of a tort committed by the company. The controllers can thus still derive some benefit from limited liability.[89]

Passive Investment

Limited liability facilitates passive investment, that is, investment on the basis that the investor will not play a part in management. Provided there is a prospect of an adequate return for the risks involved, an investor may be prepared to allow someone else to run a business using his money where there is a cap on the amount that he stands to lose if management fails. Without such a cap a prudent[90] investor might be disinclined to invest in shares at all or, at least, would expect a very high return to compensate for the risks involved. The investor might also want to monitor more closely the way in which the managers of the business conducted its affairs, and that would lead to additional costs.[91]

Because the shareholders have limited liability they may allow the managers to take greater risks in the running of the business than they would if they had to face the prospect of being personally liable without limit for the failure of that project. If the project fails, it is the creditors who will have to absorb the loss over and above the amount of share capital that has been invested. The shareholders benefit from the fact that the creditors also have something to lose, and so may engage in some degree of monitoring of management in order to protect their investment. Here, we begin to see a problem with limited liability in that it is the shareholders who reap the benefit from success because they get capital gains but they do not bear all the risk of failure (sometimes described as a 'moral hazard').[92] The adverse aspects of limited liability are considered in this chapter in the context of groups of companies.[93] For the moment, however, the focus is on successful risk-taking as a positive outcome facilitated by limited liability. Successful risk-taking, as well as benefiting shareholders and ensuring that debts to creditors can be paid when due, may also produce new jobs for employees and contribute to general economic prosperity. Thus there is a public interest in the facilitation of passive investment through the provision of limited liability.

[88] Easterbrook, FH, and Fischel, DR, *The Economic Structure of Corporate Law* (1991) 55–6.

[89] Cheffins, BR, *Company Law Theory, Structure and Operation* (1997) 500–1.

[90] A reckless investor, especially if he or she is virtually insolvent anyway, might not mind taking on such a degree of risk because there is always the option of bankruptcy.

[91] Easterbrook, FH, and Fischel, DR, *The Economic Structure of Corporate Law* (1991) 41–2. But the extent to which shareholders would intensify their monitoring of management could depend on the potential return. If high enough they might still adopt a fairly passive role: Presser, SB, 'Thwarting the Killing of the Corporation: Limited Liability, Democracy and Economics' (1992) 87 Northwestern University Law Review 148, 159.

[92] Cheffins, BR, *Company Law Theory, Structure and Operation* (1997) 497–8; Halpern, P, Trebilcock, M, and Turnbull, S, 'An Economic Analysis of Limited Liability in Corporation Law' (1980) 30 University of Toronto Law Journal 117, 144–5.

[93] See below, at 31–5 and 38–9.

Passive investment means that companies can expand their capital base whilst retaining a cohesive managerial structure involving relatively few individuals who, between them, own only a small portion of the company's issued share capital. It was exactly because large businesses, such as railway companies, needed to expand their capital base in this way that there was such pressure for the enactment of limited liability for the shareholders of registered companies in the middle of the nineteenth century.[94] When it became available under English company law it immediately prompted a spate of new incorporations.[95] The limited-liability company rapidly became the means whereby businesses could raise large amounts of finance from a large spread of investors.[96]

Portfolio Diversification

Limited liability also facilitates portfolio diversification. This is the process whereby an investor can reduce the risks involved in investing in risky securities by constructing a portfolio of investments in which those securities are balanced by others which are low risk but which offer a lower return. Portfolio diversification does not eliminate systematic risk—that is, the risk of variability in returns on investments because of the way that investment markets respond to macro-economic developments, such as changes in the tax regime, or exchange-rate and interest-rate swings. It is all about reducing the specific risks arising from factors which are unique to the individual companies whose shares are included in the portfolio.[97]

Without limited liability, portfolio diversification could not eliminate or reduce the risks associated with investing in specific companies.[98] It would have the opposite effect of increasing risk, because every time an investor added a new share to his portfolio that would expose him to the risk of being personally liable for all of that company's debts.[99] Without portfolio diversification, and in the absence of some alternative way of dealing with risk such as the purchase of insurance,[100] companies seeking to raise share capital from investors would have to offer them a return that compensated them for taking on specific risk as well as systematic risk, with the result that share capital

[94] Baskin, JB, and Miranti, PJ, *A History of Corporate Finance*, 138–45 tracing the nineteenth-century development of limited liability in the UK and the USA.

[95] Davies, PL, *Gower's Principles of Modern Company Law* (6th edn, 1997) 46, n 64; Blumberg, PI, *The Multinational Challenge to Corporation Law: The Search for a New Corporate Personality* (1993) 17–19.

[96] Posner, RA, *Economic Analysis of Law* (4th edn, 1992) 392; Halpern, P, Trebilcock, M, and Turnbull, S, 'An Economic Analysis of Limited Liability in Corporation Law' (1980) 30 University of Toronto Law Journal 117, 118–19; Knight, F, 'Risk, Uncertainty and Profit' in Putterman, L, (ed) *The Economic Nature of the Firm* (1986) 61; Radin, M, 'The Endless Problem of Corporate Personality' (1983) 32 Columbia Law Review 643, 654; Manne, HG, 'Our Two Corporation Systems: Law and Economics' (1967) 53 Virginia Law Review 259, 260.

[97] Posner, RA *Economic Analysis of Law* (4th edn, 1992) 429–34; Manne, HG, 'Our Two Corporation Systems: Law and Economics'(1967) 53 Virginia Law Review 259, 262.

[98] Easterbrook, FH, and Fischel, DR, *The Economic Structure of Corporate Law* (1991) 43.

[99] This assumes a rule of joint and several personal liability. For an analysis of portfolio diversification under a pro rata personal liability rule, see Leebron, DW, 'Limited Liability, Tort Victims, and Creditors' (1991) 91 Columbia Law Review 1565, 1597–600.

[100] On insurance as an alternative to limited liability, see Easterbrook, FH, and Fischel, DR, *The Economic Structure of Corporate Law* (1991) 47–9.

would become a more expensive form of finance. Some investors might be prompted to withdraw altogether from holding shares, which could cause the costs associated with raising capital by issuing shares to increase still further because of the diminution in the size of the pool of finance available in that form.[101] Other investors might concentrate their investment on one or two companies and engage in closer monitoring and control of the management of those companies.

Cost of Capital

The return required by the providers of a company's share capital and debt constitute its cost of capital. A well-run company will keep its cost of capital to the minimum, and corporate finance decisions such as how much debt or share capital to have in the balance sheet, or how much profit to pay out by way of dividend, are all fundamentally about cost of capital.[102] It might be argued that limited liability should not affect cost of capital because all it does is to cause part of the risk of insolvency to fall on creditors rather than shareholders. Thus, to the extent that shareholders can limit their risk, the creditors' risk is increased and that will be reflected in the interest rates charged in respect of debt finance.[103] This argument is superficially appealing but it begins to break down on closer examination.

First, if shareholders did not have limited liability and were personally liable for all of the company's debts, that would still not eliminate the risk to creditors because their chances of being repaid would depend on the creditworthiness of all of the shareholders. Checking the creditworthiness of a large number of persons would be time-consuming and costly, as would enforcing claims against a large number of shareholders in the event of default. Limited liability reduces the costs that creditors have to incur in transacting with companies because they need check only the creditworthiness of the company itself and, in the event of default, need only sue the company. In theory the reduction in transaction costs that follows from limited liability should impact positively on the rates at which the company can borrow.[104]

Secondly, a bank or other professional lender that is considering lending a large amount of money to a company will investigate the company closely and will negotiate the terms of the finance on an individual basis. This, together with the fact that it brings to any new request for finance its accumulated knowledge and experience of lending to companies, should put it in a strong position to assess the risks involved. With the benefit of the information available to it, a professional lender may take a more optimistic view of the risk for

101 Though if investors simply switched to synthetic securities devised by companies to replicate the features of share capital, query whether the overall cost of capital would increase significantly. On the response of the capital markets to the withdrawal of limited liability, see Grundfest, JA, 'The Limited Future of Unlimited Liability: a Capital Markets Perspective' (1992) 102 Yale Law Journal 387.

102 See further Ch 2 below, at 57–8.

103 Halpern, P, Trebilcock, M, and Turnbull, S, 'An Economic Analysis of Limited Liability in Corporation Law' (1980) 30 University of Toronto Law Journal 117, 126–9.

104 Clark, RC, *Corporate Law* (1986) 8–9; Halpern, P, Trebilcock, M, and Turnbull, S, 'An Economic Analysis of Limited Liability in Corporation Law (1980) 30 University of Toronto Law Journal 117, 134–5.

which it requires compensation than potential equity investors would have done.[105] This is not to suggest the equity investors do not have information on which to base their investment decisions, but a few points of contrast may serve to support the proposition that the information that they have may be less detailed than that available to at least some creditors.

The articles of association are, in theory, the contractual mechanism for shareholders to control the management of the business, but a company does not the negotiate the contents of its articles with its shareholders in the manner in which it might negotiate the terms of a major loan-agreement with its bank. The institutional investors who are the main providers of equity finance in the UK—insurance companies and pension funds—maintain an active interest in the contents of the articles of the companies in which they invest[106] and there are also certain requirements with regard to these which are imposed on listed companies by the Stock Exchange.[107] From the time when it begins to seek share capital from outside investors, it is prudent for a company to ensure that its articles meet the expectations of institutional investors and, if it seeks admission to the Stock Exchange as a means of raising capital, it will be required to comply with the requirements of that market. However, these are generally applicable expectations and requirements rather than individually negotiated terms. It is only where a company is unable to meet them in some respect that it will have to provide information to justify its departure from the norm.

A professional lender may seek detailed information about a company's existing business and its plans with a view to framing appropriate restrictive covenants in the loan agreement. It will want to prevent the company from engaging in risky activities which could jeopardise its ability to service the debt and, ultimately, to repay it. After all, its return is capped and it will not benefit from capital gains that may result from such activities. For shareholders, the arguments are the other way: they do hope for capital gain and they do not have an incentive to gather information that will enable them to insist upon the inclusion in the articles of detailed restrictions on the operation of a company's business, since those restrictions could delay the exploitation of an advantageous opportunity. Although the articles can be changed, unless there are only a few shareholders, this is a formal process requiring the convening of a general meeting on at least twenty-one days' notice and the consent of at least three-quarters of the shareholders who vote in person or by proxy at that meeting.

Another possible reason why the savings in cost of capital that flow from limited liability may not necessarily be cancelled out by higher interests rates charged by creditors to compensate them for bearing part of the risk of insolvency is that interest rates are not the only risk-management tool available to creditors. Depending on respective bargaining positions, creditors may be

[105] Clark, RC, *Corporate Law* (1986) 8.

[106] Particularly on sensitive matters such as borrowing limits, provisions requiring directors to retire by rotation and articles regulating when directors are allowed to participate in voting where they have a personal interest in the issue under consideration.

[107] *The Listing Rules*, ch 13, app 1.

able to reduce their risk by taking security or imposing contractual restrictions on the operation of the business. However, some caution is appropriate here because if one creditor accepts a lower rate of interest in return for security, another unsecured creditor may charge a higher rate to compensate it for the risk that, in insolvency, it will rank behind the secured creditor and will have to absorb loss remaining after the shareholders' funds (the equity cushion) have been wiped out. Whether alternative risk-management mechanisms that are available to creditors reduce the total amount of its interests charges is thus a debatable point. It is considered further in Chapter 15.[108]

Transferability of Shares

Unless the articles of association otherwise provide, shares in limited companies are freely transferable. Shares which are admitted to CREST, the UK's mechanism for the electronic trading of securities, are bought and sold without a document of transfer. Otherwise shares are transferred by means of an instrument of transfer[109] in accordance with the formalities prescribed in the Stock Transfer Act 1963 (where the shares have been paid for in full) or the company's articles (where they are not fully paid).[110]

If shareholders had joint and several personal liability for all of their company's debts,[111] a relevant consideration for a person investing in shares would be the ability of other shareholders to pay the company's debts. Prudent shareholders would engage in costly monitoring of each other's wealth[112] and they would want to restrict the transfer of shares so as to ensure that any new shareholders were at least as wealthy as the persons whose shares they acquired. Also, shares prices would not be uniform: the wealth of the person acquiring the shares would affect the price because a wealthy investor could expect to pay less for the same shares than an impecunious one on the basis that he or she would be taking on more of the risk in the event of corporate default.[113] With limited liability, shares are fungible securities and trading can take place on an anonymous basis. Capital markets could not function in the way that they now do without limited liability.

The functioning of the capital markets is relevant to the debate about constraining the power of those who manage companies. For companies with

108 See further Ch 15 below, at 489–490.

109 Companies Act 1985, s 183.

110 Companies Act 1985, s 182.

111 This is only one of the ways in which an unlimited-liability regime might operate. Another is that shareholders might incur liability pro rata to their investment: see Leebron, DW, 'Limited Liability, Tort Victims, and Creditors'(1991) 91 Columbia Law Review 1565, 1578–84; Hansmann, H, and Kraakman, R, 'Towards Unlimited Shareholder Liability for Corporate Torts' (1991) 100 Yale Law Journal 1879, 1892–4. Pro rata liability would remove the incentive to monitor other shareholders' wealth: Leebron, 'DW, 'Limited Liability, Tort Victims, and Creditors' (1991) 91 Columbia Law Review 1565, 1607–8; Hansmann, H, and Kraakman, R, 'Towards Unlimited Shareholder Liability for Corporate Torts' (1991) 100 Yale Law Journal 1879, 1903–6; Presser, SB, 'Thwarting the Killing of the Corporation: Limited Liability, Democracy and Economics' (1992) 87 Northwestern University Law Review 148, 160–1.

112 Easterbrook, FH, and Fischel, DR, *The Economic Structure of Corporate Law* (1991) 42.

113 Halpern, P, Trebilcock, M, and Turnbull, S, 'An Economic Analysis of Limited Liability in Corporation Law' (1980) 30 University of Toronto Law Journal 117, 130–1. Again, the position would be different under a rule of pro rata personal liability: Leebron, DW, 'Limited Liability, Tort Victims, and Creditors' (1991) 91 Columbia Law Review 1565, 1608–10.

outside investors, market forces operate as a constraint on managerial power because shareholders who are dissatisfied with the way that the company is being run can sell their shares. Widespread withdrawal from the company in response to managerial failing in this way will depress the share price and may make the company susceptible to a takeover bid. This process is generally referred to as the 'market for corporate control'.[114] How effectively the market for corporate control is at regulating the misuse of managerial power is considered in Part II of the book. Here the point is that by facilitating the transfer of shares, limited liability plays a key role in making available this control mechanism.

Tort Liabilities

Another function of limited liability is that it insulates shareholders from tort liabilities that may be incurred by their company. If, say, a company pollutes a river or one of its factories blows up, then the persons who are injured or who suffer physical damage to their property can seek compensation from the company. Depending on the seriousness of the accident and the number of victims involved, the compensation costs may be very large. Limited liability means that the shareholders do not have to meet the claims from their personal resources. The victims of the tort will be unsecured creditors in the company's insolvency. They may also have a claim against the company's directors or senior managers as joint tortfeasors but, for this to succeed, they will need to establish that those individuals owed them a duty of care and were in breach of it.[115]

There is considerable theoretical discussion about this aspect of limited liability.[116] Some commentators consider that the veil of incorporation should not be allowed to shield those involved in a company from the consequences of its hazardous activities. It is argued that preserving the veil of incorporation in this situation may encourage excessive risk-taking by companies and operate unfairly in relation to the victims of the tort who, unlike contractual creditors of the company, do not have an opportunity to protect their position through a bargaining process. Alternative ways of dealing with potential tort claims arising from risky activities, such as mandatory insurance, minimum capitalisation requirements and preferential status for tort creditors in insolvency, are examined in the literature.

For the moment it suffices to note that the present practice of the English courts is not to view tort claimants more favourably than contractual creditors

[114] The leading article on this topic is Manne, HG, 'Mergers and the Market for Corporate Control' (1965) *Journal of Political Economy* 110. For a consideration of the issues from a UK perspective see Bradley, C, 'Corporate Control: Markets and Rules' (1990) 53 MLR 170.

[115] *Williams v Natural Life Health Foods Ltd* [1998] 1 WLR 830, HL. See further Grantham, R, and Rickett, C, 'Directors "Tortious" Liability: Contract, Tort or Company Law?' (1999) 62 MLR 133.

[116] The literature includes the following: Leebron, DW, 'Limited Liability, Tort Victims, and Creditors' (1991) 91 Columbia Law Review 1565; Hansmann, H, and Kraakman, R, 'Towards Unlimited Shareholder Liability for Corporate Torts' (1991) 100 Yale Law Journal 1879; Presser, SB, 'Thwarting the Killing of the Corporation: Limited Liability, Democracy and Economics' (1992) 87 Northwestern University Law Review 148, 166–72; Goddard, D, 'Corporate Personality—Limited Recourse and its Limits' in Grantham, R, and Rickett, C (eds), *Corporate Personality in the 20th Century* (1998) 11, 39–40.

in relation to lifting the veil.[117] The debate on this topic is particularly concerned with the situation where the tortfeasor is a subsidiary within a corporate group. Accordingly we return to the issue later in the chapter and explore it further in that context.[118]

Separation of Equity Ownership and Managerial Responsibility

The traditional legal model of the management structure of a company is that the board of directors manages the business in accordance with a provision to that effect in the articles of association.[119] In performing the management function, the directors act as the agent of the company, the separate legal person. They must act in the interests of the company. The directors are not the agents of the shareholders. The constitutional position of the shareholders is that they are the owners of the company. As owners, the shareholders are entitled to exercise some control over the directors, principally through being able to appoint and remove them. The shareholders, as such, do not manage the company. Directors may also be shareholders but there is no mandatory legal rule which obliges them to hold shares in the company they manage.[120]

This model has little practical relevance in relation to one-person companies and quasi-partnership companies where most, if not all, of the shareholders are also involved in management. The formal constitutional division of functions between the board and the shareholders in the general meeting means little in this type of company, because the individuals who are the shareholders/managers are unlikely to pay much attention to whether they are acting as 'shareholders' or as 'managers' as they make the daily decisions that are necessary to the running of the company's business.

Even in its application to larger companies the model may be inaccurate. It is now widely recognised that in larger companies the constitutional managerial structure does not match reality: the board, a formal body that meets, say, once a month, does not itself manage the company on a daily basis but, instead, is concerned with the strategic direction of the company and with the supervision of its managers; the senior executives, who may or may not themselves be directors, actually manage the company. Standards of good corporate governance which were adopted by major companies in the 1990s have reinforced the trend away from direct management by the board of a company. It has become accepted practice for companies to appoint a number of non-executive directors although, in the UK, unlike North America, the present norm is for non-executive directors to be in the minority on the board. Non-executive directors are appointed as independent persons who are not directly involved in the day-to-day affairs of the company. If the board did in fact operate as a hands-on manager, the non-executive directors would rapidly lose their independence and the purpose for which they were

[117] *Adams v Cape Industries* [1990] Ch 433, CA.

[118] See below, at 31–5.

[119] Table A, art 70.

[120] Companies sometimes include a directors' shareholding requirement in their articles of association.

appointed—to provide a more detached perspective—would soon be defeated.

Yet, notwithstanding that the precise location of managerial power may lie with a company's executive officers rather than with its board, the point remains that in larger companies there is a separation of functions between management and shareholding. This separation of functions gives rise to questions about the regulation of management power. These are questions of corporate governance and they are examined more closely in Part II of the book.

THE CORPORATE GROUP

It is commonplace for business to be conducted through a network of connected companies rather than by a single corporate entity.[121] There are a variety of reasons why a structure involving a network of companies may be adopted, including tax planning, regulatory requirements and administrative convenience. Where business is diversified into a number of different and distinct activities, it may be judged to be convenient to establish separate subsidiaries to conduct those separate businesses. Companies may be brought into a corporate group by acquisition and then allowed by their new owner to retain their existing form as part of the network.[122] Analysis of business structures suggests that enterprises which are divided into separate divisions operating as separate profit centres with responsibility for their own administration may be preferable to enterprises that have one central management because the divisional structure reduces the length of chains of command and facilitates the setting of goals and consequential monitoring.[123] However, although the legal rules concerning groups of companies would seem to fit well with the achievement of a multi-divisional management structure, evidence suggests that the divisionalisation that occurs in practice within large

[121] Hadden, T, *The Control of Corporate Groups* (1983) ch 2, analyses in detail the group structure of four multi-national enterprises. Three of the four groups studied in detail comprised at least 170 active companies. The largest British groups at the time of the study (Unilever and BP) were not included in the survey but the author notes that, between them, they had some 2,100 subsidiaries. On the emergence of corporate groups in the USA: Blumberg, PI, *The Multinational Challenge to Corporation Law: The Search for a New Corporate Personality* (1993) ch 3 and Blumberg, PI, 'The American Law of Corporate Groups' in McCahery, J, Piccoitto, S, and Scott, C (eds) *Corporate Control and Accountability* (1993) 305. For comparative studies see Antunes, JE, *Liability of Corporate Groups*, ch 1 and Hadden, T, 'Regulating Corporate Groups: International Perspective' in McCahery, J, Piccoitto, S, and Scott, C (eds) *Corporate Control and Accountability* (1993) 343.

[122] Austin, RP, 'Corporate Groups' in Rickett, CEF, and Grantham, RB, *Corporate Personality in the Twentieth Century* (1998) 741; Wyatt, A, and Mason, R, 'Legal and Accounting Regulatory Framework for Corporate Groups: Implications for Insolvency in Group Operations' (1998) 16 Corporate and Securities Law Journal 424; Muscat, A, *The Liability of The Holding Company for the Debts of its Insolvent Subsidiaries* (1996) 14.

[123] Williamson, OE, 'The Modern Corporation: Origin, Evolution, Attributes' (1981) 19 *Journal of Economic Literature* 1537; Kay, N, 'Corporate Governance and Transaction Costs' in McCahery, J, Piccoitto, S, and Scott, C (eds), *Corporate Control and Accountability* (1993) 133.

organisations may be unrelated to the formal corporate structure of the group.[124]

A powerful consideration in favour of a group structure is that each company in the network is a separate legal person and its shareholders have limited liability. Thus, the corporate group is a structure that can be used to minimise liability and to insulate assets of one part of the business from claims arising from the activities of another part. For a multi-national business, a group structure may provide protection against the risks involved in operating in politically unstable countries.[125] Also, it limits the jurisdiction of the courts of a particular state only to those parts of the business which have a connection with that state. Profits can be taken out of successful companies within a group by means of intra-group dividends[126] but unsuccessful companies can be left to fail with only the loss of the original investment in its share capital and without any further liability to the creditors of those concerns.

There is no separate branch of English company law that deals with corporate groups generally,[127] but for particular purposes the Companies Act 1985 does recognise and attach legal significance to two main[128] types of corporate group: namely, the holding or parent company and its subsidiary companies, and the parent undertaking and its subsidiary undertakings. The latter type of group is relevant for the purposes of consolidated group accounts; the former is employed in other specific statutory contexts.

THE DEFINITION OF THE CORPORATE GROUP FOR ACCOUNTING PURPOSES

The purpose of group accounts is to enable shareholders and creditors of the holding company a clearer picture of the use of their investment than could be gleaned from its individual accounts.[129] The process of drawing up group accounts involves treating the assets and liabilities of all of the companies in

[124] Hadden, T, *The Control of Corporate Groups* (1983) 10, 12–13; Muscat, A, *The Liability of The Holding Company for the Debts of its Insolvent Subsidiaries* (1996) 8–10.

[125] Jones, G, 'Structuring the Relationship—the Group's Viewpoint' in Goode, RM (ed), *Group Trading and the Lending Banker* (1988) 1.

[126] Tax considerations may mean that different structures (eg administration payments) are used in order to move profits around the group: Hadden, T, 'Insolvency and the Group—Problems with Integrated Financing' in Goode, RM (ed), *Group Trading and the Lending Banker* (1988) 71.

[127] Hadden, T, *The Control of Corporate Groups* (1983) 2–3; Tunc, A, 'The Fiduciary Duties of a Dominant Shareholder' in Schmitthoff, CM, and Wooldridge F (eds), *Groups of Companies* (1991) 1–3. Prentice, DD, 'Some Comments on the Law Relating to Corporate Groups' in McCahery, J, Piccoitto, S, and Scott, C (eds), *Corporate Control and Accountability* (1993) 371, 372 argues in favour of the *status quo* and the absence of an area of law on group enterprises generally. His argument is that there is already an abundance of law relating to corporate groups, but for specific purposes and in specific contexts.

[128] Although not developed in the text, it may be noted that other groupings are also recognised (eg associated companies where one has the right to control at least one-third of the voting rights in the other) in certain contexts (eg Companies Act 1985, s 203 (attribution of interests for the purpose of disclosure obligations)).

[129] Napier, C, and Noke, C, 'Premiums and Pre-Acquisition Profits: the Legal and Accountancy Professions and Business Combinations' (1991) 54 MLR 810, 811; Hopt, KJ, 'Legal Issues and Questions of Policy in the Comparative Regulation of Groups' [1996] *I Gruppi di Societa* 45, 54–5.

the group as if they were part of the assets and liabilities of the company that heads the group. The informational value of consolidated accounts depends crucially on how the group is defined. Prior to the coming into force of new provisions in 1990, the corporate group for the purpose of consolidated accounts meant a holding company and its subsidiaries. A company was a subsidiary of another company if that other held the majority of its shares or was entitled to appoint or remove the majority in number of its directors. The definition was defective in that it looked at numerical majorities rather than actual voting control. That meant that a company could control other corporate vehicles without having to include them in its consolidated accounts by the simple device of weighted voting: a company was not a subsidiary of another entity where that other held the minority in number of its shares or had the right to appoint or remove the minority in number of its directors, notwithstanding that the shares held carried the majority of the votes in general meeting or that the directors appointed had the majority of votes at board meetings.

The Companies Act 1989 implemented the Seventh Company Law Directive on consolidated accounts[130] and as a result the definition of the corporate group for accounting purposes changed with effect from April 1990. Consolidated accounts must now be produced in respect of corporate groups comprising a parent undertaking and its subsidiary undertakings. The definitions[131] of parent undertaking and subsidiary undertaking cover parent companies and their subsidiaries using concepts of majority voting control. A company is a parent undertaking (PU) and a company is a subsidiary undertaking (SU) if: (i) PU holds a majority of the voting rights in SU; (ii) PU is a member of SU and has the right to appoint or remove the majority of its board of directors; or (iii) PU is a member of SU and controls alone, pursuant to an agreement with other shareholders, a majority of the voting rights in SU.[132] If SU in turn has a subsidiary (SSU), SSU is also a subsidiary undertaking of PU.[133] It is clear that it is voting rights that matter for this purpose. References to voting rights in a company are to rights conferred on shareholders in respect of their shares or, in the case of a company not having a share capital, on members, to vote at general meetings of the company on all, or substantially all, matters.[134] The reference to the right to appoint or remove a majority of the board of directors is to the right to appoint or remove directors holding a majority of the voting rights at meetings of the board on all, or substantially all, matters.[135]

In addition, a company is a parent undertaking and another company[136] is a subsidiary undertaking if: (i) PU has the right to exercise a dominant influence over SU by virtue of provisions contained in that other memorandum or articles or by virtue of a control contract (legal control); or (ii) PU has a participating interest in SU and actually exercises a dominant influence over it, or it

[130] Directive 83/349/EEC, [1983] OJ L193/1. [131] Companies Act 1985, s 258.
[132] Ibid, s 258. [133] Ibid, s 258 (5). [134] Ibid, sch 10, para 2.
[135] Ibid, sch 10, para 3.
[136] The text concentrates on subsidiary undertakings that are companies but partnerships and unincorporated associations can also be subsidiary undertakings: Companies Act 1985, s 259 (1).

and the other are managed on a unified basis (factual control). These two tests are derived from the Seventh Company Law Directive. Both tests recognise that a company can effectively control other entities even without majority voting control: if the majority of the shareholders are diversified passive investors, each holding a small proportion of its shares, one shareholder with a substantial shareholding may in practice (as a consequence of the voting apathy of other shareholders) be in a position to control the outcome of shareholder meetings notwithstanding that it does not formally control the majority of the votes.

The test based on factual control is more significant in practice but, looking briefly at the legal-control test, one notable feature of this is that there is no express requirement for the parent entity to hold any interest in the shares of the putative subsidiary entity. All it needs to have is the right to exercise a dominant influence.[137] A right to exercise a dominant influence is defined in the Companies Act 1985, sch 10A, para 4(1) as meaning a right to give directions with respect to the operating and financial policies of the other which its directors are obliged to comply with whether or not they are for its benefit. This right must be formally conferred either by the memorandum and articles of the subsidiary undertaking (in which case to be enforceable the parent will have to be a member) or by a control contract. A control contract is defined by the Companies Act 1985, sch 10A, para 4(2) as a contract in writing giving such a right which (i) is of a kind authorised by the memorandum and articles and (ii) is permitted by the law under which that entity is established. In the absence of tax concessions or other favourable treatment, it is difficult of conceive of circumstances where one company would want formally to give another the right to direct its operating and financial policies.[138]

The factual control test is made up of two components: (i) a participating interest; and (ii) either actual exercise of a dominant influence or management on a unified basis. A participating interest is defined in the Companies Act 1985, s 260 as an interest held in the shares of another entity on a long-term basis for the purpose of securing a contribution to that other's activities by the exercise of control or influence arising from, or related to, that interest. There is a presumption that a holding of 20 per cent or more of the shares in an undertaking is a participating interest.[139] Clearly if a company wants to avoid the existence of a parent–subsidiary undertaking relationship between itself and another entity, a sensible pre-emptive step would be to avoid having an interest of 20 per cent or more in the other's share capital; but, if the evidence supports this, a holding of less than 20 per cent may also be held to be a participating interest.

There is no statutory definition of the phrases 'held on a long-term basis', 'actual exercise of a dominant influence' and 'management on a unified

[137] Companies Act 1985, s 258 (2)(c).

[138] The concept of control contracts is derived from German law but even there, and despite attempts by the legislator to render the choice attractive, it has been estimated that in the period been 1970 and 1980 control contracts were concluded for only around 130 corporations: Hopt, KJ, 'Legal Issues and Questions of Policy in the Comparative Regulation of Groups' [1996] *I Gruppi di Societa* 45, 57.

[139] Companies Act 1985, s 260 (2).

basis'. These phrases were lifted directly from the directive in the expectation that guidance on their meaning would be given by accounting standards developed by the relevant standard-setting body, the Accounting Standards Board.[140] *Accounting for Subsidiary Undertakings*, Financial Reporting Standard 2 (FRS 2), defines actual exercise of a dominant influence as being the exercise of an influence that achieves the result that the operating and financial policies of the undertaking influenced are set in accordance with the wishes of the holder of the influence and for its benefit. The actual exercise of a dominant influence is to be identified by looking at the effect in practice. Power of veto may amount to exercise of a dominant influence in an appropriate case, although it is more likely that this would be so where the veto power is held in conjunction with other powers and no similar veto is held by anyone else. The actual exercise of dominant influence may be interventionist or non-interventionist—the latter meaning that the parent's interference occurs only rarely on critical matters. FRS 2 also defines 'managed on a unified basis'. This exists where the whole of the operations of the undertakings are integrated and they are managed as a single unit.

The Definition of the Corporate Group for Other Purposes

Other sections of the companies legislation also employ the concept of the corporate group: for example a subsidiary is prohibited from holding shares in its parent (or holding) company[141] and from giving financial assistance for the acquisition of shares in its parent.[142] Until 1990 the same, defective, definition of the corporate group applied throughout the legislation. When the definitions were changed for accounting purposes, the opportunity was also taken to revise the meaning of the corporate group for other statutory purposes. However, the definition of the corporate group that was adopted for the provisions of the Companies Act 1985 other than accounting requirements is narrower than that for accounting purposes. The narrower definition of the corporate group is that a company is a parent (or holding) company and another company is a subsidiary if (i) P holds a majority of the voting rights in S; (ii) P is a member of S and has the right to appoint or remove the majority of its board of directors; or (iii) P is a member of S and controls alone, pursuant to an agreement with other shareholders, a majority of the voting rights in S.[143] If S in turn has a subsidiary (SS), SS is also a subsidiary of P.[144] A wholly-owned subsidiary is one in which S has no members apart from P or P and other wholly-owned subsidiaries of P.[145] These tests are identical to the first set of tests that are used for the accounting definition of the corporate group and, as there, it is the control of the majority of the voting rights, not the majority in number of the shares or of the directors, that matters.[146] The accounting tests for the existence of a corporate group that are based on legal control and practical control do not apply in this context.

[140] The role of the ASB and the legal significance of accounting standards are outlined in Ch 2 below, at 65–8.

[141] Companies Act 1985, s 23.

[142] Ibid, s 151.

[143] Ibid, s 736 (1).

[144] Ibid, s 736 (1).

[145] Ibid, s 736 (2).

[146] Ibid, s 736A (2)–(3).

Where a company enters into a contract containing provisions that relate to it and other members of its group, or has such provisions in its articles, it is necessary to establish how the group is defined for this purpose. This is a matter of drafting and there is no presumption that either of the statutory definitions applies to contracts or other arrangements to which a company is a party.

The Corporate Group and Liability for the Debts of Insolvent Subsidiaries

The starting-point here is that companies which hold shares in other companies enjoy limited liability in respect of their investment. There is no legal distinction between the liability position of a parent company with respect to the debts of its subsidiaries and that of an individual investor who acquires shares: each is liable only up to the nominal amount of the shares which comprise the investment plus any premium charged in respect of the shares when they were first issued. This means that a network of companies can be formed in order to limit a group's contractual liability to outsiders and to create contractual liability within the members of the group. It also means that it is possible to limit the group's potential exposure to tort victims by conducting hazardous activities through subsidiaries. Should the risky venture end in disaster, the parent will lose the value of its investment in the subsidiary but the creditors of the subsidiary cannot look to it to make good the shortfall in the assets.

An illustration of the use of the corporate form to create contractual liabilities within a group is provided by *Re Polly Peck plc*.[147] In this case a subsidiary, incorporated in the Cayman Islands, made a public issue of debt securities and lent the proceeds to its parent company. The parent company guaranteed the issue. It was held that, as a guarantor, the parent company was a contingent creditor of its subsidiary and was entitled to lodge a proof in its liquidation on that basis. The court refused to lift the veil between the parent and subsidiary. It also rejected the argument that the subsidiary was simply acting as the agent of its parent in issuing the debt securities.

Whether a parent company should be liable for the debts of its insolvent subsidiaries is an issue that is much discussed by academics.[148] An argument for preserving the veil of incorporation between companies within a group is that this facilitates managerial risk-taking, which is important if companies are to expand for the benefit of all of the constituencies who have an interest

[147] [1996] 2 All ER 433.

[148] See in particular, Landers, JM, 'A Unified Approach to Parent, Subsidiary, and Affiliate Questions in Bankruptcy' (1975) 42 University of Chicago Law Review 589; Posner, RA, 'The Rights of Creditors of Affiliated Corporations' (1976) 43 University of Chicago Law Review 499; Landers, JM, ' Another Word on Parents, Subsidiaries and Affiliates in Bankruptcy' (1976) 43 University of Chicago Law Review 527. For an English law perspective see Schmitthoff, CM, 'The Wholly Owned and the Controlled Subsidiary' [1978] JBL 218; Lord Wedderburn, 'Multinationals and the Antiquities of Company Law' (1984) 47 MLR 87; Prentice, DD, 'Some Comments on the Law Relating to Corporate Groups' in McCahery, J, Piccoitto, S, and Scott, C (eds) *Corporate Control and Accountability* (1993) 371; Collins, H, 'Ascription of Legal Responsibility to Groups in Complex Patters of Economic Integration' (1990) 53 MLR 731.

in them and for general economic prosperity.[149] According to this argument, investors will be encouraged to invest in the shares of a holding company which caps its potential losses in respect of particularly risky activities to the amount of share capital which it invests in the subsidiaries through which those activities are conducted.[150] Another reason for preserving the veil is that contractual creditors assume that each company will be liable for its own debts but no more, and bargain accordingly. If lifting the veil within a corporate group were to become commonplace, with the result that the principle that a company's assets are only available to pay the debts owing to its own creditors could no longer be assumed, that could add to companies' costs of borrowing because creditors might want to extend their investigations into the creditworthiness of the group as a whole.[151]

At the most basic level, the argument for lifting the veil within a corporate group relates to control: a corporate group is, ultimately, an integrated economic enterprise and the parent controls, or has the power to control, its subsidiaries' activities for the benefit of the group as a whole; therefore, the parent should be liable for the activities of its subsidiaries.[152] Whilst the individuals who hold shares in a small private company may also be its controllers, their position is not analogous to that of a parent company because they could be personally ruined in the event of lifting the veil to make them liable for the company's debts; lifting the veil between parent and subsidiary company might make the parent insolvent but the shareholders in the parent would still be shielded from personal liability by the limited liability that they would continue to enjoy in respect of their investment.[153] Also, economic arguments about limited liability being necessary to enable companies to attract passive investment, to allow investors to engage in portfolio diversification and to permit the functioning of capital markets do not apply in relation to a parent company's investment in a subsidiary.[154] Strict adherence to the preservation of the veil of incorporation may encourage excessive risk-taking by managers:[155] whereas if an independent company which is not part of a group (or which is the holding company of a group) fails, the management will lose their jobs, that constraint against risk-taking is less powerful in relation to a subsidiary because there is always the possibility of its management being redeployed in other parts of the group in the event of its failure.[156] Also, although directors are legally obliged to act in the interests of their own com-

[149] Leebron, DW, 'Limited Liability, Tort Victims and Creditors' (1991) 91 Columbia Law Review 1565, 1617–18.

[150] Presser, SB, 'Thwarting the Killing of the Corporation: Limited Liability, Democracy and Economics' (1992) 87 Northwestern University Law Review 148, 174–5; Blumberg, PI, *The Multinational Challenge to Corporation Law: The Search for a New Corporate Personality* (1993) 130–3.

[151] Posner, RA, *Economic Analysis of Law* (4th edn, 1992) 409.

[152] Blumberg, PI, *The Multinational Challenge to Corporation Law: The Search for a New Corporate Personality* (1993) 123–4; Antunes, JE, *Liability of Corporate Groups* (1994) 131–2.

[153] Posner, RA, 'The Rights of Creditors of Affiliated Corporations' (1976) 43 University of Chicago Law Review 499, 511–12.

[154] Blumberg, PI, *The Multinational Challenge to Corporation Law: The Search for a New Corporate Personality* (1993) 133–40.

[155] Ibid, 134.

[156] Easterbrook, FH, and Fischel, DR, *The Economic Structure of Corporate Law* (1991) 56–7.

pany and not in the interests of the group of companies to which it may belong,[157] the distinction between group interests and those of the individual companies can easily become blurred in practice; and, except where there are insolvency concerns, irregularities or breaches of duty by the directors of a group company can, in any event, be cured by the passing of a ratifying resolution by any other companies in the group which are the owners of its shares. The net result of these considerations is that companies within a group may deal with each other otherwise than on an arms' length basis[158] to the detriment of creditors who cannot object unless they have imposed contractual restrictions on such activities, and of minority shareholders in the subsidiaries whose only effective means of redress may be to allege that such dealing constitutes unfairly prejudicial relief from which they should be granted relief under the Companies Act 1985, s 459.[159] A particular argument for lifting the veil within a corporate group is that limited liability operates unfairly in relation to the victims of torts by subsidiaries since they cannot negotiate around it.[160]

Whatever the theoretical attraction of these competing arguments, it is not the practice of the English courts to adopt a single enterprise approach[161] and to disregard the separate incorporation of each of the individual companies within the group, even where tort liability is involved. The courts emphasise the importance of maintaining the principle that the assets of a company are available to pay its creditors and no others.[162] The leading case is the decision of the Court of Appeal in *Adams v Cape Industries plc*[163] which was an attempt by victims of a tort (ie personal injuries suffered as a consequence of exposure to asbestos dust) to enforce a judgment that had been obtained in the USA. The company-law point in issue was whether the US courts could assert jurisdiction over an English company on the basis of the presence within the USA of certain subsidiaries. The court rejected the argument that the various

[157] *Lindgren v L & P Estates Ltd* [1968] Ch 572, CA.

[158] Hadden identifies intra-group lending with little or no consideration of appropriate interest charges as a particularly salient form of abuse: Hadden, T, *The Control of Corporate Groups* (1983) 15–18.

[159] *Scottish Co-operative Wholesale Society v Meyer* [1959] AC 324, HL; but contrast *Nicholas v Soundcraft Electronics Ltd* [1993] BCLC 360 CA. *Stein v Blake* [1998] 1 All ER 724, CA, illustrates the type of problems that can occur within a corporate group (transfers of assets by the controlling shareholder). The Court of Appeal held that the other shareholder had no personal common-law claim arising from the facts.

[160] Leebron DW, 'Limited Liability, Tort Victims, and Creditors' (1991) 91 Columbia Law Review 1565, 1612–26; Blumberg, PI, *The Multinational Challenge to Corporation Law: The Search for a New Corporate Personality* (1993) 135–6. But, as Blumberg notes (136–8), it may be overly simplistic to regard all contract creditors in the same way. Many contractual creditors have no real opportunity to engage in bargaining, junior employees being an example that springs readily to mind. Prentice, DD, 'Groups of Companies: The English Experience' in Hopt, KJ (ed), *Groups of Companies in European Laws* (1982) 99, 105 describes employees (and the revenue authorities) as 'quasi-involuntary creditors' who normally do not contract around limited liability. Prentice would also include unsecured trading creditors in the category of those who do not normally engage in such bargaining.

[161] Contrast Berle, AA, 'The Theory of Enterprise Entity' (1947) 47 Columbia Law Review 343 and Blumberg, PI, *The Multinational Challenge to Corporation Law: The Search for a New Corporate Personality* (1993) ch 5, both of whom discuss the increasing acceptance of enterprise principles in the US courts and legislation.

[162] See *Charterbridge Corpn v Lloyd's Bank Ltd* [1970] Ch 62; *Ford & Carter Ltd v Midland Bank Ltd* (1979) 129 NLJ 543, HL, 544 *per* Lord Wilberforce.

[163] [1990] Ch 433, CA.

companies should be treated as one group enterprise. It reaffirmed the fundamental legal principle that each company in a group of companies is a separate legal entity possessed of separate rights and liabilities.[164] It distinguished earlier cases[165] appearing to support a group-enterprise approach as being concerned with specific statutes or contracts which justified the treatment of parent and subsidiary as one unit. Rather surprisingly in view of its outright rejection in the *Adams* decision, a group-enterprise argument resurfaced in *Re Polly Peck plc*.[166] The court there regarded as persuasive the argument that in reality the issue of debt securities was by the group rather than by the Cayman Islands subsidiary through which it had been channelled but ruled that it was precluded by *Adams*, a decision of a higher court, from accepting the group-enterprise approach.[167]

The Court of Appeal in the *Adams* case confirmed[168] that the court does not have a general discretion to disregard the veil of incorporation on grounds of justice. With regard to the argument that the corporate structure in that case was a façade, because it had been adopted to remove group assets from the USA to avoid liability for asbestos claims whilst at the same time continuing to trade in asbestos there, the court concluded:

> [W]e do not accept as a matter of law that the court is entitled to lift the corporate veil as against a defendant company which is the member of a corporate group merely because the corporate structure has been used so as to ensure that the legal liability (if any) in respect of particular future activities of the group (and correspondingly the risk of enforcement of that liability) will fall on another member of the group rather than the defendant company. Whether or not this is desirable, the right to use a corporate structure in this manner is inherent in our corporate law. [Counsel] urged on us that the purpose of the operation was in substance that Cape would have the practical benefit of the group's asbestos trade in the United States of America without the risk of tortious liability. This may be so. However, in our judgment, Cape was in law entitled to organise the group's affairs in that manner.[169]

Looked at from the present English law perspective,[170] therefore, it is difficult to avoid the conclusion that lifting the veil as a means of achieving group lia-

[164] *The Albazero* [1977] AC 774, CA and HL, 807 *per* Roskill LJ.

[165] Including the notorious decision of the Court of Appeal in *DHN Food Distributors Ltd v Tower Hamlets London Borough Council* [1976] 1 WLR 852, CA. The judgment of Lord Denning MR in this case is probably the most positive endorsement of the group-enterprise approach in English law. The authority of the case is now slim: as well as being distinguished in *Adams* its correctness was doubted by the Scottish House of Lords in *Woolfson v Strathclyde Regional Council*, 1978 SLT 159, HL.

[166] [1996] 2 All ER 433.

[167] Ibid, 447. Counsel's argument was based on the acceptance in *Adams v Cape Industries plc* [1990] Ch 433, CA, of special cases where contract or statute permitted or required a group-enterprise approach, but the court refused to put the insolvency rule against double proof into this special category.

[168] *Woolfson v Strathclyde Regional Council*, 1978 SLT 159, HL.

[169] [1990] Ch 433, CA, 544.

[170] Judicial conservatism with regard to lifting the veil is not confined to the English courts. Discussing the position in Australia and New Zealand, see Baxt, R, and Lane, T, 'Developments in Relation to Corporate Groups and the Responsibilities of Directors—Some Insights and New Directions' (1998) 16 Corporate and Securities Law Journal 628; Farrar, JH, 'Legal Issues Involving Corporate Groups' (1998) 16 Corporate and Securities Law Journal 184.

bility is a non-starter even in relation to what may be considered the most deserving case, namely the tort victims of a subsidiary company.[171]

Alternatives to Lifting the Veil: Agency[172]

If it can be shown that a subsidiary acted as the agent of its parent, then, on ordinary agency principles, the liability will attach to the principal parent, not to the subsidiary.[173] However, there is no presumption that a subsidiary acts as the agent of its parent and this will depend on the facts pertaining to the relationship between parent and subsidiary.[174] Insufficient capital to engage in business independently can be an indicator that the subsidiary is an agent,[175] but capitalisation needs to be considered in conjunction with the purpose for which the subsidiary exists: for example, if a subsidiary is established purely as a vehicle for the raising of capital it may have a very small capital (with alternative forms of credit enhancement being built into the terms of the issue) but still be an independent operator rather than an agent.[176] Evidence that the subsidiary has a board of directors all or most of whom are also directors or senior executives of the holding company does not necessarily indicate an agency relationship between it and the parent company.[177]

Alternatives to Lifting the Veil: Contractual Guarantees

It is a trite observation that creditors of a failing company who are in the fortunate position of holding guarantees from other companies in its group may be able to shift the liability around the group by enforcing their contractual claims. There are some potential pitfalls that persons considering lending to a group company on the security of personal guarantees from other companies in its group need to look out for. One is that the other group companies may seek to resist giving guarantees and instead offer comfort letters in which they state that it is their policy to ensure that other companies in the group are, and will be, in a position to meet their liabilities. In *Kleinwort Benson Ltd v Malaysia Mining Corporation Bhd*[178] the Court of Appeal held that a comfort letter in these terms was merely a statement of present fact regarding intentions and that it was not a contractual promise as to future conduct. Another is that directors are required to act in the interests of their own company

[171] Prentice, DD, ' Group Indebtedness' in Schmitthoff, CM, and Wooldridge F (eds), *Groups of Companies* (1991) 77: 'piercing the corporate veil is very much the exception to the rule and probably in the majority of cases the courts will refuse to do so'.

[172] Some form of trust–beneficiary or nominator–nominee relationship between companies in a group could also suffice to shift liability.

[173] *Canada Rice Mills Ltd v R* [1939] 3 All ER 991, PC; *Firestone Tyre and Rubber Co Ltd v Lewellin (Inspector of Taxes)* [1957] 1 All ER 561, HL; *Rainham Chemical Works v Belvedere Fish Guano Co* [1921] 2 All ER 465, HL.

[174] *Adams v Cape Industries plc* [1990] Ch 433, CA.

[175] *Re FG Films* [1953] 1 All ER 615. Landers, JM, 'A Unified Approach to Parent, Subsidiary, and Affiliate Questions in Bankruptcy' (1975) 42 University of Chicago Law Review 589, 621.

[176] *Re Polly Peck plc* [1996] 2 All ER 433, 445–6.

[177] Ibid.

[178] [1989] 1 WLR 379, CA. See also *Re Atlantic Computers plc* [1995] BCC 696.

rather than that of the group as a whole.[179] If directors focus on the interests of the group and these do not coincide with the interests of their company, the guarantee will thus be tainted by breach of duty. Yet another potential pitfall is that if the solvency of the guarantor company is in doubt the guarantee may be vulnerable under provisions of the Insolvency Act 1986 concerned with preferences and transactions at an undervalue.[180]

Alternatives to Lifting the Veil: Tort Claims[181]

In particular circumstances a parent company may be jointly liable in tort with a subsidiary, or sister subsidiaries may be joint tortfeasors. Whether liability can be spread around a corporate group in this way depends on the application of the ordinary principles of the law of tort for the determination of liability. Sole personal liability may also sometimes exist, as where, for example, a parent company has deceived someone into contracting with its subsidiary by issuing spurious information about it.

Alternatives to Lifting the Veil: Insolvency Act 1986

Another way of shifting liability for the debts of an insolvent subsidiary onto its parent company under English law as it stands at present may be through the provisions of the Insolvency Act 1986 concerned with fraudulent and wrongful trading.[182] These sections were not specifically drafted with the parent–subsidiary relationship in mind. As they have been interpreted, it would seem that they will have limited application in the context of carefully managed corporate groups.

Under the Insolvency Act 1986, s 213, if it appears that any business of a company that is in the process of being wound up has been carried on with intent to defraud creditors or for any fraudulent purpose, the court, on the application of the liquidator, may declare that persons who were knowingly party to the carrying-on of the business in that manner are to be liable to make such contributions to the company's assets as the court thinks proper. A parent company could, depending on the facts, be knowingly a party to the carrying-on of the business of an insolvent subsidiary, but the limitation on the practical application of this section is that it requires fraud. Fraud in this context means 'actual dishonesty, involving real moral blame'[183] and that could be difficult to establish.[184]

[179] See further Ch 5 below, at 159–60.

[180] Insolvency Act 1986, ss 238–41. The transaction at an undervalue provision (s 238) has been interpreted restrictively: *Re MC Bacon Ltd* [1990] BCLC 324.

[181] See further, Muscat, A, *The Liability of The Holding Company for the Debts of its Insolvent Subsidiaries* (1996) 125–34.

[182] See also, Yeung, K, 'Corporate Groups: Legal Aspects of the Management Dilemma' [1997] LMCLQ 208 who considers the potential for parent-company personal liability for involvement in breaches of duty by directors of subsidiary companies under the principle in *Barnes v Addy* (1874) LR 9 Ch App 244.

[183] *Re Patrick and Lyon Ltd* [1933] 1 Ch 786.

[184] *Re Augustus Barnett & Son Ltd* (1986) 2 BCC 98,904 where an attempt to make a parent company liable under the then equivalent of s 213 failed.

The Insolvency Act 1986, s 214 allows the court to order persons who knew or ought to have concluded that the company had no reasonable prospect of avoiding insolvent liquidation to contribute to the assets of a company in liquidation unless they can establish that they took every step that ought to have been taken with a view to minimising the potential loss to the company's creditors. The judgment standards under this section are based on objective criteria rather than personal morality and honesty: a person is to be judged on the basis of his own knowledge, skill and experience and also the knowledge, skill and experience that could reasonably be expected of someone carrying out his functions in relation to the company.[185]

The limitation of the Insolvency Act 1986, s 214 is that it only applies to the directors of the failed company. Directors for this purpose include shadow directors,[186] that is, persons on whose instructions or directions the actual directors[187] are accustomed to act.[188] A parent company would not typically be a director of its subsidiaries but it could potentially be caught as a shadow director. Four facts must be established in relation to a shadow directorship allegation: (i) the identity of the actual directors; (ii) that the alleged shadow director directed the governing majority, if not all,[189] of the actual directors how to act in relation to the company or was one of the persons who did so; (iii) that those directors acted in accordance with such directions; and (iv) that they were accustomed so to act.[190] Relationships can be structured so as to minimise the risk of one party being held to be a shadow director of another: for example, a provider of finance to an ailing company should impose conditions on its offer of finance which the company is free to accept in preference to lending the money with instructions as to how it is to be used. Whether a parent company is a shadow director of its subsidiary will depend on the factual relationship between them.[191] It must be shown that it was the regular practice of the subsidiary board to follow directions from the parent.[192]

[185] Insolvency Act 1986, s 214 (4).

[186] And also de facto directors, ie persons who are not formally appointed as directors but who function as such: *Re Hydrodan (Corby) Ltd* [1994] BCC 161.

[187] Including de facto directors: *Re Hydrodan (Corby) Ltd* [1994] BCC 161.

[188] Insolvency Act 1986, s 251. There is an express exclusion of parent companies from the category of shadow director in respect of certain provisions of the Companies Act 1985 (s 741(3) of that Act) but there is no such exemption under the Insolvency Act 1986.

[189] *Re Unisoft Group Ltd (No 2)* [1994] BCC 766, 775. Harman J inclined to the view that the shadow director would have to direct the whole board but declined to exclude the possibility that direction of its governing majority might suffice.

[190] *Re Hydrodan (Corby) Ltd* [1994] BCC 161.

[191] *Shadow Directorships* (Financial Law Panel) (1994). In an Australian case the factual evidence indicated that a 42 per cent shareholder controlled the affairs of a company to such an extent that it was liable under a provision extending liability to a person in accordance with whose directions or instructions the directors were accustomed to act: *Standard Chartered Bank v Antico* (1995) 18 ACSR 1, NSW SC.

[192] *Re Unisoft Group Ltd (No 2)* [1994] BCC 766. Prentice, DD, 'Corporate Personality, Limited Liability and the Protection of Creditors' in Grantham, R, and Rickett, C, *Corporate Personality in the 20th Century* (1998) 99, 115–18.

THE CASE FOR REFORM

Although *Adams v Cape Industries plc*[193] has tilted the present attitude of English case law away from lifting the veil within corporate groups, the regulation of corporate groups and the problems of insolvent subsidiaries remain issues of concern. In the major economies of the world, including the UK, company law developed originally in relation to companies which had shareholders who were human beings and it was then applied by extension to companies whose share capital was owned by other companies.[194] Whether that extension, which permits corporate groups to exploit multiple tiers of limited liability, is appropriate or whether there should be a specific body of law on enterprise liability is the key issue.[195]

The problem of the insolvent subsidiary can be sketched in emotive terms:

> A parent company may spawn a number of subsidiary companies, all controlled directly or indirectly by the shareholders of the parent company. If one of the subsidiary companies, to change the metaphor, turns out to be the runt of the litter and declines into insolvency to the dismay of its creditors, the parent company and other subsidiary companies may prosper to the joy of the shareholders without any liability for the debts of the insolvent company.[196]

In many cases, a prosperous parent company cannot or will not abandon a failing subsidiary and its creditors, either because it has guaranteed the subsidiary's debts or is anxious not to damage the commercial reputation of the group.[197] Also, to the extent that responsibility for the failure can be placed on the shoulders of the subsidiary's board, directors'-liability insurance payments may augment the assets of the subsidiary available to pay its creditors. Nevertheless, the fact remains that in the absence of contractual guarantee obligations, a tort claim or an agency or analogous relationship, a parent company is free to walk away: where the debts of the subsidiary are of such magnitude as to threaten the solvency of the parent, the advantages of abandonment may outweigh the damage to the reputation of the group. In this respect, English law is now notably different from that in Australia and New Zealand where special rules on intra-group liability have been enacted.[198] It is also in

[193] [1990] Ch 433, CA.

[194] Antunes, JE, *Liability of Corporate Groups* (1994) 30–4; Muscat, A, *The Liability of The Holding Company for the Debts of its Insolvent Subsidiaries* (1996) ch 4.

[195] Blumberg, PI, *The Multinational Challenge to Corporation Law: The Search for a New Corporate Personality* (1993) ch 11. The author advocates a general regime of enterprise law which would include, but not be limited to, enterprise liability. See also, Blumberg, PI, 'The American Law of Corporate Groups' in McCahery, J, Piccoitto, S, and Scott, C (eds) *Corporate Control and Accountability* (1993) 305, but contrast Prentice, DD, 'Some Comments on the Law Relating to Corporate Groups' in ibid, 371; Muscat, A, *The Liability of The Holding Company for the Debts of its Insolvent Subsidiaries* (1996) ch 7.

[196] *Re Southard* [1979] 1 WLR 1198 CA.

[197] Hadden, T, *The Control of Corporate Groups* (1983) 23–4; Hopt, KJ, 'Legal Issues and Questions of Policy in the Comparative Regulation of Groups' [1996] *I Gruppi di Societa* 45.

[198] Corporations Law Pt 5.7B, div 5 (Australia); Companies Act 1993, ss 271–2 (New Zealand). On the Australian law see further: Ford, HAJ, Austin, RP, and Ramsay, IM, *Ford's Principles of Corporations Law* (8th edn, 1997) 836–40. See also, Ramsay, IM, 'Holding Company Liability for the Debts of an Insolvent Subsidiary: A Law and Economics Perspective' (1994) 17 University of New South Wales Law Journal 520.

contrast to the position in other member states of the European Union.[199] That English law may be deficient in not making special provision for group liability has been judicially acknowledged.[200]

The Cork Committee reviewed insolvency law and practice in the UK in the early 1980s and their report contained a chapter on group trading.[201] The Committee noted that 'some of the basic principles of company and insolvency law fit uneasily with the modern commercial realities of group enterprise'.[202] Intra-group transfers of assets at an undervalue, lending between group companies on other than commercial terms, gratuitous guarantees by one group company of another group company's debts and intra-group dividends paid without reference to the cash needs of the paying company were identified as the type of transactions that gave rise to concern.[203] Despite its concern and its acknowledgement that the law was defective,[204] the Committee refrained from making detailed recommendations save for one regarding the subordination of intra-group debts in the event of the insolvency of a company within the group.[205] The Committee considered that this proposal should also apply to connected persons such as directors.[206] That was clearly right since, as the saga of Mr Salomon vividly demonstrates, it is not just corporate shareholders who may finance a company mainly by means of loan finance, with a view not to achieving the best capital structure for the company but to securing a ranking in the company's insolvency higher than that afforded to providers of share capital. In US law, where equitable subordination of 'insider' debts in insolvency is established, insiders who are human beings, as well as those who are companies, are liable to have their debts subordinated to those of other creditors.[207] There is an immediate appeal in a proposal to subordinate debts owing to insiders to those of external creditors, since the lending giving rise to those debts is likely to have taken place otherwise than on an arms' length basis and on the basis of the interests of the group as a whole or of the connected person rather than that of the lending company. However, the proposal was not implemented in the insolvency legislation that followed from the report of the Cork Committee.

The Cork Committee stated a number of reasons justifying its decision to refrain from making more extensive recommendations with regard to insolvent subsidiaries in the context of its report.[208] First, an alteration of the law so as to make a parent company liable for its insolvent subsidiary's debts would

199 On the relevant French and German provisions: Wooldridge, F, *Groups of Companies The Law and Practice in Britain, France and Germany* (1981). There is a special provision for group liability in Irish companies legislation: Irish Companies Act 1990, s 140.

200 *Re Southard & Co Ltd* [1979] 1 WLR 1198, CA ; *Re Augustus Barnett & Son Ltd* (1986) 2 BCC 98,904, 98,908. See also *Qintex Australia Finance Ltd v Schroeders Australia Ltd* (1990) 3 ACSR 267, NSW SC ComD; *Re Spargos Mining NL* (1990) 3 ACSR 1, WA SC.

201 *Insolvency Law and Practice* Cmnd 8558 (1982) ch 51.

202 Ibid, para 1922. 203 Ibid, para 1926. 204 Ibid, para 1934.

205 It is established in the USA that the claims (as a creditor) of a controller of a company can be subordinated to the claims of the other creditors (the 'Deep Rock' doctrine): Landers, JM, 'A Unified Approach to Parent, Subsidiary, and Affiliate Questions in Bankruptcy' (1975) 42 University of Chicago Law Review 589, 597–606.

206 *Insolvency Law and Practice* Cmnd 8558 (1982) para 1963.

207 Clark, RC, *Corporate Law* (1986) 52–71.

208 *Insolvency Law and Practice* Cmnd 8558 (1982) paras 1390–952.

introduce a difference between types of shareholders (corporate or individual) with regard to the fundamental principle of limited liability. That could affect entrepreneurial activity as it might deter a prosperous company from embarking upon new ventures. Secondly, the Committee was concerned about the problems of allocating and apportioning liability. This concern had a number of facets: determining precisely what relationship between companies should trigger financial responsibility; to the extent that there might be financial responsibility for companies that were only partly-owned subsidiaries, whether the parent could have any claims against the minority shareholders; whether financial responsibility for an insolvent subsidiary should lie only with its parent or with all the groups in the group; and, to what extent there should be parental or group liability for debts incurred by an insolvent subsidiary at a time when it was not a member of the group. Thirdly, the Committee was also concerned about the foreign element, that is the extent to which, if at all, there should be parental or group liability for the debts of an insolvent foreign corporation. Fourthly, there were questions about the position of existing long-term creditors of companies when any changes in the law would be introduced; the creditors of, say, a parent company, would be adversely affected by a law which made the parent responsible for the debts of a subsidiary unless complex transitional arrangements could be devised to prevent the legislation operating retrospectively to the detriment of those existing creditors. In sum, the Committee concluded that the implications of a change to some form of group-enterprise liability would spread throughout company law and that a fundamental change to company law could not properly be introduced by means of proposals to change insolvency law. The Committee called for a wide review of the whole issue of group-enterprise liability with a view to the introduction of reforming legislation within the foreseeable future. Yet, almost two decades later, that review has not occurred.

As the Cork Committee noted, one of the key issues in the development of an enterprise or group-liability rule under English law would be that of control.[209] It would be obviously unwise to provide for a parent to be liable only in respect of the debts of its wholly-owned subsidiaries since the liability could be all too easily avoided by the inclusion of minority shareholders in group companies.[210] To have any real effect in practice, the legislation would need to cast the net wider. This would make it necessary to decide whether the precondition for the imposition of liability should be the existence of a parent and subsidiary relationship, a parent undertaking and subsidiary undertaking relationship, or some other formal association between the two companies.[211]

[209] Leebron, DW, 'Limited Liability, Tort Victims and Creditors' (1991) 91 Columbia Law Review 1565, 1619–23; Schmitthoff, CM, 'The Wholly Owned and the Controlled Subsidiary' [1978] JBL 218, 226–9; Muscat, A, *The Liability of The Holding Company for the Debts of its Insolvent Subsidiaries* (1996) ch 2. Avoidance of questions about the precise distribution of share ownership is one of the advantages of shadow directorship liability: Collins, H, 'Ascription of Legal Responsibility to Groups in Complex Patters of Economic Integration' (1990) 53 MLR 731, 741.

[210] Blumberg, PI, *The Multinational Challenge to Corporation Law: The Search for a New Corporate Personality* (1993) 142–7.

[211] The Irish Companies Act 1990, s 140 imposes an obligation to contribute towards the liabilities of an insolvent 'related' company. The definition of a related company includes, but is

The position of minority shareholders in a partially-owned subsidiary or subsidiary undertaking would then have to be addressed. Whatever way the group was defined at a technical level there would still be some scope for devising structures that secured 'parental' control over entities without resulting in liability, although the parent and subsidiary undertaking approach would clearly curb such creativeness more effectively than the parent and subsidiary formula. An example of a structure which might not be caught even under the parent and subsidiary undertaking formula is provided by the facts of *Multinational Gas and Petrochemical Co v Multinational Gas and Petrochemical Services Ltd.*[212] A joint venture company failed with debts amounting to nearly £114 million. Its three shareholders were international oil companies. They did not contribute to the assets of the failed venture and the liquidator's various attempts to swell its assets by alleging negligence against its directors and against the oil companies failed at an early stage. Two of the oil companies each held 40 per cent of share capital of the venture vehicle with the remaining 20 per cent being held by the third oil company. It is not apparent from the report of the case that any one of the oil companies had the right to appoint the voting majority of the directors of the venture vehicle. Accordingly that vehicle was not the subsidiary of any of the oil companies and, so, would not be caught by a liability rule based on a parent and subsidiary relationship even though its board had acted entirely at the behest of, and in accordance with directions from, the oil companies. With regard to the limb of the parent and subsidiary undertaking relationship that is concerned with practical control, the stake held by each of the oil companies was large enough to be presumed to be a participating interest, but it is not evident from the report that any one of the oil companies exercised a dominant influence over the vehicle or managed its business on a unified basis with its own.

Another factor that would need to be resolved in the formulation of a group liability rule would be whether liability should be based simply on the existence of a designated formal relationship such as parent and subsidiary, or parent and subsidiary undertaking, or should, in addition, require evidence that the parent did in fact control the operations of the subsidiary or manage it on an integrated basis with its own business.[213] The general trend in jurisdictions which have some form of group liability is for this to be triggered by factual control over other group companies rather than simply by the formal

wider than, that of parent and subsidiary. It is also different from the concept of the corporate group for the consolidated accounts requirements of the Irish legislation: Forde, M, *Company Law* (revd edn, 1992) 458–9. Generally, on formalism and legal control: McBarnet, D, and Whelan, C, 'The Elusive Spirit of the Law: Formalism and the Struggle for Legal Control' (1991) 54 MLR 848.

[212] [1983] 2 All ER 563, CA.

[213] Blumberg, PI, *The Multinational Challenge to Corporation Law: The Search for a New Corporate Personality* (1993) 245–6; Antunes, JE, *Liability of Corporate Groups* (1994) 495: 'In deciding whether the parent corporation should be made liable or not for the debts of one group affiliate, the decisive question to ask should be *whether the particular business decision(s) from which the concrete liabilities in dispute arose was (were) taken under the autonomous decision-making authority of the subsidiary corporation or under the control exercised by the parent*' (author's emphasis). The author suggests that it should be for the parent company to prove that the decision was taken autonomously by the subsidiary.

relationship. For example, the New Zealand legislation gives the court the power to order a related company of a company that is in liquidation to pay the whole or any part of the claims that have been submitted in the liquidation.[214] In deciding whether it is just and equitable to make such an order the court is directed to have regard to a number of matters, including the extent to which the related company took part in the management of the insolvent company, the conduct of the related company towards the creditors of the insolvent company and the extent to which the actions that give rise to the liquidation are attributable to the actions of the related company.[215]

Looking to Europe for Reform

In the view of one distinguished commentator on comparative company law, the problems of corporate groups are likely to languish as a backwater of reform in the UK until such time as the issue is forced upon us through membership of the European Union.[216] The draft Ninth Directive on company law[217] proposed the introduction of a regime in member states whereby, broadly, corporate groups could choose between a form of integrated operation which would entail group liability, or a form of operation in which the financial and managerial independence of the companies within the group would have to be respected and there would be no group liability.[218] The draft, which was loosely based on existing German law,[219] received a hostile reception when it was introduced, and that proposal has not been developed. Regulation of corporate groups nevertheless remains an issue that European-harmonisation initiatives may seek to address,[220] or it may be that some form of regulation could emerge as a result of decisions of the European Court of Justice. Already, in the context of European competition law, the European Court of Justice has shown a willingness to treat a corporate group as a single enterprise.[221]

An argument that is sometimes voiced is that there is little merit in overhauling domestic legislation in advance of European developments in the same field.[222] Yet waiting for Europe to lead the way in reforming the law relating to corporate groups could prove to be misguided. In other areas of English company law (such as the rules relating to share capital) the scope for radical

[214] Companies Act 1993, s 271.

[215] Ibid, s 272.

[216] Farrar, JH, 'Legal Issues Involving Corporate Groups' (1998) 16 Corporate and Securities Law Journal 184, 201.

[217] Commission Document III/1639/84-EN.

[218] Hadden, T, 'Insolvency and the Group—Future Developments' in Goode, RM (ed), *Group Trading and the Lending Banker* (1988) 101, 103–8.

[219] On which see: Hopt, KJ, 'Legal Elements and Policy Decisions in Regulating Groups of Companies' in Schmitthoff, CM, and Wooldridge F (eds), *Groups of Companies* (1991) ch V, and Wooldridge, F, *Groups of Companies The Law and Practice in Britain, France and Germany* (1981).

[220] Hopt, KJ, 'Legal Issues and Questions of Policy in the Comparative Regulation of Groups' [1996] *I Gruppi di Societa* 45.

[221] *Istituto Chemioterapio Italiano SpA and Commercial Solvents Corp v EC Commission* [1974] ECR 223; *SAR Schotte GmbH v Parfums Rothschild SARL* [1992] BCLC 235, ECJ.

[222] eg, *Comments on 'A Review of Security Interests in Property' by Professor AL Diamond* (Law Society Company Law Committee with the participation of the Joint Working Party of the Bar and the Law Society on Banking Law) (Nov 1989) (No 211) 4.

reform—as has taken place in some Commonwealth countries that, historically, had company law based closely on English law—is much reduced because of the need to ensure compliance with European directives. The inhibiting effect of European law is discussed at various points in subsequent chapters. Although directives can be amended, to date finding a space in the Union's legislative programme for amendments to company law directives has not been easy.[223] Many of the requirements in the directives were based on the company laws of other member states and some were in place even before the UK joined the European Community. This experience would seem to suggest that, rather than waiting for Europe, a preferable course might be for English law to develop its own modern rules relating to corporate groups, both for domestic purposes and also with a view to contributing effectively to the development of appropriate European law in this area.

223 The Fourth and Seventh Company Law Directives (82/891/EEC, [1982] OJ L378/47 and 83/349/EEC, [1983] OJ L193/1) on accounting requirements have been amended.

2

Corporate Finance Structure: Basic Legal, Accounting and Financing Considerations

The legal rules governing companies and corporate finance are the primary focus of this book. As a prelude to the more detailed examination of the rules which follows in later chapters, the purpose of this chapter is to outline the basic components of the financial structure of a company and to consider in a rudimentary way some of the factors that may be taken into account by the managers of a company when making financing choices. Simple illustrations of the way in which financing choices have to be recorded in a company's accounts are provided. A company's accounts play a key role in determining compliance with legal requirements on corporate capital. By giving historical information about previous financing choices and the performance of the company, the accounts also provide the data on which to base financial projections.[1]

There are basically three ways for a company to finance its operations: share issues, debt and retained profits. In an introductory exposition it is convenient to take the simplest type of share and to compare its standard features with those of the simplest type of debt instrument. This should not be allowed to obscure the great flexibility that exists in practice with regard to the characteristics of financial instruments issued by companies. It is possible to issue shares which, by their terms of issue, deviate significantly from the standard case, to structure debt financing in a way which mimics the characteristics of share capital, and to devise instruments which combine some of the features of share capital and of debt. Devising new forms of financial instrument, moulded to satisfy particular investor preferences, is a significant part of corporate-finance advisory activity.

SHARE CAPITAL TERMINOLOGY

A company limited by shares must state its **authorised share capital**[2] in its memorandum of association.[3] The amount of the authorised capital, as stated in the memorandum, represents the maximum amount of share capital that a company can issue at any given time.[4] It thus operates as a limit on the com-

[1] Houthakker, HS, and Williamson, PJ, *The Economics of Financial Markets* (1996) 182; Ross, SA, Westerfield, RW, and Jordan, BD, *Fundamentals of Corporate Finance* (4th edn, 1998) 46–7.

[2] Or nominal share capital, the terms are synonymous.

[3] Companies Act 1985, s 2 (5)(a).

[4] Provided this is authorised by the articles, the authorised share capital may be changed: Companies Act 1985, s 121.

pany's ability to raise new finance through share issues but it does not indicate how much finance has previously been raised by share issues.

The **allotted share capital** is the amount of share capital that has been allotted by a company at any time. This may also be described as the company's **issued share capital.**[5] The holders of a company's allotted shares are its shareholders, and they may also be described as its members.[6] The minimum number of allotted shares is dictated by minimum-membership requirements: a private company limited by shares must have at least one member who holds at least one share;[7] a public company must have at least two members, each of whom must hold at least one share.[8] There is no regulation of the minimum amount of a private company's allotted share capital but for a public company there is a minimum of £50,000.[9]

The minimum price at which a company may allot a share is determined by the capital clause of its memorandum: this must state the division of the authorised share capital into shares of a fixed amount.[10] The fixed amount ascribed to individual shares in the capital clause of the memorandum is known as their **par value.**[11] A company must not allot a share at less than its par value[12] but it may allot it at a higher price. The difference between the par value of a share and the allotment price is known as a **share premium**.

Shares may be allotted **fully paid** (total allotment price paid on allotment), **partly paid** (part of the allotment price paid on allotment with the balance outstanding) or **nil paid** (all of the allotment price outstanding). The amount paid up in respect of nominal amount of shares (ie excluding premiums) represents a company's **paid-up share capital**. Where shares are allotted otherwise than on a fully-paid basis, payment dates may be set by the terms of allotment or the articles; alternatively, it may be left to the discretion of the directors to call for payment in accordance with the articles. A company's **called-up share capital** is made up of the share capital that has been paid up plus any amounts in respect of share capital (ie excluding premiums) that have been called up or are due on specified future dates.[13] Allotted share capital which has not been called up is **uncalled share capital.**[14]

It might be expected that the law would regulate the amount of paid-up share capital that a company must raise before starting business, but for private companies this is not so. In theory all of shares in a private company can be allotted on a nil-paid basis. Where this is done, the shareholders can later be called upon to pay the allotment price which has to be at least equivalent to

[5] This chapter follows the common practice of using the terms 'allotted' and 'issued' interchangeably. As discussed in Ch 8, it is sometimes important to distinguish between the allotment of a share (broadly, when a person becomes entitled to be registered by the company as its holder) and the issue of a share (broadly, when registration takes place).

[6] Technically, the members of the company are the people who form it (its subscribers) and the people who are registered as its shareholders: Companies Act 1985, s 22. Where rights depends on 'membership', it is necessary to check whether a shareholder has actually been registered in respect of a share but, in loose usage, the terms 'member' and 'shareholder' are interchangeable.

[7] Companies Act 1985, ss 1 (3A) and 2 (5)(b). [8] Ibid, ss 1 (1) and 2 (5)(b).

[9] Ibid, ss 117 (2) and 118 (newly formed plc), s 45 (private company converting to plc).

[10] Ibid, s 2 (5)(a).

[11] Or nominal value. Again, the terms are interchangeable.

[12] Companies Act 1985, s 100. [13] Ibid, s 737.

[14] Ibid, s 737 (2).

the par value of the shares but, since it is for the proprietors of the company to set the par value of its shares, the amount involved may be trivial, as low as a fraction of 1p per share. To the extent that there is a constraint on private companies trading on minimal amounts of capital it is not law, but lending practice: banks may be reluctant to lend to a private company if its proprietors have not themselves demonstrated their confidence in the company's prospects by taking the risk of investing a substantial amount in its share capital. However, many private companies do in fact operate with a token amount of share capital—£100 or less.[15] An explanation for lenders' tolerance of this situation is that they can instead protect their interests by taking personal guarantees from the operators of the business and security over the assets of the company, and of the operators personally.

The paid-up share capital of public companies is regulated by the Companies Act 1985. A public company must have a paid-up share capital of at least £12,500 before it starts trading.[16] Whilst not completely trivial, this is hardly a significant amount. The dictating factors in determining the amount of the paid-up share capital of a public company's share capital stem from the commercial pressure to maintain a balance between debt and share capital that is acceptable to lenders and investors.[17] The alternative for a lender of protecting its interests by obtaining personal guarantees from the directors may be less appropriate in this context than in a private company because, first, the directors are less likely to be as closely identified with the company as in a private business and, secondly, the amount of the liabilities of the business may be far in excess of the directors' personal resources. The option of taking security over the company's property is still available to creditors that have sufficient negotiating strength to make this a condition of lending.

ACCOUNTING FOR AN ALLOTMENT OF SHARES

When a company allots shares for cash at their par value this will be recorded as an increase in the company's current assets and as an increase in share capital. In numerical terms, it will look like Figure 2.1. The amount shown in a company's accounts as its share capital is subject to the legal rules on maintenance of capital. Maintenance of capital rules are the trade-off for limited liability: shareholders cannot be held liable to contribute to the company's assets for more than they have undertaken to subscribe in respect of their shares, but in return the amounts subscribed must be maintained.

[15] Of the 1.25 million registered UK companies as at 31 March 1997, 1.1 million had an issued share capital of less than £1,000 and, of these, 80 per cent had £100 or less: *The Euro: Redenomination of Share Capital* DTI Consultative Document (1998).

[16] Companies Act 1985, s 101 (companies incorporated as public companies) and Companies Act 1985, s 45 (companies incorporated as private, which convert to public companies). The figure is reached by combining the rule in these sections with the £50,000 minimum allotted share capital requirement.

[17] If a company starts trading without an inadequate capital base and later fails, this financing structure may be a factor for the court to take into account in proceedings under Insolvency Act 1986, s 214: *Re Purpoint Ltd* [1991] BCC 121, 127 *per* Vinelott J.

Co X has a simplified balance sheet thus:

Assets		£
Cash		5,000
Financing		
Share Capital	1,000	
Reserves	4,000	5,000

Co X issues 1,000 new £1 shares at par to investors who pay cash. The result is:

Assets		£
Cash		6,000
Financing		
Share Capital	2,000	
Reserves	4,000	6,000

Figure 2.1

'Maintenance' in this context means 'not returned to the shareholders'.[18] It is not a breach of the maintenance of capital rules for a company's share capital to be wiped out by improvident trading or bad investment decisions, although such events may trigger insolvency proceedings in respect of the company.

When shares are allotted at a premium to their par value, the share premium must be credited to a separate account, as illustrated by Figure 2.2. With only a few exceptions, sums credited to a share premium account are subject to the maintenance of capital rules in the same way as paid-up share capital.

CHARACTERISTICS OF ORDINARY SHARES

The standard characteristics of a share are income in the form of dividends, capital growth and voting rights. A share with the standard characteristics is known as an **ordinary share**. Ordinary shares may also be described as **equity**.[19]

[18] *Trevor v Whitworth* (1887) 12 App Cas 409, HL, 414 *per* Lord Herschell; this analysis is echoed by Lord Watson at 423–4.

[19] Companies Act 1985, s 744 defines 'equity share capital' as being issued share capital excluding any part of the capital which, neither as respects dividends nor as respects capital, carries any right to participate beyond a specified amount in a winding-up. This brings ordinary shares within the definition but excludes preference shares unless, in additional to whatever preferential entitlements they carry, they also have the right to participate with ordinary shares in distributions of income or capital, or both.

After the share issue in Figure 2.1, Co X subsequently issues 1,000 further new shares (each with a par value of £1) at £2 each. The balance sheet after the issue will be:

Assets		£
Cash		8,000
Financing		
Share Capital	3,000	
Share Premium	1,000	
Reserves	4,000	8,000

Figure 2.2

Dividends

Dividends are distributions to shareholders which are made out of the company's profits. A company which does not have profits available for distribution cannot pay dividends. Even where profits are available, the holders of ordinary shares have no legal right to demand that dividends be paid. The payment of dividends is governed by a company's articles, which normally[20] authorise the directors to pay interim dividends at their discretion where they consider that this is justified by the company's profits, and provide for final dividends to be declared by the shareholders in general meeting on the basis of a recommendation from the directors. As a matter of legal theory, it is possible for a company to pay dividends on its ordinary shares which fluctuate widely from year to year. It is also open to a company not to pay any dividends at all and to plough back the entire profits into the future funding of its operations. Both of these possibilities give way in practice to commercial considerations which may, depending on its nature[21] or the sector in which it operates,[22] require a company to pay steady dividends out of its distributable profits in order to satisfy the expectations of persons who have invested in its shares.

Dividends are paid out of a company's post-tax profits. As from 6 April 1999, the payment of dividends does not attract a tax charge in the hands of the paying company.[23]

[20] eg, Table A, arts 102–103.

[21] In quasi-partnership companies where all of the shareholders are involved in the day-to-day running of the company, the practice may be for no dividends to be paid, the shareholders/directors instead withdrawing part of the profits in the form of remuneration.

[22] See, further, Ch 12 below, at 408–9.

[23] Prior to that date, a company paying a dividend had to make a payment to the Inland Revenue representing advance corporation tax (ACT). ACT was treated as an instalment of the company's corporation tax but could become irrecoverable where the company did not generate sufficient profits against which to offset the ACT (ACT set-off was not permitted against certain types of profit, including profits generated by overseas operations). ACT also operated so as to satisfy shareholders' basic-rate tax liability.

Capital Gains

When a company is wound up, its ordinary shareholders are entitled to any surplus that remains after all the liabilities have been paid. This means that the ordinary shareholders of a company may be described as its 'residual claimants'. The entitlement to surplus is a feature which leads to the shareholders being regarded as the legal owners of the company. The entitlement to eventual capital gains means that the company's capital growth (or contraction) is reflected in the price at which its shareholders can sell their shares during the life of the company.

Risk

When a company is wound up its ordinary shareholders are the last to be paid. Put the other way, if a company has insufficient assets to meet all of its liabilities, the shortfall must be absorbed first by the ordinary shareholders and, only when the amount that they have undertaken to subscribe in respect of the shares is wiped out, will it then pass further up the repayment ranking order. The return that a company must pay investors in its share capital must compensate them for the risk that they will not be repaid in the event of winding up.

Voting Rights

Ordinary shares usually entitle their holders to one vote per share. It is possible to have non-voting ordinary shares or ordinary shares which carry multiple votes, although, because of their distorting effect on the operation of the market for corporate control (ie, voting control of the company does not necessarily follow from acquiring the majority in number of its shares) and on corporate governance mechanisms which are based on the control that shareholders can exercise through their votes, these are unpopular with institutional investors.[24] Participants in quasi-partnership type companies or joint venture companies may favour multiple voting rights as a means of entrenching their original bargain. One familiar form of multiple voting provision used for entrenchment purposes is a clause which is triggered by a proposal to remove a shareholder from the office of director and which provides that, in that event, the votes attaching to the shares held by that shareholder will be multiplied to an extent that is sufficient to defeat the motion.[25]

[24] See eg, 'GPG Challenges Young's Over Its Share Structure' *The Times* 20 July 1998. The challenge to a multi-tiered share structure failed on this occasion: 'Challenge for Change Falls Flat at Youngs' *The Times* 22 July 1998.

[25] This is commonly described as a *Bushell v Faith* clause after the House of Lords decision which sanctioned it: [1970] AC 1099, HL.

DEBT FINANCE TERMINOLOGY

A company can borrow from banks or other lenders or can tap the capital markets by issuing **debt securities** to investors. The raising of capital by an issue of debt securities is sometimes described as **direct financing** because the company appeals directly to investors; bank borrowing is in turn described as **indirect financing** because the bank stands between the company and the providers of the funds, namely the bank's depositors and persons from whom it has raised capital via the capital markets.

There are many different types of debt instrument that companies use to raise funds from the capital markets. The terminology used to describe debt instruments tends to be driven more by market practice than by legal definition and is thus liable to fluctuate from market to market and from time to time in response to practical developments.[26] Markets devise terms to distinguish debt securities by reference to certain key characteristics such as duration (eg, **commercial paper** is commonly used to describe short-term debt securities whilst long-term debt securities are often called **bonds**) and whether they are secured (commonly described in UK markets[27] as **debentures**) or unsecured (often known as **loan stock**). Terminological variety is a particular feature of the markets in specialist debt securities (such as **eurobonds**) which are normally bought and traded in by limited numbers of expert investors.

The term **debenture** also crops up in the context of bank financing for companies. Here it tends to be used to describe a loan which is secured on the company's property. In confining the use of the term 'debenture' to secured loans, practice is narrower than legal usage. There is no exhaustive legal definition of the term 'debenture'[28] but a commonly cited description is that it encompasses any document which creates or acknowledges a secured or unsecured debt.[29]

Borrowing from banks and other lenders and issuing debt securities to investors are not the only methods for a company to raise credit to fund its operations. Other mechanisms include structures which have the same economic effect as loans but which are formally different. Prime examples are an **asset sale** which involves the company selling its assets to a financier but with an option to re-acquire them;[30] **short-term trade credit**—this, at its simplest,

[26] Cranston, R, *Principles of Banking Law* (1997) 354.

[27] But, illustrating how terminology can change from market to market, in the USA the term debenture tends to be used to describe an unsecured loan: Klein, WA, and Coffee, JC, *Business Organization and Finance* (5th edn, 1993) 236; Houthakker, HS, and Williamson, PJ, *The Economics of Financial Markets* (1996) 61–2.

[28] Companies Act 1985, s 744 and Financial Services Act 1986, sch 1, para 2, list various instruments which are debentures, but the lists are not closed. The absence of a precise definition has given rise to few practical problems: *Re SH & Co (Realisations) 1990 Ltd* [1993] BCC 60, 67 quoting Gower, LCB, *Principles of Modern Company Law* (5th edn, 1992) 379.

[29] *Levy v Abercorris Slate and Slab Co* (1887) 37 Ch D 260 See also *Edmonds v Blaina Furnaces Co* (1887) 36 Ch D 215; *Lemon v Austin Friars Investment Trust Ltd* [1926] 1 Ch 1, CA; *Knightsbridge Estates Trust v Byrne* [1940] AC 613, HL; *R v Findlater* [1939] 1 KB 594, CCA.

[30] Asset sales achieve the same economic effect as secured loans but avoid the Companies Act 1985 requirements for the registration of charges. An attempt to avoid the registration requirements by labelling a structure as a sale will not work if the legal substance of the arrangement is in fact a secured loan: *Welsh Development Agency v Export Finance Co Ltd* [1992] BCC 270, CA.

means acquiring stock on credit terms with the supplier alone bearing the risk of non-payment[31] but, at a more sophisticated level, can involve banks issuing documentary credits to ensure payment;[32] and **debt factoring**—this is the process whereby a company sells receivables (debts owing to it) to a collection agent in order to secure a cash sum which is at a discount to the face value of the receivables.[33] Reasons of space preclude separate consideration of these forms of debt financing in this book.

Accounting for Debt Finance

It can suffice here to take a simple example of a long-term loan from a bank. The accounting treatment for this is illustrated by Figure 2.3.

X Ltd has a balance sheet as follows:

Assets		£,000
Fixed Assets	500	
Current Assets	60	560
Financing		
Share Capital	100	
Reserves	420	
Long-term Liabilities	40	560

It borrows a further £80,000 by way of a 5-year fixed-term loan. The balance sheet after taking out the loan will be:

Assets		£,000
Fixed Assets	500	
Current Assets	140	640
Financing		
Share Capital	100	
Reserves	420	
Long-term Liabilities	120	640

Figure 2.3

31 The supplier may seek to reduce this risk by retaining title to the goods supplied until payment is made. On the effectiveness of retention of title provisions see McCormack, G, *Reservation of Title* (2nd edn, 1995); Wheeler, S, *Reservation of Title Clauses: Impact and Implications* (1991).

32 The leading textbooks on this subject include Gutteridge, HC, and Megrah, M, *The Law of Bankers' Commercial Credits* (7th edn, 1984); Jack, R, *Documentary Credits* (2nd edn, 1993).

33 A leading text is Oditah, F, *Legal Aspects of Receivables Financing* (1991).

CHARACTERISTICS OF SIMPLE DEBT

Interest

The rate of interest payable in respect of a loan is determined by the contract between the company and the lender. The rate of interest may be fixed (eg 6 per cent per annum on the principal amount of the loan) or may be floating and liable to be adjusted in specified circumstances. Unlike dividends, interest is normally payable whether or not the company makes profits. Interest is deductible from the company's pre-tax profits and thus goes to reduce the profits on which the company is liable to pay tax. This is one factor that makes debt a potentially cheaper source of finance for a company than share capital.

Capital Gain

A lender is entitled to the repayment of the principal amount of the loan at the end of its term, but this is the limit of the lender's claim against the company. Lenders do not share in a company's capital growth. The opportunity for capital gains for investors in debt securities lies in exploiting differences between the yield on the securities, measured by reference to their cash flows in the form of interest payments and principal repayment at maturity, and the interest rates prevailing in the market. Where the yield on debt securities is higher than market interest rates, an investor may be able to sell the securities at a premium to their face value and thereby obtain a capital gain.

Risk

Providers of debt finance rank above shareholders for repayment in the event of winding up. There is also a ranking order between debts depending on whether they are secured or unsecured and, if secured, the type of security. Certain types of debt are given a preferential ranking status by the insolvency legislation[34] whilst others are deferred.[35] Priority over share capital in winding up is another factor that reduces the cost of debt finance in comparison to share capital: providers of debt finance accept less risk and that is reflected in the return that the company has to pay for financing in this form.

Control

Contractual restrictions in the terms on which loan capital is provided are in a broad sense the debt-finance equivalent to the control that shareholders are entitled to exercise via the votes attaching to their shares. The extent of the restrictions in each case is subject to a range of variables including the duration of the loan—a long-term lender might be expected to seek to impose more stringent restrictions than a provider of short-term trade finance—and

[34] Insolvency Act 1986, sch 6 sets out the categories of preferential debt.
[35] Insolvency Act 1986, s 74 (2)(f) (sums due to a member of the company). This was considered in *Soden v British & Commonwealth Holdings plc* [1998] AC 298, CA and HL.

the respective bargaining strength of the parties. They may include limitations on the company's borrowing levels, restrictions on the payment of dividends, negative pledge clauses whereby the company promises not to grant any new security on its property, and covenants restricting disposals of the company's property or major changes in the nature of its business.[36]

HYBRID SECURITIES IN OUTLINE

A hybrid[37] security combines some of the characteristic features of share capital with some of those of debt capital. A **preference share** is a form of hybrid security. Preference shares differ from ordinary shares in that they carry the right to a fixed annual dividend and/or to a return of a fixed principal amount. Preference shares normally carry limited voting rights. The fixed dividend and/or principal is payable in priority to the return on the ordinary shares but (unless the terms on which the preference shares are issued otherwise provide) there is no right to participate over and above the fixed amount. The fixed return and the priority to ordinary shares are characteristics which resemble loan capital. Nevertheless preference shares are still shares: thus fixed dividends on preference shares can only be paid from distributable profits and, accordingly, unlike interest, will not be payable if the company does not have these profits (but so long as the entitlement is **cumulative** it can be carried forward until such time as the company does have distributable profits); capital raised through an issue of preference shares is subject to the special rules about maintenance of capital in precisely the same way as capital raised through an issue of ordinary shares.

A more sophisticated version of a preference share is the **convertible preference share** which, in addition to the rights of a normal preference share, also entitles the holder at some point in the future to convert it into another security such as an ordinary share in the company or in its holding company. The holder of a convertible preference share is entitled to a higher place on the repayment ranking order than the holder of an ordinary share but, through the conversion right, does not entirely forego the chance of capital growth.

Loan capital can also be raised on terms which provide for the investor to be able to convert his debt security into a share (of the borrower company or some other company) at some later date. This is described as **convertible debt**. Similar to a convertible debt security is a debt instrument with an attached **warrant**. The warrant gives the holder the option to subscribe shares. The debt-plus-warrant structure differs from convertible debt in that exercise of the warrant does not bring the debt instrument to an end, whereas the debt instrument disappears when a conversion right is exercised. The characteristic shared by convertible debt securities and warrants, and which makes them both hybrid securities, is that they offer their holder the opportunity to participate in capital growth.

[36] See further Ch 14 below, at 470–9.

[37] McCormick, R, and Creamer, H, *Hybrid Corporate Securities: International Legal Aspects* (1987).

Another form of loan capital that is regarded as being hybrid is **subordinated debt**. Subordinated debt is loan capital on terms providing that the principal amount of the loan (and sometimes interest as well) is not to be repaid until some or all of the company's debts have been paid in full. To compensate for the subordination a company may have to pay a higher rate of interest than it would pay on unsubordinated loan capital. To enhance the attractiveness of the investment opportunity for investors still further, it may also have to offer share options or conversion rights. Subordinated debt is thus similar to share capital in that it ranks for payment behind other debts and, if share options or conversion rights are attached, it offers the opportunity to participate in capital growth. Yet it remains loan capital, on which interest may be payable even if the company does not have distributable profits, and ranks higher on the repayment ladder than share capital.[38]

VALUATION OF SHARES[39]

The value of a share ultimately comes down to what someone is willing to pay for it, and this can depend on precisely what it is that the purchaser seeks to acquire: thus, a bidder who wants to take over a company may have to pay more for its shares than an investor who seeks to acquire a small parcel of its shares, the difference in price here being the premium that the bidder has to pay for control. Valuation is not an exact science but where shares are quoted the starting point in any valuation process is to look at the price at which they are trading in the market. For some unquoted companies it may be possible to arrive at an estimate of the value of their shares based on empirical evidence of the market value of shares in analogous quoted companies. The market price of shares may then be compared with their value on the basis of other methods of valuation. This comparison may, in different contexts, assist professional investment analysts in arriving at their recommendations whether to buy or sell securities, and enable bidders to determine the control premium they are prepared to pay. Other valuation techniques must necessarily be used to value the shares of unquoted companies where there are no appropriate quoted comparators.

The main methods of valuing shares otherwise than at the price at which they are trading in the market are as follows. All of these methods have limita-

[38] *Collins v G Collins & Sons* (1984) 9 ACLR 58, NSW SC EqD illustrates this point. A corporate rescue scheme involving the subordination of certain debts was not approved by the court but, because of the technical differences between share capital and loan capital, it was prepared to sanction an alternative arrangement in which the relevant debts would be converted into preference shares. Query, however, whether it would be possible to structure subordinated debt which ranks behind preference shares. In principle, an arrangement whereby receipts in respect of subordinated debt are turned over to the preference shareholders should be possible but, depending on the structure used, this type of arrangement could raise financial-assistance concerns or might be vulnerable as an indirect unlawful return of capital.

[39] Pike, R, and Neale, B, *Corporate Finance and Investment* (2nd edn, 1996) ch 4; Houthakker, HS, and Williamson, PJ, *The Economics of Financial Markets* (1996) ch 6; Brealey, RA, and Myers, SC, *Principles of Corporate Finance*, (5th edn, 1996) ch 4; Samuels, JM, Wilkes, FM, and Brayshaw, RE, *Management of Company Finance* (6th edn, 1995) ch 15.

tions and some are more appropriate than others for particular purposes. Where they involve assumptions or projections, there is scope for different valuers to take different views. This means that the sensible course for, say, a potential bidder, is to use a combination of valuation methodologies in order to derive a valuation range in respect of a target company.[40]

Net Asset Value

Net asset value involves dividing the total book value of the company's net assets by the number of shares in issue. Where the book values of the company's assets are out of date, it may be necessary to conduct a revaluation exercise in order to bring these into line with market values. This method of valuation is the primary tool for valuing property companies. It is inappropriate where much of the value of the business is attributable to factors which do not appear in the balance sheet, such as the skills of the staff of an advertising or design company.

Dividend Valuation

The principle underlying the dividend valuation method is that the value of a share lies in the flow of income that an investor can expect from it during its life, including any dividend paid on the liquidation of the company. Although the return to the holder of a share from time to time comes in the form of dividend plus the capital gain on the disposal of the share, the price that a purchaser is willing to pay for that share is based on expectation of future dividends, with the result that it is the value of the stream of dividends over the life of the share that represents its value. Dividend valuation methodology arrives at the present value of a share by looking at the expected flow of dividends during the life of the company and discounting future returns to reflect the time value of money and the risk that the expected cash flows may not in fact be forthcoming. The time value of money is illustrated by a simple comparison between a person who receives £100 today and invests it at an interest rate of 10 per cent so as to have £110 in one year's time with the person who receives £100 in one year's time. The second person's £100 is clearly less valuable than that of the first person. Its present value, based on an available interest rate of 10 per cent, is only £90.91—ie, £90.91 is the amount that the second person would need to receive today in order to end up in the position of having £100 in one year's time.

To use the dividend-valuation model of valuing shares, it is necessary to make assumptions about the company's future dividends: either that they will remain constant or that they will grow at a steady rate. The assumption of a steady growth rate involves further assumptions about the future availability

[40] In a different context, note *Re Macro (Ipswich) Ltd* [1994] BCC 781, where the court employed both net-asset and dividend-yield methods of valuation as the basis for arriving at the price at which a minority holding in a private company should be bought out under Companies Act 1985, s 459. Generally, on the valuation of shares in unquoted companies see Eastaway, N, Booth, H, and Eames, K, *Practical Share Valuation* (4th edn, 1998).

of projects in which the company can invest a given fraction of its profits in order to generate a constant rate of return. The nature of these assumptions means that this can be a particularly apposite method of valuation for companies which have a very stable cash flow and limited growth prospects, such as utility companies. If a company changes any of the factors on which projections are made (eg it changes its dividend policy by varying the fraction of its profits which it retains for investment) or provides information that suggests that adjustments may become necessary in the future, for example disappointing interim results which suggest that the company may have to cut its dividend, this may trigger a revaluation of its shares.

Free Cash Flow Valuation

Instead of looking at just one component of the return to shareholders (ie dividends), the free cash flow valuation method proceeds on the basis that the company's entire free cash flow (ie its income remaining net of all operating costs and investment outlays) belongs to the shareholders. Discounted cash flow methodology involves discounting future cash flows at an appropriate discount rate and relies upon projections of future cash flows. Forecasting difficulties are the main drawback of this type of valuation.

Earnings Valuation

Another way of looking at the value of shares is based on earnings per share. This popular method of assessing share values involves dividing the market price of a share by the company's last reported earnings per share[41] or its forecast[42] earnings per share in order to arrive at a price:earnings (P:E) ratio. The derivation of the P:E ratio from the existing market price means that there is an element of circularity here but it is broken by comparing that ratio with the figure that investment analysts consider to be the appropriate P:E ratio for shares in that category of company. If a particular company's P:E ratio is lower than the comparator, this is regarded as an indicator that the market may be undervaluing the shares, and conversely if it is higher. A weakness of this method of valuation is that it is based on an accounting measure of a company's earnings on which, within the overriding requirement for accounts to give a true and fair view, there can be room for considerable diversity of view depending upon the accounting method employed. Also, P:E analysis may be thought of as revealing less about the intrinsic value of a share than it does about the performance of a company relative to other companies in that sector.

[41] Listed companies are required to state their historical earnings per share in their accounts: *Earning Per Share* FRS 14. This Financial Reporting Standard is designed to bring UK accounting practice into line with an International Accounting Standard (IAS 3) on earnings per share.

[42] Based on the historical record of earnings per share and forecasts about the company's profits.

VALUATION OF DEBT SECURITIES

The value of a debt security lies is the present-day value of the stream of income payable in respect of the security. In the case of a simple debt security which has a fixed interest rate and a fixed maturity date, its value is the discounted value of the interest that is payable during the life of the loan and of the principal amount that is repayable on maturity.[43]

COST OF CAPITAL

The preceding discussion about valuation of shares and debt securities glossed over a fundamentally important point, namely, the appropriate discount rate to apply when determining the present value of expected future cash flows. The rate that is used must account for the time value of money and must reflect the risk that is inherent in any expectation of payments to be made in the future. A key element, therefore, is the evaluation of risk.[44] There are two forms of risk that are present in investing in corporate securities: risks relating to the particular companies whose securities are included in a portfolio (specific risks) and risks stemming from factors, such as the potential for changes in fiscal policy or interest rates, that are generally applicable (systematic risk). Portfolio theory dictates than an investor can eliminate specific risks by forming a diversified portfolio of investments in which risks attaching to particular securities are counterbalanced by the characteristics of other securities.[45] On this basis, it is only for systematic risk that investors can properly expect to receive compensation from the companies whose securities they hold. Accordingly, it is the valuation of systematic risk that is the focus of concern.

The Capital Asset Pricing Model (CAPM) is the most widely used technique for measuring systematic risk in equity investment and, hence, for estimating investors' required rate of return.[46] In broad terms the CAPM assesses the required rate of return on an equity investment by reference to the risk-free rate of return available to an investor, the premium required by investors to compensate them for the general systematic risk of investing in the equity

[43] Ross, SA, Westerfield, RW, and Jordan, BD, *Fundamentals of Corporate Finance* (4th edn, 1998) ch 7 applies discounted cash flow techniques to the valuation of debt securities starting with the simplest cases, such as that given in the text, to more complex examples involving loans which are repayable in instalments and loans with floating interest rates.

[44] Megginson, WL, *Corporate Finance Theory* (1997) ch 3; Ross, SA, Westerfield, RW, and Jordan, BD, *Fundamentals of Corporate Finance* (4th edn, 1998) chs 13–14.

[45] Markowitz, H, 'Portfolio Selection' (1958) 7 *Journal of Finance* 77; Houthakker, HS, and Williamson, PJ, *The Economics of Financial Markets* (1996) 106; Ross, SA, Westerfield, RW, and Jordan, BD, *Fundamentals of Corporate Finance* (4th edn, 1998) 378–80.

[46] See generally, Megginson, WL, *Corporate Finance Theory* (1997) 107–23; Houthakker, HS, and Williamson, PJ, *The Economics of Financial Markets* (1996) 150–62; Pike, R, and Neale, B, *Corporate Finance and Investment* (2nd edn, 1996) ch 11. The basic CAPM rests on a number of simplifying and restrictive assumptions. There is some empirical analysis that suggests that the CAPM may be invalid but detailed analysis of this, and of alternative asset-pricing models, are beyond the scope of this book.

market, and the undiversifiable systematic risk of a particular investment relative to the equity market. Although no investment is entirely risk-free, the rates of return on government securities (gilts) are the closest available comparator. The premium that investors require for holding a fully diversified portfolio of equity securities is determined by looking at the difference between historical gross returns on the equity market and on risk-free investments in gilts. In the UK, the historical evidence suggests that this premium lies within the range of six to ten percentage points. The undiversifiable risk inherent in holding a particular share is known as its beta. Equity betas are calculated by reference to their historical returns and the corresponding returns on the market. UK practice tends to use the equity betas produced by the risk management service of the London Business School.

In theory the CAPM can also be used to assess the required rate of return on debt securities but debt betas are not readily available. Instead, the rate of return required by investors in debt securities tends to be determined by reference to the rate of return on the existing debt securities of the company and of similar issuers. A similar process, involving examination of the company's borrowing history and comparison with analogous companies, may be used in determining the rate of return on debt finance provided by banks or other lenders.

The returns required by the providers of a company's share capital and debt constitute its cost of capital. From the viewpoint of the company assessing its cost of capital, it is necessary to make adjustments for the fact that interest is generally a deductible expense for tax purposes, with the result that the effective cost of debt is the gross rate of return on the debt net of tax at the standard corporation-tax rate. The company's cost of capital is a driving factor in decisions whether to invest in new projects because these will only be worthwhile investments where they are expected to generate returns at least equal to the company's cost of capital. Put another way, the company's cost of capital represents the cut-off rate for new projects. The average rate of a company's cost of capital is determined by the cost of its capital weighted by the proportion of funding obtained from each source (weighted average cost of capital, or WACC). Thus, if a company has outstanding debt of £1 million and its current borrowing rate is 10 per cent and it has 100,000 issued shares selling at £20 per share which is considered to represent a return on equity of 15 per cent, its weighted average cost of capital is 13.33% $((1/3 \times 0.1) + (2/3 \times 0.15)$. The next section discusses how changes in the proportion of debt to equity in a company's capital structure can affect its weighted average cost of capital. Here, it suffices to say that the weighted average cost of capital is a meaningful cut-off rate for new investment projects so long as the ratio of debt to equity remains constant. For the purposes of financial projections, companies tend to adopt a target ratio of debt to equity to cover the period of the forecasts and determine the weighted average cost of capital on that basis.[47]

[47] Ross, SA, Westerfield, RW, and Jordan, BD, *Fundamentals of Corporate Finance* (4th edn, 1998) 409–15.

CAPITAL STRUCTURE: MIX OF DEBT AND SHARE CAPITAL

This section considers the main factors that are relevant in determining the optimum long-term capital structure of a company or, to put it another way, the appropriate mix of debt and share capital. The ratio of loan capital to share capital and other reserves in a company is known as its 'gearing' ratio.[48] Debt is a superficially attractive source of corporate finance because its risk profile makes it cheaper than share capital: the return required by providers of debt is invariably lower than that required by providers of share capital because debt ranks ahead of share capital in winding up. Also interest on debt is tax deductible, unlike dividends payable on shares. However, the cost of debt cannot be looked at in isolation from the cost of share capital. Including debt in a company's capital structure increases the risk taken by the providers of share capital. Whilst companies that are funded entirely from retained earnings and share capital can become insolvent as a result of liabilities arising from their business operations, companies that rely on debt finance are more risky because there is the additional risk of default on its obligations to pay interest and repay principal to lenders. This is to be compared with a company which is funded entirely from retained earnings and share capital: failure to declare and pay a dividend is not a failure to meet an obligation because there is no obligation to declare a dividend, and capital invested in shares is permanent and does not have to be repaid.

The additional risks that flow from using debt finance are borne first by the shareholders, because it is their investment that will be wiped out first and, as rational investors, they may require additional compensation, in the form of an enhanced return on their shares, for shouldering this risk. The risk of insolvency then falls on the providers of debt finance because the limited liability of shareholders means that losses have to be absorbed by creditors once the amount contributed by the shareholders in respect of their shares is exhausted. Providers of new debt finance may thus require an enhanced return to compensate for the risks flowing from the existing levels of debt within a company's capital structure.

Figure 2.4 demonstrates the benign impact of gearing for the providers of a company's share capital. Comparing the good year to the mean year, it can be seen that the 20 per cent rise in net profits (from 10 to 12) results in a 40 per cent rise in the return on share capital in the highly geared company, whereas it results in only a 20 per cent rise in the ungeared company. This is a specific example illustrating how the benefits of a company's success, its capital growth, accrue to its shareholders whilst providers of debt finance are limited to the return that is fixed by the terms of the financing and do not share in capital growth. Figure 2.4 also shows the drawbacks of gearing in the comparison between the bad year and the mean year. Here, the drop in net profits by 20 per cent results in a 40 per cent drop in the return on equity in the highly

[48] Different users may, on the same raw figures, arrive at different ratios because of certain variable factors such as the treatment of preference share capital (some users classify it as 'loan' capital, others as share capital) and of cash and short-term loans (some users deduct these from loan capital).

Two businesses, X Ltd and Y Ltd both have financing of £100. Their simplified balance sheets are as follows:

	X Ltd	Y Ltd
Assets	100	100
Financing		
Share Capital	100	50
Borrowing (at 10% per annum)	—	50
	100	100

X Ltd is an ungeared company. Y Ltd is a highly geared company with a 1:1 debt equity ratio. There are three projections for the net profits of the business in Year 1. These are (i) £8 (bad year); (ii) £10 (mean year); and (iii) £12 (good year). The effect of these projected profits on the income attributable to the owners of the share capital is as follows:

		X Ltd	Y Ltd
Bad Year	Profit	8	8
	Interest	—	5
	Net Profit	8	3
Mean Year	Profit	10	10
	Interest	—	5
	Net Profit	10	5
Good Year	Profit	12	12
	Interest	—	5
	Net Profit	12	7

The return on share capital (net profit divided by the amount of share capital) in each of these three years for each company is:

	X Ltd	Y Ltd
Bad Year	8%	6%
Mean Year	10%	10%
Good Year	12%	14%

Figure 2.4

geared company but only a 20 per cent drop in the return in the ungeared company. The drawbacks of gearing become ever starker when an awful year is added to the picture. Say, using the simplified balance sheets in Figure 2.4, the profit is only £4. In that case there is still a 4 per cent return on the share capital in the ungeared company but the highly geared company is unable to meet its interest payment obligations out of the profit it has generated. These comparisons also demonstrate how gearing can increase the volatility of the return on equity.

In modern economics literature, analysis of capital-structure theory starts with the Modigliani-Miller (MM) theorem.[49] The main elements of the original MM theory are that (i) the total value of a company is independent of its capital structure, and (ii) the cost of a company's equity capital is a linear increasing function of its debt to equity ratio keeping the overall cost of capital constant. This theorem was developed on the basis of certain restrictive assumptions, including the absence of taxes and insolvency and transaction costs and the existence of perfect capital markets in which all investors have equal access to information. Much of the subsequent literature has evaluated MM with more realistic assumptions.[50] Once the assumptions on which the original theory was based are relaxed, in particular to take into account the fact that interest is tax deductible whereas dividends are not, it appears that it may be possible to add some debt to a company's capital structure without affecting the expected return to shareholders. Against this, the relaxation of the assumption of no insolvency costs points away from reliance on debt because, as the proportion of debt increases, the more likely it is that the company will default and enter into one of the corporate insolvency procedures within the framework of UK insolvency law.[51] These procedures are costly to implement and, as the risk of insolvency grows with the addition of more and more debt to a company's capital structure, this can eventually outweigh the tax benefit of debt. The upshot of these competing considerations is that the addition of debt to a company's capital structure will be beneficial up to the point where the tax savings resulting from debt are eclipsed by insolvency costs. On that basis, the focus then shifts to determining the proportion of debt within a company's capital structure that represents its optimal gearing level.[52]

[49] Modigliani, F, and Miller, MH, 'The Cost of Capital, Corporation Finance and the Theory of Investment' (1958) 48 *American Economic Review* 433. For an appraisal of the theorem and some of the literature spawned by it see Miller, MH, 'The Modigliani-Miller Propositions After Thirty Years' (1988) 2 *Journal of Economic Perspectives* 99 and the other symposium papers published in that edition of the journal. General overviews of the MM theorem, and subsequent literature, include the following: Klein, WA, and Coffee, JC, *Business Organization and Finance* (5th edn, 1993) 333–66; Megginson, WL, *Corporate Finance Theory* (1997) ch 7; Pike, R, and Neale, B, *Corporate Finance and Investment* (2nd edn, 1996) ch 21; Brealey, RA, and Myers, SC, *Principles of Corporate Finance* (5th edn, 1996) chs 17–18.

[50] The original authors themselves relaxed some of the original assumptions in later papers: eg, Modigliani, F, and Miller, MH, 'Corporate Income Taxes and the Cost of Capital: a Correction' (1963) 53 *American Economic Review* 261.

[51] The principal insolvency procedures in the UK are liquidation, receivership and administration. These procedures are governed by the Insolvency Act 1986 and the rules made thereunder.

[52] Ross, SA, Westerfield, RW, and Jordan, BD, *Fundamentals of Corporate Finance* (4th edn, 1998) ch 16.

The optimal level of gearing for a particular company depends on the nature of its business and investors' general expectations in respect of comparable companies. Thus companies with steady cash flows or readily realisable assets, such as utility companies and mature manufacturing companies, tend to have high gearing ratios. Companies with relatively few current tangible assets but with considerable future growth prospects, such as oil exploration companies, are likely to have low gearing ratios, as are developing companies where the reliability of profit growth is uncertain.

CAPITAL STRUCTURE AND CORPORATE GOVERNANCE

Debt as a Mechanism to Control and Monitor Management

Corporate capital structure can be analysed in terms which relate the choice of structure to the relationship between management and shareholders and the mechanisms for reducing the opportunity for management to act in ways which are not in the interests of shareholders.[53] Adding debt to a company's capital structure can be viewed as a mechanism for controlling management in that it imposes on them an obligation to make regular contractually enforceable payments of interest and principal. They are exposed to the risk of the company failing to meet its contractual commitments and, in that event, of finding themselves at the helm of a company which is put into some form of insolvency procedure, with all the damage to their professional reputation as business managers, as well as the loss of their current jobs, that this may entail. The providers of debt finance may impose contractual restrictions on the future operation of the company's business and the organisation of its capital structure, and may require management to produce regular information to facilitate monitoring of compliance with these commitments. These restrictions and monitoring activities are valuable to shareholders in that they serve as a form of guarantee of managerial diligence and they act as a counterbalance to the additional risk that is borne by shareholders once debt is included in a company's capital structure. This approach thus offers another way of explaining why adding debt to a company's capital structure does not necessarily increase the return that shareholders will expect: in effect, the shareholders 'pay' the providers of debt finance to control management by not demanding a higher return to compensate them for the additional risk to them that results from the company's reliance upon debt finance. Developing the idea slightly further, it suggests that debt should be added to the company's capital structure up to the point where the costs involved in obtaining the controlling mechanisms that are present in debt finance outweigh their

[53] The leading paper setting out the agency cost theory of financial structure is Jensen, M, and Meckling, W, 'Theory of the Firm: Managerial Behavior, Agency Costs and Ownership Structure' in Putterman, L (ed), *The Economic Nature of the Firm* (1986) 209 (reprinted in abridged form from (1976) 3 *Journal of Financial Economics* 305). An outline of the issue of agency costs and capital structure is provided by Megginson, WL, *Corporate Finance Theory* (1997) 334–8. See also Edwards, J, 'Recent Developments in the Theory of Corporate Finance' (1987) 3 *Oxford Review of Economic Policy* 1, 6–8.

benefits to the shareholders. This recognises that the interests of providers of debt finance and of shareholders are not necessarily aligned and that mechanisms which creditors may put in place to safeguard their interests may be regarded differently by shareholders. Take, as an illustration of this point, a proposal by management to invest in one of two projects, the first of which offers a modest but virtually guaranteed return, the second of which offers a 50 per cent chance of a high return but also carries a 50 per cent risk that much of the investment will be wiped out. To a potential debt financier which is considering lending to the company on the usual terms (interest payments plus repayment of the principal at the end of the term but no capital growth), so long as the expected rate of return on the first project is sufficient to enable the company to pay the interest charges on its debt obligations, the first project is preferable to the second. The chance of capital growth that is present in the second project does not matter to the debt financier because it will not see the benefit of it. From its perspective, that project represents a risk of a capital loss which it may have to absorb if it is of sufficient magnitude to wipe out the company's share capital. Accordingly, the debt financier may seek to safeguard its interests by requiring the company to promise not to invest in the second project. This type of contractual restriction is not valuable to the shareholders if it prevents the company from exploiting an opportunity which, from their perspective, offers potential returns which outweigh its inherent risks. Thus, looking at capital structure in this way, the conclusion arrived at is, again, that the financial managers of a company should aim to structure its capital on the basis of its optimal gearing ratio; that is, they should aim to borrow up to the point where the value to shareholders of the discipline that flows from adding debt becomes exhausted.

Debt as a Signal of Managerial Confidence

Another corporate governance orientated analysis of corporate capital structure is that the addition of debt to a company's capital structure can be regarded as a mechanism which operates so as to reduce the problems of asymmetric information between the managers and the shareholders of a company.[54] Managers, by virtue of their position, necessarily know more about the prospects of the business than its shareholders. By subjecting themselves to the scrutiny of providers of debt finance, the discipline of having to meet contractually enforceable payment obligations and the risk of insolvency, managers are sending out a strong and credible signal to the shareholders of their confidence in the business based on their informational advantages. The ability to send out this signal serves to distinguish their company from competitors whose financial prospects are less secure. The greater risk of insolvency that less secure companies will face if they take on additional debt constrains them from copying this signalling behaviour.

[54] A leading paper on this topic is Ross, SA, 'The Determination of Financial Structure: The Incentive-Signalling Approach' (1977) 8 *Bell Journal of Economics* 7. See also Megginson, WL, *Corporate Finance Theory* (1997) 342–3; Edwards, J, 'Recent Developments in the Theory of Corporate Finance' (1987) 3 *Oxford Review of Economic Policy* 1, 9–11.

Shareholder Control and Changes to Capital Structure

The proprietors of companies where the shareholding is concentrated in the hands of a few individuals may favour borrowing money rather than issuing shares to new investors, because this avoids the dilution of the control that they can exert via the voting rights attaching to their shares. Dilution of voting control is less of an issue in larger companies where the shareholding is already atomized—no one shareholder is likely to hold more than a small proportion of its shares and, hence, no-one is able to dictate the outcome of proposals put to the general meeting by reason of the proportion of votes that they control. Yet, notwithstanding that they do not usually have voting control, shareholders in companies whose shares are publicly traded tend to resist new share issues which are done on a non-pre-emptive basis, ie without the existing shareholders being given the right of first refusal in respect of a proportion of the new issue that is equivalent to the proportion of the existing share capital that they hold. Reasons given for this opposition are that pre-emption protects the ownership rights of shareholders and prevents the dilution of the value of their investment.[55] Analysis of an assumption that underlies this reasoning, namely that shareholders 'own' their company, can be left to a later chapter.[56] Here, it suffices to make the point that the need to satisfy investor expectations with regard to pre-emption (expectations which are supported by legal entitlement unless, or to the extent that, investors otherwise decide[57]) can act as a disincentive to raising new capital through an issue of ordinary shares and may tilt the balance in favour of loan capital.

EFFICIENT CAPITAL MARKETS

Efficient capital markets theory underpins the understanding of the pricing of securities in financial markets.[58] The efficiency of a capital market is determined by its ability to absorb and reflect information in the prices at which assets trade on that market. There are three degrees of efficiency in this context, labelled 'weak-form efficiency', 'semi-strong-form efficiency' and 'strong-form efficiency'. In a weak-form efficient market, the current prices of securities reflect all relevant historical information. A semi-strong efficient capital market is one where prices adjust rapidly in response to information as soon as it becomes available. A strong-form efficient capital market is one where the prices reflect all relevant information including information that has not yet been made public. Empirical research supports weak-form efficiency and semi-strong efficiency as explanations of how capital markets

[55] *ABI/NAPF Joint Position Paper on Pre-emption, Cost of Capital and Underwriting* (July 1996) para 1.1.

[56] See further, Ch 4 below, at 131–3.

[57] Companies Act 1985, ss 89–96, discussed in Ch 18 below, at 614–21.

[58] For an overview of the literature on this topic see Houthakker, HS, and Williamson, PJ, *The Economics of Financial Markets* (1996) 130–40.

actually work in major jurisdictions, with the semi-strong version probably being the one that is most favoured. That markets do not normally conform to the strong-form efficiency hypothesis is demonstrated by the (illegal) profits that can be made by insider trading: the opportunity for profit exists because market prices have not yet absorbed the information that has not been made public or, to put it another way, because the market is not conforming to the model of strong-form efficiency.

JUDGING FINANCIAL PERFORMANCE: FINANCIAL RATIOS AND COMPANY ACCOUNTS

The definition of an efficient capital market as one in which market prices shift rapidly in response to new information as soon as it becomes public[59] puts the spotlight onto the process whereby information is conveyed to the market and how it is interpreted and analysed. Disclosure obligations imposed by legislation or by market rules perform an important role in bringing information into the public domain: for instance the London Stock Exchange imposes a general obligation on a company whose shares are admitted to dealings on its markets to notify it of any major new development in its sphere of activity which are not public knowledge and which may lead to a substantial movement in the price of its listed securities.[60] However, whilst some information, such as a change in base lending rates announced by the Bank of England, may be absorbed very rapidly throughout the market the full impact of other 'raw' information may not be immediately apparent. It is here that the role of professional investment analysts is important: investment analysts are skilled advisers who interpret information and analyse its significance for the benefit of their clients who are usually the major participants in the markets, such as pension funds and insurance companies. The investment decisions made by major investors on the basis on the advice of their investment analysts drive market prices and in this way information, as 'decoded' by the professionals, is absorbed by the market.[61]

Information Provided by Published Accounts

Investment analysts can extrapolate a considerable amount of information from companies' published financial statements. With certain exceptions, limited companies are required by the Companies Act 1985 to publish their annual accounts comprising a balance sheet as at the end of the relevant financial period, a profit and loss account covering that period,[62] together

[59] ie the semi-strong version of market efficiency.

[60] *The Listing Rules*, ch 9, para 9.1, although there is an exception for information about impending developments or matters in the course of negotiation (para 9.4). *The Listing Rules* apply to companies on the Official List, the Exchange's main market, but there is an equivalent obligation for companies admitted to dealing on its junior market, the Alternative Investment Market: *Rules of the London Stock Exchange*, ch 16, paras 16.14–16.16.

[61] Houthakker, HS, and Williamson, PJ, *The Economics of Financial Markets* (1996) ch 7.

[62] Companies Act 1985, s 226.

with a directors' report.[63] An independent auditor must audit the accounts and the auditor's report must be published with the accounts.[64] There is an equivalent requirement for parent companies of corporate groups to publish annual audited consolidated accounts relating to the group as a whole.[65] The process for making annual accounts public is that they must be laid before a general meeting[66] and then filed with the registrar of companies so as to be available for public inspection thereafter.[67] Not less than twenty-one days before the relevant meeting, a company must send a copy of the annual accounts and reports, including consolidated accounts where relevant, to its shareholders and debenture-holders, and also to any other person who is entitled to receive notice of the general meetings.[68] Listed companies are permitted to send out summary financial statements in place of the full accounts and reports provided this is not prohibited by their articles and subject to the proviso that the full accounts and reports must be sent if this is requested by any person entitled to receive them.[69]

The form and content of individual and consolidated annual accounts are regulated by the Companies Act 1985[70] and also by accounting standards issued by the standard-setting bodies of the accounting profession. The overriding requirement is that a set of accounts should give a true and fair view of the financial position of the company or group to which it relates.[71] The detailed requirements on the form and content of individual and consolidated accounts and directors' reports are modified for small companies.[72] Small companies are companies that satisfy certain specified size criteria with regard to turnover, balance sheet total and number of employees.[73] There are special rules regarding the format and content of accounts of banking and insurance companies and groups.[74] There is an exemption from the requirement to produce consolidated accounts for small or medium-sized corporate groups.[75] The criteria for determining whether a group is small or medium-

[63] Companies Act 1985, s 234.

[64] Ibid, s 235.

[65] Ibid, s 227. Subsidiary undertakings may be excluded from consolidation in limited circumstances: Companies Act 1985, s 229. Also intermediate parent undertakings may be exempt from the requirement to produce consolidated accounts: Companies Act 1985, s 228.

[66] Companies Act 1985, ss 241–2. If all of its members who are entitled to vote agree, a private company can dispense with the requirement to lay the accounts before the AGM: Companies Act 1985, s 252. On the basis of unanimity such companies can also elect to dispense with the holding of AGMs: Companies Act 1985, s 366A. These elections are most likely to occur in wholly-owned subsidiaries and in companies with just a few shareholders, most, if not all, of whom are actively involved in its management.

[67] Companies Act 1985, s 242.

[68] Ibid, s 238. Shareholders and debentureholders can also demand a second copy free of charge: Companies Act 1985, s 239.

[69] Companies Act 1985, s 251 and the Companies (Summary Financial Statement) Regulations 1995 (SI 1995/2092).

[70] The appropriate formats are set out in Companies Act 1985, schs 4 (individual accounts) and 4A (consolidated accounts).

[71] Companies Act 1985, ss 226 (4) and 227 (3).

[72] Ibid, ss 246, 248A and sch 8. These modifications do not apply in certain circumstances: Companies Act 1985, s 247A.

[73] Ibid, s 247.

[74] Ibid, s 255–255D and schs 9 and 9A.

[75] Ibid, s 248. In certain circumstances this exemption is unavailable: Companies Act 1985, s 248 (2).

sized so as to come within this exemption are based on aggregate turnover, aggregate balance sheet total and aggregate number of employees.[76] Very small companies, determined by reference to specified turnover and balance sheet criteria,[77] and dormant companies[78] are exempted from the requirement for an independent audit.

Although publicity about a company's financial position is part of the trade-off for the benefit of limited liability, small companies, as defined by the legislation, are now allowed to keep a considerable amount of the information contained in their annual reports and accounts out of the public eye. If they wish they may instead file only a summary balance sheet[79] and a special auditors' report on it.[80] However, this privacy can only be achieved at a cost: the abbreviated accounts that may be filed with the registrar are in addition to the statutory accounts, and a company that wishes to take advantage of the publicity exemption must therefore pay for the preparation of two sets of documents. Companies that are medium-sized according to specified size criteria[81] are permitted to file an abbreviated profit and loss account as part of their annual filing. Again, the costs involved in the drawing up of this additional document, as well as the limited nature of the concession, may serve to deter qualifying companies from making significant use of this exemption.

Accounting standards are statements of accounting practice that flesh out the requirements of the companies legislation with regard to accounts for the benefit of accountants who have to interpret and apply those requirements in practice. Until 1990 these accounting standards were known as Statements of Standard Accounting Practice (or SSAPs) and they were made by the Accounting Standards Committee, a representative body of the accounting profession. SSAPs did not have any direct legal backing in the companies legislation but accountants were expected to follow them as a matter of professional practice. In 1990 a new regime came into operation when a new standard-setting body, the Accounting Standards Board was afforded statutory recognition.[82] The Accounting Standards Board is empowered by the Companies Act 1985 to make accounting standards. Its initial step was to adopt the extant SSAPs as accounting standards but it has since issued new accounting standards on certain matters and some of the SSAPs have been superseded. New accounting standards issued by the Accounting Standards Board are known as Financial Reporting Standards (or FRS). The first Financial Reporting Standard[83] obliges most companies to produce, in addition to the profit and loss account and balance sheet required by the companies legislation, a cash-flow statement explaining the difference between the cash balances on two successive balance sheets of the business. Later Financial Reports Standards have included one interpreting and amplifying the requirements of the companies legislation with regard to the entities that

[76] Ibid, s 249.
[77] Ibid, s 249A.
[78] Ibid, s 250. To avail of this exemption, a dormant company must pass a special resolution not to appoint auditors.
[79] Ibid, s 246 (5)(c) and sch 8A.
[80] Ibid, s 247B.
[81] Ibid, s 247.
[82] Ibid, s 256 and Accounting Standards (Prescribed Body) Regulations 1990 (SI 1990/1667).
[83] *Cash Flow Statements*, FRS 1.

are subsidiary undertakings to be included in group accounts[84] and one providing guidance on the accounting treatment for securities that bear some hallmarks of debt and some of those of share capital.[85] A single accounting standard specifically for companies that are small companies under the companies legislation and analogous bodies has been issued.[86]

The new regime introduced in 1990 requires companies to state whether their accounts have been prepared in accordance with applicable accounting standards and to disclose any material departures from them.[87] Although the question whether accounts give a true and fair view is a legal one for a court to decide, in reaching its conclusion on the information that is required for this purpose, the court is likely to be guided by accounting standards.[88] The task of persuading a court that accounts that are not in accordance with accounting standards nevertheless give a true and fair view is likely to be a hard one unless the matter on which the accounts are non-compliant is one where deviation from the relevant standard is common practice and is justifiable.[89]

Supplementing the statutory requirements, *The Listing Rules* of the London Stock Exchange requires the annual report and accounts of listed companies to contain certain additional information. Also listed companies must produce and publish half-yearly reports on their activities and profit and loss which must include, amongst other matters, figures for the profit or loss for the relevant period and also earnings per share.[90]

Financial Ratios

When looking at a company's financial statements, analysts employ various ratios to judge how the company is doing, both in relation to its own past performance and its budgeted performance, and against industry benchmarks for it and other comparable companies. The financial managers of a company can use the same performance ratios, and comparative analysis, to form a picture of how the market is likely to react to their capital-structure planning decisions. For managers whose remuneration includes bonus elements which are linked to performance, these measures can have even more direct personal relevance.[91]

[84] *Accounting for Subsidiary Undertakings*, FRS 2.

[85] *Accounting for Capital Instruments*, FRS 4.

[86] *Financial Reporting Standard for Smaller Entities* effective March 1999 (superseding the original *Financial Reporting Standard for Smaller Entities* issued in November 1997).

[87] Companies Act 1985, sch 4, para 36A. This requirement does not apply to small companies (Companies Act 1985, s 246) or to medium-sized companies (Companies Act 1985, s 246A(2)). It does apply to banking companies (Companies Act 1985, sch 9, para 49) and to insurance companies (Companies Act 1985, sch 9A, para 56).

[88] *Lloyd Cheyham & Co Ltd v Littlejohn & Co* [1987] BCLC 303, 306.

[89] In a published joint opinion in 1983 Leonard Hoffmann QC and Mary Arden advised that non-compliance with an SSAP would lead to a prima-facie presumption that the accounts did not give a true and fair view. In a sole opinion in 1993, Mary Arden QC advised that the statutory recognition of the ASB as a standard-setting body and the establishment of a standard-setting structure formally within company law tended to increase the presumption that compliance with accounting standards meant that the accounts gave a true and fair view.

[90] These additional requirements for annual accounts and half-yearly reports are set out in *The Listing Rules*, ch 12.

[91] Ross, SA, Westerfield, RW, and Jordan, BD, *Fundamentals of Corporate Finance* (4th edn, 1998) 67.

Two of the main performance ratios, the gearing ratio and the price:earnings ratio, have been mentioned already. Other ratios that are of particular interest to investors in shares include the following. Investors who have a preference between high income and long-term capital growth are likely to be interested in the dividend yield on a share which is determined by looking at the ratio of the dividend[92] to the market price of the share. Dividend cover, the ratio of earning per share to the dividend per share, provides investors with an indication whether the company is likely to be able to maintain its present level of dividend. A high dividend cover indicates that even if a company's profits fall substantially it should still be able to maintain its dividend; conversely a low dividend cover suggests that the company may have difficulty maintaining its dividend if it suffers a bad year.

Just as investors in shares will be interested in the company's ability to pay dividends, providers of debt finance will be concerned to see that a company has an adequate interest cover. This is measured by comparing pre-tax profits (before interest) against interest charges. A high interest cover indicates that a company should still be able to pay interest charges even if it suffers a bad year, whilst a low interest cover is an indicator that it may encounter problems if its profits fall. The interest cover ratio does not indicate whether a company can pay its debts on time. The information contained in a company's cash flow statements provides an indication of the company's ability to generate cash. The company's working capital ratio (current assets/current liabilities) is also relevant to a company short-term solvency position. Although it does not necessarily follow from the fact that the company has a large amount of current assets relative to its current liabilities that it will have the cash with which to meet future interest charges, a high ratio suggests that the company is in a relatively liquid position and is thus a guideline to its cash flow position. A variant on the working capital ratio is the quick or acid test ratio which compares current assets, excluding stock, to current liabilities. This ratio recognises that it may take some time for stock to be realised and thus may give a more accurate picture of the company's liquidity than the working capital ratio.

SOURCES OF CORPORATE FINANCE IN THE UK

Retentions

The primary source of corporate finance for established companies is retained earnings. Figures for the period 1990–94, for example, show that on average UK companies found over 50 per cent of their new finance internally.[93] This proportion has not declined since then: figures reported in 1996 indicated that UK industrial and commercial companies raised just under 60

[92] Until its abolition with effect from 6 April 1999, this calculation involved grossing up for Advance Corporation Tax.

[93] Pike, R, and Neale, B, *Corporate Finance and Investment* (2nd edn, 1996) 465, Table 18.1.

per cent of their finance from internal sources.[94] In the context of discussions about under-investment in long-term development by UK companies in comparison, say, to their German and Japanese counterparts, it may be noted that retained profits achieve this primary position notwithstanding that dividend pay-out ratios in the UK tend to be much higher than in the comparator countries.[95]

Using profits generated by the business to fund future operations avoids the administrative costs, such as lawyers' fees, that are normally incurred when a company raises finance from external sources. A second reason why managers may favour using retained profits to fund their company's future operations is that this avoids having to submit to the monitoring and discipline that adding new equity or debt finance to the company's capital structure could entail.[96] This does not mean that the managers can regard retained profits as a 'free' source of finance since they are in substance shareholders' funds which are being re-invested on their behalf by corporate management:[97] if retained profits are invested in ventures that fail to generate a sufficient return to cover the company's projected cost of capital, this will impact unfavourably on its share price and that could in turn trigger a chain of events leading ultimately to the displacement of the 'failing' management through internal control mechanisms or through the external device of a takeover.

Debt

Figures reported in 1996 indicate that the next important source of corporate finance is loan finance from banks and other lenders (ie not including debt securities).[98] This is consistent with data for earlier periods,[99] although during the recessionary conditions that existed in the UK in the early 1990s there was a trend for companies to reduce the high levels of borrowings that they had incurred during the takeover boom of the late 1980s.[100] Loan finance from

[94] Davies, H, 'Industrial Investment—Can the Market Respond?' (1996) 36 *Bank of England Quarterly Bulletin* 216.

[95] For the period 1982–88, UK pay-out ratios were around three times as high as those in Germany: Mayer, C, and Alexander, I, 'Banks and Markets: Corporate Financing in Germany and the UK' (1990) *Journal of Japanese and International Economics* 450, quoted in Mayer, C, 'Stock-Markets, Financial Institutions and Corporate Performance' in Dimsdale, N, and Prevezer, M, (eds), *Capital Markets and Corporate Governance* (1994) 179, 183–4. *Second Report: Competitiveness of UK Manufacturing Industry* (House of Commons Trade and Industry Committee) (1994) 71, quoted in Stapledon, GP, *Institutional Shareholders and Corporate Governance* (1996) 222.

[96] Samuels, JM, Wilkes, FM, and Brayshaw, RE, *Management of Company Finance* (6th edn, 1995) 621. This point can be put the other way round, ie that paying out dividends and then raising required corporate finance from other sources precipitates monitoring by external financiers for the benefit of shareholders: Easterbrook, FH, 'Two Agency-Cost Explanations of Dividends' (1984) 74 *American Economic Review* 650.

[97] Bond, S, and Jenkinson, T, 'The Assessment: Investment Performance and Policy' (1996) 12 *Oxford Review of Economic Policy* 1, 14.

[98] Davies, H, 'Industrial Investment—Can the Market Respond?' (1996) 36 *Bank of England Quarterly Bulletin* 216.

[99] Pike, R, and Neale, B, *Corporate Finance and Investment* (2nd edn, 1996) 464–5, Table 18.1.

[100] Davies, H, 'Industrial Investment—Can the Market Respond?' (1996) 36 *Bank of England Quarterly Bulletin* 216; Hoggarth, G, and Chrystal, A, 'The UK Personal and Corporate Sectors during the 1980s and 1990s: A Comparison of Key Financial Indicators' (1998) 38 *Bank of England Quarterly Bulletin* 220.

banks comes in a variety of forms, ranging from overdrafts which are repayable on demand at any time, through to long-term loans which are due for repayment only after a number of years. Borrowing from banks is a particularly important source of finance for small and medium-sized companies. The dilution of control that would result from attracting external equity investment is a factor that may discourage the founders of such a business from seeking external finance in that form. From the viewpoint of investors the risk of being locked into smaller companies whose shares are not actively traded serves as a disincentive to equity investment.[101] Also, a willingness on the part of the founders of a business to dilute their control by seeking external equity investors may be interpreted as a signal of their lack of confidence in the business on the basis that, if they were convinced of its likely profitability they would not want to share the fruits of that success.[102] The external sources of finance available to small and medium-sized businesses is an issue that has been the focus of concern in a number of official reports stretching back many years.[103] The Bank of England now compiles and publishes a regular report giving details of the financing of small firms.[104] The 1997 report indicates that the clearing banks remained the largest external source of external finance, although other sources, including short-term trade credit, asset financing (such as hire purchase), venture capital[105] and government (including EU) grants were also tapped. As at June 1996, borrowing by small businesses totalled £34.8 billion, of which 65 per cent comprised term loans rather than overdrafts. The average length of term loans was around nine years.

[101] Companies can buy back their own shares in accordance with a procedure that is set out in detail in the companies legislation. The provision of an 'exit' mechanism for external equity investors in companies whose shares were not actively traded was one of the driving factors underlying the introduction of these powers and it is only in recent years that they been actively used as a means of returning value to shareholders in companies whose shares are actively traded.

[102] Hughes, A, 'Finance for SMEs: A UK Perspective' (1997) 9 *Small Business Economics* 151, 164.

[103] *Report of the Committee to Review the Functioning of Financing Institutions*, Cmnd 7937 (1980) which, in app 2 sets out the conclusion and summary of recommendations from the Committee's interim report on the financing of small firms (Cmnd 7503) (1979). Earlier reports on the financing of British industry also noted the particular difficulties faced by small firms: *Report of the Committee on Finance and Industry*, Cmnd 3897 (1931) (Macmillan Report); *Report of the Committee on the Workings of the Monetary System*, Cmnd 827 (1959) (Radcliffe Report); *Report of the Committee of Inquiry on Small Firms*, Cmnd 4811 (1971) (Bolton Report). A general review of the financial structure of small and medium-sized enterprises (SMEs) is provided by Hughes, A, 'Finance for SMEs: A UK Perspective' (1997) 9 *Small Business Economics* 151.

[104] *Finance for Small Firms: A Fourth Report* (Bank of England, 1997). Small firms are defined for this purpose as being firms (this includes but is not limited to companies) with a turnover of up to and including £1 million. The Report notes that the issues discussed may also be relevant to some companies with a higher annual turnover.

[105] Venture capital companies provide finance for small businesses at start up, upon expansion, or as rescue capital. They also invest in management buy-outs and buy-ins. See Beecroft, A, 'The Role of the Venture Capital Industry in the UK' in Dimsdale, N, and Prevezer, M, *Capital Markets and Corporate Governance* (1994) 195; Hustler, JR, 'Venture Capital' in Rutterford, J, and Montgomerie, RR, *Butterworths Handbook of UK Corporate Finance*, (2nd edn, 1992) 59.

Public Issues of Securities

Last in the pecking order[106] as a source of corporate finance rank public issues of equity or debt securities. Within this category, equity issues are more significant than debt issues and it is on the former that this discussion is centred. There is a range of factors which influences the low position of equity issues. For a company which has not previously raised a significant amount of capital by issuing its shares to external investors, an initial public offering represents a major turning point in the life of the business. First, the legal rule that restricts the ability to make public offers of securities to public companies[107] means that there will probably need to be a change to the company's legal status.[108] Any business may adopt the form of a public company so long as the fairly small minimum capital requirement[109] and relevant formalities[110] are complied with but, because public companies are more heavily regulated by the companies legislation than private companies,[111] it is usual for businesses to operate as private companies until such time as they decide to raise capital by means of a public issue of securities. Secondly, the preparation for a forthcoming initial public offer may also involve a considerable degree of reorganisation of the company's managerial structure. To satisfy market

[106] On the pecking-order theory of corporate capital structure see Megginson, W, *Corporate Finance Theory* (1997) 338–41. The leading papers setting out this theory are Myers, SC, 'The Capital Structure Puzzle' (1984) *Journal of Finance* 575 and Myers, SC, and Majluf, NS, 'Corporate Financing and Investment Decisions When Firms Have Information Investors Do Not Have' (1984) 13 *Journal of Financial Economics* 187.

[107] Companies Act 1985, s 81. Only public companies can be listed on the London Stock Exchange: Financial Services Act 1986, s 143 (3).

[108] Conversion for private to public company status is governed by Companies Act 1985, ss 43–8.

[109] ie, at least £50,000 of allotted share capital of which a minimum of one-quarter (£12,500) must be paid up.

[110] A new plc must obtain from the registrar of companies a certificate of compliance with the minimum capital requirement before it does business or exercises any borrowing power: Companies Act 1985, s 117. For a private company converting to plc status compliance with the minimum capital requirement is a matter that the registrar must check before issuing the certificate of re-registration: Companies Act 1985, s 47 (3).

[111] There are many examples of the way in which public companies are more heavily regulated. Broadly, the rules relating to share capital and distributions are stricter in relation to plcs (eg, private companies can exclude the statutory pre-emption rights under Companies Act 1985, s 89 altogether, but plcs can only exclude them for a maximum period of 5 years at a time: Companies Act 1985, ss 91 and 95; in addition to the generally applicable restrictions on distribution of profits, there are additional restrictions on public companies: Companies Act 1985, ss 263–4, 272–3; the ratio of a plc's net assets to its called-up share capital is regulated but a private company's is not: Companies Act 1985, s 142 and s 43 (3); Companies Act 1985, ss 155–8 contain a procedure whereby private companies can sometimes give financial assistance for the acquisition of shares but there is no equivalent provision for plcs; a public company is more restricted in the circumstances in which it can purchase its own shares than a private company: Companies Act 1985, ss 171–177); some of the rules relating to administration and management are stricter in relation to plcs (eg, the rules concerning loans to directors are more detailed in the case of a public company: Companies Act 1985, ss 330–44; there are restrictions on the age of directors of plcs and the qualifications of their company secretaries: Companies Act 1985, ss 293–4, and s 286; plcs must have two directors but private companies can have only one: Companies Act 1985, s 282; the elective regime (which permits opting out of some of the procedural requirements of the legislation, such as the obligation to hold an annual general meeting) applies only to private companies: Companies Act 1985, s 379A; the statutory written resolution procedure only applies to private companies: Companies Act 1985, s 381A–C).

expectations with regard to corporate governance, independent non-executive directors may have to be appointed and the roles of chairman and chief executive separated.[112] The existing managers of the business must also make a psychological adjustment. They must be prepared for the fact that once a company's shares are in the public domain and are actively traded, their actions and decisions will be exposed to the scrutiny and discipline of the markets, and for the reality that, assuming that the market is operating efficiently, investor dissatisfaction will rapidly manifest itself in the form of a low share price.[113] Thirdly, the company's constitutional documents, its memorandum and articles, may have to be redrafted in order to remove provisions, such as weighted voting rights, that may not be appropriate to the company's new status and to add new provisions, such as more detailed powers for the regulation of company general meetings, that are suitable for it as a public company. The company will need to be guided through all of this disruptive preparation by lawyers, accountants, investment bankers and other advisers, and will incur hefty fees as a consequence. As well as its advisers' fees, the company will also have to absorb the expenses of preparing and publishing the offer documentation plus associated advertising and publicity material, and, where the issue is underwritten, underwriting fees.[114]

Although the issue costs associated with a second or subsequent public offer should not be as high as those involved in an initial public offer, they are still significant. In the UK, companies returning to the market in order to raise additional share capital by means of rights issues[115] have traditionally been expected to pay underwriting fees amounting to around 2 per cent of the proceeds of the issue. Whilst the particular matter of the fee structure for underwriting rights issues has attracted the attention of the regulatory authorities as being too high and, in response, innovative structures have been developed to enable companies to raise additional capital at a lower overall cost,[116] nevertheless this example does give a general idea of the magnitude of the fees involved.

Aside from costs, another factor that may deter a company whose shares are already in the public domain from returning to the market to raise more

[112] *The Combined Code. Principles of Good Corporate Governance and Code of Best Practice* (*Combined Code*) A.2–A.2.1 and A.3–A.3.2. The *Combined Code* is annexed to *The Listing Rules* and is effective for accounting periods ending on or after 31 December 1998. Listed companies are required to state in their annual accounts whether they comply with the *Combined Code* but non-compliance does not in itself jeopardise a company's listing: *The Listing Rules*, para 12.43A.

The *Combined Code* does not formally apply to unlisted companies but, since it embodies investor expectations with regard to good corporate governance, commercial considerations may lead them to adopt governance structures that conform to its requirements.

[113] The saga of Newcastle United plc, where directors resigned from the board in controversial circumstances but were later re-appointed and a large portion of the shares remained in the hands of the family that had controlled the company when it was private, attracted extensive critical media coverage with commentators making the point that the managers of the business seemed to have failed to adjust to their status as directors of a public company: eg, 'Newcastle Pitched Into Fresh Round of Turmoil' *Daily Telegraph* 1 June 1998.

[114] In broad terms, underwriting means agreeing to take the securities in the event of no-one else wanting them: see further, Ch 18 below, at 630–3.

[115] This is an issue of new shares offered first to the existing shareholders in proportions that are equal to their existing proportional shareholdings. See further Ch 18 below.

[116] See Ch 18 below, at 630–3.

share capital is that this may be interpreted by the market as a signal of bad news. In an earlier section it was noted that adding debt to a company's capital structure can be interpreted as a positive signal: it indicates that the managers of the company have confidence in the company's continuing ability to meet contractually enforceable obligations to pay interest and repay capital. Turning that argument around, issuing shares which do not carry contractually enforceable payment obligations may be seen as a negative sign.[117]

Liquidity and the London Stock Exchange

The liquidity of an investment, that is the ease with which it can be converted to cash, is important. An investor's decision whether to buy shares, and at what price, will necessarily be influenced by whether he will be able at a later point to realise cash quickly and easily by selling the shares. To enhance the liquidity of an issue of securities an application may be made for them to be admitted to dealings on a formal market.[118] The London Stock Exchange is the official market for the trading of shares in public companies in the UK. As well as its main market, the Exchange also operates a junior market which is known as the Alternative Investment Market.

Securities that are traded on the main market are, in formal terms, admitted to the Official List.[119] At the end of 1996 there were 2,171 UK companies on the Official List. The equity capital of these companies had a total market value of £1,011.7 billion. There were also 533 international companies listed with a total market value of £2,258.1 billion. The rules for admission to the Official List are contained in *The Listing Rules* (also known as the *Yellow Book*). The conditions for listing are set out in chapter 3 of this publication. The most important requirements are that the market value of the shares to be listed must be at least £700,000;[120] apart from special cases,[121] the company must have a trading record of at least three years and must have audited accounts for those three years; the directors and senior management of the company must collectively have appropriate expertise and experience for the management of its business and the directors must be free of conflicts of interests or duties; if the company has a controlling shareholder (ie one who can exercise, or control the exercise, of 30 per cent or more of the right to vote at general meetings or who can control the appointment of directors who are able to

117 Myers, SC, and Majluf, NS, 'Corporate Financing and Investment Decisions When Firms Have Information Investors Do Not Have' (1984) 13 *Journal of Financial Economics* 187.

118 This adds further costs such as the admission fee to join the market, and the fee payable to the sponsor that the Exchange requires an applicant to appoint to handle the application on its behalf.

119 The factual information about the Official List and the AIM are taken from the London Stock Exchange's website (www.londonstockex.co.uk).

120 In practice the market capitalisation of companies joining the Official List is likely to be much higher than this figure. At the end of 1996, the average market capitalisation of listed UK companies was £157.8 million.

121 The Exchange may waive the requirements for a minimum trading record of three years and three years of audited accounts where it is satisfied that admission to the Official List is desirable in the interests of the applicant and investors and that investors have the necessary information to arrive at an informed judgment concerning the applicant and the securities for which listing is sought: *The Listing Rules*, ch 3, paras 3.4 and 3.6A.

exercise the majority of votes at board meetings) the company must be capable at all times of operating and making decisions independently of the controlling shareholder; and at least 25 per cent of the shares must usually[122] be in the hands of the public anywhere in the European Union after the flotation. Once a company's securities have been admitted to the Official List, it must thereafter comply with continuing obligations relating to such matters as disclosure of information and treatment of, and communication with, shareholders.[123] Listed companies are subject to continuing obligations with regard to the provision of financial information over and above the requirements of the companies legislation: for instance, they have to produce half-yearly reports as well as annual accounts.[124] There are also continuing obligations relating to transactions between listed companies and their directors which are additional to legislative regulation of these matters.[125] Some large transactions by listed companies must be approved by their shareholders even though for the purposes of the Companies Act 1985 such consent is not required.[126]

The junior market of the London Stock Exchange is the Alternative Investment Market (or AIM). The AIM was launched in June 1995, although other lower-level markets had existed within the London Stock Exchange since 1980. According to data available in August 1998, there were over 260 AIM companies including international companies and the total market capitalisation of the AIM companies was nearly £6 billion. Most of the companies that had joined the AIM by that time had a market capitalisation of less than £30 million and the amounts of new capital raised on admission to the market had been up to £10 million.[127] The requirements for joining the AIM are much more relaxed than the admission criteria for the Official List.[128] This reflects the fact that the AIM is intended to be a market for smaller and younger companies. There are no minimum trading record, market capitalisation or percentage of shareholding in public hands requirements. The admission criteria are that: the company must be duly incorporated/established according to the law of the place of incorporation/establishment and must be permitted by its national law to offer securities to the public (in the UK this means that it must be a public company); the securities to be traded on the market must be freely transferable; all other issued securities of the same class must be admitted; the company must have a nominated adviser and a nominated broker;[129]

[122] A percentage lower than 25 per cent may be acceptable if the market will operate properly with a lower percentage because of a large number of shares of the class, and extent of distribution: *The Listing Rules*, ch 3, para 3.19.

[123] *The Listing Rules*, ch 9. [124] Ibid, ch 12. [125] Ibid, ch 11. [126] Ibid, ch 10.

[127] Admission to a formal market such as the AIM or the Official List is commonly linked to a new issue of securities but it need not be. A company may choose to have its existing securities admitted to a market in order to enhance their liquidity and without raising any new capital at that time.

[128] *Rules of the London Stock Exchange*, ch 16.

[129] Nominated advisers and brokers are corporate finance specialists who have been approved by the Exchange. The adviser has the task of deciding whether a company is suitable for admission to the AIM and must assist the company with compliance with the AIM rules. A company admitted to the AIM must retain its adviser and the adviser's role at that stage is to ensure that the company is aware of its continuing obligations. The role of the nominated broker is to provide a means for investors to buy and sell the company's shares.

the company's published accounts must be prepared in accordance with UK or US generally accepted accounting practice or international accounting standards; the company must ensure that appropriate settlement arrangements for its securities are in place; and a fee must be paid.[130] The company must accept continuing obligations which are principally concerned with the disclosure of information to investors.

SHORT-TERMISM

A regularly voiced criticism of the UK's financial system is that it is driven by the desire for liquidity in its capital markets which results in a short-termed orientation.[131] Short-termism on the part of large equity investors like pension funds manifests itself, it is said, in the incessant buying and selling of securities (sometimes described as 'churning'), unreasonable demands for quick profits and high dividend payouts, and ready acceptance of hostile takeover bids.[132] Short-term profits are favoured over the prospect of potentially larger profits in the longer term (the 'jam today' argument) and predicted future cash flows are discounted at a rate that is unnecessarily high given the time period and risks involved.[133] This, in turn, leads managers of businesses, who are acutely aware of the operation of efficient capital markets and who realise how investors' reactions to their decisions will soon manifest itself in the company's share price, to decline opportunities that are likely to produce high returns eventually but which will take time and investment to bring to fruition, and to prefer intrinsically less valuable projects that will produce profits over a shorter time horizon. This policy enables them to pay out a high proportion of their company's profits, as these funds are not required for long-term investment in the business. Underlying this behaviour is a relationship (or, perhaps more accurately, a lack of relationship) between investors and corporate management which is characterised by hostility and mutual suspicion. Developing the argument a little further, it is conventional to draw unfavourable comparisons between the UK position and that in Germany and Japan where different structures mean that major investors tend to take large stakes in companies on the basis of a long-term commitment, where dividend pay-out rates tend to be lower, and where hostile bids are rare. Unsurprisingly, there is a range of perspectives on whether, or to what extent, com-

[130] *Rules of the London Stock Exchange*, ch 16, para 16.1.

[131] A leading text is Hutton, W, *The State We're In* (1995) 157–61 describing the 'destructive force' of shareholders' short-termism. Stapledon, GP, *Institutional Shareholders and Corporate Governance* (1996) 212–37 provides a careful and thorough account and assessment of the relevant issues.

[132] Assessments of whether the threat of takeover contributes to short-termism include Parkinson, JE, *Corporate Power and Responsibility* (1993) 128–31; Parkinson, JE, 'The Role of "Exit" and "Voice" in Corporate Governance' in Sheikh, S, and Rees, W (eds), *Corporate Governance and Corporate Control* (1995) 75, 93–8; Cosh, A, Hughes, A, Singh, A, Carty, J, and Plender, J (eds), *Takeovers and Short-Termism in the UK* (Institute for Public Policy Research, Industrial Policy Paper No 3, 1990); Stapledon, GP, *Institutional Shareholders and Corporate Governance* (1996) 217–18.

[133] Miles, D, 'Testing for Short-Termism in the UK Stock Market' (1993) 103 *Economic Journal* 1379.

panies in the UK markets fail to make sufficient long-term investment because of the short-term myopia of large equity investors. For instance, a competing theory ascribes short-termism in the UK markets not to the attitude of large equity investors but rather to the mistaken belief of corporate managers that there is a short-term bias in share prices. This perception, it is suggested, drives them to adopt policies with a short time horizon, especially where their remuneration packages contain share options or other bonus elements which are linked to the company's share price.[134] It falls outside the scope of this book to attempt an assessment of the respective merits of these competing theories but the implications of the short- versus long-term debate for the interpretation of legal rules cannot be ignored.

Directors and senior managers are required to act in the interests of the company.[135] This duty impinges on all managerial discretionary powers and it is, for instance, the legal basis on which the directors must make their decisions concerning the proportion of the company's profits to retain within the business to finance its future operations and the proportion to distribute to shareholders. Yet the frequency with which the phrase 'interests of the company' is used belies the difficulties that beset any attempt to pinpoint its exact meaning. It is conventional to say that, as the law stands at present, the interests of the company are normally to be identified with those of shareholders. Whilst this may be helpful in removing the issue of the directors' duty to act in the interests of other constituencies, such as creditors or employees, from the field of the current inquiry in this chapter,[136] the association between corporate interests and shareholders' interests is really only a starting point. The immediately obvious next question is 'what is meant by the interests of the shareholders?' Clearly, this must denote some sort of collective interest rather than the personal preferences of individual shareholders and, in language borrowed from another discipline, the common interest of shareholders, who are presumed to be rational investors, may be assumed to be an interest in wealth maximisation.[137] At this point the long-term/short-term issue becomes relevant. If it is true that investors collectively discount prospective large future profits more heavily than is warranted by the time-period and risks involved, then a duty to maximise shareholder value would be fulfilled by following policies which are geared towards short-term profits. Since the present day value of shares reflects the discounted value of expected future cash flows, companies that pursued policies based on long-term profitability risk would be penalised by the market in terms of the trading price of their shares and would thus fail to maximise shareholder value.

134 Marsh, P, *Short-termism on Trial* (1990).

135 *Re Smith and Fawcett Ltd* [1942] Ch 304, CA.

136 Ch 4 below, at 124–40 explores the extent to which other constituencies do, or should, figure in management's assessment of how to exercise its discretionary powers.

137 It is, of course, possible to define the shareholders' common interest differently, eg, as being the 'underlying universal expectation . . . of a company governed with integrity and competence—the twin towers of an enduring business structure': Sir Owen Green, 'Corporate Governance—Great Expectations' in Sheikh, S, and Rees, W (eds), *Corporate Governance and Corporate Control* (1995) 143, 150. This formulation would seem to look more at the manner in which a company is managed than at the purpose for which it is managed.

The conclusion that directors and senior managers should pursue short-term profits so long as this is what their shareholders want is one that the courts, the agency to which the task of rounding out the duty to act in the interests of the company normally devolves, seem to have shied away from. Unfortunately there is scant authority on the point and when it has been raised the courts have failed to confront the long-term/short-term issue directly, instead resorting to convenient, but delphic, phraseology to the effect that the duty is to act in the interests of present *and future* shareholders.[138] It is presumably meant by this that long-term interests should not be sacrificed for short-term gains, but the opacity of the language in which the principle is expressed leave room for doubt on this fundamentally important point. Assuming that it is correct to say that the legal duty encompasses long-term considerations, there is, then, a divergence between the legal interpretation of the interests of the company and the interests of shareholders as they might be defined in economic terms. This divergence is difficult to explain fully, but it appears to indicate an underlying reluctance within company law to accept the full ramifications of the identification of a company's interests with those of its shareholders. It suggests a recognition of the role that company law may play in protecting the interests of other persons, such as employees, who have also made an investment in the company's affairs, although explicit endorsement of this suggestion is hard to find.[139] Yet it can hardly be claimed that the courts have done much to develop a 'stakeholder' model of company law in which shareholders are just one of the groups whose interests should drive the management of the company's affairs.[140]

Shifting at this point from the theoretical nature of the duty to act in the interests of the company to business realities, so long as markets are driven by short-term considerations[141] it makes good practical sense for corporate management to pursue[142] the goal of short-term profit maximisation: equity investors value short-term profits more than long-term prospects; companies who do not satisfy this investor preference will see the dissatisfaction expressed in a low share price; a low share price may make it harder for the company to raise new external finance at competitive rates; and, since shareholders can control management either by voting individual unsatisfactory

[138] eg *Gaiman v National Association for Mental Health* [1972] Ch 317, 330; *Brady v Brady* (1987) 3 BCC 535, CA, 552 *per* Nourse LJ; *Dawson International plc v Coats Paton plc* (1988) 4 BCC 305, Ct Sess, 313.

[139] The limitations of Companies Act 1985, s 309 are considered in Ch 4 below, at 136–7.

[140] *Fulham Football Club v Cabra Estates* [1992] BCC 863, CA, 876 *per* Neill LJ is a rare explicit judicial endorsement of the stakeholder model.

[141] Whether, or to what extent, this statement is true is a difficult issue which is considered further in Ch 7 below, at 274–5. It can suffice as an assumption here because the argument in the text is that there are powerful practical incentives for managers to serve the interests of their equity investors, whatever those may be, and that although close analysis of company law indicates that they should consider other interests this obligation cannot be effectively enforced.

[142] Or to appear to pursue. One school of thought on managerial performance is that managers, motivated by the desire for personal prestige and power, may pursue strategies which are designed more to increase the size of the company than to enhance its profitability. According to this analysis, managers tend to seek profits that are sufficient to 'satisfy' investor expectations, but no more. See further: Herman, ES, *Corporate Control, Corporate Power* (1981) 10.

performers out of office or by triggering a change in the entire management team via a takeover, it is futile, and in terms of personal job security very foolish, for management to pursue any other course. These considerations, plus the essentially subjective nature of the duty to act in the interests of the company,[143] the lack of clarity about what this means with regard to consideration of long-term interests, the reluctance of the courts to review matters of business judgment,[144] and the fact that groups, such as employees, who might be prejudiced by the pursuit of short-termist polices have no standing to complain, all combine to ensure that managers are unlikely to lose much sleep worrying about any gap between what they do and what they should do to comply fully with their legal duty. The law's insistence upon the relevance of long-term interests is, within the present environment, at best a shield against claims that management has failed in its duty by not maximising shareholder value.

There is a case for the duty of directors to act in the interests of the company to be recast in language that makes it clear that this embraces long-term considerations. However, tinkering with language would on its own be a reform with very little value. The real tension here derives from the wider framework of company law and practice in which shareholders play a central role by having the ultimate power to control the appointment and removal of the management via takeover or internal democracy. The inevitable consequence of this structure is that managers must satisfy the demands of equity investors, or risk being replaced by others who will do so more effectively. If, or so long as, equity investors have short-term preferences, these are what will hold sway. Fundamental principles of core company law and related regulatory rules would have to be opened up for reassessment in order for the law to play a normative role in shifting the orientation of management practice towards a greater emphasis on long-term considerations. Measures that could claim a place on this reform agenda would include: making it obligatory for institutional investors to cast the votes attaching to their votes as a way of becoming more actively committed to the companies in which they invest; imposing a greater transparency on the role played by institutional investors by requiring them to set out their policies in voting guidelines and to publish details of their voting record;[145] developing mechanisms to encourage dialogue between corporate management and institutional investors;[146] reassessing

143 See Ch 5 below, at 157–60.

144 *Howard Smith Ltd v Ampol Petroleum Ltd* 1974] AC 821, PC, 835 *per* Lord Wilberforce.

145 Possibly as a pre-emptive strike designed to stave off the threat of legislation, the bodies representing institutional investors have voluntarily begun to publish voting guidelines, to encourage their members actually to vote, and to disclose voting records. Voting by institutional investors is considered further in Ch 7 below, at 248–9.

146 *Investing for Britain's Future: Report of the City/Industry Task Force* (CBI) (1987) quoted in Marsh, P, 'Market Assessment of Company Performance' in Dimsdale, N, and Prevezer, M (eds), *Capital Markets and Corporate Governance* (1994) 66, 90. Involving institutional shareholders more closely in corporate strategy and information could lead to problems under the insider dealing legislation (Criminal Justice Act 1993) as this could involve disclosure of confidential information. Development of this idea would also necessitate a reappraisal of the basic principles requiring equality of treatment as between shareholders. Cheffins, BR, *Company Law Theory, Structure and Operation* (1997) 472–95 analyses in detail the application of the concept of equality to shareholders. See, in particular, 481–3 where the process of providing information to

the position of shareholders *vis-à-vis* other groups with an interest in a company, such as its employees (this could, for example, involve allowing management greater flexibility to put in place defences against hostile takeovers where they believe these to be inimical to the interests of its employees); involving institutional investors more directly in the appointment of non-executive directors; and devising fiscal changes with a view to encouraging long-term shareholding and/or discouraging takeovers. Each of these ideas raises its own difficult issues of policy and practice. Whilst not all of the proposals can be fully developed within the confines of this book, some of these issues are considered further in Part II.

analysts and fund managers via meetings and brokers' lunches is described and the impact of the insider dealing legislation on these practices is considered. See also Stapledon, GP, *Institutional Shareholders and Corporate Governance* (1996) 101–6.

3

The Company as a Business Operator

SCOPE OF CHAPTER

Any proposition about a company necessarily involves a reference to a set of rules. A company exists because there is a rule (usually in a statute) which says that a *persona ficta* shall be deemed to exist and to have certain of the powers, rights and duties of a natural person. But there would be little sense in deeming such a *persona ficta* to exist unless there were also rules to tell one what acts were to count as acts of the company.[1]

A company, being a corporation, is a legal fiction. Its existence, capacities and activities are only such as the law attributes to it. The acts and omissions attributed to a company are perforce the acts and omissions of natural persons.[2]

This chapter considers the rules that are used to determine when a company become legally bound to, and entitled to benefit from, contracts which have been concluded on its behalf by natural persons.

By statute a company can make a contract in writing under its common seal or any person acting on its authority express or implied can make a contract on its behalf.[3] Agency principles determine whether a person has authority to act on behalf of another and thus are crucial in the application of the second limb of this statutory provision. Agency principles are the primary focus of this chapter. Formal execution of documents under the common seal is considered at the end of the chapter.[4]

THE BOARD—AGENT OR ORGAN?

An agency relationship is one in which one person, the agent, has the power to alter the legal relations between another person, the principal, and outsiders.[5] When an agent, acting within the scope of authority, enters into a contract

[1] *Meridian Global Funds Management Asia Ltd v Securities Commission* [1995] 2 AC 500, PC, 506 *per* Lord Hoffmann.

[2] *Northside Developments Pty Ltd v Registrar-General and Ors* (1989–90) 2 ACSR 161, H Ct of Aust, 177 *per* Brennan J. On the theories of corporate personality and the role of the law in attributing actions and mental states to a company see: Radin, M, 'The Endless Problem of Corporate Personality' (1932) 32 Columbia LR 643; Stokes, M, 'Company Law and Legal Theory' in Wheeler, S (ed), *The Law of the Business Enterprise* (1994) 80 (reprinted from Twining, W (ed), *Legal Theory and Common Law* (1986) 155); Schane, SA, 'The Corporation as a Person: the Language of a Legal Fiction' (1987) 61 Tulane Law Review 563; Sullivan, GR, 'The Attribution of Culpability to Limited Companies' [1996] CLJ 515; Clarkson, CMV, 'Kicking Corporate Bodies and Damning Their Souls' (1996) 59 MLR 557; Wells, C, *Corporations and Criminal Responsibility* (1994).

[3] Companies Act 1985, s 36.

[4] See below, at 109–11.

[5] Dowrick, FE, 'The Relationship of Principal and Agent' (1954) 17 MLR 24.

with a third party on behalf of the principal, the legal effect is that the agent usually drops out of the picture and the contract is concluded between the principal and the outsider.[6] Agency is thus a tripartite relationship involving the principal, the agent and the outsider. In the corporate context an immediate problem in seeking to apply agency principles lies in identifying the 'principal': who, within the company, can act as principal and on what basis? Broadly, the answer to these questions lies in the company's constitution which will normally provide for the board of directors to manage the company and to appoint agents.[7] The company's constitution provides the legal basis for the board of directors either itself to make contracts on behalf of the company or to appoint others to do so on its behalf.[8]

Characterising the company's constitution as the principal is a convenient fiction to which the courts have resorted for the purpose of applying agency principles to companies. But the use of that fiction leads to problems, not least of which, as is explored in this chapter, is how to deal with situations where the company's constitution does not authorise, or even expressly prohibits, the contracts which have been made on its behalf. A strict rule which denies the company the right to enforce contracts which have been made on its behalf where they are not authorised by its constitution could result in the company losing valuable opportunities which, in commercial terms, are entirely to its benefit. A strict rule could also prejudice persons who, quite reasonably, assume that they have dealt with a company but later discover that the company is not bound because of restrictions in its constitution. To expect people to check the company's constitution before contracting is impractical; where carried out, such checks simply add to the costs of contracting with a company.

Company law has developed and refined the basic proposition that power to act on the company's behalf is derived from the company's constitution. Statute has intervened to ensure that the company can be bound even in matters which are not authorised by the memorandum and articles. This statutory intervention seeks to protect outsiders in their dealings with a company and, also (although, perhaps less clearly), to enable the company to enforce contracts against outsiders despite any restrictions in its constitution. The fact that limitations in the company's constitution have not been observed is not entirely irrelevant but, broadly speaking, this is treated as an internal matter to be resolved between the shareholders and the board without affecting the validity of the contracts that have been concluded.

At the heart of a legal rule which applies agency rules and treats the corporate constitution as principal, subject to a statutory gloss, there remains a conceptual difficulty. Consider the following extract from a key statutory provision: 'In favour of a person dealing with a company in good faith, the power of the board of directors to bind the company . . . shall be deemed to be

[6] *Montgomerie v UK Mutual Steamship Association Ltd* [1891] 1 QB 370, 371 *per* Wright J.

[7] The model is Table A, arts 70 and 71. The model is normally followed although in particular types of company, such as joint ventures, special managerial structures may be devised.

[8] *Meridian Global Funds Management Asia Ltd v Securities Commission* [1995] 2 AC 500, PC, 506 *per* Lord Hoffmann.

free of any limitation under the company's constitution.'[9] There is a problem of circularity here: if the deal is not authorised by the company's constitution, how can it be said that the dealing is with the company so as to bring the person dealing within the scope of the statutory protection? The statute does not disclose the basis on which dealings are to be attributed to a company for this purpose, and agency principles do not help. Where primary rules of attribution based on the company's constitution and agency principles fail to provide an answer, the court must fashion a special rule of attribution for the particular substantive provision.[10] For the provisions in question, one tenable interpretation is that they give effect to an organic theory:[11] the board is to be regarded as the company's organ for the purpose of the sections and not simply as its agent. An organic approach would be consistent with the First Company Law Directive, art 9 (1) which states that: 'Acts done by the organs of the company shall be binding upon it even if these acts are not within the objects of the company.'[12] The Companies Act 1985, ss 35–35B give effect to art 9 and, in accordance with the general interpretative principles applying to domestic legislation which implements a directive,[13] they must be interpreted in the light of the underlying directive and so as to give effect to it. Viewed as an organ, the board's acts would, without more, be treated as acts of the company and a person who deals with the board would thus be regarded as dealing with the company. To date, the courts have not endorsed the organic approach as the basis on which a board acts for a company, instead preferring an agency analysis in which the company's constitution assumes the role of principal.[14] However, the point has not been specifically considered in

[9] Companies Act 1985, s 35A.

[10] *Meridian Global Funds Management Asia Ltd v Securities Commission* [1995] 2 AC 500, PC. This decision rejected the application of an organic approach in favour of agency principles in the interpretation of a statutory provision concerned with disclosure of interests in shares. Although critical of metaphysical undertones to the organic approach, Lord Hoffmann's opinion does not entirely rule out the possibility of it applying, as a matter of construction of a particular statutory provision, as the basis for the attribution of an act or mental state to a company. For a defence of earlier case law supporting an organic approach in relation to questions of corporate criminal liability, see Lord Cooke of Thorndon, 'Corporate Identity' (1998) 16 Company and Securities Law Journal 160; Lord Cooke of Thorndon, *Turning Points of the Common Law* (1997) 1.

[11] Kelsen, H, *The Pure Theory of Law* (1967) 150–8; 174–8. The application of an organic theory in relation to company contracts executed under seal is supported by *Northside Developments Pty Ltd v Registrar-General and Ors* (1989–90) 2 ACSR 161, H Ct of Aust, 169 *per* Mason CJ but, in the same case, rejected at 198–9 *per* Dawson J.

[12] First Company Law Directive 68/151/EEC, [1968] OJ L65/8, art 9. Under the provision which implements the directive into Irish law it is specifically provided that the board of directors or any person registered under the regulations as being authorised to bind the company constitutes an organ of the company for this purpose: European Communities (Companies) Regulations 1973, art 6.

[13] *Pickstone v Freemans plc* [1989] AC 66, HL; *Litster v Forth Dry Dock Engineering Co Ltd* [1990] 1 AC 546, HL.

[14] See *Rolled Steel Ltd v British Steel Corporation* [1986] 1 Ch 246, CA, 295 *per* Slade LJ and at 304 *per* Browne-Wilkinson LJ; *Freeman & Lockyer (A Firm) v Buckhurst Park Properties (Mangal) Ltd* [1964] 2 QB 480, CA, 504–5 *per* Diplock LJ. When the Companies Act 1989 was passing through Parliament, Lord Wedderburn noted in debate in the House of Lords that the approach in the legislation was an attempt to adapt something that had traditionally been regarded as an agent (ie the board of directors) into an organ without saying so (*Hansard*, HL, (series 5) vol 505, cols 1248–9 (6 April 1989). The First Company Law Directive (68/151/EEC, [1968] OJ L65/8) art 2 (1)(d), as interpreted by the European Court of Justice requires the registration of the names of the organs of a company and a statement of the circumstances in which they can act as organs. The

relation to the Companies Act 1985, ss 35–35B and it is still open to a court to take an organic approach to explain the operation of the protection afforded by those sections.[15]

THE SIGNIFICANCE OF CONSTITUTIONAL LIMITS? SUMMARY AND ASSESSMENT

By statute, a person who deals with a company through its board is protected against the consequences of the deal not being authorised by the company's constitution provided there is good faith. A person who does not act in good faith cannot enforce a transaction which has exceeded constitutional limitations against the company. The statutory protections afforded to those dealing with a company do not extend to directors or persons connected to directors. Transactions purported to be concluded between such persons and a company are voidable if they are not authorised by the company's constitution. It may be a breach of duty for the directors to sanction a transaction which is not permitted by the company's constitution. Individual shareholders are, in certain circumstances, empowered to seek an order from the court restraining acts that would contravene the company's constitution. For these reasons, despite the existence of the Companies Act 1985, ss 35–35B, it remains relevant to determine what is permitted by the company's constitution.

CONSTITUTIONAL LIMITS—THE MEMORANDUM

As part of the registration process every company must deliver to the registrar of companies its memorandum of association.[16] The memorandum of every company limited by shares must state: the name of the company; the situation of the registered office (England and Wales, Wales or Scotland); the objects of the company; that the liability of the members is limited; and the amount of the share capital and its division into shares of a fixed amount.[17] A public company must also declare its status as such in its memorandum.[18] Companies can choose to include additional provisions in the memorandum.

European Commission has identified English law as being defective in not providing for this: see Wooldridge, F, 'Abolishing the Ultra Vires Rule' (1989) 133 SJ 714.

[15] In *TCB Ltd v Gray* [1986] 1 Ch 621 the court refused to accept an argument that the disputed transaction was not an act of the company on the basis that to do so would drive 'a coach and horses' through the statutory predecessor of Companies Act 1985, ss 35 and 35A. This case demonstrates that the courts are prepared to adopt a robust approach to these statutory provisions in order to make them work, although the precise analysis in that case (that the protection applies to transactions which a company *purports* to enter into and deems them to be validly entered into (at 636)) leaves unresolved questions such as: when, for this purpose, does a company purport to enter into a transaction; and on what basis does the act of natural persons on its behalf become a purported corporate act? See also Davies, PL, *Gower's Principles of Modern Company Law* (6th edn, 1997) 232.

[16] Companies Act 1985, s 10 (1). [17] Ibid, s 2 (1)–(3) and (5). [18] Ibid, s 1 (3)(a).

One reason for doing so is to entrench rights more effectively than would be possible if they were included in the articles.[19]

THE OBJECTS CLAUSE AND THE *ULTRA VIRES* RULE

The objects clause contains a statement of the purpose or purposes for which the company is formed. It is this clause therefore that needs to be considered in order to establish what the board of a company is constitutionally able to do. In addition to whatever is expressly stated in the clause as being within the objects, a company also has implied power to do anything that may fairly be regarded as incidental to, or consequential upon, its stated objects.[20] The normal practice is for a company to adopt a very long objects clause which covers all of the activities in which it may wish to engage. This practice developed in response to the decision of the House of Lords in *Ashbury Rly Carriage and Iron Co Ltd v Riche*[21] that any purported contract or act outside the company's objects was *ultra vires* and, as such, entirely void and incapable of enforcement either by or against the company. According to that decision even the unanimous consent of all of the shareholders could not suffice to permit a company to conclude a contract which was not authorised by its memorandum.

The requirement for a statement of the company's objects was originally envisaged as a means of protecting the interests of shareholders: they could learn from the statement of the objects the purposes for which their investment could properly be applied.[22] However, although the Companies Act 1856, which first introduced the requirement to state the objects, did not provide for the alteration of the objects, by the twentieth century companies were allowed to change their objects by special resolution of the shareholders.[23] Once that happened, the idea that the objects clause prevented the use of shareholders' funds in ways which they had not envisaged was undermined,[24] since new purposes could be authorised with the consent of only the requisite majority (three-quarters of those voting) of the shareholders. Moreover, accounting requirements of the companies legislation and, where relevant, Stock Exchange disclosure requirements began to give investors alternative sources of information about the activities of the companies in which they invested. With the investor demand for information met in other ways, the objects clause became, at least potentially, more of a hindrance than a help to investors because it could prevent companies from diversifying their business

[19] See further Ch 9 below, at 348–51.

[20] *Attorney General v Great Eastern Rly Co* (1880) 5 App Cas 473, HL.

[21] (1875) LR 7 HL 653, HL.

[22] *Cotman v Brougham* [1918] AC 514, HL, 520 *per* Lord Parker of Waddington.

[23] Under Companies Act 1929, s 5 any change had to be approved by the court. This was changed in the Companies Act 1948 to allow for a change to become effective unless it was challenged by an application to court within a specified time. Special resolutions altering the objects are still susceptible to challenges from dissenting shareholders or, in very limited cases, creditors: Companies Act 1985, ss 5–6.

[24] *Ashbury Rly Carriage and Iron Co Ltd v Riche* (1875) LR 7 HL 653, HL, 669–70 *per* Lord Cairns LC emphasising the (then) unalterable nature of the objects clause.

into more profitable lines of activity and thereby increasing investor returns. Investor preference for companies to have the widest possible capacity was confirmed by a consultation exercise reported in 1986.[25]

It was also said that the statement of the company's objects protected those who dealt with the company because they could infer from it the extent of the company's powers.[26] But in reality the objects clause, together with the *ultra vires* rule, formed a strange sort of protection for those dealing, or wanting to deal, with a company. Someone who wanted to deal with a company but, on checking its objects clause, discovered that the proposed transaction would be *ultra vires* was certainly protected from the consequences of *ultra vires* by being able to withdraw at that stage, but the practical result was simply to prevent the conclusion of a business contract which the parties had wished to conclude in the course of their business presumably for the purpose of making a profit. Business interests would surely have been better served if the parties had been able to conclude the deal as originally envisaged. Also, the effect of the objects clause, combined with the *ultra vires* rule, was disastrous for those who dealt with a company without checking the objects clause because, if the transaction turned out to be *ultra vires*, it could not be enforced against the company.[27] In sum, then, the protection afforded by the objects clause to those dealing with the company was illusory.[28]

The *ultra vires* rule was also said to protect creditors against the application of corporate funds on purposes which they had not envisaged when they made credit available to the company.[29] However, as with those dealing with a company, the major reason why lenders were concerned about the contents of the objects clause was not because they saw it as a source of protection—they did not need to depend on restrictions found in the company's objects clause since it was always open to them to impose contractual restrictions as conditions of making finance available—but, rather, because the *ultra vires* rule created a hazard which had to be avoided. A loan to a company which was used for purposes falling outside the scope of the objects clause risked being held to be *ultra vires* and, as such, irrecoverable.[30]

[25] *Reform of the Ultra Vires Rule* (DTI Consultative Document) (1986) (the *Prentice Report*), ch III, para 5. But, against this, note *Modern Company Law: Response to the DTI's Initial Consultation Document on Company Law Reform* (NAPF) (July 1998) 2 which refers to reinforcement of the *ultra vires* doctrine as being something that many investors might welcome.

[26] *Ashbury Rly Carriage and Iron Co Ltd v Riche* (1875) LR 7 HL 653, HL, 684–5 *per* Lord Hatherley; *Cotman v Brougham* [1918] AC 514, HL, 520 *per* Lord Parker of Waddington.

[27] eg, *Re Jon Beauforte (London) Ltd* [1953] Ch 131.

[28] *Re KL Tractors Ltd* (1960–61) 106 CLR 318, H Ct of Aust, 337–8 *per* Fullager J.

[29] The use and decline of the *ultra vires* rule as a mechanism for controlling the making of corporate gifts is considered in Ch 10 below, at 358–63. Another consideration which may have influenced the courts which developed the *ultra vires* doctrine in the nineteenth century was the sense that incorporation was a privilege which had to be rigorously controlled by the State: Getz, L, 'Ultra Vires and Some Related Problems' (1969) 3 University of British Columbia Law Review 30.

[30] *Re Introductions Ltd* [1970] Ch 199, CA. In *Rolled Steel Ltd v British Steel Corporation* [1986] 1 Ch 246, CA it was held that if a power, which was stated in the objects clause, was used otherwise than in pursuit of an object, the correct analysis was that the directors had misused their power but the transaction was not *ultra vires* the company. *Re Introductions*, which had appeared to hold that borrowing in pursuit of an unauthorised objects was indeed *ultra vires*, was explained as a case where the term *ultra vires* had been used in a loose sense as covering misuse of power by

RESPONDING TO THE *ULTRA VIRES* RULE: DRAFTING OF THE OBJECTS CLAUSE

Independent Objects Clause

In response to the *ultra vires* rule, there developed the practice for companies to adopt very long objects clauses and to include an independent objects clause. An independent objects clause is to the effect that each paragraph of the objects clause is to be given the widest interpretation and is not to be limited to or restricted by reference to, or inference from, any other object; further, no object is to be treated as being subsidiary or ancillary to another. In *Cotman v Brougham*[31] the House of Lords held that the validity of a company's registration with an objects clause containing an independent objects provision could not be challenged because, under what is now the Companies Act 1985, s 13 (7)(a), the registrar's certificate of registration in respect of the company was conclusive evidence of compliance with all of the requirements for registration. Therefore the independent objects clause had to be given its full effect. This clause is now included as a matter of course in the memoranda of trading companies; in its absence, a main object rule of construction would apply whereby there would be deemed to be one main object and all of the other paragraphs in the clause would be regarded as ancillary to that main object.[32]

Statement of Powers as well as Objects

As well as stating the types of business in which the company may wish to engage, it is also standard for the objects clause to state expressly the powers that the company may wish to be able to use in pursuit of its business. Although any power that may fairly be regarded as incidental to, or consequential upon, the stated objects will be implied,[33] it is more straightforward for a company to be able, for example, to show a potential lender an express borrowing power than to have to rely on inference.[34]

There are some difficult decisions concerning the legal effect of including a statement of corporate powers in the objects clause but, in essence, these decisions seem to establish that there is a distinction between 'true' objects and 'powers' and that an independent objects clause cannot convert something that is a power into an object.[35] The significance of the distinction—

directors. The *Rolled Steel* and *Re Introductions* decisions, both of which were Court of Appeal, sit somewhat uneasily together. The complexity of the law on this point is a particular illustration of the problems which the requirement for a statement of the objects, together with the *ultra vires* rule, can produce.

[31] [1918] AC 514, HL.

[32] *Ashbury Rly Carriage and Iron Co Ltd v Riche* (1875) LR 7 HL 653, HL, 690 *per* Lord O'Hagan; *Re Haven Gold Mining Co* (1882) 20 Ch D 151, CA; *Anglo-Overseas Agencies v Green* [1961] 1 QB 1, 8.

[33] *Attorney General v Great Eastern Rly Co* (1880) 5 App Cas 473, HL.

[34] *Cotman v Brougham* [1918] AC 514, HL, 520 *per* Lord Parker of Waddington and 522 *per* Lord Wrenbury.

[35] *Rolled Steel Ltd v British Steel Corporation* [1986] 1 Ch 246, CA explaining *Re Introductions Ltd* [1970] Ch 199, CA and *Re David Payne* [1904] 2 Ch 608, CA.

which in relation to certain paragraphs commonly included in objects clauses, such as that authorising the making of gifts[36] may be difficult to apply —is that it affects the duties of those exercising a power: it is a misuse of power to act otherwise than in pursuit of a true object, but the use of a power otherwise than in pursuit of a true object is not *ultra vires* in the narrow sense as understood in *Ashbury Rly Carriage and Iron Co Ltd v Riche*.[37] In *Rolled Steel Ltd v British Steel Corporation*, the most important modern English case on the *ultra vires* rule, Slade and Browne-Wilkinson LJJ noted that the term *ultra vires* was sometimes used to describe situations in which directors exceeded their power.[38] To avoid confusion the use of the term should be restricted to those cases where the transaction is beyond the capacity of the company under its objects clause.[39]

Subjective Incidental Clause

Supplementing the list of specific powers, there is commonly included in objects clauses a clause authorising the doing of anything else which the directors may think incidental or conducive to the stated objects. In *Bell Houses Ltd v City Wall Properties Ltd*[40] the Court of Appeal held that a clause in these terms was effective to make the bona fide opinion of the directors the determinant of whether an activity was within the company's capacity. Despite the suggestion that an objects clause containing a clause worded in such subjective terms does not satisfy the statutory requirement to state the objects,[41] it is the practice of the registrar of companies to accept memoranda in this form and the effect of the issue of the certificate of incorporation is to close the question of compliance with the statutory requirements for incorporation.[42]

RESPONDING TO THE *ULTRA VIRES* RULE: LEGISLATION PERMITTING 'SHORT FORM' OBJECTS

Companies are now permitted to state in their memorandum that their object is to 'carry on business as a general commercial company'. Where a memorandum contains this statement, by statute,[43] the effect is that (a) the object of the company is to carry on any trade or business whatsoever and (b) the com-

[36] *Re Horsley and Weight Ltd* [1982] Ch 442, CA: the making of gifts can be an independent object.

[37] (1875) LR 7 HL 653, HL.

[38] [1986] 1 Ch 246, CA, 287 *per* Slade LJ and 302–3 *per* Browne-Wilkinson LJ.

[39] *Rolled Steel Ltd v British Steel Corporation* [1986] 1 Ch 246, CA, 303 *per* Browne-Wilkinson LJ.

[40] [1966] 2 QB 656, CA. The subjective incidental clause was also accepted in British Columbia (*H & H Logging Co Ltd v Random Services Corp Ltd* (1967) 63 DLR (2d) 6, BC CA) and Australia (*HA Stephenson & Son Ltd v Gillanders, Arbuthnot & Co* (1931) 45 CLR 476, H Ct of Aust).

[41] *Re Crown Bank Ltd* (1890) 44 Ch D 634.

[42] There is one exception to this in that the certificate of incorporation is not conclusive against the Crown, but proceedings by the Attorney-General to quash the registration of a company are very rare (but note *R v Registrar of Companies ex parte Attorney-General* [1991] BCLC 476).

[43] Companies Act 1985, s 3A

pany has power to do all such things as are incidental or conducive to the carrying on of any trade or business by it. This model short form objects clause was introduced into the companies legislation in 1989[44] and it was commonly assumed that companies might adopt it instead of the traditional long objects. However, it is possible that a court could construe 'trade or business' in (a) restrictively.[45] Also, since limb (b) is worded in objective terms, it may be less flexible than the subjective incidental clause to which companies are accustomed. For these reasons, companies will hesitate to move to short form objects instead of the traditional long form. Some companies have adopted a general commercial company object in addition to their existing long objects[46] but this is an unfortunate response to a measure that was intended to reduce the length of corporate documentation. The DTI has identified the short form objects clause as an obsolescent or ineffective provision of the companies legislation which fails to achieve the purpose for which it was enacted.[47]

FULL CORPORATE CAPACITY: THE CASE FOR FURTHER REFORM

The introduction of the general commercial company object in 1989 did not go as far as had been recommended by Professor Prentice in a DTI consultation paper, *Reform of the Ultra Vires Rule*,[48] which was published in 1986. His proposal was that all companies should be deemed to have full capacity[49] and that the requirement to register objects should become optional.[50] To the extent that the abolition of a requirement to publish objects could remove a source of information about a company's affairs, Professor Prentice suggested that this could be replaced by a requirement to file an annual statement on current trading activities. For public companies the position was complicated by the requirement in the Second Company Law Directive[51] for a public company to state its objects in 'the statute or instrument of incorporation', but Professor Prentice suggested that the annual activities and business statement could be deemed to be part of the memorandum of a company so as to comply with the Second Directive.

The Government was not persuaded by Professor Prentice's views on this matter. Instead the approach taken in the reforms introduced in 1989 was to leave the requirement for companies to state their objects largely unchanged save for two relatively minor points. The first change was the introduction of

[44] Inserted by Companies Act 1989, s 110 as Companies Act 1985, s 3A with effect from 4 February 1991.

[45] For example, could a company which wished to dispose of its business safely rely on a clause which authorised it only to *carry on* a trade or business? Would such wording permit a company to make charitable donations? See further Grier, NJM, 'The Companies Act 1989—a Curate's Egg' (1995) 16 Co Law 3, 5.

[46] De Gay, S, 'Problems Surrounding the Use of the New Single Objects Clause' (1993) 137 (6) SJ 146.

[47] *Modern Company Law for a Competitive Economy* DTI Consultative Paper (1998) para 3.4.

[48] DTI Consultative Document (1986) (the *Prentice Report*).

[49] *Prentice Report*, ch IV, pt B.

[50] *Prentice Report*, ch V.

[51] 77/91/EEC, [1977] OJ L26/1, art 2 (b).

the general commercial company object, a development which has proved to have had limited practical benefit. The second development related to the procedure for changing the objects. A company can now change its objects for any reason by passing a special resolution to that effect.[52] A dissenting minority of shareholders comprising the holders of at least 15 per cent of its share capital (where the company is limited by shares) or 15 per cent of its members (where it is not) can apply to court to have the alteration cancelled.[53] The court can confirm the alteration in whole or in part and can impose conditions.[54] The considerations which the court may take into account in deciding whether to confirm an alteration are not specified.[55] Any application to challenge an alteration to the objects must be made within 21 days of the passing of the resolution, as alterations cannot thereafter be challenged.[56] Where this procedure differs from its predecessor is in the unrestricted nature of the power of alteration; previously, there was a closed list of prescribed purposes for which a company could lawfully alter its objects. The practice of drafting very long objects means that, in any event, most companies do not need to change their objects very often. Also, the old prescribed limitations had little practical impact because the 21-day time-limit on challenges applied even if the alteration was not for any of the stated purposes. Thus the reform in this respect is limited in its real effect.

Aside from the particular complication of the Second Directive requirement for public companies, what arguments are there for retaining the requirement to publish objects? Provision of information is one reason, but the efforts to ensure that an objects clause is as comprehensive as possible to avoid the effects of the *ultra vires* rule mean that the typical objects clause is not a helpful guide to the actual business of a company. Also there are other, and more effective, ways of providing information. Controlling the board is another argument for keeping the requirement to state objects.[57] The internal-control function performed by the *ultra vires* rule as applied to the object clause was used by the Government spokesperson in the House of Lords to explain the purpose of the relevant provisions in the Companies Act 1989 during their passage through Parliament: the intention was to abolish the external effects of the *ultra vires* rules but to retain it as mechanism whereby the shareholders could impose an internal control on the board.[58]

[52] Companies Act 1985, s 4.

[53] Ibid, s 5. The holders of 15 per cent of debentures issued before 1 December 1947 or of later debentures issued as part of the same series as any debentures so issued can also apply to court if this is permitted by the terms of issue.

[54] Companies Act 1985, s 5 (4).

[55] A shareholder who objects to an alteration to the objects may prefer to ventilate that objection through a petition for relief from unfairly prejudicial conduct under Companies Act 1985, s 459. S 459 petitions are not subject to a minimum shareholding requirement and, if unfair prejudice is shown, the court's powers to grant relief are very flexible. On the use of Companies Act 1985, s 459 to challenge alterations to the objects see *Hansard*, HL, (series 5) vol 504, col 533 (21 February 1989) (Lord Strathclyde).

[56] Companies Act 1985, s 6 (4).

[57] *Report of the Committee on Company Law Amendment*, Cmd 6659 (1945) para 12 (Cohen Committee); *Report of the Company Law Committee*, Cmnd 1749 (1962) para 39 (v) (Jenkins Committee); *Prentice Report* (1986) ch V, para 10.

[58] *Hansard*, HL, (series 5) vol 504, col 512 (21 February 1989) (Lord Strathclyde). See also *Hansard*, HL, (series 5) vol 505, cols 1235–6 (6 April 1989) (Lord Fraser of Carmyllie).

It is a breach of duty for the directors to use the company's property on something which is not authorised by the company's objects[59] and, although this duty is owed to the company, individual shareholders can apply to court for an order restraining the doing of any such act.[60] If a company was not required to have objects, constitutional restraints could still be imposed on directors through the articles, but the enforcement of those restraints could in theory become more difficult because there is no absolute right[61] for shareholders to seek to restrain the doing of acts which are not authorised by the articles. Although a shareholder may seek an injunction by arguing that the act would put the company in breach of the statutory contract contained in the Companies Act 1985, s 14, the court will not grant such an injunction if it considers the matter complained of to be no more than an internal irregularity.[62]

It would, however, be a mistake to overestimate the degree of shareholder control that results from the treatment of acts which exceed the limits in the objects clause under the present law. The practical impact of the shareholder's right to obtain an order restraining an unauthorised act is reduced by the fact that it is not available in respect of an act to be done in fulfilment of a previously incurred legal obligation. Thus a shareholder can seek to restrain the board from committing the company to some unauthorised activity if the plan to become involved in it is discovered whilst it is still at the negotiation stage; but, in reality, the chances of a shareholder making such a discovery are limited. Once the board has concluded a contract on the company's behalf, the individual shareholder is powerless to intervene personally because the outsider will at that point acquire a legally enforceable obligation against the company unless it is one of the rare cases where the statutory protections in favour of persons dealing with companies do not apply (ie the outsider is in bad faith or is a director or a person connected to a director). From that point onwards, it is a corporate decision whether to take action against the directors for any breach of duty they may have committed in connection with the contract.[63] There is the possibility of an individual shareholder, or group of shareholders, bringing a derivative action in respect of this breach of duty on the company's behalf, but powerful restrictions govern standing to bring a derivative action irrespective of whether it is claimed that the directors have

[59] Companies Act 1985, s 35 (3).

[60] Ibid, s 35 (2). This codifies the common-law position: see *Smith v Croft (No 2)* [1988] Ch 114.

[61] Companies Act 1985, s 35A (4) does not give the shareholder a right to bring proceedings to restrain acts which would exceed limits in the company's constitution but merely preserves any right that the shareholder may have.

[62] Much has been written about the difficulty of distinguishing between those provisions of the articles which, if breached, would amount to a contravention of the Companies Act 1985, s 14 contract and those which amount only to procedural irregularities. The case law, literature and practice is reviewed in *Shareholder Remedies: A Consultation Paper* (Law Commission Consultation Paper No 142) (1996) pt 2. The Law Commission found that no practical hardship resulted from the uncertainty surrounding the scope of the s 14 contract and made no recommendation for change: see paras 14.7–14.9 and 20.2–20.4. This recommendation is confirmed in the final report on the topic: *Shareholder Remedies* (Law Commission Report No 246) (1997) para 7.12.

[63] *Smith v Croft (No 2)* [1988] Ch 114 establishes that a shareholder does not have a personal s 14 right in respect of past acts which were not authorised by the objects clause.

exceeded their power under the memorandum or have committed some other breach of duty.[64]

Thus it would appear that removing the requirement for a company to state its objects would not in reality greatly affect the balance of power between the board and the shareholders in general meeting. In considering the possibility of further reform, it may be helpful to see what has happened in some other jurisdictions which historically followed the English *ultra vires* position but which have now departed from it.

Under the Australian Corporations Law a body corporate has the legal capacity of an individual.[65] A constitution is optional,[66] as is the inclusion of a statement of the company's objects.[67] Acts which contravene the objects or any other restrictions on the use of corporate powers which may be contained in the constitution are not invalid[68] but may in some circumstances contravene other provisions of the Corporations Law.[69] The position is similar in New Zealand. Under the New Zealand companies legislation, companies enjoy full capacity to carry on or undertake any business or activity, do any act, or enter into any transaction; and, for this purpose, they enjoy full rights, powers and privileges.[70] Companies may have, but do not have to have, a constitution.[71] A company which chooses to have a constitution may include in it restrictions on corporate capacity or corporate power;[72] thus, the onus is on the company to impose restrictions if it thinks fit. A shareholder can raise the fact that the company has acted, or is proposing to act contrary to its constitution in certain proceedings against the company or its directors but lack of capacity does not make corporate acts or transfers of property invalid.[73] It is specifically provided that the fact that an act is not, or would not be, in the best interests of a company does not affect the capacity of the company to do the act.[74] Non-compliance with the constitution cannot be asserted against a person dealing with the company or who has acquired property, rights or interests from a company.[75]

The idea that constitutional limitations can be used to enable shareholders to control the directors in their management of the company but should not affect those who deal with the company is common to English, Australian and New Zealand law. However, the Antipodean jurisdictions differ from England in that this form of control is optional rather than mandated by the companies legislation. Also, in those jurisdictions a company's constitution is one

[64] *Smith v Croft (No 2)* [1988] Ch 114. It is not necessary to show fraud on the minority where the allegation is that the directors have acted outside the objects, and to that extent the rules are different. However, in all cases the court will have regard to the views of the shareholders who are independent of the alleged wrongdoing and will allow the action to proceed only if it is supported by the majority of them: *Smith v Croft (No 2)* [1988] Ch 114.

[65] Corporations Law, s 124 (Australia).

[66] Corporations Law, ss 134–6 (Australia).

[67] Corporations Law, s 122 (Australia).

[68] Corporations Law, s 125 (Australia).

[69] Ford, HAJ, Austin, RP, and Ramsay, IM, *Ford's Principles of Corporations Law* (8th edn, 1997) 57–581.

[70] Companies Act 1993, s 16 (1) (New Zealand).

[71] Companies Act 1993, s 26 (New Zealand).

[72] Companies Act 1993, s 16 (2) (New Zealand).

[73] Companies Act 1993, s 17 (New Zealand).

[74] Companies Act 1993, s 17 (3) (New Zealand).

[75] Companies Act 1993, s 18 (1)(a) (New Zealand).

document.[76] This chapter has already discussed how, under English law, shareholder enforcement rights can differ depending on whether the constitutional provision contravened, or to be contravened, is in the memorandum or the articles. Simplification of the requirements relating to the form of a company's constitution could thus pave the way for rationalisation of shareholder rights and remedies in this respect.

The Canada Business Corporations Act 1985 provides that a corporation has the capacity, rights, powers and privileges of a natural person.[77] The articles may impose internal restrictions but no act of a corporation, including any transfer of property to or by a corporation, is invalid by reason only of the fact that it contravenes the articles.[78] A shareholder can seek a restraining order in respect of an act that would contravene limitations in the articles[79] and, although this is worded in terms that would appear to authorise a restraining order to stop a company fulfilling contractual obligations already incurred, the court can act so as to protect the interests of the person who has dealt with the company in this matter.[80]

The requirement of European law that English companies legislation must give effect to relevant underlying directives restricts the scope for reform along the lines of other Commonwealth countries. However, since the requirement to state objects only applies to public companies, it would be open to the Government to abolish the requirement for private companies to state objects and to confer on those companies the capacity to do any act whatsoever. Since private companies can already achieve that position by paying advisers to produce all-embracing objects, such a change should not have any negative corporate governance implications. Instead, bringing legal requirements and the realities of corporate practice into line in this way could be seen to be a positive corporate governance move because it would stop any misguided investor from mistakenly thinking that the objects clause was an effective form of control or a helpful source of information about a company's affairs.

It could even be argued that, although apparently paradoxical, removing the requirement to state objects could improve the effectiveness of the company's constitution as an internal-control mechanism. At present, a company's stated objects define what it can do and so there is a pressure for the clause to be as comprehensive as possible. However, if, as a matter of general law, it was provided that companies could do anything subject to any restrictions imposed by its constitution, this would allow shareholders to focus on areas where they wished to restrict corporate activity safe in the knowledge that, apart from the stated restrictions, the managers of the company would be free to direct its activities in any direction they considered appropriate.

[76] Companies Act 1993, s 29 (New Zealand); Corporations Law, s 136 (Australia).

[77] Business Corporations Act 1985, s 15 (Canada). For details and a comparison with individual Canadian provinces see Ziegel, JS, Daniels, RJ, McIntosh, JG, and Johnston, DL, *Cases and Materials on Partnerships and Canadian Business Corporations* (3rd edn, 1994) 310–21.

[78] Business Corporations Act 1985 s 16 (Canada).

[79] Business Corporations Act 1985, s 247 (Canada).

[80] Ziegel, JS, Daniels, RJ, McIntosh, JG, and Johnston, DL, *Cases and Materials on Partnerships and Canadian Business Corporations* (3rd edn, 1994) 315–6.

Bolstered by clear provisions governing enforcement of the restrictions, this approach could put shareholders in a far stronger position than they are at present.

THE OBJECTS CLAUSE AND THE PROTECTION OF PERSONS DEALING WITH A COMPANY

The all-embracing nature of a typical objects clause means that there is usually little or nothing that would not be authorised. Only in unusual circumstances therefore should recourse need to be had to the Companies Act 1985, s 35 which seeks to protect persons dealing with a company from the fact that the act in question is not authorised by its objects. The Companies Act 1985, s 35 is one of the provisions implementing the First Company Law Directive,[81] art 9 which states that acts are to be binding on a company even though they are outside its objects. To appreciate the full effect of the implementation it is necessary to read the Companies Act 1985, s 35 together with the succeeding sections, ss 35A–B. The Companies Act 1985, ss 35, 35A and 35B represent the UK's second attempt to implement art 9. The drafting of the first attempt, contained in the European Communities Act 1972, s 9 (later incorporated into the Companies Act 1985 as the original s 35) was flawed.[82] The original s 35 was replaced with effect from February 1991 by the ss 35, 35A and 35B that are now in force and which are considered in this part of this chapter.

The Companies Act 1985, s 35 (1) provides that the validity of an act done by a company shall not be called into question on the ground of lack of capacity by reason of anything in the company's memorandum. There is an unattractive argument to the effect that this wording is defective because it only insulates acts which are contrary to express restrictions in the memorandum, leaving acts which are not positively authorised by the company's memorandum still open to challenge; it seems unlikely that a court would support this argument, not least because to do so would be inconsistent with the implementation of the First Directive, art 9.[83] Equally, although there is a theoretical difficulty in identifying an 'act of the company' for this purpose,[84] the court must adopt a robust interpretation on this point, since to conclude that the act is not an act of the company because it is not authorised by the objects would defeat the whole purpose of the section and put the UK in breach of its obligations under European law. To determine what is an act of the company

[81] 68/151/151, [1968] OJ L65/8.

[82] Commentaries on the implementation of First Directive, art 9 by European Communities Act 1972, s 9 include the following: Prentice, DD, 'Section 9 of the European Communities Act' (1973) 89 LQR 518; Farrar, JH, and Powles, DG, 'The Effect of Section 9 of the European Communities Act 1972' (1973) 36 MLR 270; Collier, JG, and Sealy, LS, 'European Communities Act 1972- Company Law' [1973] CLJ 1; Wyatt, D, 'The First Directive and Company Law' (1978) 94 LQR 182.

[83] *Reducing Uncertainty, The Way Forward* Legal Risk Review Committee (February 1992) app 1, annex, para 10.

[84] This point is discussed further in Ferran, EV, 'The Reform of the Law on Corporate Capacity and Directors' and Officers' Authority' (1992) 13 Co Law 124. See also Poole, J, 'Abolition of the Ultra Vires Doctrine and Agency Problems' (1991) 12 Co Law 43.

for this purpose, reference needs to be made to the Companies Act 1985, s 35A. This provides that, in favour of a person dealing with a company in good faith, the power of the board of directors to bind the company, or to authorise others to do so, shall be deemed to be free of any limitations under the company's constitution. The familiar circularity is present—the board is deemed to have unlimited power but only in favour of a person dealing with the company—but the provision can be made to work by largely ignoring[85] the words 'dealing with a company': in favour of a person who is in good faith the board has unlimited power to act itself or to delegate.

It is open to question whether the good faith limitation in the Companies Act 1985, s 35A has much value because of the difficulties in establishing bad faith. Good faith is presumed[86] and the onus is on the company to show otherwise. It is not bad faith simply to know that the directors have breached a limit under the company's constitution.[87] There is no duty to inquire whether a transaction is permitted by the company's constitution or as to any limitation on the board's power to bind the company or to authorise others to do so.[88] A person who is aware of the contents of the company's objects clause but who does not appreciate the significance of any limitations would not be in bad faith by reason only of that knowledge. Equally, a company would not be in bad faith merely because some of its agents were aware of limitations whilst others who actually concluded the transaction on its behalf were not; nor would a company be held to be in bad faith just because information had been made known to it in the past in circumstances where its current officers and agents were personally unaware of that information.[89]

There is an old rule of company law to the effect that persons are deemed to have notice of matters that are filed with the registrar of companies.[90] This rule covers restrictions and limitations in a company's memorandum and articles. Although there is a provision in the Companies Act 1989 which is intended to override this rule, this has never been brought into force.[91] However, since knowledge or notice of limitations in a company's constitution in itself does not remove good faith,[92] the continued existence of the old rule is less important than it might otherwise have been. The Companies Act 1985, s 35B expressly provides that a party to a transaction[93] with a company is under no duty to inquire as to limitations on the power of the board.

The approach taken by the UK with regard to bad faith does not take full advantage of the derogation permitted under the First Directive, art 9 whereby it is open to Member States to provide that transactions will not be binding on

85 Under the principle of purposive construction applied to domestic legislation which implements a directive: *Pickstone v Freemans plc* [1989] AC 66, HL; *Litster v Forth Dry Dock Engineering Co Ltd* [1990] 1 AC 546, HL.

86 Companies Act 1985, s 35A (2)(c).

87 Ibid, s 35A (2)(b).

88 Ibid, s 35B.

89 See *Hansard*, HL (series 5) vol 505, col 1274 (6 April 1989) (Lord Fraser of Carmyllie).

90 *Ernest v Nicholls* (1857) 6 HL Cas 401, 10 ER 1351.

91 Companies Act 1989, s 142 inserting Companies Act 1985, s 711A.

92 First Company Law Directive (68/151/EEC, [1968] OJ L65/8) art 9.2 states that limitations on the powers of an organ (as opposed to acts outside the objects of the company) may never be relied on as against third parties even if they have been disclosed.

93 In this section the term transaction is not extended to include other acts. The significance of this omission is unclear.

a company where the person dealing knew or ought to have known that the relevant act was not within the objects.[94] Having not taken advantage of that derogation in its entirety, one might question whether there is much more than a cosmetic purpose in the retention of a good faith limitation at all.[95] It would have been preferable if the legislation had followed the model of other Commonwealth jurisdictions and taken the abolition of the *ultra vires* rule to its logical conclusion: that would mean providing simply that in favour of third parties the board has unlimited power to bind the company or to authorise others to do so (and this would amount to a statement of the organic theory in relation to the board). This would not leave the company entirely without any form of redress against persons dealing with it because it would still be possible to utilise constructive trust principles against those third parties who knowingly received company property from the directors in breach of trust or who knowingly assisted directors in a dishonest scheme.[96]

It is possible for acts which are not authorised by the company's constitution to be ratified by special resolution.[97] This reverses the decision in *Ashbury Carriage v Riche* that an act which is outside the objects is void and cannot be ratified even with the unanimous consent of all of the shareholders. One interpretation of the statutory provision permitting ratification by special resolution is that a company *must* ratify before it can enforce a transaction which is not authorised by its objects.[98] This argument is without merit: any limitations in the objects clause are there to perform an internal-control function between the shareholders and the board, not to act as impediments to enforcement by the company against the persons with whom it has dealt. A better view is that the Companies Act 1985, s 35 (3) applies where a company chooses to ratify and requires the ratification in that instance to be by special resolution. One situation where the question of ratification may be in issue is where the unauthorised transaction involves a director or a person connected with a director; such a transaction is voidable but may be ratified by the company.[99] However, it is not entirely clear that the narrow interpretation of section 35 (3) would be upheld by a court,[100] and until the point is clarified by a

[94] First Company Law Directive, art 9.1. For the purpose of limiting the extent of the protection afforded to persons who deal with a company, art 9 allows a member state to distinguish between acts outside the objects and limitations on the powers of the organs of a company. In the former case, the objective approach set out in the text may be adopted but, in the latter, the limitations may never be relied upon even if they have been disclosed: art 9.2. The Companies Act 1985 does not draw this distinction.

[95] Protection of the honest was the purpose identified by the House of Lords Government spokesperson during the passage of the Bill through Parliament: *Hansard*, HL, (series 5) vol 505, col 1274 (6 April 1989) (Lord Fraser of Carmyllie).

[96] The doctrine of the constructive trust is unaffected by the statutory provisions protecting outsiders from the consequences of *ultra vires*: *International Sales and Agencies Ltd v Marcus* [1982] 3 All ER 551. That case concerned the older version of the protection contained in European Communities Act 1972, s 9 but reforms introduced by Companies Act 1989 are not thought to affect the position: see, *Hansard*, HL, (series 5) vol 505, cols 1243–7 (6 April 1989). See also *Cooperatieve Rabobbank 'Vecht en Plassengebied' v Minderhoud* [1998] 2 BCLC 507 ECJ.

[97] Companies Act 1985, s 35 (3).

[98] Poole, J, *Abolition of the Ultra Vires Doctrine and Agency Problems* (1991) 12 Co Law 43, 45.

[99] Companies Act 1985, s 322A. This provision is discussed later in this chapter below, at 99–100.

[100] Certain comments on this clause made by the Government spokesperson during the passage of the Bill through Parliament seem to support the wider view, ie that ratification is required. See *Hansard*, HL, (series 5) vol 504, col 516 (21 Feb 1989) (Lord Strathclyde).

test case it would be prudent to consider obtaining a special resolution (although, for larger companies, the costs involved in convening a general meeting for this purpose would have to be set against the risks involved in proceeding without it).

Any breach of duty committed by the directors in relation to an act which is contrary to the company's objects may be ratified by special resolution.[101] Separate special resolutions for the ratification of the act and of the breach of duty are required.[102] This prevents the bundling together of two matters on which the shareholders may have different views.

For the sake of completeness it may be noted here that outsiders are protected not only in commercial transactions which are not authorised by the memorandum but also in respect of other corporate acts.[103] This point is most relevant to the question whether there are any grounds for challenging the validity of a corporate gift. Corporate gifts are discussed further in Chapter 10.

CONSTITUTIONAL LIMITS IN THE ARTICLES AND THEIR EFFECT ON PERSONS DEALING WITH THE COMPANY

The board of a company is normally authorised by the articles to manage the company subject to the requirements of the companies legislation and to limitations imposed by the memorandum or articles or by specific special resolution of the shareholders.[104] This part of the chapter considers situations where the board does something which is authorised by the company's memorandum but which is contrary to a limit on the power of the board under the articles. A specific example of this type of situation is where the board borrows in excess of the borrowing limit in the articles.

If the board does something which is not authorised by the articles, it steps outside the limits of its actual constitutional authority. However, the Companies Act 1985, s 35A deems the board to have unlimited[105] power to bind the company. This section operates here in the same way as it does in relation to matters that are outside the objects. Thus the deeming provision is only in favour of persons dealing with the company in good faith. A person deals with a company for this purpose if he is a party to a transaction or other act to which the company is a party.[106] The difficulties of establishing bad faith are likely to mean that the good faith limitation will prove to have little substance. The mere fact that the person dealing knows (or is put on notice of the fact) that the transaction or act is not authorised by the company's constitution, does not allow the company to disown the deal because the dealer can still be in good faith despite such knowledge.

[101] Companies Act 1985, s 35 (3).

[102] Ibid.

[103] Companies Act 1985, s 35A (2)(a).

[104] Table A, art 70.

[105] ie free of limitations imposed by the memorandum, the articles, shareholders' resolutions or shareholders' agreements: Companies Act 1985, s 35A (3).

[106] Companies Act 1985, s 35A (2)(a).

INTERPRETATION OF 'LIMITATION'

There is an ambiguity in the Companies Act 1985, s 35A which potentially limits its application. It has been queried whether the reference to 'any limitation' in s 35A (1) covers provisions of the constitution, normally the articles, which govern the process by which the board of directors makes decisions, for example, quorum requirements for board meetings, or is confined only to provisions which restrict the scope of activity of a duly constituted board. There is support for the view that the legislative protection does extend to internal requirements such as quorum provisions in a case on the statutory predecessor of s 35A.[107] However, when the issue was raised in debate in the House of Lords during the passage of the Bill containing s 35A, the Government spokesperson suggested that provisions such as quorum requirements defined the board and were not limitations on its powers. If correct, this interpretation means that a person who deals with an improperly constituted board cannot look to s 35A for protection. In that event, all is not lost because the dealer may be able to fall back on an older principle of company law which was developed by the courts to insulate persons dealing with a company from internal irregularities: so long as the dealer did not know of the irregularity and was not put on notice of it, he or she was not affected by it.[108] That principle, known as the internal management rule or the rule in *Turquand*'s case,[109] is, to a large extent, now overridden by the Companies Act 1985, ss 35 and 35A but if the term 'limitation' in s 35A is interpreted restrictively, it will remain relevant for this purpose.

The statutory provisions and the internal management rule do not give the same level of protection. The statute protects those who are in good faith and, in view of the way good faith is defined, there are likely to be few cases where lack of good faith can be successfully established. The protection afforded by the internal management is much less extensive. A person who is aware of the irregularity is not protected by the rule, nor is a person who is put on inquiry.[110] Thus, if board minutes provided to a bank in connection with a financing arrangement show that a director who had a personal interest did not abstain from the decision to approve the arrangement, as required under the quorum provision of the articles, the bank will be deemed to know of the irregularity and will lose the protection of the internal management rule.[111] An example of a situation where the dealer may be put on inquiry is where a bank, which is aware of a history of strained relations between the two directors of a company, is provided with board minutes showing that a financing arrangement has been authorised by a board meeting attended by only one of

[107] *TCB Ltd v Gray* [1986] Ch 621, 635 *per* Browne-Wilkinson VC. This is described by the Law Commission as 'the better view': *The Execution of Deeds and Documents by or on behalf of Bodies Corporate* (Law Commission Consultation Paper No 143) (1996) para 5.13.

[108] *Clarke v Imperial Gas Light and Coke Co* (1832) 4 B & Ad 315, 110 ER 473; *County of Gloucester Bank v Rudry Merthyr Steam and Home Coal Colliery Co* [1895] 1 Ch 629, CA, 636 *per* Lindley LJ; *Re County Life Assurance Co* (1870) LR 5 Ch App 288.

[109] *Royal British Bank v Turquand* (1856) 6 El & Bl 327, 119 ER 886.

[110] *Morris v Kanssen* [1946] AC 459, HL, 474–5 *per* Lord Simonds.

[111] *Rolled Steel Ltd v British Steel Corporation* [1986] 1 Ch 246, CA.

those directors and a newly appointed director; if the bank is aware that the two persons who attended the meeting are in fact related or otherwise connected,[112] it should investigate the validity of the appointment and, hence, the propriety of the board meeting as it may not be able to rely on the internal management rule in that situation. The nature of the transaction itself can be sufficient to put the dealer on inquiry, such as where a company enters into a transaction from which it gains no apparent benefit.[113]

It is difficult to find a compelling argument for treating a person who has dealt with an inquorate board more harshly than one who has dealt with a quorate board but in a transaction which is, say, not authorised by the company's objects. But that is the position that is arrived at if a restrictive interpretation of the term 'limitation' in section 35A is adopted. Laws in favour of persons dealing with a company need to achieve a balance between the promotion of business convenience and the prevention of fraud.[114] In the Companies Act 1985 the legislature has chosen to set that balance by reference to the good faith test. That test should apply to all of the provisions of a company's constitution. Requiring those dealing with a company to continue to have to look to two sets of rules for protection merely complicates the law and inconveniences business.

CONSTITUTIONAL LIMITATIONS AND TRANSACTIONS WITH DIRECTORS OR CONNECTED PERSONS

Where a director is a party to a transaction with the company in which the directors exceed any limitations on their powers under the company's constitution, the Companies Act 1985, s 35A does not apply. Instead, the transaction is voidable at the instance of the company.[115] The same rule applies to transactions between a company and persons who, as determined by statute,[116] are connected to its directors. It makes no difference for this purpose whether the director who is a party to the transaction participated in the company's decision to enter into it.[117]

Instead of voiding such a transaction, the company may choose to ratify it.[118] If the limitations which have been exceeded are in the company's memorandum, the ratification must be done by means of a special resolution.[119] If limitations in the articles have been exceeded, ratification may be effected by

[112] *B Liggett (Liverpool) Ltd v Barclays Bank Ltd* [1928] 1 KB 48.

[113] *EBM Co Ltd v Dominion Bank* [1937] 3 All ER 555, PC; *AL Underwood Ltd v Bank of Liverpool* [1924] 1 KB 775, CA; *Northside Developments Pty Ltd v Registrar-General and Ors* (1989–90) 2 ACSR 161, H Ct of Aust.

[114] *Northside Developments Pty Ltd v Registrar-General and Ors* (1989–90) 2 ACSR 161, H Ct of Aust, 171 *per* Mason CJ.

[115] Companies Act 1985, s 322A.

[116] Ibid, s 346.

[117] The common-law internal-management rule also does not protect insiders such as directors: *Howard v Patent Ivory Manufacturing Co* (1888) 38 Ch D 156. However, a much criticised decision of the Court of Appeal established that a director who did not participate in the company's decision was not to be treated as an insider for this purpose: *Hely-Hutchinson v Brayhead Ltd* [1968] 1 QB 549, CA. Companies Act 1985, s 322A overrides this distinction.

[118] Companies Act 1985, s 322A (5)(d).

[119] Ibid, s 35 (3).

means of an ordinary resolution. The significance of the requirement for a special resolution in respect of contravention of the memorandum is that one of the recognised cases where a minority shareholder can bring a derivative action on behalf of the company is where the matter complained of can only be ratified by special resolution[120] (although, even then, the action will only be allowed to proceed where it is supported by the majority of the shareholders excluding those who are implicated in the impropriety). But, if constitutional limitations are to operate as an effective internal control mechanism between the board and the shareholders in general meeting, they should be subject to the same enforcement regime irrespective of whether they are derived from the memorandum or the articles. This would suggest that a special resolution should be required in either case.

A transaction with a director or connected person in which constitutional limits have been exceeded also ceases to be voidable if: (i) restitution of any money or other asset which was the subject matter of the transaction is no longer possible; (ii) the company is indemnified for any loss or damage resulting from the transaction; or (iii) rights acquired bona fide for value and without notice by a person who is not a party to the transaction would be affected by the avoidance.[121] Whether or not the transaction is avoided, the contracting party is liable to account to the company for personal gains made directly or indirectly by the transaction and to indemnify it for any loss or damage.[122] If the contracting party is a connected person rather than director, there is a defence based on lack of knowledge that the directors were exceeding their powers.[123] The directors who authorised the transaction on the company's behalf are also liable to account to the company for any personal gains that they have made directly or indirectly by the transaction and to indemnify the company for any loss or damage.[124] The statute does not state how the company's loss or damage is to be assessed for the purpose of the indemnity mentioned in the section, but case law on another section of the Companies Act 1985 which uses the same language sheds light on the point. It has been held that where a company acquires an asset that later falls in value, its recoverable loss is not limited to the difference (if any) between the market price of the asset at the date of the transaction and the price paid but also covers loss resulting from the post-acquisition decline in the value of that asset.[125]

It would be possible for a company to enter into a contract with a number of parties, of whom some are protected by the Companies Act 1985, s 35A whilst others are not because they are directors or connected persons. Those parties who are protected by s 35A may apply to court for an order affirming, severing or setting aside the transaction on such terms as appear to the court to be just.[126]

[120] *Edwards v Halliwell* [1950] 2 All ER 1064, CA.

[121] Companies Act 1985, s 322A (5)(a)–(c).

[122] Ibid, s 322A (3).

[123] Ibid, s 322A (6).

[124] Ibid, s 322A (3).

[125] *Re Duckwari plc* [1998] 3 WLR 913, CA.

[126] Companies Act 1985, s 322 A (7). There is no equivalent provision covering the case of a multi-party transaction involving some parties who are in good faith for the purposes of Companies Act 1985, s 35A and others who are not.

INDIVIDUALS ACTING ON THE COMPANY'S BEHALF—AGENTS OR ORGANS?

Apart perhaps from the very smallest companies, it would not be practicable for the board to authorise all, or even most, of the contracts of the business. The next part of this chapter considers the circumstances in which the acts of an individual who purports to act for a company are effective to bind the company to transactions and to enable it to benefit from them.

It would be possible to view some individual corporate officers as organs of the company and, in that way, to attribute their acts to the company. This, for example, is the approach taken in the Irish legislation implementing the First Company Law directive, art 9:

> . . . any transaction entered into by any organ of the company, being its board of directors or any person registered under these regulations as a person authorised to bind the company, shall be deemed to be within the capacity of the company and any limitation of the powers of that board or person, whether imposed by the memorandum or articles of association or otherwise, may not be relied upon . . .

This is not, however, the course that has been adopted in the UK.[127] Instead, the Companies Act 1985, s 35A in effect treats the board as the organ of the company (although it does not actually say so) and individuals who act on its behalf as the company's agents. In this respect the statute reflects traditional company law as developed by the judges: it is to agency principles that the courts have generally turned when seeking to determine whether a company is bound by, and can benefit from, a contract that an individual has purported to conclude on its behalf.[128] This means that where an individual purports to act on a company's behalf but the transaction contravenes the company's constitution, say because it is not within the company's stated objects, the company may be bound, and able to benefit, but to establish whether that is the case it is necessary to consider both the statutory requirements and also agency principles as developed by the courts.

AGENCY—AN OUTLINE[129] OF THE RELEVANT PRINCIPLES

There are two main types of authority: actual authority and ostensible or apparent authority. Actual authority is authority which the principal confers, either expressly or impliedly, on the agent. An executive director appointed under a written service contract has express actual authority to bind the company to the extent that this is authorised by his contract. Where the terms of appointment to an executive position within a company are not spelt out in an express service contract, actual authority to bind the company may nevertheless be

[127] The *Prentice Report* (1986) did include a recommendation that the acts of individual directors should bind the company: ch IV, D. It appears that in practice Irish companies have not taken advantage of the provision for registration of organs other than the board: Forde, M, *Company Law* (1992) 445.

[128] *Freeman & Lockyer (A Firm) v Buckhurst Park Properties (Mangal) Ltd* [1964] 2 QB 480, CA.

[129] See Reynolds, FMB, *Bowstead and Reynolds on Agency* (16th edn, 1996); Fridman, GHL, *Law of Agency* (7th edn, 1996).

implied from the circumstances. Actual authority may also be implied where a person is allowed *de facto* to assume a position but is never expressly appointed. Thus in *Hely-Hutchinson v Brayhead Ltd*[130] the Court of Appeal held that the person who had assumed the role of managing director, but who had never been formally appointed to that position, had the authority of a managing director and, as such, was able to bind the company to contracts of guarantee and indemnity.

The crucial distinction between actual authority and ostensible authority is that actual authority is a relationship between the principal and agent and ostensible authority is the authority of an agent as it *appears* to others. Ostensible authority is created 'by a representation, made by the principal to the contractor, intended to be and in fact acted upon by the contractor, that the agent has authority'.[131] The agent is not a party to the relationship created by the principal's representation and the representation, when acted upon, acts as an estoppel preventing the principal from claiming that it is not bound.[132] Actual authority and ostensible authority can coincide[133] but ostensible authority can also exist in circumstances where the agent has no actual authority. Thus, if the company restricts the powers of an executive director in some respect, that director has no actual authority, whether express or implied, to bind the company in matters covered by the restriction; but an outsider dealing with the director who is unaware of the restriction may be able to hold the company to the transaction on the basis of ostensible authority. Ostensible authority is based on estoppel: the company is estopped from denying a representation about an individual's authority which the other party could, and reasonably did, rely upon.[134]

OSTENSIBLE AUTHORITY DERIVED FROM POSITION: USUAL AUTHORITY

Ostensible authority can derive from the position that an individual holds. The law ascribes a certain scope of authority to certain positions within a company and an individual who holds one of those positions is therefore said to have the authority attaching to the position. This form of ostensible authority is sometimes described as usual authority—the authority that is usual to the position. Some care has to be taken with regard to the use of the phrase 'usual authority' because although it is used here to denote the ostensible authority that goes with a position, it can also be used to

[130] [1968] 1 QB 549, CA.

[131] *Freeman & Lockyer (A Firm) v Buckhurst Park Properties (Mangal) Ltd* [1964] 2 QB 480, CA, 503 *per* Diplock LJ.

[132] Ibid.

[133] Ibid. *Hely-Hutchinson v Brayhead Ltd* [1968] 1 QB 549, CA, 583 *per* Lord Denning MR.

[134] *Rama Corpn Ltd v Proved Tin and General Investments Ltd* [1952] 2 QB 147; *The Raffaella* [1985] 2 Lloyd's Rep 36, CA, 41 *per* Browne-Wilkinson LJ. Although the English courts usually cite estoppel as the basis of ostensible authority, there is much argument on the point amongst commentators: see Reynolds, FMB, *Bowstead and Reynolds on Agency* (16th edn, 1996) para 8–029 and authorities cited there.

describe the implied actual authority that an individual holds by virtue of a position.[135]

A managing director or, adopting more modern terminology, chief executive officer has usual authority to bind the company in a wide variety of matters in the ordinary course of business.[136] The limits of such authority may depend on the size of the company and the type of business in which it is engaged.[137] It does not extend to authority to commence litigation in the company's name.[138] There is Australian case law to the effect that a managing director cannot commit the company to debt financing arrangements outside the ordinary course of day-to-day trading[139] nor make other critical decisions relating to the possible winding up of the company.[140]

The law does not ascribe general authority to bind the company to the position of chairman.[141] It has been said that the primary function of the chairman is to preside at meetings and that the office implies no particular authority.[142] Non-executive directors also have very limited usual authority.[143] The company secretary has usual authority to bind the company in administrative matters.[144]

OSTENSIBLE AUTHORITY DERIVED FROM HOLDING OUT

Ostensible authority can also arise from holding out.[145] This form of ostensible authority does not depend on the position which an individual holds but

[135] *First Energy UK (Ltd) v Hungarian International Bank Ltd* [1993] BCLC 1409, [1993] BCC 533, CA; *Armagas Ltd v Mundogas SA* [1986] AC 717, HL. The term 'usual authority' can also be used in a third sense in the context of the liability of an undisclosed principal for the agent's unauthorised contracts. This form of usual authority need not be explored here but for further analysis and references see Sealy, LS, and Hooley, RJA, *Text and Materials in Commercial Law* (1994) 100–4.

[136] *Freeman & Lockyer (A Firm) v Buckhurst Park Properties (Mangal) Ltd* [1964] 2 QB 480, CA, although, strictly, this was a case involving holding out rather than usual authority; *Crabtree-Vickers Pty Ltd v Australian Direct Mail Advertising & Addressing Co Pty Ltd* (1975) 133 CLR 72, H Ct of Aust; *State Bank of Victoria v Parry & Ors* (1990) 2 ACSR 15, WA SC, 29 *per* Nicholson J; *Northside Developments Pty Ltd v Registrar-General and Ors* (1989–90) 2 ACSR 161, H Ct of Aust, 201 *per* Dawson J.

[137] *CLC Group v Cambridge Gulf Holdings NL* [1997] 25 ACSR 296, Fed Ct of Aust, 323 *per* Carr J.

[138] *Mitchell & Hobbs (UK) Ltd v Mill* [1996] 2 BCLC 102.

[139] *Re Tummon Investments Pty Ltd* (1993) 11 ACSR 637, Q SC.

[140] *Re Qintex Ltd (No 2)* (1990) 2 ACSR 479, Tas SC; *Nece Pty Ltd v Ritek Incorporation* [1997] 504 FCA (11 June 1997).

[141] *Hely-Hutchinson v Brayhead Ltd* [1968] 1 QB 549, CA.

[142] *State Bank of Victoria v Parry & Ors* (1990) 2 ACSR 15, WA SC, 29 (Nicholson J).

[143] *Houghton & Co v Nothard Lowe & Wills* [1927] 1 KB 246, CA (affirmed [1928] AC 1); *Northside Developments Pty Ltd v Registrar-General and Ors* (1989–90) 2 ACSR 161, H Ct of Aust, 201 *per* Dawson J. It has been held that a single director has usual authority to sign cheques or other negotiable instruments on behalf of the company: *Re Land Credit Co of Ireland* (1869) LR 4 Ch App 460.

[144] *Panorama Developments (Guildford) Ltd v Fidelis Furnishing Fabrics Ltd* [1971] 2 QB 711, CA.

[145] Usual authority may be viewed as a form a holding out—the individual is held out as having the authority attaching to the position—but it is convenient to treat instances of specific holding out separately from the holding out involved in usual authority. See further Reynolds, FMB, *Bowstead and Reynolds on Agency* (16th edn, 1996) para 8–018 where the two forms of ostensible authority are distinguished.

on a representation arising from the factual circumstances that the person who has purported to act on behalf on the company has authority to do so. To bind the company, the general rule is that the holding out must be done by someone who has actual authority either generally or in the particular matter to which the contract relates. Managerial power in a company is ultimately traced back to the board of directors. The facts must demonstrate that the board, or someone to whom the board has delegated actual authority has held out the 'agent' as having authority in respect of this matter. An exception to the general rule must be made where the company's constitution does not empower the board to engage in transactions of the kind which the 'agent' has purported to conclude on the company's behalf, for example, where they fall outside the company's objects or they exceed limitations imposed on the board by the articles of association. In that case the holding out principle must be combined with the Companies Act 1985, s 35A which, in favour of a person dealing with a company in good faith deems the power of the board to bind the company *or to authorise others to do so* (emphasis added) to be free of any limitations under the company's constitution.

The opposite end of the spectrum from constitutional limitations are provisions, usually in the articles, permitting the board to delegate power. Table A, arts 71 and 72, for example, allow the board to appoint agents and to delegate to committees and also to individual directors. Agents may be given authority to sub-delegate.[146] The fact that the company has such provisions in its articles does not in itself amount to a basis on which the company may become bound; there is no scope for the argument that a company is bound by the actions of an individual who has purported to act on its behalf merely because authority *could have been* delegated to that individual. The facts must demonstrate an appropriate holding out, either in the form of an express representation from the board or from someone with actual authority,[147] or in the form of an inference from the circumstances.[148] Provisions in the articles permitting delegation do not create authority where it does not otherwise exist.[149] They are relevant only to the extent that if the person seeking to enforce the contract against the company was aware of them and the conduct of the representor was consistent with advantage having been taken of them, then this can help to establish that there was indeed a holding out.

[146] Table A, art 71.

[147] *Armagas Ltd v Mundogas SA* [1986] AC 717, HL.

[148] *Freeman & Lockyer (A Firm) v Buckhurst Park Properties (Mangal) Ltd* [1964] 2 QB 480, CA, 498 *per* Pearson LJ.

[149] *Northside Developments Pty Ltd v Registrar-General and Ors* (1989–90) 2 ACSR 161, H Ct of Aust, 167 *per* Mason CJ and 196 *per* Dawson J. Before the *Freeman & Lockyer* decision the cases were unclear on this point and there was an argument to the effect that a dealer could use the indoor management rule in order to bind the company, ie that it could be assumed that delegation, an internal matter, had taken place as permitted by the articles. For a discussion of that argument and the case law on which it was based see Campbell, ID, 'Contracts with Companies' (1960) 76 LQR 115; Thompson, AR, 'Company Law Doctrines and Authority to Contract' (1956) 11 University of Toronto Law Journal 248.

OSTENSIBLE AUTHORITY AND RELIANCE

The person to whom a representation of authority is made must rely on it in the dealings with the company. If that person knows or is put on notice of the fact that the individual who purported to act on the company's behalf had no actual authority he cannot claim to have relied on ostensible authority (either in the form of usual authority or on the basis of holding out) so as to bind the company. An illustration of circumstances which are sufficiently suspicious to put the third party on inquiry as to the agent's authority is provided by the facts of *AL Underwood Ltd v Bank of Liverpool*[150] where a director paid cheques which had been made out to the company into his personal account. It was held that the act of the agent in paying the principal's cheques into his own account was so unusual as to put the bank on inquiry.

It used to be the case that restrictions in a company's constitution could prevent reliance on ostensible authority. That was first because of the *ultra vires* rule: acts not authorised by the objects clause could never bind the company. It also followed from the deemed notice rule: the company's memorandum and articles were public documents filed with the registrar of companies and people could not successfully plead ostensible authority where this was inconsistent with the information that was publicly available.[151] So far as constitutional limitations on the board are concerned, the position is now governed by the Companies Act 1985, ss 35, 35A and 35B. As a result, the old limitation on reliance on ostensible authority that followed from constitutional restrictions no longer applies in relation to persons who deal in good faith, provided that the facts demonstrate an appropriate holding out by the board of directors.

It would be usual to find restrictions on the actual authority of individual directors and officers in their contracts of employment rather than in the company's constitutional documents. Contracts of employment are not filed with the registrar of companies and there is no question of the public being deemed to have notice of the contents of those documents. However, it would be open to a company to impose restrictions on its officers in its constitution, for example, by means of a provision in the articles to the effect that the specified officers cannot conclude contracts over a certain amount. There is an unresolved difficulty with regard to the situation where the board, without exceeding any direct limitation on its own powers, holds out an individual officer as having authority to conclude a contract in circumstances where this is contrary to a constitutional limit on the individual officer's authority. The Companies Act 1985, s 35A overrides constitutional limitations on the board's powers to delegate, but it is unclear whether this would extend to a provision which is expressed as a limitation on an individual. Arguably it should since there is little difference between a provision which is expressed as a restriction on the board's power to delegate authority to conclude contracts and one

150 [1924] 1 KB 775, CA. See also *EBM Co Ltd v Dominion Bank* [1937] 3 All ER 555, PC; *Rolled Steel Ltd v British Steel Corporation* [1986] 1 Ch 246, CA.

151 *Ernest v Nicholls* (1857) 6 HL Cas 401, 10 ER 1351.

which is expressed as a limitation on an individual's authority. If the Companies Act 1985, s 35A does not apply, the person dealing with the individual who has purported to act for the company would have to look to prospective s 711A (1) of the Companies Act 1985 for protection.[152] This section, which is not in force at the time of writing, is to reverse the deemed notice of the contents of public documents rule, but the effect of the reversal is uncertain because the section provides that the reversal is to be without prejudice to the question whether a person is affected by notice of any matter by reason of a failure to make such inquiries as ought reasonably to be made. What will be regarded as falling within the scope of the 'inquiries as ought reasonably to be made' is not clear and the qualified nature of the intended abolition of the notice rule may undermine the practical value of this reform.

'SELF-AUTHORISING' AGENTS

The doctrine of ostensible authority attempts to achieve a balance between the protection of persons who deal with individuals who purport to act for others and the protection of principals from being fixed with liabilities which have not been properly processed in accordance with internal authorisation procedures. The doctrine is especially important in organisations, such as many companies, that have complex management and command structures.[153] Clearly, an organisation should not be bound just because someone has purported to act on its behalf and there should be some onus on the other party to check the credentials of the individual with whom they are dealing. Equally, there has to be some limit on the extent of the inquiries that the person dealing should be required to make if contracting with a complex organisation is not to become practically impossible. To take an extreme and absurd example, a person who concludes a multimillion-pound deal with an individual who is known to be a junior clerical officer without inquiring as to his or her authority to bind the company, should bear the risk that the transaction is not authorised. In contrast, the law would not facilitate business convenience if it did not allow a dealer safely to assume that, in the absence of special facts, the managing director or chief executive officer of a company engaged in the business of selling machinery can bind the company to contracts for the sale of machines.[154]

A classic summary of the elements of ostensible authority states that the line is drawn where *the company* makes an appropriate representation which is acted upon by the person to whom it is made.[155] The company for this purpose means someone who has actual authority to act on its behalf (as modified by the Companies Act 1985, s 35A). It follows from this that an agent who

[152] To be inserted by Companies Act 1989, s 142.

[153] *Canadian Laboratory Supplies Ltd v Engelhard Industries of Canada Ltd* (1979) 97 DLR (3d) 1, SC of Can, 24 *per* Estey J.

[154] *Crabtree-Vickers Pty Ltd v Australian Direct Mail Advertising & Addressing Co Pty Ltd* (1975) 133 CLR 72, H Ct of Aust.

[155] *Freeman & Lockyer (A Firm) v Buckhurst Park Properties (Mangal) Ltd* [1964] 2 QB 480 CA, 504–5 *per* Diplock LJ.

represents himself as having more authority than is actually the case should not be able to bind the company in matters relating to that over-represented authority. Equally an agent who does not have actual authority in a particular matter cannot represent that someone else has that authority. These principles were strictly applied by the High Court of Australia in *Crabtree-Vickers Pty Ltd v Australian Direct Mail Advertising & Addressing Co Pty Ltd.*[156] In that case a director purported to conclude a contract on the company's behalf but it fell outside the scope of his actual authority to do so. The managing director had made a representation as to the director's authority but the managing director himself did not have actual authority to conclude the particular contract. It was held that in the absence of a representation from someone with actual authority the company was not bound.[157]

Crabtree-Vickers Pty Ltd v Australian Direct Mail Advertising & Addressing Co Pty Ltd[158] was a very harsh decision because the managing director in that case himself had ostensible authority to enter into the contract in question. The High Court of Australia held that a person with ostensible authority could not make a representation which could be relied upon as giving a further agent ostensible authority. Later English cases have suggested a less strict approach. In *British Bank of the Middle East v Sun Life Assurance Co of Canada (UK) Ltd*[159] it was held that the general manager of a branch office of an insurance company had no authority whatsoever to give an undertaking on the company's behalf and, equally, had no authority to represent that a more junior employee, a unit manager, had the requisite authority. However, Lord Brandon of Oakbrook stated that if the manager had had ostensible authority to make a representation about the authority of the junior employee, the consequence in law would have been that the employee would have had ostensible authority to bind the insurance company.

Just as it may be possible for an individual who has ostensible authority in a particular matter to represent that another also has authority so as to give rise to further ostensible authority, the English cases also indicate that an individual who does not have authority, actual or ostensible, to conclude a contract may sometimes be able to make representations about the approval of the transaction so as to render it enforceable against the principal. In *The Raffaella* Browne-Wilkinson LJ said:[160]

> It is obviously correct that an agent who has no actual or apparent authority either (a) to enter into a transaction or (b) to make representations as to the transaction cannot hold himself out as having authority to enter into the transaction so as to affect the principal's position. But, suppose a company confers actual or apparent authority on X to make representations and X erroneously represents to a third party that Y has authority to enter into a transaction; why should not such a representation be relied on as part of the holding out of Y by the company? By parity of reasoning, if a company confers actual or apparent authority on A to make representations on the company's behalf but no actual authority on A to enter into the specific transaction, why should a

156 (1975) 133 CLR 72, H Ct of Aust.

157 In Australia it has since been largely overridden by legislation: Tomasic, R, Jackson, J, and Woellner, R, *Corporations Law Principles, Policy and Process* (3rd edn, 1996) para 5.33.

158 (1975) 133 CLR 72, H Ct of Aust.

159 [1983] 2 Lloyd's Rep 9, HL.

160 [1985] 2 Lloyd's Rep 36, CA, 43.

representation made by A as to his authority not be capable of being relied on as one of the acts of holding out?

Representations by an individual who lacked authority to conclude a transaction were the subject of the decision of the House of Lords in *Armagas Ltd v Mundogas SA*.[161] It was held that an individual who was known not to have authority to conclude a transaction could not bind the principal by representing that the transaction had been approved at a higher level. This decision was distinguished[162] by the Court of Appeal in *First Energy (UK) v Hungarian International Bank*[163] where it was held that a bank manager who had no authority to make an offer on the bank's behalf had ostensible authority by virtue of his position (that is, what has been described in this chapter as a form of usual authority) to communicate that head office approval had been given to the transaction in question. Hence, the company was bound notwithstanding that the other party knew that the manager did not have authority to conclude the contract himself. The Court of Appeal said that the representor in *Armagas Ltd v Mundogas*[164] had not had ostensible authority to communicate decisions made by seniors and noted that the House of Lords in the earlier case had not ruled out the possibility of an individual who was known not to have actual authority to deal nevertheless being able to communicate approval. According to the Court of Appeal, commercial reality and common sense indicated that the company should be bound on the facts in question; it was in line with the parties' reasonable expectations that a bank manager should be able to communicate the fact of approval at a higher level and it would fly in the face of the way in which negotiations were conducted in practice to reach the opposite conclusion and to require the dealer to check with the managing director or with the board. On commercial grounds the decision in *First Energy* is pragmatic and sensible but it has generated some controversy amongst lawyers because, it is argued, it comes close to rendering meaningless the basic principles of ostensible authority to allow someone who knows that the agent does not have actual authority to conclude a transaction nevertheless to enforce it against the principal.[165] It has been judicially stated that cases where an agent who is known not to have authority can bind the principal through his or her own representations should be extremely rare.[166]

RATIFICATION

If an individual purports to act on behalf of a company but lacks authority to do so, it is open to the company to ratify the transaction. Ratification means

[161] [1986] AC 717, HL.

[162] Whether the decisions can properly be reconciled has been doubted: see Reynolds, FMB, 'The Ultimate Apparent Authority' (1993) 110 LQR 21 and Reynolds, FMB, *Bowstead and Reynolds on Agency* (16th edn, 1996) para 8–023.

[163] [1993] BCLC 1409, [1993] BCC 533, CA.

[164] [1986] AC 717, HL.

[165] Reynolds, FMB, *Bowstead and Reynolds on Agency* (16th edn, 1996) para 8–023.

[166] *Suncorp Insurance and Finance v Milano Assicurazioni Spa* [1993] 2 Lloyd's Rep 225, 232 *per* Waller J.

that the company adopts the contract from the time that it was first concluded. The retrospective nature of ratification means that it is not possible for a company to ratify a contract which an 'agent' purported to conclude on its behalf at a time prior to the incorporation of the company.[167]

Ratification[168] may be implied from conduct, as where the company, knowing that it could disclaim all responsibility, chooses to perform the obligations which have been incurred on its behalf or accepts performance from the other party. It may also be express in the form of a decision by a duly authorised agent or by the board. Shareholder resolutions ratifying contracts which exceed limitations in the company's constitution have been discussed in earlier parts of this chapter

CONTRACTS UNDER THE COMMON SEAL[169]

A company may make a contract in writing under its common seal.[170] Any formalities required by law in the case of a contract made by an individual also apply (unless a contrary intention appears) to a contract made by or on behalf of a company.[171]

The Companies Act 1985, s 36A provides that a company executes a document by the affixing of its common seal. It is not now obligatory for a company to have a common seal.[172] Whether or not a company has a common seal, a document signed by a director and the secretary of the company or by two directors of the company, and expressed (in whatever form of words) to be executed by the company has the same effect as if executed under the common seal of the company.[173] A document executed by a company which makes it clear on its face that it is intended by the person or persons making it to be a deed has effect, upon delivery, as a deed; and it is presumed, unless a contrary intention is proved, to have been delivered upon it being so executed.[174] A deed has been defined as a written instrument which is executed with the necessary formality and by which an interest, right or property passes or is confirmed, or an obligation binding on some person is created or confirmed.[175] Not all documents to which the common seal is commonly affixed are deeds. For example, share certificates are often sealed even though they do not confer or confirm ownership of the shares; a reason for sealing share certificates is that certificates under the common seal are prima-facie evidence of title to the shares.[176] Where a company has a common seal, it is

[167] *Kelner v Baxter* (1866) LR 2 CP 174.

[168] For a summary of the principles governing ratification see *Suncorp Insurance and Finance v Milano Assicurazioni Spa* [1993] 2 Lloyd's Rep 225, 234–5 *per* Waller J.

[169] See generally *The Execution of Deeds and Documents by or on behalf of Bodies Corporate* (Law Commission Consultation Paper No 143) (1996) and *The Execution of Deeds and Documents by or on behalf of Bodies Corporate* (Law Commission Report No 253) (1998).

[170] Companies Act 1985, s 36.

[171] Ibid.

[172] Companies Act 1985, s 36A (3) inserted by Companies Act 1989, s 130 (2).

[173] Companies Act 1985, s 36A (4).

[174] Ibid, s 35A (5).

[175] *The Execution of Deeds and Documents by or on behalf of Bodies Corporate* (Law Commission Consultation Paper No 143) (1996) para 2.6.

[176] Companies Act 1985, s 186.

permitted to have an official seal for sealing documents creating or evidencing securities. The official seal is a facsimile of the common seal with the addition on its face of the word 'Securities'. The official seal when affixed to a document has the same effect as the company's common seal.[177]

The Companies Act 1985, s 36A (6)[178] provides that in favour of a purchaser a document is deemed to have been duly executed by a company if it purports to be signed by a director and the secretary of the company and, where it makes it clear on its face that it is intended by the person or persons making it to be a deed, to have been delivered upon its being executed. A purchaser here means a purchaser in good faith for valuable consideration and includes a lessee, mortgagee or other person who for valuable consideration acquires an interest in the property. Lessors can also be purchasers for the purposes of this section.[179] It has been held that this deeming provision applies not only where a document is executed under the Companies Act 1985, s 36A (4), that is by the signature of a director and secretary or of two directors, but also where the common seal is affixed and, in accordance with the articles,[180] a director and the secretary or two directors sign to authenticate the sealing.[181]

The meaning of 'purports to be signed' is not certain. It presumably covers any lack of authority on the part of the signing officers but it is open to argument whether it also encompasses forged signatures. If it does, the effect of the Companies Act 1985, s 36A (6) in respect of documents within its scope is to reverse the position at common law, which was that a forged document would never bind the company.[182] The common-law rule certainly continues to apply to forged documents which are not within the Companies Act 1985, s 36A (6) because they do not purport to be executed by a director and secretary or by two directors. It is widely thought, however, that the common-law rule about forgeries, which itself is a qualification to the general principle that persons dealing with a company can presume that all internal procedures have been complied with (the internal-management rule) and can thus assume the validity of a sealed document,[183] should apply only where there is

[177] Companies Act 1985, s 40 provides for the official seal and specifies its effects.

[178] Companies Act 1985, s 36A (6) is in similar terms to a more limited protection for purchasers provided by Law of Property Act 1925, s 74. For a comparison of the two provisions see *The Execution of Deeds and Documents by or on behalf of Bodies Corporate* (Law Commission Consultation Paper No 143) (1996) paras 11.38–11.44.

[179] *Johnsey Estates (1990) Ltd v Newport Marketworld Ltd,* 10 May 1996, Ch D, (Judge Moseley QC). The Law Commission's view is that the point remains uncertain but, in any event, it has recommended the repeal of the irrebuttable presumption of delivery in Companies Act 1985, s 36A (6): *The Execution of Deeds and Documents by or on behalf of Bodies Corporate* (Law Commission Report No 253) (1998) paras 6.12, 6.37–6.44.

[180] See Table A, art 101.

[181] *Johnsey Estates (1990) Ltd v Newport Marketworld Ltd* ,10 May 1996 Ch D.

[182] *Ruben v Great Fingall Consolidated* [1906] AC 439, HL. The Law Commission suggests that it is unlikely that the deeming provisions in Companies Act 1985, s 36A (6) and Law of Property Act 1925, s 74 (1), would apply where signatures have been forged: *The Execution of Deeds and Documents by or on behalf of Bodies Corporate* (Law Commission Consultation Paper No 143) (1996) para 5.32 and *The Execution of Deeds and Documents by or on behalf of Bodies Corporate* (Law Commission Report No 253) (1998) paras 5.34–5.37.

[183] In *Northside Developments Pty Ltd v Registrar-General and Ors* (1989–90) 2 ACSR 161, H Ct of Aust, 168–9 Mason CJ preferred to regard the application of the internal-management rule to sealed documents as an organic principle of company law rather than a principle of the law of agency. In the same case, at 196 and 198–9, Dawson J said that the internal-management rule was

no representation that the document is genuine by someone who has authority to authenticate corporate documents.[184] Where, for example, a company secretary produces a document which he says is a copy of a board minute but which is actually a forgery, the other party should, in the absence of suspicious circumstances, be protected by the fact that it falls within the usual authority[185] of a company secretary to certify the authenticity of copies of company documents. In these circumstances the company should be estopped from denying the validity of the board minute. Any other conclusion would seem to lead to the absurd result that in a case like *First Energy* the company could be bound where its purported agent simply reports the fact of higher level approval but not bound where that person produces a forged document which purports to be evidence of higher level approval.

dependent upon the operation of ordinary agency principles. This difference in judicial approach reflects a debate that has taken place in Australia about the true nature of the internal-management rule: see, eg, Lindgreen, KE, 'History of the Rule in *Royal British Bank v Turquand*' (1975) 2 Monash University Law Review 13 and 'The Positive Corporate Seal Rule and Exceptions Thereto and the Rule in *Turquand's* Case' (1973) 9 Melbourne University Law Review 192. The relevance of the debate is said to be in relation to forgeries and documents which are not forgeries but which are executed for fraudulent purposes: *Northside Developments Pty Ltd v Registrar-General and Ors* (1989–90) 2 ACSR 161, H Ct of Aust, 205 *per* Gaudron J.

[184] *Northside Developments Pty Ltd v Registrar-General and Ors* (1989–90) 2 ACSR 161, H Ct of Aust, 166 *per* Mason CJ and 197 *per* Dawson J. Thompson, AR, 'Company Law Doctrines and Authority to Contract' (1956) 11 University of Toronto Law Journal 248, 273–8.

[185] A fraudulent act can be within the scope of an agent's authority: *Lloyd v Grace, Smith & Co* [1912] AC 716, HL.

PART II

CORPORATE GOVERNANCE

4

Management of Companies

ARTICLES OF ASSOCIATION AND THE LOCATION OF MANAGERIAL POWER

This part of the book is concerned with the way in which companies are managed and with the legal and practical controls on managerial power. According to typical articles of association, the locus of managerial power is with the board of directors. Table A, article 70 provides that:

> Subject to the provisions of the Act, the memorandum and the articles, and to any directions given by special resolution, the business of the company shall be managed by the directors who may exercise all the powers of the company.

Table A is a set of standard form articles of association which is made available, in a statutory instrument,[1] as a model which companies are free to adopt or modify in accordance with their own circumstances. The articles contained in Table A represent the default position in the sense that they will apply as a company's articles to the extent that they are not modified or excluded by the company's own tailor-made articles,[2] but it is entirely possible for a company to oust Table A entirely and to have a full set of customised articles. Private companies are commonly incorporated with Table A articles[3] and then modifications and adaptations are made over time. Fully customised articles, in which Table A is excluded in its entirety, are often adopted for the first time when a company becomes a public company in order to raise capital from the investing public. Even then, Table A continues to be influential because in many respects customised articles will tend to follow that model. This is true, for example, with regard to the managerial article which even in very large companies usually provides for the management of the business by the board.

Articles of association vesting managerial power formally in the board of directors do not necessarily reflect reality. In large companies the board is a formal body that meets at periodic intervals such as once a month. A body such as this can set and refine the strategic direction of the company and can supervise its management, but it cannot itself perform the function of managing the company on a daily basis. That task has to be devolved to the individual senior managers of the company, some of whom may be, but none of whom need be, directors of the company. Although Table A, and articles that

[1] SI 1985/805.

[2] Companies Act 1985, s 8 (2).

[3] Many companies in fact start life as 'shelf' companies incorporated by advisers, such as lawyers, for use by their clients or by firms who are simply in the business of acting as incorporation agents. The process of adaptation may start as soon as the client takes over the company from the adviser or purchases it from the incorporation agent.

follow that model, already provide for delegation of managerial power to individuals and to committees, it would be better if the English model were to be brought into line with the equivalent provisions in US states which provide for the business to be managed by *or under the direction of the board* (emphasis added).[4]

The recognition that senior managers perform the task of managing companies on a daily basis means that although the chapters in this part of the book may sometimes refer to 'directors' duties', unless otherwise stated that phrase is intended to function as a convenient shorthand for the duties that the law imposes on senior managers, whether or not they happen to be directors. 'Directors' duties' also apply to non-executive directors. Non-executive directors are not employees of the company and are not involved in the daily management. They may be former senior executives of the company or they may be brought in from outside in order to provide an independent voice. The general discussion of directors' duties that follows is relevant to non-executive directors, but the issue that is most sharply in focus in relation to them is that of the care and skill required of them in discharging their function: this requires consideration of the role that non-executive directors are expected to perform.[5]

As the focus moves away from the large company with many shareholders and few managers towards, at the opposite end of the spectrum, one-person companies and quasi-partnership companies where most, if not all, of the shareholders are also involved in management, the formal constitutional vesting of managerial functions in the board becomes increasingly unimportant. An individual who is the sole shareholder and director of a company is unlikely to pay much attention to whether decisions about the running of the company are constitutionally made as a 'shareholder' or as a 'manager/director'. Equally, market mechanisms for controlling managerial power become increasingly irrelevant as the company under consideration shrinks in size. In principle the legal rules controlling managerial power are the same irrespective of the size of the company, but these rules can be waived by the shareholders[6] and such waivers can be easily obtained where there are only a few shareholders who are in agreement about the conduct of the company's affairs. The approach in this part of the book is to examine the issues mainly as they apply in relation to large companies but, where they are also relevant to small companies, to look at any different considerations that may arise in that context.

SEPARATION OF OWNERSHIP AND CONTROL

Ever since the publication of Berle and Means' celebrated work, *The Modern Corporation and Private Property*,[7] it has become customary to start an analy-

[4] Klein, WA, and Coffee, JC, *Business Organization and Finance* (5th edn, 1993) 126–7.
[5] See Ch 6 below, at 217–23.
[6] Subject to Companies Act 1985, s 310 discussed in this chapter below, at 140–3.
[7] Berle, A, and Means, GC, *The Modern Corporation and Private Property* (1932).

sis of the structure of a large company with an examination of the proposition that control of the company has passed from the hands of the owners of the company, its shareholders, and is vested in its managers. This is the separation of ownership and control. An assumption that has historically underpinned this discussion is that the shareholders are the owners of the company. This assumption can be accepted for now but it is examined more closely later in this chapter.[8]

The process of separation of ownership and control has been described in these terms:[9]

> With larger corporate size comes a greater dispersion of stock ownership, a steady reduction in the power and interest of the shareholder, and gradual enhancement of managerial authority, that is a separation of ownership from control.

The familiar way of approaching the problems created by separation of ownership and control is to say that, because investors typically acquire only a tiny proportion of the shares in any company as part of a portfolio of investments, no one shareholder is in a position to exercise effective control through the formal process of the general meeting. Further, shareholders in public companies have little incentive to monitor the management closely since they have limited liability and they can protect themselves against company-specific risks by portfolio diversification.[10] The cost to an individual shareholder of monitoring management would normally exceed the benefit to that person and whilst other shareholders would also benefit from it they would do so at the expense of the monitoring shareholder (the free-rider problem). If investors are unhappy with the performance of the management, the capital markets provide an exit since they can simply sell their shares and invest elsewhere. It follows,[11] then, that the directors and managers of a large company enjoy managerial autonomy: they have at their disposal large sums of money which have been invested by the shareholders, and how they use those sums is for them to decide without close scrutiny or control from its providers. This structure gives scope for the managers to use the sums invested more for their benefit than for the benefit of the shareholders (conflict of interest) or they may not give the care and attention to the management of it that they would to their own money (managerial shirking).[12]

There are a number of studies which demonstrate that it is over-simplistic to assume that there is necessarily complete separation of ownership and control in all large companies.[13] For instance, where the founders of a company retain a significant proportion of the company's share capital after it has gone public, they may still be in a position to exercise considerable control in

[8] See below, at 131–3.

[9] Herman, ES, *Corporate Control, Corporate Power* (1981) 5.

[10] See Ch 1 above, at 20–1.

[11] As a starting premiss. As is explored later in this chapter, the impact of selling on the share price could trigger the market for corporate control.

[12] Eisenberg, MA, 'The Structure of Corporation Law' (1989) 89 Columbia Law Review 1461, 1471.

[13] The one that is cited most often is Herman, ES, *Corporate Control, Corporate Power* (1981). For a discussion of a number of other studies: Scott, J, *Corporations, Classes and Capitalism* (1979) ch 3.

their capacity as shareholders. In the 1990s institutional investors in the UK markets began to take a more active role in monitoring the management of large companies. That development presented a new challenge to the conventional picture of passive investors and autonomous managers.[14] Nevertheless that there is a separation of ownership and control can suffice as a starting point.

AGENCY COSTS

From an economic perspective based on the premiss that managers and shareholders will act in their own self-interest and will assume that others will do the same, there is a divergence of interest in the corporate structure.[15] Although not an accurate legal description of their relationship,[16] economists use agency concepts to describe the conflict of interest between the shareholders (the principal) and the directors/managers (the agent). In economic terms, an agency relationship gives rise to 'agency costs' which are the costs of monitoring the agents, the costs of guaranteeing that the agents will act diligently and not prefer their own interests to those of the principal, plus the residual risk that the agents will still act for their own benefit. Agency costs are factored into the price that investors are prepared to pay for shares. There is, then, an incentive for the managers of the firm to reduce agency costs in order to increase the price that investors are willing to pay.[17] The corporate governance structures that a company adopts in order to demonstrate that there are appropriate checks and balances on managerial discretion are thus inevitably intertwined with the financing of that company.

CONTROLLING MANAGERIAL PERFORMANCE BY MARKET FORCES

There are various market mechanisms that may operate so as to discipline managers and prevent them from exploiting conflicts of interest or from underperforming. The first is that managers have an incentive to perform well in order to keep their jobs: where there is competition for senior managerial positions, those responsible for the bad management of a company may find themselves replaced by other managers.[18] Although decisions to reorganise

[14] 'Managers v Shareholders Again' *Financial Times* 24 September 1998. The role of institutional investors is considered further in Ch 7.

[15] Judges, too, have adopted this view of human nature in imposing fiduciary duties on directors: *Bray v Ford* [1896] AC 44, HL, 51–2 *per* Lord Herschell.

[16] Directors are the agents of the company rather than the agents of the shareholders: *Automatic Self-Cleansing Filter Syndicate Co Ltd v Cuninghame* [1906] 2 Ch 34, CA.

[17] Jensen, M, and Meckling, W, 'Theory of the Firm: Managerial Behavior, Agency Costs and Ownership Structure' in Putterman, L (ed), *The Economic Nature of the Firm* (1986) 209 (reprinted in abridged form from (1976) 3 *Journal of Financial Economics* 305); Easterbrook, FH, and Fischel, DR, *The Economic Structure of Corporate Law* (1991) 11: 'the trick is to hold the total cost of these things as low as possible'.

[18] Fama, E, 'Agency Problems and the Theory of the Firm' in Putterman, L (ed), *The Economic Nature of the Firm* (1986) 196, 200 (reprinted with author's abridgements from (1980) 88 *Journal of Political Economy* 288).

the management would normally be taken by the board, it may be influenced by pressure from shareholders or creditors, particularly where the perceived failing is amongst the executive members of the board.[19] An alternative to the 'market for jobs' argument is provided by analysis based on the impact of organisational structure on managerial discretion: it is suggested that the separation of a company's operations into a number of distinct divisions can assist internal monitoring of managerial performance by other managers.[20]

In the last resort a badly managed company is liable to become a potential takeover target.[21] The takeover, or, as it is often referred to, the 'market for corporate control', is the second method of controlling the management of large companies through the market. The premiss on which the market for corporate control is based is that a predator can gain by securing control of an underperforming company at a price which is above the market price of the shares prior to the bid (the predator is paying a premium for control) but below the price at which they would trade if the target was managed effectively.

The third market force is closely linked to the market for corporate control. It is that the capital markets act as a constraint on managerial performance: managers have an incentive to perform well in order to minimise the costs that the company must pay in order to raise capital from the markets.

Compensation policies are the fourth market mechanism that can be employed with a view to reducing the divergence between the interests of managers and shareholders. Senior managers' remuneration packages commonly include shares and share options and, over time, an individual's shareholding and options can come to represent a significant part of his or her personal wealth.[22] Stock options work by giving the manager the right to acquire shares from the company at a specified price. There is no obligation to exercise the options but the manager can be expected to do so if, or when, the market price of the shares rises above the exercise price specified in the options. The manager is then free to make an immediate cash profit by selling the shares acquired by exercising the options. Another component of many senior managerial compensation packages is cash bonuses which are linked to the company's performance. Through shares, stock options and

[19] Departures from senior positions within public companies as a result of pressure from shareholders naturally attract the press attention: see, eg, 'McCullagh to Step Down as British Biotech Chief' (*The Times* 20 May 1998). If management does not respond to investor pressure this could ultimately result in the shareholders seeking to use their power under Companies Act 1985, s 303 to vote directors out of office.

[20] Williamson, O, 'Corporate Governance' (1984) 93 Yale Law Journal 1197, 1222–6; Williamson, O, 'The Modern Corporation: Origins, Evolution, Attributes' (1981) 19 *Journal of Economic Literature* 1537.

[21] Manne, HG, 'Mergers and the Market for Corporate Control' (1965) *Journal of Political Economy* 110; Jensen, MC, 'Agency Costs of Free Cash Flow, Corporate Finance and Takeovers' (1986) 76/2 *American Economic Review* 323; Bradley, C, 'Corporate Control: Markets and Rules' (1990) 53 MLR 170; McCahery, J, 'Risk, Trust, and the Market for Corporate Control' in McCahery, J, Picciotto, S, and Scott, C (eds), *Corporate Control and Accountability* (1993) 247; Lipton, M, and Panner, M, 'Takeover Bids and United States Corporate Governance' in Prentice, DD, and Holland, PRJ (eds), *Contemporary Issues in Corporate Governance* (1993) 115.

[22] Cosh, AD, and Hughes, A, 'The Anatomy of Corporate Control: Directors, Shareholders and Executive Remuneration in Giant US and UK Corporations' (1987) 11 *Cambridge Journal of Economics* 285, 302–5.

performance related bonuses the manager, therefore, has a direct personal interest in the profitability of the company and the performance of its securities. In these ways the managers' personal interests are brought into line with those of investor shareholders and the conflict between them is, accordingly, reduced.[23]

Fifthly, the commercial necessity of meeting consumer demands with regard to the products sold by the company is another market force that may influence managerial behaviour.[24]

The discipline of the markets is used by those who regard the company as a 'nexus of contracts' to suggest that mandatory legal rules which seek to control management may be unnecessary and potentially wasteful. They argue that the role of legal constraints on corporate managers under the general law is to supplement the parties' private bargain and the operation of market forces. The parties should be permitted to dispense with general law rules where these are unnecessary to the bargain that they have reached between themselves. This assessment, and the downplaying of the importance of general legal rules that it involves, assumes that market forces do operate effectively and that they achieve acceptable results. Both assumptions can be questioned. For example, the market for jobs may operate imperfectly at the highest level of the managerial hierarchy because the board may prefer to present a united front rather than to single out individual directors as the culprits for the under-performance of the company and to replace them with others.[25] The market for corporate control can be regarded as an effective but crude method of effecting change at board level which entails considerable cost[26] and much disruption for employees and others.[27] Also, it emerges from studies of takeover activity in the 1980s that there are many criteria other than under-performance that may influence a predator in deciding whether to

[23] Herman, ES, *Corporate Control, Corporate Power* (1981) 93–8; Megginson, WL, *Corporate Finance Theory* (1997) 74–7; Jensen, MC, and Murphy, KJ, 'Performance Pay and Top Management Incentives' (1990) 98 *Journal of Political Economy* 225; *Final Report of the Committee on Corporate Governance* (1998) (*Hampel Report*) s 4. The assumption that such mechanisms align the interests of managers and shareholders may not be true when adverse market conditions turn remuneration packages containing shares and share options into a 'depreciating currency': 'Managers v Shareholders (Again)' *Financial Times* 24 September 1998. In response to the adverse trading conditions of the late 1990s, some companies took the controversial step of adjusting the basis for calculating share option entitlements in order to preserve their value.

[24] Eisenberg, MA, 'The Structure of Corporation Law' (1989) 89 Columbia Law Review 1461, 1489.

[25] Parkinson, JE, *Corporate Power and Responsibility* (1993) 116–18.

[26] Both in terms of the fees that the bidder and target will have to pay to their advisers and the premium over the current market value of the shares that the bidder will have to pay in order to secure a controlling interest.

[27] Coffee, JC, 'Institutional Investors as Corporate Monitors: Are Takeovers Obsolete?' in Farrar, J (ed), *Takeovers, Institutional Investors and the Modernization of Corporate Laws* (1993) 12, 13; Coffee, JC, 'Regulating the Market for Corporate Control: A Critical Assessment of the Tender Offer's Role in Corporate Governance' (1984) 84 Columbia Law Review 1145.

Another factor against relying on the market for corporate control to the exclusion of other control mechanisms is that managerial policy with regard to such matters as dividend payouts may be driven by short-term considerations designed to prevent their companies from becoming takeover targets rather than by an assessment of the long-term interests of the business: Dimsdale, NH, 'The Need to Restore Corporate Accountability: An Agenda for Reform' in Dimsdale, NH, and Prevezer, M (eds), *Capital Markets and Corporate Governance* (1994).

target a particular company, such as the desire to acquire competing businesses in order to increase market power or to achieve synergies leading to lower costs.[28] Equally, studies suggest that the performance of enlarged corporate groups post-takeover does not necessarily reflect the removal of an incompetent managerial team and their replacement by more a effective group.[29] There has to be set against the controlling effect of the capital markets the fact that companies can fund at least part of their operations from retained profits. The effectiveness of incentive schemes based on compensation packages is hard to determine[30] although studies strongly suggest that the level of directors' remuneration packages may depend more on the size of the company than on performance as measured by ratios such as earnings per share.[31] Popular public perception is not that directors' remuneration packages provide them with inadequate incentives but rather that they are in fact overpaid for the job they do.[32] Stock options can have a counter-productive effect where, for instance, a senior manager fails to object to decisions about the company's strategy because of the adverse effect that this may have on the share price and on the value of the options.[33] The control exerted by the

[28] O'Sullivan, P, 'Governance by Exit: An Analysis of the Market for Corporate Control' in Keasey, K, Thompson, S, and Wright, M (eds), *Corporate Governance: Economic and Financial Issues* 122, 132–5; Deakin, S, and Slinger, G, 'Hostile Takeovers, Company Law, and the Theory of the Firm'(1997) 24 Journal of Law and Society 124, 144.

[29] Franks, J, and Mayer, C, 'Hostile Takeovers and the Correction of Managerial Failure' (1996) 40 *Journal of Financial Economics* 163; O'Sullivan, P, 'Governance by Exit: An Analysis of the Market for Corporate Control' in Keasey, K, Thompson, S, and Wright, M (eds), *Corporate Governance: Economic and Financial Issues* (1997) 122, 135–6; Deakin, S, and Slinger, G, 'Hostile Takeovers, Company Law, and the Theory of the Firm' (1997) 24 Journal of Law and Society 124, 144; 'Shareholders Should Beware of Acquisitions Warns Recent Study' (1997) 18 Co Law 329 (news digest reporting a comprehensive study of large domestic takeovers between 1984 and 1992 conducted at the University of Exeter); Plender, J, *A Stake in the Future* (1997) 66–8; Brudney, V, 'Corporate Governance, Agency Costs and the Rhetoric of Contract' (1985) 85 Columbia Law Review 1403, 1425. Parkinson, JE, *Corporate Power and Responsibility* (1993) 121–32 discusses generally the imperfections in the market for corporate control as a controlling mechanism.

[30] Parkinson, JE, *Corporate Power and Responsibility* (1993) 114–16.

[31] Gregg, P, Machin, S, and Szymanzki, S, 'The Disappearing Relationship between Directors' Pay and Corporate Performance' [1993] BJIL 1; Cosh, A, and Hughes, A, 'The Changing Anatomy of Corporate Control and the Market for Executives in the UK' (ESRC Centre for Business Research, Working Paper 49) 15; Bruce, A, and Buck, T, 'Executive Reward and Corporate Governance' in Keasey, K, Thompson, S, and Wright, M (eds), *Corporate Governance: Economic and Financial Issues* (1997) 80. For the statutory disclosure requirements in respect of directors' remuneration, see Companies Act 1985, sch 6 (as amended by The Company Accounts (Disclosure of Directors' Emoluments) Regulations 1997 (SI 1997/570). For listed companies there are also disclosure obligations in the *Combined Code* annexed to *The Listing Rules* of the London Stock Exchange. These obligations are derived from recommendations made by the Greenbury committee on directors' remuneration on best practice with regard to directors' remuneration (*Directors' Remuneration: The Report of a Study Group Chaired by Sir Richard Greenbury* (1995)). Although the *Combined Code* is not part of *The Listing Rules*, statements must be included in the annual reports and accounts with regard to the matters set out in it: *The Listing Rules* ch 12, para 12.43A. *The Listing Rules*, ch 12, para 12.43(c) requires that a company's annual reports should contain a statement of remuneration policy and details of the remuneration of each director.

[32] Kay, J, and Silberston, A, 'Corporate Governance' (1995) 3 *National Institute Economic Review* 84, 84–5: 'the issue that has made corporate governance a subject for tabloid headlines is greedy bosses'. See generally Cheffins, BR, *Company Law Theory, Structure and Operation* (1997) ch 14.

[33] eg 'Biotech Director Left Quietly to Keep Options' *The Times* 26 May 1998, reporting on the disclosure that the former research and development director of British Biotech plc did not

product market is inevitably linked to the competitiveness of the market in question and may be negligible where the company enjoys a dominant position.[34] Also such mechanisms may take considerable time to work out as losses in such markets can be sustained for long periods.

Two modern practical developments make an important contribution to the debate about the role of market forces in constraining managerial discretion. These are the role of institutional investors and the use of non-executive directors. The more active monitoring role that institutional investors began to play in the 1990s, which is explored in Chapter 7, is an alternative to the market for corporate control in that it rests on the premiss that shareholders will express their dissatisfaction with management by exercising their 'voice' (the votes attaching to their shares) rather than by exiting the company through selling their shares. The impact of institutional-investor control on managerial power remains debatable. Similarly, there are mixed views on how effective the presence of non-executive directors on a board is as a mechanism for restraining managerial autonomy.[35] The role of non-executive directors and the law's response to the functions that they perform are considered separately in Chapter 6.

LEGAL CONTROLS ON MANAGEMENT: OUTLINE

The conclusion that this discussion seems to point to is that the market mechanisms for controlling managerial conflicts of interest and shirking are important but imperfect. This conclusion then forms the point of departure for the discussion of the role of company law in controlling management. Company law seeks to control management in a variety of ways: by giving the shareholders in general meeting the right to vote on certain matters including the appointment and removal of directors; by requiring disclosure of financial information and imposing requirements for an independent audit of accounts; and by imposing fiduciary duties and duties of care and skill on directors and senior managers. In this and the following two chapters, the concern is fiduciary duties and duties of care and skill. Before proceeding to examine the substantive content of directors' duties, there are two preliminary issues to address: the identification of the groups who are intended to be protected by the rules relating to fiduciary duty and duties of care and skill; and the nature of those rules as mandatory requirements or default rules which apply only to the extent that the parties have not made alternative provision.

publicly oppose the company's strategy to commercialise its drugs in order to preserve the value of his shares on which he subsequently made a profit of more than £1 million.

[34] Eisenberg, MA, 'The Structure of Corporation Law' (1989) 89 Columbia Law Review 1461, 1489.

[35] Ghilarducci, T, Hawley, J, and Williams, A, 'Labour's Paradoxical Interests and the Evolution of Corporate Governance' (1997) 24 Journal of Law and Society 26, 31.

DUTIES OWED TO THE 'COMPANY'

The orthodox legal position is that directors, by virtue of their office, owe fiduciary duties to the company but they do not owe duties to shareholders, employees, creditors or the members of any other constituency which may have some interest in the company's affairs. This is established by *Percival v Wright*[36] where it was held that the relationship between directors and shareholders was not fiduciary and that directors therefore had no duty to inform shareholders of an impending takeover bid for the company prior to the sale of their shares to the directors. In *Multinational Gas and Petrochemical Co v Multinational Gas and Petrochemical Services Ltd*,[37] where the question of possible duties to creditors was in issue, the Court of Appeal affirmed the limited nature of the fiduciary obligation owed by directors, Dillon LJ stating: 'The directors indeed stand in a fiduciary relationship to the company, as they are appointed to manage the affairs of the company, and they owe duties to the company though not to the creditors, present or future, or to individual shareholders.' The proposition that directors owe their duties only to the company has important implications with regard to enforcement because it follows that it is for the company to decide whether or not to sue directors for breach of duty.[38] Litigation is normally a managerial function[39] but, if the wrongdoers are in control of the management, the decision whether to pursue directors through the courts for breach of fiduciary duty may devolve to the shareholders in general meeting. In exceptional circumstances, minority shareholders can bring a claim, in their own names, against wrongdoers on the company's behalf.[40] This exception does not modify the basic rule that directors owe their fiduciary duties to the company: the minority shareholder is simply allowed to bring a 'derivative' action on the company's behalf. A number of factors combine to ensure that derivative actions are rare. Minority shareholders suffer from serious informational disadvantages compared to the board and they may simply not be in a position to judge accurately the strength of a potential claim. In financial terms, although the court may order the company to fund a derivative action,[41] there is little incentive for individuals to pursue such a claim since, if it is successful, judgment will be awarded

36 [1902] 2 Ch 421. In particular circumstances directors may owe shareholders a duty of care. For example, if the directors do advise shareholders on the merits of a bid, (either through choice or in order to comply with the *Takeover Code*) they would probably be held to be in a sufficiently proximate relationship with the shareholders to give rise to a duty of care in tort in accordance with *Hedley Byrne & Co v Heller* [1964] AC 465, HL: *Dawson International plc v Coats Paton plc* (1988) 4 BCC 305, Court of Session, 314. They could also be personally liable in tort for deceit if they deliberately or recklessly give false or misleading advice: *Gething v Kilner* [1972] 1 All ER 1166. The directors may also incur direct personal obligations to the shareholders if they are appointed as the shareholders' agents: *Allen v Hyatt* (1914) 30 TLR 444, PC. Further, where there are special facts demonstrating a relationship of particular trust and confidence vested in the directors by the shareholders this may give rise to fiduciary obligations: *Coleman v Myers* [1977] 2 NZLR 298 225, NZ SC and CA; *Re Chez Nico (Restaurants) Ltd* [1991] BCC 763.

37 [1983] Ch 258, CA.

38 *Foss v Harbottle* (1843) 2 Hare 461, 67 ER 189.

39 *John Shaw and Sons (Salford) Ltd v Shaw* [1935] 2 KB 113, CA; *Breckland Group Holdings Ltd v London & Suffolk Properties Ltd* (1988) 4 BCC 542.

40 *Edwards v Halliwell* [1950] 2 All ER 1064, CA.

41 *Wallersteiner v Moir (No 2)* [1975] QB 373, CA.

in favour of the company; at most the shareholders may hope for some increase in the share price as the result of a successful action (which may be outweighed if bad publicity about the case has previously caused the price to fall) but this benefit will accrue to all shareholders whether or not they took an active part in pursuing the claim. A further disincentive is that standing to bring such an action is difficult to establish.[42]

INTERESTS OF THE 'COMPANY'

When the focus shifts from the technical question of enforcement to the issue of putting flesh onto the bare bones of directors' fiduciary obligations, there is a change of emphasis. When looking at the content of directors' duties, especially the primary duty to act in good faith in the interests of the company, the concept of the 'company' extends beyond the legal entity created by incorporation to embrace the groups who have an interest in the company, principally, its shareholders, creditors (including suppliers who provide goods on credit terms) and employees. Difficulties, however, lie in determining how the interests of these various groups, which may be in competition, are to be taken into account. This is an aspect of the stakeholder debate in the corporate context: whether, or to what extent, those who have a stake in a company are protected by fiduciary duties and duties of care and skill. The position of shareholders, creditors and employees is considered next in this chapter. The larger question, whether company law should develop a broader concept of stakeholding which, as well as employees and creditors, also recognises the interests that the wider community may have in how companies conduct their activities, is one that generates considerable debate of which only an overview can be provided here.[43]

In many instances the interests of shareholders, creditors and employees will coincide with each other and with the interests of the company as a business entity. If the directors, after balancing the risks and potential rewards, decide, say, to step up the overseas marketing of the company's products because it believes that there are valuable export opportunities which can be profitably exploited, that decision may in fact coincide with the interests of shareholders (prospect of an enhanced return on their investment), creditors (prospect of profit inflates the cushion against insolvency) and employees

[42] On the difficulties faced by minority shareholders, see generally *Shareholder Remedies: A Consultation Paper* (Law Commission Consultation Paper No 142) (1996) and *Shareholder Remedies* (Law Commission Report No 246) (1997).

[43] This is an issue which has generated a large amount of literature in recent years including the following: Kay, J, and Silberston, A, 'Corporate Governance' (1995) 3 *National Institute Economic Review* 84 *Tomorrow's Company: The Role of Business in a Changing World* (RSA Inquiry) (1995); Hutton, W, *The State We're In* (1995) ch 12; Plender, J, *A Stake in the Future* (1997); Parkinson, JE, *Corporate Power and Responsibility* (1993) ch 9 Goldenberg, P, 'Shareholders v Stakeholders: The Bogus Argument' (1998) 19 Co Law 34; Alcock, A, 'The Case Against the Concept of Stakeholders' (1996) 17 Co Law 177; Ireland, P, 'Corporate Governance, Stakeholding and the Company: Towards a Less Degenerate Capitalism?' (1996) 23 Journal of Law and Society 287; Campbell, D, 'Towards a Less Irrelevant Socialism: Stakeholding as a "Reform" of the Capitalist Economy' (1997) 24 Journal of Law and Society 65; Mitchell, A, and Sikka, *Corporate Governance Matters* (Fabian Society Discussion Paper No 24) (1996). See also Chapter 19 below, at 641–3.

(prospect of greater demand for the company's products enhances job security). But there can be other decisions where there is a potential for conflict between these constituencies. For example a decision to switch production to a third world country in order to reduce the wages bill is a move that may benefit shareholders and creditors but result in employees becoming redundant.[44] There may be conflict between the interests of the business entity and one or more of these constituencies. If, for example, the directors decide to recommend a takeover bid because the bidder is offering the existing shareholders the highest price, that may serve the interests of the shareholders well but if the bidder is planning to break up the business and dispose of it, so that eventually the company will be wound up, it can hardly be said that the decision would be taken in the interests of the company as a commercial entity. Also, decisions may impact differently on different groups within these constituencies, an example of this being a proposed re-organisation of the company capital which may affect one class of shareholders differently from other shareholders. It is where there are conflicting interests that the identification of the interests that the duties imposed by the general law are intended to protect becomes important. To the extent that potentially competing interests are to be taken into account, there is then the question of prioritising those interests in the event of conflict. Underlying the issue of the recognition of potentially competing interests lies the concern that, unless there are clear 'brightline' rules[45] about relevant interests and their priority, management will be able to play off competing interests against each other and to use them to mask its own failings.[46]

INTERESTS OF SHAREHOLDERS

The directors have a statutory duty to consider the interests of the shareholders in discharging their duty to act in the interests of the company.[47] This

[44] Kahn-Freund, O, 'Industrial Democracy' (1977) 6 ILJ 65.

[45] One such rule that is established by the cases is that where there is a conflict between groups of shareholders the directors are required to act fairly between them: *Henry v Great Northern Railway* (1987) 1 De G of J 606, 638; *Mills v Mills* (1938) 60 CLR 150, H Ct of Aust, 164 *per* Latham LJ; *Mutual Life Insurance v Bank Organization Ltd* [1989] BCLC 11; *Re BSB Holdings Ltd (No 2)* [1996] 1 BCLC 155.

[46] Ireland, P, 'Corporate Governance, Stakeholding and the Company: Towards a Less Degenerate Capitalism?' (1996) 23 Journal of Law and Society 287, 296: 'a recipe for a pig's breakfast'; Alcock, A, 'The Case Against the Concept of Stakeholders' (1996) 17 Co Law 177, 179–80; Plender, J, *A Stake in the Future* (1997) 72–3, 142–4; Karmel, RS, 'Implications of the Stakeholder Model' (1993) 61 George Washington Law Review 1156. See also Hayek, F, *Law, Legislation and Liberty* (1979) vol 3, ch 15 especially at 82.

Many US States have enacted 'other constituency' statutes which permit (or require) the directors to take into account the interests of groups other than the shareholders. Some of these statutes only apply in change of control/takeover situations but most are not so limited. The 'too many masters' argument is one of the major criticisms of these statutes. It is argued that in a takeover situation directors may use an 'other constituency' statute as a cover for actions which are, in reality, designed to bolster their own position: Solomon, LD, Schwartz, DE, Bauman, JD, and Weiss, EJ, *Corporations Law and Policy* (3rd edn, 1994) 119; Committee on Corporate Laws, 'Other Constituencies Statutes: Potential for Confusion' (1990) 45 Business Lawyer 2253.

[47] Companies Act 1985, s 309.

statutory duty to consider in itself means little: it is not enforceable by the shareholders individually and the directors are not obliged by the statute to give priority to the shareholders' interests. More important is the fact that, in general, the courts tend to treat the interests of the company as being synonymous with the interests of its shareholders with the result that the duties to consider the shareholders and to act in the interests of the company become conflated into a single duty to act in the interests of the shareholders. In some cases the interests of the company are equated with the interests of its present and future shareholders.[48] Other cases envisage only present shareholders.[49] The reference to 'future shareholders' does not mean that the directors should consider the interests of any particular persons who might invest in the company in the future. Instead, it indicates that the directors' duty is not related to the individual personal interests of the persons who happen to be shareholders at any particular time, but is concerned with the collective interest of the group over time.[50] This interpretation paves the way for the inclusion of longer term considerations in the range of factors that directors should take into account. That this is a correct assessment of the directors' legal duty is widely accepted[51] but there is a case for the inclusion of long-term considerations to be expressed more clearly than by a somewhat obscure reference to 'future shareholders' so as to remove the common, but erroneous, impression that short-term considerations are all that matter.[52] Viewing shareholders simply as investors interested in financial return, an accurate assessment at

[48] eg *Gaiman v National Association for Mental Health* [1972] Ch 317, 330; *Brady v Brady* (1987) 3 BCC 535, CA, 552 *per* Nourse LJ; *Dawson International plc v Coats Paton plc* (1988) 4 BCC 305, Ct Sess, 313.

[49] eg *Greenhalgh v Arderne Cinemas Ltd* [1951] Ch 286, CA, 291 *per* Evershed MR; *Peter's American Delicacy Co v Heath* (1939) 61 CLR 457, H Ct of Aust, 481 *per* Latham CJ, 512 *per* Dixon J; *Multinational Gas and Petrochemical Co v Multinational Gas and Petrochemical Services Ltd* [1983] 1 Ch 258, CA, 268 *per* Lawton LJ ('The plaintiff, although it had a separate existence from its oil company shareholders, existed for the benefit of those shareholders') and 288 *per* Dillon LJ ('so long as the company is solvent the shareholders are in substance the company'). Strictly, both *Greenhalgh* and *Peter's* were concerned with shareholders' power to alter articles rather than directors' duties, but the situation is analogous: *Lee Panavision Ltd v Lee Lighting Ltd* [1991] BCC 620, CA, 634 *per* Dillon LJ.

[50] Diversity of interests between groups of shareholders is another reason why shareholder interests cannot be identified with particular individual shareholders. Haskins, C, 'A Company Should Be Run Primarily in the Interests of its Shareholders' in *Proceedings of a Conference Held at the Institute of Directors* (1995) identifies five groups of shareholders: institutions, private investors, employees, predators and the state.

[51] *The Final Report of the Committee on Corporate Governance* (1998) (the *Hampel Committee Report*) para 1.16; Goldenberg, P, 'Shareholders v Stakeholders: The Bogus Argument' (1998) 19 Co Law 34, 36–7; Gower, LCB, 'Corporate Control: The Battle for the Berkeley' (1955) 68 Harv LR 1176 considering *The Savoy Hotel Limited and the Berkeley Hotel Company Limited: Investigation under Section 165(b) of the Companies Act 1948: Report of Mr E Milner Holland, QC* (HMSO, 1954) which includes the summary of an argument from Counsel that the 'Company' means the present and future members of the Company and that the board should conduct the company's business upon the footing that it would be continued as a going concern and accordingly should balance a long-term view against short-term interests of present members. See also Renard, A, 'Commentary' on Heydon, JD, 'Directors' Duties and the Company's Interests' in Finn, PD (ed), *Equity and Commercial Relationships* (1987) 137.

[52] *Tomorrow's Company: The Role of Business in a Changing World* (RSA Inquiry) (1995) calls for a re-interpretation of directors' duties to clarify this point: 11–12. On short-termism generally: Marsh, P, *Short-Termism on Trial* (1990); Charkham, J, *Keeping Good Company* (1995) 325–31.

least in ordinary public companies and larger private companies, the duty of directors translates, then, into a duty to maximise long-term shareholder value.[53]

Corporate Giving

An issue that is much discussed is how far charitable or benevolent activities by companies can be reconciled with the goal of maximisation of profits.[54] Present English company law on this is broadly consistent with the view that it is permissible for the management of companies to engage in such activities only where this is consistent with the goal of profit maximisation.[55] The courts have held that it is permissible to pay bonuses to employees where the underlying purpose is not purely philanthropic but is to encourage the employees to remain in their jobs or to become more productive: 'there are to be no cakes and ale except such as are required for the benefit of the company'.[56] This type of reasoning has been held to justify the payment of grants by a chemical company to the science departments of universities and other educational establishments for the purposes of teaching and research.[57] Since public image can affect a company's profitability, payments to charity, support for community

[53] But whether the legal rules effectively restrain corporate managers from pursuing short-term goals is doubtful: see Ch 2 above, at 76–80.

Although it is plausible here to proceed on the assumption that a company's profit maximisation strategy can be identified, this is in fact an issue that has generated a vast literature considering profit maximisation in orthodox theory under conditions of perfect competition and the implications for profit maximisation when more realistic assumptions about imperfect competition, uncertainty and risk are taken into account. For a general review see Desai, M, 'Profit and Profit Theory' in Eatwell, J, Milgate, M, and Newman, P, *The New Palgrave: A Dictionary of Economics* Vol 3 (1987) 1014–21.

[54] A classic debate on the issue took place in the pages of the Harvard Law Review in the 1930s between Berle and Dodd. Berle argued that directors acted solely for the stockholders, Dodd that they were trustees for the enterprise as a whole: Berle, A, 'Corporate Powers as Powers in Trust' (1931) 45 Harv LR 1049; Dodd, EM, 'For Whom are Corporate Managers Trustees?' (1932) 45 Harv LR 1145; Berle, A, 'For Whom Corporate Managers are Trustees' (1932) Harv LR 1365. In the 1950s Berle conceded defeat and accepted Dodd's view: Berle, A, *The Twentieth Century Capitalist Revolution* (1954). See also Dodd, EM, 'Is Effective Enforcement of the Fiduciary Duties of Corporate Trustees Practicable?' (1934) 2 University of Chicago Law Review 194 and Weiner, JL, 'The Berle–Dodd Dialogue on the Concept of the Corporation' (1964) 64 Columbia Law Review 1458. Other literature on this topic includes Herman, ES, *Corporate Control, Corporate Power* (1981) 251–64; Chayes, A, 'The Modern Corporation and the Rule of Law' in Mason, ES (ed), *The Corporation in Modern Society* (1959) 25; Rostow, EV, 'To Whom and For What End is Corporate Management Responsible?' in Mason (ed), *The Corporation in Modern Society* (1959) 46; McCabe, BJ, 'Are Corporations Socially Responsible? Is Corporate Social Responsibility Desirable?' (1992) 4 Bond LR 1; Sommer, A, 'Whom Should the Corporation Serve? The Berle–Dodd Debate Revisited Sixty Years On' (1991) 16 Delaware Journal of Corporate Law 33; Lord Wedderburn, 'The Social Responsibility of Companies' (1985) 15 Melbourne University Law Review 4; Sealy, LS, 'Directors' Wider Responsibilities—Problems Conceptual, Practical and Procedural' (1987) 13 Monash Law Review 164; Slaughter, CM, 'Corporate Social Responsibility: A New Perspective' (1997) 18 Co Law 313. See also the collection of material in a special edition of the University of Toronto Law Journal (1993) 297–796. Parkinson, JE, *Corporate Power and Responsibility* (1993) ch 9 contains a review of the issue from various perspectives, including those of academic lawyers, economists and those in business. See also Sheikh, S, *Corporate Social Responsibilities: Law and Practice* (1996).

[55] Herman, ES, *Corporate Control, Corporate Power* (1981) 255.

[56] *Hutton v West Cork Railway Co* (1883) 23 Ch D 654, CA, 673 *per* Bowen LJ.

[57] *Evans v Brunner Mond & Co Ltd* [1921] 1 Ch 35.

activities or other benevolent gestures could also be regarded as compatible with the directors' duty to maximise profits, as could payments to political parties which are perceived to have policies beneficial to the company's interests.[58]

There is a limit to what can be justified on this basis, as is illustrated by *Hutton v West Cork Railway Co*[59] and *Parke v Daily News*.[60] Both cases involved proposals to make gratuitous payments to employees who were to be made redundant by companies which had ceased to be going concerns. It was held that since these companies were moribund, the payments could not be said to be incidental to their business. The decisions in these cases have been reversed by statute since, under the Companies Act 1985, s 719, companies may make provision for the benefit of employees or former employees in connection with the cessation or transfer of the companies' business, but they still make the point that directors' power to expend the company's money on activities which are not directly a source of potential profit is narrowly prescribed.[61]

In addition to statutory provisions which expressly authorise departures from the goal of profit maximisation, a company's constitution can permit its management to behave in a more benevolent fashion than would be allowed under the general law. It is an obvious point that it is always possible for a company itself to choose not to pursue profit maximisation as its goal, as witness charitable companies. In *Re Horsley & Weight Ltd*[62] the Court of Appeal accepted that a commercial company could have a separate distinct object to make gifts or otherwise to engage in charitable or philanthropic activities. Quite what effect such an object has in relation to directors' duties has not yet arisen for determination in the courts. This object would not relieve the directors of their fiduciary duty to act in good faith in the interests of the company but would probably allow them more easily to justify social welfare activities as being matters which they genuinely believed to be in its interests, such interests being defined by the company's constitution away from the narrowest interpretation of the goal of profit maximisation. The relationship between corporate charity and the rules concerning maintenance of capital and the protection of creditors is explored further in Chapter 10.

In the UK corporate giving for social welfare purposes increased significantly from the 1980s onwards. Some companies began to make much of their support for community activities in their annual reports and accounts and other publications.[63] In some instances shareholder pressure groups sought

[58] But note *Simmonds v Heffer* [1983] BCLC 298 where payments by the League Against Cruel Sports to the Labour Party were held to be contrary to its objects. The legality of payments to political parties by companies is discussed generally in Ewing, KD, 'Company Political Donations and the Ultra Vires Rule' (1984) 47 MLR 57. An assumption that such payments are permissible underlies Companies Act 1985, sch 7, paras 3–5 which require disclosure of charitable and political gifts in directors' reports.

[59] (1883) 23 Ch D 654, CA.

[60] [1962] Ch 927.

[61] Lord Wedderburn has described the position as permitting 'a (reasonable) dash of conscientious sauce to be good for the dish of long-term profit maximisation' in 'Trust, Corporation and the Worker' (1985) 23 Osgoode Hall Law Journal 203, 227.

[62] [1982] Ch 442, CA.

[63] See the extracts from annual reports of several large companies quoted in Pettet, B, 'The Stirring of Corporate Social Conscience' (1997) 50 CLP 279, 284–6. Also *Corporate Governance: Improving Competitiveness and Access to Capital in Global Markets* (OECD Report) (1998) 32.

to encourage the trend towards corporate giving still further.[64] Whether present levels of corporate giving are within the limit of what can be justified on the grounds of self-interest is debatable[65] but a legal challenge to such practices would seem to be unlikely because of the difficulties faced by shareholders in establishing standing to bring a claim. Market forces may represent a more effective source of control here: if corporate management engages in corporate giving to an extent that becomes unacceptable to institutional investors, the sense that management is misusing 'their' money may galvanise investors into action. Market regulation is already emerging in the particular area of political donations, where influential voices in the field of corporate governance have made well-publicised calls for these to be approved in advance by the shareholders,[66] and one major pension fund has indicated that it would vote against any proposed political donations that the shareholders might be asked to approve.[67]

The trend towards greater corporate giving[68] has taken place against the general background of the stakeholder debate in company law:[69] whether, or to what extent, the interests of the wider community should figure in corporate managerial decision-making. It is unclear whether developments in corporate practice in this respect are really much more than paying lip-service to a fashion notion of corporate behaviour. The fact that influential statements of best corporate practice continue to emphasise the goal of profit maximisation and treat social responsibility only as a factor that management should consider in deciding how best to achieve that goal suggests that mainstream practice is not shifting significantly away from the self-interested philanthropy that company law has always permitted. Here it is appropriate to consider briefly the Hampel Report on Corporate Governance which was published in 1998. The report was the outcome of the deliberations of a committee comprising businessmen, lawyers, accountants and institutional investors. The committee's work was sponsored by the London Stock Exchange, the Confederation of British Industry, the Institute of Directors, the Consultative Committee of Accountancy Bodies, the National Association of Pension Funds and the Association of British Insurers. It followed on from the work of similarly constituted committees which

[64] An example of this is when certain shareholders of Shell used its AGM to pressurise the company to adopt better environmental and human rights polices: quoted in Goldenberg, P, 'Shareholders v Stakeholders: The Bogus Argument' (1998) 19 Co Law 35 at 35.

[65] In particular, Parkinson, JE, *Corporate Power and Responsibility* (1993) ch 9.

[66] 'Glaxo Attacked Over US Political Donations' *Financial Times* 15 April 1997 reporting the view of PIRC, a body that advises local authorities and other investors on corporate governance matters, that political donations should be approved by the shareholders. *The State of Corporate Governance in Britain in Britain* (1996 Survey of Directors at the Top 250 UK Companies conducted by Russell Reynolds Associates) found that 64 per cent of the directors surveyed thought that political donations should be subject to shareholder approval.

[67] *Statement on Corporate Governance and Voting Policy* issued by Hermes which manages the Post Office and BT pension funds. There are proposals for political donations by companies to be made subject to a shareholder approval requirement: *Political Donations by Companies—A Consultative Document* (DTI) (1999).

[68] Pettet, B, 'The Stirring of Corporate Social Conscience' (1997) 50 CLP 279, 286.

[69] And also labour law and industrial relations. The overlapping fields of interest for company lawyers, labour lawyers and contract lawyers may be leading to the emergence of new and distinct area of study which one commentator has described as 'the law of the productive enterprise': Collins, H, 'Organizational Regulation and the Limits of Contract' in McCahery, J, Picciotto, S, and Scott, C, *Corporate Control and Accountability* (1993) 91.

had previously considered the financial aspects of corporate governance (the Cadbury Committee) and directors' remuneration (the Greenbury Committee). All three committees produced codes of conduct. These codes occupy the realm of 'soft' law in that they are not enforceable under the general law but are followed in practice because investors expect this. In the case of companies admitted to listing on the London Stock Exchange, elements of these codes have been brought together into the *Combined Code* that is annexed to *The Listing Rules.* The *Combined Code* itself is not part of *The Listing Rules* but listed companies are required to state in their annual accounts whether they comply with it and to explain areas of non-compliance.[70]

The Hampel Committee's report states that:

> The single overriding objective shared by all listed companies, whatever their size or type of business, is the preservation and the greatest practicable enhancement over time of their shareholders' investment.[71]

To this end, the report states that the company should develop and foster relations with other groups including employees, customers, suppliers, credit providers, local communities and governments.[72] But the directors' relationship with the shareholders is, according to the report, 'different in kind' from the relationship with other stakeholders because it is to the shareholders that the directors are accountable. In all of these statements, the Hampel Committee is consistent with existing English law and is not signalling a radical change of direction. Similarly, an OECD Report on corporate governance which was published in 1998 takes long-term economic gain to enhance shareholder value as the company's central mission and builds in a recognition of societal needs as an element in the achievement of that goal.[73]

The fundamental point here is that there is a huge difference between a duty to act in the interests of certain groups and a duty to consider the interests of those groups. So long as the directors' duty to act in the interests of the company is regarded as a duty to act in the interests of the shareholders, the shareholders' interest in profit maximisation will prevail over whatever consideration may be given to wider social interests, except to the extent that the shareholders have authorised otherwise either in the company's constitution or by resolution.[74] Thus, it would seem that any proposal to amend English companies legislation to include a permission for, or obligation on, management to consider social concerns would achieve little more than a formalisation and clarification of the existing position.[75] A more radical shift towards a

[70] *The Listing Rules*, para 12.43A.

[71] *Hampel Committee Report*, para 1.16.

[72] Ibid, paras 1.16 –1.18 .

[73] *Corporate Governance: Improving Competitiveness and Access to Capital in Global Markets* (OECD Report) (1998).

[74] That the shareholders can opt out of profit maximisation is consistent with the contractual view of the company: Jensen, M, and Meckling, W, 'Theory of the Firm: Managerial Behavior, Agency Costs and Ownership Structure' in Putterman, L (ed), *The Economic Nature of the Firm* (1986) 209, 215–6 (reprinted in abridged form from (1976) 3 *Journal of Financial Economics* 305).

[75] This is consistent with the conclusion of the Committee on Corporate Laws of the American Bar Association (1990) on 'other constituency' statutes enacted in the USA. Other disagree: eg, Millon 'Redefining Corporate Law' (1991) 24 Indiana Law Review 223, 227 ('other constituency' statutes are 'manifestations of a deeper design to enhance the status of nonshareholders within the corporate enterprise').

stakeholder approach would require a reassessment of the 'company' for the purpose of the duty to act in the interests of the company[76] and the withdrawal from shareholders of the priority that they currently enjoy. Such a change could have far-reaching implications throughout company law. If shareholders were reduced to being just one of the various constituencies that directors were required to consider when determining the interests of the company, this would inevitably trigger a reconsideration of accountability issues since there would be no compelling reason for decisions whether to sue or to ratify managerial wrongdoing to devolve to the shareholders; other checks and balances on managerial discretion would have to be devised and these would have to give appropriate weight to the views of the various interested groups.[77] Provisions of the companies legislation which require shareholder approval for certain types of transaction between a company and its directors would need to be reviewed, as would the position of the shareholders as the group which, at a formal level,[78] has the power to vote directors out of office and to alter the company's capital structure and its constitution.[79] The shareholders' power to wind up the company simply by passing a resolution to that effect would also come into question and fundamental principles of corporate insolvency law would thus also need to be considered.

A less radical alternative is to impose specific social duties on companies.[80] Disclosure of policies which have social implications, such as environmental policies, is an example of this. Major companies already produce environmental reports on a voluntary basis, although this is mainly done for public relations purposes and not as an exercise in accountability.[81] An advantage of specific duties is that they can include their own enforcement mechanisms thereby avoiding the accountability problems that a move to a general stakeholder approach would entail.

Explanations of Shareholders' Preferred Status

The conventional legal explanation for the paramount position normally given to shareholders in the context of directors' duties is based on the shareholders' property rights as the 'owners' of the company. Legally, although shareholders do not own the assets of the company,[82] they tend to be regarded as the owners of the company itself.[83] The 'shareholder/ownership'

[76] Consideration of this issue is part of the agenda for the review of company law that was launched by the DTI in 1998: *Modern Company Law for a Competitive Economy* (DTI) (1998) para 3.7.

[77] Karmel, RS, 'Implications of the Stakeholder Model' (1993) 61 George Washington Law Review 1156, 1173.

[78] In practice the shareholders will normally simply endorse (or, rarely, reject) management proposals on these matters.

[79] Singer, JW, 'Jobs and Justice: Rethinking the Stakeholder Debate' (1993) 43 University of Toronto Law Journal 475, 501.

[80] eg, those discussed in Editorial Comment 'Time for Corporations to Get Responsible' (1997) 18 Co Law 161.

[81] Goldenberg, P, 'Shareholders v Stakeholders: The Bogus Argument' (1998) 19 Co Law 34, 38.

[82] *Macaura v Northern Assurance Co* [1925] AC 619, HL.

[83] Sappideen, R, 'Ownership of the Large Corporation: Why Clothe the Emperor?' (1996–97) 7 Kings College Law Journal 27; Grantham, R, 'The Doctrinal Basis of the Rights of Company Shareholders' [1998] CLJ 554.

model was the basis of Berle and Means' research on the separation of ownership and control and some of the work that succeeded it. This model continues to command support in practice: for example, the influential Cadbury Report, in dealing with the accountability of boards to shareholders, states that 'the shareholders as owners of the company elect the directors to run the business on their behalf and hold them accountable for its progress.[84] The English and Scottish Law Commissions have also viewed the shareholders as the owners of the company for the purposes of their review of directors' fiduciary and statutory duties.[85]

'Ownership' is a complex concept and in so far as it denotes having something in one's possession it is clearly inapplicable to an abstract entity such as a company. The ability to control is another feature of ownership as conventionally understood. Shareholders control companies limited by shares in the sense that it is they who enjoy the exclusive power voluntarily to form[86] and disband[87] them, and they also control management by, at a formal level, having the power to appoint and remove directors; but routine management of a company's affairs is not in the hands of the shareholders and, as a company grows in size and its shareholding becomes more widely dispersed, there is the opportunity in practice for its managers to escape from the control of the shareholders. Considerations such as these put in doubt the use of property-law concepts as the basis of a company's relationship with its shareholders.[88] Instead, shareholders come to be seen simply as providers of one form of capital.[89] This then paves the way for two distinct lines of inquiry: the first involves searching for an alternative explanation for the priority and powers that the law confers on shareholders; the second uses the proposition that shareholders are just one group of contributors to the resources of the firm to suggest that they should be displaced from the preferential position that they enjoy over other resource providers, employees and creditors, all of whom should be regarded as stakeholders whose interests should be taken into account but are not decisive. The agenda for change that is present in the

[84] *The Financial Aspects of Corporate Governance* (Report of the Cadbury Committee) (1992) para 6.1. Contrast *Enterprise with Integrity* (Institute of Directors Consultative Paper) (1994) 18: 'it is too simple to regard shareholders as 'owners' of the company' (but note Lea, R, *Directors Remuneration* (IoD Research Paper 1997) 23 which adopts the conventional model). See also Hansmann, H, 'Ownership of the Firm' in Bebchuk, LA (ed), *Corporate Law and Economic Analysis* (1990) 281 (reprinted (in abridged form) from (1988) 4 Journal of Law, Economics and Organization 267); Pennant-Rea, R, 'Punters or Proprietors? A Survey of Capitalism' *Economist*, 5 May 1990.

[85] *Company Directors: Regulating Conflicts of Interests and Formulating a Statement of Duties: A Joint Consultation Paper* (Law Commission Consultation Paper No 153; Scottish Law Commission Discussion Paper No 105) (1998) para 2.12.

[86] The subscribers to the memorandum of a company limited by shares must each take at least one share: Companies Act 1985, s 2 (5)(b). There is no equivalent requirement for a company to have creditors or employees.

[87] Insolvency Act 1986, s 84 (1)(b) and (c). Unpaid creditors of a company can only force it into liquidation with the assistance of the court: Insolvency Act 1986, s 122.

[88] Kay, J, and Silberston, A, 'Corporate Governance' (1995) 3 *National Institute Economic Review* 84, 87–8; Ireland, P, 'Company Law and the Myth of Shareholder Ownership' (1999) 62 MLR 32.

[89] Fama, E, 'Agency Problems and the Theory of the Firm' in Putterman, L (ed), *The Economic Nature of the Firm* (1986) 196, 197–8 (reprinted with author's abridgements from (1980) 88 *Journal of Political Economy* 288).

second line of inquiry has already been considered. A brief account of the first can now be given.

The main alternative explanation of shareholders' position in company law derives from the law-and-economics movement in which the company is seen as simply a shorthand term for the network of contracts between the various constituencies who have an interest in the firm. Where the personhood of the company is seen as merely a convenience to which no significance is attached,[90] there is obviously no place for 'ownership' of the company as a relevant concept.[91] Instead, shareholders are the 'residual claimants' to the firm's income. They, rather than creditors or employees, are the group who will benefit from the capital gains that flow from corporate success. Equally, it is they, rather than creditors, on whom losses will fall first. These factors give shareholders an incentive to monitor management, and company law gives them the power to do so by vesting in them the power to vote on a variety of matters including the composition of the board and the continued existence of the company.[92] Directors' duties exist within the contractual interpretation of the company as a gap-filling device: they are an alternative to elaborate promises and they are a cost-saving substitute for the bargain that investors and companies would have reached if they had engaged in a bargaining process. Shareholders, rather than creditors or employees, are the beneficiaries of fiduciary duties because of the open-ended nature of their relations and their status as residual claimants. Creditors and employees can protect their interests by contract.[93] On this view, the stakeholding debate reduces down to the simple proposition that companies can engage in activities which are not geared towards the goal of maximising shareholder value to the extent that this is bargained for by other constituencies, such as employees, or is conceded by the shareholders themselves.[94]

THE INTERESTS OF THE COMPANY AS A BUSINESS ENTITY

To speak of the interests of the business entity presupposes that the company is an autonomous institution which is capable of having interests. There is a view that it is futile to define the interests of the company by reference to the business entity because such an entity is incapable of experiencing well-being.[95] But it is possible to formulate plausible statements of corporate

[90] Easterbrook, FH, and Fischel, DR, *The Economic Structure of Corporate Law* (1991) 12.

[91] Deakin, S, and Slinger, G, 'Hostile Takeovers, Corporate Law, and the Theory of the Firm' (1997) 24 Journal of Law and Society 124, 126.

[92] Easterbrook, FH, and Fischel, DR, *The Economic Structure of Corporate Law* (1991) 67–70.

[93] Ibid, 90–3; Anderson, AG, 'Conflicts of Interest: Efficiency, Fairness and Corporate Structure' (1978) 25 UCLA Law Review 738; Fama, E, 'Agency Problems and the Theory of the Firm' in Putterman, L (ed), *The Economic Nature of the Firm* (1986) 196, 197–8 (reprinted with author's abridgements from (1980) 88 *Journal of Political Economy* 288).

[94] Easterbrook, FH, and Fischel, DR, *The Economic Structure of Corporate Law* (1991) 35–9.

[95] Parkinson, JE, *Corporate Power and Responsibility* (1993) 76. The author's view is that in this respect the corporate entity is simply a vehicle for benefiting the interests of human beings with the debate being whether it is only shareholders who count for this purpose or whether others are also to be considered. This view echoes Gower, LCB, 'Corporate Control: The Battle for the Berkeley' (1955) 68 Harv LR 1176, 1188–9. See also *Company Directors: Regulating Conflicts of*

purpose[96] and interests, such as the long-term productive use of the company's capital[97] or its survival as a thriving going concern.[98] Realist theories of the company in which the company is viewed as a real person have had a limited influence on the development of Anglo-American/Commonwealth company and corporations law but it is noticeable that in Continental Europe, where that theory has been much more significant, the idea of corporate interests being defined by reference to the business entity is not seen to be problematic. Thus, one influential French report states:

> The interest of the company may be understood as the overriding claim of the company considered as a separate economic entity, pursuing its own objectives which are distinct from those of its shareholders, employees, creditors including the internal revenue authorities, suppliers and customers.[99]

Although the courts frequently use the phrase 'interests of the company' in the context of directors' duties, it is not normally the interests of the entity, as opposed to the collective interests of the shareholders, that they have in mind.[100] Where those interests are the same, this does not matter but it is implicit in the entity approach that, although they are often synonymous, the interests of the company can be different from those of its shareholders.

Contested takeovers are one situation where the interests of the company, defined as the long-term productive use of industrial capital,[101] may be in conflict with the interests of shareholders, defined as the maximisation of the return on their investment. If the directors' duty to act in the interests of the company is interpreted as a duty to maximise shareholder value, this would suggest that, once the directors decide that the existing management is not best placed to maximise shareholder value, they should simply support the highest bidder even if that bidder is proposing to strip the company of its assets and then shut down the business. In *Heron International v Lord Grade*[102] the Court of Appeal reached precisely that conclusion: the directors,

Interests and Formulating a Statement of Duties: A Joint Consultation Paper (Law Commission Consultation Paper No 153; Scottish Law Commission Discussion Paper No 105) (1998) para 11.21. Contrast Charkham, J, *Keeping Good Company* (1994) 323: 'the company is a living organism which touches society at many points'; Sealy, LS, '"Bona Fides" and "Proper Purposes" in Corporate Decisions' (1989) 15 Monash University Law Review 265, 269–71.

[96] Though not, of course, if the personhood of the company is regarded as no more than a convenient shorthand for a network of bargains: Jensen, M, and Meckling, W, 'Theory of the Firm: Managerial Behavior, Agency Costs and Ownership Structure' in Putterman, L (ed), *The Economic Nature of the Firm* (1986) 209, 215–16 (reprinted in abridged form from (1976) 3 *Journal of Financial Economics* 305).

[97] Kay, J, and Silberston, A, 'Corporate Governance' (1995) 3 *National Institute Economic Review* 84, 89–91.

[98] *Enterprise With Integrity* (Institute of Directors Consultative Paper) (1994) 17.

[99] *The Boards of Directors of Listed Companies in France* (1995) 5 (the *Viénot Report*).

[100] The phrase 'interests of the company' is also used in relation to the power of the shareholders to alter articles by special resolution. It is possible to divide cases on the alteration of articles into those which tested the validity of the alteration against the interests of the company as a business entity and those which tested it against the collective interests of the members of the company: Rixon, FG, 'Competing Interests and Conflicting Principles: An Examination of the Power of Alteration of Articles of Association' (1986) 49 MLR 446.

[101] Ireland, P, 'Corporate Governance, Stakeholding and the Company: Towards a Less Degenerate Capitalism?' (1996) 23 Journal of Law and Society 287, 304.

[102] [1983] BCLC 244, CA.

having decided that the company should be taken over, discharged their duty by favouring the bidder offering the highest price for the company's shares. This decision seems strongly to support the argument that the interests of the company are the interests of its current shareholders, and no more.

Against the decision in *Heron International* is the decision of the Scottish Court of Session in *Dawson International plc v Coats Paton plc.*[103] This case concerned the question whether the directors of a company could validly undertake to support a particular bid, and Lord Cullen stated specifically that 'what is in the interests of the current shareholders as sellers of their shares may not necessarily coincide with what is in the interests of the company'.[104] According to Lord Cullen, possible reasons for a company, as opposed to its shareholders, to favour a particular bid were that it provided the opportunity for integrating operations or for obtaining additional resources.[105] The earlier *Heron* case was confined to its particular facts which were unusual in that the directors of the target company had power under the company's articles to decide the outcome of the takeover bid. This way of distinguishing the decision in *Heron* echoed *Re a Company No 008699 of 1985*[106] where Hoffmann J said that the judgment in the earlier case had to be read in its context and that, outside that special situation, there was no inevitable obligation on directors to facilitate whatever was the highest offer.

The decision in *Dawson* is an explicit, but rare, example of the courts using the business entity principle to override the interests of shareholders. Using the 'business entity' approach in this way can achieve the same effect as saying that the interests of the company are more than just the interests of its shareholders and encompass other constituencies such as its employees and creditors. Dicta to that effect can be found in a few cases. A potential advantage[107] of interposing the corporate vehicle between the directors and the various constituencies for the purpose of defining the content of the duty to act in the company's interest is that this opens up a way of dealing with conflicts of interest between the various constituencies and the human persons comprised in them: the interests of the company, as such, are paramount. Expansion of the business entity principle in this context could thus form the basis for further development of stakeholder concepts in English company law.[108]

[103] (1988) 4 BCC 305, Ct of Sess.

[104] Ibid, 314.

[105] Ibid, 313. See also the Australian case, *Darvall v North Sydney Brick & Tile Co Ltd* (1987–88) 12 ACLR 537, NSW SCEqD, 554, affirmed on appeal (1988–89) 15 ACLR 230, NSW CA. In the Court of Appeal Mahoney JA provided further examples of reasons why a company might concern itself with the identity of its shareholders. These included that the company might lose a government licence or a major customer if a particular person gained control of its shares. In 1988, the Takeover Panel rejected a submission that the board of IDG, which was the target of a bid, had breached the Code by recommending a bid which was not the highest where the lower bid was perceived to be the best way of providing for the future of the company.

[106] (1986) 2 BCC 99,024.

[107] Contrast Parkinson, JE, *Corporate Power and Responsibility* (1993) 79; Ireland, P, 'Company Law and the Myth of Shareholder Ownership' (1999) 62 MLR 32, 52–53.

[108] Kay, J, and Silberston, A, 'Corporate Governance' (1995) 3 *National Institute Economic Review* 84.

INTERESTS OF EMPLOYEES

The directors' statutory duty under the Companies Act 1985, s 309 to consider shareholders' interests in discharging their functions also requires them to consider the interests of employees.[109] This is not an important concession to stakeholder principles because the duty is weak:[110] it is simply to consider the employees' interests not to act in those interests; there are no instructions or guidance on balancing or prioritising employees' interests against those of the shareholders; and employees have no direct means of enforcing the duty to consider, s 309 (2) stating expressly that the duty is owed to the company alone. Unlike the position in relation to shareholders, the courts do not ordinarily seek to improve the position of employees by equating the duty to act in the interests of the company with a duty to act in the interests of the employees. One exception to this is a comment in *Fulham Football Club Ltd v Cabra Estates plc*[111] where, by reference to s 309, the Court of Appeal expressed the view that a company was more than simply the sum total of its shareholders and encompassed also employees and creditors; accordingly the Court of Appeal doubted whether the shareholders could properly adopt any breach of duty by the directors. This view, which was not vital to the decision in the case, seems seriously to overestimate the impact of the Companies Act 1985, s 309. It is very doubtful that the section was meant to have such a remarkable effect, since it would overturn much established law permitting shareholders the freedom to adopt or ratify directors' actions.[112] This dictum does, however, serve to illustrate that a shift in emphasis away from profit maximisation and towards a stakeholder theory of the company could have serious repercussions throughout company law and necessitate a fundamental reassessment of the principles on which it is based.

Greater employee involvement or representation within the corporate structure has been an important theme in European Union company law reform efforts, but proposals on this matter have proved to be very controversial. States such as the UK, which do not have a tradition of employee participation at board level, have tended to oppose proposals for greater worker involvement in that way whilst other states, such as Germany, are anxious to ensure that European measures do not erode the worker-participation structures that already exist under their national laws. The draft Fifth Company Law Directive, first proposed in 1972, which envisaged worker participation at board level or, in later versions, in other forms, generated considerable con-

[109] Companies Act 1985, s 309. The City Code on Takeovers and Mergers, which is a regulatory code that participants in the UK market are expected to follow in relation to bids for public companies contains a general principle (gen prin 9) to the effect that directors of the target company should, when advising the shareholders as they are required to do under the Code, consider employees' and creditors' interests as well as those of the shareholders themselves. Again this is a duty to consider employees' interests rather than to act in furtherance of them.

[110] Prentice, DD, 'A Company and its Employees: The Companies Act 1980' (1981) 10 ILJ 1; Birds, J, 'Making Directors Do Their Duties' (1980) 1 Co Law 67 at 73; Lord Wedderburn 'Companies and Employees: Common Law or Social Dimension' (1993) LQR 220.

[111] [1992] BCC 863, CA, 876 *per* Neill LJ.

[112] These topics are discussed later in this chapter; see below, at 144–53.

troversy and has never been adopted. More recently, attention has shifted to proposals for a European Company Statute where, again controversy about worker participation has held back development.[113]

At a national level, although the UK Government is engaged upon a review of employment law that seeks to provide a framework for the development of strong partnerships at work in place of the traditional notion of conflict between employers and employees,[114] the proposals do not signal a shift towards a stakeholder model for company law. There are no suggestions for employee participation at board level and/or enhanced priority for employee interests in the managerial decision-making process.

INTERESTS OF CREDITORS[115]

That directors should act so as to maximise profits is a maxim that becomes fairly meaningless when applied to companies in financial difficulties. Where survival of the company is in doubt, it is also rather pointless to emphasise the special position of shareholders as owners of the company since, if it fails, they will be unlikely to recover much, if any, of the original equity investment. The insolvency legislation allows for a review of the way in which a company has been managed in the twilight period before its eventual liquidation and the focus of that review is on whether creditors', not shareholders', interests have been protected. If directors of a company in insolvent liquidation are shown to have failed to take every step as ought to have been taken to minimise the loss to the company's creditors, they may be held liable for wrongful trading and required to make a personal contribution to the company's assets.[116] Specific transactions prejudicial to the general body of creditors such as transactions at an undervalue, preferences and transactions defrauding creditors are also liable to be set aside.[117]

The common-law duty to act in the interests of the company clearly could not continue to require directors to equate the company's interests with those of its shareholders at a time when the insolvency legislation dictates otherwise. Continuing to trade and incurring further debt might well be in the interests of the shareholders of an ailing company—if their investment is lost anyway, they can only gain from the keeping alive of the possibility of revival

[113] *The European Company Statute*, DTI Consultative Document (1997) which contains, in Annex C, the report of an expert group (the Davignon Group) which was asked by the European Commission to consider specifically the issue of worker-participation in the European company and to suggest possible solutions. One fear is that the formation of a European company could be a way of escaping from worker participation requirements under national law. This fear has also stalled progress on the Tenth Company Law Directive on Cross-Border Mergers, 1985 OJ C23 28/11.

[114] *Fairness at Work* Cm 3968 (1998).

[115] Grantham, R, 'The Judicial Extension of Directors' Duties to Creditors' [1991] JBL 1; Prentice, DD, 'Creditors' Interests and Directors' Duties' (1990) 10 OJLS 265; Sealy, LS, 'Directors' "Wider" Responsibilities—Problems Conceptual, Practical and Procedural' (1987) 13 Monash LR 164; Heydon, JD, 'Directors' Duties and the Company's Interests' in Finn, PD (ed), *Equity and Commercial Transactions* 120; Ziegel, JS, 'Creditors as Corporate Stakeholders. The Quiet Revolution—An Anglo-Canadian Perspective' (1993) 43 University of Toronto Law Journal 511.

[116] Insolvency Act 1986, s 214.

[117] Ibid, 238–241, 423.

through continued trading; if the gamble fails, it will be the creditors who will lose. Accordingly, in *West Mercia Safetywear Ltd v Dodd*,[118] the Court of Appeal, following Australian precedent,[119] held that in an insolvent company the interests of creditors intrude. A payment made by directors without regard to the interests of creditors amounted to a breach of duty and, because the shareholders no longer had any proprietary interest in the company's assets, they could not ratify that breach so as to make the act binding on the company.

At which point in the decline of a company do creditors' interests intrude? When they do intrude, do they oust shareholders' interests completely or merely take priority to them? What about employees' interests and the duty to consider them imposed by the Companies Act 1985, s 309? In *Kinsela v Russell Kinsela Pty Ltd*[120] Street CJ explained why these are not questions to which the courts should necessarily strive to provide definitive answers:

> I hesitate to attempt to formulate a general test of the degree of financial instability which would impose upon directors an obligation to consider the interests of creditors . . . It needs to be borne in mind that to some extent the degree of financial instability and degree of risk in the creditors are interrelated. Courts have traditionally and properly been cautious indeed in entering boardrooms and pronouncing upon the commercial justification of particular executive decisions. Wholly differing value considerations might enter into an adjudication upon the justification for a particular decision by a speculative mining company of doubtful stability on the one hand, and, on the other hand, by a company engaged in a more conservative business in a state of comparable financial instability. Moreover, the plainer it is that it is the creditors' money that is at risk, the lower may be the risk to which the directors, regardless of the unanimous support of all of the shareholders, can justifiably expose the company.
>
> The foregoing, and like, considerations point to the desirability of avoiding an attempt to enunciate principles in wide-ranging terms.

This flexible approach is echoed in the judgment of Nourse LJ in the Court of Appeal in *Brady v Brady*[121] where creditors' interests were said to predominate in circumstances of insolvency or 'doubtful' solvency.

The timing issue is thus best treated as a continuum, with creditors' interests acquiring increasing significance as the company's financial crisis deepens. Similarly, the content of the duty may depend upon the circumstances: it may be sufficient to frame the duty in terms which identify the company entirely with its creditors where what is in issue is a payment by directors in favour of themselves.[122] A genuine and careful decision by directors to sell the company's business in whole or in part, thereby saving some employees' jobs,

[118] [1988] BCLC 250 CA. See also *Facia Footwear Ltd v Hinchcliffe* [1998] 1 BCLC 218; *Re Frederick Inns Ltd* [1994] 1 ILRM 387, Ir SC.

[119] *Kinsela v Russell Kinsela Pty Ltd (in liq)* (1986) 4 NSWR 722, NSW CA.

[120] (1986) 4 NSWR 722, NSW CA.

[121] [1987] 3 BCC 535, CA, 552. Reversed by the House of Lords but not on grounds relevant to this point: [1989] AC 755, HL. See also *Re Horsley & Weight Ltd* [1982] Ch 442, CA, 455, where Templeman LJ also refers to 'doubtful' solvency. Compare *Nicholson v Permakraft (NZ) Ltd* [1985] 1 NZLR 242, NZ CA where, although Cooke J avoided a specific criterion for judging the point in time when creditors' interests became relevant, Richardson J and Somers J were more specific, favouring a balance sheet insolvency test (that is excess of liabilities over assets).

[122] As was the case in *West Mercia Safetywear Ltd v Dodd* [1988] BCLC 250, CA.

which is later challenged as a sale at too low a price, would require a more sophisticated analysis of the directors' duty. It requires an analysis which takes into account the undesirability of judging a difficult business decision harshly—because, with the benefit of hindsight, it may appear to have been unwise—and which sanctions a degree of balancing of the interests of creditors against the interests of employees.[123] The Insolvency Act 1986, s 214 may prove a helpful guide: under that section directors must minimise the loss to the company's creditors, but they are not required positively to take steps to maximise the amount available to the company from which to repay its creditors.

Some cases contain dicta suggesting that, even in a solvent company, directors must consider creditors when determining what is in the interests of the company.[124] Consideration of creditors' interests in a solvent company can be entirely comprehended within the goal of long-term profit maximisation since a prosperous company is one that will be able to pay its debts. In one sense, therefore, these dicta could be regarded as surplusage, adding nothing to the content of the duty of directors of a solvent company.[125] But there is potential (no more than that on the current authorities) for such views to be developed into a rather different version of company law from that presently established. This point is reinforced by *Fulham Football Club v Cabra Estates*[126] where the Court of Appeal doubted the ability of the shareholders to ratify on the basis that the company was more than its shareholders and extended to its employees and creditors both present and potential.

Shifting the emphasis of the directors' duty to act in the interests of the company away from shareholders in favour of creditors when insolvency looms does not, itself, affect the enforcement position: the duty is still owed to the company, not to creditors individually or collectively, and it is for the company or, more precisely, its liquidator on its behalf, to determine whether or not to sue. The possibility of directors being personally liable to creditors in tort[127] or for breach of fiduciary duty[128] has been raised, but this is open to criticism. At the heart of insolvency law is the *pari passu* principle which requires creditors to be treated equally; this principle would be undermined by a recognition of a direct duty owed by directors to creditors, since creditors who were quick off the mark could secure a significant advantage over the others. A corporate claim brought by the liquidator inures to the benefit of creditors generally[129] and, in addition, avoids the difficulty of attempting to identify

[123] Grantham, R, 'Directors' Duties and Insolvent Companies' (1991) 54 MLR 576.

[124] *Lonrho Ltd v Shell Petroleum Co Ltd* [1980] 1 WLR 627, HL, 634 *per* Lord Diplock; *Charterbridge Corpn Ltd v Lloyds Bank Ltd* [1970] Ch 62, 74; *Brady v Brady* (1987) 3 BCC 535, CA, 552 *per* Nourse LJ; *Fulham Football Club v Cabra Estates* [1992] BCC 863, CA, 876 *per* Neill LJ. *Walker v Wimborne* (1976) 137 CLR 1, H Ct of Aust recognised creditors' interests but, as was emphasised in *Equiticorp Finance Ltd v Bank of New Zealand* (1993) 11 ACSR 642, NSW CA, the relevant company in that case was insolvent.

[125] In *Brady v Brady* (1987) 3 BCC 535, CA, 552 Nourse LJ conceded that creditors' interests would count for little in a solvent company.

[126] [1992] BCC 863, CA.

[127] *Nicholson v Permakraft* [1985] 1 NZLR 242, NZ CA, 249 *per* Cooke J.

[128] *Winkworth v Edward Baron Development Co Ltd* [1986] 1 WLR 1512, HL.

[129] Leaving aside questions of security over the company's assets.

and separate individual creditors' losses from each other's, and from the loss of the company generally. The dicta in favour of a direct duty to creditors are fairly weak. As well as the arguments of principle against the recognition of such a duty, its existence was rejected by the Court of Appeal in *Re Horsley & Weight*[130] and by the Privy Council in *Kuwait Asia Bank EC v National Mutual Life Nominees.*[131] The existence of a direct duty owed by directors to creditors has also been rejected in Australia.[132] In the absence of a direct duty to creditors, the primary significance of the cases which treat the company's interests as being synonymous with those of its creditors in the event of insolvency, or doubtful solvency, is that this leads to a powerful limitation on the power of the shareholders to authorise the directors to behave in a manner which conflicts with the duties that they owe to the company under the general law, or to ratify wrongdoing after it has occurred.

LEGAL RULES: MANDATORY REQUIREMENTS OR DEFAULT PROVISIONS?

Those who view the company from the contractual perspective justify the imposition of fiduciary duties on directors on the basis that they reduce transaction costs.[133] Shareholders could seek to deal with the risk of directors preferring their personal interests or underperforming by writing out complex contracts detailing what the directors are required to do and, perhaps, also the consequences of failure to comply. In the event of breach, a director could thus be sued for breach of contract. Reliance on fiduciary duties imposed by general company law avoids the time and cost that would be involved in individual negotiation and drafting of elaborate contractual rules. Contractarians also take the view that mandatory company law should be kept to a minimum. From that perspective fiduciary duties should be regarded as standard terms supplied by the law for the purpose of economic efficiency,[134] but which the parties can depart from as they think fit.

This analysis does not appear to fit easily with present day English company law.[135] The Companies Act 1985, s 310 renders void:

> any provision, whether contained in a company's articles or in any contract or otherwise, for exempting any officer of the company or any person (whether an officer or not) employed by the company as auditor from, or indemnifying him against, any liability which by virtue of any rule of law would otherwise attach to him in respect of any negligence, default, breach of duty or breach of trust of which he may be guilty in relation to the company.

130 [1982] Ch 442, CA.

131 [1991] 1 AC 187, PC.

132 *Sycotex v Baseler* (1994) 13 ACSR 766, Fed Ct of Aust-Gen Div, 785.

133 Anderson, AG, 'Conflicts of Interest: Efficiency, Fairness and Corporate Structure' (1978) 25 UCLA Law Review 738; Easterbrook, FH, and Fischel, DR, *The Economic Structure of Corporate Law* (1991) ch 4.

134 Cheffins, BR, *Company Law: Theory, Structure and Operation* (1997) 134.

135 Bradley, C, 'Contracts, Trusts, and Companies' in McCahery, J, Picciotto, S, and Scott, C (eds), *Corporate Control and Accountability* (1993) 217, 229 where it is argued that the practical effect of Companies Act 1985, s 310 is very limited because of the procedural difficulties facing minority shareholders who seek to bring actions on the company's behalf against wrongdoing directors.

The only qualifications to this general ban on contracting out from the duties imposed by the general law are that a company may purchase liability insurance for its officers and auditors and may give indemnities in respect of any liability incurred by any officer or auditor in defending proceedings in which he is acquitted or judgment is given in his favour, or in respect of certain applications under specified sections of the companies legislation.[136]

A ban on contracting out of directors' duties was first introduced into the English companies legislation in 1928.[137] This step was taken in response to a number of cases[138] which drew public attention to articles of association which at that time commonly contained provisions exempting directors from liability except where it was due to their wilful neglect or default or, alternatively, where it was due to their actual dishonesty. The Company Law Amendment Committee which reviewed the position prior to the enactment of the ban on contracting out specifically considered and rejected the argument that a ban would cause hardship to conscientious directors or make their position more onerous, or would deter otherwise suitable persons from accepting office.[139] Arguments about the importance of not deterring suitable people from taking up office as directors continue to be voiced whenever there arises the question of imposing more onerous duties on directors or improving enforcement mechanisms.[140] The existence of liability insurance which companies can purchase on behalf of their directors should meet many of these concerns, although in practice this will depend on what is available in the insurance market with regard to such matters as the type of insurance, its cost, the liabilities that are excluded from coverage, ceilings on coverage, and the size of any deductibles which the insured is required to pay personally before the insurer will meet the claim.[141] Although many US states now permit corporations to indemnify directors for negligence liability,[142] the English position is, broadly, mirrored in other Commonwealth jurisdictions where indemnities are generally prohibited but corporations may purchase indemnity insurance for their directors.[143]

Although the ban on contracting out was first enacted to reverse the effect of articles which exempted directors from liability for negligence, Companies Act 1985, s 310 is drafted in much broader terms in that it outlaws exemptions

136 Companies Act 1985, s 310 (3).

137 Companies Act 1928, s 78.

138 *Re City Equitable Fire Insurance Co* [1925] Ch 407, CA; *Re Brazilian Rubber Plantations and Estates Ltd* [1911] 1 Ch 425.

139 *Report of the Company Law Amendment Committee*, Cmd 2657 (1926) (Greene Committee) paras 46–7.

140 *Shareholder Remedies* (Law Commission Report No 246) (1997) paras 6. 39–6.40 noting, but rejecting, the criticism of the proposed inclusion of negligence in a new statutory derivative action on the grounds that it might discourage people from becoming non-executive directors.

141 Finch, V, 'Personal Accountability and Corporate Control: The Role of Directors' and Officers' Liability Insurance' (1994) 57 MLR 880.

142 Many States amended their corporate statutes to permit this in response to the controversial decision of the Delaware Supreme Court in *Smith v Van Gorkam*, 488 A2d 858 (Del 1985) where liability was imposed on directors for breach of the duty of care: Klein, WA, and Coffee, JC, *Business Organization and Finance* (5th edn, 1993) 151–2; Romano, R, 'Corporate Governance in the Aftermath of the Insurance Crisis' (1990) 39 Emory Law Journal 1155.

143 eg, Australia: Tomasic, R, Jackson, J, and Woellner, R, *Corporations Law Principles, Policy and Process* (3rd edn, 1996) paras 7.51–7.55.

and indemnities in respect of any 'negligence, default, breach of duty or breach of trust'.[144] Commentators sought to limit the apparently sweeping scope of this provision by suggesting a number of restrictive interpretations.[145] When the matter finally came before a court in *Movitex Ltd v Bulfield*,[146] it was held that the scope of the section was indeed more limited than its drafting might appear to suggest at first glance, but the most powerful academic argument in support of that conclusion—that the section did not prohibit the reduction or abrogation of directors' duties as opposed to exclusions or indemnities in respect of breach[147]—was rejected. Instead Vinelott J held that the key to the correct interpretation of Companies Act 1985, s 310[148] lay in the proper classification of the rules governing the conduct of company directors: to the extent that those rules were 'disabilities' rather than 'duties' they were outside the scope of the section and it was therefore possible to abrogate or reduce them. The obvious question-begging aspect of this decision is how to distinguish between disabilities and duties and, on this, the *Movitex* decision provides limited guidance.[149] The case itself concerned a contract between two companies which had directors in common. The relevant directors had disclosed the nature of their interest in the purchaser company at a board meeting of the vendor company and the board had approved the contract. Although there is a legal rule prohibiting company contracts in which directors have an interest unless they have been approved by the shareholders in general meeting, it was held that the contract had been properly sanctioned by the vendor company. This was because the rule in question was a disability and it had been effectively modified by the company's articles which replaced the shareholders with the directors as the body whose consent was required.[150] Dicta in the *Movitex* decision indicate that the obligations to show due care and skill, to act in the interests of the company, to make full disclosure of interests and to prefer the company interests to personal interests in the event of conflict, are properly to be regarded as duties. The *Movitex* decision leaves in a somewhat limbo state other rules to which directors are

[144] In *Movitex Ltd v Bulfield* (1986) 2 BCC 99,403, 99,430 Vinelott J acknowledged that the scope of the section was wider than just negligence with the comment that: 'A patch may be intentionally wider than the visible hole to which it is applied.'

[145] Baker, CD, 'Disclosure of Directors' Interests in Contracts' [1975] JBL 181; Parkinson, JE, 'The Modification of Directors' Duties' [1981] JBL 335; Birds, J, 'The Permissible Scope of Articles Excluding the Duties of Company Directors' (1976) 39 MLR 394; Rule, EJ, and Brar, HS, 'Exempting the Directors' (1979) NLJ 6; Gregory, R, 'The Scope of the Companies Act 1948, Section 205' (1982) 98 LQR 413.

[146] (1986) 2 BCC 99,403. Birds, J, 'Excluding the Duties of Directors' (1987) 8 Co Law 31; Sealy, LS, 'Company Directors' "Duties" and Exempting Articles' [1987] CLJ 217.

[147] Davies, PL, *Gower's Principles of Company Law* (6th edn, 1997) 624 noting the position advocated in earlier editions of the book.

[148] Vinelott J in fact considered Companies Act 1948, s 205. That provision was consolidated into Companies Act 1985, s 310 without any change of substance.

[149] *Shareholder Remedies* (Law Commission Report No 246) (1997) para 6.26 notes that the decision in *Movitex* draws 'very difficult distinctions'.

[150] Articles of association commonly modify the 'no dealing' rule in this way: see, eg, Table A, art 84. In *Movitex* Vinelott J accepted (99,429) that the courts should, if possible, prefer a construction of s 310 which avoided a conflict with another legislative provision (art 84 is a provision in a statutory instrument).

subject, in particular the obligations to exercise their powers for proper purposes and not to make a profit from their position.[151]

As well as the distinction between disabilities and duties which was drawn in the *Movitex* decision, there are a number of other mechanisms which operate so as dilute the impact of the rules governing directors' conduct and which, in effect, can be viewed as amounting to 'opting out' of the rigour of those obligations. The first such mechanism lies in the power of the company validly to release claims that it has against miscreant directors under the general law; the second is the principle of authorisation or ratification whereby shareholders can, prospectively or retrospectively, permit directors to act in a manner that would otherwise constitute a breach of their duties. The vesting of this power in the shareholders is an example of how company law puts shareholders in a preferential position over other 'stakeholders' in a company.

A PROMISE NOT TO SUE

There is limited authority on this point but dicta in a number of cases support the proposition that a company can release a cause of action that it has against miscreant directors.[152] A valid release, if given by deed or for some consideration, would bind the company and no action could thereafter be brought even after a change of control. It appears that releases may relate to conduct that is illegal, such as the payment of unlawful dividends or the authorisation of financial assistance contrary to the Companies Act 1985.[153]

On the basis that decisions about litigation are part of the managerial function,[154] constitutionally it should be for the board to decide whether to grant a release.[155] Rules about conflicts of interest would clearly preclude miscreant directors from granting a valid release to themselves.[156] This means that it may sometimes be impossible to form a quorate board[157] made up of directors who are not implicated in the alleged wrongdoing in order to reach the decision whether to grant a release. It is established that in circumstances

[151] See also Ch 5 below, at 198–9.

[152] *Taylor v National Union of Mineworkers (Derbyshire Area)* [1985] BCLC 237, 255; *Smith v Croft (No 2)* [1988] 1 Ch 114, 180–2. See generally, Partridge, RJC, 'Ratification and the Release of Directors from Personal Liability' [1987] CLJ 122.

[153] *Smith v Croft (No 2)* [1988] 1 Ch 114 involved allegations of unlawful financial assistance.

[154] *John Shaw and Sons (Salford) Ltd v Shaw* [1935] 2 KB 113, CA; *Breckland Group Holdings Ltd v London & Suffolk Properties Ltd* (1988) 4 BCC 542. If a company is in financial difficulties its administrator, administrative receiver or liquidator will usually have the power to 'bring or defend any action or other legal proceeding in the name and on behalf of the company': Insolvency Act 1986, schs 1 and 4. Generally, see Lord Wedderburn, 'Control of Corporate Litigation' 39 MLR 327.

[155] If no consideration is provided for the release, then it would be subject to the rules on corporate gifts: see Ch 10 below.

[156] Under Table A or articles which follow that model, save for some exceptions which are not relevant here, directors cannot vote on matters in which they have a material interest or duty and which conflicts or may conflict with the interests of the company, nor may they count in the quorum (arts 94–5).

[157] Table A, arts 94–5.

where a board is disabled from acting, decision-making responsibility can constitutionally devolve to the shareholders in general meeting.[158] A release which is approved by the shareholders at a duly convened general meeting would bind the company unless there is some reason why the shareholders are also disabled from making decisions on its behalf. One such reason may be that the company is in a position of insolvency, or near insolvency, so that, under the principles established by cases such as *West Mercia Safetywear Ltd v Dodd*,[159] the shareholders are no longer an effective decision-making body. Another is that the courts may deny effect to a decision of the shareholders in general meeting, despite its constitutional propriety, in order to protect minority shareholders from misuse of power by the majority. The power of the courts to curb the extreme applications of majority rule has received more attention in relation to decisions to authorise or ratify conduct which would otherwise amount to a breach of duty. This chapter reflects that fact and considers limits on majority rule in the context of authorisation and ratification; but the principles outlined there should be equally applicable to decisions to release causes of action that the company may have against miscreant directors. In general, the relationship between binding releases and ratification is not yet entirely clear and some of the principles that have been developed in relation to ratification do not sit easily with the proposition that it is in principle possible for a company to release a cause of action arising from any type of managerial misconduct.

AUTHORISATION AND RATIFICATION

This is one of the most difficult topics in company law. The complications that beset any discussion of the topic stem from a number of different factors, including the following: (i) the underexplored nature of the relationship between the principles of authorisation and ratification and Companies Act 1985, s 310; (ii) uncertainty about terminology: in particular, the term 'ratification' can be used to denote a number of different things; (iii) the use of the concept of unratifiable wrongs; (iv) lack of clarity about the limits of the court's power to intervene to prevent the majority of the shareholders making decisions which are detrimental to the minority; (v) confusion about the constitutional requirements, in particular the extent to which the board can ratify and, when a shareholders' vote is required, the majority needed to pass a valid ratifying resolution; (vi) uncertainty concerning the relationship between ratification and the ability of minority shareholders to bring actions on the company's behalf against wrongdoing directors; and (vii) the position of other 'stakeholders', such as creditors or employees whose interests may be adversely affected by a decision of the shareholders to authorise or ratify misconduct. These points can be seen as strands in a complex tapestry: although they are separated out for the purposes of exposition here, the reality is that the issues overlap with, and impact on, each other.

[158] *Bamford v Bamford* [1969] 1 All ER 969, CA.

[159] [1988] BCLC 250, CA.

Authorisation/Ratification and the Companies Act 1985, s 310

Shareholders can authorise directors to behave in a manner which would otherwise amount to a breach of the duties which they owe to the company. This is demonstrated by *Multinational Gas and Petrochemical Co v Multinational Gas and Petrochemical Services Ltd*,[160] where the liquidator of an insolvent company failed in his attempts to sue its former directors for breach of their duties of care and skill because their actions had been authorised or ratified by the shareholders of the company. The majority of the Court of Appeal explained that the effect of authorisation or ratification was to adopt the directors' actions as acts of the company; since the alleged misconduct has thus become its own acts, the company had no grounds for complaint.

Why a contract, approved by the shareholders, which releases a director from his duty to act with due care and skill should be rendered void by Companies Act 1985, s 310, whilst a shareholders' resolution which authorises a director to take steps which would otherwise be in breach of his duty to exercise care and skill is permitted to have effect, is a question that has received little attention.[161] Similarly, scant regard is paid to the fact that, although a decision to ratify misconduct so as to preclude a claim by the company in respect of it can achieve much the same effect as a contract, or provision in the articles, which exempts the director from breach of duty, the former is permitted whilst the latter is banned. The specificity of an authorising/ratifying resolution may sometimes serve to distinguish that form of release from a provision in a contract or articles. Instinctively, there seems to be something less objectionable about resolutions which authorise directors to do particular things, or forgive them for having done them, than blanket permissions to act contrary to their obligations under the general law. In one Australian case it was said that ratification fell outside the equivalent of the Companies Act 1985, s 310 on precisely this sort of reasoning: ratification was specific absolution rather than blanket indemnification or exemption.[162] Where, however, directors' conduct is routinely submitted for shareholder authorisation or ratification, as may commonly occur where companies are wholly-owned subsidiaries or, as in the *Multinational Gas* case, have only a few shareholders, such a distinction cannot plausibly be maintained. Also, any thought that shareholders may be better placed to assess the merits of a proposal for

160 [1983] Ch 258.

161 Rogerson, P, 'Modification and Exclusion of Directors' Duties' in Rider, BAK (ed), *The Realm of Company Law* (1998) 93 considers the 'startling' possibility of authorising/ratifying resolutions falling within the 'or otherwise' category in Companies Act 1985, s 310. That such resolutions could be caught by Companies Act 1985, s 310 is rejected by other commentators: Partridge, RJC, 'Ratification and the Release of Directors from Personal Liability' [1987] CLJ 122, 144; Instone, R, 'The Scope of the Companies Act 1948, Section 205' (1982) 98 LQR 548; compare Gregory, R, 'Section 205 of the Companies Act 1948—A Reply?' (1983) 99 LQR 194. In *Burgoine v London Borough of Waltham Forest* [1997] BCC 347, 358 Neuberger J said that the words 'or otherwise' were directed towards covering an arrangement with the company which might not amount to a contract, but which might none the less give rise to an argument that the company had agreed to indemnify or exempt a director; according to the judge an example of what might be covered was an arrangement with a company amounting to an estoppel.

162 *Miller v Miller* (1995) 16 ACSR 73, NSW EqD 73, 87.

authorisation or ratification in relation to a particular matter than they would be to determine the implications of a standing contractual release must be tempered by an awareness of the problems that beset shareholder voting generally. One particular issue is the fact that the board normally convenes general meetings and, so, controls the presentation and content of the information on which shareholders are asked to make a decision.[163] With that in mind, one reform step that might usefully be considered in this context would be for legislation to set minimum disclosure requirements regarding the information to be made available to shareholders when they are asked to authorise or ratify directors' conduct.[164]

The Meaning of Ratification[165]

The first sense in which the term 'ratification' is used is to describe the process whereby a company adopts an act which originally did not bind the company because the agent who purported to act on its behalf lacked authority.[166] The only limit on ratification in this sense is that a company may not ratify an act professedly done on its behalf prior to its incorporation.[167] The reason for this limitation is that ratification in this sense is retrospective in its effect and it can therefore only operate where the person ratifying could have been a party to the contract at the time when it was first agreed.

Acts outside a company's objects clause can be ratified (in the sense of adoption) by a special resolution.[168]

The second sense in which ratification is used is to describe the situation where an act or transaction is prima facie binding on the company but is voidable. Share allotments made by directors for improper purposes to persons who are aware of the impropriety are one example of a tainted act which can be ratified in this sense.[169] Another example is provided by contracts between companies and directors which are fair in their terms but which are defective because of a failure by the directors to disclose their interests as required by the general law and the companies' articles.[170] Ratification in this sense could be used interchangeably with the term 'affirmation'.

Ratification was not in issue in *Guinness v Saunders*[171] but the facts of this case provide a good illustration of the difference between an act which is not binding on a company and therefore may require ratification in the first sense and an act which is prima facie binding but defective and, so, open to ratifica-

163 See generally, Ch 7 below, at 258–71.

164 This point has been considered in Australia: see *Company Directors and Officers: Indemnification, Relief and Insurance* (Discussion Paper No 9) (Companies and Securities Law Review Committee).

165 Partridge, RJC, 'Ratification and the Release of Directors from Personal Liability' [1987] CLJ 122; Parkinson, JE, *Corporate Power and Responsibility* (1993) 252–6.

166 eg, *Irvine v Union Bank of Australia* [1876–7] 2 AC 366, PC; *Grant v UK Switchback Railways Co* (1889) 40 Ch D 135, CA.

167 *Kelner v Baxter* (1866) LR 2 CP 174.

168 Companies Act 1985, s 35 (3).

169 *Hogg v Cramphorn* [1967] 1 Ch 254; *Bamford v Bamford* [1970] 1 Ch 212, CA.

170 *North-West Transportation Co Ltd v Beatty* (1887) 12 App Cas 589, PC; *Burland v Earle* [1902] AC 83, PC.

171 [1990] 2 AC 663, HL.

tion in the second sense. The dispute concerned the payment of a fee to a director. At first instance and on appeal, the courts held that this payment was voidable because the director had not made the requisite disclosure in accordance with the company's articles. The House of Lords identified the problem with this analysis as being that the payment had been made for services, so that restoration of the parties to their pre-contractual position which, broadly speaking, is what occurs when a voidable contract is rescinded, could not easily be effected. The House of Lords held instead that the payment was void because it had not been properly authorised and the obligation to pay it was therefore not binding on the company.[172]

Ratification in its third sense was described in one case as being the process whereby directors by making full disclosure to the shareholders 'obtain absolution and forgiveness of their sins'.[173] If a director's breach of duty is ratified by the shareholders in general meeting, the directors are absolved from liability. The Companies Act 1985, s 35 (3) distinguishes between this form of ratification and ratification in its first sense: decisions to ratify (adopt) unauthorised transactions which fall within the scope of the section must be taken separately from decisions to ratify any breach of duty which the directors may have committed in entering into those transactions on the company's behalf. This is designed to ensure that shareholders are fully aware of the position and to stop directors from securing a release from liability on the back of the adoption of a contract; it means that the shareholders cannot be forced into forgiving the directors simply as a by-product of their decision to adopt a contract.

Unratifiable Wrongs

A company cannot adopt as its own act something which it is prohibited from doing under the general law, for example an unlawful dividend[174] or financial assistance contrary to the ban in Companies Act 1985, s 151.[175] To that extent, therefore, it is sensible to speak of an 'unratifiable wrong'. However, case law and commentators use the concept of the unratifiable wrong in a broader fashion.

First, the conduct of directors in committing the company to some unlawful act also tends to be described as an unratifiable wrong. This flows from a blurring of the logical distinction between ratifying acts (adopting) and ratifying wrongdoing (forgiving). Assimilation of the two processes is commonplace in company law cases.[176]

Secondly, and again with no necessary distinction being drawn between the 'adopting' and the 'forgiving' senses of ratification, it is conventional to say that the category of unratifiable wrongs extends beyond acts which are

[172] See also *UK Safety Group Ltd v Heane* [1998] BCLC 208 (service contract containing restrictive covenants had not been approved by the board as required by the articles and was therefore not authorised but it could be ratified).

[173] *Bamford v Bamford* [1970] Ch 212, CA, 238 *per* Harman LJ.

[174] *Re Exchange Banking Co, Flitcroft's Case* (1882) 21 Ch D 519, CA.

[175] *Smith v Croft (No 2)* [1988] 1 Ch 114.

[176] Companies Act 1985, s 35 (3) is thus the exception rather than the rule. See further Yeung, K, 'Disentangling the Tangled Skein: the Ratification of Directors' Actions' (1992) 66 ALJ 343.

banned by the companies legislation and embraces certain conduct which is contrary to the obligations to which directors are subject at common law or in equity. This is the most troublesome aspect of ratification because it is not clear where the limits of the category of unratifiable wrongs are to be drawn, nor is it beyond question that any such category does, or should, in fact exist.

Failure to act in the interests of the company,[177] expropriation of the company's property,[178] and negligence from which the directors (or their associates) profit personally[179] are, on the conventional view, examples of unratifiable wrongs.[180] On the other hand, 'simple' negligence (where there is no element of personal profit for the directors or their associates)[181] and making unauthorised profits contrary to the rule that directors may not profit from their position[182] are said to be ratifiable wrongs. There are well-recognised, and much-debated, difficulties with this classification.[183] In particular, the assumption that it is possible to draw a simple, clear boundary between ratifiable profiting from position and unratifiable expropriation of property is difficult to maintain as developments in other branches of the law lead to an increasingly sophisticated and complex understanding of the nature of 'property' and the availability of proprietary remedies.[184] At an intuitive level, there is something peculiar about a judge-made category of unratifiable wrongs finding a place within a framework of company law which is, on the whole, happy to treat the shareholders as the company and to permit them to make decisions on its behalf. This is especially so now that the Companies Act 1985, s 35 even permits ratification of conduct which is not authorised by the company's objects. Nevertheless, the view that there is a category of unratifiable

177 *Atwool v Merryweather* (1867) LR 5 Eq 464.

178 *Cook v Deeks* [1916] 1 AC 554, PC; *Burland v Earle* [1902] AC 83, PC.

179 *Daniels v Daniels* [1978] 2 All ER 89.

180 Boyle, AJ, Sykes, R, and Sealy, LS, *Gore Browne on Companies* (44th edn, loose-leaf) (1986) para 27.21.1; but contrast Davies, PL, *Gower's Principles of Modern Company Law* (6th edn, 1997) 644–8 where the limits of the category of unratifiable wrongs are drawn differently. See also Parkinson, JE, *Corporate Power and Responsibility* (1993) 252–6.

181 *Pavlides v Jensen* [1956] 1 Ch 565.

182 *Regal (Hastings) Ltd v Gulliver* [1942] 1 All ER 378, [1967] 2 AC 134n, HL.

183 Davies, PL, *Gower's Principles of Modern Company Law* (6th edn, 1997) 644–8; Wedderburn, 'Shareholder Rights and the Rule in *Foss v Harbottle*' [1957] CLJ 194 and [1958] CLJ 93; Sealy, LS, 'The Director as Trustee' [1967] CLJ 83; Beck, SM, 'Corporate Opportunity Revisited' in Ziegel, JS (ed), *Studies in Canadian Company Law Vol II* (1973) 193.

184 In *Regal (Hastings) Ltd v Gulliver* [1942] 1 All ER 378, [1967] 2 AC 134n, HL, the directors took an investment opportunity which the company, because of its own financial position, could not pursue. This was held to be a breach of duty for which the directors were liable but which could have been ratified by a resolution of the shareholders in general meeting. Although this is classified as a 'profit' case (hence distinguishing it from *Cook v Deeks* [1916] AC 554, PC where the directors diverted to themselves an opportunity which the company had been pursuing and that was held to be unratifiable), it is apparent from later cases that for a fiduciary to use information which he has learnt from his position can have proprietary consequences: *Boardman v Phipps* [1967] 2 AC 46, HL. The distinction between 'profit' and 'property' is also undermined by developments in the law of restitution on proprietary restitutionary remedies which are apparent in cases such as *Attorney General for Hong Kong v Reid* [1994] 1 AC 324, PC and *Westdeutsche Landesbank Girozentrale v Islington BC* [1996] AC 669, HL. See, generally, Burrows, A, and McKendrick, E, *Cases and Materials on the Law of Restitution* (1997) ch 14, s 2.

Shareholder Remedies: A Consultation Paper (Law Commission Consultation Paper No 142) (1996) paras 5.6–5.17 seeks to distinguish *Regal (Hastings) v Gulliver* and *Cook v Deeks* in a way which avoid the property/profit dichotomy.

wrongs continues to be widely accepted.[185] In its work on shareholder remedies, the Law Commission's emphasis was on the effect of a valid ratification and its ability to bar a claim by a minority shareholder, but underpinning that discussion was an assumption, consistent with the conventional view, that there are some wrongs which are ratifiable and others which are not.[186]

Majority Rule and Protection of Minorities

The underlying purpose of the concept of the unratifiable wrong is the protection of minority shareholders against oppression by the majority. This underlying purpose was explicitly acknowledged by Vinelott J at first instance in *Prudential Assurance Co Ltd v Newman Industries Ltd (No 2)*[187] but Vinelott J rejected the notion of unratifiable wrongs. In his view, illegality aside, there was no obvious limit to the power of the majority to authorise or ratify. The important question was whether, in ratifying, the majority had an interest which conflicted with that of the minority. If the decision amounted to oppression of the minority by the majority then it would not stand. Vinelott J's denial of the category of unratifiable wrongs avoids some of the problems inherent in that theory[188] but is itself difficult to reconcile with all of the decided cases.[189] His alternative theory struggles to explain cases involving 'simple' negligence where the courts consistently deny that they have any power to review ratifying resolutions. It also sits uneasily with the principle that a vote attaching to a share is a property right which the owner can use as he or she thinks fit.[190] However, the line of cases relevant to this topic contains many inconsistencies and it is probably futile to attempt to find a theoretical framework which can accommodate all of them. Furthermore, in other branches of company law it is established that, despite the proprietary nature of voting rights, the courts can deny effect to a decision of the majority of the shareholders where it is oppressive to minority interests[191] and the

185 But see this chapter below, at 152, for the emergence of yet another view, namely, that unratifiable wrongs are in fact ratifiable but only with the unanimous consent of the shareholders.

186 *Shareholder Remedies: A Consultation Paper* (Law Commission Consultation Paper No 142) (1996) paras 5.2–5.17; *Shareholder Remedies* (Law Commission Report No 246) (1997) paras 6.80–6.86. See also *Company Directors: Regulating Conflicts of Interests and Formulating a Statement of Duties: A Joint Consultation Paper* (Law Commission Consultation Paper No 153; Scottish Law Commission Discussion Paper No 105) (1998) paras 11.30–11.38.

187 [1981] Ch 257, reversed [1982] Ch 204, CA.

188 Vinelott J distinguished *Regal (Hastings) Ltd v Gulliver* [1942] 1 All ER 378, [1967] 2 AC 134n, HL from *Cook v Deeks* [1916] AC 554, PC on the basis that the wrongdoing directors were the majority shareholders in the latter case but did not have control of the general meeting in the former case. This explanation involves an amount of reading into the facts in each case.

189 Davies, PL, *Gower's Principles of Modern Company Law* (6th edn, 1997) 646, n79 labels it 'heretical'.

190 *North-West Transportation Co v Beatty* (1887) 12 App Cas 589, PC.

191 A decision by the majority to alter the articles will not stand if it is reached otherwise than in the interests of the company as a whole: *Allen v Gold Reefs of West Africa* [1900] 1 Ch 671, CA. The 'interests of the company as a whole' is a formula which is employed to achieve the underlying purpose of protecting the minority from unconscionable conduct by the majority: *Peter's American Delicacy Co v Heath* (1939) 61 CLR 457, H Ct of Aust.

'proprietary' argument should not therefore be seen to conclude the matter against Vinelott J's approach.

Instead of attempting to find a path through a mass of what is probably irreconcilable case law, a more useful line of inquiry is to consider whether the unratifiable wrong approach is preferable in principle to Vinelott J's alternative theory, which requires an examination of the exercise of majority power on a case by case basis. There are arguments both ways.[192] In favour of the unratifiable wrong approach, it can be said that although there are doubts at the margin about what is and is not an unratifiable wrong, the general principle is clear, straightforward and easy to apply: there are some forms of conduct which the shareholders simply cannot ratify. This protects minority shareholders and also, coincidentally, creditors and employees, even though the concept of the unratifiable wrong was not developed specifically with stakeholders other than minority stakeholders in mind. A 'brightline' unratifiable wrong rule gives companies and their advisers a degree of certainty about the framework within which they operate. In the event of a purported ratification of an unratifiable wrong the court can simply strike this down without having to engage upon the difficult task of inquiring into the motives of the shareholders who voted for it. In favour of Vinelott J's approach, this theory fits more easily than its rival within the general framework of English company law relating to directors' duties in which the company is usually identified with its shareholders and the shareholders are treated as being its 'voice' for the purpose of giving consent to directors to act otherwise than in accordance with its duties. Cases which appear to hold that the majority of the shareholders can never take for themselves, or give to directors, corporate gifts and which are therefore the bedrock of the unratifiable-wrong theory[193] can be viewed as outdated relics from an earlier age in which the courts employed a variety of techniques to prevent corporate gifts. Since it is now clearly established that a company can have capacity to make gifts,[194] and corporate gifts are now controlled by a sophisticated application of a combination of rules relating to maintenance of capital, protection of creditors' interests in the event of insolvency and directors' duties, it is arguably hard to see why the shareholders in general meeting should be absolutely denied the power to exercise that power in favour of the directors. Under Vinelott J's suggested approach, the position would be that in principle directors could be forgiven for any sort of wrongdoing but, in appropriate cases, the court would be able to hold that such decisions were ineffective because they amounted to the unconscionable use of majority power contrary to the interests of the minority.

It would be clearly impossible for a court to examine the motives of individual shareholders in voting in favour of ratification. Leaving aside the share-

[192] The arguments against Vinelott J are set out by Lord Wedderburn 'Derivative Actions and *Foss v Harbottle*' (1981) 44 MLR 202.

[193] eg, *Menier v Hooper's Telegraph Works* (1873) 9 LR Ch App 350, CA; *Atwool v Merryweather* LR 5 Eq 464n; *Ngurli Ltd v McCann* (1953) 90 CLR 425, H Ct of Aust, 477. It must, however, be conceded, that the judgments in these cases do not use the *ultra vires* rule as the basis for the conclusions reached.

[194] *Re Horsley & Weight Ltd* [1982] Ch 442, CA. See further Ch 10 below.

holders who themselves are the wrongdoers, or who are clearly connected to them, the only sensible focus for the court's inquiry would have to be on the disclosure made to the shareholders in connection with the matter: provided the shareholders, other than the wrongdoers and persons connected with them, reached their decision to ratify on the basis of adequate information, then in practice their decision would stand. The courts are perfectly able to respond to the fact that management is usually in a position to control the way in which the proposal is put to the general meeting and the flow of information about it[195] and accordingly to conduct a very rigorous review of the quality of the information provided.[196] Nevertheless Vinelott J's approach could produce much greater uncertainty and unpredictability than the unratifiable-wrong theory and this in turn could diminish the protection afforded to minority shareholders (and, through them, to other constituencies).

Yet, the apparently attractive certainty of the unratifiable-wrong theory begins to look rather doubtful when there is taken into account the recognition of the effectiveness of binding releases even in respect of unratifiable wrongs. Although the unratifiable-wrong theory may say that shareholders cannot forgive certain types of breach by ratification, this will make little practical difference to the directors if they can secure forgiveness by means of a binding release of the cause of action by the company. As yet there is only limited authority on binding releases of causes of action by companies and the legal position on them is in an underdeveloped state.[197] Matters that require closer examination include: the relationship between ratification and releases of causes of action and whether, or to what extent, they are in fact distinguishable processes;[198] the limits of the power of the board of directors to grant releases bearing in mind that 'ratification' has traditionally been seen to be a shareholder function rather than a matter for the board; and the protection of minority shareholders from abuse of the power to grant releases by either the board or the majority of the shareholders in general meeting.[199]

195 Eisenberg, MA, 'The Structure of Corporation Law' (1989) 89 Columbia Law Review 1461, 1474–80; Bratton, WW, 'The Economic Structure of the Post Contractual Corporation' (1992) 87 Northwestern University Law Review 180, 193–4.

196 In this respect the non-interventionist stance of the Court of Appeal in *Prudential Assurance Co Ltd v Newman Industries Ltd* [1982] Ch 204 is hardly encouraging.

197 They are not specifically addressed by the Law Commission in its work on shareholder remedies: *Shareholder Remedies: A Consultation Paper* (Law Commission Consultation Paper No 142) (1996) and *Shareholder Remedies* (Law Commission Report No 246) (1997). The only relevant comments are in the Report at para 6.87 where it is recommended that a resolution by the majority not to sue (ie not a binding release) should be a relevant factor for the court to take into account in deciding whether to permit a minority shareholder action to proceed but that it should not be an absolute bar. In a footnote (n125, at p 95) it is accepted that a derivative action would have to be dismissed if there was a binding release of the cause of action.

198 Partridge, RJC, 'Ratification and the Release of Directors from Personal Liability' [1987] CLJ 122 suggests, for example, that ratification, in the sense of 'forgiving' is indistinguishable from resolving not to sue. The author's argument is that a binding release must be accompanied by consideration. Contrast Cranston, R, 'Limiting Directors' Liability: Ratification, Exemption and Indemnification' [1992] JBL 197, 199–200. Note *Miller v Miller* (1995) 16 ACSR 73, NSW EqD, 87–8 where it is judicially suggested that ratification does not extinguish a claim and that a binding release is required for that purpose

199 Releasing a cause of action gratuitously amounts to giving away the company's property so, once again, the problems of determining whether, or when, company property can be given away are encountered.

Constitutional Requirements: Who Can Ratify; Majority Required?

There are two main problems under this heading. The first is that company-law cases tend to assume that the power to ratify lies with the shareholders in general meeting. Whether, or to what extent, it is possible for the board to ratify wrongdoing and the compatibility of articles which permit the board to ratify with Companies Act 1985, s 310[200] are matters which are largely unexplored. This issue is seen in particularly sharp focus when ratification in the form of forgiving directors for their transgressions is considered. There is little to distinguish that form of ratification from a promise by the company to release its cause of action against the directors except that, when the process is couched in the language of giving up causes of action, ratification is somehow stripped of some of its mystery and is most easily seen to be a managerial decision about whether to litigate, something which is normally perceived to be within the role of the board.

The second issue necessitates a return to the concept of the unratifiable wrong. Aside from the Companies Act 1985, s 35 (3) which mandates a special resolution for the ratification of wrongs falling within its scope, the general rule is that ratification by ordinary resolution, that is a simple majority of those voting at a duly convened board meeting, suffices. It is possible for the shareholders to dispense with a meeting and to ratify informally but, in that case, all of the shareholders who would be entitled to vote on the matter at a meeting must consent.[201] Dicta in certain recent cases suggest a wider role for the principle of unanimous informal consent[202] and, although not expressly stated in any reported case to date, this has been interpreted by some commentators in a way which represents a retreat from the full-blown theory of unratifiable wrongs. The argument is that, if all of the shareholders consent, an unratifiable wrong can be ratified.[203] Since the unratifiable-wrong theory is a measure for the protection of minorities, this suggestion does not do violence to any underlying principles and it represents a halfway house between the rival theories considered in the previous sections.

Actions by Minority Shareholders

Ratification and the ability of minority shareholders to bring actions against miscreant directors on behalf of their company in circumstances where the wrongdoers are in control of the company and thus able to block an action by the company itself are interrelated matters.[204] Valid ratification blocks the

[200] Table A does not contain an express provision allowing the board to ratify.

[201] *Re Duomatic Ltd* [1969] 2 Ch 365. On the limits of the principle of unanimous informal consent: *Re RW Peak (Kings Lynn) Ltd* [1998] 1 BCLC 193; *Atlas Wright (Europe) Ltd v Wright* [1999] BCC 163 CA. See, generally, Grantham, R, 'The Unanimous Consent Rule in Company Law' [1993] CLJ 245.

[202] In particular *Rolled Steel Products (Holdings) Ltd v British Steel Corpn* [1986] Ch 246, CA, 296.

[203] Boyle, AJ, Sykes, R, and Sealy, LS, *Gore Browne on Companies* (44th edn, loose-leaf) (1986) para 27.21.2; Davies, PL, *Gower's Principles of Modern Company Law* (6th edn, 1997) 646.

[204] Wedderburn, KW, 'Shareholders' Rights and the Rule in *Foss v Harbottle*' [1957] CLJ 194 and [1958] CLJ 93.

ability of the minority shareholder to bring an action on the company's behalf because the effect of the ratification is to forgive the directors and to adopt their actions as corporate acts.[205] However, the converse is not necessarily true: invalid ratification or impossible ratification (using the unratifiable-wrong theory) does not, in itself, establish a minority shareholder's standing to bring an action on the company's behalf.[206] *Smith v Croft (No 2)*[207] demonstrates that the standing of a minority shareholder to pursue a derivative action on the company's behalf is not conclusively determined by reference to whether the alleged breach of duty is capable of ratification and may depend on other factors including whether the majority of the shareholders who are independent of the wrongdoing support the bringing of the claim. Treating the questions of (i) what can be ratified and (ii) when can minority shareholders sue as being one and the same has contributed to the difficulties in this area of the law.

Protection of Other Constituencies

This matter can be dealt with briefly because it has been touched upon already earlier in this chapter. The shareholders' power to ratify wrongdoing is subject to an important limitation which operates for the protection of creditors: where the company's solvency is in doubt creditors' interests intrude and the shareholders cannot effectively ratify managerial misconduct.[208] A similar limitation would undoubtedly apply to any power to release causes of action against miscreant directors, whether vested in the board or in the general meeting, to the extent that such decisions are distinguishable from decisions to ratify.

Apart from this, the position is that although other constituencies may benefit from the limitations on ratifying/releasing powers which have developed by the courts for the protection of minority shareholders, that is merely an incidental by-product and not an intended effect. Acceptance of the argument that unratifiable wrongs can be ratified with the unanimous consent of the shareholders would make it clear beyond doubt that protection of other constituencies is not intended. Although dicta in *Fulham Football Club v Cabra Estates*[209] suggest that the power to ratify may be limited by the requirement to consider employees interests which is imposed by the Companies Act 1985, s 309, this is a concession to stakeholder principles which is out of line with the body of authorities and which does not represent an accurate statement of existing law.

[205] *Shareholder Remedies* (Law Commission Report No 246) (1997) para 6.86 proposes retention of the rule that effective ratification acts as a complete bar to the continuation of a derivative action.

[206] Contrast *Estmanco (Kilner House) Ltd v GLC* [1982] 1 WLR 11.

[207] *Smith v Croft (No 2)* [1988] 1 Ch 114.

[208] See above, at 137–40.

[209] [1992] BCC 863, CA, 876 *per* Neill LJ.

5

Controlling Management: Duties of Honesty, Propriety and Loyalty

FIDUCIARY DUTIES OF DIRECTORS AND SENIOR MANAGERS

A fiduciary is someone who undertakes to act for or on behalf of someone else in circumstances which give rise to a relationship of trust and confidence between the parties.[1] Directors are in a fiduciary relationship with their company[2] and owe fiduciary duties stemming from the primary obligation of loyalty.[3] Describing a relationship as 'fiduciary' is the start, not the end, of the inquiry because the precise scope of the duties owed by a fiduciary depends on the nature of the particular relationship in question.[4] In the case of directors, there exists a large body of case law in which the nature and extent of their duties to their company have been examined and from which a picture of the parameters of the fiduciary relationship can be drawn.

The law has traditionally imposed fiduciary duties on directors on the basis of the conventional model of the corporate structure in which the directors manage the company. It may be more in line with the typical present-day management structure of larger companies to say that senior managers, not all of whom are directors, manage the company whilst the board, comprising some senior managers and some non-executive directors who are not involved in the daily operations, devises strategy, decides upon major transactions and supervises management. Where senior managers run the daily operations of a company under the supervision of the board, the relationship between them and the company may be one of trust and confidence giving rise to fiduciary duties. The fiduciary duties of senior managers who are not directors have not been litigated to the same extent as the fiduciary duties of directors, although it has been recognised in a number of cases that senior

[1] *Bristol and West Building Society v Mothew* [1998] Ch 1, CA, 18 *per* Millett LJ. Generally on fiduciary duties, see Finn, PD, *Fiduciary Obligations* (1977); Oakley, AJ, *Constructive Trusts* (3rd edn, 1997) ch 3; Goff, R, and Jones, G, *The Law of Restitution* (5th edn, 1998) ch 33; Meagher, RP, Gummow, WMC, and Lehane, JRF, *Equity Doctrine and Remedies* (3rd edn, 1992) ch 5; Sealy, LS, 'The Fiduciary Relationship' [1962] CLJ 69; Sealy, LS, 'The Director as Trustee' [1967] CLJ 83.

[2] *Regal (Hastings) Ltd v Gulliver* [1942] 1 All ER 378, [1967] 2 AC 134n, HL.

[3] *Bristol and West Building Society v Mothew* [1998] Ch 1, CA, 18 *per* Millett LJ.

[4] *Henderson v Merrett Syndicates* [1995] 2 AC 145, HL, 206 *per* Lord Browne-Wilkinson; *Re Goldcorp Exchange Ltd* [1995] 1 AC 74, PC, 98 *per* Lord Mustill; *New Zealand Netherlands Society 'Oranje' Inc v Kuys* [1973] 2 All ER 1222, PC; *Re Coomber* [1911] 1 Ch 723, CA, 728 *per* Fletcher Moulton LJ; *SEC v Chenery Corp* 318 US 80 (1943) 85–6 *per* Justice Frankfurter; *Canadian Aero Services Ltd v O'Malley* (1973) 40 DLR 371, Can SC, 391 *per* Laskin J; *Chan v Zacharia* (1983–84) 154 CLR 178, H Ct of Aust, 198–9 *per* Deane J.

managers of companies can owe fiduciary duties.[5] It can suffice as a point of departure in this chapter to say that senior managers who are not directors may be subject to fiduciary duties similar to those of directors with the consequence that the discussion of 'directors' duties' that follows should be read as being relevant to senior managers. However, the determination of the precise scope of a manager's fiduciary duties in a particular case would require an examination of the particular relationship in question and of the nature of the managerial functions that the individual in question was called upon to perform.

De Facto Directors and Shadow Directors

A de facto director is a person who acts as a director but who has never been validly appointed to that position.[6] A person can be involved in the management of a company without becoming a de facto director.[7] A definitive test for determining whether someone is a de facto director has not yet emerged, but a number of suggestions are made in the cases. It has been judicially stated that the question that has to be asked in determining whether someone is a de facto director is whether he is part of the corporate governing structure and that this is a question of degree which must take into account all relevant factors including: whether there was a holding out of the individual as a director; whether the individual used the title; whether the individual had proper information (eg management accounts) on which to base decisions; and whether the individual had to make major decisions.[8] Another judicial formulation of the test for judging whether someone is a de facto director is to ask whether he undertook functions in relation to the company which only directors could properly perform.[9] A third is to look for evidence that the individual was the sole person directing the affairs of the company or that he was acting on an equal footing with the true directors in directing its affairs.[10] A de facto director assumes the responsibilities that are attached to the office[11] and thus owes fiduciary duties to the company.

A shadow director is defined by the Companies Act 1985, s 741 as a person in accordance with whose directions or instructions the directors of the company are accustomed to act. A person is not deemed a shadow director by reason only of the fact that the directors act on advice given by him in a professional capacity. Unlike a de facto director, a shadow director does not purport to act as a director but is in the background shielding behind, and controlling, the persons who are the actual directors of the company.[12] All of the members of the board of directors, or at least the governing majority of

[5] See *Canadian Aero Services Ltd v O'Malley* (1973) 40 DLR 371, SC Can; *Green v Bestobell Industries Pty Ltd* (1982) 1 ACLC 1, WA SC; *Sybron Corporation v Rochem* [1984] Ch 112, CA, 127 *per* Stephenson LJ.

[6] *Re Hydrodan (Corby) Ltd* [1994] BCC 161, 162–3 *per* Millett J.

[7] Ibid.

[8] *Secretary of State v Tjolle* [1998] BCLC 333, 343–4 *per* Jacob J.

[9] *Re Hydrodan (Corby) Ltd* [1994] BCC 161, 163 *per* Millett J.

[10] *Re Richborough Furniture Ltd* [1996] 1 BCLC 507, 524 *per* Mr Lloyd QC (sitting as a judge).

[11] *Re Hydrodan (Corby) Ltd* [1994] BCC 161, 162 *per* Millett J.

[12] Ibid at 163, *per* Millett J.

them,[13] must as a matter of regular practice act in accordance with the directions or instructions of the person who is alleged to be a shadow director.

Shadow directorship is a statutory concept that is used to extend the application of directors' statutory duties to persons who are not directors but who control the management of companies. The categories of fiduciary relationship are not closed[14] and, in appropriate cases, a person who satisfies the statutory definition of a shadow director could be held to owe fiduciary duties to the company which he controls.

STATUTORY DUTIES BASED ON LOYALTY

Directors are subject to a variety of statutory duties which stem from the fundamental obligation of loyalty.[15] These supplement, but do not replace, directors' fiduciary duties. The statutory duties apply to persons occupying the position of director by whatever name called.[16] This would catch de facto directors but not persons holding senior managerial positions below directorship level who do not perform directorial functions. Statutory duties apply to shadow directors where this is expressly provided for in the relevant provision. Statutory duties of loyalty are considered in this chapter alongside the fiduciary duties to which they relate.

DIRECTORS AS A DISTINCT CATEGORY OF FIDUCIARY

Fiduciary duties were first developed in relation to trustees, and it was to the model of the trust that the courts looked when they sought to establish the parameters of the relationship between directors and their company.[17] There are similarities between directors and trustees with regard to their stewardship of company property. Both trustees and directors have control of a fund in which others are beneficially interested with only the technical difference between them that trust property is vested in trustees but corporate property is not vested in directors.[18] A director, like a trustee, must in principle act gratuitously unless remuneration is properly authorised.[19] However, the commercial flavour of the relationship between a director and the company distinguishes it from the trust relationship.[20] The courts have sometimes recognised that the imposition on directors of the very strict standards required of trustees could impede their management of the company's busi-

[13] *Re Unisoft Group Ltd (No 2)* [1994] BCC 766, 775 *per* Harman J.
[14] *English v Dedham Vale Properties Ltd* [1978] 1 All ER 382, 398.
[15] In particular, Companies Act 1985, Pt X (Enforcement of Fair Dealing by Directors).
[16] Companies Act 1985, s 741 (1).
[17] Sealy, LS, 'The Director as Trustee' [1967] CLJ 83.
[18] *Re Lands Allotment Co* [1894] 1 Ch 616, CA, 631 *per* Lindley LJ; *Selangor United Rubber Estates Ltd v Cradock (No 3)* [1968] 2 All ER 1073, 1092; *Re Duckwari plc* [1998] 3 WLR 913, CA, 920 *per* Nourse LJ .
[19] *Guinness plc v Saunders* [1990] 2 AC 663, HL.
[20] *Re Forest of Dean Coal Mining Co* (1878) 10 Ch D 450.

ness affairs and operate to its disadvantage.[21] One way in which the rules relating to directors reflect commercial considerations is that, unlike trustees, directors are usually permitted to act by a majority. Directors also tend to have wider discretions than trustees. Thus it has been said of directors that: 'in some respects they resemble trustees, in others they do not'.[22]

Directors are sometimes compared to other fiduciaries such as agents[23] or managing partners.[24] Directors are like agents in that, collectively, they derive their powers to act in contractual and other commercial matters from the corporate principal, the scope of the authority being specified in the corporate constitution. The power of individual directors to act on behalf of the company may also be subject to constitutional limitations. However, directors normally have much wider powers and discretions than agents.

No analogy is perfect in this context and it is now generally recognised that the relationship between directors and the company is a distinct category of fiduciary relationship. Authorities relating to duties imposed in other types of fiduciary relationship, whilst important, are thus not necessarily conclusive.[25] As was stated by Bowen LJ in *Imperial Hydropathic Hotel Co v Hampson*,[26] the point of drawing these analogies is simply to indicate 'useful points of view from which [directors] may for the moment and for the particular purpose be considered'.

DUTY TO ACT IN GOOD FAITH IN THE INTERESTS OF THE COMPANY

The classic statement of this fiduciary duty is that of Lord Greene MR in *Re Smith and Fawcett Ltd*:[27] '[Directors] must exercise their discretion bona fide in what they consider—not what a court may consider—is in the interests of the company.' A now discredited test for establishing whether an act was within a company's capacity[28] separated the elements of good faith and benefit to the company. The Court of Appeal finally established that this test had no application to questions of capacity in *Rolled Steel Products Ltd v British Steel Corpn*[29] but it was noted that the test might still be helpful in relation to

[21] *Re Faure Electric Accumulater Co* (1888) 40 Ch D 141.

[22] *Regal (Hastings) Ltd v Gulliver* [1967] 2 AC 134n, HL 147 *per* Lord Russell of Killowen.

[23] *Aberdeen Railway Co v Blaikie Bros* (1854) 1 Macq HL 461, 471–2.

[24] The similarity between a director and a managing partner of a firm was emphasised in *Automatic Self-Cleansing Syndicate Co Ltd v Cuninghame* [1906] 2 Ch 35, CA, 45 *per* Cozens-Hardy LJ.

[25] '[Fiduciary] principles . . . grew out of older cases concerned with fiduciaries other than directors or managing officers of a modern corporation, and I do not therefore regard them as providing a rigid measure whose literal terms must be met in assessing succeeding cases. . . . In this, as in other branches of the law, new fact situations may require a reformulation of existing principle to maintain its vigour in the new setting': Laskin J delivering the opinion of the Supreme Court of *Canada in Canadian Aero Service Ltd v O'Malley* (1973) 40 DLR (3d) 371, 381.

[26] 23 Ch D 1, CA, 12. See also *Mulkana Corpn NL v Bank of New South Wales* (1983) 8 ACLR 278, NSW SC.

[27] [1942] Ch 304, CA, 306 *per* Lord Greene MR.

[28] *Re Lee, Behrens & Co* [1932] 2 Ch 46; criticised in *Charterbridge Corpn Ltd v Lloyds Bank* [1970] 1 Ch 62, *Re Halt Garage (1964) Ltd* [1982] 3 All ER 1016; *Re Horsley and Weight Ltd* [1982] Ch 442, CA, *Rolled Steel Ltd v British Steel Corporation* [1986] 1 Ch 246, CA.

[29] [1986] 1 Ch 246, CA.

questions of directors' duties. In *Brady v Brady*,[30] however, Lord Oliver, who delivered the only reasoned speech in the House of Lords, did not follow the twofold test but instead held that the words 'in good faith in the interests of the company' amounted to a single composite phrase postulating a requirement that those responsible for the decision act in the genuine belief that it is in the company's interest. The context of *Brady v Brady* was a specific statutory defence to the giving of financial assistance, one of the conditions of which is that the financial assistance be given in good faith in the interests of the company, but the analysis would appear to be equally applicable to the general fiduciary duty imposed on directors.

Applying *Brady*, therefore, the duty to act in good faith in the interests of the company is an essentially subjective obligation but with a minimum threshold of genuineness. Directors who are positively dishonest will clearly be in breach of their fiduciary duty, and oppressive or extravagant conduct by directors may cast doubt on their honesty.[31] Where the circumstances are not sufficiently egregious to indicate dishonesty, directors may still be in breach of duty if their decisions are not taken genuinely in what they believe to be the interests of the company. Genuineness denotes a greater degree of objectivity than an approach which simply equates good faith with honesty,[32] and, although directors could not be held to be in breach of this duty merely because the court disagrees with their assessment of what is in the interests of the company, patent unreasonableness[33] may lead the court to conclude that the directors were not genuine in their belief concerning the company's interests.

The 'Interests of the Company'

This issue is explored in depth in Chapter 4.[34] In summary, the interests of the company for the purposes of this duty are normally equated with the long-term interests of its shareholders. By statute, the directors are required to consider employees' interests, but this does not oblige, or permit, the directors to give preference to the interests of employees.[35] The identification of a company's interests with those of its shareholders breaks down when a company's solvency is in doubt because creditors' interests intrude at that point and, if the company does become insolvent, they eventually eclipse shareholders' interests.

There are two categories of director for whom the duty to act in the interests of the company may pose particular difficulties. These are directors of subsidiary companies and nominee directors.

[30] [1989] AC 755, HL.
[31] *Shuttleworth v Cox Bros & Co (Maidenhead) Ltd* [1927] 2 KB 9, CA.
[32] Sealy, LS, 'Bona Fides and Proper Purposes in Corporate Decisions' (1989) 15 Monash ULR 265, 269. See also *Re Halt Garage (1964) Ltd* [1982] 3 All ER 1016 and *Aveling Barford Ltd v Perion Ltd* [1989] BCLC 626.
[33] *Re Halt Garage (1964) Ltd* [1982] 3 All ER 1016, 1041.
[34] See Ch 4 above, at 124–40.
[35] Companies Act 1985, s 309.

Directors of Subsidiary Companies

However much in practical terms the various companies within a corporate group are run as one enterprise, as a matter of law the directors of each company within the group are required to act in the interests of the company to which they are appointed rather than in the interests of the group as a whole.[36] Yet, if the interests of the company are treated as being synonymous with the interests of its shareholders, then, at least in wholly-owned subsidiaries, the duty of the directors of the subsidiaries should translate simply into a duty to act in the interests of the parent company. This is not the position that has been arrived at in the cases.[37] Instead, it has been held that where the parent company wants a subsidiary to do something which is outside the normal run of business matters and which does not represent a profit enhancement opportunity for the subsidiary—intra-group loans or guarantees being obvious examples—the directors of the subsidiary, even if it is a wholly-owned subsidiary, must act in the interest of their company, meaning the economic entity distinct from its shareholders, and must not sacrifice its interests in favour of the parent or the group. The only concession to the group structure is that although, strictly, directors should specifically direct their minds to their company's interests, 'in the absence of actual separate consideration . . . [the proper test] must be whether an intelligent and honest man in the position of a director of the company concerned, could, in the whole of the existing circumstances, have reasonably believed that the transactions were for the benefit of the company'.[38] This concession is a fallback which may have some use in limited cases, but properly advised directors should direct their minds specifically to the subsidiary's interests rather than risk being judged to have failed in their duty on the basis of an objective test of what the intelligent and honest director could reasonably have believed. Directors of subsidiary companies can also seek to protect themselves by having the parent company authorise or ratify their conduct.[39]

The substantial risk for directors of wholly-owned subsidiaries is that actions which are taken for the prosperity of the group as a whole but which are loss-making for the acting subsidiary may jeopardise its solvency and prejudice its creditors. Shareholder ratification will not protect the directors when the company's solvency is in doubt because creditors' interests intrude at that point. Looked at in this way, the rule which obliges subsidiary-company directors to consider the interests of the company as distinct from the group becomes, in substance,[40] part of the wider principle which treats the

[36] *Lindgreen v L & P Estates Ltd* [1968] 1 Ch 572; *Charterbridge Corpn Ltd v Lloyds Bank* [1970] 1 Ch 62.

[37] *Charterbridge Corpn Ltd v Lloyds Bank* [1970] 1 Ch 62; *Equiticorp Finance Ltd (in liq) v Bank of New Zealand* (1993) 32 NSWLR 50, NSW CA; *Farrow Finance Co Ltd v Farrow Properties Pty Ltd (in liq)* (1997–8) 26 ACSR 544, V SC.

[38] *Charterbridge Corpn Ltd v Lloyds Bank* [1970] 1 Ch 62, 74.

[39] On the limits of the protection afforded by ratification see Ch 4 above, at 144–53.

[40] *Charterbridge Corpn Ltd v Lloyds Bank* [1970] 1 Ch 62 is not limited to insolvency situations. But since, outside insolvency, the parent company can ratify any failure by directors to act

company's interests as being synonymous with those of its creditors in the event of insolvency.[41]

Nominee Directors

Nominee directors must act in the interests of the company of which they are directors, and must prefer the company's interests to those of their nominator.[42] This rule, whilst easy to state and clear in its intended effect, poses considerable practical difficulties. Typically, it is majority shareholders or major creditors who secure rights to nominate directors and they do so with a view to protecting their interest in the company; but once appointed, the nominee is largely required to ignore the underlying rationale for the appointment and to promote the company's interest even at the expense of those of the appointor. The rule is also an obstacle to the development of employee representation at board level: employee appointees would naturally incline to representing and promoting employee interests but the law, as it currently stands, would not permit them to do so.[43]

DIRECTORS MUST NOT FETTER THEIR DISCRETION[44]

Directors must make their own decisions. They are in breach of duty if they simply follow another's instructions without considering and deciding whether what is proposed is in the interests of the company.[45] Thus in *Kuwait Asia Bank EC v National Mutual Life Nominees Ltd*,[46] which concerned nominee directors of a bank, an obvious example of the type of situation where questions about fettering of discretion can arise, Lord Lowry stated:[47]

> In the performance of their duties as directors . . . [they] were bound to ignore the interests and wishes of their employer, the bank. They could not plead any instruction from the bank as an excuse for breach of their duties.

in the interests of their subsidiary and thereby cure the breach, the net result is as set out in the text.

[41] See Ch 4 above, at 137–40.

[42] *Scottish Co-operative Society v Meyer* [1959] AC 324, HL; *Boulting v ACTAT* [1963] 2 QB 606, CA, 626 *per* Lord Denning MR; *Kuwait Asia Bank EC v National Mutual Life Nominees Ltd* [1991] 1 AC 187, PC.

[43] There are indications of a more flexible approach in Australian and New Zealand case law: Boros, EJ, 'The Duties of Nominee and Multiple Directors' (1990) 10 Co Law 211 and (1989) 11 Co Law 6; Crutchfield, P, 'Nominee Directors: The Law and Commercial Morality' (1991) 12 Co Law 136. Modification of the duty to act in the interests of the company by agreement is constrained by Companies Act 1985, s 310 which is discussed in Ch 4 above, at 140–3 and this chapter, at 198–9.

[44] Courtney, TB, 'Fettering Directors' Discretion' (1995) 16 Co Law 227.

[45] *Re Englefield Colliery Co* (1878) 8 Ch D 388, CA; *Clark v Workman* [1920] 1r R 107; *Selangor United Rubber Estates Ltd v Cradock (No 3)* [1968] 2 All ER 1073; *Blackwell v Moray* (1991) 9 ACLC 924, NSW SC.

[46] [1991] 1 AC 187, PC.

[47] Ibid at 222 *per* Lord Lowry.

The Court of Appeal qualified the no-fettering rule in *Fulham Football Club Ltd v Cabra Estates plc*[48] by drawing a distinction between (i) a fetter on the future exercise of directors' discretion, and (ii) a decision by directors to bind themselves to do whatever was necessary to effectuate a contract which, at the time when the contract was negotiated, they genuinely believed to be in the interests of the company as a whole. The former was prohibited, but the latter was permissible. This case concerned a lengthy dispute between a local authority and the owners of the freehold of Fulham Football Club's ground concerning the future use of the site. The club was the lessee of the property and, as part of a package of arrangements including the payment of considerable sums to the club, the directors of the club undertook to support the freeholders' plans for redevelopment of the site. Some two and a half years later, the directors of the club had a change of heart and, in defence to the freeholders' claim that they had breached their undertakings by so doing, they claimed that the undertakings were implicitly qualified by their fiduciary duty to act in the interests of the company. The Court of Appeal, following the decision of the High Court of Australia in *Thorby v Goldberg*,[49] disagreed. The directors' undertakings were not contrary to public policy, nor were they subject to a term implied by law qualifying the promises by reference to fiduciary duty. At the time when the arrangements between the freeholders and the club had been negotiated, the directors had genuinely believed that the arrangements were in the interests of the club; accordingly, they could validly bind themselves to do whatever was necessary to effectuate those arrangements.

The decision in *Fulham* necessitates a reassessment of some earlier decisions. *Rackham v Peek Foods Ltd*[50] and *John Crowther Group plc v Carpets International plc*,[51] both first instance decisions of the English High Court, and *Dawson International plc v Coats Paton plc*,[52] a Scottish case decided by the Court of Session, Outer House, had all appeared to suggest the existence of a term implied as a matter of law qualifying, by reference to the duty to act in the interests of the company, any covenant by directors to use 'best endeavours' to ensure fulfilment of a contract or to support a transaction. The first two cases were considered in *Fulham Football Club Ltd v Cabra Estates plc*[53] where it was held that although the decisions could be justified on their particular facts, they were not to be read more widely as authority for the general proposition that directors could never bind themselves as to the future exercise of their powers.[54]

In the light of *Fulham Football Club Ltd v Cabra Estates plc*, it seems that *Rackham v Peek Foods Ltd* and *John Crowther Group plc v Carpets International plc* are best viewed as cases where, as a matter of fact rather than of law, directors' undertakings were held to be subject to an implied qualification allowing the directors to disregard them where the interests of the company so dictated. Those decisions were favourable to the directors and

[48] [1992] BCC 863. Kenyon-Slade, S, 'Improper Fettering of Directors' Discretion, or Holding Them to Their Word' [1993] CLJ 218.

[49] (1964) 112 CLR 597, H Ct of Aust.

[50] [1990] BCLC 895 (but decided in 1977).

[51] [1990] BCLC 460 (but decided in 1985).

[52] [1991] BCC 276, Ct of Sess.

[53] [1992] BCC 863, CA.

[54] Ibid at 876 *per* Neill LJ.

provided them with a let-out, but a qualification implied in fact from the circumstances of the case is no absolute guarantee of protection: in another case a court could well find that, although directors are in an impossible position because their views about the merits of a transaction have changed, the problem is of their own making and that no term can be implied with the result that they will be liable for breach of the undertaking if they act in accordance with the interests of the company, or in breach of their duty to the company if they honour their undertaking. Rather than relying on the possibility of a qualification being implied from the facts, a safer course for directors is to insist upon covenants being expressly qualified by reference to their overriding fiduciary duty to act in the interests of the company. This is a particularly important issue for directors who decide to support a takeover bid: although the decision of the Scottish Court in *Dawson International plc v Coats Paton plc*[55] suggests that such an undertaking may be subject to an implied qualification permitting the directors to withdraw their support if they believe it to be in the interests of the company to do so,[56] the circumstances in which such an implication will be made are put into some doubt by the *Fulham* decision. To protect themselves, directors who agree to support a particular bid for the company should insert an appropriate express qualification into the agreement.

DIRECTORS MUST NOT DELEGATE THEIR DISCRETIONS

Closely related to the no-fettering rule is the requirement that directors must not delegate their discretions. In practice this requirement is often overridden by a provision in the company's articles allowing the directors to delegate powers and discretions either to committees or to individual agents. The rule remains of significance to the extent that, where delegation is not provided for, any purported exercise of power which is vested in the directors under the articles by their 'delegate' will be invalid and will not bind the company.[57]

DIRECTORS MUST EXERCISE THEIR POWERS FOR PROPER PURPOSES

A director must exercise fiduciary powers for the purposes for which they were conferred,[58] but how are such purposes to be determined? The company's memorandum and articles would seem to be an obvious starting point since it is from these documents that directors derive their powers; but, typically in practice, the powers granted to directors by the company's constitution are drafted in general terms and do not expressly state the purposes for which

[55] [1991] BCC 276, Ct of Sess.

[56] It was held, in fact, that the directors had not given a contractual undertaking to recommend the bid.

[57] *Guinness plc v Saunders* [1990] 2 AC 663, HL.

[58] *Howard Smith Ltd v Ampol Petroleum Ltd* [1974] AC 821, PC, 834 *per* Lord Wilberforce; Finn, PD, *Fiduciary Obligations* (1977) 39–40.

they can be exercised; nor can such purposes be easily inferred merely from the documents themselves.

The leading authority explaining how the purposes for which a power may be exercised are to be determined is the decision of the Privy Council in *Howard Smith Ltd v Ampol Petroleum Ltd*.[59] Lord Wilberforce, delivering the judgment of Judicial Committee, emphasised that the process is not an exact one involving the laying down of precise limits beyond which the directors could not pass. Rather, the task of the court is:

> to start with a consideration of the power whose exercise is in question . . . Having ascertained, on a fair view, the nature of this power, and having defined as can best be done in the light of modern conditions that, or some, limits within which it may be exercised, it is then necessary for the court, if a particular exercise of it is challenged, to examine the substantial purpose for which it was exercised, and to reach a conclusion whether that purpose was proper or not. In doing so it will necessarily give credit to the bona fide opinion of the directors, if such is found to exist, and will respect their judgment as to matters of management; having done this, the ultimate conclusion has to be as to the side of a fairly broad line on which the case falls.[60]

This statement is in many ways typical of the courts' approach to corporate disputes, emphasising as it does due respect for directors' business judgment and eschewing close examination of their actions in favour of a more broad-brush treatment.[61] Nevertheless, it does indicate that the question whether a power has been exercised for a proper purpose is a question of law and that the directors' opinion of the propriety of their action is not conclusive.[62] The duty to use powers only for the purposes for which they were conferred thus imposes on directors a more exacting standard than the duty to act in the interests of the company, which is essentially a subjective duty though with a minimum threshold of genuineness; the courts can more readily review a decision as an improper exercise of fiduciary power than as a decision which could not have been arrived at genuinely in the interests of the company.[63]

Howard Smith v Ampol, like many of the reported decisions on the duty to exercise powers for proper purposes, was concerned with the directors' fiduciary power to issue shares. The flexible, pragmatic approach advocated by Lord Wilberforce means that it would be wrong to attempt to delimit precisely and exhaustively the purposes for which the power to issue shares may properly be exercised. Certainly, raising capital is a purpose for which the power may be exercised but there are other purposes, such as the making of bonus issues, the promotion of an employees' share scheme, the forming of a link between the allottee and the company with a view to securing the financial stability of the company,[64] or the obtaining of a valuable business

[59] [1974] AC 821, PC.

[60] Ibid at 835.

[61] Also in line with this approach is Lord Wilberforce's statement at 832: 'There is no appeal on merits from management decisions to courts of law nor will courts of law assume to act as a kind of supervisory board over decisions within the powers of management honestly arrived at.'

[62] Birds, J, 'Proper Purposes as a Head of Directors' Duties' (1974) 37 MLR 580.

[63] Nolan, RC, 'The Proper Purpose Doctrine and Company Directors' in Rider, BAK (ed), *The Realm of Company Law* (1998) 1, 7–13 considering cases which establish that the proper purpose rule is distinct from the requirement for good faith and imposes objective standards.

[64] *Harlow's Nominees Pty Ltd v Woodside (Lakes Entrance) Oil Co NL* (1968) 121 CLR 483, H Ct of Aust.

opportunity for the company,[65] for which the power may also properly be exercised. Any purpose which is expressly authorised by the company's constitution would necessarily amount to a proper purpose.[66]

Although it may not be possible to state precisely all of the purposes for which the power to issue shares may properly be exercised, it is clear from *Smith v Ampol* and earlier cases that there are certain purposes which can definitely be described as improper exercises of the fiduciary power to issue shares.[67] Directors must not 'use their fiduciary powers over the shares in the company purely for the purpose of destroying an existing majority, or creating a new majority which did not previously exist',[68] the reason being that it would be unconstitutional for the directors to use their fiduciary powers in that way.[69] The location of the ownership of the company's shares, and the power that accompanies majority share ownership, is ultimately for the shareholders, not the directors, to decide. Thus, using a takeover bid as an example, if directors genuinely believe that a bid is not in the interests of the company, they may consistently with their subjective duty of good faith advise the shareholders to reject the bid[70] but, because of the proper purpose rule, they cannot exercise their power to allot shares so as to distort the operation of the market for corporate control[71] by allotting shares to a favoured bidder and thereby thwarting a hostile bid.

The power to issue shares is now regulated by statute[72] but the analytical approach embodied in the authorities relating to share issues would seem to be equally applicable to other fiduciary powers. This is illustrated by the investigation of the affairs of the Savoy Hotel group conducted by Mr Milner

[65] *Teck Corporation Ltd v Millar* (1972) 33 DLR (3d) 288, BC SC. Although explained by Lord Wilberforce in *Howard Smith v Ampol* as being consistent with the existence of a 'proper purpose' duty separate from the duty to act in good faith in the company's interests, the reasoning in both *Harlowe* and *Teck* tends to suggest that the duties are one and the same, though expressed in different ways. The standard of review in *Teck* is unclear and has led to confusion in the Canadian courts: Ziegel, JS, Daniels, RJ, MacIntosh, JG, and Johnston, DL, *Cases and Material on Partnerships and Canadian Business Corporations* (3rd edn, 1994) Vol 1, 699–710.

[66] *Whitehouse v Carlton Hotel Pty Ltd* (1987) 162 CLR 285, H Ct of Aust; *Gaiman v National Association for Mental Health* [1972] Ch 317. A consequence of this is that the proper purpose rule should be regarded as falling outside the debate about contracting out of fiduciary duties and the limit on exemption imposed by Companies Act 1985, s 310. Provisions in the constitution provide the content of the duty by indicating, expressly or by implication, the 'proper' purposes for which powers may be exercised. They do not seek to eliminate requirements that would be imposed by the general law and it is only that type of provision that Companies Act 1985 s 310 strikes down. See also Sealy, LS, 'Company Directors' "Duties" and Exempting Articles' [1987] CLJ 217.

[67] Unless, exceptionally, the company's constitution otherwise provides.

[68] *Fraser v Whalley* (1864) 2 Hen & M 10; *Punt v Symons & Co Ltd* [1903] 2 Ch 506; *Piercy v S Mills & Co Ltd* [1920] 1 Ch 77; *Mills v Mills* (1938) 60 CLR 150, H Ct of Aust; *Ngurli v McCann* (1953) 90 CLR 425, H Ct of Aust; *Hogg v Cramphorn Ltd* [1967] Ch 254; *Pennell v Venida Investments Ltd* 24 July 1974, discussed by Burridge, SJ, 'Wrongful Rights Issues' (1981) 44 MLR 40.

[69] *Whitehouse v Carlton Hotel Pty Ltd* (1987) 162 CLR 285, H Ct of Aust, 290 *per* Mason, Deane and Dawson JJ.

[70] This assumes that the interests of the company are not simply synonymous with the interests of the shareholders. On this point see further Ch 4 above, at 133–5.

[71] This is discussed in Ch 4 above, at 118–22.

[72] Companies Act 1985, s 80 (directors' authority to allot shares) and s 89 (pre-emption rights in favour of existing shareholders). See further Ch 18 below, at 614–6.

Holland QC, the report on which was published in 1954.[73] Fearing that a bidder, if successful, would close down an important hotel within the group and redevelop the site, the directors of the various group companies devised and implemented a scheme whereby the hotel was sold to a company controlled by the trustees of the Savoy's employees' pension scheme and then leased back to the group with restrictive covenants as to user. The object of the scheme was to ensure that, even if the bid were successful, the hotel would be beyond the bidder's control, thus insulating it against a change of use. Mr Milner Holland QC accepted that the directors had proceeded with the scheme in the genuine belief that it was in the interests of their companies, but, by analogy with the share allotment cases, concluded that the directors had exercised their fiduciary powers of management for an improper purpose.

More recently, in *Lee Panavision Ltd v Lee Lighting Ltd*,[74] applying *Howard Smith v Ampol*, the Court of Appeal held that it was unconstitutional for the directors to purport to tie up the management of the company by way of a management agreement at a time when they knew that the shareholders were intending to change the managerial control of the company by removing the old board and appointing new directors. The decision of Hoffmann J in *Re a Company*[75] further supports the proposition that directors who seek to use their powers in a way which prevents shareholders from accepting an offer from a particular bidder are acting for an improper purpose. Conduct designed to frustrate a bid would also infringe the Takeover Code where that applies.[76]

The proper purpose requirement has been applied to other powers normally vested in directors by the terms of the company's articles, including the power to make calls on shares[77] and the power to forfeit shares for non-payment of calls.[78] It is also applicable to provisions in articles which empower directors to decline to register transferees of shares as the registered holders. An article entitling the directors to refuse to register the transfer of shares is commonly included in the articles of private companies. Its inclusion reflects the resemblance between some private companies and partnerships: where a company is, in effect, an incorporated partnership, the shareholder-partners are likely to be concerned about the identity of transferees of the shares, and the directors' power to refuse to register transfers provides a way of monitoring this and preventing the registration of unwelcome

[73] *The Savoy Hotel Ltd and the Berkeley Hotel Company Ltd. Investigation under Section 165(b) of the Companies Act 1948* (HMSO, 1954).

[74] [1991] BCC 620, CA.

[75] [1986] BCLC 382.

[76] *City Code on Takeovers and Mergers*, general principle 7 and r 21.

[77] *Galloway v Halle Concerts Society* [1915] 2 Ch 233.

[78] *Stanhope's Case* (1866) LR 1 Ch App 161. See further Nolan, RC, 'The Proper Purpose Doctrine and Company Directors' in Rider, BAK (ed), *The Realm of Company Law* (1998) 1, 22–35 for the drawing of a distinction between 'internal' powers (eg powers to allot shares, recommend dividends, register share transfers) and 'external' powers (eg to deal with the company's property). The author argues that the courts are, and should continue to be, more willing to review the exercise of internal rather than external powers.

persons.[79] The power to refuse registration of a transferee may be limited to particular circumstances[80] or may be drafted in unqualified discretionary terms. In the former situation, the proper purpose requirement applies but the latter course defines the proper purpose rule out of existence—directors may exercise the power for any purpose they think fit—although the obligation to act in good faith in the company's interest must still be observed.[81] A provision restricting the transfer of shares would be unusual in the articles of a public company, and, in the case of a listed company, could be incompatible with Stock Exchange requirements concerning the transferability of shares.[82]

Mixed Purposes

Directors, when exercising a power vested in them under the company's constitution, may have more than one purpose in mind. Some of those purposes may be permissible, but others may be impermissible. In that situation, the impermissible purposes will not taint the exercise of the power provided that the substantial purpose or purposes for which it was exercised were proper.[83] This concession to directors' discretion means that, for example, a transaction entered into by the directors to secure commercial advantages for the company, but which (as the directors are well aware) carries with it the incidental advantage of making the company less vulnerable to an unwelcome takeover bid could be upheld. A careful examination of the facts would be required to determine the directors' substantial purpose in entering into any such transaction:

> the court . . . is entitled to look at the situation objectively in order to estimate how critical or pressing, or substantial or, per contra, insubstantial an alleged requirement may have been. If it finds that a particular requirement, though real, was not urgent, or critical, at the relevant time, it may have reason to doubt, or discount, the assertions of

[79] *Re Smith and Fawcett Ltd* [1942] 1 Ch 304, CA, 306 *per* Lord Greene MR.

[80] *Re Bede Steam Shipping Co Ltd* [1917] 1 Ch 123, CA approving *Re Bell Brothers* (1891) 65 LT 245: power for directors to refuse to register transfer if 'in their opinion it is contrary to the interests of the company that the proposed transferee should be a member thereof' only justified refusal to register on grounds personal to the proposed transferee. See also *Australian Metropolitan Life Assurance Co Ltd v Ure* (1923) 33 CLR 199, H Ct of Aust.

[81] *Re Smith and Fawcett Ltd* [1942] 1 Ch 304, CA; *Popely v Planarrive Ltd* [1997] 1 BCLC 8.

[82] *The Listing Rules*, ch 13, app 1, paras 6–8: fully-paid shares must be freely transferable; partly-paid shares may be subject to restrictions on transfer provided the restrictions do not prevent dealings in the shares on an open and proper basis; transfer restrictions may be imposed on any shares in the event of non-compliance with a notice issued under Companies Act 1985, s 212, or in other exceptional circumstances; power can be taken to restrict the maximum number of registered shareholders in respect of a share to four.

[83] *Howard Smith Ltd v Ampol Petroleum Ltd* [1974] AC 821, PC, 835 *per* Lord Wilberforce. The 'substantial' purpose approach stems from the Australian decision, *Mills v Mills* (1938) 60 CLR 150, H Ct of Aust, 186 *per* Dixon J, but note *Whitehouse v Carlton Hotel Pty Ltd* (1987) 162 CLR 285, H Ct of Aust, 294 *per* Mason, Deane and Dawson JJ, which suggests a 'but for' test which is less favourable to directors: 'the preferable view would seem to be that, regardless of whether the impermissible purpose was the dominant one or but one of a number of significantly contributing causes, the allotment will be invalidated if the impermissible purpose was causative in the sense that, but for its presence, the power would not have been exercised'. The majority of the High Court favoured this view but it was unnecessary to reach a conclusive opinion because on the facts the only substantial purpose of the directors was the improper one of manipulating voting power.

individuals that they acted solely in order to deal with it particularly when the action they took was unusual or even extreme.[84]

Apart from unusual or extreme situations, however, the reluctance of the courts to review matters of business judgment would be likely to limit the extent of the inquiries into substantial and insubstantial purposes.[85]

Consequences of Improper Purpose

Where a fiduciary power is exercised for an improper purpose, it is possible to analyse the situation in two ways—either as an abuse of power or as a purported exercise of a power that the directors do not have, that is, as an excess of authority.[86] The share allotment cases such as *Hogg v Cramphorn*[87] and *Smith v Ampol*[88] adopt the abuse of power analysis. An allotment of shares made for an improper purpose is prima facie valid notwithstanding the directors' breach of duty but, if it is made to a person or persons who are aware of the impropriety, it is liable to be set aside at the instance of the company. On agency principles, an agent who exceeds his authority does not succeed in binding the principal; the act is void as far as the principal is concerned unless the principal chooses to adopt what was purportedly done on its behalf. In *Hogg v Cramphorn*, as well as the share allotment, the directors made a loan to trustees for a purpose which was held to be improper. Buckley J held that the loan was to be treated as having been made by the directors in excess of their powers with the result that the moneys lent remained the property of the company held by the trustees upon a resulting trust for the company. In *Lee Panavision Ltd v Lee Lighting Ltd*,[89] similarly, the Court of Appeal refused an injunction to enforce a management agreement pending full trial of the action on the grounds that the agreement, which was unconstitutional, was beyond the directors' powers. The authorities offer little guidance as to when analysis based on abuse of power is more appropriate than that based on excess of authority although it appears that this may depend on the nature of the power in question. Excess of authority and abuse of power may even coincide.[90]

As far as the directors are concerned, if they use their powers for an improper purpose and, as a result, the company loses out, they will be liable to indemnify the company for its loss.[91] If the directors benefit personally from their breach of duty, they will be liable to account to the company for the benefits that they receive. In *Bishopsgate Investment Management Ltd v Maxwell*

[84] *Howard Smith Ltd v Ampol Petroleum Ltd* [1974] AC 821, PC, 832 *per* Lord Wilberforce.

[85] *City Code on Takeovers and Mergers*, general principle 7 and r 21 further restrict the powers of the board from the time when a bona fide bid is believed to be imminent.

[86] Grantham, R, 'The Powers of Company Directors and the Proper Purpose Doctrine' (1994–95) 5 KCLJ 16; Nolan, RC, 'The Proper Purpose Doctrine and Company Directors' in Rider, BAK (ed), *The Realm of Company Law* (1998) 1.

[87] [1967] Ch 254.

[88] [1974] AC 821, PC. See also *Bamford v Bamford* [1970] Ch 212, CA; *Whitehouse v Carlton Hotel Pty Ltd* (1987) 162 CLR 285, H Ct of Aust.

[89] [1991] BCC 620, CA.

[90] *Rolled Steel Ltd v British Steel Corporation* [1986] 1 Ch 246, CA; *Advance Bank of Australia Ltd v FAI Insurances Australia Ltd* (1989) 12 ACLR 118, NSW CA, 139 *per* Kirby P.

[91] *Re Lands Allotment Co Ltd* [1894] 1 Ch 616, CA, 631 *per* Lindley LJ.

(No 2),[92] a director was held liable to compensate the company for the loss resulting from the transfer of some of the company's assets (in the form of shares) for no consideration, in circumstances where the execution of the share transfer forms amounted to an improper exercise of the director's fiduciary powers.[93] The Court of Appeal held that the burden of proof was upon the director to demonstrate the propriety of the transaction, and that it had not been discharged.

The fact that a director has misused fiduciary powers may be a factor to which the court attaches importance when considering whether to disqualify that person from being involved in the management of a company.[94] Also, improper exercise of a fiduciary power may form the basis of a petition under the Companies Act 1985, s 459 for relief from unfairly prejudicial conduct.[95]

Directors derive their fiduciary powers from the company and it is to that company that they owe the duty to exercise the powers properly. However, in one English case[96] Hoffmann J held that the real substance of a claim that directors had acted for an improper purpose was that an abuse of those powers infringed a member's contractual rights under the articles. On the particular facts, this ruling meant that the petitioner was not entitled to an order requiring the company to indemnify him as to costs—such an order would only be appropriate where he was pursuing an action on behalf of the company rather than a personal action. The wider ramifications of the reasoning are, as yet, unexplored.[97] For example, whilst it may be that shareholders have a personal right to restrain the company, acting through the directors, from a prospective improper exercise of power, if the impropriety has already occurred causing loss, it would be difficult to characterise such loss as anything other than corporate loss for which only the company can sue.[98] Another difficulty is that if an improper exercise of power amounts to a breach of a member's contractual rights, ratification of that impropriety may be impossible; but current English authorities establish that an improper exercise of power can be ratified.[99]

92 [1994] 1 All ER 261, CA.

93 Detailed examination of the permissible purposes for which the power could be exercised was unnecessary since the transactions were not in the interests of the company.

94 For example, see *Re Looe Fish Ltd* [1993] BCC 348.

95 As in *Re DR Chemicals Ltd* (1989) 5 BCC 39.

96 *Re a Company (No 005136 of 1986)* [1987] BCLC 82. Australian authority is also moving in this direction: *Residues Treatment & Trading Co Ltd v Southern Resources Ltd* (1988) 14 ACLR 569, SA SC; *Colarc Pty Ltd v Donarc Pty Ltd* (1991) 4 ACSR 155, WA SC. See further, Stapledon, GP, 'Locus Standi of Shareholders to Enforce the Duty of Company Directors to Exercise the Share Issue Power for Proper Purposes' (1990) 8 Company and Securities Law Journal 213; Yeung, K, 'Disentangling the Tangled Skein: The Ratification of Directors' Actions' (1992) 66 ALJ 343; Davies, PD, 'Directors' Fiduciary Duties and Individual Shareholders' in McKendrick, E (ed), *Commercial Aspects of Trusts and Fiduciary Relationships* (1992) 83, 99–102.

97 Nolan, RC, 'The Proper Purpose Doctrine and Company Directors' in Rider, BAK (ed), *The Realm of Company Law* (1998) 1, 30–5.

98 This is the position in respect of acts exceeding or breaching the limits of the company's objects: *Smith v Croft (No 2)* [1988] Ch 114.

99 *Hogg v Cramphorn Ltd* [1967] Ch 254; *Bamford v Bamford* [1970] Ch 212, CA. Contrast recent Australian authority to the effect that improper share allotments cannot be ratified: *Residues Treatment & Trading Co Ltd v Southern Resources Ltd* (1988) 14 ACLR 569, SA SC; *Colarc Pty Ltd v Donarc Pty Ltd* (1991) 4 ACSR 155, WA SC. See further, Stapledon, GP, 'Locus Standi of Shareholders to Enforce the Duty of Company Directors to Exercise the Share Issue Power for

CONFLICT OF DUTY AND INTEREST

The fundamental duty of a fiduciary is to be loyal to the person for whom, or on whose behalf, he acts. From this basic principle stem a number of rules which are intended to preclude a fiduciary from being swayed in his actions by considerations of personal interest or interests of third parties.[100] An underlying issue in the application of these rules to directors is whether it is appropriate to apply to directors the very strict standards that were first developed in relation to trustees, or whether the commercial nature of the relationship between the participants in a company justifies a more flexible and pragmatic approach.

DIRECTORS' INTERESTS AND COMPANY CONTRACTS

The starting point here is that a director may not enter into a contract with the company or have an interest[101] in any of the company's contracts, for example by being a partner in, or holding shares in, another firm with which the company contracts.[102] The court will not examine the fairness, or otherwise, of the terms of a contract between a director and the company and will treat the director as having infringed the rule even though the deal may be entirely favourable to the company. This rule has only to be stated, however, to see that it would be commercially impossible for it to apply entirely without qualification: that would mean, for example, that directors could not even have service contracts. The qualification that makes this rule practically operative is that a director can contract, or have an interest in a contract, with the company where either this is authorised by the company's articles or the interest has been properly disclosed to the company and the company has consented to the director's participation. The 'company' for the purposes of disclosure and consent means the shareholders in general meeting[103] but this requirement can be,[104] and normally is, modified by the articles to provide for the board to act instead of the general meeting for this purpose. The reason why the consent function is vested in the shareholders in general meeting unless the articles otherwise provide is that the company is entitled to the

Proper Purposes' (1990) 8 Company and Securities Law Journal 213; Yeung, K, 'Disentangling the Tangled Skein: The Ratification of Directors' Actions' (1992) 66 ALJ 343.

100 Finn, PD, 'Fiduciary Law and the Modern Commercial World' in McKendrick, E (ed), *Commercial Aspects of Trusts and Fiduciary Relationships* (1992) 7.

101 In determining whether the director has a disclosable interest, regard has to be had to the particular circumstances: *Cowan de Groot Properties Ltd v Eagle Trust plc* [1992] 4 All ER 700, 765–6 *per* Knox J (director who was creditor of the other contracting party held to have a disclosable interest in the particular circumstances).

102 *Aberdeen Rly Co v Blaikie Bros* (1854) 1 Macq 461; *Neptune (Vehicle Washing Equipment) Ltd v Fitzgerald (No 2)* [1995] BCC 1,000, 1,015.

103 *Imperial Mercantile Credit Association v Coleman* (1871) LR 6 Ch App 558.

104 For the purposes of Companies Act 1985, s 310, the rule that a director may not contract with the company is a disability with the consequence that the requirement for disclosure to, and consent of, the shareholders can be modified as indicated without infringing that prohibition: *Movitex v Bulfield Ltd* (1986) 2 BCC 99,403.

disinterested advice of all of its directors and this is impossible where some of them are conflicted out by their personal interest in the matter.[105]

Articles of association tend to follow the Table A model with respect to the procedure for permitting directors to contract with, or to have interests in contracts with, the company. Under Table A, a director is permitted:

(a) to be a party to, or otherwise interested in, a transaction or arrangement with the company or in which the company is otherwise interested; and
(b) to be a director, officer or employee of any body corporate promoted by the company or in which the company is otherwise interested; the director may also be a party to, or be interested in, any transaction or arrangement with such a body corporate;

provided that, in either case, the director has disclosed to the directors the nature and extent of any material interest.[106] With only a few specific exceptions, a director who has an interest in any matter must not count in the quorum or vote at any board meeting where that matter is considered.[107] Compliance with the procedure specified in the articles ensures that the director is then not accountable to the company for any benefits derived from any such transaction, arrangement, directorship, office or employment, nor is any such transaction or arrangement liable to be avoided by reason of the director's interest.[108] A director may give a general notice of interests;[109] an interest of which a director is unaware is deemed not to be his interest provided it was unreasonable to expect the director to have that knowledge.[110]

Statutory Duty of Disclosure to the Board

Statute places a further disclosure obligation on directors[111] in respect of interests that they have in company contracts.[112] Companies Act 1985, s 317 imposes a duty on directors to declare at a meeting of the directors the nature of any interest that they may have in any contract, or proposed contract, with the company. There are certain procedural requirements in this section which are not expressly[113] mirrored in the Table A disclosure obligation: the disclosure must be made at a meeting of the board[114] and, with some exceptions, it must be made at the time when the question of entering into the contract is

[105] *Benson v Heathorn* (1842) 1 Y & C CC 326, 341–2 *per* Knight-Bruce V-C; *Imperial Mercantile Credit Association v Coleman* (1871) LR 6 Ch App 558, CA, 567–8 *per* Hatherley LC. On the effectiveness of vesting the consent function in the shareholders as a mechanism for curbing misuse of power by management: Parkinson, JE, *Corporate Power and Responsibility* (1993) 214–17, 232–6; Griffiths, A, 'Regulating Directors' Self-Dealing in a Unitary Board System of Corporate Governance' [1997] CfiLR 95, 100–1.

[106] Table A, art 85. [107] Table A, art 94. [108] Table A, art 85.

[109] Table A, art 86 (a). [110] Table A, art 86 (b).

[111] Including shadow directors: Companies Act 1985, s 317 (7). The disclosure procedure is modified in this case: Companies Act 1985, s 317 (7).

[112] Defined as including any transaction or arrangement made or entered into on or after 22 December 1980: Companies Act 1985, s 317 (5).

[113] It has been said that where a company has Table A articles, or articles based on that model, Companies Act 1985, s 317 and its specific requirements for disclosure must be read into the articles: *Lee Panavision Ltd v Lee Lighting Ltd* [1991] BCC 620, Ch D and CA, 627 *per* Harman J.

[114] Companies Act 1985, s 317 (1).

first considered.[115] Unlike Table A, Companies Act 1985, s 317 does not limit the disclosure obligation to material interests and, unsatisfactorily, it does not exempt a director from doing the impossible, that is disclosing interests of which he is unaware.[116] To comply with the statute, the director must disclose the nature of an interest but there is no express requirement to disclose its extent; in this respect, however, there may be no difference of substance between it and Table A because the overriding requirement in respect of disclosure is that the declaration must make the other directors fully informed about the position and it is thus implicit in the requirement to disclose the nature of an interest that the extent of it may have to be disclosed.[117]

Failure to Comply with Disclosure Requirements

The consequence of failure to comply with the requirements of the articles with regard to disclosure of interests is that contracts between a director and the company are voidable and may be set aside at the instance of the company provided the general conditions for avoidance are satisfied.[118] The general bars to avoidance (or rescission as this process is also described) are[119] affirmation of the contract by the company, lapse of time, intervention of third-party rights and the impossibility of returning the parties substantially to their pre-contractual position. Where, for example, a director has acquired property from the company without proper disclosure of his interest but that property has since been resold to a third party who is a bona fide purchaser for value,[120] the company will not be able to avoid the contract and recover the property. Where the director's interest in the contract is indirect because it is derived from having an interest in another company (second company) with which the company (first company) enters into a contract, the principle of separate legal personality will mean that the first company will not be able to avoid the contract[121] unless either the veil of incorporation of the second

[115] Companies Act 1985, s 317 (2). Although the wording is ambiguous (see *Report of the Company Law Committee*, Cmnd 1749 (1962) paras 95 and 99 (l) (Jenkins Committee)), the better view is that a director is required to disclose all interests and not just interests in arrangements that would, apart from the director's interest, fall for consideration by the board. This view is supported by *Neptune (Vehicle Washing Equipment) Ltd v Fitzgerald* [1995] BCC 474. For the procedural requirements in respect of general notices of interest: Companies Act 1985, s 317 (3)–(4).

[116] This defect in the statutory provision was noted in the *Report of the Company Law Committee* Cmnd 1749, (1962) paras 95 and 99 (l) (Jenkins Committee). *Company Directors: Regulating Conflicts of Interests and Formulating a Statement of Duties: A Joint Consultation Paper* (Law Commission Consultation Paper No 153; Scottish Law Commission Discussion Paper No 105) (1998) asks whether the disclosure obligation should be limited to material interests: para 4.97. It also provisionally recommends that directors should not be required to disclose interests of which they are unaware: para 4.105.

[117] *Imperial Mercantile Credit Association v Coleman* (1873) LR 6 HL 189, 201 *per* Lord Chelmsford; *Gray v New Augarita Porcupine Mines* [1952] 3 DLR 1, PC, 14 *per* Lord Radcliffe; *Woolworths Ltd v Kelly* (1991) 4 ACSR 431, NSW CA; Griffiths, A, 'Regulating Directors' Self-Dealing in a Unitary Board System of Corporate Governance' [1997] CfiLR 95, 118–20.

[118] *Hely-Hutchinson v Brayhead Ltd* [1968] 1 QB 549, CA.

[119] Goff, R, and Jones, G, *The Law of Restitution* (5th edn, 1998) ch 9; Baker, PV, and Langan, P St J, *Snell's Equity* (29th edn, 1990) Pt VII, ch 2.

[120] The company could still reclaim from a person who is not a bona fide purchaser for value: *Aberdeen Town Council v Aberdeen University* (1877) 2 App Cas 544, HL.

[121] *Farrar v Farrars Ltd* (1888) 40 Ch D 395, CA, 409–10 *per* Lindley LJ.

company can be lifted[122] or the director occupies a position in relation to the second company whereby his knowledge can be attributed to it so as to prevent it from being a bona fide purchaser without notice of the contravention.[123]

The equitable remedies[124] available to the company in circumstances where the contract cannot be avoided for whatever reason, are shrouded in some obscurity. There is a line of authority to the effect that where the fiduciary acquires property in a personal capacity and then, without disclosing the interest, resells it at a profit to the company, rescission is the company's only remedy, and that the company cannot claim an account of profit.[125] This rule has been described as 'anomalous'[126] and it merits slightly closer examination. The first point to note is the limit of these authorities: they establish only that the company can recover none of the difference between the price at which the fiduciary acquired the property and the price at which it was resold to the company in circumstances where it cannot be shown that the resale price was inflated. If a director sells property to the company for more than its existing market value the director should, on normal principles, be liable to account to the company for the unauthorised profit represented by the difference between market value and the price paid.[127]

Secondly, in recent years the courts have been particularly concerned to uphold the strict prophylactic function performed by fiduciary obligations and, with that in mind, they have dealt strictly with fiduciaries who have failed to meet the high standards that the law expects of persons in that position. The older cases which limit the company's remedy in the event of non-disclosure to rescission are out of line with that trend.[128] An illustration of this strict approach is provided by *Re Duckwari plc*.[129] In this case it was held that where a director did not disclose an interest in a transaction whereby a company acquired property at a price which was a fair market price at the time of the transaction but the market in that type of property subsequently collapsed, the director was liable to make good the company's loss as represented by the

[122] eg, because it is being used to perpetrate a fraud. On lifting the veil see Ch 1 above, at 15–6.

[123] *Transvaal Lands Co v New Belgium (Transvaal) Land and Development Co* [1914] 2 Ch 488, CA.

[124] The director may be in breach of a service contract and liable accordingly. Also, remedies may lie in tort if the company has been induced to enter into the contract by misrepresentation.

[125] *Re Cape Breton* (1885) 29 Ch D 759, CA, 804 *per* Cotton LJ; *Burland v Earle* [1902] AC 83, PC; *Erlanger v New Sombrero Phosphate Co* (1878) 3 App Cas 1218, HL, 1235 *per* Lord Cairns; *Ladywell Mining Co v Brookes* (1887) 35 Ch D 400, CA; *Tracy v Mandalay Pty Ltd* (1952) 88 CLR 215, H Ct of Aust. Limiting the parties' remedies to rescission stems from a reluctance to rewrite the parties' bargain: *Re Cape Breton* (1885) 29 Ch D 759, CA, 805 *per* Cotton LJ; *Jacobus Marler Estates Ltd v Marler* (1916) 114 LT 640n, HL, 641 *per* Lord Parker of Waddington. See further Birks, P, 'Restitution Without Counter-Restitution' [1990] LMCLQ 330.

[126] Sealy, LS, *Cases and Materials in Company Law* (6th edn, 1996) 36.

[127] This situation was expressly distinguished from the previous one in *Re Cape Breton* (1885) 29 Ch D 759, CA, 805 *per* Cotton LJ and the point was left open. On undervalue transactions between a company and a director (or connected persons): *Daniels v Daniels* [1978] Ch 406; *Aveling Barford Ltd v Perion Ltd* [1989] BCLC 626. See also Hayton, DJ, *Underhill & Hayton's Law of Trusts and Trustees* (15th edn, 1995) 18.

[128] Goff, R, and Jones, G, *The Law of Restitution* (5th edn, 1998) 726.

[129] [1998] 3 WLR 913, CA.

difference between what it paid for the property and the price for which it later realised it. Although that case concerned a specific statutory obligation to indemnify the company for losses in respect of substantial property transactions which had not been properly authorised in accordance with the requirements of the companies legislation, the Court of Appeal reasoned that the conclusion so reached was consistent with the position under the general law relating to fiduciaries. The court held that, by not securing the required consents, the directors had disposed of the company's property (the purchase price) in breach of trust and that the interested director was liable[130] to indemnify the company for all loss resulting from that disposal. The Court of Appeal did not consider the line of authorities limiting the company's remedies in respect of voidable contracts to rescission. The decision indicates that the courts may now recognise that a wider range of remedies is available in respect of a contract tainted by non-disclosure than older authorities seemed to accept. Another potentially relevant remedy that is recognised in recent cases is equitable compensation,[131] although, as yet, the rules regarding issues of causation, remoteness and quantification have not been fully worked out.[132]

Although it is cited here as being indicative of a stricter approach, it should also be noted that the analysis in the *Duckwari* decision raises some difficult questions for aspects of company law discussed elsewhere in this book. Characterising a situation where a contract is voidable for non-disclosure as a breach of the directors' duty to look after the company's property as if they were trustees, may throw into doubt the availability of ratification in these circumstances.[133] It also appears to undermine the basis on which it is said that articles can modify the requirement for the shareholders to act as the consenting body in respect of contracts in which directors have a personal interest.[134]

Failure by a director to comply with Companies Act 1985, s 317 leads to a fine.[135] Although the matter is not entirely beyond doubt,[136] the better view is

[130] Jointly and severally with the corporate vehicle which contracted with the company. The director was the controller of that vehicle.

[131] *Target Holdings v Redferns* [1996] 1 AC 421, HL; *Bristol and West Building Society v Mothew* [1998] Ch 1, CA, 17 *per* Millett LJ; *Canson Enterprises Ltd v Boughton & Co* (1991) 85 DLR (4th) 129, Can SC, 163 *per* McLachlin J; *Day v Mead* [1987] 2 NZLR 443, NZ CA.

[132] Oakley, AJ, *Constructive Trusts* (3rd edn, 1997) 115–21; contrast Meagher, RP, Gummow, WMC, and Lehane, JRF, *Equity Doctrine and Remedies* (3rd edn, 1992) 52–70 where the 'fallacy' that damages are available in equity is discussed.

[133] It is traditionally said that contracts tainted by the undisclosed personal interest of a director can be ratified by the shareholders in general meeting but that misapplication of corporate property is unratifiable. See Ch 4 above, at 144–53.

[134] The 'self dealing' rule is said to be a 'disability' as opposed to a duty, but the requirement not to misapply the company's property is certainly a duty: Companies Act 1985, s 310 as interpreted in *Movitex v Bulfield Ltd* (1986) 2 BCC 99,403, following *Tito v Waddell* [1977] Ch 106, 248–9 *per* Megarry V-C. On s 310 see further, Ch. 4 above, at 140–3 and this chapter, at 198–9 below.

[135] Companies Act 1985, s 317 (7).

[136] The uncertainty stems from the decision of the House of Lords in *Guinness plc v Saunders* [1990] 2 AC 663, HL. Lord Goff's view was that failure to comply with section 317 did not render a contract voidable but Lord Templeman stated that it did.

that non-compliance with the statutory obligation does not itself make a contract voidable.[137] This may be little more than a theoretical point in the normal type of situation where the company's articles follow the form of Table A with the consequence that the disclosure requirements under the articles and Companies Act 1985, s 317 are broadly coextensive. It would be significant if the company had articles which laid down requirements with regard to company contracts which were entirely different from those in Companies Act 1985, s 317: an extreme example, and one that would be unlikely to be encountered often in practice for obvious reasons, would be a set of articles which overrode the common law rule altogether and permitted contracts between directors and the company without any disclosure or other procedural safeguards. Although Companies Act 1985, s 310 invalidates provisions in articles which seek to modify the duties to which directors are subject under the general law, the rule that a director may not contract with the company has been classified as a 'disability' rather than a 'duty' for this purpose,[138] with the consequence that articles in the form of this example may be permissible.[139] Articles could not, however, override Companies Act 1985, s 317 because that is a non-excludable 'duty'.[140] If articles were to dispense altogether with disclosure requirements in respect of directors' interest, on the basis of the view outlined in this paragraph, the effect would be that a director who did not disclose an interest in a contract would incur the statutory penalty of a fine but the contract would not be voidable.

Technical Non-compliance with Disclosure Requirements

A director may fail to comply precisely with the procedural requirements of the articles and Companies Act 1985, s 317. For example, the making of a formal declaration at a meeting may be overlooked because either the other directors are already aware of the interest or the director is the sole director of the company. What is the effect of a technical oversight such as this on the contract and with regard to Companies Act 1985, s 317?

There is a difference of view in first instance cases on this point. At one end of the spectrum is the decision in *Neptune (Vehicle Washing Equipment) Ltd v Fitzgerald*[141] where it was held that a sole director of a company who did not declare an interest at a meeting was in breach of Companies Act 1985, s 317 and that the contract between him and the contract was voidable. At the other

137 *Hely-Hutchinson v Brayhead Ltd* [1968] 1 QB 549, CA; *Lee Panavision Ltd v Lee Lighting Ltd* [1991] BCC 620, Ch D and CA; *Cowan de Groot Properties Ltd v Eagle Trust plc* [1992] 4 All ER 700, 762 *per* Knox J. Griffiths, A, 'Regulating Directors' Self-Dealing in a Unitary Board System of Corporate Governance' [1997] CfiLR 95, 101–3, *Company Directors: Regulating Conflicts of Interests and Formulating a Statement of Duties: A Joint Consultation Paper* (Law Commission Consultation Paper No 153; Scottish Law Commission Discussion Paper No 105) (1998) paras 4.78–4.80.

138 *Movitex v Bulfield Ltd* (1986) 2 BCC 99,403.

139 Unless there is an irreducible minimum duty of disclosure as argued by some commentators. eg, Griffiths, A, 'Regulating Directors' Self-Dealing in a Unitary Board System of Corporate Governance' [1997] CfiLR 95, 112–14.

140 Companies Act 1985, s 317 (1).

141 *Neptune (Vehicle Washing Equipment) Ltd v Fitzgerald* [1995] BCC 474 (interlocutory hearing); *Neptune (Vehicle Washing Equipment) Ltd v Fitzgerald* [1995] BCC 1,000.

end is *Runciman v Walter Runciman plc*[142] where Simon Brown J held that where a director failed to make formal disclosure but all the directors were aware of his interest, the breach was 'at most' technical and that it did not render the contract in question voidable. The *Neptune* decision, with its insistence on precise compliance with formal requirements, is supported by Fox LJ's judgment in the Court of Appeal in *Guinness plc v Saunders*[143] and by the first instance decision in *Lee Panavision Ltd v Lee Lighting Ltd.*[144] However, in the Court of Appeal in the *Lee* case, although it was unnecessary to decide the point, Dillon LJ stated that he would hesitate to hold that a technical failure to comply with disclosure obligations had the inevitable result, as to which the court had no discretion, of rendering the resulting contract voidable. That passage of Dillon LJ's judgment in the *Lee* case was subsequently relied upon in the *Runciman* decision. Whatever equitable discretion the courts may have in this respect, it is unlikely that it will be exercised lightly because that would be inconsistent with the courts' general insistence upon precise compliance with obligations imposed on fiduciaries without examination of the merits of their actions. Well-advised directors would proceed on the basis that disclosure is always required and would not rely on the possibility of the court exercising a discretion in favour of relieving them from the consequences of non-disclosure.[145]

The merit[146] of a strict requirement for disclosure of interests is that this provides, through the board minutes,[147] a record for subsequent controllers of the company of situations where directors had personal interests which might have been preferred over the company's interest. Although a director who is intent on defrauding the company is unlikely to give the game away by making formal disclosure of an interest, if it is later discovered that a director had a personal interest which was not disclosed and recorded in the minutes, this will act as a signal that the situation may require further investigation. In the case of a company with a single director, there is, however, a ring of absurdity about the notion that the director must go through the motions of formally declaring an interest to himself or herself at a board meeting (although, as was

142 [1992] BCLC 1084. See also *Woolworths Ltd v Kelly* (1991) 4 ACSR 431, NSW CA.

143 [1988] 2 All ER 940, CA (a passage which appears to be unaffected by the different analysis of the situation that was put forward by the House of Lords in this case).

144 [1991] BCC 620, Ch D and CA.

145 *Company Directors: Regulating Conflicts of Interests and Formulating a Statement of Duties: A Joint Consultation Paper* (Law Commission Consultation Paper No 153; Scottish Law Commission Discussion Paper No 105) (1998) para 4.102 contains a provisional recommendation that directors should be exempted from the need to make formal disclosure of their interest in their own service contracts. A further provisional recommendation is that breach of s 317 should make a contract voidable unless the court otherwise directs: para 4.113.

146 In the interlocutory proceedings in *Neptune (Vehicle Washing Equipment) Ltd v Fitzgerald* [1995] BCC 474 Lightman J gave as another reason for insisting upon formality in one-director companies the argument that the making of the declaration would be an opportunity for a statutory pause for thought about the existence of the conflict of interest and of the duty to prefer the company's interests. The idea of a statutory pause for thought is not, in terms, supported by Companies Act 1985, s 317, which simply requires the director to disclose the nature of his interest. Whether the empty formality of requiring a director to disclose his interest to himself would make him consider the conflict between his own interests and those of the company more closely than he would otherwise have done is doubtful.

147 Companies Act 1985, s 382.

accepted in the *Neptune* litigation, he need not go to the trouble of doing so out loud if no-one else is present!). In situations such as these, there is a good case for saying that the maintenance of a record of interested transactions could be achieved simply by requiring the director to lodge written notices of interests at the company's registered office and obliging the company to retain a record of such notices. With such safeguards in place, the case for dispensing with the Companies Act 1985, s 317 disclosure requirement would be compelling.[148]

Affirmation of Contract Tainted by a Director's Undisclosed Interest

A company can choose to affirm a contract which is voidable because a director failed to disclose an interest. This is one of the processes for which the term 'ratification' is sometimes used.[149] The cases establish that it is for the shareholders in general meeting to decide whether to ratify a transaction which is tainted by the undisclosed personal interest of a director.[150] If the director who failed to make the required disclosure is also a shareholder in the company, he may cast his votes in favour of the ratification of the contract. His participation in the vote to ratify the transaction will not invalidate that decision.[151]

SUBSTANTIAL PROPERTY TRANSACTIONS

The dispensation from the requirement for a director to disclose an interest to, and obtain the consent of, the shareholders in general meeting that is typically provided by articles of association is reversed by Companies Act 1985, s 320 in relation to 'substantial property transactions'. In addition to disclosure requirements imposed by Companies Act 1985, s 317 and the articles, a substantial property transaction involving a director must be approved by the shareholders in general meeting. This statutory obligation was first introduced in 1980 to implement a requirement of the Second EC Company Law Directive.[152]

[148] In a single member company where the sole member is also a director there is already a requirement for the terms of any contract between the company and that director to be in writing, set out in a written memorandum or recorded in a board minute: Companies Act 1985, s 322B. This requirement stems from the EC Directive on Single Member Companies 89/667/EEC, [1989] OJ L395/40. It has been strongly argued that Companies Act 1985 s 317 could have been dispensed with in this situation: Sealy, LS, *Cases and Materials in Company Law* (6th edn, 1996) 288. See also *Company Directors: Regulating Conflicts of Interests and Formulating a Statement of Duties: A Joint Consultation Paper* (Law Commission Consultation Paper No 153; Scottish Law Commission Discussion Paper No 105) (1998) para 4.101 which recommends that sole director companies should be exempted from Companies Act 1985, s 317.

[149] On the various interpretations of the term 'ratification' see Ch 4 above, at 146–7.

[150] *North-West Transportation Co Ltd v Beatty* (1887) 12 App Cas 589, PC.

[151] Ibid. If, however, as well as failing to disclose, the director has taken advantage of his position so as to acquire company property at an undervalue or to sell property to it at an inflated price, that may be regarded as a misappropriation of corporate property which would then involve consideration of the limits of ratification and the oppression of minorities. See also *Re Duckwari plc* [1998] 3 WLR 913 CA.

[152] 77/91/EEC, [1977] OJ L26/1.

A substantial property transaction means an arrangement[153] whereby (i) a company acquires a non-cash asset of the requisite value from one of its directors, or from a director of its holding company, or from a person connected with such a director, or (ii) a director of the company, or a director of the holding company, or a person connected with any such director acquires a non-cash asset of the requisite value from the company.[154] A 'non-cash asset' includes a lease,[155] the benefit of a contract and a beneficial interest in property[156] but not the right to a cash payment.[157] The 'requisite value' means at least £100,000 or 10 per cent of the company's asset value,[158] subject to a minimum of £2,000.[159] The value is to be taken at the time when the arrangement is entered into.[160] A shadow director is treated as a director for the purpose of this section.[161] A 'connected person' is defined for this purpose[162] and includes a director's spouse and children, bodies corporate with which the director is associated, and partners of the director.

The procedural requirements in respect of a substantial property transaction are that, unless an exception applies,[163] it must be approved by an ordinary resolution of the company in general meeting before it is concluded. Contracts that are conditional upon approval being obtained are not permitted.[164] Where the other contracting party is a director of the company's holding company or is a person connected to such a director, the contract must also be approved by an ordinary resolution of the holding company in general meeting.[165] In accordance with the general rules relating to meetings and resolutions, the notice convening a meeting to approve a substantial property transaction must give a fair, candid and reasonable explanation of what is proposed and must fully disclose the nature of the director's interest.[166]

Arrangements or transactions which are entered into in contravention of Companies Act 1985, s 320 are voidable at the instance of the company unless one or more statutory bars to rescission exists.[167] These statutory bars are: (i) restitution is no longer possible; (ii) the company has been indemnified pursuant to the statute; (iii) intervention of the rights of a bona fide purchaser for

[153] This would cover agreements and understandings without contractual effect: *Duckwari plc v Offerventure Ltd* [1995] BCC 89, Ch D and CA.

[154] Companies Act 1985, s 320 (1).

[155] *Niltan Carson Ltd v Hawthorne* [1988] BCLC 298.

[156] Companies Act 1985, s 739 (1), as interpreted in *Duckwari plc v Offerventure Ltd* [1995] BCC 89, Ch D and CA.

[157] *Lander v Premier Pict Petroleum Ltd* [1998] BCC 248, Ct of Sess.

[158] Whichever is the lesser: *Niltan Carson Ltd v Hawthorne* [1988] BCLC 298. The specified monetary limits can be changed by statutory instrument: Companies Act 1985, s 345. The company's 'asset value' is to be determined by reference to the company's last published annual accounts or, if there are none, it is the amount of the company's called-up share capital: Companies Act 1985, s 320 (2).

[159] Companies Act 1985, s 320 (2).

[160] Ibid.

[161] Companies Act 1985, s 320 (3).

[162] Ibid, s 346.

[163] Ibid, s 321.

[164] *Company Directors: Regulating Conflicts of Interests and Formulating a Statement of Duties: A Joint Consultation Paper* (Law Commission Consultation Paper No 153; Scottish Law Commission Discussion Paper No 105) (1998) para 4.192 provisionally recommends that conditional contracts should be allowed.

[165] Companies Act 1985, s 320 (1).

[166] *Kaye v Croydon Tramways* [1898] 1 Ch 358, CA.

[167] Companies Act 1985, s 322 (1).

value without notice of the contravention; (iv) affirmation by the company.[168] Whether or not the arrangement or transaction is avoided, the director and, where relevant, the connected person are liable, together with the directors who authorised it, to account to the company for any gains and, jointly and severally, to indemnify the company for any loss or damage resulting from the transaction or arrangement.[169] This is without prejudice to any liability otherwise imposed.[170] Where a director's liability is based on the fact of a connection with the contracting party, the director has a defence if he can show that he took all reasonable steps to ensure compliance with Companies Act 1985, s 320.[171] For connected persons and directors whose liability stems from the fact that they authorised the transaction or arrangement, there is a defence if they can show that, at the time it was entered into, they did not know the relevant circumstances constituting the contravention.[172]

An indemnity under this section enables the company to recover the difference between the price paid for, and the actual value of, assets which have been sold to the company at an inflated price.[173] It has also been held that the company can claim to be indemnified for losses resulting from post-acquisition falls in the market value of the assets acquired.[174]

STOCK EXCHANGE REGULATION

The London Stock Exchange imposes further safeguards against related parties (a category which includes directors[175]) taking advantage of their position.[176] The broad requirement imposed on listed companies is for transactions involving related parties to be approved by the shareholders in general meeting. There are exceptions to this requirement, including one based on the size of the transaction.[177] Where shareholder approval is required, the relevant director (and associates) must refrain from voting on the relevant resolution.[178]

168 Companies Act 1985, s 322 (2). If the other contracting party is a director of the holding company, or is connected to such a director, this affirmation must be approved by the holding company.

169 Companies Act 1985, s 322 (3)–(4).

170 Ibid, s 322 (3).

171 Ibid, s 322 (5).

172 Ibid, s 322 (6).

173 *Duckwari plc v Offerventure Ltd* [1997] Ch 201 (although reversed on appeal the point stands).

174 *Re Duckwari plc* [1998] 3 WLR 913, CA. But the indemnity does not extend to borrowing costs which the company may incur in order to enter into the transaction: *Re Duckwari plc (No 2)* 19 November 1998, CA.

175 And also substantial shareholders and associates either of directors or of substantial shareholders.

176 *The Listing Rules*, ch 11.

177 *The Listing Rules*, ch 11, para 11.7 (i) and ch 10, para 10.5.

178 *The Listing Rules*, ch 11, para 11.4 (d).

STATUTORY AND MARKET REGULATION OF SPECIFIC TYPES OF CONTRACT OR OTHER ARRANGEMENTS INVOLVING DIRECTORS

Various contracts and arrangements between directors and their companies are specifically regulated by the companies legislation. Also, for companies that raise capital from the public markets, there are also constraints stemming from the expectations of the market with regard to corporate governance. It is not intended to examine all instances of regulation closely but, in outline, the main areas are as follows.

Length of Directors' Service Contracts

The Companies Act 1985, s 319 regulates the length of directors' service contracts. The section applies to service contracts which are to incorporate a term allowing the director to serve for a period of more than five years without the company having the right lawfully to bring the contract to an early end by serving a notice of termination or limiting the right of early termination to specific circumstances. A contract in these terms must be approved in advance by the shareholders in general meeting.[179] A term incorporated in a contract in contravention of this section is, to the extent of the contravention, void;[180] and the agreement is deemed to contain a term entitling the company to terminate it at any time by the giving of reasonable notice.[181]

The length of a director's service contract is very significant because if the company terminates a director's contract before the expiry of the period of service and is in breach of contract in so doing, the basic measure of the director's compensation will be the salary for the unexpired portion of the contract.[182] Regulating the period of service is thus a way of attempting to ensure that a director does not become entrenched in office because it is simply too expensive to remove him. However, the impact of this form of regulation is somewhat diluted by the device of rolling contracts: these are contracts which are structured so as to fall outside the Companies Act 1985, s 319 but which are drafted so as to ensure that the unexpired portion of the contract at any time will be roughly five years.

There are now in place market regulatory measures which are intended to counteract the effect of rolling contracts. Although there is no direct route for shareholders to challenge the length of directors' service contracts so long as they are within the five-year limit set by Companies Act 1985, s 319, it is still important for a company to take into account the views of its shareholders on this matter. This is, first, because dissatisfaction with a company's governance structure may lead shareholders to sell their shares which may depress the

179 Companies Act 1985, s 319 (3). There are specific disclosure obligations in respect of contracts requiring approval under this section: Companies Act 1985, s 319 (5).

180 Companies Act 1985, s 319 (6).

181 Ibid.

182 *Clark v BET plc* [1997] IRLR 348 where a director's compensation for wrongful dismissal was based on his salary over three years. He had been employed on a three-year rolling contract. The total amount of the award in his favour was £2.85 million. The company appealed but later settled for £2.25 million: 'Clark Settles for Rentokil's £2.25 Million' *Financial Times*, 21 April 1997.

share price.[183] Secondly, where a director is standing for election or re-election, shareholders may vote against this simply because they object to the duration of his service contract.[184]

The length of directors' service contracts is viewed as an important matter by the institutions that are the major holders of equity share capital in UK companies. The fact that a director who is forced out of office for unsatisfactory performance, but who is not in breach of contract, can then seek[185] to claim as compensation a lump sum representing several years salary, pension rights and other benefits,[186] is regarded as being, in effect, an unwarranted reward for failure.[187] At the start of the 1990s, the practice of limiting rolling contracts to three years reflected institutional concerns on this matter.[188] During that decade, there was a shift in institutional investor expectations and the view developed that rolling contracts ought to be limited to one year or, alternatively, that longer contracts ought to contain a notice provision entitling the company to terminate the contract lawfully by giving a maximum of one-year's notice. In 1998 this view was endorsed by the London Stock Exchange. The *Combined Code* on corporate governance which is annexed to *The Listing Rules* states that there is a strong case for setting notice or contract periods at, or reducing[189] them to, one year or less, and encourages boards to set this as an objective.[190] Listed companies are required to state in their annual reports and accounts whether they have complied with the *Combined Code* and to give reasons for any areas of non-compliance, but non-compliance in itself does not jeopardise a company's listing.[191]

[183] This is shareholder control via the market by 'exit'. Exit and, as discussed next, 'voice' are considered further in Ch 7 below.

[184] In 1994, a major institutional investor PosTel (later renamed Hermes) announced that it would vote against the re-appointment of directors with rolling contracts of more than two years and expressed a preference for contracts lasting no more than 12 months: see Dow, RJ, 'Service Contracts: Golden Parachutes and Institutional Investors' (1993) 4 (6) PLC 14.

[185] The eventual award may be less than the amount that would have been earned under the unexpired portion of the contract because of mitigation principles. A dismissed director should seek to mitigate his loss by seeking alternative employment. In *Clark v BET plc* [1997] IRLR 348 a mitigating sum of £90,000 was allowed on the basis that the plaintiff was unlikely to obtain comparable employment but would hold some non-executive directorships.

[186] In *Clark v BET plc* [1997] IRLR 348 the award included compensation for the loss of life cover, and also the loss of a motor car and chauffeur.

[187] Lea, R, *Directors' Remuneration* (Institute of Directors Research Paper) (1997) 5, 9–10.

[188] *The Role and Duties of Directors—A Statement of Best Practice*, Institutional Shareholders Committee (2nd edn, August 1993), stated that contracts should not run for a period of more than three years and that there could be circumstances in which rolling contracts should be limited to one year.

[189] Directors may demand compensation for a reduction in notice periods where this amounts to a variation in their contractual rights: 'Corporate Governance' (1998) 9 (1) PLC 12.

[190] *Combined Code* B1.7–1.8. It also suggests that remuneration committees should consider providing explicitly in a contract for the amount that will be payable to a director if he is removed otherwise than for misconduct or, where there is no such provision, that they should take a robust line on reducing compensation to a departing director to reflect mitigation principles: *Combined Code* B.1.9-B.1.10.

[191] *The Listing Rules*, ch 12, para 12.43A, effective for annual reports and accounts for financial periods ending on or after 31 December 1998. The Greenbury Committee that reported on directors' remuneration in 1995 formally recommended 12-month rolling contracts or notice periods. A survey by Manifest (a proxy voting agency) that was reported in 1997 showed that the majority of the companies surveyed still had directors on two- or three-year fixed-term or rolling contracts: 'Most Directors Fail to Meet Codes of Best Practice on Pay' *The Times* 6 January 1997.

Disclosure of Directors' Service Contracts

Directors' service contracts, or written memoranda of their terms where the contracts are not in writing, must be kept available for inspection without charge by shareholders.[192] The contracts and memoranda may be kept at the registered office, at the place where the register of members is kept or at the principal place of business provided it is situated in that part of Great Britain where the company is registered;[193] but they must all be kept in the same place.[194] Contracts with less than 12 months left to run and contracts which can be lawfully terminated by the company within the next ensuing 12 months without payment of compensation are not subject to this requirement.[195] Letters of appointment not amounting to service contracts, as are sometimes given to non-executive directors, are not within the scope of this section.[196]

Removal of Directors

The company in general meeting can at any time remove a director from office by passing an ordinary resolution to that effect.[197] This is a statutory power which cannot be fettered.[198] However, this does not preclude voting agreements between shareholders in which they undertake not to vote in favour of any resolution to remove directors,[199] nor does it prevent the

[192] Companies Act 1985, s 318. For listed companies, there are additional disclosure obligations with regard to directors' service contracts under *The Listing Rules*, ch 16, paras 16.9–16.11 and ch 12, para 12.43A(c).

[193] Companies Act 1985, s 318 (3).

[194] Companies Act 1985 , s 318 (2). The company must notify the registrar of companies of the place where they are kept: s 318 (4).

[195] Companies Act 1985, s 318 (11). Note also s 318 (5) which is concerned with directors who work wholly or mainly outside the UK. *Company Directors: Regulating Conflicts of Interests and Formulating a Statement of Duties: A Joint Consultation Paper* (Law Commission Consultation Paper No 153; Scottish Law Commission Discussion Paper No 105) (1998) paras 4.140–4.147 provisionally recommends repeal of these exemptions.

[196] *Company Directors: Regulating Conflicts of Interests and Formulating a Statement of Duties: A Joint Consultation Paper* (Law Commission Consultation Paper No 153; Scottish Law Commission Discussion Paper No 105) (1998) para 41.139 provisionally recommends that the section should be extended to apply to letters of appointment (and also to contracts for services as well as service contracts).

[197] Companies Act 1985, s 303. Special notice is required: s 303 (2). On special notice: Companies Act 1985, s 379. A company's articles may additionally provide for the removal of directors by other means, eg by a resolution of the other directors, or by a special resolution of shareholders (but without special notice and the other procedural requirements relating to removal under Companies Act 1985, s 303).

[198] *Bushell v Faith* [1970] AC 1099, HL.

[199] *Russell v Northern Bank Development Corpn Ltd* [1992] 3 All ER 294, HL. Further on *Russell*: Ferran, EV, 'The Decision of the House of Lords in *Russell v Northern Bank Development Corporation Ltd*' [1994] CLJ 343; Davenport, BJ, 'What Did *Russell v Northern Bank Development Corporation Ltd* Decide?' (1993) 109 LQR 553. A vote attaching to a share is a property right which can be exercised as its owner thinks fit: *Pender v Lushington* (1877) 6 Ch D 70; *Northern Counties Securities Ltd v Jackson & Steeple Ltd* [1974] 1 WLR 1133; *North-West Transportation Co Ltd v Beatty* (1887) 12 App Cas 589, PC. The legitimacy of shareholder voting agreements has been recognised in a number of cases including *Greenwell v Porter* [1902] 1 Ch 530; *Greenhalgh v Mallard* [1943] 2 All ER 234, CA; *Ringuet v Bergeron* (1960) 24 DLR (2d) 449, C SC, 459 *per* Judson J.

inclusion of weighted votes provisions in articles which come into effect when there is a proposal to remove a shareholder from office as a director and operate so as to ensure that the targeted shareholder has the majority of votes in that situation and can thus defeat the resolution.[200] Voting agreements amongst shareholders and weighted voting provisions in articles are devices which are most likely to be found in small quasi-partnership type companies or in joint ventures.

An inhibiting factor on the use of the power contained in Companies Act 1985, s 303 which is potentially relevant to all companies is that a director who is voted out of office can seek compensation if the removal amounts to a breach of his contract with the company.[201] This point reinforces the importance of regulating the length of directors' service contracts as one way of ensuring that removal of directors who are not performing to the satisfaction of the shareholders remains an economically viable option.

Directors' Remuneration

Directors' remuneration is a difficult and sensitive issue particularly in companies that have external shareholders who are not involved in management nor connected by family or other personal relationships to management. These are usually public companies. Directors of public companies commonly receive remuneration packages comprising a fixed monetary amount, cash bonuses which are paid provided target performance ratios are met, shares and share options or other long-term incentives.[202] The inclusion of performance-related bonuses and share options, the value of which is dependent on how far the market price of the shares rises above the price at which the options can be exercised, can help to align the interests of the directors and the shareholders in the performance of their company.[203] However, there are also problems with remuneration packages in this typical form. Share options in particular present directors with the opportunity for vast personal profit and this can attract critical press and media attention, on grounds that these are examples of 'fat cats' profiting at the expense of more junior employees or of consumers.[204]

The starting point with regard to the legal controls on directors' remuneration is that it is for companies themselves to decide how much to pay their

[200] *Bushell v Faith* [1970] AC 1099, HL. Prentice, DD, 'Removal of Directors From Office' (1969) 32 MLR 693; Collier, J, 'Company: Power to Remove Directors by Ordinary Resolution: Weighted Voting: Whether Ordinary Resolution' [1970] CLJ 41; Schmitthoff, CM, 'House of Lords Sanctions Evasion of Companies Acts' [1970] JBL 1.

[201] Companies Act 1985, s 303 (5).

[202] Such as L-Tips (long-term incentive plans) which typically reward directors with shares if certain performance targets are met or deferred convertible shares which are convertible after a period of some time (such as five years) provided certain performance targets are met. L-Tips are intended to be more closely related to the performance of individual companies than share options. A problem with share options is that they are solely dependent on share-price movements and this allows directors to profit when markets are rising generally even if their company is not doing particularly well. See further: *From Greenbury to Hampel: A Mid-Term Report on Developments in Directors Remuneration* (Coopers & Lybrand Report) (1997).

[203] *Combined Code* annexed to *The Listing Rules*, B.1.4.

[204] eg, 'Zeneca Board's £23m Shares Splurge' *Guardian* 15 July 1998.

directors. It is open to a company to regulate the amount of directors' remuneration and the procedure for its payment in its articles of association. Under typical articles of association, the board is authorised to pay fees to directors up to an aggregate maximum amount authorised by the shareholders.[205] The board is also authorised to pay remuneration to executive directors[206] and this is not subject to a maximum specified by the shareholders. Directors' fiduciary duties are a constraining factor but, apart from these,[207] the only mandatory legal rules on the amounts paid to directors are indirect ones stemming from rules on maintenance of capital and protection of creditors in insolvency. In particular, if extreme, circumstances these rules may be infringed by the making of payments to directors.[208] There is at present no statutory provision which requires shareholders to approve directors' remuneration or which entitles the court, or any other agency, to strike down remuneration payments simply on the ground that the company has paid too much. Instead, the Companies Act 1985 seeks to regulate directors' remuneration through the mechanism of disclosure in accounts.[209]

For companies with external shareholders, the next layer of regulation stems from market expectations with regard to corporate governance. The regulation of executive directors' remuneration was one of the primary areas of concern of the corporate governance movement in the 1990s. The recommendations of a number of committees on the issue of directors' remuneration were consolidated by the Stock Exchange in 1998 into the *Combined Code* which is annexed to *The Listing Rules*. The framework of regulation under the *Combined Code* is that executive directors should not determine their own remuneration and that, instead, decisions about executive directors' pay should be made by a remuneration committee comprised of independent non-executive directors.[210] According to the *Combined Code* a remuneration committee should aim to set levels of remuneration that are sufficient to attract and retain the directors who are needed to run the company but

205 Table A, art 82.

206 Table A, art 84.

207 An example of a court using fiduciary duties to strike down a remuneration payment is provided by *Zemco v Jerrom-Pugh* [1993] BCC 275. The courts' reluctance to second-guess business decisions (*Howard Smith v Ampol Petroleum* [1974] AC 821, PC) means that instances of judicial interference are likely to be rare and to arise only in cases of blatant abuse. See also Griffiths, A, 'Directors' Remuneration: Constraining the Power of the Board' [1995] LMCLQ 372.

208 Excessive remuneration may also be a factor that is taken into account in proceedings under the Company Directors Disqualification Act 1986: eg, *Secretary of State for Trade and Industry v Van Hengel* [1995] BCLC 545.

209 The one direct control provided in Companies Act 1985 is s 311 which provides that it is not lawful for a company to pay a director remuneration free of income tax. *Company Directors: Regulating Conflicts of Interests and Formulating a Statement of Duties: A Joint Consultation Paper* (Law Commission Consultation Paper No 153; Scottish Law Commission Discussion Paper No 105) (1998) para 9.32 provisionally recommends the repeal of s 311. On the disclosure requirements, see Companies Act 1985, s 232 and sch 6 and also FRS 8 *Related Party Disclosures*.

210 The *Combined Code* annexed to *The Listing Rules*, B2, and B.2.1–B.2.6, set out the principle and detailed rules relating to the establishment of formal and transparent procedures for fixing executive remuneration. To facilitate the operation of a remuneration committee, the articles of association must provide for delegation of the power to fix the remuneration of executive directors to a committee: *Guinness plc v Saunders* [1990] 2 AC 663, HL. It has been reported that the government is considering asking the London Stock Exchange to add a requirement to *The Listing Rules* for shareholder approval of remuneration packages: 'Byers Seeks To Halt Big Rises in Boardroom Pay' *Financial Times* 16 February 1999.

should avoid paying more than is necessary for this purpose.[211] It recommends that a proportion of executive directors' remuneration should be structured so as to link rewards to corporate and individual performance.[212] It suggests that consideration should be given to replacing share option schemes with other forms of long-term incentive schemes and also specifically recommends that shareholders should be asked to approve new long-term incentive schemes for executive directors.[213] The status of the *Combined Code* is that it is appended to, but is not part of, *The Listing Rules* with the consequence that non-compliance with its requirements would not jeopardise a company's listing. However, listed companies are required by *The Listing Rules* to disclose any areas of non-compliance with the *Combined Code* in their annual reports and accounts and to give reasons for this;[214] unless there are good reasons, non-compliance is likely to attract criticism from institutional investors and adverse media coverage. Another obligation on listed companies under *The Listing Rules* is for the annual report and accounts to contain a specific report from the board on aspects of directors' remuneration.[215] This report should include full details of each individual director's remuneration package.

It was in the report of the Cadbury Committee on *The Financial Aspects of Corporate Governance,* published in December 1992, that the use of remuneration committees made up of non-executive directors was first formally recommended in the UK as a good corporate governance practice. The use of remuneration committees rapidly became standard practice[216] but that did not lead to a levelling off in the levels of remuneration paid to executive directors. Whilst there are many factors that might explain the upward trend in directors' remuneration, this point opens up wider concerns about relying upon non-executive directors as a mechanism for controlling and monitoring management. The wider issues relating to non-executive directors include concerns that they may not be truly 'independent' (in a worst possible case, non-executive directors who are simply 'cronies' of the executives could create an entirely misleading and damaging veneer of independent monitoring) and fears that they may be impeded from monitoring effectively because they are dependent on the executive management for information and do not have the time or resources to investigate matters themselves. These concerns about the role of non-executive directors in setting executive remuneration and more generally are developed further in Chapter 6.[217]

[211] *Combined Code*, B.1, expanded in B.1.1–B.1.6

[212] *Combined Code*, B.1, expanded in B.1.1–B.1.6. Analysis of the links between pay and performance is provided by Henry, D, and Smith, G, *Boardroom Pay and Operating Performance* (Price Waterhouse publication) (1997). See also *Boardroom Pay in UK Quoted Companies 1996* (Arthur Andersen publication) (1997).

[213] *Combined Code*, B.3.4.

[214] *The Listing Rules*, ch 12, para 12.43A (a) and (b).

[215] *The Listing Rules*, ch 12, para 12.43 (c). The scope of the auditors report must cover some of the disclosures made in the directors' remuneration report.

[216] *NAPF Corporate Governance Analysis* (1996) indicates that, at the end of 1995, 92 per cent of the UK's largest 300 companies had remuneration committees.

[217] See Ch 6 below, at 217–23.

Payments to Directors for Loss of Office[218]

The Companies Act 1985, s 312 provides that it is not lawful for a company to make any payment to a director by way of compensation for loss of office or as consideration for or in connection with his retirement, without particulars of the proposed payment (including its amount) being disclosed to the shareholders and approved by them. Although this is a safeguard against one form of abuse, the effect of this provision is limited because it does not apply to bona fide payments by way of damages for breach of contract or by way of pension in respect of past services.[219] It has also been held to be inapplicable to payments to which the director has a contractual entitlement and to payments which are made to an executive director as compensation for loss of employment as opposed to loss of office.[220]

The Companies Act 1985, ss 313–315 impose restrictions on payments to directors as compensation for loss of office or in consideration of retirement in the context of a transfer of the company's undertaking or of a takeover. The Companies Act 1985, s 313, which applies where there is a transfer of all or part of the company's undertaking or property, imposes a similar disclosure and shareholder consent requirement to that contained in the Companies Act 1985, s 312. Under the Companies Act 1985, s 314 it is the duty of a director to take reasonable steps to ensure that shareholders are notified of a payment that is proposed to be made in a takeover situation but there is no requirement for the shareholders formally to approve it.

Directors' Dealings in their Company's Securities

Directors of listed companies are prohibited from buying options to sell or buy their company's listed securities ('put' and 'call' options).[221] This specific rule in the Companies Act 1985 overlaps with the more general restrictions on insider dealing which are imposed by the Criminal Justice Act 1993.[222] Directors of listed companies are also subject to dealing restrictions under *The Listing Rules* of the London Stock Exchange.[223]

[218] For further detail on these sections and recommendations for change see *Company Directors: Regulating Conflicts of Interests and Formulating a Statement of Duties: A Joint Consultation Paper* (Law Commission Consultation Paper No 153; Scottish Law Commission Discussion Paper No 105) (1998) paras 4.11–4.61.

[219] Companies Act 1985, s 316 (3).

[220] *Taupo Totara Timber Co v Rowe* [1978] AC 537, PC.

[221] Companies Act 1985, s 323. Spouses and children of a director are also prohibited from purchasing options: Companies Act 1985, s 327. The ban applies to shadow directors: Companies Act 1985: s 327 (2)(c). The prohibition is on put and call options but not on options to subscribe: Companies Act 1985, s 323 (3). It is options to subscribe that are commonly included in directors' remuneration packages.

[222] Ss 52–64. The existence of these detailed rules in Criminal Justice Act 1993 makes Companies Act 1985, s 323 arguably redundant: *Company Directors: Regulating Conflicts of Interests and Formulating a Statement of Duties: A Joint Consultation Paper* (Law Commission Consultation Paper No 153; Scottish Law Commission Discussion Paper No 105) (1998) para 9.33 which recommends its repeal.

[223] *The Listing Rules*, ch 16, app, contains the Exchange's *Model Code.*

Directors, when they are appointed, must disclose to their company details of their holdings of the company's securities and thereafter they must notify changes in their holdings.[224] The company must keep a register of interests that are notified to it.[225] Details of subscription options granted by the company to its directors and, where relevant, details in respect of the exercise of such options must also be recorded in this register.[226] The register is to be open for inspection by any member of the company without charge and by other persons on the payment of a fee.[227] Listed companies must pass on any notification which relates to listed securities to the exchange on which they are listed.[228]

Certain details of directors' interests in the company's securities and, where relevant, in the securities of other companies in its group must be stated in the directors' annual report.[229] This report must also contain certain information about share options that have been granted to directors or to members of their immediate family.[230] The remuneration report that listed companies are required to produce in addition to their annual statutory reports and accounts must also contain information relating to share options or other long-term incentive schemes.[231]

Loans to Directors

A detailed and complex series of provisions impose restrictions on companies making loans to, providing guarantees or security for, or entering into other types of credit arrangements with, directors.[232] In outline,[233] there is a basic prohibition on any company making a loan to any of its directors or to any director of its holding company, or guaranteeing or giving security in respect of a loan made to any such director.[234] This prohibition is then qualified by a number of exceptions which, amongst other matters, permit a company to make loans of small amounts (the present limit stands at £5,000)[235] and allow a company to provide funds to a director to pay expenses or to enable the proper performance of his duties as an officer of the company provided cer-

[224] Companies Act 1985, s 324. There are also disclosure obligations in respect of spouses' and children's holdings: Companies Act 1985, s 328. The disclosure obligation applies to shadow directors: Companies Act 1985, s 324 (6). The requirements in respect of disclosure are amplified by Companies Act 1985, sch 13.

For further discussion of these disclosure obligations and consideration of proposals for change see *Disclosure of Directors Shareholdings* (DTI Consultative Document) (1996) and *Company Directors: Regulating Conflicts of Interests and Formulating a Statement of Duties: A Joint Consultation Paper* (Law Commission Consultation Paper No 153; Scottish Law Commission Discussion Paper No 105) (1998) paras 5.6–5.39.

[225] Companies Act 1985, s 325.

[226] Ibid, s 325 (3) and (4).

[227] Ibid, sch 13, Pt IV, para 25.

[228] Ibid, s 329.

[229] Ibid, s 234 and sch 7, para 2A.

[230] Ibid, s 234 and sch 7, para 2B.

[231] *The Listing Rules,* ch 12, para 12.43 (c).

[232] This includes shadow directors: Companies Act 1985, s 330 (5).

[233] Considerably more detail can be found in *Company Directors: Regulating Conflicts of Interests and Formulating a Statement of Duties: A Joint Consultation Paper* (Law Commission Consultation Paper No 153; Scottish Law Commission Discussion Paper No 105) (1998) pt 6.

[234] Companies Act 1985, s 330 (2).

[235] Ibid, s 334.

tain conditions are satisfied.[236] In the case of 'relevant companies' (public companies, subsidiaries of public companies, parent companies of public companies and sister subsidiaries of public companies),[237] the prohibition is extended to cover other types of credit arrangements and to bring within its scope arrangements with persons connected with directors.[238] A transaction or arrangement in breach of the prohibition is voidable at the instance of the company.[239] Personal liability to account to the company for gains and to indemnify the company for loss is imposed on the director for whom the transaction or arrangement is made, on the directors who authorised it and, where relevant, on connected persons.[240] Also, directors of relevant companies who authorise or permit the company to enter into an arrangement or transaction in breach of the prohibition commit a criminal offence.[241]

Loans and other credit transactions involving directors which are not prohibited must be disclosed in annual accounts.[242]

UNAUTHORISED PROFITS AND CONFLICT OF DUTY AND INTEREST

As a fiduciary, a director must not must make a profit from his position unless this has been duly authorised by the company.[243] In simple cases, for example where a director receives remuneration which has not been properly authorised in accordance with the company's constitution[244] or accepts a secret commission or bribe from an outsider in return for an undertaking to persuade the company to act in a particular fashion,[245] it is not difficult to detect a breach but in less clear-cut circumstances it can be harder to determine whether the no-profit rule has been contravened.

Profit from 'Position'

A director is not permitted to exploit that position for personal advantage. It follows from this that an important issue is whether an opportunity for

[236] Ibid, s 337. The conditions are that the advance must be approved by the shareholders or be given subject to the proviso that if shareholder approval is not forthcoming at the next AGM it will then be repaid within six months: s 337 (3). Also, if the company is a relevant company (s 331 (6)) the aggregate maximum amount that can be provided under this heading is £20,000: s 337 (3).

[237] Companies Act 1985, s 331 (6).

[238] Ibid, s 330 (3)–(4). The definition of connected persons in Companies Act 1985, s 346 applies.

[239] Companies Act 1985, s 341.

[240] Ibid, s 341 (2)–(5).

[241] Ibid, s 342.

[242] Companies Act 1985, s 232 and sch 6, pt II. Note also sch 6, pt III (details of credit transactions, arrangements and agreements involving officers who are not directors to be disclosed in accounts). For special rules relating to banks and other financial institutions: Companies Act 1985, ss 343–344.

[243] *Regal (Hastings) Ltd v Gulliver* [1942] 1 All ER 378, [1967] 2 AC 134n, HL; *Parker v McKenna* (1874) LR 10 Ch 96; *Furs Ltd v Tomkies* (1936) 54 CLR 583, H Ct of Aust; '[E]very fiduciary is under a duty not to make a profit from his position (unless such profit is authorised)': *Henderson v Merrett Syndicates* [1995] 2 AC 145, HL, 206 *per* Lord Browne-Wilkinson.

[244] *Guinness plc v Saunders* [1990] 2 AC 663, HL.

[245] eg, *Boston Deep Sea Fishing v Ansell* (1883) 39 Ch 339, CA.

personal benefit that is presented to a director can be said to derive from the position held. In *Regal (Hastings) Ltd v Gulliver* Lord Russell of Killowen said that directors would be accountable for profits which were obtained by reason of the fact that they were directors and in the course of the execution of that office.[246] Although the inherent flexibility of fiduciary duties means that they cannot properly be reduced to simple maxims,[247] the formulation that a director will be liable to account for profits derived from opportunities or information which were obtained (i) by reason of his position, and (ii) in the course of performing his functions as a director[248] can suffice as a point of departure in this discussion.[249] This is, though, only a starting point: whether in a particular case there a liability to account for an unauthorised profit will depend on the facts of the case.[250] The factors that the court may scrutinise to determine whether a director has on the particular facts breached the no-profit rule will include the nature of the opportunity, its ripeness, its specificeness, the director's relation to it, the amount of information that the director has, the nature of that information and the circumstances in which it was obtained.[251]

Profit at the Expense of the Company?

It is not a defence to a claim that a director has made an unauthorised profit that the company itself could never have obtained the profit.[252] In *Industrial Development Consultants v Cooley*[253] the former managing director of a company was held liable to account to the company for profits derived from a contract which he had taken for his personal benefit notwithstanding that the evidence established that the other contracting party would not have given the contract to the company. In *Regal (Hastings) Ltd v Gulliver*[254] the directors were liable to account for profits made on their investment in shares even though the company's financial position had made it impossible for it to take up the investment opportunity. The position was summarised by Laskin J in *Canadian Aero Service Ltd v O'Malley*[255] in these terms:

246 [1967] 2 AC 134n, HL 143, Also 153 *per* Lord Macmillan and 154 *per* Lord Wright.

247 *Canadian Aero Services Ltd v O'Malley* (1973) 40 DLR (3d) 371, Can SC, 383, 390–1 *per* Laskin J; *New Zealand Netherlands Society 'Oranje' Inc v Kuys* [1973] 2 All ER 1222, PC, 1225 *per* Lord Wilberforce; *Boardman v Phipps* [1967] 2 AC 46, HL, 123 *per* Lord Upjohn.

248 Lord Russell's approach is echoed in other cases: eg *Boardman v Phipps* [1967] 2 AC 46, HL, 103 *per* Lord Cohen; *Swain v The Law Society* [1982] 1 WLR 17, CA, 37 *per* Oliver LJ. The decision of the Court of Appeal in *Swain* was reversed by the House of Lords but Lord Brightman approved Oliver LJ's approach: [1983] AC 598, HL, 619.

249 For criticism of Lord Russell's test as being too narrow to deal effectively with the problem of profit-taking by directors see Austin, RP, 'Fiduciary Accountability for Business Opportunities' in Finn. PD, *Equity and Commercial Relationships* (1987) 141, 150–2. An alternative formulation is that of Deane J in *Chan v Zacharia* (1983–84) 154 CLR 178, H Ct of Aust, 198–9.

250 *Boardman v Phipps* [1967] 2 AC 46 HL, 102–3 *per* Lord Cohen.

251 *Canadian Aero Services Ltd v O'Malley* (1973) 40 DLR 371, Can SC, 391 *per* Laskin J.

252 *Keech v Sandford* (1726) Sel Cas 61 is the leading case establishing this principle in relation to trustees.

253 [1972] 2 All ER 162.

254 [1942] 1 All ER 378, [1967] 2 AC 134n, HL. See also *Furs Ltd v Tomkies* (1936) 54 CLR 583, H Ct of Aust.

255 (1973) 40 DLR (3d) 371, C SC, 383–4 *per* Laskin J.

The reaping of a profit by a person at a company's expense while a director thereof is, of course, an adequate ground upon which to hold the director accountable. Yet there may be situations where a profit must be disgorged, although not gained at the expense of the company, on the ground that a director must not be allowed to use his position as such to make a profit even if it was not open to the company, as for example, by reason of legal disability, to participate in the transaction.

The structure of the chapter, up to this point, has been to consider the no-profit rule under the wider principle of avoidance of conflict of interest. Here it is appropriate to question this taxonomy of the no-profit rule: if the company cannot pursue the matter itself, can it really be said that there is a conflict between the director's personal interest and the interests of the company; or, is the no-profit rule truly an independent prophylactic rule which does not require an element of conflict? Inherent in this is a further issue with regard to the strictness of any requirement for a conflict of interests: will any risk of conflict suffice or must there be a serious risk? Looking at the authorities, it is possible to find variations in approach with regard to these matters and it is important to remember that fiduciary principles based on loyalty are inherently flexible, with the consequence that the factual circumstances can affect the severity with which they are applied in any particular case.

Thus whilst some judges treat the no-profit rule as being a sub-category of the no-conflict rule,[256] others regard no-profit and no-conflict as separate, but overlapping, rules.[257] The seriousness of any conflict is clearly irrelevant to the second approach but it is central to the first. In *Boardman v Phipps*,[258] in a dissenting speech, Lord Upjohn said that there had to be 'a real sensible possibility of conflict; not that you could imagine some situation arising which might, in some conceivable possibility in events not contemplated as real sensible possibilities by any reasonable person, result in a conflict.' Despite the fact that his was a dissenting judgment,[259] Lord Upjohn's words have been influential in later cases.[260] The 'real sensible possibility of conflict' test was applied by the Privy Council in *Queensland Mines Ltd v Hudson*[261] where it was held that a director was not liable to account for a profit made in respect of an opportunity which he had exploited personally. This was so

[256] eg, *Bray v Ford* [1896] AC 44, HL, 51 *per* Lord Herschell; *Boardman v Phipps* [1967] 2 AC 46, HL, 123 *per* Lord Upjohn.

[257] eg, *Chan v Zacharia* (1983–84) 154 CLR 178, H Ct of Aust, 198–9 *per* Deane J. See further Oakley, AJ, *Constructive Trusts* (3rd edn, 1997) 111–12, 162–79; Beck, SM, 'Corporate Opportunity Revisited' in Ziegel, JS, *Studies in Canadian Company Law* (1973) 193, 204.

[258] [1967] 2 AC 46, HL, 124 *per* Lord Upjohn. See also *Boulting v ACTAT* [1963] 2 QB 606, CA, 636 where, as Upjohn LJ, he expressed a similar view on the need for a real, as opposed to theoretical or rhetorical, conflict.

[259] In *Industrial Development Consultants Ltd v Cooley* [1972] 2 All ER 162, 171–3 Roskill J quoted extensively from Lord Upjohn's judgment commenting that: 'I do not, however, detect any difference in principle between the speeches of their five Lordships but merely a difference in the application of the facts to principles which were not in dispute.'

[260] The Law Commission has adopted the 'real sensible possibility of conflict' requirement: *Fiduciary Duties and Regulatory Rules* (Law Commission Report No 236) (1995) para 1.4.

[261] (1978) 52 ALJR 399, PC. Australian case law is now generally in support of the requirement for a real rather than a theoretical risk of conflict: *Consul Development Pty Ltd v DPR Estates Pty Ltd* (1975) 132 CLR 373, H Ct of Aust, 399 *per* Gibbs J; *Chan v Zacharia* (1983–84) 154 CLR 178, H Ct of Aust, 198–9 *per* Deane J.

despite the fact that in the early stages he had been acting for the company in seeking to secure the opportunity but the company had been unable to pursue it because of financial difficulties. There are strong factual similarities between this case and the decision of the House of Lords in the *Regal* case. One way of reconciling the decisions is to say that the profit in the *Queensland* case, unlike that in *Regal*, was an authorised profit because the appropriate disclosure had been made and consent obtained. The procedural requirements for authorising the making of a profit by a corporate fiduciary are considered later in this chapter.[262] Yet notwithstanding that a close examination of the facts of the two cases can produce a point of distinction based on disclosure and consent, it would seem that in substance the decisions in *Regal* and *Queensland* represent strikingly different approaches to the application of fiduciary duty. *Regal* is the apotheosis of the application of a strict no-profit rule which is not dependent on a conflict requirement or which treats any possibility of conflict as sufficient (in cases of profiting from position this comes to much the same thing as an independent no-profit rule since there is always a possibility of some conflict of interest in a situation where a director has acted for personal rather than corporate benefit). *Queensland* demonstrates the application of the no-profit rule as an aspect of the wider principle of conflict of interests and shows the court engaging upon a close examination of the facts to determine whether there was a real conflict.

The factual circumstances[263] have weighed heavily in more recent English decisions involving allegations that directors have wrongfully profited from position. In three decisions involving directors who left their original company to engage in business personally or on behalf of another employer, the courts shied away from the extremes of a harsh application of the no-profit rule.[264] An important underlying consideration in this type of situation is that fiduciary duties should not be drawn so tightly that they in effect tie a director to one company and prevent him from ever taking the skill and general knowledge that he acquired in that position elsewhere. These decisions contrast with the very different circumstances of *Guinness v Saunders*:[265] here a director was paid an extraordinary fee of £5.2 million for his services in connection with a takeover bid mounted by the company, but that payment had not been properly authorised in accordance with the company's constitution; the director was ordered to repay the fee and, with the House of Lords emphasising the strictness of the no-profit rule, was given no allowance for the work that he had done on the company's behalf. This decision was arrived at against the background of factual circumstances involving an attempt to extradite back to

[262] See this chapter below, at 195–7.

[263] Others have also argued that decisions about the fiduciary duties applicable to directors can only properly be understood by taking a strongly contextual approach: Rider, BAK, 'Amiable Lunatics and the Rule in *Foss v Harbottle*' [1978] CLJ 279; Editorial Comment, 'There and Back Again!' (1998) 19 Co Law 97.

[264] *Island Export Finance Ltd v Umunna* [1986] BCLC 460; *Balston Ltd v Headline Filters Ltd* [1990] FSR 385; *Framlington Group plc v Anderson* [1995] BCC 611.

[265] [1990] 2 AC 663. McCormack, G, 'The Guinness Saga: In Tom We Trust' (1991) 12 Co Law 90; Hopkins, J, 'Fiduciary Duty: Receipt of Company's Property by Director: Equitable Allowance to Fiduciary' [1990] CLJ 220.

the UK the director who had received the fee in order to stand trial on a number of criminal charges arising out of the conduct of the bid.[266]

Whilst there is no closed list of circumstances that are relevant to the application of fiduciary duties, there are certain events or situations which lead to particular concerns with regard to the no-profit rule and company directors. Cases of directors profiting otherwise than at the expense of their company have been considered already. Other situations which raise similar issues include the following.

Opportunity Declined by the Management

This was precisely the factual situation in *Regal (Hastings) Ltd v Gulliver* and, on the basis of that decision, it would seem that this is a situation where the no-profit rule will be strictly applied in relation to directors: despite the fact that there is no longer any real possibility of conflict, the director has become acquainted with the opportunity by virtue of the position held and so must not profit from it unless this is authorised by the company. This case is, however, to be contrasted with the Privy Council decision in the *Queensland* case and also with the decision of the Canadian Supreme Court in *Peso Silver Mines v Cropper*,[267] where it was held that an individual director was not in breach of the no-profit rule when he exploited personally an opportunity that had been offered to the company but rejected by the board. The court reached that conclusion by taking a narrow view of the question whether the director's profit was derived from his position,[268] but it adopted[269] as a general statement of the applicable principle that a director would not be liable to account for profits made in respect of an opportunity that had been offered to the company, but which its board had decided, in accordance with their fiduciary duties of good faith and proper purpose, not to pursue.

Although not stated expressly in the judgment, the decision in *Peso* is consistent with authorities which place the no-profit rule under the umbrella of the no-conflict rule: where the conflict disappears because of the board's bona fide rejection of an opportunity, the director is then free to pursue personal interests and to use the general knowledge or information about the opportunity that he has acquired through the position in doing so. Whether that approach is preferable to the stricter standards represented by the decision of the House of Lords in *Regal* is an issue that has been much debated. The perceived problem with the approach in *Peso* is that it rests on being satisfied that the board's rejection of the opportunity was a decision made in accordance with their fiduciary duties, principally that it was made in good faith in the interests of the company.[270] The broadly subjective nature of the good-faith duty makes it difficult for the court to test, and thus there is risk

266 Goff, R, and Jones, G, *The Law of Restitution* (5th edn, 1998) 737.

267 (1966) 58 DLR (2d) 1, Can SC.

268 (1966) 58 DLR (2d) 1 Can SC, 8.

269 From the speech of Lord Greene MR in the Court of Appeal in the *Regal* case 15 Feb 1941, CA.

270 Beck, SM, 'Corporate Opportunity Revisited' in Ziegel, JS (ed), *Studies in Canadian Company Law* (1973) 193, 218–19; 231–2; Prentice, DD, '*Regal (Hastings) Ltd v Gulliver*—The Canadian Experience' (1967) 30 MLR 450.

under the *Peso* approach that situations which are in reality contrary to the fundamental duty of loyalty that is expected of directors—for example where the board have declined the opportunity either under pressure from a dominant individual director who wishes to secure it personally, or on an understanding of mutual 'backscratching'—will go unremedied. *Regal (Hastings) Ltd v Gulliver* avoids this. On the other hand, the consequence of applying *Regal* is to achieve the rather surprising result that a company can, through its board, reject an opportunity and then at a later point reap the benefits of it by pursuing the director for personal profit that has been made from it. This can be viewed as being an unfair windfall to the company which is gained at the expense of directors who, looked at sensibly and realistically, have not been disloyal to their company.[271]

Regal (Hastings) Ltd v Gulliver represents English law, and in a case with the same facts a lower court would be obliged to follow it. The elasticity of fiduciary duties and the contextual considerations that are relevant to their application may allow for the decision to be distinguished and confined, but for an honest and careful director who wants to pursue personally an opportunity in which the company had an interest, the chance that the court may take a more favourable view of the situation than the House of Lords did in *Regal* does not provide much comfort. For the prudent director, the focus should properly shift to the procedural steps that must be taken to ensure that whatever personal profit is made from the circumstances is properly authorised. These are discussed later in this chapter[272] but it is appropriate here to mention that articles of association typically bring the situation closer[273] to that achieved in *Peso* than the stricter *Regal* approach in that they allow directors to profit from opportunities in which the company had an interest where this is sanctioned by the board. Evidently, the concerns about placing undue reliance on the good faith of the board in these matters have not weighed as heavily with participants in companies as they have with the English courts.

Resigning to Pursue an Opportunity

Although the formula for testing the connection between the position and the profit that was put forward by Lord Russell in *Regal (Hastings) Ltd v Gulliver* might appear to suggest that there has to be temporal link between the holding of the directorship and the obtaining of the opportunity for profit,[274] in appropriate cases the courts have not hesitated to hold a former director liable for breach of the no-profit rule. Where a director resigns to take up personally an opportunity that the company was actively pursuing, the fact of the

[271] Jones, G, 'Unjust Enrichment and the Fiduciary's Duty of Loyalty' (1968) 84 LQR 472; Goff, R, and Jones, G, *The Law of Restitution* (5th edn, 1998) ch 33.

[272] See this chapter below, at 195–7.

[273] The situation achieved by articles such as Table A, art 85 is not quite that in *Peso*. The implication of the Canadian decision is that once the board rejects the opportunity, an individual director is then free to take it up without any further disclosure to the board. Table A, art 85 requires disclosure to the board and its consent.

[274] Austin, RP, 'Fiduciary Accountability for Business Opportunities' in Finn, PD (ed), *Equity and Commercial Relationships* (1987) 141, 180–2.

resignation will not prevent that person from being held accountable to his former company.[275] However, people do move jobs, give up being employed in favour of setting up in business for themselves and buy parts of businesses from their former employers to run them personally (management buyouts) all for perfectly legitimate reasons. The no-profit rule needs to be applied sensitively to distinguish between situations where people take with them and use the general knowledge, skill and experience that they have built up from their previous employment, and cases where people unfairly exploit the trust that was vested in them by their previous employers. There is an obvious potential here for overlapping claims based on breach of fiduciary duty, breach of confidence[276] and breach of contractual restrictive covenants.[277] Similar issues can arise under all three headings with regard to setting the boundary lines between permissible protection for former employers in respect of their trade secrets and other confidential information and measures which are anti-competitive and in restraint of trade.

The decision of the Canadian Supreme Court in *Canadian Aero Services Ltd v O'Malley*[278] is an important case on the application of fiduciary duties to resigning directors or senior officers. The court held that fiduciary duties could survive resignation and then used the concept of a 'maturing business opportunity'[279] as the basis for drawing a boundary between permissible and impermissible conduct: a resigning director would be in breach of duty to the former company where the resignation might fairly be said to have been prompted or influenced by the wish to usurp or to divert to an associated third party a maturing business opportunity that the company was actively pursuing. This was followed in *Island Export Finance Ltd v Umunna*[280] where the absence of a maturing business opportunity being actively pursued by the company at the time of resignation led the court to conclude that the former managing director of a company was not in breach of duty. The circumstances were that, after resignation, the former managing director secured a contract that was in the same line of business as a contract that had previously been held by the company. It was accepted on the evidence that the managing director's resignation had been prompted by dissatisfaction with his former company and not by a desire to usurp opportunities for himself. Also at the time of his resignation the company had not been seeking further or repeat orders.

In the *Island Exports* decision Hutchinson J explained the problems inherent in drawing the line in these situations in the following terms.[281]

Directors, no less than employees, acquire a general fund of knowledge and expertise in the course of their work, and it is plainly in the public interest that they should be

[275] eg, *Industrial Development Consultants v Cooley* [1972] 2 All ER 162.

[276] Goff, R, and Jones, G, *The Law of Restitution* (5th edn, 1998) ch 34; Burrows, A, and McKendrick, E, *Cases and Materials on the Law of Restitution* (1997) 649–61.

[277] Deakin, S, and Morris, GS, *Labour Law* (2nd edn, 1998) 338–42.

[278] (1973) 40 DLR (3d) 371, Can SC.

[279] Following US cases on the corporate opportunity doctrine.

[280] [1986] BCLC 460. See also *Balston Ltd v Headline Filters Ltd* [1990] FSR 385; *Framlington Group plc v Anderson* [1995] BCC 611.

[281] [1986] BCLC 460, 482.

free to exploit it in a new position. It is one thing to hold them accountable when, in the graphic words of Laskin J (at 391), 'they entered the lists in the heat of the maturation of the project, known to them to be under active Government consideration when they resigned from Canaero and when they proposed to bid on behalf of Terra'; but it is an altogether different thing to hold former directors accountable whenever they exploit for their own or a new employer's benefit information which, while they may have come by it solely because of their position as directors of the plaintiff company, in truth forms part of their general fund of knowledge and their stock-in-trade.

Competing with the Company

The principles that restrict directors from resigning in order to exploit opportunities that might fairly be regarded as belonging to their companies, also operate so as prevent directors from exploiting corporate opportunities and information whilst they are still in office.[282] There is no absolute rule prohibiting directors from holding multiple directorships or even from engaging in business that competes with the company,[283] but there is a tension which results from this tolerance on the one hand and the no-profit rule on the other.[284] Over and above fiduciary obligation, companies may by contract restrict their directors and employees from engaging in competing activity during the period of employment or office.[285] Equally, it may be possible for a director or senior officer who is involved with more than one company or business to limit the fiduciary obligations that would otherwise be expected by agreement with the companies or businesses involved.[286]

Opportunities Offered to a Director Otherwise than in that Capacity which might be of Interest to the Company

This is the situation where a director, acting in a personal capacity (or on behalf of someone other than the company), becomes aware of an opportunity which, if it knew about it, the company might wish to pursue. Does the director have to inform the company about this opportunity or can he simply regard it as falling outside his duty of loyalty and pursue it personally?[287] It

[282] *Green v Bestobell Industries Pty Ltd* [1982] WAR 1, WA FC; *Mordecai v Mordecai* (1987–88) 12 ACLR 751, NSW CA.

[283] *London & Mashonaland Explorations Co Ltd v New Mashonaland Exploration Co Ltd* [1891] WN 165; *Bell v Lever Bros Ltd* [1932] AC 161 HL; *Berlei Hestia (NZ) Ltd v Fernyhough* [1980] 2 NZLR 150, NZ SC. Christie, M, 'The Director's Fiduciary Duty Not to Compete' (1992) 55 MLR 506 criticises these cases and argues that directors should not be allowed to participate in competing activities.

[284] Strict application of the no-conflict rule in the circumstances discussed under the next heading (ie director acquires information otherwise than in the capacity as director but which is of interest to the company) would also lead to difficult problems in relation to multiple directorships: Prentice, DD, 'Directors' Fiduciary Duties—The Corporate Opportunity' (1972) 50 Canadian Bar Review 623, 633–5.

[285] *Hivac Ltd v Park Royal Scientific Instruments Ltd* [1946] Ch 169, CA.

[286] Based on *Kelly v Cooper* [1993] AC 205, PC. See generally *Fiduciary Duties and Regulatory Rules* (Law Commission Report No 236) (1995). Modification of fiduciary obligation in the corporate context is subject to Companies Act 1985, s 310.

[287] In theory, it could equally be asked whether a director could be liable to compensate the company for losing out on an opportunity in circumstances where the director neither discloses

cannot plausibly be argued that a director would breach the no-profit rule if he acted for himself in this situation since the opportunity had nothing to do with the position held. The issue here is where the no-conflict rule would catch the director. Existing English case law does not appear to go quite that far, although *Industrial Development Consultants v Cooley*[288] comes very close.[289] The facts of the case are consistent with the classification of this case as one where the director made an unauthorised profit from his position but the analysis in the judgment was that the director was in breach of duty because he had failed to pass on information which had come to him personally but which was of concern to the company. Whilst it is possible to conceive of circumstances where the nature of the information acquired is so important or sensitive to the company's operations that it should in fairness be disclosed, as a general rule it would seem to be taking the requirement of loyalty too far to suggest that directors are obliged to confess everything that they hear of, otherwise than in their capacity as such, which might be of interest to the company. Unduly rigorous application of the no-conflict rule in this way could make it difficult for a person to be a director of more than one company unless the businesses were wholly unrelated and that could impact unhelpfully on corporate governance mechanisms which rely on experienced and knowledgeable persons (such as persons who have experience of holding directorships) acting as non-executive directors. Also, such a harsh rule would have cost implications since directors would expect to receive remuneration packages that compensated them appropriately for totally sacrificing their personal interests in all circumstances in favour of those of the company.[290]

Authorised Profits

A director may profit from position where this is authorised by the company. Unless alternative provision is made in the company's articles,[291] it is for the shareholders to decide whether, or to what extent, directors should be allowed

to the company nor takes it up personally, but it would in practice be difficult to identify a link between a director and lost opportunities.

[288] [1972] 2 All ER 162. See Klein, WA, and Coffee, JC, *Business Organization and Finance*, (5th edn, 1993) 166–7 discussing the 'corporate opportunity' doctrine developed by the US courts which, in some versions, does require a director to tell the company about opportunities which are offered to him or her in a personal capacity where those opportunities are sufficiently closely related to the company's existing line of business. Clark, RC, *Corporate Law* (1986) ch 7 provides a more detailed analysis. On the potential for the application of principles developed by the US courts in Anglo-Australian law: Glover, J, *Commercial Equity. Fiduciary Relationships* (1995) 127–34; Bean, GMD, 'Corporate Governance and Corporate Opportunities' (1994) 15 Co Law 266.

[289] Finn, PD, *Fiduciary Obligations* (1977) 240–1; Prentice, DD, 'Directors' Fiduciary Duties—The Corporate Opportunity' (1972) 50 Canadian Bar Review 623, 626–7.

[290] Contrast Beck, SM, 'Corporate Opportunity Revisited' in Ziegel, JS (ed), *Studies in Canadian Company Law* (1973) 193, 224–5 and Austin, RP, 'Fiduciary Accountability for Business Opportunities' in Finn, PD (ed), *Equity and Commercial Relationships* (1987) 141, 147–8. Bishop, W, and Prentice, DD, 'Some Legal and Economic Aspects of Fiduciary Remuneration' (1983) 46 MLR 289, 297 provide a worked example of how a liberal incidental profits rule could lower the price of services provided by fiduciaries. But the authors argue for the maintenance of a strict rule in relation to directors: 303–4.

[291] eg, *Imperial Mercantile Credit Association v Coleman* (1871) 6 Ch App 558, CA.

to profit from position.[292] An ordinary resolution passed at a duly convened general meeting or unanimous consent informally obtained will suffice for this purpose.[293] It is common for articles of association to contain a variety of provisions permitting directors to profit from position in specified circumstances. For example, Table A, art 84 vests in the board of directors the power to appoint executive directors and to fix their remuneration. Under Table A, art 85, directors are permitted to have interests in transactions or arrangements in which the company has an interest provided the nature and extent of material interests have been disclosed to the board. This would cover at least some of the *Regal* type cases where directors exploit personally opportunities in which the company has an interest. As a general rule, directors must refrain from participating in the vote by the board (or, where permissible, a committee of the board) on any matter in which they have a personal interest.[294]

There are two notable issues in relation to such provisions in articles. The first, which is considered here, is the approach to the interpretation of such provisions. The second issue, which will be considered after discussion of the duties of directors with regard to their stewardship of the company's property, is how far articles can validly modify the fiduciary requirements imposed by the general law with respect to the no-profit rule, the no-conflict rule and stewardship obligations.[295]

It is evident from the decision of the House of Lords in *Guinness plc v Saunders*[296] that articles which permit directors to profit from their position will be interpreted very strictly and that, if a payment is to stand, there must be precise compliance with any conditions specified in the articles. In that case the director could not claim that the payment to him was properly authorised under an article which permitted the board to pay special remuneration in circumstances where a committee of the board had sanctioned the payment. Although the articles provided for delegation of powers by the board to committees, their Lordships held that this could not have been intended to apply to the power to fix remuneration which was vested in the board alone. This decision does not entirely rule out the possibility of power to fix remuneration being delegated to a committee but makes it clear that this must be specifically provided for. It is important for public companies for which market expectations about good corporate governance standards are relevant to make adequate provision for delegation with respect to the fixing of remuneration, because an important element of the framework of market regulation is that companies should have remuneration committees comprised of non-

[292] *Regal (Hastings) Ltd v Gulliver* [1942] 1 All ER 378, [1967] 2 AC 134n, HL; *Furs Ltd v Tomkies* (1936) 54 CLR 583, H Ct of Aust. This follows from the principle that the company is entitled to the unbiased advice of all of its directors with the consequence that a personal interest held by any of them disables the board from making decisions on its behalf.

[293] *Queensland Mines Ltd v Hudson* (1978) 52 ALJR 399, PC can be viewed as a case where there was in fact unanimous informal consent from the shareholders. See also *Furs Ltd v Tomkies* (1936) 54 CLR 583, H Ct of Aust, 592 *per* Rich, Dixon and Evatt JJ; *Hurley v BGH Nominees Pty Ltd* (1984) 37 SASR 499, SA SC.

[294] Table A, art 94. This article states a number of exceptions to the general rule.

[295] See this chapter below, at 198–9.

[296] [1990] 2 AC 663, HL.

executive directors whose function it is to determine the remuneration of executive directors.[297]

Authorisation for Senior Managers who are not Directors

The board of directors can authorise senior managers who are not directors but who are subject to fiduciary duties of loyalty to profit from position.[298] The board is the appropriate organ to give consent on behalf of the company because this is a managerial decision and the directors are not disabled from acting because of a conflict of interest held by any one of them.

STEWARDSHIP OF THE COMPANY'S PROPERTY

It is in relation to the company's property that the analogy between directors and trustees is at its closest.[299] Responsible directors are liable to make good misapplications of the company's property.[300] Misapplications can arise from a variety of circumstances, including: dispositions of property for purposes which are contrary to the Companies Act 1985 (eg, unlawful dividends or unlawful financial assistance); payments which are not authorised by the company's constitution; and disposals made in breach of the duty to act in good faith in the interests of the company. As well as the obligation to make good the company's losses which falls upon all of the responsible directors, where a director usurps for himself property that belongs to the company, he can be regarded as holding the property on trust for the company: *Cook v Deeks*.[301] In this case three of the four directors of a company diverted to themselves an opportunity that had been originally offered to the company. The Privy Council held that the directors were in breach of their duty to the company and that they held the benefit of the contract on trust for the company.

This account of the facts in *Cooks v Deeks* demonstrates that there can be a very significant overlap between cases which are decided on the basis that the directors have misappropriated corporate property and cases which are reasoned on the basis of unauthorised profiting from position. Where an opportunity, or information about it, is regarded as the company's property, a director who exploits it to his own advantage may be held to hold the profits that result from it on trust for the company; equally the same circumstances can be viewed as unauthorised profiting from position for which the director is liable to account to the company. Whether a case is decided on the basis of the no-profit rule or as a misappropriation of property may sometimes come

[297] Griffiths, A, 'Directors' Remuneration: Constraining the Power of the Board' [1995] LMCLQ 372, 375–6.

[298] In *Regal (Hastings) Ltd v Gulliver* [1942] 1 All ER 378, [1967] 2 AC 134n, HL the company's solicitor joined the directors in investing in the shares that the company was unable to acquire personally. It was held that the solicitor had been effectively released from his fiduciary duties to the company because he acted with the informed consent of the board.

[299] *Selangor United Rubber Estates Ltd v Cradock (No 3)* [1968] 2 All ER 1073, 1092–5.

[300] *Re Lands Allotment Co* [1894] 1 Ch 616, CA, 631 *per* Lindley LJ; *Re Sharpe* [1892] 1 Ch 154, CA, 165–6 *per* Lindley LJ; *Bishopsgate Investment Management Ltd v Maxwell (No 2)* [1994] 1 All ER 261, CA; *Re Duckwari plc* [1998] 3 WLR 913, CA.

[301] [1916] 1 AC 554, PC.

down simply to the decision of counsel as to the best way of pleading and arguing the case before the court.[302] In particular circumstances, however, it can become important to determine whether the company can bring a proprietary claim or is confined to claiming that the directors have made a personal profit for which they must account to the company. A proprietary claim is preferable to a personal claim for an account of profits where the defendant is insolvent because proprietary claims rank ahead of personal claims in bankruptcy or liquidation. A proprietary claim enables the claimant to take property which has been acquired with the original profit and any further profits which have been generated by it, whereas a personal claim, as presently recognised,[303] does not. A further advantage of a proprietary base to a claim is that this may allow the plaintiff to follow the property into the hands of third parties.[304]

THE DISTINCTION BETWEEN WRONGFUL PROFITING AND MISAPPROPRIATION OF PROPERTY AND THE COMPANIES ACT 1985, S 310

It is conventional for company lawyers to use the distinction between misappropriation of property and wrongful profiting from position to attempt to explain some of the mysteries surrounding authorisation and ratification. With regard to authorisation, it is common for articles of association to contain a provision allowing a director to profit from position on the basis of disclosure to and consent from the board. Although this derogates from the requirement imposed by the general law for disclosure to, and consent from, the shareholders, it is said that this is not rendered void by the Companies Act 1985, s 310, which precludes companies from modifying duties imposed by the general law, because the no-profit rule is a disability rather than a duty. In this respect, goes the argument, it differs from the rule preventing directors from taking for themselves the company's property, which is certainly to be classified as a duty. Similar arguments are used in relation to ratification: that it is permissible for the company to ratify unauthorised profit-taking but that misappropriation of corporate property is an unratifiable wrong. All such arguments have always had a feel of being *ex post facto* rationalisations of how the law has developed rather than being defining principles. In other words, since Table A, art 85 permits directors to profit from position, there must be

[302] Sealy, LS, *Cases and Materials in Company Law* (6th edn, 1996) 296–8. See also *Shareholder Remedies: A Consultation Paper* (Law Commission Consultation Paper No 142) (1996) paras 5.2–5.17.

[303] Claiming property which had been purchased with bribe money received by a fiduciary in breach of duty was the issue in *Attorney General for Hong Kong v Reid* [1994] 1 AC 324, PC. It has been suggested that the Privy Council could have avoided arriving at the decision that the plaintiff did have a proprietary claim in these circumstances by instead holding that the plaintiff's remedy was a personal one but that it was not limited to the amount of the original bribe and could extend to profits earned directly or indirectly from it: see, eg, Nolan, R, 'The Wages of Sin: Iniquity in Equity following *A-G for Hong Kong v Reid*' (1994) 15 Co Law 3, 7. See also Burrows, A, *The Law of Restitution* (1993) 412; Birks, P, *An Introduction to the Law of Restitution* (1985) 387–9; Goode, RM, 'Ownership and Obligation in Transactions' (1987) 103 LQR 433, 441–5.

[304] Oakley, AJ, *Constructive Trusts* (3rd edn, 1997) 12–13.

some way of reconciling it with Companies Act 1985, s 310 so as to avoid a conflict between a statutory instrument and a statute: the profit/disability and property/duty distinction can perform that function. Equally, the profit and property distinction offers a means of reconciling cases like *Cook v Deeks*,[305] where it was said that the wrongdoing was unratifiable, and *Regal (Hastings) Ltd v Gulliver*[306] where it was stated that the wrongdoing was ratifiable. The factual similarities between such cases always made that distinction rather difficult to accept. It requires reassessment in the light of developments with regard to the remedies available for breach of the no-profit rule.

REMEDIES: PROFITING FROM POSITION/MISAPPROPRIATING COMPANY PROPERTY

This is not the place for a detailed analysis of the remedies available for breach of fiduciary duties.[307] For the reasons mentioned in the previous paragraph the issue that is most relevant for company lawyers is when a proprietary remedy can be sought against a director who has profited from position in breach of his duty to the company. Certainly, such a remedy will lie where the director's profitmaking involved misappropriation of company property: the director has wrongfully taken the company's property and, so, is rightly held liable to return it. But where there is no discernible misappropriation of company property, is the company limited to seeking a personal account of profits from the director or can it look for a proprietary remedy notwithstanding the absence of an original proprietary base (ie loss of its property)?

This is a question which has divided commentators.[308] The insolvency implications of widening the availability of proprietary remedies to situations which do not have a proprietary base figure prominently in the debate: some argue that it is unfair to the general body of creditors, and contrary to the general principle of *pari passu* distribution in insolvency,[309] for the court to treat creditors who can link their claim to breach of fiduciary duty more favourably than other categories of creditor; others argue that the general body of creditors of an insolvent fiduciary should not benefit from the *pari passu* distribution of property that the fiduciary should never have obtained in the first place.[310]

At varying times, and without necessarily expressly acknowledging the

[305] [1916] AC 554, PC.

[306] [1942] 1 All ER 378, HL.

[307] See Oakley, AJ, *Constructive Trusts* (3rd edn, 1997) 114–24.

[308] The large amount of literature on this topic includes the following: Birks, P, 'Personal Restitution in Equity' [1988] LMCLQ 128; Birks, P, 'Obligations and Property in Equity: *Lister v Stubbs* in the Limelight' [1993] LMCLQ 30, 33; Goode, RM, 'Property and Unjust Enrichment' in Burrows, AS (ed), *Essays on the Law of Restitution* (1991) 215; Goode, RM, 'The Recovery of a Director's Improper Gains: Proprietary Remedies for the Infringement of Non-Proprietary Rights' in McKendrick, E, *Commercial Aspects of Trusts and Fiduciary Relationships* (1992) 137; Sir Peter Millett, 'Bribes and Secret Commissions' [1993] RLR 7; Burrows, A, *The Law of Restitution* (1993) 409–14.

[309] This is amongst the principles enumerated by Goode as justifying protection of creditors: Goode, RM, 'Property and Unjust Enrichment' in Burrows, AS (ed), *Essays on the Law of Restitution* (1991) 215, 240–1.

[310] Sir Peter Millett, 'Bribes and Secret Commissions' [1993] RLR 7, 17.

underlying policy considerations,[311] the courts seem to have adopted three different approaches to this issue in cases involving trustees and other fiduciaries including directors. The first limits the availability of proprietary remedies to circumstances where the fiduciary has misappropriated the beneficiary's property but expands the concept of property to enable it to include 'soft' assets, such as corporate opportunities or information. *Cook v Deeks*[312] is a case where an expectancy, that is an opportunity not yet secured, was regarded as the property of the company, whilst in *Boardman v Phipps*[313] the characterisation of information as property of a trust was an important factor in the speeches of some of their Lordships concerning the liability of trustees who had used that information for their own personal advantage. There is an inherent artificiality in treating opportunities or information as property, and attempts to do so can trigger a jurisprudentially complex inquiry which is ultimately unsatisfactory[314] and can leave a residual impression that the court has somehow manufactured property in order to grant a proprietary remedy. The characterisation of soft assets as property has been widely criticised[315] and currently has few supporters.[316]

The second approach is that of the Privy Council in *Attorney General for Hong Kong v Reid*.[317] This case concerned a fiduciary who had wrongfully accepted bribes. According to the English case of *Lister v Stubbs*[318] the beneficiary's remedy in these circumstances was to require the fiduciary to account personally for the amount of the bribe. *Lister v Stubbs* had supporters amongst those commentators who favoured a restrictive approach to the availability of proprietary remedies: as a general rule,[319] where the fiduciary made a wrongful profit from position but did not misuse the company's property in doing so

[311] Birks, P, 'Obligations and Property in Equity: *Lister v Stubbs* in the Limelight' [1993] LMCLQ 30, 33.

[312] [1916] AC 554, PC.

[313] [1967] 2 AC 46, HL.

[314] Lord Hodson (at 107) and Lord Guest (at 115) held that the information was trust property, Lord Cohen (at 102) that it was not property in the strict sense of the word, Lord Upjohn (at 127–8 dissenting) that it was not in any normal sense property. The differing approaches in the judgments gives the case an opacity which leaves room for disagreement whether it was decided that the trustees were personally liable to account or that they held the property acquired in breach of fiduciary obligation on trust for the beneficiaries: compare Birks, P, 'Personal Restitution in Equity' [1988] LMCLQ 128, 133 and Goff, R, and Jones, G, *The Law of Restitution* (5th edn, 1998) 735. Later cases have not brought any greater certainty to the question when information can be regarded as property: contrast, eg, *Oxford v Moss* (1978) 68 Cr App R 183 and *Nanus Asia Co Inc v Standard Chartered Bank* [1990] 1 HKLR 396, HK HC; *Satnam Investments Ltd v Dunlop, Heyward & Co Ltd* [1998] NPC 169 CA.

[315] eg, Goode, RM, 'Property and Unjust Enrichment' in Burrows, AS (ed), *Essays on the Law of Restitution* (1991) 215, 227–9; Austin, RP, 'Fiduciary Accountability for Business Opportunities' in Finn, PD (ed), *Equity and Commercial Relationships* (1987) 141, 144–6; Jones, G, 'Unjust Enrichment and the Fiduciary's Duty of Loyalty' (1968) 84 LQR 475, 484–5; Finn, PD, *Fiduciary Obligations* (1977) 131–2.

[316] Sir Peter Millett, 'Equity's Place in the Law of Commerce' (1998) 114 LQR 214, 221–2.

[317] [1994] 1 AC 324, PC.

[318] (1890) 45 Ch D 1, CA.

[319] Note Goode, RM, 'Property and Unjust Enrichment' in Burrows, AS (ed), *Essays on the Law of Restitution* (1991) 215 and Goode, RM, 'The Recovery of a Director's Improper Gains: Proprietary Remedies for Infringement of Non-Proprietary Rights' in McKendrick, E (ed), *Commercial Aspects of Trusts and Fiduciary Obligations* (1992) 437 who argues for the possibility of a remedial constructive trust where a director undertakes an activity which, if he does it at all, he should do for the benefit of the company. This is how he would deal with *Cook v Deeks* [1916] AC 554, PC.

(ie covering, but not limited to, bribes), the beneficiary should only have a personal remedy. Those who argued for a greater role for proprietary remedies opposed it. In the event the Privy Council, led by Lord Templeman, departed from *Lister v Stubbs* and held that the fiduciary held the fruits of his wrongful conduct (ie property which had been acquired with bribe money) on trust for the beneficiary. Lord Templeman invoked the principle that 'equity regards as done that which ought to be done' to reach this conclusion: the fiduciary was under a personal liability to account and therefore equity would regard the fiduciary as holding the bribe on trust for the beneficiary.

Although the Privy Council may have reached a satisfactory decision on the facts, this reasoning is open to criticism.[320] One problem with it is its apparent rigidity: it seems that, on the basis of *Attorney General for Hong Kong v Reid*,[321] a proprietary remedy will lie in every case where a fiduciary has made a wrongful profit from position without any scope for the court to examine the appropriateness of that remedy in the circumstances.[322] If *Attorney General for Hong Kong v Reid* is followed by the English courts, this will erode still further the insolvency principle of *pari passu* distribution which is already undermined by other devices, such as security interests and retention of title agreements, whereby certain creditors of an insolvent can obtain priority over the general body of creditors.

The third approach lies in the nascent doctrine in English law of the 'remedial constructive trust'. The remedial constructive trust is a proprietary remedy which lies at the discretion of the court. Its advantage over the other two approaches it that it allows the court to fashion a remedy that it considers appropriate to the circumstances: unlike the approach in *Attorney General for Hong Kong v Reid* it does not impose a proprietary straitjacket but enables the court to grant a proprietary remedy, notwithstanding that the fiduciary has not diverted trust property, where a personal remedy might not be sufficient to make the fiduciary disgorge all of the profits that can properly be regarded as having been derived from the wrongdoing. The circumstances for the court to take into account in deciding whether to grant a proprietary remedy could include its effect on other creditors of the fiduciary.[323] The disadvantage of the remedial constructive trust, especially in the commercial context, is its potential for creating uncertainty and unpredictability.[324] In *Westdeutsche Landesbank Girozentrale v Islington LBC*[325] Lord Browne-Wilkinson sug-

320 Comments on the case include: Nolan, R, 'The Wages of Sin: Iniquity in Equity Following *A-G for Hong Kong v Reid*' (1994) 15 Co Law 3; Allen, T, 'Bribes and Constructive Trusts: *A-G of Hong Kong v Reid*' (1995) 58 MLR 87; Oakley, AJ, *Constructive Trusts* (3rd edn, 1997) 134–7; Cowan, D, Edmunds, R, and Lowry, J, '*Lister & Co v Stubbs*: Who Profits?' [1996] JBL 22.

321 [1994] 1 AC 324, PC.

322 Jones, A, 'Bribing the DPP: Should He Profit from Abusing His Position?' [1994] Conv 156, 164–5. But contrast Sir Peter Millett, 'Restitution and Constructive Trusts' (1998) 114 LQR 399, 407.

323 Thus it has been argued that the remedial constructive trust could have provided a better means of achieving the result in *A-G for Hong Kong v Reid* [1994] 1 AC 324, PC where there was no evidence of the existence of competing creditors: Allen, T, 'Bribes and Constructive Trusts: *A-G of Hong Kong v Reid*' (1995) 58 MLR 87, 94. See also Goode, RM, 'Property and Unjust Enrichment' in Burrows, AS (ed), *Essays on the Law of Restitution* (1991) 215, 236, 242–4.

324 Sir Peter Millett, 'Restitution and Constructive Trusts' (1998) 114 LQR 399; McCormack, G, 'The Remedial Constructive Trust and Commercial Transactions' (1996) 17 Co Law 3; Scott, SR, 'The Remedial Constructive Trust in Commercial Transactions' [1993] LMCLQ 330.

gested that English law may be on the brink of following United States and Canada in adopting the remedial constructive trust as a restitutionary device to prevent persons profiting from their own wrongdoing, but considerations such as certainty and preservation of the statutory scheme for distribution of assets in insolvency would point towards keeping the use of the remedial constructive trust in commercial situations within narrows limits.[326]

The remedial constructive trust granted by the court at its discretion and the proprietary remedy, also conventionally described as a constructive trust, which is the means whereby a beneficiary recovers its property from a fiduciary who has wrongfully subtracted it, are different creatures. Equally, although the remedy granted in *Attorney General for Hong Kong v Reid*[327] was arrived at by a route which appears to remove any discretionary element, that too was a case where a proprietary remedy was found otherwise than to enable a beneficiary to recover its property that had been wrongly subtracted by the fiduciary. This point makes it possible to argue that the profit/property distinction relied upon by company lawyers to explain authorisation and ratification is still valid: it simply has to be fine-tuned to make it clear that it is based on cases where a proprietary remedy is available because the director has wrongfully taken the company's property, and not on those where the proprietary remedy is at the discretion of the court or follows from equitable maxims as applied in *Attorney General for Hong Kong v Reid.*[328] However, this would be to ignore the fact that the availability of proprietary remedies otherwise than as a means of recovering property wrongfully subtracted from the company removes the impetus to strain to characteristic 'soft' assets, such as opportunities or information, as property. This in turns leads back to *Cook v Deeks*,[329] a corporate opportunities case, which has traditionally been classified as a case involving the wrongful subtraction of company property,[330] which is commonly cited in support of the proposition that misappropriation of corporate property is an unratifiable wrong. All of this suggests that company lawyers should look again at authorisation and ratification. A starting point in that inquiry may be the judgment of Vinelott J at first instance in *Prudential Assurance v Newman.*[331] Although that decision was widely criticised, developments with regard to remedies may in time reveal just how perceptive was Vinelott J's rejection of the argument that limits to ratification

[325] [1996] AC 669 HL.

[326] In *Re Polly Peck International plc* [1998] 3 All ER 812, CA the court rejected a remedial constructive trust claim in precisely the most controversial situation, ie where it would operate to override the normal insolvency distribution rules. Note also the decision of the Privy Council in *Re Goldcorp Exchange Ltd* [1995] 1 AC 74, PC which predated *Westdeutsche* and which demonstrated a marked reluctance to expand the availability of proprietary claims in the commercial context.

[327] [1994] 1 AC 324, PC. [328] Ibid. [329] [1916] AC 554, PC.

[330] This classification is rejected by Goode, RM, 'Property and Unjust Enrichment' in Burrows, A (ed), *Essays on the Law of Restitution* (1991) 215, 225–7; contrast Birks, P, *An Introduction to the Law of Restitution* (1985) 137–8. Goode's argument is that cases such as *Cook v Deeks* [1916] AC 554, PC would be better dealt with by means of the remedial constructive trust: Goode, RM, 'Property and Unjust Enrichment' in Burrows, AS (ed), *Essays on the Law of Restitution* (1991) 215 and Goode, RM, 'The Recovery of a Director's Improper Gains: Proprietary Remedies for Infringement of Non-Proprietary Rights' in McKendrick, E (ed), *Commercial Aspects of Trusts and Fiduciary Obligations* (1992) 437.

[331] [1981] Ch 257, reversed in part [1982] Ch 204, CA.

lay along the boundary line between profit-taking and misappropriation of property.[332]

RELIEF FOR THE WRONGDOING DIRECTOR/RECOGNISING THE VALUE OF WORK DONE OR SERVICES PROVIDED

It is instructive here to return again to *Guinness plc v Saunders*.[333] The House of Lords ordered the director to return his fee of £5.2 million and refused to grant him any form of allowance for the work that he had done on the company's behalf. This was an extremely harsh decision because it meant that the company benefited from the work that he had done without having to pay for it. The House of Lords declined to extend the principle that the court can grant an equitable allowance to a trustee for work done or services provided on behalf of the trust.[334] Lord Templeman and Lord Goff agreed that it was not appropriate to do so on the facts, but whilst Lord Templeman could not envisage circumstances where the court would ever exercise the power in favour of a director, Lord Goff preferred to leave the point open.[335] Even if the jurisdiction is applicable to directors, it would only be exercised in an exceptional case because it is irreconcilable with the fundamental rule that a director may not profit from position unless this is authorised by the articles or by the shareholders in general meeting.

The House of Lords also rejected the director's claim for a *quantum meruit*.[336] A *quantum meruit* is a restitutionary claim based on the unjust enrichment that the recipient of work would enjoy if it is not required to pay for it. This, too, was held to be inconsistent with the fundamental no-profit rule applicable to directors.

The Companies Act 1985, s 727 permits the court to relieve, in whole or in part, an officer of a company from liability for negligence, default, breach of duty or breach of trust where it appears to the court that the officer has acted honestly and reasonably and that, having regard to all the circumstances of the case, he ought fairly to be excused. This jurisdiction was held to be unavailable in *Guinness plc v Saunders* because the nature of the company's claim was recovery of money paid without authorisation rather than breach of duty. It would be potentially applicable in a case like *Regal (Hastings) Ltd v Gulliver* where the director has, in breach of the no-profit rule, obtained a profit from a third party for which the company seeks to hold him account-

332 A further point against the proprietary/profit line of distinction is that it ignores the amounts that may be involved in the wrongdoing, ie, to take an extreme example, a director who takes home some office stationery commits an unratifiable wrong, whilst a director who makes a large unauthorised profit from position is guilty of a ratifiable wrong: Cranston, R, 'Limiting Directors' Liability: Ratification, Exemption and Indemnification' [1992] JBL 197, 201.

333 [1990] 2 AC 663, HL.

334 This principle is established by *Boardman v Phipps* [1967] 2 AC 46, HL.

335 Lord Goff's more flexible stance is supported by Birks, P, 'Restitution Without Counter-Restitution' [1990] LMCLQ 330.

336 On this aspect of the case see Beatson, J, and Prentice, DD, 'Restitutionary Claims by Company Directors' (1990) 106 LQR 365; Birks, P, 'Restitution Without Counter-Restitution' [1990] LMCLQ 330.

able. There are, however, few reported cases where claims for relief under this section have succeeded.[337]

An issue that has not been considered directly by the English courts[338] is how to deal with the situation where the director's (or other fiduciary's) own efforts or property contribute to the profit that is eventually derived from a business opportunity that was originally obtained in breach of duty. This is particularly relevant where a director breaches his duty by competing with the company or resigning to pursue an opportunity:[339] do the prophylactic and deterrence functions of fiduciary duties mean that it is justifiable in these circumstances to postulate a rule which would allow the company to reap the whole benefit of the director's efforts and of whatever personal property he has put into the venture because of the initial nexus with the fiduciary position; or is this an unfair[340] windfall that the company ought not to be permitted to claim? The approach applied to this type of situation by the High Court of Australia in *Warman International v Dwyer*[341] is compelling.[342] The court considered that where the breach consisted of the diversion of business and a proportion of the subsequent increase in profits had been generated by the skill, energy, property and resources of the errant fiduciary, it would be inappropriate and inequitable to require the fiduciary to account for the whole of it. In those circumstances (and it would be for the defendant to prove their existence), the court could either apportion the profits or make an allowance in respect of the skill, expertise and other expenses that the defendant had incurred. The order of the court on the facts was to require the former senior manager of a company who had diverted business to himself,[343] in breach of his fiduciary duties to the company, to account for profits made in the first two years after the original wrongful diversion, less an allowance for the expenses, skill, expertise, efforts and resources contributed by the defendant and his new business partner; but he was allowed to retain profits generated thereafter. It was accepted that even if the defendant had not diverted the business,

[337] One is *Re D'Jan of London Ltd* [1993] BCC 646 where the court reached the slightly odd conclusion (but one that is warranted by the wording of the section) that the director was negligent but had acted honestly and reasonably and was entitled to relief. See also *Re Brian D Pierson (Contractors) Ltd* [1999] BCC 26, where limited relief was awarded.

[338] Although it underpins much of the discussion about the appropriate remedies for breach of fiduciary duty and the potential for development of the remedial constructive trust: see, eg, Goode, RM, 'Property and Unjust Enrichment' in Burrows, AS (ed), *Essays on the Law of Restitution* (1991) 215, 236, 242–4; Beatson, J, *The Use and Abuse of Unjust Enrichment* (1991) 230–1.

[339] But, as the discussion earlier in this chapter indicates, neither competition nor resignation in itself amounts to a breach of duty.

[340] Unfair, that is, to the wronging director and also, if he is insolvent, to his creditors who are thereby deprived of the *pari passu* distribution of the elements of the director's own property that were invested in the venture: Goode, RM, 'Property and Unjust Enrichment' in Burrows, AS (ed), *Essays on the Law of Restitution* (1991) 215, 226.

[341] (1995) 128 ALR 201, H Ct of Aust.

[342] Oakley, *Constructive Trusts* (3rd edn, 1997) 174–7; Nolan, R, 'What to Take Into Account' [1996] CLJ 201.

[343] Technically, the business was diverted to two corporate vehicles which had been set up by the former manager. The order to account was made jointly against the manager (Dwyer) and the two companies, it being conceded that any award for an account of profits should be made on that basis.

in all likelihood the company would have lost it anyway within a year; the two-year limit on the order recognised that fact, but also acknowledged that the benefits from the experience, contacts and know-how gained through the company might endure beyond the initial one-year period.

6

Controlling Management: Duties of Care and Skill; Role of Non-executive Directors

DUTIES OF CARE AND SKILL: INTRODUCTION TO THE ISSUES

Those who take it upon themselves to act on behalf of or to advise others may have an equitable duty to exercise care and skill in doing so.[1] The application of this duty to company directors, which for this purpose may be taken also to include senior managers except where the contrary is indicated, is considered in this chapter.

A company can sue a director who is in breach of the equitable duty of care and skill for equitable compensation. The purpose of equitable compensation is, as might be expected, to compensate the victim of the wrongdoing. This distinguishes the duty of care and skill from the fiduciary duties outlined in Chapter 5. The primary remedy for breach of fiduciary duty is to make the wrongdoer account for the profit that he has made by wrongful exploitation of his position.[2] The modern remedy of equitable compensation is in its infancy and the detailed rules governing causation, remoteness of damage and measure of damages have still to evolve.[3] The rules governing common-law damages for breach of contractual duties of care and skill and tortious duties of care provide a model that may apply by way of analogy to the equitable duty.[4] The equitable duty of care and skill overlaps with the duty of care in tort that directors may owe to their company[5] and there is some support for the view that it is indistinguishable from it.[6]

[1] *Henderson v Merrett Syndicates Ltd* [1995] 2 AC 145, HL, 205 *per* Lord Browne-Wilkinson; *Bristol and West Building Society v Mothew* [1998] Ch 1, CA, 16–18 *per* Millett LJ; *Permanent Building Society v Wheeler* (1994) 14 ACSR 109, WA SC.

[2] *Bristol and West Building Society v Mothew* [1998] Ch 1, CA, 17 *per* Millett LJ.

[3] The cases recognising the remedy of equitable compensation include: *Target Holdings v Redferns* [1996] 1 AC 421, HL; *Bristol and West Building Society v Mothew* [1998] Ch 1, CA, 17 *per* Millett LJ; *Canson Enterprises Ltd v Boughton & Co* (1991) 85 DLR (4th) 129, Can SC, 163 *per* McLachlin J; *Day v Mead* [1987] 2 NZLR 443, NZ CA. For instance, one important question is whether breach of the equitable duty could amount to contributory negligence: Farrar, JH, 'The Duty of Care of Company Directors in Australia and New Zealand' in Ramsay, IM, *Corporate Governance and the Duties of Company Directors* (1997) 81, 88–9.

[4] *Bristol and West Building Society v Mothew* [1998] Ch 1, CA, 16–18 *per* Millett LJ.

[5] That directors owe duty of care in tort is established in Australia: *Daniels v Anderson* (1995) 16 ACSR 607, NSW CA, where it was held that directors' contributory negligence could be attributed to the company for the purposes of reducing the damages that it was entitled to claim from its auditors in respect of their negligence.

[6] *Company Directors: Regulating Conflicts of Interest and Formulating a Statement of Duties: A Joint Consultation Paper* (Law Commission Consultation Paper No 153; Scottish Law Commission Discussion Paper No 105) (1998) para 12.1 citing *Henderson v Merrett Syndicates Ltd* [1995] 2 AC 145, HL, 205 *per* Lord Browne-Wilkinson.

Historically the standard of care and skill required of directors under the duty of care and skill was low, but the traditional view has been challenged by specific legislative developments that impinge on the general law, and also by shifts in aspects of corporate governance practice and wider perception within the financial markets.

Legislative Developments

A significant catalyst for change was the insolvency legislation of the mid-1980s. Under the Insolvency Act 1986, s 214 a director who falls below an objective standard of care and skill may be held liable to contribute personally to the assets of his company. Failure to comply with the specific requirements of the companies legislation or grossly incompetent management may also result in a director becoming disqualified from acting as a director under the Company Directors Disqualification Act 1986. Both of these statutory provisions are limited in their direct effect—the Insolvency Act 1986, s 214 only applies to directors of companies in insolvent liquidation; and a director will not face disqualification if his failings amount to no more than errors of judgment—but they also have a prophylactic impact. Prudent directors would not want to be in a position where their stewardship of the company's affairs is put to the test, even if they are eventually vindicated. They would naturally prefer to set themselves high standards with a view to minimising the risk of such proceedings being brought against them.

Developments in Practice: The Emergence of Corporate Governance

The growth of interest in corporate governance in the UK markets during the 1990s focused attention on the role of directors and the standards that could be expected of them. Corporate governance may be defined as 'the system by which companies are directed and controlled'.[7] There are a variety of reasons why corporate governance assumed a greater importance in the UK in the 1990s than hitherto. One was the recession of the early 1990s and the collapse of a number of high-profile major companies during that period. Concern about the failure of some major companies was a reason for the establishment of a committee under the chairmanship of Sir Adrian Cadbury that investigated and, in 1992, reported on the financial aspects of corporate governance. The Cadbury Committee's report was the first major step in the UK towards the evolution of a broad framework of market-based corporate governance standards.

Corporate collapse is the starkest example of circumstances where the option for shareholders to withdraw from an unsatisfactory investment by selling their shares through the market is closed. The possibility of exit via the

[7] *Report of the Committee on Financial Aspects of Corporate Governance* (1992) (*Cadbury Committee Report*) para 2.5. Charkham, J, *Keeping Good Company* (1995) 248 discusses some alternative definitions but notes that: 'There is to this day some doubt about what "corporate governance" means'; Ramsay, IM, 'The Corporate Governance Debate and the Role of Directors' Duties' in Ramsay, IM (ed), *Corporate Governance and the Duties of Company Directors* (1997) 2, 2–3.

market acts as a general disincentive to investors to attach importance to the processes of corporate governance. It follows that where exit via the market is economically unattractive, such as where an investor holds a large stake in a company which it can only sell at a significant loss, the spotlight should shift onto corporate governance. The growing dominance of the UK equity markets by institutional investors to the point where at the start of 1998 they were estimated to hold 80 per cent of the market,[8] may have made exit via the market more difficult, especially in periods of dormancy in takeover activity.

The political profile of the corporate governance debate is also relevant here. Questions such as whether there is a need for fiscal or other legislative measures to curb excessive pay awards to directors of public companies, whether institutional investors have short-termist attitudes which are damaging to the long-term economic interests of the corporate economy and which ought therefore to be addressed by regulatory controls requiring institutions to take a closer interest in the management of companies in which they invest, and also the accountability of institutional investors to their clients, are all part of the agenda for possible law reform into the next century.[9] The development of market-based corporate governance codes of practice and changes in practice by institutional investors with regard to such matters as voting at general meeting can, at least in part, be viewed as pre-emptive strikes designed to stave off the threat of formal, and potentially more inflexible, legislative control.

The Role of the Non-executive Director in Corporate Governance

A central figure in the market-based system of corporate governance that has emerged in the UK is the non-executive director. Best practice[10] for the governance of public companies is that one-third of the board should comprise non-executive directors. Of these, the majority should be independent of management (this means that, for example, they should not be former executive directors of the company) and free from business or other relationships that could materially interfere with the exercise of their independent judgment. Non-executive directors are expected to discharge certain important functions in relation to the management of the companies to which they are appointed. These include, specifically, setting the remuneration of the executive directors and, more generally, monitoring the stewardship of the com-

[8] *Final Report of the Committee on Corporate Governance* (January 1998) (*Hampel Committee Report*) para 5.1 notes that 60 per cent is held by UK institutions, around 20 per cent by foreign, mainly institutional, owners and the remaining 20 per cent or so by private individuals. The DTI also estimates that around 80 per cent lies in institutional hands: *Shareholder Communications at the Annual General Meeting* (Consultative Document) (April 1996) para 1.7. See further Ch 7 below, at 241–5.

[9] *Modern Company Law For a Competitive Economy* (DTI Consultative Paper) (1998) para 3.7 notes that the government is watching developments on shareholder control over directors' pay closely and that as part of its review of company law it will examine the responsibilities of shareholders in this and other areas.

[10] The text here is based on the *Combined Code* which is appended to *The Listing Rules* of the London Stock Exchange. The legal significance of the *Combined Code* is considered further in this chapter, at 223–4 below.

pany's affairs by its executive management including the executive directors. The modern non-executive director of a public company is thus rather different from his historical counterpart. In the past a non-executive director might have been expected to do no more than to give the company the benefit of being associated with a person of his reputation and distinction but now they are expected to do rather more to justify their position.[11] This creates a new context within which the general duty of care and skill operates and makes it appropriate to consider the effectiveness of that duty as a mechanism for holding non-executives themselves accountable. It also raises the question whether the role and function of the modern day non-executive director as perceived by market standards has had an impact on the content of that duty so as to make it more rigorous than it was when non-executive directors were simply figureheads.

OVERLAP WITH CONTRACTUAL DUTIES OF CARE AND SKILL

The employees of a company owe contractual duties to their employer. These may overlap with the equitable duty of care and skill but in certain respects contractual duties can be stricter. For example, the equitable duty of care and skill as it has been developed in relation to directors does not require them to devote themselves to the company's affairs on a full-time basis but full-time employment is likely to be norm for a company's employees. Directors are not automatically employees of their company but they can become employees.[12] For directors who are employees, their contracts of employment are the primary tool for regulating the standards of care, skill and devotion to the company's affairs that they are required to demonstrate. The equitable duty of care and skill is therefore most relevant to those directors, such as non-executives, who are not employees of the company.

Executive directors of public companies typically formalise their employment relationship with the company in detailed contracts of employment, but arrangements in smaller companies may be more haphazard leading to uncertainty concerning the status of particular individuals or to doubt about the precise content of the contractual duties to which they are subject. One case where the status of a director in a public company may be unclear is with regard to the chairman, who may be described as a 'non-executive' and have no express contract, but who may in fact be involved in the management of the company to such an extent that he is actually performing executive functions.

Where not regulated by an express contract, it is a factual question whether a director is also an employee. Relevant factors include:[13]

[11] *The Changing Role of the Non-executive Director,* (ICAEW Report) (1991). The notorious *Times* advertisement for 'A titled person required to add distinction to the board of a wine company. No responsibility, investment or participation required—firm very sound', encapsulates the older view of the non-executive director's role.

[12] *Anderson v James Sutherland (Peterhead) Ltd*, 1941 SC 203; *Boulting v ACTAT* [1963] 2 QB 606, CA.

[13] *Eaton v Robert Eaton Ltd* [1988] IRLR 83 (although this was not a case of a controlling shareholder).

(i) any descriptive term attached to the directorship which is indicative of employment, such as managing or technical director; in almost all cases, a person who is the managing director of a company will be an employee;[14]
(ii) evidence, such as a board minute, which discloses an intention on the part of the company to employ the director in question;
(iii) whether remuneration is paid by way of salary, which is an indication of employment, or fees, which points the other way;[15]
(iv) whether remuneration is fixed in advance or is paid on an ad hoc basis, the latter pointing away from the relationship being one of employment;
(v) the functions actually performed by the director;
(vi) whether the director is required to devote all his time to the affairs of the company and to do all in his power to develop and extend its business.

A person can be an employee of a company even though he is also its sole director and major shareholder.[16]

THE VARIETY OF FUNCTIONS PERFORMED BY DIRECTORS: A PROBLEM FOR STANDARD SETTING

Whereas contractual duties can be tailored to apply in an appropriate fashion to each individual director, the equitable duty of care and skill has a more broad-brush application. Within a company the functions performed by the various directors may vary greatly and, when different companies are compared, the differences can become increasingly stark: for example, the function performed by the finance director of a listed international public company will obviously be very different from that of a director of a family company; and a non-executive director of a public company who is expected to perform a monitoring function will be in a very different position from a person who is appointed to a directorship of a family company largely for sentimental or ceremonial reasons. The courts recognise that directors do not form an homogenous group but in the past this has largely been used as an argument for judicial non-intervention and for adherence to a low standard in relation to the content of the equitable duty of care and skill: the range of functions carried out by directors has sometimes been said to make it impossible to formulate precise rules governing the content of their duty.[17]

[14] *Anderson v James Sutherland*, 1941 SC 203.

[15] *Parsons v Albert J Parsons & Sons Ltd* [1979] ICR 271, CA; *Folami v Nigerline (UK) Ltd* [1978] ICR 277; *Buchan v Secretary of State for Employment* [1997] BCC 145.

[16] *Lee v Lee's Air Farming Ltd* [1961] AC 12, HL. But whether a controlling shareholder is an employee depends on the context: *Buchan v Secretary of State for Employment* [1997] BCC 145.

[17] *Dovey v Cory* [1901] AC 477, HL; *Re City Equitable Fire Insurance Co* [1925] 1 Ch 407, Ch D and CA.

THE RELUCTANCE OF THE COURTS TO INTERFERE WITH SHAREHOLDERS' DECISIONS AND BUSINESS AFFAIRS

Another justification sometimes given by the courts for the low standard of care and skill that has been traditionally required of directors is that it is for the shareholders of a company to choose the directors so that, if they chose incompetent persons, that is their decision and the courts should not interfere.[18] This approach is based on the familiar model of the corporate structure in which shareholders' interests are paramount because either they are the owners of the company or, alternatively, they are the ultimate risk-bearers.[19] The adoption of a stakeholder model of corporate law, where shareholders' interests would merely rank for consideration alongside other interested groups such as employees and creditors, would obviously remove any basis for this approach. Yet it is not necessary to endorse such a radical shift in the law to criticise this justification as being too narrowly focused. It fails to take into account the fact that incompetent management may have repercussions on others who have an interest in the company, in particular its creditors and employees, as well as upon society at large.

A related factor which has inhibited the courts from setting strict standards of care and skill is the traditional reluctance of the judiciary to become embroiled in matters of business judgment.[20]

DIFFICULTIES IN ENFORCEMENT OF THE DUTY OF CARE AND SKILL

The historically low standard of care and skill expected of directors may also have had something to do with the difficulties of enforcing the duty. Put simply, the point here is that courts may have had few opportunities to develop the content of the duty because there were few cases in which the issue was actively litigated. Litigation is regarded as part of the function of management and, under most articles of association, control of managerial affairs is vested in the board. Ordinarily, the shareholders in general meeting cannot interfere with, or reverse, the board's decisions.[21] If an independent quorate board, mindful of considerations such as costs, disruption, diversion of managerial attention and the impact of bad publicity, decides that it would not be in the company's interests to pursue the claim through the courts that will normally be sufficient to dispose of the claim. However, if so many members of the board are implicated in allegations of negligence that it is impossible to form a quorate board, the decision to commence litigation may in that

[18] *Turquand v Marshall* (1869) LR 4 Ch App 376; *Daniels v Daniels* [1978] 1 Ch 406.

[19] See Ch 4 above, at 131–3.

[20] *Howard Smith v Ampol Petroleum* [1974] AC 821, PC, 835 *per* Lord Wilberforce; *Harlowe's Nominees Pty Ltd v Woodside (Lake Entrance) Oil Co NL* (1968) 121 CLR 483, H Ct of Aust, 492 *per* Barwick CJ and McTiernan and Kitto JJ.

[21] *Shaw (John) & Sons (Salford) v Shaw* [1935] 2 KB 113, CA; *Breckland Group Holdings v London & Suffolk Properties* (1988) 4 BCC 542.

situation revert to the general meeting.[22] Even if the decision falls to the general meeting, many of the shareholders, if they take an active interest in the matter at all, are likely to be influenced by the same factors as would inhibit a disinterested board from pursuing a claim. By way of exception, minority shareholders can sometimes pursue a claim on the company's behalf by bringing a derivative action but a claim against directors for negligence is not within the scope of the exception.[23]

Other remedies that are potentially available to minority shareholder prove to have a limited application where the alleged wrongdoing relates to mismanagement. A disaffected shareholder can seek relief from unfairly prejudicial conduct under the Companies Act 1985, s 459, but it has been held that mere mismanagement does not amount to unfairly prejudicial conduct, although in appropriate cases serious mismanagement may be brought within its scope.[24] It is also open to a shareholder in a solvent company to obtain an order from the court to wind up the company on just and equitable grounds,[25] but that is obviously an extreme step which, bearing in mind how liquidation costs and prior-ranking creditors' claims will eat into the return to shareholders from liquidation of the company's assets, few sensible investors are likely to want to pursue; and the court is unlikely to grant such an order merely because a company has underperformed in comparison to other similar companies because, it is alleged, its management has failed to exercise due care and skill in the management of its affairs. Equally, although shareholders can ask the DTI to appoint Inspectors to investigate the affairs of a company under the Companies Act 1985, Pt XIV,[26] this power tends only to be used where matters of serious public concern are raised and allegations of negligence or incompetence alone are unlikely to persuade the DTI to intervene.[27]

Under proposals suggested by the Law Commission,[28] negligence would be brought within the scope of a new statutory derivative action but mere mismanagement would remain outside the category of conduct that would be open to challenge by means of a petition under the Companies Act 985, s 459.

[22] *Prudential Assurance Co v Newman Industries (No 2)* [1982] Ch 204, CA, 221–2 *per* Cumming-Bruce, Templeman and Brightman LJJ (joint judgment) suggests that in some circumstances control of litigation may be a matter for the general meeting. It is not altogether clear whether this is envisaged as a concurrent power (which would be an exception to the normal position as outlined in the text) or as a power exercisable only when the board itself is disabled. On shareholder remedies generally, see *Shareholder Remedies A Consultation Paper* (Law Commission Consultation Paper No 142) (1996) and *Shareholder Remedies* (Law Commission Report No 246) (1997).

[23] *Pavlides v Jensen* [1956] Ch 565.

[24] *Re Elgindata Ltd* [1991] BCLC 959; *Re Charnley Davies* [1990] BCC 605, 625 (this case related to Insolvency Act 1986, s 27); *Re Macro (Ipswich) Ltd* 1994] 2 BCLC 354.

[25] Under Insolvency Act 1986, s 122 (1)(g).

[26] Companies Act 2985, s 431. The threshold requirement is that, in the case of a company with a share capital, the request must be from a minimum of 200 shareholders or shareholders holding not less than one tenth of the issued shares. Alternatively the company itself can apply for the appointment of Inspectors under this section. The Secretary of State can also appoint directors at his own volition or may be required to do so by the court: Companies Act 1985, s 432.

[27] Boyle, AJ, 'Draft Fifth Directive: Implications for Directors Duties, Board Structure and Employee Participation' (1992) 13 Co Law 6.

[28] *Shareholder Remedies* (Law Commission Report No 246) (1997). The proposal has the provisional support of the DTI: *Shareholder Remedies* (DTI Consultative Document) (Nov 1998).

COMPETENCE AND CARE: THE TRADITIONAL VIEW

The classic statement of the standard of care and skill required of a director by virtue of his office is that of Romer J in *Re City Equitable Fire Insurance Co.*[29] He stated that:

> a director need not exhibit in the performance of his duties a greater degree of skill than may reasonably be expected from a person of his knowledge and experience.

This requirement is essentially subjective. Although the standard is what can be *reasonably* expected of a director, this is tested by reference to the director's own knowledge and experience[30] rather than by reference to the functions which he performs as a truly objective test would require. Some older cases representing the traditional view hold that a director need bring no particular skills to his office—'he may undertake the management of a rubber company in complete ignorance of everything connected with rubber'[31]—and that errors of judgment resulting from ignorance do not result in liability.[32] With whatever level of skill he has, the director must then, according to Romer J, take such care in the conduct of the company's affairs as an ordinary man might be expected to take in the circumstances on his own behalf. Some of the older cases use the phrase 'gross negligence' to describe the degree of mismanagement that has to be established for a director to be found to have failed to discharge his duty.[33] The epitaph 'gross' has no fixed connotation[34] and in more recent cases where a distinction is drawn between 'negligence' and 'gross negligence', 'gross negligence' has tended to be used to denote conduct which amounts to more than a mere failure by a director to satisfy his duty to demonstrate appropriate skill and which involves an element of self-interest,[35] deliberateness or recklessness approaching fraud.[36]

The problem with a duty formulated as in the *Re City Equitable* decision is simple and obvious: incompetence is its own defence. Highly-qualified and skilled directors are judged by their own standards and may be liable accordingly; but the ignorant and unskilled are also judged by their own standards and, provided they do their best, they will not be held to have failed to satisfy their legal duties. This unsatisfactory position is an issue that reform bodies and commentators have grappled with over many years, with a key difficulty being the challenge of devising a test which could accommodate the very wide

29 [1925] 1 Ch 407, Ch D and CA.

30 *Lagunas Nitrate Co v Lagunas Syndicate* [1899] 2 Ch 392, CA.

31 *Re Brazilian Rubber Plantations and Estates Ltd* [1911] 1 Ch 425.

32 Ibid; *Lagunas Nitrate Co v Lagunas Syndicate* [1899] 2 Ch 392, CA; *Overend & Gurney Co v Gibb* (1872) LR 5 HL 480, HL.

33 In particular *Turquand v Marshall* (1869) LR 4 Ch App 376; *Overend & Gurney Co v Gibb* (1872) LR 5 HL 480, HL; *Sheffield and South Yorkshire Permanent Building Society v Aizlewood* (1890) 44 Ch D 412.

34 *Re City Equitable Fire Insurance Co* [1925] 1 Ch 407, Ch D and CA, 427–8 where Romer J confessed to difficulty in understanding the difference between negligence and gross negligence.

35 As in *Daniels v Daniels* [1978] 1 Ch 406 where the directors benefited from their own negligence to the tune of £115,000.

36 *Re B Johnson & Co (Builders) Ltd* [1955] Ch 634, CA; *Multinational Gas and Petrochemical Co v Multinational Gas and Petrochemical Services Ltd* [1983] 1 Ch 258, CA, 291 *per* Dillon LJ commenting on dicta in *Re Horsley & Weight Ltd* [1982] Ch 442, CA.

range of functions performed by company directors and sufficiently deter mismanagement without, at the same time, unduly inhibiting risk-taking, innovation and entrepreneurial business management.[37] Somewhat unexpectedly the enactment of wrongful trading liability in the Insolvency Act 1986, s 214 has turned out to be an important step forward in the resolution of this difficulty. The immediate background to the introduction of wrongful trading liability was the *Report of the United Kingdom Review Committee on Insolvency Law and Practice*[38] which accepted that a balance had to be struck between not discouraging the inception and growth of businesses, even though these were inevitably attended by risks to credit, and discouraging irresponsibility and ensuring that those who abused the privilege of limited liability could be held liable for the consequences of their conduct. The committee recommended that a person should be held to be personally liable to contribute to the assets of an insolvent company if, on broadly objective standards, he was considered to have been guilty of wrongful trading. With some modification this proposal was duly accepted by the government[39] and enacted.

THE INSOLVENCY ACT 1986, S 214 AND ITS IMPACT ON THE DUTY TO ACT CAREFULLY AND COMPETENTLY

The Insolvency Act 1986, s 214 applies to directors and former directors of a company which has gone into insolvent liquidation who, at some time before the commencement of the winding up of the company, knew or ought to have concluded that there was no reasonable prospect that the company would avoid going into insolvent liquidation. De facto directors and shadow directors are caught by the section, but not senior managers who do not perform directorial functions.[40] The court may order the director or former director to make such contribution to the company's assets as the court thinks appropriate,[41] except that the court must not make such an order with respect to any person who took every step with a view to minimising the potential loss to the company's creditors that (assuming him to have known that there was no rea-

[37] Leading articles are Trebilcock, MJ, 'The Liability of Company Directors for Negligence' (1969) 32 MLR 499; Mackenzie, AL, 'A Company Director's Obligations of Care and Skill' [1982] JBL 460; Finch, V, 'Company Directors: Who Cares about Skill and Care?' (1992) 55 MLR 179.

A Companies Bill introduced by a Labour Government in 1978 contained a provision (cl 45) under which a director would have been required 'to exercise such care and diligence as could reasonably be expected of a reasonably prudent person in circumstances of that description and to exercise such skill as may reasonably be expected of a person of his knowledge and experience'. This was not a radical departure from the standards in the *Re City Equitable* decision since it continued to adopt an essentially subjective standard of skill, although it did emphasise the objectivity of the care requirement.

[38] Cmnd 8558 (1982) (Cork Committee) ch 44.

[39] *A Revised Framework for Insolvency Law*, Cmnd 9175 (1984).

[40] The inclusion of shadow directors is expressly stated: Insolvency Act 1986, s 214 (7). The inclusion of de facto directors has been established by case law: *Re Hydrodan (Corby) Ltd* [1994] BCC 161. On de facto and shadow directors generally, see Ch 5 above, at 155–6.

[41] Insolvency Act 1986, s 214 (1), as drafted, leaves open the possibility that no contribution could be required even though the requirements of the section are otherwise satisfied.

sonable prospect that the company would avoid going into insolvent liquidation) he ought to have taken.[42]

The Insolvency Act 1986, s 214 (4) sets out the standard by which a director or former director is to be judged for the purpose of establishing liability under the section. It provides that:

> The facts which a director of a company ought to know or ascertain, the conclusions which he ought to reach and the steps which he ought to take are those which would be known or ascertained, or reached or taken, by reasonable diligent persons having both
> (a) the general knowledge, skill and experience that may reasonably be expected of a person carrying out the same functions as are carried out by that director in relation to the company, and
> (b) the general knowledge, skill and experience that the director has.

Limb (a) represents a significant departure from the subjective standards embodied in the *Re City Equitable* decision in that it imposes an element of objectivity. This is in addition to the subjective standard which is embodied in (b) with the consequence that, whilst inexperience or lack of skill is not a defence to a wrongful trading claim, a director who is highly skilled and greatly experienced will still be judged by his own personal standards.[43]

By referring to 'function', the minimum objective standard imposed by (a) addresses the challenge of imposing an objective standard on directors, bearing in mind the variety of activities which persons answering to that description can in practice perform. A director is to be judged by the general knowledge, skill and experience that may reasonably be expected of a person *carrying out the same functions* (emphasis added) as are carried out by that director in relation to the company. This directs the court to have regard to the particular company and its business: in *Re Produce Marketing Consortium Ltd (No 2)*[44] Knox J noted that the general knowledge, skill and experience postulated will be much less extensive in a small company in a modest way of business, with simple accounting procedures, than it will be in a large company with sophisticated procedures. The reference to function should also allow the court to distinguish between the various activities carried out by the directors within a given company so that, for example, its non-executive directors may be judged by a different objective standard from that which applies to its executive directors.[45] However, certain minimum standards will be expected

[42] Insolvency Act 1986, s 214 (3).

[43] *Re Brian D Pierson (Contractors) Ltd* [1999] BCC 26. See also Prentice, DD, 'Corporate Personality, Limited Liability and the Protection of Creditors' in Grantham, R, and Rickett, C, *Corporate Personality in the 20th Century* (1998) 99, 112.

[44] *Re Produce Marketing Consortium Ltd (No 2)* [1989] BCLC 520, 550.

[45] Faint support for this is provided by *Re Sherborne Associates Ltd* [1995] BCC 40 District Registry, although the position of non-executive directors was not subjected to detailed examination. Australian legislation provides a parallel here. This provides for corporate officers to exercise the degree of care and skill which a reasonable person in a like position in a corporation would exercise in the circumstances of the corporation (Corporations Law, s 232 (4)). Although this is an objective standard, the expressions 'a like position' and 'the corporation's circumstances' allow for the standard required to be considered in the context of the distribution of functions within a corporation. These phrases should also allow account to be taken of the special expertise of particular directors, the corporation's financial position, the size and nature of business, the urgency and magnitude of the problems it faces, and the contents of its constitution: Explanatory Memorandum to the Corporate Law Reform Bill 1992. Note also Corporations Law, s 588G which

of all directors irrespective of their particular function.[46] In particular, the Companies Act 1985 imposes obligations on all directors to maintain accounting records and, in judging what any director ought to have known, the court will consider what would have been known to that director if he had complied with these obligations.

It is only directors of companies that have gone into insolvent liquidation who are at risk of being held liable for wrongful trading. Insolvent liquidation for this purpose means liquidation at a time when the company's assets are insufficient for the payment of its debts and other liabilities and the expenses of winding up.[47] This is a form of balance-sheet insolvency. Cash-flow insolvency—that is, inability to pay debts as they fall due—may result in a company going into liquidation but, if it is not also in a state of balance-sheet insolvency, its directors are not at risk of being held liable for wrongful trading.

Although wrongful-trading liability is thus strictly limited in its direct effect, its role as a deterrent against managerial under-performance cannot be overlooked. Also, an unpredicted consequence of the enactment of the Insolvency Act 1986, s 214 is that it seems to have provided the key to reformulation of a more exacting standard in respect of the general duty of care and skill. As yet, there is only a slim body of authority, two cases, in support of this suggestion. Both of these cases are first instance decisions[48] and in one of them the relevant point was assumed without being decided. Whilst two first instance decisions on their own cannot overturn established law which is supported by decisions of the House of Lords, these cases are very significant. They represent a way forward without the need for legislative reform in an area of the law which, as traditionally interpreted, is widely regarded as outdated and inappropriate to modern commercial practice, and which would not be adhered to by those who seek to manage companies on the basis of best practice. In the view of the influential Law Commission, the modern formulation of the duty

provides for a director to be personally liable if the company incurs a debt at a time when it is insolvent (or becomes insolvent by incurring the debt, either on its own or with other debts). There must be reasonable grounds for suspecting that the company is, or would become, insolvent; and the director must be aware of such grounds, or the position must be such that a reasonable person in the position of a director of a company in the circumstances of that company would have been so aware. This formulation allows for the circumstances of the particular company to be taken into account even though it is basically an objective standard. There are some defences to this liability, one of which is that a competent and reliable subordinate was monitoring the company's solvency position and keeping the director informed.

The US Revised Model Business Corporation Act (1984), § 8.30 requires directors to act with the care an ordinarily prudent person in a like position would exercise under similar circumstances This is also required by the American Law Institute's *Principles of Corporate Governance*, § 4.01. This is a basically objective standard but the phrases 'like position' and 'similar circumstances' allow for adjustments to the standard by reference to such matters as the activities carried on by the particular corporation and the background, qualifications and management responsibilities of the particular director.

New Zealand corporate legislation is unusual in this respect because it provides simply for an objective standard of care to be exercised by the director: New Zealand Companies Act 1993, s 137.

[46] *Re Produce Marketing Consortium Ltd (No 2)* [1989] BCLC 520.

[47] Insolvency Act 1986, s 214 (6).

[48] Hoffman LJ sat as an additional judge of the Chancery Division in *Re D'Jan of London Ltd* [1993] BCC 646.

of care and skill in these two cases does indeed represent the law and would be followed by the higher courts.[49]

In *Norman v Theodore Goddard*[50] Hoffmann J held that a director had not been negligent in relying upon information provided by a professional adviser in circumstances where that information later proved to be untrue. In the course of his judgment Hoffmann J enunciated what he considered to be the extent of the skill that a director was required to use in managing the company's affairs: 'A director performing active duties on behalf of the company need not exhibit a greater degree of skill than may reasonably be expected from a person undertaking those duties.' Hoffmann J assumed, without deciding, that the standard by which a director would be judged for this purpose was accurately stated in the Insolvency Act 1986, s 214 (4). He also commented that this standard emerged clearly from the authority; but, in fact, the objective standard which he enunciated—and illustrated with the comment that 'a director who undertakes the management of the company's property is expected to have reasonable skill in property management'—contrasts sharply with the more indulgent older cases where directors were forgiven their ignorance and lack of skill with regard to the functions which they had undertaken to perform.[51]

In *Re D'Jan of London Ltd*[52] Hoffmann LJ (sitting as an additional judge of the Chancery Division) reiterated this approach and specifically held that the duty of care owed by a director at common law was accurately stated in s 214 (4). Since this statutory standard of care embodies an objective test of skill, it would now seem to be strained and artificial to attempt to distinguish 'care' from 'skill' and to postulate an objective test for the former, whilst still maintaining a subjective test for the latter.[53] For both care and skill, on the basis of these two decisions it would appear that the general duty is shifting in favour of a more objective standard, albeit one that is sensitive to the functions that the director is expected to perform.

THE FUNCTION OF NON-EXECUTIVE DIRECTORS

The emphasis on function in the development of the duty of care and skill puts the spotlight onto the role that directors are expected to play within corporate governance: what exactly is their function? The issues raised by this topic are especially pertinent for non-executive directors who do not have service contracts setting out in detailed terms their role and their duties.

[49] *Company Directors: Regulating Conflicts of Interest and Formulating a Statement of Duties: A Joint Consultation Paper* (Law Commission Consultation Paper No 153; Scottish Law Commission Discussion Paper No 105) (1998) para 15.5.

[50] [1992] BCC 14.

[51] Such as *Re Brazilian Rubber Plantations and Estates Ltd* [1911] 1 Ch 425.

[52] [1993] BCC 646 (a summons under Insolvency Act 1986, s 212).

[53] Compare the submission in *Dorchester Finance Co Ltd v Stebbing* [1989] BCLC 498 (case decided in 1977) that skill was a subjective requirement whilst care was objective. For the impracticability and the inadvisability of drawing such a distinction between the elements of 'care' and of 'skill' see *Company Directors: Regulating Conflicts of Interest and Formulating a Statement of Duties: A Joint Consultation Paper* (Law Commission Consultation Paper No 153; Scottish Law Commission Discussion Paper No 105) (1998).

Non-executive directors should bring an independent judgment to bear on issues of strategy, performance, resources, including key appointments, and standards of conduct.

This statement of the function of non-executive directors is taken from the *Code of Best Practice for Listed Companies* drawn up by the Committee on the Financial Aspects of Corporate Governance, which sat under the chairmanship of Sir Adrian Cadbury.[54] As well as this general summary of best practice with regard to the role of non-executive directors of listed companies, the *Cadbury Code* specifically endorsed the practice of having remuneration committees comprised wholly or mainly of non-executive directors to make recommendations on the pay of executive directors[55] and the establishment of audit committees comprised of non-executive directors to review the management of companies' financial operations. [56]

The *Cadbury Report,* described in a later report as a 'landmark in thinking on corporate governance',[57] was followed in 1995 by the publication of a *Report of the Study Group on Directors' Remuneration* chaired by Sir Richard Greenbury (generally known as the *Greenbury Report*) and in 1998 by the *Final Report of the Committee on Corporate Governance* chaired by Sir Ronal Hampel (generally known as the *Hampel Report*). The *Greenbury* and *Hampel Reports* built upon the foundations that had been established by Cadbury and refined them in some respects, for example by indicating that remuneration committees should comprise only (not, as has been originally suggested, mainly) non-executive directors. Later refinements such as these do not detract from the fact that it was the *Cadbury Report* that did the path-breaking work in setting the parameters for expectations of good corporate governance within modern UK business practice.[58]

The *Cadbury, Greenbury* and *Hampel Reports* were all essentially private finance initiatives. The committees comprised representatives from city, industry and investment sectors and their recommendations had no direct legal force, resting instead on the power of investing institutions to move funds away from companies that did not comply and could not offer good explanation for their failure to do so. In each case, however, the voluntary nature of the recommendations was rapidly supplemented by the adoption by the London Stock Exchange of new listing rules requiring compliance with, or at least disclosure of non-compliance with, the various codes. That process culminated in 1998

[54] *Report of the Committee on The Financial Aspects of Corporate Governance* (*Cadbury Report*) (1992). See also *The Conduct of Company Directors* Cmnd 7037 (1977) paras 19–21.

[55] *Cadbury Code,* para 3.3. See also the *Cadbury Report,* paras 4.40–4.46.

[56] *Cadbury Code,* para 4.3. See also the *Cadbury Report,* paras 4.33–4.38 and app 4.

[57] *Final Report of the Committee on Corporate Governance* (*Hampel Report*) (1998) para 1.5.

[58] Though the Cadbury Committee did itself build on earlier initiatives such as institutional investor statements on aspects of corporate governance like the ABI paper on *The Role and Duties of Directors* (1990) and the Institutional Shareholders Committee paper on *The Responsibilities of Institutional Shareholders* (1991). Before the *Cadbury Report* the best example of city, industry and investment co-operation in matters of corporate governance was *The Pre-Emption Guidelines.* The guidelines, which are still in operation, set out the circumstances in which institutional investors will support a resolution to disapply the pre-emption requirements of the Companies Act 1985, s 89. See further Ch 18 below, at 622–3.

with the adoption by the London Stock Exchange of a *Combined Code* that brings together recommendations from the three earlier reports. The status of the *Combined Code* is that it is appended to *The Listing Rules* and does not form part of them. This means that non-compliance with some aspects of the *Combined Code* does not, in itself, jeopardise a company's listing. There are, however, some specific requirements in *The Listing Rules* that relate to the *Combined Code*. In their annual reports and accounts listed companies must include statements on compliance with the *Combined Code*.[59] They must also include a specific report on directors' remuneration which must provide details on a range of matters such as the company's general policy on executive directors' remuneration and, more specifically, the amounts of individual directors' pay packages, information on share options, details of long-term incentive schemes and details of predetermined termination compensation payments.[60] These requirements apply to all annual reports and accounts published in respect of accounting periods ending on or after 31 December 1998.

It is unnecessary here to embark upon a detailed examination of the corporate governance rules relating to the operation of remuneration committees, audit committees and other committees on which non-executive directors may be expected to serve. An issue of wider significance that emerges out of the detailed rules is whether the role of non-executive directors as a matter of best practice in corporate governance is best characterised as that of a monitor of the executive management, or of a contributor to overall strategic planning and direction, or as some mix of the two. The *Hampel Report* referred to this matter, reporting that there was general acceptance that non-executive directors should have both a strategic and a monitoring function and commenting that an unintended side-effect of the earlier *Cadbury Report* might have been to emphasise the monitoring role to an unwarranted extent.[61] Some commentators have queried whether it is really possible for one person effectively to be at the same time someone who monitors the executive directors and someone who co-operates with them in the company's strategic development,[62] but suggestions that the primacy of the monitoring role should be explicitly acknowledged by the establishment of a second tier supervisory board comprising non-executive directors have not attracted support in UK practice and reform in that direction seems to be unlikely.[63]

59 *The Listing Rules*, para 12.43A (a)–(b).

60 *The Listing Rules*, para 12.43A (c).

61 *Hampel Report*, para 3.7.

62 eg, Ezzamel, M and Watson, R, 'Wearing Two Hats: The Conflicting Control and Management Roles of Non-executive Directors' in Keasey, K, Thompson, S, and Wright, M (eds), *Corporate Governance Economic, Management and Financial Issues* (1997) 54; Parkinson, JE, *Corporate Power and Responsibility* (1993) 57–8 and ch 6. Survey evidence indicates that non-executive directors also feel that their role could be more clearly defined: *The State of Corporate Governance in Britain* (Survey of directors at top 250 UK companies conducted by Russell Reynolds Associates) (1996).

63 The *Hampel Report* para 1.4 notes overwhelming support for the unitary-board system and little support for the two-tier framework. That legislation introducing two-tier boards seems to be unlikely is supported by *Modern Company Law for a Competitive Economy* (DTI Consultative Paper) (1998) paras 3.5–3.8 which declares a preference for best practice as opposed to legislation in areas of corporate governance. Papers in support of the unitary board include: *Boards Without Tiers: a CBI Contribution to the Debate* (1996); and Owen, G, *The Future of Britain's Boards of Directors: Two Tiers or One?* (Chartered Accountants in Business publication) (1995).

The balance between the monitoring and strategic functions of the modern non-executive director is an issue that has important implications when a connection is made between market expectations with regard to the role of non-executive directors and their legal duty of care and skill: viewing non-executive directors as monitors paves the way for laying blame and, potentially, legal responsibility for failure to detect and rectify underperformance or abuse by the executive management on them; but it is more difficult to say that the non-executive directors are responsible for the failings of their company when their role as strategists is emphasised in preference to their monitoring function.

Although it has become one of the key components of modern UK best practice in corporate governance, the practice of having non-executive directors on the boards of large companies that have external shareholder investors has also attracted criticism. One for the main targets for criticism is the background of typical non-executive directors and the process whereby they are selected for appointment. Non-executive directors tend to be drawn from a group comprised of persons who are themselves executive directors of other companies, or who otherwise have significant managerial experience. This has led some commentators to doubt whether, in view of the very likely professional and social contacts that potential non-executive directors have with the executive directors, as well as shared standards and perceptions of acceptable business practice, they can truly be regarded as 'independent'.[64] This criticism has to be set against the realistic practical consideration that persons who are inexperienced in business matters will probably find it extremely difficult to make a worthwhile contribution as non-executive directors. Yet, even with that point in mind, in the early 1990s it was widely thought that prevailing practices in relation to selection and appointment of non-executive directors were unsatisfactory.[65] It appeared that in many instances non-executive directors owed their position, at least in part, to personal acquaintance with the chairman or members of the executive board.[66] Since then, as the proportion of non-executive directors being appointed to the boards of companies and the role that they are expected to play have grown,[67] attempts have also

[64] Brudney, V, 'The Independent Director—Heavenly City or Potemkin Village?' (1982) 95 Harvard Law Review 597.

[65] *Research Into the Role of the Non-executive Director* (PRO NED publication) (1992). This survey of chairmen, chief executives, non-executive directors, other executive directors, directors of subsidiary companies, investment directors of institutional shareholders and senior audit partners of firms of accountants indicated widespread dissatisfaction with regard to these matters and support for the development of more rigorous selection mechanisms.

[66] Cosh, AD, and Hughes, A, 'The Anatomy of Corporate Control: Directors, Shareholders and Executive Remuneration in Giant US and UK Corporations' (1987) 11 *Cambridge Journal of Economics* 285 report that at that time the non-executive directors of UK companies appeared to be primarily either retired executive directors (often of the same company) or executive directors of other companies in the financial and industrial sectors. See also Davis, E, and Kay, J, 'Corporate Governance, Takeovers and the Role of the Non-executive Director' in Bishop, M, and Kay, J (eds), *European Mergers and Merger Policy* (1993) ch 5.

[67] By 1995/96 evidence suggested that the proportion of non-executive directors on UK company boards had risen to around 50 per cent on average: Cosh, AD, and Hughes, A, *The Changing Anatomy of Corporate Control and the Market for Executives in the UK* (ESCR Centre for Business Research Working Paper 49) (1996); 'Non-executives Fill 50% of Board Seats' *Financial Times* 15 May 1997 reporting the finding of a PRO NED survey on non-executive directors.

been made to improve the processes for the appointment of non-executives.[68] It is a principle of the *Combined Code* that the procedure for the appointment of new directors to the board of a company should be formal and transparent.[69] There is also a specific requirement[70] for the establishment of a nomination committee to make recommendations on all new board appointments.[71] A majority of this committee should be non-executive directors. Despite such initiatives, whether, or to what extent, typical non-executive directors of UK large companies (who are still commonly executive directors of other companies or former directors of the company itself) are really independent outsiders remains debatable.[72] There is a case for broadening out the discussion of this issue beyond the matter of appointment procedures to address the question of the qualities that are required of non-executive directors and whether persons other than those with direct industry experience can realistically be expected to have them.[73] This links in with, and underscores the importance of, the development of a clearer picture of the non-executive role and legal responsibilities and how an appropriate balance between the supervisory and strategic elements is to be established and maintained.

There are also concerns about whether non-executive directors can realistically be expected to form an objective picture of the company's affairs, given the time that they can devote to the company is necessarily limited. A related practical constraint is that their views have to be formed largely on the basis of a flow of information provided by the senior management and the executive directors; this means that they may not be in a position to assess properly the accuracy of the information and, moreover, that they may seek to avoid antagonistic situations which may provoke the executive directors and management to curtail the information supply. Since the appointment of non-executive directors is seen to be one way of redressing the informational asymmetries that inevitably exist between the management of a company and its shareholders,[74] difficulties with regard to access to management information that may be faced by non-executives represent a potentially

[68] The 1990s were not, however, the first time that attention focused on the role that non-executive directors might play in corporate governance. See Charkham, J, *Keeping Good Company* (1995) 268–71 discussing, amongst other matters, the establishment in 1981 of PRO NED , a body, backed by City institutions including the Bank of England and the Stock Exchange, to promote the wider use of non-executive directors.

[69] *Combined Code* A.5.

[70] *Combined Code* A.5.1.

[71] As at the end of 1995, 79 per cent of the UK's largest companies had established nomination committees: *NAPF Corporate Governance Analysis* (1996).

[72] 'Non-executives Fill 50% of Board Seats' *Financial Times* 15 May 1997. The PRO NED survey on non-executive directors reported in this article included a finding that over 50 per cent of chairmen had an individual in mind before making an appointment to a non-executive position. The conclusion drawn from the findings was that the procedures for recruiting and employing non-executives had failed to keep pace with the development of their responsibilities. Others have also doubted the independence of non-executive directors: eg, *Non-executive Directors and Their Role in Corporate Governance* (CISCO Survey) (1995).

[73] Cadbury, Sir Adrian, *The Governance Debate* (1997) 18–19 suggests that members of professions, people with experience of voluntary organisations or public life and academics may be people who are suitable for non-executive appointments. He highlights the low number of women on boards as indicating an untapped source of potential talent.

[74] Parkinson, JE, *Corporate Power and Responsibility* (1993) 174–7; 191–9.

serious problem.[75] The *Combined Code* addresses this matter by stating as a general principle that the board should be supplied in a timely manner with information in a form and of a quality appropriate to enable it to discharge its duties.[76] This admirable sentiment is bolstered by specific requirements including an obligation on the chairman to ensure that all directors are properly briefed on all matters arising at board meetings,[77] a requirement for the establishment of an agreed procedure whereby directors can take independent professional advice at the company's expense where this is necessary in the furtherance of their duties[78] and a statement that all directors should have access to the advice and services of the company secretary.[79]

The role of non-executive directors as arbiters of executive remuneration has also attracted much attention and some hostile criticism. [80] To assume that the presence of a remuneration committee will reduce the levels of pay increases of executive directors is obviously misconceived, but where evidence indicates significantly increased levels of remuneration being approved by committees comprised of non-executive directors, this does prompt concerns. [81] Put in its starkest and most extreme terms, the concern is that remuneration committees may provide a veneer of independence which cloaks a system of mutual back-scratching amongst directors.[82] Expressed less pejoratively and more specifically, it is difficult to see how non-executive directors who are also executive directors of other companies in the same sector can be truly independent if the process of setting remuneration includes use of industry comparisons on the level of executive pay awards.[83] This type of

[75] Jensen, MC, 'The Modern Industrial Revolution, Exit and the Failure of Internal Control Systems' (1993) 48 *Journal of Finance* 831, 864; Conyon, MJ, 'Institutional Arrangements for Setting Directors' Compensation in UK Companies' in Keasey, K, Thompson, S, and Wright, M (eds), *Corporate Governance Economic, Management and Financial Issues* (1997)103, 108.

[76] *Combined Code*, A.4.

[77] *Combined Code*, A.4.1.

[78] *Combined Code*, A.1.3.

[79] *Combined Code* A.1.4.

[80] There has been extensive coverage of this issue. The literature includes the following: Forbes, W, and Watson, R, 'Managerial Remuneration and Corporate Governance: A Review of the Issues, Evidence and Cadbury Committee's Proposals' (1993) 91A *Accounting and Business Research* 331; Jensen, MC, The Eclipse of the Public Corporation' (1989) October *Harvard Business Review*, 61; Cosh, AD, and Hughes, A, 'The Anatomy of Corporate Control: Directors, Shareholders and Executive Remuneration of Giant US and UK Corporations' (1987) 11 *Cambridge Journal of Economics* 285; Main, BGM, and Johnston, J, 'Remuneration Committees and Corporate Governance' (1993) 91A *Accounting and Business Research* 351; *Boardroom Pay in UK Quoted Companies* (Arthur Andersen publication) (1996); Ezzamel, M and Watson, R, 'Wearing Two Hats: The Conflicting Control and Management Roles of Non-executive Directors' in Keasey, K, Thompson, S, and Wright, M (eds), *Corporate Governance Economic, Management and Financial Issues* (1997) 54.

[81] For evidence of this see, eg, Cosh, AD, and Hughes, A, *Executive Remuneration, Executive Dismissal and Institutional Shareholdings* (ESRC Centre for Business Research Working Paper 19) (1995); Main, BGM, and Johnston, J, 'Remuneration Committees and Corporate Governance' (1993) 91A *Accounting and Business Research* 351.

[82] Lea, R, *Directors' Remuneration* (Institute of Directors Research Paper) (1997) 5, 22–3. Note 'Curtains for Corporate Back-Scratching' *The Times* 17 October 1996 reporting US proposals to curtail interlocking directorships (ie the practice of directors sitting on each other's boards).

[83] The *Greenbury Report* included a recommendation that remuneration committees should judge where to position the company relative to other companies. It stated that committees should be aware what comparable companies were paying and should take account of relative performance. In the equivalent provisions of the *Combined Code* (sch A) the emphasis shifts from comparison of remuneration levels in other companies to the development of criteria that reflect the company's performance relative to a group of comparator companies in some key variables

comparison gives non-executive directors a direct personal interest in their decision about the level of remuneration to award to the executives, since this information may feed into the data that will be used to determine their own remuneration as executive directors of other companies, thereby compromising their independence.[84]

Despite reservations such as these, having non-executive directors on the board of large companies is generally viewed as a valuable element of corporate governance structure, and institutional investors endorse the practice.[85] As at the end of 1995, 95 per cent of the UK's largest 300 companies had at least three non-executive directors[86] and by 1997 non-executive directors were reported to fill, on average, half of the places on company boards.[87]

THE IMPACT OF GOOD PRACTICE IN CORPORATE GOVERNANCE ON THE DUTY TO ACT CAREFULLY AND COMPETENTLY

An analogy can be drawn between the *Combined Code* and the *City Code on Takeovers and Mergers* (*Takeover Code*), which also carries no direct legal sanctions, although the Stock Exchange requires compliance with its provisions.[88] The attitude of the courts to accounting standards—which, at least

such as total shareholder return. Although paying competitive levels of remuneration is obviously important for companies that want to be able to attract and retain high-quality executives, it would seem preferable to emphasise company performance, as opposed to levels of remuneration, as the basis on which to make industry comparisons. The *Hampel Report* para 4.4 urged caution in the use of remuneration surveys because: 'Few remuneration committees will want to recommend lower than average salaries. There is a danger that uncritical use of comparisons will lead to an upward ratchet in remuneration with no corresponding improvement in corporate performance.' The ABI has also issued its own views on this matter in its papers *Long Term Remuneration for Senior Executives* (1994) and *Long Term Incentive Schemes—Note of Emerging Good Practice* (1996).

84 Survey evidence suggests that there can exist other arrangements between companies and their non-executive directors, such as consultancy or leasing arrangements, that may jeopardise their independent status: 'Independence of Non-executive Directors Queried' and 'Spotlight Shines on Corporate Puppeteers' *Financial Times* 6 May 1997.

85 The recommendations of the Cadbury Committee were in line with those previously expressed by the Association of British Insurers in its paper *The Role and Duties of Directors*, 1990 and by the Institutional Shareholders Committee in its paper *The Responsibilities of Institutional Shareholders* 1991.

86 *NAPF Corporate Governance Analysis* (1996). Amongst public companies outside this top group there is some resistance to the fullest application of corporate governance best practices because it is argued that these were devised with the largest companies in mind. One argument is that smaller companies face difficulties in attracting suitable non-executive directors and that the minimum number of non-executive directors in these cases should be two rather than three: see, eg, *Greenbury: The Smaller Company Perspective* (City Group for Smaller Companies (CISCO) publication) (1995); *Corporate Governance—Too Great a Burden. A Survey of Attitudes Among Quoted Companies Outside the FTSE 350* (Arthur Andersen/Binder Hamlyn publication) (1996). The *Hampel Report* paras 1.10–1.11, however, rejected the suggestion that there should be a formal distinction drawn between the governance standards expected of larger and smaller companies but it urged appropriate flexibility in the application of such standards in smaller companies.

87 Non-executives Fill 50% of Board Seats' *Financial Times* 15 May 1997.

88 In *R v Takeover Panel ex parte Datafin plc* [1987] 1 QB 815, CA, the Stock Exchange's endorsement of the *Takeover Code* was described by Nicholas LJ as a 'major element' in the enforcement of that Code. See also at 826–7 and 834–6 *per* Donaldson MR and 845 *per* Lloyd LJ. The *Takeover Code* is an endorsed code for the purposes of the Financial Services Act 1986, s 47A (2). Non-compliance by an authorised person can trigger disciplinary or intervention action under that Act.

prior to the enactment in 1989 of a specific obligation on companies to certify compliance with accounting standards,[89] had no direct legal force—also sheds some light on how the *Combined Code* may come to be regarded. In *Re Chez Nico (Restaurants) Ltd*[90] substantial infringements of the *Takeover Code*, in the words of the Vice-Chancellor 'provide strong evidence that the offer is not fairly made', and in *Re a Company*[91] Hoffmann J acknowledged that the *Takeover Code* was 'a helpful guide to the City's views on fairness'.[92] In *Lloyd Cheyham & Co v Littlejohn*[93] a negligence case, accounting standards were regarded as 'very strong evidence' as to proper standards; Woolf J stated that, unless there was some justification, a departure would be regarded as constituting a breach of duty. As yet, there is only limited reference to the *Combined Code* and its predecessors in reported decisions,[94] but in *Bishopsgate Investment Management Ltd v Maxwell*[95] Hoffmann LJ noted: 'In the older cases the duty of a director to participate in the management of a company is stated in very undemanding terms. The law may be evolving in response to changes in public attitudes to corporate governance.' This statement hints that the courts may eventually regard the *Combined Code* in the field of corporate governance in same way as they view the *Takeover Code* and accounting standards as setting out the best practice with regard to the conduct of takeovers and the preparation of accounts respectively.

DILIGENCE AND DEVOTION TO THE COMPANY'S AFFAIRS: THE TRADITIONAL VIEW

The second aspect of the duty of care and skill is the extent to which it requires a director to devote himself to the affairs of his company. Accordingly to Romer J in *Re City Equitable Fire Insurance Co*:[96]

> a director is not bound to give continuous attention to the affairs of his company. His duties are of an intermittent nature to be performed at periodical board meetings, and at meetings of any committee of the board upon which he happens to be placed. He is not, however, bound to attend all such meetings, though he ought to attend whenever, in the circumstances, he is reasonably able to do so.

[89] Companies Act 1985, sch 4, para 36A requires the inclusion of a statement in accounts, or notes thereto, indicating whether accounts have been prepared in accordance with applicable accounting standards. Certain small and medium-sized companies are exempt from this requirement. 'Accounting standards' is defined by Companies Act 1985, s 256. Companies Act 1985 s 245–245C contains a procedure whereby accounts which do not contain a true and fair view can be amended. As to whether compliance with accounting standards amounts to compliance with the statutory duty to give a true and fair view, Hoffmann QC and Mary Arden advised in a joint opinion in 1983 that accounting standards were not conclusive but that the courts would look to them for guidance. In 1993 Mary Arden QC confirmed that view in a sole opinion. See also Ch 2 above,at 65–8.

[90] [1991] BCC 736, 751 *per* Browne-Wilkinson V-C.

[91] [1986] BCLC 382, 389.

[92] But that the detailed provisions did not necessarily coincide with the requirements for fairness in Companies Act 1985, s 459.

[93] [1987] BCLC 303 QBD, 306.

[94] See *Re Macro (Ipswich) Ltd* [1994] 2 BCLC 354; *Re BSB Holdings Ltd* [1996] 1 BCLC 155. Contrast *Re Astec (BSR) plc* [1999] BCC 59.

[95] [1994] 1 All ER 261, CA, 264.

[96] [1925] 1 Ch 407, Ch D and CA, 427.

Perhaps the most notorious example of a person in a directing position[97] escaping liability for his non-involvement is that of the Marquis of Bute who was appointed a director of the Cardiff Savings Bank at the age of six months and held office for over thirty years. In that time he managed to attend only one board meeting and, although copies of annual reports and circulars were sent to him, he had no recollection of ever receiving them. The Marquis was held to be justified in relying on the active managers of the bank and incurred no liability for his own non-participation.

The courts were never entirely consistent in their attitude to non-participating directors even in the nineteenth century. A director who failed to read a prospectus prepared by his co-directors was held liable for a misrepresentation which it contained, Byrne J commenting that: 'it should be understood that a director, consenting to be a director, has assumed a position involving duties which cannot be shirked by leaving everything to others'.[98] Although a director, described as a 'country gentleman', escaped liability for not detecting financial irregularity where he relied on the chairman and the company's auditors, nevertheless he was said to be guilty of considerable negligence in the discharge of his duties and his costs were disallowed.[99] A director may not have been obliged to attend meetings, but if he chose to attend he did not escape the consequences of not attending to the company's business by being asleep at the relevant time.[100]

DEVOTION TO DUTY: MODERN DEVELOPMENTS

Nowadays a director who fails completely to participate in his company's affairs would be exposing himself to the risk of being held liable under a number of headings, including breach of the duty of care and skill. Non-involvement in the company's affairs formed the basis for attaching liability to directors for breach of their duty of care and skill in *Dorchester Finance Co Ltd v Stebbing*.[101] Two non-executive directors left the running of the company in the hands of a third director. They did not attend board meetings or monitor the company's accounting records, and even went so far as to sign blank cheques on the company's behalf when so requested by the active director. Equally, a director cannot defend himself against a wrongful trading charge by opting out of his responsibilities. Liability for wrongful trading is judged by reference to what a director ought to have known. If the director would have known that the company had no reasonable prospect of avoiding insolvent liquidation if he had familiarised himself with the company's financial

[97] Strictly, he was a trustee or manager of the bank but the court proceeded on the basis that his position was similar to that of a director of a trading company: *Re Cardiff Savings Bank* [1892] 2 Ch 100, 108–9.

[98] *Drincqbier v Wood* [1899] 1 Ch 393, 406.

[99] *Re Denham & Co* (1884) 25 Ch D 752.

[100] *Land Credit Co of Ireland v Lord Fermoy* (1870) 5 Ch App 763.

[101] [1989] BCLC 498 (case decided in 1977).

position and records to the extent required to discharge specific obligations required by the companies legislation,[102] he will be held liable accordingly.[103]

The degree of devotion to his company that a director ought to display in order to escape censure cannot be stated in absolute terms. It will depend on the circumstances and relevant variable factors, including the type of organisation and the role that the director in question can reasonably be expected to play.[104] The role of non-executive directors of a public company is necessarily an intermittent one since if non-executive directors became actively involved in the day-to-day running of the company they would lose the very independence and detachment for which they were appointed in the first place. But in smaller companies where the monitoring function of the board is less important, all directors may be expected to play a more active part in the company's affairs.[105] A director's personal qualifications and experience may also influence the amount of involvement required of him.[106]

It would be a mistake to judge the adequacy of a director's devotion to his company simply by reference to the amount of time spent on the company's affairs, since the issue is not so much the number of hours that he devotes to the company but the quality of the services that he provides. Also, there may be particular situations where, because of the director's special skills or the nature of the matter in question, the director should devote more than the usual amount of time to the company's affairs. Noteworthy in this context is the requirement of the *Takeover Code* that the board as a whole must ensure that proper arrangements are in place to enable it to monitor the conduct of the individual directors who are responsible for the day-to-day conduct of a bid.[107] This requirement is intended to prevent the recurrence of the type of situation which arose in the contested takeover of Distillers by Guinness in the 1980s, where the conduct of the bid was left entirely to three directors who were not supervised by the whole board of Guinness and where it was later discovered that the bid had involved serious breaches of legal and regulatory requirements. Thus, where their company is involved in a takeover bid, the non-executive directors may expect to be required to devote a greater proportion of their time to its affairs than would be necessary in the ordinary course of events.

The adequacy of a director's devotion to the company shades into the question of the extent to which he is justified in relying on others.

[102] Directors are subject to a number of specific obligations with regard to their company's financial records including: Companies Act 1985, s 222 (keeping of financial records); s 233 (approval and signing of accounts); and 234–234A (approval and signing of directors' report). Non-compliance with the positive obligations imposed by these sections is an offence by the directors, but individual directors can defend themselves by proving that they took all reasonable steps for securing compliance with the relevant requirements.

[103] *Re Produce Marketing Consortium Ltd (No 2)* [1989] BCLC 520. But note *Re Sherborne Associates Ltd* [1995] BCC 40.

[104] *Bishopsgate Investment Management Ltd v Maxwell* [1994] 1 All ER 261, CA, 264 *per* Hoffmann LJ.

[105] *Re Burnham Marketing Services Ltd* [1993] BCC 518 527.

[106] 'For a chartered accountant and an experienced accountant to put forward the proposition that a non-executive director has no duties to perform I find quite alarming': *Dorchester Finance Co Ltd v Stebbing* [1989] BCLC 498, 505 *per* Foster J.

[107] *City Code on Takeovers and Mergers*, app 3.

DELEGATION: THE TRADITIONAL VIEW

In respect of all duties that, having regard to the exigencies of business, and the articles of association, may properly be left to some other official, a director is, in the absence of grounds for suspicion, justified in trusting that official to perform such duties honestly.

This was the third of Romer J's propositions in *Re City Equitable Fire Insurance Co Ltd*.[108]

A director who fails to recognise his own limitations and does not seek appropriate assistance and advice may be just as much liable to censure as one who abdicates his responsibilities and leaves the running of the company entirely to others.[109] Again, the matter is more one of degree than of an absolute standard: the question is whether he is justified in relying on someone else in the first place and whether there are any grounds for suspecting the integrity of the person on whom he relies.[110] If, for example, a person is appointed as company secretary, it would not be justifiable for him to hand over responsibility for the maintenance of the company's records to someone else,[111] but the directors of the company would, barring suspicious circumstances, be justified in relying upon the secretary as having duly fulfilled his obligations with regard to those records.

DELEGATION IN THE MODERN ENVIRONMENT

In *Re City Equitable Fire Insurance Co Ltd* Romer J said that:[112]

In one company, for instance, matters may normally be attended to by the managers or other members of the staff that in another company are attended to by the directors themselves. The larger the business carried on by the company the more numerous, and the more important, the matters that must of necessity be left to the managers, the accountants and the rest of the staff. The manner in which the work of the company is to be distributed between the board of directors and the staff is in truth a business matter to be decided on business lines.

This comment about the practical necessity of delegation and reliance on others, especially as the size of a business expands, remains as true today as it was when the *Re City Equitable* case was decided. It is usually impracticable for the board of a company to make day-to-day managerial decisions, at least where the board is of any size. Instead responsibility for decision making in the ordinary course of events has to be devolved to individual directors and managers. This leaves the board free to concentrate on areas of strategy and policy, and also, through audit committees and the like, to monitor those who

108 [1925] 1 Ch 407, Ch D and CA, 427.

109 *Re New Generation Ltd* [1993] BCLC 435 (not seeking professional advice was a factor in disqualification); *Re Rolus Ltd* (1988) 4 BCC 446 (disqualification; but reliance on another was a mitigating factor).

110 See in particular *Dovey v Cory* [1901] AC 477, HL.

111 See *Re Linvale Ltd* [1993] BCLC 654.

112 [1925] 1 Ch 407, Ch D and CA, 426.

are primarily responsible for the day-to-day management of the company's affairs.

The limits of the principle of justifiable reliance on others in the context of a company run on typically modern lines, where the board performs more of a strategic and monitoring function than a direct managerial role, were considered in the Australian case of *Daniels v Anderson*.[113] The case arose from fraudulent conduct of an employee of AWA. These frauds were not detected by the auditors of AWA and, as a result, AWA later sued its auditors for negligence. The factual evidence was that the auditors had informed the individual who was chairman and chief executive (the roles were not divided)[114] of certain serious deficiencies in internal control and in the books and records, but he had failed to pass on this information to the non-executive directors. The auditors, in defending the claim, argued that there had been contributory negligence by AWA through the negligence of its chief executive and non-executive directors. The New South Wales Court of Appeal held that the chief executive had been negligent[115] but that the non-executives had not. In reaching this conclusion the court engaged upon a careful and detailed review of directors' duties of care and skill and, in particular, the extent to which non-executive directors could rely on others and trust them.

The first instance judge had held that non-executive directors were justified in trusting officers of the corporation to perform their duty and could rely without verification on the judgment, information and advice of the officers so entrusted. They could also rely on management to sift through and draw attention to any matter specifically requiring the board's attention. In relation to auditors, if the directors appointed a person of good repute and competence to audit the accounts, absent real grounds for suspecting that the auditor was wrong, the directors would have discharged their duty to the company. Generally, reliance on others would only be unreasonable where the directors were aware of circumstances that were so plain that no person with any degree of prudence, acting in his own affairs, would have done so. Although the Court of Appeal agreed with the finding on the facts that the non-executive directors had not been negligent, this analysis of the role of non-executive directors was rejected in favour of more rigorous standards as developed by the US courts. The US cases cited by the Court of Appeal[116] established that all directors had a duty to acquire at least a rudimentary

[113] (1995) 16 ACSR 607, NSW CA. This case, and subsequent Australian and New Zealand decisions are examined in Baxt, R, 'The Duty of Care of Directors—Does it Depend on the Swing of the Pendulum' in Ramsay, IM, *Corporate Governance and the Duties of Company Directors* (1997) 92.

[114] It is a tenet of good corporate governance practice in the UK that the roles of chairman and chief executive should normally be kept separate: *Combined Code* A.2. The facts of the AWA case illustrate why it can be valuable to divide these roles.

[115] It was not, however, contributory negligence for the purposes of the relevant Australian legislation.

[116] *Francis v United Jersey Bank* 432 A 2d 814 (1981); *Federal Deposit Insurance Co v Stanley* 770 F Supp 1281 (ND Ind 1991); *Stepak v Addison* 20 F 3d 398 (11th Cir 1994). Note, however, Clark, RC, *Corporate Law* 123–36 who suggests that although the US courts often 'talk tough' to warn figurehead directors, in fact this is rarely translated into holdings of liability against them. Generally on the duty of care under US law: Eisenberg, MA, 'The Duty of Care and the Business Judgement Rule in American Corporate Law' [1997] CfiLR 185.

understanding of the business and to keep themselves informed about its activities. They should attend board meeting regularly. They did not have to perform detailed inspections of the day-to-day activities but had to engage upon a general monitoring of its affairs and policies. That encompassed a duty to maintain familiarity with the financial status of the business by a regular review of its financial statements. The monitoring function could not be met solely by relying on other people.

The *Daniels* case is, broadly speaking, in tune with the English decisions which suggest that the lax standards of old have been tacitly abandoned in favour of more onerous obligations on directors. It is thus indicative of how an English court might approach the question of how far it is reasonable for a director, particularly a non-executive director, to place reliance and trust in others.[117] Notwithstanding the general trend towards stricter standards, relying on, and trusting, others should properly remain a defence to non-executive directors in appropriate cases,[118] but their role, and personal obligations, as independent monitors will not be discharged by an unquestioning acceptance of information that is presented to them in circumstances where a reasonable person would have been put in inquiry. It is impossible to state in precise terms when, or to what extent, a non-executive director will be justified in relying on others, since this will depend on a range of variables including the type of company, the skills of the director in question and the nature of the matter, although this can be expressed generally in terms of reasonableness and good faith. Yet, whilst standards cannot be set in stone, it may be that lack of clarity about the nature of the non-executive role itself exacerbates the uncertainty in this area. Perhaps if it were to be more clearly recognised that the members of the board plan the business strategy and monitor management but do not, in that capacity, manage its daily affairs,[119] then it would be seen that in allowing managers to get on with their jobs, the non-executives are not so much delegating their responsibilities as refraining from usurping functions that do not properly fall to them to perform. That would allow the focus to shift onto whether the non-executive directors have put in place systems that are appropriate and adequate for them to discharge their personal obligation to monitor and on to whether they have conducted sufficient inquiries when there are particular circumstances that would give a reasonable person cause for concern.[120]

[117] Nolan, R, 'Care and Skill in Australia' (1996) 17 Co Law 89; Alcock, A, 'Breach of Duties to Companies' [1996] LMCLQ 324.

[118] *Norman v Theodore Goddard* [1992] BCC 14 itself supports this. The allegation of wrongful trading turned on a director's reliance on a professional adviser but it was held that, provided the standard of care and skill embodied in Insolvency Act 1986, s 214 (4) was observed, the director was entitled to trust his adviser who was a person in a position of responsibility and whose previous conduct had given no grounds for suspicion. Note the Australian Corporations Law, s 588G which provides for directors' personal liability in insolvency. A director may have a defence under this section where a competent and reliable subordinate was monitoring the company's solvency.

[119] This could be effected by changes to the management articles in companies' articles of association. Reform of Table A, art 70 could lead the way in this respect.

[120] Eisenberg, MA, *The Structure of the Corporation: A Legal Analysis* (1986) is the leading proponent of explicit recognition of the monitoring role. See also Dent, GW, 'The Revolution in Corporate Governance, the Monitoring Board and the Directors' Duty of Care' (1981) 61 Boston University Law Review 623. The decision of the Delaware Court of Chancery in *Re Caremark International Inc*, 1996 Del Ch Lexis 125, emphasises the importance of establishing effective monitoring procedures in order successfully to defend claims based on breach of the duty of care.

THE IMPACT OF THE COMPANY DIRECTORS DISQUALIFICATION ACT 1986 ON STANDARDS OF CARE AND SKILL OF CORPORATE MANAGEMENT

Under the Company Directors Disqualification Act 1986 a person can be disqualified from acting as a director, liquidator or administrator of a company, or as a receiver or manager of the company's property or from being in any way, whether directly or indirectly, concerned or taking part in the promotion, formation or management of the company for a specified period.[121] There are a number of grounds on which a disqualification order may be made including conviction of offences,[122] persistent breaches of the companies legislation,[123] fraud[124] and participation in wrongful trading.[125] Under the Company Directors Disqualification Act 1986, s 11, an undischarged bankrupt commits an offence if he is involved in the promotion, formation or management of a company without the leave of the court.

A director of a company which has become insolvent (whether while he was director or subsequently) may be disqualified under the Company Directors Disqualification Act 1986, s 6 if the court is satisfied that his conduct as a director (either taken alone or together with his conduct as a director of any other company or companies) makes him unfit to be concerned in the management of a company.[126] For the purposes of the Company Directors Disqualification Act 1986, s 6, a company becomes insolvent if it goes into liquidation at a time when its assets are insufficient for the payment of its liabilities and the expenses for winding up (a form of balance sheet insolvency), or an administration order is made in relation to it or an administrative receiver is appointed to it.[127] Shadow directors and de facto directors are within the scope of this section as well as directors who have been properly appointed.[128]

The question whether, or at what level, incompetence, as opposed to fraud or other deliberate or reckless wrongdoing, should constitute unfitness to be involved in the management of the company is a difficult one which requires different and potentially conflicting interests to be balanced against each other. The underlying purpose of the disqualification legislation is to ensure that those who make use of limited liability do so with the proper sense of responsibility[129] and to protect the public against the future conduct of companies by persons whose past records as directors of insolvent companies

121 Company Directors Disqualification Act 1986, s 1.
122 Ibid, ss 2 and 5.
123 Ibid, s 3.
124 Ibid, s 4.
125 Ibid, s 10.
126 On disqualification generally, see Hicks, A, 'Disqualification of Directors—Forty Years On' [1988] JBL 27; Hannigan, BM, 'Disqualifying Company Directors' [1987] LMCLQ 188; Dine, J, 'The Disqualification of Company Directors' (1988) 9 Co Law 213; Finch, V, 'Disqualification of Directors: A Plea for Competence' (1990) 53 MLR 385; Sealy, LS, *Disqualification and Personal Liability of Directors* (3rd edn, 1993); Mithani, A, and Wheeler, S, *The Disqualification of Company Directors* (1996).
127 Company Directors Disqualification Act 1986, s 6 (2).
128 Ibid, s 6 (3) (shadow directors) and *Re Lo-Line Electric Motors Ltd* [1988] 1 Ch 477; *Re Tasbian Ltd (No 3)* [1991] BCC 435; *Re Cargo Agency Ltd* [1992] BCC 388; *Re Moorgate Metals Ltd* [1995] BCC 143; *Re Richborough Furniture Ltd* [1996] BCC 155; *Secretary of State for Trade and Industry v Hickling* [1996] BCC 678.
129 *Re Swift 736 Ltd* [1993] BCC 312, CA; *Re Sevenoaks Stationers Ltd* [1991] Ch 164, CA.

show them to be a danger to creditors, employees and investors.[130] But overly rigorous standards could inhibit the formation and expansion of new business ventures[131] and could constitute a substantial, and arguably unwarranted, interference with the liberty of individuals who want to participate in the management of companies.[132] Where the appropriate balance should be struck featured in the debate leading up to the enactment of the Company Directors Disqualification Act 1986, a piece of legislation that was designed to build upon and to strengthen existing disqualification provisions, and it has continued to attract the attention of the courts in interpreting and applying that legislation.

In 1962 the Jenkins Committee on Company Law Reform[133] had recommended that incompetent management should be a ground of unfitness, but when an opportunity for reform arose in the Insolvency Act 1976 the government at that stage concluded that to allow for disqualification solely on the grounds of incompetence 'would go unwisely far'.[134] The Insolvency Act 1976, s 9 was more restricted in its effect: it allowed for disqualification on the ground of unfitness of persons who had been directors of at least two companies which had gone into disqualification within five years of each other. That disqualification simply on the grounds of incompetence would be excessively harsh was also in essence the view of the Cork Committee which reported in 1982.[135] Whilst advocating the achievement of higher standards of corporate management through more rigorous disqualification procedures and more effective enforcement, that committee emphasised the importance of not deterring legitimate enterprise. The most extreme proposal in recent times was that put forward by the government in 1984,[136] and included in the Insolvency Bill 1985, under which every director of a company in compulsory liquidation would be disqualified unless he could disprove unfitness. This proposal attracted a welter of criticism and, after the provision in the Bill had been twice voted down by the House of Lords, it was withdrawn and what is now the Company Directors Disqualification Act 1986, s 6 was enacted instead.

Under the Company Directors Disqualification Act 1986, s 6, the court is specifically directed to consider a number of matters in determining whether the conduct of a director makes him unfit to be concerned in the management of a company. These matters, which are set out in sch 1 to the Act, include any misfeasance or breach of any fiduciary or other duty by the director in relation to the company, the extent of the director's responsibility for failure to comply with specified accounting and other provisions of the companies legislation and the extent of the director's responsibility for the causes of the company becoming insolvent. A director's lack of skill, or incompetence, is not a matter

130 *Re Grayan Building Services Ltd* [1995] BCC 554, CA, 577 *per* Henry LJ; *Re Lo-Line Electric Motors Ltd* [1988] 1 Ch 477; *Re Cedac Ltd* [1990] BCC 555, [1991] BCC 148, CA.

131 *Re Rolus Properties Ltd* (1988) 4 BCC 446.

132 Ibid.

133 *Report of the Company Law Committee*, Cmnd 1749 (1962) para 85 (b).

134 For the background to the 1980s insolvency legislation see Fletcher, I, 'The Genesis of Modern Insolvency Law—An Odyssey of Law Reform' [1989] JBL 365.

135 *Report of the Review Committee on Insolvency Law and Practice*, Cmnd 8558 (1982) ch 45.

136 *A Revised Framework for Insolvency Law*, Cmnd 9175 (1984) ch 2.

to which the court's attention is specifically drawn by the statutory guidelines; but it is clear that the court is permitted to consider other matters in addition to those specified in sch 1.[137]

There are certain types or patterns of misconduct which tend to feature in many disqualification cases. These are: (i) persistent failure to comply with the accounting requirements of the companies legislation (a matter to which the attention of the court is specifically drawn by sch 1); (ii) trading whilst insolvent without regard to creditors' interests; and (iii) diversion of corporate property or other benefits to the directors personally. Where failure to comply with accounting requirements is in issue,[138] a director's own lack of experience in financial matters has proved not to be a mitigating factor in the courts' deliberations as to unfitness.[139] At the very least directors are expected to recognise their own lack of accounting knowledge and to seek appropriate professional assistance.[140] With regard to insolvent trading, this is regarded harshly by the courts because, with the share capital already wiped out by debts, this amounts to taking unwarranted risks with creditors' money and is an abuse of limited liability.[141] Non-payment of Crown debts is one aspect of this. Although there is no absolute rule that failure to pay such debts amounts automatically to evidence of unfitness[142] the courts look severely upon this because administrative hurdles may prevent public authorities from pressing for prompt payment, thus enabling the company to continue trading at public expense. Taking unfair advantage of any creditor's forbearance to sue in this way and continuing to trade at the risk of those creditors is equally capable of amounting to evidence of unfitness.[143] Where directors engage in conduct that benefits themselves, such as by continuing to pay themselves remuneration whilst at the same time defaulting on obligations due to creditors, diverting corporate opportunities to themselves or transferring company assets to themselves at an undervalue, this, too, is the type of conduct that can lead to disqualification.[144]

[137] *Re GSAR Realisations Ltd* [1993] BCLC 409, 421.

[138] *Re Swift 736 Ltd* [1992] BCC 93, [1993] BCC 312, CA may be regarded as a leading case. Nicholas V-C in the Court of Appeal emphasises that those who persistently fail to comply with accounting obligations can expect to be disqualified.

[139] See for example *Re Rolus Properties Ltd* (1988) 4 BCC 446; *Re New Generation Engineers Ltd* [1993] BCLC 435; *Re Linvale Ltd* [1993] BCLC 654.

[140] *Re New Generation Engineers Ltd* [1993] BCLC 435; *Re Rolus Properties Ltd* (1988) 4 BCC 446 (reliance on chartered secretary who was engaged to handle paperwork was mitigating factor). Ignorance may be a slight mitigating factor in relation to the period of disqualification: *Re Melcast (Wolverhampton) Ltd* [1991] BCLC 288 but a person who does not appreciate his responsibilities as a director may, for the protection of the public, be disqualified for a significant period.

[141] *Re Synthetic Technology Ltd* [1993] BCC 549; *Re Hitco 2000 Ltd* [1995] BCC 161; *Re Living Images Ltd* [1996] BCC 112.

[142] *Re Sevenoaks Stationers Ltd* [1991] Ch 164, CA.

[143] *Re Stanford Services Ltd* [1987] BCLC 607.

[144] eg, *Re Firedart Ltd* [1994] 2 BCLC 340; *Re Moorgate Metals Ltd* [1995] BCC 143; *Re CSTC Ltd* [1995] BCC 173; *Re Ward Sherrard Ltd* [1996] BCC 418; *Re Living Images Ltd* [1996] BCC 112; *Re Park House Properties Ltd* [1997] 2 BCLC 530; *Secretary of State for Trade and Industry v McTighe (No 2)* [1996] 2 BCLC 477, CA.

Ordinary commercial misjudgment in itself is insufficient to justify disqualification.[145] The conduct complained of must display a lack of commercial probity[146] or commercial morality,[147] or incompetence or negligence in a very marked degree.[148] In each case the question of unfitness is one of fact and, although phrases such as 'incompetence or negligence in a very marked degree' may be helpful guidelines to the court in assessing the seriousness of the conduct required,[149] it has been emphasised that these phrases must not be construed as if they were themselves statutory provisions.[150] The correct approach is for the court to consider whether, as a matter of fact, the conduct complained of comes within the words of the statute.[151]

Although disqualification cases thus turn on their own facts,[152] in the context of this chapter the decision in *Re Continental Assurance Co of London plc*[153] is notable. This case concerned an insurance company which had gone into liquidation with debts in excess of £8 million. All three directors of the company were disqualified, including a non-executive director who had been appointed to that position at the request, and on behalf, of a bank which had provided finance to the parent company to enable it to acquire the now insolvent subsidiary. The court accepted that the non-executive director had not known of the misconduct in relation to the company's affairs, in particular the fact that it was lending money to its parent company to enable it to finance its bank loan in breach of the ban on financial assistance contained in Companies Act 1985, s 151. Nevertheless the court held that any competent director in his position would have known what was going on and that his failure to know displayed serious incompetence or neglect in relation to the affairs of the company that was sufficient to justify disqualification. Chadwick J said:[154]

> Those in the position of Mr Burt, being senior employees of major banks, who accept appointment as directors of client companies of those banks, are lending their name and the respectability associated with their employer to the board of directors of that client company. Those dealing with the client company are entitled to expect that external directors appointed on the basis of their apparent expertise will exercise the

[145] *Re Lo-Line Electric Motors Ltd* [1988] 1 Ch 477; approved (with some qualification) by the Court of Appeal in *Re Sevenoaks Stationers Ltd* [1991] Ch 164, CA; see also *Re Bath Glass Ltd* (1988) 4 BCC 130, 133; *Re CU Fittings Ltd* (1989) 5 BCC 210; *Re Cladrose Ltd* [1990] BCC 11; *Re ECM (Europe) Electronics Ltd* [1991] BCC 268; *Re Cedac Ltd* [1990] BCC 555, [1991] BCC 148, CA; *Re Polly Peck International plc (No 2)* [1993] BCC 890.

[146] *Re Lo-Line Electric Motors Ltd* [1988] 1 Ch 477.

[147] *Re Dawson Print Group Ltd* (1987) 3 BCC 322, and *Re Standard Services Ltd* (1987) 3 BCC 326 (decided under the Companies Act 1985, s 300) and *Re Ipcon Fashions Ltd* (1989) 5 BCC 773 and *Re Swift 736 Ltd* [1993] BCC 312, CA.

[148] Dillion LJ in *Re Sevenoaks Stationers Ltd* [1991] Ch 164, CA disagreed with the statement of the Vice Chancellor in *Re Lo-Line* that gross negligence or total incompetence was required.

[149] In *Re Polly Peck International plc (No 2)* [1993] BCC 890 Lindsey J took serious misconduct as the standard by which to judge the directors in that case.

[150] *Re Sevenoaks Stationers Ltd* [1991] Ch 164, CA.

[151] Ibid.

[152] *Re Grayan Building Services Ltd* [1995] BCC 554, CA makes it clear that it is factual evidence about the director's conduct as a director of the insolvent company that matters and that evidence that this person has, since he ceased to hold that office, shown himself to be capable of acting responsibly is not relevant. However, his conduct as a director of other companies is relevant: Company Directors Disqualification Act 1986, s 6 (1)(b).

[153] [1996] BCC 888.

[154] Ibid, 896.

competence required by the Companies Act 1985 in relation to the affairs of the company of which they have accepted office as directors. The competence required by the 1985 Act extends, at the least, to a requirement that a director who is a corporate financier should be prepared to read and understand the statutory accounts of the holding company of the company of which he is a director—*a fortiori*, whether he is a director also of that holding company—and satisfy himself that transactions between holding company and subsidiary are properly reflected in the statutory accounts of the subsidiary.

Although directed at a particular type of non-executive director, the representative of a major creditor, these comments could apply more generally. In the modern environment, the commercial expectation of investors is that non-executive directors who are appointed to the boards of public companies will discharge important functions with regard to corporate governance and will have the requisite skills to enable them to do so. Directors, especially non-executive directors, cannot safely assume that lack of involvement in, and effort to understand, their company's affairs will be a defence in disqualification proceedings.[155] This case is also significant in that it is in line with other authorities which suggest a growing judicial intolerance of honest or uninformed incompetence and a greater willingness to use the disqualification legislation in this type of case.[156]

The disqualification legislation is regarded by the judiciary as playing a real and significant role in raising the standards expected of corporate managers.[157] Henry LJ explained in one case:[158]

The Parliamentary intention to improve managerial safeguards and standards for the long term good of employees, creditors and investors is clear . . . The statutory corporate climate is stricter than it ever has been, and those enforcing it should reflect the fact that Parliament has seen the need for higher standards.

One of the most important aspects of the disqualification legislation is that it provides a more effective enforcement mechanism than the general duty of care and skill and the Insolvency Act 1986, s 214. As noted in an earlier section of this chapter,[159] there are many factors that may combine to explain why, outside insolvency situations, litigation against directors for breach of their duty of care and skill is uncommon. Costs considerations act as a disincentive to liquidators[160] from taking proceedings under the Insolvency Act 1986, s 214

[155] See also *Re Burnham Marketing Services Ltd* [1993] BCC 518 (where the director was also the proprietor of the company); *Re Majestic Recording Studios Ltd* [1989] BCLC1; *Re Stanford Services Ltd* [1987] BCLC 607, 619; *Re City Investment Centres Ltd* [1992] BCLC 956; *Re Melcast (Wolverhampton) Ltd* [1991] BCLC 288.

[156] Finch, V, 'Disqualification of Directors: A Plea for Competence' (1990) 53 MLR 385 notes, critically, a number of cases reported between 1989 and 1990 where the courts were unwilling to regard incompetence as constituting grounds for unfitness. There is a distinct difference in emphasis between those cases and later decisions such as that in the *Continental Assurance* case and *Re Grayan Building Services Ltd* [1995] BCC 554, CA.

[157] Others, though, would not necessarily agree: see, eg, Cheffins, BR, *Company Law Theory, Structure and Operation* (1997) 548–53.

[158] *Re Grayan Building Services Ltd* [1995] BCC 554, CA, 577. Also 577 *per* Neill LJ.

[159] See this chapter above, at 211–12.

[160] Individual creditors do not have standing to bring claims under this section.

except in clear cases.[161] Disqualification proceedings under the Company Directors Disqualification Act 1986, s 6, by way of contrast, are public proceedings which are commenced by, or at the direction of, the Secretary of State.[162] The costs associated with disqualification proceedings are largely[163] borne out of public funds save to the extent that these are recovered from defendants. The number of orders made under the legislation is one measure of its significance: although there was a critical official report on the work of the DTI's Insolvency Service[164] in the period between 1987 and 1993,[165] latterly its work has been more effective with the number of disqualifications on grounds of unfitness rising from 399 in 1993–4 to 1,275 in 1997–8.[166]

STRENGTHENING THE STANDARDS: AN OVERVIEW OF COUNTER-ARGUMENTS

In the USA, the business judgment rule protects directors from the consequences of wrong decisions, even those which have a serious impact on the company. The American Law Institute (a prestigious association of leading lawyers, judges and law professors) in its corporate governance project has summarised the business judgment rule by stating that a director or officer who makes a business judgment in good faith fulfils his duty if: (i) he is not interested in the subject matter of the business judgment; (ii) he is informed with respect to the matter of his business judgment to the extent he reasonably believes to be appropriate under the circumstances; and (iii) he rationally believes that his business judgment is in the best interests of the company.[167] As a result of the business judgment rule, there is said to be a presumption that directors have acted properly, so that the burden of proof lies on those who claim otherwise. The Delaware Supreme Court has said that, because of the business judgment rule, directors should only incur liability for gross negligence.[168]

Until the mid-1980s, it was generally considered that challenges to directors on grounds of lack of care were likely to fail because of the protection afforded by the business judgment rule. This perception had to be re-assessed as a result of the decision of the Delaware Supreme Court in *Smith v Van*

[161] Cheffins, BR, *Company Law Theory, Structure and Operation* (1997) 545–8.

[162] Company Directors Disqualification Act 1986, s 7. Insolvency practitioners are required to alert the Secretary of State to cases of possible unfitness: Company Directors Disqualification Act 1986, s 7 (3).

[163] Though Cheffins, BR, *Company Law Theory, Structure and Operation* (1997) 552 points out that the obligation on insolvency practitioners to report cases of possible unfitness to the Secretary of State creates a cost that has to be borne out of the funds available to pay creditors.

[164] The DTI's Insolvency Service is a specialist unit which is responsible for investigating and pursuing cases of suspected breaches that could lead to disqualification.

[165] *The Insolvency Service Executive Agency: Company Directors Disqualification* (National Audit Office) (1993).

[166] *Crackdown on Unfit Directors Nets 13% Rise and 1275 Bans* DTI Press Release 23 July 1998. This press release also reported on the 'name and shame' telephone hotline established by the DTI in January 1998 to allow members of the public to report persons believed to be involved in the management of a company in breach of a disqualification order. By the date of the press release 900 people had contacted the hotline.

[167] *Principles of Corporate Governance* (American Law Institute) § 4.01.

[168] *Aronson v Lewis* 473 A 2d 805, 812 (1984).

Gorkom,[169] a derivative suit filed by minority shareholders. The shareholders claimed that the directors had failed to exercise due care in reviewing and recommending a proposal that their company be taken over. The Delaware Supreme Court, by a majority, held that the directors had not adequately informed themselves about the proposal before voting to recommend it and that, therefore, they were not entitled to the benefit of the business judgment rule. Later decisions of the Delaware courts relating to acquisition transactions further limited the application of the business judgment rule and established that transactions involving a 'sale of control' would be subjected to particularly close scrutiny.[170] In response to the *Van Gorkom* decision and also to a reduction in the availability and coverage of insurance as well as increases in premiums and deductibles, the majority of the US states introduced legislation permitting corporations to limit or exclude the monetary liability of their directors for breaches of duties of care not involving bad faith or intentional misconduct.[171] These permissions for companies to opt out[172] of the standard established by the general law were established in order to meet concerns about individuals' unwillingness to serve as directors and about directors' unwillingness to make entrepreneurial decisions.[173]

The US experience is recounted here because it directs attention onto some of the fundamental issues raised by the enhancement of the standards expected of directors. It is a model from which the UK might learn some useful lessons in relation to the further development of its law in these respects.[174] The current position under English law is that, with limited exceptions, companies cannot exempt directors from their duties of care and skill, limit their liability or indemnify them for liabilities arising from breach of that duty;[175] but they may purchase insurance for their directors in respect of these liabilities.[176] There are no current proposals to remove the bans on exemption or limitation of liability or on the giving of indemnities, although the enact-

[169] 488 A 2d 858.

[170] In particular *Paramount Communications v QVC Network Inc* (1994) 637 A 2d 34.

[171] Gelb, H, 'Director Due Care Liability: An Assessment of the New Statutes' (1988) 61 Temple Law Review 13; DeMott, D, 'Limiting Directors' Liability' (1988) 66 Wash ULQ 295.

[172] Gelb, H, 'Director Due Care Liability: An Assessment of the New Statutes' (1988) 61 Temple Law Review 13, 29–32 notes that although an opt-in or opt-out approach is the norm, some States have mandatory statutes relieving directors of monetary liability for breach of the duty of care.

[173] Gelb, H, 'Director Due Care Liability: An Assessment of the New Statutes' (1988) 61 Temple Law Review 13, 23–4.

[174] Hamilton, RW, 'The Duties of Corporate Directors and the Draft Fifth Directive: Lessons from the United States' [1988] 4 JIBL 152 comments that 'the predominant view in the United States is that on balance it is unwise to impose monetary liability on directors—particularly outside directors—for breaches of the duty of care so long as the directors acted in good faith' and that 'if the recent history in the United States is any guide, [there is] a clear signal that there may be rocky shoals ahead for the United Kingdom'.

[175] In addition to statutes that permit corporations to exclude the duty of care entirely, US State corporations laws also contain statutes that authorise corporations to indemnify their directors to a much greater extent than is permitted under English law: Gelb, H, 'Director Due Care Liability: An Assessment of the New Statutes' (1988) 61 Temple Law Review 13, 46–9.

[176] Companies Act 1985, s 310. Reform of this section is not suggested in *Company Directors: Regulating Conflicts of Interest and Formulating a Statement of Duties: A Joint Consultation Paper* (Law Commission Consultation Paper No 153; Scottish Law Commission Discussion Paper No 105) (1998) but it is noted (at para 11.46 n 86) that this may fall within the DTI's own review of company law.

ment of a statutory business judgment rule is under active consideration. However, the US experience suggests that whether, or to what extent or by what procedures,[177] it should be possible to relieve directors from the obligation of care imposed by the general law, or the consequences of acting in breach of it, are matters that should properly be considered in conjunction with any proposals for formalising or raising those standards.

Other fundamental issues raised by making the standards required of corporate management more rigorous include the following. Against the argument that shareholders would benefit from the law's imposition of strict standards on corporate managers is the counter-argument that anxiety about possible liability could lead managers to become more risk-averse and to decline potentially valuable, but high risk, proposals in favour of safer, but less potentially profitable, ventures.[178] A related point is that able and well-qualified individuals may decline non-executive directorships for fear that acceptance might expose them to litigation about management decisions which they played a limited part in making but for which they could be held personally responsible and liable to pay vast damages.[179] Whether comprehensive liability insurance is available is obviously an important consideration in this context: studies of this aspect of the UK insurance market suggest that although directors' and officers' insurance is widely available, its coverage tends to be limited, with important categories of claim, such as in respect of environmental liabilities, being excluded.[180] More litigation against directors as a result of raising the standards expected of them could lead to insurance becoming more difficult to obtain or could trigger increases in the levels of premiums charged, further limitations in respect of coverage or increased deductibles which the insured would be required to pay himself before the insurer will pay.[181] Even if adequate insurance were to continue to be

[177] eg, whether this should be mandatory or permissive and, if permissive, what form of authorising resolutions should be required: Gelb, H, 'Director Due Care Liability: An Assessment of the New Statutes' (1988) 61 Temple Law Review 13, 29–32. This author notes (at 32–3) that another issue is whether relief should be limited to monetary liabilities or should also extend to other matters, such as claims for injunctions and rescission.

[178] Eisenberg, MA, 'Duty of Care and The Business Judgement Rule in American Corporate Law' [1997] CfiLR 185, 191; Daniels, RJ, 'Must Boards Go Overboard? An Economic Analysis of the Effects of Burgeoning Statutory Liability on the Role of Directors in Corporate Governance' in Ziegel, J (ed), *Current Developments in International and Comparative Corporate Law* (1994) 557; Gelb, H, 'Director Due Care Liability: An Assessment of the New Statutes' (1988) 61 Temple Law Review 13, 25–6; Telfer, TGW, 'Risk and Insolvent Trading' in Grantham, R, and Rickett, C, *Corporate Personality in the 20th Century* (1998) 127, 134–5; *Company Directors: Regulating Conflicts of Interest and Formulating a Statement of Duties: A Joint Consultation Paper* (Law Commission Consultation Paper No 153; Scottish Law Commission Discussion Paper No 105) (1998) paras 3.85–3.91; Cheffins, BR, *Company Law Theory Structure and Operation* (1997) 541–3.

[179] Eisenberg, MA, 'Duty of Care and The Business Judgement Rule in American Corporate Law' [1997] CfiLR 185, 192; Telfer, TGW, 'Risk and Insolvent Trading' in Grantham, R, and Rickett, C, *Corporate Personality in the 20th Century* (1998) 127, 137–8; *Company Directors: Regulating Conflicts of Interest and Formulating a Statement of Duties: A Joint Consultation Paper* (Law Commission Consultation Paper No 153; Scottish Law Commission Discussion Paper No 105) (1998) paras 3.85–3.91.

[180] Finch, V, 'Personal Accountability and Corporate Control: The Role of Directors' and Officers' Liability Insurance' (1994) 54 MLR 880; Baxter, C, 'Demystifying D&O Insurance' (1995) 15 OJLS 537.

[181] Finch, V, 'Personal Accountability and Corporate Control: The Role of Directors' and Officers' Liability Insurance' (1994) 54 MLR 880 discusses the insurance crisis (ie unavailability of

available, this might not remove all of the anxieties that may be felt by directors or prospective directors. Prudent individuals are likely to be concerned that their professional reputation could be damaged by claims of breach of duty, even if those allegations are successfully defended or the court grants relief from liability,[182] and also to be wary of taking or remaining in a position that carries with it a substantial risk of being exposed to the stresses and strains of involvement in litigation. The feeling that more rigorous standards, coupled with insurance policies that have the effect of making it financially worthwhile actually to sue directors,[183] may generate more litigation, from which lawyers would benefit far more than shareholders or any others with an interest in the company, is likely to be another concern.[184] For the management of a company in financial difficulties, the prospect of personal liability under the general duty of care and skill or the Insolvency Act 1986, s 214 and the risk of being disqualified as unfit for having gambled wrongly with creditors' money may make the option of stopping the business altogether, and thus forgoing the chance of trading out of the crisis but, at the same time, limiting their personal exposure, too appealing to resist.[185] Also, although the argument that the imposition of personal liability on the management of insolvent companies operates so as to compensate creditors for the absorption of risks for which they did not bargain is persuasive, a counter view to the effect that creditors can protect themselves by contract and do not therefore require additional support from the general law can also be put forward.[186] These arguments cannot be taken further here but it is clear that the costs and benefits of raising standards are matters that should be carefully measured in any future development of the law relating to duties of care and skill.[187]

effective cover at affordable prices) that was experienced in the USA and Canada in the 1980s. The author suggests that trends to increase directors' liabilities could create pressures within the insurance markets leading to higher premiums, restrictive coverage and larger deductibles, although she doubts the UK market would face a crisis of the severity that was felt elsewhere.

[182] Under Companies Act 1985, s 727. Such relief is not granted lightly: see Ch 5 above, at 203–5.

[183] On the possible litigation-increasing effect of insurance: Daniels, R, and Hutton, S, 'The Capricious Cushion: The Implications of the Directors and Officers' Insurance Liability Crisis on Canadian Corporate Governance' (1993) 22 Canadian Business Law Journal 182.

[184] Dent, GW, 'The Revolution in Corporate Governance, the Monitoring Board and the Directors' Duty of Care' (1981) 61 Boston University Law Review 623, 653.

[185] Cooke, T, and Hicks, A, 'Wrongful Trading—Predicting Insolvency' [1993] JBL 338, 350.

[186] See, eg, Cheffins, BR, *Company Law Theory, Structure and Operation* (1997) 547–8. An apparent difficulty with this argument is that it does not seem to take into account the position of involuntary creditors or creditors who are technically voluntary, such as employees or small trade creditors, but who do not have the bargaining strength to protect their interests by contract. On the position of such creditors see Telfer, TGW, 'Risk and Insolvent Trading' in Grantham, R, and Rickett, C, *Corporate Personality in the 20th Century* (1998) 127, 131–3.

[187] *Company Directors: Regulating Conflicts of Interest and Formulating a Statement of Duties: A Joint Consultation Paper* (Law Commission Consultation Paper No 153; Scottish Law Commission Discussion Paper No 105) (1998) ch 16 announces an empirical survey of directors to examine a range of matters including whether raising the standard of care and skill might deter directors from taking office or make it more difficult to obtain liability insurance. This work may help to shed light on some aspects of these issues.

7

Controlling Management: Corporate Democracy and the Role of Institutional Investors

OVERVIEW OF SHAREHOLDER CONTROL MECHANISMS—VOICE AND EXIT

There are two main ways in which shareholders can exert control over the managers of their company. The first control mechanism lies in the voting rights that normally attach to ordinary shares. An ordinary share usually[1] confers on its holder the right to cast one vote on all matters put to the vote at shareholders' meetings. Thus, in a company which has a conventional capital structure, every ordinary shareholder has the right to have a say in the corporate decision-making process by virtue of his shareholding. This control mechanism is sometimes referred to as control in the form of 'voice'.[2] The second form of control is based on market forces: where there is an active market in a company's shares, its shareholders from time to time can express their dissatisfaction by selling their shares. Widespread selling will trigger a fall in share price and this may ultimately result in the company becoming the target of a takeover bid. This form of control is commonly referred to as 'exit'.[3]

Exit via the market is irrelevant for smaller companies whose shares are not traded. The Companies Act 1985, s 459, which allows a shareholder to petition the court for relief from unfairly prejudicial conduct, is the primary mechanism for resolving disputes between the participants in small companies. Remedies under this section are at the discretion of the court but the remedy that is most commonly granted is for the company or some of its shareholders to buy out the shares of the petitioner. In effect the court provides exit in place of the market. Disputes ventilated through a Companies Act 1985, s 459 petition are commonly less about control of management by shareholders than they are about the breakdown of personal relations. In the type of company to which the statutory remedy is most relevant, the boundaries between the functions of shareholding and of managing are often blurred. Since they can raise issues that extend beyond its intended scope, Companies Act 1985, s 459 petitions are not considered further in this chapter. The issues discussed in this chapter are primarily relevant to larger

[1] This is the default position which will apply unless the company's articles make alternative provision: Companies Act 1985, s 370 (6).

[2] eg, Coffee, JC, 'Liquidity Versus Control: The Institutional Investor as Corporate Monitor' (1991) 91 Columbia Law Review 1277, 1288. This terminology ('voice' and, as mentioned later in the text, 'exit') derives from Hirshman, AO, *Exit, Voice and Loyalty, Responses to Decline in Firms, Organizations and States* (1970).

[3] A variant on exit is for investors to express their dissatisfaction through the market by not subscribing new shares in a rights issue: Scott, J, *Capitalist Property and Financial Power: A Comparative Study of Britain, the United States and Japan* (1986) 95.

companies with external shareholders who are not themselves involved in management nor connected by family or personal relationships to those who are. In this type of company, the legal complexities surrounding the forms of action available to shareholders help to ensure that litigation does not play an important role as a mechanism for shareholder control.[4]

The model of large company structure and organisation that has dominated modern analysis is one in which shareholders do not exercise voice and instead rely on exit as the controlling mechanism.[5] In this model, shareholders are represented as a scattered large group of investors, each holding only a tiny fraction of any one company's shares as part of a diversified portfolio. Diversification is designed to eliminate the company-specific risks that flow from holding particular shares,[6] but its effect is both to remove the incentive actively to monitor the management of the individual companies comprised in the portfolio and to make this difficult to achieve at any reasonable cost.[7] Effective monitoring requires a shareholder to devote, or to engage an agent to devote, time, effort and skill to 'decoding' information released by management and assessing its significance; all of this costs money. Every time a shareholder adds a new share to the portfolio for diversification purpose, this has the effect of multiplying potential monitoring costs. The cost issue is exacerbated by the fact that the benefits of one shareholder's active monitoring of the management of a particular company accrue to all of the shareholders and not just to the particular shareholder that incurs the expense.[8] This is known

[4] Stapledon, GP, *Institutional Shareholders and Corporate Governance* (1996) 131–2. Other considerations that inhibit other forms of shareholder activism such as costs and conflicts of interests are also relevant. These factors are considered in the course of this chapter.

In theory there are two key shareholder remedies. This first is the derivative action which allows shareholders to enforce the company's cause of action against directors who are in breach of their duties to the company. In 1997 the Law Commission concluded a comprehensive review of shareholder remedies: *Shareholder Remedies* (Law Commission Report No 246). This concluded that the existing rules relating to the derivative action were complicated and unwieldy and recommended its replacement by a new statutory derivative action. The DTI provisionally support the majority of the Law Commission's proposals although it has launched its own consultation exercise in respect of certain aspects: *Shareholder Remedies* (DTI Consultative Document) (Nov 1998). The second remedy is Companies Act 1985, s 459. Although this is extensively used by the participants in small private companies, it has proved to be less useful in the context of larger companies. One factor that limits the use of Companies Act 1985, s 459 in larger companies is that mismanagement on its own is not regarded as unfairly prejudicial conduct and informational imbalances between management and shareholders can make it difficult for shareholders to find evidence of more serious managerial misconduct.

[5] The seminal text presenting this model is Berle, AA, and Means, GC, *The Modern Corporation and Private Property* (1932). This work has had a profound influence on modern thinking about large companies: see, eg, the later work Herman, ES, *Corporate Control, Corporate Power* (1981) which follows closely the themes of the earlier work and analyses them in the light of subsequent experience. See also *Report of the Company Law Amendment Committee* Cmd 6659 (1945) para 7 (e) (Cohen Committee).

[6] See further Ch 1 above, at 20–1.

[7] Fama, E, 'Agency Problems and The Theory of the Firm' in Putterman, L (ed), *The Economies of the Firm* 196 reprinted with abridgements from (1980) 88 *Journal of Political Economy* 288. This has led some commentators to suggest legal restrictions on diversification as a means of promoting the greater use of voice by institutional investors: Coffee, JC, 'Liquidity Versus Control: The Institutional Investor as Corporate Monitor' (1991) 91 Columbia Law Review 1277, 1355–66; Charkham, JP, 'A Larger Role for Institutional Investors' in Dimsdale, N, and Prevezer, M (eds), *Capital Markets and Corporate Governance* (1994) 99, 103–4.

[8] Posner, RA, *Economic Analysis of Law* (3rd edn, 1986) 398–9.

as the 'free rider' problem: the other shareholders can hitch a free ride on the back of the active, expense-incurring, monitoring shareholder. For these reasons, in the familiar model shareholders are 'rationally apathetic': they do not vote or, if they do, they simply side with management; they rely, instead, on the market and the threat of takeover to inhibit managerial shirking or exploitation of position at the shareholders' expense.

There is a large amount of empirical and theoretical literature on the control function performed by the market in shares or, as it is often described, the market for corporate control.[9] Literature suggesting a variety of imperfections in the operation of the market for corporate control—that takeovers do not necessarily involve underperforming companies or lead to an improvement in the performance of target companies, and that they entail heavy costs and significant disruption—is considered in Chapter 4.[10] Chapter 2 considers the argument that hostile takeover activity, which is a familiar feature of market practice in the UK but not in other countries such as Germany and Japan, engenders a short-termist attitude on the part of investors and, consequently, deprives British industry of much needed finance for the long-term investment which is the determinant of economic success.[11] It is not proposed to develop these arguments further in this chapter. Instead, this chapter takes as its point of departure the proposition that there are imperfections in the market for corporate control. This throws the spotlight onto voice as a mechanism of corporate control: its existing role and the role that it might play if arguments about the adverse impact of hostile takeovers on economic performance were to be translated into regulatory curbs on the operation of the market for corporate control.

DOMINANCE OF INSTITUTIONAL INVESTORS

Institutional investors such as insurance companies and pension funds now dominate the share registers of UK public listed companies.[12] One estimate is that in January 1998 institutional investors accounted for around 80 per cent of the value of the London stock market.[13] It has also been estimated that on

9 Leading articles on this topic include Manne, HG, 'Mergers and the Market for Corporate Control' (1965) *Journal of Political Economy* 110; Easterbrook, FH, and Fischel, DR, 'The Proper Role of a Target's Management in Responding to a Tender Offer' (1981) 94 Harvard Law Review 1161; Coffee, JC, 'Regulating the Market for Corporate Control: A Critical Assessment of the Tender Offer's Role in Corporate Governance' (1984) 84 Columbia Law Review 1145. For a consideration of the issue from a UK legal perspective see Bradley, C, 'Corporate Control: Markets and Rules' (1990) 53 MLR 170; Parkinson, JE, *Corporate Power and Responsibility* (1993) 121–32; Parkinson, JE, 'The Role of 'Voice' and 'Exit' in Corporate Governance' in Sheikh, S, and Rees, W (eds), *Corporate Governance and Corporate Control* (1995) 75.

10 Ch 4 above, at 118–22.

11 Ch 2 above, at 76–80. See also Bond, S, and Jenkinson, T, 'The Assessment: Investment Performance and Policy' (1996) *Oxford Review of Economic Policy* 1, 15–17. The authors review the arguments but conclude that allegations of short-termism within the UK markets are 'not proved'.

12 Unit trusts, investment companies and investment trusts and banks also come under the heading of institutional investors but pension funds and life funds are predominant.

13 *Final Report of the Committee on Corporate Governance* (January 1998) (*Hampel Committee Report*) para 5.1 notes that 60 per cent is held by UK institutions, around 20 per cent by foreign,

the basis of January 1996 data on the ownership of the shares of the largest 300 companies, on average their twenty largest institutional shareholders accounted for between one-third and one-half of their share capital.[14] This data also indicates that direct share ownership by individual investors accounts for less than one-fifth of stock market value.[15] Since pension funds and insurance companies derive the bulk of their funds from individuals—that is, from contributors to pension plans and purchasers of insurance (in particular life assurance)—it is not accurate to say that individuals are excluded from the process of providing equity capital to companies. They do participate but it is more common for their involvement to be indirect and channelled through institutional investors than for it to be in the form of direct share ownership. This point has policy implications with regard to the responsibility and accountability of institutional investors: they are financial intermediaries investing other people's money and, as such, the principles governing their operations should be transparent so that they can be held accountable for their activities.[16]

The eclipse of the direct private investor by institutions challenges the traditional model of the big company in which a large number of disparate shareholders are rationally apathetic and rely on the market as their sole control mechanism.[17] Whilst portfolio diversification means that no one institutional shareholder may hold more than a small proportion of a company's ordinary share capital, collectively a large slice of the shares is likely to be in institutional hands, sometimes, in the case of the largest listed companies, up to nearly 50 per cent of the share capital with the five largest institutions holding up to one-quarter.[18] Institutional shareholders can communicate quite easily, both through formal committees and through more informal professional contact with each other.[19] Insurance companies' views on corporate governance tend to be channelled through the investment committees of their trade association, the Association of British Insurers (ABI). The National Association of Pension Funds Ltd (NAPF) performs the same function for pen-

mainly institutional, owners and the remaining 20 per cent or so by private individuals. The DTI also estimates that around 80 per cent lies in institutional hands: *Shareholder Communications at the Annual General Meeting* (Consultative Document) (April 1996) para 1.7.

[14] Gaved, M, *Institutional Investors and Corporate Governance* (Foundation for Business Responsibilities Issues Paper No 3) (March 1998).

[15] Gaved, M, *Institutional Investors and Corporate Governance* (Foundation for Business Responsibilities Issues Paper No 3) (March 1998) 26.

[16] Charkham, JP, 'A Larger Role for Institutional Investors' in Dimsdale, N, and Prevezer, M (eds), *Capital Markets and Corporate Governance* (1994) 99, 109–10.

[17] Scott, J, *Capitalist Property and Financial Power* (1986) ch 5; Rock, EB, 'The Logic and (Uncertain) Significance of Institutional Shareholder Activism' (1991) 79 Georgetown Law Journal 445; Jackson, T, 'Managers v Shareholders (Again)' *Financial Times* 24 Sept 1998.

[18] Gaved, M, *Institutional Investors and Corporate Governance* (Foundation for Business Responsibilities Issues Paper No 3) (March 1998) 30.

[19] Stapledon, GP, *Institutional Shareholders and Corporate Governance* (1996) ch 5 provides a detailed and helpful account of the way in which institutional shareholders operate. The Institutional Shareholders' Committee corporate governance publications include *The Role and Duties of Directors—A Statement of Best Practice* (August 1993) (2nd edn); and *The Responsibilities of Institutional Shareholders in the UK* (December 1991). On this type of industry-wide guideline see further Black, BS, 'Shareholder Passivity Reexamined' (1990) 89 Michigan Law Review 520, 580–4.

sion fund investors. Representatives of these bodies together with those of other institutional investors such as unit trusts, investment companies, investment trusts and banks sit on the Institutional Shareholders' Committee, which is a body that performs the function of developing industry-wide statements of best practice in corporate governance.[20] This type of formal and informal contact creates the potential[21] for monitoring on a more cost-efficient (they can share the costs between them) and effective (because of the proportion of voting rights held by the monitoring group) basis than could ever be achieved by individual shareholders acting independently.

This potential has been recognised for some time,[22] but it was in the 1990s that the control that could be exerted by institutional investors began to make headlines.[23] Newspaper reports during this decade detailing institutional-investor-led challenges to proposals on directors' pay increases and other controversial matters provided plenty of evidence to support the suggestion of a decline in traditional shareholder apathy.[24] Whilst being careful not to assume that occasional controversies which attract media attention amount to a fundamental change of approach by institutions, it does appear that there was some shift towards greater institutional-investor activism in the 1990s. What might explain this? Institutional dominance of the register of shareholders only recognises the *potential* for control via voice but does not explain why institutional shareholders should choose to use it. Evidence of the cyclical nature of takeover activity provides a plausible explanation: where there is no potential bidder waiting in the wings, that limits the opportunity for exit so the possibilities for control that are inherent in voice may be explored instead. Reference to efficient capital markets theory takes this idea a step further.[25] The market will quickly absorb institutional investor dissatisfaction with the performance of the management of a particular company and reflect it in its share price. In a market dominated by professionals, where all of the major participants have access to the same flow of information and can purchase the services of skilled analysts to interpret it, there is little or no legal opportunity for any one institutional investor to 'beat the market', that is to take advantage of a time-lag in the percolation of bad news down into market.

The argument that the concentration of share ownership in the hands of institutional investors restricts the opportunity for exit and increases the

[20] Stapledon, GP, *Institutional Shareholders and Corporate Governance* (1996) 52–3.

[21] But institutional investors are not a homogenous group. Also they may be business rivals. These are disincentives to collective action: Charkham, JP, *Keeping Good Company* (1995) 288; *Hampel Committee Report* para 5.2.

[22] Berle, AA, *Power Without Property: A New Development in American Political Economy* (1960) 53; *Report of the Company Law Committee* (Cmnd 1749) (1962) para 106 (Jenkins Committee).

[23] eg, 'Investors Force Out Mirror Chief' *Financial Times* 27 January 1999 reporting the resignation of a chief executive of a quoted company as a result of pressure from its institutional investors and non-executive directors. Note Stapledon, GP, *Institutional Shareholders and Corporate Governance* (1996) 122–3 who demonstrates that institutional activism was not unknown in earlier decades.

[24] See, eg, Cheffins, BR, *Company Law Theory, Structure and Operation* (1997) ch 14 discussing various high-profile battles over remuneration of executive directors of privatised utilities that took place, and were extensively reported, in the 1990s.

[25] See further Ch 2 above, at 64–5.

importance of voice is compelling.[26] It is the recognition of the growing importance of voice that forms the background to the discussion in this chapter of the legal framework governing the exercise of voice by shareholders.

Institutional investors are in a position to influence the strategic direction of the company not just by acting as watchdogs on the look-out for managerial shirking or exploitation of self-interest at the shareholders' expense, but also by positively assisting in the development of business proposals, by providing management with a sounding board for new ideas, and by giving their views on possible new appointments to the board.[27] The positive aspects of dialogue between companies and institutional investors were emphasised by various committees that reported on corporate governance in the UK in the 1990s.[28] In 1998 the London Stock Exchange put its weight formally behind this aspect of corporate governance. The *Combined Code* on corporate governance that is annexed to *The Listing Rules* states that companies and institutional investors should be ready, wherever practicable, to enter into a dialogue based on their mutual understanding of objectives.[29]

It would be wrong to suggest that the formal mechanisms of general meetings of the company represent the only means whereby institutions can exert control in the form of voice, although it is ultimately because they control a significant portion of formal voting rights that institutions can effectively ensure that their voice is heard in other ways. Institutions can achieve much through informal, behind-the-scenes dialogue with and, on controversial matters, pressure on, senior management. By definition, this extent of this type of institutional monitoring is difficult to measure[30] but statements from repre-

[26] Coffee, JC, 'Liquidity Versus Control: The Institutional Investor as Corporate Monitor' (1991) 91 Columbia Law Review 1277, 1288–89; *Hampel Committee Report* para 5.3; Cadbury, Sir Adrian, *The Governance Debate* (1997) 28 quoting Georg Siemens, founder of Deutsche Bank: 'if you cannot sell, you must care'. Another relevant factor is the development of indexed investment. These are funds held in a wide spread of companies which are not traded in order to keep the fund managers' costs at a minimum.

[27] The co-operative and mutuality-of-interests dimensions of the relationship between institutional investors and corporate management were highlighted by a report of a joint City/Industry working group chaired by Myners, P, *Developing a Winning Partnership: How Companies and Institutional Investors Are Working Together* (1995). See also *Shareholder Communications at the Annual General Meeting* (DTI Consultative Document) (April 1996) para 1.7. Gaved, M, *Institutional Investors and Corporate Governance* (1998) 36–8 provides a brief but informative account of the way in which contact between institutional investors and companies operates in practice.

A difficulty here is that if certain institutions are given access to information but that information has not been made public, they may become 'insiders' for the purposes of the insider dealing legislation and, as such, be unable to trade: *Hampel Committee Report* para 5.12

[28] *Report of the Committee on the Financial Aspects of Corporate Governance* (December 1992) (*Cadbury Committee Report*) para 6.11; *Hampel Committee Report* paras 5.10–5.12.

[29] 'The Combined Code. Principles of Good Corporate Governance and Code of Best Practice' Appendix to *The Listing Rules*, effective for accounting periods ending on or after 31 December 1998 (*Combined Code*). Listed companies are required to state in their annual accounts whether they comply with the *Combined Code* but non-compliance would not in itself jeopardise a company's listing: *The Listing Rules*, para 12.43A.

[30] Short, H, and Keasey, K, 'Institutional Shareholders and Corporate Governance in the United Kingdom' in Keasey, K, Thompson, S, and Wright, M (eds), *Corporate Governance* (1997) 18, 25; Ball, Sir James, 'Financial Institutions and Their Roles as Shareholders' in *Creative Tension* (NAPF 1990) 18, 24–5; Black, BS, and Coffee, JC, 'Hail Britannia?: Institutional Investor Behavior

sentatives of major institutions indicate that, even in controversial matters, they prefer to operate through informal contact if possible.[31] Efficient capital market theory makes it easy to understand why institutional investors might prefer to avoid the damage to the company's share price that could result from a head-to-head public confrontation between themselves and management. Yet, whilst there are advantages in behind-the-scenes contact, there is a tension between this and the pressure on institutional investors, as financial intermediaries, to behave in a transparent and accountable manner. At the end of the 1990s, these pressures led to a new emphasis on institutional participation in the formalities of company meetings.

WHY DO ORDINARY[32] SHAREHOLDERS HAVE VOTING RIGHTS?

As a matter of general law creditors and employees do not have a voice in corporate decisions, although major creditors may negotiate a contractual right to vote in respect of particularly significant matters. There is no provision for creditors or employees akin to the shareholder enfranchisement provision in the Companies Act 1985.[33] A number of different explanations of shareholder enfranchisement can be put forward. The first views the shareholders' right to vote as being an aspect of their rights as the owners of the company: the right to vote is seen to be the way in which shareholders exercise control over the persons who are managing their money.[34] The second view rejects the characterisation of shareholders as owners of a company and regards their interests as being financial rather than proprietorial. On this basis the right to vote devolves to the shareholders, rather than creditors and employees who also have a financial interest in the company, because they are the residual

Under Limited Regulation' (1994) 92 Michigan Law Review 1997, 2028–55 (an account of the public and behind-the-scenes actions of UK institutional investors based on published materials and the results of interviews with individual representing selected institutional investors); Holland, J, *The Corporate Governance Role of Financial Institutions in Their Investee Companies* (ACCA Research Report No 46) (1995) (providing six in-depth case studies of the methods of influence and intervention used by financial institution shareholders).

[31] eg, *The Responsibilities of Institutional Shareholders in the UK* (Institutional Shareholders Committee 1991) advocates informal contact, at senior executive level, between institutional shareholders and companies. Specifically with regard to the composition of the board, the paper notes that institutional shareholders should seek to identify deficiencies and initiate appropriate action at an early stage, and elaborates: 'The most effective action is taken quickly, and without publicity. It is exceptional for such initiatives to be taken collectively, because of the need for speed of action, and confidentiality. It is also undesirable for more than the minimum number of individuals to receive information or knowledge of events which at times may be highly price sensitive.'

[32] Preference shares normally carry very limited voting rights, such as the right to vote on any matter directly concerning the rights attaching to those shares plus a right to vote on all matters if the dividend in respect of the shares is in arrears.

[33] S 370 (6).

[34] The *Cadbury Committee Report* states at para 6.1: 'Thus the shareholders as owners of the company elect the directors to run the business on their behalf and hold them accountable for its progress.' The characterisation of shareholders as owners is firmly established in UK practice as well as in company law: see, eg, *ABI/NAPF Joint Position Paper on Pre-emption, Cost of Capital and Underwriting* (July 1996) para 1.1 which emphasises the function of pre-emption rights as a protection for 'company owners'.

claimants to the firm's income and, as such, are the group with the appropriate incentives to make discretionary decisions; in short they are the group with the most to gain or lose.[35] In this model, which is based on the nexus of contracts analysis of the company, shareholders' voting rights fill any gap that specific contractual provision has failed to cover; having the right to vote on residual matters which are not predetermined by contract compensates the shareholders for the risk that the company will fail and that their investment will be lost. Yet another perspective on shareholders' voting rights draws an analogy with the governance of a state, and sees voting as the way in which the electorate (the shareholders) express their control over the leaders (the directors).[36]

Whatever the theoretical basis for voting rights attaching to shares, it is clear that external investors in equity share capital have a marked preference for ordinary shares carrying one vote per share.[37] A debate about non-voting ordinary shares raged in the UK in the 1940s and 1950s when many companies, which were previously dominated by families, were first floated on the Stock Exchange. Although the movement for outlawing non-voting ordinary shares attracted some powerful support,[38] that argument did not prevail. This means that in theory non-voting ordinary shares can still be issued but commercial considerations ensure that in practice new issues of shares in this form as a means of raising capital from the public do not occur. Also, under pressure from their institutional investors, some companies that had complex share capital structures when they were first floated, involving non-voting shares or shares with weighted votes in favour of, say, the families of the controllers of the business when it was still a private concern, have since adopted straightforward structures with one vote per share.[39] The historical investor preference for exit over voice might suggest that this emphasis on voting rights is misplaced, but closer analysis demonstrates that the importance that investors have invariably given to the franchise attaching to ordinary shares is compatible with an investment strategy which relies on exit as a control mechanism. The reason for this is that the market for corporate control turns on the bidder being able to acquire a majority of the voting rights in the company in order to remove the old directors and replace them with its own team. Charkham makes the point:[40]

[35] Easterbrook, FH, and, Fischel, DR, *The Economic Structure of Corporate Law* (1991) 63–72.

[36] Stokes, M, 'Company Law and Legal Theory' included in Wheeler, S (ed), *The Law of the Business Enterprise* (1994) 80 (reprinted from Twining, W (ed), *Legal Theory and Common Law* (1986) 155).

[37] This is unequivocally stated in the Institutional Shareholders Committee's paper, *The Responsibilities of Institutional Shareholders in the UK* (1991): 'institutional investors are opposed to the creation of equity shares which do not carry full voting rights'.

[38] eg, the Note of Dissent annexed to the *Report of the Company Law Committee* (Cmnd 1749) (1962).

[39] eg, *Independent on Sunday*, Business Section, 18 July 1993, noting the proposal by GUS plc to convert its non-voting shares into voting shares; 'Whitbread Gives Equal Rights' *Financial Times* 7 October 1993; 'WH Smith to Change Share Structure' *Financial Times* 20 May 1994. But challenges to multi-tiered ordinary share capital structures do not always succeed: eg: 'Challenge for Change Falls Flat at Youngs' *The Times* 22 July 1998.

[40] Charkham, JP, 'Are Shares Just Commodities?' in *Creative Tension?* (NAPF 1990) 34, 37–8.

The stockmarket . . . has become a market for companies as well as for shares. We take it for granted that this is a natural state of affairs but it is not so. It depends on voting rights. If no shares had voting rights and companies could not be taken over in a contested bid, shareholders who felt themselves locked in would have to take action. No William Tell could ride to their rescue, bid in hand.

VOTING AS A SHAREHOLDER: AN UNFETTERED POWER

Shareholders can cast their vote as they think fit. A leading case establishing this principle is *North West Transportation Company Ltd v Beatty*[41] where the Privy Council held that, subject to contrary provision in articles, every shareholder had a right to vote on any question, irrespective of whatever personal interest he might have in the subject matter, and that the shareholder could cast votes as he thought fit. A vote is regarded as a property right and a shareholder is not to be deprived of that right by reason of the fact that the court may disapprove of the motive influencing its exercise.[42] A director who is also a shareholder is not constrained by the fiduciary duties that he owes as a director from voting as he thinks fit in his or her capacity as a shareholder.[43] A shareholder's freedom to vote as he thinks fit extends to a freedom to enter into a contract to cast votes in a particular way.[44] In *Puddephatt v Leith*[45] a mandatory injunction was granted to compel a registered shareholder to comply with an undertaking to vote in accordance with the wishes of a debtor who had previously been the registered owner of the shares and who had transferred them into the other's name as security for a loan.

Just as a shareholder has no duty to cast votes in a particular way, he has no duty to vote at all. A shareholder can be totally passive in respect of the investment or, in the words of Lord Lowry, 'the shareholder may lock away his paid-up shares and go to sleep'.[46] However, whilst shareholders are not required to vote as a matter of company law, for institutional investors, there is also the issue of their responsibility and accountability to their clients. Approaching the matter from this perspective, there is a growing acceptance in practice, although not, as yet, as a matter of law, that the obligations of institutional investors comprehend a duty to exercise the voting rights attached to the shares in their portfolio.

[41] (1887) 12 AC 589, PC, cited with approval in *Burland v Earle* [1902] AC 83, PC. Xuereb, PG, 'Voting Rights: A Comparative Review' (1987) 8 Co Law 16 compares the voting freedom of shareholders under English, French and Italian law.

[42] *Pender v Lushington* (1877) 6 Ch D 70; *Carruth v Imperial Chemical Industries Ltd* [1937] AC 707, HL.

[43] *North West Transportation Company Ltd v Beatty* (1887) 12 AC 589, PC; *Northern Counties Securities Ltd v Jackson & Steeple Ltd* [1974] 1 WLR 1133.

[44] *Greenwell v Porter* [1902] 1 Ch 530.

[45] [1916] 1 Ch 200.

[46] *Kuwait Asia Bank EC v National Mutual Life Nominees Ltd* [1991] 1 AC 187, PC.

VOTING BY INSTITUTIONAL INVESTORS

An ABI survey on Voting by Institutional Shareholders, published in July 1991, established that whilst insurance companies normally voted, practice amongst pension funds was more uneven, with over 20 per cent of them saying they never voted. A similar survey published by the NAPF in November 1995 indicated some increase in voting by pension funds, although over 20 per cent still said that they never voted. This passivity amongst major groups of institutional investors became a target for criticism during the 1990s, and the view that, as responsible investors, institutions ought to vote gained ground.[47] As well as the issue of accountability to clients, others arguments put forward in favour of voting include:[48] the addition of value—this is the argument that investors can use their votes to influence positively the strategic direction of the company and thereby increase its value; the demonstration of responsibility amongst shareholders—under English law shareholders do not owe duties to each other or to the company but some have argued that as a matter of practice shareholders have an obligation to each other to hold corporate management accountable; macro-economic responsibilities—this is the argument that when shareholders fail to hold management accountable, the result is that management becomes self-indulgent and their business becomes uncompetitive; and political considerations—following on from the last point, another argument is that, taking the lead from the USA where pension funds are required to vote as a matter of law, government should impose mandatory voting obligations to counteract the economically detrimental effects of institutional investors behaving as 'absentee landlords' who are happy to collect 'rent' in the form of dividends but who do not seek to monitor management with the result that sub-optimal managerial performance goes unchecked.

An argument against mandatory voting is that it could lead to 'box ticking' by institutional investors—that is, routine support for management proposals without any consideration of their merits. Box ticking would clearly not be a positive step forward; rather, in so far as it might create a veneer of shareholder monitoring whilst in fact the institutions were simply endorsing management proposals without an independent assessment, it could be counter-productive and could swamp the actions of genuinely active monitoring shareholders. Any legal requirement to vote would thus have to be bolstered by duties to be informed about the matter under consideration and to exercise discretion in deciding how to cast the vote. Compliance with these

[47] *The Responsibilities of Institutional Shareholders in the UK* (Institutional Shareholders' Committee) (December 1991) paras 3.1–3.3; *Cadbury Committee Report* para 6.11; *Hampel Committee Report* 5.7–5.9; *Combined Code* 2, E. Generally on voting pattern of institutional shareholders: Mallin, C, *Voting: The Role of Institutional Investors in Corporate Governance* (ICAEW publication) (1995).

[48] *Investment Committee Briefing* (NAPF) (November 1995); *Cadbury Committee Report* paras 7.4–7.5; *Developing a Winning Partnership: How Companies and Institutional Investors Are Working Together* (Report of a joint City/Industry taskforce) (1995).

duties could be difficult to police.[49] The alternative here is self regulation: so long as self regulation on voting is seen to be working, it seems unlikely that legislation on this matter will be forthcoming.[50] That institutional investors should vote has become an established aspect of good corporate governance as perceived by the market: the London Stock Exchange in the *Combined Code* annexed to *The Listing Rules* specifically states that institutional investors have a responsibility to make considered use of their votes.[51] In the 1990s the ABI and the NAPF began actively to encourage their members to participate in proxy votes at company meetings and, to counteract the problem of possible box ticking, established voting information services to assist them in doing so. Through these services, the ABI and the NAPF scrutinise notices of meetings of listed companies and provide their members with guidance whether the matters which are proposed comply with corporate governance best practice.[52] A similar voting service is also provided by Pensions Investment Research Consultants (PIRC), a body which mainly advises British local authority pension funds.[53] However, various surveys indicate that there remains a considerable gap between these initiatives and the behaviour of pension fund managers with regard to actual voting practice.[54] The gap between intention and reality is acknowledged in the *Combined Code* which exhorts institutional investors to take steps to ensure that their voting intentions are being translated into practice.[55]

THE EXTENT OF SHAREHOLDERS' VOTING CONTROL

Shareholders of a company have a right to vote where this is provided for by legislation (principally the Companies Act 1985), case law or the company's articles of association. For companies listed on the London Stock Exchange,

[49] The operation of the mandatory voting requirements to which US pension funds are subject has been criticised precisely on the grounds that this is basically a form of window dressing: Stapledon, GP, *Institutional Shareholders and Corporate Governance* (1996) 285–8 for a summary. On the difficulties of policing a duty to vote see also: Short, H, and Keasey, K, 'Institutional Shareholders and Corporate Governance in the United Kingdom' in Keasey, K, Thompson, S, and Wright, M (eds), *Corporate Governance* (1997) 18, 40–2.

[50] *Modern Company Law for a Competitive Economy* (DT1) (1998) para 3.7.

[51] *Combined Code* 2, E. *The State of Corporate Governance in Britain*, a 1996 survey of the directors of the UK's top 250 companies indicated significant demand for the more active involvement of major institutional shareholders in discussing company strategy and in using voting power. Half of those surveyed (and 71 per cent of chairmen and chief executive officers) were in favour of compulsory voting for institutions.

[52] ie, various codes that are endorsed by UK market practice plus any relevant guideline or policy that is endorsed by the body in question. The main corporate governance codes in the UK were established by the *Cadbury Committee Report*, the *Hampel Committee Report* and also the Report of the Greenbury Committee on Directors Remuneration. Elements of these various codes were consolidated into the *Combined Code* in 1998.

[53] This was the first such voting service to be established in the UK. PIRC's voting policies are set out in the *PIRC Voting Guidelines* (1996).

[54] 'Cadbury Fails to Shift Voting' *Guardian* 25 March 1997 reporting the results of a survey by PIRC indicating that the average vote for annual general meetings stood at only 39 per cent.

[55] *Combined Code* E.1.3. In June 1998 the NAPF announced that it was considering launching an independent inquiry into low levels of voting at company meetings by its members: 'Concern Over Pension Fund Voting Levels' *Independent* 22 June 1998.

The Listing Rules provide for a number of additional matters on which shareholders are also entitled to vote. The source of the right to vote on a particular matter determines whether a simple majority of those voting or some larger majority is required.

Apart from those matters which the legislation and, where relevant, *The Listing Rules* of the Stock Exchange require to be determined by the shareholders, companies are free to provide in their articles for the shareholders to have as much or as little decision-making responsibility as they think fit. The norm, as represented by Table A, art 70[56] is for the articles to vest the power to manage the company in the directors subject to the provisions of the Act, the memorandum and articles and to any directions given by special resolution. Art 70 makes clear that the shareholders' power to give directions by special resolution has prospective effect only and that the shareholders cannot, by means of a special resolution, retrospectively invalidate action that the directors have already taken.[57] In theory, a company could omit an art 70-type provision from its articles altogether so as to vest managerial power in its shareholders, but that would result in the shareholders becoming subject to the range of duties imposed on corporate management by the general law and would defeat one of the main objects of adopting the corporate form, that is to break the link between ownership of the shares in the business and responsibility for its management.

Shareholder Approval Required by Legislation

A less radical step than deviating altogether from the balance of managerial and shareholder power set by the Table A model articles, and the one that is favoured by the Companies Act 1985 and related legislation, is to focus on individual areas and to carve them out of the directors' managerial power, instead making them subject to specific shareholder approval. Relevant legislation specifies a range of matters which must be subject to shareholder approval. These include the following.

Constitutional Changes

Decisions to alter the objects[58] or articles[59] of the company must be approved by special resolution of the shareholders in general meeting. Since a change to the company's constitution affects fundamentally the bargain between shareholders and the company, and between shareholders among themselves, it is unremarkable that they should be required to approve it. More noteworthy is that the bargain can be changed without the consent of all of the shareholders:

[56] SI 1985/805. The history of the interpretation of the relevant provision is traced in *Breckland Group Holdings Ltd v London and Suffolk Properties Ltd* [1989] BCLC 100, noted Lord Wedderburn, 'Control of Corporate Actions' (1989) 52 MLR 401. The uncertainty surrounding earlier versions of Table A are discussed by Sullivan, GR, 'The Relationship Between the Board of Directors and the General Meeting in Limited Companies' (1977) 93 LQR 569.

[57] The drafting of Table A, art 70 suggests that the shareholders can direct the board to withdraw from executory contracts but such withdrawal from valid contracts would put the company in breach of its contractual obligations.

[58] Companies Act 1985, s 4.

[59] Ibid, s 9.

a special resolution, which requires the support of at least three-quarters of the votes cast,[60] not of the total electorate, will suffice to change the company's constitution.

Other constitutional changes, such as increases in authorised share capital[61] and variations of class rights[62] also require shareholder sanction.

Corporate Status

A company can change its status. For example, a company that was initially incorporated as a private company may convert into a public company in order to raise capital by offering its securities to the public. The procedure for changing status is governed by the Companies Act 1985 and normally a special resolution of the shareholders is required.[63] The one unusual case is where a limited company becomes an unlimited company. This requires the consent of all of the shareholders[64] but given that the effect of this change is to make the shareholders, who previously had limited liability, personally liable for all of the company's debts, this is hardly surprising.

Dissolution of the Company

It is for the shareholders rather than the board to decide whether to wind up their company voluntarily. The procedure requires the passing of a special or extraordinary resolution to wind up the company.[65] An extraordinary resolution is similar to a special resolution in that it requires the support of at least three-quarters of the votes cast, but it differs from a special resolution with regard to the length of notice that must be given of the intention to propose it.[66]

Authority to Allot Shares

It is a relatively recent development that directors require specific authorisation from the shareholders, either in the form of an ordinary resolution or a provision in the articles, to allot shares. This requirement, which is derived in part from the Second Company Law Directive, art 25[67] was first implemented into English law by the Companies Act 1980 and is now contained in the Companies Act 1985, s 80. The directive only applies to public companies but under the Act the directors of both public and private companies must seek authorisation. All authorisations must state the maximum amount of securities that the directors are authorised to allot[68] but the rules relating to the duration of such authorisations differ depending on the status of the company. An authorisation to the directors of a public company must be limited in duration to a maximum period of five years,[69] but in a private company, if it

[60] Ibid, s 378 (2). [61] Ibid, s 121. [62] Ibid, ss 125–127.

[63] Ibid, s 43 (private company converting to plc), s 51 (unlimited company becoming limited), s 53 (plc becoming a private company).

[64] Companies Act 1985, s 49. [65] Insolvency Act 1986, s 84.

[66] Companies Act 1985, s 378. Extraordinary resolutions require at least 14-days' notice, special resolutions require at least 21 days.

[67] 77/91/EEC, [1977] OJ L26/1. [68] Companies Act 1985, ss 80 (4) and 80A (2).

[69] Ibid, ss 80 (4) and 80A (2).

takes advantage of a special procedure,[70] the duration may be longer than five years or indefinite.

A reason for removing this power from the directors' general managerial discretion is to restrict the directors' ability to dilute the percentage interest of the shareholders at any given time. Although pre-emption requirements (which oblige the directors to offer new shares first to existing shareholders) seek to achieve the same result, pre-emption requirements on their own provide only limited protection: a right of first refusal in respect of new share issues will be of little practical value if the directors, in exercise of an unrestricted power to allot shares, have already made so many new issues that the financial resources of the existing shareholders have become strained or exhausted.

Authority to Offer New Shares Otherwise than on a Pre-emptive Basis

Again this requirement, so far as it relates to public companies, derives from the Second Directive.[71] The Companies Act 1985, s 89 contains the basic requirement for companies to give existing shareholders the right of first refusal in respect of new share issues and the immediately following sections provide for shareholders to relax that requirement. Under the Companies Act 1985, s 91, private companies may exclude the pre-emption requirement altogether by a provision to that effect in their memorandum or articles. Pre-emption rights can also be dis-applied, by both public and private companies, by passing a special resolution to that effect in accordance with the Companies Act 1985, s 95; the maximum length of a dis-application resolution under s 95 is linked in with the underlying s 80 authority in respect of the shares and, accordingly, it is five years in the case of a public company, although it can be longer, or indefinite, if the company is private.

The detailed requirements of the Companies Act 1985, ss 80 and 89 are considered further in Chapter 18 in the context of rights issues.[72] Here, it may be noted that share issues and pre-emption rights is an area where institutional investor control via voice is well developed. There are established guidelines agreed between the London Stock Exchange, the ABI, the NAPF and representatives of the corporate sector which indicate the limits within which institutional investors will support proposals by companies to dis-apply the pre-emption requirement contained in the Companies Act 1985, s 89. Although institutional investors will consider proposals for non pre-emptive issues which fall outside the limits specified in the guidelines, these have to be approved individually, whereas companies are assured of institutional investor support for proposals which are within the guidelines. These pre-emption guidelines are a model of effective institutional control: the co-ordinated approach by the ABI and NAPF[73] avoids the creation of different,

[70] Companies Act 1985, s 80A.
[71] 77/91/EEC, [1977] OJ L26/1, art 29.
[72] Ch 18 below, at 614–23.
[73] The ABI and NAPF (or predecessor bodies) have an established record of co-ordinating their efforts with regard to pre-emption: Stapledon, GP, *Institutional Shareholders and Corporate Governance* (1996) 56.

and possibly conflicting, requirements;[74] the guidelines are published, which both assists companies in assessing in advance how their proposals will be received by the market and provides a clear indication of the basis on which the institutions, as financial intermediaries, are conducting their operations.

Reduction of Capital, Share Buy Backs and Financial Assistance

Shareholder approval in the form of a special resolution is required for a reduction of capital.[75] Shareholder approval is also required for a share buy back. For the purposes of the companies legislation, the form of the approval depends on whether the buy back is to take place 'on-market' or 'off-market': an on-market share buy back requires ordinary resolution approval, that is a simple majority of the votes cast, whilst an off-market requires special resolution approval. The detail of the statutory rules governing share buy backs, including what is meant by 'on'. and 'off' market can be left to Chapter 13. In the context of this chapter, a noteworthy point is that the ABI requires approval for an on-market share buy back to be in the form of a special resolution notwithstanding that companies legislation permits an ordinary resolution. The ABI has not published formal guidelines on this point but its view is well known and can be easily discovered, for example by searching the ABI's on-line Institutional Voting Information Service.

Private companies are allowed to give financial assistance subject to certain conditions, including a requirement for shareholder approval in the form of a special resolution.[76]

Certain Transactions Involving Directors

Substantial property transactions, broadly, those exceeding £100,000 or 10 per cent of the company's asset value, between a company and any of its directors must be approved by ordinary resolution of the shareholders[77] as must advances made to a director to meet expenditure or for the purpose of enabling him properly to perform his duties as an officer of the company.[78] The making of gratuitous payments to directors for loss of office or as consideration for, or in connection with, retirement from office is also subject to prior shareholder approval given by way of ordinary resolution.[79]

Removal of Directors

Under the Companies Act 1985, s 303 the shareholders of a company can remove directors from office by passing an ordinary resolution to that effect. This power can be exercised at any time with or without cause. If a director is removed from office any service contract that he has with the company will come to an end but if the removal was not for good cause the company will be

[74] *Combined Code*, E.1.1. calls upon institutional investors to endeavour to eliminate unnecessary variations in their corporate governance and performance criteria for the companies in which they invest.

[75] Companies Act 1985, s 135.

[76] Ibid, s 155. See further, Ch 11 below, at 400–3.

[77] Companies Act 1985, s 320.

[78] Ibid, s 337.

[79] Companies Act 1985, s 312. There are also restrictions on payments in takeover situations to the outgoing directors: Companies Act 1985, ss 313–316.

liable in damages for breach of contract.[80] As a safeguard against directors entrenching themselves in office by securing long service contracts which would be prohibitively expensive for the company to break, thus rendering impotent the power to remove by ordinary resolution except where the director is guilty of a breach of duty that would justify termination of his contract, Companies Act 1985, s 319 requires all service contracts of more than five years to be approved by ordinary resolution of the shareholders in general meeting. Good corporate governance practice, as suggested by the *Combined Code* is for contract terms or notice periods to be set at a maximum of one year.[81]

Removal of unsatisfactory directors is the ultimate way in which shareholders exert control via voice. Whether, and in what circumstances, shareholders, especially institutional shareholders, are prepared to use this power and, approaching essentially the same issue from a different angle, the extent to which it operates as a real deterrent to shirking or exploitation of self-interest at shareholders' expense by corporate management, are issues that are right at the centre of the modern debate about corporate governance.

Enhancing Shareholder Control by Increasing the Range of Circumstances Where Shareholder Approval is Required

Of the matters listed above there are some, such as the powers to approve constitutional or status changes, to wind up the company, to reduce capital and to remove the directors, which are part of the fundamental framework of company law and which define basic parameters of the relationship between the directors of a company and its shareholders. In the ownership model of the company, these are matters that fall appropriately to the shareholders to decide.[82] The provisions of the companies legislation requiring shareholder approval for new share issues, for dis-application of pre-emption rights and for certain transactions involving directors are different in nature. These are all matters on which, for a long time, the companies legislation did not intervene and, although companies' articles could have imposed shareholder approval requirements, the norm was simply to leave these matters in the hands of the directors. It was largely through the European Union's programme of company law harmonisation that the companies legislation incorporated shareholder approval requirements on these matters, evidently as part of a policy to shift the balance of control more in favour of shareholders. This is a policy that could be taken further as part of a normative agenda. For instance, the Jenkins Committee in 1962 recommended that any proposal to sell the whole or substantially the whole of a company's undertaking and assets should be made subject to shareholder approval, but that suggestion was not implemented.[83] Another area where legislation could require share-

[80] Companies Act 1985, s 303 (5). [81] *Combined Code*, B.1 and B.1.7.

[82] Parkinson, JE, *Corporate Power and Responsibility* (1993) 164.

[83] *Report of the Company Law Committee* (Cmnd 1749) (1962) paras 117–18. The Committee also suggested (at para 122(h)) a reform along the lines of Companies Act 1980 but it was the obligation to incorporate the Second Company Law Directive, art 29 that finally led to

holder approval is in relation to directors' remuneration.[84] Drawbacks against multiplying the circumstances where shareholder approval is required include the costs that can be involved in the process of convening a general meeting to obtain such approval and the delay that completion of this process usually entails. There is also the issue of potential shareholder voting fatigue: shareholders invest in shares precisely because they do not want to play a part in management and if the range of matters on which their approval is required were to be increased significantly, bearing in mind that for an institutional investor holding a large diversified portfolio the impact of each new requirement would be felt many times over, that benefit might appear to disappear and could thus trigger a flight to other, less troublesome, investments. This point acquires an additional resonance if it is accepted that part of the responsibility of institutional investors should be to actively participate in the operation of the companies in which they invest by voting their shares. To facilitate this active participation, it would seem to be preferable to restrict the range of matters on which shareholder approval is required. The challenge here is to balance the range of competing considerations so that investing in shares does not become more trouble than it is worth.[85]

CASE LAW

Directors of a company owe a variety of duties to their company: they must act in good faith in its interest, exercise their powers for proper purposes, avoid conflicts of interest, not make unauthorised profits from their position, and act with due care and skill. The company can, however, release them, prospectively or retrospectively from these duties. It is the shareholders in general meeting who act as the company for this purpose. Their role in this respect and the extent to which it is permissible for articles to provide alternative release mechanisms, such as consent from disinterested directors, are complex matters that are discussed further in Chapter 4.[86]

ARTICLES OF ASSOCIATION

Table A is simply a model form of articles which companies are not obliged to adopt but in practice, it is normally taken as the starting point which companies

shareholder approval for share issues becoming part of English law. The Committee rejected (at para 118) the suggestion that fundamental changes in the company's activities, within the scope of its objects clause, should also require approval.

[84] Presently there are statutory disclosure obligations with regard to directors' remuneration but no specific approval requirements. The *Combined Code*, B.3.4 recommends that directors' long-term incentive plans be approved by shareholders. It appears that the government is inclined to favour closer regulation of directors' remuneration, in the form of shareholder approval required, imposed by the London Stock Exchange rather than legislative intervention: 'Byers Seeks To Halt Big Rises in Boardroom Pay' *Financial Times* 16 February 1999.

[85] Sealy, LS, *Company Law and Commercial Reality* (1984) 60–1.

[86] Ch 4 above, at 140–3 and 144–53.

then modify to suit their own particular requirements. Table A provides for shareholders to nominate[87] and appoint[88] directors and for shareholders to fix the remuneration of non-executive directors[89] (the salaries of executive directors are determined by the board[90]). It ensures that the shareholders will have the opportunity to consider the board's performance by requiring one-third of them to retire annually, although they may stand for re-election.[91] Shareholders sometimes vote against re-election resolutions, not because they object to a particular director as such, but in order to protest against some aspect of a company's corporate governance.[92] Another matter on which shareholders appear to have a significant say under Table A is in relation to dividends. Under article 102 it is for the shareholders to declare a dividend.[93] However, the shareholders cannot declare a dividend exceeding the amount recommended by the directors, which means that, in reality, the shareholders usually do no more than ratify a decision already made by the board.

In the articles of listed companies there is normally some deviation from Table A so as to give the shareholders greater say on certain matters. For example, the articles of listed companies normally restrict the directors' managerial power by imposing a limit on the amount that they can borrow without reverting to the shareholders for specific authorisation by ordinary resolution.[94] Although it is not a requirement of the London Stock Exchange that a company must have such a provision in its articles in order to secure, or maintain, a listing for its shares, as a matter of practice companies include it in order to meet the expectations of institutional investors.[95] The ABI is particularly involved in the scrutiny of the contents of articles of association of listed companies and, at a general level, it makes its views known via its Institutional Voting Information Service. At the company-specific level, it reviews proposed changes to articles of association of listed companies for compliance with corporate governance best practice[96] and informs subscribers[97] of the results of such reviews so that they can decide whether to support the proposals.

Generalisations about the articles of private companies are of limited value given that this category comprises an extremely large number of businesses engaged upon a wide and diverse range of activities. At the opposite end of the spectrum from the listed company is the very small 'quasi-partnership' type

[87] Table A, art 76. The board can also nominate new directors.
[88] Table A, art 78. Art 79 gives the board a limited power to appoint directors but a director appointed by the board must vacate office at the next following annual general meeting.
[89] Table A, art 82. [90] Table A, art 84. [91] Table A, art 73.
[92] eg, 'CU Investors Lose Right to Vote on Annual Report' *Financial Times* 3 April 1997, reporting PIRC's recommendation to vote against a re-election resolution as a protest against the company's decision not to put the annual report and accounts to a formal vote of approval by the shareholders.
[93] The directors may pay interim dividends without seeking shareholder approval (art 103).
[94] Versions of Table A prior to 1985 did impose a borrowing limit.
[95] The ABI suggests that the broad ballpark figure for the borrowing limits in articles of association is twice capital and reserves but there may be wide variation depending on the company and its sector.
[96] ABI guidelines together with the recommendations of the Cadbury and Greenbury committees form the basis of these reviews.
[97] Part of the IVIS service is freely available on-line but part is restricted to subscribers.

company where all of the shareholders are also intended to be involved in the management of the company. In quasi-partnership companies the idea of the shareholders, as a separate body, monitoring the activities of the board is meaningless. Table A, art 73, which requires one-third of the board to retire annually and which is intended to facilitate monitoring by the shareholders, is often excluded in the articles of this type of company. Also, although it is impossible to exclude the statutory power to remove a director by ordinary resolution,[98] the practical impact of this power can be diminished or extinguished by the clever trick of providing in the articles a formula under which any director/shareholder faced with a threat of removal is given an enhanced voting power in his or her capacity as a shareholder which is sufficient to defeat the motion. Despite the fact that this device renders the statutory power impotent it has received the sanction of the House of Lords and is effective.[99]

Another category of private company where there is likely to be some deviation from the norm of shareholder democracy as set by Table A is in joint venture companies. It may be of particular importance to the partners in a joint venture that they should be equal in which case they will want the deadlock articles so that none of them can force through certain motions, such as alterations of share capital or winding up of the company, without the consent of all of the others. Removal of the directors who are appointed as nominees of each of the partners may also be subject to special provision.

The Listing Rules and the Combined Code

The continuing obligations imposed on companies which are admitted to listing on the London Stock Exchange by *The Listing Rules* includes a requirement for shareholder approval of substantial acquisitions and disposals.[100] For the purposes of *The Listing Rules* the size of a prospective transaction must be measured by reference to a number of percentage ratios: the gross assets which are the subject of the transaction divided by the gross assets of the listed company; profits attributable to the assets which are the subject of the transaction divided by the profits of the listed company; the turnover attributable to the assets which are the subject of the transaction divided by the turnover of the listed company; the consideration divided by the market capitalisation of the listed company; and the gross capital of the company or business being acquired divided by the gross capital of the listed company. Where any of these percentage ratios is 25 per cent or more, the transaction is deemed to be a Class 1 transaction for which shareholder approval is required.

The Listing Rules overlap with the Companies Act 1985 in imposing shareholder approval requirements in relation to transactions between companies

[98] Companies Act 1985, s 303.

[99] *Bushell v Faith* [1970] AC 1099, HL. For the protection to be complete, there must also be provision for enhanced voting power with respect to any proposal to change the '*Bushell v Faith*' clause.

[100] *The Listing Rules*, ch 10.

and their directors.[101] Small transactions, which are determined by reference to the same ratios as those outlined in the previous paragraph and are when each of those ratios is below 5 per cent, are excluded from this requirement.[102] *The Listing Rules* requirement for shareholder approval also applies to transactions between a company and any of its substantial shareholders, that is any holder of 10 per cent or more of any class of capital of the company. Under the general law shareholders are normally free to vote as they please even though the effect of their vote may be to benefit themselves in another capacity, principally as directors of the company.[103] *The Listing Rules* require that the interested director or substantial shareholder should not be permitted to vote at the relevant shareholders' meeting.[104]

The *Combined Code* annexed to *The Listing Rules* suggests that shareholders should approve any new long-term incentive schemes which are included in directors' remuneration packages.[105] This is not a formal continuing obligation which, if not complied with, would jeopardise a company's listing. Its status is that listed companies must disclose whether they have complied with the requirement in their annual report and accounts, and must give reasons for any non-compliance.[106]

HOW SHAREHOLDERS EXERCISE VOICE: AN OVERVIEW AND CRITIQUE OF THE RULES RELATING TO GENERAL MEETINGS[107]

In a judgment delivered in 1933 Maugham J compared the normal procedures at company meetings in the late nineteenth century, when all of the persons concerned could go to the meeting, listen to what was said, and vote for or against the arrangement according to the views expressed at the meeting, with the position as it normally was in 1933, when only a fraction of the persons concerned could attend meetings and in the majority of cases proxies given before the meeting would in effect settle the question of voting once and for all.[108] He said:[109]

> In a sense, in all these cases, the dice are loaded in favour of the views of the directors: the notices and circulars are sent out at the cost of the company, the board have had plenty of time to prepare the circulars, all the facts of the case are known to them, proxy forms made out in favour of certain named directors . . . If we contrast with that the

[101] *The Listing Rules*, ch 11.

[102] But where any ratio is between 0.25 and 5 per cent there are disclosure obligations: *The Listing Rules*, ch 11, para 11.8.

[103] *Pender* v *Lushington* (1877) 6 Ch D 70; *Northern Counties Securities Ltd v Jackson & Steeple Ltd* [1974] 1 WLR 1133; *North-West Transportation Co Ltd v Beatty* (1887) 12 App Cas 589, PC.

[104] *The Listing Rules*, ch 11. para 11.4 (d).

[105] *Combined Code*, B.3.4.

[106] *The Listing Rules*, ch 12, para 12.43A (b).

[107] Detailed accounts of the law governing general meetings may be found in standard company law text books such as Boyle, AJ, Sykes, R, and Sealy, LS, *Gore-Browne on Companies* (44th edn, looseleaf) ch 21; Morse, G (gen ed), *Palmer's Company Law* (25th edn, loose-leaf) pt 7(B); and Pennington, RR, *Company Law* (7th edn, 1995) ch 16 and in specialist works such Shearman, I, *Shackleton on The Law and Practice of Meetings* (9th edn, 1997); Burton, M, and Patfield, F (eds), *The Conduct of Meetings* (23rd edn, 1994); Jones, M, and Jacobs, E, *Company Meetings: Law and Procedure* (1991); Janner, G, *Meetings* (1986).

[108] *Re Dorman, Long & Co Ltd* [1934] 1 Ch 635.

[109] Ibid, 657.

position of a class of objectors, it is to be observed that a member of the class who receives notice of the meeting and a circular from the directors is generally alone: he has no funds with which to fight the case and he has no information, except, sometimes, that information which has been contained in reports and balance sheets which have probably long ago been relegated to the waste paper basket. In any case, he has a minimum of information, his personal interest in the matter may be exceedingly small, probably he knows a few persons in the same position as himself and, if he manages to get in touch with them, they together have to raise funds for the purposes of an opposition, which is often an expensive matter. They have then to get the names and addresses of the members of the class who are concerned, and to frame and send out a circular representing their views. Very often there is scarcely sufficient time for those purposes between the moment when notice of the meeting reaches objectors by post and the date of the meeting. Proxies sent out by the directors can easily be lodged 48 hours before the meeting. It is quite plain that opponents may find it most difficult, after they have come together and raised the necessary funds and have agreed on a circular and have sent out their notices, to lodge such proxies as they may have been able to obtain 48 hours before the meeting.

The growing emphasis in the 1990s on the role of voice as a means of monitoring management makes it appropriate to consider whether it remains true to say that the dice are loaded in favour of the directors. Clearly, the biggest change is the emergence of the institutional investor into the role of the predominant owner of equity share capital. This development nullifies the picture of scattered shareholders who have matters sprung on them unexpectedly by the board and who are, in practical terms, incapable of engaging in collective action economically. Companies tend to be in regular dialogue with their biggest institutional shareholders; the network of formal and informal contacts between institutional investors provides the basis for potential collective action; institutional investors can absorb the cost amongst themselves; and their domination of the register of shareholder serves to restrict the problem of 'free rider' shareholders who may benefit from the collective exercise of voice but who do not have to contribute to its cost.[110] But, despite the headlines in individual cases, direct head-to-head confrontation at general meetings between corporate management and institutional investors is still uncommon.[111] Institutional preference for behind-the-scenes action goes some way towards explaining this. The mere threat of institutional shareholder opposition to a proposal can be sufficient to ensure that it is withdrawn before being put formally to the shareholders at a general meeting.[112] Whilst bearing this preference for discretion in mind, it is still pertinent to inquire whether the legal rules relating to the mechanics of the

[110] This assumes that all of a company's institutional investors would be prepared to join in collective action which is not necessarily a correct assumption: see, eg, Black, BS, and Coffee, JC, 'Hail Britannia?: Institutional Investor Behavior Under Limited Regulation' (1994) 92 Michigan Law Review 1997, 2055–9.

[111] Artus, RE, (Group Chief Investment Manager, Prudential Corporation plc (a major institutional investor)) stated in 1990: 'Some increase in institutional investors' activities aimed at bringing about more effective and better structured company boards and management may occur, but not I would suggest to a dramatic extent'; in 'Tension to Continue' in *Creative Tension?* (NAPF 1990) 12, 16.

[112] Dickins, P, 'A Voice, A Vote, A Veto' (1991) 82 *Corporate Finance* 13; Finch, V, 'Company Directors: Who Cares about Skill and Care?' (1992) 55 MLR 179.

general meeting impede, or could be redrawn so as to facilitate more effectively, the exercise of voice by institutional shareholders. The same issues need also to be addressed from the perspective of individual private investors although the fact that individual shareholders are unlikely to be in control of a sufficient number of votes to be able to influence materially the outcome of a vote means that there is another question that arises in relation to them: this is the role of general meetings as a means of conveying information to shareholders and of enabling them to ask questions about the stewardship of its affairs.[113]

Types of General Meeting

Under the Companies Act 1985 there are two types of general meeting: annual general meetings and extraordinary general meetings. Companies Act 1985, s 366 provides that every company must in each year hold an annual general meeting and that no more than 15 months must elapse between the date of one annual general meeting of a company and that of the next.[114] Any other meeting of shareholders that is held by a company during the course of a year is an extraordinary general meeting.

Calling General Meetings

Articles of association normally place the power to call company meetings in the hands of the directors.[115] This is a fiduciary power which must be exercised in good faith in the interests of the company as a whole.[116] In addition to the constraint imposed by fiduciary duty, the Companies Act 1985 provides for a variety of consequences should the directors fail to use this power correctly. First, if an annual general meeting is not held as required by the Companies Act 1985, the company and every officer of it who is in default is liable to a fine.[117] This form of default also triggers the right conferred on all shareholders of the company by the Companies Act 1985, s 367 to ask the Secretary of State to call, or direct the calling of, the meeting. Any shareholder can request this: there is no threshold level or duration of shareholding

[113] For ease of exposition the text compares the opposite ends of the spectrum, the institutional investor which has a significant proportion of a company's shares and a private shareholder who holds a tiny number of the company shares. The point has been made elsewhere that it is not in fact correct to assume that all of the institutional shareholders in a company will hold a stake that is sufficiently large to be able to influence management through informal contact or at general meetings: *Shareholder Communications At Annual General Meetings: The Manifest Response* (1996) (Manifest Voting Agency is a body that provides a voting service in respect of UK quoted companies). There is some force in this point and it means that the comments in the text about the position of private investors should be read as being capable of being extended to at least some institutional investors.

[114] Special rules govern the timing of a company's first AGM: Companies Act 1985, s 366 (2).

[115] Based on the model of Table A, art 37. This displaces Companies Act 1985, s 370 (3) which, in the absence of contrary provision in the articles, gives two or more shareholders holding not less than one-tenth of the issued share capital the right to call a meeting.

[116] *Pergamon Press Ltd v Maxwell* [1970] 1 WLR 1167.

[117] Companies Act 1985, s 366 (4). Repeated failure to call an annual general meeting as required may amount to unfairly prejudicial conduct for which members may seek a remedy under the Companies Act 1985, s 459: *Re a Company ex parte Shooter* [1990] BCLC 384.

requirement nor even a requirement that the requesting shareholder should be entitled to vote at the meeting.

The Companies Act 1985, s 368 provides a non-excludable right for shareholders themselves to requisition the calling of an extraordinary general meeting. A shareholders' requisition under s 368 means a requisition of shareholders of the company holding not less than one-tenth of the voting rights in the company. If the directors fail duly to call an extraordinary general meeting in response to a requisition from shareholders, the requisitionists may call the meeting themselves.[118] The company must reimburse any reasonable expenses incurred by the requisitionists by reason of the directors' failure duly to requisition a meeting under this section and the company must deduct the amounts so reimbursed from remuneration due to the directors who were in default. In *McGuinness v Bremner*[119] delay in holding an extraordinary general meeting in response to a member's requisition was held to amount to unfairly prejudicial conduct. The case[120] highlighted a loophole in the law as it then stood because although the directors were required to respond to the requisition by calling a meeting within a specified time there was nothing to stop the directors fixing the actual date of the meeting at some point far into the future. The loophole was closed by the Companies Act 1989 which inserted Companies Act 1985, s 368 (8) which requires the directors to fix the date of the meeting for a date not more than 28 days after the date of the notice by which the meeting is convened. The practical effect of this limitation is that it restricts the time that the directors have to prepare their response to the shareholders' motion.

Since it would be taking democracy to absurd lengths if the elaborate mechanisms for the holding of company meetings had to spring into life in response to every request from a member irrespective of how small his shareholding in the company might be, the 10-per-cent requirement is a reasonable compromise. 1996 data on the ownership of listed companies indicates that on average the largest institutional investor in a company's register of shareholders holds 8 per cent of the shares and that the largest five institutional investors hold around one-quarter of the shares.[121] This indicates that in a typical case a small group of institutional investors would be in a position to activate the procedure under Companies Act 1985, s 368. For private investors, however, the likelihood is that the 10-per-cent threshold for s 368 requisitions will represent an insurmountable hurdle.

The Companies Act 1985, s 371 allows the court to order a meeting if for any reason it is impracticable for the company itself to call or conduct it in accordance with its normal procedures. The court can act under this section of its own motion or on the application of any director of the company or of any shareholder who would be entitled to vote at the meeting. An application under this section was successful in circumstances where the company's efforts to hold a meeting in accordance with its normal procedures had failed

[118] Companies Act 1985, s 368(4).

[119] [1988] BCLC 673, Ct of Sess.

[120] So also did *Re Windward Islands (Enterprises) UK Ltd* [1983] BCLC 293.

[121] Gaved, M, *Institutional Investors and Corporate Governance* (1998) 30–1 quoting Citywatch data (January 1996).

because of the disruptive impact of a minority whose actions at attempted meetings had caused the proceedings to descend into a near riot. In these 'special and unusual circumstances', as they were described by the court, an order was granted for a meeting to be held to alter the articles to introduce voting by proxy, for entitlement to attend this meeting to be restricted to a small number of individuals, and for voting by the other members of the company to be by postal vote rather than in person as was required by the company's articles.[122] In companies with a very small number of shareholders, it may become impracticable to hold company meetings in accordance with normal procedures when the relations between those shareholders breaks down because a sufficient number of shareholders will not attend a meeting in order to satisfy quorum requirements. In that type of case, the court may make an order under Companies Act 1985, s 371 to prevent a minority shareholder from using the quorum requirement as a device to block the majority shareholders from exercising their votes;[123] but s 371 does not empower the court to make orders to break a deadlock between shareholders who have equal voting rights[124] or to override class rights.[125]

Drawing Up a Notice of a Meeting: Controlling the Agenda and the Circulation of Information

Notices of annual general meetings are normally drawn up by the directors. This is an important power because of the rule that, apart from any matters designated as ordinary business in the articles,[126] only those matters of which notice has been duly given can be discussed at a meeting.[127] There is provision in the Companies Act 1985, s 376 for shareholders to require notice to be given by the company of resolutions that they wish to put to the next annual general meeting. This provision can only be used where the number of shareholders who want the resolution to be put is either (a) any number representing not less than 5 per cent of the total voting rights of all the shareholders who would be entitled to attend and vote at the meeting on the matter to which the proposed resolution relates or (b) not less than 100 shareholders holding shares in the company on which there has been paid up an average sum, per shareholder, of not less than £100. The shareholders' requisition for the resolution to be put to the annual general meeting must be deposited at the company's registered office not less than six weeks before the meeting.[128] The costs of complying with this requisition falls on the requisitionists unless the

[122] *Re British Union for the Abolition of Vivisection* [1995] 2 Ch 1.

[123] *Re Opera Photographic Ltd* [1989] 1 WLR 634; *Re Sticky Fingers Restaurant Ltd* [1992] BCLC 84.

[124] *Ross v Telford* [1998] 1 BCLC 82, CA.

[125] *Harman v BML Group Ltd* [1994] 1 WLR 893, CA.

[126] Discussed in the following section of this chapter, at 264–6.

[127] *Kaye v Croydon Tramways* [1898] 1 Ch 358, CA; *Normandy v Ind Coope & Co* [1908] 1 Ch 84. On the general significance of the power to control the agenda and to set the date of meetings: Black, BS, 'Shareholder Passivity Reexamined' (1990) 89 Michigan Law Review 520, 592–5.

[128] But if an AGM is called for a date 6 weeks or less after a requisition is deposited the requisition is deemed to have been properly deposited: Companies Act 1985, s 377 (2).

company otherwise decides and a sum that is reasonably sufficient to cover these costs must be deposited or tendered with the requisition.[129]

The Companies Act 1985, s 376 also provides for the circulation of shareholders' statements. The fact that most shareholders do not bother physically to attend shareholders' meetings and vote by proxy, if they vote at all, means that it is important for shareholders to explain the reasons for their own resolutions or to outline their opposition to management proposals well in advance of the meeting. This highlights the significance of this aspect of s 376. With the same threshold shareholding requirement as for requiring resolutions to be put to the annual general meeting, but in relation to any meeting, requisitionists can require the company to send to its shareholders circulars relating to any matter referred to in a proposed resolution or to any business to be dealt with at a meeting.[130] The circular must not exceed 1,000 words in length[131] and must be deposited at the company's registered office not less than one week before the meeting.[132] The costs of circulation fall to the requisitionists unless the company otherwise resolves and a sum that is reasonably sufficient to meet this must be deposited or tendered with the requisition.[133] The company, or any other aggrieved person, can apply to court to be relieved of the obligation to distribute a circular which is designed to secure needless publicity for defamatory material; and the court may order the requisitionists to pay all or part of the company's costs on such an application.[134]

In 1996 the DTI published a Consultative Document seeking views on whether the Companies Act 1985 should be amended to require companies to circulate shareholders' resolutions for the annual general meeting and accompanying statements[135] without charge, provided they were submitted by a given deadline and complied with other qualifying conditions.[136] The DTI's primary concern in this paper was the difficulties faced by individual private investors in seeking to use the machinery of corporate democracy, but the fact that the costs of shareholders' resolutions and accompanying circulars falls on the requisitionists in the first place (though the shareholders can resolve that the company should meet the costs) may also be a disincentive to the use of the general meeting as the means of active monitoring by institutional investors.[137] The contrast here between the position of the board and that of shareholders who want to put forward a resolution or a counterview to that of management is stark. The directors are permitted to use the company's funds 'bona fide and reasonably for the purpose of obtaining the

129 Companies Act 1985, s 377 (1)(b).
130 Ibid, s 376 (1)(b).
131 Ibid.
132 Companies Act 1985, s 377 (1)(ii).
133 Ibid, ss 376 (1) and 377 (1)(b).
134 Ibid, s 377 (3).
135 But not for statements relating to business to be dealt with at an extraordinary general meeting. This proposed limitation has been criticised: *Shareholder Communications at Annual General Meetings: The Manifest Response* (1996) para 9.
136 *Shareholder Communications at the Annual General Meeting* (DTI Consultative Document) (April 1996). This consultative process was prompted by a Report of the House of Commons' Select Committee on Employment on *The Remuneration of Directors and Chief Executives of the Privatised Utilities* (June 1995) which suggested that Companies Act 1985, s 376 should be amended broadly as set out in the text.
137 Gaved, M, *Institutional Investors and Corporate Governance* (1998) 42–3.

best expression of the voice of the corporators in general meeting'.[138] Within the constraint of their fiduciary duties, directors can, at the company's expense and without having to obtain shareholder approval, send out circulars explaining their policies and the reasons why shareholders should support the resolutions they have put forward. In this respect, therefore, the dice is still loaded in management's favour.[139] Concerns that a change in the law in this respect could lead to a proliferation of shareholders' resolutions[140] would seem to be misplaced given that there would continue to be other qualifying conditions[141] for shareholders' resolutions and accompanying statements to be circulated at the company's expense.[142]

'Ordinary Business' at Annual General Meetings

By convention the matters normally discussed at annual general meetings are: the annual accounts and related directors' and auditors' reports;[143] the election of directors in place of those who, under the retirement by rotation provisions in the articles, are required to resign at the annual general meeting;[144]

[138] *Peel v London and NW Railway* [1907] 1 Ch 5, CA, 18 *per* Buckley LJ. In *Advance Bank of Australia Ltd v FAI Insurances Australia* (1987) 12 ACLR 118, NSW CA, the argument that the directors could never spend company funds to influence the outcome of an election to the board (based on Eisenberg, MA, 'Access to the Corporate Proxy Machinery' (1970) 83 Harvard Law Review 1489) was rejected as not being the approach adopted by the mainstream of Australian and English authority.

[139] It appears that in practice companies may be willing to include shareholders' resolutions in the AGM mailing where they are received in time and to waive the small additional cost that this entails. Essentially the DTI's proposal is to harden this practice into a legal rule. A drawback of the DTI's proposal is that it would require shareholders to draw up their resolution and any supporting statement before the publication of the company's annual report and accounts.

[140] These concerns are set out, for example, in *A Guide to Best Practice for Annual General Meetings* (ICSA) (1996) para 2.10. This is a report published by a working party established by the Institute of Chartered Secretaries and Administrators to establish and define best practice for the conduct of annual general meetings and the rights of shareholders in relation to them.

[141] *Shareholder Communications at the Annual General Meeting* (DTI Consultative Document) (April 1996) para 2.23 raises the possibility of introducing a minimum period of shareholding in addition to the qualifying threshold amount. For criticism of this proposal see *Shareholder Communications at Annual General Meetings: The Manifest Response* (1996) para 6. The DTI also suggests a re-assessment of the threshold amount (para 2.22). The limb of the present qualifying threshold which refers to 100 shareholders holding shares on which there has been paid up an average sum of £100 per share (Companies Act 1985, s 376 (2)(b)) is anomalous because 'paid up' refers to the par value of the shares which is not necessarily (and in practice is most unlikely to be) the price at which they were issued or are now trading. For example if ten £1 par value shares are issued to X at a price of £10 each, X would not satisfy s 376 (2)(b) because, although he has paid £100, the paid up value of his shares is only £10.

[142] Under present law, shareholders' resolutions are put forward infrequently: see, eg, *Shareholder Communications at the Annual General Meeting* (DTI Consultative Document) (April 1996) appendix C which provides an analysis of shareholder resolutions in the UK in 1995.

[143] Companies Act 1985, s 241 requires the accounts and reports in respect of each year to be laid before a general meeting. Although there is no Companies Act 1985 requirement for the shareholders to approve the accounts, it is usual practice for them to do so. When one company proposed to withdraw from this standard practice, this attracted strong criticism and the experiment was not repeated: 'CU Investors Lose Right to Vote on Annual Report' *Financial Times* 3 April 1997; 'CU Backs Down on Plan to Deny Vote on Accounts' *Financial Times* 4 April 1996; 'CU Says Sorry Over Vote Omission' *Financial Times* 16 April 1997.

[144] These provisions typically require one-third of the directors to retire each year but retiring directors are eligible for re-election. Under the *Combined Code* A.6, directors must be required by the articles to submit themselves for re-election at least every three years.

the appointment and fixing of remuneration of auditors;[145] and the declaration of a dividend. In some companies this convention is hardened into a more formal matter of internal administration by a provision in the articles to the effect that these matters are 'ordinary business' which need not be referred to specifically in notices convening annual general meetings. An ordinary-business provision was included in earlier versions of Table A but it is omitted from the current version.

The predictability of the main parts of the agenda for annual general meetings is helpful to shareholders. For example, the retirement by rotation provisions that must as a matter of good corporate-governance practice be included in listed companies' articles of association ensure that at each annual general meeting the composition of the board will be under review, and shareholders can thus prepare for this in advance. Case law recognises that shareholders can require a meeting to consider alternatives to proposals that were in the agenda where those alternatives can be regarded as being within the scope of the original notice of the meeting. This means that where, for example, the agenda for a forthcoming annual general meeting includes proposals for the election or re-election of directors, it is open to shareholders who want to make their own nomination to argue that the possibility of an alternative to the directors' nomination is envisaged by the original notice drawn up by the board and that it does not require separate notification.[146] In cases where this point has been considered, the courts have tended to favour shareholders in construing notices.[147] However, the prevalence of proxy voting means that it would be futile to spring a nomination on a sparsely attended meeting: to have an impact this would need to be circulated in advance so that it could be taken into account before shareholders cast their proxy votes.

Shareholders can use the predictable nature of AGM business to prepare questions in advance of the meeting. The function of the annual general meeting as a forum for shareholders to ask questions and to obtain information is more important for private investors and smaller institutional investors than for a company's major institutional investors who have the opportunity to ask

[145] Companies Act 1985, s 385 limits an auditor's tenure of office to a period starting from a general meeting at which accounts are laid until the conclusion of the next general meeting at which accounts are laid which, in effect, means from one annual general meeting to the next.

[146] Table A, art 76 (b) specifies a procedure for shareholders to nominate directors. Any member (ie no minimum shareholding) who is qualified to vote is entitled to put forward a name not less than 14 nor more than 35 clear days before the date appointed for the meeting. The company must then given notice of it to all of those persons who are entitled to receive notice of the meeting: art 77. This is a curious set of provisions which initially appear to suggest that any shareholder can require the company to consider his nomination irrespective of the size of his shareholding. This is not so. The procedure prevents shareholders from springing nominations on the company at the last moment but it does not guarantee that their nomination will be considered. If the nominating shareholders do not control a sufficient proportion of the votes to be able to force the nomination onto the agenda of a meeting and it cannot be regarded as being within the scope of the notice of a meeting drawn up by the board, then the company need not take the nomination any further.

[147] *Betts v Macnaughten* [1910] 1 Ch 430; *Choppington Collieries Ltd v Johnson* [1944] 1 All ER 762, CA. Where the company has articles based on Table A, arts 76–77, it would seem that the company should regard a shareholder nomination in accordance with the articles as being within the scope of the notice of the meeting in these circumstances.

questions and to express their views at informal meetings with management. There is at present no detailed legal mechanism governing shareholders' questions at general meetings but as a matter of practice, many companies do permit shareholders to ask questions on a wide range of matters and do not confine them to the formal resolutions on the agenda. This practice is supported in general terms by the *Combined Code* annexed to *The Listing Rules* which states that boards should use the annual general meeting to communicate with private investors and encourage their participation.[148] It requires the chairman to arrange for the chairmen of the company's audit, remuneration and nomination committees to be available to answer questions at the meeting.[149] In its review of the annual general meeting, the DTI considered the possibility of codification of practice with regard to shareholders' questions but concluded that this was a matter that should be dealt with by the development of best practice by companies themselves.[150]

Length of Notice of Meetings

The statutory minimum period of notice for annual general meetings and for extraordinary general meetings to consider passing certain types of resolution is 21 clear days.[151] Otherwise the statutory minimum period of notice is 14 clear days.[152] In addition, for listed companies the *Combined Code* states that the notice for the annual general meeting and related papers should be sent to shareholders at least 20 working days before the meeting.[153]

The Companies Act 1985 allows meetings to be held on short notice with the consent of the shareholders. For an annual general meeting all of the shareholders who are entitled to attend and vote at the meeting must consent to it being held on short notice.[154] An extraordinary general meeting[155] may be held on short notice if 95 per cent of the shareholders entitled to attend and vote on it so agree;[156] a private company can reduce the required majority to 90 per cent.[157] These provisions for shortening the period of notice are useful in smaller companies, but the high levels of shareholder support that are required for meetings to proceed on this basis mean that they become more

[148] *Combined Code*, C.2.

[149] *Combined Code*, C.2.3.

[150] *Shareholder Communications at the Annual General Meeting* (DTI Consultative Document) (April 1996) s 3. On market practice in this respect see, eg, *A Guide to Best Practice for Annual General Meetings* (ICSA) (1996) para 2.6 which states that: 'It is best practice for all Boards to provide adequate time for shareholder questions at AGMs.' This report also recommends that companies should invite (but not require) shareholders to submit questions in advance: para 2.9.

[151] Companies Act 1985, s 369 (1)(a) (annual general meeting), ss 369 (1)(b) and 378 (meetings to consider special resolutions) and s 379A (2) (meetings to consider passing elective resolutions).

[152] Companies Act 1985, s 369 (b)(ii).

[153] *Combined Code*, C.2.4. In 1998 the NAPF proposed an early-warning system whereby a company would have to give at least three-months' notice of certain proposed changes, eg, to directors' remuneration.

[154] Companies Act 1985, s 369 (3).

[155] Including one for the passing of a special resolution. But an extraordinary general meeting of a private company to pass an elective resolution can only be held on short notice with the unanimous consent of all of the members who are entitled to vote on the matter: Companies Act 1985, s 379A (2A).

[156] Companies Act 1985, s 369 (3) and (4).

[157] Ibid, ss 369 (4) and 379(A) (1)(d).

and more practically irrelevant as the number of a company's shareholders increases.

Receipt of Notices of Meetings

If the articles make no contrary provision, the default position is that all members of the company are entitled to receive notice of company meetings.[158] Under Table A, art 38, as well as all the members of the company, all persons entitled to a share in consequence of the death or bankruptcy of a member and the directors and auditors[159] are entitled to receive notice of company meetings. Art 39 provides that accidental omission to give notice of a meeting to, or the non-receipt of notice of a meeting by, any person entitled to receive notice will not invalidate the proceedings of the meeting.

Voting at Meetings

Voting at company meetings can be on a show of hands or an a poll. The procedure is governed by the company's articles in each case. It is usual to provide that on a show of hands each shareholder has one vote irrespective of the number of shares that he owns[160] and that on a poll each shareholder can cast the total number of votes that are attached to his shares.[161] A shareholder voting on a poll does not have to cast all of his votes in the same direction.[162] This is important for a shareholder who holds votes as a nominee for a number of different beneficial owners because it enables the nominee to comply with the obligation to cast votes in accordance with the preferences of the beneficial owners.

Voting usually takes place first on a show of hands. It is then for the chairman in his discretion to decide whether to proceed to a poll but, if they satisfy certain qualifying criteria under the company's articles, shareholders can demand a poll.[163] The articles cannot specify more rigorous criteria than those stated in Companies Act 1985, s 373. This section allows a minimum of five shareholders having the right to vote at a meeting, or any number of shareholders holding at least one-tenth of the voting rights or one-tenth of the paid up share capital, to demand a poll on any matter, save that the articles can exclude this in relation to the question of the election of a chairman of a meeting or the adjournment of a meeting. The chairman must demand a poll where this is necessary to give effect to the real sense of the meeting.[164] This means that he must proceed to a poll where he is aware that the number of votes cast in advance by proxy will lead to the opposite result from that which was arrived at by the vote on a show of hands.

158 Ibid, s 370(2).

159 Auditors have a statutory right to receive all notices of, and other communications relating to, general meetings and they are also entitled to attend and be heard on any matter that concerns them as auditors: Companies Act 1985, s 390.

160 eg, Table A, art 54.

161 eg, Table A, art 54. This assumes that each share carries one vote.

162 Companies Act 1985, s 374.

163 Ibid, s 373.

164 *The Second Consolidated Trust Ltd v Ceylon Amalgamated Tea and Rubber Estates Ltd* [1943] 2 All ER 567.

Attendance at Meetings/Appointment of Proxies and Corporate Representatives

Every member of the company who is entitled to attend and vote at a meeting has a statutory right to appoint a proxy to attend and vote instead of him.[165] In every notice calling a meeting of a company there must appear with reasonable prominence a statement of each member's right to appoint a proxy and an indication that a proxy need not also be a member.[166] The company can require proxy forms to be lodged at least 48 hours before the meeting but cannot impose a stricter time-limit.[167] The directors can send out proxy forms at the company's expense where this is a genuine part of carrying out their duty to promote policies which they in good faith consider to be in the company's interests.[168] However, the directors commit an offence if they try and manipulate the proxy vote by issuing, at the company's expense, invitations to appoint a proxy to selected members only.[169] Discrimination of this sort would also amount to breach of fiduciary duty by the directors.[170] If the company is listed, *The Listing Rules*[171] require proxy forms to be sent with the notice convening a meeting to all persons who are entitled to vote at the meeting. The form must make provision for two-way voting on all the resolutions intended to be proposed at the meeting; this means that the form must allow the appointing shareholder to instruct the proxy either to vote for or against each of the proposals, and must not make a proxy service available but only on condition that the shareholder votes with management. This requirement for two-way proxies serves to lessen the proxy problem that was mentioned by Maugham J in his 1933 judgment which was quoted earlier in this chapter.[172]

Modern developments give rise to new complexities with regard to the rules on proxy voting and the related topic of corporate representatives. As an alternative to appointing a proxy, a company can appoint a corporate representative to act on its behalf at company meetings.[173] A corporate representative is entitled to speak at company meetings and to vote on a show of hands as well as on a poll. This differs from the position of a proxy who, in a public company, is not allowed to speak nor to vote on a show of hands.[174] A shareholder in a public company can appoint more than one proxy[175] but it is not possible for a corporate shareholder to appoint more than one corporate representative.

It is increasingly common for shares to be registered in the names of nominee companies that provide custodian services for the beneficial owners of

[165] Companies Act 1985, s 372 (1). [166] Ibid, s 372 (3).
[167] Ibid, s 372 (5). [168] *Peel v London and NW Railway* [1907] 1 Ch 5, CA.
[169] Companies Act 1985, s 372 (6).
[170] *Peel v London and NW Railway* [1907] 1 Ch 5, CA, 21 *per* Buckley LJ.
[171] The requirements with regard to proxy forms are contained in *The Listing Rules*, ch 9, para 9.26, and ch 13, paras 13.28–13.29.
[172] *Re Dorman, Long & Co Ltd* [1934] 1 Ch 635, 657. [173] Companies Act 1985, s 375.
[174] Companies Act 1985, 372. This is subject to alternative provision in the articles but it would be unusual for articles of public companies to permit proxies to participate by speaking or by voting on a show of hands. A proxy may join in a demand for a poll: Companies Act 1985, s 373. This right may not be excluded by the articles.
[175] Companies Act 1985, s 372.

the shares. Each nominee company holding a block of shares in a company is likely to do so on behalf of a number of investors. It is usual for pension fund equity investments to be organised in this way. The structure of Personal Equity Plans (PEPs) involves the use of nominee companies. Also, private investors who want to trade through CREST, the UK's electronic trading service, tend to do so via a nominee company that is a member of CREST and which holds the title to the shares on their behalf. The nominee company, as the registered holder of the shares, has the right to vote as a matter of company law, and the beneficial owners of those shares are not entitled to attend and vote at company meetings in their own right. For institutional investors who prefer to vote by proxy anyway, this may be a point of limited significance, although it would inhibit them from taking a more active role in the discussions at a company meeting if they wanted to change their practice by moving in that direction.[176] Not being able to participate personally in company meetings is something that may be regarded as significant by private investors.[177] The device of appointing the beneficial owners as proxies is a makeshift way round this problem, but since the rights of proxies are less than those of shareholders attending company meetings in their own right, in that proxies may not speak at meetings of public companies nor vote on a show of hands, this is an imperfect solution. The alternative of appointing a corporate representative does not solve this problem: although corporate representative can speak and vote on a show of hands and on a poll, it is not possible to appoint more than one corporate representative with the consequence that only one beneficial owner of shares could be present at a meeting in this capacity. Although there have been suggestions for tinkering with the rights of proxies or with the right to appoint a corporate representative so as to ensure that shareholders whose shares are registered in the names of nominees at company meetings can participate in company meetings as if they were still registered as shareholders, there is force in the argument that as nominee shareholdings become increasingly prevalent, the issues that they raise should be separately addressed by specific legislation and not by amendment of legislation that was not drafted with that structure directly in mind.[178]

[176] The NAPF has specifically raised concerns about the inability of a company to appoint more than one corporate representative: see *Shareholder Communications at the Annual General Meeting* (DTI Consultative Document) (April 1996) s 4.

[177] As is often the case, it is convenient to take stereotypical examples but this is not meant to imply that being able to attend meetings in person is never important to institutional investors, nor that private investors always want to attend meetings in person rather than to vote by proxy.

[178] *Shareholder Communications At Annual General Meetings: The Manifest Response* (1996) para 11. The DTI and Treasury issued a joint consultative document on this issue *Private Shareholders: Corporate Governance Rights* (November 1996). See also *The ProShare Nominee Code* (August 1995) which seeks to establish best practice with regard to a variety of matters raised by nominee shareholdings. In practice, many custodians that use nominee companies do seek to pass through company membership rights to their investors. Also, as a matter of good practice, some companies do allow investors whose shares are registered in the name of a nominee company to speak at company meetings where they are present as proxies even though this is not provided for by the articles (this is supported in *A Guide to Best Practice for Annual General Meetings* (ICSA) (1996) para 2.31) and do make provision for them to receive information, such as the annual financial statements, that, as a matter of law, are only required to be distributed to registered shareholders.

Another consequence of shares being registered in the names of nominee companies which hold them on behalf of the beneficial owners is that unless, or to the extent that, the beneficial owner has delegated voting discretion, say, to the fund manager who controls the nominee company, it is necessary for the nominee to go back to the beneficial owner for instructions on how to vote: the obligation of the nominee is to exercise voting rights in accordance with the preferences of the beneficial owners. It is sometimes suggested that logistical problems about consultation between fund managers and clients may be at least a partial explanation for low levels of voting by pension fund trustees.[179] To the extent that there is force in this argument, the suggestion by the NAPF that companies should give at least three months' warning of contentious matters at forthcoming general meetings[180] would be very helpful as that would give fund managers much more time to consult with their clients on how they should vote in respect of those matters.[181]

Types of Resolution

There are two main types of shareholder resolution, the ordinary resolution which requires a simple majority of the votes cast, and the special resolution which requires a 75-per-cent majority of the votes cast.[182] At least 21 clear days' notice in writing must be given of any meeting for the passing of a special resolution.[183] There also exists the extraordinary resolution which requires a 75-per-cent majority of the votes cast. A meeting for the passing of an extraordinary resolution does not require 21 clear days' notice, unless it is also an annual general meeting.[184] Extraordinary resolutions are rarely required but an example of a situation where a decision must be in the form of an extraordinary resolution is a resolution under the Insolvency Act 1986, s 84 (1)(c) to wind up the company on the grounds that it cannot by reason of its liabilities continue its business and that it is advisable to wind up.

The final type of shareholder resolution is the elective resolution which, unlike ordinary, special and extraordinary resolutions, requires the agreement of all of the members who are entitled to attend a meeting and vote on the matter to which the resolution relates.[185] A meeting for the passing of an elective resolution requires 21 clear days' notice in writing.[186] An elective resolution is a creature of the deregulatory regime for private companies which was introduced by the Companies Act 1989. By passing an elective resolution a private company can opt out of certain of the procedural requirements that would otherwise apply, including the requirement to hold an annual general

[179] Stapledon, GP, *Institutional Shareholders and Corporate Governance* (1996) 88–92.

[180] *Investment Services Issues* (Winter 1997/98) (NAPF).

[181] Although there is still the issue of direct and indirect costs that fund managers have to incur in consulting with clients on voting policies: Black, BS, and Coffee, JC, 'Hail Britannia?: Institutional Investor Behavior Under Limited Regulation' (1994) 92 Michigan Law Review 1997, 2039.

[182] Companies Act 1985, s 378.

[183] Ibid, s 378 (2).

[184] Ibid, s 378 (1).

[185] Ibid, s 379(A) (2)(b) as amended by the Companies Act 1989.

[186] Ibid, s 379(A) (2)(a).

meeting.[187] The elective regime recognises that for small[188] private companies, the requirements relating to the holding of company meetings can be an unnecessary formality.

THE EXERCISE OF VOICE AND INSTITUTIONAL INVESTORS: AN ASSESSMENT

From this selective account of the rules relating to company meetings, it would appear that whilst there may be scope for some changes to facilitate the exercise of voice, overall it is not the technicalities of the mechanics of company meetings that inhibit greater institutional investor activism.[189] Other reasons for this must be sought. There are a number of considerations that may lead institutional investors to shy away from seeking a more extensive involvement in monitoring, especially in the form of direct intervention in the affairs of individual companies, such as by removing incumbent management and appointing new directors. First, and obviously, there are the costs entailed in monitoring: unless the benefits of monitoring are seen to outweigh its costs, there is every reason for institutional investors not to put money, time and effort into it and instead to adopt a passive investment policy even where exit is unavailable.[190] Secondly, since institutional investor expertise lies in investment rather than business management, they may hesitate to intervene.[191] Thirdly, there is consideration of the effect that public intervention may have on a company's share price[192] and the possible reluctance of institutions to become associated with unpopular management decisions

[187] Ibid, s 366A. A company can also pass an elective resolution to opt out of the requirements to lay accounts and reports before the general meeting and to appoint auditors on an annual basis: Companies Act 1985, ss 252 and 386.

[188] In principle the elective regime is open to all private companies but as the number of shareholders in a company increases the less likely it will be that the necessary unanimity can be achieved.

[189] Thus the thesis put forward by Black, BS, 'Shareholder Passivity Reexamined' (1990) 89 Michigan Law Review 520, that in the USA shareholder activism is held back by legal rules does not, it is suggested, hold good when transposed to the UK. This is an issue that has been explored by Professor Black himself: Black, BS, and Coffee, JC, 'Hail Britannia?: Institutional Investor Behavior Under Limited Regulation' (1994) 92 Michigan Law Review 1997. The authors accept that the British experience suggests limits on what legal reform can do to encourage institutional oversight in the USA. They conclude that there is more institutional activism in the UK than in the USA but that much of this takes place informally and behind the scenes. They note that there are constraints on greater institutional activism in the UK but that these do not stem from the legal rules relating to the exercise of voice but from other factors (eg the costs of establishing a coalition of shareholders, conflicts of interests, imperfect information, and limited institutional organisational capabilities to engage in monitoring).

[190] Rock, EB, ' The Logic and (Uncertain) Significance of Institutional Shareholder Activism' (1991) 79 Georgetown Law Journal 445, 455.

[191] Charkham, JP, 'A Larger Role for Institutional Investors' in Dimsdale, N, and Prevezer, M (eds), *Capital Markets and Corporate Governance* (1994) 99, 102–3 and Charkham, JP, *Keeping Good Company* (1995) 286–8. Looked at another way, it may be argued that lack of relevant skill is a reason why, as a matter of general policy, company law and practice should not be based on enhanced shareholder monitoring. Against this version of the lack of relevant skill argument see Black, BS, 'Agents Watching Agents: The Promise of Institutional Investor Voice' (1992) 39 UCLA Law Review 81, 851; Eisenberg, MA, *The Structure of the Corporation* (1976) 12.

[192] Short, H, and Keasey, K, 'Institutional Shareholders and Corporate Governance in the United Kingdom' in Keasey, K, Thompson, S, and Wright, M (eds), *Corporate Governance* (1997) 18, 26.

such as redundancies. Possible insider trading liability is another concern. Free riders—shareholders who benefit from active monitoring but who do not contribute to its costs—are yet another disincentive to increased monitoring. Whilst collective action by a group of institutional investors may be way of spreading costs and reducing the free-rider problem, business rivalries between institutions or simply differing perceptions on the seriousness of problems in particular cases, may inhibit the formation of collective action groups.[193]

Another issue that has been extensively discussed by American commentators is that greater activism may put institutional investors into a position where they face a conflict of interests.[194] An example of this is that those responsible for the investment side of an insurance company's business might hesitate to challenge the management of a company in which it is a shareholder in case this could jeopardise the selling of insurance to that company.[195] Pension fund trustees, or their external fund managers,[196] can face similar potential conflicts of interests; for instance, where, as is often the case, a fund manager is affiliated to an investment bank that has a commercial interest in maintaining good relationships with companies in which the pension fund holds shares, the manager may be reluctant to exercise any discretion it holds in respect of the voting rights on the shares against corporate management. In the absence of a clear obligation on institutional investors to make considered use of the voting rights attaching to their shares,[197] these types of potential conflict are strong factors against institutional investors taking an active stance against the management of a company on controversial matters.[198]

INSTITUTIONAL INVESTORS AND INFORMATION: THE LINK WITH NON-EXECUTIVE DIRECTORS

Reverting back to the passage from the 1933 judgment quoted above, one point made by Maugham J that has not been considered specifically in this

[193] Charkham, JP, *Keeping Good Company* (1995) 288.

[194] There is considerable literature on this topic. Recent articles include Coffee, JC, 'Liquidity Versus Control: The Institutional Investor as Corporate Monitor' (1991) 91 Columbia Law Review 1277; Black, BS, 'Shareholder Passivity Reexamined' (1990) 89 Michigan Law Review 520; Black, BS, 'Agents Watching Agents; The Promise of Institutional Investor Voice' (1992) 39 UCLA Law R 811; Rock, EB, 'The Logic and (Uncertain) Significance of Institutional Shareholder Activism' (1991) 79 Georgetown Law Journal 445.

[195] Rock, EB, 'The Logic and (Uncertain) Significance of Institutional Shareholder Activism' (1991) 79 Georgetown Law Journal 445, 471; Black, BS, 'Shareholder Passivity Reexamined' (1990) 89 Michigan Law Review 520, 601.

[196] This can be characterised as an agency costs problem, ie a divergence between the interests of the fund manager, the agent, and the pension fund, the principal. On this see Rock, EB, 'The Logic and (Uncertain) Significance of Institutional Shareholder Activism' (1991) 79 Georgetown Law Journal 445, 469–78. On agency costs generally see Ch 4 above, at 118.

[197] The duties of pension fund trustees are discussed in general terms in Nobles, RL, 'The Exercise of Trustees' Discretion under a Pension Scheme' [1992] JBL 261. See also Farrar, JH, and Russell, M, 'The Impact of Institutional Investment on Company Law' (1984) 5 Co Law 107, 108.

[198] Black, BS, and Coffee, JC, 'Hail Britannia?: Institutional Investor Behavior Under Limited Regulation' (1994) 92 Michigan Law Review 1997, 2059–61.

chapter up to now is the significance of the informational advantages that directors have over shareholders. Although regular meetings with companies give institutional investors access to more information than that which is available to private individual investors,[199] this type of contact does not eliminate information imbalances. The institutions only receive information as filtered by management: they do not have direct access to management information.[200] Also, whilst institutional investors and their advisers are experts at interpreting information from the perspective of how it will affect the price at which they can sell their investments, the assessment of information for the purposes of voice-based monitoring may require different skills to which institutions may be reluctant to devote resources to developing.[201] The effectiveness of shareholder monitoring via voice is inevitably affected by the nature of the information that is available to them and the skill with which it is interpreted. This then puts the spotlight onto the question whether it is possible to improve the flow of information available to institutional investors and the mechanisms for interpreting that information. It is at this point that the relationship between institutional investors and non-executive directors comes into focus.

In the UK in the 1990s it became an established aspect of good corporate governance practice for companies with outside investors to have a number of non-executive directors. According to the *Combined Code* annexed to *The Listing Rules* non-executive directors should comprise not less than one-third of the board of a listed company.[202] The functions of non-executive directors and of the duties to which they subject are considered generally in Chapter 6. Here the relevant issues are that non-executive directors are closer to management information than institutional shareholders (although since they are not directly involved in the daily running of the company's affairs, they are still dependent on the flow of information that management provides albeit to a different degree); they are in a position to question that information and, assuming they have been appointed because they have relevant skills, to interpret its significance. They can directly control management by taking responsibility for the setting of their remuneration. Factors such as these suggest that institutional investors should take a close interest in the appointment of non-executive directors. There have been proposals both in the UK and the USA for institutional investors to become more directly and more formally involved in the appointment of non-executive directors.[203] The

[199] For private investors, the primary sources of information are the annual accounts required by the Companies Act 1985, the interim results required by *The Listing Rules* and the information that listed companies are required to put into the public domain in accordance with their disclosure obligations under *The Listing Rules.* On communications between companies and their institutional investors see Gaved, M, *Closing the Communications Gap: Disclosure and Institutional Shareholders* (ICAEW publication) (1997) ch 3.

[200] Shareholders can inspect minute books relating to general meetings (Companies Act 1985, s 383) but there is no corresponding entitlement in respect of minutes of board meetings.

[201] Black, BS, and Coffee, JC, 'Hail Britannia?: Institutional Investor Behavior Under Limited Regulation' (1994) 92 Michigan Law Review 1997, 2068–72.

[202] *Combined Code* A.3.1.

[203] eg, Sykes, A, 'Proposals for a Reformed System of Corporate Governance to Achieve Internationally Competitive Long-Term Performance' in Dimsdale, N, and Prevezer, M (eds), *Capital Markets and Corporate Governance* (1994) 111.

proposal that has attracted most attention is that of two American professors[204] that institutional investors acting collectively should directly elect professional[205] non-executive directors. There are many potential difficulties with this type of proposal[206] including the costs that would be involved in establishing and maintaining the organisational structure for the operation of such a system of collective action by institutions, and free-rider concerns. There is also the possibility that those institutional investors who are linked to the appointment of professional non-executive directors might become insiders unable to trade in the company's shares or, as a variant on this, that they might find it difficult to trade because other investors would wrongly assume that they have access to privileged information;[207] although increased voice may be a response to reduced ability to exit, institutional investors are hardly likely to want to create a structure which removes the possibility of exit entirely or which makes it more difficult. There is no evidence of support for this type of direct linkage in UK practice.[208] The Cadbury Committee, whose Code of Best Practice published in 1992 was the first formal endorsement in the UK of the practice of appointing non-executive directors, specifically rejected the suggestion that institutional investors should be involved in corporate governance in this way. Aspects of the Cadbury Code were consolidated into the *Combined Code* in 1998 but, like its predecessor, this does not seek to promote any formal linkage between institutional investors and the appointment of non-executive directors.

ENHANCED INSTITUTIONAL SHAREHOLDER MONITORING: POSSIBLE DRAWBACKS

Placing the emphasis on the role of shareholders, especially institutional investors, as monitors of corporate management, may be challenged from a wider perspective. First, to the extent that there is weight in the allegations of short-termism on the part of institutional investors, this suggests that increasing the influence of institutional investors could lead to the economically damaging result of greater emphasis on short-term profits at the expense of long-term goals.[209] There is no conclusive view on short-termism as it affects

[204] Gilson, RJ, and Kraakman, R, 'Reinventing the Outside Director: An Agenda for Institutional Investors' (1991) 43 Stanford Law Review 863.

[205] ie, individuals whose job it is to sit as non-executive directors on the boards of a limited number of companies. This differs from the typical non-executive director under present practice: a typical NED is someone who is an executive director of another company.

[206] Although it is common for German banks that hold large stakes in German commercial companies to appoint their nominees onto the companies' supervisory boards: Parkinson, JE, 'The Role of "Voice" and "Exit" in Corporate Governance' in Sheikh, S, and Rees, W (eds), *Corporate Governance and Corporate Control* (1995) 75, 100–4.

[207] Black, BS, and Coffee, JC, 'Hail Britannia?: Institutional Investor Behavior Under Limited Regulation' (1994) 92 Michigan Law Review 1997, 2064.

[208] Although some writers have supported the principle of professional independent directors: eg, 'Redirecting Directors' *Economist* 17 November 1990, 19.

[209] Davies, PD, 'Institutional Investors in the United Kingdom' in Prentice, DD, and Holland, PRJ, *Contemporary Issues in Corporate Governance* (1993) 69, 78–81; Stapledon, GP, *Institutional Shareholders and Corporate Governance* (1996) 212–37; Ireland, P, 'Company Law and the Myth of Shareholder Ownership' (1999) 62 MLR 32.

institutional investors: statistical data demonstrating that although the size of an institution's holding of shares in a company may fluctuate regularly, it is rare for an institution to sell the whole of its holding,[210] tends to suggest that institutions are in fact more long-term investors than the trade in parts of their holding might suggest.[211] Against this, some commentators suggest that the practice of pension fund trustees of delegating investment responsibility to fund managers, who are engaged on relatively short-term contracts, typically of eighteen months to two years, and judging them by the return that they produce over that period, leads to short-termism in investment policy because of the pressure on fund managers to perform well within the contractual period.[212]

The second challenge to the assumption that enhancement of shareholder monitoring through voice or other means would be a positive outcome is that this is fundamentally misconceived, because it emphasises the position of shareholders over that of employees, creditors or others who might be said to have an interest in the company. This is an aspect of the stakeholder debate which is considered further in Chapter 4.[213] It is clear that removing shareholders from their predominant position within the corporate structure could not be done without major adjustment to the whole framework of company law. A less radical, and perhaps more realistically achievable, response to the stakeholder debate would be to bolster the range of specific obligations that management owes to employees or other groups, and also the enforcement mechanisms, whilst leaving shareholders, as owners or residual claimants, as the group that benefits most directly from the general obligations that company law imposes on management and which is most immediately concerned with monitoring the overall standard of managerial performance.

[210] This illustrates the point made earlier, namely, that institutional investors may be in effect locked in to a company because the size of their holding is too large to liquidate other than at a loss; thus, exit is blocked.

[211] See, eg, the emphasis on long-term interests in M&G's published policy statement quoted by Charkham, JP, 'A Larger Role for Institutional Investors' in Dimsdale, N, and Prevezer, M (eds), *Capital Markets and Corporate Governance* (1994) 99, 101. M&G is a major mutual fund.

[212] Charkham, JP, 'Are Shares Just Commodities?' in *Creative Tension?* (NAPF) at 38–9 but contrast, Marsh, PR, *Short-Termism on Trial* (1990). Delegation to fund managers also gives rise to agency problems as between institutional investors and the agents (fund managers) who are engaged to act on their behalf: ie, the incentive for the agent to engage in monitoring. On this, see Coffee, JC, 'Liquidity Versus Control: The Institutional Investor as Corporate Monitor' (1991) 91 Columbia Law Review 1277, 1326–7.

[213] Ch 4 above, at 124–40. An issue that is not developed there but is relevant here is the potential for inequality of treatment between institutional investors and private investors. This is considered in Stapledon, GP, *Institutional Shareholders and Corporate Governance* (1996) 249–50. The author concludes that there is no serious problem in this respect.

PART III

SHARE CAPITAL

8

Shares and Share Capital

AUTHORISED OR NOMINAL SHARE CAPITAL

The memorandum of a company limited by shares must state the total amount of the share capital and the division of the share capital into shares of a fixed amount.[1] The amount stated in the memorandum is known as the company's **authorised** or **nominal** share capital. There is no minimum authorised share capital for a private company.[2] In practice private companies are often incorporated with an original authorised share capital of £100.[3] The authorised share capital of a company which is incorporated as a public company must be at least £50,000. This limitation derives from the Companies Act 1985, ss 117 and 118. These sections require a public company to have an **allotted** share capital of at least £50,000 but, because of the way that allotted share capital is calculated, a company must have an authorised share capital of at least £50,000 if it is to have an allotted share capital of at least that amount. The requirement for a minimum authorised share capital of at least £50,000 also applies to a private company which is converting to a public company by virtue of the Companies Act 1985, s 45.

The origin of the minimum capital requirements for public companies is the Second Company Law Directive, art 6.[4] Article 6 obliges Member States to impose a minimum capital requirement on public companies. The amount of the minimum capital must be not less than 25,000 euros.[5] Article 6 expressly provides for the equivalent in national currency to be calculated initially at the rate applicable on the date of adoption of the Directive but it also envisages the possibility of a Member State having to adjust upwards the amount

[1] Companies Act 1985, s 2 (5)(a).

[2] The Jenkins Committee, a committee which reviewed and reported upon the working of the companies legislation in 1962, favoured a minimum capital requirement in principle but declined to recommend that such a requirement be enacted because it thought that its purpose would be too easy to evade, for example by the company immediately lending back to the promoters the money they had subscribed to meet the minimum capital requirement: *Report of the Company Law Committee*, Cmnd 1749, (1962) para 27. See also Prentice, DD, 'Corporate Personality, Limited Liability and the Protection of Creditors' in Grantham, R and Rickett, C, *Corporate Personality in the Twentieth Century* (1998) 99, 102.

[3] Of the 1.25 million registered UK companies as at 31 March 1997, 1.1 million had an issued share capital of less than £1,000 and, of these, 80 per cent had £100 or less: *The Euro: Redenomination of Share Capital* (DTI Consultative Document) (1998) para 1.7. The link between the issued share capital and authorised share capital is that a company cannot have an issued share capital that is greater than its authorised share capital.

[4] Second Company Law Directive 77/91/EEC, [1977] OJ L26/1.

[5] Second Company Law Directive, art 6 in its original form referred to 25,000 European units of account (ECUs). The ECU was replaced by the euro for the purposes of Community legislation including the Second Directive with effect from 1 January 1999.

expressed in its national currency because of a longstanding difference in the exchange rate between that currency and the euro.[6] Any such adjustments would be implemented in the UK by statutory instrument.[7] Article 6 also contemplates adjustments to the requisite amount: each five years the amount is to be examined and, if need be, revised in the light of economic and monetary trends in the Community and the tendency towards allowing only large and medium-sized undertakings to be public companies.[8]

Multi-Currency Authorised Share Capital and the Introduction of the Euro

The requirement for a company to state the amount of its authorised share capital in its memorandum was interpreted in *Re Scandinavian Bank Group plc*[9] where it was held that:

(i) The amount must be a monetary amount (not, for example, 100 troy ounces of gold or one ton of potatoes);[10]
(ii) It need not, subject to one suggested qualification, be a sterling amount; and
(iii) A single total amount does not have to be stated; the requirement would be satisfied by stating an authorised share capital comprised of, say, £X million, US$Y million and Swiss Francs Z million.

The suggested qualification was that for a public company the minimum capital requirement could only be satisfied in pound terms. The judge, Harman J, thought that this requirement was necessitated by references to national currencies in the Second Directive, art 6. Although this aspect of the *Scandinavian Bank* decision was criticised,[11] it was accepted as correct by the registrar of companies and the practice of Companies House was to reject applications for registration, or re-registration, of public companies which did not have an authorised minimum share capital of at least £50,000 denominated in sterling. The requirement to hold at least £50,000 of its capital in sterling creates a potential cost for companies which conduct most of their business outside the UK and, as a result, have assets and liabilities which are almost entirely denominated in currencies other than sterling. In September

[6] Second Company Law Directive, art 6.2. The value of the minimum capital expressed in national currency must be less than 25,000 euros for a period of at least one year.

[7] Companies Act 1985, s 118. [8] Art 6.3.

[9] [1987] 2 All ER 70, [1987] BCC 9; noted Thornton, L, 'The Lawfulness of Multi-currency Share Capital' (1988) 9 Co Law 51; Instone, R, 'Multi-currency Share Capital' (1987) 104 LQR 168.

[10] There are three-year transitional arrangements for national currencies which are replaced by the euro with effect from 1 January 1999. During the transitional period references to old national currencies can continue to apply but will thereafter be deemed to be references to the euro: *The Euro: Redenomination of Share Capital* (DTI Consultative Document) (1998), paras 3.4–3.9; Proctor, C, 'Share Capital and the Euro' (1998) 9 (3) PLC 17, 19. This point is relevant for companies that currently have an existing multicurrency share capital including shares which are denominated in a currency which will be replaced by the euro.

[11] In the Inaugural Lecture to the Chancery Bar Association (November 1992) Mary Arden QC described this aspect of the decision in the *Scandinavian Bank* case as 'anomalous' and suggested that, if the matter came before the European Court of Justice, the court might adopt a more purposive construction so as to hold that the minimum capital of a public company could be denominated in the currency of any Member State. It seems that the government is now persuaded that it is possible to adopt a purposive interpretation of the directive: see next footnote and accompanying text.

1998 the government announced that it would seek an amendment to the companies legislation to give companies the flexibility to denominate the whole of their authorised share capital, including the minimum amount, in currencies other than sterling.[12]

Why would a company want to have a share capital denominated in a currency other than sterling or in a mixture of currencies, of which sterling is only one? For Scandinavian Bank itself the reason was capital adequacy considerations.[13] Banks are subject to capital adequacy requirements which measure their capital against their assets. Where the capital and the assets are expressed in different currencies, the proportion of capital to assets may be eroded simply through exchange rate fluctuations. This problem can be eliminated by matching the denomination of the capital to that of the assets. Companies which are not subject to capital adequacy requirements face an identical problem if they have, in loan agreements, covenanted to maintain certain debt to equity ratios and the debt and equity are denominated in different currencies. Companies in this position may want to match the denomination or denominations of their capital to that of their debts.

A company may also want to have a multi-currency share capital in order to attract foreign investors, or to encourage foreign vendors to accept the company's shares as consideration.[14] There is no express bar on shares which are denominated in sterling being paid for in a foreign currency and whether or not this is permitted would depend on the terms of allotment. Shares which are paid up in a foreign currency will still be deemed to be paid up in cash.[15] Having the shares denominated in the currencies of the jurisdictions in which the offer is to be made avoids exchange rate complications that might arise if the terms of the allotment allowed for payment of sterling-denominated shares in other currencies.[16] However, if a company's assets and liabilities generally are denominated in sterling it may prefer nor to have part of its share capital denominated in another currency and, in that case, it will need to devise some means of resolving possible exchange rate difficulties if its shares are to be offered on the basis that they may be paid for in currencies other than sterling.

The adoption of the euro with effect from 1 January 1999 may lead some UK companies with extensive business interests in the European Union to consider redenomination of their share capital in order to match their capital base to their euro earnings, to facilitate the raising of capital from the new

[12] 'The Redenomination of Share Capital—New Legislation Proposed' DTI Press Release, 25 September 1998. The DTI proposes to bring forward proposals for change using powers available under the Deregulation and Contracting Out Act 1994.

[13] Daubney, N, and Cannon, N, 'Converting to Multi-currency Share Capital in the UK' (1987) 6(5) IFLR 7.

[14] The use of foreign currency denominated shares for this purpose is discussed by Lewis, D, 'Foreign Currency Share Capital' (1993) 4 (10) PLC 23.

[15] Companies Act 1985, s 738 (4).

[16] For example, what if the allotment terms specified an exchange rate but by the time of payment market rates have moved to such an extent that there is danger of the company not receiving, in sterling terms, the par value of the shares? See further this chapter below, at 293.

euro equity markets or to reflect their status as significant European businesses.[17]

Significance of the Amount of Authorised Share Capital Specified in the Memorandum

A company is not obliged to allot all of its authorised shares. This is one reason why it is not appropriate to look to the capital clause of the memorandum to discover how much capital a company has raised by issuing shares.[18] Shares may be authorised but remain unallotted for years or, even, forever. The significance of the capital clause is that it specifies the maximum number of shares that can be allotted at any time and it is thus a limit on the power of allotment. This limitation operates in addition to the Companies Act 1985, s 80 which requires the directors to be specifically authorised to allot shares either by an ordinary resolution or by the company's articles. Whereas failure to comply with the authorisation requirements of the Companies Act 1985, s 80 does not affect the validity of any allotment,[19] purported allotments in excess of the authorised amount are void.[20] Whether it is in principle necessary to have this dual restriction on new share issues is doubtful. In Australia and Canada companies are now not required to specify an authorised share capital.[21] It is not a requirement of the European Union's programme of harmonisation of the company laws of member states that companies should have an authorised capital.[22]

Nominal or Par Values of Individual Shares

As well as stating the total amount of the authorised share capital, the memorandum must also state the division of the share capital into shares of a fixed amount.[23] The stated fixed amount of each share is known as the **nominal** or **par** value of the share. The phrase 'fixed amount' was also considered in *Re Scandinavian Bank Group plc*[24] where it was held that:

(i) Although it had to be a monetary amount, it did not have to be an amount which was capable of being paid in legal tender; thus it could be a ½p or some other fraction or percentage; and

(ii) The fixed amount could not be stated in two currencies, i.e. a share of US$1 or £1, but could be stated in different currencies for different shares.

[17] *The Euro: Redenomination of Share Capital* (DTI Consultative Document) (1998) para 1.6; Yeowart, G, 'The Equity Markets and Company Share Capital: Planning for the Euro' [1998] 8 JIBL 269; Proctor, C, 'Share Capital and the Euro' (1998) 9 (3) PLC 17.

[18] The fact that shares can be, and often are, issued at a price that is greater than the par value stated in the memorandum is another.

[19] Companies Act 1985, s 80 (10).

[20] *Bank of Hindustan China and Japan Ltd v Alison* (1871) LR 6 CP 222; *Re A Company ex parte Shooter* [1990] BCLC 384, 389.

[21] Australia: Corporations Law, s 1431 (with effect from July 1998); Canada: Welling, BL, *Corporate Law in Canada The Governing Principles* (2nd edn, 1998) 609–12.

[22] Second Company Law Directive 77/91/EEC, [1977] OJ L26/1, art 2 imposes variable disclosure obligations depending upon whether or not a company has an authorised capital.

[23] Companies Act 1985, s 2 (5)(a).

[24] [1987] 2 All ER 70, [1987] BCC 93.

Any monetary amount will suffice; there is no prescribed minimum par value in respect of the shares of public or private companies. To encourage liquidity the ordinary shares of public companies tend to have low par values, such as 25p or lower. Liquidity is generally a less important issue in relation to the shares of a private company, and larger par values, typically £1, are common.

Why require companies to state a par value on their shares and to forbid them to issue their shares at a discount to their par value? The details of the application no-discount rule are explored later in this chapter in the section on payment for shares[25] but, here, the concern is the general underlying objective which these requirements seek to achieve. According to Lord Halsbury in *Ooregum Gold Mining Company of India v Roper*[26] the requirements first to state par values in respect of the individual shares into which the authorised share capital is divided and second not to allot shares at a price less than their individual par values are necessary because:

(i) every creditor of the company is entitled to look to a fixed and certain amount of capital as his security; and
(ii) a company should not be allowed to mislead potential shareholders and creditors about the amount of its real capital.

In other words, if a company states that its share capital is £100 divided into 100 shares of £1 each, all of which have been issued and are fully paid, creditors and potential shareholders are entitled to assume that the company has indeed received capital of £100. Both creditors and potential shareholders can take comfort from the fact that the amount raised is subject to extensive rules regarding maintenance of capital so that it cannot be freely withdrawn from the company and paid back to its existing shareholders.

These arguments, persuasive in the nineteenth century when the principles of company law and their relationship with other branches of the law were still evolving, need to be reassessed in the light of modern conditions. The key development in company law that undermined the significance of par values was the enactment of rules relating to the treatment of share premiums. Share premiums arise where shares are issued at a price that is greater than their par value. A share premium is not strictly capital and, in the company accounts, it must be shown separately from the share capital in a share premium account.[27] Yet, under rules first enacted by English companies legislation in the 1940s, for most purposes[28] it is treated as capital and is subject to the maintenance of capital principle. The resulting position, then, is that a company's financial statements must contain two entries, one for share capital and one for share premiums but the total amount is subject to the maintenance of capital rules. This, it may be thought, achieves the correct final result—that all money raised by issuing shares should be subject to the same rules—but only in a cumbersome and awkward manner.

[25] See below, at 292–303.
[26] [1892] AC 125, 133–4, HL.
[27] Companies Act 1985, s 130.
[28] Companies Act 1985, s 130 provides some limited exceptions. These are discussed in this chapter, at 305–7 below.

To suggest that par values prevent creditors and shareholders from being misled about the amount of the company's capital ignores the fact that there are remedies in tort and contract in respect of false or misleading statements. Regardless of whether shares have a par value or not, creditors and shareholders would be entitled to look to these remedies in the event of a company making inaccurate statements about the amount of finance it has raised through share issues. With regard to the argument that a minimum par value prevents one group of shareholders acquiring shares more cheaply than other groups, this is negated by the practice of issuing shares at a premium to their par value. The price that investors are willing to pay for a company's shares from time to time will fluctuate in accordance with market conditions, and it is perfectly proper for the company to adjust the issue price to meet investor demand. Thus, for perfectly legitimate reasons, some shareholders may have to pay more for their shares than others. The effect of par value requirements is to impose an arbitrary limit on the company's ability to adjust issue prices in response to investor demand and market conditions. If one group of shareholders were to be unfairly offered the opportunity to acquire shares at a lower price than that offered to another group, this discrimination could form the basis of an application for relief from unfair prejudice[29] and this would be so irrespective of whether the offer price is above or below a notional par value.

The concept of par value of share capital might have some significance if it gave some indication of the market value of the company's assets. However, it usually does not and instead may be a source of confusion. Where shares are issued at a premium, this creates an imbalance from the outset: an issue of 100 £1 shares at a premium of £1 each, gives the company a cash asset of £200 but its share capital (assuming no other issues) is £100. As time goes on, the overall net worth of the company, and the value of its individual shares depends on the success of the company's business ventures and also on general economic factors such as the effect of inflation. As a result the par value of a share commonly bears little relation to the price at which it trades in the market.

The par value requirements of English company law have been criticised frequently by review bodies. In 1945, as part of a general review of company law, the Cohen Committee reported that it saw much logic in the arguments put forward in support of having shares of no par value but because there was no public demand for, and considerable opposition to, the proposal, as well as some concerns about possible abuse, it refrained from recommending any change.[30] Less than ten years later, in 1954, a Board of Trade Committee under the chairmanship of Mr Montagu Gedge QC reported specifically on the question whether shares with no par values should be allowed.[31] On this occasion the Committee found that there was general support for the pro-

[29] Companies Act 1985, s 459.

[30] *Report of the Committee on Company Law Amendment* Cmd 6659 (1945). Previous company law amendment committees had also considered the issue: Cd 9138 (1918) (Wrenbury Committee) and Cmd 2657 (1926) (Greene Committee).

[31] *Report of the Committee on Shares of No Par Value* Cmd 9112 (1954).

posal[32] and it recommended that shares with no par value should be permitted.

The Gedge Committee accepted the following advantages claimed for no par value shares.

- They represent the share for what it is—a fraction or aliquot part of the equity—and they do not import a notional token of value.
- As there is no nominal capital and the share has no nominal value they make it impossible to relate a dividend to a nominal capital and thus avoid a potential source of misunderstanding and misrepresentation.[33]
- It is the capital employed and not the paid-up share capital which is the true value of the undertaking; an ordinary share of no par value does not purport to be anything but a share of the equity.
- Where shares do not have par values, capital reorganisations are simplified.
- Shares of no par value would in certain cases facilitate the raising of additional equity capital. The par value rules can hinder a company in financial difficulties that wants to raise new share capital where the par value of these shares is greater than the amount that anyone would be willing to pay for them.

The Gedge Committee acknowledged the need for safeguards against abuse but concluded that, provided the whole of the proceeds of any issue of shares having no par value were treated as capital money and not as distributable reserves, the position would be neither more nor less open to abuse than in respect of shares having a par value. The Jenkins Committee in 1962 also recommended that legislation should be introduced to permit shares with no par values.[34] This Committee went one step further than the Gedge Committee by recommending that no-par-value preference shares, as well as no-par-value ordinary shares, should be permitted. Despite these various recommendations, no reform has to date been enacted in the UK.[35] This is in contrast to the position in countries which historically had company law systems that largely followed the English model but which, latterly, have moved closer to the position under the corporations laws of US states. No-par-value shares are widely recognised in US states.[36] This is also now the position in Canadian jurisdictions which generally permit no-par-value shares and, in some cases, prohibit par-value shares.[37] In Australia, sweeping reform that came into force in July

[32] It was, however, opposed by the General Council of the Trades Union congress: *Report of the Committee on Shares of No Par Value* Cmd 9112 (1954) paras 29–31. Also a minority report annexed to the main report recorded one member of the committee's opposition to the proposal.

[33] Articles normally provide for dividends to be paid on the amount paid up on shares (see, eg, Table A, art 104). Where, as is the usual case, shares are fully paid up, the dividend is usually declared as a monetary amount per share (ie the amount available for distribution is divided by the number of shares in issue).

[34] *Report of the Company Law Committee* Cmnd 1749 (1962) paras 32–4.

[35] There was an attempt to include provision in the Companies Act 1967 but this failed.

[36] Brudney, V, Bratton, WW, *Brudney and Chirelstein's Corporate Finance Cases and Materials* (4th edn, 1993) 445–7; Klein, WA, and Coffee, JC, *Business Organization and Finance* (5th edn, 1993) 210–15.

[37] Welling, BL, *Corporate Law in Canada The Governing Principles* (2nd edn, 1998) 609–12.

1998 abolished the concept of par value in its entirety both for existing shares and for new share issues.[38]

In the UK simple outright abolition of the outmoded concept of par values is not possible because the Second Company Law Directive, art 8 requires public companies to attribute par values to their shares. Although art 8 provides a no-par share alternative, this alternative, which is based on a Belgian model, is unattractive because in essence it retains much of the distinction between par value and premium. It requires companies to determine for accounting purposes an 'accountable par' for its no-par-value shares. Accountable par represents the minimum price at which the shares can be issued, although they may be issued at a higher price. The government has indicated that it may raise with the European Commission the possibility of amending the Second Directive to permit 'true' no-par-value shares.[39]

Significance of Par Values in English Company Law

Apart from the rules relating to the maintenance of capital and accounting requirements which would necessarily need to be reviewed if the law were changed so as to allow no-par-value shares, other aspects of English company law that currently use the concept of par value would also need to be reconsidered. These include the following:

- the statutory entitlement to share in rights issues which is measured on the basis of the nominal value of the existing issued shares;[40]
- certain minority protection rights which have minimum shareholding thresholds and which use nominal values as a way of measuring whether such thresholds are met;[41]
- measurement of the requisite majorities for shareholder resolutions;[42] and
- requirements on disclosure of interests in shares where nominal values are used as a basis for the disclosure thresholds.[43]

ALTERING THE CAPITAL CLAUSE

The Companies Act 1985, s 121 allows a company, if so authorised by its articles, to alter its capital clause in a number of ways. These ways are:

- increasing the total amount of the share capital;

[38] Corporations Law, s 245C, ss 1443–1450 inserted by the Company Law Review Act 1998.

[39] *The Euro: Redenomination of Share Capital* (DTI Consultative Document) (1998) para 10.10.

[40] Companies Act 1985, s 89. This can be problematic if the company has ordinary shares with a low par value and participating preference shares with a high par value and is one of the reasons why a company may consider dis-application of s 89: On dis-application of s 89 for this purpose, see Ch 18 below, at 620–1.

[41] Companies Act 1985, s 5 (2) (objecting to alteration of objects); s 54 (objecting to resolution to re-register a public company as private; s 157 (2) objecting to financial assistance by private company). But contrast Companies Act 1985, s 127 (2) (objecting to variation of class rights) which sets a simpler threshold of 15 per cent of the total number of issued shares of the class.

[42] Companies Act 1985, s 125 (2) (resolution for variation of class rights); s 378 (extraordinary and special resolutions).

[43] Companies Act 1985, s 200.

- diminishing the total amount of the share capital (by cancelling shares which have not been taken or agreed to be taken by any person);[44]
- increasing the nominal value of each share (by consolidating the existing shares and then dividing them into shares of a larger nominal amount); and
- lowering the nominal value of each share (by dividing it into a number of shares each having a smaller nominal amount).

The relevant authorisation in the articles is, in the case of Table A, given by art 32 which provides for alteration of the share capital by ordinary resolution. A company may not fetter this statutory power by entering into an agreement to the effect that it will not exercise the power, or will only exercise it subject to the satisfaction of more rigorous conditions than those stipulated in its articles.[45] However, because the statutory power in this case is dependent upon the shareholder authorisation specified in the articles, it is possible to limit its exercise by specifying that the shareholder authorisation required is greater than an ordinary resolution, say a special resolution or even unanimous shareholder consent. Alternatively, the shareholders from time to time may validly covenant only to vote in favour of an alteration to the capital clause in particular circumstances[46] and, so long as this agreement is in force and is observed,[47] this will restrict the circumstances in which the authorised capital may be changed.

ALLOTTED SHARE CAPITAL

Generally the term allotment when used in respect of shares is not a term of art.[48] In *Spitzel v The Chinese Corporation Ltd*[49] Stirling J answered the general question 'What is an allotment of shares?' by saying: 'Broadly speaking, it is an appropriation by the directors or the managing body of the company of shares to a particular person.' In *Nicol's Case*[50] Chitty J, however, equated allotment with the forming of a binding contract to take shares. The key distinction between these two interpretations is that appropriation could take place before a contract is concluded: it could happen when an offer to subscribe shares is accepted but before the acceptance is communicated so as to form a contract, or it could even take place before acceptance where, as in a rights issue, the directors resolve that certain shares are to be allotted to particular persons and make an offer of those shares.[51] In line with the view that

44 This is not a reduction of capital: Companies Act 1985, s 121 (5).

45 *Russell v Northern Bank Development Corporation Ltd* [1992] 1 WLR 588, HL.

46 Ibid.

47 It is debatable whether the court will be willing to enforce such an agreement by way of injunction: *Russell v Northern Bank Development Corporation Ltd* [1992] 1 WLR 588, HL; Ferran, EV, 'The Decision of the House of Lords in *Russell v Northern Bank Development Corporation Ltd*' [1994] CLJ 343.

48 *Re Florence Land and Public Works Company, Nicol's case* (1885) 29 Ch D 421, Ch D and CA, 427 *per* Chitty J; *Re Ambrose Lake Tin and Copper Co (Clarke's Case)* (1878) 8 Ch D 635, CA; *Re Compania de Electricidad* [1980] 1 Ch 146, 182; *Whitehouse v Carlton Hotel Pty Ltd* (1987) 70 ALR 251, H Ct of Aust, 271 *per* Brennan J.

49 (1899) 80 LT 347.

50 *Re Florence Land and Public Works Company, Nicol's case* (1885) 29 Ch D 421, Ch D and CA.

51 *Spitzel v Chinese Co Ltd* (1899) 80 LT 347; *Re Compania de Electricidad* [1980] 1 Ch 146, 182.

allotment may take place before there is a binding contract to take shares is *Re The Saloon Stream Packet Co Ltd, Fletcher's Case*[52] where three stages in a contract to take shares were identified, namely an application for shares, an allotment and, finally, communication of and acquiescence in the allotment.

For the purposes of the Companies Act 1985 a share is allotted when a person acquired the unconditional right to be included in the company's register of members in respect of it.[53] A right to be included in the company's register of members would usually be derived from a contract to take shares. A contract to take shares is in essence no different from any other contract and the normal contractual rules, including those of offer and acceptance,[54] apply. Accordingly it would be possible for an offer of shares to be withdrawn before a contract is formed by communication of acceptance. If an offer is withdrawn before acceptance is communicated there would be no allotment within the Companies Act definition of that term.

Whether the company is, as a matter of contract, the offeror or the offeree of the shares will depend on the circumstances. Where a company seeks to raise capital by inviting the public to subscribe for its shares, technically the persons who respond to the invitation are the offerors. The contract is then concluded by the company's acceptance being communicated to the offerors. This communication would normally take the form of letters of allotment. Letters of allotment would normally be effective to form a binding contract, and thus constitute an allotment for the purpose of the Companies Act 1985, when the letters are posted.[55] The positions can be reversed so that the company is the offeror: this is the situation in a typical rights issue where the company offers new shares to the existing shareholders. In a rights issue the contract of allotment is concluded by it being accepted by the person to whom it is made or, where the terms of the offer allow for renunciation (as is required by *The Listing Rules* in respect of rights issues of listed companies[56]) by another person in whose favour the offer has been renounced.[57] Sometimes a contract to take shares may provide for a later allotment. In that case the arrangement is conditional and the shares will only be allotted when the conditions of the contract are fulfilled. The carrying out of an administrative act by the company, such as the issue of a formal letter of allotment, may be specified as the condition necessary to complete the allotment.

One case where a person may acquire the right to be included in the company's register of members otherwise than by contract is in a bonus issue of shares.[58] A bonus issue of shares means an issue of new shares to the existing

[52] (1867) 17 LT 136. See also *Re Scottish Petroleum Co* (1883) 23 Ch D 413, CA.

[53] Companies Act 1985, s 738 (1).

[54] *Household Fire Insurance Co v Grant* (1879) 4 ExD 216 is an example of the application of the posting rule to a contract to subscribe shares. The communication of acceptance is normally required: *Re Scottish Petroleum Co* (1883) 23 Ch D 43; *Re National Savings Bank Assurance Hebbes Case* (1867) 4 LR Eq 9.

[55] *Household Fire Insurance Co v Grant* (1879) 4 ExD 216.

[56] *The Listing Rules* ch 4, para 4.16.

[57] *Willey v Parratt* (1843) 3 Exch 211, 154 ER 819; *Ward v Lord Landesborough* 12 CB 252, 138 ER 900.

[58] The term 'issue' is used here because 'bonus issue' is common parlance. It is not meant to have any particular technical significance.

shareholders where the subscription price is met by the company out of funds which it is permitted to apply for that purpose. In *Re Cleveland Trust plc*[59] Scott J held that the relationship between company and shareholder *vis-à-vis* an authorised bonus issue may not be strictly contractual; but unless the issue is for some reason fundamentally flawed,[60] the person to whom the shares are offered, or the person to whom he has renounced the offer, acquires a right to be included in the company's register of members in respect of the bonus shares. Under the Companies Act 1985, s 359 a person whose name is wrongly omitted from a company's register of members has the right to apply to court for rectification of the register.

Amount of Allotted Share Capital

The allotted share capital of a company which is incorporated as a public company must be not less than the authorised minimum, which is currently £50,000.[61] A public company, incorporated as such, will not receive a certificate entitling it do business or to exercise any borrowing powers unless the registrar of companies is satisfied that the company's allotted share capital is not less than the authorised minimum.[62] The authorised minimum allotted capital requirement also applies to a private company which is converting to public company status.[63] The nominal value of its allotted share capital must be not less than the authorised minimum at the time when it passes a special resolution to convert to a public company.[64] Re-registration as a public company will be refused if this requirement is not satisfied.[65]

Directors' Authority to Allot Shares

Directors must be authorised to allot new shares in accordance with the Companies Act 1985, s 80. This authorisation must be given by ordinary resolution of the company in general meeting or by the articles. The maximum amount of shares that may be allotted under the authority, and its expiry date, must be stated in the resolution.[66] For a public company the maximum duration of a s 80 authority is five years.[67] A private company may elect[68] to apply the provisions of the Companies Act 1985, s 80A under which the duration of a section 80 authority may be longer than five years or unlimited. Forms of s 80 authority that are commonly used in practice are considered further in Chapter 18.[69] An allotment of shares that is not covered by an appropriate s 80 authority is not invalid for that reason[70] but the responsible directors are liable to a fine.[71]

59 [1991] BCLC 424, 434–5.
60 As in the *Cleveland* case where the purported issue was held to be void for mistake.
61 Companies Act 1985, ss 117–118. 62 Ibid, s 117. 63 Ibid, s 45.
64 Ibid. 65 Companies Act 1985, s 43. 66 Ibid, s 80 (4).
67 Ibid.
68 An elective resolution requires the consent of all of the members of the company who are entitled to vote on the matter: Companies Act 1985, s 379A.
69 See below, at 614–5.
70 Companies Act 1985, s 80 (10). 71 Ibid, s 80 (9).

Return of Allotments

Under the Companies Act 1985, s 88, within one month after the making of an allotment, a company must deliver to the registrar of companies for registration a return of the allotments which notifies details of the allotment including the number and nominal amount of the shares allotted and the price paid or payable in respect of them.

ISSUED SHARE CAPITAL AND ISSUED SHARES

The phrase 'issued share capital' is not defined by the Companies Act 1985. It may take on a meaning from the context in which it is used but prima facie it means the aggregate of the nominal or par value of the shares which the company has issued.[72]

When are shares issued? In *Levy v Abercorris Slate and Slab Co*,[73] a case which concerned an issue of debentures, Chitty J said:[74] '"issued" is not a technical term, it is a mercantile term well understood'. This comment is equally applicable to an issue of shares. Very commonly the terms 'issued' and 'allotted' are used interchangeably, as if they meant the same thing and as if both events happened at precisely the same time. However, since the word 'issued' takes its colour from the context in which it is used, in particular situations it may be used to mean something different from 'allotted'. In particular, in certain contexts a share which has been allotted may not be regarded as an issued share. The converse is generally not true—a share is normally taken to be issued at some point after it has been allotted; exceptionally, however, in *Mosely v Koffyfontein Mines Ltd*,[75] a case which concerned the construction of articles of association dealing with increase of share capital, Farwell LJ put the order of the three separate steps in the life of a new share as being creation, issue and allotment.[76]

In *Ambrose Lake Tin and Copper Co (Clarke's Case)*[77] a reference in the Companies Act 1867 to the issue of shares was taken to mean something different from, and later than, their allotment. Also in various cases concerned with construction of tax legislation employing the term, issue has been interpreted to mean something other than, and subsequent to, allotment.[78] But what does 'issued' mean where it is used to mean something other than 'allot-

[72] *Canada Safeway Ltd v IRC* [1972] 1 All ER 666. This was a decision on a Finance Act but Megarry J held that the language of that Act was entirely consonant with that of the companies legislation.

[73] (1887) 37 Ch D 260.

[74] At 264. See also *Spitzel v Chinese Co Ltd* (1899) 80 LT 347; *National Westminster Bank plc v IRC* [1995] 1 AC 119, HL.

[75] [1911] 1 Ch 73, CA.

[76] At 84. See also *Whitehouse v Carlton Hotel Pty Ltd* (1987) 70 ALR 251, H Ct of Aust, 271 *per* Brennan J.

[77] (1878) 8 Ch D 635.

[78] For example *Oswald Tillotson Ltd v IRC* [1933] 1 KB 134, CA; *Brotex Cellulose Fibres Ltd v IRC* [1933] 1 KB 158; *Murex Ltd v IRC* [1933] 1KB 173; *Agricultural Mortgage Corporation v IRC* [1978] Ch 72, CA; *Holmleigh (Holdings) Ltd v IRC* 46 TC 435.

ted', and where issue is thought to be subsequent to allotment? Again the answer to this question ultimately depends on the context in which the term is used,[79] but a view that has attracted considerable support is that the distinction between allotment and issue of a share mirrors that between being a shareholder and being a member of a company. A person to whom a share has been allotted may be a shareholder[80] but that person does not become a member until registered as such on the company's register of members.[81] A shareholder is entitled to dividends in respect of the shares but rights such as attending meetings and voting on resolutions are membership rights which are held by members and not by mere shareholders.[82] Thus in *Oswald Tillotson Ltd v IRC*[83] the Court of Appeal equated the word 'issue', as used in certain tax legislation, with the creation of a registered shareholder. In *Agricultural Mortgage Corporation v IRC*[84] Walton J, at first instance, and Goff LJ in the Court of Appeal, also inclined to the view that for the purpose of certain tax legislation 'issue' took place on registration.[85] The meaning of 'issue' for the purpose of certain tax legislation was considered by the House of Lords in *National Westminster Bank plc v IRC*.[86] As in the earlier tax cases, it was held that issue followed allotment and was completed by the entry of the names of the holders of the shares on the company's register of members.

One place where the question of a possible distinction between issued and allotted share capital arises is in the disclosure of interests in shares requirements of the Companies Act 1985, Part VI. These require a person to disclose interests in the relevant share capital of public companies which exceed certain percentage thresholds. Relevant share capital is defined, broadly, as meaning issued share capital.[87] The proper construction of the term 'issued' in this context has not arisen for decision in the courts, but in the DTI's Inspectors Report in the aftermath of the Blue Arrow affair[88] it was stated that it was understood to mean something other than, and subsequent to, allotment. The DTI Inspectors suggested that a share should be regarded as issued for this purpose when an entry was made on the register of members. The

[79] In *Central Piggery Co Ltd v McNicoll* (1949) 78 CLR 594, H Ct of Aust, 599 Dixon J interpreted the word 'issue' to mean a step after allotment whereby the shareholder is put in control of the shares allotted.

[80] Ibid at 599 *per* Dixon J. It is not, however, necessarily always the case that an allottee of shares is to be regarded as a shareholder. Thus in Companies Act 1985, s 99 it was thought to be necessary to provide expressly that references to the 'holder' of shares included persons who had an unconditional right to be registered as a member (s 99 (5)).

[81] Companies Act 1985, s 22. For the special position of subscribers to the memorandum see Smith, C, 'Subscribers: Their Status on Incorporation' (1982) 3 Co Law 99.

[82] *Spitzel v Chinese Co Ltd* (1899) 80 LT 347.

[83] [1933] 1 KB 134, CA.

[84] [1978] Ch 72, CA.

[85] 'Or possibly some other act' at 85 *per* Walton J, or 'the issue of a certificate' at 101 *per* Goff LJ. However, the view that a share is only issued when registration and the issue of a share certificate takes place has been rejected: *Re Heaton's Steel and Slab Co (Blyth's Case)* (1876) 4 Ch D 140, CA explaining *Re Imperial River Co, (Bush's Case)* (1874) 9 Ch App 554, CA; *Re Ambrose Lake Tin and Copper Co (Clarke's Case)* (1878) 8 Ch D 635, CA.

[86] [1995] 1 AC 119, HL.

[87] Companies Act 1985, s 198 (2). The full definition is that relevant share capital means the company's issued share capital of a class carrying rights to vote in all circumstances at general meetings of the company.

[88] *Report on County NatWest Ltd and County NatWest Securities Ltd, Investigation under section 432(2) of the Companies Act 1985* (1989) paras 3.05–3.06.

Inspectors recommended that the matter should be clarified in legislation but, although some aspects of the disclosure of interests requirements were amended in 1993, no amendment with regard to the meaning of issued share capital was introduced.[89]

Except in this section (or where specifically indicated) the common practice of using the terms 'issued' and 'allotted' interchangeably is adopted in this chapter.

PAYMENT FOR SHARES

The next part of this chapter is concerned with the rules governing payment for shares. This is a very detailed and complex area of company law, especially for public companies where the forms of consideration that they may accept for their shares are very closely regulated. These rules are intended to protect creditors and shareholders against companies accepting consideration that is in fact worth less than the issue price of the shares.[90] It is debatable whether such extensive regulation of public company share capital as is now contained in the companies legislation is necessary or desirable, but many of the requirements are derived from the Second Company Law Directive and, barring changes at the European level, that precludes substantive change to the domestic law.[91]

SHARES MUST NOT BE ISSUED AT A DISCOUNT

Shares may not be allotted at less than their par value. Originally this rule was established by case law[92] and it is now enshrined in the Companies Act 1985, s 100 (1). If the rule is contravened, the allottee is liable to pay the company an amount equal to the amount of the discount, together with interest.[93] Subsequent holders of shares which were allotted at less than par may also be liable to pay up the shares in full.[94] The Companies Act 1985, s 113, which permits applications to court for relief from liability arising from failure to comply with certain of the requirements of the Act regarding the allotment of shares, does not apply in this case. The directors who authorised the allot-

[89] The changes were effected by The Disclosure of Interests in Shares (Amendment) Regulations 1993 (1993/1819). A DTI consultative document that preceded the changes, *Disclosure of Interests in Shares The EC Major Shareholding Directive* (1991) para 3.3 expressly refrained from commenting on the Inspectors' interpretation.

[90] Second Company Law Directive 77/91/EEC, [1977] OJ L26/1 provides: 'whereas in order to ensure minimum equivalent protection for both shareholders and creditors of public limited companies, the co-ordination of national provisions relating to their formation, and to the maintenance, increase or reduction of their capital is particularly important'.

[91] See Klein, WA, and Coffee, JC, *Business Organization and Finance* (5th edn, 1993) 215 discussing the trend towards deregulation of share capital in the USA.

[92] *Ooregum Gold Mining Co of India v Roper* [1892] AC 125, HL; *Re Eddystone Marine Insurance Co* [1893] 3 Ch 9 CA; *Welton v Saffery* [1897] AC 299, HL.

[93] Companies Act 1985, s 100 (2). Interest is charged at 5 per cent, but there is provision for this rate to be changed: Companies Act 1985, s 107.

[94] See this chapter below, at 301.

ment at a discount may also be liable to the company for breach of fiduciary duty.[95]

A contract to allot shares at a discount at a later date is void and cannot be enforced by either party.[96]

ENSURING COMPLIANCE WITH THE NO-DISCOUNT RULE—CASH CONSIDERATION

A share is deemed to be allotted for cash if the consideration for the allotment is:

(i) cash received by the company;
(ii) a cheque received by the company in good faith which its directors have no reason for suspecting will not be paid;
(iii) a release of a liability of the company for a liquidated sum; or
(iv) an undertaking to pay cash to the company at a later date.[97]

In each of these cases 'cash' includes foreign currency.[98] The payment of cash, or any undertaking to pay cash, to any person other than the company is a form of non-cash consideration.[99] An undertaking to pay cash at a later date means an undertaking given to the company in return for the allotment; it does not include the assignment of a pre-existing debt to the company as consideration for the allotment.[100]

Payment in Foreign Currency: Exchange Rate Fluctuations

It would normally be easy to spot an infringement of the no-discount rule where shares are allotted for cash received by the company. An exceptional situation which could cause difficulties is where the terms of the allotment allow for payment to be made in a currency other than that in which the shares are denominated, with an exchange rate being stated in the allotment terms. There is a danger of the no-discount rule being infringed if generally prevailing exchange rates have moved to such an extent that the amount paid satisfies the allotment terms but is less than par value of the shares. If the terms on which shares are allotted permit payment to be made otherwise than in the currency in which they are denominated, steps must also be taken to deal with this potential problem. These measures can involve the company entering into hedging contracts to ensure that it receives the requisite sterling amount, or providing in the terms of allotment for cancellation in the event that prevailing exchange rates fluctuate to such an extent that the company will not, under the allotment terms, receive the nominal amount in respect of its shares.

[95] *Hirsche v Sims* [1894] AC 654, PC.
[96] *Re Almada and Tirito Co* (1888) 38 Ch D 415, CA.
[97] Companies Act 1985, s 738 (2).
[98] Ibid, s 738 (4).
[99] Ibid, s 738 (3).
[100] *System Controls plc v Munro Corporate plc* [1990] BCC 386.

Payment by Release of a Liability

A company could acquire assets on credit and subsequently pay for them by allotting shares to the vendor. Because 'cash' includes the release of a liability for a liquidated sum, the shares would prima facie be allotted for cash. In *Re Bradford Investments plc (No 2)*[101] Hoffmann J, referring to this type of situation, commented:'I would not wish to give the impression that an artificial resort to two documents instead of one could be used to avoid the provisions [requiring independent valuation of non-cash consideration for shares].'[102] However, whilst the courts may be expected to be vigilant to ensure that statutory requirements are not evaded, where there is no question of the two stages of the transaction being artificial or a sham, the shares will be treated as having been allotted for cash.[103]

The No-discount Rule and Convertible Securities

In *Mosely v Koffyfontein Mines Ltd*[104] the Court of Appeal analysed a proposal to issue convertible debentures at a discount to their par value where the debentures could immediately be converted into fully-paid shares having a par value equal to the par value of the debentures. The Court of Appeal held that the issue of the debentures on the proposed terms was open to abuse as it could be used to circumvent the no-discount rule and, on that basis, granted an injunction to restrain the making of the issue. Cozens-Hardy LJ expressly left open the question of a debenture issued at a discount to its par value which conferred a right at some future date to demand a fully paid share in exchange for the par value of the debenture.[105] This situation is different from that where debentures issued at a discount are immediately convertible into fully-paid shares having a par value equal to the par value of the debentures: in the former case the discount can be explained because it represents the investors' return without which, they would (presumably) have demanded a higher rate of interest; in the latter case it is difficult to find any explanation for the discount other than it being a backhanded way of allowing shares to be allotted at a discount. So interpreted, the decision in *Mosely* does not prevent the issue of convertible debentures at a discount where the conversion right is not immediately exercisable. There can be no hard and fast rule governing the length of time that would have to elapse between issue of the debentures and permitted exercise of the conversion rights. It would presumably depend on whether there is a genuine reason for the discount: if there is, even a short delay might suffice.

When shares are allotted on conversion of convertible debentures are they allotted for cash? Ultimately the answer to this question must depend on the

101 [1991] BCC 379.

102 This requirement, imposed by Companies Act 1985, s 103, is discussed further in this chapter below, at 298–301.

103 *Re Harmony and Montague Tin and Copper Mining Co, Spargo's Case* (1873) 8 Ch App 407, CA.

104 [1904] 2 Ch 108, CA.

105 [1904] 2 Ch 108, CA, 120.

conversion mechanism in the terms of the debentures. In *Mosely* Vaughan-Williams LJ thought that shares allotted upon conversion of convertible debentures were allotted for money's worth,[106] but Cozens-Hardy LJ explained the conversion as involving the cancellation of a liquidated debt.[107] Where the issuer of the convertible securities and of the shares into which they convert is the same company, an allotment of shares in exchange for the release of the liquidated debt represented by the convertibles would be an allotment for cash according to the definition of that term in the Companies Act 1985, s 738 (2).

Companies sometimes issue preference shares, or other shares carrying special rights, which are convertible at some point in the future into ordinary shares either of the same company or of another company in its group. A subscriber of share capital does not become a creditor in respect of the amount subscribed and the conversion of a share would not constitute the release of a liability of the company for a liquidated sum. The conversion terms may provide for a return of capital to the shareholders (perhaps by the redemption of their shares) and subsequent application of the redemption proceeds in the subscription of new ordinary shares and, in that case, the conversion would involve an allotment of new shares for cash consideration.

The No-discount Rule and Underwriting Commissions

A company is permitted, to a limited extent,[108] to use capital to pay underwriting commissions. Under this permission, for example, if 100 shares are issued at their par value of £1 each and the underwriter is to receive a 1-per-cent commission, the company may use up to £1 of the subscription moneys to pay the commission. If no subscribers can be found for the shares so that the underwriter has to take them itself this means, in effect, that for an issue of shares having an aggregate par value of £100 the underwriter only has to pay £99. This scenario is often said to be an exception to the rule that shares may not be issued at a discount. This is a convenient shorthand but the strict technical position is that the company and the underwriter have mutual obligations—the underwriter to pay the full subscription money and the company to pay the commission—and to the extent of the level of the commission these obligations cancel each other out.[109]

REGULATION OF NON-CASH CONSIDERATION FOR SHARES

The Companies Act 1985, s 99 (1) provides that shares of public and private companies can be paid up in money or money's worth (including goodwill and know-how). There is one exception: shares taken by a subscriber to the

[106] Ibid at 116.

[107] Ibid at 119.

[108] Companies Act 1985, ss 97–98. This is permitted by the Second Directive, art 8 (2).

[109] *Metropolitan Coal Consumers Assn v Scrimgeour* [1895] 2 QB 604, CA. The Court of Appeal had no doubt that using capital to pay commissions did not infringe the rule prohibiting the issue of shares at a discount.

memorandum of a public company must be paid up in cash.[110] At common law, despite stressing the importance of the maintenance of capital doctrine as a device for protecting creditors and shareholders, the courts were reluctant to examine the adequacy of non-cash consideration for shares. In *Re Wragg Ltd*[111] the Court of Appeal accepted that the no-discount rule applied where a company allotted shares in consideration for the acquisition of property. But

> if, however, the consideration which the company has agreed to accept as representing money's worth, the nominal value of the shares be a consideration not clearly colourable nor illusory, then, in my judgement, the adequacy of the consideration cannot be impeached . . . unless the contract can also be impeached; and I take it to be the law that it is not open to a [petitioner], unless he is able to impeach the agreement, to go into the adequacy of the consideration to show that the company have agreed to give an excessive value for what they have purchased.[112]

The Court of Appeal's approach in *Re Wragg Ltd* followed dicta in the opinions of the House of Lords in *Ooregum Gold Mining Co of India v Roper*[113] and also decisions in earlier cases[114] which established that a court could not interfere merely on the grounds that a company had, by issuing shares, overpaid for property and that only a dishonest or colourable transaction would allow the court to intervene.

Whether the consideration is colourable or illusory is one of fact to be decided by reference to the facts in each case.[115] Consideration which is clearly bad, such as past consideration[116] or consideration which permits an obvious money measure to be made showing that a discount was allowed,[117] will not be allowed to stand. The courts will not necessarily insist on a separate action to impeach a transaction involving the allotment of shares if the facts which go to establish that it is a colourable transaction are sufficiently plain to demonstrate that such an action would be little more than a technicality.[118]

However, where shares of a public company are allotted for a non-cash consideration, the traditional reluctance to interfere has been replaced by stringent statutory rules derived from the Second Company Law Directive.[119] Some of the requirements applicable to public companies are also relevant to a private company which is hoping to convert to a public company because the conversion may not proceed if those requirements have not been observed in respect of share issues in the period leading up to the proposed conversion.[120]

[110] Companies Act 1985, s 106.

[111] [1897] 1 Ch 796, CA.

[112] [1897] 1 Ch 796, CA, 836 *per* ALS Smith LJ; see also at 830 *per* Lindley LJ.

[113] [1892] AC 125, HL.

[114] Cited in the judgments in *Re Wragg* [1897] 1 Ch 796, CA. See also *Re Theatrical Trust Ltd* [1895] 1 Ch 771.

[115] *Re Innes & Co Ltd* [1903] 2 Ch 254, CA, 262 *per* Vaughan Williams LJ.

[116] *Re Eddystone Marine Insurance Co* [1893] 3 Ch 9, CA (although in Scotland past consideration for shares has been accepted: *Park Business Interiors Ltd v Park* [1990] BCC 914, Court of Session, Outer House).

[117] *Re Theatrical Trust Ltd* [1895] 1 Ch 771.

[118] *Re White Star Line Ltd* [1938] 1 Ch 458.

[119] EC/77/9, [1977] OJ L26/1.

[120] Companies Act 1985, s 44.

Undertakings to Do Work or Perform Services as Consideration for Shares in a Public Company

Under the Companies Act 1985, s 99 (2),[121] a public company is prohibited from accepting in payment up of its shares, or any premium on them, an undertaking given by any person that he or another person should do work or perform services for the company or any other person. If a company accepts such an undertaking in payment up of its shares or any premium on them, the holder of the shares when they or the premium is treated as paid up (in whole or in part) by the undertaking is liable to pay in cash to the company in respect of those shares an amount equal to the amount treated as paid up by the undertaking, together with interest.[122] The enforceability of the undertaking is unaffected[123] but it is open to a person who incurs liability resulting from a contravention of the ban on such undertakings being good consideration to apply to the court for relief.[124]

A holder of shares for this purpose includes a person who has an unconditional right to be included in the register of members in respect of the shares or to have an instrument of transfer of them executed in his favour.[125] Thus, if shares are allotted as fully paid in return from an undertaking by the allottee, or another person, to do work or to perform services, the allottee will be liable to pay for the shares in cash in accordance with the Companies Act 1985, s 99 (3). If the shares are allotted on an unpaid basis (which would be rare in practice) and the company later accepts from their then holder an undertaking to do work or perform services in payment up of the shares, that person would then become liable to pay for the shares in accordance with s 99 (3), but previous holders of the shares, including the original allottee, would not be liable. If the shares are transferred after they have been treated as paid up by such an undertaking, subsequent holders of the shares may also incur liability.[126]

Undertakings to be Performed in the Future as Consideration for Shares in a Public Company

In addition to the absolute bar on accepting undertakings to do work or perform services in consideration for their shares, public companies are also restricted with regard to accepting other types of undertaking as consideration for their shares. Under the Companies Act 1985, s 102 (1), a public company must not allot shares as fully or partly paid up (as to their nominal value or any premium on them) otherwise than in cash if the consideration for the allotment is, or includes, an undertaking which is to be, or may be, performed more than five years after the date of the allotment.[127] The effect of contravening s 102 (1) is that the allottee is still liable to pay to the company in cash

[121] This section implements into English law Second Directive, art 7.
[122] Companies Act 1985, s 99 (3).
[123] Ibid, s 115.
[124] Ibid, s 113 discussed in this chapter, at 302–3.
[125] Companies Act 1985, s 99 (5).
[126] Ibid, s 112 discussed in this chapter, at 301.
[127] The five-year rule is derived from Second Directive, arts 9.2 and 21.1.

an amount equal to the amount treated as paid up by the undertaking, with interest at the appropriate rate.[128] The enforceability of the undertaking is not affected.[129] Subsequent holders of the shares may also incur liability.[130] It is open to any person, whether allottee or subsequent holder, who incurs liability resulting from a contravention of the ban on long-term undertakings being good consideration for shares in a public company to apply to court for relief under the Companies Act 1985, s 113.[131]

The prohibition in the Companies Act 1985, s 102 extends to the variation of a contract where, if the varied terms had been the original terms, the contract would have contravened the section.[132] To cater for the case of a share allotment in consideration of an undertaking which is to be performed within five years of the allotment where the undertaking is not actually performed within the period allowed by the contract, it is provided that at the end of the period allowed by the contract, the allottee then becomes liable to pay the company the amount which was treated as paid up by the undertaking, with interest.[133] Subsequent holder liability and applications to court for relief provisions apply here just as they would to a straightforward contravention of the section.

Valuation of Non-cash Consideration for Shares in a Public Company

The Companies Act 1985, s 103 imposes a valuation requirement in respect of non-cash consideration for shares in a public company.[134] A public company must not allot shares as fully or partly paid up (as to their nominal value or any premium on them) otherwise than in cash unless the consideration has been independently valued and a valuation report has been made to the company in the six months preceding the allotment.[135] A copy of the valuation report must be sent to the proposed allottee before the allotment.[136] A copy of the valuation report must also be delivered to the registrar of companies when the company files the return of allotment of the shares required by the Companies Act 1985, s 88.[137]

The details of the valuation and report required by the Companies Act 1985, s 103 are set out in s 108.[138] The company must appoint as the independent

[128] Companies Act 1985, s 102 (2).
[129] Ibid, s 115.
[130] Ibid, s 112 discussed in this chapter, at 301.
[131] See this chapter, at 302–3.
[132] Companies Act 1985, s 102 (3). This includes a variation by a public company of the terms of a contract entered into before the company was re-registered as a public company: sub-section (4).
[133] Companies Act 1985, s 102 (5) and (6).
[134] This implements Second Directive, arts 10 and 27.2.
[135] Companies Act 1985, s 103 (1)(a)–(b). This requirement is relevant to a private company which is converting to public company status. Under Companies Act 1985, s 44 the registrar of companies is obliged not to entertain an application for re-registration if shares have been issued in a specified period prior to the application for a non-cash consideration which has not been valued in accordance with s 108.
[136] Companies Act 1985, s 103 (1)(c).
[137] Ibid, s 111.
[138] In *Re Ossory Estates plc* (1988) BCC 461, 463 Harman J described these requirements as 'curious and arcane'.

valuer[139] a person who would be qualified to be its auditor; it may appoint its current auditor. The independent valuer so appointed may delegate the task of carrying out the valuation,[140] but has a non-delegable duty to produce a report stating a range of matters including a description of the consideration, the method used to value it and the date of the valuation.[141] The independent valuer and the delegate (if any) are entitled to require from the officers of the company such information and explanations as they think necessary to enable them to carry out their responsibilities.[142] The sanction for knowingly or recklessly making a misleading, false or deceptive statement in response to a proper inquiry from a valuer or delegate is imprisonment, or a fine, or both.[143]

If the valuation requirements are not complied with, penal liability can attach to the allottee and also to subsequent holders of the shares. Even though the allottee may have duly conveyed assets of considerable value to the company, if the assets have not been duly valued, he can still be required to pay again in cash, and to pay interest. The allottee is prima facie liable to pay again in cash where the requirements for valuation have not been complied with and either (i) he has not received the valuer's report; or (ii) he knew or ought to have known that what has occurred amounted to a contravention.[144] In the latter case there must be an appreciation that the fact amounted to a contravention, but the allottee will not escape liability if he does not appreciate this in circumstances where he ought to have done. At the stage of establishing the allottee's prima-facie liability the value of any assets transferred by him to the company is not taken into account. Subsequent holders of shares allotted in contravention of the Companies Act 1985, s 103 may also be liable to pay for the shares in cash.[145]

The legislative policy underlying the penal liability that attaches to allottees, and subsequent holders, of shares in a public company which have been allotted for a non-cash consideration which has not been valued, is to prevent public companies from issuing shares at a discount.[146] The liability is harsh because, prima facie, allottees can be required to pay twice over, once in cash and once in money's worth. Subsequent holders are also in what appears to be an invidious position because they can be obliged to pay for the shares in cash even though the company may have already received, from someone else, non-cash consideration in respect of them. This harshness is mitigated by the Companies Act 1985, s 113 which allows the court to grant relief from liability in certain circumstances. The onus is on the person, whether allottee or subsequent holder, seeking relief to apply to the court, and the burden is on the applicant to satisfy the court that a case for relief is made out.[147] The circumstances in which the court may grant relief are considered in a later section of this chapter.[148]

139 It is the company's appointment: Companies Act 1985, s 103 (1)(b).
140 Companies Act 1985, s 108 (2).
141 Ibid, s 108 (1).
142 Ibid, s 110 (1).
143 Ibid, s 110.
144 Ibid, s 103 (6).
145 See this chapter, at 301.
146 *Re Bradford Investments plc (No 2)* [1991] BCC 379.
147 Ibid at 383.
148 See at 302–3.

There are two important exemptions from the general rule requiring non-cash consideration for the shares of public companies to be independently valued. These are the **takeover** exemption and the **mergers** exemption. It is also expressly provided in the Companies Act 1985, s 103 (2), presumably for the avoidance of doubt, that bonus issues fall outside the valuation requirements.

Takeover Exemption

For the takeover exemption to apply there must be an arrangement providing for the allotment of shares in a public company on terms that the whole or part of the consideration for the shares allotted is to be provided by the transfer to that company (or the cancellation) of some or all of the shares of another company (or of a class of shares in that company).[149] The arrangement must allow for participation by all of the holders[150] of the shares in the other company (or, where the arrangement is in respect of a class of shares, all of the holders of the shares in that class) save that, for this purpose, shares held by the offeror company or by its nominees, or by other companies in its group or by their nominees, are ignored.[151] Shares allotted 'in connection with'[152] an arrangement satisfying these criteria are exempt from the usual valuation requirements. This exemption is apt to cover takeover situations where the consideration offered to the shareholders of the target is, or includes, shares in the offeror but, as drafted, the exemption seems to extend far beyond straightforward share-for-share allotments.

The exemption applies to allotments 'in connection with' qualifying arrangements, so it would seem that, provided the assets to be acquired in exchange for shares include the entire share capital of another company, no valuation is required. This interpretation would permit shares to be allotted without valuation as consideration for an acquisition of assets involving many thousands or millions of pounds provided that, in addition, the vendor sold the company (which could have an allotted capital of only a few pounds). However, this exemption derives from the Second Directive[153] and the relevant provision in that Directive is cast in more restrictive terms.[154] So far as is relevant, the Second Directive, art 27 provides that Member States may provide an exemption for allotments 'made in order to give effect to a public offer for the purchase or exchange of shares'. The principle of statutory construction that domestic legislation implementing an EC Directive must be interpreted so as to give effect to the Directive if reasonably practicable is now well

[149] Companies Act 1985, s 103 (3).

[150] There is no provision defining a 'holder' for the purposes of s 103 (3) as including a person who has the right to be registered as a member or the right to have a share transfer executed in his favour. Since adjacent sections do make such provision there would seem to be an inference that the term 'holder' in this sub-section is meant to have a narrower meaning and that, for example, it does not include allottees.

[151] Companies Act 1985, s 103 (4).

[152] Ibid, s 103 (3).

[153] Second Company Law Directive 77/91/EEC, [1977] OJ L26/1.

[154] As pointed out by Mary Arden QC in the Chancery Bar Association Inaugural Lecture, 2 November 1992.

established in English law[155] and this would suggest that the takeover exemption ought to be narrowly confined.

Mergers Exemption

For the purposes of this exemption, a merger means a proposal by one company to acquire all the assets and liabilities of another company in exchange for the issue of shares or other securities of the first company to the shareholders of the other company. Shares allotted by a company in connection with such a merger are not subject to the valuation requirement.[156] Again this exemption is derived from the Second Directive, art 27 which allows a Member State to provide an exemption for an allotment 'to give effect to a merger'.

LIABILITY OF SUBSEQUENT HOLDERS

Subsequent holders of shares (of public or private companies) allotted in breach of the general no-discount rule imposed by the Companies Act 1985, s 100 are liable (jointly and severally with any other person so liable) to the company to pay the amount of the discount.[157] Subsequent holders of shares of public companies allotted in breach of the Companies Act 1985, s 99 (2) (the prohibition on consideration in the form of undertakings to do work or to perform services), s 102 (the prohibition on long-term undertakings) or s 103 (the valuation requirement) are also liable, jointly and severally with any other persons who are liable, to pay them up in cash.

A 'holder' of shares for the purpose of these liabilities includes a person who has an unconditional right to be included in the company's register of members in respect of the shares or to have an instrument of transfer of the shares executed in his favour.[158] In *System Controls plc v Munro Corporate plc*[159] a company contracted to allot shares and fulfilled its obligation by issuing a renounceable letter of allotment. Hoffmann J held that the person in whose favour the letter had been renounced was a holder of the shares for the purposes of these sections.

Subsequent holders escape liability if they are purchasers for value who, at the time of the purchase, did not have actual notice of the contravention, or are persons who derive title to the shares (directly or indirectly) from such a person.[160] In the *System Controls* case the subsequent holder was not exempt where it knew that the allotment had been effected without valuation, even though it might have been unaware of the need for such a valuation to be obtained; Hoffmann J held that actual notice in this context meant notice of the facts and need not extend to an appreciation that they constituted a contravention.

[155] *Pickstone v Freemans Plc* [1989] AC 66, [1988] 2 All ER 803, HL; *Litster v Forth Dry Dock and Engineering Co Ltd* [1990] AC 546, [1989] 1 All ER 1134, HL.

[156] Companies Act 1985, s 103 (5).

[157] Ibid, s 112.

[158] Ibid, s 112 (4).

[159] [1990] BCC 386.

[160] Companies Act 1985, s 112 (3).

RELIEF FROM LIABILITY

A company must not allot its shares at a discount to their par value. This is an absolute rule and, accordingly, if it is breached the allottee (and subsequent holders) cannot seek to be relieved of their joint and several liability to pay the whole amount.

The situation is different where what is in issue is a contravention on the bans on undertakings to do work or perform services or on long-term undertakings or a failure to comply with the valuation requirements. The allottee and subsequent holders are jointly and severally liable to pay for the shares in cash, but this does not affect the enforceability of any undertaking[161] and it does not take into account that the non-cash consideration which the company has received in respect of the shares may actually be quite valuable. In other words, the company may receive payment twice over, once in the form of cash and once in the form of an undertaking or of non-cash assets which have not been valued. The liability for failure to comply with these requirements of the Companies Act 1985 is thus penal. It is only relaxed by the Companies Act 1985, s 113 which provides for the court to be able to grant relief in certain circumstances. The court may grant relief either in relation to a liability to pay for shares in cash which is imposed by the Companies Act 1985 in circumstances where the consideration which has actually been given is for some reason unacceptable, or in relation to an undertaking given to the company in, or in connection with, payment for shares.[162]

Whether the application is for relief from liability to pay in cash or from liability resulting from an undertaking, there are two factors to which the court is required to have regard in deciding whether it should exempt the applicant in whole or in part.[163] These are:

(a) that a company which has allotted shares should receive money or money's worth at least equal in value to the aggregate of the nominal value of those shares and the whole of any premium or, if the case so requires, so much of that aggregate as is treated as paid up;
(b) subject to this, that where a company would, if the court did not grant the exemption, have more than one remedy against a particular person, it should be for the company to decide which remedy it should remain entitled to pursue.

The Companies Act 1985, s 113 (5) refers to these two factors as overriding principles. In *Re Bradford Investments plc (No 2)*[164] Hoffmann J said that the designation of (a) as an overriding principle did not mean that the court would not have jurisdiction to grant exemptions unless it was satisfied that the company had received assets worth at least the nominal value of the allotted shares and any premium. However, it did mean that very good reasons would be needed before the court could accept that it would be just and equitable to exempt an applicant from liability in circumstances where the company had not received sufficient value in respect of its shares.

[161] Companies Act 1985, s 115.
[162] Ibid, s 113 (1).
[163] Ibid, s 113 (5).
[164] [1991] BCC 379, 384.

If the application is for relief from liability imposed by the Companies Act to pay for the shares in cash the court may grant an exemption only if and to the extent that it appears to the court just and equitable to do so.[165] In determining whether it would be just and equitable the court must take into account the following:

(a) whether the applicant has paid, or is liable to pay, any amount in respect of any other liability arising in relation to the shares under any of the relevant sections, or of any liability arising by virtue of any undertaking given in or in connection with payment of those shares;
(b) whether any person other than the applicant has paid or is likely to pay (whether in pursuance of an order of the court or otherwise) any such amount; and
(c) whether the applicant or any other person has performed in whole or in part, or is likely so to perform, any such undertaking, or has done or is likely to do any other thing in payment or part payment of the shares.[166]

Where the application is for exemption from liability arising by virtue of an undertaking given to the company in, or in connection with, payment for shares the court can grant an exemption only if and to the extent that it appears just and equitable to do so having regard to:

(a) whether the applicant has paid or is liable to pay any amount in respect of any liability arising in relation to the shares under any of the relevant provisions of the Companies Act; and
(b) whether any person other than the applicant has paid or is likely to pay (whether in pursuance of order of the court or otherwise) any such amount.[167]

The burden is on the applicant to satisfy the court that a case for relief exists.[168] In *Re Ossory Estates plc,*[169] where the company had already re-sold at substantial profits properties which had been acquired in consideration for the allotment of shares and there was clear evidence that the vendor had so far complied with all of the undertakings arising from the conveyancing transactions and was likely to continue so to comply, Harman J was satisfied that a case for relief had been made out. However, in *Re Bradford Investments plc (No 2)*[170] the applicants were unable to establish that the assets transferred in consideration for shares had any net value and accordingly it was held that there was no case for relief.

CRIMINAL LIABILITY

For a company to contravene any of the statutory provisions restricting the allotment of shares for non-cash consideration is a criminal offence. The company and any officer of it who is in default is liable to a fine.[171]

[165] Companies Act 1985, s 113 (2)(a). Similarly, the court can exempt from the liability to pay interest but only where it appears just and equitable to do so: Companies Act 1985, s 113 (2)(b).
[166] Companies Act 1985, s 113 (3).
[167] Ibid, s 113 (4).
[168] *Re Bradford Investments plc (No 2)* [1991] BCC 379.
[169] (1988) 4 BCC 461.
[170] [1991] BCC 379.
[171] Companies Act 1985, s 114.

SHARE PREMIUMS: INTRODUCTION

The next part of this chapter looks at rules relating to share premiums. These rules would disappear under a no-par-value shares regime, although it would be necessary to put in place alternative safeguards in respect of sums raised through share issues.

FIXING THE ISSUE PRICE AND TREATMENT OF SHARE PREMIUMS

Shares can be issued at a price that is higher than their nominal or par value. Any excess over the nominal value of the share is called a share premium. Moneys representing share premiums must be accounted for in a share premium account and, save for certain specified purposes, they must be treated as if they were part of the company's paid-up share capital.[172] It falls to the directors as part of their general managerial power to fix the price at which shares are allotted. The safeguard against directors acting quixotically in setting issue prices is that they are fiduciaries to their company. It has been judicially stated that directors have a prima-facie duty to obtain the best price that they can for new share issues.[173] Rights issues are often made at a discount to the prevailing market price of the company's shares which is greater than is necessary to take account of the fact that the rights issues will increase the number of shares in the market. The purpose of the discount is to ensure the popularity of the issue and to prevent a commercially unacceptable proportion of it being left with the underwriters.[174] Occasionally companies dispense with underwriting altogether and make the issue at a very substantial discount to the prevailing market price. Even though directors have a prima-facie fiduciary duty to offer the shares at the maximum available price, in *Shearer v Bercain Ltd*[175] it was accepted that directors could legitimately offer a discount in order to ensure the success of a rights issue.

That share premiums should be regarded as capital was recommended by the Cohen Committee which reported in 1945.[176] The Cohen Committee's view was that the rules relating to the reduction of capital should be applied to the share premium account as if it were share capital, save for an exception allowing for the application of the share premium account in the paying up of bonus shares. Further exceptions for a company's preliminary expenses, for expenses, commissions and discounts in respect of issues of securities and for premiums payable on the redemption of securities were added to the legisla-

[172] Companies Act 1985, ss 130–134.

[173] *Lowry v Consolidated African Selection Trust Ltd* [1940] AC 648, HL, 479 *per* Lord Wright; *Shearer v Bercain Ltd* [1980] 3 All ER 295, 307–8.

[174] See further, Ch 18, at 630–33.

[175] *Shearer v Bercain Ltd* [1980] 3 All ER 295, 307: 'if a share is standing in the market at £100 and the company wishes to raise further capital from its shareholders, it may well offer them additional shares at say £90 in order to ensure that the whole of the new issue is taken up. Where there is no such reason, the directors will not be justified in issuing shares below the full value.'

[176] *Report of the Committee on Company Law Amendment* Cmd 6659 (1945) para 108.

tion which enacted the Cohen Committee's recommendations[177] during its passage through Parliament, because it was established that it was common City practice for share premiums to be used for these purposes.[178]

PERMISSIBLE USES FOR SHARE PREMIUMS

Share premiums represent a valuable source of corporate finance and they may be used by a company to finance its operations in the same way as any other fund. In specifying four uses for shares premiums, the Companies Act 1985 s 130 (2) does not preclude the application of share premiums in the normal course of business but, rather, provides special permission also to use those funds in ways that share capital cannot be used.

Bonus Issues

The share premium account may be applied by the company in paying up unissued shares to be allotted to members as fully paid shares.[179] Thus, if a company has issued 100 shares of £1 each at a premium of £1 per share, so that its share capital is £100 and it has a share premium account of £100, it may then issue a further 100 shares to its existing shareholders on the basis that the shares are to be issued fully paid by application of the share premium account; the end result is that the share premium account is reduced to zero but the company's paid-up share capital increases to £200. As far as individual shareholders are concerned the total value of their investment in the company remains constant but is made potentially more liquid by being represented by two shares, each of which has a lower individual value than the one share held before the bonus issue. A bonus issue does not result in capital leaving the company to the detriment of its creditors.

The permission in respect of bonus shares is limited to issues of fully-paid bonus shares, and does not extend to issues of partly-paid bonus shares or to issues of debentures.

The permission to use the share premium account in this way can be exploited by companies that want to return surplus cash to their shareholders. An established method of doing this is for the company to make a bonus issue of preference shares which are fully paid up by application of the share premium account and then to redeem or buy back those shares in accordance with the relevant provisions of the Companies Act 1985.[180]

Share buy backs are considered in Chapter 13.

177 Companies Act 1947, consolidated into the Companies Act 1948. Now Companies Act 1985, s 130 (2)(a) and (b).

178 *Hansard* (1946–47) Vol 146 (HL), cols 18–20 and *Hansard* (1946–47) Vol 146 (HL) col 760.

179 Companies Act 1985, s 130 (2).

180 Scott, T, 'Returning Value to Shareholders. Options for Companies' (1997) 8 (3) PLC 19.

Preliminary Expenses

The share premium account can also be used to write off a company's preliminary expenses.[181] The meaning of the phrase 'preliminary expenses' in this context has not arisen for determination by the courts. In nineteenth-century cases concerning applications by promoters of companies to be paid their preliminary expenses, such expenses were held to include the costs of obtaining a report on property to be acquired by a new company, fees paid to solicitors and brokers, and advertising and printing costs.[182] Sums paid to secure the services of certain persons as directors and fees paid to the finders of those prospective directors were also held to be allowable preliminary expenses of promoters.[183] In modern conditions, it is debatable to what extent the courts would countenance extensive use of the share premium account in writing off costs incurred in preliminary work prior to the formation of a company. Although it is in a different context and is obviously not conclusive for the purposes of the Companies Act 1985, note may be taken of the fact that for the purpose of VAT refunds[184] only certain expenses incurred before incorporation, and therefore before the company is registered for VAT, are refundable: within this category are legal and market research fees, but only if they are incurred not more than six months before the VAT registration date.

Expenses, Commissions and Discounts on Issues of Securities

The share premium account may be used to write off the expenses of an issue of shares or debentures. What would be included within the category of 'expenses of an issue' has again not attracted judicial scrutiny. Expenses incurred by a company in order to put itself in the position to issue securities—such as restructuring costs—may not be included.

The share premium account may be used to write off a commission paid on an issue of shares. Commissions on share issues are regulated by the Companies Act 1985, ss 97 and 98 where they are paid out of shares or capital money.[185] Although 'capital money' means the par value of shares and does not extend to share premiums, those restrictions are nevertheless relevant in this context. This is because the Companies Act 1985, s 130 (2)(b) allows the share premium account to be used to *write off* a commission which has been paid which implies that the commission must initially have been paid from some other fund. If it has been paid from profits the effect will simply be to reduce the amount of profit and there will be nothing to write off. However, if the commission has been paid from share capital the effect will be to create an amount in the company's accounts which may be written off. For example, if a company issues 100 shares of £1 each at a premium of 10p per share and

[181] Companies Act 1985, s 130 (2)(a).

[182] *Lydney and Wigpool Iron Ore Co v Bird* (1886) 33 Ch D 85, CA, 95 *per* Lindley LJ; *Emma Silver Mining Co v Grant* (1879) 11 Ch D 918, CA; *Bagnall v Carlton* (1877) 6 Ch D 371, CA.

[183] *Emma Silver Mining Co v Grant* (1879) 11 Ch D 918, CA, 941 *per* Jessell MR.

[184] Value Added Tax Regulations 1995 (SI 1995/2518) reg 111.

[185] Companies Act 1985, s 98 (1).

pays a commission of £10 in respect of the issue, the net result is that it has liabilities of £110 (share capital and share premium) and assets of £100 (the money raised by the issue). In order to balance the company's books £10 must be added to the assets side of the company's sheet: it is this amount which the share premium account may then be used to write off. Clearly, it is only lawful commissions, within the meaning of the Companies Act 1985, ss 97 and 98, that may be written off by application of the share premium account.

The Companies Act 1985, s 130 (2)(b) also permits the use of the share premium account to write off a discount allowed on an issue of shares or debentures. Since shares cannot be issued at a discount to their par value, the practical effect of this provision is limited to discounts on the issue of debentures. Historically, there was some uncertainty with regard to the use of the share premium account to write off such discounts.[186] The uncertainty turned on whether a discount on an issue of debentures was properly to be characterised as an incentive to take the securities—that is, a rebate on capital—or simply represented rolled-up interest. Under Financial Reporting Standard 4, *Accounting for Capital Instruments*, discounts on deep discount bonds (that is bonds which carry a low nominal rate of interest and which are issued at a discount to the value at which they will be redeemed) are to be treated as rolled up interest and, as such, charged to the profit and loss account rather than being written off directly against the share premium account.[187]

Debenture Redemption Premiums

According to the Companies Act 1985, the share premium account may also be used to provide for premiums payable on the redemption of debentures.[188] However, debenture redemption premiums are also subject to FRS 4 and must, therefore, be taken through the profit and loss account.

SHARE PREMIUMS AND NON-CASH CONSIDERATION

Until 1980 it was unclear whether a company had to create a share premium account whenever it issued shares for a non-cash consideration which was more valuable than the nominal value of the issued shares. In *Henry Head & Co Ltd v Roper Holdings Ltd*[189] a holding company acquired two companies by means of a share-for-share exchange. The actual value of the shares acquired was much greater than the nominal value of the shares issued as consideration and the directors of the holding company were advised that they had to account for this excess by crediting it to a share premium account. This advice was upheld by the court. Despite this ruling, some practitioners continued to believe the obligation to create a share premium account in this type of

[186] Johnson, B, and Patient, M, *Accounting Provisions of The Companies Act 1985* (1985) paras 9.30–9.40.

[187] Johnson, B, and Holgate, P, *The Coopers & Lybrand Manual of Accounting* (1995, looseleaf) paras 18.211–18.213.

[188] Companies Act 1985, s 130 (2).

[189] [1952] Ch 124.

situation could be avoided.[190] The arguments on which that practice was based were finally considered by the court in *Shearer v Bercain Ltd.*[191] Essentially, those arguments were: (i) it was for the company to determine the terms of issue and it was not obliged to obtain a premium merely because investors might be willing to pay it; and (ii) if the sale and purchase agreement provided for the assets to be sold at a price equal to the par value of the shares to be issued as consideration, there was no obligation on the company to create a share premium account.

Walton J rejected these arguments. In his view it was the prima-facie duty of directors to obtain the best possible price for the shares.[192] The obligation to create a share premium account was not optional and could not be avoided by stating that the shares were issued at their nominal value; if the assets acquired in consideration of the issue of shares had an actual value greater than the nominal value of the consideration shares then, irrespective of the terms on which those shares had been issued, the company was subject to a mandatory requirement to create a share premium account.

As a result of the decision in *Shearer v Bercain Ltd* pressure was brought to bear on Parliament to provide some relief from the obligation to create a share premium account. This was done in the Companies Act 1981 and the relevant reliefs are now to be found in the Companies Act 1985, ss 131 and 132.

Merger Relief: Companies Act 1985, s 131

Merger relief is available in circumstances where one company acquires the share capital of another company by issuing its shares to the shareholders of the target company. In those circumstances, provided certain conditions are satisfied, there is no obligation to credit to a share premium account the amount by which the value of the acquired shares exceeds the nominal value of the shares issued by way of consideration.[193]

The precise conditions which must be satisfied in order for merger relief to apply are:

- the issuing company must secure at least a 90 per cent equity holding in another company; and
- this holding must be secured pursuant to an arrangement[194] providing for the allotment of equity shares in the issuing company on terms that the consideration for the allotted shares is to be provided by the issue or transfer to the issuing company of equity shares in the other company; or by the cancellation of any such shares not held by the issuing company.

[190] For an account of the development of market practice and corresponding regulation in relation to share premiums see Napier, C, and Noke, C, 'Premiums and Pre-Acquisition Profits: The Legal and Accounting Professions and Business Combinations' (1991) 54 MLR 810.

[191] [1980] 3 All ER 295.

[192] Following Lord Wright in *Lowry (Inspector of Taxes) v Consolidated African Selection Trust Ltd* [1940] AC 648, HL.

[193] The issuing company's balance sheet need not record any amount representing a premium in respect of the issued shares: Companies Act 1985, s 133 (1).

[194] Companies Act 1985, s 131 (7).

Thus if a company seeks to acquire all of the equity shares in a target company and offers the shareholders in the target one of its equity shares in exchange for each of the target's equity shares, merger relief will be available if and when the issuing company acquires 90 per cent of the target's equity pursuant to the arrangement. Equity shares for this purpose are shares which in respect of either dividends or capital, or both, carry rights to participate generally in distributions.[195] If a target company's equity share capital is divided into different classes of shares (for example ordinary shares which are fully participating as to both dividends and capital and preference shares which are fully participating as to dividend but participating only for a fixed amount in any capital distribution), for merger relief to apply the conditions must be satisfied separately in respect of each class.[196] If non-equity shares[197] of the target are also included in the arrangement, the acquisition of those shares does not go towards satisfying the conditions but, if the conditions are otherwise satisfied, merger relief is extended to any shares allotted in return for the non-equity shares of the target.[198]

What is meant by securing 'at least a 90 per cent equity holding in another company in pursuance of . . . an arrangement' is amplified by the Companies Act 1985, s 131 (4). The issuing company[199] must end up holding equity shares in the target of an aggregate nominal value equal to 90 per cent or more of the nominal value of the target's total equity share capital. However, whilst the holding must be arrived at as a consequence of an acquisition or cancellation of target company shares pursuant to the arrangement, it is not required that all or any of the shares comprising the issuing company's holding of target company shares be acquired pursuant to the arrangement. Thus if the issuing company holds a number of target company shares prior to entering into an arrangement to issue its own shares in consideration for the cancellation of target company shares and, as a result of such cancellation, the size of the issuing company's original holding becomes equal to 90 per cent or more of the nominal value of the target's (diminished) equity share capital, merger relief conditions will have been satisfied. Similarly, where the arrangement is effected by means of a share-for-share exchange, the shares acquired by the issuing company pursuant to the exchange can be added to its prior holding of target company shares in order to ascertain whether the 90 per cent condition has been met.

The conditions for merger relief to apply do not preclude the acquirer from offering the target company's shareholders a mixed consideration, which is partly in the form of shares and partly in the form of cash or other assets. To the extent that shares of the acquirer are issued by way of consideration, merger relief can apply in respect of those shares.

Why is merger relief important? One reason relates to pre-acquisition profits of the target company and whether they can be made available for

[195] Ibid, ss 131 (7)(a) and 744.

[196] Ibid, s 131 (5).

[197] Defined by Companies Act 1985, s 131 (7)(b).

[198] Companies Act 1985, s 131 (3).

[199] Shares held by the issuing company's holding company or subsidiary, or by other subsidiaries of its holding company, or by its or their nominees, are to be regarded as held by the issuing company: Companies Act 1985, s 131 (6).

distribution by the acquirer.[200] If the target company has distributable profits it is free to declare a dividend after the acquisition in favour of its new parent company. However, whether the acquirer, the new parent company, can treat the dividend it has received as a realised profit which it can, in turn, distribute to its own shareholders, depends on whether the effect of the dividend paid by the target is to reduce the value of the acquirer's investment in the target company. If the acquirer's accounts have recorded the value of its investment in the target as the fair value of the consideration paid (that is share capital and share premium), it may be difficult for the company's accountants to avoid the conclusion that value taken out of the target (in the form of a dividend) must be reflected in a reduction in the value of the acquirer's investment, with the result that the intra-group dividend does not, in fact, give rise to a distributable profit. However, if merger relief is claimed so that the value of the investment in the target is recorded as being the nominal value of the consideration shares, since the actual value of the investment is likely to be significantly greater than the book value, the parent company will not have to use the dividend to reflect a diminution in the value of the investment and can instead treat it as a realised profit.

Group Relief: Companies Act 1985, s 132

A further relief from the obligation to establish a share premium account is provided by the Companies Act 1985, s 132 in respect of group reconstructions. This relief applies where the issuing company:

- is a wholly owned subsidiary; and
- allots shares to its holding company or another wholly owned subsidiary of its holding company in consideration for the transfer of assets (other than cash) to the issuing company; these assets may be assets of any company in the group comprising the holding company and all its wholly owned subsidiaries.[201]

In these circumstances, where the shares in the issuing company are issued at a premium there is no obligation to carry the premium to a share premium to the extent that it exceeds what is referred to as the minimum premium value. Broadly, the minimum premium value means the amount by which the net book value of the required assets exceeds the nominal value of the shares issued by way of consideration.

The minimum premium value is found by taking the value of the assets transferred as being the cost of those assets to the transferor company or the amount at which those assets are recorded in the transferor's books immediately before the transfer, whichever is the lesser,[202] deducting from that the value (that is the amount recorded in the company's books immediately before the transfer) of any liabilities[203] assumed by the issuing company as part of the consideration,[204] and then comparing the resulting figure to the

[200] Johnson, B, and Holgate, P, *The Coopers & Lybrand Manual of Accounting* (1995, looseleaf) paras 26.33–26.36.
[201] Companies Act 1985, s 130 (1). [202] Ibid, s 132 (5)(a). [203] Ibid, s 132 (5)(b).
[204] Ibid, s 132 (4).

nominal value of the issued shares: the minimum premium value means the amount (if any) by which the base value of the consideration for the shares allotted exceeds the aggregate nominal value of the shares.[205]

Any amount over the minimum premium value may be disregarded in determining the amount at which any shares or other consideration provided for the shares issued is to be included in the company's balance sheet.[206]

Other Reliefs

The Secretary of State is empowered[207] to make provision, by statutory instrument, for further relief from the requirement to create a share premium account, or for restricting or modifying any of the reliefs provided by the Companies Act itself.

PAID-UP SHARE CAPITAL

A company's paid-up share capital means the amount of capital money it has received in respect of its issued shares. Unless the context indicates otherwise (as in the sections of the Companies Act 1985 that are concerned with payment for shares) it does not include share premiums.[208] There is no legal requirement for a private company to have any paid-up share capital before it commences business. Such constraint as there is stems from the difficulties that the proprietors of a business may encounter in obtaining credit facilities if they have not demonstrated their own confidence in the business by investing their own money in its shares. Figures indicating that the vast majority of companies operate with a paid-up share capital of £100 or less strongly suggest that external creditors do not attach much importance to the amount of a company's paid-up share capital. They can protect their interests alternatively by taking personal guarantees from the operators of the business and security over the assets of the company and those of its operators.[209]

For public companies there is a requirement that shares must not be allotted except as paid up at least as to one-quarter of its nominal value and the whole of any premium on it.[210] The combination of this requirement with that which requires a public company to have a minimum allotted capital of at least £50,000 means that a public company must have a minimum paid-up share capital of at least £12,500. A public company, incorporated as such, will not receive the certificate entitling it to do business or to exercise any borrowing

205 Ibid, s 133 (1). 206 Ibid, s 132 (3). 207 Ibid, s 134.

208 This follows from Companies Act 1985, s 130 (3) which requires share premiums to be treated *as if they were* part of the paid-up share capital (emphasis added).

209 Of the 1.25 million registered UK companies as at 31 March 1997, 1.1 million had an issued share capital of less than £1,000 and, of these, 80 per cent had £100 or less: *The Euro: Redenomination of Share Capital* (DTI Consultative Document) (1998) para 1.7.

210 Companies Act 1985, s 101 (1). There is an exception for shares allotted in pursuance of an employees share scheme: Companies Act 1985, s 101 (2). These requirements implement Second Directive, arts 9.1 and 26.

powers if these requirements are not complied with.[211] If a public company does business or exercises borrowing powers without this certificate, it and those of its officers who are in default are liable to a fine.[212] For a private company to be re-registered as a public company, it must also have a paid-up share capital of at least £12,500 at the time when it passes the special resolution to change its status.[213]

The minimum paid-up share capital requirement for public companies is evidently intended to ensure that these companies have some substance behind them.[214] However, without a corresponding restriction concerning the amount, or proportion, of indebtedness which public companies are permitted to have, the significance of this requirement is limited. It is through covenants in loan agreements and borrowing limits in articles of association rather than the general requirements of company law that the ratio of debt to equity in public companies is typically regulated.

CALLED-UP SHARE CAPITAL

Called-up share capital means:[215]

i. so much of its share capital as equals the aggregate amount of the calls made on its shares (whether or not those calls have been paid);
ii. any share capital paid up without being called; and
iii. any share capital to be paid on a specified future date under the articles, the terms of allotment or any other arrangements for payment of those shares.

Because it is common for shares to be issued fully paid, often the amount of a company's called-up share capital will equal that of its paid-up share capital. However, it could be a larger amount where shares are issued partly paid.

Where shares are issued on a partly-paid basis, the terms of the allotment may provide for payment of the balance by instalments. In that case limb (iii) of the definition would allow the outstanding amounts to be included in the company's called-up share capital. Alternatively, no provision may be made for payment by instalments in which case the company will rely on a provision in its articles, such as Table A, art 12, which allows the directors to make calls on shares at any time. Table A, art 13 provides that the call is made when the directors pass their resolution to that effect: at that point limb (i) of the defini-

[211] Companies Act 1985, s 117. A statutory declaration confirming compliance with this requirement must be filed with the registrar of companies: Companies Act 1985, s 117 (3).

[212] Companies Act 1985, s 117 (7). The validity of transactions is not affected but directors may incur personal liability to indemnify other parties in respect of loss or damage suffered as a consequence of the company's unauthorised business or borrowing.

[213] Companies Act 1985, s 45.

[214] A share is paid up in cash, as defined in Companies Act 1985, s 738 (2), where the consideration for it is an undertaking to pay cash at a later date. Applying this definition, a public company could satisfy the minimum capital requirement without actually receiving any cash. However, it is understood that the registrar of companies will not accept for registration or re-registration as a public company a company which seeks to satisfy the minimum capital requirement in this way.

[215] Companies Act 1985, s 737. This applies except where the contrary intention appears.

tion would bring the called amounts into the company's called-up share capital. Just as share premiums are not part of a company's paid-up share capital, nor are they within its called-up share capital.

An important situation where attention has to focus on the amount of a public company's called-up share capital results from the Companies Act 1985, s 142.[216] This section provides that where the net assets of a public company are half or less of its called-up share capital, the directors must, no later than twenty-eight days from the earliest day on which that fact is known to a director of the company, duly convene an extraordinary general meeting of the company for a date not later than fifty-six days from that day. The purpose of this requirement is simply to oblige the directors to publicise the company's financial difficulties; hence, s 142 does not prescribe in detail what the company must do at this meeting beyond stating that the purpose of the meeting is to consider whether any, and if so what, steps should be taken to deal with the situation.[217]

The practical consequences for a company which is forced to publicise its financial difficulties in accordance with the Companies Act 1985, s 142 may be very serious. If the company is listed or quoted on the London Stock Exchange it will have to report the bad news through the Exchange's news service and, even if it is not listed or quoted, the news of its problems is unlikely to escape the attention of the general media unless the company is very small. How the holding of a meeting in accordance with the Companies Act 1985, s 142 can bring difficulties to a head is illustrated by the saga of Ferranti International plc. In September 1993 Ferranti plc was forced into calling an extraordinary general meeting in accordance with the section. The immediate consequence of the announcement of the need to hold this meeting was that the market value of Ferranti shares, which had been trading at 121.4p, plunged by almost one-third.[218] At the meeting, the shareholders voted in favour of the board's proposal to do nothing[219] but within a few weeks the crisis deepened with a further dramatic drop in the company's share price after the news of a tentative bid for Ferranti which valued the company at the price of 1p per share.[220]

STOCK

This is really little more than a footnote to the chapter as it is rare for UK companies to have stock. A company cannot issue stock[221] but it may, in accordance with the Companies Act 1985, s 121, convert its fully paid shares into stock. Stock is said to have two advantages over shares. First, it is possible to deal in fractions of stock but it is not possible to deal in fractions of shares. This advantage is, however, more theoretical than real. The market might want to be able to trade in a fraction of a share because the price of the whole

216 This implements Second Directive, art 17.

217 Art 17 is slightly more specific in that it states that the meeting should consider whether the company should be wound up or any other measures taken.

218 *Daily Telegraph*, 14 September 1993.

219 *The Times*, 8 October 1993.

220 *Guardian*, 27 October 1993.

221 *Re Home and Foreign Investment and Agency Co Ltd* [1912] 1 Ch 72.

unit is high. However, rather than converting its shares into stock, the company can meet this demand by sub-dividing its existing shares into new shares with lower par values that those which they replace.[222]

The second supposed advantage of stock is that stock does not have to be numbered. This is administratively more convenient than shares which do have to be numbered. However, where all of the issued shares of a class are fully paid and rank *pari passu* for all purposes, none of those shares need thereafter have a distinguishing number so long as it remains fully paid and ranks *pari passu* for all purposes with all shares of the same class for the time being issued and fully paid up.[223] It is uncommon for shares to be issued on a partly-paid basis which means that advantage can normally be taken of this exception.

In 1962 the Jenkins Committee expressed the view that since the 1948 Companies Act had introduced the exception allowing fully-paid shares not to be numbered, the advantages of converting from shares to stock had become negligible. The Committee recommended that references to stock should be eliminated from the companies legislation;[224] but this reform has never been enacted.

[222] Each share must have a par value which is a monetary amount but it need not be an amount which is capable of being paid in legal tender so it could be as little as a fraction or a percentage of 1p: *Re Scandinavian Bank Group plc* [1987] 2 All ER 70, [1987] BCC 93.

[223] Companies Act 1985, s 182 (2).

[224] *Report of the Company Law Committee*, Cmnd 1749, (1962) para 472.

9

Rights Attaching to Shares

THE LEGAL NATURE OF A SHARE

There is no comprehensive legal definition of a share[1] but in *Borland's Trustee v Steel*[2] Farwell J described a share in the following terms:

> A share is the measure of a shareholder in the company measured by a sum of money, for the purposes of liability in the first place, and of interest in the second, but also consisting of a series of mutual covenants entered into by all the shareholders inter se. The contract contained in the articles is one of the original incidents of the share. A share is not a sum of money . . . but is an interest measured by a sum of money and made up of the various rights contained in the contract.

This description makes it clear that a shareholder is an investor: he pays a sum of money in the hope of earning of return. The shareholder's financial interest is in the company itself and it does not amount to a direct interest in the company's assets. These assets belong to the company which is a separate legal person. Thus in *Macaura v Northern Assurance Co Ltd*[3] it was held that a shareholder did not have an insurable interest in the company's property.[4]

The financial rights attaching to shares are discussed in detail in this chapter. In outline, a shareholder expects to earn a return on the investment in the form of dividends and capital growth. An investment in shares is infinite and continues until the company is liquidated or effects a reduction of capital or share buy back affecting those shares.[5] Where shares have a nominal or par value, this is the minimum amount that a shareholder would hope to receive back from the company in the event of liquidation. However, unless displaced by the terms of issue, there is a presumption that all shareholders are also entitled to share equally in any surplus assets of the company which remain after all of its debts and liabilities have been discharged and the nominal amount of the share capital has been repaid to shareholders.[6]

[1] Pennington, RR, 'Can Shares in Companies be Defined?' (1989) 10 Co Law 140.

[2] [1901] 1 Ch 279, 288. This description was cited with approval in *IRC v Crossman* [1937] AC 26, HL, 66 *per* Lord Russell of Killowen.

[3] [1925] AC 619, HL.

[4] See also *Bank voor Handel en Scheepuaart NV v Slatford* [1953] 1 QB 248, CA (property held by a Dutch limited company bank with Hungarian shareholders did not fall within the scope of a provision concerned with property 'belonging to or held or managed on behalf of' a Hungarian); *John Foster & Sons Ltd v IRC* [1894] 1 QB 516, CA (conveyance of property from individuals to a company in which they held all of the shares was liable to stamp duty).

[5] The investment remains constant even though the identity of the shareholder may change from time to time as shares are bought and sold.

[6] *Birch v Cropper* (1889) 14 App Cas 525, HL.

Where shares do not have a par value, the default rule is that shareholders are entitled to share equally in whatever remains after the debts and liabilities have been paid. The amount of the return is the same in either case: if a company has assets remaining of £10,000 and ten shareholders each of whom owns one share, then each shareholder will be entitled to receive £1,000 irrespective of any par value that the shares may have. Present-day English law does not permit no-par-value shares, but they are commonplace in the USA and in some Commonwealth countries.[7] Entitlement to the residual value of an asset is viewed as a badge of ownership and this is a reason why in legal terms shareholders are generally regarded as being the owners of the company.[8]

By virtue of the Companies Act 1985, s 14 a contractual relationship subsists between a company and its members[9] and also between its members amongst themselves.[10] The persons who are members of a company are the subscribers to its memorandum and those persons who agree[11] to become members of the company and whose names are entered on the register of members. The directors should enter the names of those persons who have acquired shares in the company, through allotment or transfer, on the register of members and, if they fail to do so, the court can order that the register of members be rectified.[12] The terms of the statutory contract between a company and its members, and between the members amongst themselves, are contained in the company's memorandum and articles.[13] This statutory contract is of a special kind, its distinctive features being outlined by Steyn LJ in *Bratton Seymour Service Company Ltd v Oxborough*[14] as follows:

(i) it derives its binding force not from a bargain struck between the parties but from the terms of a statute;
(ii) it is binding only insofar as it affects the rights and obligations between the company and the members acting in their capacity as members;
(iii) it can be altered by a special resolution without the consent of all the contracting parties;

[7] See further, Ch 8 above, at 282–6.

[8] See further Ch 4 above, at 131–3.

[9] *Oakbank Oil Co v Crum* (1882) 8 App Cas 65, HL; *Welton v Saffery* [1897] AC 299, HL; *Hickman v Kent or Romney Marsh Sheepbreeders Association* [1915] 1 Ch 881; *Bratton Seymour Service Co Ltd v Oxborough* [1992] BCC 471, CA.

[10] *Wood v Odessa Waterworks Co* (1889) 42 Ch D 636, 642; *Rayfield v Hands* [1960] Ch 1. On the history of the statutory contract: *Shareholder Remedies A Consultation Paper* (Law Commission Consultation Paper No 142) (1996) paras 2.6–2.8.

[11] The agreement need not be contractual: *Re Nuneaton Borough Association Football Club* (1989) 5 BCC 377.

[12] Companies Act 1985, s 359. The names of the holders of shares that are dealt in through CREST, the electronic trading system, must still be entered on the register of members notwithstanding that the shares are in paperless form: Uncertificated Securities Regulations 1995 (SI 1995/3272) reg 19.

[13] Such terms are more commonly found in articles than in a memorandum: *Andrews v Gas Meter Co* [1897] 1 Ch 361, CA; *British and American Trustee and Finance Corporation v Couper* [1894] AC 399, HL, 416 *per* Lord Macnaghten; *Campbell v Rofe* [1933] AC 91, PC (but provisions in the memorandum, which could have been in the articles, can now be altered in accordance with Companies Act 1985, s 17).

[14] [1992] BCC 471, CA, 475 *per* Steyn LJ.

(vii) it is not defeasible on the grounds of misrepresentation, common law mistake, mistake in equity, undue influence or duress; and
(v) it cannot be rectified on the grounds of mistake.

To this list can be added the decision in *Bratton Seymour* itself: a term cannot be implied to articles of association from extrinsic circumstances on the grounds of business efficacy but this does not prevent the implication of a term purely from the language of the document itself.[15]

A distinctive feature of the statutory contract is that not all of the provisions of the memorandum and articles can be enforced. There are two limitations. First, only those rights and obligations in the memorandum and articles which affect members in their capacity as members can be enforced as part of the s 14 contract.[16] Thus if an article purports to give someone the right to hold or make appointments to an office or position in the company, such as company solicitor[17] or director,[18] those articles will not be enforceable under the statutory contract. Secondly, even a failure to comply with a provision of a memorandum and articles which does affect members in their capacity as members does not necessarily entitle an aggrieved party to seek a contractual remedy. The court will not act in vain and if the failure amounts simply to a procedural irregularity, the court will stand back and allow the company to take steps to remedy the position itself. What amounts to a procedural irregularity has to be considered on a case-by-case basis as there is little consistency in the reported decisions.[19]

A shareholder may seek a declaration[20] or an injunction against the

15 See also *Stanham v NTA* (1989) 15 ACLR 87, NSW SC EqD, 90–1 *per* Young J.

16 *Hickman v Kent or Romney Marsh Sheepbreeders Association* [1915] 1 Ch 881; *Beattie v E & F Beattie Ltd* [1938] 1 Ch 708, CA. There is extensive academic literature debating the proposition that a member should be able to enforce all articles of association (see in particular Wedderburn, KW, 'Shareholders' Rights and the Rule in *Foss v Harbottle*' [1957] CLJ 193; Goldberg, GD, 'The Enforcement of Outsider Rights under Section 20 of the Companies Act 1948' (1972) 33 MLR 362; Prentice, GN, 'The Enforcement of Outsider Rights' (1980) 1 Co Law 179; Gregory, R, 'The Section 20 Contract' (1981) 44 MLR 526; Goldberg, GD, 'The Controversy on the Section 20 Contract Revisited' (1985) 48 MLR 121; and Drury, RR, 'The Relative Nature of a Shareholder's Right to Enforce the Company Contract' [1986] CLJ 219. However, although there is a House of Lords decision which, on its facts, supports the proposition that members should be able to enforce all articles (*Quin & Axtens Ltd v Salmon* [1909] AC 442, HL), when specifically required to consider the point, the courts have tended to adopt a more restrictive approach and the accepted view is as stated by Steyn LJ in the *Bratton Seymour* decision.

17 *Eley v Positive Government Security Life Assurance Co Ltd* (1875–6) 1 Ex D 88, CA.

18 *Browne v La Trinidad* (1887) 37 Ch D 1, CA.

19 For example compare *MacDougall v Gardiner* (1876) 1 Ch D 13, CA where the court refused to declare that a poll was improperly refused and *Pender v Lushington* (1877) 6 Ch D 70 where a failure to allow certain votes to be cast was held to be remediable by way of injunction. On the same side of the line as the *MacDougall* decision are cases such as *Normandy v Ind Coope & Co Ltd* [1908] 1 Ch 84 (inadequate notice of general meeting) and *Devlin v Slough Estates Ltd* [1983] BCLC 497 (allegedly defective accounts). Cases on the *Pender* side of the line include *Kaye v Croydon Tramways Co* [1898] 1 Ch 358, CA (notice of meetings) and *Henderson v Bank of Australasia* (1890) 45 Ch D 330 (moving amendments to resolutions).

20 *Oakbank Oil Co v Crum* (1882) 8 App Cas 65, HL. For further discussion of this issue: Baxter, CR, 'Irregular Company Meetings' [1976] JBL 323; Bastin, NA, 'The Enforcement of a Member's Rights' [1977] JBL 12; Smith, RJ, 'Minority Shareholders and Corporate Irregularities' (1978) 41 MLR 147. The Law Commission, having reviewed and consulted upon this matter, has concluded that no hardship is being caused by any difficulty in identifying personal rights conferred by the articles and, accordingly, has not recommended reform: *Shareholder Remedies* (Law Commission Report No 246) (1997) para 7.12.

company for breach of the statutory contract.[21] It is possible that a shareholder may also be able to claim damages from the company. The Companies Act 1985, s 111A provides that a person is not debarred from obtaining damages or other compensation by reason only of his holding or having held shares in the company. This reverses the decision of the House of Lords in *Houldsworth v City of Glasgow Bank*[22] where it was held that a person who had been induced to take shares in a company by a fraudulent misrepresentation could not claim damages for deceit whilst he remained a shareholder. However, whilst the reversal of the *Houldsworth* decision opens up the possibility of a damages claim, there is no clear authority establishing that damages may be claimed for breach of the statutory contract and, given the special nature of this contract, it should not be assumed that damages would necessarily be available. In any event circumstances where damages for breach of the statutory contract would be more than nominal would probably be rare. The company is also entitled to seek contractual remedies against shareholders who are in breach, or may be proposing to breach, the contractual provisions of the memorandum and articles.[23]

Until the decision in *Rayfield v Hands*[24] there was a residual doubt whether individual shareholders could sue each other directly for breach of the statutory contract. Dicta in *Wood v Odessa Waterworks Co*[25] supported the view that such actions were permissible, but a comment (in a dissenting judgment) in *Welton v Saffery*[26] suggested that all actions in respect of the statutory contract had to be mediated through the company. In the *Rayfield* decision this comment was described as 'somewhat cryptic'[27] and it was held that, even where the company was not joined as a party to the action, petitioning members were entitled as against fellow members to a contractual remedy. The circumstances where a member might wish to sue fellow members are likely to be fairly limited.

Breach of the provisions of the memorandum and articles may also form the basis of a petition under the Companies Act 1985, s 459. Under this section a member of the company may apply to the court for relief where the company's affairs are being or have been conducted in a manner which is unfairly prejudicial to the interests of the members generally or some part of its members. Whilst determination of the existence or otherwise of unfairly prejudicial conduct depends on the particular facts of each case, in principle failure to comply with the company's constitution could form the basis of such a claim.[28]

A share is a chose in action[29] and it is capable of being transferred. Except for shares that have been admitted to the electronic dealing system, CREST,

[21] *Pender v Lushington* (1877) 6 Ch D 70; *Johnson v Lyttle's Iron Agency* (1877) 5 Ch D 687, CA; *Wood v Odessa Waterworks Co* (1889) 42 Ch D 636.
[22] (1880) 5 App Cas 317, HL.
[23] *Hickman v Kent or Romney Marsh Sheepbreeders Association* [1915] 1 Ch 881, 897.
[24] [1960] Ch 1.
[25] (1889) 42 Ch D 636.
[26] *Welton v Saffery* [1897] AC 299, HL, 315 *per* Lord Herschell.
[27] [1960] Ch 1, 5.
[28] *Re Saul D Harrison & Sons plc* [1995] 1 BCLC 14, CA.
[29] *Colonial Bank v Whinney* (1886) 11 App Cas 426, HL.

an instrument of transfer is required.[30] The Stock Transfer Act 1963 provides a simplified form of transfer in respect of fully paid shares. Articles of association may restrict the transferability of shares. Transfer restrictions are commonly included in the articles of private companies, for example a right of pre-emption in favour of the remaining shareholders or a power for the directors to refuse to register a transfer to a person of whom they do not approve. The purpose of such restrictions is not hard to detect: it is to prevent control of the company passing outside a limited circle.[31] In respect of shares which are listed on the London Stock Exchange *The Listing Rules* require that fully-paid shares be free from any restrictions on the right of transfer (except any restriction imposed on a shareholder who is in default in complying with a notice under the Companies Act 1985, s 212).[32] Listed partly-paid shares may be subject to restrictions provided that the restrictions are not such as to prevent dealings in the shares from taking place on an open and proper basis.[33] In exceptional circumstances approved by the Stock Exchange, a company may take powers to disapprove the transfer of any shares, provided that the exercise of such powers does not disturb the market.[34]

No share certificates are issued in respect of shares that have been admitted to CREST. For non-CREST shares, share certificates must be issued to a shareholder within two months of the allotment or, as the case may be, transfer of shares to him.[35] A share certificate executed under the common seal of the company[36] is, in England and Wales, prima-facie evidence of title.[37]

FINANCIAL INCIDENTS OF SHARES: ORDINARY SHARES

An ordinary share is the default share in the sense that the rights enjoyed by ordinary shares are those which attach to all shares unless contrary provision is made when the shares are issued or by subsequent variation of the rights attaching to the shares. A company which wants to issue shares with different rights must have power to that effect in its memorandum or articles[38] so as to displace the presumption that all shareholders are to be treated equally.[39] A company may amend its constitution to take this power if it is omitted from the constitution as originally drafted provided this amendment is not

[30] Companies Act 1985, s 183. CREST is governed by the Uncertificated Securities Regulations 1995 (SI 1995/3272) made under Companies Act 1989, s 207 (9).

[31] Until 1980 there was an obligation on private companies to include restrictions on share transfers in their articles.

[32] *The Listing Rules*, ch 13, app 1 para 6. [33] Ibid. [34] Ibid, para 7.

[35] Companies Act 1985, s 185. For the timing of the issue of share certificates where shares are withdrawn from CREST and converted into certificated form: Uncertificated Securities Regulations 1995 (SI 1995/3272) reg 26 (3).

[36] A certificate executed under the common seal includes a certificate which is signed by a director and secretary or by two directors and which is expressed to be executed by the company: Companies Act 1985, s 36A (4).

[37] Companies Act 1985, s 186.

[38] *Andrews v Gas Meter Co* [1897] 1 Ch 361, CA settled that the power did not have to be in the memorandum.

[39] *Campbell v Rofe* [1933] AC 98, PC; *British and American Trustee and Finance Corporation v Couper* [1894] AC 399, HL, 416 *per* Lord Macnaghten.

prohibited by its memorandum.[40] The power to issue shares with different rights now usually appears in articles of association rather than in the memorandum.[41]

A distinctive feature of the financial rights attaching to an ordinary share is that, in respect of both income and capital, the return to the holder is not fixed: dividends may vary depending upon the profitability of the company, and the ultimate capital return may be greater than the amount which was originally invested. This serves to distinguish ordinary shares from preference shares which in respect of dividends and/or capital may enjoy a priority to ordinary shares, but only for a fixed amount. This description of the nature of the financial rights attaching to an ordinary share would not be accurate in a company which has deferred or founders shares because in that case, the ordinary shareholders would receive only a fixed return and the balance would go to the holders of the deferred/founders shares. Deferred/founders shares are now rarely encountered and they are not discussed further.

As amongst themselves, the holders of ordinary shares are entitled to share equally in dividends and in capital distributions. This simple statement is as much as needs to be said in the straightforward, and most common, case where shares are paid up in full:[42] the return available can simply be divided by the number of shares in issue in order to arrive at each shareholder's entitlement. The position is more complicated where there are partly-paid shares because in that situation it becomes necessary to ask whether it is their nominal value or the amounts paid up on them that is to be taken as the basis for determining the return. For example, if a company has 10 ordinary shares with a nominal value of £1 each, 5 of which have paid up in full and 5 of which have been paid up as to 50p, using nominal values, the return on each share out of a total distribution of £100 would be £10 but, using paid-up amounts, it would be £13.33 on the shares that have been paid up in full and £6.66 on the partly-paid shares.

The company's articles of association may include express provision for these matters or rely on the statutory provision which makes Table A the articles of a company except in so far as it is excluded or modified.[43] Where the articles are silent, certain default rules established by case law apply.

Default Capital Rights of Ordinary Shares

The classic case which establishes the default rule applicable in respect of the distribution of any surplus which remains after paid-up capital has been

[40] *Andrews v Gas Meter Co* [1897] 1 Ch 361, CA.

[41] For example, Table A, art 2.

[42] Paid-up share capital means the amount of the nominal share capital that has been paid to the company and it does not include share premiums: see Ch 8 above, at 311–2. It would not be feasible to measure an ordinary shareholder's entitlement to income and capital by reference to an amount which included a share premium paid when the share was first subscribed. Over time, it is likely that various share issues at different prices will have taken place and it would normally be impossible to trace back to the initial price at which a share was allotted because fully-paid shares are not numbered and have no other individual distinguishing mark.

[43] Companies Act 1985, s 8.

repaid is *Birch v Cropper*.[44] In this case it was held by the House of Lords that any such surplus is distributable equally amongst the ordinary shareholders in proportion to the nominal value of their shares. Lord Macnaghten explained:[45]

> Every person who becomes a member of a company limited by shares of an equal amount becomes entitled to a proportionate part in the capital of the company and, unless it be otherwise provided by the regulations of the company, entitled, as a necessary consequence, to the same proportionate part in all of the property of the company, including its uncalled capital.[46]

Table A does not contain any provision modifying this default rule. It would, however, be open to a company to customise its own articles to provide for capital distributions to be made by reference to the amounts paid up on shares or some other basis.

Default Dividend Rights of Ordinary Shares[47]

Table A, art 104 provides for dividends to be determined by reference by the amount paid up on shares. This displaces the rule established by case law that entitlement to dividend distributions is based on the nominal value of the shares held by each shareholder.[48] The case-law rule would apply only where a company has excluded the relevant provision of Table A but has not included express provision for dividend entitlements in its customised articles. This is likely to be a rare occurrence so, in effect, Table A represents the default position. If the ordinary shares in a company are all fully paid, the dividend can be expressed simply as the amount available for distribution to the holders of the ordinary shares divided by the number of shares in issue.

Dividends must be paid in cash unless the articles otherwise provide.[49] Table A, art 105 authorises the payment of dividends in kind. Table A also sets out the standard position governing the procedural aspects of dividend payments. Art 102 provides that the company may declare a dividend in accordance with the respect of rights to the members, whilst art 103 allows the directors to pay interim dividends. Neither of these provisions means that the holder of an ordinary share has an absolute right to claim dividends. An ordinary shareholder only becomes entitled to a final dividend under art 102 when that dividend has been declared,[50] whilst the payment of interim dividends is,

44 (1889) 14 App Cas 525, HL. The default loss-sharing rule is also based on nominal values (*Re Hodges' Distillery ex parte Maude* (1870) 6 Ch App 51, CA) but this can be displaced by articles of association (*Re Kinatan (Borneo) Rubber Ltd* [1923] 1 Ch 124).

45 (1889) 14 App Cas 525, HL, 543.

46 'Amount' in this context clearly means nominal amount: *Re Driffield Gas Light Co* [1898] 1 Ch 451.

47 Dividends are considered in more detail in Ch 12.

48 *Oakbank Oil Co v Crum* (1882) 8 App Cas 65, HL. That it is possible to displace this rule is confirmed by Companies Act 1985, s 119 (c).

49 *Wood v Odessa Waterworks Co* (1889) 42 Ch D 636.

50 *Bond v Barrow Haematite Steel Co* [1902] 1 Ch 353.

under art 103, at the discretion of the board. Articles could dispense with the need for dividends to be declared[51] but that would be unusual.

In *Potel v IRC*[52] Brightman J outlined the entitlement of shareholders to dividends in the following terms.

i. If a final dividend is declared, a date when such dividend shall be paid can also be specified.[53]
ii. If a final dividend is declared by a company without any stipulation as to the date of payment, the declaration of the dividend creates an immediate debt.[54]
iii. If a final dividend is declared and is expressed to be payable at a future date a shareholder has no right to enforce payment until the due date for payment arrives.[55]
iv. In the case of an interim dividend which the board has resolved to pay, it is open to the board at any time before payment to review the decision and resolve not to pay the dividend.[56] The resolution to pay an interim dividend does not create an immediate debt.
v. If directors resolve to pay an interim dividend they can, at or after the time of such resolution, decide that the dividend should be paid at some stipulated future date. If a time for payment is so prescribed, a shareholder has no enforceable right to demand payment prior to the stipulated date.[57]

The six-year limitation period in respect of an unpaid dividend runs from the date when it is declared or any later date for payment.[58]

A shareholder is a creditor in respect of a dividend which has been declared but not paid by the due date for payment.[59] However, when a company is in liquidation any sum due to a member of the company by way of dividend is deemed not to be a debt of the company in a case of competition between the member to whom it is due and any other creditor of the company who is not a member of a company. Any such sum is to be taken into account for the purpose of the final adjustment of the rights of the contributories among themselves.[60]

In *Evling v Israel & Oppenheimer*[61] the dividend rights attaching to particular shares were exceptional in that dividends were expressed to be payable without declaration. Eve J held that the petitioning shareholder was entitled to a declaration as to his rights in the profits of the company but noted that the action could not fairly be said to be an action to recover a dividend. The difficulty which perhaps concerned Eve J in expressing this reservation is that there could be circumstances where a dividend, payable without declaration,

[51] *Bishop v Smyrna and Cassaba Railway Co* [1895] 2 Ch 265; *Paterson & Sons Ltd v Paterson* 1917 SC 13, HL; *Eveling v Israel and Oppenheimer Ltd* [1918] 1 Ch 101.
[52] [1971] 2 All ER 504.
[53] *Thairwall v Great Northern Railway Co* [1910] 2 KB 509.
[54] *Re Severn and Wye and Severn Bridge Railway Co* [1896] 1 Ch 559.
[55] *Re Kidner* [1929] 2 Ch 121.
[56] *Lagunas Nitrate Co Ltd. v Schroeder & Co and Schmidt* (1901) 85 LT 22.
[57] [1971] 2 All ER 504, 512.
[58] *Re Compania de Electricidad de la Provincia de Buenos Aires* [1980] 1 Ch 146, not following *Re Artisans' Land and Mortgage Corporation* [1904] 1 Ch 796. Compare the limitation period in respect of moneys due from a member to the company. These are treated as speciality debts (Companies Act 1985, s 14 (2)) and, as such, the limitation period is twelve years.
[59] *Re Compania de Electricidad de la Provincia de Buenos Aires* [1980] 1 Ch 146.
[60] Insolvency Act 1986, s 74 (2)(f).
[61] [1918] 1 Ch 101.

has become payable in accordance with its terms but the company is unable to pay because it has insufficient distributable profits. The solution to this problem arrived at in an Australian case was to suspend the right to payment until there were sufficient distributable profits.[62] This probably represents the position under English law but the matter is not covered by authority.

FINANCIAL INCIDENTS OF SHARES: PREFERENCE SHARES

A preference share is a share which in respect of dividends and/or capital, enjoys priority, for a limited amount, over the company's ordinary shares. The precise extent of the priority is a matter of construction of the rights attached to the shares. It is not sufficient simply to designate shares as preference shares because that expression has no precise meaning. The preferential rights that are to be attached to the shares must be spelt out precisely as they will not be implied. Once the preferential rights are specified there are certain secondary presumptions that apply unless contrary provision is made. The settling of the rights attaching to preference shares is a domestic matter in which neither creditors (unless they have specifically bargained for this) nor the outside public have an interest.[63]

Default Capital Rights of Preference Shares

There is a presumption that all shares rank equally with regard to return of capital.[64] Accordingly, any priority intended to be attached to a preference share must be expressly stated.[65] In particular, it is not to be presumed from the fact that a share has attached to it a preferential right in respect of dividend, that there is also any preferential entitlement in respect of capital.[66]

In *Scottish Insurance Corporation v Wilsons & Clyde Coal Co Ltd*[67] the articles provided that in the event of winding up, preference stock ranked before ordinary stock to the extent of repayment of the amounts called up and paid thereon. The House of Lords held that this amounted to a complete statement of the rights of the preference shares in the winding up and that they did not carry the further entitlement to share in any assets remaining after repayment of the capital paid up on the ordinary shares. Observations of Lord Macnaghten in *Birch v Cropper*[68] which suggested that preference shares were entitled to share in surplus assets unless their terms contained an express and specific renunciation of that right were criticised.[69] Thus, where a share carries a preferential right to capital on a winding up, that displaces the principle

62 *Marra Developments Ltd v BW Rofe Pty Ltd* [1977] 1 NSWLR 162, NSW Common Law Division.

63 *Birch v Cropper* (1889) 14 App Cas 525, HL.

64 *Welton v Saffery* [1897] AC 299, HL, 309 *per* Lord Watson; *Birch v Cropper* (1889) 14 App Cas 525, HL.

65 *Re London India Rubber Co* (1869) LR 5 Eq 519.

66 *Birch v Cropper* (1889) 14 App Cas 525, HL.

67 [1949] AC 462, HL.

68 *Birch v Cropper* (1889) 14 App Cas 525, HL, 546 *per* Lord Macnaghten.

69 *Scottish Insurance Corporation v Wilsons & Clyde Coal Co Ltd* [1949] AC 462, HL, 490 *per* Lord Normand.

of equality and, instead, it is presumed that the express preferential right is the sum total of the entitlement; the onus is on the preference shareholder to point to some other provision in the company's constitution or terms of issue which confers an entitlement to share in any surplus assets.[70]

As well as winding up, capital can also be returned to shareholders on a reduction of capital. In *Re Saltdean Estate Co Ltd*[71] the articles provided that preference shares carried an entitlement to priority in respect of capital on a winding up, but that those shares were not to share in surplus assets remaining after all capital had been repaid. The articles were silent with regard to the position of preference shares in the event of a reduction of capital. Buckley J held that their position mirrored the rights that would apply in a winding up and that, accordingly, the first class of capital to be repaid was the class comprising the preference shares.

The decision in *Re Saltdean Estate Co Ltd* was approved by the House of Lords in *House of Fraser plc v ACGE Investments Ltd*[72] although, in this case, the articles expressly provided that the rights attached to the preference shares on a return of capital otherwise than on winding up were the same as the rights which they enjoyed on a winding up. Lord Keith of Kinkel thought fit to quote from Buckley J's judgment in the *Saltdean* case, including the following passage:[73]

> It has long been recognised that, at least in normal circumstances, where a company's capital is to be reduced by repaying paid-up share capital in the absence of agreement of the sanction of a class meeting to the contrary, that class of capital should first be repaid which would be returned first in a winding-up of a company . . .
>
> The liability to prior repayment on a reduction of capital, corresponding to their right to prior return of capital in a winding-up . . . is part of the bargain between the shareholders and forms an integral part of the definition or delimitation of the bundle of rights which make up a preferred share.

Lord Keith described this as 'an entirely correct statement of the law'.[74]

Spens Formula

The terms on which the share is issued may provide for the payment of a premium over par value in the event of redemption of the share or other distribution of surplus capital. A term, known as a Spens Formula, is commonly attached to preference shares. The essence of the Spens Formula is that, on a repayment of capital in a liquidation or on a reduction of capital, the holders of the share capital concerned are expressly entitled to a premium if, during a defined period prior to the repayment, the shares have been standing in the market at a figure in excess of par. The premium is usually ascertained by ref-

[70] *Re National Telephone Co* [1914] 1 Ch 755, Ch D; *Re Isle of Thanet Electricity Supply Co Ltd* [1950] Ch 161, CA. In *Dimbula Valley (Ceylon) Tea Co Ltd v Laurie* [1961] Ch 353 holders of preference shares were held to be entitled in a winding up to share in surplus assets remaining after all capital in respect of preference and ordinary shares had been repaid.

[71] [1968] 1 WLR 1844.

[72] [1987] AC 387, HL.

[73] *Re Saltdean Estate Co Ltd* [1968] 1 WLR 1844, 1849—50.

[74] *House of Fraser plc v ACGE Investments Ltd* [1987] AC 387, HL, 393. This approach was not followed in *Re Northern Engineering Industries plc* [1994] BCC 618, CA where the articles made special provision with regard to the rights of the preference shares.

erence to the average middle-market quotation in excess of par during the relevant period subject to adjustments to take account of any accrued arrears of dividend which is reflected in the market price of the shares.[75]

Default Dividend Rights of Preference Shares

Whether a preference share carries a preferential right to dividends as well as capital is a matter of construction of the terms of the share. There is no presumption that a share which carries a preferential right in respect of one financial aspect of shareholding (whether it be dividend or capital) also carries a preferential right in respect of the other.[76] Commonly, however, preference shares carry preferential rights in respect of both dividends and capital.

A preferential dividend is commonly expressed as a specified percentage of the nominal value of the share; sometimes, however, it can be expressed as a specified percentage of the amount paid up on the share.[77] Preferential dividends are usually expressed to be payable only when declared,[78] but if no dividend is declared in one year (or the dividend which is declared does not fully satisfy the preference shareholders' entitlements), it is presumed that the amount which is not paid is to be carried forward into subsequent years. The presumption that preferential dividends are cumulative is well established[79] but it can be displaced by provision to that effect in the company's constitution or in the terms of issue.[80]

Preference shareholders cannot force a company to declare a dividend. Preference shares are typically issued on terms that they carry no or very limited voting rights in normal circumstances and only become fully enfranchised when the preferential dividend is in arrears. In *Re Bradford Investments plc*,[81] where the construction of such a voting provision was in issue, it was argued that a preferential dividend expressed to be payable out of profits could not be said to be in arrears when the company did not have profits. Hoffmann J rejected this argument: the dividend payment dates specified in the articles were clearly intended to allow preference shareholders to vote if the dividend was not paid on the specified dates.[82] But even if preference shareholders are entitled to vote, a further constraint is that, under normal articles, shareholders cannot declare a dividend in excess of the amount recommended by the directors.[83] If directors were to frustrate the legitimate

[75] There is an unresolved question whether the inclusion of a Spens Formula makes preference shares relevant shares for the statutory pre-emptive rights contained in Companies Act 1985, s 89. On pre-emption rights generally see Ch 18.

[76] *Birch v Cropper* (1889) 14 App Cas 525, HL.

[77] See, for example, the rights attached to the preference shares in the *House of Fraser* case (set out at [1987] AC 387, HL, 390) which included a right to a fixed cumulative dividend on the capital paid up thereon.

[78] *Bond v Barrow Haematite Steal Co* [1902] 1 Ch 362.

[79] *Henry v Great Northern Rly* (1857) 1 De G&J 606, 44 ER 858; *Webb v Earle* (1875) LR 20 Eq 556.

[80] *Staples v Eastman Photographic Materials Co* [1896] 2 Ch 303, CA.

[81] [1990] BCC 740, [1991] BCLC 224.

[82] This is a customary provision, the practice of inserting it having developed after it was held in *Re Roberts & Cooper Ltd* [1929] 2 Ch 383 that, without such provision, preferential dividends which had not been declared could not be said to be in arrears.

[83] eg, Table A, art 102.

expectations of preference shareholders by failing to recommend a dividend in circumstances where the company had sufficient distributable profits to pay it, that would probably amount to a breach of duty on their part. A breach of duty by directors does not normally entitle individual shareholders to sue the directors, because directors owe their duties to the company rather than to individual shareholders. However, the preference shareholders could petition the court for relief under the Companies Act, s 459 on the grounds that the company's affairs are being managed in a manner which is unfairly prejudicial to them,[84] or might even be able to have the company wound up on the basis of it being just and equitable to do so.[85] It has also been suggested that if directors exercise the powers which are conferred on them by the company's constitution improperly this can have the effect of putting the company in breach of the statutory contract with its members, thus giving rise to the possibility of a personal contractual action by the shareholders against the company.[86]

The general presumption of equality between shareholders is obviously displaced where certain shares are given a prior entitlement to a fixed dividend. However, once the preferential dividend has been paid, can preference shareholders invoke the equality principle so as to rank equally with the ordinary shareholders in respect of any further distribution of distributable profits? This question was answered in the negative in *Will v United Lankat Plantations Co*.[87] The shares in question had the right to a preferential dividend of 10 per cent and the House of Lords held that, as a matter of construction, that was the sum total of the holder's entitlement to dividends in respect of those shares. Articles or terms of issue could provide for preference shares to carry the right to rank equally with ordinary shares in respect of dividends in addition to a fixed preferential dividend, although a provision to that effect would be unusual and out of line with normal expectations. In commercial terms, companies and investors tend to regard preference shares as being akin to debt in the sense that the return paid to the investors is expected to be fixed or capped; if it is intended that, at some point, the investor is to be given the right to participate, that would normally be achieved by attaching a right to convert the preference share into an ordinary share at some later date. Preference shares which in respect of dividends and/or capital carry the right to participate generally in addition to the preferential entitlement are known as 'participating' preference shares.

Where cumulative preferential dividends have been in arrears for some time but distributable profits become available or the company goes into liquidation, special rules govern the entitlement of the holders of the shares in respect of those dividends. When a cumulative preference dividend is finally declared, the whole of the accumulated amount is payable to the persons who are the holders of the preference shares at that time and it does not have to be apportioned between them and the other persons (if any) who held the shares

[84] *Re Sam Weller & Sons Ltd* (1989) 5 BCC 810.
[85] *Re a Company ex parte Glossop* [1988] BCLC 570.
[86] *Re a Company* [1987] BCLC 82.
[87] [1914] AC 11, HL.

during the time when the dividends were not declared.[88] Where preference shares of the same class have been issued over a period of time and the cumulative preferential dividend has not been declared over that period, the correct approach with regard to distributing any profits that do become available is to distribute them rateably among the shareholders according to the amount of dividend that has accumulated on each of the shares.[89]

Where a company is in liquidation or is making a reduction of capital involving repayment, there is a general presumption that undeclared preference dividends are not payable. This is one aspect of the general rule that dividends are not payable until they are declared. However, express provision is often made in articles or terms of issue for the payment in a winding up or reduction of capital of a sum equal to the amount of preference dividends (whether declared or not) on preference shares calculated up to the date of the winding up or of repayment of the capital in priority to any payment to ordinary shareholders.[90]

FINANCIAL INCIDENTS OF SHARES: REDEEMABLE SHARES

Redeemable shares are shares which are issued on terms which provide for the company to redeem the shares at some point in the future. Both ordinary and preference shares can be issued on a redeemable basis provided certain conditions set out in the Companies Act 1985, Pt V, ch VII are complied with in connection with the issue. Companies were first allowed to issue redeemable preference shares by the 1929 companies legislation, and in 1981 the permission was extended so as to allow ordinary shares also to be issued on that basis.

An issue of redeemable shares allows a company to raise short-term capital. The reasons for seeking short-term capital in this form may vary from company to company. Smaller companies may favour redeemable shares because they ensure that any loss of control resulting from an issue of shares to outsiders is only temporary. Being able to offer either ordinary or preference shares on a redeemable basis gives such companies the flexibility to appeal to the widest possible range of potential investors; and, for their part, investors may be more willing to invest in redeemable shares than they would have been to invest in non-redeemable ordinary or preference shares of a company whose shares are not actively traded and for which there is no ready market.

The difficulties faced by smaller companies in raising share capital were highlighted in the late 1970s by a committee under the chairmanship of Sir Harold Wilson, and this committee recommended the extension of the power to issue redeemable shares from preference to ordinary shares.[91] This recommendation, and a specific consultation exercise culminating in the

[88] *Re Wakley* [1920] 2 Ch 205.

[89] *First Garden City Ltd v Bonham-Carter* [1928] 1 Ch 53.

[90] For example see *Re Wharfdale Brewery Co Ltd* [1952] Ch 913.

[91] *Committee to Review the Functioning of Financial Institutions Interim Report on the Financing of Small Firms* Cmnd 7503 (1979) para 17.

publication of a DTI report on the purchase by a company of its own shares,[92] were significant steps leading up to the Companies Act 1981 which, for the first time, allowed companies to issue redeemable ordinary shares.

For a company whose shares are actively traded, giving potential investors a way of realising their investment would naturally figure less prominently as a reason for issuing redeemable shares. When larger companies issue redeemable shares, they tend to be non-participating redeemable preference shares carrying a preferential entitlement in respect of dividends and capital. In economic terms an issue of redeemable preference shares on such terms is very similar to raising fixed-rate, fixed-term debt financing. However, despite that similarity, there are key legal differences between preference-share finance and all forms of debt finance: (i) capital raised through an issue of preference shares is share capital and as such, subject to the maintenance of capital rules but those rules do not apply to debt finance; (ii) raising capital by issuing preference shares may avoid borrowing limits in the company's articles or loan agreements (unless borrowing is expressly defined so as to include preference share financing); (iii) if the company is subject to capital adequacy requirements, preference-share financing may attract a more favourable treatment than debt would have done; and (iv) preference-share financing attracts a different tax and accounting treatment from that of debt.

The Companies Act 1985, s 159 allows a company to issue redeemable shares provided it is authorised to do so by its articles. To avoid the situation of a company being left with no share capital as a result of redemptions, no redeemable shares may be issued at a time when there are no issued shares of the company which are not redeemable.[93]

The Companies Act 1985, s 160 (3) provides that the redemption of shares must be effected on such terms and in such manner as may be provided by the company's articles. The correct construction of this provision is a matter of some dispute because it is unclear whether the company's articles can give a measure of discretion to the directors with regard to the detailed aspects of the redemption, such as the redemption price and the date of redemption, or whether it requires those details to be set out specifically in the articles. In general, companies would prefer the former to be the correct interpretation because it allows them the flexibility to tailor the terms of the issue to reflect market conditions immediately prior to the making of the issue. If the issue terms have to be set out in the articles, the normal timetable for convening and holding general meetings, including the setting out of the precise terms of the special resolution altering the articles in the notice convening the meeting, has to be followed with the result that the terms have to be settled many weeks before the issue can actually be made. By the time the issue is finally due to be made, changes in market conditions may have made those terms unattractive to investors.

A provision equivalent to the Companies Act 1985, s 160 (3) in Australian legislation has been interpreted as permitting the articles simply to provide

[92] *The Purchase by a Company of its Own Shares* Cmnd 7944 (1980).
[93] Companies Act 1985, s 159 (2).

for delegation to the directors.[94] However, s 160 (3) is intended to implement the Second Directive, art 39 which, in its English version, states that the terms and manner of redemption must be laid down in the company's statutes or instrument of incorporation. An English court is obliged to interpret s 160 (3) so as to give effect to art 39 if that is reasonably practicable within the confines of the language used,[95] and it is at least arguable that an article which delegates responsibility for the fixing of the terms and manner of redemption to the directors does not comply with the requirement that those matters be laid down.

At a late stage during the passage of the Companies Act 1989 through Parliament a clause was added to Bill with a view to clarifying the position. This clause, which appears on the statute books as the Companies Act 1989, s 133 allows the power to fix the redemption date to be delegated to the directors and allows the redemption price to be determined in accordance with a formula specified in the company's articles as an alternative to specifying a firm redemption price in the articles. This provision was intended to introduce some flexibility, but subsequent consultation indicated that it could create new difficulties. These potential difficulties included the fact that the new provision required a redemption date or period be specified in the articles or by the directors before the shares were issued. This was criticised on the grounds that it would preclude shares being issued on terms that they were redeemable at the option of the company and/or the holder as contemplated by the Companies Act 1985, s 159 (1), or as being redeemable as a result of specified event(s). Other objections were that the requirement to specify a date had adverse capital adequacy implications for banks,[96] and that for private companies whose shares were not actively traded it could be practically impossible to devise a viable formula which did not require a measure of discretionary judgment from its auditors or other valuers as to the value of the shares.[97] As a result, at the time of writing the DTI does not now propose to implement the Companies Act 1989, s 133, but, instead, to repeal it at the earliest opportunity. This leaves a degree of uncertainty but, in so far as it can be summarised, the current position is as follows.

The terms and manner of redemption must be provided by the company's articles before the shares are redeemed. However, such provision need not be made at the time when the shares are issued and can be inserted into the articles at a later date. The level of detail required to satisfy the requirement that the terms and manner of redemption be 'provided in' the articles is uncertain but a cautious approach is appropriate, given the background of the Second Directive. It is not essential to specify a redemption date or period: instead the articles can provide for the shares to be redeemable at any time at the option of the company and/or the holder or after the occurrence of specified event(s). However, it is questionable whether a provision to the effect that the

[94] *TNT Australia Pty Ltd v Normandy Resources NL* [1990] 1 ACSR 1, SA SC.

[95] *Pickstone v Freemans plc* [1989] AC 66, [1988] 2 All ER 803, HL; *Litster v Forth Dry Dock and Engineering Co Ltd* [1990] AC 546, [1989] 1 All ER 1134, HL.

[96] *Company Law Review: Terms and Manner of Redemption of Redeemable Shares. Sections 159A and 160(3) of the Companies Act 1985* (DTI Consultative Document) (1993).

[97] Ibid.

shares are to be redeemed by a date, or during a period, to be specified by the directors would comply with s 160 (3). Similarly, it is uncertain whether the articles can simply leave it to the directors to determine a redemption price. The articles can specify a price or a formula for determining the price; but it is doubtful whether a formula which includes a measure of discretion to be exercised, say, by the company's directors or auditors is permissible.[98]

The financial terms of redeemable shares may include a provision for the payment of a redemption premium, that is, an amount greater than the par value of the shares.

There are detailed rules concerning the financing of redemptions. Redeemable shares may be redeemed out of distributable profits of the company, or out of the proceeds of a fresh issue of shares made for the purpose of the redemption.[99] Redemption premiums must be paid from distributable profits,[100] except that in respect of redeemable shares which were issued at a premium, redemption premiums may be paid out of the proceeds of a fresh issue of shares up to an amount equal to the aggregate of the premiums received by the company on the issue of the shares redeemed, or the current amount of the company's share premium account, whichever is the less.[101] Private companies are also permitted, subject to certain conditions, to redeem shares out of capital.[102] These requirements are considered further in Chapter 13.

VOTING RIGHTS ATTACHING TO SHARES

The default position is one vote per share unless the articles make contrary provision.[103] Ordinary shares normally follow the default position, although it is possible to have non-voting ordinary shares. Preference shares normally carry only limited voting rights, but the shares may become fully enfranchised if the preference dividend is in arrears for longer than a specified period. A preference dividend which is not paid because the company has insufficient distributable profits is in arrears for this purpose if the articles provide a payment date and that date is past.[104]

INCIDENTS OF SHARES: RULES OF CONSTRUCTION OF RIGHTS ATTACHING TO SHARES

The rights attaching to shares are determined by looking at the company's constitution, any resolution authorising the issue and the issue terms, bearing in mind any default presumptions that apply where there is no express provision to the contrary. Articles of association are a commercial document and,

[98] The DTI Consultative Document also notes that even for public companies formulas relying on external mechanisms such as exchange rates would be likely to involve someone exercising discretion in checking which data out of the available range should be used.

[99] Companies Act 1985, s 160 (1)(a).

[100] Ibid, s 160 (1)(b).

[101] Ibid, s 160 (2).

[102] Ibid, s 171.

[103] Ibid, s 370 (1).

[104] *Re Bradford Investments plc* [1990] BCC 740, [1991] BCLC 224.

within the confines of the language used, are to be construed in a manner giving them reasonable business efficiency in preference to a result which would or might prove unworkable.[105] If there is any conflict between the memorandum and the articles, the memorandum prevails;[106] but reference may be made to the articles to resolve ambiguities in the memorandum.[107] The parol evidence rule generally precludes reference to a prospectus or listing particulars accompanying an issue of shares to determine their terms;[108] the parol evidence rule can be displaced, for example, where it can be shown that the prospectus contains a collateral contract.[109]

VARIATION OF RIGHTS ATTACHING TO SHARES: OUTLINE OF PROCEDURES

Where the rights attaching to shares are specified in a company's memorandum or articles they can be varied in accordance with the procedures for altering a company's constitution. Rights that are set out in the articles can be changed by special resolution of the company.[110] Where the rights are specified in the memorandum (which is a less common occurrence) they can be altered by special resolution unless the memorandum itself provides an alternative variation procedure or prohibits alteration.[111] Where a company's capital structure comprises more than one type of share, additional procedural requirements may apply because rights attaching to any class of share are specially protected and can only be changed with the consent of the class. To determine whether the additional procedural steps must be taken in any case, it is necessary to decide whether the capital structure in question does comprise classes of shares, as defined by the relevant legislation, and whether the proposed restructuring involves a variation of class rights.

A CLASS OF SHARES OR A CLASS OF MEMBERS

The phrase 'a class of shares' is used in a number of provisions of the Companies Act 1985 but it is not defined. This chapter is primarily concerned with its usage in the Companies Act 1985, s 125 which specifies a procedure for the variation of rights attaching to a class of shares.[112] In this context the judgment of Scott J in *Cumbrian Newspapers Group Ltd v Cumberland & Westmorland Herald Newspaper & Printing Co*[113] is important because it

[105] *Holmes v Keyes* [1959] 1 Ch 199, CA, 215 *per* Jenkins LJ.
[106] *Guinness v Land Corpn of Ireland* (1883) 22 Ch D 349, CA.
[107] *Angostura Bitters (Dr JGB Siegert & Sons) v Kerr* [1933] AC 550, PC.
[108] *Baily v British Equitable Assurance Co Ltd* [1906] AC 35, HL.
[109] *Jacobs v Batavia and General Plantations Trust Ltd* [1924] 2 Ch 329, CA.
[110] Companies Act 1985, s 9.
[111] Ibid, s 17.
[112] For example see Table A 1948 Act, art 4. There is no equivalent provision in the 1985 Act Table A. Articles could specifically define what is meant by a 'class of shares' but that would be unusual. In the normal case an article concerned with the variation of rights attaching to a class of shares does not define the term but leaves it to be interpreted in accordance with the general law and in a manner which is consistent with Companies Act 1985, s 125.
[113] [1987] Ch 1.

represents the first detailed judicial examination of the expression in relation to variation of rights procedures. Some guidance on the interpretation of the phrase 'class of shares' can also be derived from other cases where, without much discussion and, apparently on the basis that the position was so obvious as to require no elaboration, the courts have treated shares as being in different classes. Some of the cases which provide illustrative examples of shares being treated as being in different classes were decided in relation to reductions of capital. These cases are relevant in this context because of the prima-facie rule that reductions should be effected in a manner which conforms with class rights.[114]

Another section of the Companies Act 1985 which refers to classes of shares is s 429. Under s 429 a bidder who acquires at least 90 per cent of any class of shares in a company is, subject to satisfaction of certain requirements, allowed to buy out the remaining minority shareholders. There is no statutory or judicial interpretation of the expression 'class of shares' as used in this section.[115]

Some sections of the Companies Act 1985 use the expression 'class of members' rather than 'class of shares'. According to the *Cumbrian Newspapers* decision the reference in s 125 to 'rights attached to a class of shares' has, in relation to a company limited by shares, the same meaning as the expression 'rights of any class of members' as used in the Companies Act 1985, s 17 (2). Section 17 (2) is concerned with the variation of optional provisions in a company's memorandum. Again there is no statutory or definitive judicial interpretation of the expression 'class of members' as used in this sub-section.

The phrase 'class of members' is also relevant to the Companies Act 1985, s 425. Section 425 governs schemes of arrangement between a company and its members, or any class of them, and there are a number of cases which consider the interpretation of a 'class of members' in that context. It is doubtful whether those cases are authoritative for the purposes of interpreting the expression 'class of shares' as used in the Companies Act 1985, s 125. Under the Companies Act 1985, s 425, the courts can look through technical rights to economic interests.[116] Accordingly, members whose rights are the same but whose economic interests are different can be treated as being in difference classes for the purposes of this section.[117] The flexible and pragmatic approach of the courts in relation to s 425 cases is in marked contrast to the conventional approach to questions about variation of rights where the courts

[114] *Bannatyne v Direct Spanish Telegraph Co* (1887) 34 Ch D 287, CA, 300 *per* Cotton LJ; *Re Chatterley-Whitfield Collieries Ltd* [1948] 2 All ER 593, CA, 596; *Re Saltdean Estate Co Ltd* [1968] 1 WLR 1844, 1849–50 *per* Buckley J.

[115] Boyle, AJ, Sykes, R, and Sealy, LS, *Gore-Browne on Companies* (44th edn, looseleaf) para 30.15 doubts whether rights given to individuals as members which are not attached to particular shares would be treated as rights attaching to a class of shares for the purposes of this section even though, according to the *Cumbrian Newspapers* decision, they are for the purpose of variation of rights procedures. See also the discussion about fully-paid and partly-paid shares later in this chapter, at 335–7.

[116] *Sovereign Life Assurance Co v Dodd* [1892] 2 QB 573, CA.

[117] *Re Hellenic & General Trust Ltd* [1975] 3 All ER 382; noted Hornby, JA, 'Class Membership in a Company's Scheme of Arrangement' (1976) 39 MLR 207 and Prentice, DD, 'Corporate Arrangements—Protecting Minority Shareholders' (1976) 92 LQR 13.

tends to analyse the position from a standpoint that is entirely technical and literal. The application of s 425 cases to questions involving variation of rights cannot, therefore, be assumed.

A CLASS OF SHARES—SOME CLEAR CASES

There is no doubt that shares which have different rights attached to them are in different classes.[118] There are endless ways in which the rights attaching to shares could differ, but obvious examples of shares in different classes are preference and ordinary shares,[119] redeemable shares and non-redeemable shares,[120] and convertible shares and those which are not convertible. Preference shares carrying different rights to dividend and/or capital would be treated as being in different classes; although one case on the interpretation of an investment clause of a settlement refers to 'sub-classes' of shares,[121] the concept of a sub-class is meaningless in relation to variation of rights procedures.

These examples focus on the financial aspects of shares, but differences in the rights attaching to shares which result in the existence of separate classes of shares for the purposes of variation of rights procedures need not necessarily be financial. Thus, for instance, ordinary shares carrying limited or enhanced voting rights would comprise a class of shares separate from ordinary shares carrying a right to one vote per share. Non-voting or limited-voting ordinary shares are not common in listed companies but are often used in quasi-partnership companies or joint venture companies in order to give effect to the particular arrangements between the parties. Another familiar provision in the articles of joint venture companies is for the shares held by each of the joint venturers to be designated as 'A' shares, 'B' shares, 'C' shares, and so forth; each group of shares enjoys the same rights save that only the holder of the A shares can appoint an A director, and likewise with the other designated shares. The purpose of these arrangements is to ensure that each joint venturer has the right to appoint one member of the board; the effect of the arrangements is to create separate classes of shares.

GOLDEN SHARES

Special rights may be attached to particular shares for so long as those shares are held by a named individual. This type of right was included in the articles of association of some privatised companies at the time when the businesses were first transferred from state to private ownership. The Government retained some control over the businesses for a period of time by taking a

[118] *Cumbrian Newspapers Group Ltd v Cumberland & Westmorland Herald Newspaper & Printing Co Ltd* [1987] Ch 1, 15.

[119] *Scottish Insurance Corpn Ltd v Wilsons & Clyde Co Ltd* [1949] AC 462, HL; *White v Bristol Aeroplane Co* [1953] Ch 65, CA.

[120] *TNT Australia v Normandy Resources NL* [1990] 1 ACSR 1, SA SC.

[121] *Re Powell-Cotton's Resettlement* [1957] 1 Ch 159.

share (known as a 'golden share'), to which were attached certain rights such as the right to cast the majority of the votes on a poll at general meetings of the company in the event that any person offered to acquire more than 50 per cent of the ordinary shares;[122] but the articles provided for the determination of these rights in the event of the sale of the golden share by the Government.

In the *Cumbrian Newspapers* decision it was accepted that shares carrying defeasible rights of this type constituted a separate class of shares. Scott J considered that the fact that the special rights would determine in the event of a transfer of the shares did not prevent the special rights being rights attached to a class of shares for the purposes of variation of rights procedures.[123]

RIGHTS CONFERRED UPON AN INDIVIDUAL CONDITIONAL UPON A SHAREHOLDING

The articles that were the subject matter of the *Cumbrian Newspapers* decision conferred on a named individual the right to appoint a director, conditional upon that individual holding not less than 10 per cent in nominal value of the company's issued shares. This type of provision differs from the golden share structure because, although the right is dependent on holding a certain proportion of the company's shares, it is not attached to any particular shares. A reference to a 'class of shares' if read literally would seem to exclude rights which are not attached to particular shares, but that was not the conclusion reached by Scott J. Instead, Scott J held that where articles conferred special rights on one or more shareholders in that capacity, the shares for the time being held by that shareholder or shareholders were a class of shares.[124] This is a surprising conclusion if the expression 'class of shares', as used in the Companies Act 1985, s 125 is taken on its own.[125] The structure would more readily be described as one giving rise to a class of shareholders or members which is the phraseology used in the Companies Act 1985, s 17 (2). Scott J compared the wording of the two sections and concluded that the legislature intended to treat classes of members and classes of shares as synonymous so far as concerned companies with a share capital. Further, he considered that it would be anomalous and arbitrary not to treat rights conferred on shareholders, but not attached to particular shares, as being subject to the variation of rights procedures.[126]

Articles conferring rights on a shareholder in that capacity are to be distinguished from articles conferring rights on individuals otherwise than in that capacity and for purposes connected with the administration of the company's affairs or the conduct of its business.[127] The former are specially

[122] Graham, C, 'All that Glitters—Golden Shares and Privatised Enterprises' (1988) Co Law 23.

[123] A precedent in *Palmer's Company Precedents* (17th edn, 1956) Pt I, 818 supported this analysis.

[124] [1987] Ch 1, 22.

[125] Scott J's somewhat strained interpretation of the legislation has been criticised: Polack, K, 'Company Law—Class Rights' [1986] CLJ 399.

[126] [1987] Ch 1, 21–2.

[127] The facts of *Eley v The Positive Government Security Life Assn* (1876) 1 Ex D 88 provide an example of a right in this category. See also *Re Blue Arrow plc* [1987] BCLC 585.

protected as class rights whilst the latter do not enjoy special protection against variation and are not even enforceable under the statutory contract because they are 'outsider' rights. Distinguishing between the two is a matter of construction, but a right which is expressly stated to be dependent upon the holding of shares is clearly in the first category.

UNCERTAIN SITUATIONS: IS THERE A CLASS OF SHARES?

There remain some situations where it is not absolutely certain that the structure of a company's share capital gives rise to the existence of a number of classes of shares for the purpose of variation of rights procedures. These include the following.

Shares with Different Par Values

In *Greenhalgh v Arderne Cinemas Ltd*[128] the company's share capital included ordinary shares with a par value of 50p (converting the relevant amount to decimals) and ordinary shares with a par value of 10p. It did not fall to the Court of Appeal to decide the point but Lord Evershed MR indicated that he was included to agree with the view of the first instance judge, Vaisey J,[129] that the 10p shares formed a separate class from the 50p shares for the purpose of an article concerned with variation of rights attaching to a class of shares.

Shares on which Different Amounts Have Been Paid Up

It could happen that different amounts are paid up in respect of shares which have the same par value. If, say, some shares are fully-paid and some are partly-paid, does this give rise to two separate classes of shares? In this situation the share capital is not divided into separate identifiable classes. The distinction arises simply from the factual situation and, without any constitutional change, could disappear as circumstances change and more shares become fully-paid. The Companies Act 1985, s 125 (1) applies to the variation of the rights attached to a class of shares in a company whose share capital is divided into shares of different classes. The reference to 'division' would suggest that partly-paid and fully-paid shares are not in different classes for this purpose. But this section must now be read in the light of the *Cumbrian Newspapers* decision and, according to it, a formal division of the share capital is not required in order for the section to apply. Under the *Cumbrian Newspapers* case, as well as the conventional classes resulting from a division of the share capital, where specific rights are given to certain members in their

[128] [1946] 1 All ER 512, CA.

[129] [1945] 2 All ER 719. It must be noted that the authorities which 'fortified' Vaisey J in his conclusion were the scheme of arrangement cases, *Sovereign Life Assurance Co v Dodd* [1892] 2 QB 573, CA and *Re United Provident Assurance Co Ltd* [1910] 2 Ch 477. These cases may proceed on a different basis because consideration of economic interests as well as technical rights is permissible under Companies Act 425 which governs schemes of arrangement. On s 425 see further, Ch 10 below, at 370–1.

capacity as members or shareholders, the shares held by those members form a class of shares. Typically, articles of association draw some distinctions between the rights enjoyed by holders of fully-paid shares and those enjoyed by holders of partly paid shares. These distinctions can include restricting the right to transfer partly-paid shares,[130] and limiting the company's lien on shares to partly-paid shares.[131] Articles giving a company the right to make calls and to forfeit shares for non-payment of calls[132] necessarily only apply to partly-paid shares and (although, in this case the right is the same, its practical effect can vary significantly depending on whether shares are fully or partly-paid) dividends are usually expressed to be payable by reference to the amounts paid up on shares.[133] If, say, a company proposed to alter its articles so as to impose a lien also on fully-paid shares, might that not be treated as an alteration of the rights attached to the fully-paid shares which are to be regarded as a separate class for this purpose?[134] Applying *Cumbrian Newspapers* the answer depends on whether the freedom from lien attaching to fully-paid shares can be said to be a right given to 'certain' shareholders. It is suggested that this goes beyond what Scott J had in mind in *Cumbrian Newspapers*, which were rights given to individuals who could be identified independently from the shares that they held. Even under the extended definition of rights attaching to a class of shares provided by the *Cumbrian Newspapers* decision, partly-paid shares and fully-paid shares should not be viewed as being in different classes for the purpose of variation of rights procedures. Nevertheless the position is not free from doubt.

In *Allen v Gold Reefs of West Africa Ltd*[135] the Court of Appeal held that a company could alter its articles to extend its lien from partly-paid to fully-paid shares. Although the company's issued share capital comprised fully-paid and partly-paid shares, no mention was made of the possibility of any group of members having special class rights. At the time when this case was decided the protection afforded to class rights was not fully worked out and there was a view[136] that until 1948 (when statutory variation procedures were first introduced) class rights could never be varied except in accordance with a specific provision to that effect in the articles. On that basis, if partly-paid and fully-paid shares were indeed in different classes, it would have been remarkable for the Court of Appeal in *Allen* not to have referred to this issue and to have proceeded simply on the basis of the application of the company's power to vary its articles by special resolution. However, the *Allen* decision is not conclusive because in *Cumbrian Newspapers* Scott J rejected the non-alterability view just outlined and held that, before 1948, class rights in the articles were freely alterable by special resolution unless the articles specifically restricted the circumstances in which they could be altered.

[130] Table A, art 24. [131] Table A, art 8. [132] Table A, arts 12–22.
[133] Table A, art 104.
[134] In *Greenhalgh v Arderne Cinemas Ltd* [1945] 2 All ER 719, [1946] 1 All ER 512, CA, it was accepted that shares could be in different classes for some purposes and in the same class for others.
[135] [1900] 1 Ch 656.
[136] *Report of the Company Law Committee* Cmnd 1749 (1962) (Jenkins Committee) para 188.

Whether partly-paid and fully-paid shares should be treated as being in different classes is a question that may also arise under other sections of the Companies Act 1985. There is no authority on the point in relation to the Companies Act 1985, s 429 but it has been suggested that fully-paid and partly-paid shares should not be regarded as being in different classes for that purpose.[137] In the context of a scheme of arrangement under the Companies Act 1985, s 425, shareholders holding partly-paid shares have been held to constitute a separate class of members from shareholders holding fully-paid shares,[138] but, since the courts can consider economic interests as well as rights in that situation, this decision is not determinative in relation to other provisions which are concerned with more formal procedures and rights. The point may have limited practical significance in any event because partly-paid shares are rarely encountered.

'RIGHTS ATTACHING TO A CLASS OF SHARES' AND 'CLASS RIGHTS'

The complications in the rules relating to the variation of rights do not end with the decision that a company's share capital contains more than one class of shares. The next issue that has to be determined is whether the right that is to be varied is a 'class right' to which the variation of rights procedures apply. In the *Cumbrian Newspapers* decision Scott J said that 'rights attaching to a class of shares' and 'class rights' were synonymous terms for the purpose of the Companies Act 1985, s 125[139] but this statement merits closer examination.

There are three possible ways of interpreting the concept of a class right, even in the clearest cases where a company's share capital is divided into more than one class of shares. The first interpretation is that only those rights which are exclusive to the class and distinct from rights attaching to any other class are class rights. On this basis, for example, the only class rights attaching to ordinary shares carrying two votes are the voting rights; the dividend and capital rights, which are the same as those attached to ordinary shares which carry only one vote, are not class rights. This is the most narrow interpretation of the expression.

The second view is that class rights are all the rights which, under the company's constitution, attach to shares which are in different classes, irrespective of whether those rights are exclusive to a particular class or are also enjoyed by other classes. On this basis, taking the same example, the dividend and capital rights attaching to the two classes of ordinary share are also class rights. But, taking this interpretation to its limit, all of the other provisions[140]

[137] Pinder, M, 'Buying Out Minorities' (1992) (August) PLC 13, 21 argues for a literal approach whereby partly-paid and fully-paid shares are to be treated as being in the same class where the rights attached to them are the same. An alternative view is that the different economic interests of partly-paid and fully-paid shareholders and in particular the absence of a common system of valuation for such shares mean that they should be treated as being in different classes.

[138] *Re United Provident Assurance Co Ltd* [1910] 2 Ch 477.

[139] [1987] Ch 1, 21.

[140] Save, presumably, for those that fall to be regarded as unenforceable outsider rights under the principle in *Hickman v Kent or Romney Marsh Sheepbreeders Association* [1915] 1 Ch 881.

of the company's memorandum and articles would also be class rights, with the consequence that any alteration of the constitution would require class consent. This is the broadest interpretation of the term 'class rights'.

Lying somewhere between these two interpretations is the third approach. This is to say that any rights which are exclusive to a particular class are class rights (which is consistent with the first interpretation) but that, in addition, dividend and capital rights, rights to vote, and rights relating to protection of class rights are class rights even though in particular circumstances shares in different classes may have the same rights.

Which of these views is correct? There is no support either in the authorities or in academic writing for the second interpretation. The choice therefore seems to be between the first and the third. For a long time, the absence of authoritative case law meant that academic comment was particularly significant. A view that commanded particular respect was that expressed in the fourth edition of *Gower's Principles of Modern Company Law*[141] in favour of the third interpretation. The *Gower* view was that once a special class of shares had been created then any rights enjoyed by that class would be class rights if they were expressly described in the memorandum, articles or terms of issue as class rights or if they related to dividends, return of capital, voting rights or to the procedures for the variation of rights.[142] Rights would still be class rights if, though attached to a particular class of shares, they happened to be the same as the rights attached to another class.

The appeal of this approach lies in the sense of balance and compromise its achieves: a change to the rights which any right-minded holder of shares would regard as fundamental to his investment—namely, financial return and voting entitlements—is treated as deserving of special protection, but more peripheral rights derived from the articles, such as the right to transfer shares, can be changed more easily under the general power to alter articles[143] without requiring compliance with the variation of class rights procedures. Apart, though, from the fact that the distinction drawn accords with common sense and reflects the special importance of dividend, capital and voting rights, it is difficult to establish an altogether persuasive theoretical basis for singling out these rights in this way. It would seem to be going too far to suggest that these rights are fundamental to the nature of the share (as opposed to being matters on which an investor would place fundamental importance in determining whether the rights attaching to shares make them a good investment) given that, for example, it is perfectly possible to have non-voting shares.[144]

[141] Gower, LCB, *Principles of Modern Company Law* (4th edn, 1979) 562–3. See now Davies, PL, *Gower's Principles of Modern Company Law* (6th edn, 1997) 717–27.

[142] Companies Act 1985, s 125 (7) expressly provides that any alteration of a variation of rights clause in articles, or the insertion of such a clause into articles, is itself to be treated as a variation of class rights.

[143] *Allen v Gold Reefs of West Africa Ltd* [1900] 1 Ch 656, CA qualifies the power to alter articles by requiring it to be exercised in good faith in the best interests of the company. See also *Peter's American Delicacy Co Ltd v Heath* (1939) 61 CLR 457, H Ct of Aust.

[144] This is a view suggested by Rice, DG, 'Class Rights and their Variation in Company Law' [1958] JBL 29.

Although there is no direct judicial endorsement of the third approach, at least by implication the decision in *Greenhalgh v Arderne Cinemas Ltd*[145] provides some support for it.[146] There, the issue was whether subdivision of shares was a variation of the right of another class of shares. The two classes of shares—the 50p shares which were to be sub-divided and the original 10p shares—each carried one vote per share. The Court of Appeal held that the proposal did not vary class rights but the tacit assumption underlying the decision is that the right to cast one vote was indeed a class right, despite being equally attached to the 50p and the 10p shares. However, there is also some judicial support for the first interpretation—that rights have to be exclusive to a class in order to be class rights. In the *Cumbrian Newspapers* decision Scott J said: 'if articles provide that particular shares carry *particular rights not enjoyed by the holders of other shares*, it is easy to conclude that the rights are rights attached to a class of shares'[147] (emphasis added). Although they can be interpreted in other ways, it is possible to argue that an implication of the italicised words is that exclusivity to a particular class is the distinguishing mark of a class right. Scott J's ruling that the Companies Act 1985, ss 17 (2) and 125 are to be read together may be thought to bolster this view since s 17 (2) refers to special rights, an expression which could be thought to carry with it connotations of exclusivity and uniqueness. Yet, since it is clear that the term 'special' does not necessarily mean unique,[148] the view the exclusivity is not required in order for rights to be considered to be class rights remains tenable.

In essence, what is in issue in this debate about the interpretation of the expression 'class rights' is the extent to which minority interests are entitled to protection. Investors in share capital take the risk that the rights which they acquire under the company's constitution by virtue of becoming members of the company will be changed by a resolution of the shareholders in general meeting; typically such rights are in the articles and, under the Companies Act 1985, s 9, can be changed by a special resolution (75 per cent of those voting) of the shareholders in general meetings. Where there are class rights, this power to alter the articles is qualified by a procedure which requires the consent of a specified majority of the class also to be obtained. The more broadly the expression 'class rights' is interpreted, the more protection is afforded to minorities, and vice versa. Paradoxically, although the actual decision in *Cumbrian Newspapers* extends the scope of the protection of class rights in one (surprising) respect by including rights conferred on certain shareholders in their capacity as members or shareholders, if the dictum about exclusivity is followed, this case will also have narrowed the scope of the protection in an important and unexpected respect. Since Scott J's comment is inconsistent with the tacit assumption underlying earlier cases and has a narrowing effect,

145 [1945] 2 All ER 719, [1946] 1 All ER 512, CA.

146 Also note *Re Old Silkstone Collieries Ltd* [1954] 1 Ch 169, CA where two classes of preference shares were entitled to participate in a compensation scheme to be established under nationalisation legislation. This entitlement was held to be a special right which triggered a protective procedure under the company's articles relating to variation of class rights.

147 [1987] Ch 1, 15. See also *Re John Smith's Tadcaster Brewery Co Ltd* [1953] Ch 308, CA, 319–20 *per* Jenkins LJ.

148 See *Re Old Silkstone Collieries Ltd* [1954] 1 Ch 169, CA.

it is suggested that it should not be followed. Whilst uncertainty remains, in practice it would be prudent for companies to assume that proposals to vary dividend, capital or voting rights attaching to a class of shares would vary class rights even where the rights are equally attached to more than one class of shares.

'VARIATION' OF CLASS RIGHTS

Assuming that there is a class of shares and a proposal affecting class rights, the next issue is whether the proposal amounts to a variation of class rights. Articles of association which contain procedures for the variation of class rights may specify what, for the purpose of those articles, is meant by the term 'variation'; in that event whether a particular proposal is a variation requires close examination and construction of the particular articles. The Companies Act 1985, s 125 also makes provision for variation, and the statutory procedure applies where a company's constitution does not itself contain relevant provisions. For the purposes of the statutory procedure and also (unless the context otherwise requires) in relation to provisions for the variation of rights contained in memoranda or articles, references to variation are to be read as including 'abrogation'.[149]

Some variations are easy to detect and would not be a matter of dispute. Straightforward examples of variations of class rights would include reducing the rate of a preferential dividend and decreasing the number of votes attached to a share. Since variation includes abrogation, removing a right to a preferential dividend would amount to a variation of class rights. There are a number of cases where the courts have ruled on whether particular proposals constitute variations of class rights and some of the more significant decisions are described in the following paragraphs. These cases all related to particular provisions in articles of association but they can also be regarded as establishing general rules of construction which would apply to the extent that no contrary provision is made. Naturally, the reported cases tend not to involve obvious variations and are concerned more with doubtful situations where it is uncertain whether what is proposed amounts to a variation of class rights.

CASE LAW ON VARIATIONS OF CLASS RIGHTS

In *Re Schweppes Ltd*[150] it was held that an issue of ordinary shares did not vary the class rights of existing ordinary shares, nor those of existing preference shares. An issue of preference shares ranking *pari passu* with existing preference shares was held not to vary the class rights of the existing preference shares in *Underwood v London Music Hall Ltd.*[151] In *Dimbula Valley (Ceylon) Tea Co Ltd v Laurie*[152] the rights attached to preference shares included the right to participate in a winding up rateably with the ordinary shares in all

[149] Companies Act 1985, s 125 (8). [150] [1914] 1 Ch 322 CA. [151] [1901] 2 Ch 309.
[152] [1961] 1 Ch 353.

assets remaining after paying creditors, costs, arrears of preference dividend and repayment of all paid-up capital. It was held that a bonus issue of shares did not vary this entitlement to participate even though it might reduce individual shareholders' share of the surplus available on liquidation.

Varying the Enjoyment of a Right rather than the Right Itself

The distinction implicit in the *Dimbula* decision between varying a right and varying the enjoyment of a right was developed in a trio of cases decided by the Court of Appeal in the 1940s and 1950s. In *Greenhalgh v Arderne Cinemas Ltd*[153] the Court of Appeal held that in respect of a share capital divided into 50p and 10p shares (using decimal equivalents for the sake of simplicity), a proposal to sub-divide the 50p shares into 10p shares did not amount to a variation of the class rights of the original 10p shares even though, as a result of the sub-division, the application of the provision in the articles which provided for each share (regardless of par value) to have one vote meant that the voting strength of the holders of the original 10p shares would be greatly diminished. Formally, the rights attaching to the 10p shares were unchanged and it was simply that, through sub-division, those shareholders who could previously cast one vote in respect of each 50p shares now could cast five, with a resulting diminution in the effectiveness of the votes cast by the holders of the original 10p shares. Lord Greene MR also commented on what the position might have been if the proposal had been to give the 50p shares five votes per share, rather than so sub-divide them. In that case, his Lordship considered that the rights attaching to the 10p shares might well have been varied because one of the rights attaching to those shares was that they should have voting powers *pari passu* with the other ordinary shares.[154]

The articles in the *Greenhalgh* decision imposed a special procedure to be followed on a 'variation' of rights. In *White v Bristol Aeroplane Co Ltd*[155] the relevant articles contained a more elaborate protective procedure which was to be followed where rights attaching to a class of shares were to be 'affected, modified, varied, dealt with or abrogated in any manner'. The company's share capital comprised preference shares and ordinary shares and it proposed to increase its share capital by issuing new preference shares ranking *pari passu* with the existing preference shares and new ordinary shares ranking *pari passu* with existing ordinary shares. The question considered by the Court of Appeal was whether this clause applied on the basis that the rights of the existing preference shares would be 'affected' by a new issue of *pari passu* shares. The court held that the rights would not be affected and that, accordingly, the procedure did not apply: after the issue the rights attaching to the existing preference shares would, in formal terms, be precisely the same as they had been before the issue, the only change being in the enjoyment of, and the capacity to make effective, the voting rights attached to the shares.

In *Re John Smith's Tadcaster Brewery Co Ltd*[156] the Court of Appeal again restricted the application of special procedures for the variation of rights. In

[153] [1946] 1 All ER 512, CA.
[154] Ibid at 515.
[155] [1953] 1 Ch 65, CA.
[156] [1953] Ch 308, CA.

this case it was held that an issue of new ordinary shares did not 'affect' the voting rights attaching to preference shares so as to trigger special procedures under the company's articles. Evershed MR went so far as to express some dissatisfaction with the prolix drafting of variation of rights procedures in articles of the kind in question in *White v Bristol Aeroplane Co Ltd*[157] and the particular case before him, commenting: 'it is perhaps unfortunate that those responsible for drafting these regulations seem apt . . . to string together words without pausing to reflect what their joint or separate significance might be'.[158] Evershed MR also sought to justify the court's restrictive stance by pointing out that a loose interpretation of a word such as 'affect' would mean that any activity on the part of the directors in pursuance of their powers which could be said to affect or touch the value of the preference shares would be rendered ineffective unless the special protective procedures were adhered to—a result which, in his Lordship's view, would be absurd.[159]

There is some force in Evershed MR's justification of the restrictive approach: as Pennington has pointed out, there is very little that a company does which does not affect the value of its shares so that, if the view rejected by the Court of Appeal in these cases had instead been accepted, the holders of a class of shares could hold an effective veto over virtually all of the company's activities.[160] Nevertheless these cases have not escaped criticism for being overly legalistic and literal.[161] As a matter of drafting, it is clear that if it is intended that proposals such as that involved in the *White* case should be subject to variation procedures, those procedures must be carefully drafted such as by providing that an issue of new shares ranking *pari passu* with existing shares will be a variation of class rights. Most favourable to the holders of a class of shares would be a provision drafted in general terms, such as one which provides for the protective procedure to apply where rights are 'affected as a business',[162] but, from the company's perspective, a general formula such as this would probably be unacceptably vague.

There is one situation where there is a possibility of the literal approach not being followed in respect of articles which provide for protection in the event of class rights being 'affected'. This stems from a dictum in Evershed MR's judgment in *White v Bristol Aeroplane Co Ltd* where he said that:

> a resolution aimed at increasing the voting power of the ordinary stockholders by doubling it, so giving them twofold their present power, without altering any other of the privileges or rights attached to any class, might be said to be something so directly touching the position, and therefore the rights, of the preference stockholders . . . albeit that there was no variation of their own individual rights.[163]

[157] [1953] 1 Ch 65, CA.
[158] [1953] Ch 308, CA, 312.
[159] Ibid at 316–17.
[160] Pennington, RR, *Company Law* (7th edn, 1995) 283.
[161] These criticisms were voiced before the House of Lords in *House of Fraser plc v ACGE Investments Ltd* [1987] AC 387, HL but the House of Lords, in line with the earlier cases, adopted a narrow approach. See further Davies, PL, *Gower's Principles of Modern Company Law* (6th edn, 1997) 723–6; Farrar, JH, and Hannigan, BM, *Farrar's Company Law* (4th edn, 1998) 231–3.
[162] *White v Bristol Aeroplane Co* [1953] Ch 65, CA, 80 *per* Evershed MR.
[163] Ibid at 76–7.

The context for this statement was that Evershed MR used this example to demonstrate that meaning could be given to the term 'affected' as distinct from 'variation'. However, he emphasised that he was not deciding the point and it is therefore uncertain how much weight should be attached to this comment. Departing from the literal rule for this particular case would seem to have little merit and would serve only to create further complexity and anomaly in this already difficult area. However, applying normal principles, if the articles provide for two classes of shares to have *pari passu* voting rights and there is a subsequent proposal to increase the voting rights of one class, that would vary the *pari passu* voting right of the other class.[164]

Variation of Rights by Enhancement

Are class rights varied if the rights attached to a class are enhanced in some respect—for instance if the rate of a preferential dividend is increased or if the number of votes attached to a share is multiplied? A dictum in *Dimbula Valley (Ceylon) Teas Co Ltd v Laurie*[165] suggests that increasing rights is a reinforcement rather than a variation of those rights but, in principle, it is difficult to see why the mere fact of a change being beneficial rather than adverse should preclude it from amounting to a variation of class rights. Notably, although the point was not specifically addressed, *Rights and Issues Investment Trust Ltd v Stylo Shoes Ltd*[166] proceeded on the assumption that an alteration increasing the voting rights attached to shares required the consent of the relevant class.

CLASS RIGHTS AND REDUCTION OF CAPITAL

Cases concerning reduction of capital provide further examples of judicial consideration being given to the question of what constitutes a variation of class rights. Reductions of capital in accordance with the Companies Act 1985, s 135 are subject to the approval of the court. The established practice[167] of the court is to require a proposed reduction to be done in conformity with the class rights attached to the company's various shares[168] or, to the extent that it varies class rights, for appropriate class consents to be obtained. Well-drawn articles or issue terms may specify what is to happen in the event of a reduction of capital.[169] For

164 *Greenhalgh v Arderne Cinemas Ltd* [1946] 1 All ER 512, CA.

165 [1961] 1 Ch 353, 374.

166 [1965] 1 Ch 250.

167 Some older cases suggest that a court may approve a reduction not in conformity in class rights even though it has not been sanctioned by appropriate class consent (eg, *Carruth v Imperial Chemical Industries Ltd* [1937] AC 707, HL). Companies Act 1985, s 125 appears to be mandatory in allowing class rights only to be varied in accordance with that section or in accordance with suitable provisions in the company's constitution.

168 *Bannatyne v Direct Spanish Telegraph Co* (1887) 34 Ch D 287, CA, 300 *per* Cotton LJ; *Re Chatterley-Whitfield Collieries Ltd* [1948] 2 All ER 593, CA (affirmed *sub nom Prudential Assurance Co Ltd v Chatterley-Whitfield Collieries Ltd* [1949] AC 512, HL).

169 A provision dealing with return of capital 'on a winding up or otherwise' will be taken to refer to repayment of capital in accordance with Companies Act 1985, s 135: *House of Fraser plc v ACGE Investments Ltd* [1987] AC 387, HL.

example in *Re Northern Engineering Industries plc*[170] the articles provided that any reduction of capital would be a variation of the class rights of the preference shares.[171] If the articles or terms of isssue do not make provision, the position is that the various classes of shares are to be treated as they would be treated in the event of a winding up. What this means is that if a company's share capital comprises ordinary shares and preference shares carrying a right to priority as to return of capital (but no right to share in any surplus remaining after payment of creditors, costs, accrued unpaid dividends on preference shares (if any) and the return of paid-up capital), a reduction of share capital involving the return of capital is effected in accordance with class rights where the preference shares are paid off first[172]—they would rank before the ordinary shares on a winding up. Conversely, where the reduction involves cancellation of share capital as a result of losses, it is the ordinary shares (which would bear this loss in the event of winding up) that must be cancelled first.[173]

It is clear from the case law that the payment off and cancellation of preference shares which are non-participating as outlined in the last paragraph does not abrogate, affect, modify or deal with the rights attached to those shares. In *Re Saltdean Estate Co Ltd*[174] Buckley J explained that the rights were not abrogated; rather by paying off the preference shares first, the company was giving effect to the priority right attached to those shares. In *House of Fraser plc v ACGE Investments Ltd*[175] Lord Keith of Kinkel amplified this explanation. Paying off preference shares which were entitled to priority on a winding up or otherwise gave effect to the entitlement and did not abrogate it; and the reduction did not 'modify, commute, affect or deal with' the rights attached to the shares within the meaning of the company's articles because those words all contemplated that, after the transaction, the shareholders in question would continue to hold some rights, albeit of a different nature from those that they previously held.

The payment off and cancellation of non-participating preference shares extinguishes any further entitlement[176] to whatever fixed divided was previously attached to those shares. It is not a variation of class rights to extinguish this entitlement. It is something that the holders of the shares must be taken to have agreed to as a necessary consequence of their right to priority on a return of capital.[177]

Where a company's share capital consists of ordinary shares and preference shares which have a priority right in respect of dividends (calculated by reference to paid-up amounts) but which rank *pari passu* with the ordinary shares

170 [1993] BCC 267.

171 The argument that 'reduction' for this purpose did not include cancellation of the preference shares was rejected.

172 *Re Chatterley-Whitfield Collieries Ltd* [1948] 2 All ER 593, CA (affirmed *sub nom Prudential Assurance Co Ltd v Chatterley-Whitfield Collieries Ltd* [1949] AC 512, HL); *Scottish Insurance Corporation v Wilsons & Clyde Coal Co Ltd* [1949] AC 462, HL; *Re Saltdean Estate Co Ltd* [1968] 1 WLR 1844; *House of Fraser plc v ACGE Investments Ltd* [1987] AC 387, HL.

173 *Re Floating Dock of St Thomas Ltd* [1895] 1 Ch 691.

174 [1968] 1 WLR 1844.

175 [1987] AC 387, HL.

176 *Re Chatterley-Whitfield Collieries Ltd* [1948] 2 All ER 593, CA (affirmed *sub nom Prudential Assurance Co Ltd v Chatterley-Whitfield Collieries Ltd* [1949] AC 512, HL).

177 *House of Fraser plc v ACGE Investments Ltd* [1987] AC 387, HL .

in respect of capital, any reduction of capital must, to conform to class rights, be spread equally across both classes. A reduction will thus result in a reduction of the amounts paid up on both classes of shares, but the effect on the continuing enjoyment of the priority dividend right will be especially significant: although the rate of the dividend will remain the same, the amount that the holders of the shares actually receive will be potentially significantly less because of the reduction of the principal amount on which that dividend is based. In line with the restrictive approach that characterises case law relating to the interpretation of the term 'variation', a reduction in the amount of dividend actually received resulting not from a direct adjustment to the rate of dividend but indirectly from a reduction of the principal amount by reference to which it is calculated is not, in itself, regarded as a variation of class rights.[178]

CLASS RIGHTS AND REDEMPTION OF SHARES/SHARE BUY BACKS

Companies are permitted to issue redeemable shares and in limited circumstances they may purchase shares which were originally issued as non-redeemable.[179] Redeemed shares and shares which are purchased by the company must be cancelled,[180] and the transaction necessarily involves a diminution of the company's paid-up capital.[181] This analysis means that class rights in respect of reductions of capital are relevant even where the redemption or buy back is financed from distributable profits.

The conclusion that a redemption or buy back of shares amounts to a return of capital has various implications. Sometimes the terms on which preference shares are issued expressly anticipate further issues of redeemable issues and specify whether or not those issues will constitute a variation of the rights of the preference shares. Where no such provision is made and the company has issued preference shares which are entitled to priority on winding up or any return of capital, a subsequent issue of redeemable shares would constitute a variation of the class rights of the existing preference shares since, on redemption, capital could be returned first to the holders of the redeemable shares. Even if the terms of the preference shares simply provide for priority on a

[178] *Bannatyne v Direct Spanish Telegraph Co* (1887) 34 Ch D 287, CA; *Re Mackenzie & Co Ltd* [1916] 2 Ch 450. See also *Adelaide Electric Co Ltd v Prudential Assurance Co* [1934] AC 122, HL where the rate of dividend was unchanged but, because of a change in the place of payment and currency of payment (from English pounds to Australian pounds), shareholders actually received a much smaller amount. The House of Lords held that there was no variation of class rights. This case again illustrates the restrictive approach of the courts, but the decision does turn on the interpretation of 'pound' as used in the company's articles. A change of currency which is not within the scope of the language used in the articles could, it is suggested, constitute a variation of class rights.

[179] Companies Act 1985, Pt V, ch III.

[180] Companies Act 1985, ss 160 (4) (redeemed shares) and 162 (2) (which applies s 160 (4) to repurchased shares).

[181] The requirement to make a transfer to a capital redemption reserve is intended to ensure that the total amount of the company's undistributable reserves is maintained: Companies Act 1985, s 170. This is a creditor-protection provision. It does not function as protection for preference-shareholders' rights in this situation because, as permitted by s 170 (4), the sums credited to this account could be used to pay up a bonus issue of ordinary shares in favour of existing ordinary shareholders.

winding up and are silent with regard to returns of capital, the analysis should be the same by extension of those decisions where the court held that it is to be implied that the position on reduction of capital corresponds to the rights on winding up unless otherwise stated. Where there are preference shares which are entitled to priority on a return of capital in a winding up or otherwise, it would be a variation of their class rights for the company to purchase ordinary shares before the preference shares have been paid off. There would also be a variation of the rights of the preference shares if the company is empowered to purchase the preference shares at a price other than (whether higher[182] or lower than) their capital rights.

DEFAULT RIGHTS ATTACHING TO ORDINARY SHARES—CLASS RIGHTS?

Can the normal rights of ordinary shares—that is, the right to the whole of any declared dividend, subject to any preferential dividend, the right to any surplus capital remaining after creditors and costs have been paid and capital has been repaid in accordance with priority rights as between classes of shares, and the right to one vote per share—ever be regarded as class rights? This question is prompted by *Hodge v James Howell & Co Ltd*[183] where Jenkins LJ said:

> In general, one expects to find ordinary shares entitled to the whole of the profits and surplus assets remaining after preferences attached to any other class of shares are satisfied, and this residual right is not generally regarded as a special right or privilege or class right attached to the ordinary shares for the purposes of a modification of rights clause.

In that case the company's existing share capital comprised a class of preference shares and ordinary shares. The company's articles provided for (a) the payment of a preferential dividend on the preference shares and, subject to that, the payment of an ordinary dividend; and (b) the repayment of capital on the preference shares and, secondly, the repayment of the capital on the ordinary shares. It was argued that a proposal to create a new class of preference shares, ranking after the existing preference shares, but before the ordinary shares, varied the class rights of the ordinary shares.

The Court of Appeal rejected the argument. The fact that particular articles ranked the existing preference shares first and the ordinary shares second did not mean that the ordinary shares were forever entitled to second place. Instead, looking at the articles as a whole, it was clear that the ordinary shares were meant to be the residual class; the particular articles merely reflected the fact that, for so long as the company had only two classes of share, the ordinary shares naturally ranked second. The company was not precluded by the rights of the ordinary shares from issuing a new class of shares ranking in pri-

[182] This assumes that enhancing rights can be a variation of rights: see this chapter, at 343.
[183] [1958] CLY 446, CA.

ority to the ordinary shares; in that event the ordinary shares, as the residual class, would simply rank third.

This decision establishes that, as a normal rule, the creation of a new class of shares ranking in priority to ordinary shares would not amount to a variation of class rights attached to ordinary shares. Unless displaced by articles, the rights attached to ordinary shares are taken to be qualified by the possibility of being subsequently postponed to a class or classes of preference shares. However, the comment of Jenkins LJ quoted above is more far-reaching in that it suggests that the rights attached to ordinary shares can never be class rights. A further argument points in the same direction. Earlier, when discussing *Cumbrian Newspapers Group Ltd v Cumberland & Westmorland Herald Newspaper & Printing Co*,[184] it was noted that the Companies Act 1985, ss 17 (2) and 125 are to be read together, and that s 17 (2) refers to special rights. It is possible to argue that the normal rights of ordinary shares are not 'special' rights and that, for this reason, the procedures for variation of class rights do not apply. Further support for this argument may also be found in Romer LJ's judgment in *Hodge v James Howell & Co Ltd*[185] where he stated that the particular articles did not 'so much confer rights of any special kind as recognise the characteristics which normally attach to ordinary shares'.

Yet, taking, for example,[186] the case of a company which has two classes of ordinary shares, the shares in each class having different par values, and a proposal to remove from one class the right to cast one vote per share which is currently attached to both classes, would that not vary the class rights of the ordinary shares which are to become non-voting? In principle a variation of fundamental importance, such as a removal of voting rights, would seem to be deserving of the special protection afforded to class rights. *Greenhalgh v Arderne Cinemas Ltd*[187] lends some support to the view that changes to the one-vote-per-share default right of ordinary shares may be a variation of class rights. The state of the authorities leaves some uncertainty, but it is suggested that, although the creation of a new class of prior ranking shares would not vary the class rights of ordinary shares, there may be circumstances when rights attaching to ordinary shares may fall to be treated as class rights.

STATUTORY PRE-EMPTION RIGHTS—A CLASS RIGHT?

Is the right of pre-emption in respect of new share allotments which is conferred by the Companies Act 1985, s 89 capable of being regarded as a right which, if excluded or dis-applied, amounts to a variation of class rights? Although there is no authority on this point, it seems reasonably clear that this question should be answered in the negative. The right conferred by s 89 is expressly stated to be subject to a number of subsequent sections, including s 91, which provides for exclusion of the right by a private company, and s 95,

[184] [1987] Ch 1.

[185] [1958] CLY 446, CA.

[186] The example assumes that shares with different par values are in different classes. That point is discussed in this chapter, at 335.

[187] [1946] 1 All ER 512, CA, 516 *per* Lord Greene MR.

which provides for dis-application of the right by both public and private companies. Accordingly, the s 89 right can be viewed as being inherently defeasible in accordance with ss 91 and 95; exclusion or dis-application is therefore not a variation of the right.

Different views on this situation could, quite properly, be arrived at because of the particular terms of companies' articles of association or the terms on which shares have been issued. If the articles contain a provision entitling classes of shares to *pari passu* entitlements to offers of new shares, a proposal to limit offers to new shares to the existing holders of shares in that class would seem to vary the *pari passu* class right *under the articles* (as opposed to the statutory entitlement). However, if the articles or terms of issue do not make provision for *pari passu* entitlement to pre-emption, the position should be as outlined. In particular, a *pari passu* entitlement to dividends and capital should not be interpreted as extending to a *pari passu* entitlement to pre-emption rights in respect of new shares.

THE PROCEDURE FOR VARIATION OF CLASS RIGHTS

Where class rights are set out in the company's memorandum or articles, a variation requires an alteration to the company's constitution approved by the shareholders in general meeting. Articles of association can be altered by a special resolution of the shareholders in general meeting in accordance with s 9 of the Companies Act 1985. Unanimous consent of all of the shareholders who are entitled to vote, whether given informally[188] or in a written resolution,[189] is also effective to change the articles. The power to alter the articles by special resolution is subject to the qualification, developed by the court,[190] that it must be exercised in good faith in the interests of the company. A dissenting shareholder who is aggrieved by an alteration to the articles may seek to challenge it under the Companies Act 1985, s 459 which permits the court to grant relief from unfairly prejudicial conduct.

Provisions in the memorandum which contain class rights are alterable in accordance with the Companies Act 1985, s 17. This provides for alteration by special resolution, subject to a number of provisos. The first proviso[191] is that alterations may be challenged in court if the objecting minority holds at least 15 per cent in nominal value of the company's issued share capital and the application is made within 21 days after the resolution was passed.[192] Secondly, it is expressly provided that alterations may be challenged in court under the Companies Act 1985, s 459 on the grounds that they amount to

[188] *Cane v Jones* [1980] 1 WLR 1451.

[189] Passed in accordance with written resolution procedures in articles (such as Table A, art 53) or in accordance with the statutory written resolution procedure under Companies Act 1985, s 381A–C.

[190] *Allen v Gold Reefs of West Africa Ltd* [1900] 1 Ch 656, CA. Rixon, FG, 'Competing Interests and Conflicting Principles: An Examination of the Power of Alteration of Articles of Association' (1986) 49 MLR 446; *Shareholder Remedies A Consultation Paper* (Law Commission Consultation Paper No 142) (1996) para 9.39.

[191] Companies Act 1985, s 17 (1).

[192] Companies Act 1985, s 5 (2) applied to s 17 by s 17 (3).

unfairly prejudicial conduct.[193] The third proviso is that the power to alter conditions in the memorandum in accordance with the Companies Act 1985, s 17 can be overridden by the memorandum itself: that power does not apply where the memorandum itself provides for or prohibits the alteration of all or any of the conditions.

No alteration to the memorandum or articles can require a member to subscribe more shares or increase his liability to contribute to the company's share capital or otherwise to pay money to the company, unless the member agrees in writing, either in advance of the resolution or afterwards, to be bound by the resolution.[194]

In addition to the normal corporate consents required to change the company's constitution, variation of class rights also requires class consents. The procedure for obtaining class consents depends on where the class rights are set out. Normally class rights would be contained in the company's articles or in the terms of issue of securities or, occasionally in smaller companies, in shareholder agreements. Accordingly, this situation is considered first in the following paragraphs. There then follows a discussion of the more unusual situation, that is where the class rights are set out in the memorandum.

Class Rights Contained in Articles, Terms on which Securities are Issued, or Shareholder Agreements

In this situation, it must first be ascertained whether the articles contain provision for the class consents required to vary class rights. If the articles do make provision, that provision normally governs the variation.[195] If the articles do not make provision, the Companies Act 1985, s 125 (2) comes into play. This provides that class rights may be varied if, but only if:

> (a) the holders of three-quarters in nominal value of the issued shares of that class consent in writing to the variation; or
>
> (b) an extraordinary resolution passed at a separate general meeting of the holders of that class sanctions the variation; and
>
> any additional requirement (howsoever imposed) in relation to the variation of those rights is complied with.

The Companies Act 1985, s 125 (2) is based on the variation of rights procedure that used to be contained in Table A. The inclusion of this provision in the primary legislation renders its inclusion in articles unnecessary; accordingly the 1985 Act, Table A contains no such provision.

There is one qualification to the proposition that a provision in articles in respect of variation of rights alone governs the variation of rights contained in the articles, in the terms of issue or shareholder agreements, with the Companies Act 1985, s 125 (2) being the default provision applicable only where the articles do not otherwise provide. If the variation is connected with the giving, variation, revocation or renewal of an authority for allotment under the Companies Act 1985, s 80 or with a reduction of the company's

[193] Ibid, s 17 (2)(a). [194] Ibid, s 16. [195] Ibid, s 125 (4)(b).

share capital under the Companies Act 1985, s 135, condition (a) or (b) of s 125 (2) set out above must be satisfied in addition to any requirement of the articles or other relevant document with respect to the variation.[196]

Class Rights set out in the Memorandum

If the memorandum contains provision for the variation of the rights, that provision must be followed. Although this is not stated expressly in the Companies Act 1985, s 125, it seems to follow from the Companies Act 1985, s 17 (2) which provides for alteration of conditions in the memorandum in accordance with any procedure set out in the memorandum. If the memorandum prohibits alteration, then no variation may be effected by resolution or agreement of all or any of the members. If, in that case, the entrenched provisions in the memorandum prove to be unduly restrictive, the company's only option (apart from liquidation) is to effect a court-approved scheme of arrangement under the Companies Act 1985, s 425.

If the memorandum is silent with regard to variation of class rights set out in the memorandum, regard must then be had to the company's articles. If the articles make provision for variation, under the Companies Act 1985, s 125 (5) that provision applies but only if that provision was included in the company's articles at the time of its original incorporation.[197] There is a view that, although the Companies Act 1985, s 125 does not mention it, a provision in later articles could be relied upon if the memorandum cross-refers to a procedure set out in the articles.[198] This is an area where clarification and simplification of the rules governing the applicable provisions is desirable.

The Companies Act 1985, s 125 (5) provides that if neither the memorandum or articles contain provision for the variation of rights attached to a class of shares by the company's memorandum, the rights may only be varied with the consent of all of the members of the company. Even those members holding shares with restricted or no voting rights would be required to give their consent. A sensible construction of the Companies Act 1985, s 125 (5) is that it applies even where the articles do make provision but that provision is ineffective because it was not contained in the articles on original incorporation (or is not cross-referred to in the memorandum); however, this does involve reading s 125 (5) as if it said 'no effective provision'.

The special provision with respect to any variation connected with the giving, variation, revocation or renewal of an authority for allotment under the Companies Act 1985, s 80 or with a reduction of the company's share capital under the Companies Act 1985, s 135 also applies to the variation of rights contained in the memorandum: condition (a) or (b) of s 125 (2) set out above must be satisfied in addition to any other requirement with respect to the variation.[199]

[196] Companies Act 1985, s 125 (3).
[197] Ibid, s 125 (4)(a).
[198] That this would be effective was accepted by the courts before the enactment of the statutory procedures: *Re Welsbach Incandescent Gas Light Co Ltd* [1904] 1 Ch 87, CA.
[199] Companies Act 1985, s 125 (3).

Miscellaneous Procedural Points applicable to the Statutory Variation Procedure and to Variation Procedures set out in the Memorandum or Articles

Class meetings are governed by the procedural requirements applicable to company meetings generally (with appropriate modifications) except that: (i) the necessary quorum at any meeting (other than an adjourned meeting) is two persons holding, or representing by proxy, at least one-third in nominal value of the issued shares of the class in question, and at an adjourned meeting one person holding shares of the class in question or his proxy; and (ii) any holder of shares of the class in question present or by proxy may demand a poll. These requirements with regard to quorum and polls are imposed by the Companies Act 1985, s 125 (6) and appear to be mandatory. It is for the chairman of a class meeting to regulate its conduct but prima facie the meeting should only be attended by the members of the class so that they have an opportunity to discuss the matter privately and without their discussion being overheard by members of other classes.[200]

If a company alters it memorandum or articles this triggers extensive disclosure obligations. A copy of any special resolution or agreement which is effective to alter the articles must be forwarded to the registrar of companies,[201] as must any special resolution altering the conditions of memorandum.[202] The copy of any such resolution or agreement sent to the registrar of companies must be accompanied by a printed copy of the altered memorandum or articles.[203] The registrar of companies must then arrange for publication in the London Gazette of notice of receipt by him of the document making or evidencing the alteration in the memorandum or articles.[204] To ensure that any variation to class rights contained in the terms of issue of securities or shareholder agreements rather than in the company's constitution are also brought to the public's attention, the Companies Act 1985, s 128 (3) provides that if the relevant resolution is not otherwise subject to disclosure requirements, notification of its passing must in any event be delivered to the registrar of companies. Where a company is listed, it must also comply with the disclosure and other requirements imposed by *The Listing Rules*.[205]

200 *Carruth v Imperial Chemical Industries Ltd* [1937] AC 707, HL.

201 Companies Act 1985, s 380.

202 Ibid.

203 Companies Act 1985, s 18 (2).

204 Ibid, s 711.

205 *The Listing Rules*, ch 9, para 9.10 (c) requires a listed company to notify the Exchange (Company Announcements Office) without delay of any changes to the rights attaching to any class of listed securities. The content of circulars sent to shareholders in connection with proposals to alter the memorandum or articles is regulated (*The Listing Rules*, ch 13, para 13. 9) and the memorandum and articles must comply with certain specific requirements as to content (*The Listing Rules*, ch 13, para 13.8).

VOTING TO ALTER CLASS RIGHTS—A FETTERED POWER?

It is well established that a vote attached to a share is a property right to be exercised as its owner thinks fit.[206] In principle, a shareholder cannot be compelled to vote, nor can he be held to account for the way in which he chooses to exercise his vote. A line of authorities, however, imposes a qualification: in certain circumstances the courts will deny effect to a resolution if the shareholders who supported it were, in some sense, exercising their power inappropriately. Although some of the language in relevant judgments may suggest otherwise,[207] denying effect to a resolution is not the same thing as imposing a duty on the shareholders to vote in a particular way—shareholders may please themselves knowing that even though the court may deny effect to their decisions, they will not be held to have breached a duty, or be liable to pay compensation, to anyone who may be aggrieved by their actions.[208] However, rational shareholders would want to avoid the trouble and expense of voting in circumstances where that vote may later be held to be ineffective by a court. Accordingly, if they vote at all, they may consider themselves to be under a practical, if not a legal, duty to cast their votes in a manner which would withstand judicial scrutiny.

A class consent to the variation of rights attached to the shares comprising the class is one of the situations where the courts have been prepared to deny effect to the decision of the majority of the class. In *British American Nickel Corpn Ltd v O'Brien*[209] the company proposed a scheme for the reconstruction of the company involving mortgage bonds being exchanged for income bonds. The proposal was passed at a meeting of the mortgage bondholders but the sanction would not have been obtained but for the support of the holder of a large number of bonds who had been given an incentive to support the scheme which was not made available to other bondholders and which was not disclosed. The Privy Council held that the resolution was invalid, one reason for this invalidity being that the bondholder who had been given the incentive had not treated the interest of the whole class of bondholders as the dominant consideration.

Viscount Haldane, delivering the judgment, explained the principle applied by the court:[210]

> There is, however, a restriction of such powers, when conferred on a majority of a special class in order to enable that majority to bind a minority. They must be exercised subject to a general principle, which is applicable to all authorities conferred on majorities of classes enabling them to bind minorities; namely, that the power given must be exercised for the purpose of benefiting the class as a whole, and not merely individual members only.

[206] Leading authorities are *Pender v Lushington* (1877) 6 Ch D 70; *Northern Counties Securities Ltd v Jackson & Steeple Ltd* [1974] 1 WLR 1133; *North-West Transportation Co Ltd v Beatty* (1887) 12 App Cas 589, PC.

[207] For example, *British American Nickel Corpn v O'Brien* [1927] AC 369, PC, 378 *per* Viscount Haldane.

[208] Sealy, LS, 'Equitable and Other Fetters on a Shareholder's Freedom to Vote' in Eastham, NE, and Krivy, B (eds), *The Cambridge Lectures 1981* (1982) 80.

[209] [1927] AC 369, PC.

[210] Ibid at 371.

This principle was applied by Megarry J in *Re Holders Investment Trust Ltd*,[211] where trustees who were the holders of the majority of the preference shares in a company had supported a proposal to convert the preference shares into loan stock. The trustees also held the majority of the company's ordinary shares, and the evidence indicated that they had acted throughout on the basis of what was in the interests of trust (which, of course, as trustees they were obliged to do) and had not applied their minds to the question of what was in the interests of the preference shareholders as a class. In these circumstances, Megarry J held that the sanction given by the preference shareholders as a class was not effective.

STATUTORY PROTECTION OF MINORITIES IN A CLASS

Under the Companies Act 1985, s 127, shareholders have the right to apply to court to have a variation of class rights cancelled. There are certain requirements which must be satisfied in order to bring a claim under this provision and it is therefore limited in its effect. To have standing to bring a claim, the petitioner or petitioners must hold not less in the aggregate than 15 per cent[212] of the issued shares of the class in question.[213] The petitioner or petitioners must not have consented to or voted in favour of the resolution for the variation;[214] shareholders who have simply changed their minds may not invoke s 127.[215] The application must be made within 21 days after the date on which the consent was given or the resolution was passed;[216] a proposal made by the Jenkins Committee in 1962 that this period should be extended to 28 days has not been taken up.[217]

If a claim is properly brought, the variation has no effect until it is confirmed by the court.[218] The court may disallow the variation if it is satisfied, having regard to all the circumstances of the case, that the variation would unfairly prejudice the shareholders of the class represented by the applicant; if the court is not so satisfied, it must confirm the variation.[219] The court's decision is final[220] and a copy of the court's order must be filed with the registrar of companies.[221]

There is a dearth of reported decisions on the court's powers under the Companies Act 1985, s 127,[222] which tends to suggest that the section is not

[211] [1971] 2 All ER 289.

[212] The Jenkins Committee recommended 10 per cent instead of 15 but this suggestion was not taken up: *Report of the Company Law Committee* Cmnd 1749 (1962) para 193.

[213] Companies Act 1985, s 127 (2).

[214] Ibid.

[215] As the Jenkins Committee pointed out (*Report of the Company Law Committee* Cmnd 1749 (1962) para 193) this provision can work harshly against a nominee who holds shares on behalf of a number of persons, because assenting to the resolution on behalf of one of the persons for whom he holds shares seems to preclude the nominee from joining in a petition under s 127.

[216] Companies Act 1985, s 127 (3).

[217] *Report of the Company Law Committee* Cmnd 1749 (1962) (Jenkins Committee) para 193.

[218] Companies Act 1985, s 127 (2).

[219] Ibid, s 127 (4).

[220] Ibid.

[221] Companies Act 1985, s 127 (5).

[222] Peripheral aspects of the procedure now contained in Companies Act 1985, s 127 were litigated in *Re Suburban Stores Ltd* [1943] Ch 156 CA and *Re Sound City (Films) Ltd* [1947] Ch 169.

extensively relied upon in practice. The remedy overlaps with the Companies Act 1985, s 459. The unfair prejudice remedy in the Companies Act 1985, s 459 is not subject to such restrictive conditions; thus dissidents holding less than the 15 per cent required for the purposes of s 127 or who are outside the time-limit imposed by that section may still air their grievances in court by petitioning under s 459.[223] The court may order a buy out of the petitioning shareholders' shares or any other appropriate remedy under the Companies Act 1985, s 459. This flexibility with regard to remedies contrasts sharply with the Companies Act 1985, s 127, where the only remedy available to the court is to disallow the variation.

223 *Rights and Issues Investment Trust Ltd v Stylo Shoes Ltd* [1965] Ch 250, decided under a statutory predecessor of Companies Act 1985, s 459, arose from an alteration of class rights which was alleged to be oppressive to the minority of the class. The claim failed.

10

Maintenance and Reduction of Capital

MAINTENANCE OF CAPITAL—THE BASIC PRINCIPLE

At the heart of English company law is the recognition that there is a price to be paid for limited liability in the form of restrictions on the use of the company's capital. Creditors who deal with limited companies take the risk of the company becoming unable to pay its debts as a result of losing its capital in improvident trading, but as a matter of public policy[1] they are protected against capital being lost in other ways. Historically case law[2] established two limitations on the use of capital: (i) capital could only be applied by the company in pursuit of the objects; and (ii) capital could not be returned to shareholders without the leave of the court. The first of these limitations has been largely overridden by the development of extensive objects clauses and by the virtual abolition of the rule which rendered void acts falling outside the company's objects (the *ultra vires* rule) by the Companies Act 1985, s 35. The second limitation remains of considerable importance.

CAPITAL MUST NOT BE RETURNED TO SHAREHOLDERS

In *Trevor v Whitworth*[3] Lord Watson explained that the law prohibits

> every transaction between a company and a shareholder, by means of which the money already paid to the company in respect of his shares is returned to him, unless the Court has authorised the transaction. Paid-up capital may be diminished or lost in the course of the company's trading; that is a result which no legislation can prevent; but persons who deal with, and give credit to a limited company, naturally rely upon the fact that the company is trading with a certain amount of capital already paid, as well as upon the responsibility of its members for the capital remaining at call; and they are entitled to assume that no part of the capital which has been paid into the coffers of the company has been subsequently paid out, except in the legitimate course of its business.

Similarly in *Guinness v Land Corporation of Ireland*[4] Cotton LJ noted that paid-up capital could not be returned to shareholders because that would

[1] *MacDougall v Jersey Imperial Hotel Co Ltd* (1864) 2 H & M 528, 71 ER 568.

[2] *Trevor v Whitworth* (1887) 12 App Cas 409, HL; *Guinness v Land Corporation of Ireland* (1882) 22 Ch D 349, CA, 375.

[3] (1887) 12 App Cas 409, HL, 423–4.

[4] (1882) 22 Ch D 349, CA, 375. See also *Verner v General and Commercial Investment Trust* [1894] 2 Ch 239, CA, 264 *per* Lindley LJ; *Ammonia Soda Co Ltd v Chamberlain* [1918] 1 Ch 266, CA, 292 *per* Warrington LJ; *Hill v Permanent Trustee Co of New South Wales Ltd* [1930] 720, PC, 731 *per* Lord Russell of Killowen.

'take away from the fund to which the creditors have a right to look as that out of which they are to be paid'.

The rule prohibiting the return of capital to shareholders is now closely linked to the Companies Act 1985, Pt VIII which provides that distributions of the company's assets to members must only be made out of profits available for the purpose. The Companies Act 1985, Pt VIII does more than merely restate the underlying common-law rule because 'profits available for distribution' is a precise statutory concept. For this reason the Companies Act 1985, Pt VIII and its effect are examined separately in Chapter 12.

An unlawful return of capital can arise from a distribution of cash or other assets and can occur in circumstances where the irregularity is not immediately obvious. In *Re Halt Garage (1964) Ltd*[5] a family company was owned and managed by a husband and wife team. The company continued to pay the wife as a director of the company even after it had become apparent that she was seriously ill and would not be active again in the management of the company. The company later went into liquidation and, on the application of the liquidator, Oliver J held that the amount of remuneration so paid exceeded what could be regarded as a genuine exercise of the power to pay remuneration. To the extent that the payments exceeded genuine remuneration for the holding of the office of director, they were repayable to the liquidator because they amounted to a disguised return of capital.

The test of 'genuineness' for distinguishing between proper transactions and disguised gifts to shareholders from capital is more interventionist than a test based solely on honesty. As in the *Halt Garage* case, a payment can amount to a disguised gift from capital even where the good faith of the directors (in the sense of absence of fraudulent intent)[6] is not in doubt. The mere fact that the company has transacted on terms which appear to the court to be somewhat generous to the other party will not suffice for a transaction to be treated as a disguised gift; but evidence of patently excessive or unreasonable terms will cast doubt on the genuineness of that transaction.[7]

In *Aveling Barford Ltd v Perion Ltd*[8] the plaintiff company, at a time when it had no distributable profits, sold some of its property at a price considerably lower than that at which it had been valued by an independent valuer. The purchaser was a company, Perion Ltd, which was controlled by Dr Lee who was also the controller of the vendor company. Within a year Perion Ltd resold the property for a significant profit. The liquidator of Aveling Barford successfully sought to recover the proceeds of sale on the grounds that Perion Ltd held it on constructive trust. The court held that Dr Lee had breached his fidu-

[5] [1982] 3 All ER 1016. See also *Ridge Securities Ltd v IRC* [1964] 1 All ER 275; *Jenkins v Harbour View Courts Ltd* [1966] NZLR 1, NZ CA; *Redweaver Investments Ltd v Lawrence Field Ltd* (1990–91) 5 ACSR 438, NSW EqD.

[6] [1982] 3 All ER 1016, 1043. See also *Re National Funds Assurance Co* (1878) 10 Ch D 118, 128 *per* Jessel MR.

[7] [1982] 3 All ER 1016 Ch, 1041.

[8] [1989] BCLC 626. See also *Hickson Timber Protection Ltd (in receivership) v Hickson International plc* [1995] 2 NZLR 8, NZ CA, noted Barrett, RI, 'Diversion to Shareholders of Proceeds of Sale of Corporate Asset' (1996) 70 ALJ 43; Grantham, R, 'Corporate Groups and Informality' [1995] NZLJ 176.

ciary duty to Aveling Barford by selling the property at such a low price and that since Perion Ltd had known of the facts which made this transaction a breach of duty it was liable as a constructive trustee. Hoffmann J dealt with the argument that, if there had been a breach of fiduciary duty by Dr Lee, it was unchallengeable because it had been done with the consent of the shareholders of Aveling Barford Ltd by holding that the transaction was not a genuine exercise of the company's power under its memorandum to sell its assets, and that it amounted to an unlawful return of capital which could not be validated by shareholder authorisation or ratification.

An interesting feature of the *Aveling Barford* decision is that the purchaser company was not itself a shareholder in the vendor company, although both companies shared the same controller. Hoffmann J held that the fact that the transaction was in favour of a company controlled by, rather than directly to, Dr Lee was irrelevant because the real purpose of the transaction was to benefit Dr Lee. The *Aveling Barford* case does not extend the principle that capital must not be returned to shareholders because, by an indirect route, that was exactly the result in that case.[9] An indirect return of capital was also in issue in *Barclays Bank plc v British & Commonwealth Holdings plc*[10] where a group of banks, acting through a corporate vehicle, was required to buy a company's redeemable preference shares in the event of the company failing to redeem those shares in accordance with their terms. The company gave financial covenants to the banks so that, if it found itself unable to redeem its preference shares, it would also be in breach of covenant to the banks. The economic effect of the arrangement was that the banks had to pay for the shares but could then prove in the company's liquidation as creditors for the amount that it had paid for the shares as the sum due for breach of contract. This was held to amount to an indirect return of capital, contrary to *Trevor v Whitworth*,[11] on the basis that the rule in that case was wide enough to catch an agreement which was only likely to be called upon in the event of the company's insolvency, and which enabled shareholders in that event to obtain from third parties a payment in an equivalent amount to the payment due from the company, and for the third parties thereupon to become entitled as creditors to seek repayment from the company. Had the decision been otherwise, the effect would have been to allow a claim by shareholders to be converted into a claim by creditors ranking before shareholders' claims and equally with other creditors.

[9] The High Court of Australia has held that a scheme from which shareholders benefit indirectly can amount to an unlawful return of capital: *Australasian Oil Exploration Ltd v Lachbery* (1958) 101 CLR 119, H Ct of Aust.

[10] [1995] BCC 19 (affirmed [1995] BCC 1059, CA) following *Re Walters' Deed of Guarantee* [1933] Ch 321.

[11] (1887) 12 App Cas 409, HL.

CAPITAL AND THE OBJECTS CLAUSE[12]

Trevor v Whitworth[13] is also authority for the proposition that a company must only spend its capital in pursuit of its objects. Lord Herschell said:[14]

> The capital may, no doubt, be diminished by expenditure upon and reasonably incidental to all the objects specified. A part of it may be lost in carrying on the business operations authorised. Of this all persons trusting the company are aware, and take the risk. But I think they have a right to rely, and were intended by the Legislature to have a right to rely, on the capital remaining undiminished by any expenditure outside these limits, or by the return of any part of it to the shareholders.

The objects of a company are specified in its memorandum of association.[15] It is usual for the objects clause to be lengthy and to include within it a wide range of objects, in the sense of businesses in which the company may wish to engage, and all the powers that the company may wish to exercise in pursuit of any of these objects. A subjective object empowering the company to do 'all such other things as the directors may think incidental or conducive to any of the above objects' is one of the final provisions of a typical objects clause. To ensure that the coverage of the objects clause is as extensive as possible and is not restricted by being narrowly construed, it is also standard practice to state that the paragraphs of the objects clause are to be interpreted independently of each other and that none is subsidiary or ancillary to the others.

The development of lengthy objects clauses was the response by companies and their advisers to the *ultra vires* rule. In *Ashbury Railway Carriage and Iron Co Ltd v Riche*[16] the House of Lords held that a company only had capacity to do what was authorised by its objects clause. Anything else was totally void and could not be enforced nor become binding on the company by reason of estoppel, lapse of time, acquiescence or delay.[17] Even the approval of all of the shareholders could not make something which was outside the objects clause valid or enforceable. The harshness of the *ultra vires* rule, which was originally perceived to be a protection for shareholders and creditors in that they could discover by reading the memorandum the ways in which the funds which they made available to the company could be used, was only ameliorated by the fact that whatever could fairly be regarded as incidental to or consequential upon the specified objects would be implied into the objects clause.[18]

The companies legislation which was in force between 1856 and 1890 did not permit the objects of a company to be altered. Once it became possible to alter objects with the consent of only a majority of the shareholders and without the consent of the creditors, the idea that the objects clause was a safe-

[12] This section summarises some aspects of the law relating to the objects clause which are discussed in more detail in Ch 3 above, at 85–97. The emphasis here is on the use of the objects clause as a mechanism for controlling corporate gifts.

[13] (1887) 12 App Cas 409, HL.

[14] Ibid at 415. Also 424 *per* Lord Watson and 433 *per* Lord Macnaghten.

[15] Companies Act 1985, s 2 (1)(c). [16] (1875) LR 7 HL 653, HL.

[17] *York Corporation v Henry Leetham & Sons Ltd* [1924] 1 Ch 557, 583.

[18] *Attorney-General v Great Eastern Railway Co* (1880) 5 App Cas 473, HL.

guard against shareholders' and creditors' money being put to purposes which they had not authorised was undermined. The power to alter the objects clause has been progressively relaxed by various Companies Acts, the most recent relaxation having been effected by the Companies Act 1989 which removed limitations on the ways in which the objects can be changed: under the Companies Act 1985, s 4, a company is now free to alter its objects clause in any way by passing a special resolution to that effect. Dissenting shareholders who hold at least 15 per cent of the company's issued share capital can apply[19] to court for the alteration to the objects to be cancelled, but such applications are extremely rare.[20]

The role played by the *ultra vires* rule in protecting shareholders and creditors was also soon limited by the practice of companies adopting ever wider objects. This practice encountered some initial resistance from the courts which invoked a 'main object' rule of construction: having identified the company's main object, the other objects and powers specified in the objects clause would be regarded as ancillary to that main object.[21] Companies then sought to bypass this limitation by adopting the 'independent' object provision. In *Cotman v Brougham*,[22] albeit with some reluctance, the House of Lords accepted that this clause achieved the purpose of displacing the operation of the main object rule of construction. The 'subjective' object provision which empowers the company to do whatever *its directors* consider to be incidental or conducive to its stated objects was also eventually sanctioned by the courts.[23]

Two Court of Appeal decisions in the 1980s demonstrated how limited had become the effect of the *ultra vires* rule by that time. *Re Horsley & Weight Ltd*[24] concerned the validity of payments made by a company in respect of a pension policy. The company's objects clause authorised the granting of pensions by the company. The Court of Appeal held that the granting of pensions was an object of the company and that therefore the payments in respect of the pension could not be *ultra vires* the company. Buckley LJ commented:

> The objects of a company do not need to be commercial; they can be charitable or philanthropic; indeed, they can be whatever the original incorporators wish, provided that they are legal. Nor is there any reason why a company should not part with its funds gratuitously or for non-commercial reasons if to do so is within its declared objects.

Thus the principle of *Trevor v Whitworth*[25] was respected—a company must only spend its capital in pursuit of its objects—but it was recognised that the

[19] Under Companies Act 1985, s 5. Creditors holding at least 15 per cent of the company's debentures can also apply but only where the debentures are secured by a floating charge and were issued or first issued before 1 December 1947, or form part of the same series as any debentures so issued: Companies Act 1985, s 5 (2)(b) and (8).

[20] After an earlier relaxation made by the Companies Act 1948 there was only reported application under the relevant section: *Re Hampstead Garden Suburban Trust Ltd* [1962] Ch 806.

[21] As explained in *Anglo-Overseas Agencies v Green* [1961] 1 QB 1, 8. For cases considering whether to wind up a company on the grounds that its principal object had failed see *Re Haven Gold Mining Co* (1882) 20 Ch D 151, CA; *Re German Date Coffee Co* (1882) 20 169, CA; *Re Kitson & Co Ltd* [1946] 1 All ER 435, CA; *Re Eastern Telegraph Co Ltd* [1947] 2 All ER 104.

[22] [1918] AC 514, HL.

[23] *Bell House Ltd v City Wall Properties Ltd* [1966] 2 QB 656, CA.

[24] [1982] Ch 442, CA.

[25] (1887) 12 App Cas 409, HL.

permissible width of a company's objects meant that this could be made into an insubstantial limitation by appropriate drafting.

The second Court of Appeal decision, *Rolled Steel Products (Holdings) Ltd v British Steel Corporation*,[26] involved a guarantee and debenture given by the plaintiff company in respect of debts incurred by another company which was under the same shareholder control (ie a sister company). The company's objects clause authorised the granting of guarantees and debentures and it was held that the guarantee and debenture was not *ultra vires* the company. The Court of Appeal upheld a distinction drawn in earlier cases (including *Re Horsley and Weight Ltd*)[27] between 'true' objects and powers and accepted that, notwithstanding the existence of an independent objects clause, a provision in the memorandum would be classified as a power if either it was incapable of existing as a separate object or it could only be construed as an ancillary power. On this basis, the court held that the provision authorising the giving of guarantees and debentures was a power. It held further that a corporate power contained in the company's objects clause could only properly be exercised in pursuit of the company's true objects but that using the power for any other purpose amounted to an excess or abuse of power by the directors and did not fall outside the capacity of the company so as to be caught by the *ultra vires* rule.[28] Provided the act done in pursuit of the power was of a category which was *capable* of being performed as reasonably incidental to the attainment or pursuit of the objects, that was sufficient for it to be regarded as being within the capacity of the company.[29]

The analysis in the *Rolled Steel* decision involved a re-assessment of previous decisions[30] which had appeared to hold that exercising a power in the objects clause otherwise than in pursuit of the objects could, depending on whether the person dealing with the company was aware of the purpose for which the power was being exercised,[31] be *ultra vires*. The Court of Appeal achieved this reassessment by explaining that the term '*ultra vires*' could mean outside the authority of the directors as well as beyond the capacity of the company, and that it was in the former sense that the term had been used in earlier cases. This reasoning may not be entirely consistent with the judgments in earlier cases[32] and it must be accepted that the approach in the

[26] [1986] Ch 246, CA.

[27] *Re David Payne & Co Ltd* [1904] 2 Ch 608, CA; *Re Jon Beauforte Ltd* [1953] Ch 131; *Introductions Ltd v National Provincial Bank Ltd* [1970] Ch 199, CA.

[28] The distinction between acts beyond the company's capacity and acts which amount to an excess or abuse of power by the directors is also drawn in *Charterbridge Corp Ltd v Lloyds Bank Ltd* [1970] Ch 62 and *Re Halt Garage (1964) Ltd* [1982] 3 All ER 1016.

[29] [1986] Ch 246, CA, 295 *per* Slade LJ and 306 *per* Browne-Wilkinson LJ, applied in *Halifax Building Society v Meridian Housing Association* [1994] 2 BCLC 540.

[30] Such as *Re David Payne & Co Ltd* [1904] 2 Ch 608, CA; *Re Jon Beauforte Ltd* [1953] Ch 131; *Introductions Ltd v National Provincial Bank Ltd* [1970] Ch 199, CA .

[31] That corporate capacity could in some way depend on the knowledge of the person dealing with the company was a logically unsupportable proposition and was rightly criticised: Baxter, C, 'Ultra Vires and Agency Untwined' [1970] CLJ 280.

[32] It is particularly difficult to reconcile the *Rolled Steel* decision with that of the House of Lords in *Sinclair v Brougham* [1914] AC 398, HL. Their Lordships were mainly concerned with the consequences of *ultra vires* but accepted that the power to borrow money must be limited to borrowing for the purposes of the company, borrowing for any other purpose being *ultra*

Rolled Steel decision is difficult to square with statements such as Buckley LJ's comment in *Re Horsley and Weight Ltd*[33] that 'in the case of express "objects" which, on construction of the memorandum or by their very nature, are ancillary to the dominant or main objects of the company, an exercise of any such power can only be intra vires if it is in fact ancillary or incidental to the pursuit of some such dominant or main object'. What the decision in *Rolled Steel* demonstrates most forcefully is a willingness by the courts as a matter of policy to limit the effect of the *ultra vires* rule and to reinterpret earlier case law in a sensible, if technically questionable, manner in order to achieve that result. At least in cases involving commercial companies,[34] it would now appear to be unlikely that a court would be willing to entertain an argument based on highly technical objections to the *Rolled Steel* decision and the analysis by the Court of Appeal of earlier authorities.

A particular heresy[35] put to rest by the Court of Appeal in the *Horsley and Weight* and *Rolled Steel* decisions was that the capacity of the company to make gifts could depend upon, or be limited by, an objective test of benefit to the company. The Court of Appeal also accepted that the bona fides of the directors was irrelevant to the question of capacity to make a gift, although this was pertinent to the issue of possible breach of duty by the directors. In the *Rolled Steel* decision, Slade LJ said that these tests of 'benefit' and 'bona fides'[36] 'should, in my opinion, now be recognised as being of no assistance, and indeed positively misleading, when the relevant question is whether a particular gratuitous transaction is within the company's corporate capacity.'

The efforts of companies and their advisers and, after initial hostility, by the courts in limiting the effect of the *ultra vires* is now reinforced and, to some extent, overridden by statute. The relevant provisions are contained in the Companies Act 1985, which was significantly amended in this respect by the Companies Act 1989. Professor Prentice was asked to review the position on behalf of the DTI prior to the enactment of the Companies Act 1989 and to consult with interested persons. In his report Professor Prentice concluded that 'the doctrine of *ultra vires* no longer serves any useful purpose' because 'the doctrine is for all intents and purposes defeasible at the discretion of the draftsman'.[37] Virtually all of those consulted by Professor Prentice were of the view that the doctrine of *ultra vires* failed to provide any significant protection

vires. *Sinclair v Brougham* was not followed in *Westdeutsche Landesbank Girozentrale v Islington BC* [1996] AC 669, HL but that was with regard to the consequences of *ultra vires* rather than this point.

[33] [1982] Ch 442, CA, 449.

[34] In *Simmons Housing Ltd v UDT Ltd* [1986] 1 WLR 1440, Mervyn Davies J adopted an approach more in favour of allowing the *ultra vires* rule considerable scope but this was in relation to a charitable housing association registered under the Industrial and Provident Societies Act 1965. Contrast this with the later case of *Halifax Building Society v Meridian Housing Association* [1994] 2 BCLC 540, where Arden J applied *Rolled Steel* in relation to a housing association formed under the same Act.

[35] Derived from the judgment of Eve J in *Re Lee, Behrens & Co Ltd* [1932] 2 Ch 46 and applied in *Parke v Daily News Ltd* [1962] Ch 927; *Re W & M Roith Ltd* [1967] 1 All ER 427; criticised in *Charterbridge Corp Ltd v Lloyds Bank Ltd* [1970] Ch 62 and *Re Halt Garage (1964) Ltd* [1982] 3 All ER 1016.

[36] [1986] Ch 246, CA, 288.

[37] *Reform of the Ultra Vires Rule: A Consultative Document* (DTI) ch III, para 6.

to the interests of shareholders[38] and were critical of its operation in relation to creditors.[39] Professor Prentice concluded that the published accounts and reports of a company were a more helpful source of information than its objects clause.[40] He thought[41] that the provisions of the insolvency legislation relating to wrongful trading, preferences and transactions at an undervalue provided adequate protection to creditors against dissipation of assets without the need in addition for the *ultra vires* doctrine,[42] and that shareholders were also protected against gratuitous dispositions by fiduciary duties, rules about maintenance of capital and unlawful distributions, reporting requirements and the provisions of the Companies Act entitling them to seek relief from unfair prejudice,[43] or to have the company wound up on just and equitable grounds.[44]

Although not going so far as to provide that a company has capacity to deal in any act whatsoever (apart, of course, from those which as a legal rather than a natural person it is physically incapable of),[45] the Companies Act 1985 now provides that a company's memorandum can state that the object of the company is to carry on business as a general commercial company. The effect of this is that the object of the company is to carry on any trade or business whatsoever and the company has power to do all such things as are incidental or conducive to the carrying on of any trade or business by it. The enactment of this provision gave statutory backing to the idea of having very wide objects and sought to offer companies a way of achieving this without having to have the very long objects that had become standard. However, it soon became clear that the 'general commercial company' formula might not achieve as much as traditional long-form objects: for example, an independent charitable object such as that in *Re Horsley and Weight Ltd*[46] would not appear to be covered; and the powers limb is worded in objective terms which contrasts unfavourably with the established practice of including a subjectively worded incidental power. These considerations meant that the enactment of the general commercial company object did not lead to a significant change of practice with regard to the drafting of long objects clauses although, paradoxically, some companies chose to lengthen their objects by adopting the general commercial company object in addition to, rather than instead of, their traditional and familiar long objects. In the review of company law announced by the DTI in 1998 the short-form objects clause was identified as an ineffective provision of the companies legislation that the government wished to review.[47]

[38] *Reform of the Ultra Vires Rule: A Consultative Document* (DTI) ch III, para 3.

[39] Ibid, para 9.

[40] *Reform of the Ultra Vires Rule: A Consultative Document* (DTI) ch V, paras 7 and 11. Prentice recommended that this should be bolstered, in respect of both private and public companies, by a specific obligation to file an annual activities and business statement: ch V, paras 11, 19 and 26.

[41] Ibid, ch VI, paras 28–30.

[42] Ibid, para 25.

[43] Companies Act 1985, s 459.

[44] Insolvency Act 1986, s 122 (1)(g).

[45] Prentice recommended full corporate capacity: *Reform of the Ultra Vires Rule: A Consultative Document* (DTI) ch IV, paras 3–11.

[46] [1982] Ch 442 CA.

[47] *Modern Company Law For a Competitive Economy* (DTI Consultative Document) (1998) para 3.4.

Whilst the practice of adopting very extensive objects and powers significantly undermines the rule in *Trevor v Whitworth*[48] that a company can only apply its capital in pursuit of its objects, the final blow to that rule is contained in the Companies Act 1985, s 35 (1) which provides that 'the validity of an act done by a company shall not be called into question on the ground of lack of capacity by reason of anything in the company's memorandum'. Although the wording of s 35 is open to criticism,[49] its purpose is to ensure that it is not open, either to a company or to the person with whom it deals, to argue that an act is not binding because it is beyond the company's capacity. For the directors of a company to apply the company's funds otherwise than in pursuit of the objects is a breach of duty by them, but the breach can be ratified by the shareholders by special resolution.[50]

A COMPANY CANNOT GIVE AWAY ITS CAPITAL?

A company can have objects which are charitable or philanthropic.[51] The capacity of a company to make gifts depends on construction of its objects clause and there is no further test of 'benefit to the company' or 'bona fides by the directors' which must be satisfied.[52] It is, however, also clear that if a trading company were to apply all of its assets in making gifts (an admittedly unlikely scenario), its creditors would soon be severely prejudiced, as would those members of the company who were opposed to this generous policy. There are various ways in which company law seeks to ensure that this does not happen, such as the rules that a company must not give capital back to members and must only pay dividends from distributable profits, and the fiduciary duties imposed on directors in exercising their powers. The fiduciary duty of directors to act in the interests of the company recognises that directors must give increasing weight to the interests of its creditors as the company's financial fortune declines, and that shareholders may not release directors from their duties to the company, whether by authorisation or ratification, if the company is, or is on the verge of, insolvency.[53] Under the Insolvency Act 1986 a liquidator or administrator has power to apply to court for the reversal of gifts made, or other transactions at an undervalue entered into, in the period immediately prior to the commencement of the insolvency proceedings.[54] The Insolvency Act 1986 also allows for preferences to be set

48 (1887) 12 App Cas 409, HL.

49 Poole, J, 'Abolition of the Ultra Vires Doctrine and Agency Problems' (1991) 12 Co Law 43; Ferran, EV, 'The Reform of the Law on Corporate Capacity and Directors' and Officers' Authority' (1992) 13 Co Law 124 and 177.

50 Companies Act 1985, s 35 (3). A member can seek an injunction to restrain the directors from acting in this way: Companies Act 1985, s 35 (3); but the fact that a member may not be in a position easily to discover what the directors are proposing to do diminishes the practical significance of this power.

51 *Re Horsley and Weight Ltd* [1982] Ch 442, CA.

52 Ibid; *Rolled Steel Products (Holdings) Ltd v British Steel Corporation* [1986] Ch 246, CA.

53 See further, Ch 4 above, at 137–40.

54 Insolvency Act 1986, s 238. Note also Insolvency Act 1986, s 423 (transactions defrauding creditors) which is not subject to the time-limit imposed under Insolvency Act 1986, s 238 and enables 'victims' of the fraud to apply as well as the liquidator or administrator. This section

aside[55] and provides for directors of an insolvent company to incur personal liability in the event of wrongful trading.[56] In view of this plethora of rules and restrictions, it is therefore surprising that a further principle of company law was outlined by Harman J in *Barclays Bank plc v British & Commonwealth Holdings plc*,[57] namely, that a limited company *cannot* make gifts out of its capital even to persons who are not shareholders, unless those gifts are for the benefit of its business.[58] This principle appears to reintroduce under another guise the old learning on 'benefit to the company' which was jettisoned in relation to the *ultra vires* rule. It is impossible to square with Buckley LJ's comment in *Re Horsley and Weight Ltd* that 'nor is there any reason why a company should not part with its funds gratuitously or for non-commercial reasons if to do so is within its stated objects'.[59] It is further open to criticism on the grounds that is simply an unnecessary additional rule which serves only to complicate the position without any compensating advantage.

The authorities which, according to Harman J supported the principle that a company cannot give away its capital can be interpreted in a rather different way. In *Hutton v West Cork Railway*[60] Bowen LJ famously said:

> The law does not say that there are to be no cakes and ale, but there are to be no cakes and ale except such as are required for the benefit of the company . . . It is no charity sitting at the board of directors, because as it seems to me charity has no business to sit at boards of directors *qua* charity.

But, as Oliver J explained in *Re Halt Garage (1964) Ltd*,[61] the *Hutton* case was concerned with abuse of power and with the circumstances in which the majority in general meeting could force a particular measure on a dissentient minority; it does not support a general overriding principle that a company cannot give away its capital.

In *Re George Newman & Co*[62] Lindley LJ said:

> But to make presents out of profits is one thing and to make them out of capital or out of money borrowed by the company is a very different matter. Such money cannot be lawfully divided amongst the shareholders, nor can it be given away by them for nothing to their directors to bind the company in its corporate capacity.

The *Re George Newman & Co* case has been explained as one involving dishonesty;[63] further, there was no suggestion that the company was expressly empowered to make such gifts and, the company being insolvent, the shareholders were incompetent to approve such gifts, even by unanimous approval.[64] Consider also *Ridge Securities Ltd v IR Commrs*[65] where

require proof of intent to put assets beyond the reach of creditors or otherwise to prejudice creditors.

[55] Insolvency Act 1986, s 239.
[56] Ibid, s 214.
[57] *Barclays Bank plc v British & Commonwealth Holdings plc* [1995] BCC 19 (affirmed [1995] BCC 1059, CA).
[58] *Barclays Bank plc v British & Commonwealth Holdings plc* [1995] BCC 19, 29–31 (affirmed [1995] BCC 1059, CA).
[59] [1982] Ch 442, CA, 450.
[60] (1883) 23 Ch D 654, CA, 673.
[61] [1982] 3 All ER 1016.
[62] [1895] 1 Ch 674, CA, 686.
[63] *Re Halt Garage (1964) Ltd* [1982] 3 All ER 1016, 1033.
[64] *Re Horsley and Weight Ltd* [1982] Ch 442, CA, 450–1 *per* Buckley LJ.
[65] [1964] 1 All ER 275, 288.

Pennycuick J said that the corporators 'cannot take assets out of the company by way of voluntary disposition, however described, and if they attempt to do so the disposition is ultra vires the company'. In *Barclays Bank plc v British & Commonwealth Holdings plc*,[66] Harman J took this to mean a disposition to any person and not just to shareholders returning capital to themselves. But contrast this with Oliver J's comment in *Re Halt Garage (1964) Ltd*[67] that 'of course, when Pennycuick J referred in that passage to the corporators taking money out he was referring to payments to them qua corporators'.

Two Commonwealth decisions were also cited by Harman J in the *Barclays Bank* decision. The first, the Canadian case *Plain Ltd v Kenley & Royal Trust Co*,[68] does contain a passage to the effect that a limited company cannot lawfully give its property either to shareholders or to others, unless those gifts are prudent and proper business expenditures or are made out of profits and with the consent of the shareholders. Harman J accepted this as a correct statement of English law. However, it is plainly out of line with other English authorities. The second Commonwealth authority, the Australian case of *ANZ Executors & Trustee Co Ltd v Qintex Australia Ltd*[69] decided that a company that is insolvent or verging on insolvency may not properly make a gift out of its assets to some other person because this would be to exercise a corporate power for a non-corporate purpose. The insolvency context is an important consideration and English company law has its own established ways of dealing with gifts made in that situation: gifts paid by an insolvent, or virtually insolvent, company amount to unratifiable breaches of duty by the company's directors and may be recoverable under the insolvency legislation as preferences or as transactions at an undervalue.

This section has sought to demonstrate that the principle that a company cannot give away its capital is not part of English company law and to suggest that there is no lacuna in the law which such a principle could usefully be adopted in order to fill. However, it may be appropriate to try and set this discussion in context. In the ordinary course of events, making gifts will be only a small part of the operations of a trading company involving relatively small amounts. As Nourse LJ said in *Brady v Brady*:[70]

> in the realm of theory a memorandum of association may authorise a company to give away all its assets to whomsoever it pleases, including its shareholders. But in the real world of trading companies—charitable or political donations, pensions to widows of ex-employees and the like apart—it is obvious that such a power would never be taken.

Typical gifts made by a trading company would probably satisfy a test of benefit to the company if one were to be imposed: pensions or social welfare facilities provided to employees can be justified on the grounds of bolstering morale amongst the workforce;[71] contributions to community projects in the

[66] [1995] BCC 19 (affirmed [1995] BCC 1059, CA).

[67] [1982] 3 All ER 1016.

[68] (1931) 1 DLR 468, Ontario SC, affirmed [1931] 2 DLR 801, Ontario SC Appellate Division.

[69] (1990–1) 2 ACSR 676. Some commentators felt that the *Qintex* decision could in effect revive the doctrine of *ultra vires*: Baxt, R, 'Ultra Vires – Has it Been Revived?' (1991) C&SLJ 101.

[70] (1987) 3 BCC 535, CA, 550 (reversed [1989] AC 755, HL but not on grounds relevant to this point).

[71] *Re W & M Roith Ltd* [1967] 1 All ER 427.

areas in which the company operate can be viewed as enhancing the reputation of the company with potential commercial benefits; grants to educational establishments, even if not directed at research from which the company will immediately benefit, may be supported on the basis that these will increase the pool of educated workers from which the company can recruit its staff and also that the company may benefit from the general advancement of research;[72] and donations to political parties can, arguably,[73] be explained on the grounds that it is in the commercial interests of the company to support a Party which is advocating policies favourable to those interests. An example of a gift that could fail a benefit to the company test is one made by the company at a time when it is ceasing business, since there is no long-term benefit to the company that can be derived from this gift.[74] In the case of gifts to employees, however, this is qualified by the Companies Act 1985, s 719[75] which allows companies to make provision for employees and former employees in connection with the cessation or transfer of the company's business. This power is exercisable notwithstanding that its exercise may not be in the interests of the company.[76]

REDUCTION OF CAPITAL WITH THE APPROVAL OF THE COURT

A company may find itself in a position where it has capital which is excess to the needs of its business. For example, a rationalisation programme may lead a company to decide to sell off certain divisions of the company's business in order to concentrate on its core activities. The cash generated by selling off the divisions may then not be needed by the company to finance what has become a smaller business. A reduction of capital is one of the methods whereby the company may return this surplus to its shareholders. Other ways of returning value to shareholders are schemes of arrangement (considered in the closing section of this chapter), share buy backs (considered in Chapter 13) and special dividends (considered in Chapter 12). An advantage of returning surplus funds to shareholders in this way rather than as dividends is that, after capital has been returned, the remaining smaller business may generate a lower overall amount of profits so that, but for the reduction in its capital base, the company could in future have come under pressure to reduce its dividend. Reducing the share capital can also improve the accounting perception of the company: provided the reduction in the capital more than offsets the loss of interest on the money repaid to shareholders, the company's earnings per share, a widely-used yardstick for measuring company performance, will be improved.[77]

[72] *Evans v Brunner Mond & Co* [1921] 1 Ch 359.

[73] Ewing, KD, 'Company Political Donations and the Ultra Vires Rule' (1984) 47 MLR 57. Institutional investors have begun to raise objections to political donations by companies in which they invest where these have not been subjected to shareholder approval: see Ch 4 above, at 127–31 where government proposals to make shareholder approval of political donations mandatory are noted.

[74] *Hutton v West Cork Railway* (1883) 23 Ch D 654, CA; *Parke v Daily News Ltd* [1962] Ch 927.

[75] Also note Companies Act 1985, s 309.

[76] Ibid, s 719 (2).

[77] When it was possible to write off purchased goodwill against reserves, it was a common practice for companies to seek approval for a reduction of capital in order to write off goodwill

Another situation where a company may want to reduce its capital is where the share capital recorded in the company's books is no longer reflected by the assets of the company because of trading or other losses which the company has suffered. In this situation the company will want to cancel part of its stated capital without making any payment to its shareholders. If a company in this position did not reduce its capital it would have to make good the losses before it could resume paying dividends to its shareholders.

The Companies Act 1985, s 135 (1) provides that, subject to confirmation by the court, a limited company may, if so authorised by its articles,[78] by special resolution reduce its capital in any way. In particular, but without prejudice to the general nature of the power, the company may:[79]

—extinguish or reduce liability on any of its shares in respect of share capital not paid up;
—either with or without extinguishing liability on any of its shares, cancel any paid-up share capital which is lost or unrepresented by available assets; or
—either with or without extinguishing liability on any of its shares, pay off any paid-up share capital which is in excess of the company's wants.

Creditors' Interests

When a company has passed a resolution for reducing its share capital, it must then apply to court for an order confirming the reduction.[80] Since a reduction of capital could prejudice creditors, there are then various requirements regarding creditors which the court is required to observe. These requirements apply, unless the court otherwise directs,[81] where the reduction involves diminution of liability in respect of unpaid share capital or the payment to a shareholder of any paid-up share capital.[82] They can also apply in other types of reduction if the court so directs.[83]

The key creditor protection requirement is that every creditor who would be entitled to prove in the company's liquidation is also entitled to object to the reduction of capital.[84] The court must settle a list of creditors entitled to object.[85] An officer of the company commits an offence if he wilfully conceals the name of a creditor entitled to object to the reduction, wilfully misrepresents the nature or amount of the debt or claim of any creditor, or aids, abets or is privy to any such concealment or misrepresentation.[86] If creditors raise objections this prevents the court from confirming the reduction[87] but there is provision for the court to dispense with a creditor's consent if the company

against the share premium accounts: *Re Ratners Group plc* (1988) 4 BCC 293, 294; *Re Thorn EMI plc* (1988) 4 BCC 698. Under FRS 10, *Goodwill and Intangible Assets*, goodwill arising on an acquisition must now be treated as an asset and amortised through the profit and loss account for a period of up to 20 years.

[78] Table A, art 34 provides the relevant authorisation for companies incorporated with these articles.

[79] Companies Act 1985, s 135 (2). The general nature of the power has been emphasised by the courts on numerous occasions: eg, *Ex parte Westburn Sugar Refineries Ltd* [1951] AC 625, HL.

[80] Companies Act 1985, s 136 (1).

[81] Ibid, s 136 (6).

[82] Ibid, s 136 (2).

[83] Ibid, s 136 (2).

[84] Ibid, s 136 (3).

[85] Ibid, s 136 (4).

[86] Ibid, s 141.

[87] Ibid, s 137.

secures payment of the creditor's debt or claim by appropriating the amount of the debt or, where the debt or claim is not admitted and the company is not willing to provide for it in full, or it is contingent or not ascertained, an amount fixed by the court.[88]

In practice, however, reductions of capital are typically structured with in-built creditor protection with a view to persuading the court to order the disapplication of the statutory protections where they would otherwise apply. One such form of in-built creditor protection is for the company to demonstrate that it has, and after the reduction will continue to have, sufficient cash and readily realisable investments to pay all of its existing creditors including its contingent creditors. Another is for the company to arrange for a bank to guarantee repayment of its creditors' debts. The court will also dispense with the statutory creditor protection requirements where, or to the extent that, creditors have consented to the reduction. Widespread use of these various established mechanisms means that it is uncommon in practice for reductions of capital to involve inquiries into creditors' interests.

Shareholders' Interests

Although not specifically mentioned in the Companies Act 1985, it is clear from case law that a court which is asked to confirm a reduction of capital will also be concerned to ensure that shareholders are properly treated. The court seeks to apply broad standards of fairness, reasonableness and equity.[89] It will be concerned to see that the shareholders had the matter properly explained to them so that when it came to the general meeting at which they passed the special resolution they were fully informed about what they were doing.[90] If the company has more than one class of shares, the court will want to ensure that the reduction does not involve a variation of class rights or, if it does, that the class affected has given its consent. Broadly,[91] where the company's share capital comprises ordinary shares and preference shares with rights to a preferential dividend at a specified rate and priority with regard to the return of capital but no further rights to participate and no special terms deeming a reduction of capital to be a variation of class rights,[92] it accords with the class rights of the preference shares to repay those shares first on a reduction of capital.[93] In a reduction of capital involving no repayment but merely a cancellation of shares, it accords with their respective class rights for the ordinary shares, rather than the preference shares, to absorb this loss.[94] Some older cases suggest that the court has discretion to confirm a reduction of capital which varies or abrogates class rights even without the consent of the relevant class. However, it is doubtful whether that approach would now be followed,

[88] Companies Act 1985, s 136 (5).
[89] *Scottish Insurance Corporation v Wilsons & Clyde Coal Co Ltd* [1949] AC 462, HL.
[90] *Re Ratners Group plc* (1988) BCC 293.
[91] See further Ch 9 above, at 343–5.
[92] *Re Northern Engineering Industries plc* [1994] BCC 618, CA.
[93] *Scottish Insurance Corporation v Wilsons & Clyde Coal Co Ltd* [1949] AC 462, HL; *Re Saltdean Estate Co Ltd* [1968] 1 WLR 1844; *House of Fraser plc v ACGE Investments Ltd* [1987] AC 387, HL.
[94] *Re Floating Dock of St Thomas Ltd* [1895] 1 Ch 691.

since the Companies Act 1985, s 125, which provides a procedure for the variation of class rights, is worded in mandatory terms so that variations are only permitted where they are effected in accordance with the procedure specified in, or under, that section.

A class consent to a reduction of capital involving a variation of class rights may not be effective if those who voted in favour did not act in the interests of the class as a whole. In *Re Holders Investment Trust Ltd*[95] a class meeting of preference shareholders approved a reduction of capital which varied their class rights but this approval was held to be ineffective because the majority preference shareholders were held to have acted in what they considered to be their own best interests without asking themselves what was in the interests of the class as a whole. However, it is obviously difficult for the court to scrutinise too closely the motives which lead to votes being cast in any particular way and it is questionable how far this intervention by the court is compatible in any event with the principle that a vote attaching to a share is a right of property which the shareholder is free to exercise as he or she thinks fit.

General Powers of the Court

The court can confirm a reduction on such terms and conditions as it thinks fit. The court may order that the fact of reduction be indicated by the company adding to its name as its last words the phrase 'as reduced' for a specified period.[96] The court may also order the company to publish the reasons for the reduction of capital or such other reasons in regard to it as the court thinks expedient with a view to giving proper information to the public and (if the court thinks fit) the causes which led to the reduction.[97] The order of the court, together with a minute (approved by the court) setting out details of the company's altered share capital must be registered by the registrar of companies and it is upon registration that the reduction takes effect.[98] The registrar must certify registration of the order and minute and this certificate is conclusive evidence that all the requirements of the Act with respect to the reduction of capital have been complied with and that the company's altered share capital is as stated in the minute.[99] Notice of the registration must be published in such manner as the court may direct.[100]

The effect of a reduction of capital may be to bring the allotted share capital below the authorised minimum for a public company (currently set at £50,000). In that case the registrar of companies must not register the reduction whilst the company remains a public company unless the court otherwise directs.[101] The company should re-register as a private company. Re-registration normally requires the passing of a special resolution to alter the company's memorandum so that it no longer states that the company is to be a public company[102] but the court can order the company to be re-registered without the resolution and, where that authority is given, the court

95 [1971] 1 WLR 583.
96 Companies Act 1985, s 136 (2)(a).
97 Ibid, s 137 (2)(b).
98 Ibid, s 138 (1)–(2).
99 Ibid, s 138 (4).
100 Ibid, s 138 (3).
101 Ibid, s 139 (2).
102 Ibid, s 53.

will specify in the order the alterations to the company's constitution to be made in connection with the re-registration.[103]

Effect of a Reduction of Capital

The effect of a reduction of capital is to relieve a member of the company (past or present) for any liability in respect of any share to any call or contribution exceeding the amount that remains unpaid on the share calculated by reference to the minute showing the altered share capital.[104] This is qualified in one respect in order to protect creditors who, by reason of their ignorance of the proceedings or of their nature and effect, were not entered on the list of creditors. If, after the reduction of capital, the company is unable to pay the amount of such a creditor's debt or claim, members of the company at the time of the registration of the reduction are then liable to contribute for the payment of that debt or claim an amount not exceeding that which they would have been liable to contribute if the company had commenced to be wound up on the day before that date.[105]

REDUCTION OF CAPITAL BY A SCHEME OF ARRANGEMENT

The Companies Act 1985, s 425 provides a procedure for effecting a compromise or arrangement between a company and its creditors (or any class of them) or between a company and its members (or any class of them). A wide variety of corporate re-organisations can be effected by means of a s 425 scheme of arrangement. So long as there is some element of give and take, any type of legal transaction should fall within the term 'arrangement' which is to be broadly interpreted in this context.[106] In the UK markets in the 1990s several companies used schemes of arrangement to return value to their shareholders.[107] Schemes of arrangement can override existing class rights and they also differ from reductions of capital under the Companies Act 1985, s 135 in their tax consequences.[108]

In outline,[109] the procedure for a scheme of arrangement is that, at the first stage, the court must be asked to separate meetings of each class of shareholder or creditor affected by the proposal. It is for the company proposing the scheme to determine the compositions of the classes that should vote on

[103] Companies Act 1985, s 139 (3). The procedural steps that must be taken to complete the re-registration are specified in Companies Act 1985, s 139 (4)–(5).

[104] Companies Act 1985, s 140 (1).

[105] Ibid, s 140 (2)–(3). The court may settle a list of those liable to contribute in this way: Companies Act 1985, s 140 (4).

[106] *Re Savoy Hotel Ltd* [1981] Ch 351; *Re NFU Development Trust Ltd* [1973] 1 All ER 135 (element of give and take lacking where membership rights would be confiscated without any compensation; scheme not within the section).

[107] Hinkley, R, Hunter, D, Whittell, M, and Ziff, M, *Current Issues in Equity Finance* (1998) 23 and 51.

[108] 'Reuters Scheme of Arrangement: A Solution to the Cash Mountain' (1998) 9 (1) PLC 6.

[109] The special requirements that apply to reconstructions, amalgamations and mergers and divisions of public companies are not considered: Companies Act 1985, ss 427–427A.

the proposals. Should it get this wrong, the scheme may be challenged at a later stage. Classes of shareholders for this purpose are not determined simply by reference to class rights attaching to shares, although that is a starting point. Holders of shares of the same class can be in different classes for the purposes of s 424 because their interests are different.[110] In one case where an attempt was made to use the procedure to effect a takeover, it was held that a shareholder that was a subsidiary of the bidder had a different interest from the other shareholders and was therefore in a different class.[111] Determining the correct composition of classes of creditors can also be problematic, although there are some preliminary dividing lines that can be drawn, such as between secured and unsecured creditors and between subordinated creditors and ordinary unsecured creditors.[112]

The scheme must be approved by a majority in number representing at least three-quarters in value of those present or by proxy at each of the meetings.[113] Once the requisite approvals have been obtained, a second application must be made to court to obtain its sanction for the scheme. A scheme does not take effect until an office copy of the court's order sanctioning it has been filed with the registrar of companies; and a copy of every such order must be annexed to every copy of the company's memorandum issued thereafter.[114] The court's role in relation to this second stage application is twofold. First, it must check that the procedural requirements have been complied with.[115] Thus, for example, errors in the drawing up of the relevant classes may cause the scheme to fail at this stage. Secondly, it must satisfy itself that the scheme is fair: 'The proposal [must be] . . . such that an intelligent and honest man, a member of the class concerned and acting in respect of his interest, might reasonably approve.'[116] Interested shareholders or creditors may raise objections on either procedural or fairness grounds. Even if there are no such objections and the scheme is formally correct, the court may still decline to exercise its discretion in favour of approving the scheme if it is not satisfied as to its fairness.[117]

[110] *Sovereign Life Assurance Co v Dunn* [1892] 2 QB 573, CA, 583 *per* Bowen LJ.

[111] *Re Hellenic and General Trust Ltd* [1975] 3 All ER 382.

[112] *Re British and Commonwealth Holding plc (No 3)* [1992] BCC 58.

[113] Companies Act 1985, s 425 (2). The convening of the meetings is regulated by Companies Act 1985, s 426 which specifies the information that has to be disclosed and the manner of disclosure. For listed companies the disclosure requirements relating to circulars in *The Listing Rules*, ch 14 are also relevant.

[114] Companies Act 1985, s 425 (3).

[115] *Re Alabama, New Orleans, Texas and Pacific Junction Railway Co* [1891] 1 Ch 215, CA, 239 *per* Lindley LJ; *Re Anglo-Continental Supply Co Ltd* [1922] 2 Ch 723, 736.

[116] *Re Dorman Long & Co* [1934] Ch 635, 655–6. See also *Re Alabama, New Orleans, Texas and Pacific Junction Railway Co* [1891] 1 Ch 215, CA, 239 *per* Lindley LJ and 247 *per* Fry LJ; *Re Anglo-Continental Supply Co Ltd* [1922] 2 Ch 723, 736; *Re National Bank* [1966] 1 WLR 819.

[117] *Re ABP Holdings Ltd*, 10 April 1991 NI Ch D.

11

Financial Assistance

WHY PROHIBIT THE GIVING OF FINANCIAL ASSISTANCE?

In *Re VGM Holdings Ltd*[1] Lord Greene MR explained the mischief underlying the specific ban on the giving of financial assistance in the following terms:

> Those whose memories enable them to recall what had been happening for several years after the last war will remember that a very common form of transaction in connection with companies was one by which persons—call them financiers, speculators, or what you will—finding a company with a substantial cash balance or easily realisable assets, such as war loan, bought up the whole, or the greater part, of the shares for cash, and so arranged matters that the purchase money which they then became bound to provide was advanced to them by the company whose shares they were acquiring, either out of its cash balance or by realisation of its liquid investments. That type of transaction was a common one, and it gave rise to great dissatisfaction and, in some cases, great scandals.

Previously Lord Greene MR had chaired the Committee which recommended that such practices should be banned. In its report the Greene Committee had described the problem of financial assistance in a similar way.[2]

Reporting in 1962, the Jenkins Committee[3] also gave an example of the type of abuse that a prohibition on financial assistance was intended to correct:

> If people who cannot provide the funds necessary to acquire control of a company from their own resources, or by borrowing on their own credit, gain control of a company with large assets on the understanding that they will use the funds of the company to pay for their shares it seems to us all too likely that in many cases the company will be made to part with its funds either on inadequate security or for an illusory consideration.

At the minimum then, the giving of financial assistance is banned in order to ensure that those who buy shares in companies do so from their own resources and not from those of the company. In *Wallersteiner v Moir*[4] Lord Denning MR summed up the abuse succinctly, describing it simply as a 'cheat'.

Market Manipulation

In some circumstances, the effect of giving financial assistance may be to boost the price of the shares of the company giving the assistance. An obvious

[1] [1942] Ch 235, CA, 239.
[2] *Report of the Company Law Amendment Committee* Cmd 2657 (1926) para 30.
[3] *Report of the Company Law Committee* Cmnd 1749 (1962), para 173.
[4] [1974] 3 All ER 217, CA, 222.

example of this is a takeover situation where the consideration for the offer to the shareholders of the target takes the form of shares in the bidder and, to ensure that the price of those shares remains attractive, the bidder organises a share-support operation in which purchasers of its shares are indemnified against any losses they may suffer as a result of their purchases. Looked at from this angle, the ban on the giving of financial assistance is closely connected to the rule whereby companies are prohibited from trading in their own shares.[5] The Greene Committee referred to the practice of 'share trafficking' when recommending that financial assistance should be prohibited.[6] In *Darvall v North Sydney Brick & Tile Co Ltd*,[7] an Australian case, Kirby P expressly stated that the purposes of the prohibition on financial assistance 'include the avoidance of the manipulation of the value of shares by companies and their officers dealing in such shares'.

Unconstitutional Conduct by Management

Another reason for banning financial assistance is to prevent the management of a company from interfering with the normal market in the company's shares by providing support from the company's resources to selected purchasers. In this respect, the ban on financial assistance again complements the ban on a company purchasing its own shares, one purpose of which is to prevent the management of a company from seeking to influence the outcome of a takeover bid by purchasing its own shares.[8]

Reduction in Resources is Not Required

The ban on giving financial assistance is not limited to transactions or other acts that necessarily reduce the resources of the company that provides the assistance.[9] Where a company makes a gift to enable someone to purchase its shares, there is a clear immediate reduction in its resources. However, unlawful financial assistance can come in many forms and is not confined to simple situations where the company makes a gift of the money which is to be used to buy its shares.[10] Also included within the prohibition are loans, security, guarantees and indemnities. These types of unlawful financial assistance do not necessarily involve any reduction in the company's assets at the time when

[5] Bretten, GR, 'Financial Assistance in Share Transactions' (1968) 32 Conv (NS) 6.

[6] *Report of the Company Law Amendment Committee* Cmd 2657 (1926) para 30.

[7] (1989) 15 ACLR 230, NSW CA, 256 *per* Kirby J.

[8] *Trevor v Whitworth* (1887) 12 App Cas 409, HL.

[9] Pettet, BG, 'Developments in the Law of Financial Assistance for the Purchase of Shares' [1988] 3 JIBL 96, 100; Ford, HAJ, Austin, RP, and Ramsay, IM, *Fords' Principles of Corporations Law* (8th edn, 1997) 1091–2 discussing case law on whether a reduction in resources is required under Australian legislation relating to financial assistance. See also *Milburn v Pivot Ltd* (1997) 25 ACSR 237 Fed Ct of Aust–Cen Div.

[10] Accordingly, Lord Denning MR's description of financial assistance in *Wallersteiner v Moir* [1974] 3 All ER 217, CA, 239 ('You look to the company's money and see what has become of it. You look to the company's shares and see into whose hands they have got. You will then soon see if the company's money has been used to finance the purchase.') should be read as merely one example of financial assistance and not as illustrative of the whole category: see Farrar, JH, and Lowe, NV, 'Fraud, Representative Actions and the Gagging Writ' (1975) 38 MLR 455.

they are given. For instance, a loan does not involve any diminution in the lender's assets provided the borrower's credit is good and no provision against the likelihood of default has to be made. A contingent obligation, such as a guarantee, does not reduce the assets of the company unless some provision has to be made against the obligation being enforced. The granting of a security does not diminish or deplete the value of a company's assets and merely restricts the company from using the proceeds of the secured assets otherwise than in satisfaction of the secured debt.[11]

THE CLASS OF PERSONS PROTECTED BY THE PROHIBITION

In *Wallersteiner v Moir*[12] Scarman LJ stated that the ban on financial assistance 'must have been enacted to protect company funds and the interests of shareholders as well as creditors'. In the same case Lord Denning MR also considered that the company was included in the class of persons protected by the prohibition.[13] The Court of Appeal shared this view in a preliminary ruling in *Belmont Finance Corporation Ltd v Williams Furniture Ltd.*[14] These comments outweigh earlier pronouncements to the effect that the company was not intended to be protected by prohibition. [15]

HISTORY OF THE PROHIBITION[16]

The giving of financial assistance was first made a specific statutory[17] offence in 1928 by the Companies Act 1928, s 16. This was re-enacted without change as the Companies Act 1929, s 45.[18] Loopholes emerged in the drafting of that section[19] and it was redrafted in the Companies Act 1947 and then consolidated as the Companies Act 1948, s 54.

The Companies Act 1948, s 54 provided that:

[11] *Re MC Bacon Ltd* [1990] BCLC 324. This case concerned Insolvency Act 1986, s 238 (transactions at an undervalue).

[12] [1974] 3 All ER 217, CA, 255.

[13] Ibid at 239.

[14] [1979] 1 All ER 118, CA.

[15] *Essex Aero Ltd v Cross*, 17 November 1961, CA, where Harman LJ said '. . . the section was not enacted for the company's protection but for that of its creditors'. In *Victor Battery Co Ltd v Curry's Ltd* [1946] Ch 242 Roxburgh J was also of the view that the company was not intended to be protected.

[16] Bretten, GR, 'Financial Assistance in Share Transactions' (1968) 32 Conv (NS) 6; Morse, GK, 'Financial Assistance by a Company for the Purchase of its Own Shares' [1983] JBL 105; Pettet, BG, 'Developments in the Law of Financial Assistance for the Purchase of Shares' [1988] 3 JIBL 96.

[17] In *R v Lorang* (1931) 22 Cr App Rep 167 CCA this provision was described as declaratory and not as a new offence.

[18] It provided that: 'It shall not be lawful for a company to give, whether directly or indirectly, and whether by means of a loan, guarantee, the provision of security or otherwise, any financial assistance for the purpose of or in connection with a purchase made or to be made by any person of any shares in the company.'

[19] *Re VGM Holdings Ltd* [1942] 1 Ch 235, CA where it was held than the ban on financial assistance for the purchase of shares did not apply where the company provided financial assistance for the subscription of its shares. As a matter of construction the word 'purchase' could not be extended to include 'subscription'.

It shall not be lawful for a company to give, whether directly or indirectly, and whether by means of a loan, guarantee, the provision of security or otherwise, any financial assistance for the purpose of or in connection with a purchase or subscription made, by any person of or for any shares in the company, or, where the company is a subsidiary company, in its holding company.

As well as including the giving of financial assistance in relation to a subscription of shares within the scope of the prohibition, the prohibition was also extended to prevent subsidiary companies providing financial assistance for the purchase of, or subscription for, shares in their holding companies.

The leading case on the scope of the Companies Act 1948, s 54 was the decision of the Court of Appeal in *Belmont Finance Corporation v Williams Furniture Ltd (No 2)*.[20] In this case a company bought an asset for a price which, it later turned out, was grossly inflated and the vendors of the asset used the proceeds of the sale to buy the company. The Court of Appeal held that this was unlawful financial assistance. All members of the Court of Appeal agreed that it would have made no difference if the price which the company had paid had actually been a fair one because the company had acted without regard to its own commercial interests and with the sole purpose of putting the vendor of the assets in funds to acquire the shares. Clearly, it was not in the minds of the court that a reduction in net assets was a necessary prerequisite of unlawful financial assistance.

The ruling in *Belmont Finance* caused a re-assessment of certain assumptions on which previous market practice had been based. This resulted not so much from the decision on its facts but from the court's views on what the position would have been if the transaction had been for full value. Passages in some of the judgments with regard to the situation where a company bought an asset, genuinely and in its own commercial interests, but partly with the purpose of putting the vendor in funds to acquire its shares, were also a cause for concern: Waller LJ thought that this could infringe the Companies Act 1948, s 54, although the other two members of the Court of Appeal, Buckley and Goff LLJ, expressly chose to leave this point open. All of this came as a surprise to many practitioners who had assumed that the fairness of the price at which the transaction was done or the partially proper purpose which underlay it would be sufficient to take a transaction outside the prohibition.[21]

The next influence on the legislative history of the prohibition on financial assistance was the Second Company Law Directive.[22] The Second Directive seeks to co-ordinate on a Community-wide basis the requirements for the formation of public companies and the maintenance and alteration of their capital. As an aspect of this, the Second Directive, art 23.1 provides that, with certain exceptions, 'A company[23] may not advance funds, nor make loans, nor provide security with a view to the acquisition of its shares by a third party.'

20 [1980] 1 All ER 393, CA.

21 Counsel had advised the parties involved in the *Belmont* litigation that, provided the price was a fair one and the transaction was bona fide, it would not infringe Companies Act 1948, s 54. See also a detailed comment on s 54 and its interpretation in the *Belmont* case by Instone, R, 'Section 54 and All That' [1980] JBL 99.

22 77/91/EEC, [1977] OJ L26/1.

23 ie a public company.

This limits what a Member State may provide in its domestic legislation with regard to permitted or prohibited financial assistance, at least in relation to public companies. To comply with Community obligations, domestic legislation must prohibit financial assistance by public companies at least to the extent that this is prohibited by art 23.1, although that article sets only a minimum standard and Member States are free to impose more rigorous rules and requirements if they so desire.

Subject to the limit set by art 23.1, the 1980s companies legislation provided an opportunity in the UK to recast the prohibition on financial assistance and to clarify some of the difficulties that had been thrown up by cases and by the experience of the operation of the ban in practice. A minor change was made in the Companies Act 1980, but the modern version of the prohibition was first enacted as the Companies Act 1981, s 42. With minor drafting changes, this was re-enacted as the Companies Act 1985, s 151.

OUTLINE OF THE CURRENT LAW AND THE APPROACH TO ITS INTERPRETATION

The Companies Act 1985, s 151 contains the basic prohibition on financial assistance. The Companies Act 1985, s 152 amplifies certain key aspects of the prohibition, whilst ss 153 and 154 relax the ban in certain circumstances. Under the Companies Act 1985, ss 155–158, there is a special relaxation of the prohibition for private companies. The origin of this special private-company regime can be traced back to the report of the Jenkins Committee in 1962.[24] The Jenkins Committee suggested that the ban could be relaxed for all companies, but that recommendation was overtaken by subsequent events: the need to implement the Second Directive, art 23.1 meant that this proposal could not be implemented in relation to public companies.

Although much more extensive and detailed than their predecessors, there is sufficient similarity between the provisions of the Companies Act 1985 and earlier versions of the prohibition to mean that cases interpreting those versions can still be helpful. The version of the prohibition contained in the Companies Act 1948, s 54 was also taken as the model for similar prohibitions in other Commonwealth[25] countries and for the ban imposed by the Irish companies legislation.[26] Cases interpreting foreign legislation containing versions of the ban that were based on the English model can also help to shed some light on the scope of the current prohibition.

[24] *Report of the Company Law Committee* Cmnd 1749 (1962) paras 178–86.

[25] New Zealand Companies Act 1955, s 55 and Australian Companies Act 1961, s 67 were based on Companies Act 1948, s 54. These jurisdictions have since adopted a different approach to the regulation of the giving of financial assistance: see Corporations Law, s 260A–D (Australia) and Companies Act 1993, ss 76–81 (New Zealand).

[26] Companies Act 1963, s 60 (Ireland).

UNSATISFACTORY STATE OF THE CURRENT LAW

The relevant provisions in the Companies Act 1985 benefit from the distilled wisdom of case law and practical experience that was built up in relation to their predecessors. As a result, they are undoubtedly much more precise and focused than those which they replaced. Nevertheless, they are still not models of good drafting and they remain obscure in several key respects. Partly because of the uncertainty about the precise scope of the ban and the exceptions to it, the range of practical situations in which the possibility of there being a financial assistance problem can crop up is huge. In 1962 the Jenkins Committee described the Companies Act 1948, s 54 as 'an occasional embarrassment to the honest without being a serious inconvenience to the unscrupulous'.[27] The relevant provisions of the Companies Act 1985 have attracted similar criticism.[28] In the 1990s the DTI issued a number of consultative documents on reform of the financial assistance provisions of the companies legislation relating to financial assistance.[29] Although its original proposals were wide-ranging, it eventually concluded that the scope for reform of the provisions applying to public companies was relatively small due to the constraints of the Second Company Law Directive. It envisaged, however, enacting more extensive reforms relating to the giving of financial assistance by private companies. At the time of writing, legislation to this effect has not been forthcoming but the DTI has launched a general review of company law and reform of financial assistance will figure in this review.[30]

Unless it can be amended, the presence of the Second Directive, art 23.1 precludes the enactment of the type of root-and-branch reform of the rules relating to financial assistance that has taken place elsewhere in the Commonwealth. Australian legislation provides an example of a different approach to that which is taken by English/European law. The relevant provisions[31] permit the giving of financial assistance provided this does not materially prejudice the interests of the company or its shareholders or the company's ability to pay its creditors. Financial assistance is also permitted where it is approved by the shareholders. Certain forms of financial assistance are permissible because they are declared to be exempt.

Pending legislative reform, an analysis of English law relating to financial assistance has to be prefaced with a warning to the effect that certain key

[27] *Report of the Company Law Committee* Cmnd 1749 (1962) para 176.

[28] eg, *Section 151* (Law Society Company Law Committee Memorandum No 233) (1990); Sykes, R, 'Section 151: Crime or Civil Claim' (1991) 2(2) PLC 3.

[29] *Company Law Review: Proposals for Reform of Sections 151–158 of the Companies Act 1985* (DTI Consultative Paper) (1993); *Consultation Paper on Financial Assistance* (DTI) (1996).

[30] The DTI initially suggested removing private companies from the scope of Companies Act 1985, s 151 altogether and the enactment of a clearer set of rules for private companies on prohibited and permitted financial assistance. After consultation, however, it withdrew that suggestion and proposed instead to keep private companies with Companies Act 1985, s 151 but to provide a new exemption for small transactions and to make certain changes to the whitewash procedure: *Financial Assistance by a Company for the Acquisition of Its Own Shares: Conclusions of Consultation* (DTI) (1997).

[31] Corporations Law, Pt 2J.3 (ss 260A–260D).

points are bounded by uncertainty. This chapter attempts to pinpoint some of the uncertainties created by the sections, as presently drafted, and to suggest how they might be resolved.

THE SCOPE OF THE BAN ON THE GIVING OF FINANCIAL ASSISTANCE

The Companies Act 1985, s 151 (1) and (2) are as follows:

(1) Subject to the following provisions of this Chapter, where a person is acquiring or proposing to acquire shares in a company, it is not lawful for the company or any of its subsidiaries to give financial assistance directly or indirectly for the purpose of that acquisition before or at the same time as the acquisition takes place.

(2) Subject to those provisions, where a person has acquired shares in a company and any liability has been incurred (by that or any other person), for the purpose of that acquisition, it is not lawful for the company or any of its subsidiaries to give financial assistance directly or indirectly for the purpose of reducing or discharging the liability so incurred.

Elements of these two provisions may be separated out for particular consideration.

'Where a Person'

The ban applies to acquisitions of shares by natural persons or legal persons such as companies. Read literally, the company whose shares are to be acquired could itself be a 'person' for the purposes of the Companies Act 1985, s 51[32] but it doubtful whether this is the correct interpretation. The concept of a company providing financial assistance to itself is largely meaningless and, in any event, the funds which a company can use to purchase its own shares are closely regulated by the provisions of the Companies Act 1985 that are concerned with share buy backs.[33] This tends to suggest that the company whose shares are the subject of the acquisition should be excluded from the category of persons who can give unlawful financial assistance. The Second Directive, art 23.1 does not preclude this interpretation since it only bans financial assistance for the acquisition of shares by a third party. However, the position becomes more complicated when the possibility of a subsidiary providing financial assistance for the purpose of an acquisition by the parent of its own shares is brought into the picture. If the parent is not a 'person' for the purposes of the Companies Act 1985, s 151, it follows that its subsidiaries are not prohibited by that section from providing it with financial assistance to acquire its own shares. It could be argued that financial assistance by a subsidiary for share buy backs by its parent ought to be caught by the ban on financial assistance. However an attractive alternative view is that since assistance provided by a subsidiary directly to, or for the benefit of, its parent is within the scope of the distribution rules in the Companies Act 1985, Pt VIII

[32] Stedman, G, and Jones, J, 'Can a Company Give Financial Assistance to Itself?' (1983) LS Gaz 2419.

[33] Companies Act 1985, Pt V, ch VII.

and the general principle whereby a company must maintain its capital and, furthermore, since there are restrictions on the funds that a company may lawfully use to buy back its own shares, the matter is adequately regulated without the financial assistance rules having to apply as well.

The Companies Act 1985, s 153 (3)(d) is relevant in this context. This provides that the ban on the giving of financial assistance does not apply to a redemption or purchase of shares made in accordance with the provisions of the Companies Act 1985 which permit such acquisitions. Although it may be argued that this is an indication that the legislature must have considered that an acquisition by a company of its own shares could, if not specifically excluded, fall within the scope of the ban on the giving of financial assistance, an alternative view is that this is simply a provision which is intended to be for the avoidance of doubt. As discussed later in this chapter,[34] other parts of the Companies Act 1985, s 153 do little more than put certain matters beyond doubt and s 153 (3)(d) may simply be consistent with those parts. This is an area where the law is in need of clarification.

Must the Person be Known at the Time when the Assistance is Given?

This question could, for example, arise where the management of a company decides that its business would be more effectively conducted if it were part of a larger group and engages an investment bank or other professional adviser to find a buyer for the company's shares. Assuming for the moment that a 'finder's fee' can amount to financial assistance,[35] can it be said that the ban on the giving of financial assistance does not apply because, at the time when the company agrees to pay the fee,[36] the company is unaware of the identity of any purchaser, or aspiring purchaser, of its shares? The answer to this question is not clear from the statute but it would seem that lack of this knowledge should not be a defence to a charge of unlawful financial assistance. The mental element of this offence is that the assistance must be given for a purpose specified in the Companies Act 1985, s 151. If something that was done by a company at a time when it was totally unaware of, and had no intention of helping, a proposed acquisition, by chance happened to assist an acquisition, the situation would properly fall outside the scope of the ban on the grounds that the company's act was not done 'for the purpose of' the acquisition. The suggestion here is that the words 'proposing to acquire' do not carry with them an additional mental element involving knowledge of the identity of a potential acquirer of the shares and that it is a question of looking at the external facts, as opposed to the internal matter of the company's knowledge, to determine whether someone was proposing to acquire shares at the relevant time. The conclusion of this argument is that it is not possible to use a company's lack of knowledge of the identity of a potential acquirer to decide that

[34] See below, at 396.

[35] Relevant issues here are whether it fits within any of the categories of financial assistance as defined in Companies Act 1985, s 152 and also whether financial assistance requires an element of help given to the purchaser rather than help to the vendors.

[36] This, rather than the time when the money is actually paid, is the relevant time: *Parlett v Guppys (Bridport) Ltd* [1996] BCC 299, CA where this was common ground between the counsel in the case.

transactions such as paying a finder's fee or meeting the costs attendant upon an issue or a sale of shares are outside the ban on the giving of financial assistance.[37]

'An Acquisition of Shares'

In *NZI Bank Ltd v Euro-National Corporation Ltd*[38] it was held by the New Zealand Court of Appeal that providing money to acquire share options was not within the ban on the giving of financial assistance in the form of money for the acquisition of shares imposed by the New Zealand Companies Act 1955, s 62. The New Zealand Companies Act 1955, s 62 was based on the English Companies Act 1948, s 54 and the wording of s 62 was sufficiently close to that of s 151 to give this case some persuasive authority in relation to the interpretation of the Companies Act 1985, s 151. This line of reasoning suggests that financial assistance given in relation to the acquisition of debt securities that are convertible into shares should also fall outside the statutory ban. This is subject to the qualification that the court can look through formalities where these are inconsistent with the substance of a transaction or have been adopted in order to evade the application of a statute.[39] Thus, for example, a structure which is designed to bypass the Companies Act 1985, s 151 by the company providing financial assistance for the acquisition of convertible securities that are immediately convertible into its shares will fail to achieve the desired effect.

'Or Any of its Subsidiaries': The Position of Foreign Subsidiaries

Although a literal interpretation suggests otherwise, foreign subsidiaries are not within the scope of the ban on the giving of financial assistance.[40] This purposive interpretation of the Companies Act 1985, s 151 avoids giving extraterritorial effect to a penal section contrary to the general principles of private international law. Whether a foreign subsidiary can give financial assistance will thus depend on the law of its place of incorporation.[41]

'Financial Assistance'

In *Barclays Bank plc v British & Commonwealth Holdings plc*[42] the Court of Appeal held that the assistance has to be financial in nature and that it has to amount to help as opposed to mere co-operation. This distinction between help and co-operation is supported by Australian cases.[43] An example of non-

[37] Although it may be possible to argue that these do not fit within the categories of financial assistance mentioned in Companies Act 1985, s 152. See further this chapter below, at 385.

[38] [1992] 3 NZLR 528, NZ CA.

[39] *Welsh Development Agency v Export Finance Guarantee Co Ltd* [1992] BCC 270, CA.

[40] *Arab Bank plc v Merchantile Holdings Ltd* [1994] Ch 71.

[41] If the place of incorporation is within the European Union that law should ban financial assistance at least to the extent required by the Second Directive, art 23.1

[42] [1995] BCC 1059, CA.

[43] *Burton v Palmer* (1980) 5 ACLR 481, NSW SC, 489 *per* Mahoney J; *Industrial Equity Ltd v Tocpar Pty Ltd* [1972] 2 NSWLR 505, NSW EqD, 514 *per* Helsham J.

financial co-operation would be where a company permits a potential purchaser of its shares to inspect its books and records.[44] Australian case law also establishes that the assistance need not be help which is actively sought by the acquirer and he may be entirely indifferent to the fact that it is given.[45] With regard to timing, it is at the point when a company undertakes an obligation, rather than when it comes to be performed, that the existence or otherwise of financial assistance is to be tested.[46]

The Companies Act 1985, s 152 contains a list of transactions or other acts that are the proscribed forms of financial assistance. This section is considered separately later in this chapter.[47]

'Directly or Indirectly'

An example of direct financial assistance is where a company puts someone in funds to acquire its shares. Examples of indirect financial assistance are where the company guarantees the purchaser's borrowing or gives security on its assets for it. Whilst structures such as these fall clearly within its scope, the ban on the giving of financial assistance also snares more sophisticated schemes.

Financial assistance received by the vendor of shares may infringe the ban on the giving of financial assistance where, but for it, the vendor would not have proceeded with the sale or would only have done so at a higher price. This point is illustrated by *Armour Hick Northern Ltd v Armour Hick Trust Ltd*.[48] In this case a subsidiary paid off a debt due from its immediate holding company to the ultimate parent company and the ultimate parent company then sold the immediate holding company. If the intra-group debt had not been paid, the ultimate parent company would not have been willing to proceed with the sale at the price that the purchaser was willing to pay. Mervyn Davies QC, sitting as a judge, held that this payment was unlawful financial assistance given for the purpose of or in connection with the sale contrary to the Companies Act 1948, s 54. Another example of possible indirect financial assistance is where a company transfers assets at an undervalue to someone other than the vendor or purchaser, say to other companies within its group, and that company is then sold to the purchaser at a price which is lower than that which would have been asked if those transfers had not been made.[49]

Must the Financial Assistance Assist the Acquirer of the Shares?

A common feature of all of these examples is that they involve some form of financial help being given, directly or indirectly, to the acquirer. This financial

[44] *Burton v Palmer* (1980) 5 ACLR 481, NSW SC, 489 *per* Mahoney J.

[45] *Independent Steels Pty Ltd v Ryan* (1989) 15 ACLR 518, Vic FC.

[46] This was common ground between the counsel involved in *Parlett v Guppys (Bridport) Ltd* [1996] BCC 299, CA.

[47] See below, at 385.

[48] [1980] 3 All ER 833. The facts of this case appear to have been misunderstood in *Burton v Palmer* (1980) 5 ACLR 481, NSW SC where it was thought that it was concerned with a company paying its own debt. See also *Mercato Holding Ltd v Crown Corpn Ltd* [1989] 3 NZLR 704, NZ HC.

[49] *Charterhouse Trust Ltd v Tempest Diesels Ltd* (1985) 1 BCC 99,544.

help can come in a variety of forms including the following: the acquirer may be provided with the funds to buy the shares; liabilities which the acquirer incurs to raise the funds to buy the shares may be discharged, guaranteed or secured; value may be taken out of a target company in order to lower the purchase price that an acquirer must pay and, therefore, the amount of finance that it has to raise to finance the acquisition; or liabilities within a target company may be repaid so as to relieve the acquirer from the obligation to find the money to repay those liabilities as a condition of the acquisition agreement.[50] It is suggested that help, in a financial form, to the acquirer is an essential feature of unlawful financial assistance under section 151 (1)[51] and that if this is not present it cannot be said that there has been given 'financial assistance for the purpose of an acquisition'. Help given to enable willing vendors to sell at a higher price[52] would not amount to financial assistance on this interpretation because a disposal is not an acquisition. Although there will be an acquisition as a counterpart to the disposal, the help does not 'assist' that acquisition and indeed makes it more difficult since it makes it more expensive.

This interpretation does not find much direct support in English cases. In *Charterhouse Trust Ltd v Tempest Diesels Ltd*[53] Hoffmann J identified a reduction in the price that the purchaser would have had to have paid as being crucial to a finding that a transfer of assets out of the company to other companies in its group amounted to financial assistance.[54] In *Armour Hick Northern Ltd v Armour Hick Trust Ltd,*[55] however, Mervyn Davies QC expressly ruled that financial assistance did not have to help the purchaser to be caught by the Companies Act 1985, s 54 and that assistance to the vendor sufficed. It may be possible to explain away this statement on the grounds that the Companies Act 1985, s 54 extended to financial assistance given 'in connection with' a share purchase whereas under the Companies Act 1985, s 151 only assistance given 'for the purpose' of an acquisition is banned. A better view is that the scheme considered in the *Armour Hick* case could still fall within the current ban on the giving of financial assistance because it assisted the purchaser in cash-flow terms by relieving it of the obligation to find the cash to repay outstanding intra-group liabilities of the target company.[56]

[50] In *Armour Hick Northern Ltd v Armour Hick Trust Ltd* [1980] 3 All ER 833 there was a reduction in the net assets of the subsidiary that paid off the loan. As a result of the repayment, the position of its parent, the target company, changed from one where it had a liability to the ultimate parent but also an asset in the form of the cash in its subsidiary to one where it had neither that liability nor the cash. The financial assistance to the purchaser was that it did not have to repay the intra-group loan from its own resources.

[51] See *Charterhouse Investment v Tempest Diesels Ltd* (1985) 1 BCC 99,544, 99,552.

[52] Which could be anything from engaging advisers to advise on the merits of an offer to funding an advertising campaign to publicise the merits of the company and hence enhance its share price.

[53] (1985) 1 BCC 99,544.

[54] Although on Companies Act 1948, s 54 the reasoning in this case is equally applicable to Companies Act 1985, s 151 and the sections that follow it.

[55] [1980] 3 All ER 833.

[56] But Pennington, RR, 'The Companies Act 1981 (2)' 3 Co Law 66, 69 argues that a case such as *Armour Hick* may fall outside Companies Act 1985, s 151 because this does not contain the phrase 'in connection with'.

In an Australian case it was said that it did not matter to whom the financial assistance was given if it was given for the purpose of an acquisition.[57] The view expressed here does not dispute the correctness of that statement since, in context, the phrase 'financial assistance' there meant the particular thing which the company did, be it the making of a gift or a loan or the giving of another form of financial assistance. That the direct recipient of the form of financial assistance need not be the acquirer of the shares is not incompatible with a requirement that the financial assistance should assist the acquirer of the shares.

That there is uncertainty on such a crucial matter as whether financial assistance must involve some form of financial help to the person who acquires the shares is unfortunate. Until there is a clear ruling on this issue by the courts, in practice advisers are likely to feel uncomfortable in advising that financial help to the acquirer is a key element of the Companies Act s 151 (1) and, so, may be unwilling to absolve transactions which may help the vendor but which do not help the acquirer and may even prejudice its position by leading to an increase in the price that it has to pay in order to acquire the shares.

'Acquisition'

The Companies Act 1985, s 151 refers to an acquisition of shares unlike its predecessor, the Companies Act 1948, s 54, which referred to the purchase of, or subscription for, shares. The current wording means that an issue of shares for a non-cash consideration which is worth less than the issue price of the shares can amount to the giving of financial assistance. It would not have done so under the older legislation because the term 'subscription' means taking shares for cash.[58] A purchase of shares for non-cash consideration is also an acquisition.[59]

Timing of the Financial Assistance: Must there be an Acquisition?

The effect of the Companies Act 1985, s 151 (1) and (2) is to ban financial assistance given before, or at the same time as, or after an acquisition. But what if no acquisition ever takes place? Is financial assistance given in those circumstances caught? This is a simple question but there is no obvious answer.

A situation where this problem might arise is in a proposed management buy out where the company's board agrees to pay the legal and other costs of the buy-out team. Assuming for the moment that such an agreement can fall within the definition of financial assistance,[60] what is the position if the

[57] *EH Dey Pty Ltd v Dey* [1966] VR 464, Vic SC, 470 quoted with approval in *Armour Hick Northern Ltd v Armour Hick Trust Ltd* [1980] 3 All ER 833. But later Australian cases are clearer on the requirement for help to the purchaser: eg *Independent Steels Pty Ltd v Ryan* (1989) 15 ACLR 518 Vic FC, 524 *per* Fullagher J.

[58] *Government Stock and Other Securities Investment Co Ltd v Christopher* [1956] 1 All ER 490.

[59] *Plaut v Steiner* (1989) 5 BCC 352, decided under Companies Act 1985, s 151, involved a share-for-share exchange. It is unclear whether 'purchase' in Companies Act 1948 would have been held to be confined to cash transactions.

[60] This depends on whether the amounts involved would reduce the net assets of the company to a material extent.

buy-out team is ultimately unable to make its bid because it is unable to raise the finance, or for some other reason, but it has incurred costs up to that point? Is the company obliged to pay? One view is that financial assistance given in circumstances where an acquisition never takes place is not financial assistance given 'before' an acquisition, as the Companies Act 1985, s 151 (1) requires,[61] so that the prohibition does not bite. But the opposite view is also tenable. The principle that a company's money should not be spent in helping someone to buy shares has never been spelt out in such precise terms as to exclude cases where no acquisition actually takes place. Referring back to the management buy-out example, it could be said that what the board has done in committing the company in this way is to step outside the boundaries of their constitutional position into an unjustified effort to control the ownership of the company. This militates against the view that the ban does not bite, since prevention of unwarranted inference by the board in the ownership of the company's shares is a purpose that this ban is intended to achieve.[62]

Financial Assistance Given for Specified Purposes

To come within the Companies Act 1985, s 151, the financial assistance must be given for the purpose of an acquisition (ss (1)) or to reduce or discharge a liability incurred for the purpose of an acquisition (ss (2)). The phrase 'for the purpose' is used in a number of the sections of the Companies Act 1985 relating to financial assistance and it is considered more generally later in this chapter.[63] Here it may suffice to note that it is only financial assistance given for any of the specified purposes that is banned. This is in contrast to the Companies Act 1948, s 54 which also banned financial assistance given in connection with an acquisition. However, that provision did not expressly ban post-acquisition financial assistance and at least some of the cases that would now be caught by the Companies Act 1985 s 151 (2) would previously have been covered by the 'in connection with' element of the Companies Act 1948, s 54.[64]

Incurring a Liability/Reducing or Discharging a Liability

To see the full scope of the Companies Act 1985, s 151 (2) it is necessary to look to the amplifications provided by s 152 (3). The reference to a person 'incurring a liability' includes where he changes his financial position by making an agreement or arrangement (whether enforceable or unenforceable) and whether made on his own account or by any other means. The reference to a company giving financial assistance for the purpose of reducing or discharg-

[61] Clearly it cannot be caught as financial assistance given at the same time as an acquisition.

[62] Note a brief comment in *Parlett v Guppys (Bridport) Ltd* [1996] BCC 299, CA, 309 *per* Nourse LJ which suggests that a court is unlikely to conclude that there is no financial assistance simply on the ground that no share transfer is made.

[63] See below, at 391–4.

[64] *Juniper Pty Ltd v Grauson* (1983) 8 ACLR 212, Q SC, a decision on the Australian Uniform Companies Act, s 67 where it was held that it was immaterial that the acquisition preceded the giving of the financial assistance.

ing a liability includes the giving of such assistance for the purpose of wholly or partly restoring a person's financial position to what it was before the acquisition took place.

THE FORMS OF FINANCIAL ASSISTANCE

The Companies Act 1985, s 152 (1) provides that financial assistance means:

(i) financial assistance given by way of gift;
(ii) financial assistance given by way of
—guarantee,
—security,
—indemnity, other than an indemnity in respect of the indemnifier's own neglect or default,
—release or waiver;
(iii) financial assistance given by way of
—loan,
—any other agreement under which any of the obligations of the person giving the assistance are to be fulfilled at a time when in accordance with the agreement any obligation of another party to the agreement remains unfulfilled,
—the novation of, or the assignment of rights arising under, a loan or other such agreement; or
(iv) any other financial assistance given by a company the net assets of which are thereby reduced to a material extent or which has no net assets.

None of this helps to define the core phrase 'financial assistance' and to that extent the heading to the Companies Act 1985, s 152, which describes it as a definition section, is misleading. Although the contrary has been suggested,[65] this section does not define 'financial assistance'. All that it does is to provide a more precise list of the ways in which unlawful financial assistance can be given than its predecessor, the Companies Act 1948, s 54.[66] The term 'financial assistance' itself has no technical meaning and its frame of reference is the language of ordinary commerce.[67] With regard to the specific forms of financial assistance mentioned in the Companies Act 1985, s 152, the approach to interpretation is that since the ban on financial assistance is a penal section these should not be strained to cover transactions which are not fairly within them.[68]

[65] *Barclays Bank plc v British & Commonwealth Holdings plc* [1995] BCC 19, 37; *Arab Bank plc v Merchantile Holdings Ltd* [1994] Ch 71, 78.

[66] In *Charterhouse Investment Trust Ltd v Tempest Diesels Ltd* (1985) 1 BCC 99,544, 99,552 Hoffmann J said in relation to Companies Act 1948, s 54: 'The words have no technical meaning and their frame of reference is in my judgment the language of ordinary commerce. One must examine the commercial realities of the transaction and decide whether it can properly be described as the giving of financial assistance by the company.' Although in *Barclays Bank plc v British & Commonwealth Holdings plc* [1995] BCC 19, 37 Harman J said that Companies Act 1985, s 152 supplied the definition that was missing from the earlier legislation, as noted in the text, this is not an entirely accurate statement of the current legislative position.

[67] *Barclays Bank plc v British & Commonwealth Holdings plc* [1995] BCC 1059, CA, 1070–3 *per* Aldous LJ.

[68] *Charterhouse Investment Trust Ltd v Tempest Diesels Ltd* (1985) 1 BCC 99,544, 99,552 followed in *Barclays Bank plc v British & Commonwealth Holdings plc* [1995] BCC 19, 37.

FINANCIAL ASSISTANCE GIVEN BY WAY OF GIFT

Definition of Gift

A gift is normally taken to mean a gratuitous transfer of the ownership of property.[69] In *R v Braithwaite*,[70] a case concerned with the interpretation of the Prevention of Corruption Act 1906, Lord Lane CJ said:[71]

> The word 'gift' is the other side of the coin, that is to say it comes into play where there is no consideration and no bargain. Consideration deals with the situation where there is a contract or a bargain and something moving the other way.

The court does not generally inquire into the adequacy of consideration. This means that the term gift denotes a correspondingly limited category: if any consideration, whatever its value, is provided, the arrangement is not usually regarded as a gift. In *Barclays Bank plc v British & Commonwealth Holdings plc*,[72] the Court of Appeal held that the words used in the Companies Act 1985, s 152 had their normal legal meaning. Yet, despite this, the court then accepted that it could look to the substance of transactions rather than their form so that, for example, overpayments could be gifts depending on the circumstances of the case. This willingness to inquire into the substance of transactions is consistent with a number of company law cases where the court examined the adequacy of consideration in order to determine whether the maintenance of capital principle had been infringed.[73] It is also consistent with a previous first instance decision on financial assistance, *Plaut v Steiner*,[74] where in circumstances where the amount payable by a company was greater than the value of the assets it was to acquire, the court had held that there was financial assistance in the form of a gift to the extent of the overpayment.[75] Although the comments in the Court of Appeal in *Barclays Bank plc v British & Commonwealth Holdings plc*[76] with regard to the interpretation of the term 'gift' were thus somewhat equivocal, it would appear that a sale of assets at an undervalue, or a purchase at an inflated price, may constitute this form of financial assistance.

It may be possible to extend the idea that inadequate consideration received by a company can be regarded as a gift by the company still further in order to catch share issues for non-cash consideration worth less than the issue price of the shares. The independent valuation requirements where

[69] Bell, AP, *Modern Law of Personal Property in England and Ireland* (1989) 221.

[70] [1983] 1 WLR 385, CA.

[71] Ibid at 391.

[72] [1995] BCC 1059, CA.

[73] *Re Halt Garage (1964) Ltd* [1982] 3 All ER 1016; *Ridge Securities Ltd v IRC* [1964] 1 All ER 275; *Jenkins v Harbour View Courts Ltd* [1966] NZLR 1, NZ CA; *Redweaver Investments Ltd v Lawrence Field Ltd* (1990–91) 5 ACSR 438, NSW EqD; *Aveling Barford Ltd v Perion Ltd* [1989] BCLC 626.

[74] (1989) 5 BCC 352.

[75] The decision in *Belmont Finance Corporation v Williams Furniture Ltd (No 2)* [1980] 1 All ER 393, CA also supports this analysis on its facts. However, that case is not precisely in point because it was decided under Companies Act 1948, s 54 which did not specifically identify gifts as a forbidden form of financial assistance.

[76] [1995] BCC 1059, CA.

shares of a public company are to be allotted for non-cash consideration[77] limit the scope for this form of abuse.

Charterhouse Trust Ltd v Tempest Diesels Ltd[78] concerned the reorganisation of a corporate group prior to the disposal of one of the subsidiaries in the group. As part of this reorganisation the subsidiary in question agreed to surrender certain tax losses. Hoffmann J held that the agreement to surrender tax losses had to be considered in conjunction with the transaction as a whole to determine where the net balance of financial advantage lay and that it could amount to the giving of financial assistance if it amounted to a net transfer of value which reduced the price that the purchaser had to pay for the subsidiary company. This case was decided under the Companies Act 1948, s 54 which did not contain a list of the forms of financial assistance. This type of transaction could fall within the gift category provided this is construed as including cases where the company has transferred out more than it has received in and is not limited to situations where the company has acted gratuitously.

Gifts and Third Parties

A company may agree to pay to a third party an amount that the purchaser of shares would otherwise have to pay personally; for example it may subsidise the dealing costs incurred by shareholders who, for example, want to invest their dividends in more of the company's shares.[79] This would obviously financially assist the purchaser, but it is unclear whether this could be regarded as a gift by the company for the purposes of the Companies Act 1985, s 152. It is not a gift in the conventional sense of the word, since the company has not transferred the ownership of any property to the purchaser. Since the Court of Appeal has said, albeit with a degree of equivocation, that the forms of financial assistance mentioned in the Companies Act 1985, s 152 bear their ordinary legal meaning,[80] this would suggest that such an arrangement is not caught under this heading. Whether it amounts to another form of financial assistance is considered later in this chapter.[81]

No *De Minimis* Exception

Any gift, irrespective of its size, either in absolute terms or as a percentage of the donor company's total assets, can constitute this form of financial assistance. There is no *de minimis* exception. The Second Company Law Directive,

[77] Companies Act 1985, s 103 discussed in Ch 8 above, at 298–301. On the suggestion that a low subscription price could amount to financial assistance, see also: *Milburn v Pivot Ltd* (1997) 25 ACSR 237 Fed Ct of Aust–Gen Div.

[78] (1983–85) 1 BCC 99,544.

[79] This is an issue that may arise in practice in the context of dividend re-investment plans which are arrangements whereby a company puts in place low-cost dealing arrangements for shareholders who want to invest their dividends as described in the test. The same issue may potentially arise where a company pays costs that would otherwise fall to the vendor of shares, eg by engaging an investment bank to find a buyer for the company and paying its fees, but if financial assistance must financially assist the acquirer of shares, as suggested in the text (see above, at 381–3), this latter example is outside the scope of the ban on financial assistance altogether.

[80] *Barclays Bank plc v British & Commonwealth Holdings plc* [1995] BCC 1059, CA.

[81] See below, at 390–1.

art 23.1 in its current form precludes the enactment of such an exception for public companies, although it would be possible to provide this for private companies.[82]

FINANCIAL ASSISTANCE GIVEN BY WAY OF GUARANTEE, SECURITY, INDEMNITY, RELEASE OR WAIVER

Guarantee or Security

The company may be asked personally to guarantee the borrowings which an acquirer of its shares has incurred in order to acquire the shares or it may be asked to grant security over the company's assets for that borrowing.[83] Both of these transactions are straightforward examples of unlawful financial assistance within this category. Another type of arrangement that would also appear to be caught is where a company gives a security in respect of its own indebtedness as part of a transaction involving a sale of its shares. This might, for example, occur because the debt is owed to another company in its group and the holding company parent is willing to allow the debt to remain outstanding but, because the company is leaving the group, wants it to be converted from unsecured to secured. If the security were not granted the holding company would only be willing to proceed with the sale on the basis that the purchaser also took an assignment of those debts. The security thus provides the purchaser with a financial incentive to proceed with the deal.

Indemnity

The term 'indemnity' is used in a technical sense in the Companies Act 1985, s 152 and means a contract by one party to keep the other harmless against loss.[84] For a company, as part of a share-support operation, to undertake to make good any losses which investors in its shares may suffer as a result of having bought them would infringe this aspect of the ban on the giving of financial assistance.

Another situation where indemnities are commonly given by companies to persons who acquire, or who may acquire, its shares is in the context of underwriting agreements. This type of indemnity differs from that considered in the previous paragraph in that it is an indemnity in respect of losses that the underwriter may incur arising from the underwriting process, but not in respect of a drop in share price, which is precisely the risk that the underwriter undertakes to bear. The Companies Act 1985, s 152 (1)(ii) expressly excludes indemnities that are in respect of the indemnifier's own loss or default, but indemnities in underwriting agreements may be more extensive than this.

[82] *Financial Assistance by a Company for the Acquisition of Its Own Shares: Conclusions of Consultation* (DTI) (1997) indicated that the DTI intended at that time to introduce a *de minimis* exemption for private company financial assistance based on a 3 per cent of net assets test.

[83] One of the forms of financial assistance in *Plaut v Steiner* (1989) 5 BCC 352 was financial assistance by way of security.

[84] *Yeoman Credit Ltd v Latter* [1961] 1 WLR 828, CA, 830 *per* Pearce LJ adopted in *Barclays Bank plc v British & Commonwealth Holdings plc* [1995] BCC 1059, CA.

Where they are, there is a risk that they are caught by this aspect of the ban on financial assistance. As a matter of principle there are persuasive arguments for saying that they should not be since, unlike share-support operation indemnities, they are not given with a view to manipulating the company's share price but are an element of the costs that a company legitimately incurs as part of the process of raising capital by issuing shares to the market.[85]

Release or Waiver

The terms 'release' or 'waiver' relate to circumstances where a company relinquishes, or forbears from enforcing, rights that it has against another party. It is unclear whether contractual variations are within the scope of this category, although variation of a bilateral contract by mutual agreement of the parties is sometimes described as a waiver.[86] Even if variations can be regarded as waivers for this purpose, it may be that in many instances the mix of new benefits and burdens assumed by the parties to a varied contract will be such that it is not possible to conclude that, in commercial terms, which is how the phrase 'financial assistance' is to be interpreted,[87] a company has given assistance of a financial nature with the consequence that the situation falls outside the Companies Act 1985, s 151 on that ground.

FINANCIAL ASSISTANCE GIVEN BY WAY OF LOAN OR ANY OTHER AGREEMENT UNDER WHICH THE OBLIGATIONS OF THE PERSON GIVING THE ASSISTANCE ARE TO BE FULFILLED AT A TIME WHEN, IN ACCORDANCE WITH THE AGREEMENT, ANY OBLIGATION OF ANOTHER PARTY TO THE AGREEMENT REMAINS UNFULFILLED, OR BY WAY OF THE NOVATION OF, OR THE ASSIGNMENT OF RIGHTS ARISING UNDER, A LOAN OR SUCH OTHER AGREEMENT

Loan

The usual meaning of the term 'loan' is that it is an advance of money on terms providing for repayment.[88] An arrangement whereby a company pays off a debt that has been incurred to a third party by a purchaser of its shares on terms providing for the purchaser later to reimburse the company is not a loan

[85] *Financial Assistance by a Company for the Acquisition of Its Own Shares: Conclusions of Consultation* (DTI) (1997) stated the DTI's intention at that time to introduce an exemption from the ban on financial assistance for legitimate costs associated with the issue and transfer of shares.

[86] eg, *Brikom Investments Ltd v Carr* [1979] QB 467, CA. See generally, Guest, AG (gen ed), *Chitty on Contracts* (27th edn, 1994) 1087–90.

[87] *Barclays Bank plc v British & Commonwealth Holdings plc* [1995] BCC 1059, CA, 1070–3 *per* Aldous LJ.

[88] *Chow Yoong Hong v Choong Fah Rubber Manufactory* [1962] AC 209, PC, 216 *per* Lord Devlin; *Vigier v IRC* [1964] 1 WLR 1073, HL, 1084 *per* Lord Upjohn; *Champagne-Perrier SA v HH Finch Ltd* [1982] 3 All ER 713; *Potts v IRC* [1951] AC 443, HL. See also *Company Directors: Regulating Conflicts of Interests and Formulating a Statement of Duties* (Law Commission Consultation Paper No 153, Scottish Law Commission Discussion Paper 105) (1988) para 6.10.

within this interpretation. A loan is also to be distinguished from an transaction whereby a company buys goods on credit. Provided the form of the transaction is not a sham and its terms are consistent with the label which the parties have attached to it, buying goods on credit, or against a post-dated debt, does not give rise to a lender–borrower relationship.[89]

Any Other Agreement

This is the category that would cover such things as a tripartite arrangement whereby a company pays off the debts incurred by a purchaser of its shares against an undertaking from that person to repay at some later stage, or transactions whereby a company sells assets for deferred consideration or buys assets and pays for them in advance. If the purchaser of assets from a company were to issue loan notes or other debt securities in circumstances where there was an active market for those securities so that they could readily be converted into cash, it is conceivable that this would be regarded as falling outside the scope of the ban because the consideration which the company has received is as good as cash. The position would be different where the securities which are issued are not liquid, because there would then be a risk of the issuer being unable to meet its obligations.[90]

Novation or Assignment

If the company were, for example, to take an assignment of the debts incurred by a purchaser of its shares for the purposes of the acquisition, the assignment would amount to financial assistance within this category.

ANY OTHER FINANCIAL ASSISTANCE GIVEN BY A COMPANY THE NET ASSETS OF WHICH ARE THEREBY REDUCED TO A MATERIAL EXTENT OR WHICH HAS NO NET ASSETS

This category of financial assistance covers two distinct situations. The first is where the company providing the financial assistance has net assets. In this case the transaction or other act by the assisting company is only caught where it reduces those net assets to a material extent. The second situation is where a company has no net assets. Here any form of financial assistance is caught. 'Net assets' for the purposes of this form of financial assistance means the aggregate of the company assets less the aggregate of its liabilities.[91] It is the market value, as opposed to the book value, of those assets and liabilities, which is relevant for this purpose.[92]

[89] *Chow Yoong Hong v Choong Fah Rubber Manufactory* [1962] AC 209, PC; *IRC v Port of London Authority* [1923] AC 507, HL.

[90] Knight, WJL, *The Acquisition of Private Companies and Business Assets* (7th edn, 1997) 61 discusses this example.

[91] Companies Act 1985, s 152 (2) provides that 'liabilities' includes any provision for liabilities or charges within Companies Act 1985, sch 4, para 89.

[92] This interpretation is based on a comparison between Companies Act 1985 s 152 (2) and s 154 (2). In *Parlett v Guppys (Bridport) Ltd* [1996] BCC 299, CA it was common ground between

The materiality test is open to at least two distinct interpretations. One approach is to focus on the size of the reduction in percentage terms and to regard it as immaterial if it falls below a certain minimum threshold. The other approach is to look at the total amount involved and to regard it as material if it is large, even though it represents a tiny reduction in the company's net assets based on a percentage test. Which (if either) of these alternative approaches is correct is not clear from the wording of the legislation. It is even possible that some form of combined method in which the percentage reduction and the amount in absolute terms both feature as relevant considerations could be held to apply. In *Parlett v Guppys (Bridport) Ltd*,[93] where the question of materiality did not arise on the facts because the arrangement in issue did not reduce the net assets of the relevant company at all, Nourse LJ commented that there could be no rule of thumb in such a matter and that the question was one of degree to be answered on the facts of a particular case.

One type of transaction that could be caught under this heading is the payment by a company of the fees of the financial and other advisers who are involved in the sale of its shares.[94] It is conceivable that the amount of the fee could be sufficiently large to reduce the net assets of the paying company to a material extent. There is perhaps more likelihood of a fee satisfying the materiality test where this is based on the total amount involved than where it is judged by reference to percentages. Another potentially vulnerable category of arrangement is a contractual obligation such as a warranty or covenant. Although it was held in *Barclays Bank plc v British & Commonwealth Holdings plc*[95] that a company did not give financial assistance of this type when it undertook a contractual obligation for which in the event of breach it could be liable to pay damages, that ruling was based on the purposes for which the obligation was assumed, which was not for the purpose of the acquisition, thus leaving open the possibility that in a suitable case a covenant or warranty or other contractual commitment might be held to be financial assistance. However, whether an arrangement whereby a company undertakes an obligation or liability reduces net assets for these purposes is to be assessed on the date when the obligation or liability is assumed and not when a payment accrues due.

'FOR THE PURPOSE'

This phrase appears once in the Companies Act 1985, s 151 (1) and twice in s 151 (2). It is also used in the Companies Act 1985, s 153 (1) which provides an exemption for financial assistance given before, or at the same time as, an

the counsel in the case that it was market values that were relevant for the purposes of Companies Act 1985, s 152. But Nourse LJ commented (at 305) that whilst it was easy to speak in the abstract about the difference between actual assets and liabilities and assets and liabilities as stated in accounting records, it was less easy to disassociate an actual asset or liability from the notion of what is or ought to be in the accounting records.

93 [1996] BCC 299, CA, 308.

94 This passage assumes that, in so far as this is a necessary element of unlawful financial assistance, such payments would assist the purchaser of the shares.

95 [1995] BCC 1059, CA.

acquisition where the company's principal purpose in giving the assistance is not for the purpose of the acquisition or the giving of the assistance for that purpose, but is part of some larger purpose of the company. The Companies Act 1985, s 153 (2) provides a similarly-worded exemption for post-acquisition financial assistance: this is permitted if the company's principal purpose is not to reduce or discharge a liability incurred for the purpose of the acquisition, or if that purpose is but an incidental part of a larger purpose of the company. The Companies Act 1985, s 153 (4)(bb) provides an exemption for employees' share-dealing schemes which also uses the phrase.

In *Brady v Brady*,[96] where it was held that financial assistance had been provided after the relevant acquisition of shares, the House of Lords considered the interpretation of the ban in the Companies Act 1985, s 151 (2) and the exemption in s 153 (2) and in particular the meaning of the term 'purpose' in those provisions. In *Plaut v Steiner*[97] it was held that the reasoning in the *Brady* decision was equally applicable to the ban on financial assistance given before or at the same as an acquisition in the Companies Act 1985, s 151 (1) and the exemption from that ban in s 153 (1).

The Background of the Second Directive

Before looking at the *Brady* decision there is one preliminary issue to clear out of the way. In employing the phrase 'for the purpose', the Companies Act 1985 departs from the wording of the Second Directive, art 23.1 which prohibits, for public companies, the giving of financial assistance with a view to an acquisition of shares. It is open to the UK to impose a wider ban on the giving of financial assistance than that required by art 23.1 but a narrower ban would put the UK in breach of its Community obligation properly to implement the Second Directive. Consideration of the European law dimension leads to a number of consequences. First, it prompts the question whether the ban on financial assistance for any of the purposes specified in the Companies Act 1985, s 151 is wider than the art 23.1 prohibition on financial assistance given with a view to an acquisition.[98] This leads into the second point, which is that the Second Directive does not provide exemptions similar to those for principal or larger purposes contained in the Companies Act 1985, s 153. This suggests that the ban in the domestic legislation may be wider than that in the European law, because if the two were co-extensive there would be no scope for these exemptions. It also suggests that, to ensure compliance with European law, these exemptions should be interpreted narrowly.[99] Seen

96 [1989] AC 755, HL.

97 (1989) 5 BCC 353.

98 Note Companies Act 1985, s 154 (4)(c) which uses the phrase 'with a view to' rather than 'for the purpose'. The significance of this departure from the usual wording in the domestic statute is unclear.

99 There is now a significant body of European and domestic case law which establishes that domestic legislation enacted to implement a Directive should be interpreted in the light of the wording and the purpose of the Directive: Case 14/83 *Von Colson and Kamann v Land Nordhein-Westfalen* [1986] 2 CMLR 430, ECJ; Case 222/84 *Johnston v Chief Constable of the Royal Ulster Constabulary* [1986] 3 CMLR 240, ECJ; Case 80/86 *Officier van Justitie v Kolpinghuis Nijmegen* [1989] 2 CMLR 18, ECJ; Case 31/87 *Beentjes v Netherlands* [1990] 1 CMLR 287, ECJ; Case 125/88

against this background, the much criticised[100] *Brady* decision, where the House of Lords took a very restrictive view of the scope of the larger-purpose exemption, may take on a new light, although the Second Directive was not referred to in the opinions of their Lordships in that case.

The Interpretation of Purpose in *Brady v Brady*[101]

In the *Brady* decision Lord Oliver (with whom the other members of the House of Lords agreed) said:[102]

> 'purpose' is, in some contexts, a word of wide content but in construing it in the context of the fasciculus of sections regulating the provision of finance by a company in connection with the purchase of its own shares there has always to be borne in mind the mischief against which section 151 is aimed. In particular, if the section is not, effectively, to be deprived of any useful application, it is important to distinguish between a purpose and the reason why a purpose is formed. The ultimate reason for forming a purpose of financing an acquisition may, and in most cases probably will, be more important to those making the decision than the immediate transaction itself. But . . . 'reason' [is not] the same as 'purpose'. If one postulates the case of a bidder for control of a public company financing his bid from the company's own funds—the obvious mischief at which the section is aimed—the immediate purpose which it is sought to achieve is that of completing the purchase and vesting control of the company in the bidder. The reasons why that course is considered desirable may be many and varied. The company may have fallen on hard times so that a change of management is considered necessary to avert disasters. It may merely be thought, and no doubt would be thought by the purchaser and the directors whom he nominates once he has control, that the business of the company would be more profitable under his management than it was heretofore. These may be excellent reasons but they cannot,

Numan [1991] 1 CMLR 92; Case 106/89 *Marleasing SA v La Commercial Internacional de Alimentation SA* [1992] 1 CMLR 305, ECJ; *Pickstone v Freemans plc* [1989] AC 66,[1988] 2 All ER 803, HL; *Litster v Forth Dry Dock and Engineering Co Ltd* [1990] AC 546, [1989] 1 All ER 1134, HL; *Webb v Euro Cargo Ltd* [1993] 1 WLR 49, HL. The precise boundaries of the principle of purposive construction may not yet be entirely settled (see, eg, discussing the *Marleasing* decision: de Burca, G, 'Giving Effect to European Community Directives' (1992) 55 MLR 215; Maltby, N, '*Marleasing*: What is All the Fuss About?' (1993) 109 LQR 301; Greenwood, C, 'Effect of EC Directives in National Law' [1992] CLJ 301). One limitation is that, for reasons of legal certainty and non-retroactivity, it may not apply to domestic legislation carrying a penal sanction: Case 14/86 *Pretore di Salo v X* [1989] 1 CMLR 71, ECJ; Case 80/86 *Officier van Justitie v Kolpinghuis Nijmegen BV* (80/86) [1989] 2 CMLR 18, ECJ; Case C–168/95 *Criminal Proceedings Against Luciano Arcaro* [1996] ECR I–4705, ECJ, noted Craig, P, 'Directives, Direct Effect, Indirect Effect and the Construction of National Legislation' (1997) 22 European Law Review 519. This is relevant here because breach of the ban on financial assistance under the Companies Act 1985 is a criminal offence: Companies Act 1985, s 151 (3).

See Standing Committee A, *Hansard*, Session 1980–81, 30 June 1981 col 297 for Parliamentary discussion during the passage of the Companies Act 1981 (later consolidated as the Companies Act 1985) of the need to implement art 23.1 correctly.

[100] Only some of the criticism is directed at the restrictive nature of the House of Lords' approach: eg, Luxton, P, 'Financial Assistance by a Company for the Purchase of its Own Shares—the Principal or Larger Purpose Exception' (1991) 12 Co Law 18. Other commentators are less concerned about, or even welcome, the restrictive approach but note the difficulty of giving practical effect to it: Pettet, BG, 'Developments in the Law of Financial Assistance for the Purchase of Shares' [1988] 3 JIBL 96; Greaves, R, and Hannigan, B, 'Gratuitous Transfers and Financial Assistance after *Brady*' (1989) 10 Co Law 135; Polack, K, 'Companies Act 1985—Scope of Section 153' [1988] CLJ 359.

[101] [1989] AC 755, HL.

[102] Ibid at 779–80.

in my judgment, constitute a 'larger purpose' of which the provision of assistance is merely an incident. The purpose and the only purpose of the financial assistance is and remains that of enabling the shares to be acquired and the financial or commercial advantages flowing from the acquisition, whilst they may form the reason for forming the purpose of providing assistance, are a by-product of it rather than an independent purpose of which the assistance can properly be considered an incident.

In practice drawing a distinction between a reason and a purpose is not necessarily an easy task and, perhaps, the most that can be said with certainty is that the House of Lords has sent out a very strong signal that the term 'purpose', as used in this context, is to be narrowly interpreted.[103]

THE PRINCIPAL AND LARGER PURPOSE EXEMPTIONS

The Companies Act 1985, s 153 provides an exemption for financial assistance which is given in circumstances where the company's principal purpose is something other than the giving of financial assistance. An example of the operation of the principal purpose exemption was given by Lord Oliver in *Brady v Brady*:[104]

The [principal purpose exemption] envisages a principal and, by implication, a subsidiary purpose. The inquiry here is whether the assistance given was principally in order to relieve the purchaser of shares in the company of his indebtedness resulting from the acquisition or whether it was principally for some other purpose—for instance, the acquisition from the purchaser of some asset which the company requires for its business.

An example of the operation of the larger purpose exemption is more difficult to formulate.[105] Even Lord Oliver in the *Brady* case acknowledged that the concept of a larger corporate purpose was not easy to grasp.[106] One situation that may be covered by the larger purpose exemption is the case of a subsidiary company that provides funds to its parent company some years after its acquisition to effect a more efficient deployment of assets within the group or to improve the group's financial position. The larger purpose exemption may cover this even though the provision of such funds is used by the parent company to repay a debt incurred for the purpose of acquiring the subsidiary. The facts and decision in the *Brady* case indicate that where financial assistance is given as part of a scheme whereby some shareholders buy out other

[103] Greaves, R, and Hannigan, B, 'Gratuitous Transfers and Financial Assistance after *Brady*' (1989) 10 Co Law 135; Pettet, BG, 'Developments in the Law of Financial Assistance for the Purchase of Shares' [1988] 3 JIBL 96, 104. *Financial Assistance by a Company for the Acquisition of Its Own Shares: Conclusions of Consultation* (DTI) (1997) indicated that the DTI intended at that time to reverse the effects of the *Brady* judgment by introducing a predominant reason test in place of the larger/principal purpose exemptions.

[104] [1989] AC 755, HL, 779.

[105] Greaves, R, and Hannigan, B, 'Gratuitous Transfers and Financial Assistance after *Brady*' (1989) 10 Co Law 135, 139: 'it is difficult to envisage a situation where the section will be applicable'; Polack, K, 'Companies Act 1985—Scope of Section 153' [1988] CLJ 359, 361: 'It may be that Lord Oliver's analysis has rendered [the larger purpose] . . . exception virtually unattainable.'

[106] [1989] AC 755 HL, 779.

shareholders in order to break a deadlock in the management of the company, the aim of breaking the deadlock is not a larger corporate purpose and is merely a reason for the transaction. A discernible difference between these two examples lies in pinpointing a corporate purpose, as opposed to a purpose of individual shareholders or directors. A larger *corporate* purpose may have been what was lacking in the *Brady* case where the driving factor was the desire of the shareholders to ensure the survival of the businesses. This contrasts with the example of an intra-group transaction for which there may exist many legitimate corporate purposes that a company may seek to achieve by its participation.[107]

Establishing a principal or larger purpose does not mean that a scheme that would otherwise be unlawful financial assistance is exempt. The principal and larger purpose exemptions are both subject to a further requirement, which is that the assistance must be given in good faith in the interests of the company. In the *Brady* decision Lord Oliver held that this phrase was a single, composite expression and that it postulated a requirement that those responsible for procuring the company to provide the assistance must act in the genuine belief that it is being done in the company's interest.[108] In the Court of Appeal[109] Nourse LJ had placed particular emphasis on how the scheme would affect the company's creditors and regarded it as fatal to the claim to rely on the s 153 (2) exemption that there was no evidence that the directors had considered the interests of the creditors; whilst the directors had acted in the interests of the shareholders in not considering the creditors, they had failed to act in the interests of the company. Lord Oliver disagreed with Nourse LJ's treatment of the evidence but accepted that the interests of the creditors had to be considered at the time when the financial assistance was given: the directors had to satisfy themselves at that time that the giving of the financial assistance would not impair the company's power to pay its debts as they fell due.

In *Plaut v Steiner*[110] it was held that where a company would have been insolvent if it had given the financial assistance, the test of good faith in the interests of the company could not be satisfied. With regard to another solvent company in the same group which was also involved in group reorganisation proposals that contained elements of financial assistance, it was held that no reasonable board could have concluded that the giving of the financial assistance would be in the interests of the company in circumstances where the only justification for that company's participation was to break a managerial deadlock that was affecting other group companies but not the particular company that was to give the assistance.

[107] This suggestion derives some support from the Irish case *CH (Ireland) Ltd v Credit Suisse Canada* 12 December 1997, H Ct, LEXIS Transcript 1992/3121P where it was held that the principal purpose for the giving of a guarantee was to secure continued financial assistance for the guarantor's corporate group rather than to provide financial assistance. As so interpreted, the facts disclosed a legitimate corporate purpose.

[108] [1989] AC 755, HL, 777–8.

[109] [1988] BCLC 20, CA.

[110] (1989) 5 BCC 352.

DIVIDENDS, BONUS SHARES AND OTHER SPECIFIC EXEMPTIONS

The Companies Act 1985, s 153 (3) lists a number of specific matters which are not within the scope of the ban. This list is largely for the avoidance of doubt.[111] Thus, if read literally, a bonus issue of shares could be an 'acquisition' but it is not within the mischief of the ban that this should be caught and it is accordingly excluded.[112] In *Re Wellington Publishing Co Ltd*[113] it was held that the payment of a dividend was not something which would ordinarily be regarded as the giving of financial assistance within the meaning of the New Zealand equivalent of the Companies Act 1948, s 54. The Companies Act 1985, s 153 (3)(a) now puts this beyond doubt: a distribution of a company's assets by way of dividend lawfully made (or a distribution made in the course of the company's winding up) is not prohibited.

The other matters listed in s 153 (3) as falling outside the scope of the ban are:

- a reduction of capital confirmed by order of the court under the Companies Act 1985, s 137;[114]
- a redemption or purchase of shares made in accordance with the Companies Act 1985, Pt V, ch VII;[115]
- anything done in pursuance of an order of the court under the Companies Act 1985, s 425 (compromises and arrangements with creditors and members);[116]
- anything done under an arrangement made in pursuance of the Insolvency Act, s 10 (acceptance of shares by liquidator in winding up as consideration for sale of property);[117]
- anything done under an arrangement made between a company and its creditors which is binding on the creditors by virtue of the Insolvency Act, Pt I.[118]

All of these are matters that are regulated by other provisions of the Companies Act 1985 or the Insolvency Act 1986. Avoiding an unnecessary duplication of regulation justifies their exclusion from the financial assistance ban. Given this justification, one surprising omission from the list is the payment of underwriting commission which, within certain limits, is rendered lawful by the Companies Act 1985, s 97. Since s 97 states that it is lawful to pay commissions provided the conditions set by that section are complied with, by implication it can be taken that a payment satisfying those conditions does not infringe the ban on the giving of financial assistance, but it would be preferable for this to be stated expressly in the Companies Act 1985, s 153.[119]

[111] Standing Committee A, *Hansard*, Session 1980–81, 30 June 1981, col 301.
[112] Companies Act 1985, s 153 (5).
[113] [1973] 1 NZLR 133, NZ SC.
[114] Companies Act 1985, s 153 (3)(c).
[115] Ibid, s 153 (3)(d).
[116] Ibid, s 153 (3)(e).
[117] Ibid, s 153 (3)(f).
[118] Ibid, s 153 (3)(g).
[119] This would have been covered by the exemption for the costs of issuing and transferring shares that the DTI intended in 1997 to introduce: *Financial Assistance by a Company for the Acquisition of Its Own Shares: Conclusions of Consultation* (DTI) (1997). This specific reform initiative was not pursued after the change of government in May 1997.

EXEMPTION FOR MONEY-LENDING BUSINESSES

The Second Directive, art 23.2 provides that article 23.1 does not apply to 'transactions concluded by banks and other financial institutions in the normal course of business'. The domestic equivalent of this exemption is the Companies Act 1985, s 153 (4)(a) which provides that the ban on the giving of financial assistance does not apply to the lending of money by a company in the ordinary course of business, where the lending of money is part of the ordinary business of the company. The Companies Act 1948, s 54 had a similarly-worded exemption which was considered by the Privy Council in *Steen v Law*[120] and given a very narrow interpretation.

Viscount Radcliffe, giving the judgment of the Judicial Committee, commented that the exemption had to be read as:

> protecting a company engaged in money lending as part of its ordinary business from an infraction of the law, even though moneys borrowed from it are used and, perhaps, used to its knowledge, in the purchase of its own shares. Even so, the qualification is imposed that, to escape liability, the loan transaction must be made in the ordinary course of its business. Nothing, therefore, is protected except what is consistent with the normal course of its business and is lending which the company ordinarily practices . . . [I]t is, on the other hand, virtually impossible to see how loans, big or small, deliberately made by a company for the direct purpose of financing a purchase of its shares could ever be described as made in the ordinary course of business.

It is not sufficient that the company's ordinary business involves lending money; the particular loan must also be within the ordinary course of its business and, if it is a loan made specifically to finance a share acquisition, it will fail this test. Thus, in *Fowlie v Slater*[121] loans deliberately made by an investment bank for the purpose of financing the purchase of shares in its holding company were held to be special loans for special purposes. They could not be regarded as being within the ordinary course of business of the investment bank and, accordingly, they did not qualify for exemption.

In its application to public companies,[122] this exemption is subject to a qualification based on the application of a net-asset reduction test. This qualification also applies to the exemptions for employees which are considered next. Discussion of the net-assets qualification is postponed until after the exemptions for employees are outlined.

EXEMPTIONS FOR ACQUISITIONS OF SHARES BY EMPLOYEES

A number of overlapping exemptions are intended to allow companies to support employees' share schemes and other acquisitions of shares by employees. Again these exemptions exist against the background of a specific

120 [1964] AC 287, PC.

121 Unreported but noted by Walmsley, K, 'Lending in the "Ordinary Course of Business" ' (1979) 129 NLJ 801.

122 The limitation is required by Second Directive, art 23.2. Accordingly it must be applied to public companies but need not be applied (and has not been applied) to private companies.

exemption in the Second Directive: art 23.2 provides that art 23.1 does not apply to transactions effected with a view to the acquisition of shares by or for the company's employees or the employees of an associate company.

The Companies Act 1985, s 153 (4)(b) contains the first of the domestic exemptions. This provides that s 151 does not prohibit the provision by a company, in good faith in the interests of the company, of financial assistance for the purposes of an employees' share scheme. This provision was inserted into the Companies Act 1985 in 1989 in order to replace a more restrictively worded exemption. Previously, the exemption allowed 'money' to be provided for the 'acquisition of fully paid shares' in the company. Other forms of financial assistance—such as guaranteeing the borrowings of the trust under which the employees' share scheme was constituted—were not permitted. Also there was some doubt about whether money could be provided to cover the incidental costs of an acquisition as opposed to the cash consideration itself. Both of these limitations have now disappeared but, unlike what it replaced, it is now expressly stated that the financial assistance is only permitted where it is given in good faith and in the interests of the company. This qualification puts into statutory form the limitations to which directors are subject by virtue of their fiduciary duties. These limitations act as safeguards against corporate management manipulating employees' share schemes with a view to influencing, say, the outcome of a takeover bid for their company.

The definition of an 'employees' share scheme' is to be found in the Companies Act 1985, s 743. This provides that an employees' share scheme is a scheme for encouraging or facilitating the holding of shares or debentures in a company by or for the benefit of:

(a) the bona fide employees or former employees of the company, the company's subsidiary or holding company or a subsidiary of the company's holding company, or
(b) the wives, husbands, widows, widowers or children or step-children under the age of 18 of such employees or former employees.

NZI Bank Ltd v Euro-National Corporation Ltd[123] involved an attempt to take advantage of the employees' share scheme exemption to the ban on the giving of financial assistance under the New Zealand companies legislation. The employees' share scheme was to act as the conduit for the provision of financial assistance to certain major shareholders in the company, the aim of this being to avoid the likely effect on the company's share price if they sold their shares. The New Zealand Court of Appeal held that it was necessary to examine what the directors were in truth endeavouring to achieve in setting up the employees' share scheme so as to ensure that the exemption was not used to cover a financial engineering purpose for which it was never designed. It seems likely that the English courts would adopt a similarly inquiring approach in order to prevent manipulation or abuse of the exemption.

In the *NZI Bank* decision the New Zealand Court of Appeal also expressed the view that an arrangement could not amount to a scheme if only one employee could benefit from it. A very small class of beneficiaries would tend

[123] [1992] 3 NZLR 528, NZ CA.

to suggest that the scheme is artificial and amounts to nothing more than an attempt to take advantage of the exemption. However, there is no reason why all of the employees, former employees and connected persons of a company and its associated companies need be included in a scheme in order for it to qualify as an employees' share scheme.

There is some overlap between the Companies Act 1985, s 153 (4)(b) and s 153 (4)(c), which provides that s 151 does not prohibit the making by a company of loans to persons other than directors employed in good faith by the company with a view to enabling those persons to acquire fully paid shares in the company or a holding company to be held by them by way of beneficial ownership.

The Companies Act 1985, s 153 (4)(bb) was inserted by the Financial Services Act 1986 and later amended by the Companies Act 1989. It is still rather curiously drafted. This provision permits the provision of financial assistance by a company or any of its subsidiaries for the purposes of or in connection with anything done by the company (or another company in the same group) for the purpose of enabling or facilitating transactions in shares in the first-mentioned company between, and involving the acquisition of beneficial ownership of those shares by, the bona fide employees or former employees (or connected persons) of the company or of associated companies. The gist of this is clear: it is intended to allow companies to support internal share-dealing schemes. But the dual requirement—that only present or former employees (or connected persons) should be the beneficial participants and should be the only parties to transactions—appears to exclude common types of schemes where one of the parties to transactions can be a trust established for the benefit of employees and connected persons.[124]

NET-ASSET REDUCTION TEST FOR EXEMPTIONS FOR MONEY-LENDING BUSINESSES AND FOR EMPLOYEES

The exemptions for money-lending businesses and employees only apply where the financial assistance which is given does not reduce the company's net assets or, to the extent that those assets are reduced, the financial assistance is provided out of distributable profits.[125] For this purpose net assets are calculated by looking at the amount by which the aggregate of the company's assets exceeds the aggregate of its liabilities, taking the amount of both assets and liabilities to be as stated in the company's accounting records immediately before the financial assistance is given.[126] In other words, it is book values as opposed to market values that must be considered. The term 'liabilities' includes an amount retained as reasonably necessary for the purpose of providing for any liability or loss which is either likely to be incurred, or certain to

[124] Compare Financial Services Act 1986, sch 1, para 20 which is drafted in broader terms. *Financial Assistance by a Company for the Acquisition of Its Own Shares: Conclusions of Consultation* (DTI) (1997) indicated that the DTI intended at that time to widen this exemption to encompass transactions between employees or employee trusts and outside investors.

[125] Companies Act 1985, s 154 (1).

[126] Ibid, s 154 (2)(a).

be incurred but uncertain as to amount, or as to the date on which it will arise.[127]

Prima facie a loan would not reduce the net assets of the lender company provided the borrower's credit is good and no provision against default has to be made. Similarly, with contingent liabilities such as guarantees and indemnities, if the contingency is so remote that in accounting terms it would be valued at nil, there will be no immediate reduction in net assets.[128]

PRIVATE COMPANY WHITEWASH

In its report in 1962 the Jenkins Committee recommended that financial assistance should be permitted where it had been approved by a special resolution of the shareholders and the directors were able to make a statutory declaration of solvency. The Committee thought that the first of these requirements would afford a considerable degree of protection to minority shareholders but, to increase this further, also recommended that the dissident minority should in certain circumstances have the right to apply to the court to prohibit the proposed transaction. The second condition was designed to protect creditors.[129]

The background of the Second Directive made it impossible to implement this suggestion with regard to public companies. A special whitewash regime, based on that recommended by the Jenkins Committee, was introduced for private companies in the 1981 Companies Act. It is now contained in the Companies Act 1985, ss 155–158.

Under the Companies Act 1985, s 155, a private company is permitted to give financial assistance relating to an acquisition of shares in itself. A private company may also give financial assistance for the acquisition of shares in its holding company provided: (i) the holding company is also a private company; and (ii) no other company in the chain stretching from the holding company to the company which is to give the assistance is a public company.[130] To protect the interests of shareholders various approvals are required. The giving of financial assistance is generally only permitted where it has been approved by special resolution of the company which is to give it.[131] There is one exception to this: such approval is not required where that company is a wholly-owned subsidiary.[132] If the financial assistance relates to an acquisition of shares in a holding company, that holding company, together with any intermediate holding companies in the chain, must also pass special resolutions approving the giving of that assistance, save that no such resolution need be passed by any company which is a wholly-owned subsidiary.[133]

127 Companies Act 1985, s 154 (2)(b).

128 This is distinct from the question whether there is a possibility of a reduction in net assets at some point in the future. Companies Act 1985, s 154 is only concerned with the position at the time when the assistance is given and does not require looking ahead.

129 *Report of the Company Law Committee* Cmnd 1749 (1962) paras 178–9 and 187.

130 Companies Act 1985, s 155 (1) and (3).

131 Ibid, s 155 (4).

132 Ibid, s 155 (4).

133 Ibid, s 155 (5).

Procedural requirements regarding the passing of these resolutions are specified in the Companies Act 1985, s 157. The directors' declaration of solvency, accompanied by an auditors' report, must be available for inspection by members at the meeting at which a resolution is to be passed.[134] The resolution must be passed on the same day as that on which the directors make their declaration or within the week immediately following that date.[135]

Where such a resolution has been passed, within 28 days[136] an application may be made to the court for cancellation of the resolution by the holders of not less in the aggregate than 10 per cent in nominal value of the company's issued share capital or any class of it,[137] except that the application may not be made by a person who has consented to or voted in favour of the resolution.[138] A special resolution is not effective for the purposes of the Companies Act 1985, s 155 if it is cancelled by the court on such an application.[139]

There are two limitations which are designed to protect the interests of creditors. First, it is only possible to use the whitewash procedure where the giving of the financial assistance will not involve any immediate net-asset reduction or, to the extent that they are reduced, the assistance is provided from distributable profits.[140] This is the same net-asset reduction test as has already been considered in relation to the money-lending businesses' and employees' exemptions.[141] The second protection is the requirement for a statutory declaration of solvency.[142] The directors of the company which is to give the financial assistance must always make a statutory declaration of solvency. Where the financial assistance relates to an acquisition of shares in a holding company, the directors of that holding company must also make a statutory declaration, as must the directors of any intermediate holding companies in the chain. This declaration must be in the prescribed form and must comply with the requirements set out in the Companies Act 1985, s 156. Form 155 (6) is the 'prescribed form' but, provided all the required particulars are contained in the form and there is no failure to provide any information which is mentioned in the prescribed form, then the use of a particular piece of paper is not required.[143]

The statutory declaration must contain such particulars of the financial assistance to be given, and of the business of which they are directors, as may be prescribed, and must identify the person to whom the assistance is to be given. In *Re SH & Co (Realisations) 1990 Ltd*[144] the statutory declaration stated that financial assistance in the form of debenture was to be given but did not disclose the property charged, the kind of charge (that is, whether it was fixed or floating) or the fact that, in addition to the debenture, there was also to be financial assistance in the form of a guarantee. Mummery J held that the

134 Ibid, s 157 (4)(a).

135 Ibid, s 157 (1).

136 By virtue of Companies Act 1985, s 157 (3), the procedure in Companies Act 1985, s 54 governs this application. S 54 (3) specifies this time limit.

137 Or, if it is not limited by shares, by not less than 10 per cent of its members: Companies Act 1985, s 157(2)(b).

138 Companies Act 1985, s 157 (2).

139 Ibid, s 157 (4)(b).

140 Ibid, s 155 (2).

141 See above, at 399–400.

142 Companies Act 1985, s 155 (6).

143 *Re NL Electrical Ltd* 30 April 1992 Ch D.

144 [1993] BCC 60.

matters omitted from the particulars about the identity of the property charged, the kind of charge and the guarantee did not prevent the statutory declaration satisfying the requirements of the Companies Act 1985, s 156 (1) and that, accordingly, the guarantee and debenture were lawful financial assistance. He cautioned, though, that the case was 'close to the line' and advised that in future solicitors should err on the side of caution and provide fuller particulars.

Having given all of the requisite particulars, the directors must then make their declaration of solvency. The declaration must state that the directors have formed the opinion, as regards the company's initial situation immediately following the date on which the assistance is proposed to be given, that there would be no ground on which it could then be found to be unable to pay its debts; and either:

(a) if it is intended to commence the winding up of the company within 12 months of that date, that the company will be able to pay its debts in full within 12 months of the commencement of the winding up; or
(b) in any other case, that the company will be able to pay its debts as they fall due during the year immediately following that date.[145]

In forming this opinion, the directors must take into account the same liabilities (including contingent and prospective liabilities) as would be relevant under the Insolvency Act 1986, s 122 (which is concerned with winding up by the court) to the question whether the company is unable to pay its debts.[146]

Annexed to the directors' statutory declaration must be an auditors' report stating that they have inquired into the state of affairs of the company and that they are not aware of anything to indicate that the opinion expressed by the directors in the declaration as to any of the matters mentioned in the Companies Act 1985, s 156 (2) is unreasonable in all the circumstances.[147]

The directors' statutory declaration, together with the auditors' report, and the statutory declaration (if any) must be filed with the registrar of companies within fifteen days after the passing of the resolution or, if there is none, within fifteen days after the making of the declaration.[148] The registrar of companies will accept statutory declarations by individual directors as opposed to a joint declaration provided that the auditors' report is attached to each individual declaration. Failure to comply with filing obligation attracts a fine for the company and its directors.[149] Directors who make a false declaration without having reasonable grounds for the opinion expressed in it are liable to imprisonment or a fine or both.[150]

The Companies Act 1985, s 158 imposes time-limits. To allow for the possibility of an application to court, generally a 'wait and see' period of four weeks from the passing of the special resolution must be allowed to elapse before the financial assistance is given.[151] If an application to court is made, the financial assistance cannot be given before the final determination of the application unless the court otherwise orders.[152] Where every member of the company

[145] Companies Act 1985, s 156 (2).
[146] Ibid, s 156 (3).
[147] Ibid, s 156 (4).
[148] Ibid, s 156 (5).
[149] Ibid, s 156 (6).
[150] Ibid, s 156 (7).
[151] Ibid, s 158 (2).
[152] Ibid, s 158 (3).

which passed the resolution who is entitled to vote at general meetings of the company voted in favour of the resolution, the wait and see period does not apply.[153] This is understandable because if everyone has voted in favour there can be no application to court. In principle, though, the same reason would have justified dispensing with the wait and see period where fewer than 10 per cent of the shareholders had voted against it, but this is not the case. There is also a cut-off date. Financial assistance cannot be given after the expiry of eight weeks from the making of the statutory declaration or, if there is more than one, the making of the first of them, unless the court, on an application under the Companies Act 1985, s 157, otherwise orders.

CRIMINAL SANCTIONS FOR UNLAWFUL FINANCIAL ASSISTANCE

A company commits an offence if it gives unlawful financial assistance and is liable to a fine.[154] The persons who are intended to be protected by the ban on the giving of financial assistance include the company that provides the assistance[155] and it is therefore illogical for the company to be treated as a perpetrator of the crime.[156] Every officer of the company who is also in default is also guilty of a criminal offence. The penalty is imprisonment, up to a maximum of two years, or a fine or both.[157] These officers may also be in breach of the duties that they owe to their company by virtue of their position or under their contracts of employment. Arguments for imposing criminal as well as civil sanctions on directors include their deterrent effect and the existence of structural and commercial factors[158] that may inhibit companies from commencing litigation against their officers.[159]

CIVIL CONSEQUENCES OF UNLAWFUL FINANCIAL ASSISTANCE

The Companies Act 1985 does not refer to the civil consequences of unlawful financial assistance. These consequences are derived from case law and to

153 Ibid, s 158 (2).

154 Ibid, s 151 (3).

155 See this chapter above, at 374.

156 The reforms proposed by the DTI in 1997 included a proposal to remove the assisting company from the category of perpetrator of the crime: *Financial Assistance by a Company for the Acquisition of Its Own Shares: Conclusions of Consultation* (DTI) (1997).

157 Companies Act 1985, s 151 (3).

158 The structural factors flow from the fact that litigation is part of the managerial function, with the consequence that management rather than the shareholders in general meeting controls the initiation of litigation. Although individual shareholders can sometimes bring an action against wrongdoers on behalf of the company, and the giving of financial assistance is one of the situations where such an action is potentially available (*Wallersteiner v Moir* [1974] 3 All ER 217, CA), it is notoriously difficult for shareholders to establish standing to proceed with this type of claim. There is little financial incentive for individual shareholders to pursue such a claim because if it is successful damages will be awarded in favour of the company rather than in favour of the shareholders who brought the action.

159 Sykes, R, 'Section 151: Crime or Civil Claim' (1991) 2(2) PLC 3. *Company Directors: Regulating Conflicts of Interests and Formulating a Statement of Duties* (Law Commission Consultation Paper No 153, Scottish Law Commission Discussion Paper No 105) (1998) paras 3.79–3.84 provides a brief analysis of the economic efficiency of criminal sanctions for breach of fiduciary duty.

examine them fully would take this discussion beyond the scope of this book and into an analysis of complex issues in the fields of equity, contract and restitution where aspects of the law are still developing. It is not proposed here to attempt to give an exhaustive account of all of the remedies available in respect of, and other civil consequences of, transactions that are tainted by unlawful financial assistance. Instead, it suffices for the purposes of this book to indicate the main areas of concern and the issues that arise.

The Transaction or Other Act Constituting the Unlawful Financial Assistance

A contract to give financial assistance is an illegal contract. As such any obligations undertaken by the company providing the financial assistance are unenforceable.[160] An undertaking can be viewed as financial assistance even though it is without legal effect because, as Fisher J explained in *Heald v O'Connor*:[161]

> By the provision of a security . . . the company undoubtedly gives financial assistance to the purchaser of the shares whether the security is valid or not. All that is necessary to make the financial assistance effective is that the lender should believe the security to be valid and on the strength of it make the loan.

If all that has happened is that the company has undertaken some commitment which amounts to the giving of unlawful financial assistance, a declaration that the commitment is void may be the only remedy that the company needs. However, the position is more complicated if the company seeks to bring a personal restitutionary claim in respect of the money or other property that it has parted with in purported performance of its contractual obligations. Although a person who parts with money or other property in the mistaken belief that he is contractually obliged to do so is normally entitled to a restitutionary claim,[162] the general rule is one of no recovery in respect of obligations performed in pursuance of an illegal contract, because the court will not entertain a claim that is founded on an illegality nor assist a person who is a party to the wrongdoing.[163] An important exception to this rule is that if a contract is rendered illegal by a statute in order to protect a class of persons, a person in the protected class can recover notwithstanding the illegality. In one case it was held that a company providing financial assistance was

[160] *Brady v Brady* [1989] AC 755, HL; *Selangor United Rubber Estates Ltd v Cradock* [1968] 2 All ER 1073, 1154; *Heald v O' Connor* [1971] 2 All ER 1105; *Dressy Frocks Pty Ltd v Bock* (1951) 51 SR (NSW) 390; *EH Dey Pty Ltd (in liquidation) v Dey* [1966] VR 464, Vic SC; *Shearer Transport Co Pty Ltd v McGrath* [1956] VLR 316, Vic SC.

The DTI's abortive reform initiative in respect of the provisions of the Companies Act 1985 relating to financial assistance included a proposal to introduce a provision to the effect that a transaction would not be void solely on the grounds that it constituted unlawful financial assistance: *Financial Assistance by a Company for the Acquisition of Its Own Shares: Conclusions of Consultation* (DTI) (1997).

[161] [1971] 2 All ER 1105, 1109.

[162] *Rover International Ltd v Cannon Film Sales Ltd (No 3)* [1989] 3 All ER 423, CA; *Kleinwort Benson Ltd v Lincoln City Council* [1998] 3 WLR 1095, HL.

[163] See generally Burrows, A, *The Law of Restitution* (1993) ch 11; Goff, R, and Jones, G, *The Law of Restitution* (5th edn, 1998) ch 23.

not within the protected class and thus could not have a personal claim in respect of money that it had lent pursuant to a loan that constituted unlawful financial assistance.[164] Although later cases have established that the assisting company is within the class of persons who are intended to be protected by the ban on the giving of financial assistance,[165] to permit recovery in these circumstances a court would still somehow have to circumvent the plain fact that under the Companies Act 1985, s 151, a company is a perpetrator of the crime of giving financial assistance contrary to that section.[166]

The Acquisition of the Shares

In *Carney v Herbert*[167] it was not disputed that unlawful financial assistance in the form of mortgages had been given in relation to the sale of shares. The issue was whether this illegality tainted the whole transaction or whether the illegal mortgages could be severed from it so as to leave the sale of the shares intact. The Privy Council held that severance was possible. Lord Brightman, giving the judgment of the Judicial Committee, stated:[168]

> Subject to a caveat that it is undesirable, if not impossible, to lay down any principles which will cover all problems in this field, their Lordships venture to suggest that, as a general rule, where parties enter into a lawful contract of, for example, sale and purchase, and there is an ancillary provision which is illegal but exists for the exclusive benefit of the plaintiff, the court may and probably will, if the justice of the case so requires, and there is no public policy objection, permit the plaintiff if he so wishes to enforce the contract without the illegal provision.

In *Neilson v Stewart*[169] this dictum was quoted by Lord Jauncey in the House of Lords as authority for the proposition that a share transfer would normally be severable from surrounding unlawful financial assistance.[170]

The Assisting Company's Claims Against Its Management for Authorising Unlawful Financial Assistance and Against Third Parties who are Implicated in It

Directors act in breach of their fiduciary duties if they commit their company to a transaction which amounts to unlawful financial assistance:

> Every director who is a party to a breach of [the ban on financial assistance] is guilty of a misfeasance and breach of trust; and is liable to recoup to the company any loss occasioned to it by the default.[171]

164 *Selangor United Rubber Estates Ltd v Cradock* [1968] 2 All ER 1073. The facts and decision in the *Selangor* case are analysed in detail by Chesterman, MR, and Grabiner, AS, 'Sorting Out A Company Fraud' (1969) 32 MLR 328.

165 See further, this chapter above, at 374.

166 Bretten, GR, 'Financial Assistance in Share Transactions' (1968) 32 Conv (NS) 6, 12–15; Barrett, R, 'Financial Assistance and Share Acquisitions' (1974) 48 ALJ 6, 8–11.

167 [1985] 1 AC 301, PC.

168 [1985] 1 AC 301, PC, 317.

169 [1991] BCC 713, HL.

170 Earlier cases supporting the possibility of severance, at least in some circumstances, are *Spink (Bournemouth) Ltd v Spink* [1936] Ch 544; *South Western Mineral Water Co Ltd v Ashmore* [1967] 2 All ER 953; *Lawlor v Gray* (1980) 130 NLJ 317, CA.

171 *Wallersteiner v Moir* [1974] 3 All ER 217, CA, 239 *per* Lord Denning MR, 249 *per* Buckley LJ and 255 *per* Scarman LJ.

Committing the company's assets in this way amounts to failure to apply the assets solely for the purposes of the company and it is a breach of trust.[172] Illegality does not bar a claim by a company under this heading.[173] It seems that a director who is a party to the acts that constitute the unlawful financial assistance but who does not appreciate their legal significance cannot use his lack of understanding as a defence.[174] Third parties who are implicated in a scheme involving unlawful financial assistance or who receive money or property from the company by reason of it may also be personally liable to the company. Detailed analysis of the circumstances in which a company may have a claim against third parties shifts the focus from the relatively narrow confines of financial assistance and into much broader fields of equity and restitution that are not explored here.[175] A combination between a number of persons to procure a company to give unlawful financial assistance amounts to a conspiracy to effect an unlawful purpose. The surrounding illegality does not prevent the company from suing the conspirators in tort for compensation for loss which it suffers as a result of any such conspiracy.[176]

Disqualification

A person who is who guilty of an indictable offence in connection with the management of a company is liable to be disqualified under the Company Directors Disqualification Act 1986, s 2. Giving unlawful financial assistance is an indictable offence.[177] Failure to detect the giving of unlawful financial assistance is also a factor that can be taken into account in disqualification

[172] *Selangor United Rubber Estates Ltd v Cradock* [1968] 2 All ER 1073, 1092–4; *Steen v Law* [1964] AC 287, PC.

[173] *Selangor United Rubber Estates Ltd v Cradock* [1968] 2 All ER 1073.

[174] *Steen v Law* [1964] AC 287, PC. This is subject to Companies Act 1985, s 727 which allows the court to grant relief where a director has acted honestly and reasonably and where, having regard to all of the circumstances, he ought fairly to be excused. With regard to the criminal offence the abortive proposals of the DTI in 1997 included one to the effect that officers should have a defence where they could show that they acted in good faith, in the reasonable belief that the action did not contravene the prohibition and had taken reasonable steps to establish that this was the case: *Financial Assistance by a Company for the Acquisition of Its Own Shares: Conclusions of Consultation* (DTI) (1997).

[175] *Royal Brunei Airlines Sdn Bhd v Tan* [1995] 2 AC 378, PC establishes that a liability in equity to make good resulting losses attaches to a person who dishonestly procures or assists in a breach of trust or fiduciary duty. The trustee or fiduciary need not have been acting dishonestly although this will often be the case: 392 *per* Lord Nicholls. There is more uncertainty in the case law on when liability can attach to a third party who has received property transferred in breach of trust or fiduciary duty. A particular point of dispute is the degree of knowledge that the recipient must have in order for liability to attach. The issues and the relevant cases are discussed in the following chapters of Cornish, WR, Nolan, R, O'Sullivan, J, and Virgo, G (eds), *Restitution Past, Present and Future* (1998): Millett, Sir Peter, 'Restitution and Constructive Trusts' 199; Oakley, AJ, 'Restitution and Constructive Trusts: A Commentary' 219; Lord Nicholls, 'Knowing Receipt: The Need for a New Landmark' 231; and Harpum, C, 'Knowing Receipt: The Need for a New Landmark: Some Reflections' 247.

[176] *Belmont Finance Corporation v Williams Furniture Ltd (No 2)* [1980] 1 All ER 393, CA.

[177] Companies Act 1985, sch 24.

proceedings on grounds of unfitness under the Company Directors Disqualification Act 1986, s 6.[178]

[178] *Re Continental Assurance Co of London plc* [1996] BCC 888. This case and the Company Directors Disqualification Act 1986 are discussed further in Ch 6 above, at 230–5.

12

Distributions to Shareholders

INVESTOR EXPECTATIONS

Shareholders in British[1] companies generally expect to receive dividends in respect of their shares. This expectation is not to the exclusion of capital growth; rather, shareholders expect a return made up of two components: income, in the form of dividends, and capital gain. The commercial necessity of meeting investor expectations means that the managers of companies cannot simply distribute only that portion of the company's profits which is surplus to the continuing funding requirements of the business.[2] Instead, they may have to distribute a larger proportion of the profits to shareholders and meet the business funding requirements from borrowings or from the proceeds of issues of securities.

Investors who value income more than capital growth will be attracted to companies which have a policy of paying high levels of dividend. Conversely investors who are interested in capital growth will be less concerned about dividends and will look for corporate securities which offer capital growth. Finance directors and others who have responsibility for the financing decisions of a company obviously cannot consider the individual preferences of all of their shareholders but they must bear in mind that such preferences exist. The existence of such preferences would suggest that companies should adopt steady and predictable dividend policies so that investors have the assurance that the investment which they have chosen will continue to serve their particular needs.[3] Consistency is also important because of the way in which dividends are regarded as providing information about longer-term trends in the company's business. The information function of dividends is considered further in a later section of this chapter.[4]

Investor expectations with regard to the level of dividend depend on the nature of the company, the stage of development of its business, and the type of business in which it is engaged. Mature businesses with steady, predictable cash flows, such as utility companies, tend to pay higher dividends than the

[1] For a summary comparison of dividend polices in Britain, United States, Japan and Germany see 'Company Dividends', *The Economist* (4 June 1994) 147. For a wider comparison (geographical and by industry type) see Megginson, WL, *Corporate Finance Theory* (1997) ch 8.

[2] This is the residual theory of dividends. It is not borne out by practice which demonstrates that, in fact, companies prefer to pay steady dividends and then to make good any resulting shortfall in the available financial resources from other sources.

[3] On clientele effect see Ross, SA, Westerfield, RW, and Jaffe, BD, *Fundamentals of Corporate Finance* (4th edn, 1998) 514–15; Franks, JR, Broyles, JE, and Carleton, WT, *Corporate Finance Concepts and Applications* (1985) 418–22.

[4] See below, at 410–1.

market average. Recently-formed companies or those that are involved in exploratory work may pay only nominal dividends.[5] In the USA some companies prefer to return value to shareholders through share buy backs rather than substantial dividend payments. Although share buy backs have become much more common in the UK markets in recent years, as yet buy backs have tended to be used in addition to companies' established dividend payment policies rather than in substitution for them.[6]

In small quasi-partnership or family companies it is often the practice for no significant dividends to be paid.[7] The shareholders tend to think of themselves as owners of the business rather than as investors; as owners, long-term capital growth may be more important than the ability of the company to provide an income in the short term. There is also the fact that many, if not all, of the shareholders of such companies are likely also to be involved in its management and, as such, to be receiving an income from the company in the form of remuneration. In theory, the employment relationship between the company and its employees is entirely separate from its relationship with its shareholders, and the amount that a company pays its employees by way of remuneration is not linked to the income that its shareholders may expect to receive in respect of their shares. However, these distinctions inevitably become blurred where the same people are both shareholders and employees and the amounts paid by way of remuneration may become, at least in part, a substitute for the dividend payment that, as shareholders, they would otherwise expect to receive in respect of their investment.

Financial theorists devote considerable attention to the question of dividend policy and it has been described as one of the most thoroughly researched issues in modern finance.[8] The main issues are: whether, and if so, how dividend policy can affect the overall market value of a company; the function of dividends in conveying information or signals to investors about a company and its prospects; and the way in which the payment of dividends can help to reduce agency costs.

DIVIDENDS AND MARKET VALUE

It has been demonstrated that in theory dividend policy should not affect the overall market value of a company's shares.[9] The theory is based on the fact that shares give their holders the right to share in capital growth as well as in whatever income is distributed by the company from time to time. Shares will have a higher capital value where the company retains the profits and invests them in new profitable ventures than they would have if the company

[5] eg, oil exploration and production companies such as Lasmo plc.

[6] Hinkley, R, Hunter, D, Whittell, M, and Ziff, M, *Current Issues in Equity Finance* (1998) 55–6.

[7] This is the position in Britain and also elsewhere: Megginson, WL, *Corporate Finance Theory* (1997) ch 8.

[8] Megginson, WL, *Corporate Finance Theory* (1997) 353.

[9] Miller, MH, and Modigliani, F, 'Dividend Policy, Growth and the Valuation of Shares' (1961) 34 *Journal of Business* 411.

distributed those profits by way of dividend and then raised further capital to fund the new venture by an issue of new shares. An investor who wants cash can always sell his shares to realise a capital gain instead of relying on the company to pay him a dividend.

There are various practical difficulties with this theory. It ignores the costs involved in buying and selling shares[10] and the differing tax treatment of dividends and capital gains on the disposal of shares.[11] It assumes the existence of a liquid market for the shares which may not in fact exist. It also assumes that the new venture will be perfectly reflected in the company's share price. Although, where shares are valued on the basis of their expected dividend yield,[12] the effect of low dividends in the early years of a project should, in theory, be counterbalanced by the expected higher dividends in future years, in practice investors may view the future gains which may result from new projects funded from retained earnings as more risky than dividends paid here and now and may, as a result, undervalue the shares of a company which pays out a low level of dividends.[13] The theory also excludes the possibility of investor irrationality: irrespective of the value maximising arguments, shareholders may simply prefer to receive steady dividends than to have to sell part of their shareholding in order to generate cash. The theory of the irrelevancy of dividends becomes less sustainable once such real life considerations are taken into account.[14]

DIVIDEND POLICY AND INFORMATION ABOUT THE COMPANY AND ITS PROSPECTS

Dividends can perform an information function: healthy, consistent dividends indicate to investors who are not directly involved in managing a company that its management has confidence in the business and its prospects.[15] It is the directors of a company who normally recommend how much of its

[10] Though there has to be set against the costs for investors in realising shares the costs that a company which distributes its profits would incur in meeting its needs for capital from other sources (issues of securities and borrowing).

[11] If income gains are taxed more heavily than capital gains a generous dividend policy can reduce shareholder wealth: Brennan, MJ, 'Taxes, Market Valuation and Corporate Financial Policy' (1970) *National Tax Journal* 417; Miller, M, 'Behavioral Rationality in Finance: The Case of Dividends' in Stern, JM, and Chew, DH, *The Revolution in Corporate Finance* (2nd edn, 1992) 429 (reprinted, with some abridgment, from (1986) 59 (2) *Journal of Business* 451).

[12] This and other methods of valuation are considered in Ch 2 above, at 54–6.

[13] Cottle, S, Murray, RF, and Block, FE, *Graham and Dodd's Security Analysis* (5th edn, 1988) ch 31; Gordon, MJ, 'Dividends, Earnings and Stock Prices' (1959) 41 *Review of Economics and Statistics* 99; Keane, S, 'Dividends and the Resolution of Uncertainty' (1974) *Journal of Business Finance and Accounting* 389.

[14] *Plc UK, A Focus on Corporate Trends* Survey No 10, April 1993. See also 'Company Profitability and Finance, (1993) 33 *Bank of England Quarterly Bulletin*, 361, 367.

[15] Megginson, WL, *Corporate Finance Theory* (1997) ch 8; Bhattacharya, S, 'Imperfect Information, Dividend Policy and the "Bird in the Hand" Fallacy' (1979) *Bell Journal of Economics* 259. This is not a particularly recent phenomenon: Baskin, JB, and Miranti, PJ, *A History of Corporate Finance* (1997) 86–7 discussing dividends as a source of information in the period up to the early eighteenth century.

profits should be distributed by way of dividend. By virtue of their position, the persons responsible for the management of a company's affairs, its executive directors and senior managers, are expected to have far more information about the company's affairs than its shareholders or outside commentators, and the level of dividend which they recommend is generally seen to be an important signal of what they, with their informational advantage, think of the company's prospects. Viewed in this way, dividends act as a counterweight to the information asymmetries between managers and investors. If managers choose to increase the level of dividend, that is seen not just as an indication of the company's past profitability but also as a signal of greater dividend-paying capacity in the future. Equally, if they are forced to reduce the dividend, that is normally interpreted as a signal of long-term problems within the company rather than a temporary crisis of profitability or liquidity.[16] The result of this logic is that managers may deem it prudent to adopt a fairly conservative dividend policy in which any increases in levels of dividend are gradual and, on the basis of long-term prospects, seem capable of being sustained. This process is sometimes described as dividend 'smoothing'.[17]

The results of a survey published in 1993 indicated that the majority of finance directors who responded agreed that it had become more acceptable to cut dividends but that they would still be very reluctant to take that step. They thought that it was more justifiable to cut a dividend in response to a profit fall for reasons specific to the company rather than a profit fall generated by general economic conditions; many also thought that a cut could be justifiable if there were more important claims on cash flow. Most of those surveyed agreed that a company should aim for a consistent pay-out ratio and the pressure to maintain or increase the dividend was regarded as a useful discipline on management. The 1993 survey was conducted at a time when the UK was just beginning to emerge from a severe recession. During that recession many large companies did in fact reduce their dividends.[18]

This information function performed by dividends is obviously important in a company with a widely dispersed shareholding but it is less so where there is large overlap between the identity of the shareholders and the managers and there is no intention to seek equity investment from external investors. The absence of pressure to provide information is another reason why smaller companies may adopt a policy of paying, at most, nominal dividends.

[16] Woolridge, JR, and Ghosh, C, 'Dividend Cuts: Do They Always Signal Bad News' in Stern, JM, and Chew, DH, *The Revolution in Corporate Finance* (2nd edn, 1992) 462; Brealey, R, 'Does Dividend Policy Matter?' in Stern, JM, and Chew, DH, *The Revolution in Corporate Finance* (2nd edn, 1992) 439, 441 stating that 'unexpected changes in a company's dividend policy matter even though the expected level of dividends does not'.

[17] Ross, SA, Westerfield, RW, and Jaffe, J, *Corporate Finance, International Student Edition* (4th edn, 1996) 505.

[18] Wright, K, 'Company Profitability and Finance', (1994) 34 *Bank of England Quarterly Bulletin* 241, 247.

DIVIDENDS AND AGENCY COSTS

One way of looking at a company is to regard it as a 'nexus of contracts'.[19] Viewed this way, the shareholders provide the capital and they engage the managers as agents[20] to manage the business on their behalf. Where the managers and the shareholders do not comprise broadly the same group of people, an agency conflict arises: the shareholders fund the business but do not manage it; the managers run the business but they lack the incentive to maximise profits over the longer term and will instead act in their own self interest.[21] The agency conflict produces 'agency costs', meaning that, because of the divergence between shareholders' interests and managers' interests, investors will pay less for shares in companies where shareholding is widely dispersed and management is the responsibility of a few individuals than they will for shares in a company where the managers own a large proportion of the share capital. It follows that to improve the price which investors are willing to pay for its shares, the managers of a company should do all that they can to reduce agency costs.

Agency cost analysis suggests that companies should pay high dividends and, where necessary, raise finance from other sources: this will reduce agency costs because equity investors have the security of knowing that management will have had to expose their business record and their plans for the future to the scrutiny of lenders or to the market, and may have had to submit to restrictive covenants in order to secure the funds.[22] In Easterbrook's words: 'expected, continuing dividends compel firms to raise new money in order to carry out their activities. They therefore precipitate the monitoring and debt-equity adjustments that benefit stockholders.'[23]

[19] Easterbrook, FH, and Fischel, DR, 'The Corporate Contract' (1989) 89 Columbia Law Review 1416. See further, Ch 1 above, at 10–12.

[20] In legal terms, the directors are the agents of the company, not of the shareholders: *Automatic Self-Cleansing Filter Syndicate Co Ltd v Cuninghame* [1906] 2 Ch 34, CA.

[21] On the problem of agency conflicts and agency costs generally see Jensen, M, and Meckling, W, 'Theory of the Firm: Managerial Behavior, Agency Costs and Ownership Structure' in Putterman, L (ed), *The Economic Nature of the Firm* (1986) 209 (reprinted in abridged form from (1976) 3 *Journal of Financial Economics* 305); Fama, EF, 'Agency Problems and the Theory of the Firm' (1980) 88 *Journal of Political Economy* 288.

[22] Jensen, M, 'Agency Costs of Free Cash Flow, Corporate Finance and Takeovers' (May 1986) 76 *American Economic Review* 323; Easterbrook, FH, 'Two Agency-Cost Explanations of Dividends' (1984) 74 *American Economic Review* 650; Clark, RC, *Corporate Law* (1986) 598–9; Rozeff, M, 'How Companies Set their Dividend Payout Ratios' in Stern, JM, and Chew, DH, *The Revolution in Corporate Finance* (2nd edn, 1992) 455. A draconian proposal following this line of reasoning is that companies should be legally obliged to pay out all or a designated portion of earnings as dividends: Brewster, K, 'The Corporation and Economic Federalism' in Mason, ES (ed), *The Corporation in Modern Society* (1959) 72. A more moderate proposal is that there should be greater mandatory disclosure of the way in which management arrives at the company's dividend policy: Brudney, V, 'Dividends, Discretion and Disclosure' (1980) 66 Virginia Law Rev 85.

[23] Easterbrook, FH, 'Two Agency-Cost Explanations of Dividends' (1984) 74 *American Economic Review* 650.

DETERMINING THE LEVEL OF DIVIDENDS: THE POTENTIAL FOR ABUSE OF POWER AND HOW IT CAN BE RESTRAINED

It is for companies in their articles of association to determine the procedure for the declaration and payment of dividends. The norm is for provision to be made for both interim and final dividends.[24] Final dividends are dividends declared by shareholders in general meeting on the recommendation of the directors; the level of dividend so declared may not exceed the directors' recommendation.[25] Interim dividends are dividends paid by the directors without reference to the shareholders for approval.[26] Although the final dividend is formally determined by the shareholders, in substance the shareholders' decision is often nothing more than a rubber stamp on a decision already made by the board. This is not always the case, however, as was illustrated by one takeover battle in 1998 when the bidder, which held the majority of the shares in the target, threatened to vote against the directors' dividend recommendation. The bidder argued that the target needed to retain its profits to invest in its business but this threat was widely interpreted as a tactic designed to put pressure on the minority shareholders to sell their shares at a discounted price.[27]

The commercial necessity of meeting investor expectations with regard to dividends limits the opportunity for managerial abuse of dividend policy. Failure to meet investor expectations will have a negative effect on share price and may put the company into the frame as a potential takeover target. The individual managers who are responsible for the policy may be criticised and their job security put at risk. These market pressures are powerful but they may not entirely eliminate the risk of managerial abuse because it may be possible for directors to satisfy investor expectations by paying a reasonable dividend even though the company's performance and prospects could justify a higher payment. In such a situation, the directors may decide upon a policy of retaining profits to expand the company's business into new ventures for reasons which are more to do with the enhancement to their personal reputation resulting from the growth of the company than with the benefits that may ultimately flow to the shareholders from the company having increased in size.[28]

The presence of non-executive directors on the board can be a practical safeguard against such abuse. The legal rule whereby the general meeting declares a final dividend as recommended by the board provides a veneer of

[24] eg, Table A arts 102–3. [25] Ibid, art 102. [26] Ibid, art 103.

[27] 'Astec's Shareholders take Claim of Bullying to Court' *The Times*, 6 April 1998 (concerning Emerson Electric's bid for Astec). The claim was unsuccessful: *Re Astec (BSR) plc* [1999] BCC 59.

[28] The argument that management will pursue policies for the purposes of self-aggrandisement rather than shareholder wealth maximisation is described as the 'managerialist theory': Herman, ES, *Corporate Control, Corporate Power* (1981) 9–14; Marris, R, *The Economic Theory of Managerial Capitalism* (1964). For its application to dividend policy see Brudney, V, 'Dividends, Discretion and Disclosure' (1980) 66 Virginia Law Rev 85, 95 (criticised by Fischel, DR, 'The Law and Economics of Dividend Policy' (1981) 67 Virginia Law Rev 699, 710–14) and Jensen, MC, 'Eclipse of the Public Corporation' (Sept–Oct 1989) *Harvard Business Review* 61.

shareholder control but more often than not the general meeting will simply follow the directors' recommendation. Also, the general meeting's options are limited: it can vote down the directors' recommendation but cannot replace it with a higher level of dividend. Non-executive directors have much greater access than the shareholders in general meeting to information about the company's financial position and prospects, and are much better placed to impose pressure on the executive directors and senior management to justify their dividend policy.

Management discretion with regard to dividend policy may be constrained by covenants in the company's loan agreements which restrict dividend payments. There may also be restrictive covenants in the terms of issue of debt securities, convertible securities and warrants. The existence, and severity, of such restrictions will vary from company to company. Preference shares may carry a fixed dividend which is to be paid before any dividend on ordinary shares.

Legal rules relating to fiduciary duty have a limited role to play in preventing abuse. If directors were to manipulate the dividend policy to serve their own interests rather than those of their company, that would amount to a breach of their fiduciary duties to act in good faith in the interests of the company and to avoid conflicts of interest. The company could bring an action against its directors or former directors for breach of fiduciary duty and, in limited circumstances, individual shareholders could bring a derivative action on its behalf. Fiduciary duties have a deterrent effect but there are various factors that can be expected to operate so as to restrict the number of cases where action is actually taken. First, the powerful market and commercial constraints on dividend policy limit the scope for abuse and, hence, for legal dispute.[29] Secondly, the masking effect of a policy of paying dividends which are sufficient to satisfy investor demands even though the company's business and prospects would justify higher levels, means that it may be difficult to detect and prove wrongdoing.[30] Thirdly, even if an action did reach the courts, it is likely that, in the absence of evidence demonstrating a clear conflict of interests, the court would be reluctant to second-guess the directors' business judgment about dividend policy,[31] a reluctance that would be entirely appropriate given the complexity and commercial sensitivity of the issue.[32] As well as these factors, there are also considerations that inhibit the incidence of intra-corporate litigation generally, such as the formidable legal hurdles that have to be overcome by shareholders who seek to bring derivative actions, the availability of active stock markets on which shares can be sold thereby giving dissatisfied shareholders an alternative to pursuing grievances through the courts, and the unattractive prospect of the commencement of an action attracting media coverage that is damaging to the company's commercial interests.

[29] Fischel, DR, 'The Law and Economics of Dividend Policy' (1981) 67 Virginia Law Rev 699, 715–16.

[30] *Re a Company ex parte Glossop* [1988] 1 WLR 1068, 1076.

[31] *Burland v Earle* [1902] AC 83, PC.

[32] *Miles v Sydney Meat Preserving Co Ltd* (1912) 12 SR (NSW) 98, 103 *per* AH Simpson, CJ in E; Fischel, DR, 'The Law and Economics of Dividend Policy' (1981) 67 Virginia Law Rev 699, 715–16; Brudney, V, 'Dividends, Discretion and Disclosure' (1980) 66 Virginia Law Rev 85, 103–5.

The courts have been prepared to countenance the possibility of the Companies Act 1985, s 459 being used to challenge allegedly inadequate dividends.[33] This section allows a shareholder to petition the court for relief from unfairly prejudicial conduct. The circumstances in which a claim of unfair prejudice arising from dividend policy would be likely to succeed have not been established,[34] save that it has been indicated that the courts would not lightly interfere in such a matter.[35] Perhaps the strongest case for a potentially successful s 459 action is in a smaller company where some, but not all, of the shareholders are also involved in management. It can readily be seen that a policy of paying, at most, minimal dividends could generate serious difficulties in such a case because the manager-shareholders would be getting a return from the company in the form of remuneration whilst the other shareholders would be receiving next to no income in respect of their investment. They would probably also face difficulties in realising capital gains on their investment because there is no active market in the company's shares. In this situation the essence of the dispute that the court is asked to review is not about commercial judgment in determining dividend policy, where the court would be rightly reluctant to interfere, but about one group within a company discriminating against another, where the courts have always been ready to intervene.[36]

Broadly this situation arose in *Re Sam Weller & Sons Ltd*.[37] The shareholders who were not involved in management were dissatisfied with the company's dividend which had remained at the same level for thirty-seven years and alleged that this amounted to unfairly prejudicial conduct. Peter Gibson J held that a long-standing policy of paying only nominal dividends could amount to conduct unfairly prejudicial to the interests of those shareholders who did not receive income from the company in the form of remuneration. Peter Gibson J cautioned[38] that he did not intend to suggest that a shareholder who did not receive an income from a company except by way of dividend would always be entitled to complain whenever the company was controlled by persons who did derive an income from the company and when profits were not fully distributed by way of dividend. He considered that a court would view with great caution allegations of unfairly prejudicial conduct based on this ground.[39]

[33] *Re Sam Weller & Sons Ltd* [1990] 1 Ch 682.

[34] Under equivalent Australian legislation, failure to pay dividends has led to relief being granted: *Re Bagot Well Pastoral Co, Shannon v Reid* (1992) 9 ACSR 129, SA SC. One of the most famous examples of judicial intervention is the US case *Dodge v Ford Motor Co* 170 NW 668 (Mich 1919) where the court ordered the payment of substantial dividends contrary to the recommendation of the board of directors. This was a case where the dominant shareholder was in conflict with the minority shareholders who brought the complaint.

[35] *Re Sam Weller & Sons Ltd* [1990] 1 Ch 682, 693; *Thomas v H Thomas Ltd* [1984] 1 NZLR 686, NZ CA.

[36] In *Re Bagot Well Pastoral Co; Shannon v Reid* (1992) 9 ACSR 129, SA SC, 142 *per* Cox J the policy of not paying dividends was held to be discriminatory.

[37] [1990] 1 Ch 682.

[38] Ibid at 693.

[39] The Law Commission has reported that 25 per cent of the unfair prejudice petitions filed in 1994–5 involved allegations about non-payment of dividends: *Shareholder Remedies A Consultation Paper* (Law Commission Consultation Paper No 142) (1996) paras 9.41–9.43.

There is also the possibility of a policy of paying inadequate dividends being used as the basis for a petition that the company should be wound up on the grounds that it is just and equitable to do so.[40] Again, the possibility of winding up is likely to be of most significance in a small company where a personal relationship of trust and confidence between the shareholders has broken down,[41] but there is an indication in *Re a Company ex parte Glossop*[42] of potential judicial willingness to intervene even where the essence of the dispute is about managerial commercial judgment with regard to dividend policy rather than conflicts between groups of shareholders.[43]

SPECIAL DIVIDENDS

There are good commercial arguments for directors to pursue a policy of paying consistent dividends and for recommending increases only when they are satisfied that these can be sustained over the longer term. A consequence of such a policy is that there may be times when profits are in fact surplus to the company's present and projected needs but the directors are reluctant to distribute these in the normal way because an inflated level of dividends could not be sustained in future years. One situation where an exceptionally large profit which will not be repeated in future years may arise is where a company disposes of part of its business. A number of British companies found themselves with cash excess to the funding demands of their business in the 1990s. One response to the situation[44] was for the board to declare a special interim dividend, 'special' for this purpose meaning simply 'one-off', either as a stand-alone step or in combination with share capital restructuring.[45] In some instances, special dividends were declared by companies which were the target of takeover bids, either as a form of defence to a hostile bid[46] or as part of the terms of an agreed bid.[47]

[40] Companies Act 1985, s 122 (1)(g).

[41] *Ebrahimi v Westbourne Galleries Ltd* [1973] AC 360, HL. The Australian case, *Re City Meat Co Pty Ltd* (1983) 8 ACLR 673, SA SC, fits this analysis: the director received generous fees from the company whilst other shareholders received only minimal dividend payments; this was held to be contrary to the legitimate expectations of the shareholders and the company was ordered to be wound up.

[42] [1988] 1 WLR 1068, 1075.

[43] This approach echoes the views expressed in the US case *Knapp v Bankers Securities Corpn* (1956) 230 F 717 where it was said that minority shareholders could compel the declaration of dividends where the directors were acting fraudulently or arbitrarily in refusing to declare a dividend when the company had a surplus which it could distribute without detriment to its business.

[44] Others are reductions of capital and share buy backs. See Chs 10 and 13 respectively.

[45] eg, East Midlands Electricity plc, October 1994 (special dividend and share consolidation); The Boots Company plc, June 1997 (special dividend). Capital restructuring in the form of share consolidations may be combined with a special dividend in order to offset the negative impact on future earnings per share of taking a large amount of cash out of the business.

[46] eg Northern Electric plc, February 1995.

[47] eg, Southern Investments UK plc bid for SWEB, August 1995.

REGULATION OF DISTRIBUTIONS: THE MEANING OF 'DISTRIBUTION'

The Companies Act 1985, Pt VIII (ss 263–281) controls distributions by companies.[48] In this context a distribution means 'every description of distribution of a company's assets to its members, whether in cash or otherwise' save that four acts, which might otherwise fall within this definition, are expressly excluded.[49] These four acts are:

—an issue of shares as fully- or partly-paid bonus shares;
—the redemption or purchase of any of the company's own shares out of capital (including the proceeds of a fresh issue of shares) or out of unrealised profits in accordance with the provisions of the Act governing redemption and purchase of shares;
—the reduction of share capital by extinguishing or reducing the liability of any of the members on any of the company's shares in respect of share capital not paid up, or by paying off share capital;
—a distribution of assets to members of the company on its winding up.

Interim and final dividends paid by a company in accordance with the procedure set out in its articles are clearly distributions regulated by the Companies Act 1985, Pt VIII. If a company does something whereby its money or property ends up in the hands of its shareholders by some means other than a formally declared dividend, this may also be a regulated distribution although, in these cases, there can be difficult questions about the correct legal characterisation of the company's act and how Pt VIII applies to it if it is a distribution. A transfer of assets between companies in a corporate group where the consideration paid is less than the full market value of the assets acquired is an example of a situation where these complex questions can arise. The application of the distribution rules to intra-group transfers of assets at an undervalue is considered at the end of this chapter.[50]

In summary, the Companies Act 1985, Pt VIII provides that a company can only lawfully make distributions out of profits available for the purpose.[51] It defines distributable profits and requires the availability of distributable profits to be demonstrated by 'relevant accounts'. It imposes stricter requirements on public companies than on private companies[52] and contains special provisions for certain types of company.[53] The rules in the Companies Act 1985, Pt

[48] It fell originally to the courts to develop distribution rules out of the principle of maintenance of capital: French, EA, 'The Evolution of the Dividend Law of England' in Baxter, WT, and Davidson, S, *Studies in Accounting* (3rd edn, 1977); Yamey, BS, 'Aspects of the Law Relating to Company Dividends' (1941) 4 MLR 273. The statutory rules that now apply were first enacted in Companies Act 1980, consolidated in Companies Act 1985 and amended in various respects by a number of enactments including the Companies Act 1989. Part VIII gives effect to Second Company Law Directive 77/91/EEC, [1977] OJ L26/1, art 15 which restricts distributions by public companies.

[49] Companies Act 1985, s 263 (2).

[50] See below, at 426–9.

[51] Companies Act 1985, s 263 (1).

[52] Ibid, s 264.

[53] Ibid, ss 265–266 (investment companies) and s 268 (insurance companies). These special provisions are not considered further.

VIII are mandatory but companies can impose additional requirements in their memoranda or articles.[54]

DISTRIBUTABLE PROFITS

The profits of a company which are available for distribution are defined as its accumulated realised profits, so far as not previously utilised by distribution or capitalisation, less its accumulated realised losses, so far as not previously written off in a reduction or re-organisation of capital duly made.[55] No distinction is drawn between revenue profits and losses (profits and losses from trading) and capital profits and losses (profits and losses on the disposal of fixed assets) for this purpose.[56] Accounting standards and related materials[57] amplify the concept of 'realised' profits and losses: profits and losses which fall to be treated as realised in accordance with principles generally accepted at the time when the accounts are prepared are realised for the purpose of any accounts by which the legality of a dividend is to be determined. [58]

When fixed assets are revalued, increases in value are unrealised profits and they are not normally available for distribution.[59] Instead, they appear in the company's balance sheet as an undistributable reserve. The one exception to this rule is where a company makes a distribution of or including a non-cash asset. Any part of the amount at which the asset is shown in the relevant accounts which is an unrealised profit is to be treated as a realised profit for the purposes of determining the lawfulness of the distribution and complying with Companies Act accounting requirements.[60] Companies must pay dividends in cash unless dividends in kind are authorised by the articles.[61] Such authorisation is commonly included.[62]

Unlike revaluations of fixed assets, depreciation is taken into account in determining the profits available for distribution.[63] It is a requirement of the Companies Act 1985 that any asset with a limited economic life must be writ-

[54] Companies Act 1985, s 281. *Re Cleveland Trust plc* [1991] BCC 33—dividend unlawful because it was paid out of a realised capital profit contrary to a prohibition in the company's memorandum.

[55] Companies Act 1985, s 263 (3).

[56] Ibid, s 280 (3).

[57] See *The Determination of Realised Profits and Disclosure of Distributable Profits in the Context of the Companies Act* (ICAEW Accounting Recommendation) (Sept 1982); *Disclosure of Accounting Policies* SSAP 2; *Statement of Principles for Financial Reporting* (Accounting Standards Board Exposure Draft) (Nov 1995); *Statement of Principles for Financial Reporting—The Way Ahead* (Accounting Standards Board) (July 1996). See also Carey, A, Friel, D, and Compagnoni, M, 'Distributable Profits, Impact on Transactions' (1996) 7 (7) PLC 25.

[58] Companies Act 1985, s 262 (3). This definition applies for the purposes of Companies Act 1985, Pt VII (accounts and audit). Relevant accounts for the purposes of Pt VIII are accounts drawn up in accordance with Part VII. Accounting standards help to define 'realised profits' but may not be decisive in this respect: Nock, RS, and Nock, S, 'Illegal Dividends, Part I' (1997/8) 3 RALQ 75, 89–96.

[59] This reverses the common-law position where unrealised profits on fixed assets could be distributed: *Dimbula Valley (Ceylon) Tea Co Ltd v Laurie* [1961] Ch 353.

[60] Companies Act 1985, s 276.

[61] *Wood v Odessa Waterworks Co* (1889) 42 Ch D 636.

[62] The model is Table A, art 105.

[63] Depreciation did not have to be charged under the common-law rules: *Lee v Neuchatel Asphalte Co* (1889) 41 Ch D 1, CA.

ten down, on a systematic basis, over the course of its life to its residual value (if any).[64] Depreciation is charged to the profit and loss account and is treated as a realised loss which reduces the profits available for distribution.[65] The most common way of depreciating in the UK is the straight-line method. This works as follows: say a company acquires a machine for £10,000 and estimates that it will have a useful life of five years and will have a nil residual value at the end of that time; on the straight-line basis the company will charge a constant amount of depreciation (£2,000) to its profit and loss account in each of the five years. If, in fact, the machine is sold for more than the amount by which it has been depreciated (for example if it is sold for £9,000 in its second year) the difference between the resale price and the original cost less depreciation (ie £8,000) is a realised profit. There is a special rule for depreciation charges in respect of revalued assets where the revaluation has given rise to an unrealised profit. The Companies Act 1985 allows the difference between the depreciation charge on the revalued amount and the depreciation charge on the original amount to be treated as a realised profit.[66]

Losses incurred in previous years, so far as not previously written off, must be taken into account in determining the amount of distributable profits.[67] On the other hand, retained distributable profits from earlier years can be carried forward and used to pay dividends in years when the company makes a loss so long as the loss is not so large as to wipe out the retained distributable reserves.

ADDITIONAL REQUIREMENT FOR PUBLIC COMPANIES

For public companies there is the further requirement that a distribution may only be made when the amount of its net assets is not less than the aggregate of its called up share capital and undistributable reserves and only if, and to the extent that, the distribution does not reduce the amount of those assets to less than that aggregate.[68] This additional requirement gives effect to the Second Company Law Directive,[69] art 15.1(a) which states that 'no distribution to shareholders may be made when . . . the net assets are, or following such distribution would become, lower than the amount of the subscribed capital plus those reserves which may not be distributed under the law or the statutes'.

'Net assets' for this purpose means the aggregate of the company's assets less the aggregate of its liabilities.[70] A company's 'undistributable reserves' comprise: (i) the share premium account, (ii) the capital redemption reserve, (iii) the excess of accumulated realised profits over accumulated realised losses, and (iv) any other reserve which the company is prohibited from

[64] Companies Act 1985, sch 4, para 18, fleshed out by *Accounting for Depreciation* SSAP 12. SSAP 12 is to be superseded with effect from 23 March 2000 by *Tangible Fixed Assets*, FRS 15.

[65] Companies Act 1985, s 275 (1).

[66] Ibid, s 275 (2).

[67] This reverses the common-law position: *Lee v Neuchatel Asphalte Co* (1889) 41 Ch D 1, CA; *Ammonia Soda Co v Chamberlain* [1918] 1 Ch 266, CA.

[68] Companies Act 1985, s 264.

[69] 77/91/EEC, [1977] OJ L26/1.

[70] Companies Act 1985, s 264 (2).

distributing by any enactment or by its memorandum and articles.[71] The effect of this restriction can be illustrated by the following example. Say a company has net assets of £10 million, a share capital of £3 million, share premium account of £6 million, unrealised losses of £2 million and distributable profits of £3 million; a private company could distribute £3 million, but for a public company the effect of s 264 is to limit the amount that can be distributed to £1 million. In other words, the effect of the Companies Act 1985, s 264 is to require public companies to take unrealised losses into account in determining the maximum amount available for distribution.

RELEVANT ACCOUNTS

The amount of a distribution which may be made is to be determined by reference to the company's financial position as stated in its relevant accounts.[72] The company's last annual accounts will usually constitute the 'relevant accounts'.[73] These accounts must have been properly prepared in accordance with the requirements of the Companies Act 1985, Pt VII and must give a true and fair view of the company's financial position.[74] If the auditors have qualified their report on the accounts, they must also state in writing whether they consider the matter in respect of which the report is qualified to be relevant to the legality of the distribution.[75]

If, since publication of its last annual accounts, the company has identified surplus assets which it wants to distribute promptly by way of an interim dividend it can do so on the basis of the last annual accounts if these show sufficient retained distributable reserves. If the last annual accounts do not show adequate reserves, the company can produce interim accounts and justify the distribution by reference to those accounts.[76] Generally, the interim accounts must enable a reasonable judgment to be made as to the company's financial position[77] but there are more detailed requirements in respect of interim accounts prepared for a proposed distribution by a public company.[78]

PROCEDURE FOR DECLARING A FINAL DIVIDEND AND THE EFFECT ON SHARE PRICES

The declaration of a final dividend is a standard part of the business at the annual general meetings of companies. The directors' recommendation with regard to the dividend is included in the notice of the annual general meeting and this is accompanied by the annual accounts showing the amount of avail-

[71] Companies Act 1985, s 264 (3).
[72] Ibid, s 270 (2).
[73] Ibid, s 270 (3). Initial accounts must be produced if a company wants to declare a dividend during its first accounting reference period or before any accounts have been laid in respect of that period: Companies Act 1985, ss 270 (4)(b) and 273.
[74] Companies Act 1985, s 271 (2).
[75] Ibid, s 271 (3)–(5).
[76] Ibid, ss 270 (4) and 272.
[77] Ibid, s 270 (4).
[78] Ibid, s 272.

able distributable profits and the proposed dividend.[79] If, between the date when the notices are despatched and the holding of the meeting, it is discovered that the last annual accounts were not properly prepared then, unless the irregularity is immaterial, the dividend cannot lawfully be declared because, unless the accounts have been properly prepared they cannot be 'relevant accounts' for the purposes of the Companies Act 1985, Pt VIII.[80] The shareholders cannot sue the company for a dividend which has been recommended but not declared, because a final dividend does not become a debt payable to shareholders until it has been declared.[81] The board's decision to pay an interim dividend does not give rise to a debt and that decision can therefore be reversed at any time before payment.[82]

Shares in quoted companies are traded either cum-dividend or ex-dividend. If a share is acquired at a cum-dividend price that means that the purchaser is entitled to the dividend. Conversely, an ex-dividend price means that the vendor keeps the dividend. In the absence of any contrary provision in the company's articles, it is the person who is the registered holder of the share on the date of the declaration of a final dividend or payment of an interim dividend who is entitled to the dividend.[83] However, articles commonly authorise the board to select a date (the record date) for the payment of dividends. Shareholders on the register on the selected date receive the dividend which means that the share price goes ex-dividend on that date.

Dividends are paid on the nominal value of the shares unless the articles otherwise provide.[84] The effect of this is that the holder of a partly-paid share of a particular class would receive the same amount of dividend as the holder of a fully-paid share of that class. Companies can change the position in their articles[85] and it is commonly provided that dividends are to be calculated and paid on the amounts paid up on shares rather than their nominal value.[86]

SCRIP DIVIDENDS

The articles of association of a company may permit shareholders to elect to take additional fully-paid ordinary shares in the company in whole or in part in lieu of a cash dividend. A dividend in this form is known as a 'scrip dividend'. For listed companies, there are Stock Exchange requirements concerning the information to be given to shareholders about any entitlement to elect

[79] The amount of any dividend paid or proposed must be shown in the profit and loss account: Companies Act 1985, sch 4, para 7 (b).

[80] Companies Act 1985, s 271 (2). For the same reason directors should not declare an interim dividend on the basis of accounts which are known to be defective.

[81] *Bond v Barrow Haematite Steel Co* [1902] 1 Ch 353; *Re Accrington Corpn Steam Tramways Co* [1909] 2 Ch 40.

[82] *Lagunas Nitrate Co v Schroeder & Co and Schmidt* (1901) 85 LT 22.

[83] *Re Wakley, Wakley v Vachell* [1920] 2 Ch 205, CA; *Godfrey Phillips Ltd v Investment Trust Corpn Ltd* [1953] Ch 449.

[84] *Oakbank Oil Co Ltd v Crum* (1882) 8 App Cas 65, HL.

[85] Companies Act 1985, s 119 (c).

[86] Table A, art 104. It is a requirement for listed companies that dividends be calculated by reference to paid-up amounts only: *The Listing Rules*, ch 13, app 1, para 16.

for scrip dividends.[87] Scrip dividends enable shareholders to acquire additional shares without incurring dealing costs.

Conceptually, a scrip dividend can be characterised either as a reinvestment of the cash amount of a dividend or as a bonus issue of shares.[88] The reinvestment characterisation is appropriate where shareholders make their election after the dividend has been declared. Because the electing shareholders release the company from the obligation to pay cash, the shares are allotted for cash for the purposes of the Companies Act 1985. A consequence of this is that the pre-emption requirements of the Companies Act 1985, s 89 are relevant. For accounting purposes the new shares are deemed to be paid up out of distributable reserves. The bonus issue characterisation is appropriate where the shareholders' election is in place before the declaration of a dividend.[89] There are advantages for the company in structuring its scrip dividends election procedures so that the elections precede the dividend. Shares allotted in satisfaction of elections timed in this way are not allotted for cash and therefore the Companies Act 1985, s 89 pre-emption requirements do not apply. Also, for accounting purposes, the shares are bonus shares and can be paid up from undistributable reserves, such as the share premium account, thereby preserving the distributable reserves for subsequent dividend payments.

DIVIDEND RE-INVESTMENT PLANS

Dividend re-investment plans are like scrip dividends to the extent that they are a means whereby shareholders can acquire additional shares without having to pay the normal dealing costs, although an administration fee is usually charged. However, in a typically structured dividend re-investment plan, the company does not allot new shares to shareholders who wish to take advantage of the scheme but, instead, it arranges for their dividends to be invested in existing shares in the company that are trading in the market. Since there is no allotment of new shares, no issues with regard to pre-emption rights arise and the share purchases do not have any effect on the company's capital as recorded in its accounts. The fact that there is no dilution of the existing share capital means that there is no impact on the company's earnings-per-share or dividend-per-share ratios as there would be where there is extensive take up of scrip dividend alternatives.[90]

[87] *The Listing Rules*, ch 14, paras 14.12–14.15.

[88] Generally, *Capital Instruments* FRS 4 and Davies, M, Paterson, R and Wilson, A, *UK GAAP Generally Accepted Accounting Practice in the United Kingdom* (5th edn, 1997).

[89] Or payment where the election relates to interim as well as final dividends.

[90] Hinkley, R, Hunter, D, Whittell, M, and Ziff, M, *Current Issues in Equity Finance* (1998) 14 and 49.

CONSEQUENCES OF AN UNLAWFUL DISTRIBUTION

The courts established the principle that it was unlawful for a company to pay dividends out of capital.[91] The Companies Act 1985, Pt VIII recasts the duty in a positive, and wider, form: companies must only make distributions out of profits available for the purpose and, in making distributions, they must comply with the procedural requirements imposed by the Act. Failure to comply with the statutory requirements is also unlawful.[92] Paying an unlawful dividend attracts civil sanctions but it is not a criminal offence.

Precision Dippings Ltd v Precision Dippings Marketing Ltd[93] demonstrates the rigorous nature of the statutory obligation. Precision Dippings Ltd (PD) paid a dividend to its parent company, Precision Dippings Marketing Ltd (PDM) but subsequently went into the liquidation. The liquidator challenged the dividend payment on the grounds that the statutory requirement[94] to obtain a statement from the auditors on the materiality of a qualification in the accounts in relation to the dividend had not been satisfied. The claim was thus not that the dividend *had* been paid otherwise than from distributable profits; rather it was that the company had failed to do all that it was required to do by the Companies Act 1985 to demonstrate that the dividend was permissible.

The Court of Appeal rejected the argument that the company's failing was a mere procedural irregularity. Dillon LJ, giving the judgment of the court, stated that the group of sections now contained in the Companies Act 1985, Pt VIII constituted a major protection to creditors and that the shareholders were not free to waive or dispense with those requirements. His Lordship left open the question whether anything could be done to restore the situation in a solvent company, for example the production of an auditors' statement after the event; PD was in insolvent liquidation, so that situation did not, on the facts, arise.

In considering the remedies available in respect of the unlawful distribution, Dillon LJ looked first to the Companies Act 1985, s 277 (1). This section provides that where a distribution is made in contravention of the requirements of the Act relating to distributions, the member to whom the distribution is made is liable to repay it (or its value if it was a distribution in kind). If only part of a distribution is in contravention of the Act, the member's liability extends only to that part. In either case, a member is only personally liable under the section where he knows or has reasonable grounds for believing that the distribution is made, in whole or in part, in contravention of the Act. The fact that the section requires the recipient of the unlawful dividend to know, or to have reasonable grounds for believing, that there is a breach of the law limits the impact of the statutory liability. On the facts of the *Precision Dippings* case, PDM, through its directors, knew all the facts but did not know

[91] *Re Exchange Banking Co, Flitcroft's Case* (1882) 21 Ch D 519, CA; *Re Oxford Benefit Building and Investment Society* (1886) 35 Ch D 502.

[92] *Precision Dippings Ltd v Precision Dippings Marketing Ltd* [1986] Ch 447, CA.

[93] [1986] Ch 447, CA.

[94] Now, Companies Act 1985, s 271 (4).

the terms of the relevant statutory provisions and did not know that without the auditors' statement required by the Act, the dividend was unlawful.

The Companies Act 1985, s 277 (2) provides that the statutory liability is without prejudice to any other obligation imposed on a member to repay an unlawful distribution. Rather than determining whether PDM could be said to have had reasonable grounds for the belief that there has been a contravention of the Act so as to bring the claim within the second limb of s 277 (1), Dillon LJ turned instead to common-law liabilities in respect of unlawful dividends. His Lordship held that the dividend payment was *ultra vires*[95] PD. When it received it, PDM had notice of the facts and was a volunteer in the sense that it did not give valuable consideration for the money. As a result PDM was liable to PD as a constructive trustee and was obliged to repay the money.[96]

The failure to satisfy evidentiary requirements, namely, the absence of accounts giving a true and fair view of the company's financial position as required by the Companies Act 1985, s 272, was also held to invalidate a distribution in *Re Cleveland Trust plc*.[97] The recipient of the dividend, again a parent company, was held liable as a constructive trustee to repay the dividend to its subsidiary. These cases extend to failure to comply with the evidentiary requirements relating to distributions imposed by the Companies Act, the principle established by older authorities[98] that a shareholder who receives a distribution from capital can be held liable as a constructive trustee.

For liability as a constructive trust to arise, it must be demonstrated that the directors acted in breach of fiduciary duty and that the recipient was aware of the factual circumstances amounting to the breach of trust although, as is clear from the *Precision Dippings* decision, the recipient does not need to be aware of the law. Paying an unlawful dividend is, broadly speaking, regarded as a breach of fiduciary duty by directors. The precise degree of factual awareness that is necessary to trigger constructive-trust liability is a complex question on which there are conflicting authorities[99] but, even if it is assumed that the lowest qualifying level of knowledge which has been identified by the authorities[100]—knowledge of circumstances which would put an honest and reasonable man on inquiry—would suffice for this purpose, it can readily be seen that the practical impact of constructive-trust liability in this context is likely to be limited. Outside equity investors in a company who are not involved in management would rarely have the requisite knowledge. The remedy is most likely to work in relation to intra-group dividends or to dividends

[95] In this context this phrase means more than simply beyond the limits of the company's memorandum; it means beyond what, under the general law, companies are permitted to do.

[96] Following *Rolled Steel Products (Holdings) Ltd v British Steel Corporation* [1986] Ch 246, CA 297–8 *per* Slade LJ and 306–7 *per* Browne Wilkinson LJ.

[97] [1991] BCLC 424.

[98] Such as *Russell v Wakefield Waterworks Co* (1875) LR 20 Eq 474; *Moxham v Grant* [1900] 1 QB 88, CA.

[99] Oakley, AJ, *Constructive Trusts* (3rd edn, 1997) ch 4; Lord Nicholls, 'Knowing Receipt: The Need for a New Landmark' in Cornish, WR, Nolan, R, O'Sullivan, J, and Virgo, G (eds), *Restitution Past, Present and Future* (1998) 231.

[100] *Baden, Delvaux and Lecuit v Société Générale pour Favoriser le Développement du Commerce et de l'Industrie en France SA* [1993] 1 WLR 509n, 575–6 *per* Peter Gibson J.

paid to individual shareholders who are also closely involved in the management of the company. It is significant that in both the *Precision Dippings* and *Re Cleveland Trust* decisions the recipient of the unlawful dividend was a parent company.

There is also the possibility of the company being able to trace the unlawful dividend in the hands of the shareholders.[101] If the company can successfully trace the property, it can seek to recover the property either by a personal action (such as an action for money had and received) or an equitable proprietary claim (such as an equitable charge[102]). Tracing is the means whereby a person can identify his property in the hands of others. It is possible to trace into the hands of persons who are entirely unaware of the wrongful nature of the disposal unless they are bona fide purchasers who have given value.[103] Recipients of dividends are volunteers rather than bona fide purchasers for value.[104] A major limitation on tracing is that a person cannot trace where his property is no longer identifiable. Although it is sometimes possible to trace funds which are paid into bank accounts, [105] in reality it is very likely that unlawful dividends paid to shareholders would soon cease to be separately identifiable in the ordinary course of events. Tracing is also subject to the defence of change of position[106] so that, for example, where an individual shareholder uses a dividend to pay for a holiday, it will no longer be possible to trace. These considerations, combined with the fact that there is an argument[107] to the effect that an unlawful dividend can never be recovered from a shareholder who was totally unaware of the impropriety,[108] suggest that claims which depend on tracing are unlikely to be pursued.

The company may consider taking action against its directors to recover the unlawful dividend.[109] Directors are regarded as trustees of the company's property[110] and at common law it was regarded as a breach of trust for them to pay a dividend out of capital.[111] The breach of trust was not capable of being ratified even by all of the shareholders acting together.[112]

[101] Burrows, AS, and McKendrick, E, *Cases and Materials on the Law of Restitution* (1997) 663.

[102] Although it could not argue that the shareholder holds the dividend on trust for the company.

[103] *Re Diplock* [1948] Ch 465, CA.

[104] *Precision Dippings Ltd v Precision Dippings Marketing Ltd* [1986] Ch 447, CA. This reflects the fact that even though they may have commercial expectation to receive dividends as part of the return on their investments, legally shareholders are not entitled to dividends unless they are declared (final dividends) or paid (interim dividends).

[105] Goff, R, and Jones, G, *The Law of Restitution* (5th edn, 1998) ch 2; Burrows, AS, *The Law of Restitution* (1993) 57–76.

[106] *Lipkin Gorman v Karpnale Ltd* [1991] 2 AC 548, HL.

[107] This argument would seem to be inconsistent with *Re Diplock* [1948] Ch 465, CA unless it is said that the shareholders' commercial expectation of dividends places them in a different position from that of a recipient of a donation which is made in breach of fiduciary duty.

[108] *Segenhoe v Akins* (1989–90) 1 ACSR 691, NSW SC, 703–9 considering a statement to that effect in *Halsbury's Laws* (4th edn, 1996 re-issue) vol 7 (1) para 722.

[109] Directors who are obliged to make good the company's loss can claim an indemnity from shareholders who knowingly received the unlawful dividend: *Moxham v Grant* [1900] 1 QB 88, CA.

[110] It is only in some respects that the position of a director is equated to that of a trustee. See Sealy, LS, 'The Director as Trustee' [1967] CLJ 83.

[111] *Re Exchange Banking Co, Flitcroft's Case* (1882) 21 Ch D 519, CA; *Re Sharpe* [1892] 1 Ch 154, CA.

[112] *Re Exchange Banking Co, Flitcroft's Case* (1882) 21 Ch D 519, CA; *Re Sharpe* [1892] 1 Ch 154, CA.

Consistent with the approach in *Precision Dippings*, the principles established by the older cases should be extended to failure to comply with the detailed evidentiary and other requirements imposed by the Companies Act 1985 in respect of distributions. Accordingly, failure to comply with those requirements should be treated as a breach of trust by the company's directors. Whether such failures should necessarily be regarded as unratifiable is a different question; there would seem to be a good case for saying that where there was a failure to comply with the technical requirements of the Companies Act relating to distributions but the company did have distributable profits at the time when the dividend was declared, ratification should be possible.[113]

In some of the older cases, the liability of the directors for unlawful dividends was expressed in very strict terms: 'as soon as the conclusion is arrived at that the company's money has been applied by the directors for purposes which the company cannot sanction it follows that the directors are liable to repay the money, however honestly they may have acted'.[114] The view that prevailed,[115] however, was that directors would not be held liable where they acted under an honest and reasonable belief that the facts justified the payment. This means that the directors may escape liability where they declare an interim dividend or recommend a final dividend on the basis of accounts which are later found to have been defective provided that they had no reason to doubt the integrity, skill and competence of those responsible for the production of the accounts.[116]

DISGUISED DISTRIBUTIONS: TRANSFERS OF ASSETS AT AN UNDERVALUE

This section is concerned with payments and transfers of assets to shareholders which are not dividends formally declared by the company in accordance with the procedure in its articles but which are subject to the rules in the Companies Act 1985, Pt VIII because they are distributions. Where, for example, a company pays a shareholder for services rendered in another capacity, such as a director, but the payments are in excess of the amount that can be regarded as a genuine exercise of the power to pay remuneration, the payments will be an unlawful distribution if they are not made out of distributable

[113] In *Precision Dippings Ltd v Precision Dippings Marketing Ltd* [1986] Ch 447, CA Dillon LJ left open the question whether, in a solvent company, steps could be taken to reverse the consequences of a dividend which was unlawful only because of a failure to comply with the statutory requirements on the relevant accounts.

[114] *Re Exchange Banking Co, Flitcroft's Case* (1882) 21 Ch D 519, CA; *Re Sharpe* [1892] 1 Ch 154, CA, 165–6 *per* Lindley LJ.

[115] *Dovey v Cory* [1901] AC 477, HL, where a director escaped liability for an unlawful dividend because he had no reason to doubt the company officials on whom he relied. The cases supporting the strict approach and the approach whereby honest and reasonable directors escape liability are reviewed by Vaughan Williams J at first instance in *Re Kingston Cotton Mill Co (No 2)* [1896] 1 Ch 331, affirmed [1896] 2 Ch 279, CA.

[116] For a modern application of these principles see *Hilton International Ltd v Hilton* [1989] 1 NZLR 442, NZ H Ct: directors who did not obtain a proper set of accounts were held liable to refund the amount of the dividend.

profits.[117] The mere fact that the company has paid generously will not suffice for a transaction to be treated as a disguised gift; but evidence of patently excessive or unreasonable terms will cast doubt on the genuineness of that transaction.[118]

A company makes a distribution if it transfers assets at less than their market value to a shareholder.[119] Valuation is not an exact science and a sale to a shareholder would still be genuine even though it is priced near the bottom end of what can reasonably be regarded as the market value of the asset in question. If, however, the price is lower than the bottom of the range of market values on any reasonable assessment, it cannot be a genuine sale. In *Aveling Barford Ltd v Perion Ltd*[120] it was held that a sale at an undervalue to another company in the same group as the vendor was also a distribution even though the purchaser did not hold shares in the vendor. The vendor and purchaser companies had the same controlling shareholder and the ultimate beneficiary of the arrangement was that controller. When assets are transferred at an undervalue around a corporate group, it is usually to secure some benefit for the holding company of the group. Accordingly, on the basis of the *Aveling Barford* case, it can be assumed that the distribution rules will apply whenever there is an undervalue transaction between companies in the same group.

Transactions whereby assets are moved round corporate groups at their book value instead of their greater market value are commonplace but the application of the rules in the Companies Act 1985, Pt VIII to this type of distribution is a source of some difficulty. The difficulty stems from the underlying purpose that these rules are intended to achieve. The purpose is twofold: first, to ensure that creditors are not prejudiced by the distribution to shareholders of funds that are properly to be regarded as part of the company's capital buffer; and second, to ensure that the fact that creditors are not prejudiced is suitably evidenced by the company's accounts. It is the location of the proper limit of the second aspect that causes concern.

The easy case is where a company which does not have distributable profits makes a distribution by way of a transfer of assets at an undervalue to an associated company. This transaction is clearly an unlawful distribution contrary to the Companies Act 1985, Pt VIII and an infringement of the maintenance of capital principle. It was the situation in the *Aveling Barford* decision itself. The more complex case, which has not yet come before an English court, is where a company makes a transfer at an undervalue to an associated company in circumstances where it has some distributable profits but those profits are insufficient to cover the difference between the transfer price and the market price of the assets. Here there is scope for differing views on what is required to satisfy the Companies Act 1985, Pt VIII: one view is that the transferor company should have distributable profits at least equal to the difference between the price at which the assets are transferred and the market value of those assets

[117] *Re Halt Garage (1964) Ltd* [1982] 3 All ER 1016. See also *Ridge Securities Ltd v IRC* [1964] 1 All ER 275; *Jenkins v Harbour View Courts Ltd* [1966] NZLR 1, NZ CA; *Redweaver Investments Ltd v Lawrence Field Ltd* (1990–91) 5 ACSR 438, NSW SC—EqD; *One Life Ltd v Roy* [1996] 2 BCLC 608.

[118] *Re Halt Garage (1964) Ltd* [1982] 3 All ER 1016, 1041.

[119] *Ridge Securities Ltd v IRC* [1964] 1 All ER 275, 288.

[120] [1989] BCLC 626.

at that time; the competing view is that some distributable profits (even just a nominal £1) will suffice for this purpose.

Common to both views is the point that a transfer of assets at an undervalue by a company which has some distributable profits does not reduce its capital buffer to the prejudice of its creditors provided the sale price is at least equivalent to the book value of the assets. This is demonstrated by the following balance sheet examples.

Balance Sheet 1

Subsidiary Ltd	*£m*
Fixed Assets	5.0
Cash	1.5
Share capital	5.0
Distributable reserves	1.5

Say that Subsidiary Ltd's fixed assets have a market value of £10 million but Subsidiary wants to transfer them to Parent Ltd at their book value. Subsidiary could go through the exercise of revaluing its assets so as to produce the following balance sheet:

Balance Sheet 2

Subsidiary Ltd	*£m*
Fixed Assets	10.0
Cash	1.5
Share Capital	5.0
Revaluation Reserve	5.0
Distributable Reserves	1.5

It could then declare a dividend in specie of its fixed assets, and on the basis of the Companies Act 1985, s 276 it would treat the revaluation reserve as a realised profit for this purpose. The net result of this series of steps is exactly the same as if the company had simply transferred the assets at their original book value of £5 million. Since all of the profit on the assets is distributable to the acquiring parent anyway, allowing the subsidiary, in effect, to take the short-cut, and thereby avoid the costs of a revaluation exercise, does not prejudice the subsidiary's creditors. This contrasts with the case illustrated by the next two balance sheets:

Balance Sheet 3

Subsidiary 2 Ltd	*£m*
Fixed Assets	5.0
Liabilities	(1.0)
Share Capital	5.0
Distributable Reserves	(1.0)

Say that Subsidiary Ltd's fixed assets have a market value of £10 million but Subsidiary 2 wants to transfer them to Parent Ltd at their book value. This time, a revaluation exercise would produce the following balance sheet:

Balance Sheet 4

Subsidiary 2 Ltd	*£m*
Fixed Assets	10.0
Liabilities	(1.0)
Share Capital	5.0
Revaluation Reserves	5.0
Distributable Reserves	(1.0)

This shows that the distributable reserves available to the company (applying the Companies Act 1985, s 276), are £4 million. In these circumstances, for Subsidiary 2 Ltd to sell the assets to its parent for £5 million, thereby making a distribution of £5 million would prejudice its creditors. The subsidiary must make good the £1 million shortfall on its distributable reserves before it can make the distribution to its parent.

The difference between the two views thus lies in the interpretation of the evidentiary requirements of the Companies Act 1985, Pt VIII. Under the Companies Act 1985, s 270 (2), the amount of any distribution must be determined by reference to the following items as stated in the company's accounts: (a) profits, losses, assets and liabilities, (b) provisions of any of the kinds mentioned in specified paragraphs of sch 4 to the Act, and (c) share capital and reserves (including undistributable reserves). Since the fixed assets have a value of £5 million in the accounts, it is possible to argue that, according to the relevant accounts, the amount of the distribution is nil. This view, which amounts to permitting the short-cut described in relation to balance sheets 1 and 2 above, is persuasive but the alternative argument to the effect that the difference between book and market value must be shown to be covered by distributable profits for the distribution to be lawful also has its adherents.[121] Revaluation of assets and drawing up of accounts can be an expensive and time-consuming process. One way of pruning costs would be to revalue only those assets that are to be transferred but it is doubtful whether a company can engage in a selective revaluation because the resulting accounts may not give a true and fair view of the company's overall financial position. The Companies Act 1985, s 270 (2) is widely acknowledged to be ambiguous and the potentially serious cost implications of not permitting the short-cut, even though it does not infringe any fundamental maintenance of capital principle, provide a strong case for the enactment of clarifying legislation.

[121] Nock, RS, and Nock, S, 'Pricing of Corporate Transactions' (1995/6) 2 RALQ 203, 242–3. For discussion of this issue, see also Doran, NJL, 'Transactions at an Undervalue and the Maintenance of Capital Principle' (1991) 12 Co Law 169, 171–3; Knight, B, and Bowles, S, '*Aveling Barford:* Intra-Group Transfers and Deemed Distributions' (1996) 7 (8) PLC 13.

13

Share Buy Backs and Redeemable Shares

INTRODUCTION

The Companies Act 1985 allows a limited[1] company to purchase its own shares. Any type of share can be purchased under this power. A company may also issue shares on terms which provide for later redemption by the company. Where a share is issued on a redeemable basis it is clear from the outset that the shares are to be, or are liable to be acquired by the company at, or by, a later date. The statutory powers for companies to purchase their own shares and to issue redeemable shares are subject to extensive restrictions which are intended to prevent abuse to the prejudice of creditors or groups of shareholders.

REASONS WHY A COMPANY MAY WANT TO PURCHASE ITS OWN SHARES AND/OR ISSUE REDEEMABLE SHARES

A company may have different reasons for wanting to purchase its own shares depending on whether there is an existing active market in its shares. There would be little or no active market in the shares of a very small private company such as one which is in substance an incorporated partnership, although there may be a limited market in the shares of a larger private company.[2]

Where There is No Active Market in the Company's Shares

Attracting External Investors

A company whose shares are not actively traded is not an attractive investment prospect to external investors because of the risk of being permanently locked into that investment. Also, the income derived from such an investment may be low if, as is common practice in smaller companies, minimal, if any, dividends are paid with the bulk of the profits being re-invested or paid in the form of directors' remuneration. Whilst the other existing shareholders are the persons who are most likely to be interested in acquiring the shares of an investor who wants to leave the company, and indeed they may have pre-

[1] The maintenance of capital rules do not apply to unlimited companies but they are subject to the distribution rules in Companies Act 1985, Pt VIII. This means that unlimited companies can purchase their own shares but must finance this from distributable profits as defined by Pt VIII.

[2] See for example the private company involved in *Rutherford, Petitioner* [1994] BCC 876, Ct of Sess discussed in this chapter below, at 453–4.

emption rights in respect of the shares under the company's articles, their personal circumstances may be such that they are unwilling or unable to commit more of their own resources to an investment in the company. The risk of being locked into an investment in the shares of a company which are not actively traded is lessened if the company is able to act as an alternative purchaser and, by being able to offer this possibility, smaller companies may find it easier to raise share capital from external sources than would otherwise be the case.

Redeemable shares offer the most comfort to external investors who are concerned about becoming locked into their investment; although they are not absolutely guaranteed the return of their capital since this will depend on the company having available funds at the time of redemption, by holding redeemable shares they are assured of an exit from the company if it remains prosperous.[3]

Exit for Existing Shareholders

Being able to sell the shares back to the company also offers a way of unlocking the investment made by a proprietor of a small business who subsequently wishes to retire. The estate of a dead shareholder may similarly benefit from the company being able to purchase shares. Where the management of a smaller company is paralysed because of a dispute between its proprietors, for the company to buy only one faction's shares may be a way of resolving the deadlock without recourse to litigation (probably a petition under the Companies Act 1985, s 459).

Only Temporary Loss of Control

These powers may allow the controllers of a company to obtain an injection of capital in return for what is only a temporary dilution of control. Issuing redeemable shares is a particularly good way for controllers to raise share capital without forever forfeiting their control.

Where There is an Active Market in the Company's Shares[4]

Returning Value to Shareholders

Buying back shares is a way of returning to shareholders surplus cash that the company is unable to invest in projects that will generate a return greater than its cost of capital. A buy back of shares can prove to be a particularly useful application of surplus cash because it can have a positive impact on some of the performance ratios which are commonly used by analysts and investors to assess how well companies are doing. Any improvement in these ratios may

[3] Arrangements whereby a company tries to guarantee that investors in its redeemable shares will obtain a capital payment when the shares are due to be redeemed even though the company itself may be insolvent (eg by arranging for a third party to buy the shares in that event) need to be examined closely for potential maintenance of capital and financial assistance concerns. See *Barclays Bank plc v British & Commonwealth Holdings plc* [1995] BCC 19 (affirmed [1995] BCC 1059, CA).

[4] Hinkley, R, Hunter, D, Whittell, M, and Ziff, M, *Current Issues in Equity Finance* (1998) ch 5.

lead to an increase in share price.[5] The performance of listed companies is commonly assessed by reference to its earnings per share, that is the profits which are attributable to equity shareholders divided by the number of equity shares in issue. Buying back shares will improve this figure provided the positive effect of the reduction in the number of shares is not outweighed by the negative effect on the company's profits of the loss of interest on the cash used to finance the buy back. Certain companies, in particular property and investment companies, are also commonly measured by the yardstick of net assets per shares, that is the net assets divided by the number of equity shares in issue. Again, a buy back of shares can improve this figure.[6]

Although it was the 1981 companies legislation that first permitted companies to purchase their own shares, it was not until the 1990s that this method[7] of returning value to shareholders was extensively used in UK market practice. This was a time when factors such as the ending of recession and an inactive takeover market combined to create a build-up of surplus cash in the corporate sector. New trends in techniques for returning value, that were strongly influenced by tax considerations,[8] brought share buy backs into vogue. According to one report share repurchases in Europe rose to more than $47 billion in 1997 with most of that activity taking place in the UK.[9]

Target Capital Structures

A company may choose to buy back its shares in order to achieve a target capital structure. For example, a company may want to eliminate a particular class of shares and replace it with another class or with ordinary shares. Or, it may want to replace expensive share capital with cheaper debt. The company will need to consider the consequences of the percentage holdings of the remaining shareholders increasing as a result of the purchase. A particular point to note is that if the company is listed it must ensure that it can still comply with the London Stock Exchange's requirement that at least 25 per cent of the shares be in public hands.[10]

Investor Demand

A company whose shares are actively traded may still value the flexibility of being able to offer investors the opportunity to invest in its share capital on a temporary basis in the form of redeemable shares. Also, the fact that the com-

[5] Millerchip, CJ, 'Purchase of Own Shares' (1990) 1 (2) PLC 28; Llewellyn-Lloyd, E, *Share Buybacks* (1994, looseleaf) 1.1–1.3.

[6] The impact on earnings per share or net assets per share explains why a return of value by means of a one-off special dividend may be coupled with a reorganisation of share capital whereby existing share capital is consolidated and cancelled so that, for example, 10 existing shares are replaced by 9 new shares.

[7] Other methods include special dividends (see Ch 12) and formal reductions of capital and schemes of arrangement (see Ch 10). Generally, Scott, T, 'Returning Cash to Shareholders. Options for Companies' (1997) 8 (3) PLC 19.

[8] Tiley, J, 'The Purchase by a Company of Its Own Shares' [1992] *British Tax Review* 21; Edge, S, 'Do We Have an Imputation System on Not?' (1996) 375 *Tax Journal* 2; Edge, S, 'The Background to the Introduction of Schedule 7' [1997] *British Tax Review* 221.

[9] Hinkley, R, Hunter, D, Whittell, M, and Ziff, M, *Current Issues in Equity Finance* (1998) 12 quoting a report by JP Morgan.

[10] *The Listing Rules* ch 3, para 3.19.

pany may be able to buy back its shares at a future date may assist with the marketing of shares which are not issued as redeemable, although this benefit may be of minor significance since an active market in the company's shares should usually be sufficient to meet investors' demands for liquidity.

Discounted Repurchase of Redeemable Shares

Where redeemable shares are trading at a discount to their redemption price, being able to repurchase those shares enables the company to save money by buying up those shares at a price lower than the redemption price.

Stabilising the Share Price

A company whose shares are actively traded may further want to have the power to buy its own shares in order to bolster or stabilise their market price. However, whilst this can be presented as an argument in favour of share buy backs, allowing a company to be able to buy its own shares to bolster or stabilise the price at which they are trading in the market also raises concerns about market manipulation. Similarly, whilst, from one perspective, allowing the management of a company threatened with a takeover the power to buy back shares as a defensive tactic may be viewed positively, this also prompts the concern that unregulated use of this power could enable management to entrench themselves in position and thereby impede the functioning of the market for corporate control.[11]

Other Arguments for Permitting Share Buy Backs

These considerations may be relevant both to companies whose shares are actively traded and also to those whose shares are not.

Employee Share Schemes

Another advantage claimed for allowing companies to purchase their own shares is that this can facilitate the operation of an employee share scheme by assuring employees of a purchaser for their shares when they leave the company.[12] In larger companies it is common for employee share schemes to be operated through a trust and for the trustees to buy the shares of employees who are leaving the company, but for the company to be able to buy back the employee shares is an alternative which can be more straightforward and which can therefore make the establishment of employee share schemes less of a burden for smaller companies.

Dissident Shareholders

Buying back shares may be a way of dealing with a dissenting shareholder. However, use of the power for this purpose could clearly be open to abuse.

[11] The disciplining function performed by the market for corporate control is discussed in Ch 4 above, at 118–22.

[12] *The Purchase by a Company of its Own Shares* Cmnd 7944 (1980) para 11 also states as possible advantages that it would permit the development of open-ended investment companies and would allow companies to purchase their shares to hold in treasury and later trade. Open-ended investment companies are a form of collective investment and are an alternative to unit trusts.

Informal Reduction of Capital

A redemption or repurchase of shares could be used by a company in order to reduce its share capital without the need for court approval and the obligation to observe the other formalities attending a conventional reduction of capital under the Companies Act 1985, s 135. However, the potential for creditors to be prejudiced by an informal reduction of capital are obvious and this is a central objection to allowing companies to buy back their own shares.

OBJECTIONS TO A COMPANY BEING ABLE TO PURCHASE ITS OWN SHARES

The Maintenance of Capital Principle

Unregulated, a purchase of shares by a company would cause a reduction in its undistributable reserves and would thus operate to the detriment of the company's creditors to the extent that their interests are protected by maintenance of capital rules. In *Trevor v Whitworth*[13] the House of Lords relied on infringement of the maintenance of capital principle as the main reason for coming to the conclusion that the purchase by a company of its own shares was unlawful.

Unconstitutional Conduct by Management

The argument that a company ought to be able to purchase its own shares in order to buy out shareholders whose continued presence in the company was undesirable was accepted in some nineteenth-century cases[14] but it found little favour in the House of Lords in *Trevor v Whitworth*. Lord Macnaghten stated:[15]

> But I would ask, Is it possible to suggest anything more dangerous to the welfare of companies and to the security of their creditors than such a doctrine? Who are the shareholders whose continuance in a company the company or its executive consider undesirable? Why, shareholders who quarrel with the policy of the board, and wish to turn the directors out; shareholders who ask questions which it may not be convenient to answer; shareholders who want information which the directors think it prudent to withhold. Can it be contended that when the policy of directors is assailed they may spend the capital of the company in keeping themselves in power, or in purchasing the retirement of inquisitive and troublesome critics?

The constitutional function of the directors in a conventionally structured company is to manage the company and it is beyond their powers to seek to determine the identity of its shareholders.[16] Allowing a company to purchase its own shares could be open to abuse because directors could, by offering

13 (1887) 12 App Cas 409, HL.

14 eg, *Re Dronfield Silkstone Coal Company* (1881) 17 Ch D 76, CA.

15 (1887) 12 App Cas 409, HL, 435.

16 See further Ch 5 above, at 162–8.

them an exceptionally favourable price, use the power to secure their own control by getting rid of troublesome or disaffected shareholders who might otherwise have been tempted to make a takeover bid or to accept another's bid.[17] The directors of a company might also be tempted to pay too much for the company's shares in order to favour a selling shareholder who has a special connection to the company, such as one of its original proprietors who is retiring from the company after many years of service. If a company pays an unjustifiably high price for the shares, this may diminish the company's resources to the prejudice of its remaining shareholders.

Market Manipulation

For the company to use its own money to bolster or stabilise its share price is open to the obvious objection that this practice could mislead the investing public about the value of the company's shares and could create a false market in those shares.[18] If the risk of market manipulation were the only argument against permitting companies to buy back their own shares, it would be doubtful whether this would justify a specific ban on the practice because market manipulation is in any event prohibited by the Financial Services Act 1986, s 47.

CONSIDERATION OF THE MATTER BY REVIEW BODIES

Following the Report of the Greene Committee,[19] the Companies Act 1928, s 18 first allowed companies to issue redeemable preference shares subject to safeguards which were intended to preserve the amount of the company's share capital. The Jenkins Committee,[20] reviewing the position in 1962, compared the limited power allowed to English companies with the freedom enjoyed by US companies to repurchase shares and acknowledged the usefulness of the US position with regard to such matters as employee share schemes and the unlocking of investment in small companies. The Committee thought that if British companies were to be given a wider power to purchase their own shares it would be necessary to introduce stringent safeguards to protect creditors and shareholders but that it would be possible to devise effective safeguards and that they would not be unduly complicated. However, it refrained from recommending the general abrogation of the rule that a company could not purchase its own shares because it had received no evidence that British companies needed the power and because it identified serious tax disadvantages in selling shares back to the company rather than to a third party.

17 Brudney, V, and Bratton, WW, *Brudney and Chirelstein's Corporate Finance, Cases and Materials* (4th edn, 1993) 610–36 discussing US cases arising from the use of buy back powers in takeover situations and the unequal treatment of shareholders in the exercise of these powers. See also, Brudney, V, 'A Note on "Going Private" ' (1975) 61 Virginia Law Rev 1019, 1047–8.

18 *General Property Co Ltd v Matheson's Trustees* (1888) 16 R 82 Ct of Sess.

19 *The Report of the Committee on Company Law* Cmd 2657 (1926) para 28.

20 *Report of the Company Law Committee* Cmnd 1749 (1962) paras 167–9.

At the end of the 1970s, the problems in raising capital encountered by smaller companies were the subject of a review by a Committee under the chairmanship of Sir Harold Wilson. In its *Interim Report on the Financing of Small Firms*[21] this Committee suggested that consideration should be given to permitting such companies to issue redeemable equity shares as a means of raising capital without parting permanently with family control. During Parliamentary debates on the Bill which became the Companies Act 1980, it was announced by the Department of Trade that the Government attached high priority to relaxing the general prohibition on companies purchasing their own shares. This was then followed by the publication by the Department of Trade of a Consultative Document on *The Purchase by a Company of its Own Shares* which was written on its behalf by Professor Gower.[22] In the Consultative Document Professor Gower recommended that companies should be allowed to issue redeemable equity shares and that consideration should be given to the possibility of permitting public and private companies to repurchase their own shares.[23] He outlined safeguards intended to ensure that capital would be maintained despite repurchase or redemption of shares, but in relation to private companies he further recommended that consideration be given to allowing them to reduce their capital by repurchasing or redeeming shares.

Powers broadly in line with those recommended for consideration by Professor Gower were enacted in the Companies Act 1981 and they are now contained in the Companies Act 1985, ss 159 to 178. The safeguards which have been built into the legislation to protect creditors and shareholders have resulted in a series of provisions which are detailed and complex.[24] Broadly speaking the rules are strictest in relation to public companies but private companies operate under a slightly more relaxed regime. The Secretary of State can modify by regulations the statutory requirements governing the purchase and redemption of shares,[25] but to date this power has not been exercised.

THE EUROPEAN DIMENSION

The Second Company Law Directive[26] contains provisions regulating the redemption or repurchase of shares by public companies. This Directive does not require Member States to have laws permitting companies to issue redeemable shares or to repurchase shares but those Member States which do permit public companies to do so must observe the conditions imposed by

[21] Cmnd 7503 (1979).
[22] Cmnd 7944 (1980).
[23] *The Purchase by a Company of its Own Shares* Cmnd 7944 (1980) para 67 (Conclusions).
[24] The complexity of the legislation is criticised by Sealy, LS, *Company Law and Capitalism* (1984) 8–14. He comments: 'It is quite a challenge even for a specialist lawyer to get the drift of [the provisions] in two or three readings, and it would probably be an hour's work for him to get to the bottom of all of the qualifications and cross-references. For the businessman who wants to inform himself how the law stands, the task is plainly impossible.'
[25] Companies Act 1985, s 179.
[26] Second Company Law Directive 77/91/EEC, [1977] OJ L26/1.

the Directive. What this means is that, at least in relation to public companies, the relevant sections of the Companies Act 1985 must be read in the light of the Second Directive and so far as possible interpreted in a purposive matter in order to give effect to its provisions.[27] It is unclear whether a court would distinguish between public and private companies in interpreting these sections and apply a purposive construction when a public company is involved whilst ignoring the European dimension as regards their application to private companies. That approach would add an unfortunate additional element of complexity to what is already a formidably intricate piece of legislation.

GENERAL STATUTORY RULE AGAINST A COMPANY ACQUIRING ITS OWN SHARES

The thrust of *Trevor v Whitworth*[28] is now embodied in the Companies Act 1985, s 143 (1) which provides that a company limited by shares or by guarantee must not acquire its own shares, whether by purchase, subscription or otherwise. If a company purports to act in contravention of this rule it is liable to a fine and every officer of the company who is in default is liable to imprisonment or a fine, or both; and the purported acquisition is void.[29] The general prohibition is however qualified by the Companies Act 1985, s 143 (3) which states that it does not apply in relation to:

(a) the redemption or purchase of shares in accordance with Companies Act 1985, Pt V, ch VII;
(b) the acquisition of shares in a reduction of capital duly made;
(c) the purchase of shares in pursuance of an order of the court under Companies Act 1985, s 5 (alteration of objects), s 54 (litigated objection to resolution for company to be re-registered as private) or Part XVII (relief to members unfairly prejudiced); or
(d) the forfeiture of shares, or the acceptance of shares surrendered in lieu, in pursuance of the articles, for failure to pay any sum payable in respect of the shares.

A company limited by shares is also allowed to acquire any of its own fully-paid shares otherwise than for valuable consideration.[30]

In *Acatos and Hutcheson plc v Watson*[31] the High Court was asked to rule on whether the purchase by a company of another company whose sole asset was a substantial holding of shares in the purchasing company would infringe the prohibition contained in the Companies Act 1985, s 143 (1). Lightman J held that the proposed acquisition would not amount to a side-stepping of the prohibition which the court would prevent by lifting the veil between the purchaser and the target company. In reaching this conclusion, Lightman J

[27] *Pickstone v Freemans plc* [1989] AC 66, [1988] 2 All ER 803, HL; *Litster v Forth Dry Dock and Engineering Co Ltd* [1990] AC 546, [1989] 1 All ER 1134, HL.

[28] (1887) 12 App Cas 409, HL.

[29] Companies Act 1985, s 143 (2). But if an agreement can be performed in alternative ways, one lawful and one which would contravene s 143 (2), the court will assume that the parties intended to carry it out in the lawful manner and will give effect to it in that way: *Vision Express (UK) Ltd v Wilson* [1998] BCC 173.

[30] Companies Act 1985, s 143 (3).

[31] [1994] BCC 446.

followed three Australian cases which had adopted the same approach.[32] He noted that the opposite conclusion would enable companies to protect themselves from becoming the target of a takeover bid simply by acquiring some of the predator's shares, a result which he characterised as 'absurd'. Lightman J also drew support from the Companies Act 1985, s 23 which, although generally prohibiting an existing subsidiary from acquiring shares in its parent, in ss (5) expressly recognises the possibility of a company acquiring a new subsidiary which holds shares in it; the subsidiary may continue to hold the shares but may not exercise any votes attaching to them.

In this context may be noted the Companies Act 1985, s 144 which specifically regulates the subscription or acquisition of shares in a limited company by a nominee of that company. Subject to limited qualifications,[33] where shares are issued to a nominee of a limited company or are acquired by a nominee from a third person as partly paid up, then, for all purposes the shares are to be treated as held by the nominee on his own account and the company is to be regarded as having no beneficial interest in them.[34]

In circumstances where a company is permitted to acquire its own shares, it must then observe any limitations on what it can do with the shares so acquired. This depends on the method of acquisition.[35] The provisions of the Companies Act 1985 governing the redemption and repurchase of shares make specific provision for the cancellation of shares so acquired.[36]

SHARE BUY BACKS: AUTHORISATIONS REQUIRED BY THE COMPANIES ACT 1985

A limited company may purchase its own shares provided that it is authorised to do so by its articles. The relevant provision of Table A is art 85. The authorisation in the articles although necessary is not sufficient to enable a company to purchase its own shares. A further shareholder resolution is also required and the form of this resolution depends on whether the purchase is to take place 'on' or 'off' market.

On-Market Purchases

A purchase by a company of its own shares is on-market if it is a purchase made on a recognised investment exchange provided that the shares are subject to a marketing arrangement on that exchange. The London Stock

[32] *August Investments Pty Ltd v Poseidon Ltd* (1971) 2 SASR 71, SA SC-FC, noted Leigh French, H, 'Exceptions to Self-Purchase of Shares' (1987) 8 Co Law 88; *Dyason v JC Hutton Pty Ltd* (1935) 41 ALR 419, V SC; *Trade Practices Commission v Australian Iron & Steel Pty Ltd* (1990) 22 FCR 305.

[33] Companies Act 1985, s 145.

[34] Ibid, s 143 (1). Ss (2)–(4) make provision for other persons to be jointly and severally liable to pay any amount called for the purpose of paying up or paying any premium on shares in the event of the nominee failing to do so, and for relief from such liability.

[35] Companies Act 1985, s 146 applies where its own shares are acquired by a public company by forfeiture or otherwise than for valuable consideration (and the company has a beneficial interest in them).

[36] Companies Act 1985, s 160 (4).

Exchange is a recognised investment exchange for this purpose[37] and listed shares are always to be regarded as being subject to a marketing arrangement.[38] Accordingly, where listed shares are bought back by a company in a transaction on the Exchange, the purchase is on-market for the purposes of the Companies Act 1985. Shares which are not listed are subject to a marketing arrangement if the company has been afforded facilities for dealing in those shares to take place on the Exchange without prior permission from the Exchange and without limit as to the time during which those facilities are to be available. This would encompass shares which are admitted to dealings on the Alternative Investment Market.[39]

Ordinary or Special Resolution?

The Companies Act 1985, s 166 provides that the additional authorisation required in respect of an on-market purchase of shares is an ordinary resolution.[40] In practice listed companies which take power to purchase their own shares commonly do so by special resolution in order to comply with recommendations from the Association of British Insurers, the representative body of a major group of institutional investors.[41] An important feature of an on-market authority, whether in the form of an ordinary or a special resolution, is that it can be a general authority not linked to any particular purchase of shares. The Companies Act 1985, s 166 (3) merely requires that the authority must specify limits with regard to the maximum number of shares authorised to be acquired and the maximum and minimum prices which may be paid for the shares (such prices may be fixed or may be determined by reference to a formula, provided this is without reference to any person's discretion or opinion,[42] and must state a date on which it is to expire). The maximum length of a s 166 authority is set by ss (4) at eighteen months. The Association of British Insurers favours annual renewal of the authority and, because of this, it is the practice in some companies for a resolution to this effect to be passed regularly at their annual general meeting. Further ABI recommendations are that the number of shares covered by the authority should not exceed 10 per cent of a company's existing issued shares[43] and that the company should undertake only to exercise the power if to do so will result in an increase in earnings

37 But overseas investment exchanges are not: Companies Act 1985, s 163 (4).

38 Companies Act 1985, s 163 (2)(a).

39 This is the London Stock Exchange's junior market. See further, Ch 2 above, at 74–6.

40 It must be filed with the registrar of companies: Companies Act 1985, s 166 (7).

41 The ABI's investment committee has not issued formal guidelines on share buy backs but has requested that companies comply with certain recommendations. These recommendations, which are referred to at various points in this chapter, are available through the ABI's online Institutional Voting Information Service (IVIS). On the role of the ABI as a representative body for institutional investors and its IVIS see further Ch 7 above, at 241–5 and 248–9.

42 Companies Act 1985, s 166 (6).

43 The ABI has stated that in normal conditions authority to purchase up to 5 per cent of the issued ordinary share capital is unlikely to cause concern, although regard will be had to the effect on gearing, etc where larger amounts of capital are involved. The 10 per cent limit suggested in the text is based on the ABI's further comment that 'some offices have indicated a reluctance to accept own share purchase powers over share capital in excess of 10 per cent of the issued ordinary share capital'.

per share (or asset value per share in the case of property companies or investment trusts) and is in the best interests of shareholders generally.

A Companies Act 1985 ordinary resolution authority to purchase shares in an on-market transaction may be varied, revoked or renewed by ordinary resolution.[44] Provided this is permitted by the resolution, a company may after the expiry of an authority complete a purchase of shares arising from a contract entered into before the authority expired.[45]

Off-market Purchases

A purchase which is not a market purchase is an off-market purchase. The Companies Act 1985 requires off-market purchases of shares to be approved by special resolution.[46] In this case a general authorisation is not acceptable and the shareholders must approve the specific terms of the contract by which the shares are to be purchased.[47] A resolution approving an off-market purchase of own shares will not be effective if any shareholder holding shares to which the resolution relates exercised the voting rights carried by those shares[48] in voting on the resolution and the resolution would not have been passed if he had not done so.[49] The contract must not be entered into before it has been so authorised[50] and it (or a written memorandum of its terms) must be available for inspection by members of the company both at the company's registered office for not less than fifteen days ending with the date of the meeting at which the resolution is passed and also at the meeting itself. The names of all of the selling shareholders must be disclosed either in the contract or in a written memorandum. Non-compliance with these publicity requirements renders any resolution which is passed ineffective.[51] The disclosure requirements enable shareholders to discover the names of the selling shareholders and the terms of sale. They may help to prevent directors entering into arrangements to buy back favoured members' shares at especially favourable terms or otherwise abusing their powers. The requirement of equal treatment for shareholders is expressly backed by the Second European Community Company Law Directive, art 42.

A special resolution authorising an off-market purchase of shares may, in the case of a private company, be of unlimited duration but, given that the terms on which the sale is to take place must be settled before the resolution is passed, ordinarily the contract would be expected to be concluded fairly soon after the resolution is passed. A resolution passed by a public company must state when the authority conferred by the resolution is to expire and the

[44] Companies Act 1985, s 166 (4). The statutory time-limit of 18 months also applies to any renewal. Any such resolution must be filed with the registrar of companies: Companies Act 1985, s 166 (7).

[45] Companies Act 1985, s 166 (5).

[46] Ibid, s 164.

[47] Ibid, s 164 (2).

[48] Whether on a poll or otherwise: Companies Act 1985, s 164 (5).

[49] Ibid, s 164 (5).

[50] Any contract purported to be entered into in advance of shareholder approval would be unenforceable: *Western v Ringblast Holdings*, 1989 GWD 23–950. In principle, however, it is difficult to see why companies should be prevented from entering into purchase contracts that are conditional upon shareholder approval being forthcoming.

[51] Companies Act 1985, s 164 (6).

expiry date must be not later than eighteen months after the passing of the resolution.[52] A special resolution authorising an off-market purchase of shares can be varied, revoked or renewed by special resolution.[53] Any variation in the terms of the contract by which the shares are to be purchased must be approved by special resolution before it is agreed to by the company, and the proposed variations must be made available for inspection by members in the same way as the original contract.[54]

Private companies can use the statutory written resolution regime to pass a resolution authorising an off-market purchase of its own shares.[55] The requirement for the contract (or its terms) to be available for inspection by members is necessarily varied in this case to provide that details must have been supplied to each member before he signed the resolution. Statutory written resolutions require the unanimous consent of all of those members who are entitled to vote on the matter; the position of the shareholder holding shares to which the resolution relates is in this situation dealt with by deeming such member to be not entitled to vote on the matter.[56]

Contracts entered into by a company which do not amount to contracts to purchase those shares but under which the company may (subject to any conditions) become entitled or obliged to purchase those shares are regulated in the same way as off-market purchase contracts. Such contracts are referred to as contingent purchase contracts and an example of such a contract would be an option contract under which the company is entitled to call for the shares in specified circumstances. The terms of a contingent purchase contract must thus be approved by special resolution before the contract is entered into.[57]

The requirements for advance approval of contracts for a company to purchase its own shares are mandatory.[58] This means that they must be complied with even in circumstances where all of the shareholders would be willing to waive them. It has been held that these requirements are to be viewed in this way because their purpose extends beyond protection of the existing shareholders and encompasses protection of creditors' interests and possibly also wider public interests.[59]

OTHER STATUTORY RESTRICTIONS ON THE TERMS AND MANNER OF BUY BACKS

A company must not purchase its own shares where to do so would result in there being no member of the company holding shares other than redeemable shares.[60] The purpose of this requirement is to ensure that a

52 Ibid, s 164 (4).
53 Ibid, s 164 (3). The 18-month time-limit applies to any renewal.
54 Companies Act 1985, s 164 (7). The original contract (or a memorandum) and any previous variations must be made available.
55 Companies Act 1985, s 381A–C. But authority may not be given for this purpose by means of the unanimous informal consent of the shareholders: *Re RW Peak (Kings Lynn) Ltd* [1998] 1 BCLC 193.
56 Companies Act 1985, sch 15A, para 5.
57 Ibid, s 165.
58 *Re RW Peak (Kings Lynn) Ltd* [1998] 1 BCLC 193.
59 Ibid at 204–5.
60 Companies Act 1985, s 162 (3).

company does not end up with no members because of buy backs and later redemptions.

Shares may not be bought back unless they are fully paid (so that the valuable asset represented by uncalled capital is not lost) and the purchase price must be paid at the time of purchase.[61] The requirement for shareholders to be paid off at once ensures that members cannot be pressurised into accepting terms under which they are required to sell and thus lose their rights as members at once but not be compensated for this for some considerable time. However, having to find all of the purchase money up front rather than to agree to deferred payment by instalments may pose a difficulty to smaller companies and may inhibit the use of the buy-back power. It might have been sensible to have allowed some flexibility on this point, especially since the Companies Act 1985, s 178 already provides a solution to the potential problem of the company not having sufficient available funds at the time when payment is due by restricting the remedies that the shareholder can seek in that situation.[62]

Although not stated expressly, the Companies Act 1985 appears to require that the shares be paid for in cash.[63] There is support for the view that the term 'sale' when used in a provision of the Companies Act meant sale for cash only.[64] This may be indicative of the courts' likely approach to the interpretation of 'purchase'. Ruling out non-cash consideration prevents directors favouring some shareholders over others by acquiring their shares in return for non-cash assets of varying values.

FINANCING A BUY BACK

Only designated funds can be applied by a company in purchasing its own shares. They may be purchased out of distributable profits of the company or out of the proceeds of a fresh issue of shares made specifically for that purpose.[65] Subject to one exception, any premium payable on purchase must be paid out of distributable profits.[66] The exception is that where shares were issued at a premium, the company may pay a premium on redemption out of the proceeds of a fresh issue of shares. It may only do so up to an amount equal to the lesser of the aggregate of the premiums received by the company on the issue of the shares repurchased and the current amount of the com-

[61] Companies Act 1985, s 159 (3) as applied to the buy-back power.

[62] See this chapter, at 445.

[63] *The Purchase by a Company of its Own Shares* Cmnd 7944 (1980) para 35 recommended that repurchases should be permitted only for cash.

[64] *Re Westminster Property Group* (1983–5)1 BCC 99,355 CA. Note also *Robshaw Bros v Mayer* [1956] Ch 125 where, having reviewed earlier authorities on various statutory provisions, Upjohn J held that 'sale or purchase' in the Rules of the Supreme Court meant an exchange of property for money.

[65] Companies Act 1985, s 160 (1) (a). Where a company is about to purchase shares, it has power to issue shares up to the nominal value of the shares to be purchased as if those shares had never been issued: Companies Act 1985, s 161 (5).

[66] Ibid, s 160 (1)(b).

pany's share premium account; the company's share premium account must be reduced by the amount so paid.[67] Distributable profits for this purpose mean essentially the funds which are available to pay dividends.[68]

CANCELLATION OF PURCHASED SHARES/THE POSSIBILITY OF TREASURY SHARES

When shares are purchased they must be treated as cancelled and the amount of the company's issued share capital must be diminished by the nominal value of those shares accordingly; but the purchase and cancellation of shares is not to be taken as reducing the amount of the company's authorised share capital.[69] In requiring the shares to be cancelled, the Companies Act 1985 goes further than what is required by the Second Directive, under which public companies (the Directive not applying to private companies) are permitted to acquire and hold up to 10 per cent of the company's capital.[70] In 1980 when the government last consulted on this matter, the mood was against allowing companies to purchase shares, hold them in 'treasury' and then resell them. In 1998, however, the DTI published a new consultative document seeking views on whether there should be a change in the law to permit treasury shares.[71]

The main argument for permitting treasury shares is that this would give companies additional flexibility with regard to the management of their capital structure. Selling treasury shares back to the market would not constitute an allotment or issue of new shares. Accordingly, the statutory rules prohibiting the allotment of shares at a discount to their par value and regulating the forms of consideration for shares in public companies would not apply,[72] nor would it be necessary to comply with the statutory pre-emption rights given to shareholders in respect of new share issues.[73] However, it is debatable whether some form of pre-emptive entitlement should apply in respect of reissued treasury issues and this is a matter that would have to be examined closely if the law were to be changed to permit treasury shares.[74] The principal argument for retaining the ban on treasury shares is the potential for manipulation of share prices, although in view of the Financial Services Act 1986, s 47 which makes market manipulation a specific offence, the insider dealing

[67] Ibid, s 160 (2).
[68] Ibid, s 181.
[69] Ibid, s 160 (4).
[70] Second Company Law Directive 77/91/EEC, [1977] OJ L26/1, art 19. See also art 22 which prohibits the exercise of voting rights attaching to shares held by the company and imposes disclosure and accounting requirements.
[71] *Share Buybacks: A Consultative Document* (DTI 1998).
[72] Companies Act 1985, ss 99–116.
[73] Ibid, ss 89–96.
[74] Other relevant issues would include: disclosure of the proportion of shares held in treasury; treatment of dividend payments whilst they are so held; procedures for authorising reissue and publicising its occurrence; possible restrictions on reissue at price-sensitive times and during takeovers; whether subsidiaries should be allowed to hold shares in parent in treasury and accounting requirements: *Share Buybacks: A Consultative Document* (DTI 1998) paras 5.6–5.17.

legislation[75] and the London Stock Exchange's monitoring of share prices, this argument may carry less weight than it once did.[76] A comparison may be made here with the Irish Companies Act 1990[77] which contains provisions on the redemption and purchase of own shares which are broadly similar to those in the English legislation save that the reissue of redeemed or repurchased shares is permitted. It is provided that the reissue of treasury shares does not constitute an increase in the issued share capital for any purpose.

ACCOUNTING FOR A SHARE BUY BACK AND OTHER NOTIFICATIONS

An unregulated repurchase of shares which is funded from the company's distributable profits would have the effect of reducing the company's capital. This is shown by the following example:[78]

Company A has issued £10,000 ordinary shares and £10,000 redeemable preference shares at par. It has made realised profits of £10,000 and now has net assets of £30,000, represented by £20,000 share capital and £10,000 distributable reserves. It uses the £10,000 to redeem the preference shares. The preference shares are thereupon cancelled and the company's issued share capital is thus reduced to £10,000. In effect the company would have redeemed the preference shares from capital and would still have £10,000 free reserves available for distribution.

To ensure that this result does not occur and that the company's undistributable reserves remain intact despite the reduction in the issued share capital, the amount by which the capital is reduced must be transferred to a 'capital redemption reserve'. This reserve is to be treated as if it were share capital with the one exception that it may be used to pay up fully-paid bonus shares.[79] The requirement to make a transfer to the capital redemption reserve applies only to the extent that the buy back is funded from distributable profits. To the extent that it is funded from the proceeds of a fresh issue of shares made specifically for that purpose, the nominal amount of issued capital available to creditors remains intact, because the new shares will simply replace those which are bought back. Reverting to the above example:

The company issues new ordinary shares with a total nominal value of £10,000 at par and uses the proceeds of the issue to purchase the preference shares. At the end of the exercise the company's issued share capital remains at £20,000 although it is now comprised entirely of ordinary shares. The company's creditors have not been prejudiced because they were aware that the proceeds of the new issue were never intended to be used in the ordinary course of business and that the issue was made for a specific purpose.

The position where a private company uses it capital to finance the purchase of its shares is considered separately later in this chapter.[80]

[75] Criminal Justice Act 1993, ss 52–64 and schs 1–2.
[76] *Share Buybacks: A Consultative Document* (DTI 1998) paras 3.9–3.12.
[77] Ss 207–230.
[78] This is taken from *The Purchase by a Company of its Own Shares* Cmnd 7944 (1980) para 52.
[79] Companies Act 1985, s 170.
[80] See below, at 446–7.

Details of shares purchased in any financial year must be given in the relevant directors' report.[81] If the company is listed, additional information up to the date of the report must be included and details of any shareholders' authority for the purchase by the company of its own shares which is still valid at the end of the period under review must also be given.[82]

The company must notify the registrar of companies of any purchases of its own shares[83] and also of cancellation.[84] Copies of contracts for the purchase of shares[85] (or memoranda of their terms) must be keep at the company's registered office for ten years and must be available for inspection.[86]

CONTRACTUAL MATTERS RELATING TO SHARE BUY BACKS

The consequences of a company failing to complete its bargain to purchase shares are dealt with by the Companies Act 1985, s 178.[87] The company is not liable in damages in that event: the Companies Act 1985, s 178 (2). This is without prejudice to any other right that the shareholder may have; the shareholder may thus seek specific performance of the contract, but the court must not grant this if the company shows that it is unable to meet the costs of redeeming or purchasing the shares in question out of distributable profits.[88] The winding up of the company does not necessarily[89] preclude enforcement of a contract to purchase shares, but payment of the sums due under any such contract ranks behind the ordinary debts and liabilities of the company and any sums due in satisfaction of preferred rights attaching to other shares.[90]

The rights of a company under a contract to purchase its own shares[91] cannot be assigned.[92] Any agreement by a company to release its contractual rights relating to an off-market purchase is void unless the terms of the release have been approved in advance by special resolution.[93] Any payment by a company in respect of a release of its obligations must be made out of the company's distributable profits.[94]

[81] Companies Act 1985, s 234 and sch 7, part II.

[82] *The Listing Rules*, ch 12, para 12.43(n).

[83] Companies Act 1985, s 169 (1)–(2).

[84] Companies Act, s 122 (1)(f).

[85] Or contingent purchase contracts under Companies Act 1985, s 165.

[86] Companies Act 1985, s 169 (4)–(5). This extends to any variation of the contract as well: Companies Act 1985, s 169 (9). For the consequence of default see Companies Act 1985, s 169 (6)–(8).

[87] Considered in *Barclays Bank plc v British & Commonwealth Holdings plc* [1995] BCC 19 (affirmed [1995] BCC 1059, CA).

[88] Companies Act 1985, s 178 (3).

[89] But note Companies Act 1985, s 178 (5).

[90] Companies Act 1985, s 178 (4) and (6).

[91] Or a contingent purchase contract

[92] Companies Act 1985, s 167 (1).

[93] Ibid, s 167 (2).

[94] Ibid, s 168. This also applies to a payment made in consideration of the variation of a contract approved under Companies Act 1985, ss 164 or 165 or of the acquiring of any right with respect to the purchase of its own shares in pursuance of a contract approved under Companies Act 1985, s 165.

BUY BACK OF OWN SHARES OUT OF CAPITAL (PRIVATE COMPANIES ONLY)

Under certain conditions private companies are allowed to reduce their capital by purchasing shares. These conditions are intended to protect creditors from the risks that lie in permitting companies to use their capital in this way. They are also designed to protect dissentient members of the company.

First, the company must be authorised by the company's articles to use its capital to purchase its shares.[95] Second, recourse can only be had to the company's capital where its available profits[96] and proceeds of fresh issues made for the purpose (if any) are insufficient.[97] The amount of capital which the company can use is referred to as the 'permissible capital payment'.[98] If the permissible capital payment, together with the proceeds of a fresh issue of shares, is less than the nominal value of the shares purchased (so that the balance is funded from profits) the difference must be credited to the capital redemption reserve[99] but, if it is greater, the capital redemption reserve, share premium account, share capital account or redemption reserve may be reduced by the excess amount.[100] Third, the payment out of capital must be approved by a special resolution of the company passed within a week of the directors' statutory declaration.[101] This resolution is ineffective if any member of the company holding shares to which the resolution relates votes on it and the resolution would not have been passed if he had not done so.[102] Fourth, the directors must make a statutory declaration as to the solvency of the company.[103] The declaration must specify the amount of the permissible capital payment and must state that, having made full inquiry into the affairs and prospects of the company, they have formed the opinion:

(a) that immediately following the payment out of capital, there will be no grounds on which the company could then be found to be unable to pay its debts (taking into account contingent and prospective liabilities[104]), and
(b) that having regard to their intentions with regard to the management of the company and the amount and character of the financial resources which in their view will be available to the company throughout the year following the date on which the payment is made, the company will be able to continue to carry on its business as a going concern (and will accordingly be able to pay its debts as they fall due).

This declaration, and an accompanying auditors' report, must be filed with the registrar of companies.[105] The declaration and report must also be kept at

95 Companies Act 1985, s 171 (1). See Table A, art 35 for an authority to this effect.
96 In this context these are determined in accordance with Companies Act 1985, s 172 instead of Companies Act 1985, ss 270 to 275.
97 Companies Act 1985, s 171 (3).
98 Ibid, s 171 (3).
99 Ibid, s 171 (4).
100 Ibid, s 171 (5).
101 Ibid, ss 173 (2) and 174 (1).
102 Ibid, s 174 (2). If the company uses the statutory written resolution procedure, a member holding shares to which the resolution relates is treated as a member who is not entitled to vote on the matter: Companies Act 1985, sch 15A, para 6.
103 Ibid, s 173 (3)–(6). The special resolution is ineffective if this statutory declaration and the accompanying auditors' report are not available for inspection by members of the company at the meeting to which the resolution relates: Companies Act 1985, s 174 (4).
104 Companies Act 1985, s 171 (4).
105 Ibid, s 175 (5).

the company's registered office for a period expiring five weeks after the date of the special resolution and must be available for inspection by any member or creditor.[106] Fifth, the fact that the company has passed a special resolution for payment out of capital must be publicised in the London Gazette. The notice to this effect must also be published in an appropriate national newspaper unless the company gives such notice in writing to each of its creditors.[107]

Within five weeks of the passing of a special resolution approving a payment from capital for the purchase of shares, an application may be made to court by any creditor of the company and by any member other than one who consented to or voted in favour of the resolution.[108] On the hearing of an application the court may adjourn the proceedings to give the parties an opportunity to come to an arrangement for the purchase of the interests of dissentient members or for the protection of dissentient creditors as the case may be.[109] Without prejudice to that power, on the hearing of the application the court is required to make an order on such terms and conditions as it thinks fit either confirming or cancelling the resolution.[110] The court order can provide for the purchase by the company of the shares of any member and for the reduction accordingly of the company's capital.[111] To allow for the possibility of such an application being made, the payment out of capital must be made no earlier than five weeks after the date of the special resolution.[112]

The Insolvency Act 1986, s 76 is relevant where a company is being wound up and it has previously made a payment out of capital to purchase its own shares. If (i) the aggregate amount of the company's assets and the amounts paid by way of contribution to its assets (apart from this section) is insufficient for the payment of its debts and liabilities and the expenses of the winding up, and (ii) the winding up commenced within a year of the date on which the relevant payment was made, the person from whom the shares were purchased and the directors who signed the statutory declaration as to the company's solvency are prima facie personally liable to contribute to the company's assets to enable that insufficiency to be met. The former member who sold his shares is liable to contribute an amount not exceeding so much of the relevant payment as was made by the company in respect of his shares. The directors are jointly and severally liable with that person to contribute that amount[113] but a director can escape this liability by showing that he had reasonable grounds for forming the opinion as to the company's solvency set out in that declaration.[114]

106 Ibid, s 175 (6)–(7). This is modified where the company uses the statutory written resolution procedure: Companies Act 1985, sch 15A, s 177 (3).

107 Companies Act 1985, s 175 (2).

108 Ibid, s 176 (1).

109 Ibid, s 177 (1).

110 Ibid, s 177 (2).

111 Ibid, s 177 (2).

112 Ibid, s 174 (1). There is also a cut-off date: the payment must be made not more than seven weeks after the date of the resolution

113 Insolvency Act 1986, s 76 (3). A person who has contributed to the company's assets can ask the court for an order directing the others who are jointly and severally liable with him to pay him such amount as the court thinks just and equitable.

114 Insolvency Act 1986, s 76 (2).

LONDON STOCK EXCHANGE REQUIREMENTS ON SHARE BUY BACKS

The purchase of its own securities by a listed company is regulated by *The Listing Rules*, ch 15. These rules apply to purchases of any type of listed security and not merely to shares. The rules govern both market purchases and off-market purchases. The thrust of the requirements is mainly to require notification of proposed and actual purchases.

Any decision by the board to seek shareholder approval for the purchase of the company's own equity securities (ie ordinary shares and preference shares which, in respect of either capital or dividends, have rights to participate over and above the specified preferential amount) must be notified to the Exchange unless it is merely the renewal of an existing authority.[115] The Exchange must also be notified of the outcome of the shareholders' meeting.[116] The Exchange must be given details of actual purchases as soon as possible and in any event no later than 8.30 am on the business day following the calendar day on which the dealings took place.[117] The content of circulars seeking shareholders' authority is regulated by the Exchange[118] and where the proposed purchase is from a related party or would result in the company acquiring 15 per cent or more of the company's issued share capital the circular must be submitted in advance to the Exchange for approval.[119] A circular relating to the proposed purchase of 15 per cent or more of the issued share capital must include a statement that the working capital available to the company and its group is sufficient for present requirements or, if it is not, how it is proposed to provide the additional working capital.[120] This statement must be based on the assumption that the authority sought will be used in full at the maximum price stated, and this assumption must be stated.[121] Where a general authority is sought the circular must contain a statement from the directors regarding the use of the authority sought.[122] If the company has listed convertible securities which are convertible into, or carry a right to subscribe for, shares in the class which is to be purchased, the company must convene a separate meeting of the holders of the convertible securities and must obtain their approval by extraordinary resolution before any purchase contracts are entered into.[123] This requirement applies unless the terms on which those securities were issued expressly permit the company to acquire its own shares.

The Exchange also regulates the price at and manner in which a company purchases its own listed equity shares. Purchases by a company within a period of twelve months of less than 15 per cent of the shares may be made through the market if the price to be paid is not more than 5 per cent above the average of the market values of those shares for the ten business days preceding the purchase.[124] Purchases of more than 15 per cent must be made by way

[115] *The Listing Rules*, ch 15, para 15.3.
[116] Ibid, para 15.3.
[117] Ibid, para 15.9.
[118] Ibid, paras 15.4–15.5.
[119] Ibid, para 15.4, subject to para 15.2.
[120] Ibid, para 15.5.
[121] Ibid, para 15.5.
[122] Ibid, para 15.4 (a).
[123] Ibid, paras 15.10–15.11.
[124] Ibid, para 15.6. The ABI endorses this requirement.

of a tender or a partial offer to all shareholders.[125] A tender offer must be made on the Exchange at a stated maximum price or at a fixed price and notice of the offer must be given by advertisement in two national newspapers at least seven days before the offer closes.[126]

SHARE BUY BACKS AND INSIDER DEALING

The Listing Rules provide that a company may not purchase its own shares, either on or off market, at any time when, under the provisions of the Stock Exchange's Model Code (which regulates dealings in their company's securities by directors and certain employees[127]), a director of the company would be prohibited from dealing in its securities.[128] The effect of this is to stop a company purchasing its own listed equity shares when its directors are in possession of unpublished, price-sensitive information or in the period of up to two months immediately preceding the announcement of financial results. In this connection should also be noted the Criminal Justice Act 1993, ss 52–64 which render insider dealing in shares on a regulated market or through a professional intermediary a criminal offence punishable with up to seven-years' imprisonment. Legal persons such as companies cannot be guilty of insider dealing under this Act but the individual directors of a listed company could commit a criminal offence by procuring the purchase by the company of its own shares or by encouraging the company so to deal.

TAKEOVER CODE IMPLICATIONS OF SHARE BUY BACKS

The City Code on Takeovers and Mergers contains certain rules which are relevant to the purchase by a public[129] company of its own shares. Rule 37.3 addresses the use of the buy-back power as a defensive measure in a takeover situation. During the course of an offer, or even before the date of an offer if the board of the offeree company has reason to believe that a bona fide offer may be imminent, no redemption or purchase by the target company may be made unless it is approved by the shareholders in general meeting or it is in pursuance of a contract entered into earlier. The Panel may consent to purchases in other circumstances, for example where no formal contract has been concluded but the company nevertheless considers itself obliged to make a purchase.

The Takeover Code r 37.2 states that, subsequent to the redemption or purchase by a company of its own voting shares, all shareholders will be subject, in the making of acquisitions of shares in the company, to the provisions of r 9.1. Under r 9.1 a person who acquires 30 per cent of the voting rights in a company is generally obliged to make a general offer to shareholders. The

[125] Ibid, para 15.7. [126] Ibid, para 15.8. [127] Ibid ch 16 (App).

[128] Ibid, ch 15, para 15.1

[129] The *Takeover Code* can also apply to private companies but only where there have been public dealings in its shares in the preceding 10 years.

effect of r 37.2 is that a shareholder is not obliged to make a bid simply because the percentage size of his reaches 30 per cent as a consequence of the reduction in the total number of shares in issue by the buy back; but he will be obliged to bid if, after the buy back, he acquires shares that further increase the size of his holding. Exceptionally, where the purchase by the company of its own shares results in the increase of the shareholdings of directors and persons acting in concert with them, that increase, if it is to at least 30 per cent, does trigger r 9.1 without the need for any further acquisitions, although the Takeover Panel can be asked to waive the requirement to make a mandatory offer.[130]

As well as the *Takeover Code* itself, the Takeover Panel also applies *Rules governing the Substantial Acquisitions of Shares*. These rules regulate the timing and notification of acquisitions of shares and rights over shares carrying between 15 and 30 per cent of the voting rights of a company. The notification rules do not apply to changes in holdings resulting only from the purchase by a company of its own shares, but thereafter the rules apply on the basis of the company's latest published issued share capital.[131]

THE AUTHORISATIONS REQUIRED FOR AN ISSUE OF REDEEMABLE SHARES

A limited company which has a share capital is permitted by the Companies Act 1985, s 159 to issue redeemable shares provided this is authorised by the company's articles. The Companies Act 1985, s 159 permits shares which are to be redeemed or are liable to be redeemed at the option of the company or of the shareholder. Any class of shares may be issued as redeemable. This provision does not authorise the conversion of existing shares into redeemable form.

Table A to the Companies Act 1985, art 3 provides the relevant authorisation for the issue of redeemable shares by companies incorporated with that set of articles. It states that 'subject to the provisions of the Act, shares may be issued which are to be redeemed or are liable to be redeemed at the option of the company or the holder on such terms and in such manner as may be provided by the articles.' Table A does not make provision for the terms and manner of redemption and before making an issue of redeemable shares a company with Table A articles or with articles which follow that model would have to amend the articles to include the required provision. That the terms and manner of redemption of redeemable shares must be provided for in the company's articles and not simply in the terms of issue is required by the Companies Act 1985, s 160 (3).

The correct interpretation of the Companies Act 1985, s 160 (3) is a matter of some difficulty.[132] The issue is whether the details of the terms or manner of redemption must be specified precisely in the articles or whether it is sufficient for the articles simply to state that these details are to fixed by the direc-

[130] *The Takeover Code*, r 37.1

[131] *Substantial Acquisitions of Shares Rules*, r 3, n 2.

[132] This passage summarises a point that is discussed further in Ch 9, at 327–30.

tors at the time when the shares are issued. In *TNT Australia Pty Ltd v Normandy Resources NL*[133] general wording authorising the directors to fix the details at the time of issue of the redeemable shares was held to satisfy an identically-worded provision in Australian legislation. This is the interpretation that companies would prefer because it allows for fine-tuning of the terms on which shares are issued to reflect the market conditions at the time of issue. The alternative interpretation is inflexible because it would require the terms to be fixed far in advance of the issue date in order to be set out precisely in the circular sent with the notice convening the general meeting to consider the alteration to the articles; the normal minimum period of notice of a general meeting to consider a special resolution to change the articles is twenty-one days[134] and, in all but the smallest of companies, the convening of a meeting on short notice is unlikely to be practicable since this requires the consent of at least 95 per cent of those who are entitled to attend and vote at the meeting.[135] However, it is doubtful whether an English court could adopt the view which has found favour in Australia because of the obligation which falls on the court to consider the European dimension. The Second Company Law Directive, art 39 states that the terms and manner of redemption are to be 'laid down' in the company's statutes or instrument of incorporation. It seems that this may require the terms and manner of redemption to be expressly set out in the articles.

An attempt was made to clarify the position by a provision in the Companies Act 1989 which was intended to replace the Companies Act 1985, s 160 (3). Under this provision, the date on or by which, or the dates between which, the shares were to be or might be purchased had to be specified in the company's articles or, if the articles so provided, fixed by the directors before the shares were issued. The redemption price had also to be either specified in the articles or determined in accordance with a formula specified in the company's articles. This formula was not to depend on any person's discretion or opinion. Any other circumstances in which the shares were to be redeemed or any other terms and conditions of redemption were to be specified in the articles as well. This provision of the Companies Act 1989 is not to be brought into force because various difficulties have emerged since its enactment—for example, the requirement for a redemption date or period to be specified creates a problem for companies such as banks which are subject to capital adequacy requirements, because this results in the shares being treated less favourably for the purposes of those requirements.[136] The relevant provision of the Companies Act 1989 was inserted into the Bill at a relatively late stage and there was little opportunity for prior consultation. The speed with which

[133] *TNT Australia Pty Ltd v Normandy Resources NL* (1990) 1 ACSR 1, SA SC.

[134] Companies Act 1985, s 379 (2).

[135] A private company may elect to reduce the required percentage to 90 per cent by passing an elective resolution to that effect: Companies Act 1985, s 378 (3) (as amended). If the resolution is to be considered at the AGM all of the members entitled to attend and vote at the meeting must consent to short notice: Companies Act 1985, s 369 (3)(a).

[136] *Company Law Review: Terms and Manner of Redemption of Redeemable Shares. Sections 159A and 160(3) of the Companies Act 1985* (DTI Consultative Document) (1993).

the legislation was enacted in this case produced an unsatisfactory and uncertain result.

OTHER REQUIREMENTS OF THE COMPANIES ACT RELATING TO REDEMPTION OF REDEEMABLE SHARES

The provisions already considered in relation to the purchase of shares also apply, with appropriate contextual variations, to the redemption of redeemable shares. Redeemable shares may only be redeemed out of distributable profits or the proceeds of a fresh issue of shares made for the purpose of the redemption.[137] This is subject to the qualification that, in the circumstances considered earlier in relation to buy backs,[138] a private company may use its capital to redeem its shares.[139] Any redemption premium should usually be paid from distributable profits, but if the shares were issued at a premium the proceeds of a fresh issue can be applied for this purpose up to the aggregate of the premiums so received or the current amount of the company's share premium account whichever is the less.[140] Only fully-paid redeemable shares can be redeemed and the terms of redemption must provide for payment in full on redemption.[141] Redeemed shares must be cancelled, which has the effect of reducing the company's issued share capital; but the authorised share capital is unaffected.[142] Notice must be given to the registrar of companies of the redemption and cancellation of redeemable shares.[143]

If a company fails to redeem redeemable shares in accordance with their terms, the holder may seek specific performance but not damages. The court must not grant an order for specific performance if the company shows that it is unable to meet the costs of the redemption from its distributable profits.[144]

A company which has redeemable shares must include in the notes to its accounts details of the redemption dates and of any redemption premiums and must state whether the shares are to be redeemed in any event or are liable to be redeemed at the option of the company or of the shareholder.[145]

STOCK EXCHANGE REQUIREMENTS ON REDEMPTION

The Stock Exchange must be notified without delay of any redemption of listed securities.[146]

[137] Companies Act 1985, s 160 (1)(a).
[138] See above, at 446–7.
[139] Companies Act 1985, s 171.
[140] Ibid, s 160 (1)(b) and (2).
[141] Ibid, s 159 (3).
[142] Ibid, s 160 (4).
[143] Ibid, s 122 (1)(e) and (f).
[144] Ibid, s 178, which is discussed further in this chapter, at 445.
[145] Companies Act 1985, sch 4, para 38 (2).
[146] *The Listing Rules*, ch 9, para 9.10 (d).

SHARE BUY BACKS AND REDEEMABLE SHARES AND CLASS RIGHTS

Where a company's share capital comprises more than one class of shares, a proposal to buy back shares may amount to a variation of class rights. If it does, an appropriate class consent must be obtained in addition to the corporate consents considered in this chapter. An issue of redeemable shares may vary the class rights of existing preference shares which are entitled to priority on any return of capital and, again therefore, class consents may be required.[147]

The Association of British Insurers recommends that class meeting consent to a buy back of shares should be obtained in any case where a company has preference shares. This is a general recommendation and is not limited to instances where the buy back would amount to a variation in the rights attaching to the preference shares.

SHARE BUY BACKS AND REDEEMABLE SHARES AND PROTECTION OF MINORITIES

It would be open to a shareholder who objects to any aspect of the capital reorganisations discussed in this chapter to seek relief under the Companies Act 1985, s 459 on the grounds that the action amounts to unfairly prejudicial conduct. An unsuccessful claim arising from a proposal to buy back shares is *Rutherford, Petitioner*,[148] a decision of the Scottish Court of Session (Outer House). The company proposed to buy back a 33-per-cent interest in the company's shares. The purpose of this acquisition was to satisfy the view of most of the shareholders of the company that shareholdings should be widely spread and that there should be no dominant block of shares available to encourage individual shareholders to acquire a controlling interest. The petitioner averred that the company was proposing to pay too much for the shares because it was proposing to offer 64p per share even though the shares were trading in the market at 19p. The court held that a prima-facie case to this effect was not established on the facts, concluding that the transactions in which the shares had traded at around 19p probably involved small blocks of shares and that the value of the dominant block of shares would be likely to be materially more valuable. In this context it was held to be relevant that there was known to be an investment trust which was willing to pay up to 72p per share for a controlling interest in the company. Also, the proposed share purchase was designed to stabilise the management of the company which, the court concluded, might well elevate the price of the shares. The court held further that the petitioner would face problems in establishing the second claim, namely that the company was not in a position to fund the purchase and that interest payments on borrowings to finance the acquisition would exceed the

[147] The implications for class rights of share buy backs and issues of redeemable shares are considered in Ch 9 above, at 345–6.

[148] [1994] BCC 876 Ct of Sess.

company's annual profits. Thirdly, although the petitioner might further wish to allege that the purchase would have the effect of discouraging the investment trust which was willing to pay a premium for a controlling interest, the court thought that if this was what the majority of the shareholders wanted, it would be a fine question whether the petitioners' decreased chance of securing an offer from that bidder could be described as unfair. Taking all these factors into account in determining the balance of convenience, the court refused to grant the interdict (injunction) sought by the petitioner.

PART IV

LOAN CAPITAL

14

Debt Finance—General Considerations

FORMS OF DEBT FINANCE: OVERVIEW

The forms of corporate debt finance and the terms on which it is made available depend on agreement between borrower and lender. Provided they refrain from agreeing to something that is illegal, conceptually impossible[1] or contrary to public policy,[2] the law will give contractual effect to whatever bargain the parties arrive at. This provides great scope for variety and innovation in the corporate debt sector, but it also means that it is futile to attempt to provide an exhaustive account of all of the issues that may arise.[3] Instead, this chapter seeks to identify and consider the main points relating to unsecured debt finance, whilst the next two chapters look at the main issues arising in relation to secured debt and subordinated debt respectively.

Whilst bearing in mind that there is no closed list of the forms and terms of corporate finance, some of the main choices and structural considerations are as follows. A company may borrow from its banks, or from other lenders, on an unsecured or a secured basis. A company may secure lending facilities on which it can draw from time to time, an agreed overdraft facility being a familiar example of this type of lending arrangement,[4] or it may borrow a principal amount all at once or in agreed instalments. Interest will usually be charged on amounts borrowed and the company may also be required to pay commitment or negotiation fees in respect of lending facilities which have been made available. Interest rates may be fixed for the period of the loan or may be liable to be adjusted from time to time.[5] An alternative to interest charges is for a company to borrow less than the stated principal amount of a loan on terms that oblige it to repay the full principal amount. In this case, the discount

[1] But 'the courts should be very slow to declare a practice of the commercial community to be conceptually impossible': *Re Bank of Credit and Commerce International SA (No 8)* [1998] AC 214, HL, 228 *per* Lord Hoffmann.

[2] Historically, corporate capacity could have been another limiting factor, but the old rule that a company cannot enter into contracts that are not authorised by its memorandum (the *ultra vires* rule) has withered almost to the point of extinction. The decline of the *ultra vires* rule is considered in Ch 3 above, at 85–94.

[3] See further Wood, PR, *International Loans, Bonds and Securities Regulation* (1995) Pt 1.

[4] A more complex example is a revolving loan which enables the borrower to borrow, repay and re-borrow up to a maximum amount. A revolving loan differs from an overdraft in that it is not current account financing (and is not repayable on demand as an overdraft normally is). An ordinary term loan may allow for early repayment but will not provide for re-borrowing.

[5] Miles, D, 'Fixed and Floating-Rate Finance in the United Kingdom and Abroad', (1994) 34 *Bank of England Quarterly Bulletin*, 34, 38.

between the amount borrowed and the principal amount of the loan represents the return to the lender.[6]

The principal amount of a loan may be denominated in one currency or it may be divided into a number of portions each of which is denominated in a different currency. Principal may be repayable on demand or may be lent to the company for a set term but with provision for early repayment and for termination by the lender upon the occurrence of specified events of default. Principal may be required to be repaid in one lump sum or the agreement may provide for repayment by instalments. Loan agreements commonly contain covenants by which the company undertakes to meet performance targets, to refrain from certain activities and to provide the lender with information about its affairs. Covenants enable the lender to monitor the company while the loan is outstanding. Failure to comply with covenants will usually be an event of default which entitles the lender to terminate the loan. Other typical terms in loan agreements include conditions which must be satisfied before the company can obtain the money (or 'draw down' the funds, as this process is often referred to) and representations and warranties about the company and its affairs.

An individual bank or other lender may be unwilling to accept the whole of the risk involved in lending a very large sum of money to a company. In that event, provided the company is sufficiently creditworthy, it may still be able to obtain the required funds by entering into a syndicated loan agreement with a number of banks under which each bank in the syndicate contributes a proportion of the loan. Not surprisingly, it is normally only the largest corporate borrowers which require syndicated loans. Sovereign states and other public authorities also enter into syndicated loans.[7]

A company may also borrow from its directors or other insiders. This form of lending is most likely to be encountered in smaller or family-owned concerns where the directors and shareholders have a particularly strong personal interest in the company's affairs. Insider loans can give rise to particular points of note or concern. At one end of the spectrum, an insider loan may be made on much softer terms than would be available from a commercial lender—for example, the loan may be interest-free or may be made on the basis that the lender is to be subordinated to some or all of the company's other creditors.[8] At the other extreme, an insider may seek to exploit his position by requiring the company to accept exceptionally harsh or onerous terms, perhaps with a view to masking what is really an unlawful gift from capital by describing it as an 'interest charge'.[9]

As well as borrowing from banks or other lenders, companies can raise debt finance by issuing debt securities to investors. This form of financing is sometimes described as direct debt financing because a company raises its capital directly from the capital markets rather than going through lending interme-

[6] Megginson, WL, *Corporate Finance Theory* (1997) 404–5.

[7] On syndicated loans generally: Wood, PR, *International Loans, Bonds and Securities Regulation* (1995) ch 6; Cranston, R, *Principles of Banking Law* (1997) ch 2, V.

[8] Subordinated debt is considered in Ch 16.

[9] See, eg, *Ridge Securities Ltd v IR Comms* [1964] 1 All ER 275.

diaries. When a company borrows from a bank, it is receiving funds which the bank itself may have raised from the capital markets and, by cutting out the bank as middleman, the company may be able to secure debt finance at a cheaper rate than that offered by the bank or may be able to obtain fixed-rate funding when the bank was only willing to lend at variable rates.[10] Whatever savings there may be in interest charges have to be balanced against the significant administrative costs involved in making a public issue of securities.[11] Raising debt finance by issuing securities can also prove to be a more inflexible method of financing than bank borrowing. If circumstances change, a company may be able to renegotiate lending terms with its banks with minimum formality, but if the funds have been raised from the capital markets the process of varying the terms of the debt securities can be protracted and costly, especially if it involves the convening of a meeting of the holders of the securities to secure their consent to the variation.[12] Raising debt finance directly from the capital markets is unlikely to be a viable option for many recently-formed companies[13] or small concerns because they will not have the commercial reputation to attract investors unless they are willing to offer an exceptional rate of return which, when added to the administrative costs involved in making an issue of securities, will make this form of financing more costly than other financing options.

OVERDRAFTS

An overdraft is current account financing. It arises when a company draws on its current account to such an extent that a negative balance is produced. If the drawing which overdraws the account is met by the bank, the bank becomes the creditor of the company for the amount so overdrawn. An arrangement to overdraw up to a specified maximum amount would usually be agreed in advance between a company and its bank and the company may be required to pay a commitment fee for this facility. There is no implied term in the banker–customer relationship which permits a customer to overdraw, with the consequence that, in the absence of agreement to the contrary, the bank is not bound to meet any drawing which is not covered by funds in the

[10] Miles, D, 'Fixed and Floating-Rate Finance in the United Kingdom and Abroad', (1994) 34 *Bank of England Quarterly Bulletin*, 34.

[11] Another analysis is that bank-based financing is more efficient than financing via capital markets because banks have superior skills in collecting and monitoring information than other financial intermediaries or individual investors: Edwards, J, and Fischer, K, *Bank Finance and Investment in Germany* (1994) 35–42; Diamond, DW, 'Financial Intermediation and Delegated Monitoring' (1984) 51 *Review of Economic Studies* 393.

[12] The original terms may provide for the trustee to the issue to consent without the need for a meeting but that would only be usual in respect of minor changes.

[13] There are exceptions. For example, a special purpose vehicle company may be formed by an established company specifically in order to raise finance via an issue of debt securities. The vehicle's ability to meet interest and principal payment obligations may be secured through a variety of arrangements, such as bank guarantees, insurance policies and credit facilities and it is to these arrangements that investors will look to determine whether the issuer will be able to meet its obligations. In these circumstances the fact that the vehicle does not have a trading record is not significant.

account.[14] If a company makes an unauthorised drawing, this can be viewed conceptually as an offer by the company[15] and, if the bank meets the drawing, this constitutes an acceptance thus forming a contract between the company and the bank in respect of the overdraft.[16]

Just as a bank must pay any sums standing to the credit of a current account to the company whenever it demands it,[17] an overdraft is normally repayable on demand.[18] But, whatever its legal rights, as a matter of practice a bank would almost certainly exercise a degree of caution in demanding repayment of an overdraft in order to protect its commercial reputation:

> [I]t is obvious that neither party would have it in contemplation that when the bank had granted the overdraft it would immediately, without notice, proceed to sue for the money; and the truth is that whether there were any legal obligation to abstain from so doing or not, it is obvious that, having regard to the course of business, if a bank which had agreed to give an overdraft were to act in such a fashion, the results to its business would be of the most serious nature.[19]

What is meant by 'on demand'? According to the English cases all that the bank is required to do is to give the company time to effect the mechanics of payment, such as by arranging for the transfer of funds from one account to another. The bank is not obliged to give the customer time to raise funds which it does not have at the time when the demand is made. In *Cripps (Pharmaceutical) Ltd v Wickenden,*[20] the bank was held to be within its rights when it appointed a receiver to enforce its rights less than two hours after it had demanded repayment in circumstances where it was clear that the company did not have the money to pay. A delay of just one hour between the making of the demand and the sending in of the receivers has also been held to be justifiable.[21]

With regard to interest, it is usual for this to be calculated on the daily balance and then debited to the account on a periodic basis.[22] Once the interest

[14] *Cunliffe Brooks & Co v Blackburn Benefit Society* (1884) 9 App Cas 857, HL, 864 *per* Lord Blackburn; *Barclays Bank Ltd v WJ Simms Son & Cooke (Southern) Ltd* [1980] 1 QBD 699. An agreement to grant an overdraft may be inferred from a course of conduct: *Cumming v Shand* (1860) 5 H&N 95, 157 ER 1114.

[15] *Barclays Bank Ltd v WJ Simms Son & Cooke (Southern) Ltd* [1980]1 QBD 699; *Cuthbert v Robarts Lubbock & Co* [1909] 2 Ch 226, CA, 233 *per* Cozens Hardy MR.

[16] *Barclays Bank Ltd v WJ Simms Son & Cooke (Southern) Ltd* [1980] 1 QBD 699.

[17] *Walker v Bradford Old Bank* (1884) 12 QBD 511, 516 *per* Smith J; *Joachimson v Swiss Banking Corpn* [1921] 3 KB 110, CA.

[18] *Williams and Glyn's Bank v Barnes* [1981] Com LR 205, (1977–86) 10 Legal Decisions Affecting Bankers 220. But the parties can agree otherwise: *Williams and Glyn's Bank v Barnes* [1981] Com LR 205; *Titford Properties Co Ltd v Cannon Street Acceptances Ltd*, 22 May 1975, QBD (see Cresswell, PJ, Blair, WJL, Hill, GJS, and Wood, PR, *Encyclopaedia of Banking Law* (1982, looseleaf) div C paras 501–6); *Cryne v Barclays Bank plc* [1987] BCLC 548 CA.

[19] *Rouse v Bradford Banking Co* [1894] AC 586, HL, 596 *per* Lord Herschell LC.

[20] [1973] 1 WLR 944.

[21] *Bank of Baroda v Panessar* [1986] 3 All ER 751, noted Kay, JD, ' "On Demand" Liabilities' [1986] 4 JIBL 241 where reference is made to a number of Commonwealth cases which appear to be more generous to the borrower by allowing it a reasonable time to repay; *Sheppard & Cooper Ltd v TSB Bank plc* [1996] 2 All ER 654.

[22] *Reddie v Williamson* (1863) 1 Macph 228; *Parr's Banking Co Ltd v Yates* [1898] 2 QB 460, CA; *Yourell v Hibernian Bank Ltd* [1918] AC 372, HL, 385 *per* Lord Atkinson; *Inland Revenue Commissioners v Holder* [1931] 2 KB 81, CA, 96 *per* Lord Hanworth MR and 98 *per* Romer LJ; *Paton v Inland Revenue Commissioners* [1938] AC 341, HL.

has been debited to the account it is capitalised and thereafter interest is charged on an amount including the capitalised interest. The banking practice of charging compound interest is well-established. In *National Bank of Greece SA v Pinios Shipping Co (No 1)*,[23] where the authorities were reviewed by the House of Lords, Lord Goff, delivering the only reasoned speech, held that this practice was a general banking usage which would be implied into all contracts between banks and customers who borrowed from them unless otherwise agreed and that it continued to apply even after the bank had made a demand for repayment.[24] The cases clearly establish that the usage applies where capitalisation is to be effected at either yearly or half-yearly intervals, but whether an entitlement to capitalise on a more frequent basis can be implied was left open in the *Pinios* case because counsel conceded that the bank was entitled to capitalise interest at quarterly intervals. The practice of making express provision for the charging of compound interest and for the frequency of capitalisation has received judicial endorsement: '[Banks] should make express provisions for compound interest in their contracts. Since the repeal of the Usury Acts there has been nothing to stop them'.[25]

When money is paid into a bank account which is in debit, unless the parties have reached a contrary agreement, it is treated as discharging the earlier debit items. Applying this rule to the following facts:

- 1 January, company's current account has a debit balance of £200,000
- 15 January, the company draws on the overdraft facility for a further £150,000
- 30 January, £250,000 is paid into the account

the position is that, first, the whole of the £200,000 that was outstanding on 1 January is to be regarded as having been repaid and, second, £50,000 of the amount borrowed on 15 January is also to be treated as having been repaid; the balance of the amount borrowed on 15 January remains outstanding. This rule of appropriation of payment was established in *Devaynes v Noble; Clayton's Case*[26] and it is commonly referred to as the rule in *Clayton's Case*. It can be relevant where, for example, a bank takes security for an existing overdrawn account and the company then continues to draw on, and make payments into, that account because under the insolvency legislation a security can be held to be invalid if it is given in respect of moneys previously advanced to the borrower. The rule in *Clayton's Case* will determine whether the balance outstanding on the account at the time when the insolvency legislation falls to be applied represents new money advanced after the security was granted, in which case the security will be valid, or old money which had been lent to the

[23] [1990] 1 AC 637, HL.

[24] Thereby reversing the decision of the Court of Appeal which had held that the usage was limited to 'mercantile accounts for mutual transactions' and that it ceased to apply when the bank demanded repayment.

[25] *National Bank of Greece SA v Pinios Shipping Co (No 1)* [1990] 1 AC 637, CA and HL 659 *per* Lloyd LJ. Although the Court of Appeal's decision was reversed by the House of Lords this comment is unaffected.

[26] (1816) 1 Mer 572, 35 ER 781.

company before the security was created, in which case the security may be invalid.[27]

Small and medium businesses that require external finance rely heavily on overdraft facilities. It is debatable how far this reflects the preferences of those who run smaller businesses, who may be attracted to overdraft financing because it is simple, flexible and does not require them to surrender equity, and how far it is a function of the limited range of financing options that are offered by banks to smaller businesses and the banks' preference for on-demand financing.[28]

TERM LOANS[29]

Term loans are, as the name implies, loans for a specified period. A distinction is often drawn in practice between short-term loans (which is generally used to mean loans of up to one year), medium-term loans (between one and five years) and long-term loans (between five and ten years, or perhaps even longer).

Principal

The primary operative term of a term loan agreement is the one specifying the principal amount of the loan, the currency, or currencies, in which it is denominated[30] and the way in which it is to be made available to the borrower. The full amount of the loan may be made available to the borrower at one time or the agreement may provide for the borrower to be entitled to draw down successive tranches of the loan at, or by, specified times. The period during which the borrower is entitled to draw down (the 'availability period') may be limited so that, at the end of the period, the lender is no longer obliged to lend and any undrawn portion of the loan is no longer available to the borrower. With regard to repayment, the agreement may provide for repayment of the whole loan at one time (commonly known as bullet repayment) or for repayment in instalments over a period of time (sometimes described as amortised repayment). An instalment repayment obligation is a mechanism that allows a lender to detect early signs of a borrower's financial difficulties.[31] The borrower may be granted an option to repay early and in any well-drafted agreement the lender will be entitled to demand early repayment in the event of the occurrence of any one of a number of specified events of default. Can

[27] See Insolvency Act 1986, s 245 and the application of the rule in *Clayton's Case* in *Re Yeovil Glove Co Ltd* [1965] Ch 148, CA.

[28] Charkham, J, *Keeping Good Company* (1995) 297–8; Hughes, A, 'The "Problems" of Finance for Smaller Businesses' in Dimsdale, N, and Prevezer, M (eds), *Capital Markets and Corporate Governance* (1994) 209; Hughes, A, 'Finance for SMEs: A UK Perspective' (1997) 9 *Small Business Economics* 151.

[29] For precedents of a simple loan letter and more complex facilities see Talbot, R (ed), *Practical Lending and Security Documents* (1992, looseleaf) div A.

[30] With regard to repayment of loans denominated in a foreign currency, see Tennekoon, R, *The Law and Regulation of International Finance* (1991) 73–4.

[31] Megginson, WL, *Corporate Finance Theory* (1997) 405.

the lender insert a term to the effect that the principal amount is to be repayable on demand? Such a provision would seem to be incompatible with the nature of a term loan, the essence of which is that the loan will be made available to the borrower for a given period and, in accordance with accepted principles, a primary term should prevail over a contrary subsidiary term.[32] The lender can, however, seek to protect its interests by drafting very extensive events of default and it will then become a matter of negotiation as to whether the borrower is prepared to accept these terms.

If a lender refuses to lend in breach of contract, the borrowing company is entitled to damages. If the company can secure broadly the same lending terms from another lender the damages may be little[33] more than nominal but if, say, the first lender had agreed to an exceptionally low rate of interest the damages could be more substantial. In *South African Territories v Wallington*[34] the House of Lords refused to grant specific performance of a contract to lend money to a company. This ruling is consistent with the general rule that specific performance will not be ordered where damages are an adequate remedy,[35] but with this decision must now also be read the Companies Act 1985, s 195. This provision, which was first introduced into the companies legislation after the *Wallington* decision,[36] provides that a contract with a company to take up and pay for debentures of a company may be enforced by an order for specific performance. The term 'debenture' has no hard and fast meaning,[37] although a commonly cited description is that it encompasses any document which creates or acknowledges a debt.[38] It is debatable whether a loan agreement can be said to create or acknowledge a

[32] *Titford Properties Co Ltd v Cannon Street Acceptances Ltd*, 22 May 1987, QBD (see Cresswell, PJ, Blair, WJL, Hill, GJS, and Wood, PR, *Encyclopaedia of Banking Law* (1982, looseleaf) div C para 503); see also Hapgood, M, *Paget's Law of Banking* (11th edn, 1996) 167.

[33] The costs of negotiating a substitute loan may be recoverable: *Prehn v Royal Bank of Liverpool* (1870) LR 5 Exch 92.

[34] [1898] AC 309, HL. Also *Western Wagon and Property Co v West* [1892] 1 Ch 271, 275 *per* Chitty J; *Rogers v Challis* (1859) 27 Beav 175, 54 ER 68; *Sichel v Mosenthal* (1862) 30 Beav 371, 54 ER 932.

[35] Jones, G, and Goodhart, W, *Specific Performance* (2nd edn, 1996) 154–61 where the general principle is described as 'arguably too harsh' (155) and various recognised exceptions are discussed. See also Spry, *Equitable Remedies* (5th edn, 1997) 70–4 and *Loan Investment Corporation of Australasia v Bonner* [1970] NZLR 724, PC, 741–2 *per* Sir Garwick Berwick (dissenting) where the possibility of an order for specific performance of an obligation to lend being granted in exceptional circumstances was envisaged.

[36] Companies Act 1907, s 16.

[37] Companies Act 1985, s 744 lists various instruments which are debentures but does not contain an exhaustive definition of the term (s 744 applies only unless the contrary intention appears). This section does make clear that the term 'debenture' is not confined to secured loans. See also Financial Services Act 1986, sch 1, para 2 which lists various instruments which are included within, or excluded from the category of 'debenture'. The courts have frequently acknowledged the absence of a precise definition: see, eg, *British India Steam Navigation Co v Commissioners of Inland Revenue* [1881] 7 QBD 165; *Knightsbridge Estates Trust Ltd v Byrne* [1940] AC 613 HL, 621 *per* Viscount Maugham; *NV Slavenburg's Bank v Intercontinental Natural Resources Ltd* [1980] 1 All ER 955, 976. The absence of a precise definition has given rise to few practical problems: *Re SH & Co (Realisations) 1990 Ltd* [1993] BCC 60, 67 quoting Gower, LCB, *Principles of Modern Company Law* (5th edn, 1992) 379.

[38] *Levy v Abercorris Slate and Slab Co* (1887) 37 Ch D 260. See also *Edmonds v Blaina Furnaces Co* (1887) 36 Ch D 215; *Lemon v Austin Friars Investment Trust Ltd* [1926] 1 Ch 1, CA; *Knightsbridge Estates Trust v Byrne* [1940] AC 613, HL; *R v Findlater* [1939] 1 KB 594, CCA.

debt because in normal circumstances the debt is not actually created until after the agreement is concluded and the money is advanced. Another view is that an instrument containing a promise to pay can be a debenture.[39] This description would catch a loan agreement since it contains a promise by the borrower to repay the principal and also, usually, a promise to pay interest at specified intervals. However, it is suggested that for the purposes of the Companies Act 1985, s 195, the term 'debenture' should be more narrowly defined and should be limited to debt securities issued directly to investors and which can be traded by them.[40] This interpretation is based on the reference in that section to taking up and paying for debentures. Those words are apt to describe an investor's decision to acquire debt securities issued to the market but they do not easily fit a promise in a loan agreement to lend money. Also the context of the chapter of the Companies Act 1985 in which s 195 appears suggests that it is concerned only with debt securities issued to investors and not with loan agreements negotiated between companies and banks or other lenders.[41]

It is unlikely that a borrower would not draw down the loan having gone to the trouble of arranging it. Should this occur, it will be a matter of construction to determine whether the borrower was obliged to draw down or had simply acquired an option to do so. Even if the borrower is in breach of contract, in accordance with the general principle that specific performance of contracts to lend money will not be ordered, the lender's remedy will lie only in damages and these are likely to be minimal.[42]

In the absence of any provision to the contrary, it is unclear whether a borrower can make early repayments of borrowed money[43] but express provisions regarding early repayment are commonly included. These provisions typically require the borrower to give notice of an intended early repayment and to make the repayment on a specified date such as the last day of an interest period. Restrictions on early repayment are usually closely linked to the lender's own financing commitments. Banks themselves borrow in order to lend to their customers and this borrowing is usually done on a short-term basis on the inter-bank lending market. The short-term nature of that market means that refinancing takes place at regular intervals. By structuring its loan agreements so as to ensure that repayment is only permitted at the time when it is required to re-finance (which, for reasons discussed in the following sec-

[39] *British India Steam Navigation Co v Commissioners of Inland Revenue* [1881] 7 QBD 165, 173 *per* Lindley J. The court was required to determine whether the instrument was a debenture or a promissory note for stamping purposes.

[40] Tradability by itself does not provide the key to distinguishing between what is and is not within the scope of the term 'debenture' for the purposes of Companies Act 1985, s 195 since there are secondary markets in lenders' participations in loan agreements: Goodman, L, 'Selling Loan Participations: Impact of the Financial Services Act' (1988) 3 BJIB&FL 418.

[41] See further, Tennekoon, R, *The Law and Regulation of International Finance* (1991) 125–7; contrast Berg, A, 'Syndicated Lending and the FSA' (1991) 10 (1) IFLR 27.

[42] *Rogers v Challis* (1859) 27 Beav 175, 54 ER 68.

[43] The Australian courts have held that a borrower does not have the right to repay early unless this is provided for expressly: *Hyde Management Services (Pty) Ltd v FAI Insurances* (1979–80) 144 CLR 541, H Ct of Aust. It has also been held in England that an issuer of debt securities cannot redeem them early unless the terms of issue provide for this: *Hooper v Western Counties and South Wales Telephone Co Ltd* (1892) 68 LT 78.

tion, normally coincides with the end of an interest period), a bank seeks to avoid finding itself in a situation where it has to pay interest to its lenders but it is not earning interest because its borrower has repaid. It is usual to provide that any amount prepaid is to be applied to the repayment instalments in inverse order to their maturity. This has the effect of shortening the life of the loan.

Interest

In the absence of express agreement to the contrary or some course of dealing or custom to such effect, interest is not payable on a bank loan.[44] This point is of limited practical significance since loan agreements almost invariably make express provision for interest charges. Since the Usury Laws Repeal Act 1954, there is no statutory control with regard to interest rates charged to companies (the provisions of the Consumer Credit Act 1974 attacking 'extortionate credit bargains' apply only in favour of individuals). The rate of interest may be fixed for the term of the loan or, as is common, may be variable (or 'floating') over the life of the loan. It is theoretically possible to provide for interest to be variable entirely at the discretion of the lender,[45] but borrowers with sufficient negotiating strength would be likely to resist agreeing to this degree of uncertainty. Floating-rate loan agreements commonly provide for the interest rate to be adjusted at specified intervals (for example, three or six monthly[46]) by reference to a formula which is intended to maintain the lender's return on the loan.

The money which a bank lends to its borrowing customers may be its own money (share capital and reserves) or it may be money which it has borrowed either from depositors (the relationship between banks and depositing customers being one of debtor and creditor) or from other lenders. Banks can borrow in the inter-bank market by taking in short-term deposits. Such deposits are made for short specific periods, typically three or six months and they bear interest at a fixed rate. LIBOR, the London Inter-Bank Offered Rate, denotes the rate at which such deposits are available from time to time in the London markets. This is just one of the interest bases that may be used for calculating floating interest rates in loan agreements but it suffices for the purposes of illustration. Where a bank takes deposits in the inter-bank market and then makes a term loan to a borrower, there is an obvious mismatch between the bank's obligation to repay the deposit, in three- or six-months' time, and its rights to claim repayment in what may be many years' time: it has borrowed short to lend long. One of the ways of managing the consequences of this mismatch is for the bank to adjust the rate of interest which the borrower is required to pay to reflect LIBOR on each occasion when it is required

[44] *Chatham & Dover Rly v South East Rly* [1893] AC 429, HL.

[45] This is established practice in the UK in respect of loans to individuals for house purchase. In practice lenders in the domestic housing market operate under competitive pressures which inhibit excessive or unreasonable practices with regard to interest-rate setting, although the effectiveness of these market constraints has been questioned by the Law Commission: *Land Mortgages* (Law Commission Report No 204) (1991).

[46] The frequency of adjustment may be at the option of the borrower.

to refinance in the inter-bank market. To achieve this, the agreement should provide for the borrower to pay interest at a rate equivalent to LIBOR from time to time[47] plus an additional margin which is set at the outset and which is the bank's return on the transaction. This structure enables the bank to pass its funding costs through to the borrower.

There are various ways in which a lender may seek to protect its interests against the possibility of the company failing to make an interest payment when it is due. Failure to pay any sum, representing either interest or principal, which is due and payable is the first event of default in a typical loan agreement. Such an agreement will provide that, upon the occurrence of an event of default, the lender is entitled to terminate the agreement, to demand repayment of principal, interest and any other sums payable pursuant to the agreement, and to cancel any facilities which remain outstanding. The occurrence of an event of default thus does not, in itself, terminate the agreement but it gives the lender an option to do so.[48] The courts have a jurisdiction to hold unenforceable a contractual term which amounts to a penalty clause intended to punish the party in breach. However, it is clear that a contractual provision which entitles the lender to terminate the agreement if the borrower fails to make an interest payment when due is not a penalty clause. [49]

The rules on penalty clauses are potentially more relevant in relation to provisions which seek to impose a higher rate of interest if the borrower defaults on making a payment when due. A penalty clause is to be distinguished from a provision for liquidated damages. Into which category a particular agreement falls is a question of construction and the label attached by the parties is not conclusive.[50] In the leading case on penalties it was said that one of the indicia of a penalty was where the breach consisted only in not paying a sum of money and the sum stipulated was greater than the sum which ought to have been paid.[51] Concern that this could catch a provision for default interest led to the development of structures that achieved the same economic effect as default interest but adopted a different legal form precisely in order to fall outside the penalty clause jurisdiction. Such arrangements were held to be legally effective in a number of cases. Thus it was held that a provision specifying a high rate of interest and providing for it to be reduced to a lower specified rate in the event of punctual payment was effective even though there was no difference in substance between this and a default interest clause.[52] Another rather technical and fine distinction was upheld in *General*

[47] LIBOR is not a published rate and the loan agreement will have to include provision for how this is to be determined.

[48] This is in accordance with established general contractual principles: *Decro-Wall International SA v Practitioners in Marketing Ltd* [1971] 1 WLR 361, CA; *Photo Production Ltd v Securicor Transport Ltd* [1980] AC 827, HL.

[49] *Keene v Biscoe* (1878) 8 Ch D 201; *Wallingford v Mutual Society* (1880) 5 App Case 685, HL; *Oresundsvarvet Aktiebolag v Marcos Diamantis Lemos, The Angelic Star* [1988] 1 Lloyd's Rep 122, CA.

[50] *Dunlop Pneumatic Tyre Co Ltd v New Garage and Motor Co Ltd* [1915] AC 79, HL.

[51] Ibid at 87 *per* Lord Dunedin.

[52] *Wallingford v Mutual Society* (1880) 5 App Cas 685, HL, 702 *per* Lord Hatherley; *Herbert v Salisbury and Yeovil Railway Co* (1866) 2 LR Eq 221, 224 *per* Lord Romilly MR.

Credit and Discount Co v Glegg.[53] In this case the terms of an interest bearing loan provided for repayment by instalments. If default was made in the payment of any instalment at the due date there was also to be paid a 'commission' of 1 per cent upon what ought to have been paid for every month or part of a month from the due date to the date of payment of such instalment. This arrangement was held to be a distinct, separate, substantive contract to pay something in the event of default and not an agreement in the nature of a penalty. The court gave effect to the agreement as drafted and did not treat the commission simply as a device intended to allow the lender to increase the rate of interest on default.

The effect of default interest clauses under English law was reviewed under modern conditions in *Lordsvale Finance plc v Bank of Zambia.*[54] The court held that a provision for default interest was not an invalid penalty where it operated only with effect from the event of default and provided that the increase in the interest rate was no more than sufficient to compensate the lender for its additional funding costs and the increased credit risk involved in lending to a defaulting borrower. Apparently inconsistent older cases were distinguished[55] on the grounds that they concerned default interest clauses that operate retrospectively as well as prospectively from the date of default. The *Lordsvale* decision clarifies English law and brings it into line with that in the USA, Canada and Australia.[56]

Another way in which unpaid interest may be dealt with in a loan agreement is for the amount of the interest to be added to the principal. Thereafter interest will be charged on a sum which comprises the original amount of the principal plus the amount of the capitalised interest. The charging of compound interest is standard practice and provision for this does not constitute a penalty.[57]

Conditions Precedent

A loan agreement may require the borrower to satisfy various conditions before it can draw down the funds. For example, the company may be required to supply the lender with copies of its constitutional documents and relevant board resolutions. The purpose of this requirement is to enable the lender to check that the loan is duly authorised. This practice may not now be strictly necessary where the borrower is incorporated under the English companies legislation, given that lenders are largely protected against the lack of authorisation by the provisions of the Companies Act 1985 that operate in conjunction with established agency principles and with the rule of company law known as the internal management rule, which protects outsiders against

53 (1883) 22 Ch D 549.

54 [1996] QB 752.

55 *Holles v Vyse* (1693) 2 Vern 289, 23 ER 787; *Hunter v Seton* (1802) 7 Ves 265, 32 ER 108. In *Herbert v Salisbury and Yeovil Railway Co* (1866) 2 LR Eq 221, 224 Lord Romilly MR said: 'but if the mortgage interest is at 4 per cent, and there is an agreement that if it is not paid punctually 5 or 6 per cent interest shall be paid, that is in the nature of a penalty which this Court will relieve against'.

56 *Lordsvale Finance plc v Bank of Zambia* [1996] QB 752, 765–7.

57 *National Bank of Greece SA v Pinios Shipping Co (No 1)* [1990] 1 AC 637, HL.

internal irregularities (for example the lack of a quorum at relevant board meetings) unless they are put on notice to the contrary.[58] However, there is still something to be said for maintaining a policy of checking in advance that the loan is duly authorised because of the greater certainty that this affords; whilst the statutory protections given to persons who deal with companies are now very extensive, there would be a risk that a borrower or its liquidator (insolvency being a particular situation in which a borrower may be especially keen to escape from its obligations) might seek to challenge their application in a particular case, thereby delaying repayment. Another common condition precedent is for the borrower to be required to confirm that no events of default have occurred and that the representations and warranties are true and accurate.

The lender is only obliged to make the funds available when the borrower has fulfilled the specified conditions precedent. Can the lender withdraw completely from the agreement before the borrower has had an opportunity to satisfy those requirements? This will depend on the way the agreement is drafted.[59] The cases indicate that the effect of including conditions precedent in an agreement can, depending on the drafting, include the following: (i) the agreement is not fully binding until the conditions are fulfilled and until then either party can withdraw with impunity;[60] (ii) the main agreement is not binding but, so long as the events constituting the conditions precedent can still occur, one (or both) of the parties cannot withdraw;[61] (iii) the main agreement is not binding but neither party must do anything to prevent the occurrence of the events[62] or one of the parties undertakes to make reasonable endeavours to bring about the events.[63]

Representations and Warranties

Loan agreements commonly contain representation and warranties covering such matters as:

- the capacity of the company and the authority of its directors and officers to enter into the loan agreement;
- compliance with applicable laws and regulations;
- compliance with other contractual obligations of the company: the lender will be concerned to ensure that this loan will not, for example, trigger default under another loan agreement in which the company has covenanted to limit the amount of its borrowings;
- the accuracy of the information about the borrower that was supplied to the lender during the course of the negotiations, including confirmation that no

[58] *Royal British Bank v Turquand* (1865) 6 E&B 327, 119 ER 327; *Mahoney v East Holyford Mining Co* (1875) LR 7 HL 869. The internal management rule is discussed further in Ch 3 above, at 98–9.

[59] *Total Gas Marketing Ltd v Arco British Ltd* [1998] 2 Lloyd's Rep 209, HL; Cranston, R, *Principles of Banking Law* (1997) 339–40.

[60] *Pym v Campbell* (1856) 6 E & B 370, 119 ER 903.

[61] *Smith v Butler* [1900] 1 QB 694, CA.

[62] *Mackay v Dick* (1881) 6 App Cas 251, HL.

[63] *Hargreaves Transport Ltd v Lynch* [1969] 1 WLR 215, CA.

facts or circumstances have been omitted so as to render the information that was supplied misleading;

- the financial position of the borrower: representations and warranties on this matter would commonly take the form of a statement from the borrower to the effect that its last audited accounts represent a true and fair view of its financial position and that there has been no material adverse change since they were prepared;
- claims against the borrower: ie whether any litigation is pending or threatened which might have a material adverse effect on the borrower or on its ability to perform its obligations under the loan agreement;
- whether any event of default has occurred;
- the existing security arrangements into which the borrower has entered, including hire purchase agreement, conditional sales, factoring agreements and guarantees.

If the borrower is a holding company, representations and warranties may also relate to the other companies in its group.

Representations and warranties perform an investigative function.[64] In the negotiations leading up to the signing of the loan agreement the borrower will need to disclose any information that is inconsistent with the representations and warranties that are to be included in the agreement or risk being held liable thereafter for breach. This helps to extend the lender's knowledge and understanding of the borrowing entity. The representations and warranties that are finally agreed seek to encapsulate the factual circumstances in reliance on which the lender makes its decision to lend. As such, the truth of the matters contained in the representations and warranties is likely to remain important to a lender throughout the life of a loan and for this reason it may require the borrower to repeat the representations and warranties at specified intervals. A situation in which a lender would be likely to attach particular importance to the repetition of representations and warranties is where the loan is to be available to the borrower in instalments: the lender may require the borrower to repeat the representations and warranties before each drawing is made. Repetition can be required at more frequent intervals, for example at the beginning of each interest period. The way in which repetition will normally be effected is by a provision in the loan agreement to the effect that there is deemed repetition at the specified intervals. Representations and warranties which are required to be repeated at specified intervals are sometimes described as 'evergreen'.

Under the general law relating to liability for statements, the term 'representation' is used to denote a statement of fact which induces an innocent party to enter into a contract and which, if it is later discovered to have been untrue, gives the innocent party a remedy for misrepresentation. A 'warranty' is a contractual statement which, if untrue, allows the innocent party to sue for breach of contract; generally,[65] 'warranty' is used in contradistinction to

64 Wood, PR, *International Loans, Bonds and Securities Regulation* (1995) 29.

65 The term 'warranty' can also be used to describe an agreement which is collateral to another contract between the same parties. Breach of collateral warranty may lead to an action for damages or may be a ground on which the court refuses specific performance of the main contract. See generally Wedderburn, KW, 'Collateral Contracts' [1959] CLJ 58.

'condition' to describe a term which, if breached, allows for a claim for damages but does not entitle the innocent party to terminate the agreement. The need for detailed analysis of these technicalities is avoided in well-drafted loan agreements by stipulating expressly that it is an event of default to make a representation or warranty which is incorrect or, allowing some leeway to the borrower, which is incorrect in any material respect. If there is an event of default, the lender can call for repayment of the whole loan at once and can sue in debt for the amount due under the agreement if the borrower refuses to pay.

Covenants

The function of the covenants in a loan agreement is to seek to restrict the borrower in the conduct of its business and to give the lender some control over the way in which that business is managed. They aim to ensure that the borrower's credit rating does not decline whilst the loan is outstanding. Covenants divide, broadly, into things that the borrower promises to do (positive covenants) and things that it promises to refrain from doing (negative covenants).[66] The underlying aim is to ensure that the borrower remains able to fulfil its obligations under the loan and does not engage in conduct which would prejudice that ability. Covenants relating to the following matters are commonly included in loan agreements:

- provision of information: the borrower must supply the lender with copies of its annual audited accounts and interim financial statements (including consolidated accounts where relevant), any communications sent to the borrower's shareholders, and any other information that the lender reasonably requires;
- events of default: the borrower must notify the lender of the occurrence of an event of default or of any other event which, with the giving of notice or passage of time, would constitute an event of default;
- working capital: the borrower must ensure that its current assets exceed its current liabilities (or, where relevant, group assets and liabilities) by a specified multiple and that the ratio of current assets to current liabilities does not fall below a specified minimum;
- tangible net worth: the borrower must ensure that its (or, where relevant, its group's) paid-up share capital and reserves exceed a specified figure and that the ratio between total liabilities and total net worth (consolidated where appropriate) does not fall below a specified minimum;
- distributions: the borrower must ensure that dividends and other distributions to shareholders do not exceed a specified percentage of the company's net profits;
- disposal of assets or change of business: the borrower must not dispose of any substantial part of its undertaking or, except in the ordinary course of business, assets unless it has the lender's consent; similarly it must not, without the lender's consent, change the scope or nature of its business in a

[66] Megginson, WL, *Corporate Finance Theory* (1997) 407.

way that would have a material adverse effect on its business, assets or financial condition; if the borrower is a holding company, it may be required to undertake to procure, so far as it is able to do so,[67] that other companies within its group also abide by this covenant but the covenant, may be qualified so as to permit some intra-group transfers of assets;

- creation of security: the borrower must not create any further security over the whole or any part of its undertaking or assets without the consent of the lender (and, where relevant, the borrower may be required to undertake to procure so far as it can do so that other companies in its group will also abide by this covenant); the covenant may extend to increasing the amount secured by existing securities, entering into hire purchase, conditional sales, factoring and similar agreements, and to the giving of guarantees.

The covenants that are actually included in a particular loan agreement will depend on a number of factors including the negotiating strength of the borrowing company, the amounts involved (a lender which is advancing a relatively small amount may attach less importance to covenants than a lender which is taking a large exposure), the rate of interest (a high interest rate may compensate the lender for fewer covenants), the intended duration of the loan, whether it is to be secured or unsecured, and whether it is a bank loan or an issue of securities.[68] But even if a borrower would be willing to accept severe restrictions (or, perhaps more accurately, lack the negotiating strength to resist them), a lender might hesitate to impose them because this could backfire: if the covenants are too restrictive they may impede the borrower's operations to such an extent that its financial position is undermined rather than preserved so that, in an extreme case, its ability to meet its obligations under the loan comes under threat.[69] This issue has generated discussion, especially in relation to the drafting of terms attaching to publicly issued debt securities.[70] The potential difficulties arise most sharply in that context

[67] A parent may not have sufficient control over the operations of its subsidiary undertakings to ensure that the covenant will be complied with. The meaning of 'subsidiary undertaking' is considered further in Ch 1 above, at 27–30.

[68] Wood, PR, *International Loans, Bonds and Securities Regulation* (1995) 31; Day, J, and Taylor, P, 'Evidence on the Practice of UK Bankers in Contracting for Medium-Term Debt' [1995] 9 JIBL 394; Day, J, and Taylor, P, 'Bankers' Perspectives on the Role of Covenants in Debt Contracts' [1996] 5 JIBL 201. Wider considerations arising from market and economic conditions may also over time cause lenders to vary their perception of the importance of particular covenants: Bratton, WW, 'Corporate Debt Relationships: Legal Theory in a Time of Restructuring' [1989] Duke Law Journal 135; McDaniel, MV, 'Bondholders and Corporate Governance' (1986) 41 Business Lawyer 413; Boardman, NP, and Crosthwait, JL, 'Wither the Negative Pledge?' [1986] 3 JIBL 162; McDaniel, MV, 'Are Negative Pledge Clauses in Public Debt Issues Obsolete?' (1983) 38 Business Lawyer 867.

[69] Lister, RJ, 'Debenture Covenants and Corporate Value' (1985) 6 Co Law 209. The lender's commercial reputation may also suffer and in a competitive lending market its ability to attract new business may be undermined: Fischel, DR, 'The Economics of Lender Liability' (1989) 99 Yale Law Journal 131, 138–9.

[70] In the United States the work of the American Bar Foundation in sponsoring the development of standardised forms of debenture indentures (an indenture being the contract entered into between the issuing company and the holders of securities) has provided a focus for this debate: see Brudney, V, and Bratton, WW, *Brudney and Chirelstein's Corporate Finance*, (4th edn, 1993) 187–93. For an economic analysis of covenants see Smith, CW, and Warner, JB, 'On Financial Contracting: An Analysis of Bond Covenants' (1979) 7 *Journal of Financial Economics* 117.

because if the terms originally drafted prove to be too restrictive, the process of obtaining a relaxation may be particularly cumbersome, time-consuming and expensive as it may require the convening of a special meeting of the holders of the securities for that purpose.[71] If the terms of a loan agreement between a company and its bank prove to be too restrictive, the relaxation process, either by way of the banks consenting to occasional transactions or by way of a formal variation to the contractual terms, may be relatively straightforward. But it may be overly simplistic to draw a sharp line between debt securities and loan agreements;[72] for example, a syndicated loan involving a number of lending banks could give rise to administrative difficulties similar to, if not as severe as, those which could be encountered in the context of debt securities and, conversely, there could be situations in which an issue of debt securities has been privately placed and is held entirely by a small, and easily contactable, group of investors. Even in a straightforward case involving a loan from a single bank the debate about the approach to the drafting of covenants has relevance since it is clearly advantageous to establish from the outset a workable framework which balances the interests of the lender in minimising the risks involved in lending and the borrower's need for sufficient freedom to run its business effectively.

Reporting Covenants

Reporting covenants which require the borrower to supply the lender with copies of accounts and other information are important to the lender because they facilitate the task of monitoring the company's affairs on an ongoing basis. Information covenants supplement the disclosure of financial information and audit requirements of the Companies Act 1985 and, in relation to listed companies, *The Listing Rules*,[73] but they may be more extensive than those requirements or may require information to be updated more regularly or more swiftly. It is clearly vital for the lender to have early notice of the occurrence of an event of default so that it can consider its position and it is not unreasonable to require the borrower to notify the lender when it is in default. A requirement to notify the lender of impending events of default may create some uncertainty.

Financial Covenants

Financial covenants seek to ensure that the borrower's solvency will be maintained and that the borrower will not become too heavily dependent on debt finance: the thinking is that it will be able to pay its debts as they fall due (cash-flow solvency) because its current assets comfortably exceed its current liabilities (the working capital covenant) and it will also be solvent in a balance sheet sense because its total assets easily exceed its total liabilities (the tangible net worth covenant). The effect of financial covenants may be to oblige a

[71] Accordingly, covenants in bank loans are traditionally more restrictive than in bond issues: Wood, PR, *International Loans, Bonds and Securities Regulation* (1995) 137.

[72] But a factor that can highlight the importance of covenants in relation to debt securities is that these often have a specified term (eg 20 years) which is considerably longer than a typical bank loan.

[73] Principally Companies Act 1985, Pt VII and *The Listing Rules*, ch 9.

company to seek new equity capital for a new venture which it wants to pursue. The lender can argue that this is reasonable on the grounds that, if the venture were to be financed by additional borrowed funds, this would dilute the value of each lender's claim in the event of failure putting the company's solvency at risk, but lenders would not reap the benefits of success since they do not share in capital growth.[74] Also it can be argued that over-reliance on debt can result in companies rejecting potentially profitable opportunities because substantial benefits from those opportunities will accrue to lenders rather than to shareholders;[75] looked at in this way, covenants restricting borrowing may reduce the incentive to under-invest.[76]

A dividend covenant has the effect of increasing the company's reserves over and above those reserves which, by statute, are undistributable. It is to the company's share capital, share premium and other undistributable reserves that lenders will ultimately look for repayment in the event of a corporate borrower becoming insolvent. It has been demonstrated that a constraint on dividends can encourage new investment by the company,[77] so that although shareholders may appear to lose out in the short term (in that the company's freedom to determine whether to distribute profits or to retain them for investment is restricted) such a covenant can operate to their benefit in the longer term, where it results in enhanced capital growth. Balanced against this is the suggestion that, if a covenant is unduly onerous so that management is required to retain more of the company's profits than it can prudently invest, this could result in investments being made in risky ventures with potentially adverse consequences for both lenders and shareholders.[78] Where a company has surplus retentions, it may be possible to use these to make early repayment of expensive or restrictive debt to the extent that this is permitted by the relevant loan agreements.[79]

Disposals of Assets Covenant

A covenant restricting disposals of assets is intended to prevent asset-stripping, such as where property is sold by the borrowing company at a nominal price. Even disposals of assets at a fair market price could prejudice the lender because piecemeal sales of assets may generate significantly lower proceeds than a sale of all of the assets and undertaking of the business as a going concern. Where the borrower is a holding company, a transfer of assets between wholly-owned subsidiaries even at a nominal value does not prejudice the lender since the value remains within the group throughout. A transfer from the holding company borrower to another company in its group is however

[74] Fischel, DR, 'The Economics of Lender Liability' (1989) 99 Yale Law Journal 131.

[75] Myers, SC, 'Determinants of Corporate Borrowing' (1977) 5 *Journal of Financial Economics* 147; Sappideen, R, 'Fiduciary Obligations to Corporate Creditors' [1991] JBL 365.

[76] Smith, CW, and Warner, JB, 'On Financial Contracting: An Analysis of Bond Covenants' (1979) 7 *Journal of Financial Economics* 117, 124.

[77] Kalay, A, 'Stockholder–Bondholder Conflict and Dividend Constraints' (1982) 10 *Journal of Financial Economics* 211.

[78] Lister, RJ, 'Debenture Covenants and Corporate Value' (1985) 6 Co Law 209, 213; Sappideen, R, 'Fiduciary Obligations to Corporate Creditors' [1991] JBL 365, 378.

[79] In the case of debt securities, the borrower may be required to make payments into a sinking fund which is to be used to buy back securities before they mature.

potentially prejudicial because it means that assets that would previously have been available to repay the borrower's creditors will be claimed first by the creditors of the transferee subsidiary. A transfer from a wholly-owned subsidiary to another group company that it not wholly owned could also be problematic in that the other shareholders in the transferee company or undertaking will acquire an interest in the assets which ranks equally with that of the borrower. Hence, if the covenant is qualified so as to permit intra-group transfers, this will usually exclude transfers by the borrower itself and may also exclude or restrict transfers otherwise than between wholly-owned subsidiaries. A disposals covenant must necessarily be qualified so as to permit disposals of assets in the ordinary course of business. Disposals of insubstantial parts of the borrower's business and undertaking may also be permitted, although the introduction of a substance test may sow the seeds of potential future difficulties in interpretation and application.

Change of Business Covenant

A covenant requiring the borrower not to change its business or operations helps to preserve the identity of the borrower throughout the term of the loan. However, where, as is common, the covenant is qualified so as to restrict only changes which would have 'a material adverse effect' on its business, assets or financial condition, compliance with this covenant may prove to be difficult to monitor in practice.

Negative Pledge Covenant

The purpose of a covenant whereby the company undertakes not to create new security interests or to increase the amount secured by existing securities is to ensure that the priority position of the lender does not change whilst the loan is outstanding. The lender does not want to find itself postponed to subsequent creditors and thereby subject to the risk that the borrower's assets will be exhausted before its turn to be paid. A covenant to this effect is commonly described as a 'negative pledge' covenant.[80] Forms of negative pledge covenants can be found in both unsecured and secured loans but in this chapter[81] the focus is solely on unsecured lending. A typical clause would seek to prohibit quasi-securities (such as credit sales) as well as conventional security interests but the lender's attempts to produce an all-embracing clause may be defeated by the ingenuity of other corporate financiers who subsequently devise arrangements which perform the same economic function as a secured loan but which adopt a legal form that is unanticipated by the loan agreement.

As with any other covenant, breach of a negative pledge covenant will be a breach of contract entitling the lender to the usual contractual remedies. In a well-drafted loan agreement, breach will be an express event of default enti-

[80] American commentators distinguish between a covenant which merely prohibits the creation of new security and a covenant which attempts to be more extensive and to give the lender a security in the event of security being created in favour of another, reserving the term 'negative pledge' for the latter case: see Brudney, V, and Bratton, WW, *Brudney and Chirelstein's Corporate Finance*, (4th edn, 1993) 191.

[81] On negative pledges in secured loans see Ch 15 below, at 534–6.

tling the lender to terminate the agreement and to demand repayment of the principal and of any other sums which are outstanding. It would theoretically be possible for a lender to seek an injunction to prevent a company from granting security in breach of a negative pledge covenant, but practical difficulties in detecting whether or when a company proposes to do this are likely to preclude extensive successful recourse to this remedy. Another equitable remedy is for the court to appoint a receiver. The possibility of exercising this power in favour of a lender in the event of breach of a negative pledge in its favour was left open in one Australian decision,[82] but it seems that circumstances where it would be justifiable to grant this remedy at the behest of an unsecured lender would be rare.[83]

Does the breach of a negative pledge covenant by the granting of a subsequent security have any legal implications for the creditor in whose favour the offending security is created? In a broad sense, the answer to this question is yes, because a company that is in a position where it is prepared to break the terms of its existing financial facilities in this way is, inferentially, a company in financial difficulties. The lender in whose favour the relevant security is created, in common with the company's others creditors, may thus soon find itself embroiled in the consequences of having advanced credit to an insolvent company. In particular, should the company enter into the insolvency procedures of administration or liquidation,[84] the security may be vulnerable under those provisions of the Insolvency Act 1986 that invalidate, or authorise the court to invalidate, security that was created in the twilight period of a company's solvency.[85]

A narrower issue is whether the first lender in whose favour the covenant was given may have a claim against the subsequent lender whose security[86] was created in breach of the covenant. The point of departure here is the privity of contract rule, which is to the effect that contracts cannot give rights to, or impose burdens on, persons who are not parties to them.[87] This rule is subject to various exceptions and qualifications, but the one that is relevant in

[82] *Bond Brewing Holdings Ltd v National Australia Bank Ltd* (1989–90) 1 ACSR 445, Vic SC, App D and (1980–90) 1 ACSR 722, High Ct of Aust (refusing leave to appeal).

[83] Stone, J, 'Will a Court Appoint a Receiver at the Request of a Negative Pledge Lender?' [1991] 10 JIBL 404; Allan, DE, 'Negative Pledge Lending—Dead or Alive?' in Cranston, R, and Goode, RM (eds), *Commercial and Consumer Law* (1993) 223 (also published at [1990] 8 JIBL 330). Compare *Derby & Co Ltd v Weldon (Nos 3 and 4)* [1990] Ch 65 CA where, to prevent the withdrawal of assets from the jurisdiction, the court granted a Mareva injunction and appointed receivers in respect of the assets of defendants in an action for damages for breach of contract, negligence, breach of fiduciary duty, deceit and conspiracy to defraud.

[84] Where a company's existing facilities contain cross-default clauses, the creation of security in breach of a negative pledge covenant in one agreement will mean that it is in default under all of them and therefore that all of its lenders can call for repayment. The domino effect of a cross-default clause thus increases the likelihood of the company being unable to pay its debts as they fall due, and that will form the basis for the making of an administration order under Insolvency Act 1986, s 8 or a winding-up order under Insolvency Act 1986, s 122 (1)(f). Cross-default clauses are discussed further in this chapter, at 479–81.

[85] Especially Insolvency Act 1986, s 245 (avoidance of certain floating charges) and s 239 (preferences).

[86] Here this term is used loosely to include interests that perform the same economic function as a security but which are in a different legal form.

[87] *Privity of Contract: Contracts for the Benefit of Third Parties* (Law Commission Report No 242) (1996) provides a general review of the law in this area.

this context is the equitable principle in *de Mattos v Gibson*.[88] This principle is that where a person acquires property or an interest in property with knowledge of a previous contract affecting that property, he can be restrained by injunction from acting in a manner that is inconsistent with that contract.[89] The basis of this principle, its limits, and even whether it remains good law are issues on which the cases provide scope for different interpretations and for this reason it is unsurprising to discover that these are matters that have been extensively discussed by academic commentators.[90] One point on which there is broad agreement is that, even if it does exist as a matter of law, the principle is subject to restrictive conditions that severely limit its application. One such restriction is that it only operates against persons who know of the existence of the earlier covenant. Knowledge in this context means actual knowledge of the prior rights[91] or, possibly, recklessness as to their existence.[92] Negative pledge clauses in unsecured loan agreements are not subject to any general disclosure or registration requirement under English law but in specific instances a company may disclose the existence of such clauses in its existing facilities as part of the process of negotiating the representations and warranties of a new loan agreement.

Perhaps the strongest argument against the application of the *de Mattos v Gibson* principle to breach of negative pledge covenants is the view that the principle only operates where a person acquires property and *thereafter* seeks to deal with it in a manner which is inconsistent with an earlier contractual promise that was known about at the time of the acquisition. This interpretation excludes from the ambit of the principle situations where security is created in breach of a negative pledge because, there, it is the very acquisition of the security interest in the property rather than subsequent dealings with it that infringes the earlier covenant. The rationale for drawing this type of distinction, which is supported by the words used to describe the principle in the *de Mattos v Gibson* decision itself, is that circumstances may exist in the former case where it was part of the bargain with the acquirer that it would respect existing restrictions, and this is what the *de Mattos v Gibson* principle

[88] (1858) De G & J 276, 282, [1843–60] All ER Rep 803, 805 *per* Knight-Bruce LJ. But the principle is not a panacea for outflanking the doctrine of privity of contract: *Law Debenture Corpn v Ural Caspian Ltd* [1993] 2 All ER 355, 362 *per* Hoffmann LJ (sitting as an additional judge of the High Court). This decision was reversed on appeal ([1995] 1 All ER 157, CA) but on grounds that are not relevant to this point.

[89] *Law Debenture Corpn v Ural Caspian Ltd* [1993] 2 All ER 355, 362 *per* Hoffmann LJ.

[90] Worthington, S, *Proprietary Interests in Commercial Transactions* (1996) ch 5, provides a detailed and careful review of the authorities and the different interpretations that have been ascribed to them by numerous commentators. See also Bell, AP, *Modern Law of Personal Property in England and Wales* (1989) 210–16.

[91] *Swiss Bank Corporation v Lloyds Bank Ltd* [1979] 1 Ch 548, 575 *per* Browne-Wilkinson J (varied on appeal but on other grounds [1982] AC 584, CA and HL).

[92] This suggestion is based on the premise that the *de Mattos v Gibson* principle is the equitable counterpart of the tort of inducing breach of contract or otherwise interfering with contractual relations (see *Swiss Bank Corpn v Lloyds Bank Ltd* [1979] 1 Ch 548, 573). As discussed later in this section, recklessness may be sufficient for the purposes of this tort. However, the need for actual knowledge is emphasised in the *Swiss Bank* decision and this leaves some uncertainty about the precise relationship between the tortious and equitable principles.

seeks to enforce; whereas, in the latter case it is self-evidently not part of the bargain that the acquirer will abide by existing restrictions.[93]

A policy argument in support of the view that the equitable *de Mattos v Gibson* principle should not apply where security is created in breach of a negative pledge is that this is unnecessary because the beneficiary of the broken covenant has a potential remedy against the holder of the security in tort.[94] This remedy is to sue for the economic tort of inducing a breach of contract.[95] To succeed in this claim, the plaintiff must demonstrate that the defendant deliberately violated its contractual rights.[96] An inherent element of deliberate violation is that the defendant must be aware of the existence of the relevant contractual provision. Actual knowledge will certainly satisfy this requirement but there is some support in the cases for the view that recklessness, in the sense of turning a blind eye to the obvious, may also suffice.[97] Whether a lender that has provided a facility on the basis on a negative pledge which is later broken will be able to establish the requisite degree of knowledge is likely to depend on what it can discover about the disclosure process that preceded the subsequent secured-loan agreement.

It is sometimes the case that negative pledge lenders attempt self help by including in their loan agreements a clause to the effect that the loan will become secured in the event of breach of the negative pledge. The legal effectiveness of this form of self help is doubtful. In some cases a provision for automatic security may fail to achieve its desired effect because it does not define the subject matter of the security with sufficient certainty.[98] Careful drafting is also necessary to ensure that the security comes into existence before the security that is in breach of the negative pledge in order to win the battle for prior ranking under the first-in-time rule of priority where that is applicable.[99] Once the security created by an automatic security clause comes into existence upon satisfaction of the specified conditions,[100] it must then be

93 This places *de Mattos v Gibson* under the broader heading of prevention of unjust enrichment. For further development of this idea see Worthington, S, *Proprietary Interests in Commercial Transactions* (1996) 102–5 and the sources cited there.

94 Although *Swiss Bank Corpn v Lloyds Bank Ltd* [1979] 1 Ch 548 may suggest that the *de Mattos v Gibson* principle is simply concerned with the granting of an equitable remedy to prevent the commission of a tort, there is a compelling case for regarding that principle and tort claims as distinct: Bell, AP, *Modern Law of Personal Property in England and Wales* (1989) 210–16.

95 *Lumley v Gye* [1843–60] All ER Rep 208. Inducement to break a contract is one example of the wider principle that wrongful violation of a legal right committed knowingly gives rise to a cause of action: *Quinn v Leathem* [1901] AC 495, HL, 510 *per* Lord Macnaghten; *Law Debenture Trust Corp plc v Ural Caspian Oil Corp Ltd* [1995] 1 All ER 157, CA. Claims based on other economic torts such as conspiracy or wrongful interference with contractual relations could also be pursued. See further Stone, J, 'Negative Pledges and the Tort of Interference with Contractual Relations' [1991] 8 JIBL 310.

96 *Torquay Hotel Co Ltd v Cousins* [1969] 1 All ER 522, CA.

97 *Torquay Hotel Co Ltd v Cousins* [1969] 1 All ER 522, CA, 530 *per* Lord Denning MR; *Emerald Construction Co Ltd v Lowthian* [1966] 1 WLR 691, CA, 700–1.

98 *National Provincial Bank v Charnley* [1924] 1 KB 431, CA.

99 *Fire Nymph Products Ltd v The Heating Centre Pty Ltd* (1991–92) 7 ACSR 365, NSW CA recognises that it is possible to achieve this order of events. This was a case involving automatic crystallisation of a floating charge but the reasoning would seem to be equally applicable to unsecured negative pledge lending.

100 A contingent security which is only to come into existence if, and when, specified conditions are fulfilled is not a security prior to such fulfilment: *Re Gregory Love Ltd* [1916] 1 Ch 203.

registered within 21 days if it is a registrable charge as defined by the Companies Act 1985, s 396.[101] Although failure to register does not invalidate a security against the company itself, it does make it void against other secured creditors and this is therefore another ground on which the battle for priority may be lost. To some extent, these factors are within the control of a lender. It can employ lawyers to produce well-drafted agreements and it can engage in monitoring with a view to maximising[102] its chances of discovering breaches of its negative pledge which have triggered the existence of its security and, where relevant, the obligation to register within twenty-one days.

A further reason why provisions for automatic security in the event of breach of a negative pledge are legally doubtful stems from the uncertainty that surrounds the question whether the automatic security needs to be supported by fresh consideration provided at the time when the contingency is fulfilled. There is no clear authority on this point and commentators are divided. One view is that for an equitable charge to exist fresh value must be provided on or after fulfilment of the conditions and that the charge is only enforceable to the extent of that fresh value and not for money previously advanced.[103] If this interpretation is correct, it follows that it is conceptually impossible to achieve the desired effect of an equitable charge securing an existing unsecured loan that springs into life if the borrower breaches a negative pledge covenant. Others dispute the need for fresh value and argue that an effective equitable charge would come into operation in the event of breach of a negative pledge covenant where that is the contingency to which the charge is subject.[104] If that view is correct, it then leads on to the question whether the mismatch between the appearance that the loan is still unsecured and the reality that it has become secured affects the enforceability of the security that has sprung into existence against persons who subsequently acquire an interest in the company's property and who are unaware of the existence of that charge. This issue is discussed in more detail in the next chapter where it arises in the context of automatic crystallisation of floating charges[105] but, in summary, there is strong case for saying that principles of estoppel may preclude lenders from claiming automatic security interests that third parties cannot reasonably be expected to be aware of. The upshot of

[101] There is no registration requirement until the contingency is fulfilled: *Re Jackson and Bassford Ltd* [1906] 2 Ch 467, 476–7.

[102] For a variety of reasons, even the most rigorous monitoring could not guarantee this. Not all charges require registration and arrangements that perform a security function but are not in that legal form, such as sale and lease-back agreements, are not subject to any disclosure or registration requirements. Gaps such as these in the registration requirements provide opportunities for companies to enter into new financing arrangements that may not be easily discoverable by their existing creditors.

[103] Goode, RM, *Legal Problems of Credit and Security* (1988) 20–1, 36–7; Maxton, J, 'Negative Pledges and Equitable Principles' [1993] JBL 458. For a variant on this view which suggests that the forbearance of the lender in not calling in the loan may satisfy the fresh consideration requirement, see Cranston, R, *Principles of Banking Law* (1997) 346.

[104] Stone, J, 'The "Affirmative" Negative Pledge' [1991] JIBL 364. Without considering the issue in any detail, Gough, WJ, *Company Charges* (2nd edn, 1996) 707, n 5 assumes, on the basis of *Re Gregory Love & Co* [1916] 1 Ch 203, 211, that an equitable charge does arise on fulfilment of the contingency.

[105] Ch 15 below, at 532–3.

these various arguments is that it is unlikely that a negative pledge lender will be successful in a claim against a subsequent lender to whom security has been given in breach of the covenant. The negative pledge lender must pursue its claims against the defaulting company.

Implied Covenants

In addition to the terms expressly agreed by the parties, terms may also be implied into their contractual relationship. Terms may be implied in fact on the basis that the parties must have intended to include them but simply omitted to state this expressly. In specific contexts terms may also be implied in law (for example in relation to contracts for the sale of goods under the Sale of Goods Act 1979) or as a matter of custom. The power for banks to charge compound interest is a term that will be implied on the basis of custom unless this is excluded by an express term.[106] The court's power to imply terms is limited and it cannot imply a term simply on the grounds that it would be reasonable to do so.[107] It is not the court's function to rewrite the parties' bargain but to give effect to it as they must have intended, and for this reason it is clearly impossible for the court to imply a term which is inconsistent with an express term. The detailed and extensive drafting of a typical loan agreement will usually leave little scope for the implication of terms. There is no general implied covenant of good faith and fair dealing in contractual matters under English law.[108]

Events of Default

A well-drafted loan agreement will entitle the lender to accelerate the loan upon the occurrence of any one of a number of specified 'events of default'.[109] Typical events of default include:

- the borrower's failure to pay any sum due and payable pursuant to the agreement;
- the borrower's breach of any other obligation or undertaking under the agreement;
- any representation or warranty proving to be incorrect (or, less severe, incorrect in a material respect);
- cross-default: the borrower's failure to pay or meet any other indebtedness or financial obligation when due;
- the commencement of the winding up of the borrower or of other insolvency or re-organisation procedures;
- distress or execution being levied against any assets of the borrower;
- cessation of business by the borrower.

Where the borrower is a holding company, events of default may also relate to subsidiaries and subsidiary undertakings within its group. Grace periods of a

106 *National Bank of Greece SA v Pinios Shipping Co (No 1)* [1990] 1 AC 637, HL.
107 *Liverpool City Council v Irwin* [1977] AC 239, HL.
108 This is discussed later in this chapter, below at 481–4.
109 Youard, R, 'Default in International Loan Agreements I and II' [1986] JBL 276, 378.

number of days may be allowed to the borrower in respect of some or all of the events of default to give the borrower an opportunity to rectify the position before the lender can call in the loan, a concession that will be important to the borrower in relation to trivial or technical breaches.

When a borrower defaults, the lender, if the loan is typically drafted, will have an option whether to declare the loan due and this will not be an automatic consequence of the default.[110] Youard[111] has explained why automatic acceleration would usually be unusual:

> [S]ince the events of default (other than non-payment) simply amount to an informed guess by the parties at the time the loan is negotiated as to the events which might occur over the next (say) 10 years, and which would entitle the lender to call for immediate repayment, it would in normal circumstances be wholly inappropriate for the occurrence of those events to give rise to automatic acceleration.

The cross-default clause is especially noteworthy. Under this provision the lender is entitled to call in the loan in circumstances where the borrowing company has defaulted on its obligations *to someone else* even though (apart from the cross-default clause) the borrower has met all of its obligations to this particular lender. The rationale of the cross-default clause is that any default is a sign of trouble in response to which the lender will want to be entitled to accelerate its claim to prevent other creditors stealing a march over it with regard to enforcement or with regard to re-negotiation of terms. When a borrower is negotiating the events of default in one loan agreement, it will need to bear in mind that it may in the future enter into other loan agreements containing cross-default clauses, so that accepting very strict events of default on one occasion (for example, no grace periods or no qualifications with regard to 'materiality') could be sowing the seeds of a later catastrophe because of the 'domino' effect of cross default. Also the terms of any cross-default clause itself will need to be considered closely: if all of the borrower's obligations are included, it may find itself almost always in default and it may therefore press for a more limited clause which, perhaps, limits the cross default to failure to pay amounts exceeding a specified threshold figure or which is confined only to particular types of indebtedness.

Lenders tend to favour cross-default clauses which are drafted so as to come into effect when the relevant other indebtedness has become due or '*is capable of being declared due*'. The italicised words relate back to the fact that default does not, in normal practice, cause automatic acceleration of a loan. When a borrowing company defaults on its first loan, instead of demanding repayment, the lender may seek to impose harsher terms on the borrower, with the threat of acceleration hovering in the background should the borrower fail to comply. If the borrower's other lenders have accepted cross-default clauses which only come into effect when borrowings become 'due', those lenders are in a weaker negotiating position (unless there have been separate defaults apart from the cross-default clause) because they cannot

[110] In the event of any ambiguity, the courts will favour the interpretation that the lender has an option to accelerate and that this is not an automatic consequence of default: *Government Stock and Other Securities Investment Co v Manila Ry Co* [1897] AC 81, HL.

[111] Youard, R, 'Default in International Loan Agreements I and II' [1986] JBL 276, 278.

threaten to call in their loans under the cross-default clause as so drafted, and this may defeat the purpose of the clause which was to ensure equality amongst creditors.

LENDER LIABILITY UNDER ENGLISH LAW?[112]

Do banks or other lenders owe fiduciary duties or duties of good faith in contractual dealings to their borrowers under English law? Certainly lenders (and borrowers) must operate within the constraints of the law relating to deceit, negligence and misrepresentation, but the issue here is whether there is a wider duty requiring them to behave fairly. Under US law a wide duty of good faith in contractual dealings is recognised, and the question whether there has been a breach of this implied duty of good faith or of fiduciary duty by a lending bank has sometimes been answered in the affirmative[113] but, to date, English law has taken a different approach.[114] It has been held that a bank owes no duty of care in contract or tort to advise its customer on the prudence of a loan, nor is it subject to any fiduciary duty in this respect.[115] The relationship of lender and borrower is a normal business relationship and in ordinary circumstances it is not fiduciary.[116] There is no general power which the courts can utilise to review the fairness of terms imposed on corporate borrowers[117] and, although there are specific areas where relief from harsh bargains may be available, for example in relation to penalties, a general doctrine of 'unconscionability' is not clearly recognised to be part of English law.[118] In

[112] Lender liability for environmental matters, which has been the subject of increasing concern in recent years, is beyond the scope of this discussion. See, eg, Cromie, S, 'Contaminated Land. The Risks for Lenders' (1997) 8 (1) PLC 33; Handler, T, and Kurnatowska, M, 'Lender Liability for Environmental Damage' [1996] 10 JIBL 424.

[113] Fischel, DR, 'The Economics of Lender Liability' (1989) 99 Yale Law Journal 131, where relevant authorities are analysed and criticised. Fischel argues that covenants ('bonding mechanisms') benefit the borrower in that they enable it to obtain credit at cheaper rates and that where a lender acts pursuant to those covenants it should not be held to be in bad faith. Further, he contends that lender–borrower relations are conducted at arms' length and that the imposition of a fiduciary duty is inappropriate. See also Nicholaides, CM, 'A Survey of Lender Liability in the United States' [1988] 4 JIBL 160; Norton, JJ, 'Lender Liability in the United States' in Cranston, R (ed), *Banks, Liability and Risk* (2nd edn, 1995) 329 Cranston, R, *Principles of Banking Law* (1997) 237–45.

[114] Cranston, R, *Principles of Banking Law* (1997) 237–45.

[115] *Williams & Glyn's Bank v Barnes* [1981] Com LR 205. This case involved an individual but the reasoning would be equally applicable to a corporate borrower. Ralph Gibson J said: 'The suggestion that a Bank, dealing with a businessman of full age and competence, without being asked, or assuming the responsibility to advise, must consider the prudence from the point of view of the customer of a lending which the bank is asked to make, as a matter of obligation upon the Bank, and in the absence of any fiduciary duty, is in my judgment impossible to sustain.' See also *Goldworthy v Brickell* [1987] 1 Ch 378, CA. It has been suggested (tentatively) that a bank may owe a duty of care to a customer who is to give security to give some explanation as to the nature and effect of the security document: *Cornish v Midland Bank plc* [1985] 3 All ER 513, CA, 522–3 *per* Kerr LJ. *Verity v Lloyds Bank* [1996] Fam Law 213 indicates that a duty of care may arise on special facts.

[116] *National Westminster Bank plc v Morgan* [1985] 1 AC 686, HL.

[117] Under the Unfair Terms in Consumer Contracts Regulations 1994 (SI 1994/3159) which came into force on 1 July 1995, 'unfair' contractual terms are not binding on 'consumers' but companies are excluded from this category.

[118] In *Lloyd's Bank Ltd v Bundy* [1975] 1 QB 326, CA, 339 Lord Denning MR said that 'English law gives relief to one who, without independent advice, enters into a contract upon terms

Interfoto Library Ltd v Stiletto Ltd[119] Bingham LJ explained the approach of English law to such matters in these terms:

In many civil law systems, and perhaps in most legal systems outside the common law world, the law of obligations recognises and enforces an overriding principle that in making and carrying out contracts parties should act in good faith. This does not mean simply that they should not deceive each other, a principle which any legal system must recognise; its effect is perhaps most aptly conveyed by such metaphorical colloquialisms as 'playing fair', 'coming clean' or 'putting one's cards face upwards on the table'. It is in essence a principle of fair and open dealing . . . English law has, characteristically, committed itself to no such overriding principle but has developed piecemeal solutions in response to demonstrated problems of unfairness.

An issue which has concerned lenders to companies in recent years is whether they may be at risk of being held to be shadow directors. Under various statutory provisions shadow directors may be made liable as if they were directors.[120] One statutory provision in particular has caused concern: under the Insolvency Act 1986, s 214, directors, including shadow directors, of a company which is in insolvent liquidation[121] may be ordered by the court to make such contribution to the company's assets as the court thinks fit. Applications to court under this section may only be brought by liquidators and it must be established that the person from whom a contribution is sought knew, or ought to have concluded,[122] that there was no reasonable prospect that the company would avoid going into insolvent liquidation and that the person was a director at that time.[123] The court may not make an order against someone if it is satisfied that that person took every step with a view to minimising the potential loss to the company's creditors as (assuming him to have known that there was no reasonable prospect that the company would avoid going into insolvent liquidation) he ought to have taken.[124]

which are very unfair or transfers property for a consideration which is grossly inadequate, when his bargaining power is grievously impaired by reason of his own needs or desires, or by his own ignorance or infirmity, coupled with undue influences brought to bear on him by or for the benefit of the other.' His Lordship described this as the principle of 'inequality of bargaining power'. In *National Westminster Bank plc v Morgan* [1985] 1 AC 686, HL Lord Scarman (the other Law Lords concurring) questioned whether there was any need to erect such a doctrine. See further Beatson, J, *Anson's Law of Contract* (27th edn, 1998) 287–90; Teubner, G, 'Legal Irritants: Good Faith in British Law or How Unifying Law Ends Up in New Divergences' (1998) 61 MLR 11.

[119] [1989] 1 QB 433, CA, 439.

[120] Also shadow directors are persons connected with a company under Insolvency Act 1986, s 249 which has implications with regard to the provisions of that Act concerned with attacking transactions at undervalue (s 238), preferences (s 239) and certain floating charges (s 245) because these operate more harshly in relation to connected persons.

[121] Defined as going into liquidation 'at a time when its assets are insufficient for the payment of its debts and other liabilities and the expenses of the winding up': Insolvency Act 1986, s 214 (6).

[122] The standard by which a director is judged is based on the general knowledge, skill and experience that may reasonably be expected of a person carrying out his functions and also the director's own knowledge, skill and experience: Insolvency Act 1986, s 214 (4). Insolvency Act 1986, s 214 (4) is discussed further in Ch 6 above, at 214–7.

[123] Insolvency Act 1986, s 214 (2).

[124] Again judged by the combination of objective and subjective standards specified in Insolvency Act 1986, s 214 (4).

A shadow director in relation to a company means a person in accordance with whose directions or instructions the directors of the company are accustomed to act, but a person is not deemed a shadow director by reason only of advice given by him in a professional capacity.[125] Could a lender be caught within the scope of this definition? In *Re a Company (No 005009 of 1987)*[126] there was held to be a triable issue whether a bank had become a shadow director of an insolvent company in the context of an Insolvency Act 1986, s 214 application. Although at the trial of the action this claim was abandoned,[127] the preliminary ruling caused concern. Matters have since settled down and one leading insolvency judge, writing in his personal capacity, has stated that a bank must step outside the ordinary bank–customer relationship to be at risk of being held to be a shadow director.[128] The same judge has ruled that to establish that a defendant is a shadow director it is necessary to allege and prove: (i) who are the directors of the company, whether *de facto* or *de iure*; (ii) that the defendant directed those directors how to act in relation to the company or that he was one of the persons who did so; (iii) that those directors acted in accordance with such directions; and (iv) they were accustomed so to act.[129] A shadow director is someone who controls the whole board, or at the very least a governing majority.[130] The directors must act on that person's instructions or directions as a matter of regular practice and not just on isolated occasions.[131] These comments offer banks and other lenders considerable comfort. The essence of shadow directorship is that the directors abrogate their personal responsibility to exercise discretion and judgment in the management of the company's affairs and act as the 'puppets' or 'cat's paw'[132] of someone else. This is not what happens in a typical lending relationship. When a lender which is considering lending to a company in financial difficulties follows the usual practice of requiring the borrower to give warranties about its present circumstances and covenants as to the conduct of its affairs and imposes conditions precedent before the borrower can obtain the funds, it is not giving 'directions' or 'instructions' but is simply attaching terms and conditions to the provision and continuation of its financial support which the company is free to accept or reject. If the directors of the company choose to accept the lender's proffered terms they must then ensure compliance with those terms to prevent the occurrence of an event of default.

Probably the most sensitive time for a lender is when an event of default does occur or when it appears inevitable because it must then balance its

125 Insolvency Act 1986, s 251.

126 [1989] BCLC 13.

127 *Re MC Bacon Ltd* [1990] BCLC 324.

128 Millett, Sir P, 'Shadow Directorship—A Real or Imagined Threat to the Banks' [1991] Insolvency Practitioner 14. See also, Fidler, P, 'Banks as Shadow Directors' [1992] 3 JIBL 97; Turing, D, 'Lender Liability, Shadow Directors and the Case of Re Hydrodan (Corby) Ltd' [1994] 6 JIBL 244; Bhattacharyya, G, 'Shadow Directors and Wrongful Trading Revisited' (1995) 16 Co Law 313 commenting on *Re PFTZM Ltd* [1995] 2 BCLC 354. See also *Shadow Directorships* (Financial Law Panel) (1994) which offers banks, and others, practical assistance in dealing with the risk of shadow directorship liability.

129 *Re Hydrodan (Corby) Ltd* [1994] BCC 161, 163.

130 *Re Unisoft Group Ltd (No 2)* [1994] BCC 766, 775.

131 Ibid.

132 Ibid.

interest in ensuring repayment against the consideration that if it becomes too closely involved in attempts to rescue the business it may then risk being viewed as a shadow director.[133] In *Re a Company*[134] the circumstances which led to the shadow directorship allegation against the company's bank were ones in which the company had reached its overdraft limit and the bank has commissioned a report on its financial affairs which included recommendations which the company then took steps to implement. Although giving advice in a professional capacity is not conduct which leaves the adviser exposed as a shadow director,[135] the dividing line between 'advising' and 'instructing' or 'directing' may be difficult to draw.[136] Instead of relying on the rather uncertain 'advice' proviso, a safer course for a lender may be to express its proposals for the rehabilitation of the company in the form of conditions to the continuation of its support. This will give the borrowing company's directors a choice whether to comply with the loan or to suffer acceleration of the loan. In commercial terms, the directors may have no option but to accept the conditions, but as a matter of law this arrangement would lack the characteristics whereby the lender would be at risk of being regarded as a shadow director.[137]

In some instances a lender may seek the right to appoint its representative onto the board of a borrowing company. Nominating a few members of a larger board should not expose a lender to shadow directorship liability because the requirement for control of the whole board (or at least a governing majority of it) would not be satisfied.[138] In the absence of fraud or bad faith, a person appointing a director owes no duty to take care that the director so appointed discharges its duties as a director with due diligence and competence.[139]

LENDERS AS MONITORS OF MANAGEMENT[140]

Notwithstanding that the circumstances may not be such as to give rise to potential shadow directorship liability, a lender may be in a strong position to exercise a degree of control over corporate management and thus to play a role in corporate governance. It has the power to provide or to withhold finance and to stipulate the terms on which it is to be made available. A lender has an interest in policing the loan during its life and, as discussed earlier in

[133] An American commentator writes: 'whenever a creditor contemplates taking a hand in the management of a financially troubled debtor, it should think of its deeper pockets and keep its hands there': Douglas-Hamilton, MH, 'Creditor Liabilities Resulting From Improper Interference with the Management of a Financially Troubled Debtor' (1975) 31 Bus Law 343, 365. For illustrations of the ways in which creditors may become involved in the affairs of financially distressed companies see Herman, ES, *Corporate Control, Corporate Power* (1981) 124–6.

[134] [1989] BCLC 13.

[135] Insolvency Act 1986, s 251.

[136] *Re Tasbian Ltd (No 3)* [1992] BCC 358.

[137] Although if the arrangement is not viewed as genuine but as merely a device to avoid shadow directorship it will not be allowed to stand.

[138] *Kuwait Asia Bank EC v National Mutual Life Nominees Ltd* [1991] 1 AC 187, PC.

[139] Ibid.

[140] Generally, Traintis, GG, and Daniels, RJ, 'The Role of Debt in Interactive Corporate Governance' (1995) 83 California Law Review 1073; Cheffins, BR, *Company Law Theory, Structure and Operation* (1997) 75–9.

this chapter,[141] may take 'evergreen' warranties and covenants to enable it to do so. An events of default clause enables a lender to renegotiate its relationship with a defaulting borrower with the threat that the loan will be called in if the borrower refuses or is unable to comply with the new demands. However, the extent to which lenders can perform, or would choose to perform, the function of monitoring or controlling management must necessarily vary.[142] Factors that will influence the lender's incentive to monitor will include the size of the loan, its duration and whether or not it is secured. The identity of the borrowing company and the nature of its business are also relevant considerations. A company which has limited access to others source of finance (remembering that a small or recently-formed company may be unable to raise capital by issuing shares to the public), may have no commercial alternative but to accept short-term loans or loans which are subject to detailed restrictive covenants, although competitive pressures in the lending markets may help to constrain individual lenders from seeking to impose terms which are unreasonable or excessive.[143] Thus it has been said that: 'Bank power tends to be inversely related to borrower size, because the latter is closely correlated with credit rating and available borrowing options.'[144] As well as having more financing options available to it,[145] a large and well-established company's negotiating position may be strengthened by the sheer size of its recurring financing requirements: put simply, lending to major companies is a lucrative source of business which lenders will be anxious to maintain, especially since in addition to the profits to be derived from straightforward lending, there may also be significant opportunities to earn large fees by advising on complex and sophisticated financing structures. Competitive pressures may lead lenders to limit their initial investigations into a company's financial position and to require few covenants with the result that, so long as the company is able to meet its payment obligations and is apparently financially secure, its lenders do not actively monitor management.[146] Charkham's analysis of the relationship between banks and major corporate borrowers in the period prior to the recession in 1989–93 is telling:[147]

> It is evident from many cases where a company has collapsed that most of its lenders did not possess the full facts—severe competition had doubtless compelled them to lend without asking the right questions, however injudicious this may now with hindsight now appear. With banks lining up to lend, companies could refuse to borrow from the inquisitive, but that is no excuse.

[141] At 468–79.

[142] Levmore, S, 'Monitors and Freeriders in Commercial and Corporate Settings' (1982) 92 Yale LJ 49; Axworthy, CS, 'Corporate Directors—Who Needs Them?' (1988) 51 MLR 273, 291–2; Finch, V, 'Company Directors: Who Cares about Care and Skill?' (1992) 55 MLR 179, 189–95.

[143] Middleton, M, Cowling, M, Samuels, J, and Sugden, R, 'Small Firms and Clearing Banks' in Dimsdale, N, and Prevezer, M, *Capital Markets and Corporate Governance* (1994) 141.

[144] Herman, ES, *Corporate Control, Corporate Power* (1981) 122.

[145] Lomax, D, 'The Role of the Banks' in Dimsdale, N, and Prevezer, M (eds), *Capital Markets and Corporate Governance* (1994) 161, 173–7 outlining differences in a clearing bank's relationships with small and larger businesses.

[146] Herman, ES, *Corporate Control, Corporate Power* (1981) 123–9.

[147] Charkham, J, *Keeping Good Company* (1995) 298–9.

Just as competitive pressures made banks lower their guard, so they forced companies to hit them as hard as possible by squeezing the last ounce from every transaction. Treasury departments were turned into profit centres; relationships became secondary to securing the keenest terms.

A lender would obviously become more concerned when a borrowing company encounters financial difficulties but, even apart from the shadow directorship concern, it may still hesitate to intervene too hastily or too aggressively for fear of attracting press or public criticism and thereby undermining its commercial reputation and competitive position.

The focus of a lender's concern is to ensure that the money which it has lent is repaid, together with interest and any attendant costs. Self-interest places an inevitable limit on the role that lenders can be expected to play as monitors of corporate management: since shareholders rather than creditors benefit from capital growth, a lender has no incentive to invest resources in employing and training staff to monitor a corporate borrower beyond the extent necessary to satisfy itself that the company's ability to meet its obligations under the loan is not impaired or placed under threat.[148] Even to that extent, lenders may opt not to monitor but instead to employ other risk management techniques such as portfolio diversification principles.[149] The construction of a portfolio of loans with different risk profiles reduces a lender's incentive to monitor any one borrower and, at the same time, makes it more expensive and time-consuming to do so effectively in respect of all borrowers. It has been argued that there is a close connection between the prosperity of banks and companies, and that the management of banks owe it to their owners and depositors to be knowledgeable and concerned about the performance of industrial and commercial companies as a basis for their lending decisions, both individually and collectively. Yet the same author has conceded that at present 'in the UK the bank's role in corporate governance is negligible, except in rescue cases where they sometimes require management changes as part of the price for continuing support'.[150]

Various commentators have drawn unfavourable comparisons between the British position and that in other countries such as Germany and Japan where, according to the conventional view, closer relationships tend to exist between banks and industrial companies and banks are more willing than within the British model to provide long-term debt and equity finance and to participate in the monitoring of management through supervisory board structures.[151] However, other commentators have questioned widely-held views such as that of the powerful position of banks within the German corporate governance structure.[152] It is beyond the scope of this book to examine

[148] Charkham, J, *Keeping Good Company* (1995) 298.

[149] See further, Ch 1 above, at 20–1.

[150] Charkham, J, *Keeping Good Company* (1995) 338.

[151] eg, Hutton, W, *The State We're In* (1995) generally and ch 6 in particular; Lee, S, 'Finance for Industry' in Michie, J, and Grieve Smith, J (eds), *Creating Industrial Capacity: Towards Full Employment* (1996) 113.

[152] In particular, Edwards, J, and Fischer, K, *Bank Finance and Investment in Germany* (1994). See also Bond, S, and Jenkinson, T, 'The Assessment: Investment Performance and Policy' (1996) 12 *Oxford Review of Economic Policy* Summer 1, 11–14 questioning the classification of Germany (but not Japan) as a bank-based system of financing for industry.

recommendations to the effect that UK economic performance would be improved by a shift to greater bank-based borrowing along German or Japanese lines, and to consider the measures, including fundamental fiscal and other current legal changes, that could be adopted as government policy with a view to achieving that shift.[153] A more modest line of inquiry from the legal perspective is to look critically at any current legal rules that stand in the way of, or may inhibit, the development of closer relationships between industry and banking where, perhaps because of lessons learnt from comparative analysis of other countries' models, such relationships are seen to offer potential commercial advantages. The debate about how widely the category of shadow director is to be drawn, discussed earlier in this chapter,[154] has an obvious relevance here. In that context, after some initial concern the position that was eventually arrived at is that, ordinarily, banks should not be at risk of being held to be shadow directors. Similar questions arise when banks appoint directors to the boards of borrower companies. When looked at through the prism of the positive corporate governance role that banks have the potential to perform, the ruling that nominating banks are not responsible for the acts of their nominees is a helpful decision. As well as liability concerns, another reason why banks may eschew closer relationships with their corporate borrowers is the fear that this will give them access to inside information which will preclude them from dealing in affected securities on their own behalf or for other customers or present them with conflicts of interests in their advisory work. The problems of managing information within a multi-function financial institution are now familiar[155] although effective legal responses to these difficulties, through Chinese Walls or other measures, are still evolving.[156]

[153] See, eg, *Pre-Budget Report* (HM Treasury) Cm 4076 (1998). This Report outlines a series of measures that are under active consideration by the government with the aim of 'steering a stable course for lasting prosperity'. It includes the announcement of a wide-ranging review of the banking sector. One of the key issues to be considered in this review is the relationship between banks and small- and medium-sized business and whether there is more that banks could do to 'build on their partnership with businesses': 5 and 39–40.

[154] See above, at 481–84.

[155] McVea, H, *Financial Conglomerates and The Chinese Wall: Regulating Conflicts of Interest* (1993).

[156] The decision of the House of Lords in *HRH Prince Jefri Bolkiah v KPMG* [1999] 2 WLR 215 HL has dented confidence in the legal effectiveness of Chinese Walls as a measure for avoiding problems of conflicts of interests resulting from access to information.

15

Secured Debt

ADVANTAGES OF BEING A SECURED CREDITOR

This chapter is concerned with forms of real security which companies can give to lenders. A lender with a real security is entitled to claim the assets which are the subject-matter of the security in the event of the company failing to meet its obligations. A lender can also take guarantees in respect of the company's indebtedness from third parties (for example, from its directors or its parent company). Guarantees are sometimes described as personal security, but in this chapter the term 'security' denotes a proprietary claim, that is, a claim which involves rights in relation to a thing.[1] A guarantee is not a security as so defined because the creditor has only a personal claim against the guarantor.[2]

If a company becomes insolvent, its secured creditors are in a much stronger position than its unsecured creditors. In insolvency, unsecured debts are governed by the *pari passu* rule which means that if there are insufficient assets to meet all of the claims, they must abate rateably amongst themselves. The result of the application of the *pari passu* rule is that the company's pool of assets is distributed to its unsecured creditors in proportion to the size of their respective claims, and each of the creditors must bear a proportionate share of the shortfall. The *pari passu* rule is subject to various qualifications and exceptions.[3] For the purposes of this chapter the most important point is that the rule has no application in relation to secured debts because proprietary rights acquired before insolvency are respected and not subjected to the collective procedures of insolvency law.[4] Avoiding the *pari passu* rule and ensuring priority over unsecured creditors in the event of insolvency are compelling reasons for taking security.[5]

The options available to a secured creditor in the event of default by a borrower are greater than those available to unsecured creditors. For example, if a company disposes of assets in breach of a covenant prohibiting or restrict-

[1] Sykes, EI, and Walker, S, *The Law of Securities*, (5th edn, 1993) 9.

[2] Unless, of course, the guarantor has given the creditor a mortgage, charge or other form of security interest.

[3] For example, the Insolvency Act 1986 creates a category of preferential debts which are to be paid before ordinary unsecured debts (and also before debts secured by a floating charge). See generally, Oditah, F, 'Assets and the Treatment of Claims in Insolvency' (1992) 108 LQR 459.

[4] *Sowman v David Samuel Trust Ltd* [1978] 1 WLR 22; *Re Potters Oils Ltd* [1986] 1 WLR 201. The importance of property rights in an insolvency context are discussed generally by Goode, RM, 'Ownership and Obligations in Transactions' (1987) 103 LQR 433, 434–53.

[5] *Insolvency Law and Practice* (Report of the Review Committee under the Chairmanship of Sir Kenneth Cork) (*Cork Committee Report*) Cmnd 8558 (1982) ch 34; Allan, DE, 'Security: Some Mysteries, Myths and Monstrosities' (1989) 15 Monash Law Review 337, 343.

ing disposals, in a well-drafted loan agreement this will be an event of default which entitles the lender, whether secured or unsecured, to accelerate the loan and demand repayment. However, if the loan is secured and the assets disposed of were part of the subject-matter of the security, the secured creditor may, subject to the protections afforded to persons who acquire property in good faith, for value, and without notice of competing interests, be able to follow the assets into the hands of the person who received them or[6] to claim the proceeds of the disposal. An unsecured creditor does not have these rights.[7] In the event of default, a secured creditor may appoint a receiver to realise the security where the security provides for this or may petition the court for the appointment of a receiver (although such applications are now rare as lenders are normally adequately protected by their contractual powers of appointment). The court will not normally appoint a receiver on the application of an unsecured creditor.[8]

A further advantage of being a secured creditor is that this may entitle the creditor to block the appointment of an administrator.[9] Administration is a statutory procedure which is designed to facilitate the rescue and rehabilitation of companies which are in financial crisis. A creditor may want to oppose the appointment of an administrator by the court because there is a general moratorium on the enforcement of claims against the company whilst it is in administration.[10]

ECONOMIC PERSPECTIVES ON SECURED DEBT

There is potential for a trade off between the granting of security and the rates at which a company can borrow. Because security puts its holder in an advantageous position, it may enable the company to borrow from a particular lender which would otherwise have been unwilling to sanction the loan or, at least, to borrow at cheaper rates than that lender would otherwise have been willing to offer. Whether secured borrowing reduces a company's overall interest bill is debatable,[11] because other unsecured creditors may demand

[6] Ordinarily the creditor must choose whether to claim the proceeds or to pursue the asset: Goode, RM, *Legal Problems of Credit and Security*, (2nd edn, 1988) 16.

[7] Apart from covenants or other contractual restrictions, an unsecured creditor has no standing to object to the way in which a borrower deals with its assets: *Re Ehrmann Bros Ltd* [1906] 2 Ch 697, CA.

[8] *Harris v Beauchamp Bros* [1894] 1 QB 802, CA. See further, Ch 14 above, at 474–79.

[9] The security must be a floating charge which entitles its holder to appoint an administrative receiver, ie a receiver or manager of the whole (or substantially the whole) of the company's property appointed by or on behalf of the holders of any debentures of the company secured by a charge which, as created, was a floating charge, or by such a charge and one or more other securities: Insolvency Act 1986, ss 9 and 29.

[10] The moratorium begins when a petition is presented (Insolvency Act 1986, s 10) and is strengthened on the making of the administration order (Insolvency Act 1986, s 11).

[11] White, JJ, 'Efficiency Justifications for Personal Property Security' (1984) Vanderbilt L Rev 473; Buckley, FH, 'The Bankruptcy Priority Puzzle' (1986) 72 Virginia Law Review 1393; Kripke, H, 'Law and Economics: Measuring the Economic Efficiency of Commercial Law in a Vacuum of Fact' (1985) 133 University of Pennsylvania Law Review 929. In essence this is an application of the Modigliani-Miller theory of capital structure which is considered in Ch 2 above, at 59–62.

higher interest to compensate them for the risk of being postponed to the secured debt in the event of the borrowing company's insolvency.[12] Security has been said to be a signal of a company's creditworthiness,[13] but the effectiveness of security as a signaller has been doubted because there is some evidence that companies give security only when they are unable to borrow on an unsecured basis, so that whatever signal is sent out may be more negative than positive.[14] Another economic explanation for secured debt is that it can reduce the costs of monitoring the company, and this is a saving that will be reflected in the interest rate charged: instead of having to monitor the whole of the company's business through covenants, a secured creditor can simply check that the assets which are subject to its security have not been dissipated.[15] Again, reductions in monitoring costs so far as secured creditors are concerned have to be set against increases in unsecured creditors' monitoring costs; as one commentator has explained: 'the existence of security raises the expected cost of default for unsecured creditors by reducing the available asset pool and thus creates incentives for these parties to monitor more extensively.'[16] Yet unsecured creditors may limit their monitoring efforts where they perceive that there is some benefit to them from the existence of security, such as where it prevents the company from disposing of its existing major assets and embarking on new and more risky ventures[17] or where it is given to secure an injection of debt finance which enables the company to stay afloat.[18] Such considerations suggest that the lower monitoring costs of secured creditors may not be entirely cancelled out by the higher monitoring costs incurred by unsecured creditors when security is created.

[12] Schwartz, A, 'Security Interests and Bankruptcy Priorities: A Review of Current Theories' (1981) 10 Journal of Legal Studies 1; Schwartz, A, 'The Continuing Puzzle of Secured Debt' (1984) 37 Vanderbilt Law Review 1051.

[13] Schwartz, A, 'Security Interests and Bankruptcy Priorities: A Review of Current Theories' (1981) 10 Journal of Legal Studies 1, 14–21

[14] See Bridge, M, 'The *Quistclose* Trust in a World of Secured Transactions' (1992) 12 OJLS 333, 336–9.

[15] Jackson, TH, and Kronman, AT, 'Secured Financing and Priorities Among Creditors' (1979) 88 Yale Law Journal 1143. But where the security is a floating charge this analysis breaks down because the essence of the floating charge is that it allows the debtor to continue to deal with its assets as if they were not subject to a security.

[16] Schwartz, A, 'Security Interests and Bankruptcy Priorities: A Review of Current Theories' (1981) 10 Journal of Legal Studies 1, 10. For variations on the 'monitoring' explanation of secured debt see Levmore, S, 'Monitors and Freeriders in Commercial and Corporate Settings' (1982) 92 Yale Law Journal 49 and Scott, RE, 'A Relational Theory of Secured Financing' (1986) 86 Columbia Law Review 901, 925 *et seq.*

[17] Schwartz, A, 'Security Interests and Bankruptcy Priorities: A Review of Current Theories' (1981) 10 Journal of Legal Studies 1, 11; see also Smith, CW, and Warner, JB, 'Bankruptcy, Secured Debt, and Optimal Capital Structure: Comment' (1979) 34 *Journal of Finance* 247; Smith, CW, and Warner, JB, 'On Financial Contracting: An Analysis of Bond Covenants' (1979) 7 *Journal of Financial Economics* 117, 127 (where the authors note advantages of secured debt but also point out that secured debt involves opportunity costs by restricting the firm from potentially profitable dispositions of assets which are subject to the security).

[18] Oditah, F, *Legal Aspects of Receivables Financing,* (1991) 14–18 (this provides a valuable discussion of the various economic theories used by commentators to explain secured debt); Oditah, F, 'The Treatment of Claims in Insolvency' (1992) 108 LQR 459.

POLICY: DOMINANCE OF FREEDOM OF CONTRACT

English law allows companies to give security that extends to all of their assets. In the event of financial difficulties, the effect of all-embracing security of this type can be to allow the secured creditor to take all of the company's assets, leaving nothing or virtually nothing for the unsecured creditors. This raises policy considerations with regard to whether, or to what extent, the law should intervene to protect unsecured creditors by restricting the rights of lenders to negotiate for comprehensive security. Although some advocates of reform have from time to time suggested that there should be mandatory restrictions on the range of securities that companies can offer to their creditors,[19] the present position under English law is that freedom of contract generally prevails. The limited qualifications to this general rule stem from provisions of the Insolvency Act 1986 whereby securities created in the twilight period leading up to a company's insolvency may be invalidated[20] and certain debts are afforded a preferential status over debts secured by particular types of security.[21]

CONSENSUAL SECURITY INTERESTS

The scope of the term 'security interest' is a matter of some uncertainty, but in *Bristol Airport plc v Powdrill*[22] counsel acting for one of the parties described real security in the following terms:

> Security is created where a person ('the creditor') to whom an obligation is owed by another ('the debtor') by statute or contract, in addition to the personal promise of the debtor to discharge the obligation, obtains rights exercisable against some property in which the debtor has an interest in order to enforce the discharge of the debtor's obligation to the creditor.

Browne-Wilkinson V-C declined to hold that this was a comprehensive definition of security but confirmed that the description was certainly no wider than the ordinary meaning of the word. One way in which it may be too restrictive is that it fails to acknowledge that a third party may grant rights over

[19] In particular, the abolition of the floating charge or a limit on the scope of the assets that it can cover: see the discussion in the *Cork Committee Report* ch 36 and Diamond, AL, *A Review of Security Interests in Property* (1989) (*Diamond Report*) ch 16.

[20] Insolvency Act 1986, s 239 (avoidance of voidable preferences) and s 245 (invalidity of certain floating charges) are the key sections. These sections permit a retrospective review of security for a maximum period of two years prior to the commencement of liquidation or administration. If certain conditions are satisfied, the court can order the invalidation of a security on the grounds that it is a voidable preference. If certain conditions are satisfied, a floating charge created in the twilight period is automatically invalid under s 245. For further detail see Birds, J, Boyle, AJ, Ferran, EV, and Villiers, C, *Boyle and Birds' Company Law* (3rd edn, 1995) 632–9. A security is not a transaction at an undervalue under Insolvency Act 1986, s 238 because there is no disposal of the company's property: *Re MC Bacon Ltd* [1990] BCC 78.

[21] Insolvency Act 1986, ss 40, 175, 386 and sch 6; Companies Act 1985, s 196.

[22] [1990] Ch 744 CA, 760.

its property by way of guarantee to secure the loan to the debtor.[23] The description does highlight the essence of security, namely, that it gives the creditor proprietary and not merely personal rights in respect of a debt. The proprietary nature of security was emphasised by Lord Jauncey in *Armour v Thyssen Edelstahlwerke AG*.[24]

A right in security is a right over property given by a debtor to a creditor whereby the latter in the event of the debtor's failure acquires priority over the property against the general body of creditors of the debtor. It is of the essence of a right in security that the debtor possesses in relation to the property a right which he can transfer to the creditor, which right must be retransferred to him upon payment of the debt.

The focus of the discussion in this chapter is security interests created by agreement of the parties. Security interests can also arise by operation of law, an example being the vendor's lien on property sold which is to secure payment of the purchase price, but these types of security are not considered further.[25]

Grant and Reservation; Security Interests and Sales—Fundamental Legal Distinctions

An element of these descriptions of security that merits closer examination is the emphasis on the creditor *obtaining* rights and the debtor *granting* rights. An important distinction is conventionally[26] drawn in English law between being granted an interest to secure an obligation and reserving an interest for that purpose.[27] If, for example, a supplier sells goods to a customer on credit and title to those goods passes, the seller, if it wants to be secured in respect of the credit which it has advanced, must take an interest in the purchaser's, or some other person's, property. An alternative course for the seller would have been to reserve title to the goods until payment had been effected. An effective[28] retention of title clause has the same economic effect as taking a security but it falls into a different legal category for the purpose of English law and, in particular, it does not require registration under the company charges provisions of the Companies Act 1985.[29] Also, although this will depend on the precise wording of the provision in question, it may fall outside a covenant not

[23] A guarantor can charge its property without giving a personal undertaking to pay: *Re Conley* [1938] 2 All ER 127 CA; *Re Bank of Credit and Commerce International SA (No 8)* [1998] AC 214, HL.

[24] [1990] 3 All ER 481, HL, 486.

[25] See Worthington, S, *Proprietary Interests in Commercial Transactions* (1996) Pt II.

[26] See Goode, RM, *Legal Problems of Credit and Security*, (2nd edn, 1988) 5–9; Gough, WJ, *Company Charges*, (2nd edn, 1996) 3–4 and Sykes, EI, and Walker, S, *The Law of Securities*, (5th edn, 1993) 3 and 12–13. Contrast Oditah, F, *Legal Aspects of Receivables Financing*, (1991) 4–11 where it is argued that consensual security need not always lie in grant and that reservation can give rise to a security interest in law.

[27] A distinction clearly established by the House of Lords in *McEntire v Crossley Brothers Ltd* [1895] AC 457, HL.

[28] *Aluminium Industrie Vaassen BV v Romalpa Aluminium Ltd* [1976] 1 WLR 676, CA; *Re Peachdart Ltd* [1984] Ch 131; *Hendy Lennox Ltd v Grahame Puttick Ltd* [1984] 1 WLR 485; *Clough Mill Ltd v Martin* [1985] 1 WLR 111, CA; *Armour v Thyssen Edelstahwerke AG* [1990] 3 All ER 481, HL. Generally, on retention of title agreements, see McCormack, G, *Reservation of Title* (2nd edn, 1995) and Wheeler, S, *Reservation of Title Claims: Impact and Implications* (1991).

[29] *Clough Mill Ltd v Martin* [1985] 1 WLR 111, CA.

to create future security that was previously given by the company. The fact that by fitting the arrangement into one legal category rather than another, even though the economic effect is the same in either case, is a feature of English law which is open to criticism in that form is allowed to prevail over substance.[30] Transactions which are really very similar in nature are treated in different ways and this compartmentalisation leads to complexity.

Review bodies have proposed that English law should adopt a more flexible approach and that interests retained by the creditor should be treated as security interests in the same way as interests granted by the debtor.[31] This would bring English law into line with the US Uniform Commercial Code, art 9 where the term 'security interest' is defined broadly to include any 'interest in personal property or fixtures which secures payment or the performance of an obligation'. It is clear that this encompasses retained interests as well as interests granted by the debtor.[32] To date, successive governments have shown little willingness to bring forward legislation explicitly enacting such reform. The Companies Act 1989, Pt IV contained provisions that were intended to amend the requirements for the registration of charges as set out in the Companies Act 1985, Pt XII. For various reasons, the Companies Act 1989, Pt IV was never brought into force but it is interesting to note that some commentators sought to argue that, if it had been, retention of title agreements would have become registrable.[33] This argument was based on the definition of a 'charge' in the Companies Act 1989 as being 'any form of security interest (fixed or floating) over property, other than an interest arising by operation of law'. The term 'security interest' was not defined, but it was argued that the absence of any reference to the conferral of the interest by the company meant that reserved interests could be registrable. This interpretation of the Companies Act 1989 is very doubtful. The more natural interpretation is that the term 'security interest' was used in that legislation in its conventional sense, that is to denote consensual securities granted by the debtor.[34] Making retention of title agreements registrable would be a significant policy shift with potentially serious practical repercussions. The Companies Act 1989, Pt IV was not intended to be a vehicle for radical reform of the framework of the law relating to security but only to make various improvements to the registration requirements, broadly in line with recommendations put forward by Professor Diamond in Pt III of his *Review of Security Interests in Property*. This report, published in 1989, was the outcome of a government-backed inquiry into whether there was a need for alteration of the law relating to security over

[30] Goode, RM, 'The Modernisation of Personal Property Security Law' (1984) 100 LQR 234, 237–8; Bridge, M, 'Form, Substance and Innovation in Personal Property Security Law' [1992] JBL 1.

[31] *Report of the Committee on Consumer Credit*, Cmnd 4596 (1971) paras 5.2.8–5.2.15 (Crowther Committee); *Diamond Report* paras 3.4–3.10.

[32] Various Canadian provinces have enacted Personal Property Security Acts which are based on art 9: *Diamond Report* paras 7.1.1–7.1.10.

[33] Oditah, F, *Legal Aspects of Receivables Financing* (1991) 6; Fletcher, IF, *The Law of Insolvency* (2nd edn, 1996) 507. See generally, McCormack, G, 'Title Retention and The Company Charge Registration System' in Palmer, N, and McKendrick, E, *Interests in Goods* (2nd edn, 1998) ch 28.

[34] This argument is supported by Bridge, M, 'Form, Substance and Innovation in Personal Property Security Law' [1992] JBL 1, 21.

property other than land. Professor Diamond noted that opinions on whether retention of title agreements should become registrable differed widely and spread right across the spectrum.[35] He recommended that simple retention of title agreements should not become registrable under the system for registration of company charges.[36]

There are other types of arrangement that operate in the same way as retention of title agreements in that they give someone who has provided finance an interest in property which is not a charge and which does not therefore require registration. These include[37] agreements whereby a company obtains finance by selling its property subject to an option to re-acquire it at a later date. In economic substance, such an arrangement is the same as borrowing from the financier and using the assets as security for the loan, but its legal form, and consequences, are entirely different. The courts are obliged to respect the distinction between law and economics.[38] Accordingly they must give legal effect to an arrangement as agreed by the parties, notwithstanding that this may enable the provider of finance to achieve a position which, in economic terms, is equivalent to that of a secured lender but which avoids registration requirements or restrictive covenants that would have applied if the finance had been made available in the form of a straightforward loan. But a fraudulent attempt to bypass registration or other requirements relating to loans by attaching an inaccurate label to an arrangement will not be allowed to stand. Also, even in the absence of fraud, the parties' description of an arrangement, although important, is not conclusive and the court will reclassify it if its terms are inconsistent with the legal form in which it has been cast.[39]

SECURITY INTERESTS ARE DEFEASIBLE INTERESTS

An uncontroversial feature of a security interest is that it confers an interest in property which is defeasible or destructible on payment of the debt or performance of the obligation which was secured.[40] A borrower which gives security can always obtain the release of its property from the security by repaying the loan.[41] Subject to one exception, equity renders void any attempt to restrict

[35] *Diamond Report*, para 23.6. See also the Cork Committee's discussion of retention of title agreements: *Cork Committee Report*, ch 37.

[36] *Diamond Report*, paras 23.6.9–23.6.10. But he did suggest that legislation should draw a line between simple (unregistrable) clauses and more complex arrangements which should be registrable.

[37] Other arrangements which can have the same economic effect as a security interest but are not, technically, in that category are sales and lease-backs to the vendor, hire-purchase agreements and debt factoring agreements.

[38] *Bank of Tokyo Ltd v Karoon* [1986] 3 All ER 468, CA, 486 *per* Goff LJ.

[39] *Re George Inglefield Ltd* [1933] Ch 1, CA; *Re Curtain Dream plc* [1990] BCLC 925; *Welsh Development Agency v Export Finance Co Ltd* [1992] BCC 270, CA; *Orion Finance Ltd v Crown Financial Management Ltd* [1996] BCC 621, CA; *Re Bond Worth Ltd* [1980] Ch 228; *Borden UK Ltd v Scottish Timber Products Ltd* [1981] Ch 25, CA; *Pfeiffer E Weinkellerei-Weineinkauf GmbH & Co v Arbuthnot Factors Ltd* [1988] 1 WLR 150; *Tatung (UK) Ltd v Galex Telesure Ltd* (1989) 5 BCC 325.

[40] *Re Bond Worth Ltd* [1980] Ch 228, 248.

[41] *Re George Inglefield Ltd* [1933] Ch 1, CA, 27 *per* Romer LJ. This is one characteristic which can help to distinguish a mortgage or charge from a sale: ibid.

the borrower's right to redeem a security.[42] The exception is contained in the Companies Act 1985, s 193 which provides that a condition contained in debentures, or in a deed for securing debentures, is not invalid by reason only that the debentures are thereby made irredeemable or redeemable only on the happening of a contingency (however remote), or on the expiration of a period (however long), any rule of equity to the contrary notwithstanding. The term 'debenture' lacks a precise definition,[43] but it is clear that for the purposes of this section it includes a mortgage on land.[44] In practice, debentures which are described as 'perpetual' or 'irredeemable' may in fact give the company an option to redeem.

A SECURITY INTEREST IS AN INTEREST IN THE CHARGOR'S PROPERTY TO SECURE A DEBT

There are two issues here. The first is that a security interest is inextricably linked with the debt for which it is security. It follows from this that a creditor cannot be said to have a security interest in property at any time when there is no outstanding debt. This situation could arise, for example, where the charge predates the advance of the money or where it relates to a current account which fluctuates between being in credit and being overdrawn.

The second issue relates to the essential feature of a security interest that it gives the creditor an interest in the property of the person providing the security. This means that if the debtor[45] agrees to give security over property that it does not presently own but will acquire in the future, the creditor cannot be viewed as having a security interest in the debtor's property at the time when the agreement is concluded.[46] Adopting language that is familiar to US lawyers in the context of the Uniform Commercial Code, art 9,[47] the Crowther Committee, whose report containing a review of credit and security was published as a government command paper in 1971, described situations where there is an agreement for security but no outstanding loan or where the security is not presently owned by the debtor as being ones where the security interest has not 'attached' to the debtor's property:[48]

[42] The history of this rule of equity is traced by Viscount Haldane LC in *Kreglinger v New Patagonia Meat and Cold Storage Co Ltd* [1914] AC 25, HL. In this case the House of Lords confirmed that the rule applies to floating charges, thereby dispelling doubts raised by *De Beers Consolidated Mines v British South Africa Co* [1912] AC 52, HL.

[43] See Ch 2 above, at 50–1.

[44] *Knightsbridge Estates Trust Ltd v Byrne* [1940] AC 613, HL.

[45] This is used to include a third-party provider of security by way of guarantee.

[46] There are some exceptions to the rule that a debtor cannot give a valid security over another's property but these exceptions are of limited significance: see Goode, RM, *Legal Problems of Credit and Security*, (2nd edn, 1988) 30.

[47] Although the language of attachment is not widely used in the English courts, note *Illingworth v Houldsworth* [1904] AC 355, HL 358 where Lord Macnaghten speaks of a fixed charge 'fastening' on the subject-matter of the security.

[48] *Report of the Committee on Consumer Credit* Cmnd 4596 (1971) para 5.6.4. See also Goode, RM, *Commercial Law* (2nd edn, 1995) 734; Goode, RM, *Legal Problems of Credit and Security* (2nd edn, 1988) ch II.

The fact that there is an enforceable agreement which provides for a security interest is not by itself sufficient to make that security interest attach to a security, for the agreement may well have been entered into before the security was acquired by the debtor and/or before any advance has been made by the secured party.

Even though attachment may not have taken place, the date of an enforceable agreement for security has considerable legal significance. It is the date from which the 21-day registration period runs for the purposes of the registration requirements of the Companies Act 1985.[49] Also, as is clear from cases involving security on property not owned by the debtor at the time of the agreement but later acquired (commonly referred to as 'future property'), even though the security does not attach until the property is acquired, the creditor has more than a mere contractual right from the time when the agreement is concluded, which has important implications should the debtor become insolvent or grant someone else an interest in the same property thereby creating a potential priority dispute.

Security on Future Property

The seminal authority on the effect of an agreement for security relating to future property is the decision of the House of Lords in *Holroyd v Marshall*.[50] The indenture between the lenders and the borrower in this case provided for the lenders to have security on existing premises, machinery and other implements owned by the borrower and also on 'all machinery, implements and things, which during the continuance of this security shall be fixed or placed in or about the said mill . . . in addition to or substitution for the said premises or any part thereof'. When the borrower later defaulted on the loan, the lenders sold the machinery and effects which had been in existence at the date of the security agreement but this sale did not realise sufficient proceeds to discharge their loan. They therefore also sought to claim as part of their security machinery which had been added and substituted since the date of the security but this was also claimed by a judgment creditor. The question for the House of Lords was whether the lenders had an interest in the added and substituted machinery because, if they did, that machinery could not be taken in execution by the judgment creditor.

The House of Lords held that the lenders had an equitable interest and that their title therefore prevailed over the judgment creditor. Although the agreement to confer an interest in future property was void as law because there was nothing to convey,[51] in equity the agreement took effect so that as soon as the future property was acquired by the borrower and, without the need for

[49] Companies Act 1985, s 395. This is made even clearer by the Companies Act 1989, s 103 which was part of the series of provisions in the 1989 Act intended to amend the registration requirements of the Companies Act 1985 but which have never been brought into force.

[50] (1862) 10 HLC 191, 11 ER 999, [1861–73] All ER Rep 414, HL. This case did not lay down new doctrine but contains 'the mere enunciation of elementary principles long settled in Courts of Equity': *Tailby v Official Receiver* (1888) 13 App Cas 523, HL, 535 *per* Lord Watson; see also 546 *per* Lord Macnaghten.

[51] *Robinson v Macdonnell* (1816) 5 M&S 228, 105 ER 1034.

any new act on the part of the lenders, it became subject to the lenders' security. Lord Westbury LC said:[52]

> But if a vendor or mortgagor agrees to sell or mortgage property, real or personal, of which he is not possessed at the time, and he receives the consideration for the contract, and afterwards becomes possessed of property answering the description in the contract, there is no doubt that a court of equity would compel him to perform the contract, and that the contract would in equity transfer the beneficial interest to the mortgagee or purchaser immediately on the property being acquired.

Holroyd v Marshall was considered and in some respects clarified by the House of Lords in the later case of *Tailby v The Official Receiver*.[53] Here a bill of sale assigned (amongst other things) all of the book debts due and owing or which might during the continuance of the security become due and owing to the mortgagor. It was held that this was effective to give the creditor an equitable interest in the book debts incurred after the date of the bill of sale. The respondent's argument that the description of the security was too vague to be effective (which had found favour in Court of Appeal) was rejected. The House of Lords took the view that the Court of Appeal (and courts in some previous cases) had proceeded on a misapprehension of some observations of Lord Westbury in *Holroyd v Marshall* which had appeared to link the doctrine enunciated in that case to the class of circumstances in which a court of equity would grant specific performance.[54] Lord Macnaghten in particular sought to correct the misunderstanding. He explained that the principle of equity underlying *Holroyd v Marshall* was that equity considers as done that which ought to be done. This principle was independent of the rules relating to the granting of specific performance and applied where there was an agreement assigning future property for value with the result that, provided the consideration had passed, the agreement was binding on the property as soon as it was acquired.[55]

Tailby v Official Receiver indicates that the principle enunciated in *Holroyd v Marshall* will apply where a person has agreed to give a security interest to a lender in the following circumstances.

1. There is an agreement to confer the security interest on the lender: in *Holroyd v Marshall* this took the form of an agreement to assign by way of security whilst in *Tailby v Official Receiver* this took the form of a present assignment (by way of security) of future debts. As Lord Macnaghten stated, the principle gives effect to the parties' contractual intentions.

   > The truth is that cases of equitable assignment or specific lien, where the consideration has passed, depend on the real meaning of the agreement between the

[52] (1862) 10 HLC 191, HL, 211.

[53] (1888) 13 App Cas 523, HL.

[54] (1888) 13 App Cas 523, HL, 529 *per* Lord Hershell; 535 *per* Lord Watson. The third judge, Lord Fitzgerald did not address the point (and he neither assented to nor dissented from the decision). The opinion of the remaining judge, Lord Macnaghten, is considered next.

[55] *Metcalfe v Archbishop of York* 1 My & Cr 547. See also Sykes, EI, and Walker, S, *The Law of Securities*, (5th edn, 1993) 152–3; Keeler, JF, 'Some Reflections on *Holroyd v Marshall*' (1969) 3 Adel L Rev 360; Meagher, RP, Gummow, WMC, and Lehane, JRF, *Equity Doctrine and Remedies* (3rd edn, 1992) paras 647–54; Goode, RM, *Commercial Law* (2nd edn, 1995) 736–7.

parties. The difficulty, generally speaking, is to ascertain the true scope and effect of the agreement.[56]

2. The consideration for the security interest has been executed; ie the lender has advanced the money.
3. The borrower has acquired an interest in property matching the description of the subject-matter of the security. The subject-matter of the security may be expressed in broad terms as in the *Tailby* case where it extended to all of the borrower's future book debts. Provided the clause identifying the subject-matter of the security is not so vaguely drafted as to make it impossible to ascertain to what it is applicable, the principle will apply. Two members of the House of Lords in the *Tailby* decision adverted to the possibility of equity denying effect to a purported equitable assignment on grounds of public policy where it included all of the present and future property of the person giving it and deprived that person of the power of maintaining himself but that possible limitation has not been applied in later cases.

The position of the creditor between the conclusion of the security agreement and the acquisition of the property by the debtor is demonstrated by *Re Lind, Industrial Finance Syndicate Ltd v Lind.*[57] Lind was presumptively entitled to a share in his mother's personal estate and he used this expectancy as security for two mortgages. Later, but before his mother's death, Lind became bankrupt and obtained his discharge. He then assigned his expectancy to a syndicate. On his mother's death, the two mortgagees claimed Lind's share of the estate in priority to the syndicate and the Court of Appeal upheld their claim. The discharge in bankruptcy had discharged Lind's personal obligations but the mortgagees had a stronger claim. Bankes LJ explained: 'it is true that the security was not enforceable until the property came into existence, but nevertheless the security was there';[58] and Phillimore LJ stated, 'it is I think well and long settled that the right of the assignee is a higher right than the right to have specific performance of a contract, that the assignment creates an equitable charge which arises immediately upon the property coming into existence'.[59] An earlier decision of the Court of Appeal, *Collyer v Isaacs*,[60] had appeared to reach the opposite conclusion, but this case was distinguished on various grounds: Swinfen Eady LJ held that the agreement in question in that case did not constitute an assignment of future assets but merely gave the creditor a licence to seize assets and that, as such, it was not within the *Holroyd v Marshall* principle; Bankes LJ confined the decision to its facts; Phillimore LJ held that it was inconsistent with the current of authorities culminating in *Tailby v Official Receiver*. The way in which the *Collyer* case was distinguished in *Re Lind* has been questioned and it has been suggested that:

[56] *Tailby v Official Receiver* (1888) 13 App Cas 523, HL, 547 *per* Lord Macnaghten. Contrast *Carr v Allatt* (1858) 27 LJ (Ex) 385 and *Brown v Bateman* (1866–7) LR 2 CP 272 with *Reeve v Whitmore* (1864) 33 LJ (Ch) 63, *Thompson v Cohen* (1871–2) LR 7 QB 527; *Cole v Kernot* (1871–2) LR 7 QB 534n; *Collyer v Isaacs* (1881) 19 Ch D 342, CA (as explained in *Re Lind* [1915] 2 Ch 345 CA, 362–3 *per* Swinfen Eady LJ).

[57] [1915] 2 Ch 345, CA.

[58] Ibid at 374

[59] Ibid at 365–6.

[60] *Collyer v Isaacs* (1881) 19 Ch D 342, CA.

'It is probably more satisfactory simply to regard *Collyer v Isaacs* as no longer authoritative, and to regard *Re Lind* as expounding the present state of the law.'[61]

The precise nature of the interest held by a lender with security over future property before the property has been acquired has never been defined, but some of the consequences of *Re Lind* are reasonably clear. First, a lender which has security over future property is nevertheless a secured creditor in the chargor's liquidation and is not required to proceed as an unsecured creditor by submitting a proof. If the chargor company is in compulsory liquidation, the creditor can enforce its rights against the property when it is acquired without infringing the Insolvency Act 1986, s 127 which renders void any disposition of the company's property after the commencement of the winding up.[62] The reason for this is that the creditor's interest in the property predates the insolvency and there is therefore no disposition of the company's property at a vulnerable time. Second, for the purposes of priority rules which depend on order of creation, a security over future property is created when the agreement is concluded and not at the later date when the property is acquired. Thus, in the *Re Lind* decision itself the mortgagees took priority over a later assignment.

THE SUBJECT-MATTER OF A SECURITY INTEREST—FORMS OF PROPERTY THAT CAN BE USED AS SECURITY

The previous section made the point that a chargor can only grant security over its own property including property that it may acquire in the future. Here, the question is whether there is any limitation on the type of property owned by the chargor that can be used as security.

It is now clear that a company can use all of its present and future assets as security. Land, whether freehold or leasehold, and the fixtures and fittings attaching to it, tangible personal property such as the company's stock in trade and intangible personal property, including debts owing to the company and its intellectual property, can all be used as security. There was an old rule to the effect that a company could not charge its uncalled capital unless it had express power to do so in the objects clause of its memorandum of association,[63] but the effect of that rule is overridden by the Companies Act 1985, ss 35 and 35A which protect outsiders from the consequences of an act being outside the scope of a company's objects.[64] Also, in practice companies tend to have very extensive objects that authorise them to do virtually anything, including charging their uncalled capital.

[61] Meagher, RP, Gummow, WMC, and Lehane, JRF, *Equity Doctrine and Remedies* (3rd edn, 1992) 191.

[62] *Re Androma Pty Ltd* [1987] 2 Qd 134, Q FC. Although a decision on Australian legislation, the reasoning would seem to be equally applicable to the English statute.

[63] *Bank of South Australia v Abrahams* (1875) LR 6 CP 265.

[64] See further Ch 3 above, at 94–7.

Re Charge Card Services Ltd[65] sparked a decade of controversy. In this case Millett J said that a chargor could not use debts as security in favour of a creditor which was itself the person that owed the debts to the company; in other words, a chargor could not 'charge back' debts to the debtor because, in Millett J's view, a security in that form was conceptually impossible. The matter was extensively debated in academic journals and elsewhere.[66] When the matter finally came before the House of Lords in *Re Bank of Credit and Commerce International SA (No 8)*,[67] it was held that a charge back was not conceptually impossible and that it was open to a chargor to give security in that form. Lord Hoffmann, who delivered the only reasoned speech, accepted that a charge back lacked one of the regular features of a charge on debts—ie, the chargee could not enforce the security by suing the debtor since the chargee could not sue itself—but held that the absence of this one feature did not preclude the existence of a charge. His Lordship emphasised that where there was no threat to the consistency of the law or objection of public policy, the courts should be very slow to declare a practice of the commercial community to be conceptually impossible.

FORMS OF CONSENSUAL REAL SECURITY

Consensual real security is conventionally divided into four categories: namely, pledge, lien, mortgage and charge. Pledges and liens have limited practical significance because they require the creditor to take some form of possession of the subject-matter of the security. The forms of security that are in more widespread use in corporate financing are mortgages and charges. The terms 'mortgage' and 'charge' are often used interchangeably but there are some technical distinctions between them. For the purposes of the registration requirements of the Companies Act 1985, the term 'charge' includes mortgages.

Pledge and Lien

In a pledge, assets of the debtor are delivered to the creditor as security for the debt or other obligation.[68] The creditor is said to have a special property in the pledged property and, if the debtor fails to pay the debt when due, the creditor can sell the pledged property and use the sale proceeds to discharge the debt whilst accounting to the debtor for any surplus.[69] This distinguishes the

[65] [1987] Ch 150 (affirmed but without reference to the point relevant here at [1989] Ch 497, CA).

[66] The leading proponent of the pro charge-back view was Philip Wood: see Wood, PR, 'Three Problems of Set-off: Contingencies, Build-ups and Charge-Backs' (1987) 8 Co Law 262. Detailed analysis of the point is also to be found in Wood, PR, *English and International Set-off* (1989) paras 5.134—5.181.

[67] [1998] AC 214, HL. McCormack, G, 'Charge Backs and Commercial Certainty in the House of Lords' [1998] CfiLR 111.

[68] *Coggs v Barnard* (1703) 2 Ld Raym 909, Ct of Kings Bench; *Haliday v Holgate* (1868) LR 3 Exch 299, Exch Chamber.

[69] *Re Hardwick, ex parte Hubbard* (1886) 17 QBD 690, CA.

pledge from the lien, which at common law confers on the creditor a right to detain the debtor's property but no right of sale or disposition.[70] The creditor may use the pledged assets at its own risk. The creditor may also assign his interest as pledgee and may sub-pledge that interest.[71] The debtor is entitled to the immediate possession of the assets when he has paid the debt for which they were pledged and, if the goods have been sub-pledged, the sub-pledgee may be sued in conversion if he impedes the debtor from exercising this right. In these circumstances, the debtor can also sue the creditor for breach of the contract of pledge.[72]

A valid pledge requires an agreement between the debtor and creditor and also delivery of the assets which form the subject-matter of the security; agreement alone does not suffice.[73] In addition to actual delivery, the law has recognised constructive delivery as being effective for this purpose, an example of this being the delivery of the key to a warehouse in which goods are stored.[74] Negotiable instruments and securities, such as bearer bonds, can be pledged[75] but it has been held that the effect of depositing share certificates with a lender is to create an equitable mortgage rather than a pledge.[76] This distinction can be explained: delivery of bearer securities to a creditor constitutes delivery of the assets in the same way as delivery of goods; but delivery of share certificates, which are simply evidence of title to the shares,[77] does not amount to delivery of the shares and even the delivery of share certificates accompanied by executed share transfer forms does not complete delivery of the shares.[78]

A pledge requires agreement between debtor and creditor and there is no such thing as a pledge arising by operation of law. By way of contrast a common-law lien generally arises by operation of law[79] but it can also arise by agreement. A lien is a limited form of security which entitles the creditor to hold the assets which are the subject-matter of the security but not to sell them.[80]

[70] *Donald v Suckling* (1866) LR 1 QB 585, 604, 610, 612. [71] Ibid.

[72] See further, Sealy, LS, and Hooley, RJA, *Text and Materials in Commercial Law* (1994) 808–11.

[73] *Official Assignee of Madras v Mercantile Bank of India Ltd* [1935] AC 53, PC.

[74] *Wrightson v McArthur and Hutchinsons (1919) Ltd* [1921] 2 KB 807.

[75] *Carter v Wake* (1877) 4 Ch D 605. [76] *Harrold v Plenty* [1901] 2 Ch 314.

[77] Companies Act 1985, s 186. Compare Companies Act 1985, s 188 which is concerned with share warrants, title to which does pass by delivery.

[78] *London and Midland Bank Ltd v Mitchell* [1899] 2 Ch 161; *Stubbs v Slater* [1910] 1 Ch 632, CA. It is generally considered that legal title to shares passed only when the transferee is registered in the company's books as a member of the company: *Société Generale de Paris v Walker* (1885) 11 App Cas 20, HL, 28 *per* Lord Selborne; *Colonial Bank v Hepworth* (1887) 36 Ch D 36, 54. The judicial assumption that legal title to shares passes only on registration has been queried by Pennington, RR, *Company Law* (7th edn, 1995) 442–3.

[79] *Re Bond Worth Ltd* [1980] Ch 228, 250 *per* Slade J.

[80] *Hammonds v Barclay* (1802) 2 East 227, 102 ER 356; *Tappenden v Artus* [1964] 2 QB 185, CA. On liens see further Sealy, LS, and Hooley, RJA, *Text and Materials in Commercial Law* (1994) 814–29; Bell, AP, *Modern Law of Personal Property in England and Wales* (1989) ch 6.

Mortgage

Leaving aside statutory intervention, a mortgage is a transfer of ownership, legal or equitable, as security for a debt or other obligation with an express or implied proviso for re-transfer when the debt or obligation has been discharged.[81] A debtor may mortgage its own property as security but it is also possible for a third party to mortgage its property as security for another's debts and the third party need not itself undertake any personal obligation to pay.[82] Since 1926 mortgages of land have been subject to special statutory rules under which the creation of a mortgage does not involve a transfer of ownership. A mortgage of land must be made by a demise for a term of years absolute or by a charge by way of legal mortgage.[83] Mortgages of land and interests in land are not explored further in this chapter.

Also excluded from detailed discussion are security interests in equitable property such as beneficial interests under trusts. Although companies may hold equitable property, it is perhaps more common to think of the property that a company may use as its security as being property of which it is the legal owner such as plant, machinery and equipment, stock in trade, intellectual property, book debts and other receivables.

A legal mortgage of personal property requires the transfer to the creditor of the legal title to the assets that are to form the security. The form of the transfer depends on the nature of the assets in question. A legal mortgage of goods may be oral[84] or may be created by deed or by delivery of the goods. Whether a transaction involving the delivery of goods is a mortgage or a pledge depends on the intention of the parties.[85] Generally, a legal mortgage of a chose in action such as a debt must comply with the Law of Property Act 1925, s 136 (1) and must be in writing with written notice to the debtor,[86] but particular types of choses in action are subject to special rules: a legal mortgage of shares requires the creditor to be registered in the company's register of members in respect of the shares;[87] and a legal mortgage of negotiable instruments such as bearer securities can be created simply by delivery of the relevant documents. Future property cannot be the subject of a legal mortgage.[88] An

[81] *Santley v Wilde* [1899] 2 Ch 474, CA; *Noakes & Co Ltd v Rice* [1902] AC 24, HL, 28 *per* Earl of Halsbury LC.

[82] *Perry v National Provincial Bank of England* [1910] 1 Ch 464, CA; *Re Conley* [1938] 2 All ER 127 CA.

[83] Law of Property Act 1925, ss 85–86.

[84] *Newlove v Shrewsbury* (1888) 21 QBD 41, CA.

[85] Bell, AP, *Modern Law of Personal Property in England and Ireland* (1989) 185; Ramage, RW, 'Chattel Mortgages' (1971) 121 NLJ 291.

[86] Law of Property Act 1925, s 136 (1) refers to 'absolute' assignments and provides that it does not apply to assignments purporting to be by way of charge only. An assignment by way of mortgage is considered to be absolute and not by way of charge only: *Burlinson v Hall* (1884) 12 QBD 347; *Tancred v Delagoa Bay Co* (1889) 23 QBD 239.

[87] *General Credit and Discount Co v Glegg* (1883) 22 Ch D 549 is an example of a legal mortgage of shares. It is generally considered that legal title to shares passed only when the transferee is registered in the company's books as a member of the company: *Société Generale de Paris v Walker* (1885) 11 App Cas 20, HL, 28 *per* Lord Selborne; *Colonial Bank v Hepworth* (1887) 36 Ch D 36, 54. But note Pennington, RR, *Company Law* (7th edn, 1995) 442–3.

[88] *Holroyd v Marshall* (1862) 10 HLC 191; 11 ER 999, [1861–73] All ER Rep 414, HL; *Robinson v Macdonnell* (1816) 5 M&S 228, 105 ER 1034.

assignment of part of a debt cannot be brought within s 136 (1) with the result that it is not possible to create a legal mortgage of part of a debt.[89]

An equitable mortgage of legal property involves the transfer to the creditor of equitable ownership subject to a proviso for redemption. An equitable mortgage of legal personal property can be created in various ways. A contract to give a legal mortgage on property can give rise in equity to an equitable mortgage when the requirements for a full legal mortgage (for example registration of the creditor in the company's register of members in the case of a legal mortgage of shares or compliance with the Law of Property Act 1925, s 136 (1) in relation to the legal mortgage of a debt) have not been fulfilled. Although there are dicta that suggest otherwise,[90] it is doubtful whether, once valuable consideration has passed, an agreement needs to be specifically enforceable in order for an equitable mortgage to arise. The decision of the House of Lords in *Tailby v Official Receiver* establishes that the availability of specific performance is not a prerequisite for the intervention of equity and that it can do so where the consideration for the security had been paid on the basis simply of the maxim that equity treats as done that which ought to be done. That was a case involving the assignment, by way of security, of future property but it is difficult to think of any reason why the requirements should be different in respect of existing property. Although dicta in certain cases and some writers support the argument that to pass an equitable title under a contract the contract must be specifically enforceable, the better view is that once consideration has been executed the need for specific performance falls away and the assignment takes effect in equity on the basis that this is what ought to occur.[91] The significance of the point is apparent from the litigation in *Tailby* itself: the House of Lords rejected an argument, which had been accepted by the Court of Appeal, that the agreement did not give rise to an equitable security because the subject-matter of the security was described in terms which were too uncertain and unspecific to be capable of specific enforcement. Equitable considerations such as vagueness which were applicable to suits for specific performance were not in their Lordships' view[92] relevant to cases of equitable assignments.

Notwithstanding that the availability of specific performance may not be a prerequisite to the creation of an equitable mortgage, where that mortgage arises in circumstances where the parties intended a legal mortgage but failed to comply with the formalities required to achieve it, specific performance in a narrow sense[93] may still be relevant in that the court may be called upon to grant an order of specific performance compelling the chargor to execute a

[89] *Durham Brothers v Robertson* [1898] 1 QB 765, CA; *Re Steel Wing Co Ltd* [1921] 1 Ch 349; *Earle v Hemsworth* (1928) 44 TLR 605; *Williams v Atlantic Assurance Co* [1933] 1 KB 81, CA. Although there are authorities to the contrary, so that the point may not be regarded as being definitively settled, the view expressed in the text is widely regarded as being the better view: Marshall, OR, *Assignment of Choses in Action*, (1950) 173–4. In *Norman v FCT* (1963) 109 CLR 9, High Ct of Aust, 29 Windeyer J stated that the earlier inconsistent decisions must be taken to be overruled.

[90] *Swiss Bank Corpn v Lloyds Bank* [1982] AC 584, CA and HL, 595 *per* Buckley LJ.

[91] Meagher, RP, Gummow, WMC, and Lehane, JRF, *Equity Doctrine and Remedies* (3rd edn, 1992) ch 6.

[92] *Tailby v Official Receiver* (1888) 13 App Cas 523, HL, 547 *per* Lord Macnaghten.

[93] Spry, ICF, *The Principles of Equitable Remedies* (5th edn, 1997) 51.

legal mortgage in the required form.[94] Where an application is made for an order for specific performance in the narrow sense of requiring a particular act to establish or perfect the parties' rights, such as execution of a conveyance, less weight is attached to equitable considerations than in applications for specific performance in the broad sense of requiring performance of the contractual obligations contained in the final bargain between the parties.[95]

An equitable mortgage can also be created by the declaration of a trust with a proviso (express or implied) for termination of the trust on repayment of the debt secured.[96] A further means of creating an equitable mortgage is by depositing the title deeds to property with the creditor with the intention that they are to be held as security. Thus in *Harrold v Plenty*[97] the deposit of share certificates as security for a debt was held to amount to an equitable mortgage of the shares. There is no need for this type of arrangement to be recorded in writing for the mortgage to be effective.

Where there is no new consideration for the mortgage, as where it is given to secure existing indebtedness, it may be created by deed[98] except where the subject-matter of the security is future property, because in this case valuable consideration is always required.[99] A voluntary assignment of present property that is not contained in a deed may also give rise to an equitable mortgage where the mortgagor has done everything which, according to the nature of the property, was necessary to be done in order to transfer the property.[100] Where, for example, the subject-matter of the security is a holding of shares in a private company and the shareholder executes a transfer of those shares by way of security but the board, as it is entitled to do under the articles, declines to register the transfer, the legal transfer is incomplete, because that requires registration, but there will be an equitable transfer, notwithstanding the

[94] Goodhart, W, and Jones, G, *Specific Performance* (2nd edn, 1996) 166–8.

[95] Spry, ICF, *The Principles of Equitable Remedies* (5th edn, 1997) 51–6, 568–70.

[96] *Halsbury's Laws of England* (4th reissue, 1992) vol 4 (1) para 659.

[97] [1901] 2 Ch 314.

[98] Whether a gift can amount to an effective equitable assignment of existing property is a point which is not beyond controversy, but the view in the text is supported by Guest, AG (gen ed), *Chitty on Contracts* (27th edn, 1994) para 19–018 and Meagher, RP, Gummow, WMC, and Lehane, JRF, *Equity Doctrine and Remedies* (3rd edn, 1992) ch 6 and the cases cited there. See *Re McArdle* [1951] 1 Ch 669, CA where it was acknowledged that a document amounting to an equitable assignment (as opposed to an agreement to effect an assignment which must be supported by consideration to be effective as an equitable assignment) would not be invalid notwithstanding the absence of consideration (see also *Norman v Federal Commissioner of Taxation* (1962–3) 109 CLR 9, High Ct of Aust, 33 *per* Windeyer J). A particular issue is the equitable assignment of part of a debt, but it is considered that this can be effected by means of a gift: *Shepherd v Federal Commissioner of Taxation* (1965) 113 CLR 385, H Ct of Aust.

A deed does not take the place of consideration where that is needed to attract the aid of equity. Where value is not required but a clear expression of intention will suffice to effect an equitable assignment, the delivery of a deed couched in terms of present gift provides the best manifestation of the donor's intention: *Norman v Federal Commissioner of Taxation* (1962–3) 109 CLR 9, High Ct of Aust, 32 *per* Windeyer J.

An equitable mortgage granted otherwise than for value within the specified periods before insolvency may be liable to be set aside as a preference under Insolvency Act 1986, s 239.

[99] *Tailby v Official Receiver* (1888) 13 App Cas 523, HL; *Re Ellenborough* [1903] 1 Ch 697; *Palette Shoes Pty Ltd v Krohn* (1937) 58 CLR 1, H Ct of Aust; *Norman v Federal Commissioner of Taxation* (1962–3) 109 CLR 9, High Ct of Aust.

[100] *Milroy v Lord* (1862) 4 De G F & J 264, 45 ER 1185.

absence of consideration, because the shareholder has done everything that he can do to transfer the shares.[101]

The debtor's continuing interest in mortgaged property stems from the entitlement to require the property to be re-conveyed on the discharge of the secured debt or other obligation. This is known as the 'equity of redemption'. The equity of redemption survives default[102] and late payment or performance will still entitle the mortgagor to redeem at least until such time as the creditor enforces its security by selling the secured assets or by foreclosure. Any provision in the terms of a mortgage which purports to remove the mortgagor's right to redeem, or which would indirectly tend to have the effect of making the mortgage irredeemable is regarded in equity as a 'clog' or 'fetter' on the equity of redemption and, as such, it is void.[103] The principle that clogs on the equity of redemption are void applies to all types of mortgages and also to charges, including floating charges.[104]

The main[105] remedies that are available as a matter of law to a mortgagee in the event of default (security remedies[106]) are as follows. Legal[107] and equitable mortgagees have the power to obtain an order for foreclosure which, when granted, allows the mortgagee thereafter to hold the property free from any claim of the mortgagor. Where the mortgage (legal or equitable) is by deed, powers of sale and to appoint a receiver are implied by virtue of the Law of Property Act 1925, s 101.[108] Mortgagees can also apply to court for the appointment of a receiver or for an order for sale but, in the case of mortgages by deed, the statutory powers usually make it unnecessary to apply to court. The mortgagee's remedies may be augmented by agreement between the parties. It is common practice for mortgages given by companies to include express powers of sale and seizure and to make express provision for the appointment of receivers.

Charges

Every equitable mortgage is also an equitable charge but the converse is not true:[109] a mortgage, like a charge, appropriates property for the payment of a

[101] *Re Rose* [1952] Ch 499, CA.

[102] This was not always the case: see Simpson, AWB, *A History of the Land Law* (2nd edn, 1986) ch X.

[103] eg, *Noakes & Co Ltd v Rice* [1902] AC 24, HL, 28 *per* Earl of Halsbury LC and at 30 *per* Lord Macnaghten. There is a considerable amount of case law distinguishing valid commercial terms from void 'clogs': see Megarry, RE, and Wade, HWR, *The Law of Real Property* (5th edn, 1984) 964–71; Baker, PV, and Langan, P St J, *Snell's Equity* (29th edn, 1990) 394–7.

[104] *Kreglinger v New Patagonia Meat and Cold Storage Co Ltd* [1914] AC 25, HL dispelling doubts raised by *De Beers Consolidated Mines v British South Africa Co* [1912] AC 52, HL.

[105] See Megarry, RE, and Wade, HWR, *The Law of Real Property* (5th edn, 1984) ch 16 for a fuller account of the remedies available to mortgagees.

[106] Gough, WJ, *Company Charges* (2nd edn, 1996) 36.

[107] A legal mortgagee also has the right to claim immediate possession of the security but this right is now limited by various statutory provisions.

[108] But there is some uncertainty concerning the power of an equitable mortgagee to transfer the legal estate: *Re Hodson and Howe's Contract* (1887) 35 Ch D 668, CA (can only transfer equitable interest) contrasted with *Re White Rose Cottage* [1965] Ch 940, CA (*obiter* suggesting that equitable mortgagee now has power to transfer legal estate).

[109] *Shea v Moore* [1894] IR 158, Ir CA.

debt or the discharge of an obligation but a mortgage goes further than a charge and also operates to transfer ownership in equity to the creditor.[110] A charge gives its holder rights in relation to the property which is the subject-matter of the security but does not effect a transfer of the legal or beneficial ownership of that property.[111] Except in relation to land where, by statute, a mortgage by way of legal charge can be created,[112] a charge is a form of equitable security. A charge would normally be created by an agreement between the parties supported by consideration or in the form of a deed but, as Slade J noted in *Re Bond Worth Ltd*,[113] an equitable charge can also be created by the chargor declaring himself a trustee of the relevant assets for the purposes of the security.[114] The requirement for valuable consideration applies where the subject-matter of the charge is future property. The importance of the distinction between mortgages and charges is said to lie in the range of remedies available to the creditor in the event of default as a matter of general law.[115] A charge does not give its holder any right to foreclose.[116] A charge made by deed carries with it the implied statutory powers of sale and to appoint a receiver.[117] Irrespective of whether the charge is in the form of a deed, the holder has the right to apply to court for an order for sale or for the appointment of a receiver. The chargee's rights may be augmented by agreement between the parties and it is common practice for company charges to contain express provisions concerning the enforcement of the security by sale, appointment of a receiver and other remedies. The end result of these drafting techniques is that there is usually little difference between the remedies enjoyed by a mortgagee and by a chargee. In *Re Bond Worth Ltd*[118] Slade LJ acknowledged that the words 'mortgage' and 'charge' are often used interchangeably.[119]

FIXED AND FLOATING CHARGES: A COMPARISON OF THEIR KEY FEATURES

Fixed Charges

For companies the category of charges has to be subdivided into fixed charges and floating charges. A fixed charge is similar to a mortgage in that the holder immediately obtains rights in relation to the secured property and can restrict

[110] *Re Bond Worth Ltd* [1980] Ch 228, 250.

[111] *National Provincial and Union Bank of England v Charnley* 1924] 1 KB 431, CA, 449–50 *per* Atkin LJ; *Re Bond Worth Ltd* [1980] Ch 228, 250 *per* Slade J; *Swiss Bank Corpn v Lloyds Bank Ltd* [1982] AC 584, CA and HL, 594–5 *per* Buckley LJ; *Re Charge Card Services Ltd* [1987] Ch 150, 176 *per* Millett J.

[112] Law of Property Act 1925, s 87.

[113] [1980] Ch 228, 250.

[114] This would also be an equitable mortgage: *Halsbury's Laws of England* (4th reissue, 1992) vol 4 (1) para 659.

[115] Megarry, RE, and Wade, HWR, *The Law of Real Property* (5th edn, 1984) 926.

[116] *Carreras Rothmans Ltd v Freeman Mathews Treasure Ltd* [1985] Ch 207, 227.

[117] Law of Property Act 1925, s 205 (1)(xvi) provides that for the purposes of that Act the term 'mortgage' includes 'charge'.

[118] At 250.

[119] See also *London County and Westminster Bank v Tompkins* [1918] 1 KB 515, CA, 528–30 *per* Scrutton LJ.

the chargor company from disposing of it or destroying it. The chargee may obtain an injunction to restrain unauthorised disposals[120] and, if property which is subject to an enforceable fixed charge is wrongfully disposed of by the chargor, the person acquiring the property will take it subject to the charge unless he can claim to be a bona fide purchaser of the legal title to the property who is without notice of the existence of the fixed charge. A fixed charge is said to fasten on the assets which are the subject-matter of the security; thus in the leading case of *Illingworth v Houldsworth*[121] Lord Macnaghten described a fixed charge as 'one that without more fastens on ascertained and definite property or property capable of being ascertained or defined'. The subject-matter of a fixed charge security may extend to future property in accordance with the principles in *Holroyd v Marshall.*[122]

Floating Charges

In his speech in *Illingworth v Houldsworth*[123] Lord Macnaghten described the floating charge in these terms:

> a floating charge, on the other hand, is ambulatory and shifting in its nature, hovering over and so to speak floating with the property which it is intended to affect until some event occurs or some act is done which causes it to settle and fasten on the subject of the charge within its reach and grasp.[124]

In very broad terms the essence of the floating charge, and the factor which distinguishes it from the fixed charge, is that the chargor can continue to deal with the assets which are the subject of the security and can transfer them to third parties unencumbered by the security. However, as is discussed later in this chapter,[125] it is overly simplistic to assume that some degree of restriction on dealings by the chargor with the secured assets is incompatible with a floating charge, just as it is incorrect to assume that a degree of freedom to deal with the secured assets means that a charge cannot be classified as a fixed charge.

Floating charges can, and commonly do, extend to future property as well as to property presently owned by the chargor company. The effect of a floating charge on present and future property such as stock in trade is that as the stock turns over in the ordinary course of trade, items sold pass out of the security but new items come within the scope of the charge as soon as they are acquired by the company. A sensible lender taking a floating charge on stock will ensure that it also has a security on the debts owing to the company from customers who acquire goods on credit and on the bank account into which payments from customers are paid. The charge on the debts and their proceeds may also be a floating charge or, in certain circumstances, a fixed charge.

120 *Holroyd v Marshall* (1862) 10 HL Cas 191, HL, 211–12 *per* Lord Westbury.
121 [1904] AC 355, HL, 358.
122 (1862) 10 HLC 191, 11 ER 999, [1861–73] All ER Rep 414, HL.
123 [1904] AC 355, HL, 358.
124 Ibid.
125 See below, at 512–7.

Much of the wealth of a business may be in tied up in raw materials, goods in process of being manufactured or stock in trade. The floating charge is ideally suited to unlock the potential of items such as these as a valuable source of security. Since the items comprising raw materials, goods being manufactured or stock are circulating assets which necessarily fluctuate in the ordinary course of trade, fixed security under which the lender has power to restrain disposals is not an attractive option.[126] The floating charge was developed in the nineteenth century by the Chancery courts[127] at a time when industrial and commercial expansion meant that the demand for corporate finance was very strong and smaller companies, which were either unable or unwilling to raise it by issuing securities, were largely dependent on loans.[128] Although there is no inherent reason why individuals, partnerships and unincorporated associations should not be able to do so, the provisions of the Bills of Sale Acts 1878–1882 make it effectively impossible for them to create floating charges.[129] The Bills of Sale legislation does not apply to companies and, as a result, the ability to give a floating charge is one of the factors which may lead the founders of a business (often under pressure from their bankers) to choose to incorporate rather than to conduct the business through another form. There is no compelling reason in principle why the forms of security available to a business should depend on its organisational structure but, although there have been various proposals to extend the ability to give a floating charge to businesses other than companies, legislation to that effect has not been forthcoming.[130] There have also been calls for the floating charge to be abolished entirely and for the concept of a floating security to be subsumed within a new form of statutory security interest based on the model of the US Uniform Commercial Code, art 9.[131] Any transaction (regardless of its form) which is intended to create a security interest in personal property is an art 9 security interest. Article 9 regulates the rights of the parties and the effect of security interests on third parties. It also imposes filing requirements.

[126] *Re Woodroffes (Musical Instruments) Ltd* [1985] Ch 366, 377 *per* Nourse J.

[127] *Re Panama, New Zealand and Australia Royal Mail Co* (1870) 5 Ch App 318; *Re Florence Land and Public Works Co, ex p Moor* (1878) 10 Ch D 530, CA; *Moor v Anglo-Italian Bank* (1878) 10 Ch D 681; *Re Hamilton's Windsor Ironworks Co, ex p Pitman and Edwards* (1879) 12 Ch D 707; *Re Colonial Trusts Corporation, ex p Bradshaw* (1879) 15 Ch D 465.

[128] Pennington, RR, 'The Genesis of the Floating Charge' (1960) 23 MLR 630. Gough, WJ, 'The Floating Charge: Traditional Themes and New Directions' in Finn, PD (ed), *Equity and Commercial Relationships* (1987) 239 describes the floating charge as being 'one of the great legal success stories of Victorian times'. The contrast with the USA is striking. There it was held that there could not be an effective security interest in circulating assets (*Benedict v Ratner* 268 US 353, 45 S Ct 566, 69 L Ed 991 (1925)). The effect of that decision was reversed by legislation in the form of the Uniform Commercial Code, art 9.

[129] An exception is provided by Agricultural Credits Act 1928, s 5 which enables a farmer to give a floating charge over farming stock and other agricultural assets. Also any individual may be able to create a floating charge on present and future book debts because the Bills of Sale legislation applies only to chattels save in so far as Insolvency Act 1966, s 344 requires a general assignment of book debts to be registered under Bills of Sale Act 1878 as if it were an absolute bill of sale. See generally, Gough, WJ, *Company Charges* (2nd edn, 1996) 52–6.

[130] *Cork Committee Report*, paras 1568–9; *Diamond Report*, para 16.15.

[131] Goode, RM, 'The Exodus of the Floating Charge' in Feldman, D, and Meisel, F (eds), *Corporate and Commercial Law: Modern Developments* (1996) 193.

There is an obvious risk to a lender who takes floating as opposed to fixed security in that the company may dispose of the subject-matter of the security unprofitably thereby putting its solvency at risk. If the company does become insolvent the lender with a floating charge may find that other lenders have taken fixed charges ranking in priority to the floating charge with the consequence that the company has insufficient assets to satisfy the debt secured by the floating charge. One answer to the problem of prior ranking security may be for the lender to take fixed security whenever possible and to regard the floating charge as the appropriate form of security only in respect of assets which cannot be secured by way of a fixed charge, but a corporate borrower with sufficient bargaining strength may be able to resist demands to provide fixed security. Also there are technical reasons why, despite its limitations, a lender may favour a floating charge.[132]

For the lender which is prepared to lend on the security of a floating charge, the question, then, is how to reduce the risk of the company dissipating its assets or granting prior ranking security on them, whilst at the same time retaining the benefits of the floating charge in terms of enabling the company to continue to trade and (hopefully) to generate profits sufficient to service the interest payments on the loan and in due course to repay the principal advanced. Contractual provision is the appropriate tool. It is established that there are certain restrictions on dealings which are not incompatible with the floating nature of a floating charge and the lender can seek to include these in the charge in order to protect its interest.[133] The lender with a floating charge can also try to protect its interest through contractual provisions for crystallisation. A floating charge need not continue to float forever but can convert into a fixed charge, a process normally described as crystallisation. When a floating charge crystallises it operates as a fixed charge and, as such, it attaches to the company's existing assets which fall within the description of the subject-matter of the security and, if the security extends to future property, to property matching that description which is subsequently acquired by the company. Certain crystallising events are implied by law into a floating charge unless they are expressly excluded by the parties. It is possible to extend the range of crystallising events by express provision to that effect in the terms of the charge.[134]

THE NATURE OF THE FLOATING CHARGE

The nature of the floating charge is intriguing. It is a security interest which, as traditionally defined, means a proprietary interest held by the creditor in the

[132] In particular because it is only the holder of a certain type of floating charge who is entitled to block the appointment of an administrator: Insolvency Act 1986, s 9. This is discussed further later in this chapter, at 512–7.

[133] In particular the negative pledge whereby the company covenants not to create any new security ranking in priority to or equally with the floating charge. The priority effect of the negative pledge is discussed in this chapter, at 534–6.

[134] See further, this chapter, at 529–33.

debtor's property, yet the debtor remains, broadly, free to deal with the assets as if they were unsecured.[135] In an attempt to explain the nature of the floating charge, commentators have put forward a variety of theories. One is that a floating charge is a fixed charge combined with a licence from the creditor to the debtor to continue to deal with the assets. Although the licence theory derives some support from statements in a number of cases,[136] it has been clearly rejected in others[137] and is not now generally regarded as a satisfactory explanation of the nature of the floating charge.[138] The argument that it is not a security at all but an agreement to create a security in the future at the time of crystallisation has also been emphatically rejected.[139]

One of the most widely supported views[140] is that the floating charge is a security interest which gives the creditor an immediate proprietary interest in the property owned by the company from time to time, albeit one that does not attach specifically to any of the assets until crystallisation.[141] This approach has been described by Pennington as the 'mortgage of future assets theory'.[142] A difficulty with the mortgage of future assets theory is that it puts the nature of the proprietary interest created by the floating charge under the spotlight. Apart from acknowledging that it is different from, and lesser than, the interest created by the fixed charge,[143] it is difficult to explain the nature of the proprietary interest created by the floating charge in precise terms, but Goode, who agrees that the floating charge gives its holder a proprietary interest, suggests perhaps the most convincing analysis when he says that the floating charge gives the holder a present interest in a *fund* of assets which the

[135] This apparent paradox led the US courts to deny the effectiveness of floating security: *Benedict v Ratner* 268 US 353, 45 S Ct 566, 69 L Ed 991 (1925).

[136] Such as *Davey and Co v Williamson* [1898] 2 QB 194, CA, 200 *per* Lord Russell CJ. Farrar doubts whether there is in fact much clear-cut authority for the licence theory: Farrar, JH, 'Floating Charges and Priorities' (1974) 38 Conv 315, 316.

[137] In particular Buckley LJ in *Evans v Rival Granite Quarries Ltd* [1910] 2 KB 979, CA, 999: 'A floating charge is not a specific mortgage of the assets, plus a licence to the mortgagor to dispose of them in the course of his business.'

[138] Pennington, RR, 'The Genesis of the Floating Charge' (1960) 23 MLR 630, 646.

[139] Buckley LJ in *Evans v Rival Granite Quarries Ltd* [1910] 2 KB 979, CA, 999: 'A floating charge is not a future security; it is a present security which presently affects all of the assets of the company expressed to be included in it.' An agreement to create security in the future is not a security interest: *Re Gregory Love & Co, Francis v Gregory Love & Co* [1916] 1 Ch 203.

[140] Although there are differences of emphasis and on points of detail, the following writers agree that the holder of a uncrystallised floating charge has some form of proprietary interest: Goode, RM, *Legal Problems of Credit and Security*, (2nd edn, 1988) 48–9; Farrar, JH, 'World Economic Stagnation puts the Floating Charge on Trial' (1980) 1 Co Law 83; Ferran, EV, 'Floating Charges—The Nature of the Security' [1988] CLJ 213.

[141] Pennington, RR, 'The Genesis of the Floating Charge' (1960) 23 MLR 630, 646 and Pennington, RR, *Company Law* (7th edn, 1995) 567–9. Note Worthington, S, *Proprietary Interests in Commercial Transactions* (1996) 80 who describes this as the 'licence' theory. This description is not consistent with the explicit rejection of the licence theory by Professor Pennington in the MLR article. Equally it is not consistent with the MLR article to suggest that under the mortgage of future assets theory the chargee does not obtain a proprietary interest until crystallisation, but this is commonly asserted: eg, Calnan, RJ, 'Priorities Between Execution Creditors and Floating Chargees' (1982) 10 NZULR 111 at 121; Burns, FR, 'Automatic Crystallisation of Company Charges: Contractual Creativity or Confusion?' (1992) 20 ABLR 125, 126.

[142] Pennington, RR, *Company Law* (7th edn, 1995) 567.

[143] *Re Margart Pty Ltd; Hamilton v Westpac Banking Corpn* (1984) 9 ACLR 269, NSW SC-EqD, 272 *per* Helsham CJ ('while the charge is a floating charge that interest may or may not be an interest of the same dimension as that which he would obtain if the charge became a fixed charge').

debtor is free to manage in the ordinary course of its business.[144] The idea of a floating charge as a present security interest in a fund of assets was adopted in *Re Cimex Tissues Ltd*.[145]

The main argument against the mortgage of future assets theory is that put forward by Gough. Whilst agreeing that the floating charge is a present equitable security, Gough argues that it does not give the holder any equitable proprietary interest until crystallisation.[146] The floating charge, in his view, gives rise to a deferred equitable interest and, prior to crystallisation, the holder of a floating charge has a personal or 'mere' equity against the chargor arising under the charge contract. There are judicial statements supporting both arguments[147] and at a theoretical level the issue is unresolved. The approach of the English courts[148] when faced with questions to which the nature of the interest created by the floating charge may be thought to be relevant—such as the resolution of disputes involving competing claims against a company's property[149]—has tended to be a pragmatic, incremental one involving the consideration of one particular question: how does the floating charge operate in this specific context? The context is important.[150] There are various

[144] Goode, RM, *Legal Problems of Credit and Security*, (2nd edn, 1988) 49.

[145] [1994] BCC 626.

[146] Gough, WJ, *Company Charges* (2nd edn, 1996) 97–101 and ch 13.

[147] The cases are discussed in detail in Gough, ibid, ch 16. Even within a single judgment passages can be found to support either view: in *DCT v Lai Corporation Pty Ltd* [1987] WAR 15, WA SC, 22 Burt CJ acknowledges that a person can acquire a floating equitable interest whilst in a later passage cited by Gough in support of his analysis he states that there is no security attaching to property before the floating charge crystallises. Gough cites cases containing statements that there is no *specific* attachment to the individual assets subject to the floating charge until crystallisation in support of his analysis, but supporters of the mortgage of future assets theory do not regard those statements as being incompatible with their view which accepts that there is no specific attachment to particular assets prior to crystallisation.

[148] *Evans v Rival Granite Quarries Ltd* [1910] 2 KB 979, CA stands out as a case where the English Court of Appeal attempted to grapple with the theoretical nature of the interest created by the floating charge before proceeding to consider its effect in a particular context (competition with a judgment creditor). The Australian courts have demonstrated a willingness to embark upon a discussion of the theoretical nature of the floating charge or, at least, to acknowledge the different theories that have been put forward. The authorities in support of both arguments are reviewed in *Lyford v CBA* (1995) 17 ACSR 211, Fed Ct of Aust-GenD where the Gough view is adopted and Australian cases supporting the alternative view (*Landall Holdings Ltd v Caratti* [1979] WAR 97, WA SC; *Hamilton v Hunter* (1982) 7 ACLR 295, NSW SC EqD; *Re Margart Pty Ltd (in liq), Hamilton v Westpac Banking Corp* (1984) 9 ACLR 269, NSW SC-EqD) are not followed. *Lyford* was followed in *Wily v St George Partnership Banking Ltd* (1997–98) 26 ACSR 1, Fed Ct of Aust.

[149] On the basis that an interest must be 'proprietary' if it is to be enforceable in respect of property and against third parties: Meagher, RP, Gummow, WMC, and Lehane, JRF, *Equity Doctrine and Remedies* (3rd edn, 1992) para 425. Other situations where the nature of the interest created by an uncrystallised floating charge is relevant, but the extent of detailed judicial scrutiny of the abstract nature of that interest as opposed to examination driven by the context is variable, include the following: whether the court can appoint a receiver and manager on the application of the holder of such a charge (*Re Victoria Steamboats, Ltd, Smith v Wilkinson* [1897] 1 Ch 158 ('yes')); competing claims of floating charge holders and judgment creditors (*Evans v Rival Granite Quarries Ltd* [1910] 2 KB 979, CA); the application of particular statutory provisions (eg *Re Margart Pty Ltd; Hamilton v Westpac Banking Corpn* (1984) 9 ACLR 269, NSW SC-EqD where it was held that a payment to a creditor who held an uncrystallised floating charge did not contravene the New South Wales equivalent of the Insolvency Act 1986, s 127 because that section did not apply to the process whereby a person with a beneficial interest in property obtained the property or the proceeds of its realisation from the company; the floating charge conferred a beneficial interest for this purpose).

[150] *Re Manurewa Transport Ltd* [1971] NZLR 909, NZ SC, 915 *per* Speight J.

judicial definitions of the floating charge although, as Knox J noted in one case,[151] the concept appears to defy judicial definition without the aid of metaphor; but those definitions were mainly fashioned as part of the process of distinguishing between floating charges and fixed charges, a task of classification that can be achieved by establishing that the nature of the interest created by the floating charge is different from that created by the fixed charge, whilst leaving unresolved the underlying question of the precise nature of the floating charge and whether, or to what extent, it has a proprietary effect. The case law has thus not produced a definition of the floating charge in a general sense but has provided the raw material which commentators have endeavoured to synthesise into a broader, conceptual framework. Given the variety of questions that can arise and the mass of litigation that there has been since the nineteenth century involving the operation of the floating charge, it is unsurprising that the cases have has thrown up plenty of inconsistent judicial statements to feed different *ex post facto* theories. These theoretical uncertainties and ambiguities have not prevented the emergence of some clear and well-understood principles governing the operation of the floating charge. For example, the priority of the floating charge and the extent to which a prohibition in the terms of the charge on the subsequent creation of prior ranking security on any part of the charge property is effective to postpone such security to the floating charge, are now well-known and undisputed. This has been achieved notwithstanding the underlying theoretical dispute whether the priority effect derives from the charge, in its uncrystallised form, giving rise to some, albeit limited, equitable proprietary interest and the prohibition being an equity linked to an equitable interest,[152] or from the prohibition being an equity which can bind third parties with notice because it is linked to a claim (the floating charge) with the *potential* to mature into a proprietary interest through crystallisation.[153] Nor has the conceptual uncertainty prevented the floating charge from becoming an important element of corporate financing.

ESTABLISHING WHETHER A CHARGE IS FIXED OR FLOATING

An issue of considerable practical significance is that of distinguishing between fixed and floating charges. Both are consensual securities created by agreement between the parties. It is for the parties themselves to determine

[151] *Re New Bullas Trading Ltd* [1993] BCC 251, 260. The decision was reversed on appeal ([1994] BCC 36 CA) but this point is unaffected by the reversal.

[152] The conventional view is that an equity will only affect third parties if it is linked to an equitable interest: *National Provincial Bank Ltd v Ainsworth* [1965] AC 1175, HL; *Latec Investments Ltd v Hotel Terrigal Pty Ltd* (1965) 113 CLR 265, H Ct of Aust. McLelland, Hon Jus HL, 'Commentary' to Gough, WJ, 'The Floating Charge: Traditional Themes and New Directions' in Finn, PD (ed), *Equity and Commercial Relationships* (1987) 239, 281 doubts the Gough analysis of the floating charge for this reason.

[153] This is Gough's analysis: Gough, WJ, *Company Charges*, (2nd edn, 1996) 228–31, 392–5. It is clearly supported by a statement in the judgment of Murphy J in *DCT v Horsburgh* [1983] 2 VR 591, V SC, 603 (affirmed on different grounds: [1984] VR 773, V SC FC) accepting that a floating charge containing a prohibition could rank before a later fixed charge on the same property even though 'the fixed chargee is first with the proprietary interest'.

the form of security for a loan. It is not essential for them to label the security as a 'fixed' or, as the case may be, 'floating' charge, though it is common practice to do so. The parties' designation, if any, is a factor, but not a conclusive factor, in determining the proper classification of the charge. If, looking at the terms of the security generally, the agreement is inconsistent with the label attached to it by the parties, that description will not prevail.

Whether a charge is fixed or floating is relevant to the question of its priority against competing securities. It is also relevant for the purposes of the provisions of the Insolvency Act 1986 and the Companies Act 1985 concerning preferential debts. Preferential debts are debts which, by statute,[154] rank before debts secured by a floating charge but behind debts secured by a fixed charge in the event of the debtor company going into liquidation[155] or receivership[156] or possession being taken of property subject to the charge by or on behalf of the holders of debentures.[157] The provisions of the Insolvency Act 1986 concerned with administration procedure provide further reasons why it is important to know whether a charge is fixed or floating. Administration is a collective insolvency procedure and, once an administrator has been appointed, no one creditor, or group of creditors, is entitled to control him in the exercise of his powers. An administrator may not be appointed where an administrative receiver has been appointed to the company unless the appointor of the administrative receiver consents.[158] An administrative receiver is defined by the Insolvency Act 1986, s 29 (2) as a receiver or manager of the whole (or substantially the whole) of a company's property appointed by or on behalf of the holders of any debentures of the company secured by a charge which, as created, was a floating charge, or by such a charge and one or more other securities.[159] Lenders that want to be able to block the appointment of an administrator must thus ensure that their security includes an appropriately drafted floating charge.[160] When an administrator is appointed, he has power to dispose of property which is subject to a floating charge as if it were not secured notwithstanding that the charge may have crystallised,[161] but his power to dispose of assets which are subject to a fixed charge is dependent upon satisfying the court that the disposal would be

[154] Insolvency Act 1986, s 386, and sch 6. [155] Ibid, s 175.
[156] Ibid, s 40. [157] Companies Act 1985, s 196. [158] Insolvency Act 1986, s 9.
[159] Or a person who would be such a receiver or manager but for the appointment of some other person as the receiver of part of the company's property: s 29 (2)(b).
[160] This may be a so-called 'lightweight' floating charge: Oditah, F, 'Lightweight Floating Charges' [1991] JBL 49; Marks, D, and Emmet, D, 'Administrative Receivers: Questions of Identity and Double Identity' [1994] JBL 1. Where a company's assets consist wholly or mainly of property which is not expected to be the subject of rapid turnover, an example being a holding company with assets consisting almost entirely of shares in subsidiaries, the lender can take a fixed charge on the assets without unduly impeding the company's business affairs. This fixed charge will largely satisfy the lender's desire for control, save for the fact that it will not enable the lender to prevent the appointment of an administrator. This need can, however, be met by also taking a floating charge over the company's undertaking. This floating charge may be almost identical in scope to the fixed charge, and the detailed covenants which would usually be required from the company if the floating charge stood alone can be dispensed with, thus making the charge 'lightweight'; but a floating charge tacked onto a fixed charge in this way is not an artificial device and it is effective for the purpose of allowing its holder to block the appointment of an administrator: *Re Croftbell Ltd* [1990] BCLC 844.
[161] Insolvency Act 1986, s 15 (1) and (3).

likely to promote one or more of the purposes for which the administration order was made.[162] Other reasons why the status of a charge as fixed or floating may be important include the following: under the Insolvency Act 1986, an administrative receiver, that is a receiver appointed under a floating charge, enjoys a range of statutory powers which are not given to a receiver who is appointed under a fixed charge;[163] and under the same Act floating (but not fixed) charges may be invalid if they are created within a certain period before the onset of insolvency proceedings and other specified conditions are satisfied.[164]

When seeking to establish the characteristics of the floating charge, it is usual to cite the following passage from the judgment of Romer LJ in *Re Yorkshire Woolcombers Ltd*:[165]

> . . . I certainly think that if a charge has the three characteristics that I am about to mention, it is a floating charge.
> (1) If it is a charge on a class of assets of a company present and future;
> (2) if that class is one which, in the ordinary course of the business of the company, would be changing from time to time; and
> (3) if you find that by the charge it is contemplated that, until some future step is taken by or on behalf of those interested in the charge, the company may carry on its business in the ordinary way as far as concerns the particular class of assets I am dealing with.

These three characteristics are indicative of a floating charge but, as Romer LJ emphasised,[166] they do not amount to a precise definition of a floating charge. Vinelott J has described them as 'helpful tests or filters in deciding in a doubtful case whether a charge is fixed or floating'.[167] The absence of one or more of the stated characteristics does not mean that the charge cannot be a floating charge. This point was reiterated by Vinelott J in *Re Croftbell Ltd*[168] where a charge was held to be a floating charge notwithstanding that the secured property (shares in subsidiaries) was not expected to be the subject of regular turnover in the ordinary course of business.[169] Equally, although it would be very unusual for a floating charge not to extend to future, as well as presently owned, assets of the debtor company,[170] it has been held that a charge on present property only can be a floating charge.[171] It follows that a charge on future property only can also be a floating charge and that it is not essential to bring existing assets within the scope of the charge for it to be so classified.[172]

Ultimately it is the extent to which the charge contemplates that the company will continue to be free to deal with the assets which are the subject mat-

[162] Insolvency Act 1986, s 15 (2) and (3).
[163] Ibid, s 42 *ff* and sch 1.
[164] Ibid, s 245.
[165] [1903] 2 Ch 284 CA; affirmed *sub nom Illingworth v Houldsworth* [1904] AC 355, HL.
[166] [1903] 2 Ch 284, CA, 295. See also 298 *per* Cozens Hardy LJ.
[167] *Re Atlantic Medical Ltd* [1992] BCC 653, 658.
[168] [1990] BCLC 844.
[169] See also *Welch v Bowmaker (Ireland) Ltd* [1980] IR 251, Ir SC, where the majority of the Irish Supreme Court held that a charge secured on land could be a floating charge notwithstanding that the debtor company was not in the business of property trading and the land was not a class of asset changing from time to time in the course of the company's business.
[170] *Re Atlantic Medical Ltd* [1992] BCC 653, 658.
[171] *Re Bond Worth Ltd* [1980] 1 Ch 228, 267; *Re Cimex Tissues Ltd* [1994] BCC 626, 635.
[172] *Re Croftbell Ltd* [1990] BCLC 844, 848.

ter of the security without having to refer back to the creditor for approval and consent that is determinative of the status of the charge as fixed or floating. Expressing the distinction by reference to the preceding discussion on the nature of the floating charge, a fixed charge is specifically attached to the charged assets which means that the company cannot freely dispose of them, but a floating charge is not specifically attached to particular assets so as prevent disposals.

It is not, however, the case that any restrictions on dealings suffice to make a charge a fixed charge rather than a floating charge or, conversely, that any permitted freedom to deal with the assets under the terms of the charge mean that it must be classified as a floating charge rather than a fixed charge. In *Re Cimex Tissues Ltd*[173] the judge, Mr SJ Burnton QC explained:

> If the crucial difference between a fixed charge and a floating charge is in the nature of the interest of the chargee prior to any event of crystallisation, it would follow that a licence for the chargor to deal to some extent with the charged assets is not necessarily inconsistent with a fixed charge. If, however, the licence to deal given to the chargor is extensive, the charge will be floating, since in these circumstances there is in effect no attachment of the charge to any specific asset . . .
>
> The extent to which the licence to deal is compatible with a fixed charge must depend on all the circumstances of the case, and in particular on the nature of the charged property. Where the charged property is stock, or book debts—ie where the assets are naturally fluctuating—the court will readily conclude that a liberty for the chargor to deal with the charged assets is inconsistent with a fixed charge. Where, as in the present case, the assets are specific and do not necessarily fluctuate, some liberty to release the charged assets may not be inconsistent with a fixed charge.

Re Cimex Tissues Ltd concerned a charge on machinery. The charge, which was expressly described as a fixed charge in the charging document, was badly drafted but the case proceeded on the basis that it did permit the company to sell any part of the charged assets. This was held to be compatible with the charge being a fixed charge on the machinery. *Holroyd v Marshall*[174] was said to support that conclusion because in that case the chargor was permitted to substitute new machinery for old and it was implicit in such a covenant that the chargor might deal with the old machinery, for example by selling it, with a view to substituting new machinery. The judgments in *Holroyd v Marshall* do not explicitly indicate whether the charge in that case was fixed or floating (the case predated the recognition of the floating charge) but there are references to the chargee's interest attaching to specific property and that language is consistent with the nature of a fixed charge. Therefore Burnton QC was justified in citing that case in support of his approach.[175] That view is also supported by *Evans v Rival Granite Ltd*[176] where Buckley LJ contemplated that there could be a fixed charge coupled with a licence to deal.[177] In *Siebe*

[173] [1994] BCC 626, 635.
[174] (1862) 10 HLC 191, 11 ER 999, [1861–73] All ER Rep 414, HL.
[175] Gough, WJ, *Company Charges*, (2nd edn, 1996) 107 but compare Pennington, RR, 'The Genesis of the Floating Charge' (1960) 23 MLR 630, 634.
[176] [1910] 2 KB 979, CA.
[177] See *Re New Bullas Trading Ltd* [1993] BCC 251, [1993] BCLC 1389; although the decision was reversed on appeal ([1994] BCC 36, [1994] 1 BCLC 485, CA), this point is unaffected by the reversal.

Gorman & Co Ltd v Barclays Bank Ltd[178] where a fixed charge on debts was upheld, the argument that the fact that the charge did not preclude certain forms of dealing with the charged property meant that it could not be a fixed charge was expressly rejected.[179]

The most familiar example of a restriction that is not incompatible with a floating charge is the covenant whereby the chargor promises not to create any subsequent security on the charged assets which would rank before or equally with the floating charge. Negative pledge covenants of this type are very common and their compatibility with a floating charge is now unquestionable.[180] Another example is provided by *Re Brightlife Ltd*[181] where a prohibition on the company selling debts which were the subject matter of the security was held to be consistent with the charge being a floating charge. In *Re GE Tunbridge Ltd,*[182] which was concerned with a charge on the stock of a garage (vehicles, parts and intangibles such as book debts), the company required the chargee's consent to sell the assets but the charge was held nevertheless to be a floating charge. In *Re Cosslett (Contractors) Ltd*[183] Millett LJ made the point in general terms when he said that the essence of a floating charge was that the subject-matter of the security remained under the management and control of the chargor rather than the presence of complete freedom for the chargor to carry on business as it thought fit.

The view that emerges from cases such as *Cimex*, *Tunbridge* and *Cosslett* is that although dealing restrictions or, conversely, permissions to deal are highly relevant in determining the nature of a charge as fixed or floating, there is no absolute line to be drawn and that, in particular, the nature of the assets secured must be considered when judging whether the restrictions or permissions are sufficient to tip the balance one way or the other. This approach makes it more difficult to predict how a court will resolve a dispute on the classification of a charge than one that maintains either that the charge must be floating if the company is allowed any freedom to deal with the assets or that it must be fixed if there is any degree of restriction on what the chargor can do with the charged assets (these two options being, necessarily, mutually exclusive). This opens up the possibility of excessive litigation on the matter, but in a security system that is based on freedom of contract it is unavoidable that the ingenuity of those drafting security documentation will be tested from time to time in the courts. As Hoffmann J said, when he noted that the floating charge could not be exhaustively defined:

> All that can be done is to enumerate its standard characteristics. It does not follow that the absence of one or more of those features or the presence of others will prevent the charge from being categorised as 'floating'. There are bound to be penumbral cases in which it may be difficult to say whether the degree of deviation from the standard case is enough to make it inappropriate to use such a term. But the rights and duties which the law may or may not categorise as a floating charge are wholly derived from the agreement of the parties, supplemented by the terms implied by law. It seems to me fallacious to argue that once the parties have agreed on some terms which are thought

178 [1979] 2 Lloyd's Rep 142.
179 Ibid, 159.
180 Farrar, JH and Hannigan, BM, *Farrar's Company Law* (4th edn, 1998) 639.
181 [1987] Ch 200.
182 [1994] BCC 563.
183 [1998] Ch 495, CA, 510.

sufficient to identify the transaction as a floating charge, they are then precluded from agreeing to any other terms which are not present in the standard case.[184]

CLASSIFICATION OF A CHARGE AS FIXED OR FLOATING AND THE NATURE OF THE SECURED PROPERTY; CHARGES ON BOOK DEBTS

It is a justifiable and sensible proposition that the nature of the charged property is a relevant consideration when determining the effect of dealing restrictions or permissions on the classification of a charge. Less justifiable is the statement that the classification of a charge can be determined by reference simply to the nature of the assets charged. In some of the nineteenth-century cases there are statements to the effect that a charge must cover present and future assets if it is to be regarded as a floating charge[185] or that a charge on present and future assets must be a floating charge.[186] Whilst there remains a presumption that a floating charge is intended to extend to future assets if the charging instrument is itself silent on the point,[187] more recent cases considered in the previous section of this chapter indicate that the first of these views has not prevailed: a charge can be a floating charge even though it is confined to present assets or, as the case may be, future assets. The proposition that a charge on present and future assets *must be* a floating charge, a view that is not warranted by the cases which contain descriptions of fixed and floating charges and comparisons between them, was put to rest by the decision in *Siebe Gorman & Co Ltd v Barclays Bank Ltd.*[188]

In *Siebe Gorman & Co Ltd v Barclays Bank Ltd* the agreement between the company and its creditor, Barclays, Bank, charged the company's present and future book debts and other debts by way of first fixed charge. Under the terms of the charge, the company was required not to charge or assign any part of the charged property without the consent of Barclays. The company was permitted to continue to collect the proceeds of its book debts itself but was required to pay those proceeds into an account with Barclays. Slade J held that the restrictions on dealing with the debts (albeit that only certain forms of dealing were prohibited) together with the requirement to pay the proceeds into an account with Barclays were sufficient to constitute a fixed charge. The charging document was silent with regard to the company's access to the proceeds of the debts once they had been paid into the account, but Slade J rejected an argument from counsel that the charge gave Barclays no right to prevent withdrawals from the account and that the proceeds once paid into the account were at the free disposal of the company. Instead, Slade J held that Barclays had the right to assert a lien on the proceeds of the book debts so as to prevent the company from making withdrawals from the account. The reference to a lien in this context is open to question because a fundamental

184 *Re Brightlife Ltd* [1987] Ch 200, 214–15.
185 *Re Yorkshire Woolcombers' Association Ltd* [1903] 2 Ch 284, CA, 298 *per* Cozens Hardy LJ.
186 eg, *Evans v Rival Granite Quarries Ltd* [1910] 2 KB 979, CA, 994 *per* Fletcher Moulton LJ.
187 *Re Alfred Priestman & Co (1929) Ltd* [1936] 2 All ER 1340.
188 [1979] 2 Lloyd's Rep 142.

principle of banking law is that when money is paid into a bank account which is in credit, the legal relationship created is that of debtor (bank) and creditor (customer) and the customer does not have a claim on specific money or other property held by the bank.[189] It is established that a bank cannot have a lien, which is a possessory security, over its own indebtedness.[190] In essence, a bank's control over the proceeds of the debts which are paid into an account held with it stems simply from the fact that it is the debtor and, as such, is in a position effectively to enforce its contractual right under the terms of the charge to prevent repayment by withdrawals from the account. Another way of expressing the point would be to say that the company's chose in action—in the *Siebe Gorman* case the debt owing from Barclays Bank—becomes a flawed asset because the company cannot freely demand repayment of that debt.

Charges on Book Debts: The Approach in *Siebe Gorman & Co Ltd v Barclays Bank Ltd*

Siebe Gorman & Co Ltd v Barclays Bank Ltd was a breakthrough decision.[191] It established that a creditor can take a fixed charge on present and future book debts provided that under the terms of the charge the creditor restricts (a) dealings with the debts although such control does not need to be absolute, and (b) access to the proceeds of the debts. A perceived difficulty prior to this breakthrough stemmed from the fact that the proceeds of book debts are an important element of a company's cash flow: if, as is normally the case, a company relies on the proceeds of its book debts as a source of business finance, how can it charge its book debts without impairing its cash flow and disrupting the smooth operation of its business if not paralysing it altogether? In the *Yorkshire Woolcombers* litigation, the fact that a fixed charge on book debts could have prevented the continued operation of the company's business by depriving it of an important source of cash was regarded as significant and as pointing towards the conclusion that the parties intended to create a floating charge.[192] *Siebe Gorman & Co Ltd v Barclays Bank Ltd* confirmed that dual control—on the debts and on the proceeds of the debts—was essential to the creation of a fixed charge on book debts and that, in relation to the proceeds of the debts, the creditor had to be able to prevent withdrawals from the account into which they were paid: the cash-flow implications of that conclusion and its compatibility with the parties' evident intention that the company should continue in business despite being deprived of this source of finance were not explored.

[189] *Foley v Hill* (1848) 2 HLC 28, 9 ER 1002, HL.

[190] *National Westminster Bank v Halesowen Pressmark Assemblies Ltd* [1972] AC 785, HL.

[191] Generally, on the development of the concept of fixed charges on book debts, see: Pearce, RA, 'Fixed Charges over Book Debts' [1987] JBL 18; Pennington, RR, 'Fixed Charges Over Future Assets of a Company' (1985) 6 Co Law 9; McCormack, G, 'Fixed Charges on Future Book Debts' (1987) 8 Co Law 3.

[192] [1903] 2 Ch 284 at 288 *per* Farwell J, 296 *per* Romer LJ and 297 *per* Cozens-Hardy LJ. See also Berg, A, 'Charges Over Book Debts: A Reply' [1995] JBL 433, 436–40.

The principles established in *Siebe Gorman & Co Ltd v Barclays Bank Ltd* were soon considered in a line of cases in England and in other jurisdictions. The decision was followed in *Ex parte Copp*[193] and *Re Permanent Houses (Holdings) Ltd*[194] where the terms of the charges in question were indistinguishable from those in the seminal decision. In the Irish case of *Re Keenan Bros Ltd*[195] the charge on present and future book debts precluded specified forms of dealing with book debts and obliged the company to pay the proceeds into a separate receivables account with the creditor which, as in *Siebe Gorman & Co Ltd v Barclays Bank Ltd*, was a bank: the charge was held to be a fixed charge. In the *Keenan* decision, unlike the *Siebe Gorman* case, the charge expressly envisaged that the proceeds of the debts would indeed be frozen and rendered unusable by the company except with the creditor bank's consent. In *Re Brightlife Ltd*,[196] although the charge restricted dealing with the debts, it did not provide the creditor with any effective power to restrict the company's access to the proceeds of the debts: the charge, although described as a fixed charge, was held to be a floating charge. This was also the conclusion reached in the Northern Irish case, *Re Armagh Shoes Ltd*,[197] where the absence of any effective power to control access to the proceeds meant that a charge which the parties had described as 'fixed' was held to be a floating charge. In *William Gaskell Group v Highley*[198] and *Re CCG International Enterprises Ltd*[199] also, whether the proceeds of the charged present and future book debts were at the free disposal of the chargor company was regarded as a key factor in determining the status of the charge as fixed or floating.

Siebe Gorman & Co Ltd v Barclays Bank Ltd orthodoxy is summarised by Knox J at first instance in *Re New Bullas Trading Ltd*[200] in the following manner. The parties' description of a charge as fixed or floating is not conclusive and there are two ways for a court to discard the express description of a charge.[201] The first is where the description is a sham and does not reflect what the parties have truly agreed: 'If the transaction is a cow and has cloven hooves, the parties cannot turn it into a horse by using equine terminology or saying that it is a horse.'[202] Secondly, the court can discard the parties' description where the stated characteristics of the charge compel the court to conclude that the parties have in fact created something different from that which they had intended. The proper approach is to see whether 'the description of the transaction which the parties had adopted is necessarily to be departed from as a result of the terms of the transaction that they have provided for'.[203]

In relation to charges on book debts Knox J thought that the touchstone for determining whether a charge is fixed or floating is the extent to which the

193 [1989] BCLC 13.

194 (1989) 5 BCC 151 (in this case counsel conceded the point). See also *Re Portbase Clothing Co Ltd* [1993] Ch 388 where it was assumed, without deciding, that a charge with terms similar to those in *Siebe Gorman & Co Ltd v Barclays Bank Ltd* [1979] 2 Lloyd's Rep 142 was a fixed charge.

195 [1986] BCLC 242, Ir SC. See also *Northern Bank Ltd v Ross* [1991] BCLC 504, NI CA.

196 [1987] Ch 200.

197 [1984] BCLC 405.

198 [1994] 1 BCLC 197.

199 [1993] BCC 580.

200 [1993] BCC 251, [1993] BCLC 1389.

201 *Welsh Development Agency v Export Finance Co Ltd* [1992] BCC 270, CA.

202 [1993] BCC 251, 255.

203 Ibid.

chargor is free to deal with the debts and the proceeds if and when collected. Knox J concluded:

(i) fetters, or even a prohibition against factoring, assigning and selling, are not enough to create a fixed charge;
(ii) fetters or prohibitions on dealings combined with an obligation to pay into a particular account may be enough;
(iii) however, there has also to be sufficient restriction on dealings with the moneys in the account for the charge to be a fixed charge.

It is worth comparing the decision in *Siebe Gorman & Co Ltd v Barclays Bank Ltd* with some of the subsequent decisions to show how the line between adequate and inadequate restrictions on dealings with the proceeds can be very fine. In the *Siebe Gorman* case it was implied that the creditor could at any time prevent withdrawals from the account; although only a contractual right, the holder of the charge, in its capacity as the bank with which the account into which the proceeds of book debts were to be paid, was in a position to ensure effective enforcement and the charge was held to be fixed. In *William Gaskell Group Ltd v Highley*[204] the position at the outset was similar to that in the *Siebe Gorman* case in that the creditor (Midland Bank) required the proceeds to be paid into a Midland account, but subsequently the benefit of the charge was assigned to a third party. It was held that the effect of the assignment was to divide the identity of the person whose consent was required to draw on the account in which the proceeds of the book debts were deposited: the assignee debenture-holder had the contractual right to restrict dealings under the terms of the charge, but at the same time Midland Bank, which remained the bank with which the proceeds had to be deposited under the terms of the charge, had its right as banker to decide whether or not to meet a cheque drawn on the account when it was overdrawn. It was further held that there was nothing in the effect of the assignment to convert the fixed charge on the book debts into a floating charge. Implicit in this ruling was the acceptance that a contractual right to prevent withdrawals from an account which was drafted in mandatory and immediately operative terms—'no withdrawals unless the creditor consents'—could amount to sufficient control for the purpose of creating a fixed charge even though the creditor was not in the fortuitous position of being the bank with which the proceeds of the book debts were actually deposited.

These cases contrast with *Re Brightlife Ltd*[205] where the charge restricted dealings with the debts but the company was free to deal with the proceeds of the debts. The charge was classified as a floating charge. In *Re New Bullas Ltd*,[206] as well as restricting dealings with the book debts themselves, the charge required the company to pay the proceeds of those debts into a designated bank account with a specified bank. The creditor itself was not a bank. The charge further stipulated that, once the proceeds had been paid in, they would be released from the fixed charge on the book debts and would be sub-

[204] [1993] BCC 251, [1993] BCLC 1389.
[205] [1987] Ch 200.
[206] [1993] BCC 251, [1993] BCLC 1389 (reversed on appeal [1994] BCC 36, [1994] 1 BCLC 485, CA).

ject only to the creditor's general floating charge on the company's assets in the absence of any written directions from the creditor concerning the use of the money. At first instance, Knox J held that at the time of creation of the charge (ie at the time when its status as fixed or floating was to be determined) in the absence of directions from the creditor, the company was free to deal with the proceeds and that this freedom was inconsistent with the existence of a fixed charge. This decision contrasts with that in the *Highley* case: there an absolute contractual ban on withdrawals subject to relaxation at the discretion of the creditor was sufficient control to amount to a fixed charge, but in the *New Bullas* decision at first instance case freedom to use the proceeds subject to the possibility that the creditor might impose restrictions was insufficient control for the creation of a fixed charge. The *potential* to exert control is a feature of a floating charge: the creditor can crystallise the charge so as to convert it into a fixed charge with all the control that that entails. It is right that mere *potentiality* of control should not suffice for a fixed charge.

Control of the Proceeds of Book Debts and the Company's Cash-flow Needs

At this point we return to a key commercial difficulty with the concept of a fixed charge on book debts satisfying the requirements established by *Siebe Gorman & Co Ltd v Barclays Bank Ltd*. This is how it is possible to reconcile the creditor's need to control the proceeds of the book debts for the charge to be regarded as a fixed charge as a matter of law with the company's practical need to use the proceeds of its book debts in funding its business. The proposition that the parties to a fixed charge on book debts intend the credit balance on the blocked bank account simply to continue to grow over the life of the secured loan so that, eventually, the balance may be even larger than the amount of the loan, has only to be stated to see its obvious commercial impracticability. In commercial terms, both parties will expect the company to continue to have some access to the proceeds of its book debts. But if, in practice, the creditor does not exert the control over the proceeds to which it is entitled under the terms of the charge, does this stop the charge from being a fixed charge?

The answer to this question lies in the application of the general principles of contractual interpretation. The classification of a charge as fixed or floating is a question of construction of the parties' agreement. The principles applied by the courts in construing legal documents were reviewed by the House of Lords in *Mannai Ltd v Eagle Star Assurance Co Ltd*.[207] Lord Steyn outlined three principles: (i) in respect of contracts and contractual notices, the contextual scene is always relevant; (ii) the real question is what evidence of surrounding circumstances may ultimately be allowed to influence the question of interpretation, and that depends on what meanings the language read against the objective contextual scene will let in; and (iii) the inquiry is objective: the question is what reasonable persons, circumstanced as the actual parties were, would have had in mind. Lord Hoffmann said that: 'commercial

[207] [1997] AC 749, HL. See also *Prenn v Simmonds* [1971] 3 All ER 237, HL; *Reardon Smith Line Ltd v Yngvar Hansen-Tangen* [1976] 3 All ER 570, HL.

contracts are construed in the light of all the background which could reasonably have been expected to have been available to the parties in order to ascertain what would objectively have been understood to be their intention'.[208] Thus, evidence of the way in which the company was accustomed to use the proceeds of its book debts in the course of its business prior to the granting of the charge is a relevant consideration: where the evidence demonstrates heavy reliance on proceeds to fund the business, that may be seen as an indicator of a charge on book debts being a floating charge, on the basis that the parties' could not have intended to deprive the company of free and unrestricted access to that important source of corporate finance.[209]

Evidence of the parties' conduct after the conclusion of a contract is not admissible as an aid to interpretation of the terms of a contract,[210] although there is an exception to this principle where the evidence demonstrates that the written terms were a sham.[211] For a creditor to consent to the company drawing upon the account into which the proceeds have been paid would not be incompatible with the charge being a fixed charge, since it is a badge of a fixed security that the debtor cannot deal with the assets *without the creditor's consent*; but if in practice the creditor allows the company to have entirely free and unrestricted access to the proceeds this could amount to evidence of a sham. However, the courts have been disinclined to view arrangements whereby companies that have granted fixed charges over their book debts secure continued access to the proceeds of the debts as evidence of the sham nature of the 'fixed' charge. In *Re Keenan Bros Ltd*[212] the harsh cash-flow implications of locking up the proceeds of the book debts were later mitigated by an agreement whereby the company paid bills by drawing on another general account with the bank. From time to time sums were transferred from the separate receivables account to reduce the overdraft on the general account.[213] On normal principles of construction the supplemental agreement had no relevance to the interpretation of the original charge so long as it did not show the original agreed terms to have been a sham, and there was no suggestion to that effect. The court therefore did not attach importance to that agreement. This structure shows how, whilst complying with the principles established by *Siebe Gorman & Co Ltd v Barclays Bank Ltd*, an arrangement can be worked out which gives the creditor the benefit of fixed security on book debts, whilst still enabling the company in practice to have some access to their proceeds.

[208] [1997] AC 749, HL, 779. See also *Investors Compensation Scheme Ltd v West Bromwich Building Society* [1998] 1 WLR 896, HL, 912–13 *per* Lord Hoffmann.

[209] Berg, A, 'Charges Over Book Debts: A Reply' [1995] JBL 433, 445 argues that insufficient weight was attached to this point in *Siebe Gorman & Co Ltd v Barclays Bank Ltd* [1979] 2 Lloyd's Rep 142 and that Slade J wrongly sought to interpret the charging document divorced from the relevant factual matrix.

[210] *James Miller & Partners v Whitworth Street Estates (Manchester) Ltd* [1970] AC 583, HL; *Wickman Ltd v Schuler AG* [1974] AC 325, HL; *Re Armagh Shoes* [1984] BCLC 405; *Re Wogan's (Drogheda) Ltd* [1993] 1 IR 157, Ir SC.

[211] *AG Securities v Vaughan* [1990] 1 AC 417, HL.

[212] [1986] BCLC 242, Ir SC.

[213] In particular the judgment at first instance which is reported at [1985] BCLC 302, Ir HC (decision reversed on appeal).

A similar point emerges from *Ex parte Copp*.[214] Here the terms of the charge were indistinguishable from those in the *Siebe Gorman* case, but a factual difference at the time when the debenture was granted was that there was agreement between the bank and the company for the existing overdraft limit to remain in place. It was argued on behalf of the liquidator that this was an indication that the company should be able to deal with the proceeds of its book debts freely so long as the overdraft limit was not exceeded and that this was a badge of a floating rather than a fixed charge. Knox J rejected the argument holding that, at most, the arrangement with regard to the overdraft was a collateral arrangement which did not affect the construction of the debenture itself.

Perhaps one of the starkest illustrations of the way in which the principles governing the admissibility of evidence on the construction of contracts can have the effect of excluding from consideration evidence of the fact that in reality the company continues to have access to the proceeds of its book debts despite their payment into a bank account that is formally blocked is the decision of the Irish Supreme Court in *Re Wogan's (Drogheda) Ltd*.[215] Applying the principle that conduct after the date of the contract was not admissible in interpreting its terms, it was held that a creditor could delay the designation of a bank account into which the proceeds were to be paid or suspend for a period of time the operation of direct control over that account without the charge ceasing to be a fixed charge. Circumstances like that in fact occurred in the transaction which was litigated in *Re Keenan Bros Ltd:* the special blocked account was not opened for some five months after the charge documentation was concluded and during that period the company was apparently free to deal with the proceeds of its book debts. In the *Keenan* case the trial judge rejected the admissibility of the evidence concerning the conduct of the parties during that five months[216] and the Supreme Court did not question that approach.

Thus the fact that the creditor consents, either in a formal agreement or informally from time to time, to the company having some access to the proceeds of its book debts does not prevent the satisfaction of the *Siebe Gorman & Co Ltd v Barclays Bank Ltd* requirements for the existence of a fixed charge provided the requirement for consent is not illusory and a sham. Later events or conduct may, alternatively, be admissible to establish a subsequent variation in the terms agreed or to give rise to an estoppel against the creditor, but that will not undermine the fact that, as created, the charge was a fixed charge: the significance of this is that for the purposes of the ranking of preferential debts, these only rank before debts secured by a charge which, *as created*, was a floating charge.[217]

[214] [1989] BCLC 13.

[215] [1993] IR 157, Ir SC.

[216] Reported at [1985] BCLC 302, Ir HC.

[217] Insolvency Act 1986, ss 40, 175; Companies Act 1985, s 196.

Restricting the Impact of *Siebe Gorman & Co Ltd v Barclays Bank Ltd*

Siebe Gorman & Co Ltd v Barclays Bank Ltd was not followed in the New Zealand case *Supercool v Hoverd Industries Ltd*,[218] even though for all practical purposes the wording of the relevant provisions of the charge in that case was the same as that in the *Siebe Gorman* decision.[219] The New Zealand court did not draw the implication found in *Siebe Gorman* that the company was not free to make withdrawals from the account into which the proceeds were paid without the creditor's consent. Therefore, since the company's access to the proceeds was not restricted, the charge was only a floating charge. In Australia some courts have been very unwilling to accept the creation of a fixed charge over the present and future book debts of a business in cases where the parties contemplate the continuation of the business.[220] In Ireland the decision of the Supreme Court in *Re Holidair*[221] has limited the impact of *Siebe Gorman* and emphasised the difference between that case and the decisions in *Keenan* and *Wogan's (Drogheda)*: in the absence of express[222] restrictions on withdrawals from the designated account, a charge on present and future book debts is to be regarded as a floating charge. There are also Canadian authorities tending to support the view that a general assignment of book debts creates a floating rather than a fixed charge.[223]

Overriding *Siebe Gorman & Co Ltd v Barclays Bank Ltd*

In England the recent trend has been away from *Siebe Gorman & Co Ltd v Barclays Bank Ltd* in the sense of saying that the restrictions outlined in that case and subsequent decisions may be unnecessarily onerous and that it may be possible to create a fixed charge on book debts even though the company has more freedom to deal with the proceeds of the debts than was envisaged in the breakthrough decision. The three cases heralding this more flexible approach are *Re Atlantic Computer Systems plc*,[224] *Re Atlantic Medical Ltd*[225] and, most importantly, the decision of the Court of Appeal in *Re New Bullas Trading Ltd*[226] on appeal from Knox J. These cases are controversial and have attracted criticism.[227] Millett LJ's judgment in the more recent decision of the

[218] [1994] 3 NZLR 300, NZ HC. [219] Ibid.

[220] See *Norgard v DCT* (1986) 85 FLR 220, WA SC, where the authorities are reviewed. But note *Whitton v ACN Pty Ltd* (1997) 42 NSWLR 123 NSW EqD applying the *New Bullas* approach discussed next.

[221] [1994] 1 IR 416, Ir Sc.

[222] They were implied in the *Siebe Gorman* case and it was that fact that distinguished it from the later Irish decisions upholding fixed charges on book debts.

[223] See *Re Caroma Enterprises Ltd* (1979) 108 DLR (3d) 412, Al QB; interestingly, though, an older Canadian decision, *Evans, Coleman & Evans Ltd v RA Nelson Construction Ltd* (1958) 16 DLR (2d) 123, BC CA was the one decision cited by Slade J in *Siebe Gorman & Co Ltd v Barclays Bank Ltd* [1979] 2 Lloyd's Rep 142 in support of his conclusion in that case.

[224] [1992] Ch 505, CA. [225] [1992] BCC 653.

[226] [1994] BCC 36, [1994] 1 BCLC 485, CA.

[227] See especially, Bridge, M, 'Company Administrators and Secured Creditors' (1991) 107 LQR 394; and Goode, RM, 'Charges over Book Debts: a Missed Opportunity' (1994) 110 LQR 592. Compare Berg, A, 'Charges over Book Debts: A Reply' [1995] JBL 433 where it is argued that *Re New Bullas Trading Ltd* is a correct and helpful decision. The decision is also supported by Worthington, S, *Proprietary Interests in Commercial Transactions* (1996) para 4.2.

Court of Appeal, *Royal Trust Bank v National Westminster Bank plc*,[228] indicates that the governing principles in this field are far from settled and that there is scope for continuing discussion.

Re Atlantic Computer Systems plc[229]

Atlantic Computer Systems plc was a company in the business of leasing computers. The company generally operated by itself leasing, or acquiring on hire purchase, computers from banks or other financial institutions and then subleasing them. The company went into administration in April 1990. It stopped making payments that were due to the banks and financial institutions on the head leases and hire-purchase agreements but continued to receive payments on the subleases. Some of the banks and financial institutions applied to court. One of the claims related to an assignment of subleases and to whether that assignment amounted to a fixed or floating charge. The relevant clause in the assignment provided for the assignee to have the benefit of all rentals, claims, demands, and other moneys or claims for moneys under the subleases. No provision was made concerning the application of the proceeds of the subleases—that is, the individual instalments of rent. Nicholls LJ, delivering the judgment of the Court of Appeal, accepted that the parties might well have intended that Atlantic should be free to use the instalments until the assignee intervened but held that this feature did not result in the charge being floating rather than fixed.

Nicholls LJ drew a distinction between a charge on existing income-producing property, such as a lease, and a charge on present and future property such as a typical charge on present and future book debts. The right to receive the future income stream on a lease was a present asset of the company; it was not the same as a future book debt. In respect of a present asset only the terms governing the asset itself had to be considered. The terms did not have to extend to its proceeds for the charge to be a fixed charge. No explicit reference was made to the *Siebe Gorman & Co Ltd v Barclays Bank Ltd* line of authority in reaching this conclusion.

A striking feature of this reasoning is the emphasis placed on the nature of the property secured and, in particular, on the fact that the security related to present property only. The reasoning adopted by Nicholls LJ suggests that the charge is a fixed charge because it is a charge on present property. But, as discussed earlier in this chapter,[230] it is now established that the proper classification of a charge is to be determined by reference to whether the chargor or the chargee controls the assets. Although the nature of the assets secured may affect the extent to which ability to deal, or any restriction on dealing, is compatible with a floating or, as the case may be, fixed charge, the nature of the property does not itself determine whether a charge is fixed or floating. In this respect this decision seems to be harking back to an old-fashioned approach which is inconsistent with the modern view that the key feature that distinguishes the floating charge from fixed security is not the nature of the secured

228 [1996] BCC 613, CA.

229 [1992] Ch 505, CA.

230 See above, at 512–17.

assets but the location of the power to manage and control them in the chargor rather than the chargee.

Re Atlantic Medical Ltd[231]

This case concerned another company in the Atlantic group which had similar leasing arrangements to those that had been considered by the Court of Appeal in the previous case. The only significant point of distinction was that this time the assignment extended to subleases which might be entered into in the future. Vinelott J held that this was a 'neutral' point which did not lead to the conclusion that the charge was a floating charge. This analysis is consistent with the proposition that the nature of the assets secured does not, of itself, determine whether a charge is fixed or floating. But, having dismissed that point as a possible basis for distinguishing the Court of Appeal's decision in *Computer*, Vinelott J was, as a matter of precedent, then bound to conclude that the charge before him was a fixed charge because the terms of the assignment were otherwise indistinguishable from those considered by the Court of Appeal in the earlier case.

'Trees', 'fruit' and *Royal Trust Bank v National Westminster Bank plc*[232]

In the *Computer* decision, Nicholls LJ drew an analogy between the assignment by way of charge of the subleases and a mortgage of land. He noted that a mortgage of land did not become a floating charge by reason of the mortgagor being permitted to remain in possession and enjoy the fruits of the property charged, even where the asset charged was of a wasting character such as a short-term leasehold interest. From this he concluded in relation to the assignment of the subleases, that the mere fact that the company could continue to receive and use the instalments did not suffice to negative the fixed character of the charge. Is this a convincing analogy? If we take the example of land on which is planted an apple orchard, it is true that the owner of the land can pick the apples and consume them himself (or indeed include them in a charge on the stock of his apple-growing business in favour of the bank which is providing loan finance) without having to obtain the consent of the mortgagee of the land and without that mortgage falling to be regarded as some form of floating security. The security is the owner's freehold or leasehold interest in the land, and that is unaffected by the use of the fruits of the land:

> By leaving the mortgagor in possession, the mortgagee implicitly authorised him to carry on his business and to sell and remove the plants, trees and shrubs which, although fixed to the soil, constituted his stock in trade. This implied authority can hardly be confined to such things, but may fairly be regarded, and I thought ought to be regarded, as authorising the mortgagor whilst in possession to hire and bring and fix other fixtures necessary for his business, and to agree with their owner that he shall be at liberty to remove them at the end of the time for which they are hired.[233]

[231] [1992] BCC 653.

[232] [1996] BCC 613, CA.

[233] *Gough v Wood* [1894] 1 QB 713, CA, 720 *per* Lindley LJ; *Hobson v Gorringe* [1897] 1 Ch 182, CA; *Reynolds v Ashby* [1904] AC 466, HL; *Ellis v Glover* [1908] 1 KB 388, CA; *Rhodes v Allied Dunbar Pension Services Ltd* [1989] BCLC 318, CA.

A distinction between an asset (the 'tree') and its products (the 'fruit') is one that has been drawn elsewhere. For example, in the Australian cases of *Norman v FCT*[234] and *Shepherd v FCT*[235] the effect of purported assignments depended precisely on whether they were assignments of present property (the tree) or of future income to be derived from that property (the fruit). From these cases it appears that, in respect of shares, it is possible to separate the tree and the fruits so that a shareholder can assign the right to receive dividends in respect of shares whilst retaining the shares themselves.[236] In *Re CCG International Enterprises Ltd*[237] the same principles were applied in relation to an insurance policy although they were not specifically invoked: the policy itself was subject to a floating charge but the insurance money paid out under the policy was held to be subject to a fixed charge.

The two *Atlantic* decisions apply the 'tree' and 'fruit' analysis to finance leases and the income stream derived therefrom. Yet that they do not represent the final word on the matter is evident from *Royal Trust Bank v National Westminster Bank plc*,[238] which again concerned an assignment by way of security of hiring agreements. The security covered existing and future agreements. The assignment provided for the creditor to have the power to require the proceeds of the hiring agreements to be paid into a designated account; the charge thus reserved the power to impose control over the proceeds but did not impose direct control. At first instance it was held that the charge was a fixed charge and this point was conceded on appeal. Despite this concession, Millett LJ reviewed the terms of the charge and characterised it as a floating charge. Although the case is not mentioned by name, Millett LJ's judgment appears to mark a return to *Siebe Gorman & Co Ltd v Barclays Bank Ltd* orthodoxy in that it emphasises that a fixed charge on a receivable does arise where the proceeds of the receivable are at the free disposal of the chargor.

In a key passage Millett LJ said:[239] 'while it is obviously possible to distinguish between a capital asset and its income, I do not know how it can be possible to separate a debt or other receivable from the proceeds of its realisation.' This links back to Nicholls LJ's analysis in the *Computer* decision. It also leads the way into a discussion of the other controversial Court of Appeal decision in this field: *Re New Bullas Trading Ltd.*

Re New Bullas Trading Ltd[240]

Nourse LJ, delivering the judgment of the Court of Appeal in this case, began by saying that in the earlier cases such as *Siebe Gorman & Co Ltd v Barclays Bank Ltd* book debts and their proceeds had been regarded as being indivisible. If the two were indivisible it followed that both had to be controlled if the

[234] (1963) 109 CLR 9, H Ct of Aust.

[235] (1964) 113 CLR 385, H Ct of Aust. On this topic generally see Meagher, RP, Gummow, WMC, and Lehane, JRF, *Equity Doctrine and Remedies* (3rd edn, 1992) paras 639–45.

[236] This is apparent from *Norman v FCT* (1963) 109 CLR 9, H Ct of Aust, although the purported assignment in that case failed because the dividends were future property and the assignment was not supported by the necessary consideration.

[237] [1993] BCC 580.

[238] [1996] BCC 613, CA.

[239] Ibid at 618.

[240] [1994] BCLC 485; [1994] BCC 36, CA.

charge on them was to amount to a fixed charge.[241] However, the persons responsible for the drafting of the charge under consideration in this case had done something different—they had treated the debt and its proceeds as divisible. Nourse LJ held that it was legally possible to separate a debt from its proceeds and that, consequently, it was possible for the debts themselves to be subject to a fixed charge (with appropriate restrictions on dealings with the debts) but for the proceeds to be subject only to a floating charge once they had been paid into a designated account as required by the terms of the charge. Although not explicitly mentioned in the judgment, this is, in effect, an application of the trees and fruit analysis to book debts.

The decision has been widely criticised.[242] The main argument against Nourse LJ's approach is that the tree and fruit analogy is not apt in this context. Once a debt is paid, it ceases to exist. Proceeds of debts are not products like apples which can be removed and dealt with separately without impairing the land which is the subject-matter of security. To say that a fixed charge can be created in respect of debts even though the creditor does not control the application of the proceeds of the debts is also to accept that the debts themselves, which are the subject-matter of the security, will be destroyed by payment, an event which is outside the control of the holder of the security. This is, arguably,[243] hard to reconcile with the basic idea of a fixed charge as giving rise to a proprietary interest in the charged property which can only be released with the creditor's consent. On the other hand, accepting the conceptual possibility of separating book debts and their proceeds for charging process paves the way towards a result—continued access to the proceeds of its book debts—that is more openly in line with practical cashflow needs of a borrowing company than the *Siebe Gorman* line of authority which apparently emphasises control of, but in reality tolerates access to, proceeds because legal principles concerning contractual interpretation exclude from the factors that are relevant for testing control the actual operation and funding of the company's business after the date of the charge.

There are also policy objections to the outcome in *Re New Bullas Trading Ltd.* It has already been noted that the fixed charge enjoys certain advantages over the floating charge under the insolvency legislation. In the *New Bullas* case itself, it was important for the lender to establish that its charge on uncollected book debts was a fixed charge because, had it been only a floating charge, under the Insolvency Act 1986, s 175 its claim on those debts would have been postponed to the company's preferential debts. Charges are con-

[241] *Re Pearl Maintenance Services Ltd* [1995] BCLC 657 confirms that the *Siebe Gorman* line of authority continues to apply to charges on book debts which are not drafted in the *New Bullas* form. This means that the *Atlantic* cases do not apply to pre-*New Bullas* style charges on book debts.

[242] Goode, RM, 'Charges Over Book Debts: a Missed Opportunity' (1994) 110 LQR 592 at 601. Others have also doubted the correctness of the decision of the Court of Appeal in *Re New Bullas Trading Ltd*: Moss, G, 'Fixed Charges on Book Debts—Puzzles and Perils' (1995) 8 Insolvency Intelligence 25; Zacaroli, A, 'Fixed Charges on Book Debts—"there is nothing further that I wish to add . . ." ' (1997) 10 Insolvency Intelligence 41. A notable supporter of the case (but not the *Atlantic* decisions) is Berg, A, 'Charges Over Book Debts: A Reply' [1995] JBL 433. *New Bullas* has also been followed: *Whitton v ACN Pty Ltd* (1997) 42 NSWLR 123 NSW EqD; *Re Brumark Investments Ltd* 16 February 1999 NZ HC.

[243] See *Re Brumark Investments Ltd* 16 February 1999 NZ HC.

sensual securities and the task of the court is simply to interpret and give effect to the parties' agreement irrespective of the policy implications that this may have.[244] In this respect the *New Bullas* decision is simply the latest instalment in a saga in which the courts have recognised the supremacy of freedom of contract in this area of the law and thereby given the green light to corporate advisers to devise ever more ingenious structures which combine the advantages of fixed security so far as the creditor is concerned with the advantages of floating security from the company's perspective. *Siebe Gorman & Co Ltd v Barclays Bank Ltd* itself was an earlier stage in the same saga,[245] and it may be that the next development will be the emergence of forms of fixed security on stock which, as with book debts, have historically been regarded as not being feasible in practical terms because of the rapidity of turnover.[246] But the cumulative effect of decisions such as *Siebe Gorman* and *New Bullas* is seriously to undermine the practical effect of the preferential status intended to be enjoyed by certain debts by virtue of the insolvency legislation. There is a case here for statutory intervention, with a possible way forward being to follow the Irish model under which debts secured by fixed charges on book debts enjoy no priority over revenue debts;[247] this approach allows companies and their creditors to structure their lending arrangements as they think fit within the bounds of legal possibility but ensures that the preferential status given to certain debts by the insolvency legislation is not deprived of meaningful effect.

CRYSTALLISATION OF A FLOATING CHARGE

Until a floating charge crystallises, a company can continue to deal with the assets which are the subject-matter of the security in the ordinary course of its business.[248] The scope of a company's 'ordinary course of business' for this purpose is sometimes equated with its objects under its memorandum of association.[249] The common practice of having very extensive objects means that, adopting this approach, there is little or nothing that a company can do which would fall outside the scope of its power to continue to use assets which are the subject of a floating charge.[250] However, if a company does something

244 *Re Brightlife Ltd* [1987] Ch 200.

245 The *Cork Committee Report* para 1586 recommended statutory reversal of the *Siebe Gorman* decision.

246 See Pennington, RR, 'Fixed Charges Over Future Assets of a Company', 6 Co Law 9, 18 for a discussion of the difficulties perceived to surround the creation of fixed charges on stock.

247 Finance Act 1986, s 115.

248 *Re Panama, New Zealand & Australia Royal Mail Co* (1870) 5 Ch App 318; *Re Florence Land & Public Works Co, ex p Moor* (1878) 10 53, CA; *Wallace v Evershed* [1899] 1 Ch 189; *Re Yorkshire Woolcombers Ltd* [1903] 2 Ch 284, CA; affmd *sub nom Illingworth v Houldsworth* [1904] AC 355, HL.

249 *Re Borax Co* [1901] 1 Ch 326, CA, 342 *per* Vaughan Williams LJ; *Re Automatic Bottle Makers Ltd* [1926] Ch 412, CA, 421 *per* Warrington LJ.

250 This may be one explanation for the lack of interest in English legal practice in the theoretically interesting question whether an uncrystallised floating charge creates a proprietary interest which may be binding on persons who deal with the company in transactions falling outside the trading power. On this point see further Ferran, EV, 'Floating Charges—The Nature of the Security' [1988] CLJ 213; Worthington, S, 'Floating Charges—An Alternative Theory' [1994] CLJ 81, 99–102.

authorised by its objects which triggers the cessation of its business, this may cause the floating charge to crystallise in accordance with the principles discussed in this section. The existence of an uncrystallised floating charge does not prevent the company's debtors from claiming rights of set-off against it,[251] nor does it preclude any of the company's other creditors from enforcing judgment against its assets.[252]

When a floating charge crystallises into a fixed charge, it attaches to the existing assets of the company within the ambit of the charge and, unless the charge excludes this, all such assets that are subsequently acquired.[253] A crystallised floating charge ranks as a fixed charge for the purposes of determining its priority against others' interests in the company's property which are created or acquired after crystallisation.[254] Although there is one case to the contrary,[255] the better view is that crystallisation does not affect the priority of a floating charge against other interests in the same property which predate crystallisation. Crystallisation has the effect of postponing execution creditors to the chargee's interest,[256] and once debtors of the company have notice of crystallisation they are largely precluded from claiming rights of set-off.[257]

As charges are essentially contractual documents, it is for the parties to determine crystallising events but, in the absence of any other provision, three crystallising events will be implied.[258] These are intervention by the holder of the charge to take control of the security, such as by appointing a receiver under the terms of the charge,[259] the commencement of the winding up of the company[260] and the cessation of its business.[261] It is also possible for the parties to agree additional crystallising events in the terms of the charge. For example, a floating charge may contain a provision which entitles its holder to trigger crystallisation by serving a notice to that effect on the com-

[251] *Biggerstaff v Rowatt's Wharf Ltd* [1896] 2 Ch 93, CA.

[252] *Evans v Rival Granite Quarries Ltd* [1910] 2 KB 979, CA, not following *Davey & Co v Williamson & Sons* [1898] 2 QB 194, CA.

[253] *NW Robbie & Co Ltd v Witney Warehouse Co Ltd* [1963] 3 All ER 613, CA. But compare *Re Dex Developments Pty Ltd* (1994) 13 ACSR 485, CT SC, criticised by Tan, CH, 'Automatic Crystallisation, De-Crystallisation and Convertibility of Charges' [1998] CfiLR 41, 44.

[254] This is subject to the special considerations that may apply where there is no public indication of the fact of crystallisation. On these, see this chapter, at 532–3.

[255] *Griffiths v Yorkshire Bank plc* [1994] 1 WLR 1427.

[256] *Re Standard Manufacturing Co* [1891] 1 Ch 627, CA; *Re Opera Ltd* [1891] 3 Ch 260, CA; *Taunton v Sheriff of Warwickshire* [1895] 1 Ch 734; *Norton v Yates* [1906] 1 KB 112; *Cairney v Back* [1906] 2 KB 746. This is a complex area. The difficulties lie mainly in determining whether, for the mode of execution in question, the execution process has been completed by the time of crystallisation. See further, Gough, WJ, *Company Charges* (2nd edn, 1996) 319–28.

[257] *NW Robbie & Co Ltd v Witney Warehouse Co Ltd* [1963] 3 All ER 613, CA. This is another difficult area which is considered further in: Wood, PR, *English and International Set-Off* (1989) 925–9; Gough, WJ, *Company Charges* (2nd edn, 1996) 281–302; Derham, RS, *Set-off* (2nd edn, 1996) 606–16; Ferran, EV, 'Floating Charges—The Nature of the Security' [1988] CLJ 213, 217–27.

[258] *Edward Nelson & Co Ltd v Faber & Co* [1903] 2 KB 367.

[259] *Evans v Rival Granite Quarries Ltd* [1910] 2 KB 979, CA; *NW Robbie & Co Ltd v Witney Warehouse Co Ltd* [1963] 3 All ER 613, CA. The appointment of a receiver by the court at the instance of a debenture-holder would also trigger crystallisation but appointment of a receiver via this route would nowadays be very unusual.

[260] *Re Panama, New Zealand and Australian Royal Mail Co* (1870) 5 Ch App 318; *Re Colonial Trusts Corp; ex parte Bradshaw* (1879) 15 Ch D 465, CA, 472 *per* Jessel MR.

[261] *Re Woodroffes (Musical Instruments) Ltd* [1986] Ch 366; *William Gaskell Group Ltd v Highley* [1993] BCC 200; *Re The Real Meat Co Ltd* [1996] BCC 254.

pany.[262] Until the 1980s it was uncertain whether under English law it was possible to provide for automatic crystallisation upon the happening of an event that did not require intervention from the holder of the charge and which, unlike liquidation or cessation of business, did not signal the end of the company's business. Dicta in some old cases suggested that, outside situations of cessation of business, the holder of the charge had to intervene positively in order to bring about crystallisation.[263] In England, the powerful dicta of Hoffmann J in *Re Brightlife Ltd*[264] and his decision in *Re Permanent Houses (Holdings) Ltd*[265] heralded the acceptance of the legal effectiveness of automatic crystallisation clauses that did not require the charge-holder to intervene. Elsewhere in the Commonwealth, it has also been specifically held that automatic crystallisation in this form is possible.[266] This acceptance of non-interventionist automatic crystallisation, despite certain policy objections to it,[267] represents a triumph for freedom of contract: a floating charge is a consensual security and it is therefore for the parties to determine its features including the circumstances in which it will crystallise.

Drafting of Automatic Crystallisation Clauses

There are now two recognised forms of automatic crystallisation clause: the first is where crystallisation is to happen upon the occurrence of specified

[262] *Re Brightlife Ltd* [1987] Ch 200. The effectiveness of crystallisation notices was conceded in *Re Woodroffes (Musical Instruments) Ltd* [1986] Ch 366.

[263] In particular *Evans v Rival Granite Quarries Ltd* [1910] 2 KB 979, CA, 986–7 *per* Vaughan Williams LJ and 992–3 *per* Fletcher Moulton LJ; *Reg in right of British Columbia v Consolidated Churchill Copper Corpn Ltd* [1978] 5 WWR 652, BC SC.

[264] [1987] Ch 200. This case was actually about crystallisation by service of a notice but there is no important difference in the legal analysis between that type of clause and 'pure' non-interventionist automatic crystallisation provisions. See further, Gough, WJ, *Company Charges* (2nd edn, 1996) 233.

[265] (1989) 5 BCC 151. Counsel conceded the point but Hoffmann J reiterated the view that he had expressed in the earlier case that there was no conceptual reason why parties should not agree that any specified event should cause the charge to crystallise: 154–5.

[266] *Stein v Saywell* [1969] ALR 481, H Ct of Aust (although the point was not argued); *Fire Nymph Products Ltd v The Heating Centre Pty Ltd* (1991–92) 7 ACSR 365, NSW CA; *Re Manurewa Transport Ltd* [1971] NZLR 909, NZ SC; *DFC Financial Services Ltd v Coffey* [1991] 2 NZLR 513, PC, 518 *per* Lord Goff; *Dovey Enterprises Ltd v Guardian Assurance Public Ltd* [1993] 1 NZLR 540, NZ CA.

[267] Historically, the effect of automatic crystallisation clauses on the ranking of preferential debts was one of the issues that concerned writers on this topic. It was argued before Hoffmann J in *Re Brightlife Ltd* [1987] Ch 200. Preferential debts are debts that in the event of receivership or liquidation are by statute entitled to be paid in priority to debts secured by a floating charge even though they would on normal principles rank behind. Although these debts are preferential to ordinary unsecured debts and also to debts secured by floating charges, they are not preferential to debts secured by a fixed charge: *Re Lewis Merthyr Consolidated Collieries* [1929] 1 Ch 498, CA. Before the Insolvency Act 1986, the position was that the floating charge had to continue to float up to the date of the liquidation or receivership for preferential debts to rank for payment ahead of the debt secured by the floating charge: *Re Griffin Hotel Co Ltd* [1941] Ch 129. For the purposes of the Insolvency Act 1986, ss 40 and 175, the time of the crystallisation does not affect the ranking of the preferential debts because they are to be paid out of assets which were secured by a charge which, as created, was a floating charge.

Generally, on policy objections to automatic crystallisation see: Boyle, AJ, 'The Validity of Automatic Crystallisation Clauses' [1979] JBL 231; *Cork Committee Report* paras 1570–80. Academic opinion in favour of automatic crystallisation clauses predating the 1980s cases on the point included Farrar, JH, 'The Crystallisation of a Floating Charge' (1976) 40 Conv 397.

events without positive intervention from the holder of the charge; and the second is where crystallisation is to happen if and when the holder of the charge serves a notice to that effect. The first type of clause places the occurrence of crystallisation outside the control of the holder of the charge and, unless the clause is narrowly and carefully drafted, may result in situations where the charge crystallises even though the charge-holder is content for it to continue to exist in uncrystallised form. In anticipation of this, an automatic crystallisation clause may be coupled with an express clause entitling its holder to de-crystallise it again.[268] In the absence of such a clause, it should be possible to achieve de-crystallisation with the express or implied consent of the holder of the charge.[269] However, there is a risk that if the automatic crystallisation is so widely drafted that the holder of the charge has frequently to agree to de-crystallisation, this pattern of events may lead a court to conclude that the original agreement was later varied by the parties so as to exclude the automatic crystallisation provision.[270] The second form of automatic crystallisation clause avoids the issue of unwanted crystallisation by keeping the trigger for crystallisation within the control of the holder of the charge. On the other hand, automatic crystallisation clauses in this form have an in-built delay factor which could operate to the detriment of the holder of the charge in its claim to priority over other interests in the same property.[271]

The commencement of administration proceedings in respect of a company in accordance with the Insolvency Act 1986 does not constitute an implied crystallising event. This is an example of the type of event that could be covered by an express automatic crystallisation clause in either of the forms outlined in the previous paragraph.

A lender may seek to link an automatic crystallisation clause to a provision in a floating charge whereby the company undertakes not to create any new security ranking in priority to, or *pari passu* with, the floating charge (that is, a negative pledge). Careful drafting is needed to ensure that the automatic crystallisation is triggered before the security in breach of the negative pledge is created[272] since, if this is not achieved and the later security is a fixed charge, it will rank ahead of the crystallised floating charge under the priority rule of first in time which is discussed later in this chapter.[273] Whilst appropriate drafting can achieve this much, it must however, be borne in mind that the crystallised, and therefore now fixed, charge may lose the battle for priority despite being earlier in time because of considerations based on agency or estoppel principles.

[268] As in *Covacich v Riordan* [1994] 2 NZLR 502, NZ HC.

[269] But note Grantham, R, `Refloating a Floating Charge' [1997] CfiLR 53; Tan, CH, 'Automatic Crystallisation, De-Crystallisation and Convertibility of Charges' [1998] CfiLR 41.

[270] Goode, RM, *Legal Problems of Credit and Security* (2nd edn, 1988) 73–6; Gough, WJ, *Company Charges* (2nd edn, 1996) 404–7.

[271] However, it is doubtful whether or to what extent third parties will be affected by crystallisation if they do not know, and have no means of knowing, that it has occurred. This is because of the limitations that may result from the application of estoppel or agency principles, as discussed in the next section.

[272] *Fire Nymph Products Ltd v The Heating Centre Pty Ltd* (1991–92) 7 ACSR 365, NSW CA, recognises that it is possible to achieve this order of events.

[273] See below, at 534–6.

Automatic Crystallisation and Third Parties

An argument against automatic crystallisation provisions is that they are unfair because they can cause a charge to crystallise without that fact becoming apparent to others who deal with the company and advance credit to it. It has been suggested that any unfairness to third parties that results from recognising that automatic crystallisation clauses are effective may be mitigated by estoppel[274] or agency[275] principles: this is to say that until the fact of crystallisation has been drawn to the attention of outsiders dealing with the company, the holder of the charge may be estopped from denying that the charge remains floating or, alternatively, that outsiders can continue to rely on the company's ostensible authority to deal with its assets as if they were subject only to an uncrystallised floating charge. In circumstances where a subsequent chargee is unaware of the crystallisation of the earlier charge, on the basis of estoppel or agency principles, a debt secured by a floating charge that has crystallised into a fixed charge by operation of an automatic crystallisation notice could thus lose priority to a debt secured by a subsequent fixed charge on the same property even though, in accordance with the normal priority rules that are discussed in the next section of this chapter, it would rank ahead of it.

The operation of estoppel or agency principles in relation to automatic crystallisation contractual clauses has not been litigated.[276] It appears that these principles may protect at least some third parties who acquire an interest in the company property after crystallisation but not third parties who have only a personal claim again the company.[277] As a matter of policy, there is a strong case for saying that the important matter of the limits of the effectiveness of automatic crystallisation clauses with regard to third parties would best be dealt with by legislation specifically on the point. A system of registration of crystallisation has been advocated from time to time[278] and the Companies Act 1989 contained a provision to that effect. That provision would have authorised the Secretary of State to make regulations stipulating requirements for registration of notice of crystallising events and providing for the consequences of failure to give notice. It was specifically stated that those consequences could have included the ineffectiveness of the crystallisation against such persons as might be prescribed. This provision was part of a series of measures that were intended to revise and update the requirements of the Companies Act 1985 on the registration of charges. Various difficulties in the drafting of the new provisions emerged after the passing of the legislation and implementation of them has been shelved indefinitely.

274 Gough, WJ, *Company Charges* (2nd edn, 1996) 252–6 discusses the operation of estoppel in this context and its limits. See also Gough, WJ, 'The Floating Charge: Traditional Themes and New Directions' in Finn, PD (ed), *Equity and Commercial Relationships* (1987) 239, 251–2.

275 Goode, RM, *Legal Problems of Credit and Security* (2nd edn, 1988) 59–60, 70, 90.

276 Note, however, *Re the Real Meat Co Ltd* [1996] BCC 254 where the sale of a company's business caused the charge to crystallise under the implied ground of cessation of the company's business. It was held that the purchaser of the business prima facie took it subject to the crystallised charge.

277 Gough, WJ, *Company Charges* (2nd edn, 1996) 252–6 discusses this point in detail.

278 Boyle, AJ, 'The Validity of Automatic Crystallisation Clauses' [1979] JBL 231, 240.

PRIORITY RULES FOR COMPETING INTERESTS IN THE SAME PROPERTY

A company may use its assets as security for more than one debt. When this happens and the value of the security proves to be insufficient to pay off all of the debts that were secured on it, it becomes necessary to work out the respective priorities of the various charges. Priority disputes can also arise where a company charges property in favour of one person and then agrees to sell that property to someone else: here the issue is whether the purchaser takes the property subject to, or free from, the charge. The English courts worked out a series of rules for resolving priority disputes and these rules continue to apply to company charges even though certain aspects of them are affected by the statutory requirements for the registration of charges. English law on security interests in personal property differs from many other modern legal systems by not providing for a statutory system of priority based primarily on the timing of the registration of charges on a public register.[279] Various reform bodies[280] have considered English law to be deficient in this respect and have called for a complete overhaul of the law relating to credit and security, including the establishment of a priority system based on filing, but legislation has not been forthcoming.

There follows an outline of the various rules. At the outset of this discussion, it is pertinent to note that these priority rules are default rules that apply where the parties have not made alternative provision. It is open to secured creditors to vary the priority afforded to their charges under the general law by a priority agreement. Priority agreements between secured creditors are considered in Chapter 16. Security over land is excluded from this discussion because that is a specialist area which is affected by the requirements of the real property legislation.[281] Also, the special rules that apply where there are competing interests in debts or other forms of intangible personal property are considered separately after the general rules have been outlined.

Competing Interests in Tangible Personal Property

There are two main rules.[282] The first rule is that where the equities are equal the first in time prevails.[283] This is the priority rule that governs, for example, priority disputes between two fixed equitable charges on the same property. The charge that was created first has priority unless the equities are not equal.

[279] See, in particular the Uniform Commercial Code, art 9 (USA); the Uniform Personal Property Security Act 1982 (Canada) and the various Personal Property Security Acts, based on the model of art 9, adopted in the various provinces of Canada; Corporations Law Part 2K.3—Order of Priority (Australia). Note also Companies Act 1985, s 464 which sets out a statutory ranking order for the floating charge under Scottish law.

[280] Most recently, the *Diamond Report*. This report developed proposals that had been made in an earlier report but not implemented: *Report of the Committee on Consumer Credit* (Cmnd 4596) (1971) (the Crowther Committee report).

[281] See Tyler, ELG, *Fisher and Lightwood's Law of Mortgage* (10th edn, 1988) ch 24.

[282] For detailed treatment: Baker, PV, and Langan, P St J, *Snell's Equity* (29th edn, 1990) ch 4; Bell, AP, *Modern Law of Personal Property in England and Ireland* (1989) ch 22.

[283] *Cave v Cave* (1880) 15 Ch D 639; *Rice v Rice* (1853) 2 Drew 73, 61 ER 646.

A situation where the equities would not be equal is where the first chargee's conduct has led the second to believe that the property is unencumbered. The second rule is that a person who bona fide purchases for value a legal interest in property takes free of existing equitable interests in that property provided he does not have notice of their existence and provided there is no fraud, misrepresentation or gross negligence on his part.[284] By application of this rule a bona fide purchaser for value without notice takes property that is subject to a fixed charge free of the charge. The creditor is obliged to pursue his remedies against the company that has disposed of the security in breach of the terms of the charge.

A key feature of the floating charge is that it allows the company to continue to deal with its assets as if they were unsecured. This power to continue trading includes power to grant subsequent mortgages and charges and accordingly, although the security is first in time, the holder of a floating charge is estopped from denying the priority of later legal or fixed equitable interests.[285] A subsequent fixed chargee or purchaser takes free of an earlier floating charge even where he is aware of the existence of that charge.[286] This modification of the normal first-in-time rule does not apply as between two floating charges on the same property. Here, in accordance with the general principle, the first in time takes priority[287] unless the second charge expressly permits the creation of subsequent floating security ranking in priority to, or equally with, the first floating charge.[288] It is commonplace for floating charges to contain a promise from the chargor company not to use the assets that are the subject-matter of the security as security for any subsequent borrowing that would rank ahead of, or equally with, the floating charge, without the consent of the holder of that charge. This 'negative pledge' has a twofold purpose. Its internal purpose is to ensure that if the promise is broken, the holder of the charge can sue the company for breach of contract. In a well-drafted agreement, this breach will be an event of default which entitles the chargee to call in the loan and to appoint a receiver to enforce its security. Its external purpose is to reverse the ordinary priority rule applicable to floating charges by ensuring that the floating charge ranks ahead of the security created in breach

[284] *Pilcher v Rawlins* (1872) 7 Ch App 259.

[285] Where, as with unregistered land, the subject-matter of the security is represented by title deeds, it is possible to explain the low priority position of the floating charge by reference to the first general rule. The holder of the floating charge will leave the title deeds with the company so that it can continue to deal with the assets in the course of its business. This results in unequal equities between the first floating charge and later fixed charges which, consequently, take priority: *Re Castell & Brown Ltd* [1898] 1 Ch 315; *Re Valletort Sanitary Steam Laundry Co Ltd* [1903] 2 Ch 654.

[286] *Moor v Anglo-Italian Bank* (1878) 10 Ch D 681; *Re Hamilton's Windsor Ironworks Co, ex parte Pitman and Edwards* (1879) 12 Ch D 707; *Wheatley v Silkstone & Haigh Moor Coal Co* (1885) 29 Ch D 715; *English and Scottish Mercantile Investment Co v Brunton* [1892] 2 QB 700, CA; *Re Standard Rotary Machine Co Ltd* (1906) 95 LT 829.

[287] *Re Benjamin Cope & Sons Ltd* [1914] 1 Ch 800. *Griffiths v Yorkshire Bank plc* [1994] 1 WLR 1427, which is to the effect that a second floating charge can take priority by being the first to crystallise, is inconsistent with earlier authorities.

[288] *Re Automatic Bottle Makers Ltd* [1926] Ch 412, CA where a second floating charge on part of the property that was the subject-matter of the security in an earlier floating charge took priority to the earlier charge. This decision turned on the terms of the first floating charge, which reserved to the company the right to create certain specific charges ranking in priority. The Court of Appeal concluded that a charge in floating form could be within the scope of the reserved power.

of the covenant. Contractual promises do not normally affect third parties who are not party to the agreement but it is established that a person who obtains security, legal or equitable, on property that is already subject to a floating charge containing a negative pledge takes subject to that charge if he has notice of the existence of the negative pledge.[289] It is insufficient that the subsequent creditor has notice simply of the existence of the floating charge; he must have notice of the fact that it contains a negative pledge.[290] An explanation for the priority effect of a negative pledge in a floating charge is that it is an equity attached to an equitable interest which, on general principles, is binding on persons who have notice of it.[291]

Priority Rules for Competing Interests in Intangible Property

The priority rules for competing interests in intangible property are relevant where, for example, a company grants a series of charges, fixed or floating, on its book debts, or sells book debts that were subject to a charge. Priority here is governed by the rule in *Dearle v Hall*[292] which is that priority is governed by the order in which notice is given to the debtors. Notice does not have to be in particular form and it can be given orally.[293] Accordingly, the purchaser of the legal title to debts[294] takes them subject to an earlier fixed charge where the chargee is the first to give notice of his interest to the debtors, even though the purchaser is unaware of the existence of the fixed charge when he acquires the debts.[295] It is axiomatic that a company that has charged its debts by way of a floating charge can continue to deal with the debts and to collect their proceeds; no notice of the existence of the floating charge will be given to the company's debtors, with the consequence that the charge will rank behind notified interests.

The rule in *Dearle v Hall* is subject to the qualification that where, at the time that a person acquires an interest, he is aware of the existence of other interests, apart from floating charges, in the same property, he takes subject to those interests irrespective of the order in which notice is given.[296]

[289] *Cox v Dublin City Distillery Co* [1915] 1 IR 345, Ir CA.

[290] *Re Valletort Sanitary Steam Laundry Co Ltd* [1903] 2 Ch 654; *Siebe Gorman & Co Ltd v Barclays Bank Ltd* [1979] 2 Lloyd's Rep 142.

[291] *Rother Iron Works Ltd v Canterbury Precision Engineers Ltd* [1974] QB 1, CA. For further discussion of this explanation and alternatives to it see this chapter, at 509–12.

[292] (1823) 3 Russ 1, 38 ER 475, 492.

[293] *Lloyd v Banks* (1868) 3 Ch App 488.

[294] An assignment of the legal title to debts must comply with the formal requirements of the Law of Property Act 1925, s 136 (1). These formalities include a requirement to give written notice of the assignment to the debtors. This written notice suffices for the purposes of the rule in *Dearle v Hall* but it does not override notices, in whatever form, of prior interests that were given earlier.

[295] The displacement of the rule that a bona-fide purchaser for value of a legal interest who is without notice of a prior equitable interest takes free of it is supported by recent case law (*E Pfeiffer Weinkellerei-Weinenkauf GmbH & Co v Arbuthnot Factors Ltd* [1988] 1 WLR 150; *Compaq Computers Ltd v Abercorn Group Ltd* [1991] BCC 484). The contrary view in favour of the application of the bona-fide purchaser rule to this situation, developed by Oditah, F, (1989) OJLS 513 and recapitulated in Oditah, F, *Legal Aspects of Receivables Financing* (1991) 154–63 has not been accepted.

[296] *Re Holmes* (1885) 29 Ch D 786, CA; *Spencer v Clarke* (1878) 9 Ch D 137.

Priority of Purchase Money Security Interests

This is a special case of a priority conflict. The situation arises where a company which has created a charge covering future property acquires property fitting the description of the subject-matter of the security, but that acquisition has been funded by borrowing from a third-party lender and that lender requires an interest in the acquired property in order to secure its advance. Assuming that the bona-fide purchaser rule is inapplicable, which security interest has priority: the charge that was first in time or the later purchase money security? In *Abbey National Building Society v Cann*[297] the House of Lords resolved a conflict in decisions of lower courts on this point[298] and held that the provider of the purchase money finance took priority. Lord Jauncey stated the basis for the decision in these terms:

> a purchaser who can only complete a transaction by borrowing money . . . cannot in reality ever be said to have acquired even for a *scintilla temporis* the unencumbered freehold or leasehold interest in the land whereby he could grant interests having priority over the mortgage.

This ruling achieves a sensible result. For the benefit of the addition of that property to accrue first to the existing charge holder would constitute an unwarranted windfall in its favour.[299]

REGISTRATION OF CHARGES—OUTLINE OF REQUIREMENTS

The law relating to the registration of charges is in an unfortunate state. The Companies Act 1985, Pt XII, which contains the existing legal requirements for the registration of charges[300] has a variety of defects and lacunae. The Companies Act 1989, Pt IV, contained a proposed new Pt XII which would have corrected some of the deficiencies of the present law, but potential problems with the new regime that emerged after its enactment, including its interrelationship with other applicable registration requirements such as those relating to registered land, meant that it could not be brought into force.[301]

[297] [1991] 1 AC 56, HL. McCormack, G, 'Charges and Priorities—The Death of the Scintilla Temporis' (1991) 12 Co Law 10; Smith, RJ, 'Mortgagees and Trust Beneficiaries' (1990) 106 LQR 545; Gregory, R, 'Rompala Clauses as Unregistered Charges—A Fundamental Shift?' (1990) 106 LQR 550; de Lacy, J, 'The Purchase Money Security Interest: A Company Charge Conundrum' [1991] LMCLQ 531.

[298] *Church of England Building Society v Piskor* [1954] Ch 553, CA (favouring a *scintilla temporis* analysis that would have given priority to the chargee); *Re Connolly Brothers Ltd (No 2)* [1912] 2 Ch 25 and *Security Trust Co v Royal Bank of Canada* [1976] AC 503, PC (favouring the approach that prevailed in *Abbey National*).

[299] *Diamond Report* para 17.7.

[300] This Part applies to charges created by companies registered in England and Wales (Pt XII, ch 1) and also to charges created by companies registered in Scotland (Pt XII, ch 2). Only the former are considered here. Charges created by oversea companies which may require registration at the English companies registry are also outside the scope of the discussion in this chapter: see Companies Act 1985, s 409 and *NV Slavenburg's Bank v Intercontinental Natural Resources Ltd* [1980] 1 All ER 955.

[301] *Proposals for Reform of Part XII of the Companies Act 1985* (DTI, 1994).

The relevance of the Companies Act 1989, Pt IV now is only that it provides one possible model for reform of the registration requirements. However, it is a model which merely tinkers with some of the details of the regime and does not address some of its fundamental problems.[302]

In outline, the structure of the Companies Act 1985, Pt XII is that prescribed particulars of most, but not all, charges created by companies must be delivered to the companies registry within 21 days of creation. The facts that not all charges are registrable and that there is a 21-day registration period are key defects of the registration system but they are not matters that would have been improved by the Companies Act 1989. A person who searches the register can never be sure from that search alone[303] that he has discovered all of the charges affecting a company's property or even, because of the permitted 21-day registration period, that he has discovered all of the existing registrable charges. When this point is considered in conjunction with the priority rule of first in time, its significance can be readily appreciated. The registrar of companies is required to maintain a register of charges and this is available for public inspection. The registrar has to check whether the requirements for registration have been complied with and, if he is satisfied that they have been, his certificate of registration in respect of the charge is conclusive. Whether the registrar of companies should carry the administrative burden of filtering out defective applications is debatable, but the proposal[304] in the Companies Act 1989 to relieve him of it and, as a consequence, to remove the conclusive certificate of registration was one of the most controversial aspects of the proposed new regime.[305]

Failure to file as required by the legislation results in the charge becoming void against specified persons including subsequent secured creditors. In this respect, the registration requirements can affect priority by withdrawing from a registrable, but unregistered charge, the priority over subsequent interests that it would have enjoyed under the first-in-time rule. However, where there is proper compliance with the filing requirements, the order of priority is not affected by order of filing. This, too, is a fundamental defect in the registration requirements which would not have been corrected by the Companies Act 1989. A system of priority based on date of filing would be far more straightforward than a series of rules which depend on order of creation of competing securities, equality of equities and notice. Where the obligation to file particulars of registrable charges is overlooked, the court may authorise late filing.

[302] Companies Act 1989, Part IV was to some extent based on recommendations in the *Diamond Report*, Pt III. These recommendations were made as proposed interim measures pending the complete overhaul of the general law relating to security interests in personal property that formed the main recommendation in the report.

[303] Inquiries of the company may elicit further information. Also a company has to keep its own register of *all* charges at its registered office and this register can be searched to obtain a more complete picture (Companies Act 1985, s 407); but a charge is not rendered void if it is not entered on this register which means that there is less incentive to ensure its accuracy.

[304] This was suggested in the *Diamond Report* para 22.1.10. It was also a reform advocated previously in the *Report of the Company Law Committee*, Cmnd 1749 (1962) (Jenkins Committee) para 302.

[305] For more detailed examination of the 1989 Act see McCormack, G, 'Registration of Company Charges: The New Law' [1990] LMCLQ 520; Ferran, EV, and Mayo, C, 'Registration of Company Charges—The New Regime' [1991] JBL 152.

There is no mechanism for late filing without a court order. Here, the Companies Act 1989 would have made a positive change by providing for late filing without a court order but only on terms that would not prejudice other interests in the company's property.

REGISTRATION REQUIREMENTS—DETAILED ASPECTS

Charges Requiring Registration

Certain charges created by a company are registrable. The term 'charge' in this context includes 'mortgage'.[306] Charges arising by operation of law, as opposed to act of creation by the company, are not registrable.[307] The list of registrable charges is in Companies Act 1985, s 396. It is as follows:

(a) a charge for the purpose of securing any issue of securities
(b) a charge on uncalled share capital of the company
(c) a charge created or evidenced by an instrument which, if executed by an individual, would require registration as a bill of sale
(d) a charge on land (wherever situated) or any interest in it, but not including a charge for any rent or other periodical sum issued out of the land
(e) a charge on book debts of the company
(f) a floating charge on the company's undertaking or property
(g) a charge on calls made but not paid
(h) a charge on a ship or aircraft, or any share in a ship
(i) a charge on goodwill, or on any intellectual property.

Detailed commentaries on each of these categories of registrable charge can be found in the main company law texts.[308] Here, just a few comments are made on some of the categories of registrable charge.

Charges on Goods

(c) is the provision under which fixed charges on goods may be registrable. To determine whether a charge on goods is in fact registrable it is necessary to refer back to the Bills of Sale Acts 1878–1882 which refer to mortgages or charges on personal chattels, personal chattels being defined as goods and other articles capable of complete transfer by delivery. Amongst the categories of security excluded from the registration requirements under the bills of sale legislation are pledges. There is an obvious case for this provision to be redrafted so as to make its purpose plain and to remove the obscure reference to the bills of sale legislation. A possible model is the Companies Act 1989 which provided for the registration of charges on goods or an interest in goods other than those where the chargee was entitled to possession either of the goods or of a document of title to them. That amendment, which has never been brought into force, took the opportunity to close the gap whereby, under the present law, oral fixed charges on goods are not registrable.

[306] Companies Act 1985, s 396 (4).
[307] *London and Cheshire Insurance Co Ltd v Laplagrene Property Co Ltd* [1971] Ch 499.
[308] eg, Boyle, AJ, Sykes, R, and Sealy, LS, *Gore-Browne on Companies* (44th edn, looseleaf) para 18.9; Pennington, RR, *Company Law* (7th edn, 1995) 636–47.

Charges on Book Debts

'Debts arising in a business in which it is the proper and usual course to keep books and which ought to be entered in the books'[309] is one definition of the term 'book debts'. It has been held that where accountancy practice is not to treat certain debts as book debts, those debts should not be regarded as book debts for the purposes of the registration requirements of the companies legislation.[310] Accountancy practice is not normally to treat the credit balances on a company's bank accounts as book debts and, although there is no ruling precisely on the point, it would seem therefore that a charge on a bank account should not normally be registrable under paragraph (e).[311] In practice, however, the companies registry will accept for registration particulars of fixed charges on bank accounts.[312]

Floating Charges

All floating charges are registrable.[313] This is in contrast to fixed charges which are only registrable if they fall within one of the specific headings. Where a charge has not been registered, one of the reasons for arguing that it is a fixed charge rather than a floating charge may be to establish that the charge was outside the category of registrable charge.

Non-registrable Charges

Fixed charges on insurance policies and on shares are amongst the categories of fixed charge that fall outside the registration requirements. Those advocating reform of the system for the registration of charges have from time to time recommended that these types of fixed charge should become registrable.[314] However, Professor Diamond's *Review of Security Interests in Property,* the most recent formal review of this matter, whilst supporting the proposal for fixed charges on insurance policies to become registrable, rejected the suggestion that fixed charges on shares should be made registrable. This rejection was based on the argument that regular dealing was part of the normal

[309] *Official Receiver v Tailby* (1886) 18 QBD 25, CA, 29 *per* Lord Esher MR (affirmed *sub nom Tailby v Official Receiver* (1888) 13 App Cas 523, HL). See also *Shipley v Marshall* (1863) 14 CBNS 566, 570–1 *per* Erle CJ; *Independent Automatic Sales Ltd v Knowles and Fowler* [1962] 3 All ER 27.

[310] *Paul & Frank Ltd v Discount Bank (Overseas) Ltd* [1967] Ch 348.

[311] In *Re Brightlife Ltd* [1987] Ch 200 and *Re Permanent Houses (Holdings) Ltd* (1988) 5 BCC 151 Hoffmann J held that for the purposes of particular charging documents, credit balances were not within the scope of the charge on 'book debts'. In the latter case, however, Hoffmann J stated specifically that he was not expressing any opinion on whether credit balances were book debts for the purposes of the registration requirements of the companies legislation. As Lord Hoffmann in *Re Bank of Credit and Commerce International SA (No 8)* [1998] AC 214, HL 227, he again declined to express a view on whether charges on bank accounts were registrable as charges on book debts, since the point did not arise for decision, but he referred to *Northern Bank Ltd v Ross* [1991] BCLC 504, NI CA, with the comment that the judgment in that case 'suggests that, in the case of deposits with banks, an obligation to register is unlikely to arise'.

[312] Letter from the Companies Registration Office dated 6 August 1985.

[313] But compare Boyle, AJ, Sykes, R, and Sealy, LS, *Gore-Browne on Companies* (4th edn, looseleaf) para 18.9.6.

[314] See *Diamond Report* para 23.5 and para 23.8 considering the arguments for and against registration in these cases and the views put forward by earlier committees including the Jenkins Committee (*Report of the Company Law Committee*, Cmnd 1749 (1962)).

process of managing a portfolio of shares and that if creditors had to file new charges every time a new share was added to the portfolio this would create administrative inconvenience that could deter lenders from taking security over a portfolio of shares.[315] Professor Diamond also rejected a more restricted registration requirement—to make fixed charges on shares in subsidiary companies registrable—on the grounds that this could generate a range of difficulties, such as where a company that was not a subsidiary at the time of the charge, later became one.[316]

The Registration Requirement

The prescribed particulars of a registrable charge created by a company must be delivered to the registrar of companies for registration within 21 days after its date of creation.[317] If there is an instrument creating or evidencing the charge, that must accompany the application.[318] It is the duty of a company that creates a registrable charge to file particulars in respect of it, but this task may, instead, be carried out by any person who is interested in the charge.[319] In practice the person in whose favour the charge is created normally undertakes the task of filing the required particulars. It is in that person's interest to do so because his security will become void if the required filing is not made.[320]

The prescribed particulars of a charge created by a company, other than a charge to the benefit of which debenture holders of a series are entitled to equally, are: (i) the date of creation; (ii) the amount secured; (iii) short particulars of the property charged; and (iv) the persons entitled to the charge.[321] There are special requirements for the prescribed particulars of a charge relating to a series of debentures.[322] The existence (or not) of a negative pledge in a floating charge is not a prescribed particular, but it is common practice for details of such clauses to be included in the form by which the application for filing of a floating charge is made. Where this common practice is followed, the existence of a negative pledge in a floating charge will be included in the registered details of the charge and, so, will become known to anyone who actually searches the register.[323] The Companies Act 1989, Pt IV envisaged following Scottish law on this matter[324] by making the existence (or not) of a negative pledge a prescribed particular.[325] Whether a negative pledge is a prescribed particular is relevant to the question of the interrelationship between

315 *Diamond Report* para 23.8 316 Ibid.

317 Companies Act 1985, s 395 (1). The registration requirements are extended to cover a charge on property that is acquired by the company subject to the charge where that charge would have been registrable had it been created by the company itself: Companies Act 1985, s 400. Non-compliance with this registration requirement does not make the charge void but the company and its responsible officers are liable to a fine. This registration requirement is not considered further in this chapter.

318 Companies Act 1985, s 395 (1) and 397 (1) (deed of charge or debenture must accompany application).

319 Ibid, s 399. 320 Ibid, s 400 (2) and (4). 321 Ibid, s 401. 322 Ibid, s 397.

323 The issue of constructive notice is considered in this chapter, at 534–6.

324 Companies Act 1985, s 417 (3)(e). 325 Ibid, s 415.

the registration requirements and the priority rules and it is discussed further in that context.[326]

The Role of the Registrar and the Issue of the Certificate of Registration

The role of the registrar is to check that the application is in order. If it is not and the application is rejected, that defective filing cannot be relied upon in satisfaction of the Companies Act 1985 registration requirement and, to avoid the charge becoming void, a second, correct, application must be made within the original 21-day filing period.[327] Once correct particulars relating to a registrable charge are filed with the registrar of companies, the statutory filing obligation is fulfilled and the charge cannot thereafter be held to be void on this ground even if it does not actually appear on the register until some time after the 21-day period for filing. Upon registration of a charge, the registrar issues a certificate of registration stating the amount secured by the charge.[328] This certificate is conclusive evidence that the requirements for registration of Companies Act 1985, Pt XII have been complied with. The conclusive nature of the certificate means that, with possible exceptions for manifest error on the face of the certificate or evidence that it was obtained by fraud, it cannot be challenged by any person other than the Crown.[329] Thus, for example, where the registrar issues a certificate even though the application was in fact out of time, it is not open to any person (apart from the Crown) to argue that the charge is void for non-registration.[330]

Where the registrar fails to notice a mistake in the filed particulars and they misstate the chargee's rights, this does not estop the chargee from asserting his rights under the terms of the charge. This is illustrated by a case where the filed particulars understated the amount secured. It was held that the chargee was nevertheless entitled to enforce the charge to the full secured amount as stated in the charge.[331] This is an unfair outcome that further undermines the status of the register of charges as a source of useful information. Where the filed particulars understate a creditor's rights, he should not be entitled to assert greater rights which have not been publicly disclosed against other persons who have acquired an interest in the company's property. That was broadly the effect intended to be achieved by the relevant provisions of the Companies Act 1989 on this point.

Registration and Notice

Registration of a registrable charge serves to give constructive notice of the existence of that charge to such persons as can be reasonably expected to

[326] See below.
[327] *R v Registrar ex p Central Bank of India* [1986] QB 1114, CA.
[328] Companies Act 1985, s 401 (2).
[329] *R v Registrar ex p Central Bank of India* [1986] [1986] QB 1114, CA.
[330] *Re CL Nye* [1971] Ch 442, CA; *Re Eric Holmes Ltd* [1965] Ch 1052.
[331] *Re Mechanisations (Eaglescliffe) Ltd* [1966] Ch 20. See also *National Provincial and Union Bank of England v Charnley* [1924] 1 KB 431, CA.

search the register.[332] The category of person who could reasonably be expected to search the register includes subsequent chargees, but it is doubtful whether it covers purchasers of the company's property.[333] It does not constitute notice to debtors for the purposes of the rule in *Dearle v Hall.* Constructive notice of a charge covers the prescribed particulars of a charge, but it is widely accepted, and has been specifically so held in Ireland,[334] that it does not extend to information that chargees voluntarily include in the application for filing of a charge but which are not required to be there as a matter of law. It is at this point that the inclusion of the existence (or not) of a negative pledge in a floating charge in the list of prescribed particulars comes into sharp focus.

The Companies Act 1989 contained a helpful provision clarifying the notice effect of registration. This provided for registration to constitute notice to subsequent chargees of any matter requiring registration and disclosed on the register at the time when their charge was created. It also specifically provided for registration not to constitute notice of the registered information to persons, such as purchasers, who acquired an interest in the company's property otherwise than by way of charge.

Non-Registration

'Non-registration' in this context means failure to file correct particulars of a registrable charge within 21 days of creation of the charge. Provided filing within the 21 days has taken place, it does not matter that the charge may not actually appear on the register until some time after the 21-day registration period. Where there is non-registration in the relevant sense, the charge becomes void against the company's liquidator and administrator and also against the company's other secured creditors.[335] It is not void against purchasers of the company's property although they may take free of it under the bona-fide purchaser for value without notice rule.[336] Also, so long as it is not in liquidation or administration, the security remains valid against the company itself, although the money secured by the charge becomes immediately repayable.[337]

Late Registration

The Companies Act 1985, s 404 provides for the late registration of charges. On the application of the company, or any person interested, the court may order

[332] *Re Standard Rotary Machine Co Ltd* (1906) 95 LT 829; *Wilson v Kelland* [1910] 2 Ch 306.

[333] Goode, RM, *Legal Problems of Credit and Security* (2nd edn, 1998) 44–5 citing *Feuer Leather Corp v Frank Johnstone & Sons* [1981] Com LR 251.

[334] *Welch v Bowmaker (Ireland) Ltd* [1980] IR 251, Ir SC.

[335] Companies Act 1985, s 395 (1). This refers to creditors but it is clear from case law (*Re Cardiff's Workmen's Cottage Co Ltd* [1906] 2 Ch 627) that unsecured creditors have no standing to challenge the validity of a security that has not been registered in accordance with the Companies Act 1985. The point would have been clarified by the new regime in the Companies Act 1989. It expressly referred to secured creditors.

[336] Under the Companies Act 1989, Pt IV regime, non-registration would have rendered a charge void against purchasers.

[337] Companies Act 1985, s 395.

the extension of the time for registration. Before making such an order the court must be satisfied that the failure to register in time was accidental, or due to inadvertence or some other sufficient cause, or is not of a nature to prejudice the position of creditors or shareholders of the company, or that on other grounds it is just and equitable to grant relief. The court may impose such terms and conditions as seem to it to be just and expedient. The usual form for such orders is to extend the registration period, subject to the proviso that this 'is to be without prejudice to the rights of parties acquired during the period between the date of creation of the said charge and the date of its actual registration'.[338]

Errors in, or omissions from, a memorandum of satisfaction may also be corrected by a court order.[339] However, since charges are still fully enforceable notwithstanding errors in the registered particulars,[340] this reduces the incentive for creditors to apply to correct inaccurate particulars.

Clearing the Register—Memoranda of Satisfaction

When a debt secured by a registered charge is wholly or partly repaid, or property has been released from a registered charge or is no longer part of the company's property, that fact may be publicly advertised by filing with the registrar of companies a memorandum of satisfaction in the prescribed form.[341]

338 This proviso is derived from the decision in *Watson v Duff Morgan & Vermont (Holdings) Ltd* [1974] 1 WLR 450. On applications under this section generally, see McCormack, G, 'Extension of Time for Registration of Company Charges' [1986] JBL 282.

339 Companies Act 1985, s 404.

340 *Re Mechanisations (Eaglescliffe) Ltd* [1966] Ch 20; *National Provincial and Union Bank of England v Charnley* [1924] 1 KB 431, CA.

341 Companies Act 1985, s 403.

16

Subordination of Secured and Unsecured Debt

SCOPE OF THE CHAPTER

This chapter is concerned with contractual arrangements whereby secured or unsecured creditors vary the priority afforded to their debts by the general law by agreeing to accept lower ranking for repayment than their debts would ordinarily enjoy. Statute also makes provision for the subordination of certain debts in the event of insolvency[1] but statutory subordination is not considered further in this chapter.

WHY SUBORDINATE?

Secured Debt

Secured-debt subordination is where a secured creditor, or group of secured creditors, agrees to give up the priority which is afforded to its debt by the general law.[2] An external lender to a company may insist upon its debt ranking before existing secured loans that have been made to the company by its directors, its parent company or other insiders. This can be achieved by the parties entering into an arrangement whereby the insiders' debts, which are ordinarily entitled to priority by virtue of being first in time,[3] are postponed to the new debt.

Unsecured Debt

Unsecured-debt subordination occurs when one unsecured debt of a company is by some special arrangement made to rank as regards priority after some or all other unsecured debts of the company. The considerations that may influence the creation of secured subordination structures, such as postponement of insiders' debts, are also relevant here. For a company in financial difficulties, a subordinated loan from its directors or controlling shareholders may be a way for it to obtain additional finance where its existing creditors will not permit it to acquire new debt that ranks equally with their claims. A company that is in a position to raise capital by issuing securities to investors may offer subordinated debt securities to the markets. A higher interest rate than would be payable on the issuer's unsubordinated debts is the normal

[1] Insolvency Act 1986, s 74 (3).
[2] Goode, RM, *Legal Problems of Credit and Security* (2nd edn, 1988) 23.
[3] See Ch 15 above, at 533–37.

enticement for investors to acquire subordinated debt securities. To enhance further the appeal of subordinated debt securities to potential investors these also often contain share options or rights to convert the securities into shares of the issuer or of another company in its group. Other considerations that make issues of subordinated debt securities attractive from the viewpoint of the issuer of the securities are that since subordinated debt mimics the repayment profile of equity it may not, depending on drafting, be treated as debt for the purposes of the issuer's existing contractual restrictions on incurring new debt obligations or of the borrowing limits imposed on its board by its articles of association; where the issuer is a financial institution subject to capital adequacy requirements, its subordinated debt may, depending on its structure and the wording of the relevant rules, be treated as capital rather than as debt;[4] but, the status of the issue as debt for the purposes of company law rules means that it is not subject to the pre-emption requirements applicable to new issues of equity securities (at least where it does not carry rights to subscribe for, or to convert into, shares), nor is its repayment subject to the maintenance of capital rules.

FORM OF SECURED-DEBT SUBORDINATION

Secured-debt subordination is achieved by means of a deed of priority or priority agreement which is executed by the relevant creditors.[5] The company may, but is not required to, be a party to the arrangement. This was decided by the Privy Council in *Cheah Theam Swee v Equiticorp Finance Group Ltd*,[6] where it was held that an agreement between two mortgagees to alter the priority of the mortgagees was effective notwithstanding that the debtor was not a party to the agreement. Lord Browne-Wilkinson, delivering the judgment of the Judicial Committee, noted that this conclusion accorded with what was understood to be accepted US law on debt subordination[7] and commented that it was 'manifestly desirable that the law on this subject should be the same in all common law jurisdictions'. The aim of achieving international consistency has also been important in the development of the law relating to unsecured-debt subordination.[8] If a company wants to prevent its secured creditors from altering the priorities of its securities, it should insist upon specific contractual provisions to that effect.[9]

[4] The conditions that must be satisfied for subordinated debt issued by banks to be treated as capital are set out in the *Guide to Banking Supervisory Policy* (FSA, looseleaf) s 7.

[5] *ANZ v National Mutual Life Nominees Ltd* (1977) 137 CLR 252, H Ct of Aust, Tyler, ELG, *Fisher and Lightwood's Law of Mortgage* (10th edn, 1988) 458; Lingard, JR, *Bank Security Documents* (3rd edn, 1993) 337–41 and 438–46 (example of a priorities deed).

[6] [1992] BCC 98, PC.

[7] *Putnam v Broten* (1930) 60 ND 97; 232 NW 749.

[8] See this chapter, at 550–2.

[9] *Cheah Theam Swee v Equiticorp Finance Group Ltd* [1992] BCC 98, PC, 100.

PRIORITY AGREEMENTS AND PREFERENTIAL DEBTS

Although the precise contractual effect of a priority agreement may be a matter of dispute in a particular case, priority agreements tend to raise few issues of general legal significance. The one significant problematical area arises where a priority agreement has the effect of promoting a floating charge to rank before a fixed security that, in accordance with the normal rules, would take priority. The difficulty lies in reconciling a contractual arrangement ranking a floating charge before a fixed charge with the legislative provisions,[10] whereby preferential debts rank ahead of debts secured by a floating charge but behind debts secured by a fixed charge.

Precisely this situation arose in *Re Portbase Clothing Ltd.*[11] At some stage prior to its liquidation, Portbase Clothing Ltd had entered into a deed of priority with various of its creditors. The court's interpretation of this deed of priority and the relevant security interests was that it had the effect of postponing a fixed charge on the company's book debts (which was its only substantial asset) in favour of a bank to a later floating charge on those debts in favour of trustees. At its liquidation, the company had preferential debts outstanding to the Inland Revenue and the Commissioners of Customs and Excise. If the preferential debts were to be paid in priority to any of the claims of the secured creditors, there would be little, if any, surplus left for them. If however, the trustees, who ranked first under the deed of priority, were to be paid that would exhaust the company's assets and there would be nothing left from which to meet the preferential debts. Chadwick J held that the preferential debts were to be paid out of the realisation of the book debts before any payment was made in respect of the secured debts. Had it not been for the deed of priority, the proceeds of the book debts would not have been available to satisfy the preferential debts because they would have been subject to the prior fixed charge in favour of the bank.[12] However, the effect of the deed of priority was to make the fixed charge in favour of the bank subject to the trustees' floating charge and, consequently, this gave the preferential debts priority over the debts secured by both the fixed and the floating charges. In reaching this conclusion, Chadwick J followed Australian authority[13] in preference to the analysis in an earlier English case, *Re Woodroffes (Musical Instruments) Ltd.*[14]

Re Woodroffes (Musical Instruments) Ltd did not involve a priority agreement as such but the situation was analogous in that there were two securities, of which the one that secured a debt ranking before the preferential debts under the provisions of the insolvency legislation (call this secured debt 1)

[10] Insolvency Act 1986, ss 40 and 175; Companies Act 1985, s 196.

[11] [1993] Ch 388. There was also an issue in this case about the ranking of the payment of liquidation expenses.

[12] *Re Lewis Merthyr Consolidated Collieries* [1929] 1 Ch 498, CA.

[13] *Waters v Widdows* [1984] VR 503, V SC. Chadwick J considered that the security position in this case was indistinguishable from that in *Re Camden Brewery Ltd* (1912) 106 LT 598, CA and *Re Robert Stephenson & Corporation Ltd* [1913] 2 Ch 201, CA.

[14] [1986] Ch 366.

ranked behind the other security which secured a debt that was behind the preferential debts under the general law (call this secured debt 2). Nourse J held that the solution to the circularity conundrum was to say that secured debt 2 was to be paid first up to the point where this exhausted the assets that were the subject-matter of secured debt 1. Next ranked the preferential debts, then the remainder of secured debt 2 and, finally, secured debt 1. This case was formally distinguished in the *Portbase* decision on the grounds that the position of the preferential debts had not been in issue there,[15] the reason for this probably being that there were in any event sufficient assets to pay both the preferential debts and secured debt 2. Chadwick J, nevertheless, stated that he disagreed with the conclusion in the earlier case and that, in his view, secured debt 2 should not have had any priority over the preferential debts. On the facts present in the *Woodroffes* decision, Chadwick J's conclusion was correct. Although the situation in the *Woodroffes* decision was complicated by the methods of crystallisation of the securities and the then defective drafting of the legislation providing for the preferential status of certain debts, in essence the position there was no different to that of a floating charge which ranks ahead of a later fixed charge under general priority rules.[16] There is no question of the preferential debts not ranking ahead of the debts secured by both the fixed and the floating charge in this common and unremarkable situation.[17]

The *Portbase* decision leaves often the possibility of the parties achieving the result that had been wrongly sanctioned in the *Woodroffes* case by an appropriately drafted agreement. Whilst an agreement to postpone one security to another has the effect of making the postponed security subject to preferential debts, an agreement whereby one creditor agrees to assign its rights to receive payments to another creditor avoids that conclusion. Thus, using the example of the *Woodroffes* case and the terminology of the previous paragraph, if the holder of secured debt 1 agrees to assign the benefits of any payment received to the holder of secured debt 2 until that debt had been paid, this would allow the holder of secured debt 2 to claim payment, in right of the holder of secured debt 1, in priority to the preferential debts, or, alternatively, would permit the holder of secured debt 1 to claim payment in priority to the preferential debts subject to its obligation then to hand over the receipts to the holder of secured debt 2. Re-organisation of priorities by means of assignment would, however, give rise to other questions including whether it involves a registrable charge on the assets of the assigning creditor on the grounds that this assignment is defeasible and will come to an end if and when the senior creditor is repaid.

[15] See also *Re Fablehill Ltd* [1991] BCLC 830, 843.

[16] ie, where the floating charge contains a negative pledge and the subsequent creditor is aware of its existence when it takes its fixed charge. On general priority rules, see Ch 15, at 533–7.

[17] *Re Portbase Clothing Ltd* [1993] Ch 388. Note *Griffiths v Yorkshire Bank plc* [1994] 1 WLR 1427 but this decision is out of line with the general line of authority in assuming that the crystallisation of a floating charge can affect its priority as against other existing securities on the same property.

FORMS OF UNSECURED-DEBT SUBORDINATION

There are three established methods for achieving the postponement of one unsecured debt to other unsecured debts of a company. These are: trust subordination; contingent-debt subordination; and contractual subordination. Contractual subordination is a simpler and more straightforward concept than trust or contingent-debt subordination but it was not until 1994 that there was finally a case upholding the effectiveness of contractual unsecured-debt subordination under English law. Trust subordination and contingent-debt subordination were structures that were devised at a time when there were doubts about the effectiveness of a contractual provision subordinating a debt under English insolvency law. Now that it has been established that debts can be subordinated simply by means of a contractual agreement to that effect, trust and contingent-debt subordination have become less important.

CONTRACTUAL SUBORDINATION: THE SIMPLEST CASE

In its simplest form, contractual subordination is an agreement between a company and one creditor, or group of creditors, whereby the creditor, or group, agrees to rank behind all of the other unsecured debts of a company.[18] This agreement is designed to benefit the persons who are the company's creditors at any time but, as a fluctuating, and potentially very large, group, they are not joined as parties to the agreement. More complex agreements whereby a creditor agrees to rank behind some, but not all, of the company's debts, or a number of creditors accept a particular ranking order amongst themselves may also be possible, but those raise separate issues and it suffices for the moment to concentrate on the simplest case. The subordination may be total, as where, for example, a parent company lends to its subsidiary on the basis that no interest will be payable on the debt and the principal will not become repayable until all other debts of the subsidiary may be paid. Or it may be inchoate,[19] meaning that interest is payable and principal repayable in the normal way unless and until a specified subordinating event occurs whereupon the debt will become completely subordinated to the company's other debts. The prime example of a subordinating event is the liquidation of the debtor company.

[18] Wood, PR, *The Law of Subordinated Debt* (1990) is a leading text on the subject. The literature on the topic also includes Johnston, B, 'Contractual Debt Subordination and Legislative Reform' [1991] JBL 225; Nolan, RC, 'Less Equal Than Others—*Maxwell* and Subordinated Unsecured Obligations' [1995] JBL 484; Oditah, F, *Legal Aspects of Receivables Financing* (1991) 172–7; Goode, RM, *Legal Problems of Credit and Security* (2nd edn, 1988) 95–7; Goode, RM, *Principles of Corporate Insolvency Law* (2nd edn, 1997) 145–6; Gough, WJ, *Company Charges* (2nd edn, 1996) ch 40.

[19] Johnston, B, 'Debt Subordination: The Australian Perspective' [1987] Australian Business Law Review 80, 82; Wood, PR, *The Law of Subordinated Debt* (1990) 8 refers to this form of subordination as 'springing' subordination.

SIMPLE CONTRACTUAL SUBORDINATION: DOUBTS ABOUT ITS LEGAL EFFECTIVENESS

The starting point in considering the legal effectiveness of simple contractual subordination is to put the question: why should the law intervene to prevent an unsecured creditor doing something that a secured creditor is clearly entitled to do, that is freely to agree to take a lower place in the ranking order for repayment than that to which it is entitled as a matter of general law? Historically, the doubts about the effectiveness of contractual subordination centred on considerations of public policy and the argument that such agreements could conflict with the fundamental insolvency law principles of either *pari passu* distribution or efficient administration of insolvent estates.

Pari Passu Distribution

The principle of *pari passu* distribution is that the unencumbered assets of an insolvent company must be collected in by its liquidator and then applied in satisfaction of its liabilities *pari passu.*[20] Assets which the company holds on trust and assets which are subject to a security to the extent of that security interest are outside the reach of the *pari passu* principle. For this reason the *pari passu* principle has never been seen to be a barrier to priority agreements amongst secured creditors. Whilst agreements giving rise to proprietary interests bypass the operation of the *pari passu* principle, it is not possible by a simple contractual agreement with no proprietary effect to take assets out of the reach of the liquidator so as to prevent them from becoming available for distribution in accordance with the *pari passu* principle. This was decided by the House of Lords in the leading case on the *pari passu* rule, *British Eagle International Air Lines Ltd v Compagnie Nationale Air France.*[21] Lord Cross noted that an unsecured creditor cannot achieve by contract 'a position analogous to that of secured creditors without the need for the creation and registration of charges'.[22]

A subordination agreement does not seek to put assets of an insolvent company beyond the reach of its liquidator. It simply purports to alter the manner of distribution by ranking a liability of the company behind other unsecured liabilities. An unsecured creditor who agrees to be subordinated is not attempting to secure a better position than that which he is afforded under the insolvency law; his aim is exactly the opposite. A subordination agreement does not involve a fraud on the insolvency laws or prejudice to other creditors who have not agreed to it. Accordingly, a subordination agreement does not conflict with the *pari passu* principle in so far as this is concerned with the ascertainment of an insolvent company's estate that is available for distribu-

[20] Insolvency Act 1986, s 107 (voluntary liquidation) and Insolvency Rules 1986, r 4.181 (compulsory liquidation). The dual nature of the principle (ie ascertainment and distribution) is disputed by Oditah who argues that it has only a ascertainment effect: Oditah, F, *Legal Aspects of Receivables Financing* (1991) 174.

[21] [1975] 2 All ER 390, HL.

[22] [1975] 2 All ER 390, HL, 410.

tion to unsecured creditors. Such an agreement is not within the aspect of that principle from which the House of Lords in the *British Eagle* case said there could be no contracting out on the grounds of public policy.

That the *British Eagle* case only invalidates contractual agreements with no proprietary effect that seek to reorganise the aspect of the *pari passu* principle which is concerned with the ascertainment of the assets of an insolvent estate, and that it does not therefore apply to subordination agreements, is an interpretation that has now been accepted in England as well as in other Commonwealth jurisdictions.[23] The breakthrough English decision was *Re Maxwell Communications Corporation plc (No 2)*.[24] This case concerned a bond issue made by a vehicle company, Maxwell Finance Jersey Ltd, which was guaranteed by Maxwell Communications Corporation plc (MCC). The terms of the guarantee provided that MCC's liability to the bondholders under the guarantee was to be subordinated to MCC's liabilities to other unsecured creditors. The guarantee and the subordination agreement were subject to Swiss law. The case fell to be decided as one involving straightforward contractual subordination and, as such, it was undisputed that the arrangement was valid and effective under Swiss law. English law applied to the distribution of MCC's English assets and, to that extent, it was necessary to decide whether the agreement was effective under English law. Vinelott J, following Commonwealth authority,[25] held that it was and he distinguished *British Eagle* as being a case where the only real issue was as to the construction and effect of the agreement in that case. The principle of the *British Eagle* decision, in Vinelott J's words, was simply that 'a creditor cannot validly contract with his debtor that he will enjoy some advantage in a bankruptcy or a winding up which is denied to other creditors'.[26]

Interpreting the actual decision in *British Eagle* in this way does not end the discussion about the *pari passu* principle and its effect on subordination agreements. The principle has two aspects[27]—first, ascertainment and, second, distribution of assets—and the relevant provision of the Insolvency Act 1986 puts the distributional aspect in apparently mandatory language: thus, Insolvency Act 1986, s 107 states that a company's assets *shall be* applied in satisfaction of its liabilities *pari passu*. It is sometimes possible for the courts

[23] A line of Australian cases support the narrow interpretation of the *British Eagle* decision. These include: *Re Industrial Welding Corporation Pty Ltd* (1977–78) 3 ACLR 754, NSW SC EqD; *Re Marlborough Concrete Construction* (1977) 2 ACLR 240, Q SC; *Horne v Chester & Fein Property Development Pty Ltd & Ors* (1986–87) 11 ACSR 485, V SC.

[24] [1994] 1 All ER 737; See *Re NIAA Corporation Ltd* (1993) 33 NSWLR 344; 12 ACSR 141, NSW SC-EqD; *United States Trust Company of New York* v *Australia & New Zealand Banking Group* (1995) 17 ACSR 697, NSW CA. This is also the approach taken in South Africa: *Ex parte de Villiers, Re Carbon Developments (Pty) Ltd (in liquidation)* (1993) (1) SA 493, SA AppD. New Zealand courts have also now recognised that the *British Eagle* decision does not apply to subordination agreements: *Stotter v Ararimu Holdings Ltd* [1994] 2 NZLR 655, NZ CA, not following *Re Orion Sound Ltd* [1979] 2 NZLR 574, NZ SC.

[25] *Horne v Chester & Fein Property Development Pty Ltd & Ors* (1986–87) 11 ACSR 485, V SC; *Ex parte de Villiers, Re Carbon Developments (Pty) Ltd (in liquidation)* (1993) (1) SA 493, SA AppD, 505 *per* Goldstone JA.

[26] [1994] 1 All ER 737, 750.

[27] But for a contrary view see Oditah, F, *Legal Aspects of Receivables Financing* (1991) 174–5 who argues that: 'The principle is not at all a distributional rule. It is a rule of ascertainment of the insolvent's estate.'

to interpret mandatory language in legislation in a directory rather than an imperative sense where policy considerations do not preclude this,[28] but dicta in *British Eagle* suggested that the whole of the *pari passu* principle, rather than just the ascertainment element, was to be regarded as a mandatory requirement from which there could be no contracting out.[29] The view that the distributional element of the *pari passu* principle was mandatory also had some influential supporters.[30] In *Re Maxwell Communications Corporation plc (No 2)*,[31] however, Vinelott J reviewed the policy arguments and concluded that these were in favour of, rather than against, allowing contracting out of the *pari passu* principle by means of a simple subordination agreement postponing one creditor to all of the company's other creditors. Accordingly, he did not feel compelled by obiter observations in the *British Eagle* decision to reach the opposite conclusion.

Vinelott J identified a number of policy considerations which supported permitting contracting out of the *pari passu* principle by a subordination agreement.[32] First, since a creditor could waive his right to prove and could agree to the postponement of his debt after winding up had commenced, it was difficult to see any good reason why that creditor should not be able to reach an agreement with the debtor that, in the event of subsequent insolvency, his debt would be subordinated. The case for giving effect to such an agreement which preceded insolvency could be stronger than that for a post-insolvency agreement, since other creditors might have given credit on the assumption that the agreement would be binding. Secondly, since subordination trusts and subordination arrangements involving assignments were recognised as effective, striking down contractual subordination would represent a triumph of form over substance. Thirdly, contractual subordination was recognised as effective in other leading common-law and civil-law jurisdictions and, at a time when insolvency increasingly had international ramifications,[33] an inconsistent approach to this matter under English law would be a matter of grave concern.

[28] *National Westminster Bank Ltd v Halesowen* [1972] AC 785, HL, 805 *per* Viscount Dilhorne and 808 *per* Lord Simon.

[29] [1973] 1 Lloyd's Rep 414, 434 *per* Templeman J; [1974] 1 Lloyd's Rep 429, CA, 433 *per* Russell LJ; [1975] 2 All ER 390 HL, 403 *per* Lord Simon, 411 *per* Lord Cross.

[30] In particular, the *Report of the United Kingdom Review Committee on Insolvency Law and Practice* Cmnd 8558 (1982) paras 1448–9 (the Cork Committee) considered that the distributional element of the *pari passu* principle was mandatory: '... all unsecured debts must be paid ... *pari passu* ... It is therefore not open to a creditor to advance money on terms that the debt will be subordinated to other claims in the event of the borrower's insolvency.'

[31] [1994] 1 All ER 737; See *Re NIAA Corporation Ltd* (1993) 33 NSWLR 344; 12 ACSR 141, NSW SC-EqD; *United States Trust Company of New York* v *Australia & New Zealand Banking Group* (1995) 17 ACSR 697, NSW CA. This is also the approach taken in South Africa *Ex parte de Villiers, re Carbon Developments (Pty) Ltd (in liquidation)* (1993) (1) SA 493, SA AppD. New Zealand courts have also now recognised that the *British Eagle* decision does not apply to subordination agreements: *Stotter v Ararimu Holdings Ltd* [1994] 2 NZLR 655, NZ CA.

[32] See also *Stotter v Ararimu Holdings Ltd* [1994] 2 NZLR 655, NZ CA, 661 where Gault J said that it was 'hardly maintainable' that there could be 'any reasoned argument for striking down subordination agreements on policy grounds'; *United States Trust Corporation of New York v Australia & New Zealand Banking Group Ltd* (1995) 17 ACSR 697, NSW CA, 705 *per* Sheller JA.

[33] The collapse of the Maxwell empire being a case in point. On the international nature of this insolvency and the challenges that this presented to the courts of various jurisdictions that were called upon to handle various aspects of the multinational collapse, see Fletcher, IF, '*Floreat*

Public Policy in the Efficient Administration of Insolvent Estates

Another objection to subordination agreements on policy grounds is that they may impede the efficient administration of an insolvent estate. This argument is that the principle of equal treatment of unsecured creditors is a straightforward rule for a liquidator to apply and that requiring him to give effect to a subordination agreement would add to the complexity of his task and would place an unwarranted additional burden on him.

The leading case against contracting out in circumstances where this would be contrary to the public policy of ensuring the efficient administration of insolvent estates is the decision of the House of Lords in *National Westminster Bank Ltd* v *Halesowen*.[34] In this case the House of Lords held that insolvency set-off rules were mandatory and that there could be contracting out. Set-off, according to their Lordships, was a procedure prescribed for the orderly administration of an insolvent estate and was not a private right which those who benefited from it were free to waive. Importantly, this ruling was in the context of an agreement whereby, it was argued,[35] a creditor had given up a right of set-off to which it was entitled under the general insolvency law.[36] In that the *Halesowen* decision was concerned with the giving up of benefits, it is thus relevant to subordination agreements whereby certain creditors agree to give up the equal ranking to which they are entitled under the general law. In one New Zealand decision,[37] later departed from,[38] it was held that, on the basis of the *Halesowen* ruling, subordination agreements were also invalid.

In *Re Maxwell Communications Corporation plc (No 2)*[39] Vinelott J did not follow that approach. Instead, Vinelott J concluded that the *Halesowen* ruling on the mandatory nature of the insolvency set-off rules did not apply by analogy to the *pari passu* principle. In his view set-off and the *pari passu* principle were based on different public policy considerations. Set-off was a procedure which operated two ways. Whilst it operated to the advantage of those creditors with qualifying set-off rights, the company, and through it the general body of creditors, could also benefit. Set-off saved the company from having to take proceedings to recover debts owing to it; making it mandatory also avoided such complications as determining whether a dividend was owing in the liquidation to a creditor who had waived set-off in circumstances where proceedings against him were still on foot. The *pari passu* rule, on the other hand, was a rule from which only creditors could benefit; a waiver by a particular creditor or creditors would not affect the company or its general body of creditors. Giving effect to such an agreement would not impede the efficient administration of an insolvent estate.

Comitas: the *Maxwell* Preference Avoidance Cases in the American Courts' (1997) 10 (2) Insolvency Intelligence 11.

34 [1972] AC 785, HL.

35 The House of Lords denied that the agreement had this effect but held that, in any event, the statutory provision for set-off was mandatory.

36 The provision in force at the relevant time was the Bankruptcy Act 1914, s 31. Insolvency set-off is now governed by the Insolvency Rules, r 4.90.

37 *Re Orion Sound Ltd* [1979] 2 NZLR 574, NZ SC.

38 *Stotter v Ararimu Holdings Ltd* [1994] 2 NZLR 655, NZ CA.

39 [1994] 1 All ER 737.

The decision of the House of Lords in *Halesowen* has attracted criticism.[40] There is a case for saying that creditors should be permitted to give up rights of set-off to which they are entitled under general law and that to recognise the validity of such agreements would not necessarily impede the efficient administration of insolvent estates. Whilst further analysis of the reasons for and against permitting contracting out of insolvency set-off is beyond the scope of this chapter, the general point is that in policy terms there is everything to be said for confining the *Halesowen* decision and not using it to invalidate simple subordination agreements which, manifestly, do not add unwarranted complexity to the process of administering an insolvent estate.[41] Thus, whilst the *Maxwell* decision does sit a little uneasily with that earlier House of Lords decision, the policy arguments in favour of allowing subordination agreements are so strong that it seems unlikely that a court would strain to find that they are invalid on the grounds of precedent. This is an area where, for the avoidance of doubt, English legislation should be brought into line with that of modern corporations laws in other jurisdictions by the enactment of an express permission for subordination agreements.[42]

CONTRACTUAL-DEBT SUBORDINATION: CAN IT BE USED TO CREATE A COMPLEX RANKING ORDER AMONGST UNSECURED CREDITORS?

Re Maxwell Communications Corporation plc[43] was an example of the simplest type of contractual subordination—where one creditor agrees to rank behind all of the other creditors of a particular debtor. The next level of sophistication in subordination agreements is where a creditor agrees to rank behind some but not all of the other creditors. One example of this more complex type of arrangement is where a group of creditors agree a ranking order

[40] Derham, SR, *Set-off* (2nd edn, 1996) para 2.11.1. Earlier authorities were inconsistent on the point. *Rolls Razor Ltd v Cox* [1967] 1 QB 552, CA ruled against contracting out but other cases, reviewed by the House of Lords in *Halesowen*, contained dicta suggesting that contracting out was possible. The *Halesowen* decision has since been followed in New Zealand (*Rendell v Doors and Doors Ltd* [1975] 2 NZLR 191, NZ SC) and Australia (*Re Paddington Town Hall Centre Ltd* (1979) 41 FLR 239, NSW SC; *Gye v McIntyre* (1991) 171 CLR 609, H Ct of Aust). *Stein v Blake* [1996] AC 243, HL concerned the consequences of the mandatory nature of insolvency set-off with regard to assignment of debts. The issue of opting out of insolvency set-off did not arise on the facts. In the *Halesowen* decision itself Lord Cross dissented, saying that he could not 'see why in principle the person in whose interest it would be to invoke the rule of set-off should not be entitled to agree in advance that in the event of the bankruptcy of the other party he will not invoke it': [1972] AC 785, HL, 813 and also similar sentiments at 818. The *Report of the United Kingdom Review Committee on Insolvency Law and Practice* Cmnd 8558 (1982) (Cork Committee) para 1341 sets out commercial arguments in favour of allowing contracting out of insolvency set-off.

[41] In *Re NIAA Corporation Ltd* (1993) 33 NSWLR 344; 12 ACSR 141, NSW SC-EqD, Santow J, although agreeing with the *Maxwell* decision, was sceptical about the distinction relied upon by Vinelott J between the one-sided nature of a subordination agreement and the two-way benefits of insolvency set-off.

[42] *Report of the United Kingdom Review Committee on Insolvency Law and Practice* Cmnd 8558 (1982) (Cork Committee) para 1450(l) recommended the introduction of legislation to this effect. This has not yet occurred in the UK, but elsewhere in the Commonwealth express statutory authority for subordination agreements has been enacted: eg, Corporations Law, s 563C (Australia); Companies Act 1993, s 313 (3) (New Zealand).

[43] [1994] 1 All ER 737.

amongst themselves (eg, X, Y and Z agree to rank behind the company's general creditors but, as amongst themselves, to rank X first, Y second and Z last). Another is where a creditor agrees to rank behind some designated creditors but not others (eg, X agrees to rank behind the general body of creditors but wants to rank above Y and Z who are not party to the agreement). Each type of more complex arrangement needs to be examined against the background of the public policy of not permitting contracting out where either this would infringe the ascertainment of assets element of the *pari passu* principle or would impede the efficient administration of an insolvent estate.

An agreement of the first type—where creditors agree a ranking order amongst themselves—does not seek to remove an asset from the normal process of liquidation. It is not therefore an agreement of the type that is invalid under the *British Eagle* ruling that there can be no contracting out of the ascertainment of assets element of the *pari passu* principle. By virtue of this type of agreement some creditors (X and Y using the example in the last paragraph) gain an advantage over others (Z, and in that X ranks first, Y in the example) but this is an entirely consensual arrangement.[44] Once the principle that it is possible to contract out of the distributional element of the *pari passu* principle is accepted, this is just a variation on the simplest case which, so far as the policy of the *pari passu* principle is concerned, raises no new issues of substance. Although there is no English authority directly on the point, Commonwealth case law clearly establishes that an agreement of this kind does not infringe the public policy of the *pari passu* principle.[45]

It might be argued that giving effect to a complex subordination arrangement involving the ranking of a number of unsecured debts could impose an additional inconvenience on the liquidator which would be inconsistent with the public policy of ensuring the orderly administration of insolvent estates. The argument that no effect should be given to subordination agreements because this could lead to the liquidator becoming involved in disputes about the respective entitlements of the contracting parties was, however, rejected in the Australian case *Horne v Chester & Fein Property Development Pty Ltd & Ors.*[46] Interestingly, it was not the liquidator who raised the argument about inconvenience but one of the creditors who had agreed to be subordinated but later sought to use the argument in an unmeritorious attempt to escape his bargain. Liquidators are well-used to reviewing contractual documentation with a view to sorting out disputed proofs and there is nothing inherent in subordination agreements that would make the process of reviewing them necessarily any more difficult than in relation to other agreements.

[44] In *Re Maxwell Communications Corporation plc (No 2)* [1994] 1 All ER 737, 750 Vinelott J stated that 'a creditor cannot validly contract with his debtor that he will enjoy some advantage in bankruptcy or winding up which is denied to other creditors'. If interpreted literally, this statement of principle would strike down any subordination which was not in favour of all other unsecured debt (as was noted in *Re NIAA Corporation Ltd* (1993) 33 NSWLR 344; 12 ACSR 14, NSW SC-EqD) but the comment was made in relation to the *British Eagle* decision and should, it is suggested, be confined to that context.

[45] *Horne v Chester & Fein Property Development Pty Ltd & Ors* (1986–87) 11 ACSR 485, V SC.

[46] (1986–87) 11 ACSR 485.

Although the element of consent of all of the affected parties is absent, it is also possible to construct an agreement whereby a creditor agrees to be subordinated to some creditors but not to others in a way which does not infringe the *pari passu* principle. This is demonstrated by the decision of the Court of Appeal of New South Wales in *US Trust Corporation v Australia and New Zealand Banking Group.*[47] In this case the terms of a bond issue provided that in liquidation the bonds would be subordinated to specified senior debts but not to the company's ordinary creditors. The ordinary creditors were not parties to this arrangement. The subordination terms provided for the senior debt to be paid in full before any payment could be made in respect of the bonds and for any payments to which the holders of the bonds would have been entitled to be paid directly to the senior creditors. The Court of Appeal upheld this arrangement which, it determined, did not operate to the disadvantage of the ordinary creditors contrary to the *pari passu* principle. This conclusion was explained by reference to a numerical example,[48] as follows:

(1) assume the company assets to be nominally 100 and the claims of the senior creditor, subordinated creditor and ordinary creditors to be, respectively 200, 200 and 100;
(2) ignoring the subordination, each creditor could expect to recover one-fifth of the outstanding debt which would mean that the senior and subordinated creditors would each receive 40, and the ordinary creditors would receive 20;
(3) the effect of the subordination is that the senior creditor gets 80 (i.e. its own share plus that of the subordinated creditor) and the ordinary creditors get 20;
(4) the ordinary creditors are no better or worse off as a result of the subordination and, thus, the arrangement does not infringe the pari passu rule.

The arrangement in this case envisaged that the liquidator of the insolvent company would pay over to the designated senior creditors liquidation dividends that would ordinarily have been due to the subordinated creditor. To this extent, it required the liquidator to do something different from that which he would normally do under the general law, but the difference was hardly so significant as to impinge upon the efficient administration of the insolvent estate. No argument was raised that the agreement might be invalid as being contrary to that aspect of public policy.

In substance, the subordination structure in this case was a form of turnover subordination: the subordinated creditor was required to turn over liquidation receipts to the senior creditors, but the process of payment and handing over was short-circuited by requiring the liquidator to pay the senior creditors directly. Subordination by means of a turnover arrangement is well-established,[49] but the main potential difficulty with it is its operation in the event of the subordinated creditor becoming insolvent.

[47] (1995) 17 ACSR 697, NSW CA.
[48] Taken from Wood, PR, *The Law of Subordinated Debt* (1990)15–16.
[49] Wood, PR, *The Law of Subordinated Debt* (1990) 9–11, 27–8.

CONTRACTUAL SUBORDINATION AND THE INSOLVENCY OF THE SUBORDINATED CREDITOR

Up to this point, the focus has been on the effectiveness of a contractual subordination in the event of the insolvency of the debtor company but it is entirely possible that the subordinated creditor could also become insolvent. Whether contractual subordination, in either its simplest form or in one of the more complex variants, will survive the insolvency of the subordinated creditor is also an important consideration. The main concerns stem from the application of the *pari passu* principle in the subordinated creditor's insolvency and from the provisions of the Insolvency Act 1986 which gives the court power to invalidate transactions at an undervalue entered into, or preferences given, by the insolvent in the twilight period preceding its insolvency.[50]

A contractual turnover arrangement which involves the subordinated creditor undertaking to pay over to the senior creditors any receipts from the debtor company has the effect of making the senior creditors unsecured creditors of the subordinated creditor. In the event of the subordinated creditor becoming insolvent, the senior creditors have no claim on its assets but must instead prove in the liquidation as ordinary unsecured creditors subject to the *pari passu* principle. The variant on the turnover structure in the *US Trust* case did not require the subordinated creditor to hand over to the senior creditors receipts from the debtor company. Instead it provided for the junior creditor's dividends to be paid directly to the senior creditor. But since, apart from the contractual arrangement, those receipts would have formed part of the junior creditor's estate and, as such, would have been available for distribution amongst its unsecured creditors in accordance with the *pari passu* principle, this looks like an obvious attempt to achieve for the senior creditors by contract a position equivalent to that which they would enjoy if they were secured (or were the beneficiaries of a trust). The decision in *British Eagle* is authority that such an arrangement will not survive in the event of the promisor's insolvency because it is contrary to the mandatory dimension of the *pari passu* principle. This, therefore, is one drawback of contractual subordination. It can be used to favour selected creditors but only by means of a structure whereby the subordinated creditor turns over benefits to the designated senior creditors. If, however, the subordinated creditor becomes insolvent, a purely contractual turnover arrangement will at that point cease to operate and the senior creditors must provide in the liquidation of the subordinated creditor as unsecured creditors.

Simple contractual subordination agreements which involve one creditor agreeing to rank behind other creditors and the more complex type of arrangement in which a group of creditors agree a ranking order amongst themselves are less vulnerable to the charge of being contrary to the *pari passu* principle in the event of a subordinated creditor's insolvency. The

[50] Also of potential relevance are Insolvency Act 1986, s 178 (disclaimer of onerous property) and s 423 (transactions defrauding creditors).

distinction between these forms of subordination and that considered in the last paragraph is that there the arrangement was 'take what it is due to me and give it to someone else' whereas here the arrangement is 'nothing is due to me until others have been paid'. Certainly where the subordination has come into effect before the commencement of the subordinated creditor's insolvency, such as where it is total subordination or the subordinating event (principally the insolvency of the debtor company) has already occurred, it would seem to be difficult to argue that the arrangement infringes the *pari passu* principle as interpreted in the *British Eagle* decision. The arrangement does not in these circumstances bear the hallmark of *British Eagle* type invalidity because there is no attempt to remove an asset from the insolvent's estate after the commencement of the winding up; [51] instead, from the commencement of the insolvency of the subordinated creditor, the relevant asset, the debt due from the debtor company, is 'flawed' by being subject to postponement in favour of the senior creditors. This, however, is a difficult point on which different views are tenable.[52]

There is a risk that contractual subordination agreements whereby one creditor agrees to rank behind all of the others, or a group of creditors agree a ranking order amongst themselves, might infringe the law relating to preferences, although the conditions that must be satisfied for an action to be regarded as a voidable preference mean that this risk is small. For the purposes of the Insolvency Act 1986, s 239 a preference occurs when a company does something, or allows something to be done, which has the effect of putting any of its creditors, sureties or guarantors into a position better than the position that he would have been in if that thing had not been done. Thus this section is only of potential relevance to subordination agreements which involve a subordinated creditor agreeing to rank behind another who is both a creditor of the debtor company and also a creditor, surety or guarantor of the subordinated creditor itself.[53] Using the example in an earlier paragraph, where X, Y and Z agree to rank behind the company's general creditors but, as amongst themselves, in the order X, then Y, then Z, if, say, Z, becomes insolvent, preference law could be relevant if either X or Y is one of its creditors, sureties or guarantors. This situation is likely to be uncommon but could, for example, occur in an intra-group structure. It would then be necessary for Z's liquidator or administrator to persuade the court that the fact that Z has agreed to rank behind, say, its creditor X, for the purpose of claiming in the insolvency of the third-party debtor company's liquidation, means that X's position in Z's own insolvency is better than it would otherwise have been; this is not the most obvious example of a preferential action although it is conceivable that it could be caught. Further, it would also have to be shown that the preference was given at a relevant time, as defined by the Insolvency Act 1986,[54] and that, in giving it, Z was influenced by a desire to improve X's posi-

[51] *Carreras Rothmans Ltd v Freeman Mathews Treasure Ltd* [1985] Ch 207.

[52] Contrast Oditah, F, 'Assets and the Treatment of Claims in Insolvency' (1992) 108 LQR 459, 477–8; Johnston, B, 'Contractual Debt Subordination and Legislative Reform' [1991] JBL 225, 239–43; Wood, PR, *The Law of Subordinated Debt* (1990) 33–4.

[53] Oditah, F, 'Assets and the Treatment of Claims in Insolvency' (1992) 108 LQR 459, 478.

tion in this way.[55] A desire to prefer is presumed where the parties are connected, but this presumption can be rebutted.[56]

A transaction is also liable to be set aside by the court at the behest of an insolvent company's liquidator or administrator if it is a transaction at an undervalue as defined by the Insolvency Act 1986, s 238. A transaction at an undervalue is (i) a gift to another person, (ii) a transaction with another person on terms that provide for the company to receive no consideration, or (iii) a transaction with another person where, in terms of money or money's worth, the consideration provided by the other person is significantly less than the value of the consideration provided by the company. Where, say, in a simple subordination agreement X agrees to rank behind all of the other creditors of a company but those creditors are not parties to the agreement, this could be regarded as a gift from X to those creditors.[57] If this gift was made at a relevant time, as defined,[58] it is liable to be set aside unless the court is satisfied that X entered into the transaction in good faith and for the purpose of carrying on its business and, that at the time that it did so, there were reasonable grounds for thinking that the transaction would benefit it. An agreement between, say, X, Y and Z as to their respective ranking would presumably be supported by consideration. Thus, in the event of the insolvency of any of these parties, so far as the intra-group ranking is concerned, transaction at undervalue law would be relevant only if the agreement could be brought within limb (iii) of the definition. For this purpose the consideration provided to and received by the insolvent company must be capable of being expressed in monetary values ascertained from the company's point of view.[59] Where there is, say, an agreement by Z that its debt will rank behind X and Y's debts, it would thus be necessary to measure in monetary terms the extent to which this agreement depletes Z's assets or diminishes their value[60] and to set this against the monetary value provided to Z by X and Y.

[54] Insolvency Act 1986, s 240. 'Relevant time' means 6 months or 2 years prior to the onset of insolvency (which is defined by Insolvency Act 1986, s 240 (3)) depending on whether the parties are connected or not. The company giving the alleged preference must have been unable to pay its debts when it gave the preference or must have become so unable as a consequence of it. Companies in the same group would be connected persons: Insolvency Act 1986, ss 249 and 435.

[55] Insolvency Act 1986, s 239 (5). *Re MC Bacon Ltd* [1990] BCC 78.

[56] The presumption was successfully rebutted in *Re Fairway Magazines Ltd* [1993] BCLC 643. Cases where attempts at rebuttal were unsuccessful include: *Re Exchange Travel (Holdings) Ltd* [1996] BCC 933 and *Re Agriplant Services Ltd* [1997] BCC 842.

[57] This example is not within limb (ii) because X does not 'enter into a transaction' with the relevant persons, ie the other creditors. X's transaction is with the company but as between the company and X there is no transaction at an undervalue since both parties provide consideration and the balancing of values required for limb (iii) (as interpreted in *Re MC Bacon Ltd* [1990] BCC 78) could not take place.

[58] Insolvency Act 1986, s 240. It means two years prior to the onset of insolvency provided the company was unable to pay its debts at the time of the transaction or became unable as a consequence of it. Inability to pay debts is presumed where the parties are connected: Insolvency Act 1986, s 240 (2).

[59] *Re MC Bacon Ltd* [1990] BCC 78.

[60] The debt valuation processes that apply for the purposes of liquidation procedures may provide a useful analogy here. In *Re Maxwell Communications Corporation plc (No 2)* [1994] 1 All ER

CONTRACTUAL SUBORDINATION AND PRIVITY

Some contractual subordination arrangements may involve all of those parties who are intended to benefit, but many do not. For example, where unsecured subordinated debt securities are issued to the public, the subordination arrangement in favour of the issuer's other creditors will typically be in an agreement between the issuing company and the trustee for the issue of the securities and no other creditors will be joined as parties. *Re Maxwell Communications Corporation plc (No 2)*[61] illustrates this typical structure. Creditors who are not parties to a subordination agreement but who advance credit to a company on the basis that their claim will rank ahead of the existing subordinated debt are exposed to the risk that the company and the subordinated creditor will later agree to a variation in the terms of the debt so as to remove the subordination. A subsequent creditor may seek to protect itself by requiring the company to covenant not to change the terms of its existing borrowings without consent, but this is a limited protection because if the company decides to act in breach of covenant the creditor is unlikely to hear of this until after the event, by which time it will be too late to obtain an injunction to prevent the variation. Under current English law there is no clear way around the problem of possible variation in subordination terms contrary to the expectations of third-party creditors of the debtor company,[62] but a Bill, introduced in Parliament in December 1998 will, when enacted, restrict the rights of contracting parties to vary contracts which expressly authorise enforcement by third parties or which purport to confer benefits on third parties.[63]

Liquidation, as a collective process for the benefit of creditors generally, should put an end to privity concerns. Once a company has gone into liquidation its liquidator is bound to give effect to its contractual obligations provided they do not infringe any fundamental principle of insolvency law. The liquidator is thus bound by any subordination agreements entered into previously by the company. In the (unlikely) event of a liquidator seeking to ignore those agreements other creditors could apply to court for directions requiring the liquidator to honour the company's contractual commitments.[64]

737 the subordinated debt was held to have a nil value with the consequence that its holders could not participate in the vote on a Companies Act 1985, s 425 scheme of arrangement.

[61] [1994] 1 All ER 737.

[62] It may be that the arrangement could be entrenched by the subordinated creditor declaring a trust in respect of the promise to be postponed. But note Nolan, RC, 'Less Equal Than Others—*Maxwell* and Subordinated Unsecured Obligations' [1995] JBL 484, 495–8 who is doubtful about this and other possible solutions to the privity problem that have been suggested by various writers. Trusts of covenants and their consequences are discussed further below in the context of trust subordination.

[63] Contracts (Rights of Third Parties) Bill. See also, *Privity of Contract: Contracts for the Benefit of Third Parties* (Law Commission Report No 242) (1996).

[64] Under Insolvency Act 1986, s 112 (voluntary liquidation) and s 167 (3) (compulsory liquidation).

CONTRACTUAL SUBORDINATION AND SET-OFF

Another uncertain issue is the relationship between contractual subordination and insolvency set-off. It is contrary to public policy and therefore legally impossible for a creditor to waive the benefit of insolvency set-off.[65] However, if, by operation of the insolvency set-off rules, an amount owed to a company by a subordinated creditor is set off against the subordinated debt that will, to the extent of the set-off, defeat the subordination. This point is not covered by any clear authority but one possibility is that a court would conclude that a debt which has been postponed and which will never be paid because the company is insolvent is not due for this purpose,[66] with the consequence that there is nothing that can be set off.[67]

TRUST SUBORDINATION

Before it was established that contractual subordination agreements, whereby payment of unsecured debts was postponed, did not infringe any fundamental principle of insolvency law, commercial practice had evolved other methods of achieving debt subordination under English law. One leading form of subordination involved the use of a trust. A subordination trust typically works by the subordinated creditor proving in the debtor company's liquidation in the normal way but then holding any dividends received on trust for the senior creditors. This structure does not infringe the *pari passu* principle in the insolvency of the debtor company because the trust mechanism operates entirely outside the scope of that rule. The trust does not affect the debtor company's liquidator in the process of ascertaining and distributing its assets. It is only when the payments are made that the trust operates to divert them to the other unsecured creditors to the extent that they have not been paid by the liquidator. The process has been described as one in which the senior creditors end up with the benefit of a 'double dip' in the debtor company's insolvency: they collect their own liquidation dividends plus, to the extent necessary to clear their debts, the dividends paid to the subordinated creditor. Trust subordination is an apt method of achieving subordination in favour of selected creditors in that the intended beneficiaries of the trust can be designated in the instrument creating the trust and may be all of the other unsecured creditors of the company or only some of them. Trust subordination was held to be effective in *Re British and Commonwealth Holdings plc (No 3)*.[68]

[65] *National Westminster Bank Ltd v Halesowen* [1972] AC 785 HL.

[66] Insolvency Act 1986, s 323 (2) and Insolvency Rules 1986 r 4.90 (2) refer to set-off of sums 'due' to each party.

[67] Insolvency Act 1986, s 323 (2) and Insolvency Rules 1986 r 4.90 (2). On the operation of the set-off rules in relation to contingent debts: *Re Charge Card Services Ltd* [1987] Ch 150; *Stein v Blake* [1996] 1 AC 243 HL, 256 *per* Lord Hoffmann. See further Derham, SR, *Set-off* (2nd edn, 1996) para 2.11.3; Wood, PR, *The Law of Subordinated Debt* (1990) 47–8.

[68] [1992] BCLC 322, [1992] 1 WLR 67.

A drawback of trust subordination, in comparison to contractual subordination, is that it introduces complex trust-law considerations into what is essentially a simple concept, the ranking of debts behind each other.[69] Relevant trust-law questions include whether the trust is properly constituted and whether it conforms with rules relating to the duration of trusts.[70] Another disadvantage of the trust device is that the trust is not universally recognised, and this limits its usefulness in a business environment which is increasingly internationally orientated. *Re Maxwell Communications Corporation plc (No 2)*[71] illustrates this point. The relevant agreements in that case were subject to Swiss law which does not recognise trusts and this meant that the machinery of a subordination trust was unavailable. The case therefore fell to be decided as one involving straightforward contractual subordination. In view of these considerations and the establishment of the legal effectiveness of contractual subordination, the most pertinent question that remains worth asking about trust subordination is whether it offers advantages that cannot be achieved by contractual subordination and which therefore make it appropriate to continue to adopt that structure either as an alternative to contractual subordination or in conjunction with it.[72]

TRUST SUBORDINATION AND THE INSOLVENCY OF THE SUBORDINATED CREDITOR

Property that is held on trust is not subject to the *pari passu* principle. This means that where the aim of the subordination is to benefit selected creditors, the trust mechanism is preferable to contractual subordination involving turnover because, as discussed in an earlier section of this chapter,[73] contractual turnover subordination does not survive the insolvency of the subordinated creditor.[74] It is, however, conceivable that a subordination trust could satisfy the requirements for a voidable preference or a transaction at an undervalue that is liable to be set aside.

Whether a subordination trust, which is defeasible if and when all of the designated senior debts have been paid in full, is a charge requiring registration where the subordinated creditor is a company is a debatable point.[75] This

[69] Generally on the drawbacks of trust subordination: Johnston, B, 'Debt Subordination: The Australian Perspective' [1987] Australian Business Law Review 80, 121–4.

[70] Lingard, JR, *Bank Security Documents* (3rd edn, 1993) 333.

[71] [1994] 1 All ER 737.

[72] In the past contractual and trust subordination mechanisms have often been combined (see, eg, *Stotter v Ararimu Holding Ltd* [1994] 2 NZLR 655, NZ CA) but this may become less common with the removal of the doubts about the legal validity of contractual subordination.

[73] See above, at 557–9.

[74] This is one reason for using contractual and trust methods in conjunction with each other. The contractual turnover arrangement in *United States Trust Corporation of New York v Australia and New Zealand Banking Group Ltd* (1995) 17 ACSR 697, NSW CA was bolstered by a trust but this did not need to be tested on the facts because the subordinated creditor was not insolvent.

[75] On which see Johnston, B, 'Debt Subordination: The Australian Perspective' [1987] Australian Business Law Review 80. Related to the issue of possible registration requirements is the question of negative pledges to which the subordinated creditor may be subject. If the subordination trust creates a charge, the subordinated creditor may be in breach of those agreements.

would be an important issue in the event of the subordinated creditor becoming insolvent because registrable but unregistered charges are void against a company's liquidator and administrator.[76] The main argument against the arrangement giving rise to a registration obligation is that, even if it is a charge,[77] it is not within the list of registrable charges specified in the Companies Act 1985 because it is not a fixed charge on book debts nor is it within any of the other categories.[78]

TRUST SUBORDINATION AND PRIVITY

The intended beneficiaries of a trust can enforce it and block its variation even though they have not provided consideration where the trust is completely constituted.[79] The requirements for a trust to be completely constituted include that the subject-matter of the trust be present ascertainable property. A trust in respect of liquidation dividends that may be received at some point in the future in the event of the debtor company's insolvency would not be a trust in respect of presently ascertainable property. However, in practice this theoretical difficulty can be overcome by appropriate drafting of the trust. It is common for a subordination trust to be expressed to cover the benefit of the covenant to pay over liquidation dividends. The covenant is a present promise. This wording gives rise to a trust in respect of present property and thus ensures that the trust cannot be changed without the consent of the designated senior creditors, except to the extent that this may be authorised under the terms of the instrument by which it is created.

TRUST SUBORDINATION AND SET-OFF

One of the requirements for set-off in insolvency is that the debts in question must be mutual. An illustration of the absence of mutuality is where a debtor (D) owes money to a creditor (C) and C holds the benefit of the debt owing from D on trust for a third party (TP). If C is personally indebted to D, C cannot set off this debt against the amount owing from D to him in his capacity as trustee because that would in substance amount to using TP's money to pay off C's debt.[80] A trust attaching to a subordinated debt or its proceeds should be effective to destroy mutuality and thus to block set-off.[81] In this respect, therefore, trust subordination may be preferable to contractual subordination where the position with regard to set-off is rather more uncertain.

[76] Companies Act 1985, s 395. The types of charge that are registrable are considered in Ch 15 above, at 539–41.

[77] *Re Bond Worth Ltd* [1980] Ch 228, 248 suggests that it may be.

[78] S 396. See further Johnston, B, 'Debt Subordination: The Australian Perspective' [1987] Australian Business Law Review 80, 131–5.

[79] Baker, PV and Langan, P St J, *Snell's Equity* (29th edn, 1990) 119–27.

[80] *Jones v Mossop* (1844) 3 Hare 568, 574 *per* Wigram V-C. Generally on mutuality: Wood, PR, *English and International Set-Off* (1989) ch 14; Derham, SR, *Set-off* (2nd edn, 1996) chs 7–9.

[81] Wood, PR, *The Law of Subordinated Debt* (1990) 45–6; Wood, PR, *English and International Set-Off* (1989) 352–3; 933–5.

CONTINGENT-DEBT SUBORDINATION

The other established form of subordination before the decision in *Re Maxwell Communications Corporation plc (No 2)*[82] was to express the subordinated debt as a contingent debt, that is a debt which was only payable so long as a specified contingency (usually relating to the solvency of the company) was satisfied. This intention underlying the drafting was to ensure that amounts would be payable in respect of the subordinated obligation only and to the extent that the debtor could pay and remain solvent. This structure was thought to avoid the perceived problem of the *pari passu* principle because the obligation (and not simply payment) was made contingent. A contingent debt may be admitted to proof in a liquidation but, because of the nature of the contingency, it would probably be valued for the purpose of proof at nil or some nominal amount. Contingent-debt subordination, as so structured, was said to be different from contractual subordination in that, in the former, the debt was only ever payable when the contingency was fulfilled whereas, in the latter, the debt was payable but was simply postponed to other debts of the company. In the *Maxwell* case Vinelott J expressed little enthusiasm for the contingent-debt structure[83] and, in view of that decision there would seem to be little reason to resort to it. Accordingly, contingent-debt subordination is not explored further here.

[82] [1994] 1 All ER 737.

[83] Ibid, 752–3. A South African case relied on by Vinelott J, *Ex parte de Villiers, re Carbon Developments (Pty) Ltd* 1993 (1) SA 493, SA AppD, involved the use of a contingent-debt structure similar to that described in the text. Vinelott J doubted whether a subordinated debt could be described as a contingent debt but felt that nothing turned on the question.

PART V

RAISING FINANCE FROM CAPITAL MARKETS

17

Initial Public Offers of Securities

SCOPE OF CHAPTER

This part of the book looks at the raising of corporate finance by issuing ordinary shares to investors in the capital markets. Companies can also raise finance by issuing debt securities or other securities, such as preference shares, convertible securities and warrants that combine some of the traditional features of debt and equity. Devising new structures for corporate securities so as to meet changing investor preferences and to tap effectively into all possible sources of finance is an important area of corporate finance advisory activity, but this book does not attempt the impossible task of keeping pace with the capacity of the markets for inventiveness and innovation. At the level of detail, the application of the rules relating to public offers can vary depending on the type of security in question but the broad framework of regulation is the same in all cases.

In this chapter the focus is on the process whereby for the first time a company raises finance by offering its shares to investors in the market. An initial public offer of shares by a company, or a flotation, as this process is commonly described, is likely to be preceded by significant corporate reorganisation. The status of the company may have to change because of the rule that only public companies can offer their shares to the public.[1] It is likely that its constitutional framework, as set out in its memorandum and articles, will need to be reviewed so as to remove provisions, such as restrictions on the transfer of shares, that will cease to be appropriate once its shares are publicly traded.[2] Independent non-executive directors may have to be appointed in order to meet the expectations of the market with regard to good corporate governance and the terms of employment of existing executive directors may need to be made more transparent, particularly with regard to remuneration entitlements and notice periods. Generally, once a company has become a public company with outside investors, it will be subject to more stringent legal requirements and to the discipline imposed by market forces, as well as, specifically, the particular continuing obligations imposed by any stock exchange on which its shares are quoted. The corporate governance issues that are discussed in Part II of this book will thus become much more relevant than they were when the company was private and had fewer shareholders.

[1] Companies Act 1985, s 81. Also Financial Services Act 1986, s 143 (3)—shares of private companies cannot be accepted for listing.

[2] *The Listing Rules*, ch 13, app 1, para 6 states that the articles of listed companies must not restrict the transferability of fully-paid listed shares.

These are factors that have to be set against the advantages of widening the sources of finance that are available to a company.

FORMS OF PUBLIC OFFER OF SHARES

There are a number of ways in which a public offer of ordinary shares can be structured. In outline, the main methods are as follows.[3] First, there is an offer for sale or subscription. In an offer of sale, members of the public are given the opportunity to buy shares from an investment bank which will have agreed with the company to subscribe those shares with a view to offering them to the public. The investment bank acts as principal in this structure. In an offer for subscription, members of the public are offered the opportunity to subscribe directly for the company's shares. The investment bank acts as the company's agent in making this offer. Whether the investment bank acts as principal or as agent, the offer may include shares that were owned by existing shareholders of the company who want to realise all or part of their investment in the company at the same time as the public offer. Offers may be in the form of fixed-price offers or offers by tender where applicants are invited to tender for the shares at or above a minimum tender price.

When the investment bank acts as principal, it bears the risk that the issue will not be fully taken up by the investing public. Its return for the assumption of this risk lies in the difference between the price at which it acquires the shares and the price at which it offers them to the public. When the investment bank acts as agent, the issuing company bears the risk that the offer may not be taken up in full by the public but the company may pass on this risk to its investment bank by means of an underwriting agreement. An underwriting agreement is an agreement whereby the underwriter agrees, in return for a fee, to take up any shares that are not acquired by the general public. Issues that arise in relation to underwriting are discussed further in the next chapter on rights issues. Rights issues normally take the form of a direct offer of shares by their issuer, and underwriting is therefore an important issue in that context.

Secondly, a company may seek to raise equity share capital from the market by means of a placing. A placing is a marketing of securities to specified persons or clients of the investment bank or corporate broker that is sponsoring the issue,[4] or any securities house assisting in the placing. In one sense, it is something of a misnomer to consider placings in a section headed 'forms of *public* offer' because a placing is usually structured so as not to be an offer to the public for the purposes of the legal requirement to produce a prospectus.[5] The technical meaning of the phrase 'offer to the public' and the different marketing documents that are required in respect of offers of securities that are not public offers as so defined are discussed later in this chapter.[6] Here,

[3] Generally, *The Listing Rules*, ch 4.

[4] *The Listing Rules*, ch 2 details the role and responsibilities of the sponsor in a listed issue.

[5] *The Listing Rules*, ch 4, para 4.7 defines a placing for the purposes of explaining the methods whereby securities can be brought to listing as an offer which is not to the public.

[6] See below, at 574–7.

the relevant point is that placings are a method for a company to attract external equity investors and, so, in that looser sense, they are properly included in a discussion of public offers. The company's investment bank may act as principal or agent in the process of placing the shares. The selective marketing process that is involved in a placing means that the costs associated with it will tend to be cheaper than those involved in an offer for sale or subscription.

THE STRUCTURE OF THE LONDON STOCK EXCHANGE AND ITS ROLE

The structure of the London Stock Exchange is considered in Chapter 2.[7] In brief, it has two tiers, the main market and the Alternative Investment Market (AIM). Securities that are admitted to dealings on the main market are on the 'Official List' of the London Stock Exchange and are commonly referred to as listed securities. Applicants for admission to either of the markets must comply with certain entry requirements, although these are far more rigorous for those seeking admission to the Official List than for admission to the AIM. In both cases, there are continuing obligations that must be satisfied by companies whose securities have been admitted to dealings on the market.[8] The main market of the London Stock Exchange and the AIM are markets for investors to trade in securities, but companies can also use their facilities to raise new capital.

PROTECTION OF INVESTORS BY DISCLOSURE

Persons who provide finance to companies by investing in their securities are protected by mandatory disclosure obligations that are imposed by the general law on companies that seek to raise capital from the public. Companies must provide potential investors with detailed information about their financial and managerial structure and about the operation of their business. Failure to comply with these disclosure obligations, or the provision of false or incomplete information in purported compliance, exposes a company, its officers and advisers to a range of potential criminal and civil liabilities. The admission of the company's securities to dealing on a market such as the London Stock Exchange may be put in jeopardy and the advisers may be liable to censure by their regulatory authorities. These mandatory disclosure requirements achieve standardisation in respect of the information that must be disclosed in connection with a public issue of securities and relieve investors of the need to negotiate for the disclosure of information in respect of each individual issue. Without such requirements, disclosure would be driven by market forces and although many issuers might choose to provide broadly the same information as is presently required by the general law, others might opt to offer investors a higher return on their investment in

[7] See above, at 74–6.

[8] *The Listing Rules* set out the entry requirements and continuing obligations for the main market. The equivalent (but much less extensive) AIM rules are contained in *The Rules of the London Stock Exchange*, ch 16.

return for less disclosure. The justifications for denying companies the opportunity to bargain about the level of disclosure are debatable.[9] This issue is developed a little further later in this chapter.[10] For the present, it suffices to note that the philosophy of mandatory disclosure appears to be firmly embedded in English law.[11] Moreover, the framework of the legal rules relating to the raising of corporate finance by public offers of securities under English law, and much of their detailed content, are derived from European law. The relevant European legislation identifies a number of underlying reasons for the imposition of mandatory disclosure obligations.

EUROPEAN BACKGROUND

The programme of harmonisation of company law within the Member States of the European Union is largely based on the European Community Treaty, art 44[12] which, in art 44 (3) (g) calls for the co-ordination 'to the necessary extent the safeguards which, for the protection of the interests of members and others, are required by Member States of companies or firms . . . with a view to making such safeguards equivalent throughout the Community'. Measures relating to securities law have also been based on the European Community Treaty, art 94[13] which is concerned with 'the approximation of such provisions laid down by law, regulation or administrative action in Member States as directly affect the establishment or functioning of the common market'. There is debate about the precise nature of the aims sought to be achieved by the harmonisation measures in the field of company law[14] but one discernible purpose is to ensure that individual Member States do not seek to use a liberal legal and regulatory structure as a way of attracting businesses to incorporate in their territory rather than in other Member States which impose more rigorous requirements.[15] However, there is also the com-

[9] Easterbrook, FH, and Fischel, DR, 'Mandatory Disclosure and the Protection of Investors' (1984) 70 Virginia Law Review 669; Coffee, JC, 'Market Failure and the Economic Case for a Mandatory Disclosure System' (1984) 70 Virginia Law Review 717; Romano, R, *Foundations of Corporate Law* (1993) 313–17; Page, AC, and Ferguson, RB, *Investor Protection* (1992) 45–9; Cheffins, BR, *Company Law Theory, Structure and Operation* (1997) 163–8.

[10] See below, at 582–4.

[11] And elsewhere: see, eg, Clark, RC, *Corporate Law* (1986) 756–60.

[12] The Treaty of Amsterdam which was agreed in June 1997 and formally signed in October 1997 effects a renumbering of the various European Treaties. Under this renumbering, which takes effect in 1999, the old art 54 becomes art 44.

[13] Prior to the renumbering which takes effect from 1999 this was art 100.

[14] Detailed analysis of European Union company and securities law may be found in the following: Dine, J, *EC Company Law* (1991, looseleaf); Buxbaum, RM, and Hopt, KJ, *Legal Harmonization and the Business Enterprise* (1988); Van Hulle, *Harmonization of Company and Securities Law* (1989); Andenas, M, and Kenyon-Slade, S (eds), *EC Financial Market Regulation and Company Law* (1993); Werlauff, E, *The Development of Community Company Law* (1992) 17 European Law Rev 207.

[15] The so-called 'Delaware' effect. This description derives from the effectiveness of the lax corporate laws in Delaware in attracting business to incorporate in that case. For a comparative analysis of the US experience and the European harmonisation programme see Charny, D, 'Competition among Jurisdictions in Formulating Corporate Law Rules: An American Perspective on the "Race to the Bottom" in the European Communities' (1991) 32 Harvard Journal of International Law 423.

peting pressure to ensure that the harmonised legal rules within the European Union do not inhibit European securities markets from competing effectively with markets outside the Union: if European law is drawn too tightly, this may cause businesses to shift their capital-raising activities to other less regulated markets in non-European Union states. Some commentators have noted that, looked at in this light, harmonisation creates a strong pressure for the 'levelling down' of disclosure requirements to preserve the competitiveness of the EU markets. The protection of investors, the proper functioning and development of transferable securities markets and the development of a genuine European capital market are also identified as purposes which the company law and investment harmonisation measures seek to achieve.[16]

Harmonisation by Directives

To date, European law relating to the listing and public offer of securities has been made in the form of directives. Under the Treaty of Rome, art 249,[17] a directive is binding as to the result to be achieved upon each Member State to which it is addressed but must leave to the national authorities the choice of form and methods of implementation. This means that each Member State must pass implementing legislation to incorporate a directive into its domestic law and the directive will specify a time-limit within which this implementation should take place. The European Court of Justice has held that if a Member State fails to implement a directive before the specified time-limit, the provisions of that directive, provided they are unconditional and sufficiently clear and precise, can then be pleaded by an individual against the State and all organs of the State, although not against private persons.[18] It has also held that a claim in damages may be brought against a State which has failed to comply with a directive which has not been duly implemented.[19]

All of the existing directives relating to the public offer and listing of securities have been incorporated into English law by the passing of implementing domestic legislation. The main[20] relevant directives are as follows:

- Council Directive 79/279/EEC, co-ordinating the conditions for the admission of securities to official stock exchange listing (the Admissions Directive); [21]

[16] See the preambles to Council Directive EEC 79/269, [1979] OJ L66/21 *Admission of Securities to Stock Exchange Listing* and Council Directive 89/298, [1989] OJ L124/8 *Requirements for the Drawing-up, Scrutiny and Distribution of the Prospectus to be Published when Transferable Securities are Offered to the Public.*

[17] Under the renumbering that is effective from 1999. Previously this was art 189.

[18] Case 41/74 *Van Duyn v Home Office* [1974] ECR 1337, ECJ; Case 148/78 *Pubblico Ministero v Tullio Ratti* [1979] ECR 1629, ECJ; Case 8/81 *Becker v Finanzamt Münster-Innenstadt* [1982] ECR 53, ECJ; Case 152/84 *Marshall v Southampton and South-West Hampshire Area Health Authority (Teaching)* [1986] ECR 723, ECJ.

[19] Case C6/90 and C9/90 *Francovich and Bonifaci v Italy* [1991] ECR I–5357, ECJ; Cases C–46/93 and C–48/93 *Brasserie du Pêcheur v Germany* and *R v Secretary of State for Transport ex parte Factortame* [1996] ECR I–1029, ECJ.

[20] There have also been a number of directives amending parts of the main directives: see Council Directives 82/148/EEC, [1982] OJ L62/22; 87/345/EEC, [1987] OJ L185/81; 90/211/EEC, [1990] OJ L122/24; and Parliament Directive 94/18/EC.

[21] [1979] OJ L66/21.

- Council Directive 80/390/EEC co-ordinating the requirements for the drawing-up, scrutiny and distribution of the listing particulars to be published for the admission of securities to official stock exchange listing (the Listing Particulars Directive);[22]
- Council Directive 82/121/EEC, on information to be published on a regular basis by companies shares of which have been admitted to official stock-exchange listing (the Interim Reports Directive);[23]
- Council Directive 89/298/EEC, co-ordinating the requirements for the drawing-up, scrutiny and distribution of the prospectus to be published when transferable securities are offered to the public (the Public Offers Directive).[24]

Chronologically, harmonisation of measures relating to the listing of securities came before harmonisation of the requirements for the public offer of securities. Whilst the listing of securities need not involve any public offer of those securities, it is often the case that listing takes place at the time when securities are offered to the public.[25] Before the adoption of the Public Offers Directive, the European requirements on listing did not draw any distinction between those listings involving a public offer and those that did not. With the adoption of the Public Offers Directive, which applies to all public offers of securities whether listed or unlisted, it is important to establish whether securities which are to be listed are to be the subject of a public offer because the requirements will differ depending on the answer to that question.

Implementation into English Law

The structure of the domestic legislation that implements these directives reflects the chronological development of the European law. In 1984 the three directives on the listing of securities were implemented by regulations. The framework for implementation was subsequently incorporated into the Financial Services Act 1986, Pt IV. Within the Pt IV framework the detailed requirements of the directives are now given effect to under English law by *The Listing Rules* of the London Stock Exchange.[26] Part IV, as originally drafted, did not distinguish between listings involving a public offer and other listings. It was amended in 1995 by the Public Offers of Securities Regulations 1995[27] so as to implement into English law the Public Offers Directive in relation to securities which are to be listed and which are the subject of a public offer.[28]

[22] [1980] OJ L100/1. [23] [1982] OJ L48/26. [24] [1989] OJ L124/8.

[25] An example of a case where a company might seek a listing otherwise than in conjunction with an offer of new securities is where it has a primary listing on the securities market in its home jurisdiction but it seeks secondary listings in other countries in order to enhance the marketability of its shares.

[26] See further this chapter below, at 580–1. Provisions of the draft Financial Services and Markets Bill broadly replicate those of the Financial Services Act 1986 on official listing. The Financial Services and Markets Act is expected to be enacted and come into force in 2000.

[27] SI 1995/1537. These regulations were made under the European Communities Act 1972, s 2 (2) which allows for the implementation of Community obligations by secondary legislation.

[28] For the background to the implementation of this directive see the DTI and Treasury Consultative Documents *Listing Particulars and Public Offer Prospectuses—Implementation of Part V of the Financial Services Act 1986 and Related EC Directives* (July 1990) and *Revised Implementation of the EC Prospectus Directive* (July 1994).

Public offers of unlisted securities are regulated by the Public Offers of Securities Regulations 1995. These regulations implement for non-listed offers the requirements of the Public Offers Directive. The regulations apply to public offers of securities made through any market other than the main market of the London Stock Exchange, and thus apply to offers made through the Alternative Investment Market. The regulations also apply to offers which are entirely off-market.

Interpretation of Implementing Legislation

The European Court of Justice and the domestic courts have developed particular principles of statutory interpretation for legislation, such as the Financial Services Act 1986, Pt IV and the Public Offers of Securities Regulations 1995, which implements European measures. The European Court has held that provisions of national law which were specifically introduced in order to implement a directive must be interpreted in the light of the wording and the purpose of the directive, in so far as the courts have discretion to do so under their national law.[29] The House of Lords has held that the English courts do have discretion under national law to interpret implementing legislation purposively in order to give effect to the broad intention of Parliament to achieve full implementation of the directive, that the purposive approach should be adopted even though the domestic legislation may not, on its face, give rise to an ambiguity and that, if necessary, words can be implied into the statute to achieve the required effect.[30] This means that, in interpreting the Financial Services Act 1986, Pt IV and the Public Offers of Securities Regulations 1995 reference should be made to the underlying directives, and not only on points which are thought to be ambiguous.

OUTLINE OF THE STRUCTURE OF THE REGULATION OF PUBLIC OFFERS AND LISTING

Only public companies may offer their securities to the public in the United Kingdom[31] and only public companies may seek to have their securities listed on the Official List of the London Stock Exchange.[32] A public company which intends to make an offer of its securities to the public in the UK for the first

[29] Case 14/83 *Von Colson and Kamann v Land Nordrhein-Westfalen* [1984] ECR 1891, ECJ. For discussion of the development of this principle in European jurisprudence see Weatherill, S, *Cases and Materials on EC Law* (4th edn, 1998) 112–32; Craig, PP, and de Búrca, G, *EU Law: Text, Cases and Materials* (2nd edn, 1998) ch 4.

[30] *Pickstone v Freemans plc* [1989] 1 AC 66, HL; *Litster v Forth Dry Dock Engineering Co Ltd* [1990] 1 AC 546, HL.

[31] Companies Act 1985, s 81. The definition of an 'offer to the public' under this section is not the same as that which applies generally for the purposes of Financial Services Act 1986, Pt IV and Public Offers of Securities Regulations 1995. Share offers by private companies are not considered further in this chapter, but see Ch 18 below, at 624–5.

[32] Financial Services Act 1986, s 143 (3). Hereafter in this chapter references to sections or schedules are to sections or schedules of the Financial Services Act 1986 unless otherwise stated. References to regulations are to regulations in the Public Offers of Securities Regulations 1995.

time must produce and publish a prospectus. A prospectus is also required where the holder of securities, not being itself the issuer of those securities, intends to offer those securities to the public in the UK for the first time. Where securities are to be listed but there is no public offer triggering the requirement for a prospectus, listing particulars will usually be required instead. There is a very large overlap between the information required to be included in a prospectus and that required in listing particulars.

Where there is a public offer of securities that are not to be listed, a prospectus is required. An offer of unlisted securities that is not an offer to the public does not require a prospectus[33] but, in that case, investment advertisements relating to the offer may only be issued by or with the approval of a person who is authorised under the Financial Services Act 1986 to carry on investment business, unless an exemption applies.[34]

AN OFFER TO THE PUBLIC IN THE UNITED KINGDOM FOR THE FIRST TIME

The concept of an offer to the public in the United Kingdom for the first time is at the heart of the regulatory structure: only when there is such an offer is a prospectus required; and the person who makes such an offer, the offeror,[35] is a person who is, by statute, responsible for, and liable to compensate investors for inaccuracies in, the information contained in that prospectus. The definition of an offer to the public in the UK for the first time is, for listed offers, to be found in the Financial Services Act 1986, s 142 (7A) and sch 11A. The equivalent definition for unlisted offers is contained in the Public Offers of Securities Regulations 1995, regs 5 to 7.

The Meaning of 'Offer' and the Issue of Multiple Offerors

A person offers securities[36] if, as principal:

(i) he makes an offer which, if accepted, would give rise to a contract for their issue or sale (which for this purpose includes any disposal for valuable consideration) by him or another person with whom he has made arrangements for their issue or sale;[37] or
(ii) he invites a person to make such an offer.

An agent is not an offeror but his principal will be treated as having made the offer for this purpose. Where a number of persons simultaneously make an

[33] Unless the securities are to be admitted to the Alternative Investment Market in which case under market rules, rather than general law, a prospectus must be produced: *The Rules of the London Stock Exchange*, ch 16, para 16.7.

[34] Financial Services Act 1986, ss 57–58; Financial Services Act 1986 (Investment Advertisements) (Exemptions) Order 1996 (SI 1996/1586) and Financial Services Act 1986 (Investment Advertisements) (Exemptions) (No 2) Order 1995 (SI 1995/1536).

[35] See s 142 (7A)(a) and reg 5.

[36] This is the wording in s 142 (7A). Reg 5 states that a person 'is to be regarded as offering securities' but no change of substance appears to flow from the slightly different form of wording.

[37] Again the text tracks s 142 (7A). There are minor differences between this section and reg 5 (most obviously, reg 5 does not itself include the words in parenthesis because 'sale' is defined in reg 2 (1) as including any disposal for valuable consideration) but comparison between the two provisions does not reveal any significant variation.

offer in respect of securities of the same class—for example, in a flotation where the issuer offers new ordinary shares for sale or subscription and existing ordinary shareholders offer part of their holdings for sale—it is unclear whether this is to be regarded as one 'global' offer or as the appropriate number of separate offers. The importance of this point may be illustrated by reference to the following facts:

XYZ plc, advised by ABC Merchant Bank, offers new ordinary shares for subscription by the public at large; at the same time, ABC arranges for D's holding of existing ordinary shares in XYZ to be offered for sale to fifty of its clients and for part of E's existing ordinary shares in XYZ to be offered for sale to another fifty of its clients. The offer of either D's or E's shares, taken separately, would benefit from the exemption from the requirement to produce a prospectus where securities are offered to no more than fifty persons[38] but, viewed as one 'global offer' made by three offerors, XYZ, D and E, no exemption would be available and a prospectus would be required.

This uncertainty at the very heart of the main concept on which the regulatory structure is based is unfortunate and a review of the underlying directive does not help to resolve the difficulty.[39] The 'separate offers' approach could open up opportunities for abuse involving structures with multiple offerors designed to avoid the prospectus requirement and, even though the court could look through such a structure, this is none the less a reason why the 'global offer' interpretation seems to be preferable in principle. However it does carry with it the unfortunate consequence that persons such as the selling shareholders in the example above are, as offerors, persons who are legally responsible for the accuracy of the offer documentation, the prospectus, and may be liable in damages if it is inaccurate even though, in reality, they may have had no involvement in the drafting of that documentation and no control over the information that it contains. The potential harshness and unfairness of this outcome for certain shareholders, such as employees, has been recognised by the government and it has amended the responsibility provisions of the listed and unlisted regimes so as to exclude an offeror from informational responsibility where the securities were offered in conjunction with an offer by the issuer and the prospectus was primarily drawn up by the issuer.[40]

An 'offer' means not only a contractual offer (ie, a promise which, if accepted by the person to whom it is made, will give rise to a binding contract) but also a statement which invites the person to whom it is made to make a contractual offer (in the technical language of the law of contract, this form of invitation is known as an invitation to treat). The offer does not have to be writing since the prospectus requirement is triggered as much by an oral offer as by a formal written offer.

[38] See below, at 578.

[39] This point is not addressed in the *Guidance Note: Public Offers of Securities Regulations 1995* HM Treasury (1996).

[40] S 154A (2) and s 156A (3A) (listed issues) and reg 13 (2A) (unlisted issues) inserted by Public Offers of Securities (Amendment) Regulations 1999 (SI 1999/734) with effect from 10 May 1999.

'The Public in the UK'

The requirement to produce a prospectus only applies to offers of securities to the public in the UK.[41] There are two important elements here: first, the interpretation of 'public' and, second, the territorial limitation. An offer which is covered by one or more of the exemptions discussed later in this chapter is not an offer to the public.[42] Less clear is whether an offer which is not covered by an exemption must necessarily be regarded as an offer to the public. It is arguable that the public nature of an offer must be established independently from the availability or otherwise of an exemption,[43] and that it does not follow from the fact that an exemption does not apply that the offer is an offer to the public.[44] Applying this view, which is supported by guidance issued by the UK government,[45] it then becomes necessary to consider when, independently of possible exemptions, an offer has a public character. This is a notoriously difficult issue. The preamble to the Public Offers Directive contains the confession that 'so far, it has proved to be impossible to furnish a common definition of the term "public offer" and all its constituent parts'. The Financial Services Act 1986 and the Public Offers of Securities Regulations 1995 do no more than to provide that an offer made to any section of the public, whether selected as members or debenture-holders of a body corporate, or as clients of the person making the offer, is to be regarded as made to the public.[46] Yet, whilst this point is of theoretical interest, it is doubtful whether much of practical significance turns on it. The breadth of the exemptions is such that there would seem to be no more than a theoretical possibility of there being an offer which is not a public offer but which is not covered by an exemption. In summary then, the position would seem to be that, in view of the acknowledged difficulty of establishing what is meant by the term 'public', an offer should be regarded as an offer to the public unless an exemption applies or, exceptionally, there is otherwise felt to be a compelling case for arguing that it is not made to the public.

With regard to the territorial limitation, in deciding whether a prospectus is required when an offer is made to investors in more than one country, it is necessary to ignore the foreign investors to whom the offer is made, and to consider only the extent to which the offer is made to persons in the UK.

[41] Sch 11A, para 1(a) (listed issues) and reg 6 (unlisted issues). [42] Ibid.

[43] See sch 11A, para 1 (listed issues) which states that an offer is an offer to the public in the UK when (a) it is made to the public in the UK, and (b) an exemption does not apply.

[44] In its consultative document published in July 1990 *Listing Particulars and Public Offer Prospectuses, Implementation of Part V of the Financial Services Act 1986 and Related Directives* the DTI described the approach under which offers would be regarded as offers to the public unless covered by an exemption as the objective approach. It rejected the objective approach in favour of a hybrid approach under which, in addition to specific exemptions, there was scope for an offer to be not an offer to the public because the term 'public' was to be independently interpreted. Many of the issues considered in that consultative document were overtaken by later developments but the draft regulations based on the hybrid approach (Annex F) has some similarity to what was eventually enacted.

[45] *Guidance Note on Public Offers of Securities Amendment Regulations 1999* (HM Treasury) (1999).

[46] Sch 11A, para 1 (listed issues) and reg 6 (unlisted issues).

Hence, where an exemption depends on the identity or number of persons to whom the offer is made, it is only persons in the UK who have to be taken into account in determining whether that exemption applies.

The use of the Internet as a medium for offering securities presents difficult regulatory problems to which effective responses are still emerging. The UK's main regulatory body, the Financial Services Authority, has issued a formal Guidance on its present interpretation of the relevant law and enforcement policy.[47] This indicates that offers which may be accessed by persons in the UK are to be regarded as being made to the public in the UK, but that enforcement action is only likely where the offer is directed at persons in the UK.

'For the First Time'

Whether securities are being offered to the public in the UK for the first time is tested by asking whether any securities from the same issue were the subject of a previous public offer for which a prospectus was published; if they were, no prospectus is required.[48] Where, therefore, an issue of securities is acquired by investors in circumstances where an exemption applies and no prospectus is produced, but one of those investors later makes a public offer of its investment and no exemption is available at that point, a prospectus will be required; thereafter the other original investors can offer their investment to the public without producing a prospectus.[49]

EXEMPTIONS: OFFERS THAT ARE NOT OFFERS TO THE PUBLIC

When an exemption applies, there is no requirement to publish a prospectus in connection with an issue. There is a long list of exemptions[50] and, of these, important exemptions in relation to companies are as follows.

An Offer to Persons Whose Ordinary Activities Involve Them in Acquiring, Holding, Managing or Disposing of Investments (as principal or agent) for the Purposes of Their Businesses or Who it is Reasonable to Expect so to Acquire, Hold, Manage or Dispose of Investments, or Otherwise an Offer to Persons in the Context of Their Trades, Professions or Occupations[51]

This is the 'professionals' exemption. It is not limited to persons engaged in the ordinary business of buying and selling securities as was the case under previous law.[52] Corporate treasurers and others who perform investment

[47] *Investment Advertisements on the Internet* GR2/98 May1998.

[48] Sch 11A, para 3 (1)(s) (listed issues) and reg 7 (2)(t) (unlisted issues).

[49] This analysis is supported by *Guidance Note: Public Offers of Securities Regulations 1995* (HM Treasury) (1996) s D.

[50] Sch 11A, paras 3 and 4 (listed issues) and reg 7 (unlisted issues).

[51] Sch 11A, para 3 (1)(a) (listed issues) and reg 7 (2)(a) (unlisted issues). The underlying provision is the Public Offers Directive, art 2.1(a).

[52] Companies Act 1985, s 79 (2) (now repealed).

functions as part of a non-financial business can be included in an offer which is structured so as to take advantage of this exemption.[53]

An Offer to No More Than Fifty Persons[54]

The underlying provision of the Public Offers Directive states that the directive does not apply where securities are offered to a restricted circle of persons.[55] Under the old prospectus requirements in the Companies Act 1985, the term 'offer to the public' was used but it was not exhaustively defined and there was no specified threshold number of persons to whom the offer had to be addressed for it to amount to an offer to the public. In practice it was widely considered that an offer to fifty or fewer persons would not have been held to be an offer to the public but that was no more than a practical rule of thumb with no specific legal backing. Under the current law, in determining whether the fifty-persons exemption applies, it is the number of persons to whom the offer is made and not the number who accept it which is important. Whether joint holders, trustees and partnerships are to be treated as one person is unclear, although according to guidance issued by the UK government in March 1999, offers made to several persons jointly are to be treated as offers to a single person.

For the purpose of applying this exemption, the offer must be taken together with any other offer of the same securities which was (a) made by the same person, (b) open at any time within the preceding 12 months, and (c) not itself an offer to the public in the UK because the fifty-persons exemption applied to it.[56] This anti-avoidance measure ensures that an offeror cannot bypass the obligation to produce a prospectus by staggering an offer over a period of time with each instalment of the securities being offered to fifty or fewer investors.

An Offer to a Restricted Circle of Persons Whom the Offeror Reasonably Believes to be Sufficiently Knowledgeable to Understand the Risks Involved in Accepting the Offer[57]

In determining whether a person is sufficiently knowledgeable, any information supplied by the person making the offer must be disregarded apart from information about the issuer (which may be a different person from the offeror) and, if the securities confer the right to acquire other securities, the issuer of those securities.[58]

[53] This view is supported by *Guidance Note: Public Offers of Securities Regulations 1995* (HM Treasury) (1996) s C.
[54] Sch 11A, para 3 (1)(b) (listed issues) and reg 7 (2)(b) (unlisted issues).
[55] Public Offers Directive, art 2.1(b).
[56] Sch 11A, para (3) (listed issues) and reg 7 (6) (unlisted issues).
[57] Sch 11A, para 3 (1)(d) (listed issues) and reg 7 (2)(d) (unlisted issues). Public Offers Directive, art 2.1(b). There are some indications that the exemption is not working effectively in practice: *Public Offers of Securities: A Consultation Document* (HM Treasury) (1998) paras 3.13–3.15.
[58] Sch 11A, para 3 (4) (listed issues) and reg 7 (7) (unlisted issues).

An Offer in Connection with a Bona Fide Invitation to Enter into an Underwriting Agreement in Respect of the Securities[59]

An Offer in Connection with a Takeover Offer[60]

An Offer of Shares Made Free of Charge to Existing Shareholders[61]

This exemption would cover fully-paid bonus issues.

Other Exemptions

There are also exemptions covering offers to members of clubs and associations where the members and the club or association have a common interest[62] or to state authorities,[63] offers relating to employee schemes[64] and to mergers,[65] offers where the consideration payable, or the denomination of the securities, is above or below specified figures,[66] offers relating to the reorganisation of a company's capital structure[67] or the conversion of convertible securities (provided that appropriate documentation in respect of the convertible securities was published),[68] and offers of certain eurosecurities.[69] Offers of debentures with a maturity of less than one year from their date of issue are exempt,[70] as are offers of securities which are not transferable.[71] No prospectus is required where the securities are of the same class, and were

[59] Sch 11A, para 3 (1)(e) (listed issues) and reg 7 (2)(e) (unlisted issues). Public Offers Directive, art 2.1(b).

[60] Schedule 11A, para 3 (1)(j) (listed issues) and reg 7 (2)(k) (unlisted issues). Public Offers Directive, art 2.2(d). 'Takeover offer' is to be construed broadly in accordance with Companies Act 1985, Pt XIIIA: sch 11A, para 3 (6) and 3 (6A) (listed issues) and reg 7 (10) and (10A) (unlisted issues) (both as amended by Public Offers of Securities Amendment Regulations 1999).

[61] Sch 11A, paras 3 (1)(j) and (7) (listed issues) and reg 7 (2)(m) and (11) (unlisted issues) (both as amended by Public Offers of Securities Amendment Regulations 1999). Public Offers Directive, art 2.2(f).

[62] Sch 11A, para 3 (1)(c) (listed issues) and reg 7 (2)(c) (unlisted issues). Public Offers Directive, art 2.1(b).

[63] Sch 11A, para 3 (1)(f) (listed issues) and reg 7 (2)(g) (unlisted issues). Public Offers Directive, art 2.1(g).

[64] Sch 11A, paras 3 (1)(n) and (8) (listed issues) and reg 7 (2)(o) and (12) (unlisted issues) (both as amended by Public Offers of Securities Amendment Regulations 1999). Public Offers Directive, art 2.2(h).

[65] Sch 11A, para 3 (1)(k) (listed issues) and reg 7 (2)(l) (unlisted issues). Public Offers Directive, art 2.2(e).

[66] Sch 11A, para 3 (1)(g), (h) and (i) (listed issues) and reg 7 (2)(h), (i) and (j) (unlisted issues) (both as amended by Public Offers of Securities Amendment Regulations 1999). Public Offers Directive, art 2.1(c) and (d) and 2.2(a).

[67] Sch 11A, para 3 (1)(m) (listed issues) and reg 7 (2)(n) (unlisted issues). Public Offers Directive, art 2.2(g).

[68] Sch 11A, paras 3 (1)(o) and (2)(a) (listed issues) and reg 7 (2)(p) (unlisted issues). Public Offers Directive, art 2.2(i).

[69] Sch 11A, para 3 (1)(r) (listed issues) and reg 7 (2)(s) (unlisted issues) (both as amended by Public Offers of Securities Amendment Regulations 1999). Public Offers Directive, art 2.2(l).

[70] Sch 11A, para 3 (1)(t) (listed issues) and reg 3 (2)(a) (unlisted issues). Public Offers Directive, art 3(e).

[71] Sch 11A, para 3 (1)(v) (listed issues) and reg 7 (2)(u) (unlisted issues). Public Offers Directive, art 1.

issued at the same time, as securities in respect of which a prospectus was published.[72]

Aggregating Exemptions

Can more than one exemption be claimed in respect of the same offer? For example, if an offer is made in part to experienced investors who can reasonably be regarded as persons sufficiently expert to understand the risks involved and in part to less experienced investors who, in total, number no more than fifty, is the offer exempt from the requirement to produce a prospectus because the two parts are each covered by an exemption? The answer in relation to this specific example is yes: the two relevant exemptions can be aggregated and since each part of the offer is covered by an exemption the whole offer is deemed to be exempt.[73] Most, but not all,[74] of the exemptions are cumulative (all of the main exemptions for companies outlined above are); but if any part of an offer is not covered by a cumulative exemption a prospectus is required.

PUBLIC OFFERS OF SHARES THAT ARE TO BE LISTED: FINANCIAL SERVICES ACT 1986, PT IV AND *THE LISTING RULES*

Securities may only be admitted to the Official List of the London Stock Exchange in accordance with the provisions of the Financial Services Act 1986, Pt IV.[75] 'Securities' is a defined term for this purpose. Company shares, debentures, warrants and convertible securities are all Pt IV securities.[76] Investments which are not Pt IV securities, such as gilt-edged securities, can also be admitted to listing on a non-statutory basis. Such investments are not considered further in this chapter.

THE ROLE OF THE LONDON STOCK EXCHANGE AS 'COMPETENT AUTHORITY'

The London Stock Exchange is the UK's competent authority.[77] The term 'competent authority' is derived from the Admissions Directive which requires Member States to designate a competent authority or authorities for the purposes of admitting securities to official listing.[78] As the UK's competent authority the London Stock Exchange must act in conformity with EU or any other international obligations and must take whatever action is required for

[72] Sch 11A, para 3 (1)(s) (listed issues) and reg 7 (2)(t) (unlisted issues). Public Offers Directive, art 1.2. This is an optional provision of the directive which the UK government has chosen to adopt in full.

[73] Sch 11A, para 4, read in conjunction with paras 1 (b) and 2 (b) (listed issues) and reg 7 (3) read in conduction with reg 7 (1)(b) (unlisted issues). Public Offers Directive, art 2.

[74] Sch 11A, para 4 (listed issues) and reg 7 (3) (unlisted issues) specify the exemptions which can be aggregated.

[75] S 142 (1).

[76] S 142 (2)–(4) and sch 1, paras 1–2, 4–5.

[77] S 142 (6).

[78] Art 9.

the purpose of implementing any such obligation.[79] Thus, in exercising its power to draw up the rules which must be satisfied by applicants for listing and observed, as continuing obligations, by issuers whose securities have been admitted to listing,[80] the London Stock Exchange must give effect to the underlying directives on listing and public offers, although it may also impose additional requirements. The entry requirements and continuing obligations that are applicable to the Exchange's Official List are set out in its publication *The Listing Rules*. Where a provision in *The Listing Rules* gives effect to a European requirement this is indicated by a marginal note in that publication.

APPLICATION PROCESS

An application for listing must be made to the London Stock Exchange.[81] The application must comply with *The Listing Rules* and any extra requirements that may be imposed by the Exchange in that particular case.[82] The consent of the issuer is also a prerequisite to listing.[83] The Exchange may reject an application if (a) it considers that by reason of any matter relating to the issuer, admission of the securities would be detrimental to the interests of investors, or (b) in the case of securities already officially listed in another Member State, the issuer has failed to comply with any obligation to which it is subject by virtue of that listing.[84] The Exchange has six months within which to inform an applicant of its decision[85] and an application is to be taken as having been turned down if the Exchange does not notify the applicant otherwise during that period.[86] The Stock Exchange's decision to refuse an application may be challenged by way of judicial review,[87] but the Exchange, its members, officers and servants are not liable in damages for anything done or omitted in the discharge or purported discharge of its functions unless the act or omission is shown to have been in bad faith.[88]

Admission to listing is conclusive evidence that the listing requirements have been complied with.[89] Listing may be cancelled if the Stock Exchange is satisfied that special circumstances preclude normal dealings in the securities, and listing may also be suspended in accordance with *The Listing Rules*.[90] Other steps that may be taken by the Exchange against an issuer whose securities have been admitted to listing and which has contravened *The Listing Rules* include censuring the issuer and its responsible directors and

[79] The Secretary of State can require such action to be taken, or not taken as the case may be: s 192.

[80] S 142 (6). [81] S 143. [82] S 144 (1). [83] S 143 (2). [84] S 144 (3).

[85] S 144 (4). This period runs from the date on which the application was received or, if the Exchange required the applicant to provide further information in connection with the application, from the date when that information is furnished.

[86] S 144 (4) and (5).

[87] *R v International Stock Exchange ex parte Else* [1993] BCC 11, CA (this case involved delisting but the same principle should apply). The Admissions Directive, art 15 requires Member States to ensure that decisions of the competent authority refusing admission to official listing or discontinuing a listing to be subject to a right to apply to the courts.

[88] S 187 (4). [89] S 144 (6)).

[90] S 145. The Exchange's enforcement powers which are summarised in this paragraph are set out in detail in *The Listing Rules*, ch 1.

publishing the fact that such censure has been issued. Where a director has wilfully or persistently failed to discharge his responsibilities, the Exchange may state publicly its opinion that the retention of office by that director is prejudicial to the interests of investors and, if the director then remains in office, the Exchange may cancel or suspend the listing of the issuer's securities.

PROSPECTUSES AND LISTING PARTICULARS

Reasons of fairness and efficiency are used to justify imposing mandatory disclosure obligations on issuers. A mandatory disclosure system is said to increase public confidence in the markets, reduce fraud and protect unsophisticated investors (fairness arguments) or to be valuable because it enables information to reach the markets more efficiently than would be achieved by relying on issuers' self-interest in disclosure (efficiency arguments).[91] These justifications can be disputed.[92] Some commentators have argued that legal mandatory disclosure obligations should not be imposed on issuers and that they should be left free to decide how much they wish to disclose since, in accordance with efficient capital-markets theories that the price at which securities trade reflects all publicly available information,[93] if issuers give insufficient information to satisfy investors' expectations, this will lead to the securities being perceived to be risky and hence will increase the return that investors will expect to receive on them. Although less sophisticated investors may have difficulty in judging the adequacy of information provided, it is argued that they are protected because the actions of professional and experienced investors in response to that information will dictate the price of securities for the benefit generally of investors in the market.[94] However, those responsible for the European regulation[95] of securities offerings and listings appear, for the moment, to find fairness arguments in favour of mandatory disclosure more compelling than alternative views: the protection of investors

[91] Coffee, JC, 'Market Failure and the Economic Case for a Mandatory Disclosure System' (1984) 70 Virginia Law Review 717.

[92] Schulte, 'The Debatable Case for Securities Disclosure Regulation' (1988)13 Journal of Corporate Law 535.

[93] See further Ch 2 above, at 64–5 and also Klein, WA, and Coffee, JC, *Business Organization and Finance* (5th edn, 1993) 394–8.

[94] See, for example, Benston, G, 'The Costs and Benefits of Government-Required Disclosure: SEC and FTC Requirements' in de Mott, DA (ed), *Corporations at the Crossroads: Governance and Reform* (1980) 37; Easterbrook, FH, and Fischel, DR, 'Mandatory Disclosure and the Protection of Investors' (1984) 70 Virginia Law Review 669.

[95] In the domestic context, the DTI has also emphasised the importance of mandatory information in encouraging investor confidence: see *Financial Services in the United Kingdom—A New Framework for Investor Protection* Cmnd 9432 at paras. 3.3–3.4: 'No regulatory system can, or should, relieve the investor of responsibility for exercising judgment and care in deciding how to invest his money. If he makes a foolish decision on the basis of adequate disclosure—venturing all his savings on an avowedly speculative and high-risk proposition which fails for straightforward commercial reasons—he cannot look to any regulator to make good the losses arising from his own misjudgment . . . but . . . *caveat emptor* alone is not enough. For investors to have the confidence to venture into the market, measures are needed to reduce the likelihood of fraud and to encourage high standards in the conduct of investment business.'

and the enhancement of confidence in the markets are cited in the preambles to the Listing Particulars and Public Offers Directives as being goals, along with the development of a pan-Europe capital market, that those measures are intended to achieve.

As the UK's competent authority the London Stock Exchange is obliged to give effect to the Listing Particulars and Public Offer Directives in specifying the requirements that must be satisfied by applicants for listing. Where the securities for which admission is sought are to be offered to the public in the UK for the first time before admission, the Financial Services Act 1986, s 144 (2) and *The Listing Rules* give effect to the requirement in the Public Offers Directive for the publication of a prospectus. To determine whether a prospectus is required in conjunction with an application for listing, it is therefore necessary to ask, first, whether there is an offer of securities and, second, whether the offer is a public offer of securities to the public in the UK for the first time, so as to trigger the requirement to produce a prospectus. An example of a situation where a prospectus will not be required is where shares which are already in issue are introduced onto the Official List in order to enhance their liquidity and marketability and there is no issue of new shares. If there is no public offer triggering the requirement to produce a prospectus, the relevant document that must be produced is a set of listing particulars.[96] However, in those cases where a set of listing particulars is the relevant document, applicants may choose to publish a prospectus instead.[97]

The requirement to produce a prospectus or, as the case may be, listing particulars is subject to certain exemptions that are considered later in this chapter.[98]

Contents of Prospectuses and Listing Particulars

A prospectus must reflect the fact that there is a public offer of the securities to which it relates but, apart from this point, there is substantial similarity between the prescribed contents of prospectuses and listing particulars. This result is achieved by the Public Offers Directive, art 7 which provides that:

> Where a public offer relates to transferable securities which at the time of the offer are the subject of an application for admission to official listing on a stock exchange situated or operating within the same Member State, the contents of the prospectus and the procedures for scrutinising and distributing it shall, subject to adaptations appropriate to the circumstances of a public offer, be determined in accordance with Directive 80/390/EEC [the Listing Particulars Directive].

The Stock Exchange gives effect to the Public Offers Directive, art 7 and to the requirements of the Listing Particulars Directive, in *The Listing Rules*, chs 5 and 6.[99] These chapters set out in detailed and precise terms the information

[96] Financial Services Act 1986, s 144 (2A) and *The Listing Rules*, ch 5.
[97] *The Listing Rules*, ch 5, para 5.1 (b).
[98] See below, at 586–8 and 590–1.
[99] Special requirements applicable to certain types of issuer are set out in *The Listing Rules*, chs 17 to 24 and 26.

which prospectuses and listing particulars are required to contain. The information required for the admission of shares to listing falls under the following headings:

- the persons responsible for the prospectus or listing particulars,[100] the auditors and other advisors
- the securities for which the application is being made
- the issuer and its capital
- the group's activities
- the issuer's assets and liabilities, financial position and profits and losses
- the management
- the recent developments and prospects of the group.

The Exchange may also impose such additional requirements as it considers appropriate in any particular case.[101]

In accordance with the Listing Particulars Directive, art 5, *The Listing Rules*, ch 5 state[102] that the documents must provide factual information in as easily analysable and comprehensible a form as possible. The information must be set out in words and figures. Pictures, graphs, charts or other illustrations may not normally be included unless the Exchange is satisfied that it is the only way that the information can be clearly and fairly presented. The Exchange may require that prominence be given to important information in such manner as it considers appropriate.

GENERAL DUTY OF DISCLOSURE

In addition to the detailed requirements of *The Listing Rules* and to any conditions which the Stock Exchange may impose in a particular case, the Financial Services Act 1986, s 146 imposes a general duty of disclosure in prospectuses and listing particulars.[103] Under this section, the prospectus or listing particulars must contain all such information as investors and their professional advisors would reasonably require and reasonably expect to find there, for the purpose of making an informed assessment of:

(a) the issuer's assets and liabilities, financial position, profits and losses and prospects; and
(b) the rights attached to the securities.

The onus imposed by this obligation is mitigated in four ways. First, by specifying reasonable requirements and reasonable expectations, the Financial Services Act 1986, s 146 appears to relate the obligation of disclosure to market practice. Second, it is only information which is actually within the knowledge of any person responsible for the prospectus or which it would be

[100] The significance of being a person responsible for the documents is that such a person may be held liable to compensate investors if the information proves to have been inaccurate or incomplete: see this chapter, at 599–601.

[101] S 144 (1)(b) and *The Listing Rules*, ch 5, para 5.6 (c).

[102] *The Listing Rules*, ch 5, para 5.7.

[103] This implements Listing Particulars Directive, art 4.

reasonable for him to obtain by making inquiries, which is required to be stated.[104] Third, the content of the information required in any particular case is to be judged by reference to the nature of the securities, the issuer and the likely purchasers. Less information may need to be included in a prospectus for an issue of specialist securities, such as eurosecurities which are typically invested in by professional investors, than in a prospectus relating to the flotation of a trading company and the admission of its ordinary shares to the Official List.[105] Fourth, regard may be had to the fact that certain information may reasonably be expected to be within the knowledge of those professional advisors whom likely purchasers may reasonably be expected to consult and to the fact that certain information may be otherwise publicly available.[106]

APPROVAL, PUBLICATION AND FILING OF PROSPECTUSES AND LISTING PARTICULARS

As the competent authority, the London Stock Exchange is required to approve the contents of prospectuses or sets of listing particulars before they are published.[107] The Financial Services Act 1986, s 144 (2) and (2A) implement this requirement into domestic law whilst *The Listing Rules* set out the details of the procedure governing the submission of draft documents to the Exchange for approval prior to publication. Where a prospectus or set of listing particulars is to be published by a new applicant, the document must usually be submitted in draft to the London Stock Exchange at least twenty clear business days before the intended publication date.[108] The Exchange will review the document and amended drafts may then need to be submitted before the Exchange issues its formal approval.[109] The final form of the prospectus or listing particulars must be filed with the Exchange no later than midday at least two business days prior to the consideration of the application for admission to listing, along with the application form and other relevant documents.[110]

Subject to an exception permitting circulation of draft documents for the organisation of a placing, underwriting and other marketing arrangements,[111] prospectuses and listing particulars must not be published, advertised or circulated until they have been formally approved by the Exchange and published as required by *The Listing Rules*.[112] 'Publication' under *The Listing Rules* means making the documents available at the Company Announcements Office of the Exchange, the issuer's registered office in the UK (if any) and at the offices of any paying agent of the issuer in the UK.[113] This publication must take place at least two business days prior to the expected date of the consideration of the application for admission to listing.[114]

[104] S 146 (2).
[105] S 146 (3)(a)–(b).
[106] S 146 (3)(c)–(d).
[107] Listing Particulars Directive, art 18.
[108] *The Listing Rules*, ch 5, paras 5.9–5.10.
[109] Ibid, ch 5, paras 5.11–5.12.
[110] Ibid, ch 7, para 7.5.
[111] Ibid, ch 8, para 8.3.
[112] Ibid, ch 8, paras 8.1–8.2.
[113] Ibid, ch 8, para 8.4.
[114] Ibid, ch 8, para 8.8. The timing requirement is subject to certain exceptions: ibid, ch 8, para 8.9.

On or before the date of publication of any prospectus or set of listing particulars, a copy must be delivered to the registrar of companies and the document must state that this has been done; failure to comply with this obligation is an offence by the issuer and any other person who is knowingly a party to the publication.[115] Filing with the registrar of companies is purely an administrative requirement and the registrar plays no part in vetting the information contained in the document, that function being performed by the Stock Exchange which has seen the document in draft form.

EXEMPTIONS, OMISSIONS AND ABBREVIATIONS

In particular circumstances, an issuer of securities or an applicant for listing may seek to deviate in whole or in part from the requirements relating to the publication of a prospectus or listing particulars. The responsibility for authorising any departure from the normal requirements lies with the London Stock Exchange, but it must act within the limits set by the Financial Services Act 1986, Pt IV. These statutory limits reflect and give effect to the requirements of the Public Offers Directive and the Listing Particulars Directive.

Exemption from the Requirement to Publish a Prospectus or Set of Listing Particulars

The Listing Rules provide that no prospectus or set of listing particulars need be produced in respect of an offer of shares to be admitted to listing which are of the same class as shares already listed and which would increase that class by less than 10 per cent.[116] This exemption for small offers is permitted by the Listing Particulars Directive, art 6 and the Public Offers directive, art 11.6. As permitted by the Listing Particulars Directive, *The Listing Rules* also remove the requirement to produce listing particulars in respect of certain other share issues by an issuer whose shares are already listed, including bonus issues and allotments of shares to employees.[117] There are no precisely equivalent exemptions from the requirement to produce a prospectus because the Public Offers Directive does not permit these. Accordingly, for any of these exemptions to apply, it must first be established that the issue is a not public offer for the first time so as to trigger a requirement for a prospectus. The Exchange may also exempt an issuer from the obligation to produce listing particulars in certain particular circumstances where its existing securities are being introduced to the Official List but there is no accompanying offer of new securities (public or otherwise), such as where the company is moving up from the Alternative Investment Market to the main market of the London Stock Exchange or where its securities are already listed in another Member State.[118]

[115] S 149.

[116] *The Listing Rules*, ch 5, paras 5.1 (e) and 5.27 (e).

[117] Ibid, ch 5, paras 5.27–5.30.

[118] Ibid, ch 5, paras 5.23A–5.25.

Omission of Information

The Stock Exchange can authorise the omission of information that would ordinarily be required to be included in a prospectus or listing particulars.[119] The Exchange can authorise the omission of information which would otherwise be required if it considers that:

(a) the information is of minor importance only and is not such as will influence assessment of the assets and liabilities, financial position, profits and losses and prospects of the issuer;
(b) disclosure would be contrary to the public interest;[120]
(c) disclosure would be seriously detrimental to the issuer and omission is not likely to mislead investors with regard to facts and circumstances, knowledge of which is essential for the assessment of the securities in question; or
(d) in relation to specialist debt securities such as eurobonds, disclosure is unnecessary for persons of the kind who may normally be expected to buy or deal in the securities.

These limits are set by the Financial Services Act 1986, s 148 which, in turn, gives effect to the Listing Particulars Directive, arts 7 and 10. As drafted, s 148 is potentially ambiguous in that it can be read as being applicable only to the information required in order to fulfil the general duty of disclosure and not, so far as it is different, the specific information required to be included under *The Listing Rules*, chs 5 and 6. However, the Listing Particulars Directive, arts 7 and 10 are clearer on this point and establish that in relation to information required by the directive (ie both the general duty of disclosure and, so far as they differ, the more specific requirements incorporated into *The Listing Rules*, chs 5 and 6) the Exchange may only authorise the omission of information on one of the four specified grounds. *The Listing Rules* specify the procedure to be adopted in seeking the Exchange's permission to omit information from a prospectus or set of listing particulars.[121]

Abbreviated Prospectuses

An abbreviated prospectus can be issued in circumstances where, in the preceding twelve months, the same issuer published in the UK a full prospectus in respect of different securities and that prospectus was approved by the Exchange in accordance with *The Listing Rules*. Subject to satisfying the general duty of disclosure imposed by the Financial Services Act 1986, s 146, an abbreviated prospectus need only contain information about the changes which have arisen since the date of publication of the full prospectus (and any supplementary prospectus[122]) and which are likely to influence the value of the securities. The abbreviated prospectus must be accompanied by the full prospectus (and any supplementary prospectus) or must include a reference

[119] S 156 (2).
[120] The Secretary of State or the Treasury may certify this to be the case: s 148 (3).
[121] See *The Listing Rules*, ch 5, paras 5.17–5.18 and 5.20–5.22 and ch 23, para 23.7.
[122] See this chapter, at 588.

to it.[123] This modification of the rules that are generally applicable is permitted by the Public Offers Directive, art 6. It is only applicable in relation to prospectuses because there is no equivalent provision in the Listing Particulars Directive.

SUPPLEMENTARY PROSPECTUSES AND LISTING PARTICULARS

If, at any time between the preparation of the prospectus or listing particulars and the commencement of dealings in the securities following their admission to the Official List, there is a significant change affecting any matter contained in the document or a significant new matter arises, mention of which would have been required if it had existed when the original document was prepared, a supplementary prospectus or set of listing particulars must be published.[124] For this purpose, information is significant if it would affect the making of an informed assessment of the company's financial position or of the rights attached to the securities. For the same reasons, second, and further, supplementary prospectuses or sets of listing particulars may be required.[125] The obligation to submit a supplementary prospectus or supplementary listing particulars is imposed on the issuer but does not arise until the issuer becomes aware of the circumstances giving rise to the need for it or is informed of this by a person responsible for the prospectus or, as the case may be, listing particulars; however, it is the duty of any responsible person to inform the issuer of any such circumstances of which he is aware.[126] The Financial Services Act 1986 does not deal with the question of whose knowledge is to be attributed to the issuer for the purposes of this section.

Supplementary prospectuses and supplementary sets of listing particulars must be approved by the Exchange before publication in the same way as the original documentation.[127] They must also be published in the same way as the main documentation,[128] and they must be filed with the registrar of companies.[129]

ADVERTISEMENTS AND OTHER DOCUMENTS RELATING TO SECURITIES WHICH ARE TO BE ADMITTED TO LISTING

The Financial Services Act 1986, s 57 is the general provision regulating the publication of investments advertisements in the UK. In broad terms, the regulatory structure is that investment advertisements (a term which is broadly defined[130]) must only be issued by, or with the approval of, persons who are authorised to conduct investment business in the UK. With a view to filtering out marketing material that contains inadequate or inaccurate information, the conduct of business rules under which authorised persons operate specify matters about which an authorised person must be satisfied before issuing, or

[123] *The Listing Rules*, ch 5, para 5.23, implementing the Public Offers Directive, art 6.
[124] S 147. [125] S 147 (4). [126] S 147 (3). [127] *The Listing Rules*, ch 8.
[128] Ibid, ch 8, para 8.20. [129] S 149. [130] S 57 (2) and s 207 (2).

approving the issue of, an investment advertisement. The Financial Services Act 1986, s 57 is subject to a number of exemptions. It does not apply to prospectuses, listing particulars and supplementary prospectuses and listing particulars.[131] Where these documents are subject to extensive pre-publication vetting by the London Stock Exchange, this avoids a duplication of regulation. Secondly, where a prospectus or set of listing particulars is to be published in connection with an application for listing, the Financial Services Act 1986, s 57 does not apply to the issue in the UK of any advertisement or other information of a kind specified by *The Listing Rules* if the Stock Exchange has approved the content of such document or has authorised its issue without such approval. This exemption allows an issuer to publicise an issue or listing of its securities. The documents that may make advantage of this exemption and the procedures governing their publication are specified in *The Listing Rules*.[132] They include mini-prospectuses[133] or summary particulars[134] that contain information derived from the main prospectus or listing particulars, and also formal notices announcing the publication of a prospectus or set of listing particulars[135] and press releases. Further exemptions to the Financial Services Act 1986, s 57 that may be relevant to aspects of the marketing of an initial public offer of securities are provided by statutory instrument.[136]

PUBLIC OFFERS OF UNLISTED SHARES

Where shares offered to the public for the first time in the UK are not to be admitted to the Official List of the London Stock Exchange, the regulatory regime is that contained in the Public Offers of Securities Regulations 1995. In broad terms the regime for unlisted shares under the Public Offers of Securities Regulations 1995 mirrors that for listed shares in the Financial Services Act 1986, Pt IV. Thus, a prospectus containing specified information about the issuer, the shares and the business of the issuer must be published in conjunction with the offer of the securities.[137] As well as providing the specific information stipulated in the Regulations, the prospectus must satisfy the general duty of disclosure.[138] Supplementary prospectuses may also be required.[139] Instead of substantially repeating itself, this chapter concentrates on areas of difference between the two regimes.

[131] S 58 (1)(d)(ii). This provision also exempts any other document, publication of which is required or sanctioned in accordance with *The Listing Rules*. This would cover information which a listed company is required to publish under the continuing obligations of *The Listing Rules* such as its reports and accounts.

[132] *The Listing Rules*, ch 8, paras 8.23–8.27.

[133] Ibid, ch 8, paras 8.12–8.13.

[134] Ibid, ch 5, paras 5.32–5.33.

[135] Ibid, ch 8, para 8.10.

[136] Financial Services Act 1986 (Investment Advertisements) (Exemptions) Order 1996 (SI 1996/1586) and Financial Services Act 1986 (Investment Advertisements) (Exemptions) (No 2) Order 1995 (SI 1995/1536). eg, arts 6 and 11 of the 1996 Order which, on certain conditions, permit the circulation of advertisements to employees and experts respectively.

[137] Reg 4.

[138] Regs 8 and 9.

[139] Reg 10.

ARE THE SHARES TO BE ADMITTED TO DEALINGS ON A FORMAL MARKET?

The Public Offers of Securities Regulations 1995 apply to all offers of securities,[140] including shares, for the first time in the UK other than those where the securities are to be admitted to listing. This means that the regulations apply where an issuer is raising capital in conjunction with the admission of its shares to the Alternative Investment Market as well as where the capital-raising exercise is to take place entirely outside the framework of a formal market. The application of the regulations is the same in either case, save that certain exemptions are only available in respect of offers of securities that are being admitted to dealings on a market. An issuer that is seeking admission to the Alternative Investment Market must comply with the rules of that market as well as with the Public Offers of Securities Regulations 1995. These rules are set out in *The Rules of the London Stock Exchange,* ch 16. One requirement is that issuers seeking admission to the AIM must produce a prospectus irrespective of whether it is an offer to the public for the purposes of the Public Offers of Securities Regulations 1995.[141]

MODIFICATION OF THE GENERAL DUTY OF DISCLOSURE

The information contained in a prospectus relating to an offer of unlisted securities must satisfy the general duty of disclosure.[142] In the listed regime, the duty of disclosure is subject to four qualifications,[143] but in this context the qualifications are more restricted. Here there is no express provision permitting regard to be had to the nature of the likely purchasers or to the fact that information may already be known to their professional advisers or is otherwise already publicly available as a result of disclosure in satisfaction of applicable continuing obligations. However, the duty of disclosure is still subject to a reasonableness limitation[144] and it is only information that is known, or which ought to be known, by the persons responsible for the prospectus that must be disclosed.[145] Regard may be had to the nature of the securities and of their issuer. [146]

EXEMPTIONS AND OMISSIONS

Exemption and Omissions for Securities Admitted to the AIM

The London Stock Exchange can authorise the making of an offer without a prospectus where the securities are of the same class as securities already

[140] Reg 3 defines in precise terms the investments to which the regulations apply.

[141] *The Rules of the London Stock Exchange,* ch 16, para 16.7. However, a prospectus is not required where the issuer is applying for admission for securities of a class that is already admitted to dealings where the issuer would not be required to produce a prospectus under the Regulations: *The Rules of the London Stock Exchange,* ch 16, para 16.9.

[142] Reg 9.

[143] See this chapter, at 584–5.

[144] Reg 9 (1).

[145] Reg 9 (2).

[146] Reg 9 (3).

admitted to dealings on the AIM and would increase the class by less than 10 per cent.[147] This is subject to the proviso that up-to-date equivalent information must be available as a result of the disclosure requirements applicable to AIM companies.[148] Also, and subject to the same proviso, the Exchange may authorise the omission of information from a prospectus relating to a rights issue of securities that are to be admitted to the AIM.[149]

Offeror May Have Restricted Access to Information about the Issuer

In a public offer of unlisted securities the offeror may be acting without the consent or the active involvement of the company that is the issuer of the securities. This situation cannot arise in relation to securities which are to be admitted to listing, because listing is dependent on the consent of the issuer. An offeror of unlisted securities who is not acting in conjunction with the issuer may not have access to the detailed information about the issuer that would ordinarily be required to satisfy the duty of disclosure. For this reason it is provided that information whose inclusion would otherwise be required can be omitted from a prospectus where (a) the offeror is not the issuer, and is not acting in pursuance of an agreement with that issuer, (b) the information is not available to him because he is not the issuer, and (c) he has been unable, despite making such efforts (if any) as are reasonable, to obtain the information.[150]

Stock Exchange May Authorise Omissions

In its role as competent authority, the London Stock Exchange is authorised to permit the omission of information which would otherwise be required to be included in a prospectus on the ground that it is of minor importance only and not likely to influence assessment of the issuer's position and prospects, or that disclosure would be seriously detrimental to the issuer and its omission would not be likely to mislead investors.[151] The exemption applies to any offer of unlisted securities, whether admitted to dealings on the AIM or otherwise.

Abbreviated Prospectuses

A dispensation that is generally available is where an offer relates to a new issue of securities which is made within twelve months following the publication of a prospectus by the same offeror relating to a different class of its securities, or to an earlier issue of the same class of securities. In these circumstances the offeror may re-publish the original prospectus accompanied by a limited new prospectus which is restricted to the differences which have arisen since the publication of the main prospectus.[152]

[147] Reg 8 (5).

[148] Reg 8 (5)(b).

[149] Reg 8 (4) and *The Rules of the London Stock Exchange*, ch 16, para 16.10.

[150] Reg 11 (2).

[151] Reg 11 (3). The Treasury or the Secretary of State may also authorise the omission of information on the grounds that disclosure would be contrary to the national interest: reg 11 (1).

[152] Reg 8 (6).

NO VETTING OF INFORMATION PRIOR TO PUBLICATION

Although prospectuses relating to unlisted securities must be filed with the registrar of companies before they are published,[153] the unlisted regime does not provide for the systematic pre-publication vetting of the information contained in such prospectuses.[154] This gives rise to a particular difficulty for an offeror that wants to take advantage of mutual recognition arrangements between the states of the European Union, under which a prospectus (or set of listing particulars) which has been prepared in accordance with the requirements of one Member State may then, once translated and adjusted in certain minor respects, be deemed also to satisfy the requirements of other such States, because such arrangements depend on the prospectus having been 'vetted' in its home state. To enable advantage to be taken of the mutual recognition provisions, the Financial Services Act 1986, s 156A authorises the London Stock Exchange to approve prospectuses where there is no application for listing. The Exchange will perform this service for a fee where an application is made in accordance with the relevant requirements of *The Listing Rules*.[155]

ADVERTISEMENTS RELATING TO OFFERS OF UNLISTED SECURITIES

Prospectuses and supplementary prospectuses that comply with the requirements of the Public Offers of Securities Regulations 1995 are exempt from the Financial Services Act 1986, s 57.[156] The same exemption also applies to other advertisements which relate to a prospectus or supplementary prospectus and which contain only bare details of the offer.

An offer of unlisted securities that is not a public offer for the purposes of the Public Offers of Securities Regulations 1995 does not trigger the requirement under those regulations to produce a prospectus.[157] Advertisements relating to such offers are regulated by the Financial Services Act 1986, s 57 and will therefore need to be published by or with the approval of an authorised person unless an exemption applies.[158]

[153] Reg 4.

[154] Professor Gower's *Review of Investor Protection* Cmnd 9125 (1984) paras 9.16–9.24 was critical of the absence of pre-vetting and recommended that the Stock Exchange should undertake this role for unlisted as well as listed issues.

[155] 'Rules for Approval of Prospectuses Where No Application for Listing is Made' annexed to *The Listing Rules.* Mutally recognised prospectuses are used infrequently in practice: *Public Offers of Securities: A Consultative Document* (HM Treasury) (1998) paras 5.1–5.29. With a view to encouraging greater use, UK requirements for the translation of foreign language prospectuses into English and the inclusion and additional information on tax treatment for UK holders of the securities have been repealed: Public Offers of Securities (Amendment) Regulations 1999, reg 2 (2).

[156] Financial Services Act 1986 (Investment Advertisements) (Exemptions) (No 2) Order 1995 (SI 1995/1536), art 14.

[157] But if the securities are to admitted to the AIM a prospectus will be required under the rules of that market: see this chapter, at 590.

[158] The possible exemptions are contained in the Financial Services Act 1986 (Investment Advertisements) (Exemptions) Order 1996 (SI 1996/1586) and the Financial Services Act 1986

CIVIL LIABILITY FOR DEFECTIVE PROSPECTUSES AND LISTING PARTICULARS: RESCISSION OF CONTRACTS

An investor who is induced[159] to acquire securities on the basis of factual information which later turns out to have been false or misleading can seek rescission of the contract by which he acquired the securities. The statement complained of must have been a statement of fact not of law, intention or opinion, but a prospectus which states that it is the company's intention to do something which it has, in fact, no intention of doing contains a false statement of fact.[160] Silence in itself is not actionable as a general rule, but a claim may lie if the effect of an omission is to render what is said false or misleading.[161] In cases on the prospectus requirements of older companies legislation, it was held that failure to comply with the mandatory disclosure requirements relating to prospectuses did not entitle an investor to rescind a contract to take shares.[162] These cases still appear to represent the law. Under the modern law, as discussed later in this chapter,[163] the omission of required information can trigger a claim for statutory compensation, but the statute does not refer to the remedy of rescission,[164] and thus the rule that silence is not actionable unless it makes what is stated inaccurate or untrue should continue to apply. An ambiguous statement may be actionable but it is for the claimant to prove that he interpreted the words in their false sense and was thereby induced to take the securities.[165]

The person claiming rescission must be within the class of persons to whom the false statement was addressed.[166] Where shares are offered to the public generally, this requirement should be easily satisfied since everyone is within the category of addressee. However, a person who was unaware of the false statement or who did not rely on it cannot claim that he was induced to

(Investment Advertisements) (Exemptions) (No 2) Order 1995 (SI 1995/1536). On the conduct of business rules applicable to authorised persons approving investment advertisements see, eg, SFA Rulebook, Ch 5, Conduct of Business Rules, rs 5–9 and 5–10.

[159] The false statement need not be the sole inducement: *Re Royal British Bank, Nicol's Case* (1859) 3 De G & J 387. If a statement would have influenced a reasonable person in deciding to acquire the securities, the court will readily infer that the plaintiff was induced: *Smith v Chadwick* (1883) 9 App Cas 187, HL, 196 *per* Lord Blackburn. See further, Beatson, J, *Anson's Law of Contract* (27th edn, 1998) 238, n 37, but note *Downs v Chappell* [1997] 1 WLR 426, CA, 433 where Hobhouse LJ said that requirements of actionability in respect of a false statement included materiality, ie that, on an objective test, the natural and probable result of the statement would be to induce the representee to act on the faith of it in the way in which he did in fact act.

[160] *Edgington v Fitzmaurice* (1885) 29 Ch D 459, CA.

[161] *Derry v Peek* (1889) 14 App Cas 337, HL. See also *R v Kylsant* [1932] 1 KB 442, CCA.

[162] *Re Wimbledon Olympia Ltd* [1910] 1 Ch 630; *Re South of England Natural Gas and Petroleum Co Ltd* [1911] 1 Ch 573. In *Re Wimbledon Olympia Ltd* at 632 Neville J said: 'I cannot attribute to the Legislature the intention that the mere fact of the omission of any of the facts required by this section to be stated should give the shareholders the right to get rid of their shares.'

[163] See below, at 602–3.

[164] Save in one specific context: s 154 (5) discussed in this chapter below, at 601–2.

[165] *Smith v Chadwick* (1883) 9 App Cas 187, HL.

[166] *Peek v Gurney* (1873) LR 6 HL 377; *Al Nakib Investments (Jersey) Ltd v Longcroft* [1990] 3 All ER 321, [1990] 1 WLR 1390.

acquire the shares by reason of it.[167] Identifying the class of person to whom the statement was addressed is more problematic where the offer is directed to particular investors as, for example, in a rights issue where the offer is to the company's existing shareholders. In a typically structured rights issue, the company's offer of new securities to its existing shareholders is in a form whereby it can be renounced by those shareholders in favour of other investors. A sensible interpretation of this structure is that the offer, and the documentation supporting it, is addressed to existing shareholders and to persons in whose favour they renounce their entitlements, although there is no clear modern authority in support of this view.[168]

Rescission involves unwinding the contract and putting the parties back into their pre-contractual position. Its great advantage from an investor's perspective is that it enables the investor to recover all of the money that he paid for the shares.[169] The investor does not need to become embroiled in the complications that can arise in relation to the assessment of compensation for deceit, misrepresentation or negligence.[170] The operation of rescission in relation to modern securities markets has not produced much case law, but whether this is because the remedy is little used or rarely leads to argument when it is invoked is hard to tell.[171] Older cases suggest that the remedy of rescission may have limited practical significance in this context. As a general rule, a party seeking rescission must act promptly after the discovery of the fraud or misrepresentation and the need for swift action is particularly emphasised in nineteenth-century cases concerning contracts to take shares.

> Where a person has contracted to take shares in a company and his name has been placed on the register, it has always been held that he must exercise his right of repudiation with extreme promptness after the discovery of the fraud or misrepresentation.[172]

> If a man claims to rescind his contract to take shares in a company on the ground that he has been induced to enter into it by misrepresentation he must rescind it as soon as he learns the facts, or else he forfeits all claims to relief.[173]

> The delay of a fortnight in repudiating shares makes it to my mind doubtful whether the repudiation in the case of a going concern would have been in time. No doubt where investigation is necessary some time must be allowed[174] . . . But where, as in the

[167] *Smith v Chadwick* (1881) 9 App Cas 187, HL.

[168] The situation described in the text is different from that considered in the cases such as the *Al Nakib* decision where an investor who acquired shares in the market could not base a claim on false statements contained in a prospectus issued in connection with an offer of new shares. See further, Pennington, RR, *Company Law* (7th edn, 1995) 332–5.

[169] *Re Scottish Petroleum Co* (1883) 23 Ch D 413, CA. The investor may also recover interest: *Karberg's Case* [1892] 3 Ch 1, CA.

[170] Discussed in this chapter, at 596–604.

[171] *Smith New Court Securities Ltd v Scrimgeour Vickers (Asset Management) Ltd* [1997] AC 254, HL, 262 *per* Lord Browne-Wilkinson.

[172] *Aaron's Reefs v Twiss* [1896] AC 273, HL, 294 *per* Lord Davey.

[173] *Sharpley v Louth and East Coast Railway* (1876) 2 Ch D 663, CA, 685 *per* James LJ.

[174] As in *Central Railway Co of Veneuela v Kisch* (1867) LR 2 HL 99, HL (where two months was allowed).

present case, the shareholder is at once fully informed of the circumstances he ought to lose no time in repudiating.[175]

If, after learning that he is entitled to reject the shares, the investor does anything which amounts to accepting that he owns the shares, this will bar his right to rescind. The following acts have been held to have this effect: trying to sell the shares;[176] attending company meetings;[177] and signing proxies, paying calls or accepting dividends.[178] There are conflicting authorities on whether it is possible to rescind if some of the shares originally acquired have since been sold.[179] Since shares are fungible securities, it is doubtful in principle whether disposal of part of the original holding should bar rescission: the investor can always go into the market to buy substitute shares and in that way put himself into a position to give back the full portion of what he acquired in return for his money back.[180] If the acquirer of the shares has used them as security for its own borrowings, or third parties have otherwise acquired an interest in them, this may also bar rescission unless those rights can be unwound or arguments based on fungability are accepted. Rescission cannot be sought against a company that has gone into liquidation because, at that point, the rights of the creditors of the company intervene.[181] This bar applies even though the company which is in liquidation may be solvent.[182]

The cases referred to in the previous paragraph involved offers of shares for subscription by companies. They establish that the investor must notify the company that the shares are repudiated and take steps to have his name removed from the register[183] or some other equivalent action.[184] What if the shares are offered for sale by an investment bank acting on behalf of an issuer? The investor must first establish that there is an actionable misrepresentation

[175] *Re Scottish Petroleum Co* (1883) 23 Ch D 413, CA, 434 *per* Baggallay LJ.

[176] *Ex parte Briggs* (1866) LR 1 Eq 483.

[177] *Sharpley v Louth and East Coast Railway* (1876) 2 Ch D 663.

[178] *Scholey v Central Railway of Venezuela* (1869) LR 9 Eq 266n.

[179] *Re Metropolitan Coal Consumers' Assn Ltd* (1890) 6 TLR 416 (no rescission if part sold); *Re Mount Morgan (West) Gold Mines Ltd* (1887) 3 TLR 556 (rescission still possible despite sale of part).

[180] *Smith New Court Securities Ltd v Scrimgeour Vickers (Asset Management) Ltd* [1997] AC 254, HL, 262 *per* Lord Browne-Wilkinson.

[181] *Tennent v City of Glasgow Bank* (1879) 4 App Cas 615, HL; *Oakes v Turquand* LR 2 HL 325, HL. The investor must have repudiated the shares and taken active steps to be relieved of them (or reached some agreement with the company whereby that particular investor is dispensed from having to take active steps (eg where another investor has taken action and the result of that case will determine whether other claims stand or fall)) before the commencement of the winding up: *Re Scottish Petroleum Co* (1883) 23 Ch D 413, CA, 433–4 *per* Baggallay LJ.

[182] *Re Hull and County Bank, Burgess's Case* (1880) 15 Ch D 507.

[183] *Re Scottish Petroleum Co* (1883) 23 Ch D 413 CA. The company may agree to rectify the register (as in *Re London and Mediterranean Bank* (1871–72) 7 LR Ch App 55) but if the company disputes the claim, the investor may apply to court for rectification under Companies Act 1985, s 359. It has been said that a court order should normally be obtained: *Re Derham and Allen Ltd* [1946] 1 Ch 31, 36 *per* Cohen J.

[184] *Re General Railway Syndicate* [1900] 1 Ch 365, CA (the investor, when sued for unpaid calls, filed a counter-claim for rescission; this was held to be sufficient). Contrast *First National Reinsurance Co v Greenfield* [1921] 2 KB 260 where the defendant claimed, as a defence to an action for unpaid calls, that he was entitled to rescission but he did not, because it fell outside the jurisdiction of the court, claim rescission or rectification; his action was held to be insufficient and he was therefore liable for the calls.

of fact for which the investment bank is responsible and must then give notice to the bank of its intention to repudiate the shares.[185] If the bank does not accept the claim, the investor may seek an order for rescission from the court. The investor may have been registered by the company as the owner of the shares but this does not preclude rescission[186] and the investor can seek to have the register rectified. The Companies Act 1985, s 359 provides a summary mode of rectifying the register in any circumstances where the name of a person is, without sufficient cause, entered in the company's register of members. This power, which is discretionary,[187] is a general one and it can be exercised in circumstances where shares have been improperly transferred as well as in cases of improper allotments.[188] However, the summary procedure under the Companies Act 1985, s 359 should not be used in complicated cases, such as where the investor's right to seek rectification is disputed.[189] The bars to rescission of a contract to purchase shares from an investment bank should, on general principles, be the same as those that apply to a contract to subscribe shares and would thus include failing promptly to take steps to rescind once the false statement has been discovered or, in those circumstances, acting in a way which amounts to affirmation of the contract. If an investor successfully rescinds its contract with the investment bank, the investment bank may then seek in turn to rescind the original allotment of the securities from the company or to recover financial compensation from the company under their contractual agreement or by virtue of the remedies which are generally available.

CIVIL LIABILITY FOR DEFECTIVE PROSPECTUSES AND LISTING PARTICULARS: COMPENSATION CLAIMS

An investor who has acquired shares on the basis of a false prospectus may seek financial compensation in addition to, or instead of rescission. Anyone who is induced to enter into a contract by false statements that were addressed to him can sue the maker of those statements in tort for deceit. If there is a contractual relationship between the maker of the statements and the person seeking compensation, the innocent party may be able to seek compensation under the Misrepresentation Act 1967 and may also have a

[185] Giving notice of the intention to rescind to the other contracting party is a general requirement although it may be waived in unusual circumstances: *Car and Universal Finance Co Ltd v Caldwell* [1965] 1 QB 525, CA.

[186] See, eg, *Cory v Cory* [1923] 1 Ch 90 where the possibility of the register being rectified where a transfer which has been registered has been shown to have been induced by fraud or misrepresentation was in issue, although the judgment related only to procedural questions concerning discovery against the company.

[187] Companies Act 1985, s 359 (2); *Re Piccadilly Radio plc* [1989] BCLC 683.

[188] *Re London, Hamburgh and Continental Exchange Bank, Ward and Henry's Case* (1867) 2 Ch App 431; *Ex parte Shaw, Re Diamond Rock Boring Co* (1877) 2 QBD 463, CA; *Re Tahiti Cotton Co, ex parte Sargent* (1874) 17 Eq 273.

[189] *Reese River Co v Smith* (1869) LR 4 HL 64, HL, 80 *per* Lord Cairns; *Re Greater Britain Products Development Corpn Ltd* (1924) 40 TLR 488; *Re Hoicrest Ltd* [1998] 2 BCLC 175.

claim for breach of contract. Another possible claim is for the investor to allege that the maker of the statements is in breach of a duty of care and is liable to pay damages under the tort of negligence. These remedies are generally available and they are not unique to securities transactions. Under the Financial Services Act 1986, Pt IV (in relation to listed securities) and the Public Offers of Securities Regulations 1995 (in relation to unlisted securities) there is a further statutory claim for compensation, available only in respect of transactions regulated by those provisions. The following text concentrates on this statutory remedy because, as is explained in the text, when it is compared to the general remedies for deceit, misrepresentation or breach of duty of care, it is usually the remedy that is likely to produce the most favourable result for the investor.

Class of Persons Who Can Claim Compensation

The statutory remedy contained in the Financial Services Act 1986, s 150 (for listed securities) and the Public Offers of Securities Regulation 1995, reg 14 (for unlisted securities) allows an investor who has acquired securities and suffered loss in respect of them as a result of an untrue or misleading statement contained in the prospectus or listing particulars relating to those securities, or as a result of an omission of information required to be contained in that document, to claim compensation. It is generally accepted that claimants under the Financial Services Act 1986, s 150 may be the initial subscribers (or initial purchasers in the case of an offer structured as an offer for sale) of the securities or subsequent purchasers in the market provided, and to the extent that, they can show that their loss results from the inaccuracies in, or omissions from, the prospectus or listing particulars. There is no precise point beyond which market purchasers of shares cannot claim, but as time goes on it will become increasingly difficult to argue convincingly that the price at which the shares are trading in the market is still distorted by the false information contained in a prospectus and a claim may fail on that ground.[190] The Public Offers of Securities Regulation 1995, reg 14 does not track the wording of s 150 exactly and it has been judicially suggested that claims under that provision may be limited to initial subscribers or purchasers.[191] That comment seems to be unduly restrictive: it is not clear that the different words used in the two provisions were intended to achieve a different result, nor is it easy to see why in principle the result should be different depending on whether the securities in question are listed or unlisted.

In allowing claims by persons other than initial subscribers or purchasers, the statutory remedy under the Financial Services Act 1986, Pt IV and the Public Offers of Securities Regulations 1995 compares favourably to the remedies generally available. In an action based on deceit, the plaintiff must show that the false statement was made with the intention that it should be acted on by the plaintiff or by a class of persons of whom the plaintiff is a member. A

[190] See this chapter, at 601 and Ch 2, at 64–5.
[191] *Possfund Custodian Trustee Ltd v Diamond* [1996] 2 All ER 774.

deceit claim brought by a market purchaser of shares in respect of which a false prospectus had been issued failed on this ground because the House of Lords held that the purpose of the prospectus had been exhausted when the initial allotment was complete.[192] It is for the investor to establish that the purpose for which a prospectus was issued was to induce purchasers in the market to acquire the shares as well as initial subscribers.[193] A claim for compensation under the Misrepresentation Act 1967 depends on there being a contractual nexus between the parties and is thus limited to those who acquire the shares initially either by way of allotment from the company or who purchase from the investment bank which has offered them to the public.[194] In a claim based on breach of duty of care the claimant must establish that the maker of the statement owed him a duty of care and that maker was in breach of that duty. In the leading case of *Caparo Industries Ltd v Dickman*[195] the House of Lords held that for such a duty to arise, the following must be established: (a) foreseeability of damage to the plaintiff; (b) a relationship of proximity between the plaintiff and the defendant; and (c) that the situation is one in which it is fair, just and reasonable to impose a duty of care. The concept of 'proximity' is not one that is precisely defined: in the words of Lord Oliver of Aylmerton in the *Caparo* decision,[196] 'it is no more than a label which embraces not a definable concept but merely a description of circumstances from which, pragmatically, the courts conclude that a duty of care exists'. As such, it can overlap with, and shade into, the third criterion which explicitly acknowledges that the existence or otherwise of a duty of care is not a matter of scientific deduction and can be affected by policy considerations as perceived by the courts. The English courts are generally reluctant to impose a duty of care on the maker of statements to persons who rely on those statements and suffer economic loss. One consideration which the court regards as important in limiting the duty of care in these circumstances is the 'floodgates' argument: it is said that if the maker of a statement put into general circulation were to be held to owe a duty of care to everyone who relied on it, this would open up 'liability in an indeterminate amount for an indeterminate time to an indeterminate class'.[197] Another argument against the imposition of a duty of care is that persons who are concerned about the accuracy of statements on which they seek to rely should protect themselves by obtaining contractual warranties from the maker or by taking out insurance, and that it is beyond the proper ambit of the law of negligence to provide a claim in such circumstances.

It has been judicially stated that a relationship of proximity would typically be held to exist where:

192 *Peek v Gurney* (1873) LR 6 HL 377, HL.

193 *Andrews v Mockford* [1896] 1 QB 372, CA; *Peek v Gurney* (1873) LR 6 HL 377, HL, 412–13 *per* Lord Cairns.

194 Under Misrepresentation Act 1967, s 2 (1), a claim lies 'where a person has entered into a contract after a misrepresentation has been made to him by another party thereto and as a result thereof he has suffered loss . . .'; the claim is against the other party. Under Misrepresentation Act 1967, s 2 (2), the court may in its discretion order damages in lieu of rescission of the contract between the parties.

195 [1990] 2 AC 605, HL.

196 Ibid at 633.

197 *Ultramares Corpn v Touche* (1931) 174 NE 441, 444 *per* Cardozo CJ.

(a) the advice is required for a purpose, whether particularly specified or generally described, which is made known, either actually or inferentially, to the adviser at the time when the advice is given;
(b) the adviser knows, either actually or inferentially, that his advice will be communicated to the advisee, either specifically or as a member of an ascertainable class, in order that it should be used by the advisee for that purpose;
(c) it is known either actually or inferentially, that the advice so communicated is likely to be acted upon by the advisee for that purpose without independent inquiry, and
(d) it is so acted upon by the advisee to his detriment.[198]

The reference to the purpose of the advice echoes the requirement in claims based on deceit that the plaintiff should be a member of the class intended by the maker to be induced to act on the basis of the false statement. As in that context, this requirement can have the effect of limiting the class of persons who can sue: in *Al-Nakib Investments (Jersey) Ltd v Longcroft*[199] Mervyn Davies J struck out a claim based on breach of duty of care in respect of statements in a prospectus relating to a rights issue which was brought by an investor who acquired shares in the market (the investor was in fact a shareholder in the company which took up its own allotment and then acquired further shares in the market) because the purpose of the prospectus was to do no more than to encourage shareholders to take up their rights. This is not to say that investors in the market who rely, for example, on statements in a prospectus relating to an offer for sale could never succeed in a claim based on a duty of care—indeed, in a case decided after the *Al Nakib* decision the court held that there was an arguable case for the existence of such a duty of care to purchasers in the market and that the issues merited full consideration at trial.[200] However, the onus is on the investor who is seeking compensation to establish that such a duty exists.

Persons Who Can Be Sued

The range of potential defendants also puts the claim under the Financial Services Act 1986, Pt IV and the Public Offers of Securities Regulations 1995 into a favourable light. In both cases there is a specific statutory list of persons who are the persons responsible for the prospectus and, as such, potentially liable to compensate investors.[201] The list of responsible persons covers the issuer of the securities, its directors, other persons who are identified in the prospectus or listing particulars as persons who have agreed to become directors of the issuer, persons who are stated in the documentation as accepting responsibility for it, persons who have authorised its contents and the offeror of the securities, where different from the issuer.[202] The existence of this list

[198] *Caparo Industries Ltd v Dickman* [1990] 2 AC 605, HL, 638 *per* Lord Oliver.
[199] [1990] 3 All ER 321, [1990] 1 WLR 1390.
[200] *Possfund Custodian Trustee Ltd v Diamond* [1996] 2 All ER 774.
[201] Ss 152 and 154A (listed issues); reg 13 (unlisted issues).
[202] In the unlisted regime (but not the listed) the directors of a corporate offeror which is not the issuer and which is not acting in conjunction with it are also responsible persons: reg 13 (1)(f). In either regime, directors of the offeror will become responsible persons if they authorise the contents of the prospectus or supplementary prospectus.

relieves an investor from having to show that statements are attributable to particular persons, although those who are responsible persons may be able to escape liability by establishing that they are covered by one or more of the statutory defences.[203] Whilst investors cannot recover compensation in respect of the same loss from more than one responsible person, the fact that a range of persons are clearly identified as being liable unless they can establish a defence may increase the chances of finding a sufficiently deep financial pocket to cover the amount of the claim. The statutory defences to liability include reasonable belief in the accuracy of the particulars or prospectus,[204] reasonable reliance on the competence of an expert[205] and the taking of reasonable steps to bring a correction to the attention of likely purchasers before the securities were acquired.[206] No liability is incurred in respect of an incorrect official statement which is included in a prospectus or in listing particulars provided that it has been reproduced accurately and fairly.[207] A responsible person may also avoid liability by establishing that the investor knew about the inaccuracy in the documentation.[208] A responsible person can avoid liability for a failure to ensure the production of a supplementary prospectus or set of listing particulars by establishing that he reasonably believed that no supplementary documentation was required.[209]

In a deceit claim or a claim based on breach of duty of care, the investor must sue those who are responsible for the making of the offending statement. In respect of a prospectus or set of listing particulars relating to listed securities it is a requirement of *The Listing Rules* that the directors of the issuing company should state expressly that they take responsibility for the information contained in the document.[210] There is a broadly equivalent requirement in relation to prospectuses for unlisted securities under the Public Offers of Securities Regulations 1995.[211] The specific effect of these responsibility statements on common-law liabilities is untested but the fact that these persons have vouched for the accuracy of the information suggests that they should be liable if it proves to have been wrong, even where the information was actually provided by someone else—for example, by the company's auditors or by an expert whose report has been included in the prospectus. If the directors acting within the scope of their authority are held liable for misstatements contained in a prospectus or set of listing particulars,

[203] These defences are contained in s 151 (listed issues) and reg 15 (unlisted issues).
[204] S 151 (1) (listed issues); reg 15 (1) (unlisted issues).
[205] S 151 (2) (listed issues); reg 15 (2) (unlisted issues).
[206] S 151 (3) (listed issues); reg 15 (3) (unlisted issues).
[207] S 151 (4) (listed issues); reg 15 (4) (unlisted issues).
[208] S 151 (5) (listed issues); reg 15 (5) (unlisted issues).
[209] S 151 (6) (listed issues); reg 15 (6) (unlisted issues).
[210] *The Listing Rules*, ch 5, paras 5.2–5.5. Where the document relates to securities issued in connection with a takeover, the directors of the issuer may limit their responsibility so as to exclude responsibility for information on the target company (provided responsibility for that information is taken by the target's directors): para 5.3 (b). The company itself, rather than its directors, is required to take responsibility for information in prospectuses relating to international securities such as eurobonds: *The Listing Rules*, ch 23, para 23.11 (a).
[211] Sch 1, pt III, para 10 (as amended by Public Offers of Securities Amendment Regulations 1999).

the company will also be vicariously liable.[212] It is also established in case law that a company which issues a prospectus is responsible for all statements contained in it,[213] whether it knows them to be true or false,[214] unless—and only to the extent that statutory provisions regulating exclusion clauses permit it to do so[215]—it expressly disclaims responsibility.

The claim under the Misrepresentation Act 1967 is against the other contracting party. Statements made by an agent of a contracting party are treated as statements by that party[216] but the agent is not personally liable.[217]

Elements of the Claim

Causation

The remedies under the Financial Services Act 1986, Pt IV and the Public Offers of Securities Regulations 1995 allow an investor to claim compensation for the distortion of the operation of the market through the provision of false information.[218] The investor must show that there is a causal link between the inaccurate prospectus and the loss suffered; this means that an investor must establish that the price at which he acquired the shares was a price which reflected the wrong information. However, there is no further requirement that the investor should have been specifically aware of the false information and have relied upon it in making an investment decision. In a deceit claim or a claim under the Misrepresentation Act 1967, the investor must show that he was induced to act by the false statement and if the evidence shows that the investor was unaware of the statement or took no notice of it the claim will not succeed.[219]

Where the False Statement is Made

The statutory claim under the Financial Services Act 1986, Pt IV and the Public Offers of Securities Regulations 1995 is only available in respect of false or misleading listing particulars or prospectuses. Where the offending statement is made in some other way, perhaps in advertising material accompanying the offer,[220] the investor must pursue alternative claims. In the listed regime, if the

[212] *New Zealand Guardian Trust Co v Brooks* [1995] BCC 407, PC; *Lynde v Anglo-Italian Hemp Co* [1896] 1 Ch 178, 183: the company is liable for misrepresentation where 'the directors of a company know when allotting that an application for shares is based on the statements contained in a prospectus, even though the prospectus was issued without authority or even before the company was formed, and even if its contents are not known to the directors'.

[213] *Lynde v Anglo-Italian Hemp Co* [1896] 1 Ch 178; *Mair v Rio Grande Rubber Estates* [1913] AC 853, HL.

[214] *Collins v Grayhound Racecourses* [1930] 1 Ch 1, CA.

[215] Misrepresentation Act 1967, s 3; Unfair Terms in Consumer Contracts Regulations 1994 (1994/3159). Unfair Contract Terms Act 1977 does not apply to securities contracts: sch 1, para 1 (e). Liability for fraud cannot be excluded: *S Pearson & Son v Dublin Corporation* [1907] AC 351, HL.

[216] *Gosling v Anderson* (1972) 223 EG 1743.

[217] *Resolute Maritime Inc v Nippon Kaiji Kyokai, The Skopas* [1983] 1 WLR 857.

[218] See further, Ch 2 above, at 64–5.

[219] *Smith v Chadwick* (1881) 9 App Cas 187, HL.

[220] Financial Services Act 1986, s 154 (listed issues) regulates the issue of advertisements in connection with a set of listing particulars or a prospectus. Also investment advertisements are generally regulated under Financial Services Act 1985, s 57.

London Stock Exchange has approved the contents of such an advertisement, or has authorised its issue without such approval, no civil liability (including rescission) will arise if that advertisement, taken together with the listing particulars or the prospectus, would not be likely to mislead persons of the kind likely to consider the acquisition of the securities in question.[221]

Investor's Knowledge of Falsehood

A claim brought by an investor who knows that the information contained in a prospectus or set of listing particulars is false is likely to fail irrespective of the particular remedy pursued. An investor who knows that information is false cannot claim to have been induced to act on it and a deceit or misrepresentation claim will fail for that reason.[222] Equally, in a case based on breach of the duty of care, an investor could not credibly claim that the mistaken advice caused the loss when he or she was actually aware of the mistake and proceeded anyway. Under the Financial Services Act 1986, Pt IV and the Public Offers of Securities Regulations 1995, it is a defence for a person who would otherwise be a responsible person under those regimes to show that the investor acquired the shares with knowledge of the inaccuracy in the prospectus or listing particulars.[223]

Knowledge of Falsehood by the Persons Responsible for the Statements

An investor bringing a claim under the securities legislation is not required to show that the responsible persons knew that the offending statements were wrong. Lack of such knowledge on the part of responsible persons is relevant only to the extent that this may provide the basis for a defence where they can establish that they believed on reasonable grounds that the information was true. There are some similarities in this respect with the claim for compensation under the Misrepresentation Act 1967. There the claimant is not required to prove negligence but the defendant can escape liability by establishing that he or she reasonably believed that the statements were true.[224] The mental element is important in an action for deceit where the plaintiff must establish that the maker of a statement knew that it was false, did not have an honest belief in its truth, or was reckless as to its veracity.[225] In a claim based on breach of duty of care, it is for the claimant to show that the maker of the statement failed to act with sufficient care.

Liability for Silence

The common-law rules regarding liability for silence or failure to warn are restrictive. Keeping quiet does not, as a general rule, amount to deceit and the law of tort does not readily impose a duty of care to warn others of potential

[221] Financial Services Act 1986, s 154 (5). See *The Listing Rules*, ch 8, paras 8.23–8.27 for the procedures governing the approval and authorisation of advertisements by the Exchange.

[222] But the investor is not required to make inquiries to verify the accuracy of information: *Aaron's Reefs Ltd v Twiss* [1896] AC 273, HL, 279 *per* Lord Halsbury LC.

[223] S 151 (5) and reg 5 (5).

[224] Misrepresentation Act 1967, s 2 (1). *Howard Marine & Dredging Co Ltd v A Ogden & Sons (Excavations) Ltd* [1978] QB 574, CA.

[225] *Derry v Peek* (1889) 14 App Cas 337, HL.

dangers.[226] Equally, unless silence has the effect of making what is said untrue, there is no claim for misrepresentation under the Misrepresentation Act 1967. Under the Financial Services Act 1986 and the Public Offers of Securities Regulations 1995, inadequate information can give rise to liability even if it does not render what is said inaccurate. The omission of information required in order to satisfy the general duty of disclosure is actionable[227] as is the failure to produce supplementary prospectuses or listing particulars when required. Also, where *The Listing Rules* (in the case of listed securities) or the Public Offers of Securities Regulations 1995 (in the case of unlisted securities) require a prospectus or set of listing particulars to include information on a particular matter on the basis that there must be a specific reference to that matter or, if such is the case, a statement that there is no such matter, failure to address the matter at all is treated as a statement that there is no such matter.[228] This has the effect of turning an omission into a positive statement that there is nothing to disclose, but it only applies to claims under these statutory regimes and it does not affect the general rule that silence is not actionable. An investor who brings a claim for compensation under the securities legislation arising from the omission of information must still establish that there is a causal link between that omission and the loss he has suffered in respect of the shares.

Amount of Compensation

The rules relating to the amount of damages that may be awarded to a successful plaintiff are more generous in deceit claims than those based on breach of duty of care, because the latter are subject to remoteness rules limiting liability only to foreseeable losses; by contrast, a person who can establish that he was deceived can claim all losses flowing directly from the wrong whether or not those losses were foreseeable.[229] The deceit rules have also been held to apply to claims under the Misrepresentation Act 1967.[230] The Financial Services Act 1986 and the Public Offers of Securities Regulations 1995 provide no explicit guidance on the basis upon which compensation is to be assessed under those provisions. Cases on old companies legislation provisions that provided for compensation for untrue prospectuses applied the deceit rules.[231] Whilst the different statutory context means that such cases

[226] *Smith v Littlewoods Organization Ltd* [1987] 2 AC 241, HL.

[227] S 150 (1) and (3) and reg 14 (1) and (3).

[228] S 150 (2) and reg 14 (2).

[229] *Doyle v Olby (Ironmongers) Ltd* [1969] 2 QB 158, CA.

[230] *Royscot Trust Ltd v Rogerson* [1991] 2 QB 297, CA . This extension of the deceit rules to circumstances where the defendant has not deliberately misled the plaintiff has been criticised: Hooley, RJA, 'Damages and the Misrepresentation Act 1967' (1991) 107 LQR 547. In *Smith New Court Securities Ltd v Scrimgeour Vickers (Asset Management) Ltd* [1997] AC 254, HL, 282–3 Lord Steyn noted that there was a question whether the loose wording of the Misrepresentation Act 1967 compelled the court so to extend the deceit rules, but he expressly refrained from giving a concluded view on the correctness of the *Royscot* decision. Lord Browne-Wilkinson was equally restrained (at 267).

[231] *Clark v Urquhart* [1930] AC 28, HL. Viscount Sumner (at 56) explained that the statutory action was intended to give the remedy which in *Derry v Peek* the House of Lords had limited to those who could prove deceit. See also Lord Tomlin (at 76): 'the effect of the section is to create a statutory tort having within the ambit prescribed by the section the same characteristics and

need to be treated with some caution, there is sufficient similarity between the modern statutory regimes and their predecessors in this respect to suggest that the court may continue to apply the deceit rules.

In *Smith New Court Securities Ltd v Scrimgeour Vickers (Asset Management) Ltd*[232] the House of Lords reviewed the rules governing the assessment of damages in tort for deceit. This case involved a sale and purchase of shares that had been induced by deliberate misstatement. The House of Lords rejected a simple, but inflexible, rule to the effect that the plaintiff's basic measure of damages was the difference between the price paid for the shares and the market price that the shares would have had on that date if the market had not been distorted by the false information as being both wrong in principle and liable to produce manifest injustice. The overriding principle was that the victim of the tort was entitled to be compensated for all actual loss flowing directly from the transaction induced by the wrongdoer. In some circumstances, the difference between the price paid for property and the market price that it would have had on the date of the transaction but for the tort might be the appropriate measure of this loss, but in others a different measure, such as the difference between the price paid for the property and the price at which it was later disposed of, might be required in order to give the plaintiff full compensation in accordance with the general principle.

In ordinary circumstances,[233] an issue that is likely to concern an investor is whether he can recover for the decline in the value of the shares that reflect movements in the market generally after the acquisition as well as for the loss resulting from the distortion to the share price because of the misstatements. An inflexible date of transaction rule would preclude recovery for losses resulting from post-acquisition market movements, but under the more flexible approach adopted in the *Smith New Court* decision they are potentially recoverable. However, to succeed in this claim, the investor must still show that the defendant's misstatements caused the loss. Establishing legal causation is a complex issue of which it has been said that: 'no satisfactory theory capable of solving the infinite variety of practical problems has been found'.[234] Practical causation problems in the context of securities transactions are that an investor might not have paid the price that he did but for the misleading statement, but he might still have bought the shares for a lower price or he might have invested his money in other shares that would also have been affected by general movements in market prices. Pragmatic or common-sense solutions to practical problems such as these need to ensure that an investor does not recover for losses that he would have incurred in any event as a result of investment decisions that were entirely unaffected by the false or misleading information.[235]

consequence as the corresponding common law tort based on misrepresentation except that the complainant is relieved of the necessity of alleging and proving fraud'.

232 [1997] AC 254, HL.

233 Those in *Smith New Court Securities Ltd v Scrimgeour Vickers (Asset Management) Ltd* [1997] AC 254, HL were somewhat unusual.

234 *Smith New Court Securities Ltd v Scrimgeour Vickers (Asset Management) Ltd* [1997] AC 254, HL, 284–5 *per* Lord Steyn.

235 On how causation principles can affect the assessment of damages, see also *South*

CRIMINAL LIABILITY FOR DEFECTIVE PROSPECTUSES AND LISTING PARTICULARS

It is an offence under the Financial Services Act 1986, s 47 to make misleading statements with a view to inducing another person to enter into an acquisition agreement such as an agreement to acquire shares. This widely drafted section[236] applies to false, misleading or deceptive promises and forecasts as well as to misstatements of fact. The maker must know that what he is saying is untrue or must be reckless about this. He must act for the purpose of inducing the other party to enter into the investment agreement or must be reckless as to whether it may have this effect. Dishonest concealment of material facts for the purpose of inducing an investment agreement, or where the person effecting the concealment is reckless as to whether it may induce an investment agreement, is an offence under this section. A person who is found guilty under this section is liable to a maximum penalty of seven-years' imprisonment plus a fine.[237] The Financial Services Act 1986, s 47 is a general anti-fraud measure but its application in relation to public offers of securities is illustrated by *R v Feld*[238] where the Court of Appeal upheld a six-year sentence for breach in relation to a rights issue circular. The prospectus relating to the rights issue had contained serious misinformation overstating profits and understating liabilities. The figures had been supported by forged documents supplied to the company's auditors by its managing director, Feld. The company had raised over £20 million by the rights issue but went into insolvent liquidation the following year. In upholding the length of the conviction the court emphasised the vital importance of maintaining the confidence of the City and financial institutions in the veracity of information contained in prospectuses and similar documents.

Australian Asset Management Corpn v York Montague Ltd [1997] AC 191, HL, 214 *per* Lord Hoffmann.

[236] There are also other specific offences that may be committed in particular circumstances: eg, Theft Act 1968, s 19 which makes it an offence for an officer (or a person purporting to act as an officer) of a body corporate or unincorporated association with intent to deceive its members or creditors about its affairs, to publish or concur in the publication of a written statement or account which to his knowledge is, or may be, misleading, false or deceptive in a material particular.

[237] S 47 (6).

[238] 6 April 1998, CCA.

18

Rights Issues and Other Issues of Equity Securities

MANDATORY PRE-EMPTION RIGHTS

There are many reasons why an established company may find itself in a position where it requires additional share capital, such as to reduce its debt–equity ratio or to fund acquisition or development plans.[1] Traditionally English law and practice has favoured the rights issue method of raising additional capital through secondary offers,[2] although this has caused some tension between institutional investors, who tend to favour rights issues, and companies, which may prefer to have greater flexibility in the methods of raising capital which are open to them. Developments in recent years have enabled companies to use methods other than rights issues in certain circumstances and subject to particular limitations. In favouring rights issues as the means of raising equity capital, England is consistent with Continental[3] jurisdictions: pre-emptive rights whereby existing shareholders have the right to be offered a percentage of any new issue of shares which is equal to their existing percentage shareholdings are now enshrined in the European Union's programme of company law directives which Member States are obliged to incorporate into their domestic law. In the United States, by contrast, corporations enjoy much greater freedom in this respect: pre-emption rights are rare in the case of public corporations although they can exist in some close (private) corporations.[4]

The broad position under the Companies Act 1985, s 89 is that existing shareholders have pre-emption rights. For companies that are listed on the London Stock Exchange, this statutory requirement is reinforced by *The Listing Rules* which impose a continuing obligation on listed companies to raise additional capital by means of a rights issue. The Companies Act 1985, s 89 and the continuing obligation under *The Listing Rules* can be displaced

[1] Rawlinson, M, 'Rights Issues' (1991) 2 (5) PLC 17. On the use of a rights issue to restore a company in administration to solvency: Gregory, D, and Horton, C, 'Surviving Administration' (1993) 4 (8) PLC 15. For notes on transactions involving rights issues for other purposes (such as financing a bid, funding a dividend, transferring ownership of a football club) see Millerchip, CJ, '3i Offer: Pre-Sale Dividend Reduced Tax Charge' (1994) 5 (7) PLC 5; Godden, R, 'Financing Takeovers' (1995) 6 (8) PLC 37.

[2] As distinct from initial public offers: Ross, SA, Westerfield, RW, and Jordan, BR, *Fundamentals of Corporate Finance* (4th edn, 1998) 436 where the alternative term 'seasoned equity offering' is also noted.

[3] Xuereb, PG, 'Corporate Management and the Statutory Right of Pre-emption: A Comparative Review' (1988) 37 ICLQ 397.

[4] Clark, RC, *Corporate Law* (1986) 719; Klein, WA, and Coffee, JC, *Business Organization and Finance* (5th edn, 1993) 220.

for a limited time by special resolution of the shareholders in general meeting. Also the articles of a private company may exclude the statutory pre-emption rights in their entirety.[5] These requirements of the Companies Act 1985 and *The Listing Rules* and the extent to which they can be relaxed by shareholder resolutions or provisions in articles of association are examined closely later in this chapter but it may be helpful first to consider why pre-emption rights are afforded legal protection and to identify why investors may be loath to give up these rights.

Shareholders' Ownership Should Not Be Diluted Without Their Consent

The first argument in favour of legally protected pre-emption rights is based on the idea of the shareholders' ownership rights: their proportionate share of the ownership of the company should not be diluted without their consent.[6] Pre-emption rights give existing shareholders the opportunity to retain their proportionate share in the company's share capital and hence to prevent a watering down of their ability to control the company through the exercise of voting rights attaching to their shares. As is discussed elsewhere in this book, the law traditionally regards the shareholders as being the owners of their company, although whether the concept of ownership accurately captures the nature of the relationship between a company and its shareholders is open to debate.[7] It is not the intention here to re-open the discussion of the implications for fundamental aspects of company law that could result from a shift away from the shareholder-ownership model of the corporate structure. Instead, a narrower argument against the anti-dilutive justification for mandatory pre-emption may be noted: this is that it is sometimes argued that, to the extent that investors are concerned about holding an investment in a certain proportion of the share capital, they can always acquire shares in the market to maintain their holding.[8]

Curbing Unconstitutional Behaviour by Directors or Controllers

A second argument in favour of pre-emption rights is that they curb unconstitutional behaviour by the directors of a company which is the target of a takeover bid, because they prevent the management from facilitating or blocking the bid by, as appropriate, issuing shares to a favoured bidder or to shareholders opposed to the bid. The counter-argument here is that directors are subject to fiduciary duties to act in the interests of the company and to use their powers for proper purposes. As a number of cases clearly demonstrate, even though the directors may be acting in what they consider to be the interests of the company, it is an improper and unconstitutional use of power to

[5] S 91.
[6] *ABI/NAPF Joint Position Paper on Pre-emption, Cost of Capital and Underwriting* (July 1996) para 1.1.
[7] See Ch 4 above, at 131–3.
[8] 'Pre-emption Rights' (1987) 27 *Bank of England Quarterly Bulletin* 545, 547.

issue shares so as to influence the outcome of a bid.[9] The issue for debate is whether fiduciary duties, supplemented by the requirements of the Takeover Code, amount to an adequate constraint on the perceived abuse or whether it is necessary in addition for there to be specific control in the form of pre-emption rights.

Whilst manipulation of the outcome of a takeover bid is more of an issue for public companies than for private companies, analogous arguments about the maintenance and dilution of control can arise in private company contexts. It can be argued that, but for the requirement to honour pre-emption rights, one faction could seek to dilute the power of another group by excluding them from the opportunity to participate in a new share issue. Again, the existence of alternative control in the form of fiduciary duties is relevant. Also, if the controlling faction of a company were to behave in that way, their conduct could form the basis of a petition under the Companies Act 1985, s 459 for relief from unfairly prejudicial conduct. In *Re DR Chemicals Ltd*[10] the controllers of a small private company which had three shareholders secretly and in breach of the pre-emption requirements of the companies legislation allotted new shares to one of themselves so as to increase the allottee holding from 60 per cent to 96.1 per cent and to reduce the petitioner's interest from 40 per cent to 4 per cent. The allotment was held to constitute unfairly prejudicial conduct.

Observance of the requirement to offer new shares first to existing shareholders is not necessarily a guarantee against abuse because in circumstances where it is known that the petitioner does not have the funds to take up the offer the controllers of a company could go through the motions of complying with pre-emption rights but, in the end, achieve a watering down of the petitioner's interest. The courts have accepted that such conduct by the controllers of a company is also capable of constituting unfairly prejudicial conduct for which relief may be given under the Companies Act 1985, s 459.[11] In all, it has been reported that 10.3 per cent of the s 459 petitions filed in 1994–5 contained an allegation of unfairly prejudicial conduct involving an increase of increased share capital either in breach of, or in technical compliance only with, the statutory requirements.[12]

Preventing Transfers of Value from Existing Shareholders to New Investors

The strongest argument in favour of mandatory pre-emption rights is that they protect investors' financial interests. When a company issues new shares it usually does so at a discount to the price at which its existing shares are trading in the market which is greater than is required to reflect the increase in the

[9] *Hogg v Cramphorn Ltd* [1967] Ch 254; *Bamford v Bamford* [1970] Ch 212, CA; *Howard Smith Ltd v Ampol Petroleum Ltd* [1974] AC 821, PC.

[10] [1989] BCLC 383.

[11] *Re a Company (No 007623 of 1984)* [1985] BCLC 80 ((1986) 2 BCC 99,453 is a report of the full hearing of the case and [1986] BCLC 430, CA is a report of the hearing on appeal (*sub nom Re Cumana Ltd*)); *Re a Company (No 007623 of 1984)* [1986] BCLC 362.

[12] *Shareholder Remedies A Consultation Paper* (Law Commission Consultation Paper No 142) (1996) paras 9.36–9.38.

number of issued shares. The extra discount element is intended to encourage investors to acquire the new shares. Although directors have a fiduciary duty to obtain the best price available for new shares[13] it is justifiable for them to offer a discount in order to ensure the success of a new issue.[14] The company's financial advisers determine the appropriate level of discount by looking at a range of factors including the size of the proposed new issue, the purpose for which the new capital is to be used and the effect that this may have on the company's earnings per share, likely investor demand for new stock, prevailing general market conditions, and the discounts that were offered in recent previous share issues. The advisers often engage in advance pre-announcement marketing of the issue to the institutional investors in the issuer in order to gauge likely market reaction to the issue and to establish the price that the market would be prepared to pay. The established practices of the London capital-raising markets were considered by the Court of Appeal in *County Ltd v Girozentrale Securities*[15] and it was noted that the first stage of the marketing of an issue takes place when the issue is no more than a proposal and no issue price has been fixed. It is the job of the brokers at that stage to find out whether the issue is viable and, if it is, to form a view as to the sustainable price for the offer.[16]

It is argued that if the discount element involved in a new issue of shares is not offered to existing shareholders this will result in erosion in the value of their investment.[17] An example may help to explain this concern. This example assumes that the value of the shares remains constant save for the discount in the offer price. In the particular context of rights issues, that assumption is described by the term 'theoretical ex-rights price' which means the price at which the shares would trade in the market after the announcement of an issue if the market reacted simply to the fact of additional shares being issued and their issue price, and did not respond to other factors such as the intended use for the proceeds of the issue and the projected effect of that use on the company's earnings. For simplicity, the example also ignores tax and dealing costs and assumes that there are no share options or convertible securities of the issuer in existence with rights that will require adjustment as a consequence of the increase in the size of its share capital.

[13] *Shearer v Bercain* [1980] 3 All ER 295.

[14] Ibid at 307.

[15] [1996] 3 All ER 834 CA, 851–2 *per* Hobhouse LJ. See also Rawlinson, M, 'Rights Issues' (1991) 2(5) PLC 17, 18.

[16] Hinkley, R, Hunter, D, Whittell, M, and Ziff, M, *Current Issues in Equity Finance* (1998) 33–4 compare the traditional methods of determining rights issue prices, which are set out in the text, with book-building. Book-building is a pricing methodology that involves much more formalised pre-issue contact with investors about the price that they would be willing to pay than takes place within the traditional process. Investors are asked to indicate their demand for the new shares to be offered at different price levels. These indications are entered into a computer model (the 'book') from which can be ascertained the price at which there is sufficient demand to cover the issue. See also below, at 632–3.

[17] This problem was perceived in early US decisions developing the concept of pre-emption rights: Drinker, HS, 'The Pre-emptive Right of Shareholders to Subscribe New Shares' (1930) 43 Harvard Law Review 586. More recent expressions of this view can be found in the *ABI/NAPF Joint Position Paper on Pre-emption, Cost of Capital and Underwriting* (July 1996); Hinkley, R, Hunter, D, Whittell, M, and Ziff, M, *Current Issues in Equity Finance* (1998) ch 4.

Shareholder owns 100 XYZ plc shares currently trading at £1.85 each. The value of the holding is £185.

XYZ raises share capital by an issue of new shares which increases its share capital by 10 per cent. The new shares are offered to the market for subscription at £1.50 each.

The value of the shares in the company as a result of the issue is:

(10 x 1.50 + 100 × 1.85)/110 = £1.818
Value of holding 100 × £1.818 = £181.80
Shareholder has lost over £3 in value.

If, however, the shareholder had been given the rights to subscribe for a proportion of the new shares (one new share for every ten shares held) and had taken up those rights, paying £15 to do so, the position would have been as follows:

Value of holding 110 × £1.818 = £200
Shareholder's position is unchanged (200–15) = £185

Shareholders may not wish to, or may lack the funds to be able to, take up all or part of the shares which are offered to them on a pre-emptive basis. Under the traditional rights-issue structure they can still ensure that the issue does not adversely affect their financial position because the right to acquire the new shares at a discount is itself a tradable right. The expected value of rights to acquire the shares can, using the same example, be calculated very roughly as the difference between the issue price of the new shares and the expected value of the share price after issue, that is 32p. Provided the shareholder is able to sell those rights at a price at least equivalent to their expected value (which should be feasible so long as in fact the reaction of the market to the issue is favourable and the shares trade after the announcement at a price at or above the theoretical ex-rights price) the shareholder's position should not be adversely affected. Say, for example, a shareholder sells eight of those rights for £2.56 and takes up the balance of the entitlement for two of those rights, paying £3 to do so, the eventual outcome for the shareholder is again unchanged because:

Value of holding 102 × £1.818 = £185.44
Shareholder's position 185.44 –3 + 2.56 = £185.00

In effect the shareholder here sells part of the entitlement to fund the acquisition of the remaining part, a process that is sometimes described in practice as 'tail swallowing'. The example obviously ignores tax and dealing costs incurred in selling nil-paid rights and taking up the balance of the entitlement but it serves nevertheless to demonstrate the importance of pre-emption rights and the traditional rights-issue structure from the viewpoint of investors.

The counter-argument here is that it is an unduly short-term perspective to focus on the transfer of value resulting from the discount element in a new issue and that the longer-term financial interests of a company and its shareholders may be better served by allowing it more flexibility in the methods of raising capital. There are various facets to this argument. One is that although the discount element in a rights issue is rendered broadly neutral for shareholders through the ability to trade in nil-paid rights, for the company it means that it may be necessary to issue a larger number of shares in order to raise the desired amount of capital by a rights issue than would be involved in other methods of share issue. The significance of the number of new shares issued relates to the impact on the company's level of dividends:[18] the more shares issued the greater the pressure on the company to generate additional earnings in future so as to avoid any reduction in levels of dividend. It is theoretically possible for companies to adjust their dividend rate in response to the greater number of shares in issue. Historically, companies have been generally reluctant to cut their dividend in case this is interpreted adversely by the market, although support for the view that dividend-per-share analysis must be affected by the number of shares in issue and that adjustments to reflect an increase in that number are entirely appropriate is growing.[19] If, however, the company is not limited to offering the new shares to its existing shareholders, it may be possible for the discount to be set at a lower level than would be acceptable in a rights issue and, thus, a smaller number of shares can be issued. An issue of shares to a group of investors not limited to existing shareholders has the further advantage of broadening the investor base in the company's shares which may in the longer term open up further new sources of funding for the company. The ability to appeal to investors in jurisdictions outside those of the existing shareholders is one particular aspect of this analysis.[20]

Another aspect of the argument that it is in the financial interests of companies and their shareholders to permit as much flexibility as possible is that a rights issue can be a slow way of raising finance.[21] In a traditional rights issue the issuing company must give its shareholders a period of least 21 days to decide whether to take up their entitlements. It is only at the end of that period that shareholders who wish to take up entitlements, or the persons to whom they have transferred them, become obliged to pay the company and thus it is not until then that the subscription moneys are received. For this reason the dealings in entitlements which take place during the period when shareholders are free to decide whether to take up their rights or to sell them are

[18] Adjustments are made to the calculation of earnings per share to reflect the bonus element in rights issue and for this reason earnings per share are not disrupted despite the increased number of shares as a result of the issue: Rawlinson, M, 'Rights Issues' (1991) 2 (5) PLC 17, 18. See also the *ABI/NAPF Joint Position Paper on Pre-emption, Cost of Capital and Underwriting* (July 1996) para 2.1 which suggests that dividends per share should be adjusted after a rights issue and that this is fully recognised by institutional investors.

[19] As well as the *ABI/NAPF Joint Position Paper* see also Hinkley, R, Hunter, D, Whittell, M, and Ziff, M, *Current Issues in Equity Finance* (1998) 10–12.

[20] 'Pre-emption Rights' (1987) 27 (4) *Bank of England Quarterly Bulletin* 545, 547; Haggar, E, 'Issuing Abroad is a Risky Venture' (1993) 108 *Corporate Finance* 22; Haggar, E, 'Who Needs US Investors?' (1997) 148 *Corporate Finance* 42. The *ABI/NAPF Joint Position Paper on Pre-emption, Cost of Capital and Underwriting* (July 1996) para 2.2 argues that potential new investors can always buy shares in the market and should not have preferential access to new and usually cheaper shares. Further, it suggests that long experience demonstrates that shares placed at a discount with new investors overseas usually flow back to their domestic market.

[21] But note the *ABI/NAPF Joint Position Paper on Pre-emption, Cost of Capital and Underwriting* (July 1996) para 3.2 which identifies speed and certainty of funds for the issuing company as being advantages of the present system.

described as dealings in 'nil-paid' rights. A placing of shares with a group of investors can be a quicker method of raising capital as it does not involve the making of an offer by the company which has to remain open for a minimum period prescribed by legislation.

Underwriting Costs and Deep-Discounted Issues

One of the main expenses in a rights issue is underwriting costs. Rights issues are normally underwritten,[22] although companies sometimes dispense with underwriting and, instead, seek to ensure the success of the issue by offering the new shares at a very substantial discount. A perceived drawback of offering a very substantial discount, as noted in the last section, is that it increases the number of shares that have to be issued in order to raise the desired amount of capital which may lead to future difficulties in maintaining levels of dividend. Also there is a degree of uncertainty in a deep-discounted issue which is not underwritten because of the risk that investors may still decline to take up the new shares despite the discount. A further difficulty with deep-discounted issues is that where the company's shares are trading at only a small premium over their par value there may be little room for flexibility because of the Companies Act requirement that shares be issued at a price that is at least equivalent to their par value.[23] Underwriting costs in rights issues are substantial, with the established 'standard' underwriting commission being 2 per cent of the value of the issue for the first 30 days and 0.125 per cent for each week or part week thereafter. Recently these standard commissions have been the target of criticism from the Office of Fair Trading, which eventually referred the matter to the Monopolies and Mergers Commission for investigation. In response to the attention from regulatory authorities, the market has sought to devise new, and cheaper, underwriting structures, although the enthusiasm for deep-discounted issues expressed by the OFT has not yet been reflected in widespread market practice. The alternative underwriting structures are considered in more detail later in this chapter.[24]

OUTLINE OF THE STRUCTURE AND REGULATION OF A RIGHTS ISSUE

The paradigm example of a rights issue is an issue of new ordinary shares to existing ordinary shareholders. It is possible to have rights issues of securities other than ordinary shares and in some circumstances persons other than the existing ordinary shareholders, in particular preference shareholders and holders of convertible securities, may be entitled to be offered the new securi-

[22] Breedon, F, and Twinn, I, 'The Valuation of Sub-Underwriting Agreements for UK Rights Issues' (1996) 36 *Bank of England Quarterly Bulletin* 193.

[23] S 100. See further Marsh, P, *Underwriting of Rights Issues: A Study of the Returns Earned by Sub-Underwriters from UK Rights Issues* (OFT Research Paper 6) (Nov 1994) ch 7, para 7.2. Perceived tax disadvantages for shareholders who sell their rights is an argument against deep-discounted issues: 'MMC Report Recommends Changes to Underwriting Practices' (DTI Press Release) (24 February 1999).

[24] See below, at 632–3.

ties whether they be ordinary shares or some other type of security. The paradigm case is the central focus of the discussion in this chapter although departures from it are considered at appropriate points.

In a rights issue the company offers its shares to its existing shareholders. 'Offer' in this context is used in its narrow contractual sense as opposed to the wider approach which is adopted in the Financial Services Act 1986, s 142 (7A) and the Public Offers of Securities Regulations 1995, reg 5.[25] Shareholders who respond to the offer 'accept' it in a contractual sense and a contract to take the shares is formed by their acceptance. The form of the offer and its duration are regulated by the Companies Act 1985 and, where the company's shares are listed, by the Stock Exchange.

Although the new shares are offered first to a limited class, namely, the existing shareholders, that fact alone does not deprive the offer of its 'public' status for the purpose of regulation of public offer of securities. Accordingly, an important point for a company which is contemplating raising capital by means of a rights issue is whether it is likely to be a public offer of securities for which a prospectus is required. It may sometimes be possible to structure the issue so as to take advantage of an exemption from the requirement to produce a prospectus or listing particulars. If the company is private, there is the further consideration that it is not permitted by the Companies Act 1985 to offer its securities to the public.

The company must ensure that it has sufficient authorised but, as yet, unissued shares to make the offer. If necessary, it will have to convene a shareholders' meeting to increase its share capital and to authorise the directors to proceed with the issue. Although increasing share capital and authorising directors to issue it are general, and basic, corporate finance procedures, they tend to attract particular attention from institutional investors in the context of a rights issue and it is appropriate to examine them a little more closely here.

CORPORATE AUTHORISATIONS: AUTHORISED SHARE CAPITAL

If the issuing company does not have sufficient authorised share capital of the relevant class to cover the rights issue it will have to convene a general meeting of its shareholders to pass the appropriate resolution. The Companies Act 1985, s 121 allows a company to increase its share capital by new shares of such amount as it thinks expedient if so authorised by its articles.[26] Generally, articles of association provide for any increase to the authorised share capital

[25] SI 1995/1537. See further Ch 17 above, at 574–5.

[26] Until 1989, both the National Association of Pension Funds (NAPF) and the Association of British Insurers (ABI) (who, together, are the representative bodies of the main institutional investors) through their investment committees recommended their respective members to vote against resolutions for increases in authorised share capital which would result in more than 25 per cent of the authorised share capital remaining unissued after the completion of any transaction in contemplation, and after allowing for any part of the unissued capital reserved for issue in accordance with arrangements previously approved by shareholders. In May 1989 the NAPF withdrew this recommendation and this was followed by its withdrawal by the ABI.

to be approved by an ordinary resolution of the general meeting, although some articles require a special resolution. Notice of the increase together with a copy of the relevant resolution must be given to the registrar of companies within 15 days after the passing of the resolution.[27] A purported allotment of shares which is not supported by the amount of authorised share capital then in existence is void.[28]

CORPORATE AUTHORISATIONS: DIRECTORS' AUTHORITY TO MAKE THE RIGHTS ISSUE

Ordinary shares are relevant securities for the purposes of the Companies Act 1985, s 80 and the directors must therefore be authorised to allot the new shares in accordance with that section. Authorisation may be given by an ordinary resolution of the company in general meeting or by the articles. Common practice is for it to be given by an ordinary resolution passed at the annual general meeting, although some public companies have adopted a composite approach whereby the articles contain parts of the authority which are unlikely to change from year to year and the resolution that is passed each year simply updates the amount of the s 80 authority.

A typical s 80 authority ordinary resolution is as follows.

> That the Board be and it is hereby generally and unconditionally authorised to exercise all the powers of the Company to allot relevant securities (within the meaning of section 80 of the Companies Act 1985) up to an aggregate principal amount of £[X] PROVIDED THAT this authority shall expire at the conclusion of the next Annual General Meeting of the Company after the passing of this resolution save that the company may before such expiry make an offer or agreement which would or might require relevant securities to be allotted after such expiry and the Board may allot relevant securities in pursuance of such an offer or agreement as if the authority conferred hereby had not expired.

This is a general and unconditional authority, but it is possible to limit a s 80 authority to particular allotments and to impose conditions.[29] As is required by s 80 (4) the maximum amount of shares that may be allotted under the authority (X) and its duration (conclusion of the next AGM) are stated in the resolution. In principle, the amount specified as 'X' may be more than the existing authorised share capital but the Association of British Insurers takes the view that the maximum amount of capital in respect of which a s 80 authority is in place from time to time (other than that which is reserved for issue in connection with contractual conversion rights or options) should not exceed the lesser of the company's authorised but unissued share capital and one-third of the issued equity capital at the time the authority is given. The requirement in s 80 (4) to state an amount appears to preclude the use of a formula. The expiry date of an authority given by an ordinary resolution of a

[27] Companies Act 1985, s 123.

[28] *Bank of Hindustan China and Japan Ltd v Allison* (1871) LR 6 CP 222; *Re a Company ex parte Shooter* [1990] BCLC 384, 389.

[29] S 80 (3).

public company must be not more than five years from the date of the resolution,[30] although, as stated in the previous paragraph and as illustrated by the given resolution, s 80 authorities are in any event often updated annually to keep pace with developments in the company's capital over the course of the year and its changing needs. A private company may elect to apply the provisions of the Companies Act 1985, s 80A under which the duration of a s 80 authority may be longer than five years, or it may be unlimited (but the requirement to specify an amount remains).[31]

Where there is no s 80 authority or an existing authority is inadequate for the purposes of a proposed rights issue (perhaps because it is about to expire or the maximum amount of securities that can be allotted under it is too low or because it is subject to conditions), an ordinary resolution giving authority to the directors must be passed. Once passed, it has to be filed with the registrar of companies within 15 days.[32]

A director who knowingly and wilfully contravenes, or permits or authorises a contravention of, s 80 is liable to a fine,[33] but the validity of the allotment is not affected by the contravention.[34] If, in addition to failing to comply with s 80, the directors have acted in breach of their fiduciary duties in making the allotment, it may be liable to be set aside on that ground.[35]

PRE-EMPTION REQUIREMENTS IMPOSED BY THE COMPANIES ACT 1985, S 89

The Companies Act 1985, s 89 also requires consideration because ordinary shares are equity securities, as defined by s 94 of that Act. In broad terms, the Companies Act 1985, s 89 obliges a company which is proposing to raise capital by issuing new equity securities to offer the securities first to its existing shareholders. The conditions which have to be satisfied in order to comply with s 89 are strict, and where the circumstances of a proposed rights issue make compliance with these conditions impossible or difficult, consideration therefore has to be given to the dis-application of s 89.

Under s 89, new ordinary shares must be offered to each person who holds relevant shares or relevant employee shares. Relevant shares are defined by the Companies Act 1985, s 94 (5) as shares other than:

(i) shares which as respects dividends and capital carry a right to participate only up to a specified amount in a distribution; and
(ii) shares which are held by a person who acquired them in pursuance of an employees' share scheme, or, in the case of shares which have not been allotted, are to be allotted in pursuance of such a scheme.

[30] S 80 (4).

[31] This election requires the passing of an elective resolution and, so, is dependent on the consent of all of the members of the company who are entitled to vote on the matter: Companies Act 1985, s 379A.

[32] Companies Act 1985, s 80 (8). [33] Ibid, s 80 (9). [34] Ibid, s 80 (10).

[35] *Hogg v Cramphorn* [1967] Ch 254; *Bamford v Bamford* [1970] Ch 212, CA; *Howard Smith Ltd v Ampol Ltd* [1974] AC 821, PC.

Relevant employee shares are shares that would be relevant shares but for the fact that they are held by a person who acquired them in pursuance of an employees' share scheme.[36]

The exclusion of shares which carry limited rights to dividends and capital means that preference shareholders may have to be excluded from a right issue if it is to comply with the Companies Act 1985, s 89. Preference shares only have to be excluded, however, where both dividend and capital rights of participation are limited and not where, for example, the dividend rights are limited but the shares are fully participating with regard to capital. One situation where a company may have fully participating preference shares is where they have been issued as consideration for an acquisition. The holders of debt securities which are convertible into shares must also be excluded from a rights issue of ordinary shares if it is to comply with s 89.

The Companies Act 1985, s 89 does not apply to an issue of ordinary shares to be subscribed, wholly or partly, otherwise than in cash[37] nor to an issue of ordinary shares in pursuance of an employees' share scheme.[38] It also has no application to the issue of subscriber shares or bonus shares.[39]

Where s 89 does apply, an offer must be made to each holder of relevant shares or relevant employee shares to allot to him a proportion of the new equity securities which is as nearly as practicable equal to the proportion in nominal value held by him of the aggregate of relevant shares and relevant employee shares.[40] The record date for determining the shareholders entitled to be made an offer and their proportional entitlements may be chosen by the company but it must be a date falling in the period of 28 days immediately before the date of the offer.[41]

If s 89 is not complied with,[42] the company and every officer of it who knowingly authorised or permitted the contravention are jointly and severally liable to compensate any person to whom an offer should have been made for any loss, damage, costs or expenses which the person has sustained or incurred by reason of the contravention. A two-year cut-off point applies to the bringing of claims for compensation under this section.[43] Failure to comply with s 89 does not in itself invalidate an allotment of shares but in appropriate cases the court may exercise its power under the Companies Act 1985, s 359 to rectify the register of members by removing the names of persons to whom shares have been allotted in breach of s 89. This was done in *Re Thundercrest Ltd*[44] where the court rectified the register of members of a small private company in order to remove the names of directors of the company to whom shares had been allotted in breach of s 89. The directors were the persons responsible for the breach and the court considered that not rectifying the register in those circumstances would have enabled the directors to profit from their own wrongdoing.

[36] Companies Act 1985, s 94 (1).
[37] Ibid, s 89 (4).
[38] Ibid, s 89 (5).
[39] Ibid, s 94 (1).
[40] Ibid, s 89 (1)(a).
[41] Ibid, s 94 (7).
[42] Ibid, s 92.
[43] Ibid, s 92 (2). The time runs from the delivery to the registrar of companies of the return of allotments in question or, where equity securities other than shares are granted, from the date of the grant.
[44] [1995] BCLC 117.

DIS-APPLICATION OF THE COMPANIES ACT 1985,
S 89 PRE-EMPTION REQUIREMENTS BY LISTED COMPANIES

One of the surprising features of British corporate finance practice relating to listed companies is that they commonly pass a special resolution at their annual general meetings to dis-apply s 89 in relation to rights issues and, to a limited extent, in relation to other share issues. Why dis-apply s 89 in relation to rights issues when the purpose of that section is to require the company to raise finance by that means? The answer to this apparently puzzling question lies in the detail of s 89 and a comparison between it and the requirements in respect of rights issues which are imposed on listed companies by *The Listing Rules* of the London Stock Exchange. The two regimes are broadly very similar, but in certain important respects the Stock Exchange's requirements are more favourable to the company than those imposed by the Companies Act 1985. This means that the company may prefer to dis-apply s 89 and make its rights issue in accordance with the more flexible rules of the Stock Exchange, although, if a suitable s 89 authority is not already in place, having been passed at a previous shareholders' meeting, this will only be a worthwhile choice where the costs and administrative burden involved in obtaining the relevant dis-application resolution do not outweigh the benefits obtained by its passage.

The main areas of difficulty with the procedure required by s 89 are as follows.

The Form and Duration of the Offer

An offer in writing must be made to the existing shareholders.[45] It may be delivered to the shareholders either personally or by post; if it is sent by post it may be sent to the shareholder or to the shareholder's registered address (or, if he has no registered address in the UK, by post to the address in the UK supplied by him to the company for the giving of notices).[46] The offer must be kept open for a period of at least 21 days and the fact that it is open for that period must be stated expressly in the offer.[47] References in the companies legislation to days mean clear days.[48] Therefore the day on which the offer is made—that is, the day when it is communicated to the shareholders—must be excluded from the computation of the offer period as must the day the offer closes (since it will normally close at 3.00 pm ie part way through a day). If the offer is made by post, it is deemed to be made at the time at which the last letter to be delivered would be delivered in the ordinary course of post.[49] In accordance with a Practice Direction issued in 1985,[50] subject to proof to the contrary, delivery in the ordinary course of post is taken to be effective (a) in the case of first-class mail, on the second working day after posting, and (b) in

[45] Companies Act 1985, s 90 (2).
[46] Ibid, s 90 (2).
[47] Ibid, s 90 (6).
[48] *R v Turner* [1910] 1 KB 346, CCA; *Re Hector Whaling Ltd* [1936] Ch 208, 210 *per* Bennett J.
[49] Companies Act 1985, s 90 (2).
[50] [1985] 1 All ER 889.

the case of second-class post, on the fourth working day after posting. The Interpretation Act 1978, s 7 applies this Practice Direction to statutory provisions, such as the Companies Act 1985, s 90 (2), which require a document to be sent by post. If the postal service is disrupted when the letters are posted[51] or it is known that they did not in fact arrive,[52] the normal rule will be displaced.

The Listing Rules require an offer to be open for 21 days,[53] but in this case both the day on which the offer is delivered and the day on which is closes can by counted, thus shortening the timetable by a few days. Here, if the issuer's articles contain the commonly included provision for deemed delivery 24 or 48 hours after posting, this will determine the date of delivery. This will help to trim the length of the offer period. As well as giving the company access to the capital raised by the issue slightly earlier than would be possible under a s 89 rights issue this can also reduce the company's underwriting costs which are based on the length of the period for which the underwriter is 'on risk'. The shorter period for which the offer has to remain open under *The Listing Rules* is one of the key reasons for dis-applying s 89.

Overseas Shareholders

Sending rights issue documentation to shareholders in other jurisdictions is problematic because the distribution of such documents may contravene the securities laws of those jurisdictions unless they are in a form which complies with the local law and any requisite approvals under that law have been obtained. Also, even if relevant securities law permits the distribution of rights-issue documentation to overseas shareholders, posting it to them would have the effect of extending the offer period, since the offer would not be made until it had been deemed to be received by the most inaccessible overseas shareholder.

The Companies Act, s 90 provides a procedure which may be used in respect of overseas shareholders who do not have a registered address in the United Kingdom and who have not given the company an address in the United Kingdom for the service of notices. This procedure is known as the Gazette route. The Gazette route involves the publication of the offer, or of a notice specifying where a copy can be obtained or inspected, in the London Gazette.[54] The publication of this notice satisfies the requirement to communicate the offer to the shareholders, although where it would not infringe the domestic securities laws of the countries in which shareholders are resident, letters may also be sent. The need to avoid an extended offer-period means that, legally, care has to be taken in the drafting of such letters to ensure that the offer is clearly made in the Gazette rather than in the letters.

Resolutions dis-applying s 89 commonly permit the directors to make such arrangements as they think fit with regard to overseas shareholders who would, apart from such arrangements, be entitled to participate in a rights

51 *Bradman v Trinity Estates plc* [1989] BCLC 757.
52 *Re Thundercrest Ltd* [1995] 1 BCLC 117.
53 *The Listing Rules*, ch 13, para 13.18 (b)(viii).
54 Companies Act 1985, s 90 (5).

issue. In practice this usually means that overseas shareholders in jurisdictions where the relevant securities laws could be infringed by the offer of new shares are excluded from the offer and, instead, new shares representing their entitlements are sold on the market when dealing in the new shares commence, with the net proceeds of such sales being sent to them. This practice is sanctioned by *The Listing Rules*[55] and it has survived a challenge in the courts. In *Mutual Life Insurance Co of New York v The Rank Organisation Ltd*[56] the exclusion of shareholders holding 53 per cent of the company's equity who were resident in the United States and Canada from a rights issue was challenged as a breach of the contract between the company and its members contained in the memorandum and articles.[57] Specifically, it was alleged that the exclusion was contrary to a provision in the articles which required the company to treat all shareholders of the same class equally. Goulding J rejected the challenge for the following reasons: the directors had acted bona fide in the company's interests in making the allotment; the US and Canadian shareholders had not been treated unfairly since their exclusion from the right to acquire the new shares did not affect the existence of their shares or the rights attached to them; there was no suggestion that the terms of the offer were improvident; no shareholder in the company had the right to expect his interest to remain constant forever; and, the reason for the exclusion of the North American shareholders was because of a difficulty relating to their own personal situation.

The nature of the contract formed by a company's memorandum and articles is somewhat obscure and the extent to which the courts will enforce provisions contained in those documents is uncertain.[58] Partly for these reasons,[59] contractual actions have tended to be eclipsed in recent years by actions under the Companies Act 1985, s 459 which permits members of a company to seek relief from unfairly prejudicial conduct. However, it seems unlikely that overseas investors who are excluded from a rights issue for the reasons that the court found persuasive in the *Mutual Life* decision would fare any better if they brought a claim under this section. In the *Mutual Life* decision Goulding J said that the exclusion was not unfair and in *Re BSB Holdings Ltd (No 2)*[60] where, in reaching the conclusion that a complex capital reorganisation was not unfairly prejudicial to the petitioner, Arden J expressly adopted as applicable to the case in hand three of the reasons given by

[55] Ch 9, para 9.19 (b).

[56] [1985] BCLC 11.

[57] Companies Act 1985, s 14 gives contractual effect to these documents as between the company and its members, and between the members amongst themselves.

[58] It has generated extensive academic debate including the following articles: Wedderburn, KW, 'Shareholders' Rights and the Rule in *Foss v Harbottle*' [1957] CLJ 194; Goldberg, GD, 'The Enforcement of Outsider Rights under Section 20 of the Companies Act 1948' (1972) 35 MLR 362; Prentice, GN, 'The Enforcement of "Outsider" Rights' (1980) 1 Co Law 179; Gregory, R, 'The Section 20 Contract' (1981) 44 MLR 526; Goldberg, GD, 'The Controversy on the Section 20 Contract Revisited'(1985) 48 MLR 158; Drury, RR, 'The Relative Nature of a Shareholder's Right to Enforce the Company Contract' [1986] CLJ 219.

[59] The range of remedies open to the court on a successful petition under Companies Act 1985, s 459 is an important factor which encourages shareholders to seek relief under this section in preference to other claims that may be open to them: see, *Shareholder Remedies A Consultation Paper* (Law Commission Consultation Paper No 142) (1996) paras 20.2–20.4.

[60] [1996] 1 BCLC 155.

Goulding J in the *Mutual Life* decision as indicating an absence of unfairness: (1) the restructuring did not affect the existence of the petitioner's shares or the rights attaching to them; (2) the terms on which a rights issue which was part of the restructuring was made were not improvident; and (3) the petitioner did not have any overriding right to obtain shares.

Fractions

Shareholders may have a technical entitlement to fractions of a share (for example a shareholder who holds seven shares will be technically entitled to a fraction of a share where the basis of the rights issue is that there will be one new share for every five shares held). Before the introduction of the Companies Act 1985, s 89, the practice was to aggregate and sell the right to such fractions for the benefit of the company as soon as practicable after commencement of dealings in the new shares. This practice is not possible under s 89 because it requires the company to make an offer which is as nearly as practicable in proportion to shareholders' existing holdings. It is practicable for fractions to be rounded up or down to the nearest whole number and it seems that a company must do this in order to comply with s 89. This means that it can be practically impossible for the company to raise a round sum and the company loses the benefit that it would otherwise have had from the sale of the fractions.

If the Companies Act 1985, s 89 is dis-applied, provision can be made for fractions to be sold for the company's benefit. The dis-application resolution normally authorises the directors to aggregate them and to sell them in the market for the benefit of the company. This practice is permitted by the Stock Exchange.[61]

CREST

CREST is the electronic share dealing system in the UK markets. Although it is designed to deal with rights issues electronically, the statutory requirement for the offer of new shares to be made in writing to the existing shareholders[62] still applies, and the issuer must therefore communicate in writing with those of its shareholders who hold their shares through CREST. If s 89 is dis-applied, the offer of the new shares can be made by crediting CREST holders' stock accounts with their entitlements and without the need for any written communication to the shareholders.[63]

Warrants, Convertible Securities and Preference Shares

A right to subscribe, or convert into, shares is not a relevant share for the purposes of the Companies Act 1985, s 89. Therefore the holders of warrants or

[61] *The Listing Rules*, ch 9, para 9.19 (a).
[62] Companies Act 1985, s 90 (2).
[63] *Corporate Action Standardisation* (CREST publication) (May 1996); Knapp, V, 'CREST: Impact on Corporate Transaction' (1996) 7 (10) PLC 23; Ashurst Morris Crisp 'Payment of Rights Issues in CREST' (1997) 12 (11) BJIB&FL 552.

convertible debt securities cannot be included in a s 89 rights issues, subject to one very limited exception provided by the Companies Act 1985, s 96. However, the Stock Exchange requires an issuer of listed convertible debt securities to covenant to include holders of convertible securities in rights issues to shareholders or to make an appropriate adjustment of their conversion rights.[64] Before giving a covenant to include the holders of its listed convertible securities or warrants in rights issues, a company must therefore exclude s 89 for that purpose. In order to ensure that the company will remain able to honour its commitment to the holders of the warrants or convertible securities, the resolution dis-applying s 89 must enable the company to enter into an agreement which would or might require equity securities to be allotted after it has expired[65] and it must reserve shares sufficient to meet the commitment.

Preference shares which are participating with regard to respect to dividends or capital are relevant shares for the purposes of s 89 and the holders of such shares are therefore entitled to be included in a s 89 rights issue. Even if s 89 is dis-applied, the holders of participating preference shares in listed companies can still participate in a rights issue because participating preference shares are equity shares for the purposes of *The Listing Rules* and holders of equity shares are entitled to share in a rights issue.[66] Preference shares often have a par value much higher than that of the company's ordinary shares, a point which is relevant because proportional entitlements to the new securities are determined by reference to the par values of existing shareholdings. This can mean that a large proportion of a new offer has to be offered first to participating preference shareholders. However, if the preference shares are convertible into ordinary shares it is possible under *The Listing Rules* (but not s 89) to calculate proportionate entitlements to the new shares by reference to the par values of the ordinary shares into which the preference share are convertible. This can be a further reason for considering the dis-application of s 89.

DIS-APPLICATION OF THE COMPANIES ACT 1985, S 89 BY UNLISTED PUBLIC COMPANIES

The reasons why a listed company would consider dis-applying the Companies Act 1985, s 89 also apply to unlisted public companies. For these companies the alternative requirements imposed by *The Listing Rules* do not apply so there is scope for greater flexibility in the dis-application resolution. Even for companies whose shares are admitted to dealings on the Alternative Investment Market,[67] there are no equivalent pre-emption requirements to those imposed on companies listed on the main market.

[64] Under *The Listing Rules*, ch 13, app 2, para 4 (a)(iii) trust deeds relating to convertible listed securities must provide for the holders to be entitled to participate in rights issues or, alternatively, make provision for the appropriate adjustment of conversion rights.

[65] This extension is permitted by Companies Act 1985, s 95 (4).

[66] *The Listing Rules*, ch 9, para 9.18 and the definitions of equity shares and equity share capital.

[67] See further Ch 2 above, at 74–6.

DIS-APPLICATION OF THE COMPANIES ACT 1985, S 89 BY PRIVATE COMPANIES

Private companies can dis-apply s 89 as they think fit.

THE PROCEDURE GOVERNING DIS-APPLICATION OF THE COMPANIES ACT 1985, S 89

A private company may exclude the statutory pre-emption rights conferred on shareholders by the Companies Act 1985, s 89 either generally in relation to allotments and for a unlimited duration or in relation to particular allotments.[68] All companies, private and public, are also permitted by the Companies Act 1985, s 95 to dis-apply s 89 by a special resolution or by a provision to such effect in their articles. It is common for listed companies to dis-apply s 89 by a special resolution although, in some cases, a composite approach, whereby the parts of the dis-application which are unlikely to change from time to time are contained in the articles but the amount of the securities covered by the dis-application is updated regularly by a special resolution passed at a general meeting of the shareholders, is followed. S 95 dis-applications are linked to directors' s 80 authorities and thus, for public companies, are limited in duration to a maximum of five years.[69] All or part of the securities covered by the relevant s 80 authority may be included in the dis-application resolution and s 89 may be dis-applied altogether or it may be applied with such modifications as the shareholders may determine.[70]

The Listing Rules do not impose additional restrictions on the statutory power to dis-apply s 89.[71] The circumstances in which pre-emption rights can be dis-applied by listed companies are subject to the guidelines agreed with the investment committees of the Association of British Insurers and the National Association of Pension Funds and endorsed by the London Stock Exchange.[72] The guidelines represent an attempt to achieve a compromise between the desire of companies to have flexibility in the methods of raising capital which are open to them and institutional investors' interests in protecting pre-emption rights for the reasons discussed at the start of this chap-

[68] Companies Act 1985, s 91.

[69] Ibid, s 95 (3). If a s 80 authority is renewed so too may be the s 95 dis-application resolution: s 95 (3).

[70] Companies Act 1985, s 95 (1) and (2).

[71] *The Listing Rules*, ch 9, para 9.20. Under earlier versions of *The Listing Rules* periods of dis-application were limited to 15 months. The Exchange does, however, regulate the disclosure that must be made: a circular in connection with a resolution proposing to dis-apply pre-emption rights must include a statement of the total number of equity securities covered by the dis-application and the percentage which that number represents of the equity share capital in issue at the date of the circular: *The Listing Rules*, ch 14, para 14.8.

[72] *Stock Exchange Pre-emption Guidelines* (1987). The background to the development of these guidelines is discussed in 'Pre-emption Rights' (1987) 27 (4) *Bank of England Quarterly Bulletin* 545.

ter.[73] The guidelines are not Stock Exchange rules but companies know that if they act within them they will have the backing of their major institutional shareholders without the need for prior discussion with those shareholders. Companies can still seek dis-applications in circumstances falling outside the guidelines but their institutional investors may object unless they are persuaded that there are good reasons for the unusual course. Under the guidelines, dis-applications will be approved provided they are restricted to normal rights issues and to an amount of shares that, in any year, does not exceed 5 per cent of the issued ordinary share capital as shown by the latest published annual accounts. Companies are also expected to observe cumulative limits. A company should not without prior consultation with its institutional investors make use of more than 7.5 per cent of issued ordinary share capital shown by the latest published annual accounts by way of non-pre-emptive issues for cash in any rolling three year period.

A typical dis-application resolution complying with the pre-emption guidelines is as follows.

That the Board be and it is hereby empowered pursuant to section 95 of the Companies Act 1985 to allot equity securities (within the meaning of section 94 of the said Act) for cash pursuant to the authority conferred by the previous resolution as if sub-section (1) of section 89 of the said Act did not apply to any such allotment, PROVIDED THAT this power shall be limited:

(A) to the allotment of equity securities in connection with a rights issue, open offer or other pre-emptive offer in favour of ordinary shareholders [and in favour of all holders of any other class of equity security in accordance with the rights attached to such class] where the equity securities respectively attributable to the interests of [ordinary shareholders] / [such persons] on a fixed record date are proportionate (as nearly as may be) to the respective numbers of [ordinary shares] / [equity securities] held by them [or are otherwise allotted in accordance with the rights attaching to such equity securities] subject to such exclusions or other arrangements as the board may deem necessary or expedient to deal with fractional entitlements, legal or practical problems in any overseas territory or another other matter whatsoever; and

(B) to the allotment (otherwise than pursuant to sub-paragraph (A) above) of equity securities up to an aggregate nominal amount of £[ ]

and shall expire at the conclusion of the next Annual General Meeting of the Company after the passing of this resolution, save that the company may before such expiry make an offer or agreement which would or might require equity securities to be allotted after such expiry and the Board may allot equity securities in pursuance of such an offer or agreement as if the power conferred hereby had not expired.

Rights issues may be effected in accordance with paragraph (A) whilst paragraph (B) gives the company a limited ability to raise share capital otherwise than on a pre-emptive basis.

[73] See above, at 606–12.

SECURITIES REGULATION OF RIGHTS ISSUES[74]

Private Companies may not Offer their Shares or Debentures to the Public

The prohibition on private companies offering their shares or other securities to the public remains in the Companies Act 1985 and has not been incorporated into the legislation which governs public offers generally, namely the Financial Services Act 1986 and the Public Offers of Securities Regulations 1995. The Companies Act 1985 has its own interpretation of 'offer to the public' which is not the same as that in the 1986 Act or the 1995 Regulations.

The relevant provision is the Companies Act 1985, s 81 which provides that a private company commits an offence if it offers its shares or debentures to the public or allots, or agrees to allot, its shares or debentures with a view to all or any of those securities being offered for sale to the public. Under the Companies Act 1985, s 59 references in the Act to offering shares or debentures to the public are to be read as including a reference to offering them to any section of the public, such as the members of the company concerned. This is, however, subject to the Companies Act 1985, s 60 (1) which provides that an offer does not have to be regarded as an offer to the public if it can properly be regarded, in all the circumstances, as not being calculated to result, directly or indirectly, in the securities becoming available for subscription or purchase by persons other than those receiving the offer or otherwise as being a domestic concern of the persons receiving and making it. By virtue of the Companies Act 1985, s 60 (4)(a) an offer to existing members falls to be regarded as a domestic concern.[75]

In a public company the normal form of the offer is renounceable so that the original recipient shareholders can renounce it freely in favour of any other person and, indeed, for listed companies it is a requirement of the London Stock Exchange that rights-issues offers should be in renounceable form. A rights issue by a private company would infringe the Companies Act 1985, s 81 if the offer of new shares was made in the fully renounceable form which is employed in public-company rights issues, but a limited amount of renunciation is permitted: by virtue of the Companies Act 1985, s 60 (7) an offer is still to be regarded as being a domestic concern so long as the class of persons to whom the offer may be renounced does not extend beyond other existing shareholders, existing employees, members of the families of such members or employees, or existing debenture holders.

[74] The general requirements relating to public offers of securities are considered in Ch 17. This chapter identifies, and concentrates on, the requirements that are of particular importance in relation to rights issues.

[75] Companies Act 1985, s 60 (4) and also s 60 (7) which is considered in the next paragraph of the text, apply only 'unless the contrary is proved': s 60 (3). The circumstances in which the contrary could be proved have not been tested. The discrepancy between the concept of a 'public offer' in the Companies Act 1985, s 81 and the Public Offers of Securities Regulations 1995 is a source of confusion. The Treasury has consulted on this but, to date, has not published any specific proposed amendments: *Public Offers of Securities: A Consultation Document* (HM Treasury) (1998) paras 4.1–4.25.

A rights issue by a private company which is structured so as to avoid the Companies Act prohibition on public offers will not trigger the requirement to produce a prospectus under the Public Offers of Securities Regulations 1995. This is because there is an express exemption in that legislation in respect of offers of securities of a private company to members or employees or the company, or their families, or the holders of debentures issued by the company.[76] Private companies cannot be listed,[77] so the requirements of Part IV of the Financial Services Act 1986 are not relevant.

An offer of new securities is an investment advertisement as defined by the Financial Services Act 1986, s 57 (2) because it contains an offer to enter into an agreement to acquire shares which is an investment agreement as defined for that purpose.[78] The Financial Services Act 1986, s 57 states that investment advertisements can only be issued by or with the approval of an authorised person, that is a person who is authorised under the Financial Services Act 1986 to carry on investment business in the UK, but this requirement is subject to a number of exemptions provided by or under s 58 of that Act. Where a rights issue is structured so as to avoid the prohibition on offers to the public which is imposed by the Companies Act 1985, s 81, it should also be exempt from the Financial Services Act 1986, s 57 by virtue of regulations made under s 58.[79]

Rights Issues by Unlisted Public Companies are Regulated by the Public Offers of Securities Regulations 1995 and the Requirements of any Market on which the Shares are to be Quoted

A rights issue by an unlisted public company is subject to the Public Offers of Securities Regulations 1995. The detailed discussion in Chapter 17 of the concept of an offer to the public for the purpose of these regulations is not repeated here:[80] in summary, for all practical purposes any offer of securities in the UK for the first time triggers the requirement under the Regulations to register and publish a prospectus unless it is covered by an appropriate exemption. There are certain general exemptions from the requirement to produce a prospectus which, depending on the structure adopted, could apply to a rights issue, such as the offer to no more than fifty persons exemption[81] (where, to ensure compliance, the offer would have to be made in a non-renounceable form). A specific exemption for rights issues made by companies quoted on the Alternative Investment Market is provided by the Public Offers of Securities Regulations 1995, reg 8 (5) which permits the London Stock Exchange to authorise the making of an offer on a pre-emptive basis without a prospectus where up-to-date information equivalent to that required to be included in a prospectus is available as a result of the requirements of the Exchange. Documents issued in connection with a rights issue

[76] Reg 7 (1)(f).
[77] Financial Services Act 1986, s 143 (3).
[78] By Financial Services Act 1986, s 44 (9).
[79] Financial Services Act 1986 (Investment Advertisements) (Exemptions) Order 1996 (SI 1996/1586), art 12 (advertisements relating to matters of common interest).
[80] See Ch 17 above, at 574–7.
[81] Reg 7 (2)(b).

which is exempt from the requirement to produce a prospectus remain subject to the Financial Services Act 1986, s 57 unless an appropriate exemption applies.

Rights Issues by Listed Companies are Regulated by the Financial Services Act 1986, Pt IV and the Requirements of the London Stock Exchange's Listing Rules

In the case of a listed company, it is a condition of admission to listing for securities which are to be offered to the public in the UK for the first time before admission that a prospectus, approved by the Exchange, be published.[82] In circumstances where the requirement to produce a prospectus is not triggered—for example where admission precedes the offer (although this would be unusual in a rights issue)—there is still a general requirement to produce listing particulars. As permitted by the Listing Particulars Directive,[83] art 6, para 3 (a) and the Public Offers Directive, art 11.6,[84] the Stock Exchange normally waives the requirement to produce a prospectus or listing particulars for new issues of shares which would increase the shares of a class already listed by less than 10 per cent.[85] Many rights issues by listed companies are too large to be able to take advantage of these small issues exemptions, so a prospectus is usually required.

CONTENTS OF A RIGHTS-ISSUE PROSPECTUS

Specific items of information required to be included in a rights-issue prospectus issued by a listed company are set out in *The Listing Rules*.[86] The matters on which information is required include the following:[87]

the pro rata entitlement to the new shares to be issued by way of rights;
the last date on which transfers were or will be accepted for registration for participation in the issue;
how the new shares rank for dividend or interest;
whether the new shares rank *pari passu* with any existing listed securities;
the nature of the document of title and its proposed date of issue;
the treatment of any fractions; and
how shares not taken up will be dealt with and the time, not being less than 21 days, in which the offer can be accepted.

A rights-issue circular relating to securities that are to be listed must also contain a table of market values for securities of the class to which the rights issue relates for the first dealing day in each of the six months before the date of the circular, for the last dealing day before the announcement of the rights issue and (if different) the latest practicable date prior to despatch of the circular.[88] Statements on the amount of borrowings must be included and the issuer must give an opinion on the adequacy of its working capital.[89] The general

[82] Financial Services Act 1986, s 144 (2).
[83] 80/390/EEC, [1980] OJ L100/1.
[84] 89/298/EEC, [1989] OJ L124/8.
[85] *The Listing Rules*, ch 5, para 5.27 (e).
[86] Ibid, ch 5, app I, tab 1 col 2.
[87] Ibid, ch 6, para 6.b.23.
[88] Ibid, ch 6, para 6.B.27.
[89] Ibid, ch 6, paras 6.E.15–16.

duty of disclosure under the Financial Services Act 1986, s 146, the general nature of which is discussed in Chapter 17,[90] applies, but in determining the information that is required to be included in order to satisfy this duty regard can be had to information that is already available to investors or their professional advisers by virtue of the continuing obligations to which the issuer is subject under *The Listing Rules*.[91]

Detailed items of information which are required to be included in a prospectus for a rights issue of unlisted securities are set out in the Public Offers of Securities Regulations 1995.[92] Under reg 9 there is a general duty of disclosure in relation to a rights-issue prospectus which is to be published by an unlisted company. This is substantially equivalent to the duty of disclosure in the listed regime although there are certain differences in the details.[93] One difference flows from the fact that offerors of unlisted securities may not be quoted on a market and, so, may not be subject to continuing obligations. This precludes a general qualification permitting regard to the fact that information is already available to investors because it has been disclosed in that way. However, the Stock Exchange is permitted by the Public Offers of Securities Regulations 1995, reg 8 (4) to authorise the omission of information in a prospectus for a rights issue by a company that is quoted on the Alternative Investment Market provided that equivalent up-to-date information is available as a result of requirements imposed by that market.

INACCURATE INFORMATION: INVESTORS' REMEDIES

The remedies that are generally available to investors who have acquired securities on the basis of false or incomplete information given about those securities when they were offered to the public are considered in Chapter 17.[94] A few points of specific relevance to shares offered by way of rights may be made here.

In a rights issue the new shares are offered by the company for subscription. The provisional allotment letters sent to the existing shareholders are offers.[95] The contract to take the shares is between the company and the investor and it would be against the company that the investor would seek to exercise any right of rescission. The initial investor in the shares may be the existing shareholder to whom they were first offered or another person, or persons, in

[90] See Ch 17 above, at 584–5.
[91] Financial Services Act 1986, s 146 (3)(d).
[92] Reg 8, and sch 1.
[93] See Ch 17 above, at 590 where the differences between the duties of disclosure in the listed and unlisted regimes are examined further.
[94] See Ch 17 above, at 593–604.
[95] This is the point of distinction between a rights issue and the situation in *Collins v Associated Greyhound Racecourses Ltd* [1930] 1 Ch 1, CA where individuals applied for shares (offer) and the company allotted them (acceptance) on terms whereby they could then be renounced. In that case, the person in whose favour the shares were renounced was in a position analogous to that of a purchaser rather than an original allottee and therefore he could not claim rescission as against the company.

whose favour the offer has been renounced. To rescind, the innocent person must demonstrate 'inducement' to take the shares and for this purpose must show that he was within the class of persons to whom the inducement was addressed. There is clearly no difficulty about this where the initial investor is an existing shareholder who took up rights, but what if the initial investor is a person in whose favour rights have been renounced? Given that the company knows from the outset that the shares offered might be taken by the existing shareholders or by person(s) in whose favour the offer was renounced it would seem reasonable to regard renouncees as being included in the class of persons to whom the inducement was directed.

Initial subscribers and subsequent market purchasers of the shares should be able to pursue a statutory claim for compensation under, as the case may be, the Financial Services Act 1986 or the Public Offers of Securities Regulations 1995. It has been held, however, that the sole purpose of a rights-issue prospectus is to facilitate the initial allotment of the shares and that no claim in tort may be brought in respect of subsequent market purchases of shares, even by persons who were existing shareholders prior to the rights issue.[96]

THE MECHANICS OF ISSUE

The offer of the new shares is normally made by way of a renounceable letter of allotment known as a provisional allotment letter (or PAL). For listed companies, it is a requirement of *The Listing Rules* that rights issues normally be made by renounceable letter or other negotiable document.[97] These requirements do not apply to the new shares offered in respect of existing holdings that are held in uncertificated form in CREST. CREST has been designed to accommodate rights issues and its procedures mimic electronically those that apply to certificated shares.[98]

Where no increase in the authorised share capital or other shareholder approval is required to implement the rights issue, the shareholders will normally receive a PAL simultaneously with the circular letter comprising the prospectus for the issue. Where a general meeting is required, the circular letters will usually be sent out together with notice of an EGM. The PALs will be sent out after the passing at the EGM of the resolutions increasing the authorised share capital and providing any other shareholder consents that are required for the rights issue.

A PAL is, essentially, an offer document. Each PAL will give details of the number of shares provisionally allotted and the basis on which the provi-

[96] *Al Nakib Investments (Jersey) Ltd v Longcroft* [1990] 3 All ER 321, [1990] 1 WLR 1390: no duty of care owed by directors in respect of market purchases by existing shareholder. This approach is consistent with the 'exhaustion of the purpose of the prospectus' analysis used to defeat a deceit claim by market purchasers in *Peek v Gurney* (1873) LR 6 HL 377, HL.

[97] *The Listing Rules* ch 4, para 4.16.

[98] *Corporate Action Standardisation* CREST publication (May 1996); Knapp, V, 'CREST: Impact on Corporate Transaction' (1996) 7 (10) PLC 23; Ashurst Morris Crisp 'Payment of Rights Issues in CREST' (1997) 12 (11) BJIB&FL 552.

sional allotment has been made.[99] Each shareholder must be given three options:

(i) to take up his rights fully; or
(ii) to take up his rights in part only and to renounce the rest; or
(iii) to renounce his rights in full.

A shareholder who chooses option (i) must lodge the PAL together with his payment for the shares with the company's registrars by the latest date for acceptance. A shareholder who chooses to split his entitlement (option (ii)) must do so by the date and in accordance with the procedure specified in the PAL. The specified procedure will involve the returning of the PAL to the company's registrars, its cancellation and the issue of split letters of allotment. For the period of the offer, 'nil-paid' dealings in the shares which are provisionally allotted can take place by means of renunciation of whole or partial entitlements by the persons entitled (options (ii) and (iii)). A person in whose favour a renunciation has been made and who wishes to take up the offer must accept the offer by lodging the PAL together with his payment for the shares with the registrars by the latest date for acceptance.

Once the offer period has expired, the provisional allotment of those shares which have been accepted must be confirmed by the board, or by a committee of the board. The allotment letters will then be returned to the allottees stamped 'fully paid'. There then usually follows a fully-paid renounceable dealing period. During this period the fully-paid allotment letters constitute the transferable documents of title to the new shares. The company will then require them to be submitted for registration when they will be replaced by share certificates; from the close of the renounceable dealing period, dealings in the shares will take place in registered form.

If all of the shares offered by way of rights have not been subscribed by the close of the subscription period, *The Listing Rules* require them to be disposed of for the benefit of the holders entitled, unless arrangements to the contrary have been approved by the shareholders in general meeting.[100] However, by way of qualification, it is expressly provided that where the proceeds to which a holder would be entitled does not exceed £3, those proceeds may be sold for the benefit of the company.[101] The exercise of selling the shares not taken up (commonly referred to as the 'rump' or the 'stick') will be undertaken by brokers acting on behalf of the lead underwriter. If there is no premium available in the market, the shares can be allotted to the underwriters themselves.[102] Provided this is authorised by the Exchange, other shareholders may be allowed to acquire any rights that have not been taken up by shareholders.[103]

The existence or size of a rump could well constitute 'inside information' as defined by the Criminal Justice Act 1993, s 56. However, that Act provides a special 'market information' defence to charges of insider dealing which should cover underwriters who dispose of securities comprised in the rump of an issue without disclosing its existence or size.[104] It is also conceivable that

[99] *The Listing Rules*, ch 13, para 13.18 (b)(viii).
[100] Ibid, ch 4, para 4.19
[101] Ibid, ch 4, para 4.19 (a).
[102] Ibid, ch 4, para 4.19 (b).
[103] Ibid, ch 4, para 4.19 (c).
[104] Criminal Justice Act 1993, sch 1, para 2.

the failure to announce the result of a rights issue before the rump is placed in the market could in certain circumstances constitute the offence of creating a false market contrary to the Financial Services Act 1986, s 47 (2). In the UK markets it is common practice for this information to be disclosed if the portion of the issue that has not been taken up is material.

UNDERWRITING OF RIGHTS ISSUES

Although there have been examples of rights issues done at a deep discount to the prevailing market price and not underwritten, it is more common for rights issues to be underwritten. Underwriting performs the function of ensuring that the company receives all of the capital intended to be raised by the rights issue even if it is not fully subscribed by the existing shareholders:

> An underwriting agreement means an agreement entered into before the shares are brought before the public that in the event of the public not taking up the whole of them, or the number mentioned in the agreement, the underwriter will, for an agreed commission, take an allotment of such part of the shares as the public has not applied for.[105]

> In return for a percentage fee the underwriter undertakes to take up any of the shares offered which have not been applied for by the closing date.[106]

In practice the underwriter normally passes on[107] most of the obligation to take the shares if they are not subscribed by the public to sub-underwriters who are typically institutions such as pension funds and insurance companies. The process of passing on the risk to sub-underwriters came under judicial scrutiny in *Eagle Trust plc v SBC Securities Ltd*.[108] In this case SBC, the underwriter of a rights issue, accepted a director of the company as a sub-underwriter. The director used company money to pay for the shares and was later convicted of theft. The company sought to make SBC liable to repay the money which had been mis-applied by its former director. The claim failed but, in coming to that conclusion, the court analysed closely the role of the underwriter and the duties to which it is subject when arranging sub-underwriting. Arden J concluded that an underwriter acts in its own interests when arranging sub-underwriting and that it is under no duty to the company to choose any particular type of sub-underwriter for the benefit of the company. Unless specifically agreed with the company to the contrary, the underwriter is therefore free to accept a director as a sub-underwriter. This is the position even where, as is common, the underwriter not only undertakes the obligation to take the shares as a last resort but also acts as financial adviser to the company in relation to the issue because the underwriting function, including related matters such as sub-underwriting, is distinct and separate from the

[105] *Re Licensed Victuallers' Mutual Trading Association, ex parte Audain* (1889) 42 Ch D 1, CA, 6 *per* Cotton LJ.

[106] *County Ltd v Girozentrale* [1996] 3 All ER 834, CA, 850 *per* Hobhouse LJ.

[107] The underwriter may be subject to capital adequacy requirements which make it important for it to pass on the risk.

[108] [1995] BCC 231.

function of the financial adviser. In the *Eagle Trust* case the further argument that SBC had acted in breach of its duty of care as financial adviser by failing to disclose the fact that it had accepted a director as a sub-underwriter to the issuing company's board was also rejected on the facts.

For many years underwriting commissions on rights issues in the UK market were fixed at the fairly standard level of 2 per cent of the proceeds of the issue divided up as follows: 0.25 per cent to the broker; 0.5 per cent to the lead underwriter; and 1.25 per cent to the sub-underwriters. An extra 0.125 per cent was charged for each seven days or part of seven days for which the underwriting continued beyond the initial thirty days. Underwriting commissions at these levels were tolerated by the investment committees of the Association of British Insurers and the National Association of Pension Funds and were well within the limits on lawful commissions out of capital prescribed by the Companies Act 1985. Section 97 of that Act allows a commission to be paid provided payment is authorised by the company's articles and the amount paid does not exceed the amount or rate authorised by the articles or 10 per cent of the issue price, whichever is the less.

However, in the 1990s, the Office of Fair Trading began to scrutinise the established underwriting practices in the UK markets on competition grounds. This review first came into prominence in November 1994 when the OFT published a research report which it had commissioned and which concluded that the fees charged by sub-underwriters greatly exceeded the value of the insurance of the success of the issue which they provided.[109] The report made the point that institutional investors were major participants in sub-underwriting activity. This consideration, combined with the fact that, even if some institutional investors were not themselves direct participants in the sub-underwriting of a particular issue, they might well hold shares in other institutions which were, led the author to conclude that:

> Over time, and across different issues, the losses suffered by institutional investors from companies overpaying for sub-underwriting may be more than counterbalanced by the profits they earn from sub-underwriting.

In this scenario the losers were the issuing company's private investors and smaller institutions which were unable to participate in sub-underwriting.

Over the following few years, there were a number of further OFT publications that continued to express dissatisfaction with market processes with regard to underwriting.[110] This dissatisfaction culminated in November 1997 with the matter of underwriting commissions being referred to the Monopolies and Mergers Commission for investigation.

[109] Marsh, P, *Underwriting of Rights Issues: A Study of the Returns Earned by Sub-Underwriters from UK Rights Issues* (OFT Research Paper No 6) (November 1994). Previous research dating back to 1963 pointed towards the same conclusion: see ch 2 of the Marsh Research Paper. See also Breedon, F, and Twinn, I, 'The Valuation of Sub-Underwriting Agreements for UK Rights Issues' (1996) 36 *Bank of England Quarterly Bulletin* 193.

[110] *Underwriting of Equity Issues* (Report by the Director General of Fair Trading) (March 1995) announcing a two-year monitoring period; *Underwriting of Equity Issues* (OFT Report) (December 1996) containing a survey showing little evidence of change in market practices; 'Last Chance for Underwriters' (OFT Press Release) (2 July 1997) indicating continuing dissatisfaction at the absence of vigorous competition in the underwriting market.

The MMC Report on the matter was published in February 1999. The MMC found that complex monopoly situations existed in established underwriting practice and that the standard practice operated against the public interest. Yet it did not suggest that direct legal measures to curb the practice were required. Instead, its recommendations sought to use information disclosure and accountability requirements as mechanisms for shifting market practice. Its first recommendation was that the Securities and Futures Authority (and relevant recognised professional bodies) should issue guidance to corporate financial advisers reminding them of the Financial Services Authority's principle on information for customers and recommending that they should advise their clients of alternatives to underwriting at standard fees. Secondly, it recommended that the London Stock Exchange should change *The Listing Rules* to require directors to explain their choice in those cases where their company undertook an underwritten share issue on the standard basis without incorporating the competitive tender process which is described in the next section of this chapter for at least two-thirds of the sub-underwriting. The third recommendation was that the Bank of England should publish guidance for companies on share-issuing good practice which should encourage the use of tendering and explain the advantages of deep discounting. These recommendations were adopted by the Secretary of State and, at the time of writing, discussions are ongoing with the relevant authorities with a view to their implementation. Also at the recommendation of the MMC, the Secretary of State has referred to the general review of company law which is outlined in Chapter 19 of this book the question whether there is scope for reducing the minimum length of the offer period for a rights issue which, under the Companies Act 1985, s 89, presently stands at 21 days. The perceived tax disadvantages of deep-discounted issues for investors (which, broadly, stem from the capital-gain tax rules that apply when shareholders sell their rights) are to be examined further by the Treasury.

Innovations in Rights-Issues Structures

The scrutiny of established practices by the competition authorities acted as the catalyst for the development of innovative structures designed to reduce underwriting costs.[111] A central feature of the modern underwriting structures is a competitive-tender process to set commission rates rather than the fixed-commission rates that were previously charged. Also, in some cases institutional investors have been asked to indicate in advance whether they will take up their entitlements. An issue does not need to be underwritten to the extent that there are advance commitments to take up entitlements and this will thus reduce underwriting costs. Within certain limits,[112] the Stock Exchange permits a pre-issue placing of those entitlements which investors have indicated in advance that they will not take up. Entitlements that are pre-placed in this way do not need to be underwritten and this, again, can help to trim underwriting costs. The competition authorities have expressed support

[111] Hinkley, R, Hunter, D, Whittell, M, and Ziff, M, *Current Issues in Equity Finance* (1988) 34–5.
[112] *The Listing Rules*, ch 4, para 4.17.

for deep-discounted rights issues which dispense altogether with underwriting. To date, however, these have not become popular within the UK practice market although the investment committees of the ABI and the NAPF have issued a paper that signals a willingness to support greater flexibility in the structuring of rights issues including the use of non-underwritten deep-discount issues with an appropriate consequential adjustment to dividend payments and to dividend-per-share analysis. [113]

ALTERNATIVES TO STANDARD RIGHTS ISSUES

Vendor Placings

Rights issues are sometimes effected in order to fund acquisitions. An alternative way of structuring the financing of an acquisition is to do a vendor placing. In a vendor placing the acquiring company allots its shares as the consideration for the acquisition but then arranges for the shares to be sold in the market for the benefit of the vendor. The net result of the vendor placing is that the vendor receives cash for the assets which have been sold but because, technically, the acquiring company allots its shares for a non-cash consideration, namely the assets acquired, the pre-emption requirements do not apply since they only come into operation when shares are allotted for cash.[114] The non-application of the Companies Act 1985, s 89 to issues of shares for non-cash consideration is based on the practical consideration that there may be circumstances when a company wants to acquire a unique piece of property but its owner will only give it up in return for shares.[115] This is not the case in a vendor placing where the vendor actually wants cash and the allotment of shares is little more than a device designed to put the transaction outside the scope of s 89 pre-emption requirements. For this reason, the practice of vendor placings has been criticised by institutional investors on the grounds that it is prejudicial to the interest of existing shareholders, as (i) others are being given an opportunity to acquire shares in the company often at a discount to the market price; and (ii) the holdings of existing shareholders are being diluted without an opportunity being given to them to maintain their percentage stakes in the issuer (this opportunity being described in practice as a 'clawback'). The current view of institutional investors[116] is that shareholders are entitled to expect a right of clawback for any issues of significant size or

[113] *ABI/NAPF Joint Position Paper on Pre-emption, Cost of Capital and Underwriting* (July 1996).

[114] Companies Act 1985, s 89 (4). Shareholder approval may be required under *The Listing Rules* if the transaction is of sufficient magnitude to constitute a Class 1 transaction or if the vendor is a Related Party ('Class 1' and 'Related Party' are defined in *The Listing Rules*, chs 10 and 11 respectively). Apart from such cases, however, there is no formal requirement to seek shareholder approval provided the company has sufficient authorised but unissued share capital to effect the transaction and the directors are authorised to issue those shares in accordance with Companies Act 1985, s 80.

[115] Drinker, HS, 'The Pre-emptive Right of Shareholders to Subscribe to New Shares' (1930) 43 Harvard Law Review 586 at 607.

[116] *Stock Exchange Pre-emption Guidelines* (1987) as amended by *Shareholders' Pre-emption Rights and Vendor Placings* (1992, minor revision 1993).

which are offered at more than a very modest discount to market price. It is expected that issues involving more than 10 per cent of issued equity share capital or a discount greater than 5 per cent will be placed on a basis which leaves existing shareholders with a right to claw back their pro rata share of the issue if they so wish. In cases where the limits are exceeded an open offer may be made instead of a rights issue in the traditional form.

Open Offers

Another variant on a rights issue is an open offer which is a form of offer sanctioned by *The Listing Rules.*[117] Like a rights issue, an open offer is an offer of new securities to existing shareholders in proportion to their existing holdings. It differs from a rights issue in that the minimum offer period is only fifteen business days. Also the offer is not made by means of a renounceable letter and no arrangements are made to sell shares which are not taken up for the benefit of shareholders. From the company's viewpoint the main advantages of open offers are the shorter offer period (with a corresponding saving in underwriting costs) and the fact that the discount on shares offered by way of an open offer is usually less than the equivalent rights-issue discount would be. Under *The Listing Rules* an open offer of equity securities of a class already listed may not be made if the price is to be at a discount of more than 10 per cent to the middle market price of the securities at the time of announcing the terms of the offer, unless the Exchange is satisfied that the issuer is in severe financial difficulties or that there are other exceptional circumstances.

The Companies Act 1985, s 89 must be dis-applied before an open offer can be made. Dis-application resolutions now commonly contain wording authorising open offers (see, for example, the dis-application resolution given earlier in this chapter[118]). Institutional investors have not raised formal objections to the use of open offers,[119] but this is not surprising given that they tend to take up their rights anyway. The categories of investor who may lose out if a company raises capital by means of an open offer rather than a rights issue are smaller and private shareholders, who either lack the resources to take up their rights or who are apathetic. This is because the structure of an open offer does not permit renunciation of offers; nor is there any requirement for the company to arrange for the sale of the new securities for the benefit of shareholders who take no action themselves in respect of their entitlements.

Open offers are normally combined with a placing.[120] The shares are placed with institutions subject to recall and then offered to the existing shareholders in proportion to their existing holdings.

[117] *The Listing Rules,* ch 4, paras 4.22–4.26.

[118] See above, at 622–3.

[119] Although it is reported in Millerchip, CJ, 'British Land Placing and Open Offer' (1995) 6 (3) PLC 6, 8 that the ABI has indicated that it would be concerned if there was to be a concerted move towards the use of open offers as opposed to rights issues for larger equity capital raising.

[120] See Ch 17 above, at 568–9.

Trombone Rights Issues

A trombone rights issue was first used in relation to the Dixons acquisition of Cyclops in 1987 and it has now become an established method of financing a bid for another company. In the context of a bid, a traditional rights issue suffers from the disadvantage that the issuer will receive the full amount of cash needed to finance the bid but may not in fact need that cash if the bid proves to be unsuccessful.

In a typical trombone rights issue there is an issue of convertible loan stock which is in two parts, the first instalment being unconditional and the second being conditional on the success of the bid. The first instalment is payable at the end of the offer period (as in a normal rights issue) and the second instalment is payable only if and when the bid becomes unconditional. If the bid does not succeed the unpaid stock is cancelled. The reasoning behind the issue of loan stock rather than shares is that cancellation of nil- or partly-paid shares amounts to a formal reduction of capital which must be approved by the court in accordance with the Companies Act 1985, s 135 but no such formality is imposed in respect of the cancellation of unpaid loan stock. Another reason for using convertible loan stock is that the Stock Exchange normally refuses to permit shares to be admitted to listing whilst the issue remains subject to conditions, although there have been exceptions to this general rule.[121]

[121] Creamer, H, and Mullen, 'Rights Issues' in Barc, S (gen ed), *Tolley's Company Law* (looseleaf) para R5011.

PART VI

THE FUTURE

19

The Strategic Framework of Modern Company Law

PUBLICATION OF CONSULTATION DOCUMENT

When the manuscript of this book was with the publishers, the Company Law Review Steering Group established by the DTI in 1998 to conduct a fundamental review of core company law[1] published its first consultation document entitled *Modern Company Law for a Competitive Economy: The Strategic Framework.*[2] The consultation document is concerned with the overall strategic framework of company law. As such, it raises fundamental policy issues for consideration. It does not contain detailed suggestions for change but initial preferences in some areas are indicated. Detailed proposals are expected to follow later, with the intention being to present a final report in 2001. Although timing considerations precluded a critical evaluation of the consultation document here, in the circumstances this book would have been incomplete without some reference to this important publication that is likely to shape the direction and content of company law in this country into the next millennium. Accordingly, there follows a summary of the main features of the consultation document which highlights aspects of it which are particularly relevant within the context of this book.

PRESUMPTIONS

The consultation document sets out four presumptions that should govern the formulation of modern company law.[3] These are (1) against interventionist legislation and in favour of facilitating markets, including provision for transparency of information, wherever possible; (2) in favour of minimising complexity and maximising accessibility of the rules; (3) against creating criminal offences unless the subject-matter demands it; and (4) in favour of allocating jurisdiction to the most suitable regulatory body, avoiding duplication and conflict.

[1] This review was announced in a DTI consultative paper: *Modern Law for a Competitive Economy* (1998). The commencement of the review process is noted at various points in the book.
[2] February 1999. In this chapter, references to chapters and paragraphs mean chapters and paragraphs of the Steering Group's consultation document unless otherwise stated.
[3] Consultation document, executive summary, para 2.

Non-intervention and the Role of Market Forces

In line with the first presumption, the important role that contractual principles and the operation of market forces play in regulating the relationship between participants in companies is emphasised.[4] Yet, the deregulatory agenda that is implicit in the first presumption is not unqualified, since it is accepted that the presumption must yield in circumstances where markets, combined with accountability mechanisms, cannot be expected to work.[5]

Minimising Complexity and Maximising Accessibility

This presumption is developed into a proposal for a radical restructuring of the companies legislation which is summarised in the consultation document as 'think small first'. This phrase is intended to mean that the companies legislation should be drawn up with the small company in mind as the basic entity with additional requirements being added on, in discrete layers, for larger, more sophisticated or exceptional entities.[6] If implemented, this would be a broad reversal of the current position, which is largely[7] that the same rules apply to all companies irrespective of their profits, turnover, number of shareholders or employees or other measurement criteria but with some derogations and provisions for opting-out that can be utilised by smaller companies.

In general, the consultation document devotes considerable attention to the needs of small and closely-held companies[8] and to how these might best be catered for within a new legal framework. Wider questions about legal forms of organisation, with and without limited liability, are to be addressed in the next phase of the review.[9]

Jurisdiction to the Most Suitable Regulatory Body

The multi-layered nature of the regulation applicable to companies is explored in the consultation document.[10] It is noted that those involved with companies may need to consider not only the companies legislation itself but

[4] eg, paras 2.7 and 2.22.

[5] Para 2.23. On the role, and limits, of contract and market forces in company law see this book, Ch 1 above, at 10–12 and Ch 4 above, at 118–22.

[6] Para 2.25.

[7] The main exception to this is in the area of share capital and maintenance of capital where more stringent rules tend to apply to public companies than to private companies. The basis for the distinction between the rules applicable to private and public companies in these respects is often to be found in the company law directives that the UK, as a member state of the European Union, must give effect to under its domestic law.

[8] This term is used in the consultation document to describe companies where often all of the shareholders are involved in management: para 5.2.1. In this book this type of company tends to be described as a 'quasi-partnership' company which is consistent with existing practice (see, eg, Ch 1 above, at 1–5). In this respect the Steering Committee's consultation document may cause a shift in terminological usage.

[9] Para 5.2.11.

[10] See also this book, Ch 1 above, at 6–8.

also accounting standards, the *Listing Rules* of the London Stock Exchange, the City Code on Takeovers and Mergers and the Combined Code on Corporate Governance.[11] The consultation document explains that it is intended to review the present regulatory structure and distribution of functions which have developed on a piecemeal rather than systematic basis. However, in an early indication of the Steering Group's thinking on this matter, such review is not expected to lead to rationalisation of the system by means of more statutory regulation but, rather, for the trend to be away from prescriptive rules set out in statute towards more flexible rules in the form of codes of practice.[12] This suggestion links in with the presumption that the law should be broadly non-interventionist: in those circumstances where market forces alone do not work effectively, a code of practice from a regulatory body may be preferable to full-blown statutory regulation.[13]

KEY ISSUES

As well as the needs of small companies and the jurisdiction of regulatory and self-regulatory bodies, the consultation document identifies six other key areas. These are (1) the scope of company law; (2) company formation; (3) company powers; (4) capital maintenance; (5) electronic communications and information; and (6) the international aspects of the law.[14] Accounting and reporting issues are also singled out as being deserving of early attention.[15] The internal constitutional structure of companies—meaning the respective functions, powers and duties of those who exercise authority and control within a company's constitutional structure—is identified as probably the most difficult, important and wide-ranging area still to be covered.[16]

Scope of Company Law[17]

It is under this heading that the content of the duty of directors to act in the interests of the company is explored.[18] The consultation document recognises that the extent to which the present-day duty of directors in this respect embraces longer-term considerations is widely misunderstood and that, in practice, this lack of clarity may tend to lead to an undue focus on short-term issues.[19] The consultation document supports the view that the current duty of directors is to maximise value in the longer term but takes mutual trust and co-operation between shareholders and other 'constituencies', such as employees, suppliers and customers, as being the basis on which such value maximisation can best be achieved. Accordingly, to discharge their duties properly, directors should take into account all of the considerations which contribute to the success of their enterprise. The duty imposed by the

[11] Ch 5.5 generally and para 5.5.1 in particular. [12] Para 5.5.5. [13] Ibid.
[14] Para 2.31. [15] Para 2.32 and Ch 6. [16] Para 2.33. [17] Ch 5.1.
[18] Some of the issues raised under this heading in the consultation document are considered in this book, Ch 2 above, at 78–80 and Ch 4 above, at 124–40.
[19] Para 5.1.7.

Companies Act 1985, s 309 to consider the interests of employees is one aspect of this duty to consider. This inclusive approach is described in the consultation document as the 'Enlightened Shareholder Value' approach. According to the consultation document, under this approach there is no need to reform the fundamentals of directors' duties,[20] although it accepts that there is a case for the duty to consider all relevant interests to be made clearer either by primary legislation or by some form of non-legally binding but nevertheless authoritative public statement.[21]

The Enlightened Shareholder Value approach is contrasted to the 'Pluralist' approach. The Pluralist approach is broadly equivalent to what has been described in this book as the stakeholder model of company law,[22] in which shareholder interests are downgraded from their present overriding position and become only one of the considerations that the management of a company should consider, alongside those of others who make commitments to it such as its employees. The consultation document recognises that adoption of the Pluralist approach would involve a need to balance potentially conflicting interests, would require reform of the law of directors' duties and might require changes in shareholder control over the company through their ability to determine the composition of the board. The discussion in Chapter 4 of this book[23] suggests that fundamental aspects of company law would indeed need to be reviewed if a stakeholder or Pluralist approach were to be adopted.

Although it is emphasised that much work remains to be done in this area before any final recommendation can properly be made, the indications in the consultation document are that the Steering Group does not favour the Pluralist approach. Early responses in the media to the publication of the consultation document tended to favour the view that discussion of the Pluralist approach was probably included precisely in order for it to be shot down. The consultation document seems, however, to be more positive about the possibility of achieving the objectives of the Pluralist approach within the framework of Enhanced Shareholder Value through the mechanism of enhanced reporting obligations. These could, for example, require greater disclosure of relationships and dependencies and their value to the business, and mandatory reports on such matters as relations with employees, philanthropic activity and environmental performance.[24]

The consultation document also expresses little enthusiasm for mandatory reform of board structures to achieve wider representation of employee or other interests, but it acknowledges that that there may be a case for enabling

[20] Para 5.1.17.

[21] Paras 5.1.22–5.1.23.

[22] See this book, Ch 1 above, at 12–13. On pluralism, see further, Kelly, G, and Parkinson, J, 'The Conceptual Foundations of the Company: A Pluralist Approach' [1998] CfiLR 174.

[23] Particularly at 125–33. See also Ch 2 above, at 78–80

[24] Paras 5.1.44–5.1.47 and 5.1.50, question 6. Arguments for the de-regulation of disclosure requirements on the grounds that this can be regulated by market forces (ie that in accordance with efficient capital markets theory, share prices will reflect market (dis)satisfaction with the amount and quality of information disclosed (see further this book, Ch 17 above, at 582–3)) do not appear to have found favour with the Steering Group. The consultation document emphasises the importance of statutory and regulatory disclosure requirements.

companies to adopt alternative structures if there is a strong demand for an optional regime to this effect.[25] Although stated at a high level of generality, if developed this suggestion could result in a change to the law relating to the duties of directors who are appointed as nominees of a particular group to allow them more easily to discharge their representative function.[26] Whether directors should be empowered or required to subordinate shareholder interests to wider ethical considerations or to engage in charitable activity at shareholder expense are other issues that are raised for consideration.[27]

Company Formation and Powers

Although the provisions of the Companies Act 1985 relating to company powers and the effect of constitutional limits on persons dealing with companies were amended in 1989, the changes that were enacted then were not as far-reaching as some had hoped for.[28] In particular, the requirement for companies to register an objects clause was retained and old doctrines about the public being deemed to have notice of information filed with the registrar of companies were only partially swept away. The consultation document recognises that the 1989 changes did not solve all of the problems and puts forward suggestions for radical simplification as follows:[29] in their dealings with third parties companies should be deemed to have the capacity to do anything which a legal person could do; there should be no obligation to register an objects clause; constitutional restrictions limiting the authority of directors (including those in the objects clauses of existing companies that could be retained if their operators thought fit[30]) should not affect independent outsiders dealing with a company; the abolition of deemed notice should be implemented in full; and shareholders should be able to bring proceedings to restrain directors, or a person authorised by them, from acting beyond their constitutional powers save that this could not affect the validity of any commitment entered into already.

If these proposals—and also the related suggestion that, in the interests of simplification, the distinction between the memorandum and articles should disappear and that companies should have one constitutional document—were to be implemented, English law would be brought more closely into line with Commonwealth countries such as Australia and New Zealand which have modernised their own corporate laws in recent years.[31] Generally, the consultation document acknowledges the importance to the review process

[25] Para 5.133.

[26] On the position of nominee directors see this book, Ch 5 above, at 160.

[27] Paras 5.1.40–5.1.43. Present-day controls on corporate philanthropy are considered in this book, Ch 4 above, at 127–31.

[28] Generally on the imperfections of the existing law in this respect see this book, Ch 3 above, at 84–97.

[29] Para 5.3.18.

[30] A related proposal is for the abolition of the special minority protection in relation to resolutions to alter a company's objects (Companies Act 1985, s 5).

[31] See further this book, Ch 3 above, at 89–94.

of learning from other countries' experience and provides a summary of key developments in certain Commonwealth and continental European countries and in the USA.[32]

The point has been made at various places in this book that the obligation on the UK as a member state of the European Union to implement company law directives into its law limits the scope for reform at a purely domestic level. The proposal to abolish the requirement for companies to file an objects clause is one illustration of this point, because it is uncertain whether for public companies this would be compatible with the Second Company Law Directive.[33] The Steering Group plans to investigate further the question of compatibility but, importantly, the consultation document also raises the possibility of seeking an amendment to European law in this and other areas (principally capital maintenance) where it constrains meritorious reform initiatives.[34] It is noted that the DTI has begun the process of bilateral discussions with other Member States to see if there is common ground on the need for reform.[35] The consultation document also notes that rights grants under the European Convention on Human Rights, such as the right to freedom of association and to peaceful enjoyment of possessions, impose constraints on UK legislation and the operation of the corporate regulatory system.[36]

Capital Maintenance

The consultation document makes three radical proposals under this heading: (1) to permit companies to reduce their capital, without court approval, but subject to shareholder approval by special resolution and a declaration of solvency by the directors; (2) to permit companies to give financial assistance subject to approval by disinterested shareholders by ordinary resolution and solvency certification; and (3) the abolition of the requirement for shares to have a nominal or par value. To implement these proposals in relation to public companies it would be necessary to consider seeking amendments to the relevant provisions of the Second Company Law Directive.[37] These proposals reflect widespread acceptance that the detailed body of law governing capital maintenance is outmoded in many respects[38] and that creditors' interests may be better served by other mechanisms such as solvency declarations. The suggestions broadly follow the pattern of de-regulation in other Commonwealth countries. That the law in the UK should not retain anachronistic requirements which have been abandoned elsewhere is important because of the need, emphasised in the consultation document, to ensure

[32] Ch 4.

[33] Para 5.3.19. The relevant provision is Second Company Law Directive, 77/91/EEC, [1977] OJ L26/1, art 2(b).

[34] Para 5.3.19 (objects clause), para 5.4.10 (reduction of capital), para 5.4.2 (financial assistance) and para 5.4.28 (par values).

[35] Ch 3 and para 3.5 in particular.

[36] Para 3.8.

[37] 77/91/EEC, [1977] OJ L26/1, art 32 (reduction of capital), art 23 (financial assistance) and art 8 (par values).

[38] See in relation to par values the discussion in this book at Ch 8 above, at 282–6.

that the law provides a competitive infrastructure which is attractive to internationally mobile business and an efficient regime for domestic companies.[39]

Information and Communications Technology

Modern electronic methods of communicating and storing information are capable of transforming the means whereby companies make information publicly available and the way in which the participants in companies relate to each other. An example of how information technology might impact upon the mechanisms for corporate governance is that the ability to use electronic means to communicate quickly and cheaply is something that could be exploited by shareholders who are opposed to management proposals to disseminate their views to other shareholders.[40] The barriers to effective communication by shareholders within the traditional setting of paper-based documents sent by post are examined in Chapter 7 of this book.[41] To date there is limited explicit recognition of the use of electronic data storage and retrieval systems within the existing companies legislation,[42] but the potential for electronic methods to supplant traditional forms of information storage and communication is already actively recognised in practice.[43]

The broad approach suggested by the consultation document[44] in this area is that the law should facilitate, rather than require, the use of modern electronic methods for the storage, publication and communication of information relating to companies. However, it is recognised that the permissive rather than prescriptive approach may need to change over time if it becomes the norm for individuals, as well as businesses, to have access to these methods. Particular proposals that are put forward for consideration include: that electronic means should be permitted for all information required to be sent to, or maintained by, the registrar of companies; and that electronic communications between companies and members should be expressly permitted.[45] The impact of technological advances on company meetings, including the

[39] Para 5.6.1 and Ch 5.6 generally on international issues.

[40] Boyce, GR, and Hewitt, S, 'Proxy Season In an Electronic Environment' (1997) New York Law Journal (accessed via: www.ljx.com/practice/securities/0508proxy.html); Silverman, AJ, 'Electronic Proxies: Are They in Your Future' (accessed via: www.e-counsel.com/electron.html).

[41] In particular, at 262–4.

[42] These are discussed in the consultation document, paras 5.7.13–5.7.16.

[43] An illustration of this is the E-Vote electronic proxy voting system which at the time of writing (March 1999) is undergoing trials with a view to being launched in the UK in the near future. This system, which is designed to allow shareholders to register their proxy votes electronically, has been broadly welcomed by institutional investors. The suggestion in the consultation document that it is arguable whether the Companies Act 1985, ss 372 and 373 permit the communication of proxies in digital form is unhelpful in this context. Although these sections refer to an 'instrument' or 'other document' it is difficult to see why an appointment of a proxy that is delivered electronically should not fall within the scope of these terms. Contrast, eg, the Securities and Exchange Commission's Interpretative Release, *Use of Electronic Media for Delivery Purposes* Release No 33–7233; 34–36345; IC–21399 (1995) which refers to electronically delivered documents and which states, broadly, that delivery of information through an electronic medium should satisfy delivery obligations under federal securities law.

[44] Para 5.7.11.

[45] Para 5.7.18.

scope for 'virtual meetings', is to be explored generally in the next phase of the review, when wider policy issues surrounding the role of the general meeting are to be examined.[46]

ONGOING REFORM: A STANDING COMPANY LAW COMMITTEE

The traditional approach to company law reform in this country has been for general reviews to be conducted on an infrequent basis (the last such general review being in 1962) with piecemeal changes being made between such reviews in response to particular situations, such as the need to implement a new directive, the emergence of a new problem in practice or the outcome of a government-appointed review of the law in a particular area. The consultation document suggests that consideration should be given to the establishment of a standing committee charged with the task of reviewing company law. This is not the first time that a suggestion to this effect has been put forward[47] and, as is noted in the consultation document, such bodies already exist in some other comparable countries.[48]

[46] Para 5.7.18.
[47] See, eg, *Report of the Committee on Company Law Amendment* Cmd 6659 (1945) para 176 (Cohen Committee).
[48] Para 8.12.

Index